The British
BOXING
Board of Control
YEARBOOK
1998

Edited and compiled by
Barry J. Hugman

Queen Anne Press

First published in 1997

© Barry J. Hugman

Barry J. Hugman has asserted his right under
the Copyright, Designs and Patent Act, 1988
to be identified as the author of this work

First published in Great Britain in 1997 by
Queen Anne Press
a division of Lennard Associates
Mackerye End, Harpenden
Hertfordshire, AL5 5DR

A CIP catalogue record for this book
is available from the British Library

ISBN 1 85291 582 X

Typeset and designed by Typecast (Artwork and Design)
8 Mudford Road
Yeovil, Somerset, BA21 4AA

Printed and bound in Great Britain by
Butler & Tanner, London and Frome

Front cover: Naseem Hamed (John Gichigi/Allsport)
Back cover: Robin Reid (right) and Henry Wharton (John Gichigi/Allsport)

Contents

BRITANNIA BOXING EQUIPMENT (PRESTON) LTD
UNIT 4, THORN BUILDING, KENT STREET, PRESTON, LANCASHIRE, PR1 1PJ

SUPPLIERS THROUGHOUT THE WORLD OF TOP QUALITY BOXING EQUIPMENT

FOR EXPERT ADVICE OF OUR FULL RANGE OF EQUIPMENT
CONTACT OUR SALES TEAM ON

PRESTON   01772 - 201711
OR FAX   01772 - 201770

AS WELL AS OUR OWN "BBE" QUALITY PRODUCTS
WE ARE ALSO DISTRIBUTORS AND SUPPLIERS OF
"CLETO REYES" BOXING EQUIPMENT,
"TOP TEN"
AND MANY OTHERS.

Approved by the
International Amateur
Boxing Association

Official Suppliers to the
British Boxing Board of Control

Acknowledgements

I take great pleasure in yet again thanking all the people who participate in helping to make the *British Boxing Yearbook*, now in its 14th year, a must for all followers of the sport.

As in previous editions, I start with the BBBoC, without whose support the Yearbook would be sadly lacking. John Morris, the General Secretary, has always given me every assistance when it comes to producing the Yearbook and, as a friend, his encouragement was again invaluable. Others at the Board I would like to thank personally for their help and attention to detail are Simon Block, John's assistant, and Robert Smith, formerly a leading welter and now the Southern Area Secretary. And last but not least the ladies, Debbie Wilkinson, Christine Venturelli, and Jean Jeeves, who put in a lot of hard work in an effort to make sure that the Yearbook maintained its eye for detail, especially in the area of licenseholders and boxers' key data.

Despite his health problems, I am again indebted to Ron Olver, who has been with me as Assistant Editor since the first edition of the Yearbook and who, as ever, was a great source of inspiration. Ron again produced the Directory of Ex-Boxers' Associations and Obituaries for the 1998 Yearbook. A former Assistant Editor of both *Boxing News* and *Boxing World*, he is also well known for being the British correspondent of *The Ring*; the author of *The Professionals*; for producing the boxing section within *Encyclopedia Britannica*; his work on *Boxing*, Foyle's library service; and as the former co-editor of the *Boxing News Annual*. His honorary work, which includes being the Chairman of the BBBoC Benevolent Fund Grants' Committee; the Vice President of many ex-boxers' associations; the Public Relations Officer of the London Ex-Boxers' Association; and membership of the Commonwealth Boxing Council and the International Hall of Fame, has, in the past couple of years, been honoured by the Boxing Writers' Club and the BBBoC. Ron is the man who first recognised that there was a common bond between old fighters and it was with his prompting and support that the ex-boxers' associations came into being. He will always be identified within the pages of the trade paper, *Boxing News*, as the man responsible for the "Old Timers". Long may his good work continue.

Interestingly, three well established Yearbook contributors, Bob Lonkhurst, John Jarrett, and Ralph Oates, have all recently published books of their own. Bob, who is a BBBoC Southern Area Inspector, has produced *Man of Courage: The Life and Career of Tommy Farr* (for further details see page 34); John, the Northern Area Secretary, is responsible for *Byker to Broadway: The Fighting Life and Times of Seaman Tommy Watson* (for further details see page 46); and Ralph Oates, the leading boxing quiz book specialist, has surpassed himself again with *Boxing Shadows* (for further details see page 24). In producing articles such as No Substitute for Experience; Home and Away with British Boxers During 1996-97; and Howard Winstone: The Welsh Dragon, Tania Follett: Britain's First Woman Boxing Manager, and The Triple Hitters' Quiz, respectively, all of these men have again proved their great value to maintaining standards within the Yearbook.

I would also like to acknowledge the articles produced by Eric Armit – A-Z of Current World Champions – a leading authority on boxer's records, worldwide, who is also responsible for *Boxing News'* World Scene; David Prior – Highlights From the 1996-97 Amateur Season – who is the Press Liaison Officer for the Amateur Boxing Association and who formerly covered amateur boxing for the *Amateur Boxing Scene* and *Boxing News*; Bob Yalen – World Title Bouts During 1996-97; Robert Soderman – The American Invasion of Bombardier Billy Wells; Derek O'Dell – Don Cockell and High Wycombe Remembered; Harold Alderman – Imperial British Empire Title Bouts, 1887-1954; and Les Clark – A Boxing Quiz With a Few Below the Belt.

Other much-needed editorial help came from Neil Blackburn, who again pieced together information required to make Obituaries as complete as possible; Mrs Enza Jacoponi, the Secretary of the EBU (EBU championship data); Patrick Myler (Irish amateur boxing); Ray Allen (Welsh amateur boxing); and Dai Corp, Tommy Gilmour, David Hall, John Jarrett, Robert Smith, and Paul Thomas (Area title data).

As in previous years, the largest chunk of research, as far as I was personally concerned, was in the World Title Bouts Since Gloves' section. For work involved in this edition, I would like to thank Professor Luckett Davis, Herb Goldman, Paul Zabala, Robert Soderman, and Harold Alderman. Now down to assessing the final 200 fights, as mentioned in the Introduction, hopefully, Robert Soderman and myself will "crack" it during the next 12 months.

Regarding photographs, as in previous years, the majority were produced by Les Clark (where would I be without him), who has built up a large library of both action and poses from British rings. If anyone requires a photo that has appeared in the Yearbook, or requires a list, Les can be reached at 352 Trelawney Avenue, Langley, Bucks SL3 7TS. Other photographs were supplied by my good friends, Harry Goodwin, Chris Bevan, and Derek Rowe.

Others who should be mentioned are: Bernard Hart, the Managing Director of Lonsdale Sports Equipment Ltd, who sponsors the BBBoC Awards and the launch of the Yearbook at a special luncheon; Jean Bastin, who continued to set high standards in typesetting and design despite ill health; my wife Jennifer, who looks after the proof reading; and the sponsor, Jonathan Ticehurst, Managing Director of the Sports Division of Windsor Insurance Brokers, whose generous support and enthusiasm continued to help the *British Boxing Yearbook* maintain the standards required of it.

Barry J. Hugman (Editor)

18.11.1990	Chris Eubank	WBO Middleweight Champion
21.09.1991	Chris Eubank	WBO Super-Middleweight Champion
03.10.1992	Nigel Benn	WBC Super-Middleweight Champion
15.05.1993	Paul Weir	WBO Mini-Flyweight Champion
15.05.1993	Baby Jake Matlala	WBO Flyweight Champion
19.05.1993	Chris Pyatt	WBO Middleweight Champion
16.10.1993	Eamonn Loughran	WBO Welterweight Champion
19.03.1994	Herbie Hide	WBO Heavyweight Champion
11.05.1994	Steve Collins	WBO Middleweight Champion
23.11.1994	Paul Weir	WBO Light-Flyweight Champion
18.03.1995	Steve Collins	WBO Super-Middleweight Champion
18.11.1995	Baby Jake Matlala	WBO Light-Flyweight Champion
22.11.1995	Paul Jones	WBO Light-Middleweight Champion
13.04.1996	Jose Luis Lopez	WBO Welterweight Champion

Producing World Champions - Year After Year, After Year

MATCHROOM BOXING LIMITED, 10 WESTERN ROAD, ROMFORD, ESSEX RM1 3JT
Telephone: 01708 788770 Facsimile: 01708 760066

ST. ANDREW'S SPORTING CLUB
EXCLUSIVE GENTLEMEN'S CLUB
AND
THE HOME OF SCOTTISH BOXING

Team 1997-98

Flyweight
PAUL WEIR, *Former WBO Mini-Flyweight and Light-Flyweight Champion of the World*
KEITH KNOX, *Former ABA Champion*

Bantamweight
DREW DOCHERTY, *British Champion*
SHAUN ANDERSON

Super-Bantamweight
WILSON DOCHERTY   ALSTON BUCHANAN

Featherweight
BILLY HARDY, *European Champion*
IAN McLEOD, *Undefeated*   GARRY BURRELL

Super-Featherweight
DAVIE McHALE

Lightweight
HUGH COLLINS
BRADLEY WELSH, *Former ABA Champion*

Light-Welterweight
MARK BRESLIN, *Undefeated*   JAN CREE, *New Pro*

Welterweight
JOHN DOCHERTY

Light-Middleweight
JOE TOWNSLEY,
Commonwealth Games Bronze Medallist
BILLY COLLINS

Light-Heavyweight — STEVEN WILSON

Cruiserweight — COLIN BROWN

Co-Manager:
ADEY LEWIS, *British Flyweight Champion*
DEREK ROCHE, *Undefeated*
CHARLES SHEPHERD
BOBBY VANZIE, *Undefeated*   MICHAEL GALE

1997-98 Fixture List

Monday 22nd September 1997

Monday 27th October 1997

Monday 24th November 1997

Saturday 13th December 1997
(Ladies Night
Dinner, Dance & Cabaret)

Monday 26th January 1998
(Silver Jubilee Evening)

Monday 23rd February 1998

Monday 23rd March 1998

Monday 27th April 1998

Monday 1st June 1998

ADMINISTRATIVE OFFICES:
FORTE POSTHOUSE, BOTHWELL STREET, GLASGOW G2 7EN, SCOTLAND
Telephone: +44 141 248 5461 and +44 141 248 2656   Fax: +44 141 248 5922   TELEX: 77440

DIRECTOR: TOMMY GILMOUR JNR.

Introduction

by Barry J. Hugman

I think it is fair to say that for the past 14 years, the *British Boxing Yearbook* has not only recorded faithfully what has happened during the previous 12 months, but has also prided itself in keeping its patrons abreast of any additional historical information as it comes to light, especially in the field of championship boxing dating back to early gloved fights.

The 1998 Yearbook has continued in this vein, with additional world title bout input covering the period, 1892-1941, along with a complete examination by the boxing historian, Harold Alderman, of the Imperial British Empire title, which first came to fruition in 1887.

Regarding the early world championship scene, for the past five years I have personally carried out much research in the libraries of North America and this country, helped by many students of boxing history, including Americans, Professor Luckett Davis, Bob Soderman, Paul Zabala, Gary Phillips, Herb Goldman, the editor of the *International Boxing Digest* magazine, and Harold Alderman and Derek O'Dell from this side of the Atlantic. More recently, further no-decision fights involving all so-called champions and claimants (these are men who had realistic claims throughout the world) have been identified and analysed after assessing pre-fight weights and status. Now down to examining the final 200 fights from records that have been faithfully recorded for leading fighters by Luckett Davis and his team of researchers over the years, Bob Soderman is processing 75 of them through individual libraries throughout America, while I am now concentrating my energies on Ohio, Indiana, Pennsylvania, and New York City. Hopefully, following the 1999 edition of the Yearbook, all the supplementary work will come together in a compendium titled the *History of World Championship Boxing*.

Harping back to the Imperial British Empire title fights' section compiled by Harold Alderman for this edition, this is a much needed and much fairer reflection of how it really was than what was first listed in the *Boxing News Annual* just after the last war, which was predominately British related. It is also interesting to note that prior to 1954, there was no official body organising title bouts throughout the Empire and countries, such as Australia, Canada, and South Africa, as well as Britain, carried their own versions of the title. In compiling this listing, Harold Alderman has utilised 30/40 years of diligent research carried out at the British Newspaper Library in Colindale, and many other more localised libraries.

Apart from the current boxers' records (vital to the people involved in the sport), other ongoing record sections, and the Licenseholders' Directory, the Yearbook once again offers up a selection of interesting and topical articles, such as Howard Winstone: The Welsh Dragon (Another story by Ralph Oates of a much-liked and respected world champion, this time from Wales); Tania Follett: Britain's First Woman Boxing Manager (Ralph Oates interviews a recent addition to the BBBoC's list of licenseholders); No Substitute for Experience (Bob Lonkhurst evaluates the qualities of two famous ex-amateur boxers who have since become Class "A" Star referees); Home and Away with British Boxers During 1996-97 (A regular feature from the pen of John Jarrett, covering last season, month by month); Don Cockell and High Wycombe Remembered (A walk down memory lane with Derek O'Dell); A-Z of Current World Champions (The synopsis and seasonal record for all of the current non-British IBF, WBA, WBC, and WBO champions, including those who first won and lost titles in 1996-97, prepared by Eric Armit); The American Invasion of Bombardier Billy Wells (An American perspective of England's "Great White Hope" by Bob Soderman); Highlights From the 1996-97 Amateur Season (The regular amateur feature by David Prior); Obituaries (A brief synopsis of the leading boxing personalities who passed away between July 1996 and going to press); and two boxing quizzes presented by Les Clark and Ralph Oates, a man who is well known for producing boxing quiz books.

Finally, I would like to send my good wishes to all those involved in the sport of boxing, especially to those who continue to support the *British Boxing Yearbook*.

Abbreviations and Definitions used in the record sections of the Yearbook: PTS (Points), CO (Count Out), RSC (Referee Stopped Contest), RTD (Retired), DIS (Disqualified), NC (No Contest), ND (No Decision).

British Boxing Board of Control Ltd: Structure

(Members of the World Boxing Council, World Boxing Association, International Boxing Federation, World Boxing Organisation, Commonwealth Boxing Council and European Boxing Union)

PRESIDENT	
VICE PRESIDENT	Leonard E. Read, QPM
CHAIRMAN	Leonard E. Read, QPM
VICE CHAIRMAN	Dr Adrian Whiteson
GENERAL SECRETARY	John Morris
ADMINISTRATIVE STEWARDS	Dr Oswald Ross William Sheeran Dennis Lockton Lincoln Crawford Frank Butler, OBE Tom Pendry, MP Cliff Curvis Bill Martin Lord Brooks of Tremorfa Charles Giles Sebastian Coe, OBE Judge Alan Simpson John Clifford Robert Graham BEM
HONORARY STEWARDS*	Dr James Shea Mary Peters, CBE, MBE
STEWARDS OF APPEAL*	Robin Simpson, QC John Mathew, QC Nicholas Valios, QC Robert Harman, QC William Tudor John Geoffrey Finn Judge Brian Capstick, QC Colin Ross Munro, QC Peter Richards Lord Meston
HONORARY CONSULTANT*	Ray Clarke, OBE
HEAD OFFICE	Jack Petersen House 52a Borough High Street London SE1 1XW Tel. 0171 403 5879 Fax. 0171 378 6670 Telegrams: BRITBOX, LONDON

* Not directors of the company

AREA COUNCILS - AREA SECRETARIES

AREA NO 1 (SCOTLAND)
Brian McAllister
11 Woodside Crescent, Glasgow G3 7UL
Telephone 0141 3320392

AREA NO 2 (NORTHERN IRELAND)
John Campbell
8 Munt Eden, Belfast, Northern Ireland BT9 6RA
Telephone 01232 683310

AREA NO 3 (WALES)
Dai Corp
113 Hill Crest, Brynna, Pontyclun, Mid Glamorgan
CF7 9SN
Telephone 0144 3226465

AREA NO 4 (NORTHERN)
(Northumberland, Cumbria, Durham, Cleveland, Tyne and Wear, North Yorkshire [north of a line drawn from Whitby to Northallerton to Richmond, including these towns].)
John Jarrett
5 Beechwood Avenue, Gosforth, Newcastle NE3 5DM
Telephone 0191 2856556

AREA NO 5 (CENTRAL)
(North Yorkshire [with the exception of the part included in the Northern Area - see above], Lancashire, West and South Yorkshire, Greater Manchester, Merseyside and Cheshire, Isle of Man, North Humberside.)
Ron Hackett
38 Grangethorpe Road,
Urmston, Manchester,
Lancashire M31 1HT
Telephone 0161 7483545

AREA NO 6 (SOUTHERN)
(Bedfordshire, Berkshire, Buckinghamshire, Cambridgeshire, Channel Islands, Isle of Wight, Essex, Hampshire, Kent, Hertfordshire, Greater London, Norfolk, Suffolk, Oxfordshire, East and West Sussex.)
Robert W. Smith
British Boxing Board of Control
Jack Petersen House, 52a Borough High Street, London SE1 1XW
Telephone 0171 4035879

AREA NO 7 (WESTERN)
(Cornwall, Devon, Somerset, Dorset, Wiltshire, Avon, Gloucestershire.)
Dai Corp
113 Hill Crest, Brynna, Pontyclun, Mid Glamorgan
CF7 9SN
Telephone 0144 3226465

AREA NO 8 (MIDLANDS)
(Derbyshire, Nottinghamshire, Lincolnshire, Salop, Staffordshire, Herefordshire and Worcestershire, Warwickshire, West Midlands, Leicestershire, South Humberside, Northamptonshire.)
Alec Kirby
105 Upper Meadow Road, Quinton, Birmingham B32
Telephone 0121 4211194

Foreword

by John Morris *(General Secretary, British Boxing Board of Control)*

Just another year in boxing's magnificent but ever turbulent history and what a year. Mike Tyson took to chewing ears, Oliver McCall shed tears of anguish in an unprecedented breakdown in the ring and Henry Akinwande opted to cling rather than fight with the WBC world heavyweight crown on offer.

For the moment forget the big fellas, though we grieve for Lennox Lewis as he seeks the glory he deserves and which has been cruelly denied him thus far. There is so much else to applaud in Britain and Europe with the emergence of exciting, talented young men and so many quality championship fights.

A year ago I wrote that boxing faced a crucial period and nothing has changed. We are not much further forward, but at least things are no worse and in several areas progress is being made, particularly with regard to relations between the Board and the ABA of England. Talks proceed in a most friendly and encouraging way, not to bring sweeping changes, but to identify specific areas where pros and amateurs can work happily together.

The action of the year will nowhere be reflected better than here in the pages of Barry Hugman's latest Yearbook, the 14th in a series that began in 1985. The Book is recognised across the world as the finest of its kind and British boxing is fortunate to have a chronicle of this quality to record its performances.

These jottings are not intended as a boxing state-of-the-nation statement – I leave that to my dedicated chairman, "Nipper" Read, at annual meetings – but there are a few points to note. Last year, the Board brought in mandatory annual MRI brain scans for all British boxers thanks to the benevolence of promoter, Frank Warren, whose donations have started the fund through which the Board subsidises scans for all but the top-earning boxers. However, the sport must help itself as well, and the Board will soon be launching a campaign to build a Trust Fund to be combined with the existing Board Benevolent Fund whose grants committee, led by Ron Olver, assists so many former fighters each year.

I appeal now to all supporters of professional boxing to back the campaign as much as possible. We will be asking all license holders and supporters to fund raise across the nation once the details are in place.

The medium of television brings more tournaments onto our screens than ever before, but almost entirely through the satellite and cable channels. The terrestrial channels, BBC and ITV, free to the general public, have turned their backs on boxing despite the huge audience that exists for the sport. Viewing figures have soared as high as 16 million for the biggest fights, and yet these channels now ignore us. Do they take the view that if they are outpriced for the very best then they will not screen any boxing?

If this is the case then I feel they are failing in their duty to the sporting public and indeed to the sport. Their support for what are termed "small hall" promotions would be welcomed hugely. While the major entrepreneurs corner the TV market and draw in the top boxers, many other promoters are desperate to keep public hall boxing going all over the country. I am pleased to report that groups of these promoters have drawn together to plan concerted action and have chosen to consult the Board as well. The Board Stewards are keen to work with them to keep the grass roots of the sport not just alive but flourishing.

Looking back over recent months many boxers stand out. We have seen the superb form of British and European light-heavyweight champion, Crawford Ashley, the thrilling performances of Robin Reid as WBC super-middleweight champion, and the magical skills and show biz verve of Naseem Hamed. Then there has been the emergence of the likes of Spencer Oliver, Ryan Rhodes and the "Mighty Atom", Ady Lewis.

In spite of all the pressures and problems I look ahead with eager anticipation, and, while there is much yet to do, there is plenty of goodwill on which to build. Enjoy the book.

Sir David Hopkin: Long May He Rest

by Leonard "Nipper" Read *(Chairman, British Boxing Board of Control)*

The death in August of Sir David Hopkin, the President of the British Boxing Board, was a tremendous blow to all connected or concerned in boxing.

His presence at ringside for so many championship contests was an indication of his interest and love of the sport.

He often joked that due to his lack of height he was able to get a better view than the rest of the officials, as he was able to see *under* the bottom rope.

David may have been short in stature but he was a giant of a man in other ways, as anyone who saw him officiate at a Board Meeting can testify.

He first became involved with the Boxing Board in the early 1950s when he joined the Southern Area Council.

At that time, Jack Solomons, the famous promoter, was predominant in the Area and David, who was then working at the Director of Public Prosecutions' office, soon found himself deeply involved in the politics of boxing administration.

His love of the sport and his skill at legal argument and disputation quickly identified his potential and he progressed through the various stages until 1983 when he was appointed Chairman of the Board.

Consequently, he became senior Vice-President of The World Boxing Council, where his influence in determining policy was considerable. His sometimes lengthy exchanges of views with the president of that organisation, Jose Sulaiman, were anticipated with relish by all those attending and often provided the highlight of the conventions.

I had the great good fortune to know David Hopkin for over 40 years. We met in the early '50s when I was a young detective and he was a legal attache at the Director of Public Prosecutions' Office.

From that time on we were concerned together in the prosecution of a number of serious cases, culminating with the conviction of the Kray brothers and members of their "firm" in 1969.

David's work on this case was commendable and there is no doubt that he was instrumental in a very positive way in so preparing the cases that convictions resulted.

David could always be relied upon in a crisis, so, when the judge late on Friday night at the commencement of the Kray trial, ordered the jury to be inoculated he rose to the occasion. One telephone call secured the services of the Board's Senior Medical Officer, Dr Adrian Whiteson, who, deserting a waiting-room full of patients, presented himself at the Old Bailey with his black bag to ensure that none of the jurors would fall foul of the epidemic then sweeping the country.

David was a most enthusiastic supporter of the European Boxing Union and was for many years a forceful member of the EBU Council. His fluency in Italian was of considerable advantage to him in this regard.

He was also always a major player on the international scene, where he was one of the first senior executives in boxing to advocate a common set of medical and boxing rules.

Not a demonstrative man, but one who made others aware of the fact that, like them, he was a devotee who loved the sport of boxing, to which he gave his time and his considerable talents, Sir David will be sadly missed by so many boxing people who held him in great respect and affection.

His contributions to boxing at domestic and international level were often underrated, but those who knew and worked with him were aware of the tremendous impression he was able to assert through his dynamic leadership and feeling for the sport he loved.

British Boxing Board of Control Awards

The Awards, inaugurated in 1984 in the form of statuettes of boxers, and designed by Morton T. Colver, the manufacturer of the Lonsdale Belt, are supplied by Len Fowler Trophies of Holborn. Len was an early post-war light-heavyweight favourite. As in 1996, the Awards Ceremony, which has reverted back to a luncheon format, is due to be held this coming Autumn in London and will again be hosted by the Lonsdale International Sporting Club's Bernard Hart, the Managing Director of Lonsdale Sports Equipment Ltd, and sponsor of the Awards.

British Boxer of the Year: The outstanding British Boxer at any weight. 1984: Barrry McGuigan. 1985: Barry McGuigan. 1986: Dennis Andries. 1987: Lloyd Honeyghan. 1988: Lloyd Honeyghan. 1989: Dennis Andries. 1990: Dennis Andries. 1991: Dave McAuley. 1992: Colin McMillan. 1993: Lennox Lewis. 1994: Steve Robinson. 1995: Nigel Benn. 1996: Prince Naseem Hamed.

British Contest of the Year: Although a fight that took place in Europe won the 1984 Award, since that date, the Award, presented to both participants, has applied to the best all-action contest featuring a British boxer in a British ring. 1984: Jimmy Cable v Said Skouma. 1985: Barry McGuigan v Eusebio Pedroza. 1986: Mark Kaylor v Errol Christie. 1987: Dave McAuley v Fidel Bassa. 1988: Tom Collins v Mark Kaylor. 1989: Michael Watson v Nigel Benn. 1990: Orlando Canizales v Billy Hardy. 1991: Chris Eubank v Nigel Benn. 1992: Dennis Andries v Jeff Harding. 1993: Andy Till v Wally Swift Jnr. 1994: Steve Robinson v Paul Hodkinson. 1995: Steve Collins v Chris Eubank. 1996: P. J. Gallagher v Charles Shepherd.

Overseas Boxer of the Year: For the best performance by an overseas boxer in a British ring. 1984: Buster Drayton. 1985: Don Curry. 1986: Azumah Nelson. 1987: Maurice Blocker. 1988: Fidel Bassa. 1989: Brian Mitchell. 1990: Mike McCallum. 1991: Donovan Boucher. 1992: Jeff Harding. 1993: Crisanto Espana. 1994: Juan Molina. 1995: Mike McCallum. 1996: Jacob Matlala.

Special Award: Covers a wide spectrum, and is an appreciation for services to boxing. 1984: Doctor Adrian Whiteson. 1985: Harry Gibbs. 1986: Ray Clarke. 1987: Hon. Colin Moynihan. 1988: Tom Powell. 1989: Winston Burnett. 1990: Frank Bruno. 1991: Muhammad Ali. 1992: Doctor Oswald Ross. 1983: Phil Martin. 1994: Ron Olver. 1995: Gary Davidson. 1996: Reg Gutteridge and Harry Carpenter.

Sportsmanship Award: This Award recognises boxers who set a fine example, both in-and-out of the ring. 1986: Frank Bruno. 1987: Terry Marsh. 1988: Pat Cowdell. 1989: Horace Notice. 1990: Rocky Kelly. 1991: Wally Swift Jnr. 1992: Duke McKenzie. 1993: Nicky Piper. 1994: Francis Ampofo. 1995: Paul Wesley. 1996: Frank Bruno.

Prince Naseem Hamed seen receiving the 1996 British Boxer of the Year award from the BBBoC's Vice-President, "Nipper" Read

Les Clark

Insure You Keep Your Guard Up

Insurance Brokers and Insurance Consultants to the:-
British Boxing Board of Control, Football Association,
F.A. Premier League, Football League, British Olympic Association,
Professional Board Sailors Association, Cricketer's Association,
Spanish Basketball Association, St Moritz Tobogganing Club.

Windsor is one of the world's largest specialist sports, leisure and entertainment brokers, servicing national sports associations, leagues, clubs and players throughout the U.K., Europe, and North America.

While Personal Accident forms the major part of our sports related business, the group can also offer many other types of insurance cover, including Stadium Risks, Commercial Fire, High-Risk Liability, Professional Indemnity, Marine and Aviation - at highly competitive rates.

For sponsors and event organisers we offer wide experience of contingency risks such as Event Cancellation/Abandonment, Prize Indemnity, Death and Disgrace, Bonus Protection, and other insurance-protected sponsorship enhancements and marketing initiatives.

A separate group company provides consultancy on Life Assurance, Group Pensions and Personal Financial Planning.

WINDSOR
Windsor Insurance Brokers Ltd

Lyon House, 160/166 Borough High Street, London SE1 1JR
Tel: 0171 - 407 7144 Fax: 0171 - 378 6676 Telex: 889360
For further infomation ring Jonathan Ticehurst on:
+44(0)171 - 407 7144

Boxing and the Need for Insurance

by Jonathan Ticehurst (Managing Director, Sports Division of Windsor Insurance Brokers Ltd)

To all of us in the insurance industry, our clients are of paramount importance. But, in our case, not only are they important, they are also in the public eye – because our speciality is professional sports and, in particular, boxing.

Boxing is, of course, a national sport, enjoyed at amateur level through schools and clubs by thousands of people and watched at top professional level by millions worldwide through the eyes of television.

How many of us see claims, or potential claims, occurring on television, or read about them in the papers before we get to the office? Millions have seen both promising, mature and lucrative careers ended in a matter of seconds as we have watched late night title fights and supporting bouts from our sitting room chairs.

Many people might wonder how such a direct contact sport can possibly qualify for Accident and Injury insurance cover. The answer lies in the definition of "injury" and the definition of "disablement". For many years, the British Boxing Board of Control has provided and paid for a Personal Accident Policy for every one of its licensed boxers. This includes overseas boxers who have acquired a temporary licence for the purposes of fighting in this country in specific bouts. Traditionally, that policy provided cover for death, blindness, deafness and loss of limbs or parts of limbs whilst the licensed boxer was in the ring or climbing into or out of the ring.

Windsor have been managing the insurance affairs of the world of professional football and cricket for 20 years or more. During this time, various policies have paid out millions of pounds against claims by the national associations, the leagues, the clubs and counties, in respect of players who have gone out of the game early through injury. Some names you will only remember, others you may well have seen or, in early days, even played with, like Ian Storey-Moore, Steve Coppell, Gary Bailey, Alan Brazil, John O'Neill, Norman Whiteside, Gary Stevens, Siggi Jonsson, Mick McCarthy, Paul Elliott, John Fashanu, "Syd" Lawrence, Paul Downton, Nigel Felton, Rodney Ontong and many others.

It was, perhaps, no surprise, therefore, that the Board should turn to Windsor in the course of its review of the insurance cover which has been available historically for boxers. The London insurance market is nothing if not imaginative and when brokers who are experts in their field put their heads together with underwriters who have made it their business to specialise in a particular class of insurance worldwide, then almost anything is possible at an affordable premium. The result was that the Board has now been able to include within their policy the all-important additional cover of Permanent & Total Disablement.

Experience has taught us that where an association, a federation, or affinity body takes out insurance for the benefit of its membership, then any individual member who needs additional or more wide-ranging cover for his own particular needs, should be able to buy his or her own cover as an extension to the group cover. That is what happens in football, cricket and many other sports. The Board's policy provides basic benefits for its licensed members and, although the benefits could not be, and, as is generally known, was never intended to be, regarded as a "retirement fund", the policy is a very important starting point.

The Professional Boxers' Association recognised the hard work and imagination that the Board put into their new policy and were quick to endorse its value to all their members. Perhaps, more importantly, the PBA then worked closely with Windsor in designing tailor-made additional insurance cover which could be purchased, through their association, by members individually.

It is an ideal arrangement. The British Boxing Board of Control, through their own funds, are providing a general benefit for all their licensed boxers which can act as a platform for individual members to buy top-up cover, at their own expense, to suit their own particular requirements and financial obligations. The insurance wraps itself around the actual business of boxing and those in it and responds directly to the risks associated with it. It may be marginally more expensive than "off the shelf" Accident & Injury policies, but then "off the shelf" policies will not respond to the peculiarities and the particular risks associated with a sport having such pugnacious characteristics.

Between them, the Board and the PBA have taken a giant leap forward for the benefit of all professional boxers. We, at Windsor, are happy that another high profile professional sport has the protection from the insurance market that it needs and deserves.

DAI GARDINER BOXING STABLE

sponsored by

Empress Car Sales

PRINCE OF WALES INDUSTRIAL ESTATE, CWMCARN, GWENT.
TEL: 01495 248882

ROBBIE REGAN	Bantamweight (World WBO Champion)
STEVE ROBINSON	Featherweight (WBO Inter-Continental Champion)
NEIL SWAIN	Super-Bantamweight
CHRIS WILLIAMS	Super-Bantamweight
MICHAEL SMYTH	Welterweight
GARETH LAWRENCE	Super-Featherweight
L. A. WILLIAMS	Heavyweight
NICKY HOWARD	Heavyweight
JOHN JANES	Welterweight
HARRY WOODS	Flyweight
JASON THOMAS	Flyweight
CHRIS THOMAS	Flyweight
MARK SAWYERS	Light-Middleweight
KEITH JONES	Featherweight
DAVID ANDREWS	Light-Middleweight
TOMMY JANES	Lightweight
DAVID JAY	Super-Featherweight
HARRY BUTLER	Light-Middleweight
GRANT BRIGGS	Super-Middleweight
IAN TURNER	Bantamweight

LICENCED MANAGER - DAI GARDINER

- TRAINERS -

PAT CHIDGEY

GARY THOMAS ∎ BILLY SUMMERS

Howard Winstone: The Welsh Dragon

by Ralph Oates

It would not be an exaggeration to say that Howard Winstone was without doubt one of the finest post-war fighters to emerge from these shores. The Welshman was a superb boxer with an immaculate left jab which found it's target with uncanny accuracy, often leaving his opponent bemused and the watching fans transfixed with admiration. Complimenting his talent with an abundance of courage and durability, the only weakness in his armour was the absence of a big punch. Had Howard possessed the necessary power to put his opponents away early he would have been practically unbeatable and his name would have been linked with the immortals of the division. However, even without the said knockout punch, he was able to box his way to the top of a very difficult and hazardous mountain, overcoming his share of problems and obstacles, to confirm that he had the heart of the Welsh Dragon.

Howard, born on 15 April 1939 in Merthyr Tydfil, South Wales, to proud parents Howard and Katie, embarked upon the amateur side of boxing at a young age and was showing a great deal of promise. However, fate took a tragic turn during 1956. While at work in a factory, Howard caught his right hand in a machine which resulted in him losing the tops of three fingers. The hands are the very tools of the fighter - and many a boxer would have called it a day and walked away from the sport - yet Winstone showed the fighting spirit which creates champions and decided to continue. Prior to the accident, he was able to punch, but now it was clear that the power would no longer be there and in the future he would have to concentrate more on his boxing skills rather than look for the dynamic knockout.

In this area, Winstone was most fortunate, his mentor being former European, British and Empire Welterweight Champion, Eddie Thomas, a man who knew his boxing and who, in his time, had fought against some of the best fighters at his weight. Thomas helped Winstone to overcome his handicap and thus cultivated his talent to such a degree, that 1958 saw his young charge win the ABA bantamweight title and the gold medal at the Empire Games (now called Commonwealth) which were held in Wales.

The logical step now seemed to be a move into the professional ranks with Eddie Thomas at the managerial helm. Winstone duly made his professional debut at Wembley on 24 February 1959, outpointing his opponent, Billy Graydon, over six rounds and despite being only weeks away from his 20th birthday, his vast potential shone like a bright light in a dark room - clear and obvious for all to see. Even at this early stage, the connoisseurs of boxing were nodding their heads in approval over the performance of the new fistic talent from Merthyr Tydfil.

That same year, Winstone had a further nine bouts, winning them all in style, and displaying the kind of class which suggested a good future was waiting for the Welshman in the 126lbs division.

1960 also proved to be a very busy and successful period, as he continued his winning sequence with 13 bouts against a mixture of fighters who possessed a variation of both style and ability. Thomas was attempting to ensure that Howard's ring education would be complete and full.

On 19 January 1961, Winstone was given his first big test, when matched over ten rounds against Floyd Robertson, the reigning Empire featherweight champion. In his previous contest, Robertson had won the Empire crown, by outpointing the defending title holder, Percy Lewis, over 15 rounds in Belfast. The Ghanaian was an ambitious fighter who had every intention of defeating the Welshman to further his own ring career. The non-title contest went the full distance at Cardiff with Winstone giving his fans a night to remember by winning a good, solid points decision. It was not an easy bout, but once again he had proved that he was a little bit special, with a fine display of boxing against a very good opponent.

After the defeat by Winstone, Robertson went on to challenge twice for the World featherweight crown, being outpointed over 15 rounds by defending champion, Sugar Ramos, in 1964, while a second attempt, which took place in 1966, also ended in failure when the then title holder, Vicente Saldivar, knocked him out in two rounds.

Howard, wearing his Welsh Empire Games attire, proudly shows off his world featherweight championship trophy

Winstone's big chance came in his next contest on 2 May when he challenged Terry Spinks for the British championship at the Wembley Pool. Spinks, from London, was a most accomplished boxer with an impressive amateur record, winning the ABA flyweight crown and the Melbourne Olympic Games gold medal to score a magnificent 1956 double. Spinks brought to the championship contest a professional record of 39 bouts, with 34 wins, four defeats, and one draw.

Terry had won the British crown on 27 September 1960 when he stopped defending titleholder, Bobby Neill, in seven rounds and had retained the championship in a return bout with Neill on 22 November 1960 with a knockout in the 14th. A victory over Winstone would have given Spinks a third notch on the Lonsdale Belt, thus making it his own property.

However, on the night in question, the championship changed hands when Howard proved to be the superior fighter, with the extremely brave Spinks retiring in round ten. They say that Wales is the land of song, well on this occasion Winstone certainly gave his Welsh fans plenty to sing about with a mercurial performance. After the contest, the Lonsdale Belt was presented to Howard, along with a few words of congratulations from the then President and Chairman of the British Boxing Board of Control, J. Onslow Fane.

Winstone then had a deserved break from the ring and did not box again until 24 August, whereupon he outpointed Ghana's Aryee Jackson over ten rounds. Next up came the American, Gene Fossmire, on 4 September. He also went down to a ten-round points loss, but not before giving the Welshman a few problems to overcome. Finland's Olli Maki was next on the busy agenda, meeting Winstone on 20 November. At the end of their eight-round contest, Howard's arm was raised in victory. Once again he had outlined his talent when calling upon his vast repertoire of boxing skills to ensure victory. The Howard Winstone show was still on the road and other major titles looked certain to follow in the future.

The victory over Maki proved to be one of great value for Winstone, since the Finnish boxer went on to challenge Davey Moore for the world featherweight championship in Helsinki on 17 August 1962, where his attempt at the title ended in defeat when stopped in round two. Yet Maki fought on and made boxing history by becoming the first holder of the European light-welterweight title (140lbs).

Howard, now undefeated in 28 fights and his reputation growing with every victory achieved, opened his 1962 account with an eight-round points win over Oripes Dos Santos on 9 January. This was followed by a first defence of the British title on 10 April and although the challenger, Derry Treanor, from Scotland, gave his all, he found that Winstone had an answer to every move he made. Howard thus retained his championship in round 14 and now had a second notch on the Lonsdale Belt.

There was no point in keeping the crown in cold storage and he was quickly back in action the following month, defending the championship against fellow-Welshman, Harry Carroll, on 30 May in Cardiff. Carroll

was a worthy challenger, full of ambition and confidence, undefeated in 18 bouts, with 17 wins and one draw. However, once again Winstone put on a brilliant boxing exhibition to retain his title when Carroll retired from the contest at the end of round six after being given a complete lesson in the noble art.

Howard had now won the Lonsdale Belt outright and was looking towards the European championship held by Gracieux Lamperti of France. Lamperti was a good fighter, but Howard appeared to have all the necessary skills to take the crown from the Frenchman, keeping punch sharp by having two winning bouts in August and one in September.

Then, on 5 November, the unexpected happened, Howard being stopped in two rounds by big punching American, Leroy Jeffrey, in Leeds. This was a shocking setback for Winstone, a man who looked to be heading for the top. Now the Welshman had to somehow pick up the pieces of his shattered career and thus attempt to make some sort of sense of his defeat. When a fighter suffers his first loss in such dramatic circumstances he often has to overcome a psychological barrier of self doubt. The confidence must be restored and he must be able to realise that such a defeat is not the end of the world. However, this can often prove to be very tricky and indeed delicate, since the wrong move can ruin the career of the fighter. This was a fact that Eddie Thomas was well aware of, so his next course of action would be planned with great care. Thomas thus decided to get his charge back into the ring as soon as possible and during the month of December Winstone fought twice, stopping both his opponents in the third round. Eddie did not give his fighter time to ponder or indeed brood over the Jeffrey encounter, a ploy which clearly worked since Howard showed no signs of hesitancy or doubt in his two winning bouts, the magic being still there, along with the confidence.

Come 31 January 1963, Winstone put his British featherweight title on the line against Scotland's Johnny Morrissey in Glasgow, the latter finding the skills of the Welshman too hot to handle before being rescued by the referee in round 11.

On 29 April, Winstone was back in the fray, this time against former European featherweight title holder, Gracieux Lamperti, of France. Although the Frenchman had earlier lost his EBU crown on 19 August 1962, when Italy's Alberto Serti outpointed him over 15 rounds in San Remo, Winstone needed to put on an impressive show. The Welshman did not disappoint, stopping his opponent in round eight.

After a routine eight-round points victory in May against Juan Cardenas the stage was set for Howard to advance his world ranking by challenging for the European title, meeting Serti on 9 July at Maindy Stadium, Cardiff. At the start of the first round it seemed very clear that Howard's concentration was one hundred per cent, with his superb left jab finding its mark with constant regularity. The Italian could not cope with the Welshman, who fought in a world-class manner and was clearly outboxed and outfought in all aspects, the contest being terminated in round 14, with Winstone being declared the new champion of Europe much to the delight of his many fans. Howard thus became the first British holder of the EBU featherweight title since Ronnie Clayton and looked to be a real threat to champion, Sugar Ramos, who had taken the crown from Davey Moore on 21 March.

Billy Calvert was the next man to cross gloves with Winstone, their contest being booked to take place on 20 August in Porthcawl. Calvert had already fought Howard twice in 1959, losing on a seven-round stoppage in the first encounter and an eight-round points decision in their second meeting. He was an experienced fighter who had mixed it with class men like Freddie Gilroy, Love Allotey, Percy Lewis, Floyd Robertson, Olli Maki and Ray Nobile, and, just to add little spice to the proceedings, he had outpointed Leroy Jeffrey over ten rounds on 26 November 1962, a matter of weeks after the American had destroyed Winstone's undefeated record. With the stage set for an interesting battle involving the British and European featherweight championships, could Calvert make it third time lucky in their series of fights, or would Winstone make it a hat-trick?

Although winning clearly, for the first time in his career, Howard was forced to go the full distance of 15 rounds to retain his titles. Despite being given a most difficult time by a determined Calvert, who gave it his very best shot, Winstone was too clever and built up the points as the rounds progressed to put a second notch on Lonsdale Belt number two.

After outpointing Miguel Kimbo Calderin over ten rounds on 20 September, on 9 December Winstone put his British and European titles on the line yet again, this time against the Scot, John O'Brien, in London. Once again emerging supreme, with a clear victory on points over 15 rounds, Winstone won his second Lonsdale Belt outright and looked more and more like a world champion in waiting.

However, 1964 started badly for Winstone when he met world-ranked American, Don Johnson, on a Harry Levene card at the Olympia in London on 28 January. Johnson was a class man who tested Winstone to the full, but the Welshman appeared to have the moves to contain the American and at the end of the ten-round contest looked a good winner, but referee Jack Hart saw it differently and gave the points decision to the visitor. This was without doubt a shock, but since the verdict was a controversial one it did not really do any harm to Howard's reputation on the boxing stock-market. Winstone and manager, Eddie Thomas, were not the kind to sit back and let a slight setback put them off their goal - which was the world title. In their view, and that of many other followers of boxing, Howard was most unlucky not to get the nod over Johnson.

The 24th March saw the Welshman back inside the ring, his opponent being yet another world-ranked man in the shape of Rafiu King of Nigeria. The "Welsh Dragon" pulled off a brilliant ten-round points victory and thus recovered a little lost ground from the Johnson defeat.

Winstone next saw action on 12 May when he defended his European crown against Italy's Lino Mastellaro at the Empire Pool, London. Mastellaro had previously challenged for the European title against the then title holder, Gracieux Lamperti. On that occasion the Italian failed to lift the crown, when Lamperti retained the championship by virtue of a 15 round draw. To his credit, Mastellaro had also defeated John O'Brien on a ten-round points decision during 1963, so the Italian knew his way around the ring and would not be an easy touch. However, once again, Winstone proved that he was without doubt the king of Europe with yet another great performance and retained his title when Mastellaro retired in round eight. The Italian was not in Howard's league and was given a complete boxing lesson.

To complete 1964 there were a further four winning bouts, but the major news in the nine stone division that year was the crowning of a new world champion. On 26 September, a Mexican southpaw by the name of Vicente Saldivar had won the title when forcing the holder, Sugar Ramos, to retire in round 11. So now the Welshman had a new target to aim for in the shape of Saldivar, a man who was going to be a most difficult proposition to handle in the ring.

On 22 January 1965, Winstone once again defended his European crown and for the first time in his professional career he had to travel abroad to Rome in Italy. His challenger was the Frenchman, Yves Desmarets, and under normal circumstances Howard would have been a safe bet to retain his championship. However, past events had proven time after time that when boxing in Europe there was no such thing as a sure thing, a fact confirmed by the many British fighters who had been victims of a bad decision. So Winstone was in a precarious position, not only having to win, but having to win well to ensure that he was given the just verdict. The contest was clearly an incredibly risky one, yet true to form the Welshman put on a sterling performance to outbox the Frenchman over 15 rounds and thus retained his title on points. At that particular moment in time, Europe appeared to have two grades of featherweights operating, Winstone and the rest, the Welshman being way out in front in a class of his own. On the continent he was the master, the undisputed king.

Next, on 29 March, it was time to balance the books - time to put the record straight and right a wrong. At Carmarthen, Howard had a return contest with Don Johnson, winning a ten-round points decision to gain revenge for the defeat he had previously suffered at the hands of the American. This time, Winstone left nothing to chance, using his vast skills to the very full to clinch the verdict. Johnson, to his credit, also contributed much to the contest, having wanted to prove that his victory over the Welshman in 1964 was not just a lucky fluke, giving his all but to no avail. Winstone was on top form, much to the delight of the partisan fans who cheered him all through the exciting encounter.

On 1 June, Winstone crossed gloves with Mexico's Lalo Guerero, an opponent who was not an easy touch. However, after putting up a worthy display, Guerero found that the skill of the Welshman was too much for him to deal with, the referee stopping the contest in round five.

On his way to a seventh-round win over the capable Phil Lundgren (right) in June 1964, this picture shows just what an effective weapon Howard's jab was

The ever busy Winstone had yet another contest on 22 June against Jose Legra. Legra, born in Cuba but based in Spain, was a very talented and dangerous fighter who had ambitions of his own. He was not a journeyman and in Howard he saw a way to the top, a chance to elevate his own position in the world rankings. The pressure was all on Winstone and he was now so close to a world title challenge that a defeat at this stage was unthinkable. Legra, however, gave him a tough night and made him fight for every point of each respective round. Although Winstone was declared the victor on points at the end of ten rounds, the bout provided the many fans in attendance at the Winter Gardens in Blackpool with a fine display of boxing between two men of real class.

Winstone did not go into battle again until 7 September and then it was for the world featherweight championship. Harry Levene had signed reigning title holder, Vicente Saldivar, to defend his crown against Winstone at the Exhibition Hall, Earls Court, London. Fight fans were full of anticipation and Howard, at long last, was going to be given his chance to prove that he was the premier nine stone man in the world. The task, however, would be far from easy, since Saldivar was a magnificent fighter. Since taking the world title from Sugar Ramos, he had defended his Mexican featherweight crown against Delfino Rosales, stopping him in round 11, and while the world title was not officially at stake, a defeat would have put the crown at risk.

The Mexican's first defence of the world title took place on 7 May 1965 against highly-regarded American, Raul Rojas, whose attempt at the championship proved futile when referee, Tommy Hart, stopped the contest in Saldivar's favour during round 15 at the Coliseum, Los Angeles.

Vicente had started his pro career on 18 February 1961, aged just 17 years old, knocking out Babe Palacious in the first round. Born on 3 May 1943, he was a southpaw who would put immense pressure on his opponents during the course of the fight, giving no quarter in the ring and expecting none in return. The fact that the Mexican agreed to defend against Winstone in Britain spoke volumes about the man and the faith he had in his own ability.

The big question mark against the Welshman was his lack of punching power. There was no doubting that Howard had sufficient boxing know-how to account for his opponents in Europe and he also had the necessary skills to outscore many world-ranked men from various other parts of the globe, yet would his expertise in ring science be enough to keep a man like Saldivar at bay for 15 rounds? The Mexican had already shown in previous fights that he could take punishment from opponents with a solid punch and still walk through them to win, leaving Howard's chances looking very slim.

So, at fight time, it was no surprise to find that Saldivar was the firm favourite to retain his title. The Welsh camp was of course confident and Winstone looked in excellent shape. Eddie Thomas had brought his man to peak fitness at the right time, nothing had been left to chance. Some experts held the opinion that Winstone just might be able to both outbox and outspeed the Mexican, but there were just as many sceptics who felt the Welshman would be lucky to last the full distance of 15 rounds. Howard was clearly facing a mission which seemed impossible, against a man considered to be one of the better world titleholders around at the time. That was some tribute when one considers the quality, and indeed calibre, of the other champions at the time, men like Muhammad Ali (heavyweight), Jose Torres (light-heavyweight), Joey Giardello (middleweight), Nino Benvenuti (junior-middleweight), Emile Griffith (welterweight), Carlos Hernandez (junior-welterweight), Ismael Laguna (lightweight), Gabriel "Flash" Elorde (junior-lightweight), Masahiko "Fighting" Harada (bantamweight), and Salvatore Burruni (flyweight). At the time of the fight the United Kingdom did not have one world title holder to boast of and the only British-European champion was Winstone. So a win for the Welshman would give British boxing a massive and much-needed boost.

At the sound of the bell to start round one, Winstone shocked the fans by taking the fight to Saldivar, punch after punch being thrown by the Welshman. Those who expected Winstone to use his fine boxing skill to contain Saldivar could not quite understand the tactics employed by the Welshman, but they seemed to be working since Howard was outpunching and outworking the Mexican world champion and winning the rounds. Many boxers would rather walk on hot coals with their bare feet than fight a southpaw, yet Winstone was handling Saldivar without too many problems, despite taking his share of punches from the Mexican. However, in the later rounds Saldivar started to score with two-fisted attacks, punishing a tired Winstone who was fast running out of steam and, although the fight was close, at the end of the 15-round thriller Saldivar's arm was raised in victory by referee, Bill Williams. The Mexican was still champion of the world.

Howard had been defeated by a fine fighter and while there was an obvious feeling of disappointment in his camp, there was also one of hope - since all was not lost. The Welshman had fought well in his first world title fight and, with a few more impressive wins under his belt, there was every chance that another world championship opportunity would be forthcoming sometime in the future.

Resuming ring action on 13 December against Birmingham's Brian Cartwright, after taking part in a very important, high profile world title bout which attracted a great deal of media cover, the Midlands area featherweight champion was the ideal opponent for Winstone at this stage. Brian was a solid professional who had taken part in 60 bouts, with 41 wins, 16 defeats and three draws. The Birmingham boxer had also contested the vacant British flyweight title, losing a 15-round points decision to Jackie Brown, and had crossed gloves with men like Piero Rollo, Felix Brami, George Bowes, Alan Rudkin, Salvatore Burruni, Evan Armstrong, Lennie Williams, Billy Calvert, Floyd Robertson, Rafiu King, Billy Williams, and Dai Corp. However, when the contest started, he found, like so many before him, that Winstone was in a different class and try as he did he just could not cope with the talented Welshman, with only courage and dignity keeping him going until the referee stopped the contest in round nine. Howard was back on the winning trail, confirming that the defeat by Vicente Saldivar had not hurt his fighting spirit - the "Welsh Dragon" was still very much in contention.

Winstone did not box again until 7 March 1966 and the occasion was a defence of the European title, his opponent being Italy's Andrea Silanos. On the surface, the contest did not look too demanding. However, for the second time during his career Howard had to venture abroad into the lion's den to face his challenger, this time the battleground was to be Sassari in Italy. Winstone and his manager, Eddie Thomas, were fully aware of the dangers of fighting on the other man's turf and of the fact that few if any favours would be given their way. Indeed, the previous British boxer to challenge for a European crown was Scotland's Walter McGowan, who had met Tommaso Galli in Rome, Italy. Galli, defending his European bantamweight title against the Scot, was cheered on by his many fans, yet at the end of the 15-round encounter McGowan appeared to have well won the championship with his clever brand of boxing. Surprisingly, though, Galli kept his title when the bout was declared a draw, so the warning signs were clearly there for Winstone to see. A defeat would not only see him lose his European crown, but also a second chance of challenging for the world title, so the stakes were high.

In the early rounds of the contest, Silanos gave Winstone a few problems, but the Welshman was pure world class and eventually started to box to perfection, giving his challenger little chance of victory. Silanos fought very hard to bring the European featherweight crown back to Italy but his brave attempt came to an end in round 15 when the referee stopped the contest. Howard was still the king of the featherweight division in Europe and this latest victory kept him well in the running for another shot at Vicente Saldivar.

Due to a foot injury, Winstone did not see any ring action until 6 September, when he defended his European championship against Jean de Keers of Belgium. The title bout took place at Wembley and it was clear from the first bell that the Belgian challenger had come to fight and had every confidence of taking the crown back home with him. Making the sixth defence of the European championship, Howard had other ideas on the subject, thus the bout came to an end in round three when the referee stepped in to stop the contest in his favour, De Keers having sustained a badly cut eye and taking heavy punishment when the end came.

The next opponent was old rival, Don Johnson, from America. The two had, of course, fought twice before with the score standing at one win each, the rubber match was to take place in Manchester on 10 October.

Prior to meeting Winstone on this occasion, Johnson had lost his two previous bouts, a ten-round points decision to Borge Krogh in Copenhagen and an eight-round points defeat to Jesus Zarco in San Remo. So it was possible that the American had slipped a little, but a good contest was expected just the same.

Sadly, the fight failed to catch alight and proved to be a disappointment when Johnson was declared a loser in round four by way of a disqualification. The American had landed a series of low blows during the contest and the referee decided that he had no option but to take the necessary action. It was not the ideal victory for Howard, but a win is a win and the Welshman was still very much on course for another world title chance.

The next major challenge for Winstone came from fellow-Welshman, Lennie Williams, an all-action fighter, nicknamed "The Lion". Williams would throw plenty of leather during a contest and was always a danger. The contest which involved both the European and British titles took place on 7 December at Aberavon. Lennie, the Welsh featherweight champion, had taken part in 36 pro bouts, with 33 wins, one draw and two defeats and would not be intimidated by Winstone's reputation, being ready to take over from the defending champion. The "Welsh Dragon", however, was not yet ready to step down. At the Wyvern Sporting Club, Howard introduced Williams to world class boxing, every jab, every move proving to be a painful lesson for the challenger. Williams was brave and kept on going, where a lesser man would have given up the task much earlier, before the referee came to his rescue in round eight. Howard was still the champion of both Britain and Europe and, remarkably, he had also managed to put the first notch on a third Lonsdale Belt.

On 17 January 1967, he accounted for world-ranked Chinese-American, Richie Sue, whom he outpointed over ten rounds at the Albert Hall in London. Sue gave Winstone a tough, competitive fight, but the Welshman boxed his way to a good victory.

Winstone's second attempt at Vicente Saldivar and the world featherweight title took place at Ninian Park, Cardiff on 15 June 1967. Since the pair had last fought, the Mexican had successfully defended his crown three times. Once again Saldivar was the firm favourite to retain the championship and he looked too strong for Winstone. An interesting side-line to the fight was the appointment of referee, Wally Thom, a man who had outpointed Winstone's manager, Eddie Thomas, over 15 rounds in 1951 to take the British and Empire welterweight titles.

Once the contest began, Howard immediately went to work boxing most brilliantly. Saldivar was the bull to Winstone's matador, the Welshman was poetry in motion, working his left hand beautifully, perpetually jabbing it into the Mexican's face. Saldivar just could not pin his man down, while Howard was able to block, slip and roll away from his attacks. Yet, after setting such a fast pace at the start of the contest, Winstone started to slow a little as the rounds progressed and started to take blows to both head and body. However, much to the delight of the fans, the end of the contest was now in sight and the Welshman was still giving Saldivar all kinds of nightmares. The Mexican and his cornermen looked most concerned, the fight being much too close for their comfort and Saldivar knew he had to do something spectacular to save his title.

In round 14, he made his big effort to end the fight, attacking in a whirlwind manner, driving his challenger across the ring and raining punches on Winstone repeatedly to send him down for a count. At times like this it is so very tempting for a fighter to stay down and thus enlist the warm comfort and safety of the canvas while the referee tolls out the full ten seconds. The body is painful and every muscle appears to ache, yet this is the ultimate test - the moment of truth. It was now not just the winning of the championship for the Welshman, it was a matter of pride and courage and he again showed he had more than his share of these two attributes, standing up on legs of jelly as the count reached eight and bravely lasting out the round. After avoiding a number of Saldivar's damaging blows in the 15th and final round with his clever footwork and defensive skills, there was a buzz of excitement amongst the spectators who optimistically felt that, despite the bad 14th round, Winstone had scored sufficient points in the early stages of the contest to take the decision, and the unhappy look in the Mexican corner seemed to confirm that view. Although the fans were fully expecting to see a new world champion crowned, there was to be no coronation on this night, Thom raising the arm of Saldivar, who was still king of the featherweights.

Many fight experts felt that Howard was more than just a little unlucky not to have taken the decision, but Winstone, ever the gentleman and good sportsman, accepted the result with good grace. Both men had given their all in a punishing contest and in so doing had built a bridge of mutual respect and friendship.

Following his great performance, the Welshman was given a third opportunity to win the world title on 14 October. This time, Howard had to travel to Mexico City to face Saldivar and thus had the difficult task of getting acclimatised to the high altitude of the country. As before, Saldivar was the firm favourite to retain his crown. After all, if Winstone could not defeat the Mexican on British soil, what possible chance would he have in the champion's backyard?

As in their previous contests, Howard fought well from the first round, giving the Mexican a boxing lesson - he was the teacher and Saldivar the pupil. However, in round 12, the firepower of the champion brought the contest to a close. Floored for a count, upon getting back to his feet and walking into further punishment, Eddie Thomas threw in the towel to save his gladiator from further pain. It now seemed that Winstone's world title aspirations were finally over, if not his career.

Then Saldivar shocked the world by announcing his retirement from the ring, a decision which gave Winstone's boxing career a new lease of life as both the World Boxing Council and the World Boxing Association versions were now vacant.

Howard was duly matched by the WBC with Japan's Mitsunori Seki for their version of the crown. Seki, like Winstone, was a man who had chased a world-title dream for a number of years without success, his first attempt having taken place in 1961 against Pone Kingpetch for the flyweight crown, when he fought well but lost a 15-round points decision. He next retired in round six against Sugar Ramos in 1964, in a futile challenge for the world featherweight crown, before being outpointed over 15 rounds in 1966 and then stopped in round seven in 1967 by Saldivar. It was felt that the pairing of Winstone and Seki was a championship contest between two men who were surely getting their last chance to win a world title.

The two boxers met at the Royal Albert Hall in London on 23 January 1968 and this time Winstone was the favourite to capture the title. However, Seki was no soft touch and for a time he gave Winstone a few problems. Howard did not seem to have the same snap or sharpness of old, even his left jab seemed slower, and it was more than possible that the three gruelling wars with Saldivar had taken quite a lot out of him. The Welshman eventually started to get his boxing together and began to dictate the contest, the bout being over in round nine when referee Roland Dakin stepped in to stop the proceedings in Howard's favour, with Seki being too badly cut over the right eye to continue. The enthusiastic fans invaded the ring - at long last Howard Winstone had made it, he was the world featherweight champion. Winstone's old opponent, and now good friend, Vicente Saldivar, the former title holder, presented Howard with his world title trophy.

After Raul Rojas won the vacant WBA version of the world title by outpointing Enrique Higgins over 15 rounds in Los Angeles, the ideal contest would have been a Winstone v Rojas WBC - WBA championship bout to produce an undisputed world title holder.

Sadly, that was not to be as Howard was ordered to defend his WBC crown against Jose Legra, an opponent he had outpointed over ten rounds in 1965.

Before that, though, on 9 April 1968, Howard engaged in a ten-round non-title contest at Wembley, his opponent being Jimmy Anderson, a hard-punching fighter who had put his name in the record books by becoming the first-ever holder of the British junior-lightweight title (now called super-featherweight). Anderson, full of confidence and fire, proved just how dangerous a puncher he was by flooring Winstone in the first round, before Howard boxed his way to a good ten-round points victory.

While brilliant by normal standards, Winstone still appeared to be missing a little of the old magic and, at the age of 29, it seemed that the sun was beginning to set on his career. The Welshman had been a professional for nine years and had taken part in 66 bouts. The skills were still there, but the moves were a little slower than they once were.

Sometime later, Howard was awarded the MBE in the Queen's Birthday list, an honour which was well deserved.

On 24 July, Winstone made the first defence of his title against Jose Legra at the Coney Beach area in Porthcawl. There was every indication that the championship would change hands, since Legra was a very talented boxer who was at his peak, while the champion was showing signs of deterioration. The fans hoped for the best but, in truth, feared the worst.

The tension before the fight was terrific with every boxing enthusiast in Britain willing the Welshman on, hopeful that he could dig down once more into his fighting soul and produce another winning performance. His chances of doing that looked distinctly bleak when moments after the bell sounded to start round one Legra sent him crashing to the canvas with a well delivered bolo blow, the punch immediately closing his left eye, thus reducing even further the odds of a Welsh victory. Winstone beat the count and took the fight to Legra, only to be floored for a second time and at this stage a first round defeat looked more than a possibility.

Although somehow making it to the bell, Winstone looked a beaten fighter, but did not recognise the word "quit", it not being part of his boxing vocabulary. In the rounds which followed, Howard fought back bravely and at

Howard and Bronwen in relaxing mood

times appeared to turn back the clock, with his left jab giving Legra problems. However, it was to be a lost cause. Defeating the Cuban with two good eyes was a tough enough task, but with just one good eye, it was impossible and he was in a sorry state when Harry Gibbs stepped in to stop the contest in round five, awarding the world title to Legra.

It was a heart-breaking moment, yet Howard, who had given his very best, had nothing to be ashamed of and had lost like a champion, fighting to the very end.

Winstone later retired from the sport, leaving a void which would be very difficult to fill, having served boxing well over the years. His name going hand in hand with pride and honour - a fine advertisement for the game.

I recently asked former fighter and now Welsh Area secretary, Dai Corp, his opinion about Howard. "When people talk and try to compare Howard with today's champions they should first take a look at his record, which speaks for itself. Sixty-seven contests, of which he lost six, and no "padded record", how many "class" boxers have that many bouts today? Seventeen British, European and world championship contests, all over 15-rounds, or less, ten wins inside the distance. Two Lonsdale Belts outright, one notch on the third. Howard was a credit to boxing inside the ring and a gentleman outside. Many of today's so-called "world" champions would do well to follow in the Merthyr Marvel's footsteps." Few, if any, would argue with Dai's sentiments.

I then spoke to Howard on behalf of the Yearbook. The former world champion, who has three sons, Howard jnr, Wayne and Roy, twin daughters Fay and Benita, and stepson Alan, still lives in Merthyr with his second wife, Bronwen.

(Ralph Oates) Why did you choose not to box on after the Legra defeat and thus attempt to win a third Lonsdale Belt outright, since you only needed two more victories to accomplish the said task?

(Howard Winstone) To be honest, I was having weight problems and felt it was best to call it a day, rather than continue. After all, I had been boxing for a long time.

(RO) Was there a reason for not meeting Leroy Jeffrey again?

(HW) We did try to get a return with Jeffrey, but the fight just did not come off. However, Billy Calvert beat him and I defeated Billy three times, so I draw some consolation from that fact.

(RO) During your career you won, of course, the British, world and European titles. Why didn't you challenge Floyd Robertson for the Empire crown after outpointing him in a non-title bout?

(HW) Yes, I would have liked to have fought Floyd again, with the championship on the line, but the fight just was not made.

(RO) What are your views about the many and various boxing organisations which operate today?

(HW) I prefer to see one champion at each weight, it's less confusing, but if this situation gives the fighters a chance to make more money, then good luck to them.

(RO) Who was your favourite old-time boxer?

(HW) I have two – Sugar Ray Robinson and Muhammad Ali – and both were a joy to watch.

(RO) Do you have a modern-day favourite?

(HW) There are a number of boxers whom I like, but Robbie Regan rates high on my list.

After I bid farewell to Howard, I started to think about the critics who from time to time knock boxing for one reason or another. However, while the game produces men like Howard Winstone the sport will always be able to hold its head high.

Although Vicente Saldivar sadly passed away in 1985, his name will always be linked with Howards, since both he and the Welshman fought to the very limit in their three world championship bouts.

The Welshman is a walking example of all that is good in boxing, and thus deserves all the joy and honours which have come his way over the years. Wales, and indeed the whole of Britain, can feel very proud of Howard Winstone, "The Welsh Dragon".

Tania Follett: Britain's First Woman Boxing Manager

by Ralph Oates

In the 1995 British Boxing Board of Control Yearbook I interviewed Carol Polis (First American female boxing judge), Lisa Budd (First British MC), Tania Follett (Britain's first woman to be licensed as a second), Katherine Morrison (first Scottish lady promoter), and Jackie Kallen (a female American boxing manager).

Since that occasion, Tania Follett has once again made history when she became Britain's first woman boxing manager in 1997. On behalf of the Yearbook, I contacted Tania and asked for her opinions about various aspects of the game.

(Ralph Oates) Were you confident that your application to become a manager would be successful or did you have any self doubt?

(Tania Follett) I was always confident and positive that I would succeed in obtaining my manager's license, because I felt that it was a natural progression from my seconds' and agents' licenses.

(RO) Having worked your way through the boxing ranks, so to speak, you clearly know the fight game. However, do you feel that your dealings with promoters will be more difficult than that of your male counterparts?

(TF) I imagine a lot of promoters will see me as a soft touch to begin with, and may not take me seriously. As a manager, my main concern will be for my boxer and his career and I will be as ruthless as I have to be to obtain the best deal possible for him. So don't say you haven't been warned.

(RO) When you sign on a fighter, what attributes will you look for?

(TF) The basic attributes I will be looking for are a good all-round boxing foundation which you can build upon, a high standard of fitness, determination, dedication, and a good attitude.

(RO) Do you feel that you will be able to bring something new to boxing management?

(TF) Yes, I think I can. I would like to see the role of the manager perceived by boxers as being an enhancement to their career, rather than a hindrance. I believe that managers should work for the boxer, and that everybody in a team is equal and all play a part in obtaining the best results. I am also willing to try new ideas, rather than stick with the more traditional ways, and feel I am very approachable. I listen to the individual's needs and never lose sight of the fact that I am dealing with people's lives.

(RO) Who in boxing do you look up to most and why?

(TF) Evander Holyfield. He is the true example of what a champion should be, having great presence, deep beliefs in himself, spurred on by his faith, and a strong commitment to boxing. A fantastic role model and ambassador for the sport.

(RO) What is the best advice you have ever been given?

(TF) Nothing really comes to mind, but people have always given me little pointers and suggestions, the common theme being to basically keep working hard.

(RO) What is the worst advice you have ever been given?

(TF) Nothing I could say in a book which could be printed.

(RO) Have you ever had moments of doubt and felt that, in boxing, you had picked the wrong career?

(TF) Sometimes, when things go wrong, we all have moments of doubt, but something good is always around the corner which picks you up and drives you on. I have never felt that boxing was not right for me, or that I was not right for boxing.

(RO) What did you do before you entered the world of boxing?

(TF) I worked with animals and in the sport and leisure industry. I would love to make a full-time career out of boxing one day.

(RO) What is your opinion about the various different boxing organisations, such as the WBC, WBA, IBF, and WBO. Do you feel that boxing would be better served to go back to the one champion, one weight situation or do you see any advantage in there being at least four champions at each weight?

(TF) In light of the recent mismatches and fight fiascos, the alphabet organisations need a good kick up their own complacency to show them the way. As for the one champion, one weight situation, unfortunately, I cannot see it working today. Obviously, with more than one champion at each weight, more title fights mean more boxers get the chance to earn good money, and more media interest in the sport is generated.

(RO) Do you have a view with regards to the age limit of boxers, bearing in mind that George Foreman is still in action?

(TF) My view is that if it is not detrimental to their health or to boxing in general, it's fine by me, although George Foreman is an exception to the rule.

(RO) In our last interview you stated that your favourite boxers were James Toney and Evander Holyfield. do you have any others that you might now like to add to the list?

(TF) I'm afraid it's another American – Ronald "Winky" Wright. I love that style of fighter.

(RO) Do you have a favourite old-time fighter?

(TF) The man who was probably the most complete fighter of all time - Sugar Ray Robinson.

(RO) When you watch old films and videos of fighters

of the past in action how do you feel they compare with boxers of today with regards to skill, technique, and fitness?

(TF) I do not feel that you can compare modern-day boxers with the boxers of yesteryear in any way. Today's boxers are the best of their generation, just as boxers of the '30s, '40s, and '50s were the best of their times.

(RO) What annoys you most in boxing?

(TF) Politics, time wasting, two-faced people, and those who are narrow minded.

(RO) Have you noticed a change in attitude towards you since your appointment to the management side of boxing?

(TF) Ask me the same question when I have had a year as a manager and I am sure the answer will be yes, but at the moment the answer is no.

(RO) Would you like to see other women involved in boxing and what is your view about women boxing?

(TF) Of course I would, there is a lot of room in the sport for everyone. Womens' boxing has become very popular in America and in Europe, where it seems to be accepted. I do not think it could support itself in Britain without being affiliated to mens' professional boxing, something I feel has already been proven. When the first womens' show was held in this country there was only a novelty interest, but this could change if they were shown on the same bills as the men. The other problem is the quality of the opponent. There are only a handful of good women boxers in the world and only the fight fans can determine if it is to be accepted in Britain.

(RO) I know you have a great interest in music, what is your favourite style of music?

(TF) I like most kinds, but my favourites are R'n'B and dance.

(RO) Do you have any other favourite sports?

(TF) My other sporting interest is football, and I love Arsenal with a passion - C'mon you "Gunners".

(RO) What ambitions do you have for the future?

(TF) My main ambitions are obviously to manage a world champion, but at this stage of my career a Southern Area champ would do nicely.

(RO) Now the million dollar question. What made you want to become a boxing manager?

(TF) Because I wanted to be involved with the best sport in the world at a higher level than I already was. If someone had predicted to me that in January 1993 I would be interviewing Lennox Lewis, in March 1993 I would be assistant press co-ordinator of the Lennox Lewis tour of Great Britain, and within another six months I would make history by becoming the first woman to be licensed to work in the corner, I would have said they were barking mad. It paved the way for the start of the arduous task of being accepted and allowed to work in what is a male-dominated sport. Upon reflection, in the beginning it was unbelievably hard to make any headway and I still think women in boxing will never truly become accepted. This is not a feminist issue, just an observation based on experience. My initial breakthrough, gaining a seconds license, at the time was something I just strove towards. However, it really was a bigger issue for many reasons. For myself, it became a foundation from which to build my boxing career, while for women who wanted to pursue a career in the sport, I suppose it opened a door, or gave them some sort of lever. Sadly, those of preformed opinions showed their bias towards the change, something which became apparent when opportunities presented themselves to me.

Becoming a manager, hopefully, means that I will now be more in control over my own destiny.

(RO) On behalf of the Yearbook I thank you for your time and wish you well in the future.

There is no doubt that Tania will have some very difficult times ahead - a fact that she is fully aware of. However, Britain's first woman boxing manager has a keen sense of purpose and is more than capable of being very successful in time.

Tania: Striking a pose outside the ring

No Substitute For Experience

by Bob Lonkhurst

Whatever the sport, officials at all levels are frequently subjected to criticism and abuse. In Britain, however, criticism of professional boxing referees is extremely rare. This is due largely to the fact that we have some of the finest in the world and yet there is justifiable concern that our top officials receive too few world title appointments in the United States. Two of the top British referees are Roy Francis and Larry O'Connell, who, between them, have officiated as referees or judges at more than 70 world championship contests. Both were top class amateur boxers, who, during their careers, beat some of the best men in the world.

Between them they had more than 350 contests, including many at international level. Both also spent several years coaching at top London amateur clubs before being appointed as referees.

In his days as a fighter, Roy Francis of Brixton was one of the finest amateurs in Britain. Now, more than 40 years later, he is one of the most respected referees in the world. Very much the man in charge, he stands no nonsense during the course of battle. He is a commanding figure with the bark of a sergeant major, yet he is highly respected by the men who fight. His story is a moving one; that of a hard working man, who, throughout his life, has been dedicated to the sport of boxing.

Brought up in the Old Kent Road area of south-east London, Roy was taught to box by his father when he was a boy. Frequently they had sessions with the gloves in the living room of their terraced house at 5 Lorncliffe Road, just behind the Thomas A' Becket pub. Often, Roy was not allowed to go out until he had done a stint with his dad.

As a youngster, Roy was a keen all-round sportsman. By the age of 15 he was a fine swimmer, had won schoolboy and Federation of Boys Club boxing championships, and represented London schools at football. After being invited to Chelsea Football Club for a trial, a career within soccer was a distinct possibility. The great Ted Drake, who ran the youth set-up at the club was impressed with Roy, but advised him that he would have to make a choice between football and boxing. He chose the latter, and it is a decision he has never regretted.

Born on 14 March 1935, Roy started boxing at the age of 12. His first amateur club was the Lynn at Walworth Road, but, when he became unhappy there, he moved to Battersea. Then, after winning a couple of open competitions staged by the Brixton Ivy Leaf Club, he was invited to join them on a permanent basis. It proved to be a successful move, and in 1953, just before his 18th birthday, Roy Francis exploded on to the amateur scene in a big way.

In March he won the London South-East Divisional light-middleweight championship by stopping Leo Steinbrecker in the opening round, having knocked out reigning champion, Terry Wakeling of Lynn, in the semi final. The following month his big punching brought him the London title with second-round stoppages over Ron Garnett (semi-final) and J. O'Connor (final).

At this point in time, Francis was employed as an eel dresser, and a few weeks earlier had unsuccessfully challenged the TV Panel in "What's My Line".

Back in the ring, he progressed to the 1953 ABA light-middleweight final by beating Peter Sellick (Sidmouth). Big swinging right handers caused serious damage to his opponents mouth, and the fight was stopped in the third round. In the final, Roy came up against the talented Bruce Wells (RAF), whose skills were sufficient to overcome the Brixton boy's aggression and enthusiasm to take a points decision.

The ability of the youngster was duly recognised, and, even before his defeat by Wells, he was selected to represent London ABA against Holland in Amsterdam and Rotterdam on 11 and 12 May. To his dismay, both matches were cancelled due to the fact that no suitable halls could be found. On 29 May, however, he received just reward, winning his first full international vest when he represented England against Wales at Cardiff, and beat John Warren on points.

Bruce Wells, meanwhile, had gone to Warsaw, where after four hard-fought contests, he became Britain's lone gold medal winner at the European Championships. On returning home he represented the Royal Air Force against London ABA at an open-air show on Clapham Common on 4 June. His opponent was Roy Francis, fresh from his international debut, and anxious to avenge the defeat suffered in the ABA final.

Wells clearly won the opening session with skilful boxing, but Francis began to take over in the second. Throwing punches from every angle, he roughed up the European champion and completely unsettled him. Suddenly, with about 30 seconds of the final round left, a cut appeared under Wells' right eye and the referee promptly stopped the fight. The crowd were stunned, but Roy had achieved what he set out to do.

Shortly after the Wells' contest, he was called up for National Service and enlisted as a trooper with the Royal Tank Regiment. With his considerable boxing experience, he settled in well and was selected for trials at Tidworth, staged to select an Army team to meet Wales. Although confidently expecting to be picked, he suffered a shock defeat to staff sergeant, Colin Melville, which set him back quite a bit. He did represent the British Army against Ulster in Belfast in January 1954, but lost on points to Martin Loughran. Two months later he was outpointed by lance corporal Bernard Waters (Royal Signals) in the British Army light-middleweight final at Tidworth.

Early in 1955, Francis returned to his best form. He represented the Army against Wales in Cardiff, and against Ulster in Belfast, and then boxed for the 20th Armoured Brigade against the Rest of BAOR in Rome, winning all contests on points. In January, he also boxed for the ABA against Scotland and stopped Jim Doig in the first round.

In April the same year, Roy won the Army light-middleweight title at Bristol by outpointing old foe, Peter Sellick (2nd Battalion REME). Two weeks later, however, he suffered a shock defeat in the BAOR inter-unit final at Demold in Germany when he was knocked out in the first round by the comparatively unknown, Lieutenant Kelly of the Lancashire Fusiliers. Boxing at full middleweight, Roy put Kelly down for a short count, but when the action resumed, both threw heavy right hooks which connected. Both men hit the canvas and, although Kelly struggled up, Roy failed to beat the count. His defeat was one of the biggest shocks in Army boxing that season.

The result proved to be just a temporary setback, and before the end of the month, Francis won the Imperial Services title at Aldershot by stopping Ken Cook (RAF) in the second round. The victory took him to the semi-finals of the 1955 ABA Championships and by this stage of his career Roy had lost just 18 of more than 200 contests. That season alone he had won 28 out of his last 30.

In the ABA semi-final, Francis faced former champion, Bernard Foster, from the Birmingham-based Mitchell Butler Amateur Boxing Club. Foster was a known hitter who caused a sensation when he stopped Bruce Wells in 92 seconds of the first round to win the 1952 ABA light-middleweight title. At the time it was his 31st first-round victory in his last 41 contest. Despite his own big-hitting capabilities, Roy Francis went the same way, and was knocked out by two tremendous right hooks after just 50 seconds of the opening round.

After being discharged from the Army in the summer of 1955, Roy became a lift engineer, and resumed his amateur career with the Brixton Ivy Leaf Club. He was soon winning again and was selected to represent the ABA against Denmark. Bernard Foster, meanwhile, had been chosen to box in the international against Russia at Wembley on 12th October, but when he failed to make the light-middleweight limit, Francis was promoted to take his place.

Roy faced the experienced Carlos Dzhanerjan who was completely lacking in confidence, being continually forced back by the Brixton man's southpaw jab. When the Russian did get close, he ducked his head and closed his eyes like a novice. In the second round a flurry of left hooks crashed on to Dzhanerjan's nose sending blood spurting everywhere. More big hooks floored the Russian and had him hanging on grimly on a number of occasions. In the final round, Roy became a little too confident and left himself open to heavy counters from the Russian. Despite being staggered a couple of times, Roy recovered well and regained the initiative to finish well on top. Then, to the amazement of all, the Russian judges gave a split decision against him. The crowd were so incensed that there was a demonstration of slow hand-clapping, stamping and booing which lasted for several minutes, and the MC was unable to announce the next contest.

Roy's performance made him an automatic choice to represent the ABA against the United States at Wembley just two weeks later. Although his opponent was the highly talented Frankie Davis, the star of the American team, Roy turned in a performance which was the high point of his fine career. Davis was a tremendous hitter who had won 66 contests in a row, mostly inside the distance, and was expected to add the Brixton man to his long list of victims. Francis, however, hadn't read the script, and ended the fight after just 56 seconds of the first round. Davis had backed him against the ropes with hefty left hooks, and, as he confidently moved in for the kill, Roy let go a mighty right hook. It crashed against the American's jaw sending him spinning to the canvas. When the count reached ten he was still motionless. Roy's victory was one of amateur boxing's greatest upsets of all time, and won him the admiration of millions of live television viewers.

Roy Francis (left) meets the American, Frankie Davis

The following week, Roy proved that his victory over Davis was no fluke when he knocked out Tommy Evans at Eltham in the opening round. Evans, an Australian from HMS Vengence, was another knock-out specialist who had beaten middle and cruiserweights.

Before the end of the year, Francis appeared in three further representative matches. Boxing for England against Wales on 9 November, he outpointed C. Wood, and three weeks later beat H. Studemund on points, whilst representing London against Berlin. He then suffered a setback, losing on points to corporal Ted Batterham when boxing for London against the Army at Seymour Hall. Representing England against Scotland at the Royal Albert Hall in January 1956, Roy suffered another shock defeat when he was outpointed by Hugh Clowes, a hard puncher who had also floored the American, Frankie Davis.

Although he lost on points to South-Eastern Counties champion, Chalky White, Roy recovered some of his form to win the 1956 London South-East Divisional light-middleweight title by stopping Neville Axford in two rounds. In the London semi-finals at the Royal Albert Hall, however, he again met with disaster, being stopped in the second round by Ron Garnett (Earlsfield). The end came after Roy had been hit low. Garnett was severely cautioned by the referee, who then ordered them to box on. Still suffering from the effects of the low blow, Roy was a sitting target and Garnett finished it quickly.

Although he won the Territorial Army title in May 1956, Roy Francis was coming to the end of his amateur career. He had become disillusioned with the ABA over internationals and eventually decided to turn professional. He had a good international record and would undoubtedly have won more representative honours but for being in the same weight division as Bruce Wells, who was always the automatic first choice.

Although he turned professional under Jim Wicks, it was not a successful move, and he had just three pro contests. The first was at Harringay on 2 October 1956 on the undercard of the Dick Richardson v Ezzard Charles bill. He met Freddie Cross of Nuneaton, and was knocked out in the fifth round. Despite stopping Ron Wild in three at the Royal Albert Hall the following month, Roy was knocked out in the second round by Dennis Booty (Stepney) early in 1957 and decided it was time to quit. He had just got married and openly admits, "You have to be honest with yourself if you don't think you can make it in this game."

With boxing in his blood, it was important that Roy stayed in the sport. Shortly after retiring he was offered the job of coach at the Robert Browning Boys Club at Walworth, a post he readily accepted, and literally ran the club for 26 years. Not only did he train youngsters seven evenings a week, he did almost everything else as well to keep the club running. When he eventually called it a day, the club only survived for another two years.

Roy had been one of the finest amateur coaches in Britain, having trained the England team for six years and travelled the world with them. He coached 11 junior and senior ABA champions, including John H Stracey, who he had for five years before John joined Repton, and Johnny Clark for 11 years until he turned professional. When Mark Rowe was a promising young professional, Roy frequently sparred with him.

It was in 1980 when Roy was persuaded to turn to refereeing by his good friend, and former amateur international, Larry O'Connell. The first contests he handled were two six rounders between Tony Britton and Gary Cooper, and Prince Wilmot and Casley McCallum, at the Anglo American Sporting at Mayfair on 16 March 1981. As a trialist referee, he did not score the contests, this being done by qualified referee, Mike Jacobs, from ringside.

Roy was appointed as a Class "A" Star referee in 1989 and, in November that year, officiated at his first title contest when Donovan Boucher took the Commonwealth welterweight title from Gary Jacobs at Motherwell on 23 November. In March 1990, Roy took charge of his first British title fight, that between Kirkland Laing and Trevor Smith for the welterweight crown.

In September 1991, he took charge of his first world title contest. It was the ill-fated Chris Eubank - Michael Watson bout at Tottenham, which he stopped early in the final round to save Watson from further punishment. Everyone knows of the tragic consequences to Watson, but absolutely no blame lay with Roy, whose stoppage looked perfectly timed. In fact, Watson and his handlers protested bitterly when Roy stepped in.

Working for the WBO, Roy has been a judge or referee for more than 30 world-title fights, duties which have taken him to South Africa, America, France, Italy, Germany, and Ireland. Since becoming a "third man", he has been in the thick of the action on more than one occasion. In 1992, he was hit solidly on the chin (accidentally), by Herbie Hide during his fight with Jean Chanet. "The biggest surprise to Herbie was the fact that I didn't go down," said Francis dryly when recalling the incident. He did, however, finish on the floor at York Hall, Bethnal Green on 1 July 1995, amid a rough and tumble between Julius Francis and Scott Welch for the Southern Area heavyweight title.

Courage and determination, alertness, and the ability to make split second decisions, are essential qualities for anyone actively involved in boxing. Roy Francis possesses all of those qualities in abundance, and has used them to good effect on at least two occasions outside the ring.

During 1956, Roy and a colleague were working on a lift in a high building at Clerkenwell when they heard screams for help. On going to a window, Roy saw a man hanging by his collar from scaffolding which was starting to collapse. Risking their lives, Roy and his pal climbed to the 14th floor, only to find that the victim had a scaffold pole impaled in the back of his head.

As they climbed through a bathroom window, the scaffolding started to pull away from the building. Whilst the dangerous structure swayed and creaked around them, they managed to strap the injured man to some boards and manoeuvre him through the window and into the building. Firemen were called, and rescued Roy and his mate just before the scaffolding collapsed. Although an ambulance conveyed the victim to hospital, he died later that day.

Roy's bravery was officially recognised, and he was awarded the Queen's Commendation for Bravery. This was published in the London Gazette on 12 February 1957 and he was presented with a certificate commemorating the award at a ceremony at the Ministry of Labour.

During the mid-1980's, Roy was on holiday in Spain when his bravery and quick thinking saved a young man from drowning in a hotel swimming pool. Roy was fast asleep at the pool side when his wife woke him because the lad was in serious difficulty at the deep end. The unfortunate swimmer had just arrived at the hotel on his honeymoon, and jumped straight into the pool. The sudden change of temperature of the water effected him and he lost control. Whilst the others watched, Roy dived straight into the pool and brought the youngster to the side, where he administered first aid. A British Government Official who was holidaying at the hotel, praised Roy for his quick thinking action, but, despite promising to put him forward for an award, Roy heard no more of the incident.

Outside boxing, Roy was employed as a security officer with the De Beer Diamond Company at Hatton Garden for more than 20 years until he retired in March 1995. He has been married to Jean for 40 years, having met her when he was just 13 years old and they have three grown-up children and five grandchildren. Roy is a member of the London Ex-Boxers Association and amongst his hobbies is golf.

The efficiency with which Roy controls a fight attracted the attention of the producers of the classic apartheid film "The Power of One", which was shot at Charterhouse School. It depicted the story of a youngster brought up in a prison camp in South Africa, who becomes a good fighter. The climax of the film was a fight under rules, and Roy played the part of the referee. It was a totally new experience, and the fight scene alone took eight hours to film.

The importance of the referee within boxing can never be understated and it is worth recalling the words of Mr Eugene Corri, himself a highly repected official at the turn of the century;

"The referee is the most important personage of the trio in the ring. Yet he must be the least conspicuous. A busybody of a referee is a poor referee, not sometimes, but all of the time."

Roy Francis has never been a busybody referee. He is firm, efficient, and, above all, highly respected by everyone within boxing. He is a fine man, one of great experience as a fighter, trainer, and now as a world-class official. He is a credit to himself and the sport he represents.

Roy Francis counts Manuel Hernandez out in the sixth round at the London Arena in November 1994, leaving his oppenent, Billy Schwer, the victor   Les Clark

Although he was never a professional fighter, Larry O'Connell was a tremendous amateur and beat many of the best men in Britain and Europe in his day. During a long and distinguished career he won a host of titles and, when he retired from boxing at the age of 27, he had won 122 of his 155 contests.

Born at Belvedere, Kent, in 1938, Larry first became involved in boxing at the age of 11 when he joined the Erith Amateur Boxing Club. Having taken part in his first contest a year later, losing on points, he then made steady progress, and, in 1955, became London Junior champion at nine stone seven pounds in Class "B" when he stopped Terry Cole (Hampstead) in two rounds.

Larry remained with the Erith club until he was 17 and then moved to Royal Ordinance Factories (ROF), where he trained under Jimmy McCarthy. "He was the most influential man in my boxing upbringing," recalls O'Connell more than 40 years later. McCarthy had seen Larry box for Erith on many occasions and when he joined ROF told him, "You have a brilliant jab son, use it more often. Why have a fight?" In order to develop Larry's natural weapon to near perfection, McCarthy then tied up his right arm and made him jab with his left for three rounds. Larry was then made to jab in front of a mirror for two hours in order to develop the basics of boxing he had avoided for years.

The move to ROF soon proved a rewarding one because in March 1958, Larry won the London South-East Division lightweight title, following points victories over Len Mills (Lynn) in the semi-final, and George Smith (Sir Phillip Game) in the final. Two weeks later, in the London Championships at the Royal Albert Hall, he beat Paul Warwick (West Ham) in the semi-final, but sustained a cut eye. In the lightweight final, the cut failed to stand up to the big punching of Alex Dunning (Battersea), and the fight was stopped in the first round.

Away from boxing, Larry left Picardy Secondary School at the age of 15 to do a five-year apprenticeship as a hand engraver. In December 1957, at the age of 19, he was married to Beryl, before enlisting for National Service and joining the Royal West Kent Regiment. He subsequently became a Physical Training instructor, which enabled him to progress with his boxing.

In 1960, he won both the Army and Imperial Services championships at light-welterweight. In the Army championships, O'Connell faced stocky Ted Carter (RAOC), the end coming in dramatic fashion. During the first two rounds, despite a considerable reach advantage, Larry had difficulty in coping with his shorter opponent. Only in the final session did he get on top. Then, with just 35 seconds to go, Carter's head smashed into Larry's face and blood poured from an eye injury. The referee stepped in and immediately disqualified Carter.

Although the victory automatically qualified him for the Imperial Services Championships at Portsmouth the following week, the eye injury made this look extremely doubtful. Larry, however, remained optimistic because of a treatment prescribed by Jimmy McCarthy. The injury was bathed with hot and cold water to get the bruising out and then treated with olive oil. Boraxic powder and vaseline were then applied. Not one stitch was inserted and Larry was fit to box just seven days later. It was a treatment he would use for cuts throughout his career.

O'Connell drew a bye in the semi-final and then in the final boxed cleverly and carefully to outpoint Alan Pheby (Navy) to take his second title in a week. The victory took him forward to the ABA finals at Wembley in May.

Although he had won 13 of 15 contests during the season, Larry failed to reach the light-welterweight final, being narrowly oupointed in the semi by the talented 18-years-old Tony Lewis (St Pancras), who was unbeaten in 59 contests.

Two weeks later, O'Connell put up one of the most courageous displays of his career. Representing the British Army against the Polish Army at the Royal Albert Hall, he faced Jerzy Kulej, one of the finest amateurs in Europe, and a man who would go on to win gold medals at the European Championships in 1963 and 1965 in Moscow and East Berlin, respectively. Floored in the opening round, Larry fought back strongly, pushing the great Pole all the way, only to lose an extremely close decision.

Despite his recent defeats, Larry was in good form and turned down the chance of an England international vest to box in the Olympic trials during a match between the Army and Wales at Cwnbran. When his original opponent, Bobby Putz of Cardiff withdrew, Larry faced Bobby Kelsey (Monteagle), a man who was rated as the number one light-welterweight in Britain. Although beaten on points, he came out of the contest with tremendous credit, having made Kelsey work extremely hard for victory.

When the new season commenced, O'Connell's fine form continued. In October, boxing for the Army against the rest at the Garrison Theatre, Tidworth, he outpointed Brian Brazier (1st Queens/Surrey's Regiment). He beat Brazier again three weeks later on a Woolwich Recreation show at Eltham. In November, representing the Army against London ABA, Larry caused a real upset by outpointing Jimmy Davison (Fisher), a recent conquerer of Bobby Kelsey. Boxing brilliantly, he frequently made Davison miss, whilst scoring with his own sharp jabs and counter punches. It was Larry's last contest before being discharged from the Army.

Resuming his ring career with the famous Fitzroy Lodge Club, he was selected to represent England against Scotland at Glasgow on 5 January 1961. He put up a fine performance when stopping Norrie McCulloch in two rounds, although England lost the match 6-4.

Two weeks later, Larry claimed his greatest scalp to date when he outpointed the fine West German, Gerhard Dieter, in an international against Germany at the Royal Albert Hall. He boxed magnificently and, after his victory, Boxing News rated him as the number one light-welterweight in Great Britain.

Larry confirmed his top rating when he outpointed triple schoolboy champion, Richard Atkins (Eltham), in a tight contest at Bermondsey Baths. The following month they met again in the London South-East Divisional Championships at Eltham. The light-welter division was the toughest of the championships and brought together the top men in Britain in O'Connell, Atkins, Jimmy Davison, Eric Russell (ROF), and Eric Cartmel (Covent Garden). Larry beat Davison in a vigorously contested preliminary round, and then outpointed Cartmel in the semi-final. However, when facing Atkins in the final, after three fiercely contested rounds he lost on points.

Larry was extremely disappointed and disillusioned and shortly afterwards announced his retirement from

boxing. After about six months, however, he missed the sport so much that he returned. Following several victories, he won the London South-East Divs light-welterweight title, stopping Terry Clarkson (BRS) in three rounds in the semi-final and outpointing Ian McDonald (Downham Community) in the final.

The following month, Hampstead southpaw, Ronnie Smith, caused a big upset when he stopped Larry in the third round in the London semi-final at the Royal Albert Hall. Having been badly wobbled by a heavy right in the opening round, Larry was floored for a count of eight in the third. When he rose, the contest was stopped, although many onlookers thought it premature because it was a fight he was winning.

At the beginning of 1963, Larry was fourth in the light-welter ratings, having beaten new international, Len Wilson, and regular soldier, Brian Brazier, the ABA champion for the past two years, on two occasions. An eagerly awaited third meeting between them took place at Manor Place Baths. Striving to regain international recognition, Larry attacked throughout the three rounds. At the final bell though, Brazier got the decision, but it was so close it could have gone either way.

Larry O'Connell in fighting pose

Consistent good form earned the Fitzroy Lodge star a recall to the England team, albeit as a late substitute for flu victim Brazier. Boxing against Ireland at the Albert Hall on 31 January 1963, Larry became very much the hero of the night. After being contacted at work during the afternoon of the fight, he had to shed two pounds before entering the ring to face Des Leahy. Then, due to a timekeeper's error, he had to box a four-minute second round. At the end of a hard-fought contest, however, Larry was rewarded with a well-earned decision.

The victory put O'Connell immediately behind Brazier and Dick McTaggart in the ratings, although February turned out to be a month of mixed fortunes. After stopping Steve Cassidy (Liverpool Transport) in two rounds, Larry boxed for a West Ham team against a French invitation squad. Deputising for injured international, Len Wilson, the Fitzroy Lodge boxer sustained a cut right eye against Jacques Bottier and was stopped in the second round. Although the injury was a bad one, Larry again treated it himself using the method learned from Jimmy McCarthy. Incredibly, it healed sufficiently for him to box in the London South-East Divisional Championships at Eltham Baths the following week. He again displayed too much class for Ian McDonald, jabbing with power and accuracy to retain his title on points.

On 11 April, he won the London title at the Royal Albert Hall with points victories over Dennis Delbridge (semi-final) and Lionel Baldwin (final) and, by this stage of his career, had won 103 of 130 contests. In winning the London title, Larry again qualified for the ABA finals at Wembley the following month. In the semi-final, he cleverly out-thought and outboxed Les McAteer (Buckley), but in the final had to bow to the superiority of the legendary Dick McTaggart. The Scot was just too skilful for the young Londoner and his points victory gave him his fourth ABA title.

On 11 July, Larry was the only winner for London ABA against an Italian "B" team at Jessolo, Venice. The team lost 9-1, but he was a unanimous points winner over Sergio Panerini.

In October, he was the only London champion in a match between London and Paris at the Royal Albert Hall. In a 7-3 defeat, he was London's most impressive performer, stopping experienced Paul Cosentino in two rounds. Although the win came by courtesy of a cut eye, the Londoner was well on the way to victory.

On 7 November, boxing for England against Hungary, O'Connell faced yet another top European amateur. Istvan Toth was a powerfully built, hard-hitting, and experienced campaigner, but the Fitzroy Lodge man matched him in every department. Previously unbeaten in internationals, Larry was extremely unlucky to be adjudged a loser on this occasion. When the verdict was announced he shook his head in disbelief, because Toth had been outboxed for most of the fight. Boos from the crowd echoed around the arena and continued well into the next contest.

Two weeks later, representing London ABA against the Army at Manor Place Baths, Larry boxed badly by his standards, but was still good enough to outpoint lance corporal Phil Taylor (RAOC). He was, however, unhappy with his form and, after losing a decision to unheralded Dave Sharrard (Hove) on a small club show, he considered withdrawing from the England team due to face Russia in December.

Fortunately, he changed his mind and, in fact, turned in two solid performances, despite losing on points on each occasion. In Moscow, he was beaten by Yuri Polyakov in a 9-1 defeat and three days later lost to Yevgeny Frolov in Tbilisi. Frolov, another great Eastern block amateur, would go on to win a European gold medal in 1967 by beating another old foe, Jerzy Kulej.

On 30 January 1964, boxing for England against Scotland, Larry was again sadly below his best. Although he just scraped through against the relatively inexperienced 17-years-old Willie Appleby, he needed a big rally in the final round to do so. He did recover some of his form a couple of weeks later, when he outpointed Jimmy Jennings on a West Ham Club show, but in doing so sustained a badly damaged hand. The injury did not respond to treatment, and Larry was forced to withdraw from the London South-East Divisional Championships in March. The injury kept him out of action for some months and it was not until October 1964, when he beat old opponent Dave Sharrard on points, that he looked anything like his old self.

The good form continued and, on 22 February 1965, on a Fitzroy Lodge club show at Manor Place Baths, Larry faced Dick McTaggart in the principle contest of the evening. It was a fight he had been pressing for since their meeting in the 1963 ABA final. In what was his finest performance for a long time, Larry unsettled the brilliant Scot from the start, pressing forward throughout the fight and scoring with good punches to head and body. Despite his considerable skills, Dick found it difficult to respond and Larry's fine display earned him the decision.

The victory over McTaggart was just the tonic he needed after an unsettled period. In March, he again won the London South-East Divisional light-welterweight title by beating Kevin McGee (Fisher), an 18-years-old prospect who had won 51 of 53 contests. O'Connell went on to take the London Championship the following month by outpointing Jimmy Tresham (Chiswick General) in the semi-final, and then taking the decision from fellow-international, Brian Anderson (Middle Row), in the final. What was expected to be a classic turned out to be a tame affair, due to a clash of styles between two vastly experienced men.

The victory took Larry back to the ABA finals at Wembley, where, after beating David Hughes (Bynea), he again faced McTaggart in the final. In an attempt to overcome the southpaw stance of the Scot, Larry was assisted in his corner by Roy Francis. Although Boxing News tipped Larry to take the title, McTaggart showed that he could still turn on the class. He made the Londoner do all the attacking, yet moved out of range to avoid his punches. Despite an aggressive display, O'Connell again found himself on the wrong end of the decision. After the fight he was taken to hospital with a damaged shoulder.

Larry had reached his peak and, despite being selected to box for the London ABA in Frankfurt and Hanover, he announced his retirement after more than 15 years in the amateur game. He did not turn professional because in his words, "My style was not suited to the pro game." More importantly, his hands were extremely important in his skilled career as an engraver and he did not want to risk any serious damage. Instead, he became a coach at the Fitzroy Lodge club for four years. Among the good lads he trained were Jimmy Revie, Johnny Clark, and Johnny Cheshire, all of whom would develop into fine professionals.

In 1977, Larry was granted a British Boxing Board of Control referees' license and the first contest he took charge of was at the Hilton Hotel in London. He was a natural "third man" and after just two years as a Class "B" referee, was promoted to Class "A". Six years later, he was appointed to Class "A" Star, the top grade for a British official.

A striking man, with silver hair and film star looks, Larry O'Connell is now regarded as one of the finest professional officials in the world. Working for the World Boxing Council (WBC), he has officiated at over 40 world title fights as either referee or judge and duties have taken him to Korea, Japan, United States, Ghana, Italy, France, and Mexico. He has also taken charge of numerous European, Commonwealth, and British title fights, as well as continuing to officiate on small hall shows in the Southern Area.

Larry has refereed contests involving George Foreman, Pernell Whitaker, and Mike McCallum, whom he regards as his favourite boxer of all time. Barry McGuigan is his favourite British boxer because; "In my opinion, he was the best pressure fighter Britain has ever had." Amongst contests Larry has judged have been Julio Cesar Chavez v Oscar de la Hoya, Lennox Lewis v Oliver McCall, and Mike Tyson v Frank Bruno (2). He regards the highlight of

his refereeing career as the night he took charge of the Nigel Benn v Chris Eubank (2) contest. He considers that the decision of a draw was absolutely correct.

Larry's expertise as a "third man" was typified in March 1991 when the Sunday Mirror Sports Editorial team selected his handling of the British heavyweight title fight between Lennox Lewis and Gary Mason as the Carlsberg Sports Performance of the Week. He was presented with an engraved tankard and the award was announced in the Sunday Mirror on 10 March.

Larry loves boxing and the people involved in it. "It is essential for the fabric of our society," he remarked convincingly when I asked him for his opinion of the sport. "It provides the best discipline on earth." He loves reunions with old opponents, and two have been very special to him. In 1990, Scottish promoter, Tommy Gilmour, invited Larry to dinner in Glasgow, where he was reunited with Dick McTaggart. It was the first time they had met since their ABA final in 1965. "A reunion with an old opponent is one of the big pleasures in boxing," Larry told me. "No other sport can match the camaraderie."

Another very special reunion for Larry was with the great Pole, Jerzy Kulej, in 1990. They had not seen each other since their fight in 1960, but, one night in 1990, when Larry was refereeing at Battersea Town Hall, Kulej was introduced from the audience. At the time, Larry was unaware of his presence, but the two great ex-amateurs immediately recognized each other. As they came face to face, they opened their arms and fell into a warm embrace. The two men have been friends ever since and have visited

Larry O'Connell, the referee, comes to the rescue of Robert Wright during the third round of his fight with Darren Dyer at York Hall on 26 November 1991
Les Clark

Larry (right) seen with fellow referees, John Keane (left) and Sid Nathan   Les Clark

each others homes with their wives. As a result of their meeting, Larry was invited to Poland in 1993 to referee on the first professional boxing promotion in that country.

Away from boxing, Larry is the president of Erith & Belvedere Association Football Club, vice-president of the Freddie Mills Boys Club, and part of the support group for ex-boxer, Gary Davidson, a long-time sufferer of moto-neurones disease. Larry's hobbies include oil painting and golf and he frequently plays in charity tournaments. He also does after-dinner speaking about his exploits within boxing.

Already a Freeman of Goldsmiths of the City of London, he was made a Freeman of the City of London in 1994 and is also a fellow of the Institute of Professional Goldsmiths. With a full-time profession as an engraver, a career he embarked on in 1953, for the past 27 years he has had his own business, O'Connell & Yardley, currently situated at Mill Street in the fashionable Mayfair district of London.

Larry's skills have brought him work from the Royal Family, being engaged to engrave a fabulous piece to commemorate the wedding of the Prince and Princess of Wales. He has also done work for the Sultan of Brunei and other members of royalty in the Middle East. He has twice entered a national competition for the Goldsmith's Engraving Award and won it on each occasion.

A devoted family man, Larry has been married to Beryl since 1957 and, on 27 December, this year, they celebrate their ruby wedding anniversary. they have a son aged 39, a daughter aged 38, and five grandchildren.

A professional man in every respect, Larry O'Connell is still some years away from retirement, which is good for British and, indeed, world boxing. One of the most popular and respected individuals within the professional game, his understanding of boxers and the sport in general make him a role model for any aspiring young official.

Their knowledge of boxing picked up from years in the sport, firstly as contestants, then as coaches, make Roy Francis and Larry O'Connell ideal candidates for the role of professional boxing referees. They know the sport inside out, know how to control a fight, and, most importantly, have the respect of the fighters. For an official in the dangerous, competitive sport of professional boxing, there is no substitute for experience.

"MAN OF COURAGE"
The Life and Career of Tommy Farr,
by Bob Lonkhurst

A deeply researched biography of the man regarded by many followers of boxing as Britain's finest heavyweight. Details of more than 60 of his fights, never before recorded, are contained in the story of Farr's battle to survive as a boy, his rise to fame, and of his many battles in the courts. It is a remarkable story of a true man of courage.

Published in March 1997 by THE BOOK GUILD, Temple House, 25 High Street, Lewes, East Sussex BN7 2LU. Price £18.50.

Home and Away with British Boxers During 1996-97

by John Jarrett

JULY

Dublin's darling boy, Steve Collins, is neither a brilliant boxer nor a dynamic puncher, but he has enough stuff in his toolbox to get the job done as he proved once again at the Nynex Arena in Manchester. Hired by promoter, Frank Warren, to go 12 rounds with Nigel Benn, the Irishman finished work early when Benn was forced to pull out with a twisted right ankle.

As strong as a horse and as fit as a butcher's dog, Collins' combative instincts had seen him prevail in all but three of his 35 pro fights and the three men who beat him were all champions. He became a champion himself, collecting the WBO, USBA, WBO Penta-Continental and All-Ireland titles at middleweight.

He had to beat the charismatic Chris Eubank, however, before anyone took any notice. That was in March 1995 when he moved up to super-middleweight to take Eubank's WBO title and hand him his first defeat in 44 contests. He did it again six months later to finally land in the big time at the age of 31. Bring on Nigel Benn! Hell, bring on Roy Jones!

Unfortunately, before Steve could get to Benn the South African, Sugar Boy Malinga, disarmed the London warrior at Newcastle and walked off with his WBC title. Disgusted with his performance Nigel promptly retired, but was soon talking comeback, thus persuading Warren to make Collins an offer he could not refuse – a fight with Benn in Manchester.

The crowds rolled up to see the "Dark Destroyer" do battle with the "Celtic Warrior" but the fireworks fizzled out in round four when Benn missed with a big right-hand shot and fell to the canvas, twisting his right ankle in the process. Despite getting up and gamely trying to carry on, he was forced to strike his colours and limp back to his corner, leaving Steve Collins the winner and still champion.

Although the ending was unsatisfactory, Collins had looked the bigger and stronger of the two and was leading on the scorecards after the three completed rounds. But he was more than ready to give Benn another chance to settle what was obviously unfinished business, and Benn, after retiring again, reconsidered and said he would like a rematch.

It was a big night for Salford's 15-year veteran, Steve Foster, as he collected a unanimous decision and the Commonwealth light-middleweight title from Chris Pyatt in a war of attrition that could have gone either way. Pyatt was the better boxer of the two, but the 35-year-old "Viking" refused to be beaten and what he lacked in technique he made up for in tenacity and it paid off on the night.

Sixteen months after losing his WBO heavyweight title to Riddick Bowe, Herbie Hide started again, walloping former victim, Michael Murray, on the Nynex show. Herbie was off his game but he was still too much for Murray, who was stopped after six painful rounds.

Light-heavyweight, Mark Prince, took his undefeated record (13-0) to Manchester and added the scalp of former British champion, Maurice Core, to his belt, while scooping up the vacant WBO Inter-Continental title. Prince, with a cut on the left eye that posed a stoppage threat, turned on the power that had ended ten of his fights early to bring the referee's intervention in round seven.

When two big punchers meet, it is not just a question of who has the better punch, but, rather, who has the better chin. Such was the scenario at the York Hall when former British light-welterweight champion, Andy Holligan, clashed head on with Paul "Scrap Iron" Ryan with the latter's British and Commonwealth title on the line. The Hackney tearaway had stopped 20 of his 22 victims against one defeat, but that loss had been in his last fight when Jonathan Thaxton took him out in the first with a devastating left-hand shot.

The Liverpool ex-champ had powered his way to 18 early wins against two losses in a 25-fight career and after sampling what Ryan had on offer closed the show after just two minutes and nine seconds with two crushing left hooks that left Paul down on the canvas and his future up in the air.

Belfast's American-based WBC bantamweight champion, Wayne McCullough, was due to meet Britain's former three-time world champ, Duke McKenzie, in Denver in a non-title scrap but it did not happen. Duke felt that there was not enough time to become acclimatised to the rarefied Denver air, did not think his purse (£60,000) was big enough, and, in any case, the American immigration authorities were unhappy with his visa, so no fight! a pity, because McCullough looked less than sensational in taking the ten-rounds decision over Mexican substitute, Julio Cesar Cardona.

There will soon be enough titles to go around so that every boxer can have one. A boxing Utopia! Not every fighter could become the champion in the old days, now many have a better than even chance of becoming a champion. Kevin Lueshing had one genuine title, the British welterweight championship, and in New York he won the vacant IBO title stopping Mexican, Cirilo Nino, inside two rounds. Okay, we should now just record the winning of a championship, whatever the initials, and delete "..of the world!"

AUGUST

From the moment he entered the ring at the Point Depot in Dublin waving the Irish tricolour, the Mexican, Manuel Medina, had the near capacity crowd with him all the way in his challenge to WBO featherweight champion, Naseem Hamed. In the final analysis, however, it failed to help the former IBF and WBC champion as Hamed turned on the power to bring a stoppage just as the bell ended round 11.

Medina, with a 52-7 pro log that included ten title

fights, figured to be Hamed's toughest opponent in his 22-fight career and he proved to be just that, giving his new fans plenty to cheer about, although it must be said that Hamed's performance was possibly his worst since becoming champion. With his timing and accuracy woefully lacking, Naz blamed a heavy cold for which he had been prescribed antibiotics.

In fact, had Medina packed a punch he might have left Dublin once again wearing the purple, but he had only stopped 23 of his 52 victims and it was Hamed's power that finally decided the match, when dropping the Mexican three times on his way to the finish in the penultimate round.

On the undercard, local favourite, Michael Carruth, had too much of everything as he stopped American, Mark Brannon, inside three rounds of a welterweight bout. The 60-fight veteran from Indianapolis had no answer to the southpaw skills of the former Olympic gold medallist and was down twice before it was called off, while Robin Reid, marking time before making his challenge to WBC super-middleweight champion, Vincenzo Nardiello, beat Don Pendleton, who quit after four rounds of a disgraceful mismatch, the man from Milwaukee coming to the ring with only one win in his last 35 fights!

It used to be that you got the experience and then, if you were good enough, you got a shot at the title. But, 'fings ain't what they used to be, as the song says, and that goes in boxing as in almost everything else today. A case in point is Camberwell cruiserweight, Chris Okoh, who rocketed to the top when he stopped Franco Wanyama in only his eighth pro fight to become Commonwealth champion. That was in September 1995 and Chris has looked less than sensational since then against men like Darren Westover and Gypsy Carman, mainly because he still has not got the experience. This time round, journeyman Nigel Rafferty made Chris look bad for three rounds at Windsor before being stopped in the fourth.

Liverpool middleweight, Paul Wright, took his 16-2-2 pro log along to the Adelphi Hotel and went home with the Central Area title after a close decision over Colin Manners. The 34-year-old Leeds' fighter had been out for a year and a half and probably could have used a warm-up fight. As it was he gave Paul a stubborn argument.

One of the fight game's oldest cliches, they never come back, is booked for boxing's dustbin. These days they always come back! This month saw Chris Eubank and Herol Graham announce they were ready to rumble again. Eubank, of course, had not been away long, his last fight being his second WBO super-middleweight title defeat by Steve Collins in September 1995. Now, just turned 30, he was back with a date in Cairo of all places!

Herol Graham had not boxed since losing his British middleweight title to Frank Grant in 1992. The Sheffield stylist had all sorts of problems in his life and his comeback was thwarted when he failed to satisfy the Board's medical regulations. But he persevered and finally got the green light, although, at 37, the comeback road could be a short one.

SEPTEMBER

An an amateur, Keith Knox won the ABA flyweight title in 1992 and when the gritty little Scot finished strongly against Mickey Cantwell in their fight for the British championship some four years later he looked to have completed the double, this time as a professional. But it was not to be when the Londoner took a controversial decision and the title.

Now the Bonnyrigg battler was going for the European title, meeting Jesper Jensen in Copenhagen. The Danish southpaw was undefeated in 17 fights and at the final bell he was still unbeaten, still the flyweight champion of Europe. Keith gave it all he had but Jensen was too fast, too clever, and the Scot finished second, again.

Keighley hard man, Peter Judson, came through a scare over his brain scan, a second scan proving to be okay, before surviving a tough scrap with Welshman, Dean Phillips, to win the vacant IBF Inter-Continental super-featherweight title at Bowlers Club in Manchester. Judson's 34-fight background helped him outlast Phillips, who was out in front when he caved in halfway through round ten. The Yorkshireman had lost 13 fights going in, but came out a winner in the one that mattered.

At Tylorstown, with the ghost of Jimmy Wilde sitting ringside, former WBO featherweight champion, Steve Robinson, stepped out against Midlands Area champion, Kelton McKenzie, to see if there was life after Naz. A year since the traumatic loss of his title to Hamed, Steve had enough to beat McKenzie over eight competitive rounds, dropping his man in round six, although looking in need of more work before going into a proposed European title challenge against Billy Hardy.

The selection of Commonwealth title challengers is something that needs looking at, especially those from the African continent. Kenya's James Wanene, aged 35 and with only six wins in six fights, was allowed to challenge Peter Culshaw for the flyweight title the young Liverpool boy had won with a stunning kayo of Daniel Ward. Peter was 23, unbeaten in 11 fights (one draw), and stopped his man in the seventh. Wanene, albeit a substitute, shaped like a novice and only his unorthodox style let him survive as long as he did.

Another seven-day sub in Trust Ndlovu, this time from Zimbabwe, was no match for former WBO, British, and Commonwealth featherweight champion, Colin McMillan, at York Hall. The British champion stopped his man in seven rounds of a contest labelled a final eliminator for the Commonwealth title, but would have a tougher job with contender, Paul Ingle, who kept his unbeaten certificate (13-0) on the undercard with a second-round stoppage of Brian Robb.

Former British and WBC International heavyweight champion, James Oyebola, was starting out again, going for the Southern Area title at the Broadway Theatre in Barking. But champion, Julius Francis, was not about to lose his title again. A tremendous right to the head in the fifth round toppled the giant and although Oyebola beat the count he had nothing left and it was called off.

Back in action after a year out, British lightweight champion, Michael Ayers, looked sharp in stopping Tony Swift in the fifth round of a light-welterweight match and looked forward to a title defence against Southern Area champion, Colin "Dynamo" Dunne, while the British super-bantamweight champion, Richie Wenton, had to climb off the deck to take the decision against gritty Mexican, Efren Gonzalez, at Manchester.

Chicago tough guy, Anthony Ivory, had never been knocked out in 50 pro fights, but then he had never fought Ensley Bingham. So the American had two new experiences to remind him of his trip to Manchester when being bombed out inside two rounds by the British light-middleweight champion. Live and learn!

London postal worker, Bernard Paul, failed to deliver when meeting Jonathan Thaxton in Sheffield and Brendan Ingle's entry scooped the vacant WBA Inter-Continental light-welterweight title to add to the IBF title he already held, when coming out with the 12-rounds decision. On the same card, 19-year-old Ryan Rhodes racked up an impressive six-threes win over former British welter champ, Del Bryan, for his tenth straight win.

Former British light-middleweight title challenger, Paul Wesley, came in as a late sub, conceded 17 pounds to Nigel Rafferty, and held the Wolverhampton strong man to a draw over six rounds at Walsall. In the main event, Carl Allen dropped Matthew Harris twice on his way to a hard-fought decision victory that gave him the Midland Area super-bantamweight title and revenge for three amateur defeats.

Two Central Area titles also went on the block this month. At Bradford, Trevor Meikle lost his welterweight crown to Leeds'-based Irishman, Derek Roche, in a tough ten rounder, while at Hull, Manchester's Wayne Rigby beat the local favourite, Jimmy Phelan, in a bruising battle to take his lightweight championship.

OCTOBER

The cards were stacked against Robin Reid long before the first bell rang for his challenge to WBC super-middleweight champion, Vincenzo Nardiello. He would be fighting the Italian in Milan and the record book showed only two Britons ever winning a world title in Italy – Maurice Hope and Nigel Benn, and they did not rely on the judges. Neither did Reid! The former bookie's clerk from Runcorn upset the odds with a tremendous victory, powering his way to a seventh-round knockout of the Italian veteran to bring the title back to Britain.

Richie Woodhall was not so successful in his shot at a WBC title on foreign soil, but maybe the outcome of his challenge to middleweight champion, Keith Holmes, in a little town in Maryland was decided before he even flew the Atlantic. Two weeks earlier he had an operation on his right elbow and the sensible thing to do would have been to postpone the biggest fight of his life.

But Richie had been messed about the best part of two years and he did not want to risk losing this opportunity. So he fought, and he lost, which was not surprising since his right hand, the punch we are told you need most when fighting a southpaw, was not doing its job. Even so the Englishman went into the last round before Holmes got to him – the referee stopping it just 28 seconds before the final bell.

Well, he came back! Former WBO middle and super-middleweight champion, Chris Eubank, was back in the ring as a light-heavyweight and promoting his own show in Cairo where he racked up a predictable fifth-round knock-out of Argentine middleweight, Luis Dionisio Barrera.

After two defeats in world title bouts, against Chris Eubank and Nigel Benn, Henry Wharton hopes it will be third time lucky when he meets, well, whoever. The big-punching Yorkshireman kept his name in the frame with a confident display against Rick Thornberry, who came all the way from Australia to Halifax to challenge the Commonwealth super-middleweight champion. Henry retained his title for the sixth time, dropping Rick twice before he pulled out after five rounds claiming a damaged shoulder.

Almost a year after beating Fitzgerald Bruney for the vacant Commonwealth middleweight title on a controversial decision, Robert McCracken made no mistake in the return with the Canadian at Birmingham, coming out a good winner to keep his unbeaten record (28-0) intact. The Brummie was hoping to land a European title shot, which was what took Carl Wright from Liverpool to Vejle in Denmark where he challenged Soren Sondergaard for his light-welterweight title. Carl did us proud in a hectic battle and the Dane had to get off the deck before winning the decision.

Wright's Liverpool neighbour, Shea Neary, won himself a title right in his own backyard when he beat veteran American, Darryl Tyson, in a thriller for the vacant WBU light-welterweight championship, the first to be held in this country. If you can't beat 'em (and you can't) then join 'em!

When boxing at super-bantam, Paul Lloyd had been stopped in the fifth round of a British title challenge to Richie Wenton, so the boy from Ellesmere Port dropped down to the bantamweight class for his next opportunity. This time round, new manager, Frank Maloney, came up with a fight for the vacant Commonwealth title and Paul seized his chance to stop the Tasmanian, Nathan Sting, in six rounds at Catford. Michael Smyth was not so lucky when he clashed with Andrew Murray for his Commonwealth welterweight title in Cardiff, the Guyanese having too much of everything and finishing a clear winner over 12 rounds.

Another vacant Commonwealth title found a home when Jonjo Irwin took the featherweight crown back to Doncaster after beating Ghana's Smith Odoom in a so-so fight at the London Hilton. On the undercard, former WBO strawweight and light-flyweight champion, Paul Weir, on the comeback trail, was too clever for Lyndon Kershaw in a six-threes.

Basingstoke super-middleweight, Dean Francis, collected the vacant WBO Inter-Continental title with an easy four-rounds stoppage of Mexican, Rolando Torres, at Bristol to take his pro log to 15-1, 13 early. And, when opportunity knocks, you had better be at home. Hartlepool lightweight, Alan Temple, took his chance with both fists when offered a fight with former British and Commonwealth champion, Billy Schwer, and did himself proud despite a 6-3 pro record, a last round knockdown sealing victory for the latter.

After carrying off the English ABA flyweight championship three times, little Danny Costello stepped out as a bantamweight to win his pro debut with a third round stoppage of Henry Jones at Liverpool, while another former ABA champion, Peter Richardson, had his unbeaten run snapped at ten when Lithuanian light-welterweight, Rimvidas Billius, had his glove raised in round six after a nasty gash on the Middlesbrough southpaw's left eyebrow brought about the referee's intervention.

Northern Area welterweight champion, Paul King, scored his hat trick over Wallsend rival, Hugh Davey, in the Newcastle ring to retain his title and make the Camerons Brewery belt his own. Davey thought he had done enough, but King's superior boxing carried the day, although Paul admitted it had been the toughest of their three fights.

Shea Neary (right) stepped up in class to win the WBU light-welterweight title, thanks to a clear points win over the veteran American, Darryl Tyson   Les Clark

NOVEMBER

It was a sorry night at the Nynex in Manchester as Nigel Benn reached the end of the road, beaten for the third time in three fights (twice by Steve Collins), and when the "Dark Destroyer" announced his retirement for the third time, this time he meant it. In their previous fight, Benn had quit in the fourth after suffering a damaged ankle. This time he gave it all he had left, but it was not nearly enough to stop the "Celtic Warrior" and Steve's hold on the WBO super-middleweight title was never threatened before Benn's corner pulled him out after six rounds, much to the disgust of the fans who booed long and loud when Nigel left the ring for the last time. It was a sad exit for one of Britain's most exciting champions, a man who captured the WBO middleweight and WBC super-middleweight titles in his 42-5-1 career.

As one star blinked and went out for the last time, another shone brightly in the fistic firmament. Prince

Naseem Hamed regally dismissed the fourth challenger for his WBO featherweight crown, destroying Remigio Molina inside two rounds. The unbeaten Argentine (27-0) did not land a punch in the opening round and failed to finish the second. Naz turned on the heat and when Molina rose unsteadily after taking a seven count he had to be rescued by the referee. Promoter Frank Warren promised that the IBF champ, Tom "Boom Boom" Johnson, would be next for Naz.

A third title bout on the Manchester card saw local favourite Ensley Bingham given a boxing lesson by American southpaw stylist, Ronald "Winky" Wright, who retained his WBO light-middleweight championship with a lop-sided decision. Big-punching Bingham was never allowed to land his vaunted left hook and was always running in second place.

Former WBO heavyweight champion, Herbie Hide, does not believe in working longer than he has to. In taking his record to 28-1, the Norwich man had veteran American, Frankie Swindell, on his way back to the dressing room after just 59 seconds for his 27th win via the short route! One of these days he may have to face young Brixton heavyweight, Danny Williams, who took out former British title challenger, Michael Murray, in 2.05 of the first round to run his pro log to 7-0.

In Las Vegas that same night, another two of Britain's big men were in action. Henry Akinwande retained his WBO title, stopping Alexander Zolkin in ten rounds to remain unbeaten in 32 fights (1 draw), while Scott Welch, the British and Commonwealth champion, failed to impress in taking a decision over Argentine veteran, Daniel Netto.

One British fighter who did impress in a foreign ring was the Bracknell welterweight, Geoff McCreesh, who upset the odds in Hammanskraal where he knocked out Dingaan Thobela in two rounds. The African, a former WBO and WBA lightweight champion, had just been ranked number one for the WBO light-welter title. Then the roof fell in!

They called him Colin "Dynamo" Dunne and he had won 21 straight fights on his way to meeting British lightweight champ, Michael Ayers, for the title at Wembley. Although the London-based Liverpudlian fought his heart out, Ayers was on top of his game to force a stoppage in round nine of a tremendous scrap to keep his belt.

At the age of 30, with ambitions of a third crack at a world title, Welshman Nicky Piper retained his Commonwealth light-heavyweight championship with a seventh-round stoppage of Hackney-based Jamaican, Bruce Scott, at Tylorstown. Scott survived a first round knockdown to fight back, but by the seventh a grotesque swelling over his left eye prompted the referee's intervention.

There was a time when Herol Graham could thread his jab through the eye of a needle and you could not hit him with a handful of rice. As the champion of Britain, the Commonwealth, and Europe, at light-middle, and of Britain and Europe at middleweight, he was a star of the '80s, but this was November 1996 and Graham, aged 37, had not fought in four years, and had had to fight the Board to get his licence back. Although the fans turned up at the Concord Leisure Centre in Sheffield to see him outbox American, Terry Ford, over eight rounds, it was not the old Herol Graham and next morning his trainer, Glyn Rhodes, told him not to come back to his gym, telling reporters, "He just has not got it anymore."

Bethnal Green fans were spoiled for choice with two shows on two nights! On Tuesday night at the York Hall, a cut right eye ended Vince Feeney's worthy challenge to Willie Perdomo for the Dominican's WBC International bantamweight title in round ten, but the main event on Wednesday night was all over in 86 seconds! That is all it took for Adrian Dodson to take care of Trinidad's Anthony Joseph, as the unbeaten (16-0) WBO Inter-Continental light-middleweight champion defended his title for the third time. Joseph was down twice and could not get up the second time as he suffered a damaged ankle.

At the Ice Stadium in the German town of Garmisch-Partenkirchen, Derby heavyweight, Clifton Mitchell, wore his bowler into the ring to challenge European champion, Zeljko Mavrovic, only to have his ambitions knocked into a cocked hat by the Croat, who decked him twice in the second round and prompted the referee's intervention, much to the disgust of Clifton and his mentor, Brendan Ingle. But, to impartial observers, the champion was on top of the action and the referee acted correctly. You just can't please everyone!

Challenging for the British lightweight title, the unbeaten Colin Dunne (left) was stopped in the ninth by the defending champion, Michael Ayers　　　　　Les Clark

DECEMBER

Sheffield light-middleweight, Ryan Rhodes, just could not wait to become a British champion. Some three weeks after attaining eligibility, his 20th birthday, he answered the opening bell against former WBO champ, Paul "Silky" Jones, at the Ponds Forge International Leisure Centre in their hometown. Half-an-hour later, however, Rhodes was the new champ and Jones was telling the fans they had just watched his last fight. There was nothing in the scoring after seven rounds but, in the eighth, Ryan rendered the arithmetic redundant with a thudding right that took Jones out of the fight and out of boxing.

Another former champion reaching the end of the road that night was Dennis Andries. From Guyana via Hackney, the unfashionable Andries fought at championship level an incredible 17 years and in Sheffield he was still at it, taking on Johnny Nelson for the vacant British cruiserweight title. But the desire and durability that took Dennis to the top as a light-heavyweight, winning Southern Area, British, WBC titles (3 times), before becoming British cruiser champ, was sadly missing, and, at 43, the veteran was an easy mark for Nelson, who made full use of his talents to regain the title. There was also a victory for Jonjo Irwin at the Dome in Doncaster as he retained his Commonwealth featherweight title against Australian, Ricky Rayner, with a convincing points decision. Stopped by Billy Hardy when challenging for the same title just over four years previously, Ricky at least went the distance this time, but the local favourite was a good winner.

Liverpool super-featherweight, Gary Thornhill, survived a first-round blitz from Justin Juuko to give the Commonwealth champion a stubborn argument before being rescued in the eighth with his right eye almost closed.

With an 8-1-2 pro log, Bargoed flyweight, Harry Woods, jumped at the chance of a shot at the WBC International title, even if it did mean travelling to Accra for the fight with Alex Baba. Harry did not win but he pushed the local hero all the way in what manager, Dai Gardiner, called one of the best fights he had ever seen.

Back in the ring after a short spell as a guest of Her Majesty, Chatham southpaw, John Armour, stopped Lyndon Kershaw with a cut on the left eyebrow in round eight at York Hall to take his record to 21-0 and set his sights on the Commonwealth and European bantamweight titles he never lost in the ring.

A few weeks after giving former British lightweight champion, Billy Schwer, all sorts of problems, Alan Temple was back home in Hartlepool to fight local rival, Harry Escott. Although southpaw Alan did not beat Schwer, he did beat Escott over eight rounds to keep his name in the frame.

Southern Area titles had an airing this month, with Matt Brown stopping south-London rival, Marcus McCrae, in the ninth to claim the vacant super-featherweight crown, while Howard Eastman, who had stopped 11 of his 12 victims on the way to a fight for the vacant middleweight title, stopped Sven Hamer, but it was halfway through the tenth and final round before his big punches paid off this time. The vacant light-heavyweight title also found a home, as Stevenage's Monty Wright dropped Eddie Knight in the fifth round of a lively battle at York Hall. Eddie got up but was pulled out by the referee.

Another vacant title, this time in the Central Area, was claimed when southpaw Stefy Bull overcame Robert Braddock in round four of their bout at The Dome in Doncaster to become featherweight champion. It was win number eight for the unbeaten Denaby lad, with one draw.

Marking time for bigger things, former British light-heavyweight champion, Crawford Ashley, barely worked up a sweat in a mismatch with Hull veteran, Tony Booth, at

Southwark. Booth was down four times and on his way back to the dressing room inside three minutes!

Another guy in a hurry was Darren Corbett. At Doncaster, the heavy-handed Belfast cruiserweight bombed Chris Woollas to the deck twice in the opening round for a stoppage, improving on the seven rounds it took him to beat the local man three months previously.

Up there in Glasgow, Scottish featherweight champion, Brian Carr, kept his unbeaten record intact as he made veteran loser, Pete Buckley, his 12th straight victim with a lopsided decision over six rounds.

Coventry super-featherweight, Dean Pithie, chalked up another win when Marty Chestnut suffered a cut on his right eyebrow, prompting the referee's intervention in round three of a scheduled eight in Sheffield. Pithie took his pro log to nine wins and a draw and needs stiffer opposition.

Exactly three years after retiring with a 32-95-14 record, Doncaster veteran, Dean Bramhald, bounced back with a points win over Chris Price at The Dome in his hometown. At 33, in fight number 142, Dean is not going anywhere, but he enjoyed the evening and so did his fans.

After losing 19 of his 22 fights, Camberwell welterweight, George Wilson, set up shop in France, giving up his British licence. Boxing on a French ticket, Georgie won his first fight in three and a half years when he took a six-rounds decision from Stephane Galtier.

Wallsend welterweight, Hughie Davey, has one ambition – to beat Newcastle arch rival, Paul King. In a six-rounder at Hartlepool, the Northern Area champion made it 4-0 in their series, but Hughie is still not convinced!

Stopped inside seven rounds of a contest for the vacant British cruiserweight title, Dennis Andries (right) has surely come to the end of the road. The new champion, Johnny Nelson, won going away   Les Clark

JANUARY

Shades of Bob Fitzsimmons! For 100 years, give or take a few days, we Brits just could not get our hands on the world heavyweight championship. Today, thanks to the proliferation of titles sanctioned by the various governing bodies, we are knee-deep in "world" heavyweight champions! Lennox Lewis, Frank Bruno, Michael Bentt, Herbie Hide, and Henry Akinwande, hell, we've even had Brits

fighting each other for one or other of the titles. This month we had Akinwande v Scott Welch topping the hit parade in Nashville, a place where the folks would rather see you belting out a country and western number. Maybe the Brighton bomber had that in mind when he answered the bell against Akinwande, because he allowed the big fellow to call the tune all the way, giving what Frank Warren called, "one of the worst performances I have ever seen from a British fighter." In the land of baseball, Big Henry pitched a shutout in retaining his WBO title.

On the same show, British welterweight champion, Kevin Lueshing, at least tried to take the IBF title off Felix Trinidad, dropping the Puerto Rican with two left hooks in the second round. The thing is with Felix, he always gets knocked down in the second round of his title fights, but he always gets up again. And that is when this guy is dangerous. Like a wounded animal, Trinidad came out for round three to smash Lueshing to the canvas three times, prompting the referee to call a halt.

Over in Boston, Belfast's "Pocket Rocket" misfired when Wayne McCullough went after Daniel Zaragoza's WBC super-bantamweight title. The 39-year-old veteran turned in a punch-perfect performance to hold off McCullough's big finish and hand the Las Vegas-based Irishman his first defeat in 21 fights. Mac thought he won and so did one of the judges, but it was not to be his night.

They say youth will be served. That was the message hammered home to Colin McMillan in Bethnal Green by Scarborough's Paul Ingle, as the unbeaten Yorkshireman ended Mac's second reign as British featherweight champion. Colin had held WBO, as well as Commonwealth, titles in his 31-3 pro career, but he was pushing 31 and Paul Ingle was just 24 and had stopped his last seven opponents. On this night at the York Hall he stopped McMillan in round eight and, on the way home, Colin was thinking this was a tough racket and maybe it was time to hang them up.

At Swadlincote a week later, another 24-year-old challenger went up against another 30-year-old British champion when Willie Quinn tried to take Neville Brown's middleweight title. He came close when a whistling right to the head sent the champion tumbling to the canvas in round two, but Brown got up and in the fourth set up a blistering attack that brought about the referee's intervention. It was still a commendable effort from the Scot, who went into the ring knowing his younger brother Tommy had been taken to hospital after being knocked out in his fight with Jimmy Vincent. Happily, Tommy recovered, which more than compensated for Willie's disappointment.

The Scots lost another British title challenge when their flyweight, Keith Knox, was adjudged a points loser to little Ady Lewis at Glasgow. Beaten by Mickey Cantwell in a previous British title fight, and by Jesper Jensen when challenging for the European crown, Keith figured he had won this one, but Lewis, Britain's smallest pro (4' 10½"), has a big talent and his work convinced the referee, Dave Parris, that he was the winner and new champion.

British light-heavyweight champion, Crawford Ashley, had another one-sided win at Bethnal Green when Peter

Kamarenko failed to last out the first round. The outgunned and outclassed Ukranian had no answer to Ashley's firepower and was rescued after just 118 seconds!

John Armour was still undefeated (22-0) and he was a champion again, but he'll never be so glad to hear the final bell as he was this night at York Hall after 12 bloody, bruising rounds with unsung Romanian, Petrica Paraschiv. WBC International bantamweight champion, Willie Perdomo, was unable to make the trip due to visa problems so they called this one for the interim title and brought in Paraschiv with his 6-3-1 record to make up the numbers. On paper, the Chatham southpaw looked a banker, but at the end he looked more like a traffic accident victim.

On the same card, Adrian Dodson retained his unbeaten record (17-0) when Frenchman, Rachid Serdjane, was disqualified for what the referee, Marcus McDonnell, called "ungentlemanly conduct" in the fifth round. Serdjane had collapsed from an obviously low left-hand shot and when he did not or could not get up, McDonnell ruled him out instead of Dodson! This was one for Ripley's "Believe it or Not!"

Newbridge southpaw, Joe Calzaghe, is a good fighter, but the three-time ABA champion, and former undefeated British super-middleweight boss, is in need of a stiffer test than that posed by the likes of Carlos Christie, who was bounced off the canvas five times before being counted out in round two of their bout at Bristol. It was Christie's 23rd defeat in 37 fights, while Calzaghe went to 20-0, 19 early.

A couple of months after his stunning knockout of Dingaan Thobela in South Africa, Geoff McCreesh returned to fight national champion, Peter Malinga, in Durban. Unfortunately, the Bracknell welterweight found Malinga too hot to handle in the DLI Hall where the temperature under the ring lights was estimated at a stifling 40 degrees, being floored in the first and baled out at the end of the fifth, while claiming he was unable to breathe.

During the month of January, the British middleweight champion, Neville Brown (left), came off the floor to stop his challenger, Willie Quinn, in round four   Les Clark

FEBRUARY

Lennox Lewis regained the WBC heavyweight title when he beat his former conqueror, Oliver McCall, inside five rounds in Las Vegas, but the fans were not buzzing over his victory as they made their way back to the casino.

The name of everyone's lips was that of his victim, McCall, whose bizarre performance prompted the referee, Mills Lane, to pull him out after 55 seconds of round five. The big American gave Lewis a fight for three rounds before the wheels came off. Instead of returning to his corner, McCall walked around the ring looking like he wished he was somewhere else and, when the bell rang for the fourth round, he refused to fight, just walking away from Lewis who did not quite know what to make of it all. Was McCall faking or setting a trap? Lennox hit his man when he could catch up with him and when things got no better in the fifth, McCall was sent to his corner. With a history of drug abuse, Oliver had come into the fight from rehab and was already talking of retiring as he had found God. So once again, through no fault of his own, Lennox Lewis was denied his moment of glory.

Meanwhile, in London, Prince Naseem Hamed was becoming a king again, adding the IBF featherweight title to his WBO belt with a stunning victory over the American, Tom Johnson. This time, Naz had a fight on his hands, but he was more than equal to the occasion and when he set up a big attack in the eighth round, Johnson had nothing left. A wicked right uppercut sent him sprawling on the canvas and it was all over for the veteran American.

South African, Giovanni Pretorius, survived a first-round blitz to hold off Robin Reid until the seventh when a thudding right took him out of the fight, as Reid made a first successful defence of his WBC super-middleweight championship on the London Arena mega-show.

WBO super-middle champ, Steve Collins, was hoping to entice Roy Jones into the ring, but on this night had to make do with gutsy French challenger, Frederic Seillier. The veteran visitor was cut on the left eyebrow in the third and when Collins sliced his nose open in the fifth the doctor advised the referee to call a halt. It was not vintage Collins, but it was good enough to secure his belt for another night.

Tiny terror, Jake Matlala, had beaten Paul Weir, Pat Clinton, and Francis Ampofo on previous visits to Britain and looked set for another triumph when matched to defend his WBO light-flyweight title against former British flyweight champion, Mickey Cantwell. The veteran South African beat Mickey as expected, but the Londoner gave him a stiff argument and his fine showing convinced one judge he had done enough to win. But the casting votes were for the little South African, 35 years old and still winning.

Another veteran with a few more miles left on his tyres was Billy Hardy, who delighted his hometown fans in Sunderland as he defended his European featherweight title against former WBO champion, Steve Robinson, coming out with a comfortable points win to keep alive his shot at Naz. On his last visit to the north-east, Steve came in as a substitute and beat John Davison for the vacant WBO title, but he was out of luck this time.

Ryan Rhodes, Brendan Ingle's latest star, was not tested in the first defence of his British light-middleweight title at Sheffield, Central Area champion, Peter Waudby, being blasted to the canvas three times inside round one, leaving Rhodes with the second notch on his belt in 1.58.

Ryan's stablemate, heavyweight, Pele Reid, was in no mood to hang about either. His match with former British title challenger, Michael Murray, lasted just nine seconds, a British record, with the latter's right arm out of joint, forcing a stoppage.

Over in Vienna, Julius Francis did not enjoy his waltz with European heavyweight champion, Zeljko Mavrovic. The Croat with the Mohawk haircut was too strong for the Southern Area champion and Francis took a standing count in round seven before being dropped with a body shot in the eighth. When he got up the referee waved it over.

Glasgow lightweight, Tanveer Ahmed, had lost only one of his 16 fights, to Hartlepool's Sean Armstrong, and now he was meeting Alan Temple, another lad from Hartlepool, in a final eliminator for the British title. Fighting on home turf this time, Ahmed nearly blew this one as Temple went for the double and crashed home a superb left to the chin in the second round. However, the bell rang before Alan could cash in and Tanveer fought back to stop his man in round eight of a bloody battle.

Another British title final eliminator, at light-heavy, thrilled Sunderland fans as Mark Prince survived Michael Gale's punches to stop his man in the sixth. Prince took a few rounds to wake up and as round six got underway was almost put to sleep. Gale, bleeding from a bad cut on his right eye, ripped into the unbeaten Londoner and had him on the brink of a knockout, only to walk into a right hand that stretched him out. It should have been all over, but the Yorkshireman hauled himself up at eight and Prince finished the job with a left hook.

Popular Spencer Oliver took the vacant Southern Area super-bantamweight title with a scorching ten-rounds stoppage of Patrick Mullings at Cheshunt to stay unbeaten at 10-0. Bernard Paul had to climb off the deck to win a hard-fought decision victory over Richie Edwards in their battle for the vacant Southern Area light-welterweight title. Paul Lloyd had it easy making the first defence of his Commonwealth bantamweight title as Lybo Nkoko folded in 101 seconds from a body shot.

MARCH

Having failed in two European title challenges, British light-heavyweight champion, Crawford Ashley, finally nailed it down at Liverpool when he squared up to Spanish puncher, Roberto Dominguez, for the vacant crown. The Latin had stopped 15 of his 22 victims, but was not in Ashley's class and the Leeds' man ended matters in round three with a cracking right uppercut. Having failed in two world title challenges, maybe Crawford could make it third time lucky.

Over in Denmark, British bantamweight champion, Drew Docherty, went after the European title and this one also ended in round three. But this time it was the British boy who came in second as the local hero, Johnny Bredahl, took care of business. With only one defeat in 32 fights, the Dane was on top when the referee called it off and sent the Scot back to his corner.

Manchester super-bantamweight, Michael Brodie, sent his fans home happy after a tremendous fight at the Wythenshawe Forum for the vacant British title against the Commonwealth champion, Neil Swain. The Welshman's title was not on the line, but would be declared vacant after his crushing tenth-round defeat. Brodie, unbeaten in 18 fights going in, was favoured over Swain who brought a 17-6 record to the ring, but not the Commonwealth title which he had won for the second time. From the opening bell both lads set a cracking pace and there was nothing in it going into round ten, but it was Brodie who had the power and a crunching right to the head knocked Swain out before he hit the floor.

Former British super-middleweight champion, Joe Calzaghe, racked up another easy one as America's Tyler Hughes folded in just 2.04 of round one to give Joe his 21st straight win on the Manchester card.

It's a good job Ryan Rhodes is not superstitious. Having already become the youngest post-war British champion at 20, the Sheffield blade was out to win the Lonsdale Belt in record time – 90 days against the 95 it took Michael Ayers to win his lightweight belt in 1995. But this was fight number 13 for Ryan and coming out of the other corner at the Rivermead Leisure Centre in Reading was former two-time British welterweight champion, Del Bryan, a 50-fight veteran with ten years on the kid. Well the kid was up to it, he was too fast, hit too hard, and in round seven youth was served as Roy Francis stopped the fight.

Chris Okoh successfully defended his Commonwealth cruiserweight title for the third time, beating Denzil Browne of Leeds on a decision at Lewisham, and that was all you can say about this fight. Browne failed in a British light-heavyweight title challenge against Dennis Andries two years previously and there was no way he was going to win this one either. Having said that, Okoh did not exactly sparkle. He won. End of story.

The fans had a better night at Norwich where they turned out in force to watch local hero, Jon Thaxton, retain his IBF and WBO Inter-Continental light-welterweight belts with a ninth-round victory over former British and Commonwealth lightweight champion, Paul Burke. At 30, Burke was moving up a division, and those two factors decided this fight as the more powerful Thaxton gradually wore him down, dropping him twice in the ninth to force the stoppage.

On the Norwich card, Jason Matthews picked up the vacant WBO Inter-Continental middleweight title with a fine win over Liverpool's Paul Wright, the referee calling a halt in the third round after Wright had been decked for eight. Matthews, from Hackney, chalked up his 14th straight victory, all but two inside schedule.

Approaching his 28th birthday, Cornelius Carr was a former British super-middleweight champion and had taken Irish hard man, Steve Collins, the distance in a WBO title fight. With a respectable 27-2 pro log, he climbed into the ring at Reading to do battle with Dean Francis for the Basingstoke man's WBO Inter-Continental championship, knowing that victory would put him back on top. But Mr

Francis had other ideas! How Carr survived the first two rounds only he knows, yet the lad from Middlesbrough boxed his way back into it with commendable courage. In the seventh, however, Francis stepped on the gas again and the referee called a halt.

Five weeks after losing a title bid against European champion, Billy Hardy, Cardiff's former WBO feather-weight champion, Steve Robinson, grabbed the chance of what he admitted was a "Second Division title" at Brentwood, meeting Tomas Serrano for the vacant WBO Inter-Continental crown. The Mexican was on his way home after just 2.07 of round one as Robinson smashed him to the canvas with a crippling left hook to the body.

Liverpool is firmly back on the boxing scene thanks to the dramatic punching power of Shea Neary, which had brought him 15 inside schedule wins in his 18-0 pro career. Defending his WBU light-welterweight title for the first time, the local favourite was hardly tested by the unsung African, Jeremiah Malinga, who was hammered inside three rounds.

The Chris Eubank roadshow hit Dubai, good fight, shame about the crowd, actually no crowd at all, which was hardly surprising. Horse racing, okay. Boxing? Forget it! The former WBO middle and super-middleweight champion racked up a fourth-round stoppage win over tough Colombian light-heavyweight, Camilo Alarcon, to take his record to 45-2-2. At 30, the man from Brighton looked good and said he was after Steve Collins.

APRIL

A puncher is always in with a chance. British middleweight champion, Neville Brown, learned that lesson at Swadlincote when making his second bid for the European title. Coming from the other corner was the Frenchman, Hassane Cherifi, boasting a 23-1-1 record with 16 early wins. In a sensational opening round, Brown looked all over a winner, sending the champion crashing to the floor with a right to the head. When he got up, Brown nailed him again with the right and he was on the ropes taking a standing count. Round three and Cherifi was on the deck again from that right hand, but got up and when he hit Brown he hurt him. In the sixth he landed his own right and Brown was on the canvas. Although getting up at six, the Frenchman did not let him off the hook and Brown was again in trouble when the referee called it off. The winner, and still champion of Europe, Hassane Cherifi!

Warming up for his British featherweight title challenge to Paul Ingle, Michael Alldis got Ervine Blake out of there inside three rounds, but three weeks later at the Ice Arena in Hull, he received a chilly welcome from the champion who was making his first defence after thrashing Colin McMillan. Ingle turned in a brilliant performance to force a retirement in round 11 and the future looked bright indeed for him as he took his pro record to 16-0.

Another lad with loads of potential was David Starie, who took the vacant British super-middleweight title when former champion, Sam Storey, was stopped inside seven rounds at the York Hall in Bethnal Green. The Belfast southpaw gave it a shot but, at 33, his future was behind him and the new kid on the block, 22-year-old Starie, was still unbeaten in 14 pro fights, with ten via the short route.

British light-middleweight champion, Ryan Rhodes, added the IBF Inter-Continental crown to his Lonsdale Belt, but jumped-up welterweight, Lindon Scarlett, was no match for the Sheffield puncher and the local fans stayed away from the Hillsborough Leisure Centre. Scarlett was dumped twice and on his way back to the dressing room after 2.54 of round one. A much better fight on the card saw the clever Welshman, Barry Jones, claim the IBF Inter-Continental super-featherweight title with a split decision over rugged Yorkshireman, Peter Judson.

In an all-action thriller at the York Hall, Liverpool's Paul Lloyd came through the first defence of his Commonwealth bantamweight title when the referee took African, Simphiwe Pamana, out of the fight in round 11. It could well have ended in the opener when Lloyd dropped Pamana with a left hook to the body, but the challenger was up at six and firing back, and in the seventh took Paul's legs from under him with a left hook – right cross. Lloyd beat the count and fought back well enough to keep his title.

A week later in the same ring, Tottenham's Bernard Paul won the vacant Commonwealth light-welterweight title in the opinion of referee Larry O'Connell, and practically nobody else! Zambian, Felix Bwalya, survived a rocky tenth round and looked to have outboxed and outpunched Paul most of the way, only to finish second at the final bell.

With Commonwealth cruiserweight champion, Chris Okoh, sitting ringside at the Ulster Hall in Belfast, Darren Corbett showed the champ what was in store for him when he retained his All-Ireland title with a crushing kayo of Noel Magee. The former Commonwealth light-heavy-weight champion was blasted to the canvas twice in the second round and announced his retirement as promoter, Barry Hearn, booked Okoh for Corbett at the new Waterfront Hall on 2 June.

Big-punching British light-welterweight champion, Andy Holligan, had to go all the way to take a points decision from the Lithuanian, Rimvidas Billius, at Hull, while at Swadlincote, Holligan's last victim, Paul "Scrap Iron" Ryan, came roaring back at welterweight to stop Nottingham's Michael Monaghan in two rounds.

Busy fists in the Southern Area with four championship contests being decided. West Ham southpaw, Steve Roberts, stayed unbeaten (13-0) as he took the vacant light-middleweight crown with a points win over Gilbert Jackson at York Hall, while, on the same bill, former British flyweight champ, Francis Ampofo, put in a late burst but was unable to overhaul Vince Feeney, who claimed the vacant bantamweight title. Back in action after his terrific losing challenge to British champion, Michael Ayers, Colin "Dynamo" Dunne kept his lightweight title with a crushing fourth-round knockout of Lewis Reynolds in Mayfair, while, at Enfield, Chris Henry captured the vacant cruiserweight title when he forced Darren Westover, claiming a damaged hand, to retire after four rounds, but the Ilford man looked well beaten by then.

Mixed fortunes in foreign rings for British boxers, with Manchester's Carl Thompson warming up for a mandatory challenge to WBO cruiserweight champion, Ralf Rocchigiani, with an easy four-rounds victory in Zurich over American, Keith McMurray. Nigel Wenton was in good form in Milan as he kept in shape for his crack at WBO light-welterweight champion, Giovanni Parisi, stopping American, Craig Houk, in the first round. Former Commonwealth heavyweight champion, Derek Williams, looked at the end of the road when he blew a six-rounds decision to Carlos Monroe at Inglewood in California. The sun was shining, but it was fast going down on the big fellow's career.

It looks like Neville Brown has just won the European middleweight title in this shot, but, in truth, he was banged out by the defending champion, Hassane Cherifi, in the sixth
Les Clark

MAY

Every now and then a good match is made between two fighters that has the boxing world counting the minutes to the first bell. Such a match was that between WBC super-middleweight champion, Robin Reid, and former British, Commonwealth, and European champion, Henry Wharton, at the Nynex Arena in Manchester. The main event that night was Naseem Hamed's mandatory WBO feather-weight title defence against European champion, Billy Hardy, with Naz's IBF crown also in the pot, but for most people the fight to see was Reid versus Wharton. Reid was making the second defence of his title and was unbeaten at 23-01-1, while Wharton was hoping to make it third time lucky after world title failures against Chris Eubank and Nigel Benn, his only defeats in 28 fights (one draw).

Well, this one lived up to the hype. Most of us figured Reid would be too clever and so it proved, but the gutsy Yorkshireman never stopped trying in a fascinating contest that held everyone spellbound to the final bell. Henry fought valiantly, as always, and even convinced the Mexican judge that he had held Reid even, but his vaunted left hook would not be the match winner this night, the night Robin Reid came of age. The champion, a puncher in his own right, with 18 early wins, turned in a brilliant boxing performance that delighted his followers and removed any doubts as to his standing on the world stage.

By contrast, Naz versus Hardy was an anti-climax. The little hard man from Sunderland deserved his shot, but Hamed, forced to take the fight, was in no mood to hang about and he made it a power show from the off. It was all over in 93 seconds with Billy down twice and stopped, albeit on his feet, but by then a firm believer in the power of Naseem Hamed.

Steve Foster was another fighter who reached too far that night at the Nynex, going after the WBO light-middleweight title held by the classy champion, Ronald "Winky" Wright. The American southpaw had too much of everything for the Salford veteran and Steve knew it. Decked twice in the sixth round by body shots before the referee led him back to his corner, the 36-year-old Foster announced, "That's it for me. The Viking is hanging up his gloves." In his 19-14-2 pro career, the Lancastrian earned a Commonwealth and an IBF Inter-Continental title and to his legion of fans will always be a champion.

European super-bantamweight champion, Martin Krastev, came to London with a respectable 19-2-1 pro log and the smart money said he would return home to Bulgaria still wearing his crown after his fight with Spencer Oliver at Edmonton. The 22-year-old Barnet boy had won the Southern Area title in a sizzler with Patrick Mullings last time out, but still had only ten pro fights on his rèsumè going in and you wondered whether this was too much too soon. In round four, the kid they call "The Omen" gave his answer with a thudding right to the head that dropped the champion on all fours. Krastev hauled himself up at seven, but he was still rocky and the referee counted him out.

A workman is no good without his tools and European light-heavyweight champion, Crawford Ashley, was severely handicapped in his title defence against French-man, Pascal Warusfel, in Paris, his left hand sustaining damage that troubled him from the third round. The challenger fought above himself as fighters often do when given a shot at a title, but the Leeds' veteran was still good value for his points decision, even if one judge saw them even at the finish. The French champion was tough and soaked up enough right hands to finish half-a-dozen men, but it was Ashley's fight.

Just 19 days after beating Steve Williams in an eliminator, Sudbury flyweight, Mark Reynolds, climbed in there with British champion, Ady Lewis, at the Marriott Hotel in London's Mayfair. The little Bury bomber had stopped nine in his 12 winning fights, but he could not stop Reynolds, who was still plugging away at the final bell.

At Reading, Dean Francis was in sparkling form as he took out Canadian champion, Kit Munro, in two rounds to retain his WBO Inter-Continental super-middleweight title and chalk up his 17th win in 18 pro fights. However, he had to climb off the deck himself in a sensational opening round that saw him twice drop the visitor. Dean wasted no time in the second, having Munro down three times for the mandatory stoppage.

Former WBO featherweight champion, Steve Robinson, got back some of his old fire in destroying Mexican challenger, Julio Cesar Sanchez, inside seven rounds at Mansfield to retain his WBO Inter-Continental belt. The payoff punch was Robbo's pet left hook to the body. End of fight! Another WBO Inter-Continental title fight saw Hackney's unbeaten Jason Matthews put his middleweight crown on the line in London against Patrick Swann, but the American was not up for the job and had enough after five one-sided rounds as Matthews racked up his 15th straight win, 13 early.

Paul Weir had won WBO titles at two weights when barely out of his amateur vest, but struggled against European flyweight champion, Jesper Jensen, who kept his title when the referee sent the little Scot back to his corner in round eight of their fight in Randers. Paul protested at the stoppage, but he had been down twice and was bleeding from a cut on his cheek and defeat was staring him in the face. At 29, with a 12-4 scorecard, Paul's options would appear limited, especially in view of Jensen's subsequent knockout by Frenchman, David Guerault.

With Martin Krastev on the floor in the fourth round, Spencer Oliver is just seconds away from winning the European super-bantamweight crown   Les Clark

JUNE

Heavyweights hogged the headlines this month with Herbie Hide on top again following his dramatic two-rounds demolition of former IBF champion, Tony Tucker, at the Sports Village in Norwich. Hide's sensational victory gave him back the WBO crown he had worn for a 12-month period in 1994-95 and which had been vacated by Henry Akinwande when he signed to fight WBC champion, Lennox Lewis.

To put matters in their proper context, the veteran American had seen better days and, at 38, was long past his sell-by date. However, he had only been stopped once in 59 fights and that was with an eye injury, and Mike Tyson and Lennox Lewis were two of the guys he stood up against. But there was no way Tucker was going to stand up against Hide, whose accurate, thudding punches sent Tony rolling on the canvas three times in the second round for an automatic stoppage. Herbie rides again.

On the undercard that night, former British and Commonwealth heavyweight champion, Scott Welch, came roaring back with a 64-second blitz of Ukranian, Yuri Yelistratov, who was blasted to the canvas twice before the referee had to call it off. Welch had been slated by the critics for his dreary showing when going for Akinwande's WBO title in his last fight. This was more like it!

Birmingham banger, Pele Reid, was another heavyweight in a hurry, but then he always is. His nine winning fights had lasted less than 11 rounds and Ricardo Kennedy, a Jamaican based in Florida, was the latest to feel the venom in his fists, it being all over in 2.43 of round one. It is difficult to assess Pele's potential, you don't see him in the ring long enough! Bang, bang, goodnight!

A four rounder on the Norwich card saw Joe Bugner junior, back in action after a three-year layoff. He probably figured if the old man can still make a few bob on the other side of the world at his age, why not? Joe outpointed Rob Albon, but gave no hint he could emulate his famous father.

Julius Francis gave the leaders in the heavyweight division no cause for alarm with his showing against Joseph Chingangu at the York Hall. His victory by the decision route brought him the vacant Commonwealth title but precious little else. The only time Francis looked likely to end matters early was in round six when he sent the Zambian through the ropes, but the African survived to go the distance.

In Belfast, big Kevin McBride, all 6'7" and 17 stone of him, stopped Paul Douglas in a contest billed for the All-Ireland heavyweight title, yet scheduled for only eight-threes. In the event, the distance proved academic as Douglas found McBride too big and too heavy and it was called off in the fifth round.

The Belfast fans soon forgot McBride's lacklustre display and went home talking about Darren Corbett's explosive win over Chris Okoh. The former heavyweight ripped the Commonwealth cruiserweight crown off the Croydon man with a dynamic three knockdowns, three-rounds victory, as the fans threatened to lift the roof off the brand new Waterfront Arena.

The dark spectre that haunts boxing every now and then hung over the ring in the Grundy Park Leisure Centre at Cheshunt when Dominic Negus challenged Chris Henry for his Southern Area cruiserweight championship. An excellent contest ended dramatically in the tenth round as Negus sent Henry crashing to the floor and on to the hospital to begin another fight, this time for his life. Fortunately, with the help of the surgeons he survived, but would never fight in a ring again!

There has been a big increase in the number of fighters from Eastern Europe, especially since the fragmentation of the Soviet Republic, which is great news for British promoters, but bad news for British ring announcers. Just imagine being beaten by a guy whose name you cannot pronounce! Down in Bristol, the local favourite, Glenn Catley, was doing very nicely thank you, for six rounds, but in round seven, an Hungarian, Andras Galfi, crashed over a right to the head and Glenn crashed to the canvas. Despite managing to beat the count, another right-hand bomb landed and the referee had to stop it.

On the comeback trail as a welterweight, former British and Commonwealth light-welter champion, Ross Hale, chalked up a lop-sided decision over Shaun Stokes in a mismatch, while Joe Calzaghe racked up another meaningless victory when Brazilian, Luciano Torres, was saved by the referee in round three.

A couple of Sky TV pundits, Nicky Piper and Duke McKenzie, did not seem able to make their minds up as to which side of the screen they wish to work from. The Duke, a former three-time champion, struggled with Midlands Area super-bantamweight champion, Carl Allen, before taking the points, while Piper, still the Commonwealth light-heavyweight champion, had to climb off the deck to outpoint Frenchman, Stephane Nizard, at Norwich. McKenzie had just turned 34, while Welshman, Piper, was hoping for a crack at WBA/WBO champion, Dariusz Michalczewski. And there was yet another one of those names to wrap your tongue around – Gagik Chachatrian. The Armenian living in Hamburg, came to Norwich to fight Jon Thaxton for his WBO and IBF Inter-Continental light-welterweight titles, but was out of it after two rounds, a big left hook doing the job.

Byker to Broadway
The Fighting Life and Times of Seaman Tommy Watson
by John Jarrett

Well researched and well written in an easy on the eye style, this is the story of the Geordie boxing hero whose hammering fists took him from the grimy streets of Newcastle to the glittering concrete canyons of New York City and from back-street scraps in Byker to a world championship fight in Madison Square Garden against the legendary Cuban, Kid Chocolate. To this day, he is still recognised as the greatest fighter to come out of the north east.

Published by Bewick Press, with signed copies available from the author, 5 Beechwood Avenue, Gosforth, Newcastle NE3 5DM. Price £9.95 + £1.50 postage & packing.

Facts and Figures, 1996-97

There were 658 (685 in 1995-96) British-based boxers who were active between 1 July 1996 and 30 June 1997, spread over 210 (223 in 1995-96) promotions held in Britain, not including Eire, during the same period. The above figure comprised 527 boxers already holding licenses or having been licensed previously, three foreign-born boxers who started their careers elsewhere, and 128 new professionals, a decrease of 15 on the previous season.

Unbeaten during season (minimum qualification: 6 contests): 10: Esham Pickering. 7: Jason Booth. 6: Steve Conway, Darren Corbett, Scott Dixon, Dominic Negus, Kelly Oliver.

Longest unbeaten sequence (minimum qualification: 10 contests): 33: Henry Akinwande (1 draw). 29: Robert McCracken. 26: Prince Naseem Hamed. 25: Justin Juuko (1 draw), Robin Reid (1 draw). 23: John Armour. 22: Joe Calzaghe. 19: Michael Brodie. 18: Adrian Dodson, Shea Neary. 17: Barry Jones (1 draw), Robert Norton (1 draw). 16: Tanveer Ahmed (2 draws), Paul Ingle, Derek Roche, Nicky Thurbin, Clinton Woods. 15: Terry Dunstan, Howard Eastman, Jason Matthews, Mark Prince. 14: Steve Collins, Wayne Llewelyn, Ryan Rhodes, David Starie. 13: Mark Baker, Mark Breslin, Brian Carr, Ady Lewis, Dean Pithie (1 draw), Steve Roberts. 12: Peter Culshaw (1 draw), Scott Dixon (1 draw), Paul Griffin, Georgie Smith. 11: Darren Corbett, Spencer Oliver, Mark Winters. 10: Danny Peters, Esham Pickering.

Most wins during season (minimum qualification: 6 contests): 10: Esham Pickering. 7: Jason Booth. 6: Steve Conway, Darren Corbett, Eamonn Magee, Dominic Negus, Kelly Oliver, George Richards.

Most contests during season (minimum qualification: 10 contests): 16: Pete Buckley, Brian Coleman. 14: Graham McGrath. 13: Keith Jones. 12: Michael Alexander, Ervine Blake, Tony Booth, Dean Bramhald, Martin Jolley, Nigel Rafferty, Chris Woollas. 11: Benny Jones, Miguel Matthews. 10: Howard Clarke, Henry Jones, Prince Kasi Kaihau, Esham Pickering, Chris Price.

Most contests during career (minimum qualification: 50 contests): 153: Shamus Casey. 148: Dean Bramhald. 117: Des Gargano. 103: Miguel Matthews. 100: Pete Buckley. 92: John Smith. 79: Graham McGrath. 74: Nigel Rafferty. 72: Tony Booth. 70: Brian Coleman. 69: Ernie Loveridge. 67: Steve Pollard. 65: Dennis Andries. 64: Trevor Meikle. 61: Tony Foster. 57: Kid McAuley, Steve Osborne. 56: Ray Newby. 55: Neil Parry. 53: Paul Wesley. 52: Gary Jacobs, Phil Lashley. 51: Herol Graham, Colin Innes, Martin Jolley, Chris Pyatt. 50: Del Bryan, Karl Taylor.

Diary of British Boxing Tournaments, 1996-97

Tournaments are listed by date, town, venue, and promoter, and cover the period 1 July 1996 - 30 June 1997

Code: SC = Sporting Club

Date	Town	Venue	Promoters
03.07.96	Wembley	Brent Town Hall	National Promotions
06.07.96	Manchester	Nynex Arena	Sports Network
09.07.96	Bethnal Green	York Hall	Panix Promotions
13.07.96	Bethnal Green	York Hall	Sports Network
19.07.96	Ystrad	Rhondda Leisure Centre	Gardiner
29.07.96	Skegness	Festival Pavilion	Frater
16.08.96	Liverpool	Adelphi Hotel	Vaughan
22.08.96	Salford	Willows Hotel	Wood
27.08.96	Windsor	Blazers Night Club	Panix Promotions/Evans
03.09.96	Bethnal Green	York Hall	Panix Promotions
03.09.96	Belfast	Ulster Hall	Matchroom
06.09.96	Liverpool	Everton Park Sports Centre	Munro & Hyland
12.09.96	Doncaster	The Dome	Rushton
14.09.96	Sheffield	Concord Leisure Centre	Sports Network
18.09.96	Tylorstown	Rhondda Fach Sports Centre	Gardiner
19.09.96	Manchester	Bowler's Arena	Sports Network
20.09.96	Glasgow	Thistle Hotel	Morrison
20.09.96	Tooting	Leisure Centre	Noble Arts Promotions
23.09.96	Cleethorpes	Winter Gardens	Dalton
23.09.96	Bradford	Stakis Hotel	Yorkshire Executive SC
23.09.96	Glasgow	Forte Post House Hotel	St Andrew's SC
26.09.96	Glasgow	Forte Post House Hotel	St Andrew's SC
26.09.96	Walsall	Town Hall	Cowdell/Gray
27.09.96	Stevenage	Leisure Centre	Matchroom
27.09.96	Hull	Country Park Inn	Hull & District SC
28.09.96	Barking	Broadway Theatre	Panix Promotions
30.09.96	Manchester	Piccadilly Hotel	Trickett
01.10.96	Birmingham	Aston Villa Leisure Centre	National Promotions
02.10.96	Cardiff	Sophia Gardens	Gardiner
02.10.96	Stoke	North Staffs Hotel	Brogan
03.10.96	Sunderland	Swallow Hotel	Conroy
04.10.96	Pentre Halkyn	Springfield Hotel	Davies
04.10.96	Wakefield	Lightwaves Leisure Centre	Callighan
07.10.96	Lewisham	Lewisham Theatre	Panix Promotions
07.10.96	Birmingham	Forte Post House Hotel	Cowdell/Gray
08.10.96	Battersea	Town Hall	Panix Promotions
09.10.96	Stoke	Trentham Gardens	North Staffs SC
10.10.96	Newcastle	Mayfair Ballroom	Fawcett
11.10.96	Mayfair	Hilton Hotel	Matchroom
13.10.96	Shaw	Tara Sports & Leisure Complex	Tara Promotions
14.10.96	Mayfair	Marriott Hotel	National Promotions
15.10.96	Wolverhampton	Park Hall Hotel	Wolverhampton SC
18.10.96	Barnstaple	Barnstaple Hotel	Adair
19.10.96	Bristol	Whitchurch Leisure Centre	Sports Network
23.10.96	Halifax	North Bridge Leisure Centre	National Promotions
24.10.96	Lincoln	Drill Hall	Dalton
24.10.96	Birmingham	Forte Post House Hotel	Cowdell/Gray
24.10.96	Wembley	Brent Town Hall	National Promotions

DIARY OF BRITISH BOXING TOURNAMENTS, 1996-97

Date	Town	Venue	Promoters
24.10.96	Mayfair	Hilton Hotel	Nordoff Robbins Trust
25.10.96	Mere	Golf & Country Club	Wood
26.10.96	Liverpool	Everton Park Sports Centre	Munro & Hyland
28.10.96	Bradford	Norfolk Gardens Hotel	Yorkshire Executive SC
28.10.96	Leicester	Grand Hotel	Griffin
28.10.96	Glasgow	Forte Post House Hotel	St Andrew's SC
01.11.96	Mansfield	Leisure Centre	Ashton
05.11.96	Belfast	Ulster Hall	Matchroom
06.11.96	Glasgow	Kelvin Hall	Sports Network
06.11.96	Hull	Ice Arena	Panix Promotions
06.11.96	Tylorstown	Rhondda Fach Sports Centre	Gardiner
07.11.96	Battersea	Town Hall	Holland
09.11.96	Manchester	Nynex Arena	Sports Network
10.11.96	Glasgow	Forte Post House Hotel	St Andrew's SC
12.11.96	Dudley	Town Hall	National Promotions
14.11.96	Sheffield	Pinegrove Country Club	Hobson
18.11.96	Glasgow	Forte Post House Hotel	St Andrew's SC
20.11.96	Wembley	Conference Centre	National Promotions
21.11.96	Solihull	Conference Centre	Cowdell/Gray
22.11.96	Liverpool	Adelphi Hotel	Vaughan
22.11.96	Hull	Country Park Inn	Hull & District SC
25.11.96	Cleethorpes	Beachcomber Club	Frater
26.11.96	Bethnal Green	York Hall	Panix Promotions
26.11.96	Sheffield	Concord Leisure Centre	Brogan
26.11.96	Wolverhampton	Park Hall Hotel	Wolverhampton SC
27.11.96	Bethnal Green	York Hall	Matchroom
27.11.96	Swansea	Brangwyn Hall	Sporting Club of Wales
28.11.96	Hull	Quality Royal Hotel	Ulyatt
29.11.96	Glasgow	Thistle Hotel	Morrison
30.11.96	Tylorstown	Rhondda Fach Leisure Centre	Sports Network
01.12.96	Shaw	Tara Sports & Leisure Complex	Tara Promotions
02.12.96	Birmingham	Forte Post House Hotel	Cowdell/Gray
03.12.96	Yarm	Tall Trees Hotel	Spensley
03.12.96	Liverpool	Everton Park Sports Centre	Munro & Hyland
04.12.96	Hartlepool	Borough Hall	Robinson
04.12.96	Stoke	Trentham Gardens	North Staffs SC
04.12.96	Stoke	North Staffs Hotel	Brogan
05.12.96	Sunderland	Swallow Hotel	Conroy
06.12.96	Leeds	Queen's Hotel	Sportsman Promotions
09.12.96	Bradford	Norfolk Gardens Hotel	Yorkshire Executive SC
09.12.96	Chesterfield	Bradbury Hall	Dalton
09.12.96	Leicester	Grand Hotel	Griffin
09.12.96	Bristol	Odyssey Night Club	Sanigar
10.12.96	Plymouth	New Continental Hotel	Christian
11.12.96	Southwark	Elephant & Castle Leisure Centre	Panix Promotions
14.12.96	Sheffield	Ponds Forge Leisure Centre	Sports Network
16.12.96	Cleethorpes	Winter Gardens	Dalton
17.12.96	Bethnal Green	York Hall	National Promotions
17.12.96	Doncaster	The Dome	Matchroom/Rushton
22.12.96	Salford	Willows Hotel	Wood
22.12.96	Glasgow	Thistle Hotel	Morrison
11.01.97	Bethnal Green	York Hall	Panix Promotions
16.01.97	Solihull	Conference Centre	Cowdell/Gray
18.01.97	Manchester	New Century Hall	Phoenix Camp Promotions

Date	Town	Venue	Promoters
18.01.97	Swadlincote	Green Bank Leisure Centre	Sports Network
21.01.97	Bristol	Whitchurch Leisure Centre	Sports Network/Sanigar
27.01.97	Glasgow	Forte Post House Hotel	St Andrew's SC
28.01.97	Belfast	Ulster Hall	Matchroom
28.01.97	Piccadilly	Cafe Royal	Panix Promotions
29.01.97	Bethnal Green	York Hall	National Promotions
29.01.97	Stoke	Trentham Gardens	North Staffs SC
31.01.97	Pentre Halkyn	Springfield Hotel	Davies
03.02.97	Sunderland	Crowtree Leisure Centre	Sports Network
03.02.97	Leicester	Grand Hotel	Griffin
08.02.97	Millwall	London Arena	Sports Network
11.02.97	Wolverhampton	Park Hall Hotel	Wolverhampton SC
11.02.97	Bethnal Green	York Hall	National Promotions
12.02.97	Glasgow	Kelvin Hall	Sports Network/Morrison
15.02.97	Tooting	Leisure Centre	Noble Art Promotions
17.02.97	Bradford	Norfolk Gardens Hotel	Yorkshire Executive SC
18.02.97	Cheshunt	Grundy Park Leisure Centre	Panix Promotions/Harding
19.02.97	Acton	Town Hall	Cameron
20.02.97	Mansfield	Leisure Centre	Ashton
24.02.97	Glasgow	Forte Post House Hotel	St Andrew's SC
24.02.97	Manchester	Piccadilly Hotel	Trickett
25.02.97	Sheffield	Hillsborough Leisure Centre	Sports Network/Ingle
26.02.97	Cardiff	National Ice Rink	Gardiner
27.02.97	Sunderland	Swallow Hotel	Conroy
27.02.97	Hull	Quality Royal Hotel	Ulyatt
28.02.97	Kilmarnock	Grand Hall	St Andrew's SC
01.03.97	Liverpool	Everton Park Sports Centre	Munro & Hyland/Panix Promotions
03.03.97	Leicester	Grand Hotel	Griffin
03.03.97	Birmingham	Forte Post House Hotel	Cowdell/Gray
04.03.97	Southwark	Elephant & Castle Leisure Centre	Panix Promotions
04.03.97	Yarm	Tall Trees Hotel	Spensley
07.03.97	Northampton	Danes Camp Leisure Centre	Shinfield
07.03.97	Weston super Mare	Winter Gardens	Queensbury Yeo
08.03.97	Brentwood	International Centre	Matchroom
12.03.97	Stoke	North Staffs Hotel	Brogan
14.03.97	Reading	Rivermead Leisure Centre	Sports Network/Sanigar
14.03.97	Irvine	Volunteer Rooms	St Andrew's SC
14.03.97	Hull	Country Park Inn	Hull & District SC
16.03.97	Shaw	Tara Sports & Leisure Complex	Tara Promotions
17.03.97	Glasgow	Forte Post House Hotel	St Andrew's SC
17.03.97	Mayfair	Marriott Hotel	National Promotions
19.03.97	Stoke	Trentham Gardens	North Staffs SC
20.03.97	Doncaster	The Dome	Rushton
20.03.97	Solihull	Conference Centre	Cowdell/Gray
20.03.97	Salford	Willows Hotel	Wood
20.03.97	Newark	Spring Grove Leisure Centre	Dalton
22.03.97	Wythenshawe	The Forum	Sports Network
24.03.97	Bristol	Odyssey Night Club	Sanigar
25.03.97	Lewisham	Lewisham Theatre	Panix Promotions
25.03.97	Wolverhampton	Park Hall Hotel	Wolverhampton SC
27.03.97	Norwich	Sports Village	Sports Network
03.04.97	Wembley	Brent Town Hall	National Promotions
04.04.97	Liverpool	Adelphi Hotel	Vaughan
04.04.97	Brighton	Hove Town Hall	Peacock Promotions

Date	Town	Venue	Promoters
04.04.97	Glasgow	Thistle Hotel	Sports Network/Morrison
08.04.97	Bethnal Green	York Hall	Panix Promotions/Matchroom
10.04.97	Sheffield	Pinegrove Country Club	Hobson
11.04.97	Barnsley	Metrodome	Munro & Hyland
12.04.97	Sheffield	Hillsborough Leisure Centre	Sports Network/Ingle
14.04.97	Bradford	Norfolk Gardens Hotel	Yorkshire Executive SC
15.04.97	Edgbaston	Tower Ballrooms	Cowdell/Gray
16.04.97	Bethnal Green	York Hall	National Promotions
19.04.97	Plymouth	Mayflower Centre	Sanigar
20.04.97	Leeds	Rothwell Sports Centre	Callighan
22.04.97	Bethnal Green	York Hall	Matchroom
24.04.97	Mayfair	Hilton Hotel	National Promotions
25.04.97	Mere	Golf & Country Club	Wood
25.04.97	Cleethorpes	Beachcomber Club	Frater
26.04.97	Swadlincote	Green Bank Leisure Centre	Sports Network
28.04.97	Hull	Ice Arena	Panix Promotions
28.04.97	Enfield	Starlight Rooms	Harding
28.04.97	Glasgow	Forte Post House Hotel	St Andrew's SC
29.04.97	Belfast	Ulster Hall	Matchroom
29.04.97	Manchester	Holiday Inn	Cross
30.04.97	Acton	Town Hall	Cameron
01.05.97	Newcastle	Mayfair Ballroom	Fawcett
01.05.97	Hull	Quality Royal Hotel	Ulyatt
03.05.97	Manchester	Nynex Arena	Sports Network
08.05.97	Mansfield	Leisure Centre	Matchroom/Ashton
10.05.97	Nottingham	Clifton Leisure Centre	Dalton
12.05.97	Leicester	Grand Hotel	Griffin
15.05.97	Reading	Rivermead Leisure Centre	Sports Network/Sanigar
15.05.97	Sunderland	Swallow Hotel	Conroy
16.05.97	Glasgow	Thistle Hotel	Morrison
16.05.97	Hull	Country Park Inn	Hull & District SC
19.05.97	Cleethorpes	Winter Gardens	Dalton
20.05.97	Edmonton	Lee Valley Leisure Centre	Panix Promotions/Harding
20.05.97	Gillingham	Black Lion Leisure Centre	National Promotions
21.05.97	Liverpool	Moat House Hotel	Munro & Hyland
22.05.97	Southwark	Elephant & Castle Leisure Centre	Panix Promotions
22.05.97	Solihull	Conference Centre	Cowdell/Gray
27.05.97	Mayfair	Marriott Hotel	Matchroom
29.05.97	Mayfair	Hilton Hotel	Sports Network
02.06.97	Belfast	Waterfront Hall	Matchroom/Panix Promotions
02.06.97	Glasgow	Forte Post House Hotel	St Andrew's SC
05.06.97	Bristol	Whitchurch Leisure Centre	Sports Network/Sanigar
08.06.97	Shaw	Tara Sports Leisure Complex	Tara Promotions
09.06.97	Birmingham	Forte Post House Hotel	Cowdell/Gray
09.06.97	Bradford	Stakis Hotel	Yorkshire Executive SC/St Andrew's SC
13.06.97	Leeds	Queen's Hotel	Sportsman Promotions
13.06.97	Paisley	Town Hall	Morrison
17.06.97	Cheshunt	Grundy Park Leisure Centre	Panix Promotions
19.06.97	Scunthorpe	Baths Hall	Woollas
21.06.97	Cardiff	Star Leisure Centre	Sports Network
26.06.97	Salford	Willows Hotel	Wood
26.06.97	Sheffield	Pinegrove Country Club	Hobson
28.06.97	Norwich	Sports Village	Sports Network
30.06.97	Bethnal Green	York Hall	Panix Promotions

Current British-Based Champions: Career Records

Shows the complete record of all British champions, or British boxers holding Commonwealth, European, IBF, WBA, WBC and WBO titles, who have been active between 1 July 1996 and 30 June 1997. Names in brackets are real names, where they differ from ring names, and the first place name given is the boxer's domicile. Boxers are either shown as self managed, or with a named manager, the information being supplied by the BBBoC shortly before going to press. Also included are the Ugandan, Justin Juuko, the Commonwealth super-featherweight champion, who currently holds a BBBoC licence, and Robbie Regan, the WBO bantamweight champion, despite his inactivity.

(Gary) Crawford Ashley (Crawford)

Leeds. *Born* Leeds, 20 May, 1964
British & European L. Heavyweight Champion. Former Undefeated Central Area L. Heavyweight Champion. Ht. 6'3"
Manager Self

26.03.87 Steve Ward W RSC 2 Merton
29.04.87 Lee Woolis W RSC 3 Stoke
14.09.87 Glazz Campbell L PTS 8 Bloomsbury
07.10.87 Joe Frater W RSC 4 Burnley
28.10.87 Ray Thomas W RSC 1 Stoke
03.12.87 Jonjo Greene W RSC 7 Leeds
04.05.88 Johnny Nelson L PTS 8 Solihull
15.11.88 Richard Bustin W CO 3 Norwich
22.11.88 Cordwell Hylton W CO 3 Basildon
24.01.89 John Foreman W RSC 4 Kings Heath
08.02.89 Lavell Stanley W CO 1 Kensington
28.03.89 Blaine Logsdon L RSC 2 Glasgow
10.05.89 Serg Fame W RTD 7 Solihull
31.10.89 Carl Thompson W RSC 6 Manchester
(Vacant Central Area L. Heavyweight Title)
24.01.90 Brian Schumacher W RSC 3 Preston
(Central Area L. Heavyweight Title Defence)
25.04.90 Dwain Muniz W RSC 1 Brighton
26.11.90 John Williams W RSC 1 Mayfair
12.02.91 Melvin Ricks W CO 1 Belfast
01.03.91 Graciano Rocchigiani L PTS 12 Dusseldorf, Germany
(Vacant European L. Heavyweight Title)
25.07.91 Roy Skeldon W RSC 7 Dudley
(Vacant British L. Heavyweight Title)
30.01.92 Jim Peters W RSC 1 Southampton
(British L. Heavyweight Title Defence)
25.04.92 Glazz Campbell W RSC 8 Belfast
(British L. Heavyweight Title Defence)
23.09.92 Yawe Davis DREW 12 Campione d'Italia, Italy
(Vacant European L. Heavyweight Title)
23.04.93 Michael Nunn L RSC 6 Memphis, USA
(WBA S. Middleweight Title Challenge)
29.01.94 Dennis Andries L RTD 4 Cardiff
19.11.94 Nicky Piper W PTS 12 Cardiff
(Vacant British L. Heavyweight Title)
25.02.95 Hunter Clay W RTD 3 Millwall
01.04.95 Virgil Hill L PTS 12 Stateline, USA
(WBA L. Heavyweight Title Challenge)
01.07.95 Lenzie Morgan W PTS 8 Kensington
24.11.95 Jesus Castaneda W RSC 3 Manchester
10.02.96 Frank Minton W RSC 1 Cottbus, Germany
02.03.96 Ray Kane W CO 2 Newcastle
11.12.96 Tony Booth W RSC 1 Southwark
11.01.97 Peter Kamarenko W RSC 1 Bethnal Green

01.03.97 Roberto Dominguez W CO 3 Liverpool
(Vacant European L. Heavyweight Title)
31.05.97 Pascal Warusfel W PTS 12 Paris, France
(European L. Heavyweight Title Defence)
Career: 36 contests, won 28, drew 1, lost 7.

Crawford Ashley   Les Clark

Michael Ayers

Tooting. *Born* London, 26 January, 1965
British Lightweight Champion. Former Undefeated WBC International & Southern Area Lightweight Champion. Ht. 5'8"
Manager B. Hearn

16.05.89 Young Joe Rafiu W RSC 5 Wandsworth
27.06.89 Greg Egbuniwe W CO 1 Kensington
15.11.89 Mille Markovic W RSC 2 Lewisham
05.12.89 Darren Mount W RSC 2 Catford
26.04.90 Nick Hall W CO 3 Wandsworth
04.06.91 Stuart Rimmer W CO 1 Bethnal Green
22.06.91 Wayne Weekes W RSC 6 Earls Court
(Vacant Southern Area Lightweight Title)
21.09.91 Peter Till W RSC 5 Tottenham
(Elim. British Lightweight Title)
28.01.92 Jorge Pompey W PTS 8 Hamburg, Germany

19.02.92 Rudy Valentino W RSC 7 Muswell Hill
(Southern Area Lightweight Title Defence. Elim. British Lightweight Title)
27.06.92 Sugar Gibiliru W RSC 6 Quinta do Lago, Portugal
13.10.92 Scott Brouwer W RSC 4 Mayfair
(Vacant WBC International Lightweight Title)
20.02.93 Danny Myburgh W RSC 5 Earls Court
(WBC International Lightweight Title Defence)
16.04.93 Giovanni Parisi L PTS 12 Rome, Italy
(WBO Lightweight Title Challenge)
24.05.94 Karl Taylor DREW 8 Sunderland
30.09.94 John O. Johnson W RSC 3 Bethnal Green
07.11.94 Bamana Dibateza W PTS 6 Bethnal Green
17.02.95 Paul Burke W RSC 6 Crawley
(Vacant British Lightweight Title)
31.03.95 Karl Taylor W RSC 8 Crystal Palace
(British Lightweight Title Defence)
23.05.95 Charles Shepherd W RSC 3 Potters Bar
(British Lightweight Title Defence)
30.09.95 Dave Anderson W RTD 7 Basildon
(British Lightweight Title Defence)
27.09.96 Tony Swift W RSC 5 Stevenage
20.11.96 Colin Dunne W RSC 9 Wembley
(British Lightweight Title Defence)
Career: 23 contests, won 21, drew 1, lost 1.

Michael Ayers   Les Clark

Michael Brodie   Harry Goodwin

Michael Brodie

Manchester. *Born* Manchester, 10 May,
1974
British S. Bantamweight Champion. Ht.
5'6"
Manager J. Trickett

03.10.94	Graham McGrath W RSC 5 Manchester
20.10.94	Chip O'Neill W CO 3 Middleton
28.11.94	Muhammad Shaffique W CO 2 Manchester
13.12.94	Pete Buckley W PTS 6 Potters Bar
16.02.95	G. G. Goddard W PTS 6 Bury
03.04.95	Garry Burrell W RSC 4 Manchester
05.05.95	G. G. Goddard W PTS 6 Swansea
17.05.95	Ian Reid W RSC 3 Ipswich
10.06.95	Chris Clarkson W PTS 6 Manchester
14.11.95	Niel Leggett W CO 1 Bury
25.11.95	Karl Morling W RSC 1 Dagenham
18.12.95	Marty Chestnut W RTD 3 Mayfair
26.02.96	Bamana Dibateza W PTS 6 Manchester
13.04.96	John Sillo W CO 1 Liverpool
07.05.96	Elvis Parsley W RSC 1 Mayfair
06.07.96	Colin Innes W RSC 2 Manchester
19.09.96	Ervine Blake W RSC 4 Manchester
09.11.96	Miguel Matthews W PTS 6 Manchester
22.03.97	Neil Swain W RSC 10 Wythenshawe *(Vacant British S. Bantamweight Title)*

Career: 19 contests, won 19.

Neville Brown

Burton. *Born* Burton, 26 February, 1966
British Middleweight Champion. Ht. 5'10"
Manager F. Warren

08.11.89	Spencer Alton W RSC 4 Wembley
10.01.90	Colin Ford W RTD 3 Kensington
27.03.90	Jimmy McDonagh W RSC 2 Mayfair
09.05.90	William Pronzola W RSC 3 Wembley
13.09.90	Anthony Campbell W RSC 2 Watford
10.10.90	Nigel Moore W CO 1 Kensington
13.12.90	Chris Richards W RSC 2 Dewsbury
17.01.91	Shamus Casey W RSC 4 Alfreton
13.02.91	Jimmy Thornton W RSC 1 Wembley
28.03.91	Tony Booth W PTS 6 Alfreton
12.04.91	Winston Wray W RSC 1 Willenhall
04.07.91	Paul Wesley L RSC 1 Alfreton
29.08.91	Paul Smith W RSC 3 Oakengates
03.10.91	Paul Wesley W PTS 8 Burton
21.11.91	Colin Pitters W RSC 3 Burton
26.03.92	Paul Murray W CO 3 Telford
01.10.92	Ernie Loveridge W CO 4 Telford
02.11.92	Horace Fleary W PTS 8 Wolverhampton
04.12.92	Karl Barwise W RSC 6 Telford
20.01.93	Graham Burton W CO 4 Wolverhampton
16.03.93	Paul Busby W PTS 10 Wolverhampton *(Elim. British Middleweight Title)*
10.11.93	Frank Grant W RSC 7 Bethnal Green *(British Middleweight Title Challenge)*
26.01.94	Andrew Flute W RTD 7 Birmingham *(British Middleweight Title Defence)*
16.03.94	Wallid Underwood W PTS 10 Birmingham
20.07.94	Agostino Cardamone L RSC 7 Solofra, Italy *(European Middleweight Title Challenge)*
29.10.94	Colin Pitters W CO 2 Cannock
29.11.94	Antonio Fernandez W RSC 9 Cannock *(British Middleweight Title Defence)*
10.02.95	Steve Goodwin W RSC 3 Birmingham
03.03.95	Carlo Colarusso W RSC 7 Bethnal Green *(British Middleweight Title Defence)*
22.07.95	Anthony Ivory L PTS 8 Millwall
02.09.95	Trevor Ambrose W PTS 8 Wembley
10.11.95	Shaun Cummins W CO 5 Derby *(British Middleweight Title Defence)*
09.03.96	Steve Collins L RSC 11 Millstreet *(WBO S. Middleweight Title Challenge)*
18.01.97	Willie Quinn W RSC 4 Swadlincote *(British Middleweight Title Defence)*
26.04.97	Hassine Cherifi L RSC 6 Swadlincote *(European Middleweight Title Challenge)*

Career: 35 contests, won 30, lost 5.

Neville Brown   Les Clark

Steve Collins   Les Clark

Steve Collins

Dublin. *Born* Dublin, 21 July, 1964
WBO S. Middleweight Champion. Former
Undefeated WBO, USBA, WBO, Penta-
Continental & All-Ireland Middleweight
Champion. Ht. 5'11"
Manager Self

24.10.86	Julio Mercado W RSC 3 Lowell, USA
26.11.86	Mike Bonislawski W PTS 4 Dorchester, USA
20.12.86	Richard Holloway W RSC 2 Dorchester, USA
10.10.87	Jim Holmes W CO 1 Attleboro, USA
20.10.87	Harold Souther W PTS 8 Lowell, USA
20.11.87	Mike Williams W PTS 6 Atlantic City, USA
09.12.87	Benny Sims W PTS 8 Atlantic City, USA
18.03.88	Sammy Storey W PTS 10 Boston, USA *(Vacant All-Ireland Middleweight Title)*
26.05.88	Lester Yarborough W PTS 10 Boston, USA
30.07.88	Mike Dale W PTS 8 Brockton, USA
22.10.88	Muhammad Shabbaz W RSC 4 Salem, USA
10.12.88	Jesse Lanton W PTS 10 Salem, USA
07.02.89	Paul McPeek W RSC 9 Atlantic City, USA
09.05.89	Kevin Watts W PTS 12 Atlantic City, USA *(USBA Middleweight Title Challenge)*
26.07.89	Tony Thornton W PTS 12 Atlantic City, USA *(USBA Middleweight Title Defence)*
21.11.89	Roberto Rosiles W RSC 9 Las Vegas, USA
03.02.90	Mike McCallum L PTS 12 Boston, USA *(WBA Middleweight Title Challenge)*
16.08.90	Fermin Chirino W RSC 6 Boston, USA
24.11.90	Eddie Hall W PTS 10 Boston, USA
11.05.91	Kenny Snow W RSC 3 Belfast

25.05.91	Jean-Noel Camara W CO 3 Brest, France
11.12.91	Danny Morgan W RSC 3 Dublin
22.04.92	Reggie Johnson L PTS 12 East Rutherford, USA *(Vacant WBA Middleweight Title)*
22.10.92	Sumbu Kalambay L PTS 12 Verbania, Italy *(European Middleweight Title Challenge)*
06.02.93	Johnny Melfah W RSC 3 Cardiff
20.02.93	Ian Strudwick W RSC 7 Kensington
26.06.93	Gerhard Botes W RSC 7 Kensington *(Vacant WBO Penta-Continental Middleweight Title)*
30.11.93	Wayne Ellis W RSC 9 Cardiff *(WBO Penta-Continental Middleweight Title Defence)*
22.01.94	Johnny Melfah W RSC 4 Belfast
09.02.94	Paul Wesley W PTS 8 Brentwood
11.05.94	Chris Pyatt W RSC 5 Sheffield *(WBO Middleweight Title Challenge)*
18.03.95	Chris Eubank W PTS 12 Millstreet *(WBO S. Middleweight Title Challenge)*
09.09.95	Chris Eubank W PTS 12 Cork *(WBO S. Middleweight Title Defence)*
25.11.95	Cornelius Carr W PTS 12 Dublin *(WBO S. Middleweight Title Defence)*
09.03.96	Neville Brown W RSC 11 Millstreet *(WBO S. Middleweight Title Defence)*
06.07.96	Nigel Benn W RSC 4 Manchester *(WBO S. Middleweight Title Defence)*
09.11.96	Nigel Benn W RTD 6 Manchester *(WBO S. Middleweight Title Defence)*
08.02.97	Frederic Seillier W RSC 5 Millwall *(WBO S. Middleweight Title Defence)*

Career: 38 contests, won 35, lost 3.

Darren Corbett

Belfast. *Born* Belfast, 8 July, 1972
Commonwealth & All-Ireland
Cruiserweight Champion. Ht. 5'11"
Manager B. Hearn

10.12.94	David Jules W RSC 1 Manchester

13.12.94	Carl Gaffney W RSC 1 Potters Bar
21.02.95	Steve Garber W PTS 6 Sunderland
18.03.95	Gary Williams DREW 6 Millstreet
14.04.95	Dennis Bailey W RSC 2 Belfast
27.05.95	R. F. McKenzie L PTS 6 Belfast
26.08.95	Nigel Rafferty W PTS 6 Belfast
07.10.95	Nigel Rafferty W PTS 6 Belfast
02.12.95	Bobbi Joe Edwards W PTS 6 Belfast
07.05.96	Cliff Elden W RSC 1 Mayfair
28.05.96	Darren Fearn W RSC 1 Belfast
03.09.96	Chris Woollas W RSC 7 Belfast
05.11.96	Ray Kane W RSC 5 Belfast *(Vacant All-Ireland Cruiserweight Title)*
17.12.96	Chris Woollas W RSC 1 Doncaster
28.01.97	Nigel Rafferty W PTS 10 Belfast *(All-Ireland Cruiserweight Title Defence)*
29.04.97	Noel Magee W CO 2 Belfast *(All-Ireland Cruiserweight Title Defence)*
02.06.97	Chris Okoh W RSC 3 Belfast *(Commonwealth Cruiserweight Title Challenge)*

Career: 17 contests, won 15, drew 1, lost 1.

Darren Corbett   Les Clark

Peter Culshaw

Liverpool. *Born* Liverpool, 15 May, 1973
Commonwealth Flyweight Champion.
Former Undefeated Central Area Flyweight
Champion. Ht. 5'6"
Manager S. Vaughan

02.07.93	Graham McGrath W PTS 6 Liverpool
28.09.93	Vince Feeney W PTS 6 Liverpool
11.12.93	Nick Tooley W RSC 1 Liverpool
25.02.94	Des Gargano W PTS 6 Chester
06.05.94	Neil Swain W PTS 6 Liverpool
26.09.94	Daryl McKenzie W PTS 6 Liverpool
20.04.95	Rowan Williams W CO 6 Liverpool
29.09.95	Maxim Pougatchev DREW 8 Liverpool
05.03.96	Louis Veitch W RSC 3 Barrow *(Central Area Flyweight Title Challenge)*

53

13.04.96 Lyndon Kershaw W RSC 3 Liverpool
25.06.96 Danny Ward W RSC 3 Stevenage
(Commonwealth Flyweight Title Challenge)
27.09.96 James Wanene W RSC 7 Stevenage
(Commonwealth Flyweight Title Defence)

Career: 12 contests, won 11, drew 1.

Peter Culshaw   Les Clark

(Andrew) Drew Docherty

Condorrat. *Born* Glasgow, 29 November, 1965
British Bantamweight Champion. Ht. 5'6"
Manager T. Gilmour

14.09.89 Gordon Shaw W PTS 6 Motherwell
23.11.89 Chris Clarkson W PTS 6 Motherwell
09.05.90 Rocky Lawlor DREW 8 Solihull
03.10.90 Steve Robinson W PTS 8 Solihull
21.11.90 Pete Buckley W PTS 8 Solihull
14.11.91 Stevie Woods W RSC 1 Edinburgh
27.01.92 Neil Parry W RSC 4 Glasgow
27.04.92 Pete Buckley W PTS 8 Glasgow
01.06.92 Joe Kelly W RSC 5 Glasgow
(British Bantamweight Title Challenge)
25.01.93 Donnie Hood W PTS 12 Glasgow
(British Bantamweight Title Defence)
26.04.93 Russell Davison W PTS 8 Glasgow
25.10.93 Pete Buckley W PTS 8 Glasgow
02.02.94 Vincenzo Belcastro L PTS 12 Glasgow
(European Bantamweight Title Challenge)
09.07.94 Conn McMullen W PTS 8 Earls Court
20.09.94 Miguel Matthews W PTS 8 Musselburgh
23.11.94 Ady Benton W PTS 12 Irvine
(British Bantamweight Title Defence)
17.02.95 Alfred Kotey L RSC 4 Cumbernauld
(WBO Bantamweight Title Challenge)
13.10.95 James Murray W CO 12 Glasgow
(British Bantamweight Title Defence)
20.01.96 Daniel Jimenez L PTS 12 Mansfield
(WBO Bantamweight Title Challenge)
14.03.97 Johnny Bredahl L RSC 3 Odense, Denmark
(European Bantamweight Title Challenge)

Career: 20 contests, won 15, drew 1, lost 4.

Julius Francis

Woolwich. *Born* Peckham, 8 December, 1964
Commonwealth Heavyweight Champion.
Former Undefeated Southern Area Heavyweight Champion.
Ht. 6'2"
Manager F. Maloney

23.05.93 Graham Arnold W RSC 5 Brockley
23.06.93 Joey Paladino W CO 4 Edmonton
24.07.93 Andre Tisdale W PTS 4 Atlantic City, USA
28.08.93 Don Sargent W RSC 2 Bismark, USA
01.12.93 John Keeton W PTS 4 Bethnal Green
27.04.94 Manny Burgo W PTS 4 Bethnal Green
25.05.94 John Ruiz L CO 4 Bristol
12.11.94 Conroy Nelson W RSC 4 Dublin
23.11.94 Gary Charlton W RSC 1 Piccadilly
23.02.05 Damien Caesar W RSC 8 Southwark
(Vacant Southern Area Heavyweight Title)
27.04.95 Keith Fletcher W PTS 10 Bethnal Green
(Southern Area Heavyweight Title Defence)
25.05.95 Steve Garber W PTS 8 Reading
01.07.95 Scott Welch L RSC 10 Kensington
(Southern Area Heavyweight Title Defence. Final Elim. British Heavyweight Title)
24.10.95 Neil Kirkwood W RSC 7 Southwark
30.11.95 Nikolai Kulpin L PTS 10 Saratov, Russia
05.02.96 Michael Murray L PTS 10 Bexleyheath
(Elim. British Heavyweight Title)
09.04.96 Damien Caesar W CO 1 Stevenage
(Vacant Southern Area Heavyweight Title)

Drew Docherty (right) in action against Conn McMullen

Les Clark

07.05.96 Darren Fearn W PTS 8 Mayfair
09.07.96 Mike Holden W PTS 10 Bethnal Green
28.09.96 James Oyebola W RSC 5 Barking
(Southern Area Heavyweight Title Defence)
15.02.97 Zeljko Mavrovic L RSC 8 Vienna, Austria
(European Heavyweight Title Challenge)
30.06.97 Joseph Chingangu W PTS 12 Bethnal Green
(Vacant Commonwealth Heavyweight Title)

Career: 22 contests, won 17, lost 5.

Julius Francis　　　　　　　　　Les Clark

Prince Naseem Hamed

Sheffield. *Born* Sheffield, 12 February, 1974
WBO & IBF Featherweight Champion. Former Undefeated WBC International S. Bantamweight Champion. Former Undefeated European Bantamweight Champion. Ht. 5'3"
Manager B. Ingle

14.04.92 Ricky Beard W CO 2 Mansfield
25.04.92 Shaun Norman W RSC 2 Manchester
23.05.92 Andrew Bloomer W RSC 2 Birmingham
14.07.92 Miguel Matthews W RSC 3 Mayfair
07.10.92 Des Gargano W RSC 4 Sunderland
12.11.92 Pete Buckley W PTS 6 Liverpool
24.02.93 Alan Ley W CO 2 Wembley
26.05.93 Kevin Jenkins W RSC 3 Mansfield
24.09.93 Chris Clarkson W CO 2 Dublin
29.01.94 Pete Buckley W RSC 4 Cardiff
09.04.94 John Miceli W CO 1 Mansfield
11.05.94 Vincenzo Belcastro W PTS 12 Sheffield
(European Bantamweight Title Challenge)
17.08.94 Antonio Picardi W RSC 3 Sheffield
(European Bantamweight Title Defence)
12.10.94 Freddy Cruz W RSC 6 Sheffield
(Vacant WBC International S. Bantamweight Title)

19.11.94 Laureano Ramirez W RTD 3 Cardiff
(WBC International S. Bantamweight Title Defence)
21.01.95 Armando Castro W RSC 4 Glasgow
(WBC International S. Bantamweight Title Defence)
04.03.95 Sergio Liendo W RSC 2 Livingston
(WBC International S. Bantamweight Title Defence)
06.05.95 Enrique Angeles W CO 2 Shepton Mallet
(WBC International S. Bantamweight Title Defence)
01.07.95 Juan Polo Perez W CO 2 Kensington
(WBC International S. Bantamweight Title Defence)
30.09.95 Steve Robinson W RSC 8 Cardiff
(WBO Featherweight Title Challenge)
16.03.96 Said Lawal W RSC 1 Glasgow
(WBO Featherweight Title Defence)
08.06.96 Daniel Alicea W RSC 2 Newcastle
(WBO Featherweight Title Defence)
31.08.96 Manuel Medina W RSC 11 Dublin
(WBO Featherweight Title Defence)
09.11.96 Remigio Molina W RSC 2 Manchester
(WBO Featherweight Title Defence)
08.02.97 Tom Johnson W RSC 8 Millwall
(WBO Featherweight Title Defence. IBF Featherweight Title Challenge)
03.05.97 Billy Hardy W RSC 1 Manchester
(WBO & IBF Featherweight Title Defences)

Career: 26 contests, won 26.

Prince Naseem Hamed　　　　Les Clark

Billy Hardy

Sunderland. *Born* Sunderland, 5 September, 1964
European Featherweight Champion. Former Undefeated British & Commonwealth Featherweight Champion. Former Undefeated British Bantamweight Champion. Ht. 5'6"
Manager T. Gilmour

21.11.83 Kevin Downer W PTS 6 Eltham
03.12.83 Brett Styles W PTS 6 Marylebone
27.01.84 Keith Ward W PTS 6 Longford
13.02.84 Johnny Mack W RSC 5 Eltham
01.03.84 Graham Kid Clarke W PTS 8 Queensway
27.03.84 Glen McLaggon W PTS 6 Battersea
06.04.84 Graham Kid Clarke W RSC 7 Watford
25.04.84 Anthony Brown W RSC 5 Muswell Hill
04.06.84 Roy Webb L PTS 6 Mayfair
06.09.84 Les Walsh W PTS 8 Gateshead
10.10.84 Jorge Prentas L RSC 5 Shoreditch
12.02.85 Ivor Jones W PTS 8 Kensington
17.04.85 Ivor Jones W PTS 10 Bethnal Green
08.06.85 Valerio Nati L RSC 4 Florence, Italy
10.10.85 Keith Wallace W RSC 7 Alfreton
(Final Elim. British Bantamweight Title)
02.06.86 Rocky Lawlor W PTS 8 Mayfair
19.02.87 Ray Gilbody W RSC 3 St Helens
(British Bantamweight Title Challenge)
23.04.87 Rocky Lawlor W RSC 7 Newcastle
04.06.87 Brian Holmes W PTS 10 Sunderland
17.03.88 John Hyland W CO 2 Sunderland
(British Bantamweight Title Defence)
11.05.88 Luis Ramos W RSC 2 Wembley
29.09.88 Jose Gallegos W RSC 4 Sunderland
02.11.88 Vincenzo Belcastro L PTS 12 Paolo, Italy
(European Bantamweight Title Challenge)
14.02.89 Ronnie Carroll W PTS 12 Sunderland
(British Bantamweight Title Defence)
29.03.89 Jose Soto W PTS 8 Wembley
28.06.89 Vincenzo Belcastro DREW 12 Pavia, Italy
(European Bantamweight Title Challenge)
10.10.89 Brian Holmes W CO 1 Sunderland
(British Bantamweight Title Defence)
24.01.90 Orlando Canizales L PTS 12 Sunderland
(IBF Bantamweight Title Challenge)
22.05.90 Miguel Pequeno W RSC 4 Stockton
29.11.90 Ronnie Carroll W RSC 8 Sunderland
(British Bantamweight Title Defence)
28.02.91 Francisco Ortiz W RSC 7 Sunderland
04.05.91 Orlando Canizales L RSC 8 Laredo, USA
(IBF Bantamweight Title Challenge)
03.03.92 Chris Clarkson W RSC 5 Houghton le Spring
07.10.92 Ricky Raynor W RSC 10 Sunderland
(Vacant Commonwealth Featherweight Title)
19.05.93 Barrington Francis W PTS 12 Sunderland
(Commonwealth Featherweight Title Defence)
15.06.93 Angel Fernandez W PTS 10 Hemel Hempstead
30.11.93 Mustapha Hame L PTS 8 Marseilles, France
24.05.94 Alan McKay W RSC 8 Sunderland
(Vacant British Featherweight Title. Commonwealth Featherweight Title Defence)
15.10.94 Stanford Ngcebeshe W PTS 12 Sun City, South Africa
(Commonwealth Featherweight Title Defence)
21.02.95 Percy Commey W RSC 11 Sunderland
(Commonwealth Featherweight Title Defence)

04.03.95 Fabrice Benichou DREW 10 St
Quentin, France
28.10.95 Mehdi Labdouni W PTS 12 Fontenay
sous Bois, France
*(European Featherweight Title
Challenge)*
14.02.96 Michael Alldis W PTS 12 Sunderland
*(Commonwealth Featherweight Title
Defence)*
20.06.96 Stefano Zoff W PTS 12 San Remo,
Italy
*(European Featherweight Title
Defence)*
03.02.97 Steve Robinson W PTS 12 Sunderland
*(European Featherweight Title
Defence)*
03.05.97 Prince Naseem Hamed L RSC 1
Manchester
*(WBO & IBF Featherweight Title
Challenges)*
Career: 46 contests, won 36, drew 2, lost 8.

Billy Hardy

Herbie Hide

Norwich. *Born* Nigeria, 27 August, 1971
WBO Heavyweight Champion. Former
Undefeated British, WBC International &
Penta-Continental Heavyweight Champion.
Ht. 6'1½"
Manager F. Warren

24.10.89 L. A. Williams W CO 2 Bethnal Green
05.11.89 Gary McCrory W RTD 1 Kensington
19.12.89 Steve Osborne W RSC 6 Bethnal Green
27.06.90 Alek Penarski W RSC 3 Kensington
05.09.90 Steve Lewsam W RSC 4 Brighton
26.09.90 Jonjo Greene W RSC 1 Manchester
17.10.90 Gus Mendes W RSC 2 Bethnal Green
18.11.90 Steve Lewsam W RSC 1 Birmingham
29.01.91 Lennie Howard W RSC 1 Wisbech
09.04.91 David Jules W RSC 1 Mayfair
14.05.91 John Westgarth W RTD 4 Dudley
03.07.91 Tucker Richards W RSC 3 Brentwood
15.10.91 Eddie Gonzalez W CO 2 Hamburg,
Germany
29.10.91 Chris Jacobs W RSC 1 Cardiff
21.01.92 Conroy Nelson W RSC 2 Norwich
*(Vacant WBC International
Heavyweight Title)*
03.03.92 Percell Davis W CO 1 Amsterdam,
Holland

Herbie Hide   Les Clark

08.09.92 Jean Chanet W RSC 7 Norwich
06.10.92 Craig Peterson W RSC 7 Antwerp,
Belgium
*(WBC International Heavyweight Title
Defence)*
12.12.92 James Pritchard W RSC 2 Muswell
Hill
30.01.93 Juan Antonio Diaz W RSC 3
Brentwood
*(Vacant Penta-Continental
Heavyweight Title)*
27.02.93 Michael Murray W RSC 5 Dagenham
(Vacant British Heavyweight Title)
11.05.93 Jerry Halstead W RSC 4 Norwich
*(Penta-Continental Heavyweight Title
Defence)*
18.09.93 Everett Martin W PTS 10 Leicester
06.11.93 Mike Dixon W RSC 9 Bethnal Green
*(Penta-Continental Heavyweight Title
Defence)*
04.12.93 Jeff Lampkin W RSC 2 Sun City,
South Africa
*(WBC International Heavyweight Title
Defence)*
19.03.94 Michael Bentt W CO 7 Millwall
(WBO Heavyweight Title Challenge)
11.03.95 Riddick Bowe L CO 6 Las Vegas, USA
(WBO Heavyweight Title Defence)
06.07.96 Michael Murray W RSC 6 Manchester
09.11.96 Frankie Swindell W CO 1 Manchester
28.06.97 Tony Tucker W RSC 2 Norwich
(Vacant WBO Heavyweight Title)
Career: 30 contests, won 29, lost 1.

Paul Ingle

Scarborough. *Born* Scarborough, 22 June,
1972
British Featherweight Champion. Ht. 5'5"
Manager F. Maloney

23.03.94 Darren Noble W RSC 3 Cardiff
27.04.94 Graham McGrath W PTS 4 Bethnal
Green
25.05.94 Neil Swain W CO 4 Bristol
03.08.94 Anthony Hanna W PTS 6 Bristol
24.11.94 Graham McGrath W PTS 6 Hull
23.02.95 Pete Buckley W PTS 8 Southwark
27.04.95 Pete Buckley W PTS 8 Bethnal Green
16.06.95 Des Gargano W RSC 2 Southwark
29.09.95 Miguel Matthews W RSC 4 Bethnal
Green

15.12.95 Damir Nanev W RSC 5 Bethnal Green
05.02.96 Greg Upton W RSC 10 Bexleyheath
29.06.96 Ervine Blake W RSC 2 Erith
03.09.96 Brian Robb W RSC 2 Bethnal Green
06.11.96 Chris Jickells W RSC 4 Hull
11.01.97 Colin McMillan W RSC 8 Bethnal
Green
(British Featherweight Title Challenge)
28.04.97 Michael Alldis W RTD 11 Hull
(British Featherweight Title Defence)
Career: 16 contests, won 16.

Paul Ingle   Les Clark

(John) Jonjo Irwin

Doncaster. *Born* Denaby, 31 May, 1969
Commonwealth Featherweight Champion.
Former British Featherweight Champion.
Former Undefeated WBO Inter-Continental
Featherweight Champion. Former
Undefeated WBO Penta-Continental S.
Featherweight Champion. Former
Undefeated All-Ireland Featherweight
Champion. Ht. 5'8"
Manager J. Rushton

08.09.92	Kid McAuley W PTS 6 Doncaster	
30.09.92	Miguel Matthews W PTS 6 Solihull	
24.11.92	Colin Lynch W RSC 4 Doncaster	
20.01.93	Mark Hargreaves W RSC 4 Solihull	
23.02.93	G. G. Goddard W RSC 8 Doncaster	
16.03.93	Kid McAuley W PTS 10 Mayfair	

(Vacant All-Ireland Featherweight Title)

28.04.93 Kevin Middleton L RSC 6 Solihull
06.10.93 Pete Buckley W PTS 8 Solihull
21.12.93 Peter Harris W PTS 8 Mayfair
22.01.94 Derek Amory L RSC 2 Belfast
10.05.94 Michael Armstrong W PTS 12 Doncaster
(Vacant WBO Penta-Continental S. Featherweight Title)
04.10.94 Harry Escott W PTS 12 Mayfair
(WBO Penta-Continental S. Featherweight Title Defence)
13.12.94 Bamana Dibateza W PTS 12 Potters Bar
(WBO Penta-Continental S. Featherweight Title Defence)
30.06.95 Manuel Calvo W PTS 12 Doncaster
(Vacant WBO Inter-Continental Featherweight Title)
17.07.95 Learie Bruce W RSC 8 Mayfair
(WBO Inter-Continental Featherweight Title Defence)
20.09.95 Mike Deveney W PTS 12 Potters Bar
(British Featherweight Title Challenge)
18.12.95 Elvis Parsley W RSC 8 Mayfair
(British Featherweight Title Defence)
14.05.96 Colin McMillan L PTS 12 Dagenham
(British Featherweight Title Defence)
11.10.96 Smith Odoom W PTS 12 Mayfair
(Vacant Commonwealth Featherweight Title)
17.12.96 Rick Raynor W PTS 12 Doncaster
(Commonwealth Featherweight Title Defence)

Career: 20 contests, won 17, lost 3.

Jonjo Irwin   Les Clark

Justin Juuko   Les Clark

Justin Juuko

Millwall. *Born* Musaka, Uganda, 21 September, 1972
Commonwealth & WBC International S. Featherweight Champion. Ht. 5'7"
Manager Self

18.03.91 Gilbert Diaz W RSC 3 Las Vegas, USA
26.03.91 Jorge Lopez W PTS 4 Las Vegas, USA
02.06.91 Kevin Childrey W RSC 2 Las Vegas, USA
12.06.91 Juan Carlos Lopez W CO 4 Irvine, USA
06.07.91 Norberto Bravo L RSC 2 Las Vegas, USA
29.10.91 Danny Gonzalez W RSC 1 Phoenix, USA
30.11.91 Ruben Rivera W RSC 5 Las Vegas, USA
14.02.92 Chris Crespin W RSC 3 Las Vegas, USA
28.03.92 Amador Martinez W RSC 2 Las Vegas, USA
24.05.92 Mario Lozano W CO 2 Las Vegas, USA
26.06.92 Victor Miranda T DREW 2 Las Vegas, USA
21.08.92 Jose Manjarez W RSC 6 Las Vegas, USA
21.10.92 Roberto Torres W RSC 2 Las Vegas, USA
26.12.92 Roberto Torres W RSC 1 Las Vegas, USA
24.01.93 Cesar Guzman W CO 3 Lynwood, USA
24.02.93 Abe Gomez W PTS 8 Las Vegas, USA
17.04.93 Russell Mosley W CO 4 Sacramento, USA
28.11.93 Derek Amory W RSC 1 Southwark
09.02.94 Charles Shepherd W RSC 5 Bethnal Green
09.04.94 Bamana Dibateza W RSC 5 Mansfield
12.10.94 Juan Amando Reyes W PTS 8 Sheffield

18.02.95 Alberto Lopez W RTD 3 Shepton Mallet
13.05.95 Peter Till W RTD 4 Glasgow
07.07.95 Mark Smith W RSC 4 Cardiff
30.09.95 Tony Pep W PTS 12 Cardiff
(Commonwealth S. Featherweight Title Challenge)
26.01.96 Jackie Gunguluza W RSC 7 Brighton
(Commonwealth S. Featherweight Title Defence)
11.12.96 Gary Thornhill W RSC 8 Southwark
(Commonwealth S. Featherweight Title Defence)
22.02.97 Martin Ramirez W CO 1 Kampala, Uganda
08.04.97 Rakhim Mingaleev W RSC 2 Bethnal Green
22.05.97 David Ouma W PTS 12 Southwark
(Commonwealth S. Featherweight Title Defence. Vacant WBC International S. Featherweight Title)

Career: 30 contests, won 28, drew 1, lost 1.

(Adrian) Ady Lewis

Bury. *Born* Bury, 31 May, 1975
British Flyweight Champion. Former Undefeated Central Area Flyweight Champion. Ht. 4'10½"
Manager J. Doughty/B. Hearn

25.04.94 Darren Greaves W RSC 1 Bury
02.06.94 Dave Campbell W RSC 1 Middleton
22.09.94 Neil Parry W RSC 3 Bury
21.11.94 Daryl McKenzie W RSC 4 Glasgow
17.01.95 Yusuf Vorajee W RSC 2 Worcester
16.02.95 Chip O'Neill W RSC 1 Bury
06.03.95 Mark Cokely W RSC 5 Mayfair
09.05.95 Pete Buckley W PTS 4 Basildon
25.06.96 Graham McGrath W RSC 1 Stevenage
13.10.96 Gary Hickman W RSC 3 Shaw
01.12.96 Louis Veitch W PTS 10 Shaw
(Vacant Central Area Flyweight Title)
27.01.97 Keith Knox W PTS 12 Glasgow
(Vacant British Flyweight Title)
27.05.97 Mark Reynolds W PTS 12 Mayfair
(British Flyweight Title Defence)

Career: 13 contests, won 13.

Ady Lewis   Harry Goodwin

57

Lennox Lewis   Les Clark

Lennox Lewis
Crayford. *Born* London, 2 September, 1965
WBC Heavyweight Champion. Former
Undefeated British, European &
Commonwealth Heavyweight Champion.
Ht. 6'4¾"
Manager F. Maloney

27.06.89 Al Malcolm W CO 2 Kensington
21.07.89 Bruce Johnson W RSC 2 Atlantic City,
USA
25.09.89 Andrew Gerrard W RSC 4 Crystal
Palace
10.10.89 Steve Garber W CO 1 Hull
05.11.89 Melvin Epps W DIS 2 Kensington
18.12.89 Greg Gorrell W RSC 5 Kitchener,
Canada
31.01.90 Noel Quarless W RSC 2 Bethnal Green
22.03.90 Calvin Jones W CO 1 Gateshead
14.04.90 Mike Simwelu W CO 1 Kensington
09.05.90 Jorge Dascola W CO 1 Kensington
20.05.90 Dan Murphy W RSC 6 Sheffield
27.06.90 Ossie Ocasio W PTS 8 Kensington
11.07.90 Mike Acey W RSC 2 Mississuaga,
Canada
31.10.90 Jean Chanet W RSC 6 Crystal Palace
*(European Heavyweight Title
Challenge)*
06.03.91 Gary Mason W RSC 7 Wembley
*(British Heavyweight Title Challenge.
European Heavyweight Title Defence)*
12.07.91 Mike Weaver W CO 6 Lake Tahoe,
USA
30.09.91 Glenn McCrory W CO 2 Kensington
*(British & European Heavyweight Title
Defence)*
21.11.91 Tyrell Biggs W RSC 3 Atlanta, USA
01.02.92 Levi Billups W PTS 10 Las Vegas,
USA
30.04.92 Derek Williams W RSC 3 Kensington
*(British & European Heavyweight Title
Defence. Commonwealth Heavyweight
Title Challenge)*

11.08.92 Mike Dixon W RSC 4 Atlantic City,
USA
31.10.92 Razor Ruddock W RSC 2 Earls Court
*(Final Elim. WBC Heavyweight Title &
Commonwealth Heavyweight Title
Defence)*
08.05.93 Tony Tucker W PTS 12 Las Vegas,
USA
(WBC Heavyweight Title Defence)
01.10.93 Frank Bruno W RSC 7 Cardiff
(WBC Heavyweight Title Defence)
06.05.94 Phil Jackson W RSC 8 Atlantic City
(WBC Heavyweight Title Defence)
24.09.94 Oliver McCall L RSC 2 Wembley
(WBC Heavyweight Title Defence)
13.05.95 Lionel Butler W RSC 5 Sacramento,
USA
(Elim. WBC Heavyweight Title)
02.07.95 Justin Fortune W RSC 4 Dublin
07.10.95 Tommy Morrison W RSC 6 Atlantic
City, USA
10.05.96 Ray Mercer W PTS 10 New York City,
USA
07.02.97 Oliver McCall W RSC 5 Las Vegas,
USA
(Vacant WBC Heavyweight Title)
Career: 31 contests, won 30, lost 1.

Paul Lloyd   Les Clark

Paul Lloyd
Ellesmere Port. *Born* Bebington, 7
December, 1968
Commonwealth Bantamweight Champion.
Former Undefeated Central Area S.
Bantamweight Champion. Ht. 5'7"
Manager J. Hyland

25.09.92 Graham McGrath W RSC 3 Liverpool
23.10.92 Kid McAuley W PTS 4 Liverpool
20.11.92 Des Gargano W PTS 4 Liverpool
15.12.92 Glyn Shepherd W RSC 1 Liverpool
27.02.93 Miguel Matthews W PTS 6 Ellesmere
Port
04.05.93 Andrew Bloomer W PTS 6 Liverpool
02.07.93 Ronnie Stephenson W RTD 1
Liverpool

30.10.93 Marty Chestnut W RSC 1 Chester
11.12.93 Gerald Shelton W RSC 3 Liverpool
25.02.94 Ady Benton W RSC 5 Chester
*(Vacant Central Area S. Bantamweight
Title)*
06.05.94 Pete Buckley W RTD 4 Liverpool
26.09.94 Chris Clarkson L RSC 4 Liverpool
25.03.95 Richie Wenton L RSC 5 Chester
*(British S. Bantamweight Title
Challenge)*
16.06.95 Garry Burrell W RSC 2 Liverpool
24.11.95 Michael Parris L RSC 4 Chester
03.02.96 Julian Gomez W CO 2 Liverpool
07.10.96 Nathan Sting W RSC 6 Lewisham
*(Vacant Commonwealth Bantamweight
Title)*
18.02.97 Lybo Nkoko W CO 1 Cheshunt
*(Commonwealth Bantamweight Title
Defence)*
16.04.97 Simphiwe Pamana W RSC 11 Bethnal
Green
*(Commonwealth Bantamweight Title
Defence)*
Career: 19 contests, won 16, lost 3.

Kevin Lueshing   Les Clark

Kevin Lueshing
Beckenham. *Born* Beckenham, 17 April,
1968
British & IBO Welterweight Champion.
Former Undefeated Southern Area L.
Middleweight Champion. Ht. 5'11"
Manager F. Warren

30.09.91 John McGlynn W RSC 2 Kensington
23.10.91 Julian Eavis W RSC 2 Bethnal Green
14.12.91 Trevor Meikle W CO 3 Bexleyheath
18.01.92 Simon Eubank W CO 4 Kensington
25.03.92 Tracy Jocelyn W RSC 3 Dagenham
30.04.92 Newton Barnett W PTS 6 Kensington
03.02.93 Ian Chantler W RSC 2 Earls Court
17.02.93 Leigh Wicks W PTS 6 Bethnal Green
31.03.93 Ernie Loveridge W RSC 5 Bethnal
Green

14.04.93 Marty Duke W RSC 2 Kensington
23.06.93 Kirkland Laing W RSC 5 Edmonton
(Vacant Southern Area L. Middleweight Title)
03.03.94 Chris Saunders L RSC 4 Ebbw Vale
30.07.94 Dennis Berry W CO 2 Bethnal Green
25.10.94 Peter Waudby W RSC 2 Middlesbrough
17.06.95 Michael Smyth W RSC 3 Cardiff
(Final Elim. British Welterweight Title)
30.09.95 Danny Quacoe W PTS 8 Cardiff
09.12.95 Steve Goodwin W RTD 2 Bethnal Green
13.02.96 Chris Saunders W RSC 3 Bethnal Green
(British Welterweight Title Challenge)
08.06.96 Paul King W RSC 2 Newcastle
17.07.96 Cirilo Nino W RSC 2 New York City, USA
(Vacant IBO Welterweight Title)
11.01.97 Felix Trinidad L RSC 3 Nashville, USA
(IBF Welterweight Title Challenge)
Career: 21 contests, won 19, lost 2.

Robert McCracken

Birmingham. *Born* Birmingham, 31 May, 1968
Commonwealth Middleweight Champion. Former Undefeated British L. Middleweight Champion. Ht. 6'0"
Manager M. Duff

24.01.91 Mick Mulcahy W RSC 1 Brierley Hill
13.02.91 Gary Barron W RTD 2 Wembley
06.03.91 Tony Britland W RSC 2 Wembley
12.04.91 Dave Andrews W RSC 4 Willenhall
08.05.91 Tony Gibbs W CO 1 Kensington
30.05.91 Paul Murray W RSC 2 Birmingham
04.07.91 Marty Duke W RSC 1 Alfreton
25.07.91 John Smith W RTD 1 Dudley
31.10.91 Newton Barnett W DIS 2 Oakengates
28.11.91 Michael Oliver W RSC 3 Liverpool
12.02.92 Paul Lynch W RSC 4 Wembley
01.10.92 Horace Fleary W PTS 8 Telford
02.11.92 Ensley Bingham W RSC 10 Wolverhampton
(Elim. British L. Middleweight Title)
20.01.93 Leigh Wicks W PTS 8 Wolverhampton
17.02.93 Ernie Loveridge W CO 4 Bethnal Green
24.04.93 Martin Smith W RSC 10 Birmingham
(Final Elim. British L. Middleweight Title)
29.06.93 Steve Langley W RSC 4 Edgbaston
01.12.93 Chris Peters W PTS 8 Kensington
23.02.94 Andy Till W PTS 12 Watford
(British L. Middleweight Title Challenge)
10.09.94 Steve Foster W PTS 12 Birmingham
(British L. Middleweight Title Defence)
11.10.94 Dean Cooper W RSC 4 Bethnal Green
10.02.95 Paul Wesley W PTS 12 Birmingham
(British L. Middleweight Title Defence)
21.04.95 Sergio Medina W RSC 7 Dudley
01.09.95 Jorge Sclarandi W PTS 10 Wolverhampton
03.11.95 Fitzgerald Bruney W PTS 12 Dudley
(Vacant Commonwealth Middleweight Title)
03.04.96 Paul Busby W RTD 7 Bethnal Green
(Commonwealth Middleweight Title Defence)

Robert McCracken   Les Clark

15.05.96 Humberto Aranda W RSC 5 Cardiff
01.10.96 Fitzgerald Bruney W PTS 12 Birmingham
(Commonwealth Middleweight Title Defence)
12.11.96 Glen Odem W PTS 10 Dudley
Career: 29 contests, won 29.

Johnny Nelson   Les Clark

Johnny Nelson

Sheffield. *Born* Sheffield, 4 January, 1967
British & European Cruiserweight Champion. Former WBF Heavyweight Champion. Former WBF Cruiserweight Champion. Former Undefeated Central Area Cruiserweight Champion.
Ht. 6'2"
Manager B. Ingle/F. Warren

18.03.86 Peter Brown L PTS 6 Hull
15.05.86 Tommy Taylor L PTS 6 Dudley
03.10.86 Magne Havnaa L PTS 4 Copenhagen, Denmark
20.11.86 Chris Little W PTS 6 Bredbury
19.01.87 Gypsy Carman W PTS 6 Mayfair
02.03.87 Doug Young W PTS 6 Huddersfield
10.03.87 Sean Daly W RSC 1 Manchester
28.04.87 Brian Schumacher L PTS 8 Halifax
03.06.87 Byron Pullen W RSC 3 Southwark
14.12.87 Jon McBean W RSC 6 Edgbaston
01.02.88 Dennis Bailey L PTS 8 Northampton
24.02.88 Cordwell Hylton W RSC 1 Sheffield
25.04.88 Kenny Jones W CO 1 Liverpool
04.05.88 Crawford Ashley W PTS 8 Solihull
06.06.88 Lennie Howard W CO 2 Mayfair
31.08.88 Andrew Gerrard W PTS 8 Stoke
26.10.88 Danny Lawford W RSC 2 Sheffield
(Vacant Central Area Cruiserweight Title)
04.04.89 Steve Mormino W RSC 2 Sheffield
21.05.89 Andy Straughn W CO 8 Finsbury Park
(British Cruiserweight Title Challenge)
02.10.89 Ian Bulloch W CO 2 Hanley
(British Cruiserweight Title Defence)
27.01.90 Carlos de Leon DREW 12 Sheffield
(WBC Cruiserweight Title Challenge)
14.02.90 Dino Homsey W RSC 7 Brentwood
28.03.90 Lou Gent W CO 4 Bethnal Green
(British Cruiserweight Title Defence)
27.06.90 Arthur Weathers W RSC 2 Kensington
05.09.90 Andre Smith W PTS 8 Brighton
14.12.90 Markus Bott W RSC 12 Karlsruhe, Germany
(Vacant European Cruiserweight Title)
12.03.91 Yves Monsieur W RTD 8 Mansfield
(European Cruiserweight Title Defence)
16.05.92 James Warring L PTS 12 Fredericksburg, USA
(IBF Cruiserweight Title Challenge)
15.08.92 Norbert Ekassi L RSC 3 Ajaccio, France
29.10.92 Corrie Sanders L PTS 10 Morula, South Africa
30.04.93 Dave Russell W RSC 11 Melbourne, Australia
(WBF Cruiserweight Title Challenge)
11.08.93 Tom Collins W RSC 1 Mansfield
(WBF Cruiserweight Title Defence)

01.10.93 Francis Wanyama L DIS 10 Waregem, Belgium
(WBF Cruiserweight Title Defence)
20.11.93 Jimmy Thunder W PTS 12 Auckland, New Zealand
(WBF Heavyweight Title Challenge)
05.04.94 Henry Akinwande L PTS 10 Bethnal Green
05.11.94 Nikolai Kulpin W PTS 12 Bangkok, Thailand
(WBF Heavyweight Title Defence)
22.08.95 Adilson Rodrigues L PTS 12 Sao Paulo, Brazil
(WBF Heavyweight Title Defence)
03.12.95 Adilson Rodrigues L PTS 12 Sao Paulo, Brazil
(WBF Heavyweight Title Challenge)
20.01.96 Tony Booth W RSC 2 Mansfield
14.12.96 Dennis Andries W RSC 7 Sheffield
(Vacant British Cruiserweight Title)
22.02.97 Patrice Aouissi W RSC 7 Berck sur Mer, France
(Vacant European Cruiserweight Title)
Career: 41 contests, won 28, drew 1, lost 12.

Spencer Oliver

Barnet. *Born* Barnet, 27 March 1975
European S. Bantamweight Champion.
Former Undefeated Southern Area S.
Bantamweight Champion. Ht. 5'4½"
Manager J. Harding

17.02.95 Des Gargano W PTS 4 Cumbernauld
13.04.95 Marty Chestnut W RSC 4 Bloomsbury
23.05.95 Pete Buckley W PTS 4 Potters Bar
20.09.95 Karl Morling W RSC 5 Potters Bar
25.11.95 Shaun Anderson W RSC 3 Dagenham
23.01.96 Ricky Beard W RSC 3 Bethnal Green
09.04.96 Gary Hickman W PTS 6 Stevenage
25.06.96 Lyndon Kershaw W RSC 3 Stevenage
27.09.96 Rowan Williams W RTD 3 Stevenage
18.02.97 Patrick Mullings W RSC 10 Cheshunt
*(Vacant Southern Area
S. Bantamweight Title)*
20.05.97 Martin Krastev W RSC 4 Edmonton
*(European S. Bantamweight Title
Challenge)*
Career: 11 contests, won 11.

Spencer Oliver　　　　　Les Clark

Bernard Paul　　　　　Les Clark

Bernard Paul

Tottenham. *Born* Mauritius, 22 October, 1965
Commonwealth L. Welterweight
Champion. Former Undefeated Southern
Area L. Welterweight Champion. Ht. 5'7½"
Manager Self

01.05.91 Trevor Royal W CO 1 Bethnal Green
04.06.91 Dave Jenkins W RSC 1 Bethnal Green
24.09.91 Pat Delargy W RSC 5 Basildon
26.10.91 Gordon Webster W RSC 4 Brentwood
26.11.91 John O. Johnson W PTS 6 Bethnal Green
19.02.92 Rick North W PTS 6 Muswell Hill
17.03.92 Mick Mulcahy W PTS 6 Mayfair
16.06.92 Brendan Ryan W CO 6 Dagenham
13.10.92 Dean Bramhald DREW 6 Mayfair
10.11.92 Ray Newby DREW 6 Dagenham
12.12.92 Michael Driscoll L RSC 2 Muswell Hill
20.04.93 Ray Newby DREW 6 Brentwood
28.09.93 Dean Bramhald W PTS 8 Bethnal Green
06.11.93 Shaun Cogan DREW 6 Bethnal Green
11.01.94 Shaun Cogan L PTS 6 Bethnal Green
09.07.94 Carlos Chase W RSC 2 Earls Court
30.09.94 Richard Swallow L PTS 8 Bethnal Green
13.12.94 Steve Burton W PTS 6 Potters Bar
21.02.95 Mark Legg W RSC 4 Sunderland
18.03.95 Jean Chiarelli W RTD 4 Millstreet
23.05.95 Keith Marner W PTS 10 Potters Bar
*(Southern Area L. Welterweight Title
Challenge)*
20.09.95 John Smith W PTS 6 Potters Bar
29.11.95 Jason Rowland W CO 1 Bethnal Green
*(Southern Area L. Welterweight Title
Defence. Elim. British L. Welterweight
Title)*
20.04.96 Micky Hall W RSC 3 Brentwood
14.09.96 Jonathan Thaxton L PTS 12 Sheffield
*(Vacant WBO Inter-Continental
L. Welterweight Title)*
27.11.96 Brian Coleman W PTS 6 Bethnal Green

18.02.97 Richie Edwards W PTS 10 Cheshunt
*(Vacant Southern Area L. Welterweight
Title)*
22.04.97 Felix Bwalya W PTS 12 Bethnal Green
*(Vacant Commonwealth L.
Welterweight Title)*
Career: 28 contests, won 20, drew 4, lost 4.

Nicky Piper　　　　　Les Clark

Nicky Piper

Cardiff. *Born* Cardiff, 5 May, 1966
Commonwealth L. Heavyweight
Champion. Former Undefeated WBO Inter-
Continental L. Heavyweight Champion.
Former Undefeated WBA Penta-
Continental S. Middleweight Champion.
Ht. 6'3"
Manager Self

06.09.89 Kevin Roper W CO 2 Aberavon
17.10.89 Gus Mendes W RSC 3 Cardiff
19.12.89 Dave Owens W CO 1 Gorleston
17.04.90 Darren McKenna W RTD 4 Millwall
22.05.90 Maurice Core DREW 6 St Albans
23.10.90 Paul McCarthy W RSC 3 Leicester
12.11.90 John Ellis W CO 1 Norwich
05.03.91 Johnny Held W RSC 3 Millwall
08.05.91 Serge Bolivard W RSC 1 Millwall
22.05.91 Martin Lopez W CO 1 Millwall
03.07.91 Simon Harris W RSC 1 Reading
04.09.91 Carl Thompson L RSC 3 Bethnal Green
29.10.91 Franki Moro W RSC 4 Kensington
20.11.91 Carlos Christie W CO 6 Cardiff
22.01.92 Frank Eubanks W PTS 10 Cardiff
(Elim. British S. Middleweight Title)
11.03.92 Ron Amundsen W PTS 10 Cardiff
16.05.92 Larry Prather W PTS 8 Muswell Hill
25.07.92 Johnny Melfah W RSC 5 Manchester
(Elim. British S. Middleweight Title)
12.12.92 Nigel Benn L RSC 11 Muswell Hill
(WBC S. Middleweight Title Challenge)
13.02.93 Miguel Maldonado W PTS 12 Manchester
*(Vacant WBA Penta-Continental S.
Middleweight Title)*

10.04.93 Chris Sande W RSC 9 Swansea
(WBA Penta-Continental S. Middleweight Title Defence)
10.07.93 Trevor Ambrose W RSC 5 Cardiff
23.10.93 Frank Rhodes DREW 8 Cardiff
29.01.94 Leonzer Barber L RSC 9 Cardiff
(WBO L. Heavyweight Title Challenge)
21.09.94 Charles Oliver W RSC 5 Cardiff
19.11.94 Crawford Ashley L PTS 12 Cardiff
(Vacant British L. Heavyweight Title)
17.06.95 Tim Bryan W RSC 1 Cardiff
07.07.95 John Keeton W RTD 2 Cardiff
30.09.95 Noel Magee W CO 9 Cardiff
(Commonwealth L. Heavyweight Title Challenge. Vacant WBO Inter-Continental L. Heavyweight Title)
26.04.96 Danny Juma W RTD 2 Cardiff
30.11.96 Bruce Scott W RSC 7 Tylorstown
(Commonwealth L. Heavyweight Title Defence)
28.06.97 Stephane Nizard W PTS 8 Norwich
Career: 32 contests, won 26, drew 2, lost 4.

11.02.92 Juan Bautista W CO 1 Cardiff
19.05.92 James Drummond W RSC 9 Cardiff
(British Flyweight Title Defence)
14.11.92 Salvatore Fanni W PTS 12 Cardiff
(European Flyweight Title Challenge)
30.03.93 Danny Porter W RSC 3 Cardiff
(European Flyweight Title Defence)
26.06.93 Adrian Ochoa W PTS 10 Earls Court
29.01.94 Michele Poddighe W PTS 10 Cardiff
12.03.94 Mauricio Bernal W PTS 8 Cardiff
01.10.94 Shaun Norman W RSC 2 Cardiff
19.11.94 Luigi Camputaro W PTS 12 Cardiff
(European Flyweight Title Challenge)
17.06.95 Alberto Jimenez L RTD 9 Cardiff
(WBO Flyweight Title Challenge)
16.12.95 Ferid Ben Jeddou W RSC 2 Cardiff
(Vacant Interim IBF Flyweight Title)
26.04.96 Daniel Jimenez W PTS 12 Cardiff
(WBO Bantamweight Title Challenge)
Career: 22 contests, won 17, drew 3, lost 2.

Robin Reid
Runcorn. Liverpool, 19 February, 1971
WBC S. Middleweight Champion. Ht. 5'9"
Manager F. Warren

27.02.93 Mark Dawson W RSC 1 Dagenham
06.03.93 Julian Eavis W RSC 2 Glasgow
10.04.93 Andrew Furlong W PTS 6 Swansea
10.09.93 Juan Garcia W PTS 6 San Antonio, USA
09.10.93 Ernie Loveridge W PTS 4 Manchester
18.12.93 Danny Juma DREW 6 Manchester
09.04.94 Kesem Clayton W RSC 1 Mansfield
04.06.94 Andrew Furlong W RSC 2 Cardiff
17.08.94 Andrew Jervis W RSC 1 Sheffield
19.11.94 Chris Richards W RSC 3 Cardiff
04.02.95 Bruno Westenberghs W RSC 1 Cardiff
04.03.95 Marvin O'Brien W RSC 6 Livingston
06.05.95 Steve Goodwin W CO 1 Shepton Mallet

Robbie Regan   Les Clark

Robbie Regan
Cefn Forest. *Born* Caerphilly, 30 August, 1968
WBO Bantamweight Champion. Former Undefeated British, European & Welsh Flyweight Champion. Ht. 5'4"
Manager Self

19.08.89 Eric George DREW 6 Cardiff
06.03.90 Francis Ampofo W PTS 6 Bethnal Green
26.04.90 Kevin Downer W RSC 4 Merthyr
20.06.90 Dave McNally DREW 6 Basildon
19.11.90 Ricky Beard W RSC 6 Cardiff
21.12.90 Michele Poddighe DREW 6 Sassari, Italy
12.02.91 Kevin Jenkins W PTS 10 Cardiff
(Vacant Welsh Flyweight Title)
28.05.91 Joe Kelly W PTS 12 Cardiff
(Vacant British Flyweight Title)
03.09.91 Francis Ampofo L RSC 11 Cardiff
(British Flyweight Title Defence)
17.12.91 Francis Ampofo W PTS 12 Cardiff
(British Flyweight Title Challenge)

Robin Reid   Harry Goodwin

61

10.06.95	Martin Jolley W CO 1 Manchester
22.07.95	John Duckworth W PTS 8 Millwall
15.09.95	Trevor Ambrose W CO 5 Mansfield
10.11.95	Danny Juma W PTS 8 Derby
26.01.96	Stinger Mason W RSC 2 Brighton
16.03.96	Andrew Flute W RSC 7 Glasgow
26.04.96	Hunter Clay W RSC 1 Cardiff
08.06.96	Mark Dawson W RSC 5 Newcastle
31.08.96	Don Pendleton W RTD 4 Dublin
12.10.96	Vincenzo Nardiello W CO 7 Milan, Italy
	(WBC S. Middleweight Title Challenge)
08.02.97	Giovanni Pretorius W RSC 7 Millwall
	(WBC S. Middleweight Title Defence)
03.05.97	Henry Wharton W PTS 12 Manchester
	(WBC S. Middleweight Title Defence)

Career: 25 contests, won 24, drew 1.

Ryan Rhodes

Sheffield. *Born* Sheffield, 20 November, 1976
British & IBF Inter-Continental L. Middleweight Champion. Ht. 5'8½"
Manager B. Ingle/F. Warren

04.02.95	Lee Crocker W RSC 2 Cardiff
04.03.95	Shamus Casey W CO 1 Livingston
06.05.95	Chris Richards W PTS 6 Shepton Mallet
15.09.95	John Rice W RSC 2 Mansfield
10.11.95	Mark Dawson W PTS 6 Derby
20.01.96	John Duckworth W RSC 2 Mansfield
26.01.96	Martin Jolley W CO 3 Brighton
11.05.96	Martin Jolley W RSC 2 Bethnal Green
25.06.96	Roy Chipperfield W RSC 1 Mansfield
14.09.96	Del Bryan W PTS 6 Sheffield
14.12.96	Paul Jones W RSC 8 Sheffield
	(Vacant British L. Middleweight Title)
25.02.97	Peter Waudby W CO 1 Sheffield
	(British L. Middleweight Title Defence)
14.03.97	Del Bryan W RSC 7 Reading
	(British L. Middleweight Title Defence)
12.04.97	Lindon Scarlett W RSC 1 Sheffield
	(Vacant IBF Inter-Continental L. Middleweight Title)

Career: 14 contests, won 14.

Ryan Rhodes   Les Clark

David Starie

Bury St Edmunds. *Born* Bury St Edmunds, 11 June, 1974
British S. Middleweight Champion. Ht. 6'0"
Manager G. Holmes

24.09.94	Paul Murray W RSC 2 Wembley
25.10.94	Dave Owens W PTS 6 Southwark
07.02.95	Marvin O'Brien W PTS 6 Ipswich
30.03.95	Mark Dawson W RSC 1 Bethnal Green
17.05.95	Marvin O'Brien W RSC 5 Ipswich
14.09.95	John Duckworth W PTS 6 Battersea
20.10.95	Hunter Clay W PTS 8 Ipswich
15.12.95	Carlos Christie W CO 4 Bethnal Green
21.03.96	Paul Murray W RSC 1 Southwark
14.05.96	Phil Ball W RSC 1 Dagenham
09.07.96	John Duckworth W RSC 1 Bethnal Green
03.09.96	Pascal Mercier W RSC 3 Bethnal Green
26.11.96	Ray Webb W RSC 6 Bethnal Green
08.04.97	Sammy Storey W RSC 7 Bethnal Green
	(Vacant British S. Middleweight Title)

Career: 14 contests, won 14.

David Starie   Les Clark

Henry Wharton

York. *Born* Leeds, 23 November, 1967
Commonwealth S. Middleweight Champion. Former Undefeated British & European S. Middleweight Champion. Ht. 5'10½"
Manager M. Duff

21.09.89	Dean Murray W RSC 1 Harrogate
25.10.89	Mike Aubrey W PTS 6 Wembley
05.12.89	Ron Malek W RSC 1 Dewsbury
11.01.90	Guillermo Chavez W CO 1 Dewsbury
03.03.90	Joe Potts W CO 4 Wembley
11.04.90	Juan Elizondo W RSC 3 Dewsbury
18.10.90	Chuck Edwards W RSC 1 Dewsbury
31.10.90	Dino Stewart W PTS 8 Wembley
21.03.91	Francisco Lara W CO 1 Dewsbury

09.05.91	Frankie Minton W CO 7 Leeds
27.06.91	Rod Carr W PTS 12 Leeds
	(Vacant Commonwealth S. Middleweight Title)
30.10.91	Lou Gent DREW 12 Leeds
	(Commonwealth S. Middleweight Title Defence)
23.01.92	Nicky Walker W PTS 10 York
19.03.92	Kenny Schaefer W CO 1 York
08.04.92	Rod Carr W RSC 8 Leeds
	(Commonwealth S. Middleweight Title Defence)
23.09.92	Fidel Castro W PTS 12 Leeds
	(Commonwealth S. Middleweight Title Defence. British S. Middleweight Challenge)
07.04.93	Ray Domenge W RSC 3 Leeds
01.07.93	Royan Hammond W RSC 3 York
07.10.93	Ron Amundsen W RSC 8 York
26.02.94	Nigel Benn L PTS 12 Earls Court
	(WBC S. Middleweight Title Challenge)
10.09.94	Guy Stanford W RTD 3 Birmingham
26.10.94	Sipho Moyo W CO 1 Leeds
	(Commonwealth S. Middleweight Title Defence)
10.12.94	Chris Eubank L PTS 12 Manchester
	(WBO S. Middleweight Title Challenge)
08.07.95	Mauro Galvano W CO 4 York
	(Vacant European S. Middleweight Title)
11.11.95	Sammy Storey W CO 4 Halifax
	(European & Commonwealth S. Middleweight Title Defence)
13.01.96	Vincenzo Nardiello W RSC 6 Halifax
	(European S. Middleweight Title Defence)
04.06.96	Stephane Nizard W PTS 10 York
23.10.96	Trevor Thornberry W RTD 5 Halifax
	(Commonwealth S. Middleweight Title Defence)
03.05.97	Robin Reid L PTS 12 Manchester
	(WBC S. Middleweight Title Challenge)

Career: 29 contests, won 25, drew 1, lost 3.

Henry Wharton   Les Clark

Active British-Based Boxers: Career Records

Shows the complete record for all British-based boxers, excluding those currently holding British, Commonwealth, European, IBF, WBA, WBC and WBO titles, who have been active between 1 July 1996 and 30 June 1997. Names in brackets are real names, where they differ from ring names, and the first place name given is the boxer's domicile. Boxers are either shown as being self-managed or with a named manager, the information being supplied by the BBBoC shortly before going to press. Also included are foreign-born fighters who made their pro debuts in Britain, along with others like Bamana Dibateza (Zaire) and Peter Oboh (Nigeria), who, although starting their careers elsewhere, now hold BBBoC licenses and had three or more fights in this country last season in order to qualify for this section.

Ojay Abrahams
Watford. *Born* Lambeth, 17 December, 1964
Welterweight. Ht. 5'8½"
Manager B. Hearn

21.09.91	Gordon Webster W RSC 3 Tottenham
26.10.91	Mick Reid W RSC 5 Brentwood
26.11.91	John Corcoran W PTS 6 Bethnal Green
21.01.92	Dave Andrews DREW 6 Norwich
31.03.92	Marty Duke W RSC 2 Norwich
19.05.92	Michael Smyth L PTS 6 Cardiff
16.06.92	Ricky Mabbett W PTS 6 Dagenham
13.10.92	Vince Rose L RSC 3 Mayfair
30.01.93	Vince Rose DREW 6 Brentwood
19.05.93	Ricky Mabbett L RSC 4 Leicester
18.09.93	Ricky Mabbett L PTS 6 Leicester
09.12.93	Nick Appiah W PTS 6 Watford
24.01.94	Errol McDonald W RSC 2 Glasgow
09.02.94	Vince Rose W PTS 6 Brentwood
23.05.94	Spencer McCracken L PTS 6 Walsall
11.06.94	Darren Dyer W RSC 1 Bethnal Green
29.09.94	Gary Logan L PTS 10 Bethnal Green *(Southern Area Welterweight Title Challenge)*
13.12.94	Geoff McCreesh L PTS 6 Potters Bar
11.02.95	Gary Murray L PTS 8 Hamanskraal, South Africa
17.07.95	Andreas Panayi L PTS 8 Mayfair
02.10.95	Larbi Mohammed L RTD 5 Mayfair
08.12.95	Jason Beard W CO 2 Bethnal Green
09.04.96	Kevin Thompson W RSC 3 Stevenage
07.05.96	Harry Dhami L RSC 5 Mayfair *(Vacant Southern Area Welterweight Title)*
12.11.96	Spencer McCracken L PTS 8 Dudley
22.04.97	Paul King W RSC 4 Bethnal Green
29.05.97	Paul Ryan L RSC 3 Mayfair
30.06.97	Ahmet Dottuev L RSC 4 Bethnal Green

Career: 28 contests, won 12, drew 2, lost 14.

Danny Adams
Basildon. *Born* Basildon, 20 August, 1973
S. Featherweight. Ht. 5'8½"
Manager G. Moughton

22.05.97	Robert Grubb W PTS 4 Southwark

Career: 1 contest, won 1.

Kevin Adamson
Walthamstow. *Born* Hackney, 29 February, 1968
L. Middleweight. Ht. 6'0½"
Manager F. Warren

17.07.89	Carlton Myers W RSC 1 Stanmore
04.12.90	Darron Griffiths L RSC 4 Southend
12.11.91	Danny Shinkwin W RSC 4 Milton Keynes

30.04.92	Wayne Appleton W RSC 2 Bayswater
03.02.93	Joel Ani W RSC 6 Earls Court
27.02.93	Robert Whitehouse W RSC 1 Dagenham
31.03.93	Russell Washer W PTS 6 Barking
07.09.93	Bullit Andrews W PTS 6 Stoke
22.09.93	Russell Washer W PTS 6 Bethnal Green
27.10.93	Mick Duncan W RSC 3 Stoke
10.11.93	Clayon Stewart W RSC 1 Bethnal Green
01.12.93	Dave Maj W RSC 2 Stoke
19.01.94	Spencer Alton W RSC 1 Stoke
26.02.94	Lloyd Honeyghan L RSC 6 Earls Court *(Commonwealth L. Middleweight Title Challenge)*
25.05.94	Chris Richards W RSC 2 Stoke
17.08.94	Ernie Loveridge W RSC 2 Sheffield
25.02.95	Ensley Bingham L CO 5 Millwall
28.07.95	Glenn Catley L CO 1 Bristol
13.07.96	Brendan Ryan W RSC 2 Bethnal Green
25.02.97	Jimmy Vincent L PTS 6 Sheffield
27.03.97	Nicky Thurbin L PTS 8 Norwich

Career: 21 contests, won 15, lost 6.

Tanveer Ahmed (Niazi)
Glasgow. *Born* Glasgow, 25 October, 1968
Lightweight. Ht. 5'10"
Manager A. Morrison

22.10.92	John T. Kelly W PTS 6 Glasgow
01.12.92	Shaun Armstrong L PTS 6 Hartlepool
26.03.93	David Thompson W PTS 6 Glasgow
14.05.93	Dean Bramhald W PTS 6 Kilmarnock
09.09.93	Brian Wright W RTD 5 Glasgow
21.10.93	Martin Campbell W PTS 6 Glasgow
21.03.94	Chris Aston W CO 5 Glasgow

06.06.94	Chris Aston W CO 4 Glasgow
28.09.94	Norman Dhalie W CO 5 Glasgow
10.12.94	Kevin McKillan W PTS 6 Manchester
16.01.95	Micky Hall W RSC 4 Musselburgh
13.05.95	John O. Johnson W CO 3 Glasgow
01.07.95	Cham Joof W PTS 6 Kensington
16.03.96	Kevin McKillan W PTS 4 Glasgow
24.05.96	Kevin McKillan DREW 8 Glasgow
06.11.96	Floyd Churchill W RTD 5 Glasgow
12.02.97	Alan Temple W RSC 8 Glasgow *(Elim. British Lightweight Title)*
04.04.97	David Armstrong DREW 12 Glasgow *(Vacant WBO Inter-Continental Lightweight Title)*

Career: 18 contests, won 15, drew 2, lost 1.

Chris Ainscough
Liverpool. *Born* Liverpool, 24 January, 1971
Featherweight. Ht. 5'6"
Manager S. Vaughan

16.08.96	Chris Lyons W PTS 6 Liverpool

Career: 1 contest, won 1.

Israel Ajose
Belsize Park. *Born* Westminster, 6 October, 1974
Heavyweight. Ht. 6'1½"
Manager F. Maloney

26.11.96	Gary Williams W CO 2 Bethnal Green
11.01.97	Zak Goldman W CO 1 Bethnal Green
26.04.97	Albert Call W PTS 4 Swadlincote
26.06.97	Mike Holden L RSC 1 Salford

Career: 4 contests, won 3, lost 1.

Israel Ajose (left) in action against Albert Call at Swadlincote last April

Les Clark

Henry Akinwande

Lewisham. *Born* London, 12 October, 1965
Former Undefeated WBO, European &
Commonwealth Heavyweight Champion.
Ht. 6'7"
Manager Self

04.10.89	Carlton Headley W CO 1 Kensington
08.11.89	Dennis Bailey W RSC 2 Wembley
06.12.89	Paul Neilson W RSC 1 Wembley
10.01.90	John Fairbairn W RSC 1 Kensington
14.03.90	Warren Thompson W PTS 6 Kensington
09.05.90	Mike Robinson W CO 1 Wembley
10.10.90	Tracy Thomas W PTS 6 Kensington
12.12.90	Francois Yrius W RSC 1 Kensington
06.03.91	J. B. Williamson W RSC 2 Wembley
06.06.91	Ramon Voorn W RSC 2 Barking
28.06.91	Marshall Tillman W PTS 8 Nice, France
09.10.91	Gypsy John Fury W CO 3 Manchester *(Elim. British Heavyweight Title)*
06.12.91	Tim Bullock W CO 3 Dussledorf, Germany
28.02.92	Young Joe Louis W RSC 3 Issy les Moulineaux, France
26.03.92	Tucker Richards W RSC 2 Telford
10.04.92	Lumbala Tshimba W PTS 8 Carquefou, France
05.06.92	Kimmuel Odum W DIS 6 Marseille, France
18.07.92	Steve Garber W RTD 2 Manchester
19.12.92	Axel Schulz DREW 12 Berlin, Germany *(Vacant European Heavyweight Title)*
18.03.93	Jimmy Thunder W PTS 12 Lewisham *(Vacant Commonwealth Heavyweight Title)*
01.05.93	Axel Schulz W PTS 12 Berlin, Germany *(Vacant European Heavyweight Title)*
06.11.93	Frankie Swindell W PTS 10 Sun City, South Africa
01.12.93	Biagio Chianese W RSC 4 Kensington *(European Heavyweight Title Defence)*
05.04.94	Johnny Nelson W PTS 10 Bethnal Green
23.07.94	Mario Schiesser W CO 7 Berlin, Germany *(European Heavyweight Title Defence)*
08.04.95	Calvin Jones W CO 2 Las Vegas, USA
22.07.95	Stanley Wright W RSC 2 Millwall
16.12.95	Tony Tucker W PTS 10 Philadelphia, USA
27.01.96	Brian Sergeant W RSC 1 Phoenix, USA
23.03.96	Gerard Jones W DIS 7 Miami, USA
29.06.96	Jeremy Williams W CO 3 Indio, USA *(Vacant WBO Heavyweight Title)*
09.11.96	Alexander Zolkin W RSC 10 Las Vegas, USA *(WBO Heavyweight Title Defence)*
11.01.97	Scott Welch W PTS 12 Nashville, USA *(WBO Heavyweight Title Defence)*

Career: 33 contests, won 32, drew 1.

Rob Albon

Hayes. *Born* Hayes, 21 April, 1964
Heavyweight. Ht. 6'1½"
Manager D. Currivan

10.05.89	Massimo Mighaccio L RSC 3 Tallin, Estonia

15.09.89	L. A. Williams DREW 6 High Wycombe
20.02.90	Steve Osborne W PTS 6 Brentford
03.04.90	Dennis Bailey L RSC 4 Canvey Island
08.05.90	Steve Yorath W PTS 6 Brentford
12.09.90	Phil Soundy L RSC 1 Bethnal Green
18.02.91	Des Vaughan W PTS 6 Windsor
25.01.95	Darren Fearn L PTS 6 Cardiff
03.03.95	Keith Fletcher L RSC 3 Bracknell
09.05.95	Darren Westover L RSC 2 Basildon
28.07.95	Shane Woollas L RTD 4 Epworth
10.12.96	Gary Cavey L RTD 3 Plymouth
19.02.97	Jim Pallatt W PTS 6 Acton
04.03.97	Mika Kihlstrom L PTS 6 Southwark
28.06.97	J. A. Bugner L PTS 4 Norwich

Career: 15 contests, won 5, drew 1, lost 9.

Michael Alexander

Doncaster. *Born* Doncaster, 31 August,
1971
L. Middleweight. Ht. 5'9"
Manager Self

25.01.93	Tim Hill W PTS 6 Bradford
09.03.93	J. T. Kelly L PTS 6 Hartlepool
29.04.93	Pete Roberts W RSC 2 Hull
06.05.93	Ian Noble W PTS 6 Hartlepool
28.06.93	Mick Hoban W PTS 6 Morecambe
04.10.93	Micky Hall L CO 1 Bradford
28.11.93	Everald Williams L PTS 6 Southwark
28.02.94	Paul Hughes W PTS 6 Manchester
28.03.94	Laurence Roche W PTS 6 Cleethorpes
20.05.94	Andrew Morgan W PTS 6 Neath
13.06.94	Laurence Roche L PTS 6 Bradford
26.09.94	Derek Roche L RSC 6 Bradford
21.11.94	Alan Peacock L RSC 1 Glasgow
06.03.95	Brian Dunn L CO 5 Bradford
26.02.96	Charlie Paine W PTS 6 Manchester
05.03.96	John Jones L PTS 6 Barrow
29.03.96	Cam Raeside L PTS 6 Doncaster
22.04.96	Peter Reid L PTS 6 Cleethorpes
03.05.96	Andy Davidson W RTD 2 Sheffield
10.05.96	Tony Mock W PTS 6 Liverpool
03.06.96	Tommy Quinn L PTS 6 Glasgow
24.06.96	Lee Murtagh L PTS 6 Bradford
29.07.96	Brian Dunn W PTS 6 Skegness
06.09.96	Paul Burns L RSC 4 Liverpool
28.10.96	Stuart Dunn W PTS 6 Leicester
10.11.96	Joe Townsley L PTS 8 Glasgow
26.11.96	George Richards W PTS 8 Wolverhampton
03.12.96	James Donoghue L PTS 6 Yarm
21.01.97	Anthony van Niekerk L PTS 8 Hammanskraal, South Africa
17.02.97	Derek Roche L DIS 4 Bradford
03.03.97	George Richards L PTS 8 Birmingham
14.03.97	Joe Townsley L PTS 6 Irvine
15.04.97	Darren Sweeney L RSC 6 Edgbaston *(Vacant All-Ireland Middleweight Title)*
22.05.97	Howard Clarke L RSC 3 Solihull

Career: 34 contests, won 13, lost 21.

Wayne Alexander

Croydon. *Born* Tooting, 17 July, 1973
L. Middleweight. Ht. 5'8¾"
Manager F. Warren

10.11.95	Andrew Jervis W RTD 3 Derby
13.02.96	Paul Murray W PTS 4 Bethnal Green
11.05.96	Jim Webb W RSC 2 Bethnal Green
13.07.96	John Janes W RSC 3 Bethnal Green
05.06.97	Prince Kasi Kaihau W CO 4 Bristol

Career: 5 contests, won 5.

Raziq Ali

Bradford. *Born* Wakefield, 14 September,
1972
Middleweight. Ht. 6'0"
Manager C. Aston

08.09.92	Wayne Panayiotiou W PTS 6 Doncaster
05.10.92	Sean Baker L PTS 6 Bristol
24.05.93	David Sumner W PTS 6 Bradford
25.04.94	Billy Collins L PTS 6 Glasgow
07.03.97	Martin Jolley W PTS 6 Northampton
14.04.97	Darren Rees W PTS 6 Bradford
13.06.97	James Lowther L PTS 6 Leeds

Career: 7 contests, won 4, lost 3.

Michael Alldis

Crawley. *Born* London, 25 May, 1968
Featherweight. Ht. 5'6"
Manager B. Hearn

15.09.92	Ceri Farrell W RSC 3 Crystal Palace
10.11.92	Kid McAuley W PTS 6 Dagenham
12.12.92	Kid McAuley W CO 1 Muswell Hill
16.02.93	Ceri Farrell W CO 1 Tooting
29.06.93	Ady Benton L DIS 3 Mayfair
28.09.93	Alan Ley W PTS 6 Bethnal Green
06.11.93	Pete Buckley W PTS 8 Bethnal Green
09.04.94	Fernando Lugo W CO 1 Bethnal Green
11.06.94	Conn McMullen W PTS 8 Bethnal Green
20.12.94	Pete Buckley W PTS 6 Bethnal Green
17.02.95	Miguel Matthews W PTS 8 Crawley
25.03.95	Chip O'Neill W RSC 2 Chester
13.06.95	Laureano Ramirez L PTS 12 Basildon *(Vacant WBO Inter-Continental S. Bantamweight Title)*
25.11.95	Conn McMullen W CO 4 Dagenham
13.01.96	Garry Burrell W RSC 7 Halifax
14.02.96	Billy Hardy L PTS 12 Sunderland *(Commonwealth Featherweight Title Challenge)*
04.04.97	Ervine Blake W RSC 3 Brighton
28.04.97	Paul Ingle L RTD 11 Hull *(British Featherweight Title Challenge)*

Career: 18 contests, won 14, lost 4.

Carl Allen

Wolverhampton. *Born* Wolverhampton, 20
November, 1969
Midlands Area S. Bantamweight
Champion. Ht. 5'7¼"
Manager Self

26.11.95	Gary Jenkinson W PTS 6 Birmingham
29.11.95	Jason Squire L PTS 6 Solihull
17.01.96	Andrew Robinson W PTS 6 Solihull
13.02.96	Ervine Blake W RSC 5 Wolverhampton
21.02.96	Ady Benton L PTS 6 Batley
29.02.96	Chris Jickells W PTS 6 Scunthorpe
27.03.96	Jason Squire DREW 6 Whitwick
26.04.96	Paul Griffin L RSC 3 Cardiff
30.05.96	Roger Brotherhood W RSC 5 Lincoln
26.09.96	Matthew Harris W PTS 10 Walsall *(Midlands Area S. Bantamweight Title Challenge)*
07.10.96	Emmanuel Clottey L RTD 3 Lewisham
21.11.96	Miguel Matthews W PTS 8 Solihull
30.11.96	Floyd Havard L RTD 3 Tylorstown
29.01.97	Pete Buckley W PTS 8 Stoke
11.02.97	David Morris DREW 8 Wolverhampton
28.02.97	Ian McLeod L RTD 3 Kilmarnock
21.05.97	David Burke L PTS 4 Liverpool
30.06.97	Duke McKenzie L PTS 8 Bethnal Green

Career: 18 contests, won 7, drew 2, lost 9.

Mark Allen (Hodgson)

Denaby. *Born* Mexborough, 11 January, 1970
L. Welterweight. Ht. 5'11"
Manager Self

24.03.92	Jamie Morris L PTS 6 Wolverhampton
04.06.92	Blue Butterworth L RSC 5 Burnley
10.11.92	Bobby Guynan L RSC 2 Dagenham
09.12.92	Simon Hamblett DREW 6 Stoke
09.02.93	Simon Hamblett W PTS 6 Wolverhampton
23.02.93	Simon Hamblett L PTS 6 Doncaster
11.03.93	Jamie Morris DREW 6 Walsall
20.04.93	Paul Knights L PTS 6 Brentwood
06.05.93	Brian Coleman L PTS 6 Walsall
28.05.93	Nick Boyd L CO 2 Middleton
29.06.93	Robbie Sivyer W PTS 6 Edgbaston
14.08.93	Cham Joof L RSC 3 Hammersmith
28.10.93	Paul Bowen L RSC 2 Walsall
09.02.94	Paul Knights L RSC 2 Brentwood
18.04.94	Patrick Parton L PTS 6 Walsall
23.05.94	Patrick Parton L PTS 6 Walsall
13.06.94	James Jiora L PTS 6 Bradford
21.07.94	Bradley Welsh L PTS 6 Edinburgh
11.10.94	Marc Smith L PTS 6 Wolverhampton
20.10.94	Marc Smith W PTS 6 Walsall
02.11.94	Mark Breslin LPTS 6 Solihull
29.11.94	Simon Hamblett L PTS 6 Wolverhampton
18.12.94	Gordon Blair L RSC 3 Glasgow
09.03.95	Patrick Parton L PTS 6 Walsall
16.03.95	Tim Hill L PTS 6 Sunderland
11.05.95	Shaun O'Neill L PTS 6 Sunderland
18.05.95	Scott Walker L RSC 2 Middleton
06.07.95	Shaun Stokes L PTS 6 Hull
29.07.95	Paul Scott L RSC 5 Whitley Bay
22.01.96	John Stovin L PTS 6 Glasgow
26.02.96	Shaun Gledhill L RSC 3 Manchester
24.04.96	Kid McAuley L PTS 6 Stoke
27.02.97	Brian Booth L PTS 6 Sunderland
12.03.97	Peter Gabbitus L PTS 6 Stoke
03.04.97	Daniel James L RSC 4 Wembley

Career: 35 contests, won 3, drew 2, lost 30.

Francis Ampofo

Bethnal Green. *Born* Ghana, 5 June, 1967
Bantamweight. Former Undefeated British Flyweight Champion. Former Commonwealth Flyweight Champion. Ht. 5'1½"
Manager B. Hearn

30.01.90	Neil Parry W PTS 6 Bethnal Green
06.03.90	Robbie Regan L PTS 6 Bethnal Green
29.05.90	Eric George W RSC 3 Bethnal Green
12.09.90	Eric George W CO 2 Bethnal Green
26.03.91	Ricky Beard W PTS 8 Bethnal Green
22.06.91	Neil Johnston W RSC 2 Earls Court
03.09.91	Robbie Regan W RSC 11 Cardiff *(British Flyweight Title Challenge)*
17.12.91	Robbie Regan L PTS 12 Cardiff *(British Flyweight Title Defence)*
25.02.92	Ricky Beard W PTS 8 Crystal Palace
16.06.92	Shaun Norman RSC 4 Dagenham
12.12.92	James Drummond W PTS 12 Mayfair *(Vacant British Flyweight Title)*
17.02.93	Alberto Cantu W RSC 5 Bethnal Green
29.06.93	Albert Musankabala W RSC 3 Mayfair *(Vacant Commonwealth Flyweight Title)*
11.06.94	Jacob Matlala L RTD 9 Bethnal Green *(WBO Flyweight Title Challenge)*
20.09.94	James Drummond W RSC 3 Musselburgh *(British Flyweight Title Defence)*
20.12.94	Daren Fifield W RSC 2 Bethnal Green *(British Flyweight Title Defence. Commonwealth Flyweight Title Challenge)*
06.03.95	Danny Ward L CO 12 Mayfair *(Commonwealth Flyweight Title Defence)*
27.11.96	Rowan Williams W PTS 6 Bethnal Green
08.04.97	Vince Feeney L PTS 10 Bethnal Green *(Vacant Southern Area Bantamweight Title)*

Career: 19 contests, won 14, lost 5.

Francis Ampofo   Les Clark

Shaun Anderson

Maybole. *Born* Girvan, 20 September, 1969
Featherweight. Ht. 5'5"
Manager T. Gilmour

29.05.92	Tucker Thomas W RSC 1 Glasgow
11.09.92	Mark Hargreaves W PTS 6 Glasgow
10.12.92	Graham McGrath W PTS 6 Glasgow
29.01.93	Graham McGrath W PTS 6 Glasgow
26.03.93	Dave Campbell W RSC 5 Glasgow
30.04.93	Paul Kelly W RSC 5 Glasgow
14.05.93	Kid McAuley W PTS 8 Kilmarnock
29.05.93	Ronnie Stephenson W PTS 6 Paisley
09.09.93	Graham McGrath W PTS 8 Glasgow
19.12.93	Pete Buckley W PTS 6 Glasgow
13.04.94	Paul Wynn DREW 6 Glasgow
13.05.94	Paul Wynn W PTS 8 Kilmarnock
08.09.94	Graham McGrath W PTS 8 Glasgow
23.09.94	Johnny Armour L RSC 11 Bethnal Green *(Commonwealth Bantamweight Title Challenge)*
18.11.94	James Murray L PTS 10 Glasgow *(Vacant Scottish Bantamweight Title)*
21.01.95	Brian Carr L PTS 6 Glasgow
04.03.95	Shaun Norman W PTS 6 Livingston
21.04.95	Donnie Hood W PTS 8 Glasgow
12.05.95	Warren Bowers L RSC 7 Bethnal Green
25.11.95	Spencer Oliver L RSC 3 Dagenham
16.03.96	Colin Innes W PTS 4 Glasgow
24.04.96	Ady Benton L PTS 6 Solihull
06.11.96	Donnie Hood W PTS 6 Glasgow
27.01.97	Lyndon Kershaw L PTS 8 Glasgow
28.02.97	Benny Jones W PTS 6 Kilmarnock
17.03.97	Neil Parry W RTD 4 Glasgow
20.04.97	Noel Wilders L PTS 6 Leeds
28.04.97	Graham McGrath W PTS 6 Glasgow

Career: 28 contests, won 18, drew 1, lost 9.

Dave Andrews

Trelewis. *Born* Merthyr, 22 July, 1968
L. Middleweight. Ht. 5'11"
Manager Self

12.09.88	Ian Midwood-Tate L RTD 4 Northampton
05.12.88	Robert Dugdale W PTS 6 Northampton
16.01.89	Graham Burton L PTS 6 Northampton
06.03.89	Jimmy Thornton W PTS 6 Northampton
28.03.89	Jim Beckett L PTS 6 Chigwell
08.06.89	John Davies L RSC 3 Cardiff
26.02.90	Rocky Bryan L RSC 2 Crystal Palace
17.09.90	Julian Eavis W PTS 6 Cardiff
19.11.90	Andy Williams W RSC 1 Cardiff
05.03.91	Brian Cullen W RSC 1 Cardiff
12.04.91	Robert McCracken L RSC 4 Willenhall
19.11.91	Paul Dyer L PTS 6 Norwich
17.12.91	Mark Atkins W RSC 3 Cardiff
21.01.92	Ojay Abrahams DREW 6 Norwich
09.02.92	Paul Burke L PTS 6 Bradford
03.03.92	Howard Clarke L RSC 3 Cradley Heath
22.04.96	Anthony McFadden L RSC 2 Crystal Palace
15.04.97	Steve Levene L PTS 6 Edgbaston
22.05.97	George Richards L PTS 6 Solihull

Career: 19 contests, won 6, drew 1, lost 12.

Karl Andrews

Bristol. *Born* High Wycombe, 21 March, 1975
Heavyweight. Ht. 6'4¾"
Manager C. Sanigar

19.10.96	Gary Cavey L CO 1 Bristol

Career: 1 contest, lost 1.

Karl Andrews   Les Clark

Simon Andrews

Plymouth. *Born* Birmingham, 24 April, 1970
S. Middleweight. Ht. 5'9½"
Manager G. Mitchell

19.09.95 J. P. Matthews L RSC 3 Plymouth
13.11.95 Carl Winstone L PTS 6 Barnstaple
03.12.95 Jason Hart L PTS 6 Southwark
12.02.96 Neville Smith L RSC 3 Heathrow
04.04.96 Jetty Williams W PTS 6 Plymouth
10.05.96 Graham Townsend L RSC 5 Wembley
18.10.96 Gareth Thomas W RSC 5 Barnstaple
07.11.96 Gary Reyniers DREW 6 Battersea
10.12.96 Gareth Thomas W RSC 4 Plymouth
15.02.97 Neville Smith L PTS 4 Tooting
19.04.97 Peter Vosper L PTS 10 Plymouth
(Vacant Western Area L. Heavyweight Title)

Career: 11 contests, won 3, drew 1, lost 7.

Dennis Andries

Hackney. *Born* Guyana, 5 November, 1953
Former British Cruiserweight Champion.
Former WBC L. Heavyweight Champion.
Former Undefeated WBC International L.
Heavyweight Champion. Former
Undefeated British & Southern Area L.
Heavyweight Champion. Ht. 5'11"
Manager Self

16.05.78 Ray Pearce W CO 2 Newport
01.06.78 Mark Seabrook W RSC 1 Heathrow
20.06.78 Bonny McKenzie L PTS 8 Southend
18.09.78 Ken Jones W PTS 6 Mayfair
31.10.78 Neville Estaban W PTS 6 Barnsley
14.11.78 Les McAteer DREW 8 Birkenhead
22.11.78 Glen McEwan W RSC 7 Stoke
04.12.78 Tom Collins W PTS 8 Southend
22.01.79 Bunny Johnson L PTS 10 Wolverhampton
30.01.79 Tom Collins W CO 6 Southend
05.04.79 Francis Hand W RSC 8 Liverpool
06.06.79 Bonny McKenzie W PTS 8 Burslem
17.09.79 Johnny Waldron W RTD 10 Mayfair
(Southern Area L. Heavyweight Title Challenge)
27.02.80 Bunny Johnson L PTS 15 Burslem
(British L. Heavyweight Title Challenge)
17.04.80 Mustafa Wasajja L PTS 8 Copenhagen, Denmark
18.06.80 Chris Lawson W RSC 8 Burslem
23.03.81 Shaun Chalcraft W PTS 10 Mayfair
(Southern Area L. Heavyweight Title Challenge)
16.09.81 Liam Coleman W RSC 6 Burslem
12.10.81 David Pearce L RSC 7 Bloomsbury
23.11.81 Alek Penarski W PTS 10 Chesterfield
15.03.82 Tom Collins L PTS 15 Bloomsbury
(Vacant British L. Heavyweight Title)
10.08.82 Keith Bristol W PTS 10 Strand
(Southern Area L. Heavyweight Title Defence)
28.02.83 Karl Canwell W CO 4 Strand
(Southern Area L. Heavyweight Title Defence & Elim. British L. Heavyweight Title)
19.05.83 Chris Lawson W CO 4 Queensway
22.09.83 Keith Bristol W CO 4 Strand
(Southern Area L. Heavyweight Title Defence & Elim. British L. Heavyweight Title)

26.01.84 Tom Collins W PTS 12 Strand
(British L. Heavyweight Title Challenge)
06.04.84 Tom Collins W PTS 12 Watford
(British L. Heavyweight Title Defence)
10.10.84 Devon Bailey W CO 12 Shoreditch
(British L. Heavyweight Title Defence)
23.03.85 Jose Seys W RSC 3 Strand
07.05.85 Jeff Meacham W CO 4 New Orleans, USA
25.05.85 Tim Broady W RSC 5 Atlantic City, USA
06.06.85 Marcus Dorsey W CO 3 Lafayette, USA
11.12.85 Alex Blanchard DREW 12 Fulham
(European L. Heavyweight Title Challenge)
13.02.86 Keith Bristol W RSC 6 Longford
(British L. Heavyweight Title Defence)
30.04.86 J. B. Williamson W PTS 12 Edmonton
(WBC L. Heavyweight Title Challenge)
10.09.86 Tony Sibson W RSC 9 Muswell Hill
(WBC & British L. Heavyweight Title Defence)
07.03.87 Thomas Hearns L RSC 10 Detroit, USA
(WBC L. Heavyweight Title Defence)
06.10.87 Robert Folley W PTS 10 Phoenix, USA
20.02.88 Jamie Howe W PTS 10 Detroit, USA
22.05.88 Bobby Czyz W PTS 10 Atlantic City, USA
10.09.88 Tony Harrison W RTD 7 Detroit, USA
17.10.88 Paul Maddison W RSC 4 Tucson, USA
21.02.89 Tony Willis W RSC 5 Tucson, USA
(Vacant WBC L. Heavyweight Title)
24.06.89 Jeff Harding L RSC 12 Atlantic City, USA
(WBC L. Heavyweight Title Defence)
26.10.89 Art Jimmerson W PTS 10 Atlantic City, USA
20.01.90 Clarismundo Silva W RSC 7 Auburn Hills, USA
(Vacant WBC International L. Heavyweight Title)
28.07.90 Jeff Harding W CO 7 Melbourne, Australia
(WBC L. Heavyweight Title Challenge)
10.10.90 Sergio Merani W RTD 4 Kensington
(WBC L. Heavyweight Title Defence)
19.01.91 Guy Waters W PTS 12 Adelaide, Australia
(WBC L. Heavyweight Title Defence)
11.09.91 Jeff Harding L PTS 12 Hammersmith
(WBC L. Heavyweight Title Defence)
15.11.91 Ed Neblett W RSC 4 Tampa, USA
11.12.91 Paul Maddison W RTD 8 Duluth, USA
27.02.92 Akim Tafer L PTS 12 Beausoleil, France
(Vacant European Cruiserweight Title)
27.02.93 David Sewell W PTS 10 Dagenham
31.03.93 Willie Jake W RTD 6 Barking
29.01.94 Crawford Ashley W RTD 4 Cardiff
26.02.94 Mike Peak W PTS 4 Earls Court
23.03.94 Chemek Saleta L PTS 12 Cardiff
(Vacant WBC International Cruiserweight Title)
01.10.94 Sylvester White W RSC 5 Carpentras, France
21.01.95 Denzil Browne W RSC 11 Glasgow
(Vacant British Cruiserweight Title)
04.03.95 Mike Peak W CO 4 Livingston
13.05.95 Terry Dunstan L PTS 12 Glasgow
(British Cruiserweight Title Defence)
28.10.95 Artis Pendergrass W PTS 8 Bristol

13.02.96 Terry Dunstan L PTS 12 Bethnal Green
(British Cruiserweight Title Challenge)
14.12.96 Johnny Nelson L RSC 7 Sheffield
(Vacant British Cruiserweight Title)

Career: 65 contests, won 49, drew 2, lost 14.

(Mohammed) Naveed Anwar

Rochdale. *Born* Pakistan, 14 August, 1970
Cruiserweight. Ht. 5'11¼"
Manager A. Talbot

08.06.96 Peter Mason L RSC 4 Newcastle
25.10.96 Pele Lawrence L PTS 6 Mere
09.12.96 Phill Day L PTS 6 Bristol
11.01.97 Dominic Negus L RTD 2 Bethnal Green
29.04.97 Lee Swaby L PTS 6 Manchester

Career: 5 contests, lost 5.

Wayne Appleton

Pontefract. *Born* Hemsworth, 9 November, 1967
L. Middleweight. Ht. 5'10"
Manager Self

13.11.90 Bullit Andrews W RSC 5 Edgbaston
26.11.90 Stuart Good W CO 4 Lewisham
10.12.90 Wayne Timmins W CO 4 Birmingham
15.03.91 Andre Wharton L RSC 7 Willenhall
14.11.91 Dave Hindmarsh W RSC 8 Edinburgh
30.04.92 Kevin Adamson L RSC 2 Bayswater
01.03.93 Hughie Davey W PTS 6 Bradford
12.05.93 Richard O'Brien W RTD 2 Sheffield
25.10.93 Errol McDonald W PTS 8 Glasgow
04.12.93 Gary Murray L RTD 7 Sun City, South Africa
18.01.95 Delroy Waul L PTS 6 Solihull
10.06.95 Joni Nyman L PTS 6 Pori, Finland
26.01.96 Leigh Wicks W PTS 6 Brighton
11.01.97 Jamie Robinson DREW 4 Bethnal Green

Career: 14 contests, won 8, drew 1, lost 5.

John Armour

Chatham. *Born* Chatham, 26 October, 1968
Former Undefeated European &
Commonwealth Bantamweight Champion.
Ht. 5'4¾"
Manager M. Duff

24.09.90 Lupe Castro W PTS 6 Lewisham
31.10.90 Juan Camero W RSC 4 Crystal Palace
21.01.91 Elijro Mejia W RSC 1 Crystal Palace
30.09.91 Pat Maher W CO 1 Kensington
29.10.91 Pete Buckley W PTS 6 Kensington
14.12.91 Gary Hickman W RSC 6 Bexleyheath
25.03.92 Miguel Matthews W PTS 6 Dagenham
30.04.92 Ndabe Dube W RSC 12 Kensington
(Vacant Commonwealth Bantamweight Title)
17.10.92 Mauricio Bernal W PTS 8 Wembley
03.12.92 Albert Musankabala W RSC 5 Lewisham
(Commonwealth Bantamweight Title Defence)
28.01.93 Ricky Romero W CO 1 Southwark
10.02.93 Morgan Mpande W PTS 12 Lewisham
(Commonwealth Bantamweight Title Defence)
09.06.93 Boualem Belkif W PTS 10 Lewisham
01.12.93 Karl Morling W CO 3 Kensington

14.01.94 Rufus Adebayo W RSC 7 Bethnal
Green
*(Commonwealth Bantamweight Title
Defence)*
23.09.94 Shaun Anderson W RSC 11 Bethnal
Green
*(Commonwealth Bantamweight Title
Defence)*
14.02.95 Tsitsi Sokutu W RSC 7 Bethnal Green
*(Commonwealth Bantamweight Title
Defence)*
19.04.95 Antonio Picardi W RSC 8 Bethnal
Green
(Vacant European Bantamweight Title)
19.05.95 Matthew Harris W RSC 3 Southwark
29.11.95 Redha Abbas W CO 5 Bethnal Green
*(European Bantamweight Title
Defence)*
17.12.96 Lyndon Kershaw W RSC 8 Bethnal
Green
29.01.97 Petrica Paraschiv W PTS 12 Bethnal
Green
*(Vacant Interim WBC International
Bantamweight Title)*
20.05.97 Anatoly Kvitko W RSC 8 Gillingham
Career: 23 contests, won 23.

(Shaun) Lee Armstrong
Huddersfield. *Born* Hartlepool, 18 October,
1972
Featherweight. Ht. 5'8"
Manager C. Aston

26.04.96 Daryl McKenzie W RSC 4 Glasgow
10.05.96 Charlie Rumbol W PTS 6 Wembley
23.05.96 Ian Richardson W PTS 6 Queensferry
04.10.96 Michael Gibbons L RSC 3 Wakefield
18.11.96 Garry Burrell W PTS 6 Glasgow
20.02.97 Carl Greaves W RSC 4 Mansfield
10.04.97 Chris Lyons W PTS 6 Sheffield
28.04.97 Hugh Collins W RTD 5 Glasgow
26.06.97 Garry Burrell W PTS 6 Sheffield
Career: 9 contests, won 8, lost 1.

Neil Armstrong
Paisley. *Born* Glasgow, 19 June, 1970
Bantamweight. Ht. 5'5"
Manager J. McIntyre

31.01.92 Mark Robertson W RSC 6 Glasgow
04.03.92 Des Gargano W PTS 6 Glasgow
12.03.92 Louis Veitch W PTS 6 Glasgow
10.04.92 Shaun Norman DREW 8 Glasgow
11.09.92 Louis Veitch W PTS 6 Glasgow
10.12.92 L. C. Wilson W PTS 6 Glasgow
29.01.93 Louis Veitch W PTS 6 Glasgow
04.03.93 Shaun Norman W RSC 8 Glasgow
26.03.93 Conn McMullen L RSC 5 Glasgow
29.05.93 Louis Veitch W PTS 10 Paisley
21.10.93 Shaun Norman W RSC 7 Glasgow
10.02.94 Rowan Williams W PTS 6 Glasgow
21.03.94 James Drummond L RSC 5 Glasgow
*(Elim. British Flyweight Title. Vacant
Scottish Flyweight Title)*
24.02.97 Sean Green W PTS 6 Glasgow
13.06.97 Gary Hickman W PTS 4 Paisley
Career: 15 contests, won 12, drew 1, lost 2.

Shaun Armstrong
Hartlepool. *Born* Hartlepool, 22 September,
1968
Welterweight. Ht. 5'8"
Manager T. Conroy

05.10.92 Shea Neary L RSC 6 Liverpool
01.12.92 Tanveer Ahmed W PTS 6 Hartlepool
24.04.97 Dennis Griffin W PTS 6 Mayfair
Career: 3 contests, won 2, lost 1.

Darren Ashton
Stoke. *Born* Stoke, 26 February, 1969
L. Heavyweight. Ht. 6'1"
Manager Self

13.10.93 Tony Colclough W RSC 1 Stoke
08.12.93 Nigel Rafferty W PTS 6 Stoke
23.03.94 L. A. Williams W PTS 6 Stoke
23.05.94 Nigel Rafferty W PTS 6 Walsall
30.11.94 Carlos Christie L PTS 6 Solihull
04.03.95 John Wilson NC 3 Livingston
06.05.95 Dale Nixon W RSC 4 Shepton Mallet
13.05.95 Stefan Wright W PTS 6 Glasgow
11.10.95 Neil Simpson L RSC 3 Solihull
17.11.95 Mark Baker L RSC 1 Bethnal Green
12.01.96 Frederic Alvarez L PTS 6 Copenhagen,
Denmark
27.05.96 Harri Hakulinen L PTS 4 Helsinki,
Finland
09.07.96 Chris Johnson L RSC 1 Bethnal Green
08.02.97 Paul Bowen L PTS 4 Millwall
04.04.97 Mark Snipe W RSC 2 Brighton
26.06.97 Clinton Woods L PTS 6 Sheffield
Career: 16 contests, won 7, lost 8, no contest 1.

David Bain   Les Clark

David Bain
Wolverhampton. *Born* Peterborough, 2
October, 1966
L. Middleweight. Ht. 5'8"
Manager C. Flute

29.03.94 Warren Stephens W PTS 6
Wolverhampton
23.05.94 Andy Peach W RSC 6 Walsall
11.10.94 Warren Stephens W PTS 6
Wolverhampton
07.02.95 Peter Reid L PTS 6 Wolverhampton
28.03.95 Prince Kasi Kaihau W PTS 6
Wolverhampton
11.05.95 Howard Clarke L RSC 1 Dudley

03.11.95 Rob Stevenson W PTS 6 Dudley
28.11.95 Nick Ingram L PTS 8 Wolverhampton
26.09.96 Jimmy Vincent L RSC 3 Walsall
25.03.97 George Richards L PTS 6
Wolverhampton
Career: 10 contests, won 5, lost 5.

Mark Baker
Sidcup. *Born* Farnborough, 14 July, 1969
S. Middleweight. Former Undefeated
Southern Area Middleweight Champion.
Ht. 5'9½"
Manager Self

07.09.92 Jason McNeill W RSC 2 Bethnal Green
15.10.92 Graham Jenner W RTD 4 Lewisham
03.12.92 Adrian Wright W RSC 1 Lewisham
10.02.93 Paul Hanlon W RSC 2 Lewisham
26.04.93 Karl Mumford W CO 1 Lewisham
15.06.93 Alan Baptiste W PTS 6 Hemel
Hempstead
14.01.94 Karl Barwise L PTS 6 Bethnal Green
11.03.94 Graham Jenner W RSC 2 Bethnal
Green
26.04.94 Jerry Mortimer W PTS 6 Bethnal
Green
23.09.94 Alan Baptiste W RSC 1 Bethnal Green
17.10.94 Steve Thomas W RSC 5 Mayfair
27.10.94 Chris Richards W PTS 6 Milwall
13.12.94 Stinger Mason W RSC 4 Ilford
20.01.95 Mark Dawson W RSC 3 Bethnal Green
17.11.95 Darren Ashton W RSC 1 Bethnal
Green
13.01.96 Mark Dawson W RSC 3 Halifax
05.03.96 Sven Hamer W PTS 10 Bethnal Green
*(Vacant Southern Area Middleweight
Title)*
14.10.96 John Duckworth W RSC 6 Mayfair
27.03.97 Heath Todd W RSC 5 Dubai
30.06.97 Mark Delaney W PTS 10 Bethnal
Green
(Elim. British S. Middleweight Title)
Career: 20 contests, won 19, lost 1.

David Baptiste
Balham. *Born* Luton, 5 March, 1966
Welterweight. Ht. 5'7"
Manager G. Steene

20.09.96 Robbie Dunn W CO 2 Tooting
Career: 1 contest, won 1.

David Baptiste   Les Clark

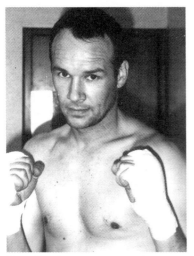

Dean Barclay   Les Clark

Dean Barclay

Enfield. *Born* Ponders End, 12 April, 1964
Middleweight. Ht. 6'0"
Manager Self

30.10.85	Nick Harty W RSC 3 Basildon
16.01.86	Karl Ince W PTS 6 Preston
21.04.86	Gary Flear W RSC 1 Birmingham
29.09.86	Dean Murray W RSC 3 Mayfair
13.10.86	Wally Swift Jnr DREW 8 Dulwich
11.03.87	Ian Chantler L PTS 8 Kensington
21.03.88	Kesem Clayton DREW 8 Bethnal Green
25.04.88	Kevin Hayde W PTS 6 Bethnal Green
29.06.88	Ken Foreman W PTS 6 Basildon
02.05.89	Jason Rowe W PTS 8 Chigwell
17.11.95	Ernie Loveridge W PTS 4 Bethnal Green
08.02.97	Paul Carr W PTS 4 Millwall

Career: 12 contests, won 9, drew 2, lost 1.

Nicky Bardle

Ware. *Born* Ware, 30 January, 1972
L. Welterweight. Ht. 5'9½"
Manager H. Holland

07.11.91	Michael Clynch W RSC 4 Peterborough
12.02.92	Steve Hearn W RSC 1 Watford
30.04.92	James Campbell L CO 1 Watford
17.09.92	Brian Coleman W RSC 4 Watford
19.11.94	Anthony Campbell W PTS 6 Heathrow
21.09.95	Andy Davidson W CO 1 Battersea
30.10.95	Paul Salmon W CO 1 Heathrow
03.12.95	Vince Burns W RSC 1 Southwark
12.02.96	Richard Swallow L RSC 4 Heathrow
25.06.96	John Smith W PTS 4 Stevenage
27.09.96	Brian Coleman W PTS 4 Stevenage
07.11.96	John Harrison W PTS 6 Battersea
18.02.97	Steve Tuckett L CO 2 Cheshunt

Career: 13 contests, won 10, lost 3.

Jason Barker

Sheffield. *Born* Chesterfield, 1 June, 1973
L. Middleweight. Ht. 6'0"
Manager Self

30.01.92	Nicky Lucas W PTS 6 Southampton

12.02.92	Roger Hunte L RTD 4 Wembley
29.04.92	Dave Lovell L PTS 6 Stoke
03.06.92	John O. Johnson L PTS 6 Newcastle under Lyne
07.07.92	Patrick Loughran L PTS 6 Bristol
21.10.92	Brian Coleman L PTS 6 Stoke
02.11.92	Shea Neary L RSC 3 Liverpool
09.12.92	John O. Johnson L PTS 8 Stoke
28.01.93	Jason Beard L RSC 3 Southwark
22.04.93	Marco Fattore L PTS 6 Mayfair
12.05.93	Shaba Edwards W PTS 6 Stoke
14.06.93	Delroy Leslie L RTD 3 Bayswater
21.09.95	Jamie Gallagher W RSC 2 Sheffield
20.10.95	Wesley Jones W RSC 2 Mansfield
22.11.95	Darren Covill W PTS 4 Sheffield
08.12.95	James Donoghue L PTS 6 Leeds
05.02.96	Darren Covill L RSC 1 Bexleyheath
03.05.96	Shamus Casey W RSC 1 Sheffield
09.05.96	Hughie Davey L PTS 6 Sunderland
08.10.96	Alvar Coppard W RSC 3 Battersea
26.11.96	Ray Newby W PTS 6 Sheffield
03.12.96	Phil Epton W RSC 1 Yarm
24.02.97	Humphrey Harrison W CO 6 Manchester
03.03.97	Ricky Mabbett W PTS 6 Leicester
17.03.97	Billy Collins L PTS 6 Glasgow
20.05.97	Panayiotis Panayiotiou L PTS 6 Edmonton

Career: 26 contests, won 11, lost 15.

Chris Barnett

Manchester. *Born* Coventry, 15 July, 1973
L. Welterweight. Ht. 5.5½"
Manager F. Warren

18.02.95	Wayne Jones W RSC 5 Shepton Mallet
24.11.95	Brian Coleman W PTS 6 Manchester
09.04.96	Charlie Paine W RSC 2 Salford
25.10.96	John Smith W PTS 6 Mere
22.12.96	Wayne Shepherd W PTS 6 Salford
18.01.97	Kid McAuley W RTD 3 Manchester
24.02.97	Jay Mahoney L PTS 6 Manchester
20.03.97	Mike Watson W RSC 2 Salford

Career: 8 contests, won 7, lost 1.

(Martin) Wee Barry (Moore)

Staines. *Born* Limavaay, Ireland, 5 April, 1971
Lightweight. Ht. 5'6½"
Manager Self

30.10.95	Martin Evans L PTS 6 Heathrow
12.02.96	Martin Evans W RSC 4 Heathrow
07.11.96	Dean Murdoch L PTS 6 Battersea

Career: 3 contests, won 1, lost 2.

Owen Bartley

Croydon. *Born* Jamaica, 26 March, 1970
Heavyweight. Ht. 6'0"
Manager F. Rix

22.05.94	Art Stacey W PTS 6 Crystal Palace
27.11.94	Steve Yorath DREW 6 Southwark
03.09.96	Mika Kihlstrom L PTS 6 Bethnal Green
08.10.96	Gary Williams W PTS 4 Battersea

Career: 4 contests, won 2, drew 1, lost 1.

Ricky Beard

Dagenham. *Born* Hackney, 1 March, 1963
S. Bantamweight. Former Southern Area
Flyweight Champion. Ht. 5'7½"
Manager Self

02.05.89	Ged Goodwin W RSC 1 Chigwell

06.06.89	Ged Goodwin W RTD 1 Chigwell
19.09.89	Eric George L PTS 6 Bethnal Green
04.10.89	Gordon Shaw L PTS 6 Basildon
03.10.90	Neil Johnston DREW 6 Basildon
19.11.90	Robbie Regan L RSC 6 Cardiff
26.03.91	Francis Ampofo L PTS 8 Bethnal Green
30.09.91	Mickey Cantwell L PTS 8 Kensington
25.02.92	Francis Ampofo L PTS 8 Crystal Palace
14.04.92	Prince Naseem Hamed L CO 2 Mansfield
20.04.93	Tim Yeates L PTS 6 Brentwood
11.05.93	Mickey Bell W RSC 2 Norwich
29.06.93	James Drummond W PTS 8 Mayfair
05.09.94	Shaun Norman L PTS 8 Brentwood
16.09.94	Jesper D. Jensen L RTD 2 Aalborg, Denmark
23.11.94	James Drummond W RSC 2 Irvine
30.03.95	Daren Fifield W RSC 8 Bethnal Green *(Vacant Southern Area Flyweight Title)*
20.10.95	Mark Reynolds L PTS 10 Ipswich *(Southern Area Flyweight Title Defence)*
18.11.95	Lehlohonolo Ledwaba L RSC 3 Glasgow
23.01.96	Spencer Oliver L RSC 3 Bethnal Green
04.05.96	Graham McGrath L PTS 6 Dagenham
17.03.97	Wilson Docherty L RSC 4 Glasgow
20.05.97	Patrick Mullings L RTD 3 Edmonton

Career: 23 contests, won 6, drew 1, lost 16.

Gary Beardsley

Belper. *Born* Belper, 18 July, 1968
Welterweight. Ht. 5'10"
Manager Self

09.02.95	Shaun Stokes W RSC 3 Doncaster
01.03.95	Eddie Haley W RSC 1 Glasgow
06.03.95	Stefan Scriggins L PTS 6 Leicester
15.03.95	Jamie Gallagher W PTS 6 Stoke
20.10.95	Dewi Roberts W PTS 6 Mansfield
22.11.95	Richard Swallow DREW 6 Sheffield
06.12.95	John Smith W PTS 8 Stoke
06.02.96	Georgie Smith L RSC 1 Basildon
22.03.96	Mark Legg W PTS 6 Mansfield
09.12.96	Derek Roche L RSC 2 Bradford
16.01.97	Steve Levene L PTS 6 Solihull
29.01.97	Howard Clarke L PTS 6 Stoke

Career: 12 contests, won 6, drew 1, lost 5.

Clinton Beeby   Les Clark

Clinton Beeby

Northolt. *Born* Hillingdon, 1 March, 1976
S. Bantamweight. Ht. 5'4"
Manager D. Currivan

27.08.96	Marty Chestnut W PTS 6 Windsor
18.01.97	Danny Ruegg L RSC 2 Swadlincote
30.04.97	Anthony Hanna DREW 6 Acton

Career: 3 contests, won 1, drew 1, lost 1.

Gordon Behan

Leamington. *Born* Dublin, 13 February, 1976
Middleweight. Ht. 5'10¾"
Manager M. Shinfield

24.04.96	Michael Pinnock W PTS 6 Solihull
03.06.96	Peter Mitchell DREW 6 Birmingham
07.03.97	James Lowther L PTS 6 Northampton

Career: 3 contests, won 1, drew 1, lost 1.

Steven Bendall

Coventry. *Born* Coventry, 1 December, 1973
Middleweight. Ht. 6'0"
Manager C. Sanigar/F. Warren

15.05.97	Dennis Doyley W RSC 2 Reading

Career: 1 contest, won 1.

Steven Bendall   Les Clark

Nigel Benn

Ilford. *Born* Ilford, 22 January, 1964
Former WBC S. Middleweight Champion.
Former WBO & Commonwealth
Middleweight Champion. Ht. 5'9½"
Manager P. De Freitas

28.01.87	Graeme Ahmed W RSC 2 Croydon
04.03.87	Kevin Roper W RSC 1 Basildon
22.04.87	Bob Niewenhuizen W RSC 1 Kensington
09.05.87	Winston Burnett W RSC 4 Wandsworth
17.06.87	Reggie Marks W RSC 1 Kensington
01.07.87	Leon Morris W CO 1 Kensington
09.08.87	Eddie Smith W CO 1 Windsor

16.09.87	Winston Burnett W RSC 3 Kensington
13.10.87	Russell Barker W RSC 1 Windsor
03.11.87	Ronnie Yeo W RSC 1 Bethnal Green
24.11.87	Ian Chantler W CO 1 Wisbech
02.12.87	Reggie Miller W CO 7 Kensington
27.01.88	Fermin Chirinos W CO 2 Bethnal Green
07.02.88	Byron Prince W RSC 2 Stafford
24.02.88	Greg Taylor W RSC 2 Aberavon
14.03.88	Darren Hobson W CO 1 Norwich
20.04.88	Abdul Amoru Sanda W RSC 2 Muswell Hill
	(Vacant Commonwealth Middleweight Title)
28.05.88	Tim Williams W RSC 2 Kensington
26.10.88	Anthony Logan W CO 2 Kensington
	(Commonwealth Middleweight Title Defence)
10.12.88	David Noel W RSC 1 Crystal Palace
	(Commonwealth Middleweight Title Defence)
08.02.89	Mike Chilambe W CO 1 Kensington
	(Commonwealth Middleweight Title Defence)
28.03.89	Mbayo Wa Mbayo W CO 2 Glasgow
21.05.89	Michael Watson L CO 6 Finsbury Park
	(Commonwealth Middleweight Title Defence)
20.10.89	Jorge Amparo W PTS 10 Atlantic City, USA
01.12.89	Jose Quinones W RSC 1 Las Vegas, USA
14.01.90	Sanderline Williams W PTS 10 Atlantic City, USA
29.04.90	Doug de Witt W RSC 8 Atlantic City, USA
	(WBO Middleweight Title Challenge)
18.08.90	Iran Barkley W RSC 1 Las Vegas, USA
	(WBO Middleweight Title Defence)
18.11.90	Chris Eubank L RSC 9 Birmingham
	(WBO Middleweight Title Defence)
03.04.91	Robbie Sims W RSC 7 Bethnal Green
03.07.91	Kid Milo W RSC 4 Brentwood
26.10.91	Lenzie Morgan W PTS 10 Brentwood
07.12.91	Hector Lescano W CO 3 Manchester
19.02.92	Dan Sherry W RSC 3 Muswell Hill
23.05.92	Thulani Malinga W PTS 10 Birmingham
03.10.92	Mauro Galvano W RTD 3 Marino, Italy
	(WBC S. Middleweight Title Challenge)
12.12.92	Nicky Piper W RSC 11 Muswell Hill
	(WBC S. Middleweight Title Defence)
06.03.93	Mauro Galvano W PTS 12 Glasgow
	(WBC S. Middleweight Title Defence)
26.06.93	Lou Gent W RSC 4 Earls Court
	(WBC S. Middleweight Title Defence)
09.10.93	Chris Eubank DREW 12 Manchester
	(WBC S. Middleweight Title Defence. WBO S. Middleweight Title Challenge)
26.02.94	Henry Wharton W PTS 12 Earls Court
	(WBC S. Middleweight Title Defence)
10.09.94	Juan Carlos Gimenez W PTS 12 Birmingham
	(WBC S. Middleweight Title Defence)
25.02.95	Gerald McClellan W CO 10 Millwall
	(WBC S. Middleweight Title Defence)
22.07.95	Vincenzo Nardiello W RTD 8 Millwall
	(WBC S. Middleweight Title Defence)
02.09.95	Danny Ray Perez W CO 7 Wembley
02.03.96	Thulani Malinga L PTS 12 Newcastle
	(WBC S. Middleweight Title Defence)

06.07.96	Steve Collins L RSC 4 Manchester
	(WBO S. Middleweight Title Challenge)
09.11.96	Steve Collins L RTD 6 Manchester
	(WBO S. Middleweight Title Challenge)

Career: 48 contests, won 42, drew 1, lost 5.

Andrew Benson

Mile End. *Born* Islington, 8 May, 1969
Cruiserweight. Ht. 6'0"
Manager F. Warren

02.09.94	Trevor Small W PTS 6 Spitalfields
18.11.94	Gypsy Carman W PTS 6 Bracknell
26.04.95	Martin Langtry L PTS 6 Solihull
17.05.95	Paul Lawson L RSC 2 Ipswich
13.04.96	Kelly Oliver L PTS 4 Wythenshawe
27.08.96	Jacklord Jacobs W CO 2 Windsor
01.10.96	Robert Norton L RSC 6 Birmingham
29.04.97	Ray Kane W RSC 6 Belfast

Career: 8 contests, won 4, lost 4.

(Adrian) Ady Benton

Dewsbury. *Born* Dewsbury, 26 August, 1973
S. Bantamweight. Ht. 5'6"
Manager K. Tate

27.04.92	Mark Hargreaves W PTS 6 Bradford
29.10.92	Vince Feeney DREW 6 Bayswater
09.11.92	Stevie Woods W PTS 6 Bradford
25.01.93	Neil Parry W RSC 6 Bradford
26.02.93	James Drummond DREW 6 Irvine
08.03.93	Dave Campbell W PTS 6 Leeds
29.06.93	Michael Alldis W DIS 3 Mayfair
20.09.93	Mike Deveney L PTS 8 Glasgow
08.11.93	Chip O'Neill W RSC 5 Bradford
24.01.94	Mike Deveney W PTS 6 Glasgow
25.02.94	Paul Lloyd L RSC 5 Chester
	(Vacant Central Area S. Bantamweight Title)
25.04.94	Pat Clinton W RSC 1 Glasgow
16.09.94	Johnny Bredahl L PTS 8 Aalborg, Denmark
23.11.94	Drew Docherty L PTS 12 Irvine
	(British Bantamweight Title Challenge)
21.04.95	James Murray L RSC 7 Glasgow
14.06.95	Louis Veitch L RSC 2 Batley
11.10.95	Lyndon Kershaw W RTD 6 Solihull
18.10.95	Graham McGrath W PTS 6 Batley
29.11.95	Greg Upton L PTS 6 Solihull
21.02.96	Carl Allen W PTS 6 Batley
24.04.96	Shaun Anderson W PTS 6 Solihull
11.04.97	Matthew Harris W PTS 8 Barnsley

Career: 22 contests, won 13, drew 2, lost 7.

Dennis Berry

Derby. *Born* Birmingham, 4 April, 1967
Welterweight. Ht. 5'8"
Manager F. Maloney

01.04.93	Lee Renshaw W RSC 3 Evesham
08.06.93	David Sumner W PTS 6 Derby
04.11.93	Andy Peach W PTS 6 Stafford
17.03.94	Rick North L PTS 6 Lincoln
16.05.94	Rick North W RSC 6 Cleethorpes
24.05.94	Norman Hutcheon W RSC 2 Leicester
28.06.94	Howard Clarke W RSC 3 Edgbaston
30.07.94	Kevin Lueshing L CO 2 Bethnal Green
07.11.94	Vince Rose L PTS 6 Bethnal Green
15.12.94	Warren Stephens W PTS 6 Evesham
25.01.95	Howard Clarke W PTS 8 Stoke

03.03.95 Geoff McCreesh W RTD 5 Bracknell
01.09.95 Gordon Blair W RSC 3 Wolverhampton
25.10.95 Rick North W PTS 6 Telford
18.03.96 Brian Dunn W RSC 2 Glasgow
03.09.96 Neil Sinclair W PTS 6 Belfast
06.11.96 Vince Rose W RSC 3 Hull
01.03.97 Lindon Scarlett L DIS 6 Liverpool
28.04.97 Spencer McCracken L RSC 10 Hull
(Final Elim. British Welterweight Title)

Career: 19 contests, won 14, lost 5.

Dennis Berry   Les Clark

Ensley Bingham

Manchester. *Born* Manchester, 27 May, 1963
Former Undefeated British L. Middleweight Champion.
Ht. 5'8½"
Manager F. Warren

20.11.86 Steve Ward W CO 5 Bredbury
16.12.87 Tony Britland W CO 1 Manchester
23.02.88 Franki Moro W PTS 6 Oldham
01.03.88 Kelvin Mortimer W PTS 8 Manchester
26.04.88 Clinton McKenzie L PTS 8 Bethnal Green
18.10.88 Kostas Petrou L RSC 7 Oldham
22.03.89 Gary Cooper L PTS 8 Reading
26.09.89 Wally Swift Jnr W PTS 10 Oldham
(Elim. British L. Middleweight Title)
28.03.90 Fernando Alanis L RSC 3 Manchester
06.06.90 Andy Till W DIS 3 Battersea
(Final Elim. British L. Middleweight Title)
19.03.91 Wally Swift Jnr L RSC 4 Birmingham
(Vacant British L. Middleweight Title)
29.11.91 Russell Washer W RSC 4 Manchester
29.05.92 Graham Jenner W CO 5 Manchester
18.07.92 Gordon Blair W CO 2 Manchester
02.11.92 Robert McCracken L RSC 10 Wolverhampton
(Elim. British L. Middleweight Title)
28.05.93 Mark Kelly W RSC 5 Middleton
14.08.93 Robert Peel W RTD 3 Hammersmith
25.02.95 Kevin Adamson W CO 5 Millwall
28.07.95 Mark McCreath W RSC 2 Bristol

13.01.96 Gilbert Jackson W RSC 3 Manchester
(Vacant British L. Middleweight Title)
13.04.96 Garry Logan W RSC 6 Wythenshawe
(British L. Middleweight Title Defence)
19.09.96 Anthony Ivory W RSC 2 Manchester
09.11.96 Ronald Wright L PTS 12 Manchester
(WBO L. Middleweight Title Challenge)

Career: 23 contests, won 16, lost 7.

Lee Bird

Doncaster. *Born* Doncaster, 17 June, 1971
Middleweight. Ht. 5'6"
Manager T. Petersen

13.02.96 Paul Bowen L RSC 2 Bethnal Green
27.09.96 Mark Owens W PTS 6 Hull
24.10.96 Michael Monaghan L RSC 6 Lincoln
19.06.97 Shaun O'Neill L PTS 6 Scunthorpe

Career: 4 contests, won 1, lost 3.

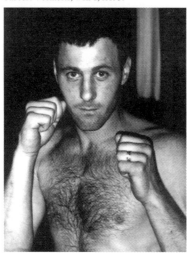

Lee Bird   Les Clark

Ervine Blake

Worcester. *Born* Belfast, 17 February, 1966
S. Featherweight. Ht. 5'7½"
Manager Self

08.10.90 Colin Innes W PTS 6 Bradford
16.10.91 Barrie Kelley L PTS 6 Evesham
07.10.91 Derek Amory W PTS 6 Birmingham
13.02.96 Carl Allen L RSC 5 Wolverhampton
27.03.96 Michael Edwards W RSC 2 Stoke
24.04.96 Steve Conway L PTS 6 Solihull
10.05.96 Mark Bowers W RSC 3 Wembley
03.06.96 Wayne Jones W RSC 1 Birmingham
29.06.96 Paul Ingle L RSC 2 Erith
31.08.96 Paul Griffin L PTS 4 Dublin
19.09.96 Michael Brodie L RSC 4 Manchester
01.11.96 Roger Brotherhood L PTS 6 Mansfield
26.11.96 Jamie Morris W CO 1 Wolverhampton
04.12.96 Kid McAuley W PTS 6 Stoke
09.12.96 Kelton McKenzie L PTS 6 Leicester
29.01.97 Dean Bramhald L RSC 1 Stoke
01.03.97 David Burke L PTS 4 Liverpool
19.03.97 Jason Squire W RTD 6 Stoke
04.04.97 Michael Alldis L RSC 3 Brighton
22.05.97 Chris Price W PTS 6 Solihull
08.06.97 Dave Clavering DREW 6 Shaw

Career: 21 contests, won 9, drew 1, lost 11.

Jason Blanche

Leeds. *Born* New Ross, 29 April, 1972
Lightweight. Ht. 5'4"
Manager J. Celebanski

25.09.95 T. J. Smith W PTS 6 Bradford
30.10.95 Muhammad Shaffique W CO 2 Bradford
11.11.95 Brian Robb W RSC 4 Halifax
11.12.95 Colin Innes W PTS 6 Bradford
13.01.96 Alan Bosworth L PTS 6 Halifax
07.03.96 John T. Kelly DREW 6 Bradford
01.04.96 John T. Kelly DREW 6 Bradford
20.05.96 G. G. Goddard W RSC 4 Bradford
24.06.96 Kid McAuley W PTS 6 Bradford
23.09.96 Vic Broomhead W PTS 6 Bradford
09.12.96 Bamana Dibateza W RSC 4 Bradford
17.02.97 Dean Bramhald W PTS 4 Bradford

Career: 12 contests, won 9, drew 2, lost 1.

Lee Blundell

Wigan. *Born* Wigan, 11 August, 1971
S. Middleweight. Ht. 6'2"
Manager Self

25.04.94 Robert Harper W RSC 2 Bury
20.05.94 Freddie Yemofio W RSC 6 Acton
08.09.94 Gordon Blair DREW 6 Glasgow
07.12.94 Kesem Clayton W RTD 2 Stoke
18.02.95 Glenn Catley L RSC 6 Shepton Mallet
11.12.95 Martin Jolley W PTS 6 Morecambe
16.03.97 Martin Jolley W PTS 6 Shaw
08.05.97 Paul Jones L RSC 4 Mansfield

Career: 8 contests, won 5, drew 1, lost 2.

Stevie Bolt

Plymouth. *Born* Hanover, Germany, 13 April, 1968
S. Featherweight. Ht. 6'0"
Manager Self

29.09.94 Alan Temple L CO 2 Bethnal Green
20.12.94 Georgie Smith L RSC 2 Bethnal Green
24.02.95 Trevor Royal L RSC 5 Weston super Mare
20.09.96 Brian Gentry L RSC 3 Tooting

Career: 4 contests, lost 4.

Paul Bonson

Featherstone. *Born* Castleford, 18 October, 1971
L. Heavyweight. Ht. 5'10"
Manager T. Callighan

04.10.96 Michael Pinnock W PTS 6 Wakefield
14.11.96 Michael Pinnock DREW 6 Sheffield
22.12.96 Pele Lawrence DREW 6 Salford
20.04.97 Shamus Casey W PTS 6 Leeds
26.06.97 Andy Manning L PTS 6 Sheffield

Career: 5 contests, won 2, drew 2, lost 1.

Brian Booth

South Shields. *Born* Jarrow, 3 May, 1973
Welterweight. Ht. 5'9"
Manager T. Callighan

10.10.96 Shaun O'Neill L PTS 6 Newcastle
27.02.97 Mark Allen W PTS 6 Sunderland
01.05.97 Paul Scott W PTS 6 Newcastle
15.05.97 Phil Molyneux W PTS 6 Sunderland
08.06.97 Scott Walker L PTS 6 Shaw

Career: 5 contests, won 3, lost 2.

(Gary) G. L. Booth

Manchester. *Born* Manchester, 30 July, 1963
L. Middleweight. Ht. 6'0"
Manager S. Foster

22.01.86	Clayon Stewart W PTS 6 Stoke
10.02.86	Ned Newbold W PTS 6 Manchester
24.02.86	Trevor Grant DREW 6 Coventry
04.03.86	Gerard Treble L RSC 1 Liverpool
22.05.86	Sean Leighton L RSC 3 Horwich
25.09.86	Nigel Fairbairn L PTS 6 Peterborough
27.10.86	Steve Harwood W PTS 6 Liverpool
01.12.86	Paul Gillings W PTS 6 Manchester
12.01.87	Ian Midwood-Tate W PTS 6 Manchester
09.02.87	Oliver Henry L PTS 6 Manchester
04.03.87	Peter Elliott L PTS 6 Stoke
13.04.87	Kid Carnall W RSC 5 Manchester
15.06.87	Andy Sumner L CO 3 Manchester
25.04.88	Steve Hogg W PTS 6 Liverpool
16.05.88	Barry Messam W CO 4 Manchester
10.10.88	Ian Midwood-Tate L RTD 3 Manchester
14.11.88	Spencer Alton W RSC 7 Manchester
13.02.89	Chris Richards L RSC 8 Manchester
08.05.89	Chris Richards L RSC 2 Manchester
27.11.90	Skip Jackson W PTS 6 Liverpool
25.04.97	Chris Vassiliou W PTS 6 Mere
26.06.97	Pedro Carragher W CO 1 Salford

Career: 22 contests, won 12, drew 1, lost 9.

Jason Booth

Nottingham. *Born* Nottingham, 7 November, 1977
Flyweight. Ht. 5'4"
Manager M. Shinfield

13.06.96	Darren Noble W RSC 3 Sheffield
24.10.96	Marty Chestnut W PTS 6 Lincoln
27.11.96	Jason Thomas W PTS 4 Swansea
18.01.97	David Coldwell W PTS 4 Swadlincote
07.03.97	Pete Buckley W PTS 6 Northampton
20.03.97	Danny Lawson W RSC 3 Newark
10.05.97	Anthony Hanna W PTS 6 Nottingham
19.05.97	Chris Lyons W PTS 6 Cleethorpes

Career: 8 contests, won 8.

Jason Booth   Les Clark

Tony Booth

Hull. *Born* Hull, 30 January, 1970
Former Undefeated Central Area Cruiserweight Champion. Ht. 5'11¾"
Manager Self

08.03.90	Paul Lynch L PTS 6 Watford
11.04.90	Mick Duncan W PTS 6 Dewsbury
26.04.90	Colin Manners W PTS 6 Halifax
16.05.90	Tommy Warde W PTS 6 Hull
05.06.90	Gary Dyson W PTS 6 Liverpool
05.09.90	Shaun McCrory L PTS 6 Stoke
08.10.90	Bullit Andrews W RSC 3 Cleethorpes
23.01.91	Darron Griffiths DREW 6 Stoke
06.02.91	Shaun McCrory L PTS 6 Liverpool
06.03.91	Billy Brough L PTS 6 Glasgow
18.03.91	Billy Brough W PTS 6 Glasgow
28.03.91	Neville Brown L PTS 6 Alfreton
17.05.91	Glenn Campbell L RSC 2 Bury *(Central Area S. Middleweight Title Challenge)*
25.07.91	Paul Murray W PTS 6 Dudley
01.08.91	Nick Manners DREW 8 Dewsbury
11.09.91	Jim Peters L PTS 8 Hammersmith
28.10.91	Eddie Smulders L RSC 6 Arnhem, Holland
09.12.91	Steve Lewsam L PTS 8 Cleethorpes
30.01.92	Serg Fame W PTS 6 Southampton
12.02.92	Tenko Ernie W RSC 4 Wembley
05.03.92	John Beckles W RSC 6 Battersea
26.03.92	Dave Owens W PTS 6 Hull
08.04.92	Michael Gale L PTS 8 Leeds
13.05.92	Phil Soundy W PTS 6 Kensington
02.06.92	Eddie Smulders L RSC 1 Rotterdam, Holland
18.07.92	Maurice Core L PTS 6 Manchester
07.09.92	James Cook L PTS 8 Bethnal Green
30.10.92	Roy Richie DREW 6 Istrees, France
18.11.92	Tony Wilson DREW 8 Solihull
25.12.92	Francis Wanyama L PTS 6 Izegem, Belgium
09.02.93	Tony Wilson W PTS 8 Wolverhampton
01.05.93	Ralf Rocchigiani DREW 8 Berlin, Germany
03.06.93	Victor Cordoba L PTS 8 Marseille, France
23.06.93	Tony Behan W PTS 6 Gorleston
01.07.93	Michael Gale L PTS 8 York
17.09.93	Ole Klemetsen L PTS 8 Copenhagen, Denmark
07.10.93	Denzil Browne DREW 8 York
02.11.93	James Cook L PTS 8 Southwark
12.11.93	Carlos Christie W PTS 6 Hull
28.01.94	Francis Wanyama L RSC 2 Waregem, Belgium *(Vacant Commonwealth Cruiserweight Title)*
26.03.94	Torsten May L PTS 6 Dortmund, Germany
21.07.94	Mark Prince L RSC 3 Battersea
24.09.94	Johnny Held L PTS 8 Rotterdam, Holland
07.10.94	Dirk Wallyn L PTS 6 Waregem, Belgium
27.10.94	Dean Francis L CO 1 Bayswater
23.01.95	Jan Lefeber L PTS 8 Rotterdam, Holland
07.03.95	John Foreman L PTS 6 Edgbaston
27.04.95	Art Stacey W PTS 10 Hull *(Vacant Central Area Cruiserweight Title)*
04.06.95	Montell Griffin L RSC 2 Bethnal Green
06.07.95	Nigel Rafferty W RSC 7 Hull
22.07.95	Mark Prince L RSC 2 Millwall
06.09.95	Leif Keiski L PTS 8 Helsinki, Finland
25.09.95	Neil Simpson W PTS 8 Cleethorpes
06.10.95	Don Diego Poeder L RSC 2 Waregem, Belgium
11.11.95	Bruce Scott L RSC 3 Halifax
16.12.95	John Marceta L RSC 2 Cardiff
20.01.96	Johnny Nelson L RSC 2 Mansfield
15.03.96	Slick Miller W PTS 6 Hull
27.03.96	Neil Simpson L PTS 6 Whitwick
17.05.96	Mark Richardson W RSC 2 Hull
13.07.96	Bruce Scott L PTS 8 Bethnal Green
03.09.96	Paul Douglas L PTS 4 Belfast
14.09.96	Kelly Oliver L RSC 2 Sheffield
06.11.96	Martin Jolley W PTS 4 Hull
22.11.96	Slick Miller W RSC 5 Hull
11.12.96	Crawford Ashley L RSC 1 Southwark
18.01.97	Kelly Oliver L RSC 4 Swadlincote
27.02.97	Kevin Morton L PTS 6 Hull
25.03.97	Nigel Rafferty DREW 8 Wolverhampton
04.04.97	John Wilson L PTS 6 Glasgow
16.04.97	Robert Norton L RSC 4 Bethnal Green
15.05.97	Phill Day W PTS 4 Reading

Career: 72 contests, won 23, drew 7, lost 42.

John Bosco (Waigo)

Bermondsey. *Born* Uganda, 16 July, 1967
L. Middleweight. Ht. 5'8½"
Manager M. Duff

05.12.91	Tony Kosova W CO 2 Peterborough
17.02.92	Gilbert Jackson W PTS 6 Mayfair
03.09.92	Russell Washer W RSC 2 Dunstable
19.10.92	Steve Goodwin W RSC 2 Mayfair
07.12.92	Griff Jones W RSC 1 Mayfair
28.01.93	Jerry Mortimer W RSC 4 Southwark
15.02.93	Mark Dawson W PTS 6 Mayfair
29.03.93	Winston May W RSC 3 Mayfair
10.11.93	Mark Dawson W RTD 4 Watford
26.01.94	Julian Eavis W RSC 1 Birmingham
14.03.94	Carlo Colarusso W PTS 6 Mayfair
28.04.94	Chris Peters W PTS 8 Mayfair
05.10.94	Robert Wright L RSC 7 Wolverhampton
16.10.95	J. P. Matthews DREW 6 Mayfair
17.11.95	Harry Dhami W PTS 6 Bethnal Green
04.05.96	Adrian Dodson L RSC 7 Dagenham *(WBO Inter-Continental L. Middleweight Title Challenge)*
08.02.97	Harry Simon L RSC 2 Millwall

Career: 17 contests, won 13, drew 1, lost 3.

Alan Bosworth

Northampton. *Born* Northampton, 31 December, 1967
Lightweight. Ht. 5'7"
Manager M. Shinfield

17.10.95	Simon Hamblett W RSC 2 Wolverhampton
29.10.95	Shaun Gledhill W PTS 6 Shaw
16.11.95	Brian Coleman W PTS 6 Evesham
23.11.95	David Thompson W RSC 4 Tynemouth
13.01.96	Jason Blanche W PTS 6 Halifax
31.01.96	Arv Mittoo W PTS 6 Stoke
16.02.96	John Docherty W PTS 6 Irvine
24.03.96	Scott Walker DREW 6 Shaw
16.05.96	Yifru Retta W PTS 6 Dunstable
07.03.97	Wayne Rigby L RSC 5 Northampton

Career: 10 contests, won 8, drew 1, lost 1.

Michael Bowen

West Ham. *Born* Forest Gate, 14
November, 1974
L. Heavyweight. Ht. 6'1/2"
Manager P. De Freitas

02.06.95 Robert Harper W PTS 6 Bethnal Green
09.12.95 Peter Varnavas W CO 3 Bethnal Green
13.02.96 Henry Price W RSC 1 Bethnal Green
13.04.96 Danny Ryan W RSC 2 Wythenshawe
11.05.96 Mark Dawson W PTS 4 Bethnal Green
25.02.97 Mark Dawson W RSC 4 Sheffield
Career: 6 contests, won 6.

Paul Bowen

West Ham. *Born* Barking, 14 May, 1973
S. Middleweight. Ht. 6'0"
Manager P. De Freitas

13.02.96 Lee Bird W RSC 2 Bethnal Green
13.04.96 Pat Durkin W RSC 3 Wythenshawe
13.07.96 Mark Dawson W RSC 3 Bethnal Green
08.02.97 Darren Ashton W PTS 4 Millwall
Career: 4 contests, won 4.

Craig Bowen-Price

Blackpool. *Born* Blackpool, 20 May, 1969
Heavyweight. Ht. 6'4 3/4"
Manager A. Talbot

18.01.97 Gary Williams W CO 1 Manchester
28.04.97 Waldemar Framas W PTS 4 Hull
Career: 2 contests, won 2.

Craig Bowen-Price   Les Clark

Nick Boyd

Bolton. *Born* Bolton, 11 October, 1966
L. Welterweight. Ht. 5'10"
Manager Self

05.02.93 Mark O'Callaghan W PTS 6
            Manchester
28.05.93 Mark Allen W CO 2 Middleton
25.07.93 Trevor Royal W PTS 6 Oldham
17.02.94 Chris Aston W CO 3 Bury
25.04.94 Brian Wright W CO 2 Bury

02.06.94 John Stovin W RSC 5 Middleton
06.07.96 Brian Coleman W PTS 4 Manchester
Career: 7 contests, won 7.

Robert Braddock

Doncaster. *Born* Mexborough, 14 January,
1971
Featherweight. Ht 5'7"
Manager J. Rushton

03.04.89 Ronnie Stephenson L CO 4 Manchester
13.10.89 Dave McNally L PTS 6 Preston
23.10.89 John Whitelaw W PTS 6 Hull
30.10.89 Pete Buckley L PTS 6 Birmingham
28.06.90 Pete Buckley L RSC 5 Birmingham
10.06.91 Tony Smith DREW 6 Manchester
23.09.91 Al Garrett DREW 6 Glasgow
07.10.91 Glyn Shepherd DREW 6 Bradford
13.11.91 Chris Morris L RSC 5 Liverpool
16.12.91 Carl Roberts L PTS 6 Manchester
28.04.92 Chip O'Neill L PTS 6 Houghton le
            Spring
01.06.92 Alex Docherty L PTS 6 Glasgow
08.09.92 Chris Lyons W CO 5 Doncaster
05.10.92 Karl Morling L PTS 6 Northampton
09.11.92 Chip O'Neill W RSC 3 Bradford
23.11.92 Ian McLeod DREW 6 Glasgow
07.12.92 Gary White L PTS 6 Manchester
20.09.93 Hugh Collins L PTS 8 Glasgow
06.10.93 Ian McGirr L PTS 8 York
07.11.93 Wilson Docherty L RSC 3 Glasgow
07.12.93 Yifru Retta L RSC 2 Bethnal Green
23.09.96 Ian McLeod L RSC 3 Glasgow
28.10.96 Jason Squire L PTS 6 Leicester
26.11.96 Graham McGrath W PTS 6
            Wolverhampton
17.12.96 Stefy Bull L RSC 4 Doncaster
            (Vacant Central Featherweight Title)
20.03.97 Esham Pickering L RSC 6 Newark
Career: 26 contests won 4, drew 4, lost 18.

Nigel Bradley

Sheffield. *Born* Sheffield, 24 February,
1968
Welterweight. Ht. 5'8"
Manager Self

14.12.87 Lee Amass L RSC 4 Piccadilly
29.01.88 John Townsley L PTS 6 Durham
23.03.88 Darren Darby W RSC 1 Sheffield
28.03.88 Adam Muir NC 4 Glasgow
18.04.88 Mark Kelly L PTS 6 Manchester
08.06.88 Mike Russell W PTS 6 Sheffield
09.09.88 David Bacon W RSC 5 Doncaster
26.10.88 Dean Dickinson W PTS 6 Sheffield
23.02.89 Chris Mulcahy W RSC 2 Stockport
09.03.89 Michael McDermott W RSC 5
            Glasgow
04.04.89 John Mullen W RSC 6 Sheffield
08.10.90 John Townsley DREW 8 Glasgow
14.11.90 B. F. Williams W CO 2 Sheffield
29.01.91 Sugar Gibiliru L PTS 8 Stockport
11.02.92 Dean Hollington L PTS 6 Barking
18.03.92 Kris McAdam W CO 2 Glasgow
14.04.92 Dave Whittle W CO 3 Mansfield
29.09.92 Tony Swift L PTS 8 Stoke
08.02.94 Howard Clarke L RTD 6
            Wolverhampton
17.11.94 John Smith W PTS 6 Sheffield
03.03.95 Jason Rowland L RSC 3 Bethnal Green
13.04.95 Allan Hall L RSC 2 Bloomsbury
08.09.95 Shea Neary L RSC 2 Liverpool
            (Vacant Central L. Welterweight Title)

25.10.95 Michael Smyth L RSC 4 Cardiff
12.05.97 Richard Swallow L PTS 6 Leicester
Career: 25 contests, won 11, drew 1, lost 12, no
            contest 1.

Nigel Bradley   Les Clark

Thomas Bradley

Sheffield. *Born* Sheffield, 29 August, 1972
Lightweight. Ht. 5'7"
Manager B. Ingle

15.05.95 Simon Hamblett W PTS 6 Cleethorpes
15.09.95 Mark Haslam L CO 4 Mansfield
14.11.95 Ian Richardson W PTS 6 Yarm
06.12.95 Scott Marshall W RSC 5 Stoke
13.06.96 Ram Singh W RSC 1 Sheffield
23.09.96 Arv Mittoo DREW 6 Cleethorpes
14.11.96 Arv Mittoo W RSC 4 Sheffield
25.02.97 Chris Lyons W PTS 4 Sheffield
20.03.97 Pete Buckley L PTS 6 Newark
10.04.97 Vic Broomhead W CO 3 Sheffield
26.06.97 Kid McAuley W PTS 6 Sheffield
Career: 11 contests, won 8, drew 1, lost 2.

Christian Brady

Birmingham. *Born* Birmingham, 23 July,
1970
L. Welterweight. Ht. 5'8"
Manager P. Cowdell/R. Gray

02.12.96 Shaun Gledhill W RTD 3 Birmingham
03.03.97 Vic Broomhead W PTS 6 Birmingham
09.06.97 Tony Smith W RSC 4 Birmingham
Career: 3 contests, won 3.

Dean Bramhald

Doncaster. *Born* Balby, 25 May, 1963
L. Welterweight. Former Central Area
Lightweight Champion. Ht. 5'7½"
Manager J. Rushton

25.01.84 Wayne Trigg L CO 3 Stoke
22.02.84 Andy Deabreu L PTS 6 Evesham
27.02.84 Billy Joe Dee W PTS 6 Nottingham
19.03.84 Billy Joe Dee L PTS 6 Bradford

27.03.84	Neville Fivey DREW 6 Wolverhampton
04.04.84	Peter Bowen L PTS 6 Evesham
12.04.84	Andy Deabreu L PTS 6 Piccadilly
09.05.84	Wayne Trigg DREW 4 Leicester
21.05.84	Doug Munro L PTS 6 Aberdeen
11.06.84	Glenn Tweedie L PTS 6 Glasgow
06.08.84	Andy Williams L PTS 6 Aintree
21.09.84	Clinton Campbell W PTS 6 Alfreton
02.10.84	John Doherty L PTS 8 Leeds
10.10.84	Rocky Lawler W RSC 5 Stoke
22.10.84	John Maloney DREW 6 Mayfair
29.10.84	Ray Newby L PTS 6 Nottingham
19.11.84	Dave Adam L PTS 6 Glasgow
27.11.84	Mickey Markie DREW 6 Wolverhampton
05.12.84	Neville Fivey W PTS 6 Stoke
17.12.84	John Maloney DREW 6 Mayfair
18.01.85	Mark Reefer L RSC 8 Bethnal Green
20.02.85	Stuart Carmichael DREW 6 Stafford
01.03.85	Craig Windsor DREW 6 Glasgow
13.03.85	Dave Adam L PTS 8 Stoke
25.03.85	Michael Marsden W PTS 8 Huddersfield
05.04.85	Bobby McDermott L PTS 8 Glasgow
18.04.85	John Doherty L PTS 8 Halifax
04.06.85	Pat Doherty L CO 6 Streatham
31.07.85	Robert Dickie L RSC 7 Porthcawl
23.09.85	Kevin Taylor L RSC 1 Bradford
21.10.85	Kevin Taylor L PTS 6 Bradford
21.11.85	Russell Jones L PTS 8 Blaenavon
30.11.85	Floyd Havard L RSC 3 Cardiff
20.01.86	Paul Downie L PTS 8 Glasgow
06.02.86	Stuart Carmichael W PTS 8 Doncaster
20.02.86	Floyd Havard L PTS 6 Halifax
10.03.86	Peter Bradley L PTS 8 Glasgow
17.03.86	Paul Downie L CO 5 Glasgow
27.04.86	Andrew Pybus W PTS 6 Doncaster
20.05.86	Eamonn McAuley L PTS 6 Wembley
02.06.86	Peter Bradley L PTS 8 Mayfair
13.06.86	Peppy Muire L RSC 7 Gloucester
30.07.86	Steve James L PTS 8 Ebbw Vale
17.11.86	Jim Moffat L PTS 8
25.11.86	Joey Joynson L PTS 8 Wolverhampton
03.12.86	Steve Brown L PTS 6 Stoke
15.12.86	Rocky Lester W PTS 6 Loughborough
26.01.87	Tony Swift L PTS 8 Birmingham
09.02.87	Peter Crook L PTS 8 Manchester
16.02.87	Nigel Senior L PTS 8 Glasgow
04.03.87	Tony Swift L RSC 5 Dudley
06.04.87	Drew Black L PTS 8 Glasgow
27.04.87	Kevin Spratt L PTS 8 Bradford
06.05.87	Peter Bradley L RSC 4 Livingston
04.06.87	David Maw L PTS 8 Sunderland
13.06.87	Michael Betts DREW 6 Great Yarmouth
04.09.87	David Maw L PTS 6 Gateshead
14.09.87	John Bennie W PTS 6 Glasgow
07.10.87	Tony Swift L PTS 8 Stoke
19.10.87	Peter Till L PTS 8 Birmingham
11.11.87	Ron Shinkwin W PTS 8 Stafford
24.11.87	Peter Till L PTS 8 Wolverhampton
02.12.87	Tony Swift L PTS 8 Stoke
14.12.87	Ron Shinkwin L PTS 8 Bradford
20.01.88	Davy Robb L PTS 8 Stoke
29.01.88	Frankie Lake L PTS 8 Torquay
07.02.88	Damien Denny L PTS 4 Stafford
24.02.88	David Lake L PTS 8 Southend
09.03.88	Mickey Vern W CO 5 Stoke
23.03.88	Frankie Lake DREW 8 Evesham
13.04.88	Davy Robb W RSC 5 Wolverhampton
25.04.88	Nigel Senior W PTS 8 Nottingham
16.05.88	Ronnie Campbell L RSC 7 Wolverhampton

16.06.88	Mark Dinnadge W PTS 8 Croydon
26.09.88	Dave Croft DREW 4 Bradford
06.10.88	Ronnie Campbell W RSC 6 Dudley
17.10.88	Dave Griffiths L RSC 5 Mayfair
17.11.88	Tony Feliciello L PTS 8 Weston super Mare
29.11.88	Neil Foran L PTS 6 Manchester
16.12.88	Brian Sonny Nickels L PTS 6 Brentwood
26.01.89	George Baigrie W PTS 6 Newcastle
14.02.89	Steve Hogg W PTS 6 Wolverhampton
06.03.89	Pat Barrett L PTS 8 Manchester
03.04.89	Brian Cullen W RSC 3 Manchester
19.04.89	Calum Rattray W PTS 6 Doncaster
26.04.89	Michael Driscoll L RSC 2 Southampton
29.05.89	Peter Hart L RSC 2 Liverpool
25.09.89	Ian Honeywood L RTD 4 Crystal Palace
25.10.89	Oliver Henry L PTS 6 Doncaster
28.11.89	Shaun Cooper L CO 2 Wolverhampton
17.01.90	Peter Bowen W PTS 6 Stoke
24.01.90	Paul Bowen L PTS 8 Solihull
07.03.90	Andrew Robinson L PTS 6 Doncaster
14.03.90	Shaun Cogan L PTS 8 Stoke
04.04.90	Dave Croft W PTS 6 Stafford
26.04.90	Seamus O'Sullivan L PTS 6 Wandsworth
21.05.90	Brendan Ryan DREW 6 Grimsby
05.06.90	Billy Couzens L PTS 6 Nottingham
22.06.90	Mark Dinnadge L PTS 6 Gillingham
14.11.90	Jim Lawlor DREW 8 Doncaster
13.12.90	Andrew Morgan DREW 8 Cleethorpes
10.12.90	Colin Sinnott W PTS 6 Bradford
17.12.90	Sugar Gibiliru L PTS 8 Manchester
17.01.91	Richard Burton L RTD 1 Alfreton
05.03.91	Charlie Kane L RSC 6 Glasgow
10.04.91	Ronnie Campbell W PTS 6 Wolverhampton
24.04.91	Dave Jenkins L PTS 8 Aberavon
13.05.91	Andrew Robinson L RTD 1 Birmingham
17.06.91	Malcolm Melvin L PTS 6 Edgbaston
04.07.91	Shane Sheridan L PTS 6 Alfreton
10.09.91	Mark Elliot L CO 5 Wolverhampton
08.10.91	Colin Sinnott L PTS 8 Wolverhampton
21.10.91	Colin Sinnott W PTS 6 Cleethorpes
20.11.91	Rocky Feliciello L PTS 6 Solihull
04.12.91	Ron Shinkwin W PTS 8 Stoke
22.01.92	Ray Newby L PTS 8 Solihull
30.01.92	Ron Shinkwin L PTS 6 Southampton
11.02.92	Ray Newby L RSC 7 Wolverhampton
11.03.92	Andreas Panayi W PTS 8 Stoke
24.03.92	Richard Swallow L PTS 8 Wolverhampton
06.04.92	Richard Swallow L PTS 6 Northampton
28.04.92	Darren McInulty L PTS 6 Wolverhampton
11.05.92	Darren McInulty L PTS 6 Coventry
12.06.92	Carl Wright L PTS 6 Liverpool
15.09.92	Mike Morrison W PTS 6 Crystal Palace
30.09.92	Barrie Kelley L PTS 6 Solihull
13.10.92	Bernard Paul DREW 6 Mayfair
26.11.92	Kevin Toomey W PTS 10 Hull (Central Area Lightweight Title Challenge)
12.12.92	Mark Tibbs L PTS 6 Muswell Hill
20.01.93	Dean Amory L PTS 6 Solihull
18.02.93	Kevin Toomey L PTS 10 Hull (Central Area Lightweight Title Defence)
23.03.93	Alan Peacock W PTS 6 Wolverhampton

01.04.93	Shane Sheridan W PTS 6 Evesham
30.04.93	Alan McDowall L PTS 6 Glasgow
14.05.93	Tanveer Ahmed L PTS 6 Kilmarnock
07.06.93	Howard Clarke L RTD 2 Walsall
06.09.93	Joey Moffat L PTS 6 Liverpool
20.09.93	Rick North L PTS 6 Cleethorpes
28.09.93	Bernard Paul L PTS 8 Bethnal Green
28.10.93	Gary Hiscox L RSC 5 Walsall
13.12.93	Jamie Morris L PTS 6 Doncaster
17.12.96	Chris Price W PTS 6 Doncaster
29.01.97	Ervine Blake W RSC 1 Stoke
17.02.97	Jason Blanche L PTS 4 Bradford
20.03.97	Wayne Windle L RSC 4 Doncaster (Vacant Central Area L. Welterweight Title)
25.04.97	Tony Smith W PTS 6 Cleethorpes
08.05.97	Chris Pegg W RSC 5 Mansfield
16.05.97	Scott Dixon L PTS 6 Glasgow

Career: 148 contests, won 36, drew 14, lost 98.

James Branch

Woodford. *Born* Bethnal Green, 3 February, 1974
L. Heavyweight. Ht. 6'3"
Manager F. Warren

31.08.96	Chris Davies W PTS 4 Dublin
19.09.96	Stinger Mason DREW 4 Manchester
30.11.96	Trevor Small L CO 1 Tylorstown
27.03.97	Toks Owoh L RSC 1 Norwich

Career: 4 contests, won 1, drew 1, lost 2.

Dave Brazil

Aldershot. *Born* Liskeard, 27 March, 1972
L. Welterweight. Ht. 5'8"
Manager J. Evans

03.07.96	Andy Martin W RSC 3 Wembley
27.08.96	Brian Coleman W PTS 6 Windsor
26.09.96	Steve McLevy L RSC 1 Glasgow
11.12.96	Pat Larner L PTS 6 Southwark
08.03.97	Paul Knights W RSC 2 Brentwood
16.04.97	Dennis Griffin L RSC 1 Bethnal Green

Career: 6 contests, won 3, lost 3.

Mark Breslin

Barrhead. *Born* Paisley, 5 January, 1972
L. Welterweight. Ht. 5'9½"
Manager T. Gilmour

19.09.94	Brian Coleman W CO 1 Glasgow
02.11.94	Mark Allen W PTS 6 Solihull
23.11.94	Kevin McKenzie W PTS 6 Irvine
05.04.95	T. J. Smith W PTS 6 Irvine
01.06.95	T. J. Smith W RSC 3 Musselburgh
18.09.95	Mike Watson W PTS 6 Glasgow
18.11.95	Paul Scott W PTS 6 Glasgow
22.04.96	Mark Legg W PTS 8 Glasgow
23.09.96	Dean Nicholas W PTS 8 Glasgow
18.11.96	Anthony Campbell W PTS 6 Glasgow
28.02.97	Karl Taylor W RSC 6 Kilmarnock
14.03.97	Paul Scott W RTD 3 Irvine
28.04.97	David Kirk W PTS 8 Glasgow

Career: 13 contests, won 13.

John Briffa

Salford. *Born* Salford, 23 October, 1970
L. Welterweight. Ht. 5'7"
Manager S. Foster

22.08.96	Chris Price W RSC 2 Salford
25.10.96	Mike Watson L RSC 1 Mere

Career: 2 contests, won 1, lost 1.

73

Grant Briggs

Cilfyndd. *Born* Aberdare, 20 November, 1971
S. Middleweight. Ht. 6'3"
Manager D. Gardiner

19.07.96 Paul Matthews W PTS 4 Ystrad
18.09.96 Carlton Williams W RTD 3 Tylorstown
02.10.96 P. R. Mason W CO 2 Cardiff
06.11.96 Ernie Loveridge W PTS 4 Tylorstown
30.11.96 Brian Galloway W PTS 4 Tylorstown
15.05.97 Bruce Scott L RSC 2 Reading
Career: 6 contests, won 5, lost 1.

Grant Briggs   Les Clark

Steve Bristow

Liverpool. *Born* Northwich, 27 February, 1970
Cruiserweight. Ht. 6'0"
Manager S. Vaughan

10.05.96 David Jules W RSC 2 Liverpool
16.08.96 John Pierre W PTS 6 Liverpool
11.10.96 Chris Henry W PTS 4 Mayfair
Career: 3 contests, won 3.

Vic Broomhead

Buxton. *Born* Buxton, 20 March, 1974
Lightweight. Ht. 5'5"
Manager J. Ashton

24.04.96 Dave Madden W RSC 3 Stoke
13.06.96 Chris Lyons L PTS 6 Sheffield
12.09.96 Peter Gabbitus W RSC 3 Doncaster
23.09.96 Jason Blanche L PTS 6 Bradford
02.10.96 Stuart Rimmer L CO 5 Stoke
03.03.97 Christian Brady L PTS 6 Birmingham
20.03.97 Marc Smith W PTS 6 Solihull
10.04.97 Thomas Bradley L CO 3 Sheffield
13.06.97 Franny Hogg L RSC 2 Leeds
Career: 9 contests, won 3, lost 6.

Roger Brotherhood

Mansfield. *Born* Mansfield, 10 June, 1971
Featherweight. Ht. 5'7½"
Manager J. Ashton

07.04.94 Robert Grubb W PTS 6 Walsall
05.12.94 Garry Burrell W PTS 6 Bradford
09.02.95 Kid McAuley L PTS 6 Doncaster
07.04.95 Paul Wynn W RSC 5 Sheffield
22.03.96 Marty Chestnut W PTS 6 Mansfield
30.05.96 Carl Allen L RSC 5 Lincoln
01.11.96 Ervine Blake W PTS 6 Mansfield
Career: 7 contests, won 5, lost 2.

Colin Brown

Edinburgh. *Born* Glasgow, 14 March, 1969
Cruiserweight. Ht. 5'11¼"
Manager T. Gilmour

18.09.95 Declan Faherty W RSC 4 Cleethorpes
18.11.95 David Flowers W DIS 3 Glasgow
19.02.96 Sean Daly W RTD 4 Glasgow
18.03.96 Albert Call W PTS 6 Glasgow
22.04.96 John Pierre W PTS 6 Glasgow
28.10.96 Chris Woollas W PTS 8 Glasgow
27.01.97 Chris Henry L RSC 3 Glasgow
Career: 7 contests, won 6, lost 1.

Matt Brown

Walworth. *Born* Camberwell, 17 February, 1971
Southern Area S. Featherweight Champion. Ht. 5'6"
Manager F. Maloney

15.06.94 Chris Lyons W CO 3 Southwark
25.10.94 Jason Hutson W PTS 4 Southwark
23.01.95 Andrew Reed W PTS 4 Bethnal Green
21.09.95 Niel Leggett W PTS 4 Battersea
24.10.95 Jason Hutson W RSC 3 Southwark
05.02.96 Des Gargano W RSC 4 Bexleyheath
02.04.96 Marco Fattore W PTS 4 Southwark
29.06.96 Pete Buckley L RSC 1 Erith
11.12.96 Marcus McCrae W RSC 9 Southwark
(Vacant Southern Area S. Featherweight Title)
04.03.97 Wayne Jones W RSC 3 Southwark
30.06.97 Rudy Valentino W PTS 10 Bethnal Green
(Southern Area S. Featherweight Title Defence)
Career: 10 contests, won 9, lost 1.

Tim Brown

Dolgellau. *Born* Wrexham, 27 November, 1973
Cruiserweight. Ht. 5'10½"
Manager D. Davies

11.04.97 Nigel Selby L PTS 6 Barnsley
Career: 1 contest, lost 1.

Denzil Browne

Leeds. *Born* Leeds, 21 January, 1969
Central Area Cruiserweight Champion. Ht. 6'2½"
Manager M. Duff

18.10.90 Mark Bowen W PTS 6 Dewsbury
29.11.90 R. F. McKenzie L PTS 6 Sunderland
13.12.90 Gary Railton W RSC 2 Dewsbury
21.02.91 Mark Bowen W PTS 6 Walsall
21.03.91 R. F. McKenzie W PTS 6 Dewsbury
09.05.91 Darren McKenna W PTS 6 Leeds
27.06.91 Steve Yorath W PTS 6 Leeds
01.08.91 Tony Colclough W RSC 1 Dewsbury
09.10.91 R. F. McKenzie L PTS 6 Manchester

30.10.91 Gus Mendes W RSC 6 Leeds
23.01.92 Darren McKenna W PTS 6 York
19.03.92 Ian Bulloch W PTS 8 York
23.09.92 Steve Yorath W PTS 8 Leeds
29.10.92 Sean O'Phoenix W RSC 4 Leeds
25.02.93 Cordwell Hylton W PTS 8 Bradford
22.04.93 Dave Muhammed W PTS 8 Mayfair
01.07.93 Steve Osborne W RSC 1 York
07.10.93 Tony Booth DREW 8 York
01.12.93 Lennie Howard W RSC 6 Kensington
26.10.94 Steve Lewsam W CO 2 Leeds
21.01.95 Dennis Andries L RSC 11 Glasgow
(Vacant British Cruiserweight Title)
08.07.95 Bobbi Joe Edwards L PTS 8 York
11.11.95 John Keeton L RSC 4 Halifax
13.01.96 Albert Call W PTS 6 Halifax
04.06.96 Bobbi Joe Edwards W PTS 10 York
(Vacant Central Area Cruiserweight Title)
25.03.97 Chris Okoh L PTS 12 Lewisham
(Commonwealth Cruiserweight Title Challenge)
Career: 26 contests, won 19, drew 1, lost 6.

(Delroy) Del Bryan

Birmingham. *Born* Nottingham, 16 April, 1967
L. Middleweight. Former British Welterweight Champion. Former Undefeated Midlands Area Welterweight Champion. Ht. 5'8"
Manager M. Shinfield

21.04.86 Wil Halliday W PTS 6 Birmingham
15.05.86 Gary Sommerville L PTS 6 Dudley
28.05.86 Trevor Hopson W RTD 4 Lewisham
26.06.86 Gary Sommerville L PTS 8 Edgbaston
26.09.86 Gary Cass W PTS 6 Swindon
06.10.86 Gary Sommerville W PTS 8 Birmingham
14.10.86 Mickey Lerwill W PTS 8 Wolverhampton
04.11.86 George Collins L RSC 4 Oldham
16.12.86 Ray Golding W PTS 6 Alfreton
08.01.87 Darren Dyer W PTS 6 Bethnal Green
17.02.87 Tommy Shiels L RSC 2 Alfreton
30.09.87 Peter Ashcroft W PTS 8 Solihull
26.10.87 Gary Sommerville W RSC 7 Birmingham
(Vacant Midlands Area Welterweight Title)
03.12.87 Mickey Hughes W PTS 8 Southend
15.12.87 Lloyd Christie W PTS 8 Bradford
24.02.88 Gary Jacobs L PTS 10 Glasgow
(Final Elim. British Welterweight Title)
09.03.88 Michael Justin DREW 8 Wembley
20.04.88 Kelvin Mortimer W RSC 4 Stoke
04.05.88 Gary Sommerville W PTS 8 Solihull
09.08.88 Jimmy Thornton W PTS 6 St Helier
28.09.88 Ossie Maddix W PTS 8 Solihull
12.12.88 Michael Justin W RSC 8 Nottingham
(Midlands Area Welterweight Title Defence)
22.03.89 Lenny Gloster W PTS 8 Solihull
10.05.89 Crisanto Espana L PTS 8 Kensington
19.08.89 Javier Castillejos W PTS 8 Benidorm, Spain
04.09.89 Joni Nyman L PTS 8 Helsinki, Finland
30.01.90 Simon Eubank W PTS 6 Battersea
16.02.90 Arvey Castro W RSC 1 Bilbao, Spain
17.04.90 Damien Denny W PTS 10 Millwall
(Final Elim. British Welterweight Title)

30.09.90	Phumzile Madikane L RSC 6 Capetown, South Africa	
16.01.91	Kirkland Laing W PTS 12 Kensington	
	(British Welterweight Title Challenge)	
16.04.91	Anthony Ivory W PTS 10 Nottingham	
26.11.91	Mickey Hughes W RSC 3 Bethnal Green	
	(British Welterweight Title Defence)	
20.02.92	Gary Jacobs L PTS 12 Glasgow	
	(British Welterweight Title Challenge)	
12.05.92	Darren Dyer L RSC 10 Crystal Palace	
29.09.92	Chris Peters W PTS 10 Stoke	
02.01.93	Godfrey Nyakana L PTS 8 Differdange, Luxembourg	
05.05.93	Oscar Checca W CO 2 Belfast	
11.08.93	Sidney Msutu W PTS 10 Durban, South Africa	
22.09.93	Pat Barrett W PTS 12 Bethnal Green	
	(Vacant British Welterweight Title)	
17.02.94	Derek Grainger W CO 7 Dagenham	
	(British Welterweight Title Defence)	
11.05.94	Paul Lynch W PTS 8 Sheffield	
10.09.94	Lindon Scarlett W PTS 12 Birmingham	
	(British Welterweight Title Defence)	
17.12.94	Jose Luis Navarro L RSC 10 Cordoba, Spain	
	(Vacant European Welterweight Title)	
02.06.95	Gary Logan W RSC 11 Bethnal Green	
	(British Welterweight Title Defence)	
15.09.95	Chris Saunders L PTS 12 Mansfield	
	(British Welterweight Title Defence)	
12.05.96	Nika Kumalo L PTS 10 Cape Town, South Africa	
06.07.96	Harry Simon L RSC 6 Manchester	
14.09.96	Ryan Rhodes L PTS 6 Sheffield	
14.03.97	Ryan Rhodes L RSC 7 Reading	
	(British L. Middleweight Title Challenge)	

Career: 50 contests, won 32, drew 1, lost 17.

Brendan Bryce

Birmingham. *Born* Berwick on Tweed, 18 October, 1973
S. Bantamweight. Ht. 5'6"
Manager Self

06.09.95	Shaun Norman L PTS 6 Stoke
02.10.95	Darren Greaves W PTS 6 Birmingham
26.10.95	Graham McGrath W PTS 6 Birmingham
03.12.95	Dave Martin L PTS 6 Southwark
20.12.95	Henry Jones L PTS 6 Usk
27.03.96	Chris Lyons W PTS 6 Whitwick
02.04.96	Dharmendra Singh Yadav L PTS 4 Southwark
14.05.96	Vince Feeney L PTS 6 Dagenham
09.07.96	Mark Reynolds L PTS 4 Bethnal Green
23.09.96	Esham Pickering L RSC 5 Cleethorpes

Career: 10 contests, won 3, lost 7.

Alston Buchanan

Glasgow. *Born* Glasgow, 25 December, 1972
S. Bantamweight. Ht. 5'5"
Manager T. Gilmour

26.04.96	Amjed Mamond W RTD 1 Glasgow
24.05.96	Marty Chestnut W PTS 6 Glasgow
20.09.96	Gary Hickman W PTS 6 Glasgow
29.11.96	Pete Buckley W PTS 6 Glasgow
12.02.97	Benny Jones L CO 5 Glasgow
02.06.97	Jason Whitaker W RSC 6 Glasgow

Career: 6 contests, won 5, lost 1.

Pete Buckley

Birmingham. *Born* Birmingham, 9 March, 1969
Featherweight. Former Undefeated Midlands Area S. Featherweight Champion. Former Midlands Area S. Bantamweight Champion. Ht. 5'8"
Manager Self

04.10.89	Alan Baldwin DREW 6 Stafford
10.10.89	Ronnie Stephenson L PTS 6 Wolverhampton
30.10.89	Robert Braddock W PTS 6 Birmingham
14.11.89	Neil Leitch W PTS 6 Evesham
22.11.89	Peter Judson W PTS 6 Stafford
11.12.89	Stevie Woods W PTS 6 Bradford
21.12.89	Wayne Taylor W PTS 6 Kings Heath
10.01.90	John O'Meara W PTS 6 Kensington
19.02.90	Ian McGirr L PTS 6 Birmingham
27.02.90	Miguel Matthews DREW 6 Evesham
14.03.90	Ronnie Stephenson DREW 6 Stoke
04.04.90	Ronnie Stephenson L PTS 8 Stafford
23.04.90	Ronnie Stephenson W PTS 6 Birmingham
30.04.90	Chris Clarkson L PTS 8 Mayfair
17.05.90	Johnny Bredahl L PTS 6 Aars, Denmark
04.06.90	Ronnie Stephenson W PTS 8 Birmingham
28.06.90	Robert Braddock W RSC 5 Birmingham
01.10.90	Miguel Matthews W PTS 6 Cleethorpes
09.10.90	Miguel Matthews L PTS 8 Wolverhampton
17.10.90	Tony Smith W PTS 6 Stoke
29.10.90	Miguel Matthews W PTS 8 Birmingham
21.11.90	Drew Docherty L PTS 8 Solihull
10.12.90	Neil Leitch W PTS 8 Birmingham
10.01.91	Duke McKenzie L RSC 5 Wandsworth
18.02.91	Jamie McBride L PTS 8 Glasgow
04.03.91	Brian Robb W RSC 7 Birmingham
26.03.91	Neil Leitch DREW 8 Wolverhampton
01.05.91	Mark Geraghty W PTS 8 Solihull
05.06.91	Brian Robb W PTS 10 Wolverhampton
	(Vacant Midlands Area S. Featherweight Title)
09.09.91	Mike Deveney L PTS 8 Glasgow
24.09.91	Mark Bates W RTD 5 Basildon
29.10.91	John Armour L PTS 6 Kensington
14.11.91	Mike Deveney L PTS 6 Edinburgh
28.11.91	Craig Dermody L PTS 6 Liverpool
19.12.91	Craig Dermody L PTS 6 Oldham
18.01.92	Alan McKay DREW 8 Kensington
20.02.92	Brian Robb W RSC 10 Oakengates
	(Midlands Area S. Featherweight Title Defence)
27.04.92	Drew Docherty L PTS 8 Glasgow
15.05.92	Ruben Condori L PTS 10 Augsburg, Germany
29.05.92	Donnie Hood L PTS 8 Glasgow
07.09.92	Duke McKenzie L RTD 3 Bethnal Green
12.11.92	Prince Naseem Hamed L PTS 6 Liverpool
19.02.93	Harald Geier L PTS 12 Vienna, Austria
	(Vacant WBA Penta-Continental S. Bantamweight Title)
26.04.93	Bradley Stone L PTS 8 Lewisham
18.06.93	Eamonn McAuley L PTS 6 Belfast

01.07.93	Tony Silkstone L PTS 8 York
06.10.93	Jonjo Irwin L PTS 8 Solihull
25.10.93	Drew Docherty L PTS 8 Glasgow
06.11.93	Michael Alldis L PTS 8 Bethnal Green
30.11.93	Barry Jones L PTS 4 Cardiff
19.12.93	Shaun Anderson L PTS 6 Glasgow
22.01.94	Barry Jones L PTS 6 Cardiff
29.01.94	Prince Naseem Hamed L RSC 4 Cardiff
10.03.94	Tony Falcone L PTS 4 Bristol
29.03.94	Conn McMullen W PTS 6 Bethnal Green
05.04.94	Mark Bowers L PTS 6 Bethnal Green
13.04.94	James Murray L PTS 6 Glasgow
06.05.94	Paul Lloyd L RTD 4 Liverpool
03.08.94	Greg Upton L PTS 6 Bristol
26.09.94	John Sillo L PTS 6 Liverpool
05.10.94	Matthew Harris L PTS 6 Wolverhampton
07.11.94	Marlon Ward L PTS 4 Piccadilly
23.11.94	Justin Murphy L PTS 4 Piccadilly
29.11.94	Neil Swain L PTS 6 Cardiff
13.12.94	Michael Brodie L PTS 6 Potters Bar
20.12.94	Michael Alldis L PTS 6 Bethnal Green
10.02.95	Matthew Harris W RSC 6 Birmingham
	(Midlands Area S. Bantamweight Title Challenge)
23.02.95	Paul Ingle L PTS 8 Southwark
20.04.95	John Sillo L PTS 6 Liverpool
27.04.95	Paul Ingle L PTS 8 Bethnal Green
09.05.95	Ady Lewis L PTS 4 Basildon
23.05.95	Spencer Oliver L PTS 4 Potters Bar
01.07.95	Dean Pithie L PTS 4 Kensington
21.09.95	Patrick Mullings L PTS 6 Battersea
29.09.95	Marlon Ward L PTS 4 Bethnal Green
25.10.95	Matthew Harris L PTS 10 Telford
	(Midlands Area S. Bantamweight Title Defence)
08.11.95	Vince Feeney L PTS 8 Bethnal Green
28.11.95	Barry Jones L PTS 6 Cardiff
15.12.95	Patrick Mullings L PTS 4 Bethnal Green
05.02.96	Patrick Mullings L PTS 8 Bexleyheath
09.03.96	Paul Griffin L PTS 4 Millstreet
21.03.96	Colin McMillan L RSC 3 Southwark
14.05.96	Venkatesan Deverajan L PTS 4 Dagenham
29.06.96	Matt Brown W RSC 1 Erith
03.09.96	Vince Feeney L PTS 4 Bethnal Green
28.09.96	Fabrice Benichou L PTS 8 Barking
09.10.96	Gary Marston DREW 8 Stoke
06.11.96	Neil Swain L PTS 4 Tylorstown
29.11.96	Alston Buchanan L PTS 8 Glasgow
22.12.96	Brian Carr L PTS 6 Glasgow
11.01.97	Scott Harrison L PTS 4 Bethnal Green
29.01.97	Carl Allen L PTS 8 Stoke
12.02.97	Ronnie McPhee L PTS 6 Glasgow
25.02.97	Dean Pithie L PTS 4 Sheffield
07.03.97	Jason Booth L PTS 6 Northampton
20.03.97	Thomas Bradley W PTS 6 Newark
08.04.97	Sergei Devakov L PTS 6 Bethnal Green
25.04.97	Matthew Harris L PTS 6 Cleethorpes
08.05.97	Gregorio Medina L RTD 2 Mansfield
13.06.97	Mike Deveney L PTS 6 Paisley

Career: 100 contests, won 22, drew 6, lost 72.

(Joe) J. A. Bugner

St Ives. *Born* St Ives, 12 August, 1970
Heavyweight. Ht. 6'6"
Manager Self

12.11.91 Denroy Bryan W PTS 4 Milton Keynes
06.02.92 Gary Railton W CO 3 Peterborough
05.03.92 John Harewood W PTS 4 Battersea
22.04.92 Gary McCrory W PTS 4 Wembley
07.09.92 Gary Williams W PTS 4 Bethnal Green
17.10.92 Steve Gee W PTS 6 Wembley
17.12.92 Chris Coughlan W RSC 3 Wembley
24.02.93 Steve Garber L RSC 6 Wembley
22.09.93 Gary Charlton W RSC 1 Wembley
11.05.94 Wayne Buck DREW 6 Stevenage
28.06.97 Rob Albon W PTS 4 Norwich
Career: 11 contests, won 9, drew 1, lost 1.

J. A. Bugner   Les Clark

(Andrew) Stefy Bull (Bullcroft)

Doncaster. *Born* Doncaster, 10 May, 1977
Central Area Featherweight Champion. Ht.
5'10"
Manager J. Rushton

30.06.95 Andy Roberts W PTS 4 Doncaster
11.10.95 Michael Edwards W PTS 6 Stoke
18.10.95 Alan Hagan W RSC 1 Batley
28.11.95 Kevin Sheil W PTS 6 Wolverhampton
26.01.96 Robert Grubb W PTS 6 Doncaster
12.09.96 Benny Jones W PTS 6 Doncaster
15.10.96 Kevin Sheil DREW 6 Wolverhampton
24.10.96 Graham McGrath W PTS 6
           Birmingham
17.12.96 Robert Braddock W RSC 4 Doncaster
           (Vacant Central Area Featherweight
           Title)

Career: 9 contests, won 8, drew 1.

David Burke

Liverpool. *Born* Liverpool, 3 February,
1975
S. Featherweight. Ht. 5'9"
Manager J. Hyland

01.03.97 Ervine Blake W PTS 4 Liverpool
21.05.97 Carl Allen W PTS 4 Liverpool
Career: 2 contests, won 2.

David Burke   Les Clark

Paul Burke

Preston. *Born* Preston, 25 July, 1966
L. Welterweight. Former British &
Commonwealth Lightweight Champion. Ht.
5'10"
Manager Self

21.01.87 Steve Brown W CO 4 Stoke
30.01.87 Paul Marriott L PTS 6 Kirkby
02.03.87 Brian Murphy W CO 2 Marton
06.04.87 Paul Marriott W PTS 6 Newcastle
30.04.87 Paul Gadney W PTS 6 Bethnal Green
01.06.87 Pat Barrett W PTS 6 Bradford
15.09.87 Marvin P. Gray L RSC 6 Batley
18.11.87 Rudy Valentino W PTS 6 Bethnal
           Green
15.12.87 James Jiora L PTS 4 Bradford
11.02.88 Paul Gadney DREW 8 Gravesend
25.01.89 Paul Charters W PTS 6 Bethnal Green
23.02.89 Mark Kelly L DIS 5 Stockport
07.03.89 Tony Connellan W RSC 5 Manchester
11.04.89 Billy Buchanan W RSC 4 Oldham
21.10.89 Aaron Kabi DREW 8 Middlesbrough
09.12.89 Angel Mona L RSC 3 Toulouse, France
23.04.90 Tony Richards L PTS 10 Glasgow
           (Elim. British Lightweight Title)
25.09.90 Robert Harkin W PTS 8 Glasgow
21.01.91 Peter Bradley W PTS 10 Glasgow
           (Elim. British Lightweight Title)
31.05.91 Art Blackmore W RSC 3 Manchester
20.09.91 Tony Richards W PTS 8 Manchester
09.02.92 Dave Andrews W PTS 6 Bradford
28.04.92 Paul Charters W RSC 7 Houghton le
           Spring
           (Final Elim. British Lightweight Title)
28.09.92 Marcel Herbert W PTS 6 Manchester
17.11.92 Jean-Baptiste Mendy L PTS 12 Paris,
           France
           (European Lightweight Title
           Challenge)
24.02.93 Billy Schwer W RSC 7 Wembley
           (British & Commonwealth Lightweight
           Title Challenge)
25.07.93 Lyndon Paul Walker W PTS 8 Oldham
10.11.93 Billy Schwer L PTS 12 Watford
           (British & Commonwealth Lightweight
           Title Defence)

22.04.94 Racheed Lawal L RSC 4 Aalborg,
           Denmark
           (European Lightweight Title
           Challenge)
04.10.94 Rudy Valentino W PTS 6 Mayfair
17.02.95 Michael Ayers L RSC 6 Crawley
           (Vacant British Lightweight Title)
27.05.95 Patrick Gallagher W PTS 8 Belfast
13.01.96 Cham Joof W RSC 2 Manchester
13.04.96 Peter Till W PTS 8 Wythenshawe
18.01.97 Brian Coleman W PTS 6 Manchester
27.03.97 Jonathan Thaxton L RSC 9 Norwich
           (IBF & WBO Inter-Continental
           L. Welterweight Title Challenges)

Career: 36 contests, won 23, drew 2, lost 11.

Paul Burns

Liverpool. *Born* Liverpool, 15 July, 1971
Welterweight. Ht. 5'9½"
Manager J. Hyland

16.06.95 Mick Mulcahy W RSC 3 Liverpool
08.09.95 Peter Varnavas W RSC 3 Liverpool
24.11.95 Donovan Davey W PTS 6 Chester
03.02.96 Rick North W PTS 4 Liverpool
06.09.96 Michael Alexander W RSC 4 Liverpool
03.12.96 Charlie Paine W PTS 6 Liverpool
Career: 6 contests, won 6.

Vince Burns

Battersea. *Born* Paddington, 27 July, 1970
L. Welterweight. Ht. 5'7"
Manager B. Dawson

29.04.93 Jason Hutson W RSC 1 Hayes
04.10.93 Yifru Retta L PTS 6 Mayfair
17.10.94 Danny Lutaaya L RSC 6 Mayfair
25.03.95 Lewis Reynolds L RSC 4 Millwall
17.06.95 Mervyn Bennett L CO 4 Cardiff
03.12.95 Nicky Bardle L RSC 1 Southwark
03.09.96 Richie Edwards L CO 1 Bethnal Green
28.01.97 Marco Fattore L PTS 6 Piccadilly
11.02.97 Daniel James L CO 2 Bethnal Green
Career: 9 contests, won 1, lost 8.

Garry Burrell

Kirkcaldy. *Born* Musselburgh, 9 July, 1965
Featherweight. Ht. 5'7½"
Manager T. Gilmour

21.09.92 Alan Graham W PTS 6 Glasgow
09.11.92 Alan Graham L PTS 6 Bradford
22.02.93 Tim Hill L PTS 6 Glasgow
23.03.93 Yusuf Vorajee L PTS 6
           Wolverhampton
26.04.93 Robbie Sivyer W PTS 6 Glasgow
20.09.93 Phil Found L RSC 4 Glasgow
25.11.93 Colin Innes L PTS 6 Newcastle
24.05.94 Alan Graham L PTS 6 Sunderland
29.09.94 Tim Hill L PTS 6 Tynemouth
07.10.94 Dennis Holbaek Pedersen L PTS 6
           Copenhagen, Denmark
05.12.94 Roger Brotherhood L PTS 6 Bradford
23.01.95 Trevor George L PTS 6 Glasgow
24.02.95 Colin Innes W PTS 6 Irving
16.03.95 Liam Dineen L PTS 6 Sunderland
25.03.95 John Sillo L PTS 6 Chester
03.04.95 Michael Brodie L RSC 4 Manchester
15.05.95 Paul Goode W RSC 1 Bradford
22.05.95 Trevor Sumner L PTS 6 Morecambe
01.06.95 Marty Chestnut W RTD 3 Musselburgh
05.06.95 Robert Hay L PTS 6 Glasgow
16.06.95 Paul Lloyd L RSC 2 Liverpool

05.10.95 Ram Singh W PTS 8 Glasgow
23.10.95 Ian Richardson W PTS 6 Glasgow
20.11.95 Glen Hopkins W PTS 6 Glasgow
13.01.96 Michael Alldis L RSC 7 Halifax
16.02.96 Ian Richardson W PTS 8 Irvine
19.03.96 Shaun Hall W PTS 6 Leeds
02.04.96 Venkatesan Deverajan L RSC 1
          Southwark
09.05.96 Richard Vowles W PTS 8 Glasgow
28.05.96 Paul Ireland L PTS 6 Belfast
23.09.96 Neil Parry W PTS 6 Glasgow
10.10.96 Harry Escott L PTS 6 Newcastle
18.11.96 Lee Armstrong L PTS 6 Glasgow
29.11.96 Benny Jones W PTS 6 Glasgow
04.03.97 Michael Gibbons L PTS 6 Yarm
14.03.97 Colin Innes W PTS 6 Irvine
20.04.97 Nigel Leake L PTS 6 Leeds
01.05.97 Colin Innes W PTS 6 Newcastle
27.05.97 Gregorio Medina L RSC 3 Mayfair
26.06.97 Lee Armstrong L PTS 6 Sheffield
Career: 40 contests, won 15, lost 25.

Graham Burton

Chesterfield. *Born* Chesterfield, 16 June,
1964
Middleweight. Ht. 5'10"
Manager M. Shinfield

10.10.88 Frank Mobbs W RSC 3 Manchester
03.11.88 Terry French W RSC 3 Manchester
16.01.89 Dave Andrews W PTS 6 Northampton
04.04.89 Spencer Alton W RSC 3 Sheffield
06.12.89 Dave Brosnan W RSC 6 Stoke
29.01.90 Darren McKenna W PTS 4 Hull
23.04.90 Stevie R. Davies W PTS 6 Bradford
05.06.90 Nick Gyaamie W PTS 6 Eltham
18.09.90 Wayne Timmins W PTS 6
          Wolverhampton
17.01.91 John Ashton L PTS 10 Alfreton
12.03.91 Peter Gorny W PTS 6 Mansfield
13.06.91 Michael Gale L CO 4 Hull
12.11.91 Paul Busby L RSC 3 Wolverhampton
04.02.92 Richie Woodhall L RSC 2 Alfreton
17.03.92 Andrew Flute L PTS 8 Wolverhampton
13.10.92 Richard Carter DREW 8
          Wolverhampton
24.11.92 Nigel Rafferty L PTS 8
          Wolverhampton
20.01.93 Neville Brown L CO 4 Wolverhampton
24.04.93 Cornelius Carr L PTS 6 Birmingham
26.05.93 Jason McNeill W RSC 3 Mansfield
11.08.93 Tony Behan W PTS 6 Mansfield
16.03.94 Andrew Flute L PTS 6 Birmingham
18.04.94 Nigel Rafferty L PTS 8 Walsall
19.05.97 Shamus Casey W PTS 6 Cleethorpes
08.06.97 Jeff Finlayson L PTS 6 Shaw
Career: 25 contests, won 13, drew 1, lost 11.

Kevin Burton

Doncaster. *Born* Doncaster, 20 February,
1965
L. Heavyweight. Ht. 5'10½"
Manager J. Rushton

10.05.93 Pat McNamara W RSC 2 Cleethorpes
07.06.93 Tony Colclough W PTS 6 Walsall
20.09.93 Bullit Andrews W PTS 6 Cleethorpes
30.09.93 Tony Colclough W DIS 5 Walsall
13.12.93 Tony Colclough W RSC 3 Doncaster
07.03.94 Bullit Andrews W RSC 1 Doncaster
07.04.94 Johnny Hooks L PTS 6 Walsall
10.05.94 Declan Faherty L RSC 4 Doncaster
12.10.94 Tony Colclough W PTS 6 Stoke
25.10.94 Chris Nurse W RSC 1 Edgbaston

12.12.94 Jem Jackson W RSC 4 Doncaster
09.02.95 Dave Battey L PTS 6 Doncaster
05.05.95 Dave Battey L PTS 6 Doncaster
16.05.95 Clinton Woods L PTS 6 Cleethorpes
14.06.95 Clinton Woods L RSC 6 Batley
28.07.95 Paul Murray W PTS 6 Epworth
25.09.95 Robert Harper W DIS 4 Cleethorpes
11.10.95 John Kaighin L CO 1 Stoke
26.01.96 Paul Murray W PTS 6 Doncaster
26.02.96 Lee Whitehead L PTS 6 Manchester
24.04.96 David Jules L PTS 6 Stoke
11.05.96 Frederik Alvarez L RSC 1 Bethnal
          Green
09.10.96 Zak Goldman W PTS 6 Stoke
09.12.96 P.R. Mason L PTS 6 Bradford
24.03.97 Harri Hakulinen L RSC 3 Helsinki,
          Finland
16.05.97 Alex Carey W PTS 6 Hull
Career: 26 contests, won 14, lost 12.

Paul Busby

Worcester. *Born* Worcester, 20 April, 1966
S. Middleweight. Former WBO Inter-
Continental Middleweight Champion.
Former Undefeated WBO Penta-
Continental Middleweight Champion. Ht.
5'11½"
Manager Self

18.11.90 Carlos Christie W PTS 6 Birmingham
04.12.90 Marty Duke W PTS 6 Bury St Edmunds
23.01.91 Tony Wellington W RSC 2 Brentwood
27.02.91 Paul Murray W PTS 6 Wolverhampton
19.03.91 Paul Smith W PTS 6 Leicester
10.09.91 Nigel Rafferty W RSC 2
          Wolverhampton
12.11.91 Graham Burton W RSC 3
          Wolverhampton
17.12.91 Paul Murray W CO 3 Cardiff
01.02.92 John Kaighin W PTS 4 Birmingham
23.05.92 Stinger Mason W RSC 2 Birmingham
06.10.92 Chris Richards W PTS 6 Antwerp,
          Belgium
14.11.92 Paul Wesley W PTS 8 Cardiff
19.01.93 Stan King W PTS 8 Cardiff
16.03.93 Neville Brown L PTS 10
          Wolverhampton
          (Elim. British Middleweight Title)
10.07.93 Wayne Ellis L RSC 5 Cardiff
03.11.93 Spencer Alton W RTD 4 Worcester
19.01.94 Colin Manners DREW 8 Solihull
15.03.94 Colin Manners W PTS 8 Mayfair
28.06.94 Wayne Ellis L TD 4 Mayfair
          *(Vacant WBO Penta-Continental
          Middleweight Title)*
29.10.94 Wayne Ellis W PTS 12 Cannock
          *(WBO Penta-Continental Middleweight
          Title Challenge)*
17.01.95 Warren Stowe W PTS 12 Worcester
          *(WBO Penta-Continental Middleweight
          Title)*
01.06.95 Willie Quinn L RTD 8 Musselburgh
          *(Vacant WBO Inter-Continental
          Middleweight Title)*
28.11.95 Barry Thorogood W PTS 8 Cardiff
03.04.96 Robert McCracken L RTD 7 Bethnal
          Green
          *(Commonwealth Middleweight Title
          Challenge)*
24.03.97 Leif Keiski L RSC 4 Helsinki, Finland
26.04.97 Orhan Delibas L PTS 8 Leipzig,
          Germany
01.06.97 Marcus Beyer L PTS 8 Riesa, Germany
Career: 27 contests, won 18, drew 1, lost 8.

(Barrie) Blue Butterworth

Burnley. *Born* Lambeth, 5 October, 1970
Welterweight. Ht. 5'8½"
Manager Self

31.03.92 Brian Coleman W PTS 6 Stockport
04.06.92 Mark Allen W RSC 5 Burnley
14.09.92 Lee Soar W CO 4 Bradford
12.11.92 Dave Madden W PTS 6 Burnley
25.02.93 Ian Thomas W PTS 6 Burnley
27.05.93 Brian Coleman W PTS 6 Burnley
13.09.93 Kevin McKenzie L PTS 6 Middleton
11.11.93 Jamie Davidson W RSC 3 Burnley
25.04.94 Rob Stewart L PTS 6 Bury
20.10.94 Wahid Fats DREW 6 Middleton
03.04.95 Jay Mahoney L PTS 6 Manchester
16.03.97 Shaun O'Neill DREW 6 Shaw
Career: 12 contests, won 7, drew 2, lost 3.

Albert Call

Grimsby. *Born* Grimsby, 17 April, 1967
Cruiserweight. Ht. 6'2"
Manager Self

21.09.92 John Pierre W PTS 6 Cleethorpes
14.12.92 Art Stacey W PTS 6 Cleethorpes
22.03.93 Kenny Sandison W PTS 6 Liverpool
25.08.93 Peter Smith L PTS 6 Hammanskrall,
          South Africa
20.09.93 Trevor Small DREW 6 Cleethorpes
28.09.93 Dennis Bailey DREW 6 Liverpool
30.10.93 Kenley Price DREW 6 Chester
13.12.93 Trevor Small W RSC 5 Cleethorpes
17.03.94 Art Stacey W PTS 6 Lincoln
15.04.94 Cordwell Hylton L RSC 4 Hull
          *(Vacant Midlands Area Cruiserweight
          Title)*
11.12.95 Art Stacey W RSC 3 Cleethorpes
13.01.96 Denzil Browne L PTS 6 Halifax
18.03.96 Colin Brown L PTS 6 Glasgow
13.04.96 Carl Thompson L RTD 4
          Wythenshawe
20.05.96 Nigel Rafferty DREW 6 Cleethorpes
29.07.96 Tony Dowling W RSC 4 Skegness
19.10.96 Rudiger May L PTS 6 Frankfurt,
          Germany
25.11.96 Chris Woollas W PTS 6 Cleethorpes
08.02.97 Antoine Palatis L PTS 8 St Pierre
          D'Albigny, France
26.04.97 Israel Ajose L PTS 4 Swadlincote
03.05.97 Danny Williams L RSC 4 Manchester
Career: 21 contests, won 8, drew 4, lost 9.

Joe Calzaghe

Newbridge. *Born* Hammersmith, 23 March,
1972
Former Undefeated British S. Middleweight
Champion.
Ht. 5'11"
Manager M. Duff/T. Lawless

01.10.93 Paul Hanlon W RSC 1 Cardiff
10.11.93 Stinger Mason W RSC 1 Watford
16.12.93 Spencer Alton W RSC 2 Newport
22.01.94 Martin Rosamond W RSC 1 Cardiff
01.03.94 Darren Littlewood W RSC 1 Dudley
04.06.94 Karl Barwise W RSC 1 Cardiff
01.10.94 Mark Dawson W RSC 1 Cardiff
30.11.94 Trevor Ambrose W RSC 2
          Wolverhampton
14.02.95 Frank Minton W CO 1 Bethnal Green
22.02.95 Bobbi Joe Edwards W PTS 8 Telford
19.05.95 Robert Curry W RSC 1 Southwark

77

Anthony Campbell (right) sets up Brian Coleman with a right over the top   Les Clark

08.07.95 Tyrone Jackson W RSC 4 York
30.09.95 Nick Manners W RSC 4 Basildon
28.10.95 Stephen Wilson W RSC 8 Kensington
(Vacant British S. Middleweight Title)
13.02.96 Guy Stanford W RSC 1 Cardiff
13.03.96 Anthony Brooks W RSC 2 Wembley
20.04.96 Mark Delaney W RSC 5 Brentwood
(British S. Middleweight Title Defence)
04.05.96 Warren Stowe W RTD 2 Dagenham
15.05.96 Pat Lawlor W RSC 2 Cardiff
21.01.97 Carlos Christie W CO 2 Bristol
22.03.97 Tyler Hughes W CO 1 Wythenshawe
05.06.97 Luciano Torres W RSC 3 Bristol
Career: 22 contests, won 22.

Anthony Campbell

Shepherds Bush. *Born* Kensington, 20
January, 1967
L. Welterweight. Ht. 5'6"
Manager D. Currivan

05.04.94 Andrew Reed W PTS 6 Bethnal Green
20.05.94 Malcolm Thomas W PTS 6 Acton
29.09.94 P. J. Callagher L PTS 6 Bethnal Green
19.11.94 Nicky Bardle L PTS 6 Heathrow
25.01.95 Gareth Lawrence L PTS 6 Cardiff
07.02.95 Anthony Maynard L PTS 8
Wolverhampton
26.05.95 M. T. Atkin DREW 6 Norwich
09.09.95 Mark Winters L PTS 4 Cork
30.09.95 Bobby Guynan W RSC 5 Basildon
21.10.95 Dean Pithie L PTS 4 Bethnal Green
30.10.95 Wayne Jones W RSC 1 Heathrow
02.11.95 Marc Smith W PTS 6 Mayfair
24.11.95 Mark Haslam W PTS 4 Manchester
19.01.96 Tommy Lawler W PTS 4 Bracknell
15.03.96 Roger Hunte DREW 4 Dunstable
24.04.96 Neil Smith W PTS 8 Solihull

04.05.96 Bobby Guynan W RSC 4 Dagenham
02.06.96 Bobby Vanzie L PTS 6 Shaw
09.09.96 Jyrki Vierela DREW 8 Helsinki,
Finland
18.11.96 Mark Breslin L PTS 6 Glasgow
01.12.96 Scott Walker W RSC 4 Shaw
19.02.97 Brian Coleman W PTS 6 Acton
03.04.97 Gareth Jordan L PTS 6 Wembley
30.04.97 Mark Ramsey W PTS 6 Acton
Career: 24 contests, won 12, drew 3, lost 9.

Jason Campbell

Brighton. *Born* Northampton, 12
November, 1970
L. Welterweight. Ht. 5'8"
Manager D. Currivan

06.05.93 Adrian Chase L CO 2 Bayswater
07.12.93 Jason Beard L RSC 2 Bethnal Green
15.03.94 M. T. Atkin L RSC 5 Mayfair
22.04.96 Craig Stanley L RSC 2 Crystal Palace
27.08.96 Danny Lutaaya L RSC 3 Windsor
28.09.96 Costas Katsantonis L PTS 6 Barking
Career: 6 contests, lost 6.

Mickey Cantwell

Eltham. *Born* London, 23 November, 1964
Former Undefeated British Flyweight
Champion. Former Undefeated Southern
Area Flyweight Champion. Ht. 5'2½"
Manager F. Maloney

21.01.91 Eduardo Vallejo W RSC 4 Crystal
Palace
26.03.91 Mario Alberto Cruz W PTS 6 Bethnal
Green
30.09.91 Ricky Beard W PTS 8 Kensington

23.10.91 Carlos Manrigues W RSC 5 Bethnal
Green
14.12.91 Shaun Norman W PTS 8 Bexleyheath
16.05.92 Louis Veitch W PTS 6 Muswell Hill
10.02.93 Louis Veitch DREW 8 Lewisham
14.04.93 Daren Fifield W PTS 10 Kensington
(Vacant Southern Area Flyweight Title)
15.09.93 Pablo Tiznado L PTS 12 Bethnal Green
*(Vacant WBC International L.
Flyweight Title)*
03.11.93 Anthony Hanna W PTS 8 Bristol
27.04.94 Luigi Camputaro L PTS 12 Bethnal
Green
(European Flyweight Title Challenge)
15.06.94 Lyndon Kershaw L PTS 8 Southwark
27.04.95 Anthony Hanna W PTS 6 Bethnal
Green
02.07.95 Anthony Hanna W PTS 6 Dublin
21.03.96 Keith Knox W PTS 12 Southwark
(Vacant British Flyweight Title)
29.06.96 Krasimir Tcholakov W PTS 6 Erith
08.02.97 Jacob Matlala L PTS 12 Millwall
(WBO L. Flyweight Title Challenge)
03.05.97 David Coldwell W PTS 8 Manchester
Career: 18 contests, won 13, drew 1, lost 4.

Alex Carey

Sheffield. *Born* Trowbridge, 25 March,
1976
Middleweight. Ht. 5'10"
Manager B. Ingle

14.03.97 Pat Durkin W RSC 6 Hull
16.05.97 Kevin Burton L PTS 6 Hull
09.06.97 Carlton Williams DREW 6
Birmingham
Career: 3 contests, won 1, drew 1, lost 1.

Brian Carr

Moddiesburn. *Born* Glasgow, 20 June, 1969
S. Bantamweight. Scottish Featherweight Champion. Ht. 5'6"
Manager A. Morrison

18.12.94 Fred Reeve W CO 2 Glasgow
21.01.95 Shaun Anderson W PTS 6 Glasgow
04.03.95 G. G. Goddard W PTS 8 Livingston
13.05.95 Paul Wynn W RTD 2 Glasgow
08.06.95 Abdul Manna W PTS 6 Glasgow
13.10.95 Muhammad Shaffique W PTS 6 Glasgow
17.12.95 Abdul Mannon W PTS 8 Glasgow
16.03.96 Chip O'Neill W PTS 4 Glasgow
26.04.96 Mike Deveney W PTS 10 Glasgow
(*Vacant Scottish Featherweight Title*)
20.09.96 Fred Reeve W RSC 3 Glasgow
06.11.96 Mike Deveney W PTS 10 Glasgow
(*Scottish Featherweight Title Defence*)
22.12.96 Pete Buckley W PTS 6 Glasgow
04.04.97 Lyndon Kershaw W PTS 10 Glasgow
(*Elim. British S. Bantamweight Title*)
Career: 13 contests, won 13.

(John) Cornelius Carr

Middlesbrough. *Born* Middlesbrough, 9 April, 1969
Former Undefeated British S. Middleweight Champion. Ht. 5'9½"
Manager Self

22.09.87 Paul Burton W RSC 5 Bethnal Green
28.11.87 Dave Heaver W RSC 2 Windsor
12.01.88 Shamus Casey W RSC 6 Cardiff
27.01.88 Kesem Clayton W PTS 6 Bethnal Green
29.03.88 Darren Parker W RSC 1 Bethnal Green
12.04.88 Franki Moro W PTS 6 Cardiff
10.05.88 Andy Catesby W RSC 5 Tottenham
15.11.88 Skip Jackson W CO 1 Norwich
20.12.88 Kevin Hayde W PTS 6 Swansea
22.03.89 George Bocco L RSC 3 Reading
24.10.89 Carlo Colarusso W RTD 4 Watford
20.02.90 Peter Gorny W RSC 4 Millwall
21.04.90 Franki Moro W PTS 8 Sunderland
26.09.90 John Maltreaux W CO 1 Metairie, USA
27.10.90 Jerry Nestor W CO 1 Greenville, USA
16.02.91 Frank Eubanks W RSC 5 Thornaby
02.03.91 Carlo Colarusso W PTS 8 Darlington
18.05.91 Paul Burton W RSC 3 Verbania, Italy
06.09.91 Marvin O'Brien W RSC 7 Salemi, Italy
29.10.92 Alan Richards W PTS 8 Bayswater
24.04.93 Graham Burton W PTS 6 Birmingham
19.05.93 Stan King W PTS 8 Sunderland
22.09.93 Horace Fleary W PTS 8 Wembley
11.03.94 James Cook W PTS 12 Bethnal Green
(*British S. Middleweight Title Challenge*)
04.02.95 Colin Manners W PTS 8 Cardiff
13.05.95 Chris Richards W RTD 3 Glasgow
07.07.95 Barry Thorogood W RSC 6 Cardiff
25.11.95 Steve Collins L PTS 12 Dublin
(*WBO S. Middleweight Title Challenge*)
02.03.96 Danny Juma W PTS 8 Newcastle
14.03.97 Dean Francis L RSC 7 Reading
(*WBO Inter-Continental S. Middleweight Title Challenge*)
Career: 30 contests, won 27, lost 3.

Paul Carr

Sidcup. *Born* Basildon, 16 April, 1973
L. Middleweight. Ht. 5'10"
Manager F. Warren

02.06.95 Dave Curtis W PTS 6 Bethnal Green
01.07.95 Rob Stevenson W PTS 6 Kensington
22.07.95 Wesley Jones W RSC 3 Millwall
21.10.95 Andrew Jervis L RSC 3 Bethnal Green
13.02.96 Ernie Loveridge W PTS 4 Bethnal Green
13.07.96 Clayon Stewart L RSC 1 Bethnal Green
08.02.97 Dean Barclay L PTS 4 Millwall
05.06.97 Darren Dorrington L PTS 6 Bristol
Career: 8 contests, won 4, lost 4.

(Peter) Pedro Carragher

Knottingley. *Born* Pontefract, 13 January, 1975
Welterweight. Ht. 6'0"
Manager T. Callighan

20.04.97 C. J. Jackson DREW 6 Leeds
01.05.97 Robbo Johnson W PTS 6 Hull
26.06.97 G. L. Booth L CO 1 Salford
Career: 3 contests, won 1, drew 1, lost 1.

Michael Carruth

Dublin. *Born* Dublin, 9 July, 1967
Welterweight. Ht. 5'8"
Manager Self

26.02.94 George Wilson W PTS 6 Earls Court
21.05.94 Ricky Mabbett W CO 3 Belfast
17.08.94 Mark Antony W RSC 3 Sheffield
17.09.94 Kim-Ken Jackson W RSC 4 Las Vegas, USA
12.10.94 Rick North W PTS 6 Sheffield
19.11.94 Dave Lovell W RSC 2 Cardiff
21.01.95 Gordon Blair L PTS 6 Glasgow
17.03.95 Vernice Harvard W RSC 3 Worcester, USA
17.06.95 Steve McGovern W RSC 4 Cardiff
09.09.95 John Smith W PTS 8 Cork
25.11.95 Paul Denton W PTS 8 Dublin
09.03.96 Gordon Blair W RTD 3 Millstreet
25.06.96 Chris Saunders W RSC 10 Mansfield
31.08.96 Mark Brannon W RSC 3 Dublin
08.02.97 Paul Dyer W PTS 4 Millwall
Career: 15 contests, won 14, lost 1.

Shamus Casey (West)

Alfreton. *Born* Pinxton, 13 January, 1960
Middleweight. Ht. 5'11"
Manager Self

25.01.84 Tony Burke L CO 1 Solihull
16.04.84 Ronnie Fraser L RSC 3 Nottingham
05.07.84 Craig Edwards L PTS 6 Prestatyn
21.09.84 Dave Foley W PTS 6 Alfreton
28.09.84 Dennis Boy O'Brien L PTS 6 Longford
11.10.84 Terry Gilbey L PTS 6 Barnsley
22.10.84 Dave King W PTS 6 South Shields
09.11.84 Reuben Thurley W CO 4 Alfreton
16.11.84 Tucker Watts L PTS 6 Leicester
26.11.84 Terry Gilbey L RSC 1 Liverpool
14.01.85 Mark Walker L PTS 6 Manchester
24.01.85 Tommy Campbell L PTS 8 Manchester
11.02.85 Paul Smith W PTS 6 Manchester
18.02.85 John Graham L PTS 6 Mayfair
01.03.85 Dennis Sheehan W PTS 6 Mansfield
11.03.85 Sean O'Phoenix L PTS 6 Manchester
20.03.85 Sean O'Phoenix L PTS 6 Stoke
15.04.85 Ronnie Tucker L PTS 6 Manchester
14.05.85 Dennis Sheehan L PTS 10 Mansfield
(*Midlands Area L. Middleweight Title Challenge*)
05.06.85 Gary Stretch L RSC 2 Kensington
02.09.85 Newton Barnett DREW 8 Coventry
12.09.85 Cliff Curtis W RSC 7 Swindon
23.09.85 Danny Quigg L PTS 8 Glasgow
10.10.85 Davey Cox W PTS 6 Alfreton
22.10.85 Mick Mills L RSC 3 Hull
02.12.85 Newton Barnett DREW 8 Dulwich
09.12.85 Steve Ward L PTS 6 Nottingham
16.12.85 Robert Armstrong W PTS 6 Bradford
20.01.86 Billy Ahearne L PTS 8 Leicester
06.02.86 Denys Cronin L RSC 6 Doncaster
10.03.86 Neil Munn L PTS 8 Cardiff
20.03.86 Andy Wright L RSC 4 Merton
22.04.86 Franki Moro L PTS 8 Carlisle
29.04.86 John Graham L PTS 8 Piccadilly
08.05.86 Randy Henderson L PTS 8 Bayswater
19.05.86 Joe Lynch W RSC 3 Plymouth
28.05.86 Andy Wright L PTS 6 Lewisham
15.09.86 Gerry Sloof L PTS 6 Scheidam, Holland
23.09.86 Derek Wormald L PTS 8 Batley
06.10.86 David Scere L PTS 6 Leicester
21.10.86 David Scere W PTS 8 Hull
29.10.86 Peter Elliott W PTS 6 Stoke
25.11.86 Steve Foster L PTS 8 Manchester
15.12.86 Tucker Watts DREW 6 Loughborough
13.01.87 Robert Armstrong L PTS 6 Oldham
26.01.87 Richard Wagstaff W PTS 8 Bradford
05.02.87 Neil Patterson L PTS 6 Newcastle
20.02.87 Dennis Boy O'Brien L PTS 8 Maidenhead
02.03.87 Roddy Maxwell L PTS 6 Glasgow
24.03.87 Ian Chantler L PTS 8 Nottingham
07.04.87 Richard Wagstaff L PTS 8 Batley
28.04.87 Sean Leighton DREW 8 Manchester
05.05.87 Dave Owens L PTS 6 Leeds
12.05.87 Jason Baxter L PTS 6 Alfreton
23.06.87 Terry Magee L CO 6 Swansea
(*Vacant All-Ireland L. Middleweight Title*)
31.07.87 Cyril Jackson L RSC 5 Wrexham
22.09.87 Brian Robinson L PTS 6 Bethnal Green
28.09.87 Sean Leighton L PTS 8 Bradford
19.10.87 Sammy Storey L PTS 6 Belfast
10.11.87 Peter Brown L PTS 8 Batley
19.11.87 Kid Murray W PTS 6 Ilkeston
26.11.87 Trevor Smith L CO 4 Fulham
12.01.88 Cornelius Carr L RSC 6 Cardiff
15.02.88 Leigh Wicks L PTS 6 Copthorne
25.02.88 R. W. Smith L RSC 3 Bethnal Green
28.03.88 Tony Britton L PTS 8 Birmingham
13.06.88 Jim Kelly L PTS 6 Glasgow
25.06.88 Wayne Ellis L PTS 6 Luton
12.09.88 Shaun Cummins L CO 3 Northampton
17.10.88 Jim Kelly L PTS 6 Glasgow
01.11.88 Brian Robinson L PTS 6 Reading
17.11.88 Mark Howell L CO 1 Ilkeston
16.12.88 Conrad Oscar L PTS 6 Brentwood
25.01.89 Tony Velinor L RTD 3 Basildon
22.02.89 Mickey Murray DREW 6 Doncaster
01.03.89 Nigel Fairbairn L PTS 6 Stoke
21.03.89 Dave Thomas L PTS 6 Cottingham
29.03.89 W. O. Wilson L RSC 5 Wembley
08.05.89 Antonio Fernandez L PTS 6 Edgbaston
31.05.89 Ossie Maddix L CO 3 Manchester
11.09.89 Terry French W PTS 6 Nottingham
18.09.89 Skip Jackson W PTS 6 Northampton
26.09.89 Theo Marius L PTS 8 Chigwell
05.10.89 Val Golding L PTS 6 Stevenage

17.10.89 Carl Harney L PTS 4 Oldham
13.11.89 Ian Vokes W RSC 5 Bradford
29.11.89 Ray Close L CO 2 Belfast
21.06.90 Skip Jackson W RSC 6 Alfreton
04.09.90 Pete Bowman W PTS 6 Southend
14.09.90 Chris Richards L PTS 6 Telford
08.10.90 Billy Brough W PTS 6 Leicester
22.10.90 Gordon Blair L RSC 3 Glasgow
22.11.90 Jimmy Thornton W PTS 6 Ilkeston
14.12.90 Stefan Wright L PTS 6 Peterborough
17.01.91 Neville Brown L RSC 4 Alfreton
21.02.91 Richie Woodhall L RSC 3 Walsall
28.03.91 Pete Bowman W PTS 6 Alfreton
12.04.91 Martin Rosamond W PTS 6 Willenhall
13.05.91 Paul King W PTS 6 Northampton
04.07.91 Dave Hall W PTS 6 Alfreton
11.09.91 Clay O'Shea L PTS 6 Hammersmith
10.10.91 Dave Johnson L PTS 6 Gateshead
17.10.91 Tyrone Eastmond L PTS 6 Mossley
14.11.91 Dave Johnson L PTS 6 Gateshead
28.11.91 Ian Vokes W PTS 6 Hull
07.12.91 Steve Foster L PTS 8 Manchester
17.03.92 Gary Osborne L RSC 5
          Wolverhampton
          *(Vacant Midlands Area L.
          Middleweight Title)*
28.05.92 Mark Jay L PTS 8 Gosforth
25.07.92 Warren Stowe L CO 2 Manchester
16.10.92 Terry Morrill L PTS 6 Hull
23.10.92 Fran Harding L PTS 6 Liverpool
12.11.92 Gypsy Johnny Price L PTS 6 Burnley
14.12.92 Peter Waudby L PTS 6 Cleethorpes
22.02.93 Lee Ferrie L CO 3 Bedworth
07.06.93 Stephen Wilson L PTS 6 Glasgow
16.09.93 Peter Waudby L PTS 6 Hull
03.11.93 Warren Stephens W PTS 6 Worcester
13.11.93 Terry Morrill L PTS 8 Hull
30.11.93 Stuart Dunn L PTS 6 Leicester
13.12.93 Glenn Catley L PTS 4 Bristol
20.01.94 Darren Dorrington L PTS 6 Battersea
26.02.94 Adrian Dodson L CO 1 Earls Court
21.04.94 Mark Jay L PTS 6 Gateshead
16.05.94 Peter Waudby L PTS 6 Cleethorpes
02.06.94 Eric Noi L PTS 6 Middleton
02.07.94 Paul Wright L RSC 1 Liverpool
12.09.94 Phil Ball L PTS 6 Doncaster
20.09.94 Willie Quinn RSC 3 Musselburgh
24.10.94 John Stronach L PTS 6 Bradford
31.10.94 Jon Stocks L PTS 6 Liverpool
07.11.94 Sven Hamer L PTS 4 Piccadilly
24.11.94 Peter Waudby L PTS 6 Hull
05.12.94 Derek Roche L PTS 6 Bradford
15.12.94 Ray Golding L PTS 6 Evesham
16.01.95 Billy Collins L PTS 6 Musselburgh
30.01.95 Shaun Hendry L PTS 6 Bradford
16.02.95 Darren Swords L PTS 6 Bury
04.03.95 Ryan Rhodes L CO 1 Livingston
19.09.95 Justin Simmons L PTS 6 Plymouth
05.10.95 Andy Neri W RSC 4 Queensferry
29.10.95 Darren Swords L PTS 6 Shaw
11.12.95 Wayne Shepherd W PTS 6 Morecambe
13.01.96 Derek Roche L PTS 6 Halifax
05.02.96 Lee Murtagh L PTS 6 Bradford
14.02.96 Joe Townsley L PTS 6 Sunderland
26.02.96 Rob Stevenson L PTS 6 Hull
16.03.96 Tommy Quinn L PTS 4 Glasgow
24.03.96 Jeff Finlayson L PTS 6 Shaw
03.05.96 Jason Barker L RSC 1 Sheffield
03.06.96 Joe Townsley L PTS 6 Glasgow
26.11.96 Panayiotis Panayiotiou L CO 1 Bethnal
          Green
20.04.97 Paul Bonson L PTS 6 Leeds
19.05.97 Graham Burton L PTS 6 Cleethorpes
Career: 153 contests, won 28, drew 5, lost 120.

Ross Cassidy

Derby. *Born* Derby, 12 February, 1978
Bantamweight. Ht. 5'4"
Manager J. Ashton

20.02.97 David Coldwell W PTS 6 Mansfield
27.02.97 Darren Noble W RSC 5 Sunderland
08.05.97 Sean Green DREW 6 Mansfield
Career: 3 contests, won 2, drew 1.

Glenn Catley

Bristol. *Born* Sodbury, 15 March, 1972
Former WBC International Middleweight
Champion. Ht. 5'8"
Manager C. Sanigar/F. Warren

27.05.93 Rick North W PTS 4 Bristol
26.06.93 Chris Vassiliou W CO 2 Keynsham
31.08.93 Marty Duke W RSC 2 Croydon
13.09.93 Barry Thorogood W PTS 4 Bristol
03.11.93 Marty Duke W RSC 1 Bristol
13.12.93 Shamus Casey W PTS 4 Bristol
10.03.94 Mark Cichocki W PTS 6 Bristol
23.03.94 Carlo Colarusso L RSC 5 Cardiff
25.05.94 Chris Davies W RSC 1 Bristol
02.07.94 Martin Jolley W RSC 1 Keynsham
22.11.94 Kirkland Laing W RSC 5 Bristol
18.02.95 Lee Blundell W RSC 6 Shepton Mallet
06.05.95 Mark Dawson W RSC 5 Shepton
          Mallet
28.07.95 Kevin Adamson W CO 1 Bristol
02.09.95 Quinn Paynter W RSC 1 Wembley
30.09.95 John Duckworth W RSC 3 Cardiff
28.10.95 Carlos Christie W PTS 8 Bristol
10.11.95 Carlos Christie W CO 3 Bristol
16.12.95 Peter Vosper W RSC 2 Cardiff
26.04.96 Lee Crocker W RSC 2 Cardiff
19.10.96 Paul Wesley W RSC 7 Bristol
21.01.97 George Bocco W RTD 4 Bristol
          *(Vacant WBC International
          Middleweight Title)*
05.06.97 Andras Galfi L RSC 7 Bristol
          *(WBC International Middleweight Title
          Defence)*
Career: 23 contests, won 21, lost 2.

Gary Cavey   Les Clark

Gary Cavey

Plymouth. *Born* Plymouth, 13 March, 1973
Heavyweight. Ht. 5'10½"
Manager N. Christian

19.10.96 Karl Andrews W CO 1 Bristol
10.12.96 Rob Albon L RTD 3 Plymouth
Career: 2 contests, won 1, lost 1.

Adrian Chase

St Albans. *Born* St Albans, 18 October,
1968
Welterweight. Ht. 5'9"
Manager H. Holland

06.05.93 Jason Campbell W CO 2 Bayswater
24.06.93 Delwyn Panayiotiou W CO 1 Watford
23.02.94 Dennis Griffin W PTS 6 Watford
16.05.94 Tony Gibbs W PTS 6 Heathrow
21.07.94 Steve Burton W PTS 6 Battersea
19.11.94 Wayne Jones W PTS 6 Heathrow
21.04.95 Juha Temonen L PTS 4 Pori, Finland
28.10.95 Tom Welsh L RSC 2 Bristol
03.12.95 Delroy Leslie L RSC 4 Southwark
12.02.96 Marc Smith W CO 1 Heathrow
21.03.96 Peter Richardson L RSC 2 Southwark
07.11.96 Gary Hiscox W PTS 4 Battersea
15.02.97 Ray Newby L PTS 6 Tooting
Career: 13 contests, won 8, lost 5.

(Martin) Marty Chestnut (Concannon)

Birmingham. *Born* Birmingham, 8 March,
1968
Featherweight. Ht. 5'8"
Manager Self

29.04.93 Fred Reeve L PTS 6 Hull
07.06.93 Ian McGirr L PTS 6 Glasgow
30.10.93 Paul Lloyd L RSC 1 Chester
11.12.93 John Sillo L PTS 6 Liverpool
25.01.94 Anthony Hanna L PTS 4 Piccadilly
10.02.94 James Murray L PTS 6 Glasgow
01.03.94 Chris Lyons W PTS 6 Dudley
27.04.94 Chris Lyons L RSC 3 Bethnal Green
02.06.94 Des Gargano L PTS 6 Middleton
02.09.94 Tiger Ray W PTS 4 Spitalfields
17.09.94 Stephen Smith L RSC 5 Leverkusen,
          Germany
27.10.94 Abdul Mannon W DIS 2 Millwall
30.11.94 Matthew Harris L RSC 3
          Wolverhampton
23.01.95 Paul Webster L RSC 3 Bethnal Green
20.02.95 Paul Hamilton W PTS 6 Manchester
09.03.95 Graham McGrath W PTS 6 Walsall
20.03.95 Graham McGrath L PTS 6 Birmingham
13.04.95 Spencer Oliver L RSC 4 Bloomsbury
01.06.95 Garry Burrell L RTD 3 Musselburgh
08.09.95 Alex Moon L RSC 3 Liverpool
07.10.95 Paul Ireland L RSC 6 Belfast
21.11.95 Graham McGrath W PTS 6 Edgbaston
02.12.95 Frankie Slane L PTS 4 Belfast
18.12.95 Michael Brodie L RTD 3 Mayfair
31.01.96 Anthony Hanna DREW 6 Stoke
22.03.96 Roger Brotherhood L PTS 6 Mansfield
24.05.96 Alston Buchanan L PTS 6 Glasgow
19.07.96 Ian Turner L PTS 6 Ystrad
27.08.96 Clinton Beeby L PTS 6 Windsor
23.09.96 David Coldwell L PTS 6 Cleethorpes
08.10.96 Anthony Hanna L PTS 6 Battersea
24.10.96 Jason Booth L PTS 6 Lincoln
14.12.96 Dean Pithie L RSC 3 Sheffield
Career: 33 contests, won 6, drew 1, lost 26.

Roy Chipperfield   Les Clark

Roy Chipperfield

Bury. *Born* Radcliffe, 29 April, 1965
Middleweight. Ht. 5'10¾"
Manager B. Myers

22.09.94	Darren Swords L PTS 6 Bury
30.11.94	Eddie Haley L RSC 3 Solihull
27.02.95	Jon Stocks L RSC 3 Barrow
09.10.95	Lee Whitehead L RSC 2 Manchester
23.11.95	Mark Owens W RSC 6 Marton
07.12.95	Mark Cichocki L RSC 5 Sunderland
14.02.96	David Maw L PTS 6 Sunderland
25.03.96	Darren Sweeney L CO 1 Birmingham
29.04.96	Steve McNess L RSC 3 Mayfair
25.06.96	Ryan Rhodes L RSC 1 Mansfield
23.09.96	Robert Harper W DIS 2 Bradford
23.10.96	Ron Hopley L PTS 6 Halifax
06.11.96	Terry Morrill L RSC 1 Hull
09.12.96	Darren Rees L PTS 6 Bradford
28.01.97	Jim Rock L RTD 2 Belfast
27.02.97	Rob Stevenson L RSC 5 Hull

Career: 16 contests, won 2, lost 14.

(Peter) Carlos Christie

Birmingham. *Born* Birmingham, 17
August, 1966
Former Undefeated Midlands Area S.
Middleweight Champion. Ht. 6'0"
Manager C. Sanigar

04.06.90	Roger Wilson L PTS 6 Birmingham
17.09.90	John Kaighin W PTS 6 Cardiff
27.09.90	Colin Manners W PTS 6 Birmingham
29.10.90	Paul Murray W PTS 6 Birmingham
18.11.90	Paul Busby L PTS 6 Birmingham
27.11.90	Nigel Rafferty W PTS 8 Wolverhampton
06.12.90	Nigel Rafferty W PTS 6 Wolverhampton
10.01.91	Ray Webb L PTS 6 Wandsworth
28.01.91	Gil Lewis W PTS 8 Birmingham
04.03.91	Nigel Rafferty W PTS 8 Birmingham
14.03.91	Michael Gale L PTS 8 Middleton
01.05.91	Peter Elliott W RSC 9 Solihull *(Vacant Midlands Area S. Middleweight Title)*

11.05.91	Ray Close L PTS 6 Belfast
07.09.91	Ray Close L PTS 6 Belfast
20.11.91	Nicky Piper L CO 6 Cardiff
10.03.92	Glenn Campbell DREW 8 Bury
15.09.92	Roland Ericsson W RSC 4 Crystal Palace
28.01.93	James Cook L PTS 8 Southwark
28.04.93	Sammy Storey L RSC 8 Dublin
31.08.93	Simon Harris L CO 3 Croydon
12.11.93	Tony Booth L PTS 6 Hull
28.11.93	Ali Forbes L CO 4 Southwark
22.01.94	Darron Griffiths L PTS 8 Cardiff
21.02.94	Stephen Wilson L RSC 2 Glasgow
15.06.94	William Joppy L PTS 6 Southwark
27.08.94	Antonio Fernandez L PTS 8 Cardiff
26.09.94	Paul Wright L PTS 6 Liverpool
29.10.94	Andrew Flute W PTS 8 Cannock
30.11.94	Darren Ashton W PTS 6 Solihull
23.01.95	Robert Allen L CO 2 Bethnal Green
16.03.95	Mark Delaney L CO 1 Basildon
20.10.95	Richard Bustin W PTS 6 Ipswich
28.10.95	Glenn Catley L PTS 8 Bristol
10.11.95	Glenn Catley L CO 3 Bristol
15.12.95	David Starie L CO 4 Bethnal Green
24.10.96	Andrew Flute W PTS 10 Mayfair *(Midlands Area S. Middleweight Title Defence)*
21.01.97	Joe Calzaghe L CO 2 Bristol

Career: 37 contests, won 13, drew 1, lost 23.

Floyd Churchill

Kirkby. *Born* Liverpool, 19 January, 1969
L. Welterweight. Former Undefeated
Central Area S. Featherweight Champion.
Ht. 5'4"
Manager T. Miller

29.04.92	T. J. Smith W RSC 2 Liverpool
14.05.92	Jamie Davidson W RSC 4 Liverpool
12.06.92	Kevin McKillan L PTS 6 Liverpool
26.09.92	Richie Wenton W RSC 2 Earls Court
12.11.92	Brian Hickey W CO 1 Liverpool
04.05.93	Jimmy Owens W CO 1 Liverpool *(Vacant Central Area S. Featherweight Title)*
02.07.94	Mark Antony L RSC 1 Liverpool
09.11.94	Jason Rowland L RSC 2 Millwall
25.03.95	Tony Mock L PTS 6 Chester
08.06.95	Dave Anderson L PTS 8 Glasgow
15.09.95	Alan McDowall L RSC 5 Glasgow
06.11.96	Tanveer Ahmed L RTD 5 Glasgow

Career: 12 contests, won 5, lost 7.

Mark Cichocki (Weatherill)

Hartlepool. *Born* Hartlepool, 18 October, 1967
Northern Area L. Middleweight Champion.
Ht. 5'7"
Manager T. Conroy

01.12.92	Tony Trimble W PTS 6 Hartlepool
29.01.93	Gordon Blair W PTS 8 Glasgow
09.03.93	Rob Pitters W RSC 10 Hartlepool *(Vacant Northern Area L. Middleweight Title)*
06.05.93	Mick Duncan W RSC 7 Hartlepool *(Northern Area L. Middleweight Title Defence)*
12.05.93	Glyn Rhodes L PTS 6 Sheffield
02.12.93	Mark Jay W RSC 4 Hartlepool *(Northern Area L. Middleweight Title Defence)*
22.01.94	Anibal Acevedo L RTD 3 Cardiff

10.03.94	Glenn Catley L PTS 6 Bristol
07.12.95	Roy Chipperfield W RSC 5 Sunderland
14.02.96	Craig Winter L PTS 6 Sunderland
19.03.97	Howard Clarke L PTS 6 Stoke

Career: 11 contests, won 6, lost 5.

Howard Clarke

Warley. *Born* London, 23 September, 1967
Welterweight. Ht. 5'10"
Manager Self

15.10.91	Chris Mylan W PTS 4 Dudley
09.12.91	Claude Rossi W RSC 3 Brierley Hill
04.02.92	Julian Eavis W PTS 4 Alfreton
03.03.92	Dave Andrews W RSC 3 Cradley Heath
21.05.92	Richard O'Brien W CO 1 Cradley Heath
29.09.92	Paul King W PTS 6 Stoke
27.10.92	Gordon Blair L RSC 4 Cradley Heath
16.03.93	Paul King W PTS 6 Edgbaston
07.06.93	Dean Bramhald W RTD 2 Walsall
29.06.93	Paul King W PTS 6 Edgbaston
06.10.93	Julian Eavis L PTS 8 Solihull
30.11.93	Julian Eavis W PTS 8 Wolverhampton
08.02.94	Nigel Bradley W RTD 6 Wolverhampton
18.04.94	Andy Peach W PTS 6 Walsall
28.06.94	Dennis Berry L RSC 3 Edgbaston
12.10.94	Julian Eavis W PTS 8 Stoke
25.10.94	Andy Peach W RSC 3 Edgbaston
02.11.94	Julian Eavis W PTS 8 Birmingham
29.11.94	Julian Eavis W PTS 6 Cannock
07.12.94	Peter Reid W PTS 6 Stoke
25.01.95	Dennis Berry L PTS 8 Stoke
08.03.95	Andrew Jervis W PTS 6 Solihull
11.05.95	David Bain W RSC 1 Dudley
20.09.95	Michael Smyth DREW 6 Ystrad
02.10.95	Nigel Wenton L PTS 6 Mayfair
02.12.96	Martin Smith L PTS 8 Birmingham
29.01.97	Gary Beardsley W PTS 6 Stoke
11.02.97	Prince Kasi Kaihau L RSC 4 Wolverhampton
19.03.97	Mark Cichocki W PTS 6 Stoke
15.04.97	Prince Kasi Kaihau W PTS 6 Edgbaston
30.04.97	Allan Gray W PTS 8 Acton
22.05.97	Michael Alexander W RSC 3 Solihull
21.06.97	Paul Samuels L PTS 8 Cardiff

Career: 33 contests, won 24, drew 1, lost 8.

Howard Clarke   Les Clark

Dave Clavering

Bury. *Born* Bury, 21 October, 1973
Lightweight. Ht. 5'6"
Manager J. Doughty

16.05.94	Al Garrett W RTD 4 Morecambe
22.09.94	Ian Richardson W RSC 1 Bury
26.09.94	Chris Jickells W PTS 6 Morecambe
16.02.95	Trevor George W PTS 6 Bury
18.05.95	Kid McAuley W PTS 6 Middleton
29.10.95	John T. Kelly W PTS 6 Shaw
14.11.95	Dave Madden W RSC 1 Bury
24.03.96	Frankie Foster W RSC 4 Shaw
08.06.97	Ervine Blake DREW 6 Shaw

Career: 9 contests, won 8, drew 1.

Edwin Cleary

Leamington. *Born* Leamington, 8 January, 1973
L. Heavyweight. Ht. 5'10½"
Manager B. Ingle

20.03.97	Gary Reyniers W PTS 6 Newark
16.05.97	Slick Miller DREW 6 Hull

Career: 2 contests, won 1, drew 1.

David Coldwell

Sheffield. *Born* Calcutta, India, 6 July, 1975
Flyweight. Ht. 5'3"
Manager B. Ingle

23.09.96	Marty Chestnut W PTS 6 Cleethorpes
24.10.96	Benny Jones L PTS 6 Lincoln
16.12.96	Darren Noble L PTS 6 Cleethorpes
18.01.97	Jason Booth L PTS 4 Swadlincote
20.02.97	Ross Cassidy L PTS 6 Mansfield
14.03.97	Willie Smith W RSC 5 Hull
25.03.97	Graham McGrath L PTS 6 Wolverhampton
03.05.97	Mickey Cantwell L PTS 8 Manchester

Career: 8 contests, won 2, lost 6.

David Coldwell   Les Clark

Brian Coleman

Birmingham. *Born* Birmingham, 27 July, 1969
L. Welterweight. Ht. 5'11"
Manager Self

21.11.91	Jamie Morris DREW 6 Stafford
11.12.91	Craig Hartwell DREW 6 Leicester
22.01.92	John O. Johnson L PTS 6 Stoke
20.02.92	Davy Robb L PTS 6 Oakengates
31.03.92	Blue Butterworth L PTS 6 Stockport
17.05.92	Korso Aleain L RSC 5 Harringay
17.09.92	Nicky Bardle L RSC 4 Watford
21.10.92	Jason Barker W PTS 6 Stoke
10.12.92	A. M. Milton DREW 4 Bethnal Green
31.03.93	A. M. Milton L PTS 4 Bethnal Green
26.04.93	Jason Beard L PTS 6 Lewisham
06.05.93	Mark Allen W PTS 6 Walsall
18.05.93	Sean Metherell DREW 6 Kettering
27.05.93	Blue Butterworth L PTS 6 Burnley
23.06.93	Jonathan Thaxton L PTS 8 Gorleston
11.08.93	Steve Howden L RSC 4 Mansfield
13.09.93	Mick Hoban L PTS 6 Middleton
01.12.93	A. M. Milton L PTS 4 Bethnal Green
08.12.93	Chris Pollock W PTS 6 Stoke
16.12.93	Mark Newton L PTS 6 Newport
11.01.94	Paul Knights L RSC 4 Bethnal Green
08.02.94	Andy Peach W PTS 6 Wolverhampton
18.02.94	Cam Raeside L PTS 6 Leicester
08.03.94	Chris Pollock L PTS 6 Edgbaston
29.03.94	P. J. Gallagher L PTS 6 Bethnal Green
14.04.94	Cham Joof L CO 3 Battersea
02.06.94	Scott Walker L CO 1 Middleton
12.09.94	Shabba Edwards L PTS 6 Mayfair
19.09.94	Mark Breslin L CO 1 Glasgow
09.11.94	Kenny Scott L PTS 6 Stafford
23.11.94	Billy McDougall W PTS 4 Piccadilly
29.11.94	Warren Stephens W PTS 6 Wolverhampton
09.12.94	Danny Stevens L RTD 2 Bethnal Green
24.01.95	Wayne Jones L PTS 6 Piccadilly
07.02.95	Alan Temple L PTS 6 Ipswich
23.02.95	Darren Covill L PTS 4 Southwark
16.03.95	Paul Knights L RSC 2 Basildon
02.07.95	Tommy Lawler L PTS 4 Dublin
08.09.95	George Naylor L PTS 6 Liverpool
27.09.95	Allan Gray L PTS 6 Bethnal Green
20.10.95	Mikael Nilsson L PTS 4 Ipswich
02.11.95	Marco Fattore W PTS 6 Mayfair
16.11.95	Alan Bosworth L PTS 6 Evesham
24.11.95	Chris Barnett L PTS 6 Manchester
02.12.95	Neil Sinclair L RTD 1 Belfast
20.01.96	James Hare L PTS 6 Mansfield
29.01.96	Dave Fallon L PTS 6 Piccadilly
13.02.96	Martin Holgate L PTS 4 Bethnal Green
21.02.96	Marco Fattore W PTS 6 Piccadilly
13.03.96	Paul Samuels L PTS 6 Wembley
03.04.96	Ian Honeywood L PTS 6 Bethnal Green
20.04.96	Ray Robinson L PTS 6 Brentwood
24.05.96	Scott Dixon L PTS 8 Glasgow
08.06.96	Mark Winters L PTS 4 Newcastle
06.07.96	Nick Boyd L PTS 4 Manchester
16.08.96	Charlie Paine W PTS 6 Liverpool
27.08.96	Dave Brazil L PTS 6 Windsor
19.09.96	Ricky Sackfield W RSC 3 Manchester
27.09.96	Nicky Bardle L PTS 4 Stevenage
08.10.96	Marcus McCrae W PTS 6 Battersea
09.11.96	Mark Haslam L PTS 6 Manchester
27.11.96	Bernard Paul L PTS 6 Bethnal Green
09.12.96	Wayne Windle L PTS 6 Chesterfield
18.01.97	Paul Burke L PTS 6 Manchester
19.02.97	Anthony Campbell L PTS 6 Acton
25.03.97	Craig Stanley DREW 4 Lewisham
03.04.97	Kevin McCarthy L PTS 6 Wembley
22.04.97	Georgie Smith L PTS 6 Bethnal Green
19.05.97	John O.Johnson DREW 6 Cleethorpes
02.06.97	Steve McLevy W RSC 5 Glasgow

Career: 70 contests, won 12, drew 6, lost 52.

Billy Collins

Stirling. *Born* Stirling, 20 May, 1968
L. Middleweight. Ht. 5'9"
Manager T. Gilmour

25.04.94	Raziq Ali W PTS 6 Glasgow
16.01.95	Shamus Casey W PTS 6 Musselburgh
23.01.95	Eddie Haley W RSC 4 Glasgow
24.02.95	Rob Stevenson W PTS 6 Irvine
24.04.95	Phil Epton W RSC 3 Glasgow
05.06.95	Ernie Loveridge W PTS 8 Glasgow
20.11.95	Brian Dunn L PTS 8 Glasgow
28.10.96	James Donoghue L PTS 6 Glasgow
17.03.97	Jason Barker W PTS 6 Glasgow
16.05.97	Anthony van Nierkerk L RTD 5 Hammanskraal, South Africa

Career: 10 contests, won 7, lost 3.

Hugh Collins

Stirling. *Born* Stirling, 17 August, 1969
S. Featherweight. Ht. 5'6"
Manager T. Gilmour

29.03.93	Tim Hill W PTS 6 Glasgow
20.09.93	Robert Braddock W PTS 8 Glasgow
24.11.93	Paul Bowen W PTS 6 Solihull
24.01.94	Colin Innes W PTS 6 Glasgow
21.02.94	Norman Dhalie W RTD 4 Glasgow
28.03.94	Trevor Royal W RSC 2 Musselburgh
25.04.94	Miguel Matthews W PTS 8 Glasgow
20.09.94	Russell Davison W RTD 4 Musselburgh
02.11.94	Michael Hermon L RSC 3 Solihull
16.01.95	John T. Kelly W PTS 6 Musselburgh
17.02.95	Paul Wynn W RSC 3 Cumbernauld
05.04.95	Kid McAuley W PTS 6 Irvine
05.06.95	Wayne Rigby L RSC 4 Glasgow
18.11.95	John T. Kelly W PTS 6 Glasgow
18.03.96	Kid McAuley W PTS 8 Glasgow
28.04.97	Lee Armstrong L RTD 5 Glasgow

Career: 16 contests, won 13, lost 3.

Steve Conway

Dewsbury. *Born* Hartlepool, 6 October, 1977
Featherweight. Ht. 5'8"
Manager K. Tate

21.02.96	Robert Grubb W PTS 6 Batley
24.04.96	Ervine Blake W PTS 6 Solihull
20.05.96	Chris Lyons W PTS 6 Cleethorpes
30.05.96	Ram Singh W PTS 6 Lincoln
03.02.97	Jason Squire W PTS 6 Leicester
11.04.97	Marc Smith W PTS 4 Barnsley

Career: 6 contests, won 6.

Jason Cook

Newport. *Born* Maesteg, 27 February, 1975
Lightweight. Ht. 5'9"
Manager B. Hearn

11.10.96	Brian Robb W RSC 2 Mayfair
27.11.96	Andrew Reed W RSC 3 Bethnal Green
27.05.97	Marc Smith W PTS 4 Mayfair

Career: 3 contests, won 3.

Jason Cook   Les Clark

Jarrod Corrigan   Les Clark

Steve Cranston
Woolwich. *Born* Jamaica, 4 May, 1971
Heavyweight. Ht. 6'7"
Manager B. Hearn

20.09.96 R. F. McKenzie L DIS 5 Tooting
15.02.97 Keith Long L PTS 4 Tooting
Career: 2 contests, lost 2.

Steve Cranston   Les Clark

Alvar Coppard
Crawley. *Born* Crowborough, 18 August, 1970
L. Middleweight. Ht. 5'8"
Manager J. Evans

08.10.96 Jason Barker L RSC 3 Battersea
28.01.97 Chris Vassiliou L RSC 6 Piccadilly
04.03.97 Ed Robinson W RSC 1 Southwark
Career: 3 contests, won 1, lost 2.

Maurice Core (Coore)
Manchester. *Born* Manchester, 22 June, 1965
Former Undefeated British L. Heavyweight Champion. Ht. 6'5"
Manager Self

15.01.90 Dennis Banton W PTS 6 Mayfair
03.05.90 Everton Blake W PTS 8 Kensington
22.05.90 Nicky Piper DREW 6 St Albans
22.02.91 Everton Blake W RSC 8 Manchester
12.04.91 Glazz Campbell W CO 2 Manchester
31.05.91 Rodney Brown W RSC 6 Manchester
29.11.91 Steve Osborne W PTS 6 Manchester
31.01.92 Denroy Bryan W RSC 1 Manchester
05.04.92 Willie Ball W RSC 3 Bradford
18.07.92 Tony Booth W PTS 6 Manchester
28.09.92 Noel Magee W RSC 9 Manchester
          (Vacant British L. Heavyweight Title)
05.02.93 Larry Prather W PTS 10 Manchester
25.07.93 John Kaighin W PTS 6 Oldham
01.12.93 Simon Harris W RSC 11 Bethnal Green
          (British L. Heavyweight Title Defence)
25.10.94 Fabrice Tiozzo L RSC 4 Besancon,
          France
          *(European Light-Heavyweight Title
          Challenge)*
10.06.95 Eric French W RSC 2 Manchester
21.10.95 Frank Minton W RSC 5 Ronse, Belgium
06.07.96 Mark Prince L RSC 7 Manchester
          *(Vacant WBO Inter-Continental L.
          Heavyweight Title)*
Career: 18 contests, won 15, drew 1, lost 2.

Jarrod Corrigan
Bridlington. *Born* Bridlington, 3 April, 1973
Heavyweight. Ht. 6'1"
Manager S. Pollard/F. Maloney

28.04.97 Gary Williams L RSC 4 Hull
Career: 1 contest, lost 1.

Danny Costello
Camberwell. *Born* Lambeth, 21 August, 1975
Bantamweight. Ht. 5'6¹/₂"
Manager J. Hyland

26.10.96 Henry Jones W RSC 3 Liverpool
Career: 1 contest, won 1.

Danny Costello   Les Clark

Ryan Cummings
Islington. *Born* Lancaster, 17 November, 1973
L. Heavyweight. Ht. 5'11"
Manager F. Warren

10.03.94 Terry Duffus W PTS 6 Watford
07.11.94 Mark Hale W RSC 6 Bethnal Green
10.06.95 Mark Dawson L PTS 6 Manchester
11.05.96 Nicky Wadman W RSC 2 Bethnal Green
14.12.96 Steve Osborne W RSC 4 Sheffield
Career: 5 contests, won 4, lost 1.

(Gerardo) Jezz D'Agostino
Peterborough. *Born* Peterborough, 4 September, 1972
Featherweight. Ht. 5'5"
Manager A. Urry

03.04.97 David Jeffrey L PTS 6 Wembley
Career: 1 contest, lost 1.

Jezz D'Agostino   Les Clark

Shaune Danskin

Peterborough. *Born* Spalding, 28
December, 1975
S. Featherweight. Ht. 5'5"
Manager K. Whitney

08.12.95 Gary Jenkinson L PTS 6 Leeds
19.02.96 Paul Hamilton L CO 2 Glasgow
04.10.96 Nicky Wilders L PTS 6 Wakefield
Career: 3 contests, lost 3.

Donovan Davey

Bradford. *Born* Shipley, 20 July, 1967
L. Middleweight. Ht. 5'7"
Manager B. Myers

14.11.95 Shaun Marsh W PTS 6 Yarm
24.11.95 Paul Burns L PTS 6 Chester
11.12.95 Lee Murtagh L PTS 6 Bradford
13.02.96 George Richards L PTS 6
Wolverhampton
06.03.96 George Richards L PTS 6 Solihull
20.11.96 Kevin McCarthy L PTS 6 Wembley
04.12.96 John Green L PTS 6 Hartlepool
13.06.97 Steve Tuckett L PTS 6 Leeds
Career: 8 contests, won 1, lost 7.

Hughie Davey   Les Clark

Hughie Davey

Newcastle. *Born* Wallsend, 27 January, 1966
Welterweight. Ht. 5'8"
Manager N. Fawcett

30.03.92 Wayne Shepherd W PTS 6 Bradford
28.04.92 Benji Joseph W RSC 4 Houghton le
Spring
10.09.92 Darren McInulty W PTS 6 Southwark
21.09.92 Rick North DREW 6 Cleethorpes
23.10.92 Richard O'Brien W PTS 6 Gateshead
01.03.93 Wayne Appleton L PTS 6 Bradford
29.04.93 Paul King L PTS 6 Newcastle
11.06.93 Wayne Shepherd W PTS 6 Gateshead
04.10.93 Steve Scott W PTS 6 Bradford
08.11.93 Warren Bowers W RSC 2 Bradford
13.12.93 Sean Baker L PTS 4 Bristol
03.03.94 Paul King L PTS 10 Newcastle
*(Vacant Northern Area Welterweight
Title)*

06.10.94 Mick Hoban W PTS 6 Cramlington
24.11.94 John Stronach W PTS 6 Newcastle
10.12.94 Craig Winter L PTS 6 Manchester
21.02.95 David Maw W RSC 3 Sunderland
20.03.95 Joe Townsley W PTS 6 Glasgow
22.06.95 David Maw W PTS 6 Houghton le
Spring
29.07.95 Kevin McKenzie W RSC 5 Whitley Bay
25.09.95 Derek Roche L PTS 6 Bradford
22.10.95 Peter Malinga L PTS 10 Durban, South
Africa
02.03.96 Craig Lynch W PTS 4 Newcastle
13.04.96 Neil Sinclair L PTS 6 Liverpool
09.05.96 Jason Barker W PTS 6 Sunderland
08.06.96 Craig Lynch W PTS 4 Newcastle
10.10.96 Paul King L PTS 10 Newcastle
*(Northern Area Welterweight Title
Challenge)*
04.12.96 Paul King L PTS 6 Hartlepool
03.02.97 John Green L PTS 4 Sunderland
01.05.97 Dewi Roberts W PTS 6 Newcastle
02.06.97 Joe Townsley L PTS 8 Glasgow
Career: 30 contests, won 17, drew 1, lost 12.

Chris Davies

Blaencldach. *Born* Pontypridd, 24 August,
1974
L. Heavyweight. Ht. 5'9"
Manager D. Gardiner

27.04.94 Craig Joseph L PTS 6 Solihull
25.05.94 Glenn Catley L RSC 1 Bristol
29.05.96 Mark Hickey W RSC 1 Ebbw Vale
19.07.96 Michael Pinnock W PTS 6 Ystrad
31.08.96 James Branch L PTS 4 Dublin
02.10.96 Neil Simpson L PTS 4 Cardiff
Career: 6 contests, won 2, lost 4.

Johnny Davison

Swansea. *Born* Whitehaven, 13 September,
1969
Heavyweight. Ht. 6'2"
Manager D. Davies

09.12.96 Greg Wedlake L PTS 6 Bristol
21.01.97 Greg Wedlake L RSC 2 Bristol
19.02.97 Michael Sprott L CO 2 Acton
11.04.97 Neil Kirkwood L RSC 3 Barnsley
Career: 4 contests, lost 4.

Johnny Davison   Les Clark

(Anthony) Jarral Dawson

Manchester. *Born* Birmingham, 21 March,
1966
L. Welterweight. Ht. 5'8"
Manager T. Miller

29.11.96 Frank O'Connor DREW 6 Glasgow
Career: 1 contest, drew 1.

Mark Dawson (Lee)

Burton. *Born* Burton, 26 February, 1971
S. Middleweight. Ht. 5'8"
Manager W. Swift

03.06.92 Rick North W PTS 6 Newcastle under
Lyme
09.09.92 Jimmy Vincent W PTS 6 Stoke
29.09.92 Steve Goodwin L RSC 1 Stoke
28.10.92 Steve McNess W RSC 2 Kensington
07.12.92 Steve Goodwin W PTS 6 Mayfair
27.01.93 Rick North W PTS 8 Stoke
15.02.93 John Bosco L PTS 6 Mayfair
27.02.93 Robin Reid L RSC 1 Dagenham
30.03.93 Matthew Turner L PTS 6 Cardiff
12.05.93 Steve Goodwin L PTS 10 Stoke
*(Vacant Midlands Area L.
Middleweight Title)*
27.05.93 Derek Wormald L RTD 5 Burnley
10.11.93 John Bosco L RTD 4 Watford
15.03.94 Stinger Mason W RSC 6 Stoke
22.03.94 Geoff McCreesh L PTS 6 Bethnal
Green
05.09.94 Tony Griffiths W PTS 6 Brentwood
17.09.94 Mark Delaney L PTS 6 Crawley
01.10.94 Joe Calzaghe L RSC 1 Cardiff
29.11.94 Andrew Flute L PTS 8 Cannock
07.12.94 John Duckworth W PTS 6 Stoke
20.01.95 Mark Baker L RSC 3 Bethnal Green
08.03.95 Lester Jacobs L PTS 6 Bloomsbury
30.03.95 David Starie L RSC 1 Bethnal Green
06.05.95 Glenn Catley L RSC 5 Shepton Mallet
10.06.95 Ryan Cummings W PTS 6 Manchester
01.07.95 Shaun Cummins L PTS 8 Kensington
22.07.95 Lester Jacobs L PTS 4 Millwall
06.09.95 Robert Harper W PTS 6 Stoke
15.09.95 Jason Matthews L RSC 3 Mansfield
25.10.95 Jetty Williams W PTS 6 Telford
10.11.95 Ryan Rhodes L PTS 6 Derby
25.11.95 Danny Ryan L PTS 4 Dublin
02.12.95 Frederik Alvarez L RTD 6 Belfast
13.01.96 Mark Baker L RSC 3 Halifax
04.03.96 Harri Hakulinen L PTS 4 Helsinki,
Finland
13.04.96 Paul Wright L PTS 6 Liverpool
11.05.96 Michael Bowen L PTS 4 Bethnal Green
31.05.96 Peter H. Madsen L PTS 4 Copenhagen,
Denmark
08.06.96 Robin Reid L RSC 5 Newcastle
13.07.96 Paul Bowen L RSC 3 Bethnal Green
18.01.97 Lee Whitehead L PTS 6 Manchester
03.02.97 Peter Mason L PTS 4 Sunderland
25.02.97 Michael Bowen L RSC 4 Sheffield
Career: 42 contests, won 11, lost 31.

Phill Day

Swindon. *Born* Swindon, 5 November,
1974
Cruiserweight. Ht. 5'11½"
Manager C. Sanigar

07.07.95 Tim Redman L RSC 2 Cardiff

21.09.95 John Pettersson L RSC 4 Battersea
10.11.95 L. A. Williams W PTS 6 Bristol
21.02.96 Carl Heath L PTS 6 Piccadilly
18.10.96 David Jules W RSC 1 Barnstaple
09.12.96 Naveed Anwar W PTS 6 Bristol
24.03.97 Jim Pallatt W CO 1 Bristol
15.05.97 Tony Booth L PTS 4 Reading
Career: 8 contests, won 4, lost 4.

Phill Day   Les Clark

Jason Dee (Davies)
Neath. *Born* Londonderry, 18 August, 1972
Featherweight. Ht. 5'7"
Manager F. King

11.10.96 Danny Thomas W RSC 3 Mayfair
28.04.97 David Jay W RSC 3 Enfield
Career: 2 contests, won 2.

Garry Delaney
West Ham. *Born* Newham, 12 August, 1970
Cruiserweight. Former Commonwealth L. Heavyweight Champion. Former Undefeated WBO Penta-Continental, WBO Inter-Continental & Southern Area L. Heavyweight Champion. Ht. 6'3"
Manager F. King

02.10.91 Gus Mendes W RSC 1 Barking
23.10.91 Joe Frater W RSC 1 Bethnal Green
13.11.91 John Kaighin W PTS 6 Bethnal Green
11.12.91 Randy B. Powell W RSC 1 Basildon
11.02.92 Simon Harris DREW 8 Barking
12.05.92 John Williams W PTS 6 Crystal Palace
16.06.92 Nigel Rafferty W CO 5 Dagenham
15.09.92 Gil Lewis W CO 2 Crystal Palace
06.10.92 Simon McDougall W PTS 8 Antwerp, Belgium
10.11.92 John Oxenham W CO 5 Dagenham
12.12.92 Simon McDougall W PTS 8 Muswell Hill
30.01.93 Simon Collins W PTS 8 Brentwood
28.09.93 Glazz Campbell W CO 6 Bethnal Green
(Southern Area L. Heavyweight Title Challenge)

06.11.93 John Kaighin W CO 1 Bethnal Green
21.12.93 Ray Albert W RSC 3 Mayfair
(Vacant WBO Penta-Continental L. Heavyweight Title)
11.01.94 Jim Murray W RSC 7 Bethnal Green
(WBO Penta-Continental L. Heavyweight Title Defence)
09.04.94 Simon Harris W CO 6 Bethnal Green
(WBO Penta-Continental & Southern Area L. Heavyweight Title Defence)
09.07.94 Sergio Merani W PTS 12 Earls Court
(WBO Penta-Continental L. Heavyweight Title)
30.09.94 Arigoma Chiponda W CO 2 Bethnal Green
(Vacant Commonwealth L. Heavyweight Title)
18.03.95 Ernest Mateen W RTD 7 Millstreet
(Vacant WBO Inter-Continental L. Heavyweight Title)
09.05.95 Noel Magee L RTD 7 Basildon
(Commonwealth L. Heavyweight Title Defence)
06.02.96 Francis Wanyama W PTS 6 Basildon
09.04.96 Joey Paladino W RSC 1 Stevenage
07.02.97 John Kiser W PTS 6 Las Vegas, USA
04.03.97 Peter Oboh W DIS 8 Southwark
Career: 25 contests, won 23, drew 1, lost 1.

Mark Delaney
West Ham. *Born* London, 1 December, 1971
Former Undefeated WBO Inter-Continental S. Middleweight Champion. Ht. 5'11"
Manager F. King

05.10.93 Lee Sara W RTD 5 Mayfair

Mark Delaney (left) on his way to a fifth-round win over John Duckworth   Les Clark

11.01.94	Jason McNeill W RSC 2 Bethnal Green	
22.01.94	Graham Jenner W RTD 3 Belfast	
09.02.94	Tony Colclough W RSC 4 Brentwood	
19.03.94	Paul Murray W CO 3 Millwall	
09.04.94	Tim Robinson W RSC 2 Bethnal Green	
11.06.94	Ernie Loveridge W RSC 5 Bethnal Green	
09.07.94	Eddie Knight W CO 4 Earls Court	
17.09.94	Mark Dawson W PTS 6 Crawley	
30.09.94	Jerry Mortimer W RSC 3 Bethnal Green	
07.11.94	Martin Jolley W RSC 3 Bethnal Green	
23.11.94	Marvin O'Brien W RTD 1 Irvine	
20.12.94	Martin Jolley W RSC 4 Bethnal Green	
17.02.95	Peter Vosper W RSC 1 Crawley	
16.03.95	Carlos Christie W CO 1 Basildon	
31.03.95	Trevor Ambrose W RSC 1 Crystal Palace	
09.05.95	Eddie Knight W RSC 2 Basildon	
30.09.95	Andrew Flute W PTS 12 Basildon	
	(Vacant WBO Inter-Continental S. Middleweight Title)	
28.10.95	Hunter Clay W RTD 2 Kensington	
14.11.95	Armando Rodriguez W PTS 12 Bury	
	(WBO Inter-Continental S. Middleweight Title Defence)	
23.01.96	Darron Griffiths W PTS 12 Bethnal Green	
	(WBO Inter-Continental S. Middleweight Title Defence)	
20.04.96	Joe Calzaghe L RSC 5 Brentwood	
	(British S. Middleweight Title Challenge)	
27.11.96	John Duckworth W RSC 5 Bethnal Green	
08.03.97	Butch Lesley W PTS 6 Brentwood	
30.06.97	Mark Baker L PTS 10 Bethnal Green	
	(Elim. British S. Middleweight Title)	

Career: 25 contests, won 23, lost 2.

Paul Denton (Ramsey)

Birmingham. *Born* Birmingham, 12 April, 1970
L. Welterweight. Ht. 5'10"
Manager B. Ingle

18.03.93	Mark O'Callaghan W RSC 4 Lewisham	
29.04.93	Dave Maj DREW 6 Mayfair	
11.08.93	Billy McDougall W PTS 6 Mansfield	
01.10.93	Ferid Bennecer W CO 3 Waregem, Belgium	
01.12.93	Brian Hickey W CO 1 Kensington	
28.01.94	Youssef Bakhouche L PTS 6 Waregem, Belgium	
07.05.94	Viktor Fesechko L PTS 6 Dnepropetrousk, Ukraine	
23.09.94	Roy Rowland W RSC 5 Bethnal Green	
03.01.95	Patrick Charpentier L RSC 4 Epernay, France	
25.02.95	Paul Ryan L RSC 4 Millwall	
25.11.95	Michael Carruth L PTS 8 Dublin	
03.02.96	George Naylor W RSC 3 Liverpool	
26.04.96	Ross Hale W RSC 4 Cardiff	
15.11.96	Frank Olsen L RSC 4 Nestved, Denmark	
14.03.97	Mark Winters L PTS 8 Reading	
13.06.97	Alan McDowall DREW 6 Paisley	

Career: 16 contests, won 7, drew 2, lost 7.

Mike Deveney

Paisley. *Born* Elderslie, 14 December, 1965
Former British Featherweight Champion.
Ht. 5'5"
Manager N. Sweeney

18.02.91	John George W PTS 6 Glasgow	
18.03.91	Frankie Ventura W PTS 6 Piccadilly	
22.04.91	Neil Leitch W PTS 6 Glasgow	
09.09.91	Pete Buckley W PTS 8 Glasgow	
19.09.91	Noel Carroll L PTS 6 Stockport	
14.11.91	Pete Buckley W PTS 6 Edinburgh	
28.01.92	Graham O'Malley L RSC 1 Piccadilly	
28.02.92	Gary Hickman W PTS 6 Irvine	
14.09.92	David Ramsden L PTS 6 Bradford	
07.10.92	Mark Hargreaves L RSC 7 Glasgow	
07.12.92	Carl Roberts W PTS 6 Manchester	
27.01.93	Barry Jones L PTS 6 Cardiff	
26.02.93	Alan Graham W PTS 6 Irvine	
23.03.93	Colin Lynch W PTS 6 Wolverhampton	
29.05.93	Dave Buxton W PTS 6 Paisley	
20.09.93	Ady Benton W PTS 8 Glasgow	
30.11.93	Elvis Parsley L PTS 6 Wolverhampton	
24.01.94	Ady Benton L PTS 6 Glasgow	
02.03.94	Yusuf Vorajee W PTS 6 Solihull	
21.03.94	Chris Jickells W RSC 5 Glasgow	
15.04.94	Chris Clarkson W RSC 3 Hull	
06.06.94	Mark Hargreaves W PTS 6 Manchester	
15.06.94	Justin Murphy L PTS 6 Southwark	
29.09.94	Henry Armstrong W PTS 8 Tynemouth	
24.10.94	Henry Armstrong W PTS 10 Glasgow	
	(Elim. British Featherweight Title)	
23.01.95	Wilson Docherty W PTS 12 Glasgow	
	(Vacant British Featherweight Title)	
04.03.95	Dean Phillips L PTS 8 Livingston	
20.09.95	Jonjo Irwin L PTS 12 Potters Bar	
	(British Featherweight Title Defence)	
16.03.96	Abdul Mannon W RSC 2 Glasgow	
26.04.96	Brian Carr L PTS 10 Glasgow	
	(Vacant Scottish Featherweight Title)	
29.06.96	Welcome Ncita L PTS 8 East London, South Africa	
06.11.96	Brian Carr L PTS 10 Glasgow	
	(Scottish Featherweight Title Challenge)	
26.04.97	Esham Pickering L PTS 4 Swadlincote	
29.05.97	Paul Griffin L PTS 6 Mayfair	
13.06.97	Pete Buckley W PTS 6 Paisley	

Career: 35 contests, won 20, lost 15.

Venkatesan Deverajan

Plaistow. *Born* India, 22 July, 1973
S. Featherweight. Ht. 5'9"
Manager F. Maloney

02.04.96	Garry Burrell W RSC 1 Southwark	
14.05.96	Pete Buckley W PTS 4 Dagenham	
09.07.96	Michael Wright L RSC 3 Bethnal Green	

Career: 3 contests, won 2, lost 1.

Norman Dhalie

Birmingham. *Born* Birmingham, 24 March, 1971
S. Featherweight. Ht. 5'7"
Manager Self

06.04.92	Karl Morling L PTS 6 Northampton	
27.04.92	Wilson Docherty L RSC 2 Glasgow	
02.07.92	John White L RSC 6 Middleton	
29.09.92	Gary Marston DREW 6 Stoke	
07.10.92	Jacob Smith W PTS 6 Sunderland	
03.12.92	Bradley Stone L CO 4 Lewisham	
26.01.93	Neil Smith L PTS 4 Leicester	
13.02.93	John White L CO 2 Manchester	
20.04.93	Bobby Guynan L PTS 6 Brentwood	
29.04.93	Kevin Toomey L PTS 6 Hull	
23.05.93	Mike Anthony Brown W PTS 4 Brockley	

09.06.93	Joey Moffat L RTD 4 Liverpool	
30.09.93	Simon Frailing W PTS 6 Hayes	
06.10.93	Kevin McKillan L RSC 1 Solihull	
06.12.93	Colin Innes W PTS 6 Bradford	
16.12.93	Peter Till L PTS 8 Walsall	
19.01.94	John Naylor L RSC 3 Stoke	
21.02.94	Hugh Collins L RTD 4 Glasgow	
14.04.94	Mike Anthony Brown L PTS 6 Battersea	
28.04.94	John Stovin DREW 6 Hull	
06.05.94	Sugar Gibiliru L RTD 5 Liverpool	
02.09.94	Dave Fallon L DIS 4 Spitalfields	
28.09.94	Tanveer Ahmed L CO 5 Glasgow	
24.11.94	Tony Foster L RTD 7 Hull	
17.02.95	Paul Knights L RTD 5 Crawley	
16.06.95	George Naylor L PTS 6 Liverpool	
25.10.95	Joe Donohoe W PTS 6 Stoke	
20.12.95	J. T. Williams L CO 2 Usk	
16.03.96	Robbie Sivyer L CO 4 Barnstaple	
15.10.96	Wayne Windle W PTS 6 Wolverhampton	
02.12.96	Andrew Robinson W PTS 6 Birmingham	

Career: 31 contests, won 7, drew 2, lost 22.

(Hardip) Harry Dhami

Gravesend. *Born* Gravesend, 17 April, 1972
Southern Area Welterweight Champion.
Ht. 5'10"
Manager T. Toole

29.10.92	Johnny Pinnock W PTS 6 Hayes	
20.05.94	Nick Appiah W RSC 4 Acton	
27.05.94	Chris Vassiliou W RSC 5 Ashford	
11.10.94	Steve McNess DREW 6 Bethnal Green	
09.11.94	Clay O'Shea L PTS 6 Millwall	
30.11.94	Robert Wright L PTS 8 Wolverhampton	
17.11.95	John Bosco L PTS 6 Bethnal Green	
08.12.95	Nicky Thurbin L PTS 8 Bethnal Green	
25.04.96	Chris Pollock W PTS 6 Mayfair	
07.05.96	Ojay Abrahams W RSC 5 Mayfair	
	(Vacant Southern Area Welterweight Title)	
20.11.96	Andy Peach W RTD 3 Wembley	
14.03.97	Paul Dyer W PTS 10 Reading	
	(Southern Area Welterweight Title Defence)	
20.05.97	Paul Miles W RTD 2 Gillingham	
	(Southern Area Welterweight Title Defence)	

Career: 13 contests, won 8, drew 1, lost 4.

(Guillaume) Bamana Dibateza

Dagenham. *Born* Kinshasha, Zaire, 27 June, 1968
Lightweight. Ht. 5'5"
Manager T. Toole

13.12.88	Nicola Cara L PTS 6 San Pellegrino	
27.12.88	Massimo Spinelli W PTS 6 San Pellegrino	
21.01.89	Nicola Cara L PTS 6 Vasto	
10.03.90	Djamel Ayed W PTS 6 Brest, France	
20.04.90	Abdelac Lahmeri L PTS 6 Istres	
10.05.90	Zahir Nemer W PTS 6 Vaulk	
30.09.90	Boualem Belkif L PTS 8 Calais, France	
02.03.91	Pascal Ragaut W PTS 6 Salon	
12.04.91	Didier Schaeffer W PTS 6 Elbeuf	
25.05.91	Santiago Galan L PTS 8 Mondragon	
07.06.91	Frederic Malesa W PTS 6 La Seyne, France	
23.11.91	Mustapha Hame W PTS 6 Beziers	

13.02.93 Alain Pernice W PTS 6 Narbonne, France
09.04.94 Justin Juuko L RSC 5 Mansfield
11.05.94 Yifru Retta L PTS 6 Stevenage
04.10.94 Michael Armstrong W RSC 3 Mayfair
07.11.94 Michael Ayers L PTS 6 Bethnal Green
13.12.94 Jonjo Irwin L PTS 12 Potters Bar
(WBO Penta-Continental S. Featherweight Title Challenge)
08.03.95 Charles Shepherd L PTS 8 Solihull
24.03.95 Dean Phillips L PTS 6 Swansea
03.11.95 Yifru Retta L PTS 6 Dudley
13.02.96 Gareth Jordan L PTS 8 Cardiff
26.02.96 Michael Brodie L PTS 6 Manchester
26.04.96 Dean Phillips L PTS 6 Cardiff
24.10.96 Colin Dunne L PTS 8 Wembley
09.12.96 Jason Blanche L PTS 4 Bradford
27.01.97 Dave McHale L PTS 6 Glasgow
18.02.97 P. J. Gallagher W PTS 8 Cheshunt
25.03.97 Duke McKenzie L PTS 8 Lewisham
08.06.97 Gary Hibbert L PTS 4 Shaw
30.06.97 Tontcho Tontchev L PTS 4 Bethnal Green

Career: 31 contests, won 10, lost 21.

Liam Dineen

Peterlee. *Born* Horden, 17 October, 1972
L. Welterweight. Ht. 5'10"
Manager T. Conroy

24.05.94 Carl Roberts W PTS 6 Sunderland
05.12.94 Ram Singh W PTS 6 Houghton le Spring
21.02.95 T. J. Smith W PTS 6 Sunderland
16.03.95 Garry Burrell W PTS 6 Sunderland
09.05.96 Ram Singh W PTS 6 Sunderland
02.06.96 Scott Walker L RSC 1 Shaw
05.12.96 Phil Molyneux W PTS 6 Sunderland

Career: 7 contests, won 6, lost 1.

Scott Dixon

Hamilton. *Born* Hamilton, 28 September, 1976
L. Welterweight. Ht. 5'9"
Manager A. Morrison

13.10.95 Andrew Smith W PTS 4 Glasgow
17.12.95 Martin Evans W RSC 4 Glasgow
12.02.96 Colin Innes W PTS 6 Glasgow
16.03.96 Ian Richardson W PTS 4 Glasgow
26.04.96 Andy Green W RSC 5 Glasgow
24.05.96 Brian Coleman W PTS 8 Glasgow
20.09.96 Alan Temple W PTS 4 Glasgow
06.11.96 Rocky Ferrari DREW 6 Glasgow
22.12.96 Marc Smith W PTS 6 Glasgow
04.04.97 Jimmy Phelan W PTS 6 Glasgow
16.05.97 Dean Bramhald W PTS 6 Glasgow
13.06.97 Chris Price W PTS 6 Paisley

Career: 12 contests, won 11, drew 1.

Trevor Dixon

Birmingham. *Born* Marston Green, 2 October, 1969
L. Welterweight. Ht. 5'7"
Manager B. Hearn

18.06.93 Elvin Battle W DIS 4 Woodbridge, USA
05.08.93 Darryl Jacobs W PTS 6 Fort Eustis, USA
04.11.93 James Furr W PTS 4 Washington, USA
16.03.94 Dale Lepariz W CO 1 Raleigh, USA

26.08.94 Lou Dews W PTS 4 Upper Marlboro, USA
20.09.94 James Furr W PTS 4 Washington, USA
22.04.97 Kevin McKillan L PTS 6 Bethnal Green

Career: 7 contests, won 6, lost 1.

Trevor Dixon   Les Clark

John Docherty

Edinburgh, *Born* Edinburgh, 10 December, 1974
Welterweight. Ht. 5'11"
Manager T. Gilmour

05.10.95 Chris Aston W PTS 6 Glasgow
22.01.96 Wahid Fats DREW 6 Glasgow
16.02.96 Alan Bosworth L PTS 6 Irvine
09.05.96 Dean Nicholas W PTS 6 Glasgow
26.09.96 Wayne Shepherd W PTS 6 Glasgow
28.10.96 Shaun O'Neill W RSC 5 Glasgow
10.11.96 Wayne Shepherd W PTS 6 Glasgow
24.02.97 Shaun O'Neill W PTS 6 Glasgow
14.03.97 Ali Khattab L PTS 4 Odense, Denmark

Career: 9 contests, won 6, drew 1, lost 2.

Wilson Docherty

Condorrat. *Born* Glasgow, 15 April, 1968
S. Bantamweight. Former Undefeated WBO Penta-Continental Featherweight Champion.
Ht. 5'6"
Manager T. Gilmour

27.04.92 Norman Dhalie W RSC 2 Glasgow
09.07.92 Graham McGrath W RSC 4 Glasgow
26.04.93 Des Gargano W PTS 6 Glasgow
07.06.93 Chris Jickells W RSC 5 Glasgow
14.07.93 Anton Gilmore L PTS 8 Marula, South Africa
07.11.93 Robert Braddock W RSC 3 Glasgow
24.01.94 Paul Harvey W PTS 12 Glasgow
(Vacant WBO Penta-Continental Featherweight Title)
27.08.94 Peter Harris W PTS 12 Cardiff
(WBO Penta-Continental Featherweight Title Defence)

23.01.95 Mike Deveney L PTS 12 Glasgow
(Vacant British Featherweight Title)
24.04.95 Peter Harris L PTS 10 Glasgow
(Final Elim. British Featherweight Title)
06.02.96 Richie Wenton L PTS 12 Basildon
(British S. Bantamweight Title Challenge)
09.05.96 John T. Kelly W PTS 8 Glasgow
18.11.96 Colin Innes W PTS 8 Glasgow
17.03.97 Ricky Beard W RSC 4 Glasgow

Career: 14 contests, won 10, lost 4.

Adrian Dodson

Islington. *Born* Georgetown, Guyana, 20 September, 1970
WBO Inter-Continental L. Middleweight Champion. Ht. 5'10"
Manager Self

31.03.93 Chris Mulcahy W RSC 1 Bethnal Green
14.04.93 Rick North W RTD 1 Kensington
06.05.93 Greg Wallace W RSC 3 Las Vegas, USA
23.06.93 Russell Washer W PTS 6 Edmonton
22.09.93 Robert Peel W CO 1 Bethnal Green
23.10.93 Julian Eavis W RSC 4 Cardiff
26.02.94 Shamus Casey W CO 1 Earls Court
12.03.94 Danny Juma W PTS 6 Cardiff
09.04.94 Stuart Dunn W RSC 1 Mansfield
04.06.94 Andrew Jervis W RSC 2 Cardiff
10.09.94 Colin Pitters W PTS 6 Birmingham
25.05.95 Lloyd Honeyghan W RSC 3 Millwall
07.10.95 Hughes Daigneault W RSC 4 Belfast
(Vacant WBO Inter-Continental L. Middleweight Title)
02.12.95 Craig Snyder W RSC 8 Belfast
(WBO Inter-Continental L. Middleweight Title Defence)
04.05.96 John Bosco W RSC 7 Dagenham
(WBO Inter-Continental L. Middleweight Title Defence)
27.11.96 Anthony Joseph W CO 1 Bethnal Green
(WBO Inter-Continental L. Middleweight Title Defence)
29.01.97 Rachid Serdjane W DIS 5 Bethnal Green
29.04.97 Viktor Fessetchko W RSC 3 Belfast

Career: 18 contests, won 18.

James Donoghue

Middlesbrough. *Born* Middlesbrough, 12 January, 1973
L. Middleweight. Ht. 5'9"
Manager T. O'Neill

15.09.95 George Wilson W PTS 6 Darlington
08.12.95 Jason Barker W PTS 6 Leeds
19.03.96 Ernie Loveridge W PTS 6 Leeds
28.10.96 Billy Collins W PTS 6 Glasgow
03.12.96 Michael Alexander W PTS 6 Yarm
04.03.97 Andrew Jervis W RSC 4 Yarm

Career: 6 contests, won 6.

Darren Dorrington

Bristol. *Born* Bristol, 24 July, 1968
Middleweight. Western Area
S. Middleweight Champion. Ht. 5'11"
Manager C. Sanigar

13.09.93 Justin Smart DREW 4 Bristol

03.11.93	Russell Washer W PTS 4 Bristol
20.01.94	Shamus Casey W PTS 6 Battersea
29.01.94	Barry Thorogood DREW 6 Cardiff
10.03.94	Ray Price W RSC 6 Bristol
25.05.94	Steve Thomas W PTS 4 Bristol
02.07.94	Paul Murray W RSC 3 Keynsham
03.08.94	Gary Pemberton W CO 4 Bristol
07.10.94	Peter Vosper W RSC 6 Taunton
	(Vacant Western Area S. Middleweight Title)
27.10.94	Russell Washer W PTS 8 Bayswater
22.11.94	Robert Allen L RSC 5 Bristol
21.03.95	Lee Crocker L PTS 6 Swansea
19.10.96	Peter Vosper W RSC 3 Bristol
09.12.96	Ernie Loveridge W PTS 6 Bristol
21.01.97	Peter Mitchell W RSC 5 Bristol
24.03.96	Peter Mitchell W RSC 7 Bristol
05.06.97	Paul Carr W PTS 6 Bristol

Career: 17 contests, won 13, drew 2, lost 2.

Paul Douglas

Belfast. *Born* Belfast, 2 May, 1964
Heavyweight. Ht. 6'0"
Manager B. Hearn

03.09.96	Tony Booth W PTS 4 Belfast
05.11.96	Chris Henry L PTS 4 Belfast
22.05.97	Marat Tekouev DREW 4 Southwark
02.06.97	Kevin McBride L RSC 5 Belfast
	(Vacant All-Ireland Heavyweight Title)

Career: 4 contests, won 1, drew 1, lost 2.

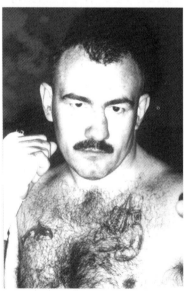

Paul Douglas   Les Clark

Tony Dowling

Lincoln. *Born* Lincoln, 5 January, 1976
Cruiserweight. Ht. 6'2"
Manager J. Ashton

22.03.96	Slick Miller W RSC 4 Mansfield
30.05.96	Nigel Rafferty W PTS 6 Lincoln
29.07.96	Albert Call L RSC 4 Skegness

Career: 3 contests, won 2, lost 1.

Dennis Doyley

Ilford. *Born* Hackney, 25 January, 1967
Middleweight. Ht. 5'11½"
Manager M. Holland

20.09.96	Gary Reyniers W RSC 2 Tooting
15.05.97	Steven Bendall L RSC 2 Reading

Career: 2 contests, won 1, lost 1.

Dennis Doyley   Les Clark

John Duckworth

Burnley. *Born* Burnley, 25 May, 1971
S. Middleweight. Ht. 6'2"
Manager B. Myers

04.04.92	Warren Stephens W RSC 5 Cleethorpes
13.04.92	Steve Goodwin L PTS 6 Manchester
04.06.92	Phil Foxon W RSC 4 Burnley
05.10.92	Dave Maj DREW 6 Manchester
29.10.92	Tony Massey W RTD 4 Leeds
20.01.93	James McGee W PTS 6 Solihull
25.02.93	Tony Trimble W PTS 6 Burnley
31.03.93	Jamie Robinson L RSC 3 Barking
27.05.93	Warren Stephens W RSC 5 Burnley
15.09.93	Mark Jay W RSC 4 Newcastle
11.11.93	Darren Pilling W PTS 6 Burnley
02.03.94	Dave Johnson L PTS 8 Solihull
15.03.94	Andrew Jervis W PTS 6 Stoke
18.04.94	Craig Winter L RSC 5 Manchester
26.09.94	Danny Peters L PTS 6 Liverpool
26.10.94	Darren Littlewood L PTS 6 Stoke
07.11.94	Paolo Roberto DREW 6 Piccadilly
28.11.94	Carl Harney L PTS 6 Manchester
07.12.94	Mark Dawson L PTS 6 Stoke
27.02.95	Paul Wright DREW 6 Barrow
05.04.95	Willie Quinn L PTS 8 Irvine
12.06.95	Carl Smith W PTS 6 Manchester
20.06.95	Andy McVeigh DREW 6 Birmingham
22.07.95	Robin Reid L PTS 8 Millwall
02.09.95	Jason Matthews L PTS 4 Wembley
14.09.95	David Starie L PTS 6 Battersea
30.09.95	Glenn Catley L RSC 3 Cardiff
24.11.95	Eric Noi L PTS 6 Manchester
06.12.95	Stinger Mason L PTS 6 Stoke
17.12.95	John McAlpine DREW 6 Glasgow
20.01.96	Ryan Rhodes L RSC 2 Mansfield

16.03.96	Clinton Woods L PTS 8 Sheffield
29.04.96	Howard Eastman L RSC 5 Mayfair
09.07.96	David Starie L RSC 1 Bethnal Green
31.08.96	Pascal Collins L PTS 4 Dublin
14.10.96	Mark Baker L RSC 6 Mayfair
27.11.96	Mark Delaney L RSC 5 Bethnal Green
28.01.97	Noel Magee L PTS 6 Belfast
18.02.97	Howard Eastman L CO 7 Cheshunt

Career: 39 contests, won 10, drew 5, lost 24.

Marty Duke

Yarmouth. *Born* Yarmouth, 19 June, 1967
L. Middleweight. Ht. 5'9"
Manager Self

16.05.88	Wayne Timmins L PTS 6 Wolverhampton
06.09.88	Tony Cloak W PTS 6 Southend
26.09.88	Tony Cloak L RSC 2 Bedford
27.10.88	Matthew Jones L PTS 6 Birmingham
06.12.88	Peter Mundy W PTS 6 Southend
25.01.89	Tony Hodge W RSC 2 Basildon
07.02.89	Dennis White L PTS 6 Southend
04.04.89	Tony Cloak W RSC 5 Southend
27.04.89	Steve West L RSC 1 Southwark
03.10.89	Colin Ford L PTS 6 Southend
23.10.89	Andy Catesby W PTS 6 Mayfair
19.12.89	Mike Jay DREW 6 Gorleston
08.02.90	Dean Lake L RSC 4 Southwark
14.03.90	Ahmet Canbakis L RSC 6 Battersea
12.11.90	Chris Haydon W PTS 6 Norwich
04.12.90	Paul Busby L PTS 6 Bury St Edmunds
29.01.91	Paul Smith L PTS 6 Wisbech
15.04.91	James McGee W PTS 6 Leicester
08.05.91	Martin Rosamond DREW 8 Millwall
16.05.91	Danny Shinkwin L PTS 6 Battersea
30.05.91	Richie Woodhall L RSC 4 Birmingham
04.07.91	Robert McCracken L RSC 1 Alfreton
03.09.91	Eamonn Loughran L PTS 6 Cardiff
26.09.91	Adrian Riley L PTS 6 Dunstable
05.11.91	Tony McKenzie L RSC 7 Leicester
31.03.92	Ojay Abrahams L RSC 2 Norwich
08.09.92	Ricky Mabbett DREW 6 Norwich
14.11.92	Vince Rose L PTS 6 Cardiff
26.01.93	Ricky Mabbett W CO 1 Leicester
14.04.93	Kevin Lueshing L RSC 2 Kensington
23.06.93	Billy McDougall W PTS 6 Gorleston
31.08.93	Glenn Catley L RSC 2 Croydon
03.11.93	Glenn Catley L RSC 1 Bristol
28.03.94	Spencer McCracken L RSC 2 Birmingham
27.11.94	Maurice Forbes L PTS 6 Southwark
09.12.94	Jason Beard L PTS 6 Bethnal Green
20.01.95	Nicky Thurbin L PTS 6 Bethnal Green
06.03.95	Howard Eastman L RSC 1 Mayfair
14.04.95	Neil Sinclair L RSC 2 Belfast
12.05.95	Nicky Thurbin L RSC 3 Bethnal Green
29.04.96	Paul Webb W PTS 6 Mayfair
16.05.96	Paul Webb W PTS 6 Dunstable
07.10.96	Anthony McFadden L CO 1 Lewisham
08.03.97	Richard Williams L RSC 3 Brentwood

Career: 44 contests, won 11, drew 3, lost 30.

Marcus Duncan

Morecambe. *Born* Blackpool, 9 January, 1971
Former Central Area Bantamweight Champion. Ht. 5'6"
Manager Self

12.11.92	Andrew Bloomer W PTS 6 Burnley
22.04.93	Chris Lyons W RSC 2 Bury
27.05.93	Neil Swain L PTS 6 Burnley

28.06.93	Neil Parry L RSC 2 Morecambe
13.09.93	Neil Parry W PTS 6 Middleton
11.11.93	Dave Campbell W PTS 6 Burnley
17.02.94	Jason Morris W RSC 6 Bury
21.03.94	Graham McGrath W PTS 6 Bradford
16.05.94	Daryl McKenzie W PTS 6 Morecambe
13.06.94	Matthew Harris L RSC 1 Bradford
26.09.94	Dave Campbell W PTS 6 Morecambe
22.05.95	Robert Hay L RSC 3 Morecambe
30.06.95	Luigi Mancini L RSC 4 Vigneux, France
11.12.95	Lyndon Kershaw W RSC 6 Morecambe
	(*Vacant Central Area Bantamweight Title*)
20.03.97	Andy Roberts L PTS 10 Doncaster
	(*Central Area Bantamweight Title Defence*)

Career: 15 contests, won 9, lost 6.

Brian Dunn

Immingham. *Born* Cleethorpes, 16 July, 1969
L. Middleweight. Ht. 5'10"
Manager L. Billany

15.04.94	Warren Stephens W PTS 6 Hull
16.05.94	Peter Reid W RSC 4 Cleethorpes
06.06.94	Eddie Haley L PTS 6 Glasgow
26.09.94	Japhet Hans L PTS 6 Cleethorpes
26.10.94	Ron Hopley W PTS 6 Leeds
12.12.94	Japhet Hans W PTS 6 Cleethorpes
06.03.95	Michael Alexander W CO 5 Bradford
05.04.95	Joe Townsley L RSC 3 Irvine
16.05.95	Andy Peach L RSC 1 Cleethorpes
22.09.95	Rob Stevenson W PTS 6 Hull
02.11.95	Mickey Johnson W RSC 3 Houghton le Spring
20.11.95	Billy Collins W PTS 8 Glasgow
11.12.95	Carlton Williams W RSC 4 Cleethorpes
18.03.96	Dennis Berry L RSC 2 Glasgow
22.04.96	Paul Webb W PTS 6 Cleethorpes
27.05.96	Joni Nyman L PTS 8 Helsinki, Finland
29.07.96	Michael Alexander W CO 3 Skegness
25.11.96	Cam Raeside L RSC 3 Cleethorpes
	(*Vacant Midlands Area Welterweight Title*)
25.04.97	Prince Kasi Kaihau L RSC 1 Cleethorpes

Career: 19 contests, won 10, lost 9.

Robbie Dunn

Plymouth. *Born* Mexborough, 29 May, 1969
Welterweight. Ht. 5'10½"
Manager N. Christian

24.01.95	Chris Vassiliou L PTS 6 Piccadilly
03.03.95	Dennis Gardner L RSC 4 Bracknell
13.06.95	Steve Roberts L RSC 3 Basildon
28.07.95	Andy Edge L RSC 2 Bristol
25.06.96	Pat Wright L RSC 2 Stevenage
20.09.96	David Baptiste L CO 2 Tooting
15.02.97	Pat Larner L RSC 2 Tooting

Career: 7 contests, lost 7.

Stuart Dunn

Leicester. *Born* Leicester, 19 January, 1970
L. Middleweight. Ht. 5'10½"
Manager J. Griffin

15.10.91	Spencer McCracken DREW 6 Dudley
09.12.91	Wayne Panayiotiou W CO 4 Brierley Hill
23.01.92	Charlie Moore L RSC 3 York

27.10.92	Andy Peach W RSC 3 Leicester
26.01.93	Wayne Panayiotiou W RSC 2 Leicester
28.04.93	Barry Thorogood W RSC 2 Solihull
19.05.93	Matthew Turner W RSC 3 Leicester
18.09.93	Lee Ferrie L RSC 1 Leicester
10.11.93	Jamie Robinson L PTS 6 Bethnal Green
30.11.93	Shamus Casey W PTS 6 Leicester
18.02.94	Jimmy Alston W RSC 1 Leicester
09.04.94	Adrian Dodson L RSC 1 Mansfield
18.02.95	Dean Cooper L RSC 1 Shepton Mallet
20.04.95	Howard Eastman L RSC 2 Mayfair
22.07.95	Jason Matthews L CO 1 Millwall
28.10.96	Michael Alexander L PTS 6 Leicester
09.12.96	Prince Kasi Kaihau L RSC 2 Leicester

Career: 17 contests, won 7, drew 1, lost 9.

Colin Dunne

Holloway. *Born* Liverpool, 19 September, 1970
Southern Area Lightweight Champion.
Ht. 5'6"
Manager T. Toole

07.12.93	Mark O'Callaghan W RSC 1 Bethnal Green
14.01.94	Wayne Jones W RSC 3 Bethnal Green
04.03.94	Malcolm Thomas W CO 1 Bethnal Green
26.04.94	Steve Burton W CO 2 Bethnal Green
17.05.94	Phil Found W PTS 6 Kettering
23.09.94	Steve Howden W CO 1 Bethnal Green
11.10.94	Jimmy Phelan W PTS 6 Bethnal Green
09.11.94	Mark O'Callaghan W RSC 2 Millwall
09.12.94	David Thompson W RSC 3 Bethnal Green
20.01.95	Chris Aston W RSC 4 Bethnal Green
03.03.95	Marco Fattore W RSC 3 Bethnal Green
19.04.95	Rudy Valentino W PTS 6 Bethnal Green
12.05.95	Chris Aston W RSC 4 Bethnal Green
27.09.95	Steve Howden W RSC 4 Bethnal Green
28.10.95	Chris Clarkson W RSC 4 Kensington
08.12.95	Jonathan Thaxton W RSC 5 Bethnal Green
	(*Vacant Southern Area Lightweight Title*)
05.03.96	Rudy Valentino W RSC 4 Bethnal Green
03.04.96	Kino Rodriguez W RSC 2 Bethnal Green
10.05.96	Lajos Nagy W RSC 5 Wembley
03.07.96	Marian Stoica W PTS 8 Wembley
24.10.96	Bamana Dibateza W PTS 8 Wembley
20.11.96	Michael Ayers L RSC 9 Wembley
	(*British Lightweight Title Challenge*)
24.04.97	Lewis Reynolds W CO 4 Mayfair
	(*Southern Area Lightweight Title Defence*)
30.06.97	Demir Nanev W RSC 8 Bethnal Green

Career: 24 contests, won 23, lost 1.

Terry Dunstan

Vauxhall. *Born* London, 21 October, 1968
Former Undefeated British Cruiserweight Champion. Ht. 6'3"
Manager F. Warren

12.11.92	Steve Osborne W PTS 6 Bayswater
25.11.92	Steve Yorath W PTS 8 Mayfair
31.03.93	Lee Prudden W PTS 6 Barking
15.09.93	Paul McCarthy W RSC 3 Ashford

02.12.93	Devon Rhooms W CO 2 Sheffield
30.09.94	Michael Murray W PTS 8 Bethnal Green
20.12.94	Trevor Small W RTD 4 Bethnal Green
04.03.95	Art Stacey W CO 1 Livingston
13.05.95	Dennis Andries W PTS 12 Glasgow
	(*British Cruiserweight Title Challenge*)
09.09.95	Dave Robinson W RSC 5 Cork
25.11.95	Jimmy Bills W RSC 7 Dublin
13.02.96	Dennis Andries W PTS 12 Bethnal Green
	(*British Cruiserweight Title Defence*)
11.05.96	John Keeton W RSC 1 Bethnal Green
	(*British Cruiserweight Title Defence*)
09.11.96	Sergio Merani W CO 3 Manchester
12.04.97	Art Jimmerson W RSC 1 Sheffield

Career: 15 contests, won 15.

Pat Durkin

Southport. *Born* Southport, 15 February, 1969
L. Heavyweight. Ht. 6'2"
Manager N. Basso

28.10.87	Paul Jones L PTS 4 Sheffield
09.11.87	Michael Justin L PTS 4 Leicester
16.11.87	Michael McDermott L PTS 4 Glasgow
30.11.87	Mike Snagg W RSC 6 Manchester
14.12.87	Dave Kettlewell L PTS 4 Bradford
18.01.88	Frank Harrington L PTS 4 Bradford
29.01.88	Dave Kettlewell L PTS 4 Durham
08.02.88	Adrian Din L CO 2 Nottingham
11.03.88	Frank Mobbs L RSC 3 Cottingham
03.11.88	Chris Mulcahy L RSC 2 Manchester
09.10.90	Trevor Meikle L DIS 3 Liverpool
07.02.91	Phil Epton L PTS 6 Watford
25.02.91	Willie Yeardsley L PTS 6 Bradford
05.03.91	Chris Mulcahy L PTS 6 Leicester
06.04.94	Laurence Rowe L PTS 6 Manchester
15.12.94	Chris Nurse L PTS 6 Walsall
09.02.95	Phil Ball L PTS 6 Doncaster
15.03.95	Steve Loftus L PTS 6 Stoke
13.04.96	Paul Bowen L RSC 3 Wythenshawe
30.09.96	Mike Whittaker L PTS 6 Manchester
26.11.96	Danny Southern L PTS 6 Sheffield
14.03.97	Alex Carey L RSC 6 Hull

Career: 22 contests, won 1, lost 21.

Paul Dyer

Portsmouth. *Born* Portsmouth, 11 July, 1970
Welterweight. Ht. 5'11½"
Manager C. Sanigar

24.09.91	Mick Reid W PTS 6 Basildon
19.11.91	Dave Andrews W PTS 6 Norwich
23.02.92	Kevin Mabbutt L PTS 6 Kettering
17.06.94	Dewi Roberts W PTS 6 Plymouth
27.10.94	George Wilson W PTS 4 Bayswater
25.01.95	John Janes W PTS 6 Cardiff
08.03.95	Anthony Huw Williams W PTS 6 Cardiff
06.05.95	Wahid Fats W PTS 4 Shepton Mallet
15.09.95	Mark Ramsey W PTS 6 Mansfield
16.12.95	Dennis Gardner W RSC 1 Cardiff
26.01.96	Danny Quacoe W PTS 6 Brighton
30.11.96	Mark Winters L PTS 6 Tylorstown
09.12.96	Paul Miles W PTS 6 Bristol
08.02.97	Michael Carruth L PTS 6 Millwall
14.03.97	Harry Dhami L PTS 10 Reading
	(*Southern Area Welterweight Title Challenge*)

Career: 15 contests, won 11, lost 4.

Paul Dyer   Les Clark

Gilbert Eastman

Battersea. *Born* Guyana, 16 November, 1972
Welterweight. Ht. 5'10"
Manager F. Maloney

22.04.96	Wayne Shepherd W PTS 4 Crystal Palace	
09.07.96	Costas Katsantonis W RSC 1 Bethnal Green	
11.01.97	Mike Watson W RSC 1 Bethnal Green	
25.03.97	Danny Quacoe W RSC 3 Lewisham	

Career: 4 contests, won 4.

Howard Eastman   Les Clark

Howard Eastman

Battersea. *Born* New Amsterdam, Guyana,
8 December, 1970
Southern Area Middleweight Champion.
Ht. 5'11"
Manager D. Mancini/M. Duff

06.03.94	John Rice W RSC 1 Southwark
14.03.94	Andy Peach W PTS 6 Mayfair
22.03.94	Steve Phillips W RSC 5 Bethnal Green
17.10.94	Barry Thorogood W RSC 6 Mayfair
06.03.95	Marty Duke W RSC 1 Mayfair
20.04.95	Stuart Dunn W RSC 2 Mayfair
23.06.95	Peter Vosper W RSC 1 Bethnal Green
16.10.95	Carlo Colarusso W RSC 1 Mayfair
29.11.95	Brendan Ryan W RSC 2 Bethnal Green
31.01.96	Paul Wesley W RSC 1 Birmingham
13.03.96	Steve Goodwin W RSC 5 Wembley
29.04.96	John Duckworth W RSC 5 Mayfair
11.12.96	Sven Hamer W RSC 10 Southwark
	(Vacant Southern Area Middleweight Title)
18.02.97	John Duckworth W CO 7 Cheshunt
25.03.97	Rachid Serdjane W RSC 7 Lewisham

Career: 15 contests, won 15.

Darrell Easton

New Addington. *Born* Croydon, 27
February, 1970
Featherweight. Ht. 5'7"
Manager D. Powell

25.03.97	Benny Jones W PTS 4 Lewisham
22.05.97	Keith Jones W PTS 4 Southwark

Career: 2 contests, won 2.

Darrell Easton   Les Clark

Andy Edge

Reading. *Born* Manchester, 8 April, 1971
L. Middleweight. Ht. 5'11"
Manager C. Sanigar

28.07.95	Robbie Dunn W RSC 2 Bristol
14.09.95	Andy Ewen L PTS 4 Battersea
20.10.95	Andy Ewen L PTS 4 Ipswich
28.10.95	Barrie Bessant W PTS 6 Bristol
05.02.96	Steve Ford L CO 1 Bexleyheath
27.08.96	Clayon Stewart L PTS 4 Windsor

Career: 6 contests, won 2, lost 4.

Richie Edwards

Greenford. *Born* Ealing, 25 March, 1969
L. Welterweight. Ht. 5'8"
Manager F. Maloney

30.03.95	John O. Johnson W PTS 4 Bethnal Green
04.06.95	Seth Jones W RSC 4 Bethnal Green
16.06.95	Mikael Nilsson W PTS 4 Southwark
24.10.95	John Smith W PTS 4 Southwark
02.04.96	Delroy Leslie W RSC 3 Southwark
03.09.96	Vince Burns W CO 1 Bethnal Green
07.10.96	Marco Fattore W PTS 6 Lewisham
18.02.97	Bernard Paul L PTS 10 Cheshunt
	(Vacant Southern Area L. Welterweight Title)
30.06.97	Georgie Smith L RSC 10 Bethnal Green
	(Vacant Southern Area L. Welterweight Title)

Career: 9 contests, won 7, lost 2.

Shaba Edwards

Clapham. *Born* Clapham, 29 April, 1966
Welterweight. Ht. 5'7½"
Manager B. Padget

12.05.93	Jason Barker L PTS 6 Stoke
23.06.93	Steve Howden L RSC 1 Gorleston
12.09.94	Brian Coleman W PTS 6 Mayfair
29.09.94	Everald Williams L CO 1 Bethnal Green
30.11.94	Clayton Hollingsworth L PTS 6 Wolverhampton
22.05.95	Clayton Hollingsworth L PTS 6 Telford
16.03.95	Georgie Smith L CO 2 Basildon
29.11.95	Chris Francis DREW 6 Bethnal Green
12.01.96	Lars Myrberg L RSC 3 Copenhagen, Denmark
24.10.96	Daniel James L PTS 6 Wembley

Career: 10 contests, won 1, drew 1, lost 8.

Matthew Ellis   Les Clark

Matthew Ellis

Blackpool. *Born* Oldham, 12 April, 1974
Heavyweight. Ht. 5'11¾"
Manager J. Hyland

03.02.96	Laurent Rouze W CO 1 Liverpool	
01.04.96	Ladislav Husarik W RTD 4 Den Bosch, Holland	
06.09.96	Darren Fearn W RSC 6 Liverpool	
26.10.96	Daniel Beun W RSC 1 Liverpool	
01.03.97	Yuri Yelistratov L RSC 5 Liverpool	

Career: 5 contests, won 4, lost 1.

Phil Epton (Hampton)

Doncaster. *Born* Doncaster, 14 June, 1968
Middleweight. Ht. 5'8"
Manager T. Petersen

18.10.90	Mark Jay W PTS 6 Dewsbury
15.11.90	Paul King L PTS 6 Oldham
07.02.91	Pat Durkin W PTS 6 Watford
21.03.91	Paul King L PTS 6 Dewsbury
13.06.91	Willie Yeardsley W RSC 3 Hull
23.01.92	Carl Hook W PTS 6 York
19.03.92	Ricky Mabbett L RSC 3 York
23.09.92	Jimmy Vincent L RSC 6 Leeds
08.12.94	David Maw L PTS 6 Hull
24.04.95	Billy Collins L RSC 3 Glasgow
24.06.95	Warren Bowers W PTS 6 Cleethorpes
08.07.95	Ron Hopley W RSC 4 York
15.09.95	Robbie Bell L PTS 6 Darlington
11.12.95	John Stronach L PTS 6 Bradford
09.03.96	Jim Webb L PTS 4 Millstreet
03.12.96	Jason Barker L RSC 1 Yarm
20.03.97	Rob Stevenson W PTS 6 Doncaster

Career: 17 contests, won 7, lost 10.

Harry Escott

Sunderland. *Born* West Germany, 17 October, 1969
S. Featherweight. Ht. 5'8"
Manager N. Fawcett

26.02.87	Kenny Walsh W RSC 4 Hartlepool
06.04.87	Gypsy Finch W PTS 4 Newcastle
23.04.87	Gypsy Finch W PTS 4 Newcastle
30.04.87	Craig Windsor W RSC 3 Washington
22.05.87	Ginger Staples W RSC 1 Peterlee
04.06.87	Barry Bacon W RSC 2 Sunderland
04.09.87	Kevin Plant L RSC 4 Gateshead
26.01.88	Michael Howell W RSC 4 Hartlepool
17.03.88	Ian Honeywood W RSC 4 Sunderland
25.04.88	Les Walsh W PTS 8 Bradford
23.05.88	Tony Foster L RSC 6 Bradford
22.09.88	Dave Kettlewell W PTS 6 Newcastle
14.11.88	John Townsley W PTS 8 Glasgow
30.01.89	Tony Dore DREW 8 Glasgow
14.02.89	Kevin Pritchard W RSC 3 Sunderland
13.03.89	Young Joe Rafiu W PTS 8 Glasgow
11.04.89	Muhammad Lovelock W PTS 6 Oldham
05.06.89	Gary Maxwell W PTS 8 Glasgow
11.09.89	Gary Maxwell W PTS 8 Nottingham
19.10.89	Rudy Valentino W RTD 4 Manchester
07.12.89	Joey Jacobs W PTS 6 Manchester
24.01.90	Tomas Arguelles W PTS 6 Sunderland
15.05.90	Kevin Pritchard L PTS 8 South Shields
13.11.90	Brian Roche L RSC 3 Hartlepool
02.03.91	Steve Walker DREW 6 Darlington
06.04.91	Darren Elsdon L RSC 2 Darlington
06.07.91	Jackie Gunguluza L CO 6 Imperia, Italy
20.09.91	Steve Walker DREW 6 Manchester
04.02.92	Neil Smith W PTS 8 Alfreton
17.03.92	Floyd Havard L RSC 7 Mayfair
27.05.92	Wilson Rodriguez L PTS 10 Cologne, Germany
07.10.92	Dominic McGuigan W RTD 5 Sunderland
30.10.92	Eugene Speed L PTS 8 Istres, France
01.12.92	Neil Haddock L PTS 10 Liverpool
18.06.93	Medhi Labdouni L PTS 8 Fontenay Sous Bois, France
21.07.93	Phillip Holiday L PTS 8 Marula, South Africa
01.12.93	Floyd Havard L PTS 8 Bethnal Green
27.04.94	Kid McAuley W RTD 6 Solihull
10.05.94	Kelton McKenzie W PTS 6 Doncaster
04.10.94	Jonjo Irwin L PTS 12 Mayfair *(WBO Penta-Continental S. Featherweight Title Challenge)*
04.02.95	Colin McMillan L PTS 8 Cardiff
01.04.95	Julien Lorcy L RSC 1 Levallois Perret, France
20.05.95	Jimmy Bredahl L PTS 8 Copenhagen, Denmark
10.10.96	Garry Burrell W PTS 6 Newcastle
28.10.96	Charles Shepherd L PTS 8 Glasgow
04.12.96	Alan Temple L PTS 8 Hartlepool
18.01.97	Dean Pithie L RSC 4 Swadlincote

Career: 47 contests, won 24, drew 3, lost 20.

Chris Eubank

Brighton. *Born* Dulwich, 8 August, 1966
L. Heavyweight. Former WBO S. Middleweight Champion. Former Undefeated WBO Middleweight Champion. Former Undefeated WBC International Middleweight Champion. Ht. 5'10"
Manager Self

03.10.85	Tim Brown W PTS 4 Atlantic City, USA
07.11.85	Kenny Cannida W PTS 4 Atlantic City, USA
08.01.86	Mike Bragwell W PTS 4 Atlantic City, USA
25.02.86	Eric Holland W PTS 4 Atlantic City, USA
25.03.87	James Canty W PTS 4 Atlantic City, USA
15.02.88	Darren Parker W RSC 1 Copthorne
07.03.88	Winston Burnett W PTS 6 Hove
26.04.88	Michael Justin W RSC 5 Hove
04.05.88	Greg George W RSC 5 Wembley
18.05.88	Steve Aquilina W RSC 4 Portsmouth
31.01.89	Simon Collins W RSC 4 Bethnal Green
08.02.89	Anthony Logan W PTS 8 Kensington
01.03.89	Franki Moro W PTS 8 Bethnal Green
26.05.89	Randy Smith W PTS 10 Bethnal Green
28.06.89	Les Wisniewski W RSC 2 Brentwood
04.10.89	Ron Malek W RSC 5 Basildon
24.10.89	Jean-Noel Camara W RSC 2 Bethnal Green
05.11.89	Johnny Melfah W CO 4 Kensington
20.12.89	Jose da Silva W RTD 6 Kirkby
16.01.90	Denys Cronin W RSC 3 Cardiff
06.03.90	Hugo Corti W RSC 8 Bethnal Green *(WBC International Middleweight Title Challenge)*
25.04.90	Eduardo Contreras W PTS 12 Brighton *(WBC International Middleweight Title Defence)*
05.09.90	Kid Milo W RSC 8 Brighton *(WBC International Middleweight Title Defence)*
22.09.90	Reginaldo Santos W CO 1 Kensington

Martin Evans

Taunton. *Born* Liverpool, 3 August, 1967
S. Featherweight. Ht. 5'7½"
Manager N. Christian

27.03.90	Tony Doyle L RSC 3 Leicester
04.05.90	Jimmy Owens L RSC 2 Liverpool
05.06.90	Tony Ward L RSC 3 Liverpool
09.10.90	Neil Berry W RSC 2 Liverpool
10.11.90	Jimmy Owens L RSC 3 Liverpool
24.01.91	Barrie Kelley L PTS 6 Gorseinon
06.06.91	Nicky Lucas L PTS 6 Barking
20.06.91	Charlie Coke L RTD 3 Liverpool
19.09.95	Dave Hinds L RSC 5 Plymouth
30.10.95	Wee Barry W PTS 6 Heathrow
29.11.95	Eddie Sica W RSC 2 Southwark

The following relates to the Nigel Benn column on the right side:

18.11.90	Nigel Benn W RSC 9 Birmingham *(WBO Middleweight Title Challenge)*
23.02.91	Dan Sherry W TD 10 Brighton *(WBO Middleweight Title Defence)*
18.04.91	Gary Stretch W RSC 6 Earls Court *(WBO Middleweight Title Defence)*
22.06.91	Michael Watson W PTS 12 Earls Court *(WBO Middleweight Title Defence)*
21.09.91	Michael Watson W RSC 12 Tottenham *(Vacant WBO S. Middleweight Title)*
01.02.92	Thulani Malinga W PTS 12 Birmingham *(WBO S. Middleweight Title Defence)*
25.04.92	John Jarvis W CO 3 Manchester *(WBO S. Middleweight Title Defence)*
27.06.92	Ronnie Essett W PTS 12 Quinta do Lago, Portugal *(WBO S. Middleweight Title Defence)*
19.09.92	Tony Thornton W PTS 12 Glasgow *(WBO S. Middleweight Title Defence)*
28.11.92	Juan Carlos Giminez W PTS 12 Manchester *(WBO S. Middleweight Title Defence)*
20.02.93	Lindell Holmes W PTS 12 Earls Court *(WBO S. Middleweight Title Defence)*
15.05.93	Ray Close DREW 12 Glasgow *(WBO S. Middleweight Title Defence)*
09.10.93	Nigel Benn DREW 12 Manchester *(WBO S. Middleweight Title Defence, WBC S. Middleweight Title Challenge)*
05.02.94	Graciano Rocchigiani W PTS 12 Berlin, Germany *(WBO S. Middleweight Title Defence)*
21.05.94	Ray Close W PTS 12 Belfast *(WBO S. Middleweight Title Defence)*
09.07.94	Mauricio Amaral W PTS 12 Earls Court *(WBO S. Middleweight Title Defence)*
27.08.94	Sammy Storey W RSC 7 Cardiff *(WBO S. Middleweight Title Defence)*
15.10.94	Dan Schommer W PTS 12 Sun City, South Africa *(WBO S. Middleweight Title Defence)*
10.12.94	Henry Wharton W PTS 12 Manchester *(WBO S. Middleweight Title Defence)*
18.03.95	Steve Collins L PTS 12 Millstreet, Eire *(WBO S. Middleweight Title Defence)*
27.05.95	Bruno Godoy W RSC 1 Belfast
29.07.95	Jose Barruetabena W CO 1 Whitley Bay
09.09.95	Steve Collins L PTS 12 Cork *(WBO S. Middleweight Title Challenge)*
19.10.96	Luis Dionisio Barrera W CO 5 Cairo, Egypt
27.03.97	Camilo Alarcon W RSC 4 Dubai

Career: 49 contests, won 45, drew 2, lost 2.

17.12.95 Scott Dixon L RSC 4 Glasgow
12.02.96 Wee Barry L RSC 4 Heathrow
04.06.96 Michael Gibbons L RSC 2 York
03.07.96 Charlie Rumbol L PTS 6 Wembley
19.09.96 Michael Gomez L RSC 1 Manchester
10.12.96 Dean Murdoch L RSC 4 Plymouth
Career: 17 contests, won 3, lost 14.

Richard Evatt
Coventry. *Born* Coventry, 26 August, 1973
Featherweight. Ht. 5'6"
Manager B. Hearn

18.12.95 Kevin Sheil W RSC 1 Mayfair
06.02.96 Joe Donohoe W RSC 2 Basildon
09.04.96 Fred Reeve W RSC 1 Stevenage
20.04.96 Wayne Jones W RSC 2 Brentwood
04.05.96 Miguel Matthews W PTS 6 Dagenham
27.11.96 Brian Robb W RSC 2 Bethnal Green
17.12.96 Andrew Robinson W RSC 2 Doncaster
08.03.97 Brian Robb W CO 3 Brentwood
Career: 8 contests, won 8.

Andy Ewen
Ipswich. *Born* Ipswich, 12 January, 1966
Middleweight. Ht. 5'9"
Manager Self

12.10.94 Peter Mitchell W PTS 6 Sheffield
23.11.94 Sven Hamer L RSC 1 Piccadilly
07.02.95 Russell Washer W PTS 4 Ipswich
31.03.95 Jason Hart L PTS 6 Crystal Palace
17.05.95 Robert Peel W RSC 4 Ipswich
16.06.95 Lee Crocker L RSC 3 Southwark
14.09.95 Andy Edge W PTS 4 Battersea
20.10.95 Andy Edge W PTS 4 Ipswich
08.11.95 Panayiotis Panayiotiou L PTS 4 Bethnal Green
22.11.95 Clinton Woods L RSC 3 Sheffield
26.11.96 Anthony McFadden L PTS 6 Bethnal Green
04.03.97 Enzo Giordano L RSC 3 Southwark
08.04.97 Jason Ratcliff L RSC 4 Bethnal Green
Career: 13 contests, won 5, lost 8.

Barry Exton
Lincoln. *Born* Lincoln, 27 December, 1970
Middleweight. Ht. 6'0"
Manager J. Gaynor

20.06.95 Robert Harper W PTS 6 Birmingham
21.09.95 P. R. Mason DREW 6 Sheffield
26.10.95 Carlton Williams DREW 6 Birmingham
23.02.96 Peter Vosper W PTS 6 Weston super Mare
24.10.96 Ernie Loveridge W PTS 6 Lincoln
Career: 5 contests, won 3, drew 2.

(Antonio) Tony Falcone
Chippenham. *Born* Chippenham, 15 October, 1966
Former Western Area S. Bantamweight Champion. Ht. 5'6"
Manager C. Sanigar

22.10.90 Karl Morling L PTS 6 Mayfair
21.11.90 Barrie Kelley L PTS 6 Chippenham
18.02.91 Barrie Kelley W PTS 6 Mayfair
28.02.91 Paul Wynn W PTS 6 Sunderland
21.03.91 Tony Silkstone L PTS 6 Dewsbury
22.04.91 Alan Smith L RSC 5 Mayfair
30.05.91 Alan Smith W PTS 6 Mayfair

11.12.91 Dennis Adams W RTD 4 Basildon
30.04.92 Andrew Bloomer W PTS 6 Mayfair
07.07.92 Miguel Matthews W PTS 6 Bristol
05.10.92 Andrew Bloomer W PTS 8 Bristol
13.12.93 Des Gargano W PTS 4 Bristol
23.02.94 Conn McMullen DREW 4 Watford
10.03.94 Pete Buckley W PTS 4 Bristol
29.03.94 Justin Murphy L RSC 2 Bethnal Green
22.11.94 Fred Reeve W PTS 6 Bristol
18.02.95 Danny Ruegg W PTS 10 Shepton Mallet
(Vacant Western Area S. Bantamweight Title)
06.05.95 Danny Lawson W RSC 2 Shepton Mallet
28.07.95 Neil Swain L RSC 5 Bristol
(Commonwealth S. Bantamweight Title Challenge)
18.10.96 Danny Ruegg L PTS 10 Barnstaple
(Western Area S. Bantamweight Title Defence)
Career: 20 contests, won 12, drew 1, lost 7.

Anthony Farnell
Manchester. *Born* Manchester, 1 July, 1978
Welterweight. Ht. 5'10"
Manager F. Warren

03.05.97 Lee Molyneux W PTS 4 Manchester
Career: 1 contest, won 1.

John Farrell
Bootle. *Born* Bootle, 11 November, 1968
Featherweight. Ht. 5'6¼"
Manager B. Ingle

22.03.97 Michael Gomez L RSC 2 Wythenshawe
12.05.97 Graham McGrath W RSC 4 Leicester
21.06.97 Delroy Pryce DREW 4 Cardiff
Career: 3 contests, won 1, drew 1, lost 1.

Marco Fattore
Watford. *Born* Italy, 17 October, 1968
L. Welterweight. Ht. 5'8"
Manager Self

03.09.92 Jason White W RSC 1 Dunstable
19.10.92 Carlos Domonkos W RTD 4 Mayfair
07.12.92 Steve Patton W RSC 6 Mayfair
15.02.93 Jason Hutson W PTS 6 Mayfair
29.03.93 T. J. Smith DREW 6 Mayfair
22.04.93 Jason Barker W PTS 6 Mayfair
04.10.93 Andrew Bloomer W PTS 6 Mayfair
10.11.93 Lee Fox W PTS 6 Watford
09.12.93 Jason Hutson DREW 6 Watford
10.03.94 Simon Frailing DREW 6 Watford
28.04.94 Andrew Reed DREW 6 Mayfair
12.09.94 Keith Jones W PTS 6 Mayfair
30.11.94 Kid McAuley L PTS 6 Solihull
03.03.95 Colin Dunne L RSC 3 Bethnal Green
25.05.95 P. J. Gallagher L RSC 5 Reading
02.11.95 Brian Coleman L PTS 6 Mayfair
22.11.95 Marc Smith L PTS 6 Mayfair
29.01.96 Ram Singh DREW 6 Piccadilly
21.02.96 Brian Coleman L PTS 6 Piccadilly
02.04.96 Matt Brown L PTS 4 Southwark
07.10.96 Richie Edwards L PTS 6 Lewisham
11.12.96 Craig Stanley L PTS 4 Southwark
28.01.97 Vince Burns W PTS 6 Piccadilly
24.03.97 Jose Tuominen L RSC 3 Helsinki, Finland
Career: 24 contests, won 9, drew 5, lost 10.

Darren Fearn
Carmarthen. *Born* Carmarthen, 21 February, 1969
Heavyweight. Ht. 6'2"
Manager D. Gardiner

25.06.94 Keith Fletcher W PTS 6 Cullompton
25.01.95 Rob Albon W PTS 6 Cardiff
12.04.95 L. A. Williams W PTS 6 Llanelli
19.01.96 Mika Kihlstrom L PTS 4 Bracknell
07.05.96 Julius Francis L PTS 8 Mayfair
28.05.96 Darren Corbett L RSC 1 Belfast
06.09.96 Matthew Ellis L RSC 6 Liverpool
26.11.96 Nicolai Valouev L RTD 1 Bethnal Green
Career: 8 contests, won 3, lost 5.

Spencer Fearon
Forest Hill. *Born* London, 20 December, 1973
L. Middleweight. Ht. 6'0"
Manager F. Warren

28.06.97 Mark Sawyers W PTS 4 Norwich
Career: 1 contest, won 1.

Spencer Fearon   Les Clark

Peter Federenko
Sheffield. *Born* Rotherham, 17 May, 1978
L. Middleweight. Ht. 5'9"
Manager D. Ingle

22.05.97 Chris Pollock W CO 2 Solihull
Career: 1 contest, won 1.

Vince Feeney
Sligo. *Born* Sligo, 12 May, 1973
Southern Area Bantamweight Champion. Ht. 5'4"
Manager Self

29.10.92 Ady Benton DREW 6 Bayswater
06.02.93 Kevin Jenkins W PTS 6 Cardiff
29.03.93 Andrew Bloomer W PTS 6 Mayfair
29.04.93 Neil Swain L PTS 6 Mayfair
28.09.93 Peter Culshaw L PTS 6 Liverpool
30.11.93 Tiger Singh W PTS 6 Leicester

18.02.94 Shaun Norman W RSC 2 Leicester
09.04.94 Neil Swain W PTS 6 Mansfield
24.05.94 Louis Veitch W PTS 6 Leicester
07.10.94 Jesper D. Jensen L PTS 6 Copenhagen, Denmark
12.11.94 Mark Reynolds W PTS 6 Dublin
02.07.95 Louis Veitch W PTS 4 Dublin
08.11.95 Pete Buckley W PTS 8 Bethnal Green
15.12.95 Willy Perdomo L RSC 6 Bethnal Green
(WBC International Bantamweight Title Challenge)
30.03.96 Rowan Williams W RSC 6 Dublin
14.05.96 Brendan Bryce W PTS 6 Dagenha
03.09.96 Pete Buckley W PTS 4 Bethnal Green
26.11.96 Willy Perdomo L RSC 10 Bethnal Green
(WBC International Bantamweight Title Challenge)
08.04.97 Francis Ampofo W PTS 10 Bethnal Green
(Vacant Southern Area Bantamweight Title)
Career: 19 contests, won 13, drew 1, lost 5.

(Robert) Rocky Ferrari (Ewing)

Glasgow. *Born* Glasgow, 27 October, 1972
Lightweight. Ht. 5'7"
Managers Self

25.01.91 James Hunter W CO 1 Stoke
11.02.91 Sol Francis W RSC 5 Glasgow
05.03.91 Chris Saunders W PTS 4 Glasgow
11.09.92 Mick Mulcahy W PTS 6 Glasgow
28.02.94 Kevin McKenzie L PTS 6 Marton
13.05.94 Colin Innes W PTS 6 Kilmarnock
02.03.95 Kevin McKenzie DREW 6 Glasgow
21.04.95 Jyrki Vierela L RTD 3 Glasgow
06.11.96 Scott Dixon DREW 6 Glasgow
29.11.96 Stuart Rimmer L RSC 5 Glasgow
Career: 10 contests, won 5, drew 2, lost 3.

Jeff Finlayson   Les Clark

Jeff Finlayson

Manchester. *Born* Manchester, 12 March, 1968
Middleweight. Ht.5'7¼"
Manager J. Doughty

04.12.95 Earl Ling W PTS 6 Manchester
24.03.96 Shamus Casey W PTS 6 Shaw
02.06.96 Carlton Williams L PTS 6 Shaw
28.11.96 Terry Morrill L PTS 6 Hull
03.03.97 Carlton Williams L PTS 6 Leicester
29.04.97 Humphrey Harrison L PTS 6 Manchester
27.05.97 Jason Ratcliff L PTS 4 Mayfair
08.06.97 Graham Burton W PTS 6 Shaw
Career: 8 contests, won 3, lost 5.

Stuart Fleet

Grimsby. *Born* Grimsby, 15 January, 1963
Midlands Area L. Heavyweight Champion. Ht. 6'0"
Manager Self

09.12.91 Rocky Shelly L RSC 1 Cleethorpes
16.09.93 Lee Avery W RSC 1 Hull
30.09.93 Robert Norton L CO 2 Walsall
12.11.93 Richard Atkinson W CO 1 Hull
10.02.94 Eddie Pyott W RSC 2 Hull
26.02.96 Nigel Williams W RSC 1 Hull
22.04.96 Mark Hale W PTS 6 Cleethorpes
29.07.96 Michael Pinnock W RSC 3 Skegness
25.11.96 Steve Osborne W PTS 6 Cleethorpes
25.04.97 Neil Simpson W PTS 10 Cleethorpes
(Midlands Area L. Heavyweight Title Challenge)
Career: 10 contests, won 8, lost 2.

Andy Fletcher

Leigh. *Born* Leigh, 20 February, 1965
S. Middleweight. Ht. 5'8"
Manager F. Britton

02.06.96 Lee Whitehead L RSC 2 Shaw
01.12.96 Mike Whittaker L CO 1 Shaw
Career: 2 contests, lost 2.

Andrew Flute

Coseley. Born Wolverhampton, 5 March, 1970
S. Middleweight. Ht. 6'1"
Manager T. Toole

24.05.89 Stinger Mason W PTS 6 Hanley
24.10.89 Paul Murray W RSC 3 Wolverhampton
22.03.90 Dave Maxwell W RSC 5 Wolverhampton
24.05.90 Spencer Alton L RSC 1 Dudley
18.09.90 Tony Hodge W CO 2 Wolverhampton
24.10.90 Nigel Rafferty W CO 6 Dudley
27.11.90 Paul Burton L PTS 6 Stoke
13.03.91 Robert Peel W PTS 6 Stoke
10.04.91 Russell Washer W PTS 6 Wolverhampton
14.05.91 Alan Richards W PTS 8 Dudley
16.10.91 Karl Barwise L RSC 8 Stoke
05.12.91 Richard Okumu DREW 8 Cannock
17.03.92 Graham Burton W PTS 8 Wolverhampton
28.04.92 Paul Smith W RSC 5 Wolverhampton
20.01.93 Glen Payton W RSC 4 Wolverhampton
16.03.93 Mark Hale W RSC 2 Wolverhampton
24.04.93 Steve Thomas W RSC 1 Birmingham
21.10.93 Terry Magee W RSC 6 Bayswater
26.01.94 Neville Brown L RTD 7 Birmingham
(British Middleweight Title Challenge)
16.03.94 Graham Burton W PTS 6 Birmingham
29.10.94 Carlos Christie L PTS 8 Cannock
29.11.94 Mark Dawson W PTS 8 Cannock
17.01.95 Chris Richards W PTS 6 Worcester

11.05.95 Paul Murray W PTS 6 Dudley
30.09.95 Mark Delaney L PTS 12 Basildon
(Vacant WBO Inter-Continental S. Middleweight Title)
16.03.96 Robin Reid L RSC 7 Glasgow
25.05.96 Norbert Nieroba L RTD 4 Leipzig, Germany
28.09.96 Leif Keiski L PTS 8 Barking
24.10.96 Carlos Christie L PTS 10 Mayfair
(Midlands Area S. Middleweight Title Challenge)
15.02.97 Markus Beyer L PTS 6 Vienna, Austria
01.06.97 Sven Ottke L PTS 6 Riesa, Germany
Career: 31 contests, won 18, drew 1, lost 12.

Maurice Forbes

Brixton. *Born* Jamaica, 24 June, 1968
L. Middleweight. Ht. 5'10½"
Manager Self

23.05.93 Michael Dick W RSC 1 Brockley
25.06.93 Kenny Scott W RSC 2 Battersea
14.08.93 Phil Found W PTS 4 Hammersmith
14.04.94 Dave Maj W RTD 2 Battersea
22.05.94 Trevor Meikle W RTD 3 Crystal Palace
21.07.94 Michael Smyth L RSC 3 Battersea
27.11.94 Marty Duke W PTS 6 Southwark
31.03.95 Steve McGovern W PTS 6 Crystal Palace
02.06.95 Gordon Blair W RSC 4 Bethnal Green
03.05.97 Chris Pyatt L PTS 8 Manchester
Career: 10 contests, won 8, lost 2.

Steve Ford

Cirencester. *Born* Swindon, 9 March, 1971
L. Middleweight. Ht. 5'8"
Manager W. Ball

05.02.96 Andy Edge W CO 1 Bexleyheath
27.08.96 Anthony McFadden L RSC 4 Windsor
Career: 2 contests, won 1, lost 1.

Steve Foster

Salford. *Born* Salford, 28 December, 1960
Former Undefeated Commonwealth & IBF Inter-Continental L. Middleweight Champion. Ht. 5'8½"
Manager F. Warren

09.02.81 Pat McCarthy W RSC 3 Manchester
16.03.81 Dave Dunn L PTS 6 Manchester
26.03.81 John Lindo L RSC 1 Newcastle
28.11.85 Malcolm Melvin DREW 6 Ilkeston
06.03.86 Taffy Morris L PTS 6 Manchester
17.04.86 Martin Kielty W RSC 3 Wolverhampton
25.11.86 Shamus Casey W PTS 8 Manchester
28.04.87 Cyril Jackson W RSC 7 Manchester
11.05.87 Fidel Castro L PTS 8 Manchester
19.10.87 Cyril Jackson W RTD 3 Manchester
14.12.87 Sean Leighton L PTS 8 Bradford
27.01.88 Sammy Storey L RSC 4 Belfast
20.04.88 Tony Collins L PTS 4 Muswell Hill
19.10.88 Ray Close L RSC 2 Belfast
14.12.88 Fran Harding L PTS 6 Kirkby
01.03.89 Dario Deabreu W RSC 2 Cardiff
06.03.89 Steve Aquilina W PTS 6 Manchester
03.12.89 Antonio Fernandez W PTS 8 Birmingham
06.02.90 Sean O'Phoenix W RSC 4 Oldham
14.03.90 Andy Till L RTD 5 Battersea
02.06.90 Ian Chantler DREW 4 Manchester
22.02.91 Kesem Clayton W CO 6 Manchester

20.09.91 Colin Pitters W RTD 5 Manchester
07.12.91 Shamus Casey W PTS 8 Manchester
10.03.92 Mike Phillips W RSC 4 Bury
25.04.92 Mark Jay W RSC 7 Manchester
28.11.92 Shaun Cummins L PTS 12 Manchester
          (Vacant WBA Penta-Continental L.
          Middleweight Title)
25.07.93 Russell Washer W PTS 6 Oldham
18.12.93 Kevin Sheeran W RSC 3 Manchester
10.09.94 Robert McCracken L PTS 12
          Birmingham
          (British L. Middleweight Title
          Challenge)
10.06.95 Tony Enna W RSC 6 Manchester
02.09.95 Bahri Ahmeti L RSC 4 Wembley
          (Vacant IBF Inter-Continental
          L. Middleweight Title)
24.11.95 Bahri Ahmeti W PTS 12 Manchester
          (IBF Inter-Continental L. Middleweight
          Title Challenge)
06.07.96 Chris Pyatt W PTS 12 Manchester
          (IBF Inter-Continental L. Middleweight
          Title Defence. Commonwealth
          L. Middleweight Title Challenge)
03.05.97 Ronald Wright L RSC 6 Manchester
          (WBO L. Middleweight Title
          Challenge)

Career: 35 contests, won 19, drew 2, lost 14.

Tony Foster

Hull. *Born* Hull, 9 July, 1964
L. Welterweight. Former Central Area
Lightweight Champion. Ht. 5'7"
Manager S. Pollard

04.09.87 Paul Kennedy L PTS 6 Gateshead
17.09.87 Ian Hosten L PTS 6 Gravesend
28.09.87 Steve Winstanley L PTS 6 Bradford
06.10.87 Roy Doyle L PTS 6 Manchester
03.11.87 Darren Darby L PTS 6 Cottingham
25.11.87 Kevin McCoy W RSC 4 Cottingham
02.12.87 Alan Roberts W RSC 5 Piccadilly
11.12.87 Mitchell King DREW 8 Coalville
11.01.88 Paul Chedgzoy W PTS 6 Manchester
25.01.88 Johnny Walker L PTS 6 Glasgow
01.02.88 Sean Hogg W PTS 6 Manchester
11.02.88 Lee Amass L RSC 6 Gravesend
28.03.88 Darryl Pettit W PTS 6 Bradford
22.04.88 Paul Charters L PTS 6 Gateshead
09.05.88 Gary Maxwell L PTS 6 Nottingham
17.05.88 Warren Slaney W PTS 6 Leicester
23.05.88 Harry Escott W RSC 6 Bradford
26.09.88 Peter Bradley L PTS 8 Piccadilly
17.10.88 John Townsley L PTS 8 Glasgow
15.11.88 Steve Pollard W RSC 3 Hull
12.12.88 Mark Kelly W PTS 6 Nottingham
08.02.89 Paul Gadney W PTS 6 Kensington
03.04.89 Jari Gronroos W PTS 4 Helsinki,
          Finland
15.04.89 Paul Moylett W PTS 6 Salisbury
27.06.89 Ian Honeywood L PTS 6 Kensington
10.10.89 Steve Pollard W RSC 3 Hull
16.11.89 Sugar Gibiliru W PTS 8 Manchester
30.11.89 Joey Jacobs L CO 4 Oldham
30.01.90 Sugar Gibiliru W PTS 10 Manchester
          (Vacant Central Area Lightweight
          Title)
21.04.90 Marvin P. Gray DREW 6 Sunderland
22.05.90 Marvin P. Gray L PTS 6 Stockton
15.06.90 Marcel Herbert L RSC 4 Telford
15.02.91 Jimmy Bredahl L PTS 6 Randers,
          Denmark
05.03.91 Floyd Havard L PTS 8 Millwall

15.04.91 Dave Anderson L PTS 8 Glasgow
12.05.91 Alain Simoes W PTS 8 Voiron, France
11.09.91 Billy Schwer L PTS 8 Hammersmith
21.11.91 Giovanni Parisi L RSC 6 Perugia, Italy
31.01.92 Angel Mona L PTS 8 Esch,
          Luxembourg
30.03.92 Ian Honeywood L RSC 4 Eltham
13.06.92 Pierre Lorcy L PTS 8 Levallois Perret,
          France
16.10.92 Tony Doyle W PTS 8 Hull
31.10.92 Dingaan Thobela L PTS 8 Earls Court
14.01.93 Allan Hall L PTS 6 Mayfair
27.02.93 Steve Foran DREW 6 Ellesmere Port
09.07.93 Giorgio Campanella L PTS 8
          Barisardo, Italy
12.11.93 Micky Hall W PTS 8 Hull
10.02.94 Kid McAuley W RTD 4 Hull
18.02.94 Racheed Lawal L PTS 8 Randers,
          Denmark
21.04.94 Charles Shepherd W PTS 10 Hull
          (Vacant Central Area Lightweight
          Title)
24.11.94 Norman Dhalie W RTD 7 Hull
07.12.94 Shea Neary L RSC 2 Stoke
25.02.95 Cham Joof L PTS 8 Millwall
11.05.95 Spencer McCracken L PTS 6 Dudley
30.06.95 Andy Holligan L CO 2 Liverpool
22.09.95 Jimmy Phelan L PTS 10 Hull
          (Central Area Lightweight Title
          Defence)
29.09.95 Peter Richardson L RSC 1 Bethnal
          Green
02.03.96 Alan Temple L PTS 6 Newcastle
13.03.96 Yifru Retta L RSC 3 Wembley
06.11.96 Wayne Windle L PTS 4 Hull
28.11.96 Sean Morrison DREW 6 Hull

Career: 61 contests, won 20, drew 4, lost 37.

Simon Frailing

Hayes. *Born* London, 13 June, 1966
Lightweight. Ht. 5'7"
Manager D. Currivan

29.04.93 Bruce Ruegg DREW 6 Hayes
15.06.93 Bruce Ruegg L PTS 6 Hemel
          Hempstead
14.08.93 Mike Anthony Brown L RSC 4
          Hammersmith
30.09.93 Norman Dhalie L PTS 6 Hayes
09.12.93 Andrew Reed W PTS 6 Watford
25.01.94 Craig Kelley L PTS 4 Piccadilly
10.03.94 Marco Fattore DREW 6 Watford
17.05.94 T. J. Smith L RSC 1 Kettering
03.03.95 Jason Lepre W PTS 6 Bracknell
25.05.95 Lewis Reynolds L CO 1 Reading
06.02.96 David Kehoe L CO 1 Basildon
01.10.96 Robbie Sivyer L PTS 6 Birmingham
24.10.96 Charlie Rumbol W PTS 6 Wembley
28.01.97 Danny Lutaaya W PTS 6 Piccadilly
25.02.97 Martin Renaghan L RSC 3 Sheffield
22.05.97 Danny Lutaaya L RSC 2 Southwark

Career: 16 contests, won 4, drew 2, lost 10.

Dean Francis

Basingstoke. *Born* Basingstoke, 23 January,
1974
WBO Inter-Continental S. Middleweight
Champion. Ht. 5'10½"
Manager C. Sanigar

28.05.94 Darren Littlewood W PTS 4
          Queensway
17.06.94 Martin Jolley W PTS 6 Plymouth

21.07.94 Horace Fleary W RSC 4 Tooting
02.09.94 Steve Osborne W RTD 4 Spitalfields
27.10.94 Tony Booth W CO 1 Bayswater
22.11.94 Darron Griffiths W RTD 1 Bristol
30.03.95 Paul Murray W RSC 2 Bethnal Green
25.05.95 Hunter Clay W RSC 8 Reading
16.06.95 Paul Murray W RTD 3 Southwark
20.10.95 Zafarou Ballogou L RSC 10 Ipswich
          (WBC International S. Middleweight
          Title Challenge)
16.12.95 Kid Milo W RSC 3 Cardiff
13.02.96 Mike Bonislawski W RSC 2 Bethnal
          Green
26.04.96 Neil Simpson W RSC 3 Cardiff
08.06.96 John Marceta W RSC 8 Newcastle
14.09.96 Larry Kenny W RSC 3 Sheffield
19.10.96 Rolando Torres W RSC 4 Bristol
          (Vacant WBO Inter-Continental
          S. Middleweight Title)
14.03.97 Cornelius Carr W RSC 7 Reading
          (WBO Inter-Continental
          S. Middleweight Title Defence)
15.05.97 Kit Munro W RSC 2 Reading
          (WBO Inter-Continental
          S. Middleweight Title Defence)

Career: 18 contests, won 17, lost 1.

Les Frost

Doncaster. *Born* Doncaster, 27 October,
1972
L. Welterweight. Ht. 5'10½"
Manager T. Petersen

06.12.96 Franny Hogg L PTS 6 Leeds
22.12.96 Frank O'Connor L PTS 6 Glasgow
12.02.97 Scott McQueen L RSC 3 Glasgow
17.03.97 John Paul Temple L CO 4 Mayfair
01.05.97 Ivan Walker L CO 1 Newcastle

Career: 5 contests, lost 5.

Peter Gabbitus

Doncaster. *Born* Cantley, 23 January, 1963
Lightweight. Ht. 5'5¼"
Manager J. Rushton

20.05.80 Iggy Jano W PTS 4 Southend
11.06.80 George Bailey W PTS 4 Morecambe
30.07.80 Bryn Jones W PTS 4 Doncaster
22.10.80 Steve Sims L PTS 4 Doncaster
25.11.80 Jim Harvey W PTS 4 Doncaster
19.01.81 Jim Harvey W PTS 4 Bradford
02.03.81 Paul Huggins L RSC 1 Brighton
10.06.81 Selvin Bell L PTS 6 Brodsworth
17.05.82 Lou Buttice W RSC 2 Windsor
28.06.82 Ian Murray W PTS 6 Bradford
07.09.82 Joey Joynson L RSC 2 Hornsey
19.01.83 Alan Tombs W RSC 2 Stoke
25.02.83 Paul Keers W RSC 4 Doncaster
10.10.83 Steve Topliss W PTS 8 Birmingham
20.03.85 Alec Irvine W PTS 8 Evesham
09.09.88 Steve Winstanley W PTS 6 Doncaster
29.09.88 Phil Lashley W CO 2 Stafford
14.11.88 Jimmy Vincent W PTS 6 Stratford on
          Avon
22.02.89 Craig Windsor W RTD 2 Doncaster
19.04.89 Mike Close W CO 3 Doncaster
25.10.89 Dave George W RSC 6 Doncaster
07.03.90 Sugar Gibiliru L RTD 6 Doncaster
          (Vacant Central Area S. Featherweight
          Title)
24.04.91 Paul Harvey L RSC 5 Preston
12.09.96 Vic Broomhead L RSC 3 Doncaster

Dean Francis (left) trades punches with Cornelius Carr at Reading last March   Les Clark

11.02.97   Jamie Morris W RSC 1
Wolverhampton
12.03.97   Mark Allen W PTS 6 Stoke
20.03.97   Chris Price W PTS 6 Doncaster
01.04.97   Bruno Wartelle L RTD 3 Marseille,
France
Career: 28 contests, won 20, lost 8.

Michael Gale

Leeds. *Born* Cardiff, 28 October, 1967
Central Area L. Heavyweight Champion.
Ht. 5'11"
Manager T. Callighan/T. Gilmour

21.09.89   Dave Lawrence W RTD 4 Harrogate
13.11.89   Coco Collins W CO 1 Manchester
05.12.89   Randy B. Powell W RSC 1 Dewsbury
11.01.90   Cliff Curtis W RSC 2 Dewsbury
24.01.90   Andy Marlow W RSC 2 Sunderland
03.03.90   Peter Vosper W RSC 2 Wembley
11.04.90   Teo Arvizu W PTS 6 Dewsbury
18.10.90   Mick Queally W RSC 5 Dewsbury
15.11.90   Steve Osborne W PTS 6 Oldham
14.03.91   Carlos Christie W PTS 8 Middleton
21.03.91   David Haycock W RSC 2 Dewsbury
09.05.91   Steve Osborne W RSC 2 Leeds
13.06.91   Graham Burton W CO 4 Hull
27.06.91   Mark Bowen W PTS 8 Leeds
30.10.91   Denys Cronin DREW 8 Leeds
23.01.92   John Kaighin W PTS 8 York
08.04.92   Tony Booth W PTS 8 Leeds
29.10.92   Bobbi Joe Edwards W PTS 10 Leeds
*(Vacant Central Area L. Heavyweight
Title)*

07.04.93   Brent Kosolofski L RSC 9 Leeds
*(Vacant Commonwealth L.
Heavyweight Title)*
01.07.93   Tony Booth W PTS 8 York
07.10.93   John Kaighin W PTS 8 York
26.10.94   Bobbi Joe Edwards W PTS 8 Leeds
22.11.95   Simon McDougall W PTS 10 Sheffield
*(Central Area L. Heavyweight Title
Defence)*
10.11.96   Chris Woollas DREW 6 Glasgow
03.02.97   Mark Prince L RSC 6 Sunderland
(Elim. British L. Heavyweight Title)
Career: 25 contests, won 21, drew 2, lost 2.

(Patrick) P. J. Gallagher

Wood Green. *Born* Manchester, 14
February, 1973
Former Undefeated British & WBC
International S. Featherweight Champion.
Former Undefeated Southern Area S.
Featherweight Champion. Ht. 5'7"
Manager F. Maloney

15.09.93   John T. Kelly W RSC 2 Bethnal Green
13.10.93   Mike Morrison W PTS 4 Bethnal
Green
01.12.93   Mark Antony W PTS 4 Bethnal Green
09.02.94   Simon Hamblett W RSC 1 Bethnal
Green
29.03.94   Brian Coleman W PTS 6 Bethnal
Green
15.06.94   Mark O'Callaghan W RSC 4
Southwark

29.09.94   Anthony Campbell W PTS 6 Bethnal
Green
12.11.94   Karl Taylor W PTS 6 Dublin
23.01.95   David Thompson W RSC 1 Bethnal
Green
30.03.95   Phil Found W PTS 6 Bethnal Green
25.05.95   Marco Fattore W RSC 5 Reading
02.07.95   Chris Clarkson W RSC 3 Dublin
29.09.95   Marc Smith W RSC 3 Bethnal Green
08.11.95   Justin Murphy W RSC 6 Bethnal Green
*(Vacant Southern Area
S. Featherweight Title & Elim. British
S. Featherweight Title)*
19.01.96   Rakhim Mingaleev W PTS 12
Bracknell
*(Vacant WBC International
S. Featherweight Title)*
22.04.96   Dave McHale W RSC 10 Crystal
Palace
(Vacant British S. Featherweight Title)
29.06.96   Charles Shepherd W PTS 12 Erith
*(British S. Featherweight Title
Defence)*
18.02.97   Bamana Dibateza L PTS 8 Cheshunt
Career: 18 contests, won 17, lost 1.

Brian Galloway

Sheffield. *Born* West Germany, 4 June,
1964
S. Middleweight. Ht. 6'0"
Manager Self

02.11.95   Ernie Loveridge W PTS 6 Mayfair
08.12.95   Shaun Hendry L RSC 3 Leeds

95

19.09.96 Lee Whitehead L PTS 4 Manchester
30.11.96 Grant Briggs L PTS 4 Tylorstown
03.02.97 Carlton Williams W PTS 6 Leicester
14.03.97 Sven Hamer L CO 1 Reading
Career: 6 contests, won 2, lost 4.

Des Gargano (Southern)

Manchester. *Born* Brighton, 20 December, 1960
S. Bantamweight. Ht. 5'5"
Manager Self

25.01.85 Sugar Gibiliru L PTS 4 Liverpool
18.03.85 Sugar Gibiliru L PTS 6 Liverpool
24.04.85 Glen McLaggon L PTS 6 Stoke
03.06.85 Anthony Wakefield DREW 6 Manchester
17.06.85 Anthony Wakefield W PTS 6 Manchester
03.10.85 Anthony Brown L PTS 6 Liverpool
13.10.85 Gary Maxwell L PTS 6 Sheffield
09.12.85 Robert Newbiggin W PTS 6 Nottingham
16.12.85 Gypsy Johnny W PTS 6 Bradford
24.02.86 Kevin Taylor W PTS 6 Bradford
01.04.86 Carl Cleasby L PTS 6 Leeds
07.04.86 Gerry McBride W PTS 6 Manchester
29.04.86 Pat Clinton L PTS 6 Manchester
23.09.86 David Ingram L PTS 6 Batley
24.11.86 Andrew Steadman L PTS 6 Leicester
03.12.86 Sean Murphy L PTS 6 Muswell Hill
15.12.86 Tony Heath L PTS 8 Loughborough
30.01.87 Nigel Crook L PTS 6 Kirkby
16.02.87 Pat Clinton L PTS 6 Glasgow
13.04.87 Jimmy Lee W PTS 6 Manchester
26.05.87 John Green L PTS 6 Oldham
19.10.87 John Green L PTS 6 Manchester
28.10.87 Paul Thornton W RSC 6 Stoke
09.11.87 Tony Heath L PTS 6 Leicester
26.01.88 Graham O'Malley L PTS 4 Hartlepool
23.03.88 Lambsy Kayani L PTS 6 Sheffield
29.03.88 Graham O'Malley L PTS 8 Marton
25.04.88 Ronnie Stephenson W PTS 8 Bradford
06.06.88 Darryl Pettit W PTS 6 Manchester
13.06.88 Joe Mullen L PTS 6 Glasgow
05.09.88 Wull Strike DREW 6 Glasgow
22.09.88 John Davison L PTS 8 Newcastle
29.09.88 John Davison L PTS 8 Sunderland
10.10.88 Shane Silvester L PTS 8 Edgbaston
18.10.88 Peter English L PTS 4 Oldham
28.10.88 Eyub Can L PTS 6 Copenhagen, Denmark
21.11.88 Ronnie Stephenson W PTS 6 Leicester
29.11.88 Chris Clarkson W PTS 6 Manchester
07.12.88 Renny Edwards L PTS 6 Aberavon
16.12.88 Jimmy Clark L PTS 6 Brentwood
14.02.89 Nigel Crook L PTS 10 Manchester
17.03.89 Jimmy Bredahl L PTS 6 Braedstrup, Denmark
17.04.89 Mark Priestley W PTS 8 Middleton
10.05.89 Mark Goult L PTS 8 Solihull
17.05.89 Mark Geraghty L PTS 8 Glasgow
12.06.89 Neil Parry W PTS 6 Manchester
11.07.89 Chris Clarkson L PTS 6 Batley
04.09.89 Ronnie Stephenson W PTS 6 Hull
11.09.89 Paul Dever W RSC 1 Manchester
20.09.89 Miguel Matthews W PTS 6 Stoke
05.10.89 Wayne Windle W PTS 6 Middleton
16.10.89 Wayne Windle L PTS 6 Manchester
31.10.89 Dave McNally L PTS 6 Manchester
10.11.89 Kruga Hydes L PTS 6 Liverpool
20.11.89 Dave Buxton L PTS 6 Leicester

30.11.89 Noel Carroll L PTS 6 Oldham
11.12.89 Joe Kelly L PTS 6 Bayswater
14.02.90 Danny Porter L PTS 6 Brentwood
06.03.90 Bradley Stone L PTS 6 Bethnal Green
17.03.90 John Lowey L RSC 6 Belfast
24.04.90 Jamie Morris W PTS 4 Stoke
09.05.90 Terry Collins L PTS 6 Kensington
16.05.90 Tony Doyle W PTS 6 Hull
11.06.90 Steve Armstrong W PTS 6 Manchester
05.09.90 John George L PTS 6 Stoke
01.10.90 Tony Smith W PTS 6 Cleethorpes
09.10.90 Brian Robb L PTS 6 Wolverhampton
22.10.90 John George L PTS 6 Cleethorpes
26.11.90 Tony Smith W PTS 8 Bury
03.12.90 Tony Smith W PTS 6 Cleethorpes
11.12.90 Stewart Fishermac W PTS 8 Evesham
16.01.91 Tony Smith W PTS 6 Stoke
06.02.91 Tim Driscoll L PTS 6 Bethnal Green
28.02.91 Carl Roberts W PTS 6 Bury
07.05.91 James Drummond L PTS 8 Glasgow
16.05.91 Jimmy Owens L RSC 2 Liverpool
19.08.91 Petteri Rissanen L PTS 4 Helsinki, Finland
02.10.91 Eric George L PTS 6 Solihull
24.10.91 Edward Cook L RSC 5 Glasgow
29.11.91 Harald Geier L DIS 8 Frohsdorf, Austria
31.01.92 Edward Cook L PTS 6 Glasgow
24.02.92 Colin Lynch L PTS 6 Coventry
04.03.92 Neil Armstrong L PTS 6 Glasgow
11.03.92 Dennis Oakes L PTS 6 Stoke
27.04.92 David Ramsden L PTS 6 Bradford
01.06.92 Mark Hargreaves L PTS 6 Manchester
08.06.92 David Ramsden L PTS 6 Bradford
07.10.92 Prince Naseem Hamed L RSC 4 Sunderland
20.11.92 Paul Lloyd L PTS 4 Liverpool
26.02.93 Alex Docherty W RSC 4 Irvine
04.04.93 Rowan Williams L PTS 4 Brockley
26.04.93 Wilson Docherty L PTS 6 Glasgow
01.06.93 Neil Parry W PTS 6 Manchester
09.09.93 James Murray L PTS 6 Glasgow
13.11.93 Richie Wenton L PTS 8 Cullompton
13.12.93 Tony Falcone L PTS 4 Bristol
17.02.94 Daryl McKenzie DREW 6 Bury
25.02.94 Peter Culshaw L PTS 6 Chester
15.03.94 Gary Marston L PTS 8 Stoke
02.06.94 Marty Chestnut W PTS 6 Middleton
20.10.94 Paul Quarmby W PTS 6 Middleton
05.12.94 Chip O'Neill L PTS 6 Houghton le Spring
23.01.95 Patrick Mullings L PTS 4 Bethnal Green
17.02.95 Spencer Oliver L PTS 4 Cumbernauld
03.03.95 Mark Bowers L RTD 2 Bracknell
18.05.95 Paul Quarmby W PTS 6 Middleton
04.06.95 Patrick Mullings L PTS 6 Bethnal Green
16.06.95 Paul Ingle L RSC 2 Southwark
22.11.95 Abdul Mannon W PTS 6 Mayfair
29.11.95 Brian Gentry L PTS 4 Southwark
08.12.95 Gary Thornhill L RTD 2 Liverpool
(Vacant Central Area S. Featherweight Title)
05.02.96 Matt Brown L RSC 4 Bexleyheath
30.09.96 Lyndon Kershaw L PTS 6 Manchester
06.11.96 Ronnie McPhee L RTD 5 Glasgow
04.12.96 Carl Greaves L PTS 6 Stoke
09.12.96 Esham Pickering L RTD 2 Chesterfield
28.02.97 Louis Veitch L PTS 6 Kilmarnock
Career: 117 contests, won 32, drew 3, lost 82.

(Terrance) Terry Gaskin

Doncaster. *Born* Doncaster, 20 October, 1974
Bantamweight. Ht. 5'4"
Manager H. Hayes

28.03.94 Keith Knox L PTS 6 Musselburgh
09.05.94 Tiger Singh L RSC 2 Bradford
26.09.94 Ian Baillie W RSC 3 Bradford
29.10.94 Neil Parry L PTS 6 Cannock
28.11.94 Tiger Singh L PTS 6 Manchester
08.12.94 Ian Baillie W RTD 3 Hull
11.03.95 Neil Parry DREW 6 Barnsley
22.03.95 Neil Parry L PTS 8 Stoke
19.05.95 Shaun Hall L RSC 3 Leeds
21.09.95 Darren Noble DREW 6 Sheffield
20.10.95 Steve Williams L PTS 6 Mansfield
12.05.97 Paul Squire DREW 6 Leicester
Career: 12 contests, won 2, drew 3, lost 7.

Brian Gentry

Morden. *Born* Balham, 2 January, 1975
S. Featherweight. Ht. 5'6"
Manager Self

29.11.95 Des Gargano W PTS 4 Southwark
20.09.96 Stevie Bolt W RSC 3 Tooting
07.11.96 Wayne Jones L PTS 6 Battersea
15.02.97 David Jeffrey W PTS 6 Tooting
Career: 4 contests, won 3, lost 1.

Brian Gentry　　　　　　　　Les Clark

Michael Gibbons

Middlesbrough. *Born* Middlesbrough, 24 December, 1970
Featherweight. Ht. 5'4"
Manager T. Callighan

04.06.96 Martin Evans W RSC 2 York
04.10.96 Lee Armstrong W RSC 3 Wakefield
03.12.96 Neil Parry W PTS 6 Yarm
04.03.97 Garry Burrell W PTS 6 Yarm
14.04.97 John Matthews L PTS 6 Bradford
Career: 5 contests, won 4, lost 1.

Enzo Giordano

Islington. *Born* London, 15 April, 1971
Middleweight. Ht. 5'11"
Manager Self

29.09.95	John Janes W RSC 4 Bloomsbury	
09.07.96	Andy Gray DREW 6 Bethnal Green	
28.09.96	Ernie Loveridge W PTS 6 Barking	
11.01.97	Jimmy Steel W PTS 4 Bethnal Green	
04.03.97	Andy Ewen W RSC 3 Southwark	
08.04.97	Johnny Hooks W PTS 4 Bethnal Green	

Career: 6 contests, won 5, drew 1.

Shaun Gledhill

Oldham. *Born* Oldham, 22 April, 1976
L. Welterweight. Ht. 5'8"
Manager N. Basso

12.06.95	Tom Welsh L RSC 4 Manchester
06.09.95	Chris Price W PTS 6 Stoke
29.10.95	Alan Bosworth L PTS 6 Shaw
20.11.95	Dean Nicholas L RSC 4 Glasgow
26.02.96	Mark Allen W RSC 3 Manchester
30.09.96	Phil Molyneux DREW 6 Manchester
02.12.96	Christian Brady L RTD 3 Birmingham
29.04.97	Chris Price W PTS 6 Manchester

Career: 8 contests, won 3, drew 1, lost 4.

(Robert) Zak Goldman

Doncaster. *Born* Ainwick, 19 July, 1964
Cruiserweight. Ht. 6'2"
Manager J. Rushton

07.12.92	Paul Hanlon L PTS 6 Birmingham
15.12.92	Kenley Price L RTD 2 Liverpool
09.02.93	Lee Archer L CO 3 Wolverhampton
12.05.93	Steve Loftus L PTS 6 Stoke
08.03.94	Justin Clements L RSC 3 Edgbaston
09.10.96	Kevin Burton L PTS 6 Stoke
28.10.96	Michael Pinnock DREW 6 Leicester

11.01.97	Israel Ajose L CO 1 Bethnal Green

Career: 8 contests, drew 1, lost 7.

Michael Gomez (Armstrong)

Manchester. *Born* Dublin, 21 June, 1977
Featherweight. Ht. 5'5"
Manager F. Warren

10.06.95	Danny Ruegg W PTS 6 Manchester
15.09.95	Greg Upton L PTS 4 Mansfield
24.11.95	Danny Ruegg L PTS 4 Manchester
19.09.96	Martin Evans W RSC 1 Manchester
09.11.96	David Morris W PTS 4 Manchester
22.03.97	John Farrell W RSC 2 Wythenshawe
03.05.97	Chris Williams L PTS 4 Manchester

Career: 7 contests, won 4, lost 3.

Steve Goodwin

Derby. *Born* Derby, 17 February, 1966
Midlands Area L. Middleweight Champion.
Ht. 5'11"
Manager Self

13.04.92	John Duckworth W PTS 6 Manchester
29.04.92	John Corcoran W PTS 8 Stoke
03.09.92	Steve McNess L PTS 6 Dunstable
29.09.92	Mark Dawson W RSC 1 Stoke
19.10.92	John Bosco L RSC 2 Mayfair
07.12.92	Mark Dawson L PTS 6 Mayfair
12.02.93	Said Bennajem L PTS 6 Aubervilliers, France
12.05.93	Mark Dawson W PTS 10 Stoke *(Vacant Midlands Area L. Middleweight Title)*
28.07.93	Gary Stretch L PTS 6 Brixton
07.09.93	Wally Swift Jnr W RSC 7 Stoke *(Midlands Area L. Middleweight Title Defence)*
02.11.93	Lloyd Honeyghan L RSC 6 Southwark
25.05.94	Wally Swift Jnr L PTS 8 Stoke

10.02.95	Neville Brown L RSC 3 Birmingham
06.05.95	Robin Reid L CO 1 Shepton Mallet
27.09.95	Nicky Thurbin L PTS 8 Bethnal Green
25.10.95	Ernie Loveridge W PTS 4 Stoke
10.11.95	Brendan Ryan L RSC 4 Derby
09.12.95	Kevin Lueshing L RTD 2 Bethnal Green
19.01.96	Geoff McCreesh W DIS 5 Bracknell
13.03.96	Howard Eastman L RSC 5 Wembley
07.02.97	Oliver Duprez L PTS 8 Amiens, France

Career: 21 contests, won 7, lost 14.

Lee Gordon (Corden)

Nottingham. *Born* Nottingham, 6 April, 1978
S. Middleweight. Ht. 6'0¾"
Manager W. Wigley

08.06.97	Mike Whittaker L RSC 1 Shaw

Career: 1 contest, lost 1.

Mike Gormley

Manchester. *Born* Salford, 2 November, 1965
S. Middleweight. Ht. 6'0"
Manager S. Foster

25.04.97	Robert Peel W PTS 6 Mere

Career: 1 contest, won 1.

Herol Graham

Sheffield. *Born* Nottingham, 13 September, 1959
S. Middleweight. Former British & European Middleweight Champion. Former Undefeated British, Commonwealth & European L. Middleweight Champion. Ht. 5'11"
Manager Self

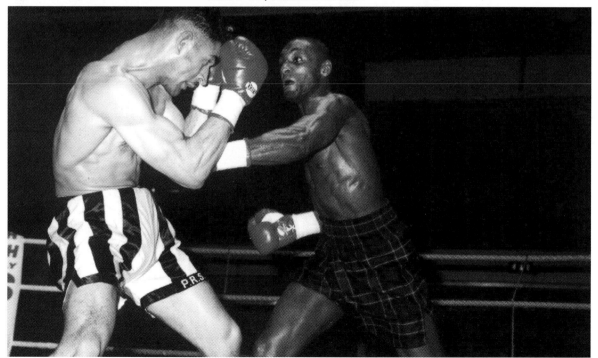

Herol Graham (right) en route to an eight-round points win over Craig Joseph

Les Clark

97

28.11.78 Vivian Waite W PTS 6 Sheffield
04.12.78 Curtis Marsh W RTD 1 Southend
22.01.79 Jimmy Roberts W RSC 2 Bradford
12.02.79 Dave Southwell W PTS 8 Reading
28.02.79 Dave Southwell W PTS 8 Burslem
27.03.79 George Walker W PTS 8 Southend
27.04.79 Mac Nicholson W PTS 8 Newcastle
16.05.79 Gordon George W PTS 8 Sheffield
26.09.79 Lloyd James W PTS 8 Sheffield
27.10.79 Billy Ahearne W RSC 3 Barnsley
27.11.79 Errol McKenzie W PTS 8 Sheffield
12.02.80 Glen McEwan W PTS 8 Sheffield
22.04.80 George Danahar W PTS 8 Sheffield
09.09.80 Joey Mack W PTS 8 Sheffield
30.10.80 Larry Mayes W RSC 4 Liverpool
22.01.81 Lancelot Innes W PTS 10 Liverpool
24.03.81 Pat Thomas W PTS 15 Sheffield
    (British L. Middleweight Title
    Challenge)
17.06.81 Prince Rodney W RSC 1 Sheffield
25.11.81 Kenny Bristol W PTS 15 Sheffield
    (Commonwealth L. Middleweight Title
    Challenge)
24.02.82 Chris Christian W RSC 9 Sheffield
    (British & Commonwealth
    L. Middleweight Title Defence)
22.04.82 Fred Coranson W PTS 10 Liverpool
30.09.82 Hunter Clay W PTS 15 Lagos, Nigeria
    (Commonwealth L. Middleweight Title
    Defence)
15.03.83 Tony Nelson W RTD 5 Wembley
23.05.83 Clemente Tshinza W CO 2 Sheffield
    (Vacant European L. Middleweight
    Title)
11.10.83 Carlos Betancourt W CO 1 Kensington
09.12.83 Germain le Maitre W RSC 8 St
    Nazaire, France
    (European L. Middleweight Title
    Defence)
22.07.84 Lindell Holmes W RSC 5 Sheffield
25.09.84 Irwin Hines W CO 2 Wembley
16.10.84 Jose Seys W RSC 6 Kensington
26.11.84 Liam Coleman W RSC 3 Sheffield
06.03.85 Jose Rosemain W CO 5 Kensington
24.04.85 Jimmy Price W CO 1 Shoreditch
    (Vacant British Middleweight Title)
16.10.85 Roberto Ruiz W RSC 2 Kensington
03.12.85 Sanderline Williams W PTS 10 Belfast
05.02.86 Ayub Kalule W RSC 10 Sheffield
    (European Middleweight Title
    Challenge)
23.06.86 Ernie Rabotte W RSC 1 Las Vegas,
    USA
04.11.86 Mark Kaylor W RTD 8 Wembley
    (European Middleweight Title Defence)
17.01.87 Charlie Boston W RTD 7 Belfast
26.05.87 Sumbu Kalambay L PTS 12 Wembley
    (European Middleweight Title Defence)
05.12.87 Ricky Stackhouse W RSC 8 Doncaster
08.06.88 James Cook W RSC 5 Sheffield
    (Vacant British Middleweight Title)
23.11.88 Johnny Melfah W RSC 5 Bethnal
    Green
    (British Middleweight Title Defence)
10.05.89 Mike McCallum L PTS 12 Kensington
    (Vacant WBA Middleweight Title)
25.10.89 Rod Douglas W RSC 9 Wembley
    (British Middleweight Title Defence)
11.04.90 Ismael Negron W CO 3 Dewsbury
24.11.90 Julian Jackson L CO 4 Benalmadena,
    Spain
    (Vacant WBC Middleweight Title)
10.12.91 John Ashton W RSC 6 Sheffield
    (British Middleweight Title Defence)

12.03.92 Sumbu Kalambay L PTS 12 Pesaro,
    Italy
    (European Middleweight Title
    Challenge)
23.09.92 Frank Grant L RSC 9 Leeds
    (British Middleweight Title Defence)
26.11.96 Terry Ford W PTS 8 Sheffield
04.03.97 Craig Joseph W PTS 8 Southwark
Career: 51 contests, won 46, lost 5.

Allan Gray

Putney. *Born* Roehampton, 4 August, 1971
Welterweight. Ht. 5'9"
Manager D. Mancini/M. Duff

19.05.95 Darren Covill W PTS 6 Southwark
23.06.95 Wayne Jones W PTS 6 Bethnal Green
27.09.95 Brian Coleman W PTS 6 Bethnal
    Green
28.10.95 John O. Johnson W PTS 6 Kensington
29.11.95 Justin Simmons L PTS 6 Bethnal
    Green
08.12.95 Mike Watson W PTS 8 Bethnal Green
15.03.96 Mike Watson DREW 6 Dunstable
29.04.96 Mike Watson W PTS 6 Mayfair
03.07.96 John Harrison W PTS 6 Wembley
24.10.96 Costas Katsantonis W PTS 6 Mayfair
29.01.97 Gary Hiscox W PTS 6 Bethnal Green
19.02.97 Costas Katsantonis W PTS 6 Acton
30.04.97 Howard Clarke L PTS 8 Acton
Career: 13 contests, won 10, drew 1, lost 2.

Allan Gray   Les Clark

Andy Gray

Great Yarmouth. *Born* Great Yarmouth, 19
February, 1966
S. Middleweight. Ht. 5'10"
Manager T. Toole

15.03.96 Robert Harper W DIS 6 Dunstable
25.04.96 Jimmy Steel L PTS 6 Mayfair
09.07.96 Enzo Giordano DREW 6 Bethnal
    Green
15.11.96 Peter H. Madsen L PTS 4 Nestved,
    Denmark

01.12.96 Johnny Whiteside L PTS 6 Shaw
08.03.97 Jason Ratcliff L PTS 4 Brentwood
08.04.97 Panayiotis Panayiotiou L PTS 6
    Bethnal Green
28.06.97 Zoltan Sarossy L RTD 2 Norwich
Career: 8 contests, won 1, drew 1, lost 6.

Andy Gray   Les Clark

Carl Greaves

Newark. *Born* Nottingham, 12 June, 1976
S. Bantamweight. Ht. 5'7"
Manager J. Ashton

22.03.96 Paul Hamilton W PTS 6 Mansfield
30.05.96 Kevin Sheil W PTS 6 Lincoln
02.10.96 Robert Grubb W PTS 8 Stoke
01.11.96 Benny Jones W PTS 6 Mansfield
26.11.96 Danny Ruegg W RTD 4 Sheffield
04.12.96 Des Gargano W PTS 6 Stoke
20.02.97 Lee Armstrong L RSC 4 Mansfield
10.04.97 Kevin Sheil W PTS 6 Sheffield
08.05.97 Benny Jones L RSC 4 Mansfield
Career: 9 contests, won 7, lost 2.

Andy Green

Middlesbrough. *Born* Middlesbrough, 31
December, 1970
Lightweight. Ht. 5'8"
Manager F. Warren

22.02.96 Wayne Pardoe W RSC 3 Walsall
19.03.96 Ram Singh W PTS 6 Leeds
27.03.96 Neil Smith L RSC 3 Whitwick
26.04.96 Scott Dixon L RSC 5 Glasgow
03.12.96 Fred Reeve W CO 2 Yarm
04.03.97 Rudy Valentino W PTS 6 Yarm
Career: 6 contests, won 4, lost 2.

John Green

Middlesbrough. *Born* Middlesbrough, 23
August, 1969
Welterweight. Ht. 5'8"
Manager G. Robinson

04.12.96 Donovan Davey W PTS 6 Hartlepool
03.02.97 Hughie Davey W PTS 4 Sunderland
04.03.97 Junior Witter L PTS 6 Yarm
13.06.97 Ali Khattab L RTD 3 Slagelse, Denmark

Career: 4 contests, won 2, lost 2.

Sean Green
Doncaster. *Born* Doncaster, 2 November, 1977
Bantamweight. Ht. 5'6"
Manager J. Rushton

17.12.96 Willie Smith W PTS 6 Doncaster
17.02.97 Jason Whitaker W PTS 6 Bradford
24.02.97 Neil Armstrong L PTS 6 Glasgow
08.05.97 Ross Cassidy DREW 6 Mansfield

Career: 4 contests, won 2, drew 1, lost 1.

Dennis Griffin
Stepney. *Born* Stepney, 9 June, 1965
Welterweight. Ht. 5'9"
Manager Self

31.08.93 Trevor Royal W RSC 1 Croydon
09.12.93 Keith Marner L PTS 6 Watford
19.12.93 Dave Madden W RSC 1 Northampton
23.02.94 Adrian Chase L PTS 6 Watford
19.11.94 Danny Quacoe L RSC 5 Heathrow
13.07.96 James Hare L RSC 4 Bethnal Green
04.04.97 Pat Larner L PTS 6 Brighton
16.04.97 Dave Brazil W RSC 1 Bethnal Green
24.04.97 Shaun Armstrong L PTS 6 Mayfair

Career: 9 contests, won 3, lost 6.

Paul Griffin
Dublin. *Born* Dublin, 3 June, 1971
Featherweight. Ht. 5'7"
Manager F. Warren

04.03.95 Chris Jickells W RSC 5 Livingston
10.06.95 Andrew Reed W RSC 5 Manchester
09.09.95 G. G. Goddard W PTS 4 Cork
25.11.95 Michael Hermon W PTS 4 Dublin
13.01.96 Jason Thomas W RSC 2 Manchester
09.03.96 Pete Buckley W PTS 4 Millstreet
26.04.96 Carl Allen W RSC 3 Cardiff
25.06.96 Miguel Matthews W PTS 6 Mansfield
31.08.96 Ervine Blake W PTS 4 Dublin
14.12.96 Miguel Matthews W PTS 4 Sheffield
25.02.97 Elvis Parsley W PTS 8 Sheffield
29.05.97 Mike Deveney W PTS 6 Mayfair

Career: 12 contests, won 12.

Darron Griffiths
Porth. *Born* Pontypridd, 11 February, 1972
Welsh S. Middleweight Champion. Ht. 6'0"
Manager Self

26.11.90 Colin Ford DREW 6 Mayfair
04.12.90 Kevin Adamson W RSC 4 Southend
23.01.91 Tony Booth DREW 6 Stoke
06.03.91 Barry Messam W PTS 6 Croydon
10.04.91 John Kaighin W PTS 6 Newport
25.04.91 Michael Graham W RSC 2 Mayfair
02.05.91 Carlton Myers W RTD 5 Kensington
21.10.91 John Ogiste W PTS 6 Mayfair
11.12.91 Adrian Wright W PTS 6 Stoke
22.01.92 Richard Okumu W PTS 8 Solihull
17.02.92 John Ogiste W RSC 5 Mayfair
29.04.92 Colin Manners DREW 8 Solihull
30.09.92 Colin Manners W PTS 10 Solihull
         (Elim. British Middleweight Title)

28.10.92 Antonio Fernandez W PTS 10 Cardiff
         (Elim. British Middleweight Title)
24.03.93 John Kaighin W RSC 6 Cardiff
         (Vacant Welsh S. Middleweight Title)
22.01.94 Carlos Christie W PTS 8 Cardiff
09.02.94 Paul Hitch W PTS 6 Bethnal Green
23.03.94 Karl Barwise W PTS 8 Cardiff
27.04.94 Ray Webb W RSC 6 Bethnal Green
         (Elim. British S. Middleweight Title)
15.06.94 Nigel Rafferty W RSC 4 Southwark
29.09.94 Ali Forbes L PTS 12 Bethnal Green
         (Final Elim. British S. Middleweight Title)
22.11.94 Dean Francis L RTD 1 Bristol
05.05.95 Wayne Ellis W PTS 10 Swansea
         (Welsh S. Middleweight Title Defence)
29.05.95 Andy Till W RSC 3 Bethnal Green
23.01.96 Mark Delaney L PTS 12 Bethnal Green
         (WBO Inter-Continental S. Middleweight Title Challenge)
02.04.96 Chris Johnson L RTD 3 Southwark
26.02.97 Yuri Filipko W PTS 8 Cardiff

Career: 27 contests, won 20, lost 4, drew 3.

Darron Griffiths   Les Clark

Robert Grubb
Tipton. *Born* Stourbridge, 18 April, 1972
Lightweight. Ht. 5'4"
Manager Self

17.02.94 Paul Wynn L PTS 6 Walsall
07.04.94 Roger Brotherhood L PTS 6 Walsall
11.10.94 Chris Lyons L PTS 6 Wolverhampton
20.10.94 Andy Roberts DREW 6 Walsall
07.12.94 Fred Reeve L RSC 3 Stoke
09.02.95 Andy Roberts DREW 6 Doncaster
09.03.95 Andrew Smith DREW 6 Walsall
28.03.95 Andrew Smith L PTS 6 Wolverhampton
14.06.95 Chris Aston L CO 1 Batley
17.10.95 Andy Roberts W PTS 6 Wolverhampton
25.10.95 Brian Robb L PTS 6 Telford
08.11.95 Paul Hamilton L PTS 6 Walsall

04.12.95 Robbie Sivyer L PTS 6 Birmingham
26.01.96 Stefy Bull L PTS 6 Doncaster
21.02.96 Steve Conway L PTS 6 Batley
27.03.96 Phil Lashley W PTS 6 Stoke
03.04.96 Charlie Rumbol L PTS 6 Bethnal Green
24.04.96 Johnny Miller L PTS 6 Stoke
15.05.96 David Jay L RSC 4 Cardiff
26.09.96 Jimmy Singh W RSC 2 Walsall
02.10.96 Carl Greaves L PTS 8 Stoke
06.11.96 Keith Jones L PTS 4 Tylorstown
22.11.96 John Sillo L RSC 2 Liverpool
03.03.97 Kevin Sheil L DIS 3 Birmingham
22.05.97 Danny Adams L PTS 4 Southwark

Career: 25 contests, won 3, drew 3, lost 19.

Robert Grubb   Les Clark

Mark Hale
Nuneaton. *Born* Nuneaton, 13 October, 1969
L. Heavyweight. Ht. 5'11"
Manager Self

07.10.91 Andy Manning L PTS 6 Liverpool
07.11.91 Marc Rowley W PTS 6 Peterborough
15.01.92 Paul Murray W PTS 6 Stoke
25.03.92 Marc Rowley W PTS 6 Hinckley
11.05.92 Martin Jolley L PTS 6 Coventry
21.05.92 Tony Colclough DREW 6 Cradley Heath
01.06.92 Tony Colclough L PTS 6 Solihull
05.10.92 Martin Jolley L RSC 4 Bardon
16.03.93 Andrew Flute L RSC 2 Wolverhampton
11.05.93 Earl Ling W RSC 2 Norwich
08.12.93 Dean Ashton L RSC 1 Stoke
25.05.94 Steve Loftus L PTS 6 Stoke
06.09.94 Steve Loftus L PTS 6 Stoke
17.09.94 Eddie Knight L PTS 6 Crawley
12.10.94 Phil Ball W RSC 3 Stoke
07.11.94 Ryan Cummings L RSC 6 Bethnal Green
15.12.94 Darren Sweeney L PTS 6 Walsall

17.03.95 Frederik Alvarez L CO 1 Copenhagen, Denmark
26.04.95 Steve Loftus L PTS 6 Stoke
15.05.95 Dave Battey L PTS 6 Bradford
29.09.95 Kenley Price L RSC 1 Liverpool
22.04.96 Stuart Fleet L PTS 6 Cleethorpes
21.05.96 Darren Sweeney L RSC 8 Edgbaston
12.03.97 P. R. Mason L PTS 6 Stoke
20.03.97 Carl Nicholson L RSC 3 Salford
Career: 25 contests, won 5, drew 1, lost 19.

Ross Hale

Bristol. *Born* Bristol, 28 February, 1967
Welterweight. Former British &
Commonwealth L. Welterweight
Champion. Former Undefeated Western
Area Welterweight Champion. Ht. 5'9"
Manager C. Sanigar

16.11.89 Dave Jenkins W PTS 6 Weston super Mare
30.11.89 Tony Gibbs W PTS 6 Mayfair
12.12.89 Chris McReedy W RSC 4 Brentford
13.03.90 Davey Hughes W RSC 3 Bristol
30.04.90 Andy Robins W RSC 4 Bristol
12.09.90 Derrick Daniel W PTS 6 Bethnal Green
21.11.90 Mark Kelly W PTS 8 Chippenham
29.11.90 Chris Saunders W PTS 6 Bayswater
24.10.91 Greg Egbuniwe W RSC 4 Bayswater
22.01.92 Tony Borg W PTS 6 Cardiff
30.04.92 J. P. Matthews W RSC 3 Bayswater
12.05.92 John Smith W CO 1 Crystal Palace
07.07.92 Julian Eavis W RSC 8 Bristol
(Vacant Western Area Welterweight Title)
05.10.92 Malcolm Melvin W PTS 10 Bristol
(Elim. British L. Welterweight Title)
01.12.92 Sugar Gibiliru W RSC 1 Bristol
27.01.93 Andreas Panayi L RSC 3 Cardiff
26.06.93 Mark Antony W RSC 1 Keynsham
28.07.93 Gary Barron W CO 2 Brixton
01.10.93 Carlos Chase W RTD 8 Cardiff
(Elim. British L. Welterweight Title)
03.11.93 Regino Caceres W CO 2 Bristol
11.12.93 Stephen Schramm W RSC 4 Dusseldorf, Germany
22.01.94 Michael Driscoll W RSC 7 Cardiff
(Elim. British L. Welterweight Title)
25.05.94 Andy Holligan W RSC 3 Bristol
(British & Commonwealth L. Welterweight Title Challenge)
03.08.94 Hugh Forde W RSC 7 Bristol
(British L. Welterweight Title Defence)
18.02.95 Malcolm Melvin W PTS 12 Shepton Mallet
(British & Commonwealth L. Welterweight Title Defence)
06.05.95 Shaun Cogan W RSC 4 Shepton Mallet
(Commonwealth L. Welterweight Title Defence)
28.10.95 Charlie Kane W CO 2 Bristol
(British & Commonwealth L. Welterweight Title Defence)
09.12.95 Paul Ryan L CO 1 Bethnal Green
(British & Commonwealth L. Welterweight Title Defence. WBO Inter-Continental L. Welterweight Title Challenge)
26.04.96 Paul Denton L RSC 4 Cardiff
24.03.97 Leigh Wicks W PTS 6 Bristol
05.06.97 Shaun Stokes W PTS 8 Bristol
Career: 31 contests, won 28, lost 3.

Paul Halpin   Les Clark

Paul Halpin

Brighton. *Born* Brighton, 4 August, 1974
Featherweight. Ht. 5'5"
Manager J. Bowers

04.04.97 Graham McGrath W PTS 6 Brighton
20.05.97 David Jeffrey W PTS 6 Gillingham
Career: 2 contests, won 2.

Sven Hamer

Margate. *Born* Margate, 6 June, 1973
S. Middleweight. Ht. 5'11"
Manager C. Sanigar

25.10.94 Eddie Haley W RSC 4 Southwark
07.11.94 Shamus Casey W PTS 4 Piccadilly
23.11.94 Andy Ewen W RSC 1 Piccadilly
20.12.94 Tony Velinor W RSC 4 Bethnal Green
24.01.95 Delroy Matthews L PTS 6 Piccadilly
28.07.95 Russell Washer W PTS 6 Bristol
09.12.95 Jason Matthews L RSC 6 Bethnal Green

05.03.96 Mark Baker L PTS 10 Bethnal Green
(Vacant Southern Area Middleweight Title)
11.12.96 Howard Eastman L RSC 10 Southwark
(Vacant Southern Area Middleweight Title)
14.03.97 Brian Galloway W CO 1 Reading
15.05.97 Stinger Mason W CO 5 Reading
Career: 11 contests, won 7, lost 4.

Anthony Hanna

Birmingham. *Born* Birmingham, 22
September, 1974
Midlands Area Flyweight Champion.
Ht. 5'6"
Manager Self

19.11.92 Nick Tooley L PTS 6 Evesham
10.12.92 Daren Fifield L RSC 6 Bethnal Green
11.05.93 Tiger Singh W PTS 6 Norwich
24.05.93 Lyndon Kershaw L PTS 6 Bradford
16.09.93 Chris Lyons W PTS 6 Southwark
06.10.93 Tiger Singh W PTS 6 Solihull
03.11.93 Mickey Cantwell L PTS 8 Bristol
25.01.94 Marty Chestnut W PTS 4 Picaddilly
10.02.94 Allan Mooney W RTD 1 Glasgow
13.04.94 Allan Mooney L PTS 6 Glasgow
22.04.94 Jesper D. Jenson L PTS 6 Aalborg, Denmark
03.08.94 Paul Ingle L PTS 6 Bristol
01.10.94 Mark Hughes L PTS 4 Cardiff
30.11.94 Shaun Norman W PTS 10 Solihull
(Vacant Midlands Area Flyweight Title)
24.02.95 Darren Greaves W RSC 5 Weston super Mare
06.03.95 Mark Hughes L PTS 6 Mayfair
27.04.95 Mickey Cantwell L PTS 6 Bethnal Green
05.05.95 Mark Cokely W RSC 4 Swansea
04.06.95 Mark Reynolds L PTS 10 Bethnal Green
(Elim. British Flyweight Title)
02.07.95 Mickey Cantwell L PTS 6 Dublin
02.11.95 Shaun Norman DREW 10 Mayfair
(Midlands Area Flyweight Title Defence)

Anthony Hanna (left) shows a tight defence during his six-round draw against Northolt's Clinton Beeby   Les Clark

31.01.96	Marty Chestnut DREW 6 Stoke
20.03.96	Harry Woods L PTS 6 Cardiff
22.04.96	Neil Parry W PTS 6 Manchester
14.05.96	Dharmendra Singh Yadav L PTS 4 Dagenham
08.10.96	Marty Chestnut W PTS 6 Battersea
11.12.96	Mark Reynolds DREW 8 Southwark
28.01.97	Colin Moffett L PTS 4 Belfast
28.02.97	Paul Weir L PTS 8 Kilmarnock
14.03.97	Jesper Jensen L PTS 6 Odense, Denmark
30.04.97	Clinton Beeby DREW 6 Acton
10.05.97	Jason Booth L PTS 6 Nottingham
02.06.97	Keith Knox L PTS 6 Glasgow

Career: 33 contests, won 10, drew 4, lost 19.

James Hare

Robertown. *Born* Dewsbury, 16 July, 1976
L. Welterweight. Ht. 5'6"
Manager B. Ingle/F. Warren

20.01.96	Brian Coleman W PTS 6 Mansfield
25.06.96	Mike Watson W PTS 4 Mansfield
13.07.96	Dennis Griffin W RSC 4 Bethnal Green
14.09.96	Paul Salmon W RSC 4 Sheffield
14.12.96	John Harrison W PTS 4 Sheffield
25.02.97	Kid McAuley W PTS 4 Sheffield
12.04.97	Andy Peach W RSC 1 Sheffield

Career: 7 contests, won 7.

Robert Harper

Doncaster. *Born* Doncaster, 1 April, 1969
Middleweight. Ht. 5'8"
Manager Self

16.09.93	Smokey Enison L RSC 1 Hull
02.12.93	Kevin Bailey L PTS 6 Sheffield
24.02.94	Dave Proctor L PTS 6 Hull
08.03.94	Chris Nurse L PTS 6 Edgbaston
25.04.94	Lee Blundell L PTS 2 Bury
25.01.95	Steve Loftus L PTS 6 Stoke
07.03.95	Andy McVeigh L RSC 5 Edgbaston
13.04.95	Russell Washer L PTS 6 Bloomsbury
	Freddie Yemofio L PTS 6 Norwich
02.06.95	Michael Bowen L PTS 6 Bethnal Green
20.06.95	Barry Exton L PTS 6 Birmingham
06.09.95	Mark Dawson L PTS 6 Stoke
25.09.95	Kevin Burton L DIS 4 Cleethorpes
06.12.95	Steve Loftus L PTS 6 Stoke
26.01.96	Mark Snipe L PTS 6 Brighton
12.02.96	John McAlpine L PTS 6 Glasgow
15.03.96	Andy Gray L DIS 6 Dunstable
12.09.96	Paul Webb NC 3 Doncaster
23.09.96	Roy Chipperfield L DIS 2 Bradford •
04.10.96	Craig Winter L RSC 5 Pentre Halkyn

Career: 20 contests, lost 19, no contest 1.

Matthew Harris

Aldridge. *Born* Brownhills, 2 May, 1971
Bantamweight. Former Midlands Area S.
Bantamweight Champion. Ht. 5'7"
Manager M. Shinfield

23.03.94	Yusuf Vorajee W PTS 6 Stoke
13.06.94	Marcus Duncan W RSC 1 Bradford
02.09.94	Karl Morling W CO 5 Spitalfields
	(Vacant Midlands Area S. Bantamweight Title)
05.10.94	Pete Buckley W PTS 6 Wolverhampton
30.11.94	Marty Chestnut W RSC 3 Wolverhampton
15.12.94	Kid McAuley W PTS 6 Evesham
10.02.95	Pete Buckley L RSC 6 Birmingham
	(Midlands Area S. Bantamweight Title Defence)

21.04.95	Chris Lyons W PTS 6 Dudley
19.05.95	John Armour L RSC 3 Southwark
26.08.95	Lehlohomolo Ledwaba L CO 2 Durban, South Africa
25.10.95	Pete Buckley W PTS 10 Telford
	(Midlands Area S. Bantamweight Title Challenge)
19.02.96	Robert Hay L RTD 5 Glasgow
26.09.96	Carl Allen L PTS 10 Walsall
	(Midlands Area S. Bantamweight Title Defence)
27.11.96	Harry Woods L PTS 8 Swansea
11.04.97	Ady Benton L PTS 8 Barnsley
25.04.97	Pete Buckley W PTS 6 Cleethorpes

Career: 16 contests, won 9, lost 7.

Peter Harris

Swansea. *Born* Swansea, 23 August, 1962
Welsh Featherweight Champion. Former
British Featherweight Champion. Ht. 5'6½"
Manager Self

28.02.83	Dave Pratt L PTS 6 Birmingham
25.04.83	Jim Harvey DREW 6 Aberdeen
27.05.83	Brett Styles W PTS 8 Swansea
20.06.83	Danny Knaggs W PTS 6 Piccadilly
19.12.83	Kevin Howard W PTS 8 Swansea
06.02.84	Ivor Jones DREW 8 Bethnal Green
27.03.84	Johnny Dorey W RSC 6 Bethnal Green
13.06.84	Keith Wallace W PTS 10 Aberavon
28.09.84	Ray Minus L PTS 10 Nassau, Bahamas
21.11.84	John Farrell L PTS 8 Solihull
20.03.85	Kid Sumali W PTS 8 Solihull
09.05.85	John Feeney L PTS 10 Warrington
09.11.85	Antoine Montero L PTS 8 Grenoble, France
26.03.86	Steve Pollard W RSC 3 Swansea
22.04.86	Roy Webb W RTD 8 Belfast
18.11.86	Kelvin Smart W PTS 10 Swansea
	(Vacant Welsh Featherweight Title)
30.04.87	Albert Parr W RSC 3 Newport
30.09.87	John Farrell W PTS 12 Solihull
	(Final Elim. British Featherweight Title)
15.12.87	Roy Williams W RSC 2 Cardiff
24.02.88	Kevin Taylor W PTS 12 Aberavon
	(Vacant British Featherweight Title)
18.05.88	Paul Hodkinson L RSC 12 Aberavon
	(British Featherweight Title Defence)
06.09.89	Paul Hodkinson L RSC 9 Aberavon
	(British & European Featherweight Title Challenge)
24.04.91	Colin Lynch W PTS 8 Aberavon
18.07.91	Steve Robinson L PTS 10 Cardiff
	(Welsh Featherweight Title Defence)
05.06.92	Stephane Haccoun L PTS 8 Marseille, France
22.12.92	Paul Harvey L PTS 8 Mayfair
21.12.93	Jonjo Irwin L PTS 8 Mayfair
20.05.94	Nigel Haddock W PTS 10 Neath
	(Vacant Welsh Featherweight Title)
27.08.94	Wilson Docherty L PTS 12 Cardiff
	(WBO Penta-Continental Featherweight Title Challenge)
24.04.95	Wilson Docherty W PTS 10 Glasgow
	(Final Elim. British Featherweight Title)
26.09.95	Welcome Ncita L RSC 3 Hammanskraal, South Africa
31.05.96	Jimmy Bredahl L PTS 8 Copenhagen, Denmark
06.07.96	Cassius Baloyi L PTS 6 Manchester

Career: 33 contests, won 16, drew 2, lost 15.

Humphrey Harrison

Manchester. *Born* Jamaica, 25 September, 1958
L. Middleweight. Ht. 5'8"
Manager N. Basso

05.10.87	Steve Hogg W RSC 1 Manchester
11.01.88	Paul Jones W PTS 8 Manchester
07.03.88	Eddie Collins W RSC 2 Manchester
29.03.88	Dave Hindmarsh W RSC 3 Marton
06.06.88	Davey Hughes W PTS 8 Manchester
11.10.88	Phil Walters W RSC 1 Wolverhampton
14.04.89	Tony Ekubia W RSC 5 Manchester
	(Central Area Welterweight Title Challenge)
12.06.89	Tony Swift L PTS 8 Manchester
04.10.89	Tony Richards W RSC 7 Solihull
10.11.89	Tony Brown W PTS 6 Liverpool
27.02.90	Willie Beattie W RSC 2 Manchester
17.04.91	Derek Grainger W RSC 7 Kensington
01.05.91	Julian Eavis W PTS 6 Solihull
31.01.92	Dave Binsteed W CO 1 Manchester
25.03.92	Roy Rowland L CO 7 Dagenham
24.02.97	Jason Barker L CO 6 Manchester
29.04.97	Jeff Finlayson W PTS 6 Manchester

Career: 17 contests, won 13, lost 4.

John Harrison

Plymouth. *Born* Scunthorpe, 18 March, 1977
L. Welterweight. Ht. 5'11½"
Manager G. Mitchell

13.01.96	Mark Haslam L PTS 6 Manchester
13.02.96	Paul Samuels L CO 1 Cardiff
16.05.96	Dave Fallon W RSC 4 Dunstable
03.07.96	Allan Gray L PTS 6 Wembley
01.10.96	Cam Raeside L PTS 6 Birmingham
07.11.96	Nicky Bardle L PTS 6 Battersea
14.12.96	James Hare L PTS 4 Sheffield
19.04.97	Jason Williams W PTS 6 Plymouth

Career: 8 contests, won 2, lost 6.

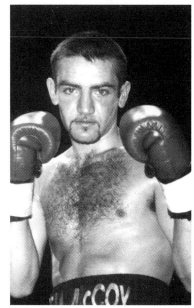

Scott Harrison   Les Clark

101

Scott Harrison

Cambuslang. *Born* Bellshill, 19 August, 1977
Featherweight. Ht. 5'7"
Manager F. Maloney

07.10.96 Eddie Sica W RSC 2 Lewisham
11.01.97 Pete Buckley W PTS 4 Bethnal Green
25.03.97 David Morris W PTS 4 Lewisham
Career: 3 contests, won 3.

Jason Hart

Tooting. *Born* Beckenham, 23 January, 1970
S. Middleweight. Ht. 5'9½"
Manager T. Toole

02.06.94 Paul Matthews L RSC 3 Tooting
28.07.94 Julian Eavis W PTS 6 Tooting
30.09.94 Freddie Yemofio W PTS 6 Bethnal Green
31.03.95 Andy Ewen W PTS 6 Crystal Palace
20.09.95 Steve Roberts L RSC 5 Potters Bar
03.12.95 Simon Andrews W PTS 6 Southwark
30.01.96 Ernie Loveridge W PTS 6 Barking
05.03.96 Martin Jolley W PTS 6 Bethnal Green
03.04.96 Michael Pinnock W PTS 6 Bethnal Green
24.10.96 Graham Townsend L RSC 5 Mayfair
          (Vacant Southern Area S. Middleweight Title)
13.04.97 Sven Ottke L RSC 2 Cologne, Germany
20.05.97 Johnny Hooks W PTS 6 Gillingham
Career: 12 contests, won 8, lost 4.

Craig Hartwell

Rugby. *Born* Rugby, 24 August, 1968
Welterweight. Ht. 5'9"
Manager J. Weaver

11.12.91 Brian Coleman DREW 6 Leicester
25.03.92 Benji Joseph L PTS 6 Hinckley
18.05.92 Dean Hiscox L PTS 6 Bardon
19.10.93 Warren Bowers L PTS 6 Cleethorpes
01.10.96 Mark Richards L PTS 6 Birmingham
14.10.96 Danny Stevens L CO 2 Mayfair
05.12.96 Shaun O'Neill L PTS 6 Sunderland
29.01.97 Kevin McCarthy L RSC 1 Bethnal Green
Career: 8 contests, drew 1, lost 7.

Mark Haslam

Manchester. *Born* Bury, 20 October, 1969
Lightweight. Ht. 5'8"
Manager N. Basso/F. Warren

12.06.95 Steve Burton W PTS 6 Manchester
15.09.95 Thomas Bradley W CO 4 Mansfield
24.11.95 Anthony Campbell L PTS 4 Manchester
13.01.96 John Harrison W PTS 6 Manchester
09.04.96 Pete Roberts W CO 2 Salford
25.10.96 Andrew Robinson W RTD 4 Mere
09.11.96 Brian Coleman W PTS 6 Manchester
22.03.97 Mark Richards DREW 4 Wythenshawe
Career: 8 contests, won 6, drew 1, lost 1.

Floyd Havard

Swansea. *Born* Swansea, 16 October, 1965
Featherweight. Former Undefeated British S. Featherweight Champion. Ht. 5'8"
Manager Self

30.11.85 Dean Brahmald W RSC 3 Cardiff
22.01.86 Sugar Gibiliru W PTS 6 Muswell Hill
20.02.86 Dean Brahmald W PTS 6 Halifax
10.03.86 Russell Jones W PTS 8 Cardiff
28.04.86 Tony McLaggon W CO 2 Cardiff
24.05.86 Sugar Gibiliru W PTS 8 Manchester
20.09.86 George Jones W RSC 4 Hemel Hempstead
25.10.86 Joe Duffy W RSC 3 Stevenage
29.11.86 Marvin P. Gray W RSC 2 Wandsworth
14.03.87 Nigel Senior W RSC 5 Southwark
14.04.87 Ray Newby W RSC 7 Cumbernauld
28.04.87 Hector Clottey W RSC 5 Halifax
19.05.87 Kid Sumali W RTD 2 Cumbernauld
22.09.87 Frank Loukil W RSC 4 Bethnal Green
11.11.87 Cedric Powell W PTS 8 Usk
12.01.88 Mario Salazar W RSC 2 Cardiff
24.02.88 Richard Fowler W RSC 1 Aberavon
20.04.88 Benji Marquez W PTS 8 Muswell Hill
18.05.88 Pat Cowdell W RSC 8 Aberavon
          (British S. Featherweight Title Challenge)
15.11.88 John Kalbhenn W PTS 10 Norwich
11.04.89 Idabeth Rojas W PTS 10 Aberavon
06.09.89 John Doherty L RTD 11 Aberavon
          (British S. Featherweight Title Defence)
05.03.91 Tony Foster W PTS 8 Millwall
29.10.91 Thunder Aryeh W RTD 6 Cardiff
17.12.91 Patrick Kamy W DIS 5 Cardiff
17.03.92 Harry Escott W RSC 7 Mayfair
01.12.93 Harry Escott W PTS 8 Bethnal Green
22.01.94 Juan Molina L RTD 6 Cardiff
          (IBF S. Featherweight Title Challenge)
23.03.94 Neil Haddock W RSC 10 Cardiff
          (British S. Featherweight Title Challenge)
29.09.94 Edward Lloyd W RSC 4 Bethnal Green
13.12.94 Dave McHale W RSC 10 Ilford
          (British S. Featherweight Title Defence)
24.03.95 Elvis Parsley W RSC 6 Swansea
05.05.95 Michael Armstrong W CO 9 Swansea
          (British S. Featherweight Title Defence)
16.03.96 Sergio Pena W PTS 8 Glasgow
19.10.96 Efren Gonzalez W PTS 6 Bristol
30.11.96 Carl Allen W RTD 3 Tylorstown
Career: 36 contests, won 34, lost 2.

Chris Henry

Tottenham. *Born* London, 21 July, 1966
Former Southern Area Cruiserweight Champion. Ht. 6'1"
Manager J. Harding

06.11.93 Chris Okoh L RSC 2 Bethnal Green
11.10.96 Steve Bristow L PTS 4 Mayfair
26.10.96 Alexander Jacob W PTS 4 Liverpool
05.11.96 Paul Douglas W PTS 4 Belfast
27.01.97 Colin Brown W RSC 3 Glasgow
28.04.97 Darren Westover W RTD 4 Enfield
          (Vacant Southern Area Cruiserweight Title)
17.06.97 Dominic Negus L RSC 10 Cheshunt
          (Southern Area Cruiserweight Title Defence)
Career: 7 contests, won 4, lost 3.

Ian Henry

Gateshead. *Born* Gateshead, 8 May, 1967
Cruiserweight. Ht. 6'1½"
Manager T. Conroy

26.04.90 Willy James W RSC 3 Manchester
15.05.90 Mark Whitehouse W RSC 4 South Shields
24.04.90 Paul Hendrick L PTS 6 Manchester
19.11.90 Shaun McCrory W PTS 6 Manchester
14.12.90 Eddie Collins W PTS 6 Peterborough
21.01.91 Shaun McCrory W PTS 6 Glasgow
28.01.91 Simon McDougall L PTS 8 Bradford
18.03.91 Ian Vokes W RSC 2 Manchester
25.03.91 Dave Lawrence W PTS 6 Bradford
10.05.91 Simon McDougall W PTS 6 Gateshead
10.10.91 Chris Walker W PTS 6 Gateshead
14.11.91 Dave Owens W PTS 8 Gateshead
27.11.91 John Oxenham W PTS 6 Marton
11.03.92 Simon McDougall W PTS 8 Solihull
05.05.92 Glenn Campbell L RSC 1 Preston
23.10.92 Lee Archer W RTD 1 Gateshead
01.03.93 Lee Prudden W PTS 6 Bradford
17.03.93 Lee Archer L PTS 6 Stoke
11.06.93 Art Stacey W PTS 6 Gateshead
22.09.93 Mohammed Isaacs L RSC 5 Eldorado Park, South Africa
02.12.93 Paul McCarthy W PTS 6 Hartlepool
19.03.94 Gary Ballard L RSC 4 Millwall
21.04.94 Terry French L PTS 10 Gateshead
          (Northern Area L. Heavyweight Title Challenge)
15.05.97 Danny Southern DREW 6 Sunderland
19.06.97 Chris Woollas L PTS 6 Scunthorpe
Career: 25 contests, won 16, drew 1, lost 8.

Gary Hibbert

Oldham. *Born* Oldham, 5 February, 1975
Lightweight. Ht. 5'8½"
Manager R., Tindall

02.06.96 John T. Kelly W PTS 6 Shaw
13.10.96 Sean Morrison W RSC 2 Shaw
16.03.97 David Kirk W PTS 6 Shaw
08.06.97 Bamana Dibateza W PTS 4 Shaw
Career: 4 contests, won 4.

Gary Hickman

Sunderland. *Born* Easington, 9 April, 1970
Bantamweight. Ht. 5'6"
Manager Self

06.06.88 Darren Weller L PTS 4 Northampton
17.10.88 Brian Connal W RSC 2 Glasgow
28.10.88 Jimmy Clark L PTS 6 Brentwood
13.12.88 Joe Mullen L PTS 4 Glasgow
14.02.89 Mark Geraghty W PTS 6 Sunderland
30.10.89 Phil Lashley W RSC 4 Piccadilly
30.11.89 Jimmy Clark L PTS 6 Barking
18.12.89 Tommy Graham W RTD 3 Glasgow
26.02.90 Marvin Stone L RSC 5 Crystal Palace
03.05.90 Alan McKay L PTS 8 Kensington
29.05.90 Bradley Stone DREW 6 Bethnal Green
20.06.91 Craig Dermody L RSC 2 Liverpool
14.12.91 John Armour L RSC 6 Bexleyheath
28.02.92 Mike Deveney L PTS 6 Irvine
02.03.96 Colin Innes L PTS 4 Newcastle
09.04.96 Spencer Oliver L PTS 6 Stevenage
08.06.96 Colin Innes L PTS 4 Newcastle
20.09.96 Alston Buchanan L PTS 6 Glasgow
13.10.96 Ady Lewis L RSC 3 Shaw
28.01.97 Paul Ireland L RSC 4 Belfast
29.04.97 Colin Moffett L PTS 4 Belfast
13.06.97 Neil Armstrong L PTS 4 Paisley
Career: 22 contests, won 4, drew 1, lost 17.

Gary Hiscox

Dudley. *Born* Dudley, 25 May, 1970
Welterweight. Ht. 5'7¾"
Manager Self

14.10.92 Alan Ingle L PTS 6 Stoke
12.11.92 Shane Sheridan W PTS 6 Stafford
27.01.93 Dave Madden W PTS 6 Stoke
03.03.93 Erwin Edwards W PTS 6 Solihull
26.06.93 Mark Tibbs L RSC 4 Earls Court
28.10.93 Dean Bramhald W RSC 5 Walsall
04.11.93 Paul Hughes W PTS 6 Stafford
25.11.93 Mark Legg L RSC 3 Tynemouth
01.03.94 Gary Cogan W PTS 6 Dudley
29.09.94 Patrick Parton W PTS 6 Walsall
26.10.94 Steve Howden W RSC 4 Stoke
09.02.95 Cam Raeside W RSC 5 Doncaster
06.03.95 Neil Smith W PTS 6 Leicester
11.05.95 Anthony Maynard L RSC 4 Dudley
03.11.95 Mike Watson W PTS 6 Dudley
11.12.95 Rick North W PTS 6 Cleethorpes
15.05.96 Paul Samuels L RSC 3 Cardiff
07.11.96 Adrian Chase L PTS 4 Battersea
22.11.96 Tony Mock W PTS 6 Liverpool
04.12.96 Lee Molyneux W PTS 6 Stoke
17.12.96 Pat Wright L PTS 6 Bethnal Green
29.01.97 Allan Gray L PTS 6 Bethnal Green
29.05.97 Martin Holgate L PTS 4 Mayfair
Career: 23 contests, won 14, lost 9.

Mark Hobson

Huddersfield. *Born* Workington, 7 May, 1976

L. Heavyweight. Ht. 6'5"
Manager C. Aston

09.06.97 Michael Pinnock W PTS 6 Bradford
Career: 1 contest, won 1.

(Francis) Franny Hogg

Leeds. *Born* Belfast, 8 March, 1973
Lightweight. Ht. 5'8"
Manager T. O'Neill

06.12.96 Les Frost W PTS 6 Leeds
16.12.96 Gary Jenkinson W RSC 2 Cleethorpes
24.03.97 Tomas Jansson L PTS 4 Helsinki, Finland
13.06.97 Vic Broomhead W RSC 2 Leeds
Career: 4 contests, won 3, lost 1.

Mike Holden

Manchester. *Born* Ashton under Lyme, 13 March, 1968
Heavyweight. Ht. 6'4"
Manager B. Hearn

04.10.94 Gary Williams W RSC 4 Mayfair
20.12.94 Pat Passley L RTD 3 Bethnal Green
07.10.95 R. F. McKenzie W RSC 2 Belfast
14.11.95 Michael Murray L PTS 6 Bury
09.07.96 Julius Francis L PTS 10 Bethnal Green
28.09.96 Mikael Lindblad W PTS 6 Barking
26.06.97 Israel Ajose W RSC 1 Salford
Career: 7 contests, won 4, lost 3.

Gary Hiscox   Les Clark

Mike Holden (right) looks to set up Mikael Lindblad for the left hook   Les Clark

Martin Holgate

Walthamstow. *Born* Waltham Forest, 24 November, 1968
Welterweight. Ht. 5'6½"
Manager F. Warren

02.06.95	Adam Baldwin W PTS 6 Bethnal Green
22.07.95	Mike Watson W PTS 6 Millwall
02.09.95	Trevor Smith W RSC 2 Wembley
21.10.95	John O. Johnson W PTS 4 Bethnal Green
09.12.95	Andrew Reed W RSC 1 Bethnal Green
13.02.96	Brian Coleman W PTS 4 Bethnal Green
13.07.96	John Smith W PTS 4 Bethnal Green
27.03.97	Danny Stevens W RSC 3 Norwich
29.05.97	Gary Hiscox W PTS 4 Mayfair

Career: 9 contests, won 9.

Andy Holligan

Liverpool. *Born* Liverpool, 6 June, 1967
Former Undefeated British & Commonwealth L. Welterweight Champion. Ht. 5'5¾"
Manager S. Vaughan

19.10.87	Glyn Rhodes W PTS 6 Belfast
03.12.87	Jimmy Thornton W RTD 2 Belfast
27.01.88	Andrew Morgan W RSC 5 Belfast
26.03.88	Tony Richards W RSC 2 Belfast
08.06.88	David Maw W RSC 1 Sheffield
19.10.88	Lenny Gloster W PTS 8 Belfast
14.12.88	Sugar Gibiliru W PTS 8 Kirkby
16.03.89	Jeff Connors W RSC 5 Southwark
19.09.89	Billy Buchanan W RSC 4 Belfast
25.10.89	Tony Adams W RSC 5 Wembley
26.09.90	Mike Durvan W CO 1 Mayfair
31.10.90	Eric Carroyez W RTD 2 Wembley
17.04.91	Pat Ireland W RSC 1 Kensington
16.05.91	Simon Eubank W RSC 2 Liverpool
20.06.91	Tony Ekubia W PTS 12 Liverpool *(British & Commonwealth L. Welterweight Title Challenge)*
28.11.91	Steve Larrimore W RSC 8 Liverpool *(Commonwealth L. Welterweight Title Defence)*
27.02.92	Tony McKenzie W RSC 3 Liverpool *(British & Commonwealth L. Welterweight Title Defence)*
15.09.92	Tony Ekubia W CO 7 Liverpool *(British & Commonwealth L. Welterweight Title Defence)*
07.10.92	Dwayne Swift W PTS 10 Sunderland
12.11.92	Mark Smith W PTS 10 Liverpool
26.05.93	Lorenzo Garcia W RSC 2 Mansfield
18.12.93	Julio Cesar Chavez L RTD 5 Puebla, Mexico *(WBC L. Welterweight Title Challenge)*
26.02.94	Massimo Bertozzi W CO 5 Earls Court
25.05.94	Ross Hale L RSC 3 Bristol *(British & Commonwealth L. Welterweight Title Defence)*
30.06.95	Tony Foster W CO 2 Liverpool
04.11.95	Allan Hall W RSC 2 Liverpool *(Final Elim. British L. Welterweight Title)*
05.03.96	Karl Taylor W PTS 6 Barrow
13.07.96	Paul Ryan W CO 1 Bethnal Green *(British & Commonwealth L. Welterweight Title Challenge)*
28.04.97	Rimvidas Billius W PTS 8 Hull

Career: 29 contests, won 27, lost 2.

Donnie Hood

Glasgow. *Born* Glasgow, 3 June, 1963
Former Undefeated WBC International & Scottish Bantamweight Champion. Ht. 5'5"
Manager Self

22.09.86	Stewart Fishermac W PTS 6 Glasgow
29.09.86	Keith Ward W PTS 6 Glasgow
08.12.86	Jamie McBride DREW 8 Glasgow
22.12.86	Keith Ward L PTS 8 Glasgow
27.01.87	Chris Clarkson W PTS 6 Glasgow
09.02.87	Danny Porter W RSC 4 Glasgow
24.02.87	Danny Lee W PTS 8 Glasgow
07.09.87	Kid Sumali W PTS 8 Glasgow
15.09.87	David Ingram L PTS 8 Batley
26.10.87	Jimmy Lee W PTS 8 Glasgow
25.11.87	Brian Holmes W PTS 10 Bellahouston *(Vacant Scottish Bantamweight Title)*
28.03.88	Nigel Crook W CO 2 Glasgow
12.05.88	Eyup Can L PTS 8 Copenhagen, Denmark
17.06.88	Fransie Badenhorst L RSC 7 Durban, South Africa
05.09.88	Gerry McBride W RTD 7 Glasgow
25.10.88	Graham O'Malley W RSC 9 Hartlepool *(Elim. British Bantamweight Title)*
06.03.89	Francisco Paco Garcia W RSC 6 Glasgow
28.03.89	John Vasquez W RSC 5 Glasgow
27.06.89	Ray Minus L RSC 6 Glasgow *(Commonwealth Bantamweight Title Challenge)*
22.01.90	Dean Lynch W PTS 8 Glasgow
26.03.90	Keith Wallace W RTD 8 Glasgow *(Elim. British Bantamweight Title)*
09.10.90	Samuel Duran W PTS 12 Glasgow *(WBC International Bantamweight Title Challenge)*
10.12.90	David Moreno W RSC 4 Glasgow
25.01.91	Dave Buxton W RSC 5 Shotts
05.03.91	Virgilio Openio W PTS 12 Glasgow *(WBC International Bantamweight Title Defence)*
31.05.91	Willie Richardson W PTS 8 Glasgow
24.09.91	Rocky Commey W PTS 12 Glasgow *(WBC International Bantamweight Title Defence)*
24.10.91	Vinnie Ponzio W PTS 8 Glasgow
14.03.92	Johnny Bredahl L RSC 7 Copenhagen, Denmark *(Vacant European Bantamweight Title)*
29.05.92	Pete Buckley W PTS 8 Glasgow
25.01.93	Drew Docherty L PTS 12 Glasgow *(British Bantamweight Title Challenge)*
11.03.94	Kid McAuley W PTS 8 Glasgow
02.03.95	Rowan Williams W PTS 8 Glasgow
21.04.95	Shaun Anderson L PTS 8 Glasgow
06.11.96	Shaun Anderson W PTS 6 Glasgow

Career: 35 contests, won 25, drew 1, lost 9.

Johnny Hooks

Nottingham. *Born* North Shields, 9 March, 1968
S. Middleweight. Ht. 6'1"
Manager J. Gill

26.01.87	Young Gully L RSC 2 Nottingham
02.03.87	Jim Conley L RSC 2 Nottingham
18.02.94	Jim Pallatt W RSC 1 Leicester
07.04.94	Kevin Burton W PTS 6 Walsall
24.05.94	Dave Battey W PTS 6 Leicester
20.10.94	Neil Simpson L RSC 2 Walsall
27.09.96	Peter Mason L PTS 6 Hull

04.10.96	Carl Nicholson L PTS 6 Wakefield
13.10.96	Darren Swords W PTS 6 Shaw
04.12.96	Rocky Shelly L RSC 6 Stoke
19.03.97	Chris Pollock L PTS 6 Stoke
08.04.97	Enzo Giordano L PTS 4 Bethnal Green
10.05.97	Martin Jolley DREW 6 Nottingham
20.05.97	Jason Hart L PTS 6 Gillingham

Career: 14 contests, won 4, drew 1, lost 9.

Johnny Hooks   Les Clark

Ron Hopley

Ripon. *Born* Ripon, 3 April, 1969
Middleweight. Ht. 5'8½"
Manager D. Mancini

27.11.91	William Beaton W RSC 2 Marton
23.01.92	Rick North W PTS 6 York
08.04.92	Steve Howden L PTS 6 Leeds
25.02.93	Rob Stevenson DREW 6 Bradford
07.04.93	Warren Stephens W PTS 6 Leeds
01.07.93	Rob Stevenson W PTS 6 York
07.10.93	Warren Bowers W PTS 6 York
28.02.94	Warren Bowers W RSC 1 Marton
26.10.94	Brian Dunn L PTS 6 Leeds
08.07.95	Phil Epton L RSC 4 York
04.06.96	Paul Webb W PTS 6 York
23.10.96	Roy Chipperfield W PTS 6 Halifax

Career: 12 contests, won 7, drew 1, lost 4.

Steve Howden

Sheffield. *Born* Sheffield, 4 June, 1969
L. Welterweight. Ht. 5'8¾"
Manager Self

08.04.92	Ron Hopley W PTS 6 Leeds
01.06.92	Kevin McKillan L RSC 2 Manchester
07.07.92	Mike Morrison L CO 3 Bristol
01.10.92	Jimmy Reynolds L RTD 2 Telford
23.06.93	Shaba Edwards W RSC 1 Gorleston
11.08.93	Brian Coleman W RSC 4 Mansfield
30.11.93	Colin Anderson W PTS 6 Leicester
17.08.94	Rick North L PTS 6 Sheffield
23.09.94	Colin Dunne L CO 1 Bethnal Green
26.10.94	Gary Hiscox L RSC 4 Stoke
25.01.95	Mike Watson W RSC 2 Stoke
10.02.95	Clayton Hollingsworth L PTS 6 Birmingham

03.03.95 Danny Stevens L RSC 2 Bethnal Green
26.04.95 Mark Legg L RTD 2 Stoke
01.09.95 Patrick Parton L PTS 6 Wolverhampton
27.09.95 Colin Dunne L RSC 4 Bethnal Green
25.10.95 Dave Madden W PTS 6 Stoke
22.08.96 Ricky Sackfield W PTS 6 Salford
15.10.96 Andy Peach L RSC 6 Wolverhampton
14.11.96 Steve Tuckett L RSC 1 Sheffield
Career: 20 contests, won 7, lost 13.

Roger Hunte
Leyton. *Born* London, 28 October, 1971
L. Welterweight. Ht. 5'6"
Manager Self

12.02.92 Jason Barker W RTD 4 Wembley
25.03.92 Phil Cullen W RSC 3 Kensington
15.03.96 Anthony Campbell DREW 4 Dunstable
16.05.96 Paul Salmon W RSC 5 Dunstable
17.12.96 Jay Mahoney L RSC 5 Bethnal Green
Career: 5 contests, won 3, drew 1, lost 1.

Geoff Hunter
Manchester. *Born* Runcorn, 28 October, 1969
Heavyweight. Ht. 6'0¾"
Manager T. Miller

13.01.96 Slick Miller DREW 6 Halifax
04.10.96 Tim Redman L CO 5 Pentre Halkyn
20.11.96 Michael Sprott L RSC 1 Wembley
15.05.97 Gavin McGhin L PTS 6 Sunderland
Career: 4 contests, drew 1, lost 3.

Colin Innes
Newcastle. *Born* Newcastle, 24 July, 1964
S. Featherweight. Northern Area Featherweight Champion. Ht. 5'6"
Manager N. Fawcett

10.09.90 Lee Christian W RSC 5 Northampton
24.09.90 Steve Armstrong W PTS 6 Manchester
08.10.90 Ervine Blake L PTS 6 Bradford
22.10.90 Steve Armstrong W RSC 6 Manchester
26.11.90 Carl Roberts L RSC 3 Bury
11.02.91 Steve Armstrong W PTS 6 Manchester
18.02.91 Ian McGirr L PTS 6 Glasgow
02.03.91 Tommy Smith W PTS 6 Darlington
28.03.91 Darryl Pettit W RTD 3 Alfreton
30.04.91 Noel Carroll L PTS 4 Stockport
19.09.91 Carl Roberts L PTS 4 Stockport
12.12.91 Tommy Smith L PTS 6 Hartlepool
24.02.92 Mark Geraghty L PTS 8 Glasgow
30.03.92 Chris Jickells L RSC 3 Bradford
28.05.92 Tommy Smith L PTS 6 Gosforth
05.10.92 Wayne Rigby L PTS 6 Manchester
18.11.92 Al Garrett DREW 6 Solihull
15.09.93 Chris Bennett DREW 6 Newcastle
25.11.93 Garry Burrell W PTS 6 Newcastle
06.12.93 Norman Dhalie L PTS 6 Bradford
24.01.94 Hugh Collins L PTS 6 Glasgow
03.03.94 Leo Turner DREW 6 Newcastle
21.04.94 Leo Turner W PTS 6 Gateshead
13.05.94 Rocky Ferrari L PTS 6 Kilmarnock
13.06.94 Leo Turner L PTS 6 Bradford
12.09.94 Kid McAuley L PTS 6 Doncaster
06.10.94 Chip O'Neill DREW 6 Cramlington
24.11.94 Paul Goode W PTS 6 Newcastle
24.02.95 Garry Burrell L PTS 6 Irvine
11.03.95 Trevor Sumner L PTS 6 Barnsley
25.03.95 Paul Hamilton L PTS 6 Rothwell
05.04.95 Ian McLeod L RSC 5 Irvine

11.05.95 Chip O'Neill L PTS 6 Sunderland
05.06.95 Paul Watson L RSC 4 Glasgow
15.09.95 Paul Hamilton W PTS 6 Darlington
05.10.95 Fred Reeve L PTS 6 Hull
14.11.95 Chris Price L PTS 6 Yarm
11.12.95 Jason Blanche L PTS 6 Bradford
12.02.96 Scott Dixon L PTS 6 Glasgow
02.03.96 Gary Hickman W PTS 4 Newcastle
16.03.96 Shaun Anderson L PTS 4 Glasgow
25.04.96 Chip O'Neill W RSC 9 Newcastle
(*Vacant Northern Area Featherweight Title*)
08.06.96 Gary Hickman W PTS 4 Newcastle
06.07.96 Michael Brodie L RSC 2 Manchester
10.10.96 Neil Parry W PTS 6 Newcastle
18.11.96 Wilson Docherty L PTS 8 Glasgow
05.12.96 John T. Kelly L PTS 8 Sunderland
03.02.97 John T. Kelly L PTS 6 Sunderland
14.03.97 Garry Burrell L PTS 6 Irvine
01.05.97 Garry Burrell L PTS 6 Newcastle
16.05.97 Ronnie McPhee L RSC 2 Glasgow
Career: 51 contests, won 15, drew 4, lost 32.

Richard Inquieti
Mansfield. *Born* Langley Mill, 19 October, 1968
Welterweight. Ht. 6'3¼"
Manager J. Ashton

30.09.96 Peter Varnavas L CO 2 Manchester
20.02.97 Paul Johnson W PTS 6 Mansfield
12.03.97 Tony Smith W RSC 2 Stoke
19.03.97 Andy Peach L RSC 1 Stoke
Career: 4 contests, won 2, lost 2.

Paul Ireland   Les Clark

Paul Ireland
Belfast. *Born* Belfast, 22 April, 1970
S. Bantamweight. Ht. 5'7"
Manager B. Hearn

26.08.95 Graham McGrath W PTS 4 Belfast
07.10.95 Marty Chestnut W RSC 6 Belfast
20.04.96 Graham McGrath W PTS 6 Brentwood

28.05.96 Garry Burrell W PTS 6 Belfast
03.09.96 Miguel Matthews W PTS 6 Belfast
28.01.97 Gary Hickman W RSC 4 Belfast
29.04.97 Danny Ruegg W RSC 6 Belfast
27.05.97 Ricardo Martinez W RSC 2 Mayfair
02.06.97 John Matthews W RSC 4 Belfast
Career: 9 contests, won 9.

(Carl) C. J. Jackson
Manchester. *Born* Manchester, 21 January, 1973
Welterweight. Ht. 5'9¼"
Manager J. Doughty

13.10.96 Lee Molyneux L PTS 6 Shaw
01.12.96 Dean Nicholas DREW 6 Shaw
16.03.97 Wayne Shepherd W PTS 6 Shaw
20.04.97 Pedro Carragher DREW 6 Leeds
08.06.97 Bobby Vanzie L RSC 3 Shaw
Career: 5 contests, won 1, drew 2, lost 2.

Gilbert Jackson (Amponsan)
Battersea. *Born* Ghana, 21 August, 1970
L. Middleweight. Ht. 5'10"
Manager A. Gee

17.02.92 John Bosco L PTS 6 Mayfair
05.03.92 Tony Wellington W CO 2 Battersea
22.04.92 Russell Washer W PTS 6 Wembley
08.09.92 Paul Gamble W RSC 1 Norwich
05.02.93 Carl Harney W CO 3 Bayswater
14.06.93 Lee Crocker W RSC 2 Bayswater
16.09.93 Alan Baptiste W RSC 5 Southwark
02.11.93 Ernie Loveridge W RTD 3 Southwark
01.12.93 Jerry Mortimer W RSC 3 Kensington
16.02.94 Chris Richards W RSC 2 Stevenage
14.03.94 Mark Atkins W PTS 6 Mayfair
13.04.94 Gordon Blair W RTD 1 Glasgow
23.09.94 Martin Jolley W CO 3 Bethnal Green
09.11.94 Chris Peters W RSC 3 Millwall
14.02.95 Chris Richards W RTD 2 Bethnal Green
21.04.95 Paul Wesley W RSC 6 Dudley
(*Elim. British L. Middleweight Title*)
13.01.96 Ensley Bingham L RSC 3 Manchester
(*Vacant British L. Middleweight Title*)
08.04.97 Steve Roberts L PTS 10 Bethnal Green
(*Vacant Southern Area L. Middleweight Title*)
Career: 18 contests, won 15, lost 3.

Gary Jacobs
Glasgow. *Born* Glasgow, 10 December, 1965
L. Middleweight. Former European & Commonwealth Welterweight Champion. Former Undefeated British, IBF Inter-Continental, WBC International & Scottish Welterweight Champion. Ht. 5'7½"
Manager Self

20.05.85 John Conlan W PTS 6 Glasgow
03.06.85 Nigel Burke W PTS 6 Glasgow
12.08.85 Mike McKenzie W PTS 6 Glasgow
07.10.85 Albert Buchanan W PTS 6 Cambuslang
11.11.85 Tyrell Wilson W CO 5 Glasgow
02.12.85 Dave Heaver W PTS 6 Glasgow
10.02.86 Courtney Phillips W RSC 5 Glasgow
10.03.86 Alistair Laurie W PTS 8 Glasgow
14.04.86 Billy Cairns W PTS 8 Glasgow
24.06.86 Dave Douglas L PTS 10 Glasgow
(*Vacant Scottish Welterweight Title*)

15.09.86	Jeff Connors W RSC 3 Glasgow
20.10.86	Kelvin Mortimer W RSC 5 Glasgow
27.01.87	Dave Douglas W PTS 10 Glasgow
	(Scottish Welterweight Title Challenge)
24.02.87	Gary Williams W CO 7 Glasgow
06.04.87	Robert Armstrong W RTD 5 Glasgow
19.05.87	Gary Williams W RSC 3 Cumbernauld
08.06.87	Tommy McCallum W RSC 5 Glasgow
	(Scottish Welterweight Title Defence)
26.11.87	Jeff Connors W PTS 8 Fulham
24.02.88	Del Bryan W PTS 10 Glasgow
	(Final Elim. British Welterweight Title)
19.04.88	Wilf Gentzen W PTS 12 Glasgow
	(Commonwealth Welterweight Title Challenge)
06.06.88	Juan Alonzo Villa W RSC 5 Mayfair
16.09.88	Javier Suazo W CO 10 Las Vegas, USA
	(Vacant WBC International Welterweight Title)
29.11.88	Richard Rova W CO 4 Kensington
	(Commonwealth Welterweight Title Defence)
14.02.89	Rocky Kelly W RTD 7 Wandsworth
	(Commonwealth & WBC International Welterweight Title Defence)
05.04.89	George Collins W PTS 12 Kensington
	(Commonwealth & WBC International Welterweight Title Defence)
27.06.89	Rollin Williams W RSC 1 Kensington
27.08.89	James McGirt L PTS 10 New York, USA
23.11.89	Donovan Boucher L PTS 12 Motherwell
	(Commonwealth Welterweight Title Defence)
26.04.90	Pascal Lorcy W RSC 2 Wandsworth
09.05.90	Mike Durvan W CO 1 Kensington
17.10.90	Mickey Hughes L CO 8 Bethnal Green
05.03.91	Kenny Louis W CO 2 Glasgow
20.11.91	Peter Eubank W PTS 8 Kensington
20.02.92	Del Bryan W PTS 12 Glasgow
	(British Welterweight Title Challenge)
25.03.92	Tommy Small W RSC 2 Kensington
22.04.92	Cirillo Nino W PTS 10 Wembley
09.07.92	Robert Wright W RSC 6 Glasgow
	(British Welterweight Title Defence)
16.10.92	Ludovic Proto L PTS 12 Paris, France
	(Vacant European Welterweight Title)
06.02.93	Ludovic Proto W RTD 9 Paris, France
	(European Welterweight Title Challenge)
19.05.93	Horace Fleary W RTD 4 Sunderland
22.09.93	Daniel Bicchieray W RSC 5 Wembley
	(European Welterweight Title Defence)
01.02.94	Tek Nkalankete W PTS 12 Paris, France
	(European Welterweight Title Defence)
13.04.94	Alessandro Duran W CO 8 Glasgow
	(European Welterweight Title Defence)
05.10.94	Rusty deRouen W RSC 6 Wolverhampton
09.11.94	Marcelo di Croce W PTS 10 Millwall
04.03.95	Jose Miguel Fernandez W PTS 10 Atlantic City, USA
26.08.95	Pernell Whitaker L PTS 12 Atlantic City, USA
	(WBC Welterweight Title Challenge)
18.11.95	Leigh Wicks W RTD 3 Glasgow
13.03.96	Edwin Murillo W CO 5 Wembley
	(IBF Inter-Continental Welterweight Title Challenge)
14.06.96	Patrick Charpentier L RSC 7 Gravelines, France
	(European Welterweight Title Challenge)
25.03.97	Jimmy Vincent W RSC 1 Lewisham
16.04.97	Viktor Fessetchko W PTS 8 Bethnal Green

Career: 52 contests, won 45, lost 7.

Jacklord Jacobs

London. *Born* Nigeria, 1 January, 1970
Cruiserweight. Ht. 6'1"
Manager Self

03.03.94	Cordwell Hylton W RSC 3 Ebbw Vale
30.07.94	Cordwell Hylton W RSC 4 Bethnal Green
01.11.94	Bobby Anderson DREW 4 Las Vegas, USA
14.11.95	John Pierre W PTS 6 Yarm
05.02.96	Tim Redman DREW 6 Bexleyheath
22.04.96	Chris Woollas DREW 4 Crystal Palace
27.08.96	Andrew Benson L CO 2 Windsor

Career: 7 contests, won 3, drew 3, lost 1.

Daniel James

Newmarket. *Born* Lincoln, 15 December, 1975
L. Welterweight. Ht. 5'9"
Manager T. Lawless

24.10.96	Shaba Edwards W PTS 6 Wembley
20.11.96	Costas Katsantonis W PTS 6 Wembley
11.02.97	Vince Burns W CO 2 Bethnal Green
03.04.97	Mark Allen W RSC 4 Wembley

Career: 4 contests, won 4.

Daniel James   Les Clark

John Janes

Cardiff. *Born* Worcester, 3 March, 1974
L. Middleweight. Ht. 5'7"
Manager D. Gardiner

29.11.94	Steve Burton W PTS 6 Cardiff
25.01.95	Paul Dyer L PTS 6 Cardiff
06.05.95	Sean Baker L PTS 4 Shepton Mallet
20.09.95	Gavin Lane W PTS 6 Ystrad
29.09.95	Enzo Giordano L RSC 4 Bloomsbury
13.11.95	Justin Simmons L PTS 6 Barnstaple
28.11.95	Mark McGowan W PTS 6 Cardiff

19.01.96	Paul Miles W PTS 4 Bracknell
29.05.96	Gavin Lane W PTS 6 Ebbw Vale
13.07.96	Wayne Alexander L RSC 3 Bethnal Green

Career: 10 contests, won 5, lost 5.

Tommy Janes

Cardiff. *Born* Cardiff, 28 November, 1976
Lightweight. Ht. 5'10"
Manager D. Gardiner

20.12.95	Craig Kelley W PTS 6 Usk
13.02.96	Arv Mittoo W PTS 6 Cardiff
20.03.96	Marc Smith L RSC 6 Cardiff
15.05.96	Chris Price W RSC 4 Cardiff
19.07.96	Barrie Kelley W RSC 3 Ystrad
18.09.96	Gary Jenkinson W RSC 1 Tylorstown
06.11.96	Terry Whittaker W RSC 4 Tylorstown
27.11.96	Lewis Reynolds L RSC 1 Swansea

Career: 8 contests, won 6, lost 2.

David Jay

Cefn Hengoed. *Born* Merthyr Tydfil, 4 May, 1971
S. Featherweight. Ht. 5'10"
Manager D. Gardiner

15.05.96	Robert Grubb W RSC 4 Cardiff
29.05.96	Gary Jenkinson DREW 6 Ebbw Vale
18.09.96	David Morris L PTS 4 Tylorstown
28.04.97	Jason Dee L RSC 3 Enfield

Career: 4 contests, won 1, drew 1, lost 2.

David Jeffrey

Bournemouth. *Born* Edgware, 22 May, 1969
Featherweight. Ht. 5'7"
Manager N. Christian

15.02.97	Brian Gentry L PTS 6 Tooting
01.03.97	Alex Moon L RSC 2 Liverpool
03.04.97	Jezz D'Agostino W PTS 6 Wembley
19.04.97	Greg Upton L RSC 5 Plymouth
20.05.97	Paul Halpin L PTS 6 Gillingham

Career: 5 contests, won 1, lost 4.

David Jeffrey   Les Clark

Gary Jenkinson

Lincoln. *Born* Lincoln, 16 January, 1969
S. Featherweight. Ht. 5'5½"
Manager J. Gaynor

26.10.95	Carl Allen L PTS 6 Birmingham
02.11.95	Paul Quarmby W PTS 6 Houghton le Spring
08.12.95	Shaune Danskin W PTS 6 Leeds
23.02.96	Wayne Jones DREW 6 Weston super Mare
16.03.96	Chris Lyons W PTS 6 Barnstaple
29.05.96	David Jay DREW 6 Ebbw Vale
18.09.96	Tommy Jeans L RSC 1 Tylorstown
24.10.96	Craig Kelley W PTS 6 Lincoln
16.12.96	Franny Hogg L RSC 2 Cleethorpes
19.06.97	Andy Ross W PTS 6 Scunthorpe

Career: 10 contests, won 5, drew 2, lost 3.

Andrew Jervis

Liverpool. *Born* Liverpool, 28 June, 1969
L. Middleweight. Ht. 5'11"
Manager Self

05.10.92	Rick North W PTS 6 Liverpool
02.11.92	Shaun Martin W CO 2 Liverpool
01.12.92	Cliff Churchward W PTS 6 Liverpool
27.01.93	Mark Ramsey L PTS 6 Stoke
22.02.93	Alan Williams W PTS 6 Liverpool
29.03.93	Bullit Andrews W PTS 6 Liverpool
09.06.93	Chris Mulcahy W PTS 6 Liverpool
15.03.94	John Duckworth L PTS 6 Stoke
25.05.94	Sean Baker DREW 4 Bristol
04.06.94	Adrian Dodson L RSC 2 Cardiff
17.08.94	Robin Reid L RSC 1 Sheffield
26.10.94	David Larkin L CO 5 Leeds
08.03.95	Howard Clarke L PTS 6 Solihull
22.03.95	Andy Peach W PTS 6 Stoke
03.04.95	Andy Davidson W CO 3 Manchester
27.05.95	Neil Sinclair W RSC 3 Belfast
22.09.95	Peter Waudby L PTS 10 Hull
	(Vacant Central Area L. Middleweight Title)
21.10.95	Paul Carr W RSC 3 Bethnal Green
10.11.95	Wayne Alexander L RTD 3 Derby
23.01.96	Steve Roberts L PTS 6 Bethnal Green
04.03.97	James Donoghue L RSC 4 Yarm

Career: 21 contests, won 10, drew 1, lost 10.

Chris Jickells

Brigg. *Born* Scunthorpe, 26 March, 1971
Former Undefeated Central Area
Featherweight Champion.
Ht. 5'5"
Manager J. Rushton

18.11.91	Tony Smith W RSC 4 Manchester
09.12.91	Al Garrett W RSC 2 Bradford
15.01.92	Ronnie Stephenson L PTS 6 Stoke
30.03.92	Colin Innes W RSC 3 Bradford
29.04.92	Kevin Middleton W RSC 6 Solihull
01.06.92	Dave McHale L RSC 4 Glasgow
12.10.92	Ian McGirr W RSC 3 Bradford
10.02.93	Kevin Middleton L CO 1 Lewisham
07.06.93	Wilson Docherty L RSC 5 Glasgow
02.11.93	Mark Bowers L RSC 3 Southwark
21.03.94	Mike Deveney L RSC 5 Glasgow
26.09.94	Dave Clavering L PTS 6 Morecambe
11.10.94	Yifru Retta L PTS 6 Bethnal Green
11.11.94	Dennis Holback Pedersen L PTS 6 Randers, Denmark

(Continued second column)

23.11.94	Ian McLeod L PTS 6 Irvine
04.02.95	Neil Swain L PTS 6 Cardiff
04.03.95	Paul Griffin L RSC 5 Livingston
30.06.95	Graham McGrath W PTS 4 Doncaster
28.07.95	Graham McGrath W PTS 6 Epworth
11.10.95	Gary Marston L PTS 8 Stoke
25.10.95	Barry Jones L PTS 6 Cardiff
29.11.95	Miguel Matthews L PTS 6 Solihull
22.01.96	Ian McLeod L PTS 8 Glasgow
29.02.96	Carl Allen L PTS 6 Glasgow
01.04.96	Kid McAuley W PTS 6 Bradford
03.05.96	Trevor Sumner W RSC 5 Sheffield
	(Vacant Central Area Featherweight Title)
25.05.96	Stephen Smith L RSC 3 Leipzig, Germany
25.06.96	Gary Thornhill L PTS 6 Stevenage
06.11.96	Paul Ingle L RSC 4 Hull

Career: 29 contests, won 9, lost 20.

(Paul) John O. Johnson (Johnson)

Nottingham. *Born* Nottingham, 2
November, 1969
Lightweight. Ht. 5'5"
Manager W. Swift

29.08.91	Seth Jones W DIS 1 Oakengates
09.10.91	James Jiora W PTS 6 Manchester
24.10.91	Carl Hook L PTS 6 Dunstable
31.10.91	Darren Morris W PTS 6 Oakengates
26.11.91	Bernard Paul L PTS 6 Bethnal Green
22.01.92	Brian Coleman W PTS 6 Stoke
30.01.92	Chris Saunders W PTS 6 Southampton
20.02.92	Alan Peacock W PTS 6 Glasgow
09.03.92	Ricky Sackfield W PTS 6 Manchester
26.03.92	Davy Robb L PTS 6 Telford
03.06.92	Jason Barker W PTS 6 Newcastle under Lyme
09.09.92	Chris Saunders DREW 6 Stoke
05.10.92	Andreas Panayi L RTD 1 Liverpool
09.12.92	Jason Barker W PTS 8 Stoke
10.02.93	Dean Hollington L PTS 6 Lewisham
17.03.93	Jonathan Thaxton L PTS 6 Stoke
19.01.94	Billy McDougall L RSC 3 Stoke
10.03.94	Keith Marner L RSC 5 Watford
10.05.94	Mark Legg W RSC 6 Doncaster
11.06.94	Paul Knights W PTS 6 Bethnal Green
28.06.94	Andreas Panayi L RSC 5 Mayfair
30.09.94	Michael Ayers L RSC 3 Bethnal Green
23.02.95	Peter Richardson L RSC 5 Southwark
30.03.95	Richie Edwards L PTS 4 Bethnal Green
20.04.95	Carl Wright L PTS 6 Liverpool
13.05.95	Tanveer Ahmed L CO 3 Glasgow
21.09.95	Paul Miles L PTS 4 Battersea
21.10.95	Martin Holgate L PTS 4 Bethnal Green
28.10.95	Allan Gray L PTS 6 Kensington
25.11.95	Mark Winters L RSC 2 Dublin
13.01.96	Ricky Sackfield L PTS 6 Manchester
20.01.96	Jonathan Thaxton L RSC 4 Mansfield
10.05.97	Marc Smith W PTS 6 Nottingham
19.05.97	Brian Coleman DREW 6 Cleethorpes

Career: 34 contests, won 12, drew 2, lost 20.

(Paul) Robbo Johnson

Doncaster. *Born* Doncaster, 30 April, 1977
Welterweight. Ht. 5'11¾"
Manager H. Hayes

20.02.97	Richard Inquieti L PTS 6 Mansfield
01.05.97	Pedro Carragher L PTS 6 Hull

Career: 2 contests, lost 2.

Martin Jolley

Alfreton. *Born* Chesterfield, 22 November, 1967
S. Middleweight. Ht. 5'11½"
Manager Self

10.03.92	Gypsy Johnny Price W RSC 3 Bury
06.04.92	Sean Byrne L RSC 6 Northampton
11.05.92	Mark Hale W PTS 6 Coventry
08.09.92	Brian McGloin W PTS 6 Doncaster
05.10.92	Mark Hale W RSC 4 Bardon
14.10.92	Carl Smallwood W PTS 6 Stoke
02.11.92	Bobby Mack L PTS 6 Wolverhampton
24.11.92	Phil Ball DREW 6 Doncaster
02.02.93	Mark McBiane W RSC 2 Derby
23.02.93	Phil Ball W RSC 5 Doncaster
12.05.93	Marvin O'Brien W PTS 6 Sheffield
08.06.93	Paul Hanlon W PTS 6 Derby
22.09.93	Nigel Rafferty L PTS 6 Chesterfield
29.10.93	Mads Larsen L CO 2 Korsoer, Denmark
02.12.93	Darren Littlewood L PTS 6 Evesham
17.03.94	Paul Hitch W RSC 2 Lincoln
25.04.94	Derek Wormald L RSC 4 Bury
24.05.94	Dave Johnson L PTS 6 Sunderland
17.06.94	Dean Francis L PTS 6 Plymouth
02.07.94	Glenn Catley L RSC 1 Keynsham
23.09.94	Gilbert Jackson L CO 3 Bethnal Green
24.10.94	Craig Joseph L PTS 6 Bradford
07.11.94	Mark Delaney L RSC 3 Bethnal Green
12.12.94	Darren Littlewood L PTS 6 Cleethorpes
20.12.94	Mark Delaney L RSC 4 Bethnal Green
17.02.95	Willie Quinn L CO 5 Cumbernauld
11.05.95	Darren Sweeney L PTS 6 Dudley
19.05.95	Steve McNess L PTS 6 Southwark
10.06.95	Robin Reid L CO 1 Manchester
27.09.95	Steve McNess W RTD 4 Bethnal Green
29.10.95	Warren Stowe L PTS 6 Shaw
13.11.95	Peter Vosper W PTS 6 Barnstaple
23.11.95	Dave Johnson L PTS 6 Tynemouth
11.12.95	Lee Blundell L PTS 6 Morecambe
26.01.96	Ryan Rhodes L CO 3 Brighton
05.03.96	Jason Hart L PTS 6 Bethnal Green
16.03.96	Willie Quinn L RSC 4 Glasgow
11.05.96	Ryan Rhodes L RSC 2 Bethnal Green
25.06.96	Jason Matthews L RSC 3 Mansfield
20.09.96	Neville Smith L RSC 3 Tooting
06.11.96	Tony Booth L PTS 4 Hull
06.12.96	James Lowther L PTS 6 Leeds
22.12.96	Lee Whitehead DREW 6 Salford
31.01.97	Craig Winter L RSC 3 Pentre Halkyn
07.03.97	Raziq Ali L PTS 6 Northampton
16.03.97	Lee Blundell L PTS 6 Shaw
20.04.97	David Radford L PTS 8 Leeds
03.05.97	Pascal Collins L PTS 6 Manchester
10.05.97	Johnny Hooks DREW 6 Nottingham
20.05.97	Eddie Knight L PTS 6 Gillingham
26.06.97	Lee Whitehead L PTS 6 Salford

Career: 51 contests, won 12, drew 3, lost 36.

Barry Jones

Cardiff. *Born* Cardiff, 3 May, 1974
IBF Inter-Continental S. Featherweight
Champion. Ht. 5'7"
Manager F. Warren

28.10.92	Conn McMullen W PTS 6 Cardiff
14.12.92	Miguel Matthews W PTS 6 Cardiff
27.01.93	Mike Deveney W PTS 6 Cardiff
24.03.93	Greg Upton W RSC 2 Cardiff
28.04.93	Kid McAuley W PTS 8 Solihull
09.10.93	John White W PTS 4 Manchester

10.11.93 Neil Swain W PTS 6 Ystrad
30.11.93 Pete Buckley W PTS 4 Cardiff
16.12.93 Elvis Parsley W PTS 6 Newport
22.01.94 Pete Buckley W PTS 6 Cardiff
27.08.94 Kelton McKenzie W PTS 6 Cardiff
25.05.95 Justin Murphy W PTS 10 Reading
          (Elim. British Featherweight Title)
25.10.95 Chris Jickells W PTS 6 Cardiff
28.11.95 Pete Buckley W PTS 6 Cardiff
30.11.96 David Morris DREW 6 Tylorstown
12.04.97 Peter Judson W PTS 12 Sheffield
          (IBF Inter-Continental
          S. Featherweight Title Challenge)
21.06.97 Affif Djelti W PTS 12 Cardiff
          (IBF Inter-Continental S.
          Featherweight Title Defence)

Career: 17 contests, won 16, drew 1.

Barry Jones   Les Clark

Benny Jones   Les Clark

108

(John) Benny Jones

Birmingham. *Born* Birmingham, 6 April, 1978
Featherweight. Ht. 5'10"
Manager N. Nobbs

12.09.96 Stefy Bull L PTS 6 Doncaster
07.10.96 Graham McGrath L PTS 6 Birmingham
24.10.96 David Coldwell W PTS 6 Lincoln
01.11.96 Carl Greaves L PTS 6 Mansfield
29.11.96 Garry Burrell L PTS 6 Glasgow
11.12.96 Francky Leroy L CO 5 Southwark
12.02.97 Alston Buchanan W CO 5 Glasgow
28.02.97 Shaun Anderson L PTS 6 Kilmarnock
25.03.97 Darrell Easton L PTS 4 Lewisham
24.04.97 Rudy Valentino L PTS 6 Mayfair
08.05.97 Carl Greaves W RSC 4 Mansfield

Career: 11 contests, won 3, lost 8.

Henry Jones

Pembroke. *Born* Haverfordwest, 23 December, 1975
Bantamweight. Ht. 5'0"
Manager Self

17.06.95 Abdul Mannon W PTS 6 Cardiff
07.07.95 Harry Woods L PTS 4 Cardiff
07.10.95 Frankie Slane L PTS 4 Belfast
28.11.95 Jason Thomas L PTS 4 Cardiff
20.12.95 Brendan Bryce W PTS 6 Usk
20.03.96 Danny Lawson W CO 1 Cardiff
29.05.96 Ian Turner L PTS 6 Ebbw Vale
02.10.96 Jason Thomas W PTS 4 Cardiff
26.10.96 Danny Costello L RSC 3 Liverpool
29.04.97 Tommy Waite L PTS 4 Belfast
19.05.97 Francky Leroy L RSC 1 Coudekerque, France

Career: 11 contests, won 4, lost 7.

John Jones

Liverpool. *Born* Liverpool, 13 July, 1968
Welterweight. Ht. 5'9"
Manager S. Vaughan

29.09.95 John Smith W PTS 6 Liverpool
05.03.96 Michael Alexander W PTS 6 Barrow
10.05.96 Charlie Paine W PTS 6 Liverpool
04.09.97 Shaun Stokes W PTS 6 Liverpool

Career: 4 contests, won 4.

Keith Jones

Cefn Hengoed. *Born* Bradwell, 4 December, 1968
S. Featherweight. Ht. 5'5¾"
Manager Self

17.05.94 Abdul Mannon L PTS 6 Kettering
13.06.94 G. G. Goddard L PTS 6 Liverpool
21.07.94 G. G. Goddard L RSC 1 Battersea
12.09.94 Marco Fattore L PTS 6 Mayfair
29.09.94 Marlon Ward L PTS 4 Bethnal Green
21.10.94 James Murray L CO 3 Glasgow
27.11.94 Daniel Lutaaya L CO 1 Southwark
03.09.96 Benny May W RSC 2 Bethnal Green
18.09.96 Kevin Sheil W PTS 4 Tylorstown
04.10.96 Andy Ross DREW 6 Pentre Halkyn
18.10.96 Wayne Jones DREW 6 Barnstaple
06.11.96 Robert Grubb W PTS 4 Tylorstown
22.11.96 Tony Mulholland L PTS 4 Liverpool
03.12.96 Alex Moon L RTD 5 Liverpool
21.01.97 Greg Upton DREW 6 Bristol
26.02.97 Greg Upton L PTS 4 Cardiff

07.03.97 Dean Murdoch L PTS 6 Weston super Mare
20.03.97 Kevin Sheil DREW 8 Solihull
04.04.97 Tony Mulholland L PTS 4 Liverpool
22.05.97 Darrell Easton L PTS 4 Southwark

Career: 20 contests, won 3, drew 4, lost 13.

Paul Jones

Sheffield. *Born* Sheffield, 19 November, 1966
Middleweight. Former Undefeated WBO, WBO Inter-Continental & Central Area L. Middleweight Champion. Ht. 6'0"
Manager B. Hearn

08.12.86 Paul Gillings W PTS 6 Liverpool
28.10.87 Pat Durkin W PTS 4 Sheffield
10.11.87 David Binns L PTS 6 Batley
11.01.88 Humphrey Harrison L PTS 8 Manchester
27.09.88 George Sponagle DREW 8 Halifax, Canada
07.12.88 Jimmy Thornton W PTS 6 Stoke
23.01.89 Donovan Boucher L DIS 6 Toronto, Canada
13.03.89 Dale Moreland W PTS 6 Toronto, Canada
30.03.89 Benoit Boudreau W PTS 10 Moncton, Canada
19.04.89 Tony Collier W CO 3 Toronto, Canada
06.06.89 George Sponagle L PTS 8 Halifax, Canada
06.09.89 Kid Ford W PTS 6 Mississouga, Canada
13.11.89 Ian Midwood-Tate W RSC 4 Manchester
08.12.89 Antoine Tarver L PTS 4 Doncaster
06.03.90 Antonio Fernandez W PTS 8 Stoke
22.03.90 Darren Pilling W RTD 7 Gateshead
26.04.90 Newton Barnett W PTS 8 Mayfair
20.05.90 Jim Beckett W CO 1 Sheffield
22.05.90 Wayne Ellis L PTS 6 St Albans
14.11.90 Jason Rowe W PTS 10 Sheffield
          (Central Area L. Middleweight Title Challenge)
12.03.91 Tony Velinor W PTS 8 Mansfield
16.08.91 Hugo Marinangelli L CO 2 Marbella, Spain
01.10.91 Simon Eubank W CO 6 Sheffield
14.04.92 Paul Lynch W RSC 3 Mansfield
19.05.92 Trevor Ambrose W PTS 6 Cardiff
02.06.92 Patrick Vungbo W PTS 10 Rotterdam, Holland
19.09.92 Ernie Loveridge W PTS 6 Glasgow
24.11.92 Paul Wesley L RSC 2 Doncaster
17.01.95 Julian Eavis W RSC 4 Worcester
06.03.95 Peter Waudby W PTS 6 Mayfair
14.04.95 Damien Denny W CO 1 Belfast
          (Vacant WBO Inter-Continental L. Middleweight Title)
26.08.95 Danny Juma W PTS 12 Belfast
          (WBO Inter-Continental L. Middleweight Title Defence)
02.10.95 Eric Spalding W RSC 2 Mayfair
          (WBO Inter-Continental L. Middleweight Title Defence)
22.11.95 Verno Phillips W PTS 12 Sheffield
          (WBO L. Middleweight Title Challenge)
14.12.96 Ryan Rhodes L RSC 8 Sheffield
          (Vacant British L. Middleweight Title)
08.05.97 Lee Blundell W RSC 4 Mansfield

Career: 36 contests, won 26, drew 1, lost 9.

Wayne Jones   Les Clark

Wayne Jones

Saltash. *Born* Halifax, 6 October, 1968
S. Featherweight. Ht. 5'8"
Manager Self

13.11.93	Robbie Sivyer W PTS 6 Cullompton
14.01.94	Colin Dunne L RSC 3 Bethnal Green
04.03.94	Robbie Sivyer W PTS 6 Weston super Mare
17.06.94	Trevor Royal W PTS 6 Plymouth
09.07.94	Bobby Guynan L PTS 6 Earls Court
30.07.94	Sean Knight L RSC 2 Bethnal Green
01.10.94	Gareth Jordan L RSC 2 Cardiff
19.11.94	Adrian Chase L PTS 6 Heathrow
27.11.94	Everald Williams L RSC 2 Southwark
24.01.95	Brian Coleman W PTS 6 Piccadilly
18.02.95	Chris Barnett L RSC 5 Shepton Mallet
25.03.95	Danny Lutaaya L RSC 3 Millwall
09.05.95	Georgie Smith L RSC 3 Basildon
16.06.95	Lewis Reynolds L PTS 4 Southwark
23.06.95	Allan Gray L PTS 6 Bethnal Green
02.09.95	A. M. Milton L RSC 1 Wembley
30.10.95	Anthony Campbell L RSC 1 Heathrow
06.02.96	Michael Wright L PTS 4 Basildon
23.02.96	Gary Jenkinson DREW 6 Weston super Mare
16.03.96	Phil Lashley W PTS 6 Barnstaple
20.04.96	Richard Evatt L RSC 2 Brentwood
03.06.96	Ervine Blake L RSC 1 Birmingham
18.10.96	Keith Jones DREW 6 Barnstaple
07.11.96	Brian Gentry W PTS 6 Battersea
22.11.96	Tommy Peacock L RSC 4 Liverpool
28.01.97	Eddie Sica L PTS 6 Piccadilly
04.03.97	Matt Brown L RSC 3 Southwark
28.04.97	Tontcho Tontchev L RSC 1 Hull

Career: 28 contests, won 6, drew 2, lost 20.

Gareth Jordan

Monmouth. *Born* Usk, 19 December, 1971
Lightweight. Ht. 5'6¾"
Manager M. Duff

02.11.92	Con Cronin W RSC 2 Wolverhampton
04.12.92	Jason White W RSC 2 Telford
16.03.93	Lee Fox W RSC 3 Wolverhampton
26.05.93	Mark O'Callaghan W RSC 3 Mansfield
27.10.93	Dave Madden W RSC 5 West Bromwich
16.12.93	Phil Found W PTS 6 Newport
04.06.94	T. J. Smith W RSC 1 Cardiff
01.10.94	Wayne Jones W RSC 2 Cardiff
30.11.94	Kevin McKenzie W PTS 6 Wolverhampton
04.02.95	Mark O'Callaghan W RSC 2 Cardiff
21.04.95	Peter Till W PTS 6 Dudley
07.07.95	Kelton McKenzie W PTS 4 Cardiff
25.10.95	Mervyn Bennett L PTS 10 Cardiff *(Welsh Lightweight Title Challenge)*
13.02.96	Bamana Dibateza W PTS 8 Cardiff
16.05.96	Billy Schwer L RSC 3 Dunstable
03.04.97	Anthony Campbell W PTS 6 Wembley

Career: 16 contests, won 14, lost 2.

Craig Joseph

Bradford. *Born* Bradford, 15 December, 1968
S. Middleweight. Ht. 6'0"
Manager J. Doughty

04.10.93	Pat McNamara W RSC 2 Bradford
07.02.94	Jimmy Tyers W PTS 6 Bradford
27.04.94	Chris Davies W PTS 6 Solihull
13.06.94	Spencer Alton W PTS 6 Bradford
24.10.94	Martin Jolley W PTS 6 Bradford
20.02.95	Ray Webb L PTS 6 Glasgow
26.04.95	Neil Simpson W PTS 6 Solihull
20.10.95	Thomas Hansvoll L PTS 4 Copenhagen, Denmark
07.03.96	P. R. Mason W PTS 6 Bradford
09.04.96	Fran Harding DREW 6 Salford
14.11.96	Clinton Woods L PTS 10 Sheffield *(Vacant Central Area S. Middleweight Title)*
04.03.97	Herol Graham L PTS 8 Southwark

Career: 12 contests, won 7, drew 1, lost 4.

Peter Judson

Keighley. *Born* Keighley, 14 January, 1970
S. Featherweight. Former IBF Inter-Continental S. Featherweight Champion. Ht. 5'7"
Manager F. Warren

24.04.89	Darryl Pettit DREW 6 Bradford
11.07.89	Neil Leitch W PTS 6 Batley
18.09.89	Phil Lashley W PTS 6 Mayfair
02.10.89	Stevie Woods L PTS 6 Bradford
22.11.89	Pete Buckley L PTS 6 Stafford
19.02.90	Phil Lashley W CO 6 Nottingham
08.03.90	Wayne Goult L PTS 6 Peterborough
19.03.90	Andrew Robinson W PTS 6 Grimsby
26.03.90	Wayne Marston W PTS 6 Nottingham
30.04.90	Derek Amory L PTS 6 Brierley Hill
09.05.90	Brian Robb W PTS 6 Solihull
04.06.90	Jamie McBride L PTS 8 Glasgow
17.09.90	Mark Geraghty W PTS 8 Glasgow
26.09.90	Carl Roberts W PTS 6 Manchester
08.10.90	Mark Geraghty L PTS 8 Glasgow
19.11.90	Russell Davison L PTS 8 Manchester
27.11.90	Rocky Lawlor W PTS 8 Wolverhampton
29.01.91	Russell Davison L PTS 10 Stockport *(Vacant Central Area Featherweight Title)*
21.02.91	Noel Carroll W PTS 8 Leeds
20.03.91	Colin Lynch W RTD 5 Solihull
01.05.91	Jimmy Owens L PTS 6 Liverpool
28.05.91	Scott Durham W PTS 6 Cardiff
24.09.91	Ian McGirr L PTS 6 Glasgow
11.11.91	Miguel Matthews W PTS 6 Stratford upon Avon
18.11.91	Jamie McBride DREW 6 Glasgow
09.02.92	Ceri Farrell W PTS 6 Bradford
05.04.92	Barrie Kelley W PTS 6 Bradford
14.11.92	J. T. Williams DREW 6 Cardiff
25.02.93	Dominic McGuigan DREW 6 Bradford
16.05.94	Carlos Chase W PTS 4 Heathrow
25.03.95	Sugar Gibiliru W PTS 6 Chester
06.05.95	Colin McMillan L PTS 8 Shepton Mallet
30.09.95	Daniel Alicea L PTS 6 Cardiff
16.03.96	Cassius Baloyi L PTS 6 Glasgow
19.09.96	Dean Phillips W RSC 10 Manchester *(Vacant IBF Inter-Continental S. Featherweight Title)*
12.04.97	Barry Jones L PTS 12 Sheffield *(IBF Inter-Continental S. Featherweight Title Defence)*

Career: 36 contests, won 18, drew 4, lost 14.

David Jules

Doncaster. *Born* Doncaster, 11 July, 1965
Heavyweight. Ht. 6'2"
Manager J. Rushton

12.06.87	Carl Timbrell W CO 5 Leamington
07.10.87	Carl Timbrell L RSC 3 Stoke
17.03.88	Peter Fury W RTD 2 Sunderland
21.03.88	Jess Harding L RSC 2 Bethnal Green
29.09.88	Gary McCrory L PTS 6 Sunderland
22.11.88	Gary McCrory L PTS 6 Marton
05.12.88	Denroy Bryan DREW 6 Dudley
18.01.89	Denroy Bryan W RSC 2 Stoke
22.02.89	Tony Hallett W RSC 1 Doncaster
19.04.89	Rocky Burton L RSC 3 Doncaster
11.11.89	Jimmy di Stolfo W RSC 1 Rimini, Italy
30.11.89	Biagio Chianese L RSC 2 Milan, Italy
19.02.90	Vance Idiens L PTS 6 Birmingham
07.05.90	Ramon Voorn L RSC 3 Arnhem, Holland
12.11.90	Steve Garber L RSC 6 Bradford
09.04.91	Herbie Hide L RSC 1 Mayfair
05.12.91	Vance Idiens L RSC 4 Cannock
24.02.92	Rocky Burton W CO 1 Coventry
05.04.92	Steve Garber L RSC 4 Bradford
08.09.92	Wayne Buck L RSC 3 Doncaster
09.12.92	Vance Idiens L PTS 8 Stoke
10.05.93	Steve Lewsam L CO 6 Cleethorpes
28.10.93	Joey Paladino L RSC 2 Walsall
10.12.94	Darren Corbett L RSC 1 Manchester
14.06.95	Martin Langtry L RSC 3 Batley
08.11.95	Shane Woollas L PTS 6 Scunthorpe
15.12.95	Mika Kihlstrom L RSC 2 Bethnal Green
31.01.96	Shane Woollas W PTS 6 Stoke
16.03.96	Chris Woollas L PTS 6 Sheffield
25.03.96	Andy Lambert L RSC 1 Birmingham
24.04.96	Kevin Burton W PTS 6 Stoke
10.05.96	Steve Bristow L RSC 2 Liverpool
29.07.96	Shane Woollas W PTS 6 Skegness
09.09.96	Marko Valtonen L RSC 1 Helsinki, Finland
18.10.96	Phill Day L RSC 1 Barnstaple
10.05.97	Jim Pallatt W RSC 1 Nottingham
05.06.97	Greg Wedlake L RSC 3 Bristol

Career: 37 contests, won 10, drew 1, lost 26.

John Kaighin

Swansea. *Born* Brecknock, 26 August, 1967
Cruiserweight. Ht. 5'11¼"
Manager P. Boyce

17.09.90 Carlos Christie L PTS 6 Cardiff
24.09.90 James F. Woolley L PTS 6 Lewisham
15.10.90 Max McCracken L PTS 6 Brierley Hill
22.10.90 Stefan Wright L PTS 6 Peterborough
15.11.90 Tony Wellington W PTS 6 Oldham
13.12.90 Nick Manners L CO 3 Dewsbury
24.01.91 Robert Peel L PTS 6 Gorseinon
12.02.91 Robert Peel W PTS 6 Cardiff
15.03.91 Max McCracken DREW 6 Willenhall
10.04.91 Darron Griffiths L PTS 6 Newport
24.04.91 Paul Murray W PTS 6 Aberavon
08.05.91 Benji Good W RSC 3 Kensington
15.05.91 Robert Peel L PTS 8 Swansea
06.06.91 Peter Vosper DREW 6 Barking
30.06.91 John Ogistie L PTS 6 Southwark
29.08.91 Adrian Wright W PTS 6 Oakengates
09.09.91 Terry Johnson W RTD 2 Liverpool
11.09.91 Lester Jacobs L RSC 2 Hammersmith
22.10.91 Andy Wright DREW 6 Wandsworth
13.11.91 Garry Delaney L PTS 6 Bethnal Green
20.11.91 Keith Inglis W RSC 1 Kensington
23.01.92 Michael Gale L PTS 8 York
01.02.92 Paul Busby L PTS 4 Birmingham
25.02.92 Andy Wright L PTS 6 Crystal Palace
05.03.92 Lester Jacobs L RSC 1 Battersea
27.04.92 Bruce Scott L CO 4 Mayfair
18.07.92 Carl Harney L PTS 6 Manchester
15.09.92 Paul Wright L DIS 5 Liverpool
26.09.92 Shaun Cummins L RTD 4 Earls Court
28.10.92 Joey Peters DREW 4 Kensington
12.11.92 Graham Jenner L RSC 5 Baywater
01.12.92 Peter Vosper W RSC 4 Bristol
22.12.92 Darrit Douglas W PTS 6 Mayfair
14.01.93 Ole Klemetsen L RTD 3 Mayfair
24.03.93 Darron Griffiths L RSC 6 Cardiff
(Vacant Welsh S. Middleweight Title)
28.04.93 Ray Kane L PTS 6 Dublin
23.05.93 Mark Prince L RSC 3 Brockley
25.07.93 Maurice Core L PTS 6 Oldham
22.09.93 Sammy Storey L PTS 6 Bethnal Green
07.10.93 Michael Gale L PTS 8 York
16.10.93 Noel Magee L PTS 6 Belfast
08.11.93 Garry Delaney L CO 1 Bethnal Green
18.12.93 Fran Harding L PTS 6 Manchester
16.02.94 Shaun Cummins L RSC 3 Stevenage
11.10.95 Kevin Burton W CO 1 Stoke
27.11.96 Tim Redman L PTS 4 Swansea

Career: 46 contests, won 11, drew 4, lost 31.

Prince Kasi Kaihau

Doncaster. *Born* Doncaster, 3 October, 1967
L. Middleweight. Ht. 5'11"
Manager J. Rushton

12.10.93 Prince Louis W PTS 6 Wolverhampton
24.11.93 Steve Levene W PTS 6 Solihull
13.12.93 Rob Stevenson W RSC 5 Doncaster
07.03.94 Steve Levene W RSC 3 Doncaster
10.05.94 Billy McDougall W RTD 4 Doncaster
12.09.94 Rick North W PTS 6 Doncaster
12.10.94 Andy Peach W PTS 6 Stoke
30.11.94 Billy McDougall W PTS 6 Solihull
12.12.94 Andy Peach W PTS 6 Doncaster
28.03.95 David Bain W PTS 6 Wolverhampton
05.05.95 Andy Peach W PTS 6 Doncaster
02.11.95 Robbie Bell L PTS 6 Houghton le Spring
26.01.96 Ozzy Orrock W RSC 5 Doncaster
29.03.96 Chris Pollock L RSC 2 Doncaster
10.05.96 Jon Stocks L PTS 6 Liverpool

28.05.96 Neil Sinclair L RSC 2 Belfast
26.09.96 Joe Townsley L PTS 8 Glasgow
07.10.96 Carl Winstone W RSC 5 Birmingham
24.10.96 George Richards L PTS 6 Birmingham
09.12.96 Stuart Dunn W RSC 2 Leicester
16.01.97 George Richards L PTS 8 Solihull
11.02.97 Howard Clarke W RSC 4 Wolverhampton
27.02.97 Terry Morrill L PTS 6 Hull
15.04.97 Howard Clarke L PTS 6 Edgbaston
25.04.97 Brian Dunn W RSC 1 Cleethorpes
05.06.97 Wayne Alexander L CO 4 Bristol

Career: 26 contests, won 15, lost 11.

Charlie Kane

Glasgow. *Born* Glasgow, 2 July, 1968
L. Welterweight. Ht. 5'10½"
Manager Self

05.03.91 Dean Bramhald W RSC 6 Glasgow
21.10.91 James Jiora W PTS 6 Glasgow
24.02.92 Karl Taylor W PTS 8 Glasgow
10.12.92 Mick Mulcahy W RSC 2 Glasgow
07.11.93 Mick Mulcahy W RSC 2 Glasgow
25.11.93 John Smith W PTS 6 Tynemouth
02.03.94 Micky Hall W RSC 2 Glasgow
28.03.94 John Smith W PTS 6 Musselburgh
24.10.94 Shaun Cogan W PTS 10 Glasgow
(Elim. British L. Welterweight Title)
28.10.95 Ross Hale L CO 2 Bristol
(British & Commonwealth L. Welterweight Title Challenge)
22.04.96 Paul King W PTS 8 Glasgow
23.09.96 Shaun Stokes W RSC 6 Glasgow

Career: 12 contests, won 11, lost 1.

Ray Kane

Dublin. *Born* Dublin, 4 June, 1968
Cruiserweight. Ht. 6'0"
Manager Self

07.09.91 R. F. McKenzie W PTS 4 Belfast
11.12.91 Chris Coughlan W PTS 6 Dublin
28.04.93 John Kaighin W PTS 6 Dublin
05.05.93 Johnny Uphill W CO 2 Belfast
16.10.93 Jason McNeill W PTS 6 Belfast
12.03.94 Kent Davis W PTS 6 Cardiff
21.05.94 Nicky Wadman W PTS 6 Belfast
12.11.94 Steve Osborne W PTS 6 Dublin
14.04.95 Bobbi Joe Edwards W PTS 6 Belfast
27.05.95 Bobbi Joe Edwards W PTS 6 Belfast
02.03.96 Crawford Ashley L CO 2 Newcastle
05.11.96 Darren Corbett L RSC 5 Belfast
(Vacant All-Ireland Cruiserweight Title)
29.04.97 Andrew Benson L RSC 6 Belfast

Career: 13 contests, won 10, lost 3.

Costas Katsantonis

London. *Born* London, 16 October, 1970
L. Welterweight. Ht. 5'8"
Manager A. Urry

09.07.96 Gilbert Eastman L RSC 1 Bethnal Green
28.09.96 Jason Campbell W PTS 6 Barking
24.10.96 Allan Gray L PTS 6 Mayfair
20.11.96 Daniel James L PTS 6 Wembley
19.02.97 Allan Gray L PTS 6 Acton
30.04.97 Kevin McCarthy W RSC 6 Acton

Career: 6 contests, won 2, lost 4.

John Keeton

Sheffield. *Born* Sheffield, 19 May, 1972
Cruiserweight. Ht. 6'0"
Manager Self

11.08.93 Tony Colclough W RSC 1 Mansfield
15.09.93 Val Golding L PTS 6 Ashford
27.10.93 Darren McKenna W RSC 3 Stoke
01.12.93 Julius Francis L PTS 4 Bethnal Green
19.01.94 Dennis Bailey W RTD 2 Stoke
17.02.94 Dermot Gascoyne L RSC 1 Dagenham
09.04.94 Eddie Knight W RTD 5 Mansfield
11.05.94 John Rice W RSC 5 Sheffield
02.06.94 Devon Rhooms W RSC 2 Tooting
06.09.94 Mark Walker W RSC 5 Stoke
24.09.94 Dirk Wallyn L CO 3 Middlekerke, Belgium
26.10.94 Lee Archer W PTS 6 Stoke
09.12.94 Bruce Scott L CO 2 Bethnal Green
11.02.95 Rudiger May L PTS 6 Frankfurt, Germany
06.03.95 Simon McDougall W RSC 5 Mayfair
07.07.95 Nicky Piper L RTD 2 Cardiff
15.09.95 Steve Osborne W RSC 4 Mansfield
27.10.95 Nicky Wadman W RSC 1 Brighton
03.11.95 Monty Wright W RSC 4 Dudley
11.11.95 Denzil Browne W RSC 4 Halifax
30.01.96 Cesar Kazadi W RSC 3 Lille, France
11.05.96 Terry Dunstan L RSC 1 Bethnal Green
(British Cruiserweight Title Challenge)
14.09.96 John Pierre W PTS 4 Sheffield
14.12.96 Nigel Rafferty W RTD 3 Sheffield
12.04.97 Nigel Rafferty W RSC 6 Sheffield

Career: 25 contests, won 17, lost 8.

David Kehoe

Northampton. *Born* Northampton, 24 December, 1972
L. Welterweight. Ht. 5'10½"
Manager F. King

06.02.96 Simon Frailing W CO 1 Basildon
20.04.96 Paul Salmon W PTS 6 Brentwood
12.11.96 Peter Nightingale L PTS 6 Dudley
28.04.97 Craig Kelley L DIS 3 Enfield

Career: 4 contests, won 2, lost 2.

Barrie Kelley

Llanelli. *Born* Llanelli, 14 February, 1972
Former Welsh S. Featherweight Champion.
Ht. 5'6"
Manager Self

16.10.90 Ervine Blake W PTS 6 Evesham
21.11.90 Tony Falcone W PTS 6 Chippenham
29.11.90 John O'Meara W RSC 5 Bayswater
24.01.91 Martin Evans W PTS 6 Gorseinon
18.02.91 Tony Falcone L RSC 6 Mayfair
26.03.91 Dennis Adams W PTS 6 Bethnal Green
18.07.91 Robert Smyth DREW 6 Cardiff
16.09.91 Dominic McGuigan DREW 6 Mayfair
14.10.91 Michael Armstrong L CO 4 Manchester
20.11.91 Neil Haddock L PTS 6 Cardiff
03.02.92 Noel Carroll L PTS 8 Manchester
18.03.92 Mark Geraghty L PTS 8 Glasgow
05.04.92 Peter Judson L PTS 6 Bradford
30.09.92 Dean Bramhald W PTS 6 Solihull
28.10.92 Derek Amory W PTS 6 Cardiff
19.01.93 Edward Lloyd W PTS 10 Cardiff
(Vacant Welsh S. Featherweight Title)
10.11.93 J. T. Williams L RTD 3 Ystrad
(Welsh S. Featherweight Title Defence)

24.02.94 Peter Till L PTS 6 Walsall
19.11.94 Marcus McCrae W PTS 6 Cardiff
31.03.95 Mike Anthony Brown L RSC 2 Crystal
          Palace
04.06.95 Paul Webster L RTD 1 Bethnal Green
10.11.95 Michael Hermon DREW 8 Bristol
12.01.96 Dennis Pedersen L RSC 4 Copenhagen,
          Denmark
19.07.96 Tommy Janes L RSC 3 Ystrad
Career: 24 contests, won 9, drew 3, lost 12.

Craig Kelley
Llanelli. *Born* Swansea, 6 November, 1975
S. Featherweight. Ht. 5'8"
Manager G. Davies

25.01.94 Simon Frailing W PTS 4 Piccadilly
25.02.94 John Sillo L PTS 6 Chester
27.08.94 Dean Phillips L RSC 4 Cardiff
20.01.95 Jason Hutson W RSC 2 Bethnal Green
25.03.95 Gary Thornhill L PTS 6 Chester
20.09.95 Marc Smith L RSC 1 Ystrad
20.12.95 Tommy Janes L PTS 6 Usk
24.10.96 Gary Jenkinson L PTS 6 Lincoln
04.04.97 Tommy Peacock L PTS 6 Liverpool
28.04.97 David Kehoe W DIS 3 Enfield
21.06.97 Byron Pryce DREW 4 Cardiff
Career: 11 contests, won 3, drew 1, lost 7.

Brendan Kelly
Shepherds Bush. *Born* Hammersmith, 30
October, 1970
Lightweight. Ht. 5'7"
Manager J. Evans

19.02.97 Mark O'Callaghan W PTS 6 Acton
03.04.97 Kid McAuley W RSC 3 Wembley
30.04.97 Andrew Reed W PTS 6 Acton
Career: 3 contests, won 3.

Brendan Kelly   Les Clark

John T. Kelly
Hartlepool. *Born* Hartlepool, 12 June, 1970
Lightweight. Ht. 5'7"
Manager T. Conroy

22.10.92 Tanveer Ahmed L PTS 6 Glasgow

02.11.92 Kevin Lowe W PTS 6 Liverpool
01.12.92 Wayne Rigby W PTS 6 Hartlepool
15.02.93 Kevin McKillan L PTS 6 Manchester
09.03.93 Michael Alexander W PTS 6
          Hartlepool
17.04.93 Micky Hall DREW 4 Washington
06.05.93 Alan Graham W PTS 6 Hartlepool
15.09.93 P. J. Gallagher L RSC 2 Bethnal Green
02.12.93 Brian Wright W PTS 6 Hartlepool
02.02.94 Dave McHale L CO 1 Glasgow
13.04.94 Bradley Welsh L PTS 6 Glasgow
06.10.94 Chris Aston DREW 6 Hull
13.10.94 Tim Hill W PTS 6 Houghton le Spring
24.11.94 Dominic McGuigan L PTS 6
          Newcastle
05.12.94 Glen Hopkins W PTS 6 Houghton le
          Spring
16.01.95 Hugh Collins L PTS 6 Musselburgh
16.02.95 Scott Walker L PTS 6 Bury
06.03.95 Steve Tuckett L RSC 3 Bradford
18.05.95 Wayne Rigby L PTS 6 Middleton
22.06.95 Dave Madden W PTS 6 Houghton le
          Spring
28.09.95 Ram Singh W PTS 6 Sunderland
09.10.95 T. J. Smith DREW 6 Manchester
29.10.95 Dave Clavering L PTS 6 Shaw
18.11.95 Hugh Collins L PTS 8 Glasgow
07.12.95 Kid McAuley W PTS 6 Sunderland
22.02.96 G. G. Goddard W PTS 6 Sunderland
07.03.96 Jason Blanche DREW 6 Bradford
01.04.96 Jason Blanche DREW 6 Bradford
22.04.96 Ram Singh W PTS 6 Manchester
09.05.96 Wilson Docherty L PTS 8 Glasgow
02.06.96 Gary Hibbert L PTS 6 Shaw
03.10.96 Arv Mittoo W PTS 6 Sunderland
05.12.96 Colin Innes W PTS 8 Sunderland
03.02.97 Colin Innes W PTS 6 Sunderland
28.04.97 Dave McHale L RSC 4 Glasgow
Career: 35 contests, won 15, drew 5, lost 15.

Lyndon Kershaw
Halifax. *Born* Halifax, 17 September, 1972
S. Bantamweight. Ht. 5'6"
Manager T. Callighan

19.10.92 Stevie Woods W PTS 6 Glasgow
14.12.92 Louis Veitch DREW 6 Bradford
26.04.93 Golfraz Ahmed W PTS 6 Bradford
24.05.93 Anthony Hanna W PTS 6 Bradford
07.10.93 Louis Veitch L PTS 10 Hull
          (Vacant Central Area Flyweight Title)
06.12.93 Ian Baillie W PTS 6 Bradford
02.03.94 Tiger Singh W PTS 6 Solihull
27.04.94 Mark Cokely W PTS 6 Solihull
09.05.94 Ian Baillie W PTS 6 Bradford
15.06.94 Mickey Cantwell W PTS 8 Southwark
02.11.94 Louis Veitch L PTS 10 Solihull
          (Central Area Flyweight Title
          Challenge)
13.01.95 Jesper D. Jensen L PTS 6 Aalborg,
          Denmark
20.02.95 Keith Knox DREW 6 Glasgow
08.03.95 Tiger Singh W PTS 6 Solihull
21.05.95 Jaji Sibali L RTD 8 Cape Town, South
          Africa
11.10.95 Ady Benton L RTD 6 Solihull
11.12.95 Marcus Duncan L RSC 6 Morecambe
          (Vacant Central Area Bantamweight
          Title)
22.02.96 Chip O'Neill W PTS 6 Sunderland
13.04.96 Peter Culshaw L RSC 3 Liverpool
25.06.96 Spencer Oliver L RSC 3 Stevenage
30.09.96 Des Gargano W PTS 6 Manchester

11.10.96 Paul Weir L PTS 6 Mayfair
06.12.96 Nicky Wilders L PTS 6 Leeds
17.12.96 John Armour L RSC 8 Bethnal Green
27.01.97 Shaun Anderson W PTS 8 Glasgow
04.04.97 Brian Carr L PTS 10 Glasgow
          (Elim. British S. Bantamweight Title)
Career: 26 contests, won 12, drew 2, lost 12.

Paul King
Newcastle. *Born* Newcastle, 3 June, 1965
Northern Area Welterweight Champion. Ht.
5'8½"
Manager Self

04.09.87 Willie MacDonald W PTS 6 Gateshead
03.11.87 Mick Mason L PTS 6 Sunderland
24.11.87 Mick Mason L PTS 6 Marton
31.01.89 Jim Larmour W RTD 4 Glasgow
27.02.90 Ian Thomas W PTS 6 Marton
06.03.90 Mick Duncan W PTS 6 Newcastle
15.11.90 Phil Epton W PTS 6 Oldham
28.02.91 Dave Kettlewell W RSC 1 Sunderland
21.03.91 Phil Epton W PTS 6 Dewsbury
13.05.91 Shamus Casey L PTS 6 Northampton
31.05.91 Gordon Blair L PTS 8 Glasgow
09.10.91 Delroy Waul L RSC 6 Manchester
29.09.92 Howard Clarke L PTS 6 Stoke
16.03.93 Howard Clarke L PTS 6 Edgbaston
29.04.93 Hughie Davey W PTS 6 Newcastle
29.06.93 Howard Clarke L PTS 6 Edgbaston
14.08.93 Gary Logan L CO 2 Hammersmith
28.11.93 Gary Logan L CO 4 Southwark
03.03.94 Hughie Davey W PTS 10 Newcastle
          (Vacant Northern Area Welterweight
          Title)
02.03.95 Peter Reid W RSC 3 Cramlington
20.04.95 Craig Winter L RSC 4 Liverpool
12.06.95 Derek Roche L PTS 6 Bradford
23.11.95 Kevin McKenzie L PTS 10 Marton
          (Northern Area Welterweight Title
          Defence)
12.01.96 Frank Olsen L RTD 4 Copenhagen,
          Denmark
02.03.96 Kevin McKenzie W RSC 2 Newcastle
          (Northern Area Welterweight Title
          Challenge)
22.04.96 Charlie Kane L PTS 8 Glasgow
08.06.96 Kevin Lueshing L RSC 2 Newcastle
10.10.96 Hughie Davey W PTS 10 Newcastle
          (Northern Area Welterweight Title
          Defence)
04.12.96 Hughie Davey W PTS 6 Hartlepool
24.01.97 Paolo Roberto L PTS 6 Copenhagen,
          Denmark
26.02.97 Michael Smyth L CO 1 Cardiff
22.04.97 Ojay Abrahams L RSC 4 Bethnal
          Green
Career: 32 contests, won 13, lost 19.

David Kirk
Sutton in Ashfield. *Born* Mansfield, 5
October, 1974
L. Welterweight. Ht. 5'8"
Manager J. Ashton

01.11.96 Arv Mittoo W PTS 6 Mansfield
04.12.96 Stuart Rimmer W PTS 6 Stoke
20.02.97 Chris Price W PTS 6 Mansfield
16.03.97 Gary Hibbert L PTS 6 Shaw
25.03.97 Miguel Matthews W PTS 6
          Wolverhampton
28.04.97 Mark Breslin L PTS 8 Glasgow
Career: 6 contests, won 4, lost 2.

Neil Kirkwood

Barnsley. *Born* Barnsley, 30 November, 1969
Central Area Heavyweight Champion.
Ht. 6'4"
Manager Self

17.03.94	Gary Williams W RSC 1 Lincoln	
16.05.94	Joey Paladino W RSC 2 Cleethorpes	
26.08.94	Shane Woollas W RSC 6 Barnsley	
11.03.95	Carl Gaffney W RSC 2 Barnsley	
	(Vacant Central Area Heavyweight Title)	
24.10.95	Julius Francis L RSC 7 Southwark	
08.10.96	Nikolai Valouev L RSC 2 Battersea	
11.04.97	Johnny Davison W RSC 3 Barnsley	

Career: 7 contests, won 5, lost 2.

Eddie Knight

Ashford. *Born* Ashford, 4 October, 1966
L. Heavyweight. Ht. 5'11"
Manager T. Toole

05.10.92	Shaun McCrory L PTS 6 Bristol
29.10.92	Adrian Wright L PTS 6 Bayswater
25.11.92	Julian Johnson L RSC 2 Mayfair
15.09.93	Terry Duffus W PTS 6 Ashford
09.04.94	John Keeton L RTD 5 Mansfield
27.05.94	Lee Sara W CO 2 Ashford
09.07.94	Mark Delaney L CO 4 Earls Court
17.09.94	Mark Hale W PTS 6 Crawley
13.12.94	Tim Robinson W RTD 2 Potters Bar
09.05.95	Mark Delaney L RSC 2 Basildon
30.01.96	Graham Townsend W PTS 4 Barking
04.03.96	Marko Salminen W RSC 2 Helsinki, Finland
17.12.96	Monty Wright L RSC 5 Bethnal Green
	(Vacant Southern Area L. Heavyweight Title)
20.05.97	Martin Jolley W PTS 6 Gillingham

Career: 14 contests, won 7, lost 7.

Paul Knights

Redhill. *Born* Redhill, 5 February, 1971
L. Welterweight. Ht. 5'10"
Manager B. Hearn

26.11.91	Steve Hearn W RSC 4 Bethnal Green
19.02.92	Seth Jones W RSC 5 Muswell Hill
16.06.92	Seth Jones W PTS 6 Dagenham
10.11.92	Alex Moffatt W CO 3 Dagenham
30.01.93	Dave Lovell W PTS 6 Brentwood
20.04.93	Mark Allen W PTS 6 Brentwood
26.06.93	Paul Found W PTS 4 Earls Court
28.09.93	Pat Delargy W RSC 3 Bethnal Green
11.01.94	Brian Coleman W RSC 4 Bethnal Green
09.02.94	Mark Allen W RSC 2 Brentwood
19.03.94	Alan Peacock W PTS 6 Millwall
11.06.94	John O. Johnson L PTS 6 Bethnal Green
17.09.94	Dewi Roberts W PTS 6 Crawley
17.02.95	Norman Dhalie W RTD 5 Crawley
16.03.95	Brian Coleman W RSC 2 Basildon
09.05.95	Alan Peacock W PTS 6 Basildon
28.10.95	Tony Swift W PTS 6 Kensington
23.01.96	Karl Taylor DREW 6 Bethnal Green
08.03.97	Dave Brazil L RSC 2 Brentwood
22.04.97	Peter Nightingale W PTS 6 Bethnal Green

Career: 20 contests, won 17, drew 1, lost 2.

Keith Knox   Les Clark

Keith Knox

Bonnyrigg. *Born* Edinburgh, 20 June, 1967
Scottish Flyweight Champion. Ht. 5'3"
Manager T. Gilmour

04.03.94	Ian Bailie W CO 3 Irvine
28.03.94	Terry Gaskin W PTS 6 Musselburgh
20.09.94	Tiger Singh W PTS 6 Musselburgh
21.11.94	Neil Parry W PTS 6 Glasgow
16.01.95	Neil Parry W PTS 6 Musselburgh
20.02.95	Lyndon Kershaw DREW 6 Glasgow
05.04.95	Louis Veitch DREW 6 Irvine
18.09.95	Shaun Norman W PTS 8 Glasgow
20.11.95	Louis Veitch W RSC 6 Glasgow
	(Vacant Scottish Flyweight Title. Elim. British Flyweight Title)
21.03.96	Mickey Cantwell L PTS 12 Southwark
	(Vacant British Flyweight Title)
13.09.96	Jesper Jensen L PTS 12 Ringsted, Denmark
	(European Flyweight Title Challenge)
27.01.97	Ady Lewis L PTS 12 Glasgow
	(Vacant British Flyweight Title)
02.06.97	Anthony Hanna W PTS 6 Glasgow

Career: 13 contests, won 8, drew 2, lost 3.

Andy Lambert

Birmingham. *Born* Selly Oak, 22 July, 1962
Heavyweight. Ht. 6'4"
Manager E. Cashmore

25.03.96	David Jules W RSC 1 Birmingham
21.05.96	Jim Pallatt W RSC 1 Edgbaston
25.06.96	Pele Reid L CO 1 Mansfield
31.08.96	Danny Williams L RSC 2 Dublin
03.12.96	Peter Oboh L CO 1 Liverpool

Career: 5 contests, won 2, lost 3.

David Larkin

Doncaster. *Born* Pontefract, 26 April, 1972
S. Middleweight. Ht. 5'10½"
Manager H. Hayes

29.10.92	Rick North W PTS 6 Leeds
07.04.93	Cliff Churchward W RSC 4 Leeds
19.05.93	Ray Golding W PTS 6 Sunderland
01.07.93	David Sumner W CO 5 York
07.10.93	Lee Crocker W RSC 5 York
26.10.94	Andrew Jervis W CO 5 Leeds
03.03.95	Robert Peel L PTS 6 Bethnal Green
08.07.95	Carl Winstone W RSC 2 York
28.09.95	Mickey Johnson L PTS 6 Sunderland
16.10.95	Butch Lesley W RSC 4 Mayfair
06.03.96	Darren Sweeney L PTS 6 Solihull
24.03.96	Scott Beasley W RTD 3 Shaw
03.05.96	Michael Pinnock DREW 6 Sheffield
04.10.96	David Radford L PTS 8 Wakefield

Career: 14 contests, won 9, drew 1, lost 4.

Pat Larner

Bognor. *Born* Chichester, 22 February, 1976
L. Welterweight. Ht. 6'0"
Manager P. Newman

07.11.96	Paul Salmon W PTS 6 Battersea
11.12.96	Dave Brazil W PTS 6 Southwark
15.02.97	Robbie Dunn W RSC 2 Tooting
04.04.97	Dennis Griffin W PTS 6 Brighton

Career: 4 contests, won 4.

Pat Larner   Les Clark

Phil Lashley

Birmingham. *Born* Birmingham, 1 May, 1965
S. Featherweight. Ht. 5'5"
Manager Self

27.04.86	Ronnie Stephenson L PTS 4 Doncaster
30.05.86	David Beech L PTS 6 Stoke
10.09.86	Gypsy Johnny W RSC 1 Stoke
17.09.86	Paul Hodkinson L RSC 2 Kensington
10.11.86	Roy Williams W CO 1 Birmingham
18.11.86	Dean Lynch L PTS 6 Swansea
08.12.86	Frank Monkhouse L RSC 4 Birmingham
28.01.87	Shane Porter L RSC 1 Dudley
03.03.87	John Carlin L PTS 6 Livingston
24.03.87	John Carlin W RSC 1 Wolverhampton
08.04.87	Gary King L CO 1 Evesham
13.10.87	Mick Greenwood L PTS 6 Wolverhampton

09.11.87	Ronnie Stephenson DREW 4 Birmingham
24.11.87	Mark Goult L CO 1 Wisbech
14.02.88	Steve Pike L CO 1 Peterborough
21.03.88	Dean Lynch L PTS 6 Bethnal Green
13.04.88	Paul Bowen W RSC 1 Wolverhampton
20.04.88	Chris Cooper W PTS 6 Torquay
23.05.88	Roy Williams W RSC 2 Mayfair
09.09.88	Ronnie Stephenson W PTS 6 Doncaster
29.09.88	Peter Gabbitus L CO 2 Stafford
14.11.88	Mark Antony L RSC 2 Stratford upon Avon
02.02.89	Lester James L PTS 4 Wolverhampton
28.02.89	Lester James L PTS 6 Dudley
15.03.89	Andrew Robinson L PTS 6 Stoke
17.04.89	Lester James L RSC 5 Birmingham
28.06.89	Jamie Morris L RSC 1 Kenilworth
18.09.89	Peter Judson L PTS 6 Mayfair
04.10.89	Craig Garbutt L PTS 6 Stafford
16.10.89	Neil Leitch L PTS 6 Manchester
30.10.89	Gary Hickman L RSC 4 Piccadilly
28.11.89	Neil Leitch L PTS 6 Wolverhampton
04.12.89	Neil Leitch L PTS 6 Grimsby
12.12.89	John O'Meara L CO 3 Brentford
08.02.90	Jason Primera L PTS 6 Southwark
19.02.90	Peter Judson L CO 6 Nottingham
19.03.90	Neil Leitch L PTS 6 Grimsby
27.03.90	Ronnie Stephenson W PTS 6 Wolverhampton
21.05.90	Ronnie Stephenson L PTS 6 Grimsby
04.06.90	Elvis Parsley L RSC 3 Birmingham
23.01.91	Mark Bates L RTD 3 Brentwood
04.03.91	Dave Annis W CO 2 Birmingham
01.05.91	Mark Bates L PTS 6 Bethnal Green
04.06.91	Paul Donaghey L CO 1 Bethnal Green
21.10.91	Ronnie Stephenson L PTS 6 Cleethorpes
21.11.91	Ronnie Stephenson L PTS 6 Stafford
30.03.92	Jamie McBride L RSC 1 Glasgow
05.10.92	Chip O'Neill L PTS 6 Manchester
12.05.93	Gary Marston L RSC 2 Stoke
16.03.96	Wayne Jones L PTS 6 Barnstaple
27.03.96	Robert Grubb L PTS 6 Stoke
11.12.96	Patrick Mullings L RSC 3 Southwark

Career: 52 contests, won 9, drew 1, lost 42.

Gareth Lawrence

Gilfach Goch. *Born* Pontypridd, 1 February, 1975
Featherweight. Ht. 5'6½"
Manager D. Gardiner

25.01.95	Anthony Campbell W PTS 6 Cardiff
08.03.95	Phil Found W PTS 6 Cardiff
17.06.95	Dean Amory W RSC 2 Cardiff
08.11.95	Nelson Ide W RSC 5 Bethnal Green
20.12.95	Kid McAuley W PTS 6 Usk
25.05.96	Ruslan Smolenkov W PTS 6 St Petersburg, Russia
19.07.96	Willy Perdomo W PTS 8 Ystrad
06.11.96	Angel Vasilev W CO 4 Tylorstown

Career: 8 contests, won 8.

Patrick Lawrence

Hayes. *Born* Sligo, 30 June, 1966
Cruiserweight. Ht. 6'1"
Manager D. Currivan

28.09.96	Dominic Negus L RSC 2 Barking
15.04.97	Steve Pettit L PTS 6 Edgbaston

Career: 2 contests, lost 2.

(Ian) Pele Lawrence

Sheffield. *Born* Sheffield, 20 November, 1968
L. Heavyweight. Ht. 6'0"
Manager S. Foster

06.04.90	P. D. Taylor W PTS 6 Telford
24.04.90	Mark Bowen L CO 5 Eltham
18.09.90	Adrian Wright L CO 2 Stoke
15.02.96	Chris Woollas L RSC 6 Sheffield
25.10.96	Naveed Anwar W PTS 6 Mere
22.12.96	Paul Bonson DREW 6 Salford
25.04.97	Slick Miller W PTS 6 Mere

Career: 7 contests, won 3, drew 1, lost 3.

Danny Lawson

Plymouth. *Born* Plymouth, 27 May, 1971
Bantamweight. Ht. 5'5¾"
Manager D. Sullivan

17.06.94	Danny Ruegg W PTS 6 Plymouth
07.10.94	Jobie Tyers L PTS 6 Taunton
07.02.95	Mark Reynolds L PTS 4 Ipswich
06.05.95	Tony Falcone L RSC 2 Shepton Mallet
20.03.96	Henry Jones L CO 1 Cardiff
20.03.97	Jason Booth L RSC 3 Newark

Career: 6 contests, won 1, lost 5.

Nigel Leake

Wakefield. *Born* Normanton, 13 June, 1969
S. Featherweight. Ht. 5'6"
Manager T. Callighan

31.01.97	Andy Ross W PTS 6 Pentre Halkyn
11.02.97	Charlie Rumbol W RSC 3 Bethnal Green
20.04.97	Garry Burrell W PTS 6 Leeds

Career: 3 contests, won 3.

Nigel Leake Les Clark

(Herbert) Butch Lesley

Islington. *Born* Chelmsford, 21 April, 1973
S. Middleweight. Ht. 6'2½"
Manager J. Harding

02.09.95	Lester Jacobs L PTS 4 Wembley

16.10.95	David Larkin L RSC 4 Mayfair
23.01.96	Michael Pinnock W PTS 4 Bethnal Green
09.04.96	Jerry Mortimer W RSC 3 Stevenage
25.06.96	Graham Townsend L PTS 6 Stevenage
05.11.96	Sammy Storey L DIS 3 Belfast
08.03.97	Mark Delaney L PTS 6 Brentwood

Career: 7 contests, won 2, lost 5.

Butch Lesley Les Clark

Steve Levene

Birmingham. *Born* Birmingham, 23 September, 1969
L. Middleweight. Ht. 5'8½"
Manager Self

27.10.92	Steve Scott L RSC 1 Cradley Heath
07.12.92	Warren Stephens W CO 2 Birmingham
16.03.93	Alan Williams W RSC 1 Edgbaston
24.03.93	Sean Baker DREW 6 Belfast
19.04.93	Bullit Andrews W PTS 6 Northampton
18.05.93	Mark Antony L RSC 1 Edgbaston
06.09.93	Danny Peters L RSC 4 Liverpool
24.11.93	Prince Kasi Kaihau L PTS 6 Solihull
06.12.93	Bullit Andrews W RSC 6 Birmingham
17.02.94	Bullit Andrews W PTS 6 Walsall
07.03.94	Prince Kasi Kaihau L RSC 3 Doncaster
20.06.95	Paul Webb W PTS 6 Birmingham
17.10.95	Ozzy Orrock W RSC 1 Wolverhampton
21.11.95	Roy Gbasai W CO 2 Edgbaston
22.02.96	Andy Peach W PTS 6 Walsall
21.05.96	James McGee L PTS 6 Edgbaston
21.11.96	Paul Webb W RSC 2 Solihull
16.01.97	Gary Beardsley W PTS 6 Solihull
15.04.97	Dave Andrews W PTS 6 Edgbaston

Career: 19 contests, won 12, drew 1, lost 6.

Darren Littlewood

Sheffield. *Born* Sheffield, 6 November, 1974
S. Middleweight. Ht. 6'0"
Manager Self

24.11.93	Mark Smallwood L PTS 8 Solihull

02.12.93 Martin Jolley W PTS 6 Evesham
01.03.94 Joe Calzaghe L RSC 1 Dudley
28.05.94 Dean Francis L PTS 4 Queensway
17.08.94 Chris Woollas L RSC 4 Sheffield
26.10.94 John Duckworth W PTS 6 Stoke
24.11.94 Tim Robinson W PTS 6 Hull
12.12.94 Martin Jolley W PTS 6 Cleethorpes
23.01.95 Roland Ericsson W RSC 4 Bethnal Green
11.11.95 Jetty Williams L PTS 6 Halifax
06.07.96 Pascal Collins W PTS 4 Manchester
17.09.96 Roberto Dominguez L RSC 5 Porrino, Spain
10.04.97 Clinton Woods L RSC 6 Sheffield
(Central Area S. Middleweight Title Challenge)
Career: 13 contests, won 6, lost 7.

Wayne Llewelyn

Beckenham. *Born* Greenwich, 20 April, 1970
Heavyweight. Ht. 6'3½"
Manager F. Warren

18.01.92 Chris Coughlan W RSC 3 Kensington
30.03.92 Steve Stewart W RSC 4 Eltham
23.04.92 Gary Charlton W RSC 6 Eltham
10.12.92 Gary McCrory W RSC 2 Glasgow
23.05.93 Cordwell Hylton W PTS 6 Brockley
01.12.93 Manny Burgo W PTS 6 Bethnal Green
14.04.94 Vance Idiens W RSC 1 Battersea
22.05.94 Cordwell Hylton W CO 2 Crystal Palace
03.05.95 Mitch Rose W PTS 4 New York City, USA
07.07.95 Vance Idiens W RSC 1 Cardiff
11.08.95 Carlos Monroe W RSC 3 Louisiana, USA
26.04.96 Steve Garber W CO 1 Cardiff
08.06.96 Dermot Gascoyne W RSC 4 Newcastle
22.03.97 Mike Sedillo W CO 2 Wythenshawe
Career: 14 contests, won 14.

Gary Lockett   Les Clark

Gary Lockett

Cwmbran. *Born* Pontypool, 25 November, 1976
L. Middleweight. Ht. 5'10"
Manager J. Hyland

06.09.96 Ernie Loveridge W PTS 4 Liverpool
26.10.96 Charlie Paine W RSC 4 Liverpool
Career: 2 contests, won 2.

Keith Long

Brixton. *Born* Greenwich, 30 July, 1968
Heavyweight. Ht. 5'11½"
Manager C. Carew

15.02.97 Steve Cranston W PTS 4 Tooting
Career: 1 contest, won 1.

Keith Long   Les Clark

Ernie Loveridge

Stourport. *Born* Bromsgrove, 7 July, 1970
S. Middleweight. Former Undefeated Midlands Area Welterweight Champion. Ht. 5'10"
Manager Self

06.02.89 Ricky Nelson L RSC 6 Nottingham
17.04.89 Martin Robinson L PTS 4 Birmingham
08.05.89 Bullit Andrews W PTS 6 Edgbaston
05.06.89 Alan Richards L PTS 6 Birmingham
19.06.89 Ian Thomas DREW 6 Manchester
28.06.89 Barry Messam L PTS 6 Kenilworth
10.10.89 Matt Sturgess W RSC 1 Wolverhampton
25.10.89 Darren Mount L PTS 6 Stoke
11.12.89 Cliff Churchward W PTS 6 Birmingham
27.02.90 Julian Eavis W PTS 6 Evesham
14.03.90 Mickey Lerwill W PTS 6 Stoke
27.03.90 Eddie King W PTS 6 Wolverhampton
24.04.90 Mark Jay W PTS 6 Stoke
24.05.90 Mickey Lerwill DREW 6 Dudley
18.09.90 Ronnie Campbell W PTS 6 Wolverhampton
24.10.90 Trevor Meikle W PTS 6 Dudley
23.01.91 Cliff Churchward W PTS 6 Solihull
27.02.91 Ronnie Campbell W PTS 8 Wolverhampton
13.03.91 John Corcoran W RSC 4 Stoke
10.04.91 Julian Eavis DREW 8 Wolverhampton
14.05.91 Paul Murray W PTS 8 Dudley
05.06.91 Cliff Churchward W PTS 8 Wolverhampton
10.09.91 Gary Osborne W RSC 1 Wolverhampton
(Midlands Area Welterweight Title Challenge)
12.11.91 Mickey Lerwill W PTS 6 Wolverhampton
05.12.91 Jim Lawlor W PTS 8 Cannack
01.02.92 Michael Oliver W PTS 8 Birmingham
19.09.92 Paul Jones L PTS 6 Glasgow
01.10.92 Neville Brown L CO 4 Telford
20.01.93 Lee Crocker L PTS 6 Wolverhampton
17.02.93 Robert McCracken L CO 4 Bethnal Green
31.03.93 Kevin Lueshing L RSC 5 Bethnal Green
18.05.93 Antonio Fernandez L PTS 8 Edgbaston
10.07.93 Michael Smyth L RSC 6 Cardiff
09.10.93 Robin Reid L PTS 4 Manchester
02.11.93 Gilbert Jackson L RTD 3 Southwark
11.06.94 Mark Delaney L RSC 5 Bethnal Green
28.07.94 Dave Cranston L PTS 6 Tooting
17.08.94 Kevin Adamson L RSC 2 Sheffield
01.03.95 Dave Johnson L PTS 6 Glasgow
17.03.95 Mads Larsen L RSC 3 Copenhagen, Denmark
20.04.95 Danny Peters L PTS 6 Liverpool
05.06.95 Billy Collins L PTS 8 Glasgow
16.06.95 Craig Winter L PTS 6 Liverpool
08.09.95 Craig Winter L PTS 6 Liverpool
21.09.95 Paolo Roberto L PTS 4 Battersea
29.09.95 Panayiotis Panayiotiou L PTS 4 Bethnal Green
16.10.95 Vince Rose L PTS 4 Heybridge
25.10.95 Steve Goodwin L PTS 4 Stoke
02.11.95 Brian Galloway L PTS 6 Mayfair
17.11.95 Dean Barclay L PTS 4 Bethnal Green
25.11.95 Steve Roberts L PTS 4 Dagenham
15.12.95 Luan Morena L PTS 4 Bethnal Green
19.01.96 Toks Owoh L PTS 4 Bracknell
30.01.96 Jason Hart L PTS 6 Barking
13.02.96 Paul Carr L PTS 4 Bethnal Green
23.02.96 Carl Winstone W PTS 8 Weston super Mare
05.03.96 Paul Wright L PTS 6 Barrow
19.03.96 James Donoghue L PTS 6 Leeds
30.03.96 Anthony McFadden L PTS 4 Dublin
14.05.96 Panayiotis Panayiotiou L PTS 4 Dagenham
13.06.96 Clinton Woods L PTS 6 Sheffield
06.09.96 Gary Lockett L PTS 4 Liverpool
28.09.96 Enzo Giordano L PTS 6 Barking
24.10.96 Barry Exton L PTS 6 Lincoln
01.11.96 Rocky Shelly W RTD 3 Mansfield
06.11.96 Grant Briggs L PTS 4 Tylorstown
27.11.96 Jason Ratcliff L PTS 4 Bethnal Green
09.12.96 Darren Dorrington L PTS 6 Bristol
08.02.97 Jason Matthews L CO 5 Millwall
Career: 69 contests, won 20, drew 3, lost 46.

James Lowther

Leeds. *Born* Leeds, 28 June, 1976
Middleweight. Ht. 5'11"
Manager G. Lockwood

12.01.95 Warren Stephens W CO 4 Leeds
25.03.95 Scott Doyle W PTS 6 Rothwell
19.05.95 Eddie Haley W RSC 5 Leeds
19.03.96 Earl Ling W RSC 4 Leeds
06.12.96 Martin Jolley W PTS 6 Leeds
07.03.97 Gordon Behan W PTS 6 Northampton
13.06.97 Raziq Ali W PTS 6 Leeds
Career: 7 contests, won 7.

Danny Lutaaya

Canning Town. *Born* Uganda, 23
December, 1971
Ugandan Lightweight Champion. Ht. 5'5½"
Manager Self

17.10.94 Vince Burns W RSC 6 Mayfair
27.11.94 Keith Jones W CO 1 Southwark
23.01.95 Elvis Parsley L RSC 3 Bethnal Green
25.03.95 Wayne Jones W RSC 3 Millwall
16.06.95 Dean Phillips L RSC 2 Southwark
14.09.95 Jason Hutson L RSC 2 Battersea
21.02.96 Arv Mittoo W PTS 6 Piccadilly
27.08.96 Jason Campbell W RSC 3 Windsor
24.10.96 Mark O'Callaghan W RSC 1 Mayfair
28.01.97 Simon Frailing L PTS 6 Piccadilly
22.02.97 Polly Kommankado W PTS 10
　　　　　Kampala, Uganda
　　　　　(Ugandan Lightweight Title Challenge)
22.05.97 Simon Frailing W RSC 2 Southwark

Career: 12 contests, won 8, lost 4.

Craig Lynch

Edinburgh. *Born* Edinburgh, 22 July, 1974
Welterweight. Ht. 6'1"
Manager Self

13.05.95 James Clamp DREW 6 Glasgow
08.06.95 Gary Silvester W RSC 3 Glasgow
15.09.95 Adam Baldwin W PTS 6 Glasgow
25.11.95 Jim Rock L PTS 4 Dublin
02.03.96 Hughie Davey L PTS 4 Newcastle
08.06.96 Hughie Davey L PTS 4 Newcastle
24.10.96 Pat Wright L PTS 6 Wembley

Career: 7 contests, won 2, drew 1, lost 4.

Craig Lynch　　　　　　　　Les Clark

Chris Lyons

Birmingham. *Born* Birmingham, 2
September, 1972
S. Featherweight. Ht. 5'9"
Manager Self

02.12.91 Ronnie Sephenson L PTS 6
　　　　　Birmingham

09.12.91 Ronnie Stephenson L PTS 6
　　　　　Cleethorpes
22.01.92 Dennis Oakes L RSC 3 Stoke
17.05.92 Dave Martin DREW 6 Harringay
08.09.92 Robert Braddock L CO 5 Doncaster
13.10.92 Paul Kelly W PTS 6 Wolverhampton
30.10.92 Paul Kelly W CO 1 Birmingham
17.12.92 Mark Bowers L CO 2 Wembley
08.03.93 Chip O'Neill L PTS 6 Leeds
22.04.93 Marcus Duncan L RSC 2 Bury
26.06.93 Tim Yeates L PTS 4 Earls Court
16.09.93 Anthony Hanna L PTS 6 Southwark
30.11.93 Kid McAuley L RSC 5
　　　　　Wolverhampton
01.03.94 Marty Chestnut L PTS 6 Dudley
27.04.94 Marty Chestnut W RSC 3 Bethnal
　　　　　Green
06.05.94 John Sillo L RSC 3 Liverpool
15.06.94 Matt Brown L CO 3 Southwark
19.09.94 Daryl McKenzie L PTS 6 Glasgow
11.10.94 Robert Grubb W PTS 6
　　　　　Wolverhampton
02.11.94 Daryl McKenzie L PTS 6 Solihull
16.11.94 Danny Ruegg L PTS 6 Bloomsbury
28.11.94 Andrew Bloomer W PTS 6
　　　　　Northampton
24.01.95 Abdul Mannon L PTS 6 Piccadilly
07.02.95 Michael Edwards W PTS 6
　　　　　Wolverhampton
21.04.95 Matthew Harris L PTS 6 Dudley
26.08.95 Eamonn Brolly L PTS 4 Belfast
11.10.95 Jason Squire L PTS 6 Solihull
24.10.95 Eddie Sica L PTS 4 Southwark
21.11.95 Andrew Smith L PTS 6 Edgbaston
07.12.95 Fred Reeve L PTS 6 Hull
31.01.96 Brian Robb L PTS 6 Birmingham
16.03.96 Gary Jenkinson L PTS 6 Barnstaple
27.03.96 Brendan Bryce L PTS 6 Whitwick
03.05.96 Sean Morrison L PTS 6 Sheffield
20.05.96 Steve Conway L PTS 6 Cleethorpes
13.06.96 Vic Broomhead W PTS 6 Sheffield
16.08.96 Chris Ainscough L PTS 6 Liverpool
28.09.96 Thomas Jansson L PTS 4 Barking
04.12.96 Gary Marston L PTS 8 Stoke
25.02.97 Thomas Bradley L PTS 4 Sheffield
10.04.97 Lee Armstrong L PTS 6 Sheffield
24.04.97 John Paul Temple L PTS 6 Mayfair
19.05.97 Jason Booth L PTS 6 Cleethorpes

Career: 43 contests, won 7, drew 1, lost 35.

Ricky Mabbett

Leicester. *Born* Leicester, 27 November,
1971
L. Middleweight. Ht. 5'9"
Manager J. Griffin

19.03.92 Phil Epton W RSC 3 York
16.06.92 Ojay Abrahams L PTS 6 Dagenham
08.09.92 Marty Duke DREW 6 Norwich
27.10.92 Steve McGovern DREW 6 Leicester
26.01.93 Marty Duke L CO 1 Leicester
16.03.93 Spencer McCracken L PTS 6
　　　　　Edgbaston
26.04.93 Darren McInulty W CO 3 Cleethorpes
19.05.93 Ojay Abrahams W RSC 4 Leicester
18.09.93 Ojay Abrahams W PTS 6 Leicester
21.05.94 Michael Carruth L CO 3 Belfast
03.03.97 Jason Barker L PTS 6 Leicester

Career: 11 contests, won 4, drew 2, lost 5.

(Colin) Kid McAuley

Doncaster. *Born* Liverpool, 6 June, 1968
Lightweight. Ht. 5'6"
Manager J. Rushton

08.09.92 Jonjo Irwin L PTS 6 Doncaster
19.09.92 Alex Docherty L PTS 6 Glasgow
30.09.92 Yusuf Vorajee W PTS 6 Solihull
13.10.92 John White L PTS 4 Bury
23.10.92 Paul Lloyd L PTS 4 Liverpool
10.11.92 Michael Alldis L PTS 6 Dagenham
24.11.92 Miguel Matthews W PTS 6 Doncaster
12.12.92 Michael Alldis L CO 1 Muswell Hill
27.01.93 Yusuf Vorajee L RSC 5 Stoke
03.03.93 Kevin Middleton L PTS 8 Solihull
16.03.93 Jonjo Irwin L PTS 10 Mayfair
　　　　　*(Vacant All-Ireland Featherweight
　　　　　Title)*
28.04.93 Barry Jones L PTS 8 Solihull
14.05.93 Shaun Anderson L PTS 8 Kilmarnock
29.05.93 James Murray L PTS 6 Paisley
28.06.93 Carl Roberts W PTS 6 Morecambe
25.07.93 Mario Culpeper L PTS 6 Oldham
12.10.93 Elvis Parsley L PTS 6 Wolverhampton
30.11.93 Chris Lyons W RSC 5 Wolverhampton
22.01.94 Eamonn McAuley L PTS 6 Belfast
10.02.94 Tony Foster L RTD 4 Hull
11.03.94 Donnie Hood L PTS 8 Glasgow
27.04.94 Harry Escott L RTD 6 Solihull
02.06.94 Wayne Rigby L PTS 6 Middleton
10.06.94 Bradley Welsh L RTD 1 Glasgow
12.09.94 Colin Innes W PTS 6 Doncaster
30.11.94 Marco Fattore W PTS 6 Solihull
15.12.94 Matthew Harris L PTS 6 Evesham
09.02.95 Roger Brotherhood W PTS 6 Doncaster
17.02.95 Dean Pithie L RSC 3 Cumbernauld
28.03.95 Anthony Maynard L PTS 8
　　　　　Wolverhampton
05.04.95 Hugh Collins L PTS 6 Irvine
13.04.95 Dean Pithie L RSC 1 Bloomsbury
11.05.95 Glen Hopkins DREW 6 Sunderland
18.05.95 Dave Clavering L PTS 6 Middleton
06.06.95 Neil Smith L RTD 1 Leicester
28.09.95 Glen Hopkins L PTS 6 Sunderland
18.10.95 Terry Whittaker L PTS 6 Batley
04.11.95 Gary Thornhill L PTS 6 Liverpool
29.11.95 Terry Whittaker DREW 6 Solihull
07.12.95 John T. Kelly L PTS 6 Sunderland
20.12.95 Gareth Lawrence L PTS 6 Usk
17.01.96 Wayne Rigby L PTS 6 Solihull
17.02.96 Stephen Smith L RSC 4 Dortmund,
　　　　　Germany
18.03.96 Hugh Collins L PTS 8 Glasgow
01.04.96 Chris Jickells L PTS 6 Bradford
24.04.96 Mark Allen W PTS 6 Stoke
30.05.96 Terry Whittaker L PTS 6 Lincoln
13.06.96 Robbie Sivyer L PTS 6 Sheffield
24.06.96 Jason Blanche L PTS 6 Bradford
22.11.96 Chris Price DREW 6 Hull
04.12.96 Ervine Blake L PTS 6 Stoke
17.12.96 Danny Stevens L DIS 3 Bethnal Green
18.01.97 Chris Barnett L RTD 3 Manchester
25.02.97 James Hare L PTS 4 Sheffield
14.03.97 Jimmy Phelan L PTS 6 Hull
03.04.97 Brendan Kelly L RSC 3 Wembley
26.06.97 Thomas Bradley L PTS 6 Sheffield

Career: 57 contests, won 8, drew 3, lost 46.

Kevin McBride

Clones. *Born* Monaghan, 10 May, 1973
All-Ireland Heavyweight Champion. Ht.
6'5"
Manager Self

17.12.92 Gary Charlton DREW 6 Barking
13.02.93 Gary Williams W PTS 4 Manchester
15.09.93 Joey Paladino W CO 2 Bethnal Green

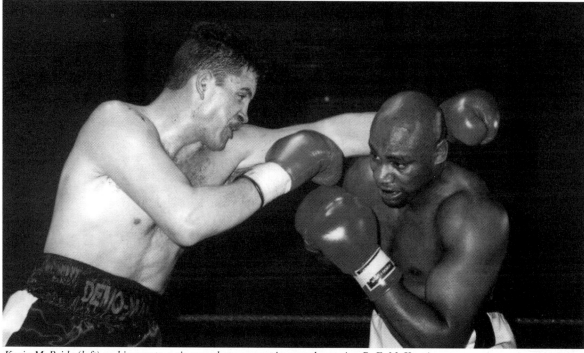

Kevin McBride (left) on his way to a six-round stoppage win over the ageing R. F. McKenzie   Les Clark

13.10.93	Chris Coughlan W PTS 4 Bethnal Green
01.12.93	John Harewood W RSC 3 Bethnal Green
06.05.94	Edgar Turpin W RSC 1 Atlantic City, USA
04.06.94	Roger Bryant W CO 1 Reno, USA
17.06.94	Stanley Wright W PTS 6 Atlantic City, USA
26.08.94	James Truesdale W RSC 3 Upper Marlboro, USA
24.09.94	Graham Arnold W RSC 2 Wembley
12.11.94	Dean Storey W RSC 3 Dublin
10.12.94	John Lamphrey W RSC 1 Portland, USA
07.02.95	Carl Gaffney W RSC 1 Ipswich
03.03.95	Carl McGrew W RSC 5 Boston, USA
22.04.95	Jimmy Harrison W RSC 1 Boston, USA
13.05.95	Atelea Kalhea W CO 1 Sacramento, USA
02.07.95	Steve Garber W RSC 7 Dublin
06.11.96	Shane Woollas W RSC 2 Hull
03.12.96	R.F. McKenzie W RSC 6 Liverpool
21.01.97	Tui Toia W RSC 2 Kansas City, USA
07.02.97	Louis Monaco L RSC 5 Las Vegas, USA
28.04.97	Stoyan Stoyanov W RSC 1 Hull
02.06.97	Paul Douglas W RSC 5 Belfast
	(Vacant All-Ireland Heavyweight Title)

Carrer: 23 contests, won 21, drew 1, lost 1.

Kevin McCarthy

Bletchley. *Born* Bletchley, 10 March, 1972
Welterweight. Ht. 5'9½"
Manager D. Mancini

03.07.96	Paul Webb W RSC 2 Wembley

24.10.96	Peter Nightingale DREW 6 Wembley
20.11.96	Donovan Davey W PTS 6 Wembley
29.01.97	Craig Hartwell W RSC 1 Bethnal Green
03.04.97	Brian Coleman W PTS 6 Wembley
30.04.97	Costas Katsantonis L RSC 6 Acton

Career: 6 contests, won 4, drew 1, lost 1.

Peter McCormack

Birmingham. *Born* Birmingham, 9 March, 1974
Middleweight. Ht. 5'10"
Manager P. Cowdell

07.10.96	Paul Webb DREW 6 Birmingham
21.11.96	Ozzy Orrock W RSC 2 Solihull
04.12.96	Lee Simpkin L PTS 6 Stoke
11.02.97	Mark Sawyers L RSC 2 Wolverhampton

Career: 4 contests, won 1, drew 1, lost 2.

Spencer McCracken

Birmingham. *Born* Birmingham, 8 August, 1969
Welterweight. Ht. 5'9"
Manager M. Duff

15.10.91	Stuart Dunn DREW 6 Dudley
09.12.91	Seth Jones W RSC 2 Brierley Hill
27.10.92	Dave Lovell W PTS 4 Cradley Heath
07.12.92	Mark Antony W CO 1 Birmingham
22.02.93	Rick North W PTS 8 Birmingham
16.03.93	Ricky Mabbett W PTS 6 Edgbaston
18.05.93	Tony Britland W CO 1 Edgbaston
06.12.93	Jimmy Thornton W PTS 6 Birmingham
19.01.94	Julian Eavis W PTS 8 Solihull
28.03.94	Marty Duke W RSC 2 Birmingham

23.05.94	Ojay Abrahams W PTS 6 Walsall
25.10.94	Julian Eavis W PTS 6 Edgbaston
11.05.95	Tony Foster W PTS 6 Dudley
05.06.95	Stefan Scriggins L PTS 8 Birmingham
01.10.96	Danny Quacoe W RTD 3 Birmingham
23.10.96	Shaun Stokes W PTS 8 Halifax
12.11.96	Ojay Abrahams W PTS 8 Dudley
28.04.97	Dennis Berry W RSC 10 Hull
	(Final Elim. British Welterweight Title)

Career: 18 contests, won 16, drew 1, lost 1.

Spencer McCracken   Les Clark

Marcus McCrae

Brixton. *Born* London, 13 November, 1969
S. Featherweight. Ht. 5'7"
Manager Self

22.09.93	Miguel Matthews W PTS 6 Bethnal Green
10.11.93	Ian Reid W PTS 6 Bethnal Green
17.02.94	Thomas Bernard W RSC 1 Dagenham
04.06.94	Andrew Reed W PTS 6 Cardiff
01.10.94	Ceri Farrell W RTD 1 Cardiff
19.11.94	Barrie Kelley L PTS 6 Cardiff
25.02.95	Andrew Reed W RSC 4 Millwall
07.07.95	Daniel Alicea L RSC 3 Cardiff
08.10.96	Brian Coleman L PTS 6 Battersea
11.12.96	Matt Brown L RSC 9 Southwark *(Vacant Southern Area S. Featherweight Title)*

Career: 10 contests, won 6, lost 4.

Geoff McCreesh   Les Clark

Geoff McCreesh

Bracknell. *Born* Stockton, 12 June, 1970
Former Undefeated Southern Area L. Middleweight Champion. Ht. 5'10"
Manager J. Evans

16.02.94	Tony Walton W PTS 6 Stevenage
12.03.94	Barry Thorogood W PTS 6 Cardiff
22.03.94	Mark Dawson W PTS 6 Bethnal Green
20.05.94	Robert Peel W RSC 2 Acton
02.07.94	Julian Eavis W PTS 4 Keynsham
18.11.94	Andrew Furlong W PTS 6 Bracknell
13.12.94	Ojay Abrahams W PTS 6 Potters Bar
20.01.95	Clay O'Shea W RSC 1 Bethnal Green *(Vacant Southern Area L. Middleweight Title)*
03.03.95	Dennis Berry L RTD 5 Bracknell
16.12.95	Michael Smyth L DIS 4 Cardiff
19.01.96	Steve Goodwin L DIS 5 Bracknell
02.03.96	Peter Varnavas W PTS 4 Newcastle
13.03.96	Kevin Thompson W PTS 6 Wembley
09.04.96	Vince Rose W RSC 4 Stevenage
10.05.96	George Wilson W PTS 6 Wembley
25.06.96	Wayne Shepherd W PTS 4 Stevenage

27.08.96	Jimmy Vincent W RSC 1 Windsor
28.09.96	George Wilson W PTS 4 Barking
05.11.96	Dingaan Thobela W CO 2 Hammanskraal, South Africa
19.01.97	Peter Malinga L RTD 5 Durban, South Africa

Career: 20 contests, won 16, lost 4.

Simon McDougall

Blackpool. *Born* Manchester, 11 July, 1968
Cruiserweight. Ht. 5'10½"
Manager Self

14.11.88	Andrew Bravardo W CO 4 Manchester
16.01.89	Steve Osborne L PTS 6 Bradford
25.01.89	Steve Osborne L PTS 6 Stoke
20.02.89	Willie Connell W RSC 4 Bradford
04.04.89	Lee Woolis L PTS 6 Manchester
12.10.89	George Ferrie W PTS 6 Glasgow
30.11.89	Jimmy Cropper W PTS 6 Oldham
07.12.89	Sean O'Phoenix L PTS 6 Manchester
07.04.90	Eddy Smulders L PTS 6 Eindhoven, Holland
15.05.90	Terry French W PTS 4 South Shields
12.10.90	Ray Alberts L PTS 6 Cayenne, France

Simon McDougall   Harry Goodwin

22.10.90	Glenn Campbell L RSC 4 Manchester
10.12.90	Morris Thomas W RSC 2 Bradford
28.01.91	Ian Henry W PTS 8 Bradford
28.02.91	Glenn Campbell L PTS 10 Bury *(Central Area S. Middleweight Title Challenge)*
23.04.91	Paul Burton L PTS 8 Evesham
10.05.91	Ian Henry L PTS 6 Gateshead
30.09.91	Doug Calderwood W RSC 4 Liverpool
10.10.91	Terry French L PTS 6 Gateshead
19.10.91	Andrea Magi L RSC 5 Terni, Italy
03.03.92	Paul Hitch L PTS 6 Houghton le Spring
11.03.92	Ian Henry L PTS 8 Solihull
30.03.92	Nigel Rafferty L PTS 8 Coventry
08.06.92	Mark McBiane W PTS 6 Bradford
06.10.92	Garry Delaney L PTS 8 Antwerp, Belgium
12.12.92	Garry Delaney L PTS 8 Muswell Hill
04.03.93	Alan Smiles L PTS 6 Glasgow
26.03.93	Roland Ericsson W RSC 5 Copenhagen, Denmark
17.04.93	Terry French L PTS 6 Washington
12.05.93	Martin Langtry L PTS 6 Sheffield
14.08.93	Mark Prince L PTS 6 Hammersmith
04.10.93	Bruce Scott L PTS 6 Mayfair

15.10.93 Christophe Girard L PTS 8 Romorantin, France
08.12.93 Stevie R. Davies W RSC 5 Hull
29.01.94 Ole Klemetsen L RTD 5 Cardiff
08.03.94 John Foreman W RSC 6 Edgbaston
11.05.94 Monty Wright W PTS 6 Stevenage
19.09.94 Stephen Wilson L RTD 3 Glasgow
21.01.95 Sean Heron L PTS 4 Glasgow
16.02.95 Glenn Campbell L PTS 6 Bury
06.03.95 John Keeton L RSC 5 Mayfair
17.04.95 Stefan Angehrn W RSC 5 Berne, Switzerland
22.11.95 Michael Gale L PTS 10 Sheffield
(Central Area L. Heavyweight Title Challenge)
01.06.97 Rudiger May L PTS 6 Riesa, Germany
Career: 44 contests, won 14, lost 30.

Alan McDowall

Renfrew. *Born* Renfrew, 29 September, 1967
L. Welterweight. Ht. 5'10"
Manager A. Morrison

24.09.91 Johnny Patterson W PTS 4 Glasgow
28.11.91 Johnny Patterson W PTS 6 Glasgow
31.01.92 Charles Shepherd W RSC 3 Glasgow
20.02.92 Mark O'Callaghan W PTS 6 Glasgow
12.03.92 James Jiora W CO 2 Glasgow
29.05.92 Karl Taylor W PTS 6 Glasgow
22.10.92 Robert Lloyd W RTD 4 Glasgow
30.04.93 Dean Bramhald W PTS 6 Glasgow
29.05.93 Rob Stewart DREW 6 Paisley
19.12.93 Dean Amory W PTS 8 Glasgow
10.06.94 Mark Antony W PTS 8 Glasgow
08.09.94 Peter Till L PTS 6 Glasgow
15.09.95 Floyd Churchill W RSC 5 Glasgow
13.10.95 Peter Till W RSC 5 Glasgow
12.02.96 Mark Ramsey W PTS 8 Glasgow
16.03.96 Mark Ramsey W PTS 6 Glasgow
12.02.97 Kevin McKillan W RTD 1 Glasgow
13.06.97 Paul Denton DREW 6 Paisley
Career: 18 contests, won 15, drew 2, lost 1.

Anthony McFadden

Donegal. *Born* Leeds, 21 December, 1971
L. Middleweight. Ht. 5'10"
Manager F. Maloney

30.03.96 Ernie Loveridge W PTS 4 Dublin
22.04.96 Dave Andrews W RSC 2 Crystal Palace
29.06.96 Peter Vosper W PTS 4 Erith
27.08.96 Steve Ford W RSC 4 Windsor
07.10.96 Marty Duke W CO 1 Lewisham
26.11.96 Andy Ewen W PTS 6 Bethnal Green
04.03.97 Clayon Stewart W RSC 6 Southwark
20.05.97 Jamie Robinson W PTS 8 Edmonton
Career: 8 contests, won 8.

James McGee

Bedworth. *Born* Nuneaton, 9 May, 1968
L. Middleweight. Ht. 6'1"
Manager Self

19.03.91 Adrian Din W PTS 6 Leicester
15.04.91 Marty Duke L PTS 6 Leicester
20.05.91 Cliff Churchward W PTS 6 Leicester
11.06.91 Julian Eavis W PTS 6 Leicester
01.10.91 Trevor Meikle L PTS 6 Bedworth
21.10.91 Crain Fisher L RSC 4 Bury
11.12.91 Julian Eavis DREW 6 Leicester
11.02.92 Chris Mulcahy W PTS 6 Wolverhampton

25.03.92 Darren Morris DREW 6 Hinckley
11.05.92 Julian Eavis W RSC 3 Coventry
05.10.92 Julian Eavis L PTS 6 Bardon
23.11.92 James Campbell DREW 6 Coventry
20.01.93 John Duckworth L PTS 6 Solihull
22.02.93 Julian Eavis W PTS 6 Bedworth
24.03.93 Damien Denny L CO 2 Belfast
(Final Elim. All-Ireland L. Middleweight Title)
16.12.93 Anthony Lawrence DREW 6 Walsall
26.01.94 Wayne Shepherd L PTS 6 Stoke
26.03.96 Gavin Lane L PTS 6 Wolverhampton
21.05.96 Steve Levene L PTS 6 Edgbaston
09.10.96 George Richards L PTS 6 Stoke
Career: 20 contests, won 7, drew 4, lost 9.

Gavin McGhin

Sunderland. *Born* Sunderland, 22 June, 1970
Heavyweight. Ht. 6'5½"
Manager T. Conroy

15.05.97 Geoff Hunter W PTS 6 Sunderland
Career: 1 contest, won 1.

Steve McGovern

Bembridge. *Born* Newport, IOW, 17 April, 1969
Welterweight. Ht. 5'9"
Manager J. Bishop

21.09.89 Mike Morrison W PTS 6 Southampton
17.04.90 Justin Graham W PTS 6 Millwall
21.01.91 Mark Dinnadge W PTS 6 Crystal Palace
23.02.91 Tim Harmey W PTS 6 Brighton
23.04.91 Frank Harrington W PTS 6 Evesham
08.05.91 A.M.Milton W PTS 6 Millwall
16.12.91 Chris Mylan W PTS 8 Southampton
03.03.92 Tony Swift L RSC 4 Cradley Heath
27.10.92 Ricky Mabbett DREW 6 Leicester
29.04.93 Michael Dick W PTS 6 Hayes
23.06.93 Joel Ani W PTS 6 Edmonton
23.02.94 David Lake W PTS 6 Watford
17.12.94 Ahmet Katejev L RSC 4 Berlin, Germany
31.03.95 Maurice Forbes L PTS 6 Crystal Palace
19.04.95 Jason Beard L PTS 6 Bethnal Green
17.06.95 Michael Carruth L RSC 4 Cardiff
19.01.96 Dennis Gardner L PTS 6 Bracknell
09.03.96 Eamonn Magee L PTS 4 Millstreet
04.04.96 Justin Simmons DREW 6 Plymouth
10.12.96 Justin Simmons L RSC 2 Plymouth
Career: 20 contests, won 10, drew 2, lost 8.

Mark McGowan

Plymouth. *Born* Plymouth, 5 February, 1972
Lightweight. Ht. 5'7½"
Manager C. Sanigar/N. Christian

10.06.95 Mark Winters L PTS 6 Manchester
28.11.95 John Janes L PTS 6 Cardiff
20.12.95 Phil Found W PTS 6 Usk
19.04.97 Mark Richards W PTS 6 Plymouth
Career: 4 contests, won 2, lost 2.

Graham McGrath

Warley. *Born* West Bromwich, 31 July, 1962
S. Bantamweight. Ht. 5'4"
Manager Self

21.05.92 Paul Kelly W RSC 2 Cradley Heath
01.06.92 Greg Upton L PTS 6 Solihull
09.07.92 Wilson Docherty L RSC 4 Glasgow
25.09.92 Paul Lloyd L RSC 3 Liverpool
02.11.92 Dennis Oakes L PTS 4 Liverpool
01.12.92 Leo Beirne W PTS 6 Liverpool
10.12.92 Shaun Anderson L PTS 6 Glasgow
14.01.93 Daren Fifield L PTS 4 Mayfair
29.01.93 Shaun Anderson L PTS 6 Glasgow
23.02.93 Ian Baillie W PTS 6 Kettering
29.03.93 Ian McLeod L PTS 6 Glasgow
19.04.93 Karl Morling L RSC 6 Northampton
23.06.93 Rowan Williams L PTS 4 Edmonton
02.07.93 Peter Culshaw L PTS 6 Liverpool
09.09.93 Shaun Anderson L PTS 8 Glasgow
28.09.93 John Sillo L PTS 6 Liverpool
06.10.93 Neil Parry DREW 6 Glasgow
21.10.93 James Murray L PTS 6 Glasgow
28.10.93 Greg Upton L PTS 8 Torquay
07.11.93 Alex Docherty L RSC 3 Glasgow
06.12.93 Darren Greaves DREW 6 Birmingham
16.12.93 Darren Greaves W PTS 6 Walsall
19.01.94 Gary White L PTS 6 Solihull
21.02.94 Ian McLeod L CO 6 Glasgow
21.03.94 Marcus Duncan L PTS 6 Bradford
28.03.94 Jason Morris W PTS 6 Birmingham
27.04.94 Paul Ingle L PTS 4 Bethnal Green
20.05.94 Mark Cokely W PTS 6 Neath
10.06.94 James Murray L PTS 8 Glasgow
08.09.94 Shaun Anderson L PTS 8 Glasgow
21.09.94 Mark Hughes L PTS 4 Cardiff
03.10.94 Michael Brodie L RSC 5 Manchester
02.11.94 Darren Greaves W RSC 4 Birmingham
24.11.94 Paul Ingle L PTS 6 Hull
05.12.94 Darren Greaves W PTS 6 Birmingham
13.12.94 Patrick Mullings L PTS 4 Ilford
18.01.95 Rowan Williams L CO 6 Solihull
(Vacant Midlands Area Bantamweight Title)
14.02.95 Mark Bowers L PTS 6 Bethnal Green
09.03.95 Marty Chestnut L PTS 6 Walsall
20.03.95 Marty Chestnut W PTS 6 Birmingham
30.03.95 Patrick Mullings L RSC 3 Bethnal Green
11.05.95 Jon Pegg W PTS 6 Dudley
05.06.95 Jon Pegg W PTS 6 Birmingham
20.06.95 Jon Pegg W PTS 6 Birmingham
30.06.95 Chris Jickells L PTS 4 Doncaster
28.07.95 Chris Jickells L PTS 6 Epworth
26.08.95 Paul Ireland L PTS 4 Belfast
20.09.95 Neil Swain W PTS 6 Ystrad
18.10.95 Ady Benton L PTS 6 Batley
26.10.95 Brendan Bryce L PTS 6 Birmingham
08.11.95 Andy Roberts L PTS 6 Scunthorpe
21.11.95 Marty Chestnut L PTS 6 Edgbaston
28.11.95 Andy Roberts W PTS 6 Wolverhampton
04.12.95 Andrew Robinson L PTS 6 Birmingham
18.12.95 Miguel Matthews L PTS 8 Mayfair
24.01.96 Michael Edwards L PTS 6 Stoke
22.02.96 Michael Edwards L PTS 6 Walsall
06.03.96 Michael Edwards W PTS 6 Solihull
15.03.96 Mark Bowers L PTS 6 Dunstable
29.03.96 Andy Roberts W PTS 6 Doncaster
20.04.96 Paul Ireland L PTS 6 Brentwood
04.05.96 Ricky Beard W PTS 6 Dagenham
28.05.96 Tommy Waite L PTS 6 Belfast
04.06.96 Noel Wilders L PTS 6 York
25.06.96 Ady Lewis L RSC 1 Stevenage
16.08.96 Tony Mulholland L RSC 3 Liverpool
07.10.96 Benny Jones W PTS 6 Birmingham
24.10.96 Stefy Bull L PTS 6 Birmingham
05.11.96 Tommy Waite L PTS 4 Belfast

26.11.96 Robert Braddock L PTS 6 Wolverhampton
09.12.96 Jason Squire L PTS 8 Leicester
16.12.96 Esham Pickering L PTS 6 Cleethorpes
07.03.97 Anthony Norbury L PTS 6 Weston super Mare
25.03.97 David Coldwell W PTS 6 Wolverhampton
04.04.97 Paul Halpin L PTS 6 Brighton
12.04.97 Esham Pickering L PTS 4 Sheffield
28.04.97 Shaun Anderson L PTS 6 Glasgow
12.05.97 John Farrell L RSC 4 Leicester
26.06.97 Esham Pickering L PTS 6 Salford
Career: 79 contests, won 18, drew 2, lost 59.

Dave McHale

Glasgow. *Born* Glasgow, 29 April, 1967
S. Featherweight. Ht. 5'7"
Manager T. Gilmour

08.10.90 Sol Francis W RSC 2 Glasgow
25.11.91 Eddie Garbutt W RSC 1 Liverpool
30.03.92 Kevin Lowe W RSC 5 Glasgow
01.06.92 Chris Jickells W RSC 4 Glasgow
09.07.92 G. G. Goddard W RTD 4 Glasgow
19.10.92 Lee Fox W RSC 3 Glasgow
23.11.92 Karl Taylor W PTS 8 Glasgow
15.05.93 Miguel Matthews W RSC 4 Glasgow
02.02.94 John T. Kelly W CO 1 Glasgow
21.03.94 Frankie Foster W PTS 8 Glasgow
13.12.94 Floyd Havard L RSC 10 Ilford
 (British S. Featherweight Title Challenge)
23.10.95 Chris Aston W RTD 3 Glasgow
22.04.96 P. J. Gallagher L RSC 10 Crystal Palace
 (Vacant British S. Featherweight Title)
27.01.97 Bamana Dibateza W PTS 6 Glasgow
28.04.97 John T. Kelly W RSC 4 Glasgow
Career: 15 contests, won 13, lost 2.

Duke McKenzie

Croydon. *Born* Croydon, 5 May, 1963
Former Undefeated British Featherweight Champion. Former WBO S. Bantamweight & Bantamweight Champion. Former IBF Flyweight Champion. Former Undefeated British & European Flyweight Champion. Ht. 5'7"
Manager Self

23.11.82 Charlie Brown W RSC 1 Wembley
24.01.83 Andy King W RSC 2 Mayfair
27.02.83 Dave Pearson W RSC 1 Las Vegas, USA
03.03.83 Gregorio Hernandez W RSC 3 Los Angeles, USA
19.03.83 Lupe Sanchez W CO 2 Reno, USA
18.10.83 Jerry Davis W RSC 2 Atlantic City, USA
22.11.83 Alain Limarola W PTS 6 Wembley
15.01.84 David Capo W PTS 4 Atlantic City, USA
23.05.84 Gary Roberts W CO 1 Mayfair
06.03.85 Julio Guerrero W PTS 8 Kensington
05.06.85 Danny Flynn W RSC 4 Kensington
 (Vacant British Flyweight Title)
16.10.85 Orlando Maestre W PTS 8 Kensington
19.02.86 Sonny Long W PTS 10 Kensington
20.05.86 Charlie Magri W RTD 5 Wembley
 (British Flyweight Title Defence & European Flyweight Title Challenge)
19.11.86 Lee Cargle W PTS 10 Atlantic City, USA

17.12.86 Piero Pinna W PTS 12 Acqui Terme, Italy
 (European Flyweight Title Defence)
24.03.87 Jose Manuel Diaz W PTS 8 Wembley
02.12.87 Juan Herrera W PTS 10 Wembley
09.03.88 Agapito Gomez W CO 2 Wembley
 (European Flyweight Title Defence)
04.05.88 Jose Gallegos W PTS 10 Wembley
05.10.88 Rolando Bohol W CO 11 Wembley
 (IBF Flyweight Title Challenge)
30.11.88 Artemio Ruiz W PTS 10 Southwark
08.03.89 Tony de Luca W RSC 4 Kensington
 (IBF Flyweight Title Defence)
07.06.89 Dave Boy McAuley L PTS 12 Wembley
 (IBF Flyweight Title Defence)
12.10.89 Dave Moreno W PTS 10 Southwark
08.11.89 Memo Flores W PTS 8 Wembley
30.09.90 Thierry Jacob L PTS 12 Calais, France
 (Vacant European Bantamweight Title)
10.01.91 Pete Buckley W RSC 5 Wandsworth
07.02.91 Julio Blanco W RSC 7 Watford
04.04.91 Chris Clarkson W RSC 5 Watford
30.06.91 Gaby Canizales W PTS 12 Southwark
 (WBO Bantamweight Title Challenge)
12.09.91 Cesar Soto W PTS 12 Wandsworth
 (WBO Bantamweight Title Defence)
25.03.92 Wilfredo Vargas W RSC 8 Kensington
 (WBO Bantamweight Title Defence)
13.05.92 Rafael del Valle L CO 1 Kensington
 (WBO Bantamweight Title Defence)
07.09.92 Pete Buckley W RTD 3 Bethnal Green
15.10.92 Jesse Benavides W PTS 12 Lewisham
 (WBO S. Bantamweight Title Challenge)
09.06.93 Daniel Jimenez L PTS 12 Lewisham
 (WBO S. Bantamweight Title Defence)
18.12.93 John Davison W RSC 4 Manchester
 (Vacant British Featherweight Title)
29.01.94 Marcelo Rodriguez W PTS 8 Cardiff
17.08.94 Mark Hargreaves W RSC 3 Sheffield
01.10.94 Steve Robinson L CO 9 Cardiff
 (WBO Featherweight Title Challenge)
28.04.95 Mehdi Labdouni L PTS 12 Fontenay sous Bois
 (European Featherweight Title Challenge)
25.06.96 Elvis Parsley W RSC 1 Mansfield
25.03.97 Bamana Dibateza W PTS 8 Lewisham
30.06.97 Carl Allen W PTS 8 Bethnal Green
Career: 45 contests, won 39, lost 6.

Kelton McKenzie

Leicester. *Born* Leicester, 18 September, 1968
S. Featherweight. Midlands Area Featherweight Champion. Ht. 5'7"
Manager J. Griffin

18.10.90 Tony Silkstone L PTS 6 Dewsbury
29.11.90 Neil Leitch DREW 6 Marton
11.12.90 Sylvester Osuji W PTS 6 Evesham
21.01.91 J. T. Williams DREW 6 Crystal Palace
14.03.91 Craig Dermody L RSC 3 Middleton
01.05.91 Tim Yeates W PTS 6 Bethnal Green
17.06.91 Derek Amory W RSC 6 Edgbaston
05.11.91 Richard Woolgar W RSC 5 Leicester
22.01.92 Colin Lynch W RSC 5 Solihull
26.03.92 Brian Robb W RSC 4 Telford
29.04.92 Elvis Parsley W RSC 5 Solihull
 (Vacant Midlands Area Featherweight Title)

18.07.92 Steve Walker W CO 2 Manchester
27.10.92 Alan McKay L PTS 10 Cradley Heath
 (Elim. British Featherweight Title)
28.04.93 Richie Wenton L PTS 8 Dublin
19.05.93 Paul Harvey L RSC 7 Leicester
04.10.93 Mehdi Labdouni L PTS 8 Paris, France
10.05.94 Harry Escott L PTS 6 Doncaster
27.08.94 Barry Jones L PTS 6 Cardiff
31.10.94 Sugar Gibiliru L PTS 6 Liverpool
09.12.94 Yifru Retta L PTS 4 Bethnal Green
06.03.95 Wayne Rigby W PTS 8 Leicester
26.04.95 Charles Shepherd L RSC 7 Solihull
07.07.95 Gareth Jordan L PTS 4 Cardiff
29.07.95 Dominic McGuigan DREW 6 Whitley Bay
08.09.95 Dennis Holbaek Pedersen L RSC 5 Aalborg, Denmark
10.11.95 Dean Pithie DREW 6 Derby
01.12.95 Arlindo de Abreu L PTS 8 Gien, France
26.04.96 Dean Pithie L PTS 6 Cardiff
18.09.96 Steve Robinson L PTS 8 Tylorstown
26.10.96 Alex Moon L RSC 3 Liverpool
09.12.96 Ervine Blake W PTS 6 Leicester
03.02.97 Jimmy Phelan W RSC 5 Leicester
03.03.97 Marc Smith W PTS 8 Leicester
12.05.97 Miguel Matthews W PTS 6 Leicester
Career: 34 contests, won 13, drew 4, lost 17.

(Roger) R. F. McKenzie

Croydon. *Born* Croydon, 3 October, 1965
Former Southern Area Heavyweight Champion. Ht. 6'2"
Manager G. Steene

31.01.89 Gerry Storey W PTS 6 Bethnal Green
24.09.90 Mark Bowen L RSC 1 Mayfair
29.11.90 Denzil Browne W PTS 6 Sunderland
12.02.91 Noel Magee L PTS 6 Belfast
21.03.91 Denzil Browne L PTS 6 Dewsbury
28.05.91 Steve Yorath L PTS 6 Cardiff
07.09.91 Ray Kane L PTS 4 Belfast
09.10.91 Denzil Browne W PTS 6 Manchester
28.10.91 Pedro van Raamsdonk W CO 7 Arnhem, Holland
12.12.91 Norbert Ekassi L RSC 3 Massy, France
14.03.92 Neils H. Madsen L PTS 6 Copenhagen, Denmark
25.04.92 Noel Magee L PTS 8 Belfast
31.10.92 Warren Richards DREW 6 Earls Court
13.02.93 Magne Havnaa W RTD 5 Randers, Denmark
31.03.93 Warren Richards W RSC 8 Bethnal Green
 (Vacant Southern Area Heavyweight Title)
17.09.93 Brian Neilsen L PTS 6 Copenhagen, Denmark
13.10.93 James Oyebola L RSC 1 Bethnal Green
 (Southern Area Heavyweight Title Defence)
11.12.93 Bernd Friedrich W RSC 2 Dusseldorf, Germany
25.03.94 Mark Hulstrom L PTS 6 Bernholme, Denmark
17.09.94 Scott Welch L RSC 1 Crawley
27.05.95 Darren Corbett W PTS 6 Belfast
07.10.95 Mike Holden L RSC 2 Belfast
20.09.96 Steve Cranston W DIS 5 Tooting
03.12.96 Kevin McBride L RSC 6 Liverpool
Career: 24 contests, won 9, drew 1, lost 14.

Kevin McKillan

Manchester. *Born* Belfast, 1 March, 1969
L. Welterweight. Ht. 5'8"
Manager T. Miller

28.10.91	Michael Byrne W PTS 6 Leicester	
13.11.91	Barry Glanister W PTS 6 Liverpool	
22.01.92	Sugar Boy Wright W PTS 6 Solihull	
10.02.92	Jamie Davidson L PTS 6 Liverpool	
11.03.92	Jamie Davidson DREW 6 Stoke	
01.06.92	Steve Howden W RSC 2 Manchester	
12.06.92	Floyd Churchill W PTS 6 Liverpool	
25.09.92	John Smith W PTS 6 Liverpool	
07.10.92	J. T. Williams L PTS 6 Barry	
20.11.92	Steve Foran L PTS 6 Liverpool	
15.02.93	John T. Kelly W PTS 6 Manchester	
19.04.93	Simon Hamblett W CO 2 Manchester	
26.04.93	Steve Walker DREW 8 Manchester	
01.06.93	Micky Hall W PTS 6 Manchester	
06.10.93	Norman Dhalie W RSC 1 Solihull	
29.10.93	Soren Sondergaard L CO 2 Korsoer, Denmark	
26.01.94	Dean Amory W PTS 8 Stoke	
06.06.94	Micky Hall W PTS 6 Manchester	
22.09.94	Kevin McKenzie W PTS 6 Bury	
10.12.94	Tanveer Ahmed L PTS 6 Manchester	
18.05.95	Shaun Stokes DREW 8 Middleton	
29.09.95	Alan Temple L PTS 6 Hartlepool	
28.10.95	Georgie Smith L CO 2 Kensington	
16.03.96	Tanveer Ahmed L PTS 4 Glasgow	
10.05.96	Carl Wright L PTS 8 Liverpool	
24.05.96	Tanveer Ahmed DREW 8 Glasgow	
29.06.96	Peter Richardson L CO 2 Erith	
03.09.96	Eamonn Magee L RTD 4 Belfast	
06.11.96	Steve McLevy L PTS 6 Glasgow	
12.02.97	Alan McDowall L RTD 1 Glasgow	
27.03.97	Jason Rowland L PTS 8 Norwich	
22.04.97	Trevor Dixon W PTS 6 Bethnal Green	
02.06.97	Eamonn Magee L RSC 3 Belfast *(Elim. All-Ireland L. Welterweight Title)*	

Career: 33 contests, won 14, drew 4, lost 15.

Ian McLeod

Kilmarnock. *Born* Edinburgh, 11 June, 1969
S. Featherweight. Ht. 5'9"
Manager T. Gilmour

23.11.92	Robert Braddock DREW 6 Glasgow	
29.03.93	Graham McGrath W PTS 6 Glasgow	
21.02.94	Graham McGrath W CO 6 Glasgow	
04.03.94	Chip O'Neill W RSC 2 Irvine	
23.11.94	Chris Jickells W PTS 6 Irvine	
05.04.95	Colin Innes W RSC 5 Irvine	
22.01.96	Chris Jickells W PTS 8 Glasgow	
23.09.96	Robert Braddock W RSC 3 Glasgow	
28.02.97	Carl Allen W RTD 3 Kilmarnock	

Career: 9 contests, won 8, drew 1.

Steve McLevy

Glasgow. *Born* Glasgow, 23 September, 1972
Scottish L. Welterweight Champion.
Ht. 5'8"
Manager Self

22.11.93	Dewi Roberts W RSC 1 Glasgow	
02.02.94	Kevin McKenzie W PTS 6 Glasgow	
28.03.94	Mark Antony W CO 1 Musselburgh	
20.09.94	Dave Curtis W RTD 3 Musselburgh	
21.11.94	Mark Legg W RSC 5 Glasgow	
24.02.95	John Smith W PTS 6 Irvine	

01.06.95	Micky Hall L RSC 1 Musselburgh	
23.10.95	Alan Peacock W RSC 6 Glasgow *(Vacant Scottish L. Welterweight Title)*	
22.01.96	Tony Swift L PTS 8 Glasgow	
03.06.96	Wahid Fats W RSC 3 Glasgow	
26.09.96	Dave Brazil W RSC 1 Glasgow	
06.11.96	Kevin McKillan W PTS 6 Glasgow	
18.11.96	John Smith W PTS 8 Glasgow	
24.02.97	Shaun Stokes W RSC 1 Glasgow	
02.06.97	Brian Coleman L RSC 5 Glasgow	

Career: 15 contests, won 12, lost 3.

Colin McMillan

Barking. *Born* London, 12 February, 1966
Former WBO & British Featherweight
Champion. Former Undefeated
Commonwealth Featherweight Champion.
Ht. 5'5¼"

Manager Self

29.11.88	Mike Chapman W PTS 6 Battersea	
10.12.88	Aldrich Johnson W PTS 6 Crystal Palace	
31.01.89	Alan McKay L RSC 3 Bethnal Green	
12.06.89	Miguel Matthews W RSC 3 Battersea	
19.09.89	Graham O'Malley W PTS 8 Millwall	
11.10.89	Marcel Herbert W PTS 6 Millwall	
30.11.89	Sylvester Osuji W RSC 4 Barking	
14.02.90	Vidal Tellez W RSC 2 Millwall	
17.04.90	Jesus Muniz W PTS 8 Millwall	
03.05.90	Steve Walker W PTS 6 Kensington	
05.07.90	Tyrone Miller W CO 2 Greensville, USA	
17.07.90	Malcolm Rougeaux W CO 1 Lake Charles, USA	
25.09.90	Darren Weller W RSC 2 Millwall	
10.10.90	Graham O'Malley W PTS 6 Millwall	
12.11.90	Mark Holt W PTS 8 Norwich	
05.03.91	Russell Davison W PTS 6 Millwall	
26.04.91	Willie Richardson W PTS 8 Crystal Palace	
22.05.91	Gary de Roux W RSC 7 Millwall *(British Featherweight Title Challenge)*	
03.07.91	Herbie Bivalacqua W RSC 3 Reading	
04.09.91	Kevin Pritchard W RSC 7 Bethnal Green *(British Featherweight Title Defence)*	
29.10.91	Sean Murphy W PTS 12 Kensington *(British Featherweight Title Defence)*	
18.01.92	Percy Commey W PTS 12 Kensington *(Vacant Commonwealth Featherweight Title)*	
25.03.92	Tommy Valdez W CO 6 Dagenham	
16.05.92	Maurizio Stecca W PTS 12 Muswell Hill *(WBO Featherweight Title Challenge)*	
26.09.92	Ruben Palacio L RSC 8 Earls Court *(WBO Featherweight Title Defence)*	
23.10.93	Steve Robinson L PTS 12 Cardiff *(WBO Featherweight Title Challenge)*	
04.02.95	Harry Escott W PTS 8 Cardiff	
25.02.95	Mark Hargreaves W RSC 4 Millwall	
06.05.95	Peter Judson W PTS 8 Shepton Mallet	
22.07.95	Dean Phillips W PTS 8 Millwall	
30.01.96	Justin Murphy W RSC 4 Barking	
21.03.96	Pete Buckley W RSC 3 Southwark	
14.05.96	Jonjo Irwin W PTS 12 Dagenham *(British Featherweight Title Challenge)*	
03.09.96	Trust Ndlovu W RSC 7 Bethnal Green *(Final Elim. Commonwealth Featherweight Title)*	
11.01.97	Paul Ingle L RSC 8 Bethnal Green *(British Featherweight Title Defence)*	

Career: 35 contests, won 31, lost 4.

Steve McNess

Bethnal Green. *Born* Bow, 17 November, 1969
Middleweight. Ht. 5'10½"
Manager Self

22.04.92	Rick North W PTS 6 Wembley	
13.05.92	Mark Verikios L RSC 5 Kensington	
03.09.92	Steve Goodwin W PTS 6 Dunstable	
28.10.92	Mark Dawson L RSC 2 Kensington	
28.01.93	Steve Scott W PTS 6 Southwark	
26.04.93	Bullit Andrews W RSC 3 Lewisham	
15.06.93	Martin Rosamond L RSC 5 Hemel Hempstead	
07.12.93	Robert Whitehouse W RSC 3 Bethnal Green	
16.02.94	Billy McDougall W PTS 4 Stevenage	
11.03.94	Tony Walton W PTS 4 Bethnal Green	
11.10.94	Harry Dhami DREW 6 Bethnal Green	
23.02.95	Julian Eavis W PTS 6 Southwark	
25.03.95	Peter Vosper W RSC 5 Millwall	
20.04.95	Spencer Alton W RSC 2 Mayfair	
19.05.95	Martin Jolley W PTS 6 Southwark	
27.09.95	Martin Jolley L RTD 4 Bethnal Green	
29.04.96	Roy Chipperfield W RSC 3 Mayfair	
14.10.96	Tony Walton W PTS 6 Mayfair	
17.03.97	Kevin Thompson L RSC 1 Mayfair	

Career: 19 contests, won 13, drew 1, lost 5.

Steve McNess   Les Clark

Ronnie McPhee

Glasgow. *Born* Stirling, 1 August, 1976
S. Bantamweight. Ht. 5'6½"
Manager A. Morrison

06.11.96	Des Gargano W RTD 5 Glasgow	
22.12.96	Amjed Mamond W RSC 3 Glasgow	
12.02.97	Pete Buckley W PTS 6 Glasgow	
16.05.97	Colin Innes W RSC 2 Glasgow	

Career: 4 contests, won 4.

Scott McQueen

Saltcoats. *Born* Irvine, 13 June, 1978
L. Welterweight. Ht. 5'10"
Manager A. Morrison

12.02.97 Les Frost W RSC 3 Glasgow
16.05.97 Ivan Walker L PTS 6 Glasgow
Career: 2 contests, won 1, lost 1.

Eamonn Magee
Belfast. *Born* Belfast, 13 July, 1971
L. Welterweight. Ht. 5'9"
Manager M. O'Callaghan

25.11.95 Pete Roberts W CO 4 Dublin
09.03.96 Steve McGovern W PTS 4 Millstreet
28.05.96 John Stovin W RSC 2 Belfast
03.09.96 Kevin McKillan W RTD 4 Belfast
05.11.96 Shaun Stokes W RSC 2 Belfast
28.01.97 Karl Taylor W PTS 6 Belfast
03.03.97 Troy Townsend W RSC 1 Austin, USA
28.03.97 Teddy Reid L PTS 6 Boston, USA
29.04.97 Peter Nightingale W RTD 2 Belfast
02.06.97 Kevin McKillan W RSC 3 Belfast
(Elim. All-Ireland L. Welterweight Title)

Career: 10 contests, won 9. lost 1.

Noel Magee
Belfast. *Born* Belfast, 16 December, 1965
Cruiserweight. Former Commonwealth L.
Heavyweight Champion. Ht. 6'1"
Manager Self

22.05.85 Nigel Prickett W CO 1 Stoke
12.09.85 Dave Furneaux W RSC 3 Swindon
28.10.85 Eddie Chatterton W RSC 1 Stoke
06.11.85 Winston Burnett W PTS 8 Nantwich
11.12.85 Winston Burnett W PTS 8 Stoke
22.01.86 Blaine Logsdon W PTS 8 Stoke
20.02.86 Barry Ahmed W PTS 8 Newcastle
05.03.86 Winston Burnett W PTS 8 Stoke
23.04.86 Barry Ahmed W RSC 7 Stoke
30.05.86 Geoff Rymer W CO 1 Stoke
13.10.86 Jimmy Ellis W PTS 8 Dulwich
17.11.86 Serg Fame W PTS 8 Dulwich
24.02.87 Lennie Howard W RSC 1 Ilford
03.08.87 Jimmy Ellis W RSC 6 Stoke
20.10.87 Johnny Held L PTS 8 Stoke
13.02.88 Rufino Angulo DREW 8 Paris, France
03.05.88 Mike Brothers W CO 6 Stoke
15.11.88 Ian Bulloch DREW 10 Hull
15.02.89 Yves Monsieur L RSC 5 Stoke
02.10.89 Paul McCarthy W CO 2 Hanley
29.11.89 Sammy Storey L RSC 9 Belfast
(British S. Middleweight Title Challenge)
15.09.90 Glazz Campbell W PTS 8 Belfast
30.10.90 Johnny Melfah W PTS 6 Belfast
12.02.91 R. F. McKenzie W PTS 6 Belfast
11.05.91 Simon Collins W PTS 8 Belfast
13.11.91 Frank Minton W RSC 3 Belfast
11.12.91 Tony Wilson W RSC 3 Dublin
25.04.92 R. F. McKenzie W PTS 8 Belfast
28.09.92 Maurice Core L RSC 9 Manchester
(Vacant British L. Heavyweight Title)
22.05.93 Dariusz Michalczewski L RSC 8 Aachen, Germany
(Vacant IBF Inter-Continental L. Heavyweight Title)
16.10.93 John Kaighin W PTS 6 Belfast
21.05.94 John J. Cooke W PTS 6 Belfast
05.03.95 Fabrice Tiozzo L RSC 4 Vitrolles, France
(European L. Heavyweight Title Challenge)
09.05.95 Garry Delaney W RTD 7 Basildon
(Commonwealth L. Heavyweight Title Challenge)

30.09.95 Nicky Piper L CO 9 Cardiff
(Commonwealth L. Heavyweight Title Defence. Vacant WBO Inter-Continental L. Heavyweight Title)
28.01.97 John Duckworth W PTS 6 Belfast
29.04.97 Darren Corbett L CO 2 Belfast
(All-Ireland Cruiserweight Title Challenge)

Career: 37 contests, won 27, drew 2, lost 8.

Jay Mahoney
Peterborough. *Born* Peterborough, 21
September, 1971
L. Welterweight. Ht 5'8"
Manager Self

05.12.94 Shaun O'Neill W PTS 6 Houghton le Spring
20.02.95 David Thompson W RSC 4 Manchester
08.03.95 Peter Hickenbottom W PTS 6 Solihull
03.04.95 Blue Butterworth W PTS 6 Manchester
02.10.95 Anthony Maynard L PTS 8 Birmingham
17.12.96 Roger Hunte W RSC 5 Bethnal Green
24.02.97 Chris Barnett W PTS 6 Manchester

Career: 7 contests, won 6, lost 1.

Shane Mallon
Kingston. *Born* Chertsey, 26 June, 1974
Flyweight. Ht. 5'10"
Manager J. Evans

05.11.96 Colin Moffett L RSC 2 Belfast

Career: 1 contest, lost 1.

Amjed Mamond
Rochdale. *Born* Pakistan, 7 February, 1972
Featherweight. Ht. 5'7"
Manager Self

26.04.96 Alston Buchanan L RSC 1 Glasgow
22.11.96 Esham Pickering L RSC 2 Hull
22.12.96 Ronnie McPhee L RSC 3 Glasgow

Career: 3 contests, lost 3.

Colin Manners
Leeds. *Born* Leeds, 4 July, 1962
Middleweight. Ht. 5'10"
Manager J. Rushton

26.04.90 Tony Booth L PTS 6 Halifax
27.09.90 Carlos Christie L PTS 6 Birmingham
18.10.90 Carlton Myers W CO 2 Dewsbury
25.10.90 Colin Ford L PTS 6 Bayswater
12.12.90 Tony Kosova W PTS 6 Leicester
31.01.91 Lee Crocker W PTS 6 Bredbury
18.02.91 John Ogiste L PTS 6 Mayfair
14.03.91 John Ogiste L PTS 8 Middleton
01.05.91 Darren Parker W CO 2 Solihull
05.06.91 Richard Carter W CO 1 Wolverhampton
03.09.91 Wayne Ellis W RSC 1 Cardiff
29.04.92 Darron Griffiths DREW 8 Solihull
14.07.92 Stan King W PTS 8 Mayfair
30.09.92 Darron Griffiths L PTS 10 Solihull
(Elim. British Middleweight Title)
23.02.93 Chris Pyatt L CO 3 Doncaster
15.07.93 Juan Medina Padilla L PTS 8 La Linea, Gibralter
19.01.94 Paul Busby DREW 8 Solihull
15.03.94 Paul Busby L PTS 8 Mayfair
11.05.94 Shaun Cummins W RSC 6 Sheffield
17.01.95 Antonio Fernandez L PTS 8 Worcester

04.02.95 Cornelius Carr L PTS 8 Cardiff
18.03.95 Sammy Storey L PTS 8 Millstreet, Eire
16.08.96 Paul Wright L PTS 10 Liverpoool
(Vacant Central Area Middleweight Title)
24.10.96 Darren Sweeney L PTS 8 Birmingham
16.05.97 Willie Quinn L PTS 6 Glasgow

Career: 25 contests, won 8, drew 2, lost 15.

Colin Manners   Les Clark

Andy Manning
Sheffield. *Born* Sheffield, 1 June, 1970
L. Heavyweight. Ht. 5'7¹/₂"
Manager G. Rhodes

07.10.91 Mark Hale W PTS 6 Liverpool
04.11.91 Steve Thomas L PTS 6 Merthyr
02.12.91 Marc Rowley W PTS 6 Liverpool
03.03.92 Justin Clements DREW 6 Cradley Heath
18.03.92 Willie Quinn L PTS 6 Glasgow
29.04.92 Adrian Wright W PTS 6 Stoke
11.05.92 Julian Johnson W PTS 6 Llanelli
18.05.92 John Oxenham L PTS 6 Marton
25.01.93 Joe McCluskey L PTS 6 Glasgow
26.06.97 Paul Bonson W PTS 6 Sheffield

Career: 10 contests, won 5, drew 1, lost 4.

Gary Marston
Stoke. *Born* Taunton, 11 December, 1966
Featherweight. Ht. 5'4"
Manager Self .

29.09.92 Norman Dhalie DREW 6 Stoke
17.03.93 Jason Morris W PTS 6 Stoke
12.05.93 Phil Lashley W RSC 2 Stoke
07.09.93 Joe Fannin W RSC 2 Stoke
27.10.93 Jobie Tyers W PTS 6 Stoke
01.12.93 Dougie Fox W RSC 1 Stoke
15.03.94 Des Gargano W PTS 8 Stoke
11.10.95 Chris Jickells W PTS 8 Stoke
06.12.95 Miguel Matthews W PTS 8 Stoke
24.01.96 Miguel Matthews L PTS 8 Stoke
27.03.96 Joe Donohoe W PTS 8 Stoke
24.04.96 Miguel Matthews W PTS 8 Solihull
09.10.96 Pete Buckley DREW 8 Stoke
04.12.96 Chris Lyons W PTS 8 Stoke

Career: 14 contests, won 11, drew 2, lost 1.

121

Andy Martin

Hull. *Born* Hull, 2 November, 1966
L. Welterweight. Ht. 5'6"
Manager M. Brooks

03.07.96 Dave Brazil L RSC 3 Wembley
31.08.96 Martin Renaghan L RSC 2 Dublin
Career: 2 contests, lost 2.

Alex Mason

Wolverhampton. *Born* Wolverhampton, 27 February, 1975
Middleweight. Ht. 5'11"
Manager P. Cowdell/R. Gray

09.12.96 Carlton Williams L PTS 6 Leicester
16.01.97 Lee Simpkin W PTS 6 Solihull
29.01.97 Chris Pollock W RSC 5 Stoke
07.03.97 Mark Sawyers W PTS 6 Weston super Mare
20.03.97 Carlton Williams W PTS 6 Solihull
15.04.97 Mike Thompson W RSC 2 Edgbaston
Career: 6 contests, won 5, lost 1.

(Paul) P. R. Mason

Sheffield. *Born* Sheffield, 18 October, 1965
L. Heavyweight. Ht. 6'0"
Manager Self

21.09.95 Barry Exton DREW 6 Sheffield
29.09.95 Mark Owens W RSC 3 Hartlepool
16.11.95 Mark Hopkins W PTS 6 Evesham
05.02.96 Michael Joyce W RSC 4 Bradford
15.02.96 Scott Beasley W PTS 6 Sheffield
07.03.96 Craig Joseph L PTS 6 Bradford
09.09.96 Harri Hakulinen DREW 6 Helsinki, Finland
02.10.96 Grant Briggs L CO 2 Cardiff
09.12.96 Kevin Burton W PTS 6 Bradford
12.03.97 Mark Hale W PTS 6 Stoke
20.04.97 Carl Nicholson L PTS 6 Leeds
Career: 11 contests, won 6, drew 2, lost 3.

Peter Mason

Hartlepool. *Born* Hartlepool, 19 March, 1971
L. Heavyweight. Ht. 6'1"
Manager G. Robinson

08.06.96 Naveed Anwar W RSC 4 Newcastle
22.08.96 Lee Whitehead L PTS 6 Salford
27.09.96 Johnny Hooks W PTS 6 Hull
04.12.96 Marvin O'Brien W CO 5 Hartlepool
03.02.97 Mark Dawson W PTS 4 Sunderland
Career: 5 contests, won 4, lost 1.

(Paul) Stinger Mason

Sheffield. *Born* Sheffield, 27 February, 1964
L. Heavyweight. Ht. 5'8"
Manager Self

19.04.89 Sean Stringfellow W PTS 6 Stoke
24.05.89 Andrew Flute L PTS 6 Hanley
16.11.89 Tony Lawrence DREW 4 Ilkeston
27.01.90 Ian Vokes W PTS 6 Sheffield
28.03.90 Cliff Curtis W PTS 6 Bethnal Green
20.05.90 Tony Hodge W CO 2 Sheffield
11.06.90 Glenn Campbell L RTD 5 Manchester
12.11.90 Adrian Wright L RSC 4 Stratford upon Avon
13.03.91 Mike Phillips DREW 6 Stoke

13.05.91 Doug Calderwood L CO 3 Manchester
23.10.91 Roger Wilson DREW 6 Stoke
11.11.91 Russell Washer W PTS 4 Stratford upon Avon
23.05.92 Paul Busby L RSC 2 Birmingham
28.09.92 Quinn Paynter L CO 1 Manchester
20.09.93 Stephen Wilson L RSC 6 Glasgow
10.11.93 Joe Calzaghe L RSC 1 Watford
15.03.94 Mark Dawson L RSC 6 Stoke
02.06.94 Luan Morena L PTS 6 Tooting
05.10.94 Lee Archer L PTS 6 Wolverhampton
16.11.94 Lester Jacobs L PTS 6 Bloomsbury
05.12.94 Jason Brown W RSC 2 Cleethorpes
13.12.94 Mark Baker L RSC 4 Ilford
23.01.95 Naveed Mirza W RSC 3 Bethnal Green
07.03.95 Justin Clements L RSC 4 Edgbaston
02.07.95 Pascal Collins L PTS 4 Dublin
09.09.95 Danny Ryan L PTS 6 Cork
27.10.95 Mark Snipe DREW 6 Brighton

06.12.95 John Duckworth W PTS 6 Stoke
26.01.96 Robin Reid L RSC 2 Brighton
20.03.96 Greg Scott-Briggs L PTS 6 Stoke
09.07.96 Mervyn Penniston-John L PTS 4 Bethnal Green
19.09.96 James Branch DREW 4 Manchester
23.11.96 Leif Keiski L RSC 4 Munich, Germany
14.03.97 Thomas Hansvoll L PTS 6 Odense, Denmark
04.04.97 Willie Quinn L RSC 6 Glasgow
15.05.97 Sven Hamer L CO 5 Reading
Career: 36 contests, won 8, drew 5, lost 23.

Jason Matthews

Hackney. *Born* London, 20 July, 1970
WBO Inter-Continental Middleweight Champion. Ht. 5'10½"
Manager F. Warren

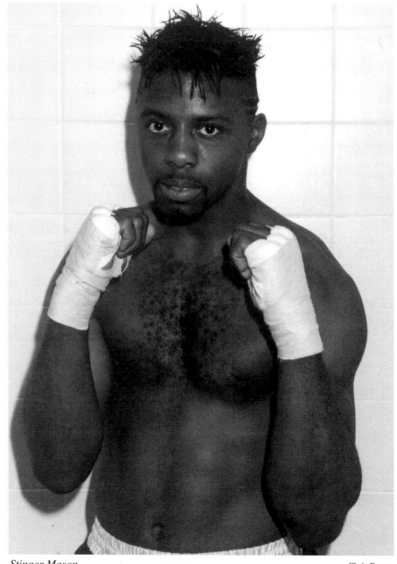

Stinger Mason   Chris Bevan

01.07.95	Chris Richards W CO 4 Kensington
22.07.95	Stuart Dunn W CO 1 Millwall
02.09.95	John Duckworth W PTS 4 Wembley
15.09.95	Mark Dawson W RSC 3 Mansfield
30.09.95	Marvin O'Brien W PTS 6 Cardiff
09.10.95	Salah Eddine Kobba W RSC 1 San Benedetto, Italy
27.10.95	Russell Washer W RSC 5 Brighton
09.12.95	Sven Hamer W RSC 6 Bethnal Green
16.03.96	John McAlpine W RSC 1 Glasgow
11.05.96	Peter Vosper W RSC 1 Bethnal Green
25.06.96	Martin Jolley W RSC 3 Mansfield
19.10.96	Danny Ryan W CO 5 Bristol
08.02.97	Ernie Loveridge W CO 5 Millwall
27.03.97	Paul Wright W RSC 3 Norwich
	(Vacant WBO Inter-Continental Middleweight Title)
29.05.97	Patrick Swann W RTD 5 Mayfair
	(WBO Inter-Continental Middleweight Title Defence)

Career: 15 contests, won 15.

John Matthews

Aldershot. *Born* Guildford, 13 January, 1969
Bantamweight. Ht. 5'6½"
Manager J. Evans

26.02.97	Chris Williams W RSC 1 Cardiff
12.03.97	Noel Wilders L PTS 6 Stoke
14.04.97	Michael Gibbons W PTS 6 Bradford
02.06.97	Paul Ireland L RSC 4 Belfast

Career: 4 contests, won 2, lost 2.

John Matthews — Les Clark

(Nicholas) Miguel Matthews

Ystalfera. *Born* Glanamman, 22 December, 1965
S. Featherweight. Ht. 5'7"
Manager R. Gray/P. Cowdell

21.09.88	Terry Collins L PTS 6 Basildon
28.09.88	Eugene Maloney DREW 6 Edmonton
25.10.88	Hugh Ruse L PTS 6 Pontadawe
15.11.88	Tommy Bernard W RSC 2 Chigwell
14.12.88	Richie Wenton L CO 2 Kirkby

14.02.89	Brian Robb W RSC 2 Wolverhampton
06.03.89	Mickey Markie L PTS 8 Northampton
21.03.89	Ronnie Stephenson DREW 6 Wolverhampton
11.04.89	Hugh Ruse W PTS 6 Aberavon
05.06.89	Lester James DREW 6 Birmingham
12.06.89	Colin McMillan L RSC 3 Battersea
06.09.89	Marcel Herbert L PTS 6 Aberavon
20.09.89	Des Gargano L PTS 6 Stoke
28.09.89	Steve Walker L PTS 6 Cardiff
17.10.89	Alan Roberts W PTS 6 Cardiff
24.10.89	Jimmy Clark L PTS 6 Watford
06.11.89	Mickey Markie DREW 8 Northampton
03.12.89	Johnny Bredahl L PTS 6 Copenhagen, Denmark
19.02.90	Mickey Markie L PTS 8 Kettering
27.02.90	Pete Buckley DREW 6 Evesham
21.03.90	Rocky Lawlor L PTS 8 Solihull
03.09.90	Derek Amory L PTS 6 Dudley
01.10.90	Pete Buckley L PTS 8 Cleethorpes
09.10.90	Pete Buckley W PTS 8 Wolverhampton
29.10.90	Pete Buckley L PTS 8 Birmingham
21.11.90	Jason Primera L PTS 8 Solihull
12.12.90	Paul Harvey L PTS 6 Basildon
19.12.90	Paul Forrest L PTS 6 Preston
07.03.91	Bradley Stone L RSC 4 Basildon
04.04.91	Mark Tierney L PTS 6 Watford
16.04.91	Craig Dermody L PTS 6 Nottingham
25.04.91	Bradley Stone L PTS 6 Basildon
23.05.91	Jason Lepre L PTS 6 Southampton
31.05.91	Danny Connelly L PTS 8 Glasgow
13.06.91	Tony Silkstone L PTS 6 Hull
24.06.91	Jimmy Owens L PTS 6 Liverpool
09.09.91	Moussa Sangare L RSC 5 Forges les Eux, France
09.10.91	Mark Loftus DREW 6 Manchester
24.10.91	Kevin Middleton L PTS 6 Dunstable
31.10.91	Brian Robb DREW 6 Oakengates
11.11.91	Peter Judson L PTS 6 Stratford on Avon
21.11.91	Craig Dermody L PTS 6 Burton
28.11.91	Dave Hardie L PTS 6 Glasgow
11.12.91	Jimmy Clark Ł PTS 6 Basildon
08.01.92	Ceri Farrell W PTS 6 Burton
31.01.92	John Green DREW 6 Manchester
20.02.92	Edward Cook L PTS 6 Glasgow
27.02.92	Craig Dermody L PTS 6 Liverpool
25.03.92	John Armour L PTS 6 Dagenham
01.06.92	Danny Porter L PTS 6 Bristol
07.07.92	Tony Falcone L PTS 6 Bristol
14.07.92	Prince Naseem Hamed L RSC 3 Mayfair
30.09.92	Jonjo Irwin L PTS 6 Solihull
17.10.92	Mark Bowers L PTS 6 Wembley
24.11.92	Kid McAuley L PTS 6 Doncaster
14.12.92	Barry Jones L PTS 6 Cardiff
30.01.93	Tim Yeates L PTS 6 Brentwood
27.02.93	Paul Lloyd L PTS 6 Ellesmere Port
18.03.93	Kevin Middleton L PTS 6 Lewisham
17.04.93	Fabian Zavattini L PTS 6 Lausanne, Switzerland
05.05.93	Conn McMullen DREW 6 Belfast
15.05.93	Dave McHale L RSC 4 Glasgow
10.07.93	Russell Rees L PTS 6 Cardiff
22.09.93	Marcus McCrae L PTS 6 Bethnal Green
06.10.93	Mark Geraghty L PTS 6 Glasgow
30.10.93	Gary Thornhill L PTS 6 Chester
22.11.93	Ian McGirr L PTS 6 Glasgow
29.11.93	Tim Yeates DREW 6 Ingatestone
18.12.93	John White L PTS 6 Manchester
14.01.94	Kevin Middleton L PTS 6 Bethnal Green
28.01.94	Frederic Perez L PTS 8 Sete, France

10.04.94	Mark Geraghty L PTS 8 Glasgow
25.04.94	Hugh Collins L PTS 8 Glasgow
22.05.94	Mike Anthony Brown W RSC 5 Crystal Palace
06.06.94	Russell Davison W PTS 6 Glasgow
21.07.94	Mike Anthony Brown L PTS 6 Battersea
20.09.94	Drew Docherty L PTS 8 Musselburgh
17.02.95	Michael Alldis L PTS 8 Crawley
06.03.95	Michael Armstrong L PTS 6 Mayfair
09.06.95	Moussa Sangare L CO 2 Grande Synthe, France
29.09.95	Paul Ingle L RSC 4 Bethnal Green
29.11.95	Chris Jickells W PTS 6 Solihull
06.12.95	Gary Marston L PTS 8 Stoke
18.12.95	Graham McGrath W PTS 8 Mayfair
24.01.96	Gary Marston W PTS 8 Stoke
13.02.96	Dean Amory L PTS 8 Wolverhampton
21.02.96	Terry Whittaker L PTS 6 Batley
06.03.96	Fred Reeve W PTS 6 Solihull
24.04.96	Gary Marston L PTS 8 Solihull
04.05.96	Richard Evatt L PTS 6 Dagenham
14.05.96	Patrick Mullings L PTS 6 Dagenham
25.06.96	Paul Griffin L PTS 6 Mansfield
03.09.96	Paul Ireland L PTS 6 Belfast
14.09.96	Dean Pithie L PTS 4 Sheffield
28.09.96	Frederic Perez L PTS 8 Barking
15.10.96	Elvis Parsley L PTS 8 Wolverhampton
09.11.96	Michael Brodie L PTS 6 Manchester
21.11.96	Carl Allen L PTS 8 Solihull
04.12.96	Elvis Parsley L PTS 6 Stoke
14.12.96	Paul Griffin L PTS 4 Sheffield
25.03.97	David Kirk L PTS 6 Wolverhampton
12.05.97	Kelton McKenzie L PTS 6 Leicester
21.05.97	Alex Moon DREW 4 Liverpool

Career: 103 contests, won 12, drew 11, lost 80.

Paul Matthews

Pontardulais. *Born* Gorseinon, 26 September, 1968
Middleweight. Ht. 5'8"
Manager Self

23.03.94	Steve Thomas W PTS 6 Cardiff
02.06.94	Jason Hart W RSC 3 Tooting
21.09.94	Peter Mitchell L PTS 6 Cardiff
12.11.94	Mads Larsen L RTD 4 Randers, Denmark
08.03.95	Barry Thorogood L PTS 4 Cardiff
12.04.95	Carl Winstone L PTS 6 Llanelli
06.05.95	Danny Ryan L PTS 6 Shepton Mallet
29.05.96	Carl Winstone W PTS 6 Ebbw Vale
19.07.96	Grant Briggs L PTS 4 Ystrad

Career: 9 contests, won 3, lost 6.

Benny May

Peckham. *Born* Dulwich, 19 August, 1976
Featherweight. Ht. 5'6"
Manager F. Maloney

05.02.96	Abdul Mannon W PTS 4 Bexleyheath
02.04.96	Eddie Sica L RSC 1 Southwark
03.09.96	Keith Jones L RSC 2 Bethnal Green

Career: 3 contests, won 1, lost 2.

Anthony Maynard

Birmingham. *Born* Birmingham, 12 January, 1972
L. Welterweight. Ht. 5'8"
Manager Self

17.10.94	Malcolm Thomas W PTS 6 Birmingham

123

02.11.94	Dean Phillips W PTS 6 Birmingham	
25.01.95	Neil Smith L PTS 6 Stoke	
07.02.95	Anthony Campbell W PTS 8 Wolverhampton	
08.03.95	Scott Walker W PTS 6 Solihull	
28.03.95	Kid McAuley W PTS 8 Wolverhampton	
11.05.95	Gary Hiscox W RSC 4 Dudley	
06.06.95	Richard Swallow L RSC 2 Leicester	
02.10.95	Jay Mahoney W PTS 8 Birmingham	
26.10.95	Ray Newby W PTS 8 Birmingham	
17.01.96	Tom Welsh W RSC 8 Solihull	
06.03.96	G. G. Goddard W RSC 3 Solihull	
20.03.97	Richard Swallow W PTS 6 Solihull	

Career: 13 contests, won 11, lost 2.

Trevor Meikle

Scunthorpe. *Born* Scunthorpe, 29 January, 1967
Former Central Area Welterweight Champion. Ht. 5'9"
Manager J. Rushton

16.05.89	Lewis Welch DREW 6 Halifax
12.06.89	Chris Mulcahy L PTS 6 Manchester
19.06.89	Anthony Lawrence L PTS 6 Manchester
11.07.89	Chris Mulcahy L PTS 6 Batley
16.10.89	Steve Hardman DREW 6 Manchester
23.10.89	Mick Mulcahy W PTS 6 Cleethorpes
06.11.89	Ian Thomas W PTS 6 Northampton
14.11.89	Cliff Churchward W PTS 6 Evesham
22.11.89	Cliff Churchward W PTS 6 Stafford
11.12.89	Barry Messam L CO 5 Nottingham
05.02.90	Malcolm Melvin L PTS 6 Brierley Hill
19.02.90	Gordon Blair L PTS 6 Glasgow
27.02.90	Dave Whittle DREW 8 Marton
14.03.90	Carlos Chase L PTS 6 Battersea
27.03.90	Barry Messam W PTS 6 Leicester

30.04.90	Young Gully L PTS 6 Brierley Hill
21.05.90	Frank Harrington W RSC 5 Hanley
30.05.90	Mark Jay DREW 6 Stoke
15.06.90	Mark Jay W RSC 5 Telford
14.09.90	Mickey Lerwill DREW 8 Telford
03.10.90	Jim Lawlor L PTS 6 Solihull
09.10.90	Pat Durkin W DIS 3 Liverpool
24.10.90	Ernie Loveridge L PTS 6 Dudley
06.11.90	Stuart Good L PTS 6 Southend
21.11.90	Jim Lawlor L PTS 6 Solihull
29.11.90	Dave Whittle L PTS 6 Marton
10.12.90	Kevin Spratt L PTS 6 Bradford
11.02.91	Steve Hardman L PTS 6 Manchester
21.02.91	Colin Sinnott W PTS 6 Leeds
27.02.91	Andreas Panayi W PTS 6 Wolverhampton
03.04.91	Mick Mulcahy W PTS 6 Manchester
10.04.91	Wayne Timmins L PTS 6 Wolverhampton
22.04.91	Nick Cope W RSC 2 Glasgow
01.05.91	Tommy Milligan L PTS 6 Liverpool
09.05.91	Tod Riggs L PTS 6 Leeds
03.06.91	Tommy Milligan L PTS 6 Glasgow
10.06.91	Chris Mulcahy DREW 6 Manchester
14.08.91	Efren Calamati L RSC 4 Alcamo, Italy
23.09.91	Alan Peacock W PTS 6 Glasgow
01.10.91	James McGee W PTS 6 Bedworth
05.11.91	Lee Ferrie L PTS 6 Leicester
25.11.91	Mark Kelly W PTS 8 Cleethorpes
05.12.91	Mickey Lerwill L PTS 6 Oakengates
14.12.91	Kevin Lueshing L CO 3 Bexleyheath
28.01.92	Alan Peacock L PTS 8 Piccadilly
29.02.92	Andre Kimbu L RTD 5 Gravelines, France
13.04.92	Crain Fisher L PTS 6 Manchester
30.04.92	B. F. Williams L PTS 6 Watford
14.09.92	Kevin Spratt W RSC 4 Bradford
23.10.92	Andreas Panayi L PTS 6 Liverpool
26.11.92	Willie Yeardsley W PTS 6 Hull
03.02.93	Derek Grainger L RSC 6 Earls Court

13.12.93	Rick North L PTS 6 Cleethorpes
22.05.94	Maurice Forbes L RTD 3 Crystal Palace
23.09.94	Clay O'Shea L RSC 1 Bethnal Green
08.11.95	Andy Peach W PTS 6 Scunthorpe
06.12.95	Andy Peach W RSC 3 Stoke
29.02.96	Kevin Toomey W PTS 10 Scunthorpe *(Vacant Central Area Welterweight Title)*
14.05.96	Peter Richardson L RSC 2 Dagenham
23.09.96	Derek Roche L PTS 10 Bradford *(Central Area Welterweight Title Defence)*
06.11.96	Steve Pollard W RSC 6 Hull
28.11.96	Peter Waudby L PTS 8 Hull
21.01.97	Michael Schultz L PTS 6 Hammanskraal, South Africa
25.04.97	Junior Witter L PTS 6 Mere

Career: 64 contests, won 21, drew 6, lost 37.

Malcolm Melvin

Birmingham. *Born* Birmingham, 5 February, 1967
All-Ireland & Midlands Area L. Welterweight Champion. Ht. 5'7"
Manager W. Swift

28.11.85	Steve Foster DREW 6 Ilkeston
04.12.85	Simon Collins L PTS 6 Stoke
24.03.86	Rocky McGran L PTS 6 Mayfair
10.04.86	Lincoln Pennant W PTS 6 Leicester
21.04.86	Malcolm Davies W PTS 6 Birmingham
07.05.86	Julian Monville W PTS 6 Solihull
19.01.88	Antonio Fernandez L RSC 4 Kings Heath
07.03.88	John Ellis L PTS 6 Piccadilly
03.12.89	Dave Jenkins W PTS 6 Birmingham
05.02.90	Trevor Meikle W PTS 6 Brierley Hill
22.02.90	Chris Saunders L PTS 4 Hull
19.03.90	Barry North W PTS 6 Brierley Hill

Paul Miles (right) storms into the attack during his losing six rounder against Pat Wright at York Hall last January

Les Clark

30.04.90	Andy Kent W RSC 5 Brierley Hill
04.06.90	Brendan Ryan L RSC 7 Edgbaston
03.09.90	Dave Jenkins W PTS 8 Dudley
13.11.90	Brendan Ryan W PTS 10 Edgbaston
	(Vacant Midlands Area L. Welterweight Title)
18.03.91	Carl Brasier W PTS 6 Piccadilly
17.06.91	Dean Bramhald W PTS 6 Edgbaston
21.05.92	Mark Kelly W PTS 8 Cradley Heath
05.10.92	Ross Hale L PTS 10 Bristol
	(Elim. British L. Welterweight Title)
17.11.92	Tusikoleta Nkalankete DREW 8 Paris, France
16.03.93	Shaun Cogan W PTS 10 Edgbaston
	(Vacant All-Ireland L. Welterweight Title & Midlands Area L. Welterweight Title Defence)
29.06.93	Mark Kelly W PTS 6 Edgbaston
24.11.93	Alan Peacock W PTS 8 Solihull
08.03.94	Julian Eavis W PTS 6 Edgbaston
28.06.94	John Smith W PTS 6 Edgbaston
18.02.95	Ross Hale L PTS 12 Shepton Mallet
	(British & Commonwealth L. Welterweight Title Challenge)
21.05.96	Karl Taylor W PTS 10 Edgbaston
	(Midlands Area L. Welterweight Title Defence)
03.06.96	Jamie Morris W RSC 2 Birmingham
09.06.97	Jimmy Phelan W RSC 2 Birmingham

Career: 30 contests, won 20, drew 2, lost 8.

Paul Miles

Walton on Thames. *Born* Coventry, 6 February, 1974
Welterweight. Ht. 5'9¼"
Manager D. Currivan

21.09.95	John O. Johnson W PTS 4 Battersea
08.11.95	Adam Baldwin W RSC 2 Bethnal Green
29.11.95	John Smith W PTS 4 Southwark
19.01.96	John Janes L PTS 4 Bracknell
21.03.96	Darren Covill W PTS 4 Southwark
14.06.96	Jyri Kjall L RSC 4 Gravelines, France
23.10.96	Derek Roche L RSC 2 Halifax
09.12.96	Paul Dyer L PTS 6 Bristol
21.01.97	Justin Simmons L PTS 4 Bristol
29.01.97	Pat Wright L PTS 6 Bethnal Green
15.02.97	Danny Quacoe W PTS 6 Tooting
20.03.97	Michael Monaghan L PTS 6 Newark
20.05.97	Harry Dhami L RTD 2 Gillingham
	(Southern Area Welterweight Title Challenge)

Career: 13 contests, won 5, lost 8.

(Alvin) Slick Miller

Doncaster. *Born* Doncaster, 12 May, 1968
Cruiserweight. Ht. 6'2"
Manager T. Petersen

28.04.94	Declan Faherty L RSC 2 Hull
06.10.94	Kent Davis L PTS 6 Hull
17.11.94	Graham Wassell L RSC 1 Sheffield
29.09.95	Mark Richardson L PTS 6 Hartlepool
13.01.96	Geoff Hunter DREW 6 Halifax
13.02.96	Danny Williams L RSC 1 Bethnal Green
15.03.96	Tony Booth L PTS 6 Hull
22.03.96	Tony Dowling L RSC 4 Mansfield
26.09.96	Steve Pettit L PTS 6 Walsall
22.11.96	Tony Booth L RSC 5 Hull
17.03.97	Michael Sprott L CO 1 Mayfair
25.04.97	Pele Lawrence L PTS 6 Mere
16.05.97	Edwin Cleary DREW 6 Hull

Career: 13 contests, drew 2, lost 11.

Clifton Mitchell

Derby. *Born* Derby, 29 October, 1965
Heavyweight. Ht. 6'2½"
Manager F. Warren

06.04.91	John Harewood W RSC 2 Darlington
01.08.91	John Harewood W CO 1 Dewsbury
03.10.91	Tucker Richards W PTS 6 Burton
21.11.91	Tucker Richards W RSC 6 Burton
14.04.92	Michael Murray W RSC 8 Mansfield
16.03.93	Vivian Schwalger W CO 1 Wolverhampton
26.05.93	John Harewood W RSC 4 Mansfield
18.12.93	Jim Huffman W CO 3 Manchester
29.01.94	Cordwell Hylton W RSC 1 Cardiff
26.02.94	Jean Chanet W RSC 2 Earls Court
11.05.94	Emanuel Brites Camargo W RSC 1 Sheffield
21.05.94	Steve Garber W CO 1 Belfast
17.08.94	Carl Gaffney W CO 1 Sheffield
10.09.94	Jeff Williams W CO 1 Birmingham
19.11.94	James Oyebola L CO 4 Cardiff
	(WBC International Heavyweight Title Challenge & Vacant British Heavyweight Title)
10.11.95	Brian Sargent W CO 2 Derby
20.01.96	Jimmy Bills W CO 1 Mansfield
09.03.96	Rick Sullivan W RSC 3 Millstreet
08.06.96	Levi Billups W PTS 8 Newcastle
02.11.96	Zeljko Mavrovic L RSC 2 Garmish, Germany
	(European Heavyweight Title Challenge)

Career: 20 contests, won 18, lost 2.

Clifton Mitchell   Chris Bevan

125

Kevin Mitchell (George)

Brockley. *Born* Greenwich, 13 March, 1970
Cruiserweight. Ht. 6'2"
Manager T. Toole

25.04.96 Carl Nicholson W RSC 4 Mayfair
15.11.96 Patrick Akerlund L RSC 1 Nestved, Denmark
11.04.97 Danny Southern L RSC 3 Barnsley
Career: 3 contests, won 1, lost 2.

Peter Mitchell

Southampton. *Born* Southampton, 26 May, 1967
Middleweight. Ht. 5'10½"
Manager J. Bishop

21.09.94 Paul Matthews W PTS 6 Cardiff
12.10.94 Andy Ewen L PTS 6 Sheffield
08.03.95 Paul Webb W RSC 1 Bloomsbury
19.04.95 Nicky Thurbin L PTS 6 Bethnal Green
02.06.95 Danny Ryan L PTS 6 Bethnal Green
13.11.95 Barrie Bessant W RSC 2 Barnstaple
04.12.95 Darren Sweeney L PTS 8 Birmingham
09.03.96 Jim Rock L PTS 6 Millstreet
03.06.96 Gordon Behan DREW 6 Birmingham
21.01.97 Darren Dorrington L RSC 5 Bristol
07.03.97 Peter Vosper W PTS 8 Weston super Mare
24.03.97 Darren Dorrington L RSC 7 Bristol
29.04.97 Danny Ryan DREW 6 Belfast
Career: 13 contests, won 4, drew 2, lost 7.

Arv Mittoo   Les Clark

(Arvill) Arv Mittoo

Birmingham. *Born* Birmingham, 8 July, 1971
L. Welterweight. Ht. 5'8"
Manager N. Nobbs

31.01.96 Alan Bosworth L PTS 6 Stoke
13.02.96 Tommy Janes L PTS 6 Cardiff
21.02.96 Danny Lutaaya L PTS 6 Piccadilly
20.05.96 Terry Whittaker L CO 5 Cleethorpes
29.06.96 Craig Stanley L PTS 4 Erith

23.09.96 Thomas Bradley DREW 6 Cleethorpes
03.10.96 John T. Kelly L PTS 6 Sunderland
01.11.96 David Kirk L PTS 6 Mansfield
14.11.96 Thomas Bradley L RSC 4 Sheffield
22.05.97 Craig Stanley W RSC 3 Southwark
Career: 10 contests, won 1, drew 1, lost 8.

Tony Mock

Liverpool. *Born* Liverpool, 3 May, 1969
Welterweight. Ht. 5'8"
Manager S. Vaughan

30.10.93 Tony Britland W PTS 6 Chester
11.12.93 Mark Antony W RSC 4 Liverpool
25.02.94 Mike Morrison W PTS 6 Chester
06.05.94 Scott Doyle W PTS 6 Liverpool
31.10.94 Charlie Paine W PTS 6 Liverpool
25.03.95 Floyd Churchill W PTS 6 Chester
30.06.95 Kevin McKenzie W PTS 6 Liverpool
10.05.96 Michael Alexander L PTS 6 Liverpool
22.11.96 Gary Hiscox L PTS 6 Liverpool
Career: 9 contests, won 7, lost 2.

Colin Moffett

Belfast. *Born* Belfast, 15 April, 1975
Flyweight. Ht. 5'6"
Manager B. Hearn

05.11.96 Shane Mallon W RSC 2 Belfast
28.01.97 Anthony Hanna W PTS 4 Belfast
29.04.97 Gary Hickman W PTS 4 Belfast
02.06.97 Jason Thomas L RSC 3 Belfast
Career: 4 contests, won 3, lost 1.

Lee Molyneux

Liverpool. *Born* Liverpool, 19 April, 1970
Welterweight. Ht. 5'9¾"
Manager P. Dwyer

13.10.96 C. J. Jackson W PTS 6 Shaw
04.12.96 Gary Hiscox L PTS 6 Stoke
20.03.97 Junior Witter L RSC 6 Salford
03.05.97 Anthony Farnell L PTS 4 Manchester
Career: 4 contests, won 1, lost 3.

Phil Molyneux (Lynch)

St Helens. *Born* St Helens, 3 February, 1971
Welterweight. Ht. 5'8"
Manager R. Jones

30.09.96 Shaun Gledhill DREW 6 Manchester
05.12.96 Liam Dineen L PTS 6 Sunderland
24.02.97 Ram Singh W PTS 6 Manchester
01.05.97 David Thompson W CO 1 Hull
15.05.97 Brian Booth L PTS 6 Sunderland
Career: 5 contests, won 2, drew 1, lost 2.

Michael Monaghan

Nottingham. *Born* Nottingham, 31 May, 1976
L. Middleweight. Ht. 5'10¾"
Manager B. Ingle

23.09.96 Lee Simpkin W PTS 6 Cleethorpes
24.10.96 Lee Bird W RSC 6 Lincoln
09.12.96 Lee Simpkin W PTS 6 Chesterfield
16.12.96 Carlton Williams W PTS 6 Cleethorpes
20.03.97 Paul Miles W PTS 6 Newark
26.04.97 Paul Ryan L RSC 2 Swadlincote
Career: 6 contests, won 5, lost 1.

Alex Moon

Liverpool. *Born* Fazackerley, 17 November, 1971
Featherweight. Ht. 5'7½"
Manager J. Hyland

08.09.95 Marty Chestnut W RSC 3 Liverpool
24.11.95 G. G. Goddard L RTD 2 Chester
03.02.96 Chris Price W RSC 2 Liverpool
06.09.96 Jason Squire W PTS 4 Liverpool
26.10.96 Kelton McKenzie W RSC 3 Liverpool
03.12.96 Keith Jones W RTD 5 Liverpool
01.03.97 David Jeffrey W RSC 2 Liverpool
21.05.97 Miguel Matthews DREW 4 Liverpool
Career: 8 contests, won 6, drew 1, lost 1.

Terry Morrill

Hull. *Born* Hull, 2 February, 1965
Middleweight. Former Central Area L. Middleweight Champion. Ht. 5'10¼"
Manager S. Pollard

10.12.88 Chris Richards W PTS 6 Crystal Palace
08.02.89 Newton Barnett W PTS 6 Kensington
28.03.89 Skip Jackson L RSC 5 Glasgow
27.06.89 Mark Howell W PTS 6 Kensington
10.10.89 Spencer Alton W PTS 6 Hull
15.11.89 Davey Hughes DREW 4 Lewisham
08.12.89 Tony Baker W PTS 6 Doncaster
22.02.90 Mark Holden W RSC 7 Hull
          (Central Area L. Middleweight Title Challenge)
10.04.90 Ernie Noble W RSC 7 Doncaster
20.05.90 Jason Rowe L CO 6 Sheffield
          (Central Area L. Middleweight Title Defence)
31.10.90 Shaun Cummins L RSC 1 Crystal Palace
14.03.91 Delroy Waul DREW 8 Middleton
28.05.91 Eamonn Loughran L CO 1 Cardiff
16.10.92 Shamus Casey W PTS 6 Hull
16.09.93 Des Robinson W PTS 8 Hull
12.11.93 Shamus Casey W PTS 8 Hull
09.05.96 Lee Simpkin W RSC 5 Hull
06.11.96 Roy Chipperfield W RSC 1 Hull
28.11.96 Jeff Finlayson W PTS 6 Hull
27.02.97 Prince Kasi Kaihau W PTS 6 Hull
Career: 20 contests, won 14, drew 2, lost 4.

Terry Morrill   Les Clark

David Morris   Les Clark

David Morris
Cardiff. *Born* Birmingham, 1 September, 1975
Featherweight. Ht. 5'5"
Manager G. Watts

18.09.96	David Jay W PTS 4 Tylorstown
01.10.96	Danny Thomas W PTS 6 Birmingham
09.11.96	Michael Gomez L PTS 4 Manchester
30.11.96	Barry Jones DREW 6 Tylorstown
11.02.97	Carl Allen DREW 8 Wolverhampton
25.03.97	Scott Harrison L PTS 4 Lewisham
26.04.97	Dean Pithie L PTS 8 Swadlincote

Career: 7 contests, won 2, drew 2, lost 3.

Jamie Morris
Nuneaton. *Born* Nuneaton, 15 February, 1970
L. Welterweight. Ht. 5'9"
Manager P. Byrne

28.06.89	Phil Lashley W RSC 1 Kenilworth
05.09.89	Carl Brasier L RSC 3 Southend
10.10.89	Andrew Robinson L PTS 6 Wolverhampton
06.12.89	Wayne Taylor L RSC 5 Leicester
17.01.90	Lee Ahmed L PTS 6 Stoke
05.02.90	Lee Ahmed W PTS 6 Leicester
27.02.90	Lee Ahmed W PTS 6 Evesham
26.03.90	George Bailey W PTS 6 Bradford
06.04.90	Rick Dimmock L PTS 6 Stevenage
24.04.90	Des Gargano L PTS 4 Stoke
30.04.90	Neil Leitch L PTS 6 Nottingham
14.05.90	Tony Heath L PTS 6 Leicester
01.10.91	Michael Byrne DREW 4 Bedworth
16.10.91	Michael Byrne W PTS 6 Stoke
11.11.91	Mitchell Barney DREW 6 Stratford upon Avon
21.11.91	Brian Coleman DREW 6 Stafford
04.12.91	Sugar Boy Wright L PTS 6 Stoke
20.01.92	Mark Antony L RSC 5 Coventry
24.02.92	Simon Hamblett DREW 6 Coventry
11.03.92	Razza Campbell L PTS 6 Stoke

24.03.92	Mark Allen W PTS 6 Wolverhampton
27.01.93	Billy McDougall L PTS 6 Stoke
11.03.93	Mark Allen DREW 6 Walsall
17.06.93	Chris Pollock L RSC 2 Bedworth
13.12.93	Dean Bramhald L RSC 3 Doncaster
26.03.96	Patrick Parton L PTS 6 Wolverhampton
03.06.96	Malcolm Melvin L RSC 2 Birmingham
26.11.96	Ervine Blake L CO 1 Wolverhampton
11.02.97	Peter Gabbitus L RSC 1 Wolverhampton

Career: 29 contests, won 6, drew 5, lost 18.

Sean Morrison
Sheffield. *Born* Sheffield, 6 November, 1972
Lightweight. Ht. 5'7"
Manager G. Rhodes

15.02.96	Hurricane Hughes W PTS 6 Sheffield
03.05.96	Chris Lyons W PTS 6 Sheffield
13.10.96	Gary Hibbert L RSC 2 Shaw
28.11.96	Tony Foster DREW 6 Hull

Career: 4 contests, won 2, drew 1, lost 1.

Kevin Morton
Leicester. *Born* Leicester, 17 April, 1969
Cruiserweight. Ht. 6'0"
Manager M. Shinfield

06.02.91	Dennis Afflick W PTS 6 Liverpool
28.02.91	Stevie R. Davies W RSC 3 Bury
04.04.91	Johnny Uphill W CO 1 Watford
02.05.91	Alan Baptiste W RSC 2 Northampton
30.10.91	Nick Manners W PTS 8 Leeds
03.06.92	Mark Pain W PTS 6 Newcastle under Lyme
09.09.92	Adrian Wright W PTS 6 Stoke
20.09.96	John Wilson L PTS 8 Glasgow
27.02.97	Tony Booth W PTS 6 Hull

Career: 9 contests, won 8, lost 1.

Tony Mulholland
Liverpool. *Born* Liverpool, 24 November, 1972
Featherweight. Ht. 5'6¾"
Manager S. Vaughan

16.08.96	Graham McGrath W RSC 3 Liverpool
22.11.96	Keith Jones W PTS 4 Liverpool
04.04.97	Keith Jones W PTS 4 Liverpool

Career: 3 contests, won 3.

Michael Murray   Harry Goodwin

127

Patrick Mullings

Harrow. *Born* Harlesden, 19 October, 1970
S. Bantamweight. Ht. 5'4½"
Manager F. Maloney

13.12.94	Graham McGrath W PTS 4 Ilford
23.01.95	Des Gargano W PTS 4 Bethnal Green
30.03.95	Graham McGrath W RSC 3 Bethnal Green
04.06.95	Des Gargano W PTS 6 Bethnal Green
21.09.95	Pete Buckley W PTS 6 Battersea
15.12.95	Pete Buckley W PTS 4 Bethnal Green
05.02.96	Pete Buckley W PTS 8 Bexleyheath
21.03.96	Danny Ruegg W RSC 3 Southwark
14.05.96	Miguel Matthews W PTS 6 Dagenham
11.12.96	Phil Lashley W RSC 3 Southwark
18.02.97	Spencer Oliver L RSC 10 Cheshunt *(Vacant Southern Area S. Bantamweight Title)*
20.05.97	Ricky Beard W RTD 3 Edmonton

Career: 12 contests, won 11, lost 1.

Dean Murdoch

Plymouth. *Born* Plymouth, 3 March, 1970
S. Featherweight. Ht. '5'7¾"
Manager G. Mitchell

07.11.96	Wee Barry W PTS 6 Battersea
10.12.96	Martin Evans W RSC 4 Plymouth
07.03.97	Keith Jones W PTS 6 Weston super Mare

Career: 3 contests, won 3.

Gerard Murphy

Uddingston. *Born* Glasgow, 5 October, 1977
L. Welterweight. Ht. 5'10"
Manager B. Ingle

13.06.97	Ivan Walker W PTS 6 Paisley

Career: 1 contest, won 1.

Michael Murray

Manchester. *Born* Preston, 3 September, 1964
Former Undefeated Central Area Heavyweight Champion. Ht. 6'1"
Manager Self

23.02.88	Gypsy John Fury L PTS 6 Oldham
28.04.88	Ian Nelson W RSC 6 Manchester
17.11.88	Steve Garber W PTS 6 Stockport
07.02.89	Rocky Burton W PTS 6 Manchester
10.05.89	Barry Ellis W RSC 3 Solihull
08.09.89	Noel Quarless L PTS 8 Liverpool
17.10.89	John Westgarth W RTD 4 Oldham
06.02.90	Al Malcolm W RSC 5 Oldham
02.06.90	Gypsy John Fury L RTD 6 Manchester
30.04.91	Steve Garber W CO 1 Stockport
19.09.91	Carl Gaffney W RSC 8 Stockport *(Vacant Central Area Heavyweight Title)*
22.10.91	Markus Bott W RSC 7 Hamburg, Germany
07.12.91	Steve Gee W RSC 7 Manchester
14.04.92	Clifton Mitchell L RSC 8 Mansfield
28.11.92	Ricky Sekorski W PTS 8 Manchester
27.02.93	Herbie Hide L RSC 5 Dagenham *(Vacant British Heavyweight Title)*
30.09.94	Terry Dunstan L PTS 8 Bethnal Green

Shea Neary   Les Clark

10.12.94	Scott Welch L PTS 8 Manchester
23.02.95	Derek Williams W PTS 8 Southwark
17.05.95	John Ruiz L RSC 4 Ipswich
14.10.95	Zeljko Mavrovic L RSC 4 Munich, Germany
14.11.95	Mike Holden W PTS 6 Bury
16.12.95	Keith Fletcher W DIS 3 Cardiff
05.02.96	Julius Francis W PTS 10 Bexleyheath *(Elim. British Heavyweight Title)*
31.05.96	Mark Hulstrom L RSC 2 Copenhagen, Denmark
06.07.96	Herbie Hide L RSC 6 Manchester
09.11.96	Danny Williams L CO 1 Manchester
25.02.97	Pele Reid L RSC 1 Sheffield

Career: 28 contests, won 15, lost 13.

Lee Murtagh

Leeds. *Born* Leeds, 30 September, 1973
L. Middleweight. Ht. 5'9¼"
Manager J. Celebanski

12.06.95	Dave Curtis W PTS 6 Bradford
25.09.95	Roy Gbasai W PTS 6 Bradford
30.10.95	Cam Raeside L PTS 6 Bradford
11.12.95	Donovan Davey W PTS 6 Bradford
13.01.96	Peter Varnavas W PTS 6 Halifax
05.02.96	Shamus Casey W PTS 6 Bradford
20.05.96	Shaun O'Neill W PTS 6 Bradford
24.06.96	Michael Alexander W PTS 6 Bradford
28.10.96	Jimmy Vincent L RSC 2 Bradford
14.04.97	Lee Simpkin W PTS 6 Bradford

Career: 10 contests, won 8, lost 2.

(Jimmy) Shea Neary

Liverpool. *Born* Liverpool, 18 May, 1968
WBU L. Welterweight Champion. Former
Undefeated Central Area L. Welterweight
Champion. Ht. 5'7½"
Manager B. Devine/J. Hyland

03.09.92 Simon Ford W RSC 1 Liverpool
05.10.92 Shaun Armstrong W RSC 6 Liverpool
02.11.92 Jason Barker W RSC 3 Liverpool
01.12.92 Chris Saunders W PTS 6 Liverpool
22.02.93 Vaughan Carnegie W RSC 1 Liverpool
29.03.93 John Smith W PTS 6 Liverpool
06.09.93 Wayne Shepherd W RTD 2 Liverpool
25.10.93 Mark Antony W RSC 1 Liverpool
13.06.94 Mark Pearce W RSC 4 Liverpool
07.12.94 Tony Foster W RSC 2 Stoke
25.01.95 John Smith W RSC 5 Stoke
15.03.95 Tony Swift W RSC 3 Stoke
16.06.95 Hugh Forde W RTD 6 Liverpool
08.09.95 Nigel Bradley W RSC 2 Liverpool
(Vacant Central Area L. Welterweight Title)
24.11.95 Mark Richardson W CO 1 Chester
03.02.96 Terry Sutherland W CO 2 Liverpool
26.10.96 Darryl Tyson W PTS 12 Liverpool
(Vacant WBU L. Welterweight Title)
01.03.97 Jeremiah Malinga W RSC 3 Liverpool
(WBU L. Welterweight Title Defence)
Career: 18 contests, won 18.

Dominic Negus   Les Clark

Dominic Negus

Havering. *Born* Bethnal Green, 28 July,
1970
Southern Area Cruiserweight Champion.
Ht. 6'2"
Manager F. Maloney

03.09.96 Gareth Thomas W RSC 2 Bethnal
Green
28.09.96 Patrick Lawrence W RSC 2 Barking
11.01.97 Naveed Anwar W RTD 2 Bethnal
Green
04.03.97 Nigel Rafferty W PTS 4 Southwark
20.05.97 Nigel Rafferty W PTS 4 Edmonton

17.06.97 Chris Henry W RSC 10 Cheshunt
(Southern Area Cruiserweight Title Challenge)
Career: 6 contests, won 6.

Ray Newby

Nottingham. *Born* Sunderland, 16
December, 1963
Welterweight. Former Midlands Area
Lightweight Champion. Ht. 5'7"
Manager J. Griffin

20.09.84 Rocky Lawlor DREW 6 Dudley
10.10.84 Jeff Rumdan W RSC 3 Evesham
29.10.84 Dean Bramhald W PTS 6 Nottingham
07.11.84 Gary Flear L PTS 6 Evesham
21.11.84 Glenn Tweedie W PTS 6 Solihull
10.12.84 Wayne Trigg W RSC 6 Nottingham
04.02.85 Peter Bowen W PTS 8 Nottingham
07.03.85 Steve Cooke L PTS 8 Nottingham
25.09.85 Billy Laidman W RSC 2 Stoke
03.10.85 John Faulkner W PTS 8 Nottingham
21.11.85 Michael Marsden L PTS 6
Huddersfield
20.01.86 Steve Griffith L RSC 3 Mayfair
24.02.86 Ian Harrison W PTS 6 Coventry
05.03.86 Mark Pearce DREW 6 Stoke
24.03.86 Paul Dawson W RSC 3 Wandsworth
07.04.86 Wayne Cooper W RSC 2 Nottingham
14.04.86 Les Remikie L PTS 6 Mayfair
03.06.86 Peter Till W PTS 10 Wolverhampton
(Vacant Midlands Area Lightweight Title)
15.09.86 George Baigrie W PTS 8 Coventry
06.10.86 Muhammad Lovelock W PTS 8
Leicester
29.10.86 Andrew Williams L PTS 8 Ebbw Vale
01.12.86 George Baigrie W DIS 1 Nottingham
11.12.86 Ian McLeod L PTS 8 Livingston
16.02.87 Mervyn Bennett W CO 8 Glasgow
24.03.87 Joey Joynson L PTS 8 Wembley
07.04.87 Mark Pearce L PTS 8 West Bromwich
14.04.87 Floyd Havard L RSC 7 Cumbernauld
12.10.87 Brian Nickels L PTS 8 Mayfair
19.10.87 Tony Borg L PTS 8 Nottingham
11.12.87 Joey Dee W PTS 8 Coalville
17.02.88 Wayne Weekes W PTS 8 Bethnal Green
08.03.88 Darren Connellan W RSC 7 Batley
10.04.88 Aladin Stevens L RSC 8 Eldorado
Park, South Africa
09.05.88 Ian Honeywood W RSC 1 Nottingham
14.06.88 Peter Till L PTS 10 Dudley
(Midlands Area Lightweight Title Defence)
31.10.88 Les Remikie W PTS 8 Leicester
11.11.88 Mahjid Mahdjoub L PTS 8
Vennissieux, France
25.09.90 Rocky Milton L PTS 6 Millwall
12.11.90 Brian Cullen W PTS 6 Stratford on
Avon
30.11.90 Peter Till L PTS 8 Birmingham
12.04.91 Henry Armstrong L PTS 8 Manchester
22.01.92 Dean Bramhald W PTS 8 Solihull
11.02.92 Dean Bramhald W RSC 7
Wolverhampton
24.03.92 Ronnie Shinkwin W PTS 8
Wolverhampton
18.05.92 Ronnie Shinkwin W RSC 5 Bardon
02.07.92 Richard Burton L PTS 6 Middleton
10.11.92 Bernard Paul DREW 6 Dagenham
20.01.93 Richard Swallow L PTS 8 Solihull
03.03.93 Richard Swallow W PTS 8 Solihull
20.04.93 Bernard Paul DREW 6 Brentwood
19.05.93 Michael Driscoll L RTD 2 Leicester
26.10.95 Anthony Maynard L PTS 8 Birmingham

02.10.96 Paul Street W CO 2 Stoke
26.11.96 Jason Barker L PTS 6 Sheffield
15.02.97 Adrian Chase W PTS 6 Tooting
10.05.97 Cam Raeside L PTS 10 Nottingham
(Midlands Area Welterweight Title Challenge)
Career: 56 contests, won 28, drew 4, lost 24.

Dean Nicholas

South Shields. *Born* South Shields, 9 May,
1973
Welterweight. Ht. 5'9"
Manager T. Callighan

22.09.95 David Thompson W PTS 6 Hull
02.11.95 Paul Scott W PTS 6 Houghton le
Spring
20.11.95 Shaun Gledhill W RSC 4 Glasgow
14.02.96 Shaun O'Neill W PTS 6 Sunderland
22.04.96 John Smith W PTS 6 Glasgow
09.05.96 John Docherty L PTS 6 Glasgow
23.09.96 Mark Breslin L PTS 8 Glasgow
01.12.96 C. J. Jackson DREW 6 Shaw
27.02.97 Keith Scott L PTS 6 Sunderland
Career: 9 contests, won 5, drew 1, lost 3.

Carl Nicholson

Wakefield. *Born* Dewsbury, 19 May, 1974
L. Heavyweight. Ht. 6'1"
Manager T. Callighan

22.03.96 Rocky Shelly W RTD 3 Mansfield
25.04.96 Kevin Mitchell L RSC 4 Mayfair
04.10.96 Johnny Hooks W PTS 6 Wakefield
18.10.96 Thomas Hansvoll L CO 1 Vejle,
Denmark
20.03.97 Mark Hale W RSC 3 Salford
20.04.97 P. R. Mason W PTS 6 Leeds
Career: 6 contests, won 4, lost 2.

Peter Nightingale   Les Clark

Peter Nightingale

Tipton. *Born* Tipton, 20 January, 1969
L. Welterweight. Ht. 5'10"
Manager D. Bradley

24.10.96 Kevin McCarthy DREW 6 Wembley

129

12.11.96 David Kehoe W PTS 6 Dudley
08.03.97 Georgie Smith L RSC 1 Brentwood
22.04.97 Paul Knights L PTS 6 Bethnal Green
29.04.97 Eamonn Magee L RTD 2 Belfast
Career: 5 contests, won 1, drew 1, lost 3.

Darren Noble

North Shields. *Born* Newcastle, 2 October, 1969
Bantamweight. Ht. 5'3"
Manager T. Callighan

21.10.93 Allan Mooney W PTS 6 Glasgow
23.03.94 Paul Ingle L RSC 3 Cardiff
26.04.95 Tiger Singh L PTS 6 Solihull
21.09.95 Terry Gaskin DREW 6 Sheffield
22.03.96 Steve Williams L PTS 6 Mansfield
13.06.96 Jason Booth L RSC 3 Sheffield
16.12.96 David Coldwell W PTS 6 Cleethorpes
27.02.97 Ross Cassidy L RSC 5 Sunderland
Career: 8 contests, won 2, drew 1, lost 5.

Anthony Norbury

Merthyr. *Born* Merthyr, 19 March, 1974
Featherweight. Ht. 5'9"
Manager D. Gardiner

07.03.97 Graham McGrath W PTS 6 Weston
super Mare
Career: 1 contest, won 1.

Robert Norton

Stourbridge. *Born* Dudley, 20 January, 1972
Cruiserweight. Ht. 6'2"
Manager D. Bradley/M. Duff

30.09.93 Stuart Fleet W CO 2 Walsall
27.10.93 Kent Davis W PTS 6 West Bromwich
02.12.93 Eddie Pyatt W RSC 2 Walsall
26.01.94 Lennie Howard W PTS 6 Birmingham
17.05.94 Steve Osborne W PTS 6 Kettering
05.10.94 Chris Woollas DREW 6 Wolverhampton
30.11.94 L. A. Williams W RSC 2 Wolverhampton
10.02.95 Newby Stevens W RSC 3 Birmingham
22.02.95 Steve Osborne W PTS 6 Telford
21.04.95 Cordwell Hylton W PTS 6 Dudley
25.10.95 Nigel Rafferty W RSC 6 Telford
31.01.96 Gary Williams W RSC 2 Birmingham
25.04.96 Steve Osborne W RSC 5 Mayfair
01.10.96 Andrew Benson W RSC 6 Birmingham
12.11.96 Nigel Rafferty W PTS 8 Dudley
11.02.97 Touami Benhamed W RSC 5 Bethnal Green
16.04.97 Tony Booth W RSC 4 Bethnal Green
Career: 17 contests, won 16, drew 1.

Peter Oboh

London. *Born* Nigeria, 6 September, 1968
Cruiserweight. Ht. 6'2"
Manager M. Duff

12.05.93 Antonio Russo W RSC 5 Cassino, Italy
14.01.94 Ridha Soussi W PTS 6 Tagliacozzo, Italy
13.05.94 Antonio Pasqualino W RSC 2 Avellino, Italy
16.10.95 Tim Redman W RTD 2 Mayfair
09.07.96 Yuri Yelistratov W PTS 6 Bethnal Green
27.08.96 Joe Siluvangi L RSC 6 Windsor

03.12.96 Andy Lambert W CO 1 Liverpool
04.03.97 Garry Delaney L DIS 8 Southwark
Career: 8 contests, won 6, lost 2.

(David) Marvin O'Brien (Powell)

Leeds. *Born* Leeds, 3 September, 1966
L. Heavyweight. Ht. 5'11"
Manager T. Miller

31.01.90 Tony Hodge L RSC 3 Bethnal Green
04.04.90 Gary Osborne L CO 2 Stafford
07.09.90 Mike Phillips L RSC 1 Liverpool
12.11.90 Mike Phillips W PTS 6 Liverpool
17.01.91 Barry Messam L PTS 6 Alfreton
21.02.91 Russell Washer DREW 6 Walsall
02.03.91 Quinn Paynter DREW 6 Irvine
21.03.91 Nick Manners L CO 2 Dewsbury
31.05.91 Carl Harney W RSC 5 Manchester
24.06.91 Frank Eubanks L PTS 6 Liverpool
06.09.91 Cornelius Carr L RSC 7 Salemi, Italy
02.03.92 John Oxenham L PTS 6 Marton
26.03.92 John Ashton L PTS 8 Telford
05.04.92 Quinn Paynter L PTS 6 Bradford
17.05.92 Lester Jacobs L PTS 6 Harringay
20.11.92 Fran Harding L RSC 4 Liverpool
16.02.93 Andy Wright L PTS 6 Tooting
12.05.93 Martin Jolley L PTS 6 Sheffield
15.09.93 Paul Hitch L PTS 4 Newcastle
15.10.93 Bruno Girard L PTS 6 Romorantin, France
03.12.93 Mads Larsen L PTS 6 Randers, Denmark
02.02.94 Willie Quinn L PTS 6 Glasgow
06.06.94 Willie Quinn L RSC 4 Glasgow
20.10.94 Derek Wormald L PTS 6 Middleton
23.11.94 Mark Delaney L RTD 1 Irvine
18.01.95 Mark Smallwood L PTS 6 Solihull
07.02.95 David Starie L PTS 6 Ipswich
04.03.95 Robin Reid L RSC 6 Livingston
17.05.95 David Starie L RSC 5 Ipswich
01.09.95 John Wilson L PTS 6 Wolverhampton
15.09.95 John Wilson L PTS 6 Glasgow
30.09.95 Jason Matthews L PTS 6 Cardiff
24.10.95 Toks Owoh L RSC 2 Southwark
25.11.95 Pascal Collins L PTS 4 Dublin
09.03.96 Danny Ryan L PTS 4 Millstreet
16.03.96 Kelly Oliver L RSC 2 Glasgow
04.12.96 Peter Mason L CO 5 Hartlepool
Career: 37 contests, won 2, drew 2, lost 33.

Mark O'Callaghan

Tunbridge Wells. *Born* Tunbridge Wells, 17 January, 1969
Lightweight. Ht. 5'7"
Manager F. Turner

03.10.91 Chris Mylan DREW 6 Burton
24.10.91 Nicky Lucas W PTS 6 Dunstable
11.12.91 Richard Joyce L RSC 3 Stoke
20.02.92 Alan McDowall L PTS 6 Glasgow
12.11.92 Erwin Edwards L RSC 6 Bayswater
20.01.93 Sugar Boy Wright W CO 1 Wolverhampton
05.02.93 Nick Boyd L PTS 6 Manchester
18.03.93 Paul Denton L RSC 4 Lewisham
22.04.93 Trevor Royal W PTS 6 Mayfair
26.05.93 Gareth Jordan L RSC 3 Mansfield
22.09.93 Dean Hollington L CO 1 Wembley
07.12.93 Colin Dunne L RSC 1 Bethnal Green
15.06.94 P. J. Gallagher L RSC 4 Southwark
09.11.94 Colin Dunne L RSC 2 Millwall
04.02.95 Gareth Jordan L RSC 2 Cardiff
23.05.95 Andrew Reed L PTS 4 Potters Bar

30.09.95 Michael Wright W RSC 1 Basildon
07.10.95 Eamonn Brolly L PTS 4 Belfast
25.11.95 Michael Wright L PTS 4 Dagenham
02.12.95 Eamonn Brolly L RTD 3 Belfast
06.02.96 Bobby Guynan L RSC 3 Basildon
24.10.96 Danny Lutaaya L RSC 1 Mayfair
11.02.97 John Paul Temple L PTS 6 Bethnal Green
19.02.97 Brendan Kelly L PTS 6 Acton
Career: 24 contests, won 4, drew 1, lost 19.

Frank O'Connor

Motherwell. *Born* Bellshill, 23 August, 1975
L. Welterweight. Ht. 5'11"
Manager A. Morrison

29.11.96 Jarral Dawson DREW 6 Glasgow
22.12.96 Les Frost W PTS 6 Glasgow
Career: 2 contests, won 1, drew 1.

Nick Odore

Hayes. *Born* Nairobi, Kenya, 24 February, 1965
L. Middleweight. Ht. 5'11"
Manager G. Taylor/H. Holland

07.05.96 Errol McDonald W RSC 4 Mayfair
20.09.96 Hunter Clay W RTD 5 Tooting
03.05.97 Harry Simon L RSC 5 Manchester
Career: 3 contests, won 2, lost 1.

Nick Odore   Les Clark

Chris Okoh

Camberwell. *Born* Carshalton, 18 April, 1969
Former Commonwealth Cruiserweight Champion. Former Undefeated WBO Inter-Continental Cruiserweight Champion. Former Undefeated Southern Area Cruiserweight Champion. Ht. 6'2"
Manager D. Powell

16.03.93 Lee Prudden W PTS 6 Mayfair
10.07.93 Steve Yorath W PTS 6 Cardiff

28.09.93	Steve Osborne W RSC 5 Bethnal Green	
06.11.93	Chris Henry W RSC 2 Bethnal Green	
09.04.94	Art Stacey W RSC 6 Bethnal Green	
17.09.94	Art Stacey W PTS 6 Crawley	
23.02.95	Paul Lawson W RSC 5 Southwark	

(Vacant Southern Area Cruiserweight Title)

29.09.95	Francis Wanyama W RSC 8 Bethnal Green

(Commonwealth Cruiserweight Title Challenge)

08.11.95	Paul Lawson W RSC 1 Bethnal Green

(Commonwealth Cruiserweight Title Defence)

05.02.96	Darren Westover W RSC 2 Bexleyheath

(Vacant WBO Inter-Continental Cruiserweight Title)

22.04.96	Gypsy Carman W RSC 6 Crystal Palace

(WBO Inter-Continental Cruiserweight Title Defence)

27.08.96	Nigel Rafferty W RSC 4 Windsor
06.11.96	Tosca Petrides W PTS 12 Hull

(Commonwealth Cruiserweight Title Defence)

25.03.97	Denzil Browne W PTS 12 Lewisham

(Commonwealth Cruiserweight Title Defence)

02.06.97	Darren Corbett L RSC 3 Belfast

(Commonwealth Cruiserweight Title Defence)

Career: 15 contests, won 14, lost 1.

Kelly Oliver   Les Clark

Kelly Oliver

Lincoln. *Born* Lincoln, 11 November, 1973
Cruiserweight. Ht. 6'3"
Manager C. Sanigar

20.01.96	Steve Osborne W RSC 4 Mansfield	
16.03.96	Marvin O'Brien W RSC 2 Glasgow	
13.04.96	Andrew Benson W PTS 4 Wythenshawe	
06.07.96	John Pierre W PTS 4 Manchester	
14.09.96	Tony Booth W RSC 2 Sheffield	
30.11.96	Nigel Rafferty W PTS 6 Tylorstown	

18.01.97	Tony Booth W RSC 4 Swadlincote	
14.03.96	Chris Woollas W PTS 6 Reading	
05.06.97	Darren Westover W RTD 1 Bristol	

Career: 9 contests, won 9.

(Mike) Chip O'Neill

Sunderland. *Born* Sunderland, 10 December, 1963
Featherweight. Ht. 5'6½"
Manager Self

28.06.82	Charlie Brown L PTS 6 Bradford
20.09.82	Danny Flynn L RSC 2 Glasgow
07.03.83	Charlie Brown L RSC 3 Glasgow
28.04.92	Robert Braddock W PTS 6 Houghton le Spring
10.09.92	Vince Wilson W RSC 1 Sunderland
21.09.92	Ian McGirr L PTS 6 Glasgow
05.10.92	Phil Lashley W PTS 6 Manchester
09.11.92	Robert Braddock L RSC 3 Bradford
19.01.93	Russell Rees L RSC 1 Cardiff
08.03.93	Chris Lyons W PTS 6 Leeds
29.04.93	Paul Wynn L PTS 6 Newcastle
07.10.93	Fred Reeve W RSC 2 Hull
08.11.93	Ady Benton L RSC 5 Bradford
13.12.93	Paul Richards L PTS 6 Bristol
04.03.94	Ian McLeod L RSC 2 Irvine
24.05.94	Paul Wynn W PTS 6 Sunderland
06.10.94	Colin Innes DREW 6 Cramlington
20.10.94	Michael Brodie L CO 3 Middleton
05.12.94	Des Gargano W PTS 6 Houghton le Spring
16.02.95	Ady Lewis L RSC 1 Bury
25.03.95	Michael Alldis L RSC 2 Chester
11.05.95	Colin Innes W PTS 6 Sunderland
30.06.95	Gary Thornhill L RTD 3 Liverpool
22.02.96	Lyndon Kershaw L PTS 6 Sunderland
16.03.96	Brian Carr L PTS 4 Glasgow
25.04.96	Colin Innes L RSC 9 Newcastle

(Vacant Northern Area Featherweight Title)

03.10.96	Andy Roberts L PTS 6 Sunderland

Career: 27 contests, won 8, drew 1, lost 18.

Shaun O'Neill

Sunderland. *Born* Sunderland, 21 December, 1968
Welterweight. Ht. 5'9"
Manager T. Conroy

13.10.94	Trevor George W RSC 6 Houghton le Spring
05.12.94	Jay Mahoney L PTS 6 Houghton le Spring
16.03.95	Scott Marshall W RSC 3 Sunderland
11.05.95	Mark Allen W RSC 6 Sunderland
22.06.95	Jamie Gallagher W PTS 6 Houghton le Spring
29.07.95	Wayne Shepherd W PTS 4 Whitley Bay
18.09.95	Tommy Quinn L PTS 6 Glasgow
02.11.95	James Clamp W PTS 6 Houghton le Spring
04.12.95	Wahid Fats L RSC 5 Manchester
14.02.96	Dean Nicholas L PTS 6 Sunderland
09.05.96	Mark Owens W RTD 2 Sunderland
20.05.96	Lee Murtagh L PTS 6 Bradford
03.10.96	Lee Simpkin W PTS 6 Sunderland
10.10.96	Brian Booth W PTS 6 Newcastle
28.10.96	John Docherty L RSC 5 Glasgow
05.12.96	Craig Hartwell W PTS 6 Sunderland
03.02.97	Keith Scott L PTS 4 Sunderland
24.02.97	John Docherty L PTS 6 Glasgow

16.03.97	Blue Butterworth DREW 6 Shaw
01.05.97	Keith Scott L PTS 6 Newcastle
19.06.97	Lee Bird W PTS 6 Scunthorpe

Career: 21 contests, won 11, drew 1, lost 9.

(Brendan) Ozzy Orrock

Nottingham. *Born* Barnsley, 4 June, 1971
L. Middleweight. Ht. 5'8¾"
Manager Self

17.10.95	Steve Levene L RSC 1 Wolverhampton
06.12.95	George Richards L RSC 3 Stoke
26.01.96	Prince Kasi Kaihau L RSC 5 Doncaster
26.03.96	Andy Peach L RSC 2 Wolverhampton
12.09.96	Shaun Stokes L CO 1 Doncaster
21.11.96	Peter McCormack L RSC 2 Solihull

Career: 6 contests, lost 6.

Steve Osborne

Nottingham. *Born* Nottingham, 27 June, 1965
Cruiserweight. Ht. 5'9"
Manager Self

28.05.87	Gary Railton L PTS 6 Jarrow
09.06.87	Ian Bulloch L PTS 6 Manchester
24.09.87	Bobby Frankham L PTS 6 Glasgow
05.10.87	Ray Thomas L RSC 8 Piccadilly
14.12.87	Branko Pavlovic L RSC 3 Bedford
16.01.89	Simon McDougall W PTS 6 Bradford
25.01.89	Simon McDougall W PTS 6 Stoke
02.02.89	Dave Furneaux W CO 4 Southwark
13.02.89	Carl Thompson L PTS 6 Manchester
06.03.89	Jimmy Cropper W PTS 6 Manchester
05.04.89	Jimmy Cropper L PTS 6 Halifax
16.05.89	Henry Brewer W PTS 6 Halifax
12.06.89	Carl Thompson L PTS 8 Manchester
16.11.89	Dave Lawrence W PTS 6 Ilkeston
19.12.89	Herbie Hide L RSC 6 Bethnal Green
05.02.90	Dave Lawrence W PTS 8 Piccadilly
20.02.90	Rob Albon L PTS 6 Brentford
03.03.90	Darren Westover L RSC 6 Wembley
15.11.90	Michael Gale L PTS 6 Oldham
08.12.90	Neils H. Madsen L RSC 5 Aalborg, Denmark
16.04.91	Art Stacey DREW 6 Nottingham
09.05.91	Michael Gale L RSC 2 Leeds
11.11.91	Art Stacey L PTS 6 Bradford
21.11.91	Bruce Scott L PTS 6 Burton
29.11.91	Maurice Core L PTS 6 Manchester
12.02.92	Phil Soundy L PTS 6 Wembley
12.11.92	Terry Dunstan L PTS 6 Bayswater
10.12.92	Ole Klemetsen L RSC 1 Bethnal Green
27.01.93	Darren McKenna L PTS 6 Stoke
22.02.93	Nicky Wadman L PTS 6 Eltham
26.04.93	Joe Frater W PTS 6 Cleethorpes
01.07.93	Denzil Browne L RSC 1 York
28.09.93	Chris Okoh L RSC 5 Bethnal Green
10.11.93	Monty Wright L RSC 3 Watford
13.12.93	Martin Langtry L PTS 6 Cleethorpes
28.03.94	Joe Frater W RSC 6 Cleethorpes
05.04.94	Bruce Scott L RSC 5 Bethnal Green
17.05.94	Robert Norton L PTS 6 Kettering
28.07.94	Devon Rhooms W PTS 6 Tooting
26.08.94	Martin Langtry L PTS 8 Barnsley
02.09.94	Dean Francis L RTD 4 Spitalfields
27.10.94	Phil Soundy L PTS 6 Millwall
12.11.94	Ray Kane L PTS 6 Dublin
26.11.94	Rudiger May L PTS 6 Wuppertal, Germany
05.12.94	Justin Clements L PTS 6 Birmingham
22.02.95	Robert Norton L PTS 6 Telford
03.03.95	Gypsy Carman L PTS 6 Bracknell
30.03.95	John Pettersson L PTS 4 Bethnal Green

02.06.95 Mark Prince L RSC 3 Bethnal Green
17.07.95 Darren Westover L RSC 5 Mayfair
15.09.95 John Keeton L RSC 4 Mansfield
18.10.95 Martin Langtry L RSC 6 Batley
29.11.95 Luan Morena L PTS 4 Southwark
20.01.96 Kelly Oliver L RSC 4 Mansfield
25.04.96 Robert Norton L RSC 5 Mayfair
25.11.96 Stuart Fleet L PTS 6 Cleethorpes
14.12.96 Ryan Cummings L RSC 4 Sheffield
Career: 57 contests, won 10, drew 1, lost 46.

Anas Oweida

Sheffield. *Born* Syria, 16 August, 1971
L. Middleweight. Ht. 5'9½"
Manager B. Ingle

08.02.97 Chris Vassiliou W PTS 4 Millwall
03.05.97 Tony Smith W RSC 1 Manchester
Career: 2 contests, won 2.

Mark Owens

Billingham. *Born* Stockton, 25 January, 1973
L. Middleweight. Ht. 5'8"
Manager G. Robinson

29.09.95 P. R. Mason L RSC 3 Hartlepool
23.11.95 Roy Chipperfield L RSC 6 Marton
22.02.96 Norman Mitchell W PTS 6 Sunderland
25.04.96 Lee Herman L PTS 6 Newcastle
09.05.96 Shaun O'Neill L RTD 2 Sunderland
27.09.96 Lee Bird L PTS 6 Hull
04.12.96 Keith Scott L PTS 6 Hartlepool
Career: 7 contests, won 1, lost 6.

(Tokunbo) Toks Owoh (Owomoyela)

Belsize Park. *Born* Newham, 21 July, 1972
L. Heavyweight. Ht. 5'10½"
Manager Self

24.10.95 Marvin O'Brien W RSC 2 Southwark
08.11.95 Dave Fulton W RSC 1 Bethnal Green
29.11.95 Nicky Wadman W PTS 6 Southwark
19.01.96 Ernie Loveridge W PTS 4 Bracknell
27.03.97 James Branch W RSC 1 Norwich
Career: 5 contests, won 5.

James Oyebola

Paddington. *Born* Nigeria, 10 June, 1961
Former British & WBC International
Heavyweight Champion. Former
Undefeated Southern Area Heavyweight
Champion. Ht. 6'9"
Manager Self

01.07.87 Andrew Gerrard W PTS 6 Kensington
16.09.87 Ian Priest W RSC 2 Kensington
03.11.87 Carl Timbrell W CO 2 Bethnal Green
24.11.87 Mike Jones L RSC 2 Wisbech
09.02.88 Denroy Bryan W RSC 6 Bethnal Green
10.05.88 Andrew Gerrard DREW 6 Tottenham
07.09.88 Tee Lewis W CO 1 Reading
01.11.88 Dorcey Gayman W RSC 1 Reading
23.11.88 Everton Christian W CO 1 Bethnal Green
31.01.89 John Westgarth W CO 3 Reading
15.02.89 Art Terry W CO 5 Bethnal Green
07.03.89 John Westgarth L RSC 5 Wisbech
12.04.91 Stan Campbell W CO 1 Greenville, USA

18.05.91 Bonyongo Destroyer W CO 1 Harare, Zimbabwe
(*Final Elim. African Heavyweight Title*)
15.09.93 Denroy Bryan W RSC 5 Bethnal Green
13.10.93 R. F. McKenzie W RSC 1 Bethnal Green
(*Southern Area Heavyweight Title Challenge*)
01.12.93 Jimmy Bills W PTS 8 Bethnal Green
09.02.94 Ladislao Mijangos W RSC 2 Bethnal Green
06.05.94 Scott Welch W CO 5 Atlantic City, USA
(*Vacant WBC International Heavyweight Title*)
19.11.94 Clifton Mitchell W CO 4 Cardiff
(*WBC International Heavyweight Title Defence & Vacant British Heavyweight Title*)
07.02.95 Keith McMurray W RSC 7 Ipswich
27.10.95 Scott Welch L RSC 10 Brighton
(*British Heavyweight Title Defence. Vacant Commonwealth & WBO Inter-Continental Heavyweight Titles*)
28.09.96 Julius Francis L RSC 5 Barking
(*Southern Area Heavyweight Title Challenge*)
Career: 23 contests, won 18, drew 1, lost 4.

Charlie Paine (Bird)

Liverpool. *Born* Liverpool, 27 August, 1970
L. Middleweight. Ht. 5'7"
Manager Self

09.06.93 Delwyn Panayiotiou W PTS 6 Liverpool
13.10.94 Micky Hall L PTS 6 Houghton le Spring
31.10.94 Tony Mock L PTS 6 Liverpool
20.01.95 Dennis Gardner L RSC 1 Bethnal Green
23.02.95 Derek Roche L CO 1 Hull
30.06.95 Andreas Panayi L CO 1 Liverpool
26.02.96 Michael Alexander L PTS 6 Manchester
09.04.96 Chris Barnett L RSC 2 Salford
10.05.96 John Jones L PTS 6 Liverpool
16.08.96 Brian Coleman L PTS 6 Liverpool
26.10.96 Gary Lockett L RSC 4 Liverpool
03.12.96 Paul Burns L PTS 6 Liverpool
Career: 12 contests, won 1, lost 11.

Jim Pallatt

Leicester. *Born* Leicester, 8 September, 1969
Heavyweight. Ht. 6'0"
Manager Self

18.02.94 Johnny Hooks L RSC 1 Leicester
21.05.96 Andy Lambert L RSC 1 Edgbaston
19.02.97 Rob Albon L PTS 6 Acton
24.03.97 Phill Day L CO 1 Bristol
10.05.97 David Jules L RSC 1 Nottingham
Career: 5 contests, lost 5.

Andreas Panayi

St Helens. *Born* Cyprus, 14 July, 1969
Welterweight. Ht. 5'6"
Manager Self

21.11.90 Trevor Ambrose L RSC 5 Solihull

04.02.91 Cliff Churchward W PTS 6 Leicester
12.02.91 Eddie King W CO 2 Wolverhampton
27.02.91 Trevor Meikle L PTS 6 Wolverhampton
15.04.91 Mick Mulcahy W RSC 2 Leicester
24.04.91 Darren Morris DREW 6 Stoke
11.09.91 Robert Riley W PTS 6 Stoke
30.09.91 Steve Hardman W RSC 5 Liverpool
23.10.91 Darren Morris W PTS 6 Stoke
25.11.91 Marvin P. Gray W PTS 8 Liverpool
11.12.91 Mark Kelly DREW 8 Stoke
11.03.92 Dean Bramhald L PTS 8 Stoke
14.05.92 Dave Maj W CO 6 Liverpool
03.09.92 Rick North DREW 6 Liverpool
05.10.92 John O. Johnson W RTD 1 Liverpool
23.10.92 Trevor Meikle W PTS 6 Liverpool
20.11.92 Rick North W PTS 6 Liverpool
15.12.92 Mark Kelly W PTS 6 Liverpool
27.01.93 Ross Hale W RSC 3 Cardiff
27.02.93 Darren McInulty W PTS 6 Ellesmere Port
04.05.93 Jimmy Thornton W CO 2 Liverpool
02.07.93 Mark Ramsey DREW 6 Liverpool
28.09.93 Hugh Forde W PTS 8 Liverpool
11.12.93 Bobby Butters W CO 3 Liverpool
09.04.94 Tony Swift L PTS 8 Bethnal Green
10.05.94 Shaun Cogan W RSC 7 Doncaster
11.06.94 Tony Swift W PTS 8 Bethnal Green
28.06.94 John O. Johnson W RSC 5 Mayfair
17.09.94 Sammy Fuentes L RSC 4 Crawley
(*Vacant WBC Penta-Continental L. Welterweight Title*)
11.02.95 Dingaan Thobela L CO 1 Hammanskraal, South Africa
20.04.95 John Smith W RSC 4 Liverpool
30.06.95 Charlie Paine W CO 1 Liverpool
17.07.95 Ojay Abrahams W PTS 8 Mayfair
15.05.97 Junior Witter L RSC 5 Reading
Career: 34 contests, won 23, drew 4, lost 7.

Panayiotis Panayiotiou

Stratford. *Born* Limassol, Cyprus, 18 September, 1973
Middleweight. Ht. 5'11"
Manager B. Lynch

29.09.95 Ernie Loveridge W PTS 4 Bethnal Green
08.11.95 Andy Ewen W PTS 4 Bethnal Green
05.03.96 Michael Pinnock W PTS 4 Bethnal Green
03.04.96 Peter Varnavas W PTS 4 Bethnal Green
14.05.96 Ernie Loveridge W PTS 4 Dagenham
26.11.96 Shamus Casey W CO 1 Bethnal Green
08.04.97 Andy Gray W PTS 6 Bethnal Green
20.05.97 Jason Barker W PTS 6 Edmonton
Career: 8 contests, won 8.

Neil Parry

Middlesbrough. *Born* Middlesbrough, 21 June, 1969
Bantamweight. Ht. 5'5"
Manager T. Callighan

12.06.89 Des Gargano L PTS 6 Manchester
21.12.89 Kevin Jenkins L PTS 6 Kings Heath
31.01.90 Francis Ampofo L PTS 6 Bethnal Green
12.03.90 Paul Dever W PTS 6 Hull
19.03.90 James Drummond L RSC 4 Glasgow
27.11.90 Stevie Woods W PTS 6 Glasgow
04.12.90 Conn McMullen L RSC 2 Southend

21.01.91	Stevie Woods L PTS 8 Glasgow
06.02.91	Paul Dever W PTS 6 Liverpool
05.03.91	Tony Smith DREW 6 Leicester
24.04.91	Paul Dever DREW 6 Stoke
17.05.91	Gary White L PTS 6 Bury
03.06.91	Stevie Woods W RSC 2 Glasgow
20.06.91	Tony Smith W PTS 6 Liverpool
12.09.91	Mark Tierney L PTS 6 Wandsworth
21.10.91	Neil Johnston L PTS 8 Glasgow
27.01.92	Drew Docherty L RSC 4 Glasgow
28.02.92	Stevie Woods W PTS 6 Irvine
11.05.92	Tim Yeates L PTS 6 Piccadilly
21.09.92	Paul Weir L RSC 4 Glasgow
27.11.92	Eyup Can L PTS 6 Randers, Denmark
25.01.93	Ady Benton L RSC 6 Bradford
29.03.93	Louis Veitch L PTS 6 Glasgow
01.06.93	Des Gargano L PTS 6 Manchester
28.06.93	Marcus Duncan W RSC 2 Morecambe
13.09.93	Marcus Duncan L PTS 6 Middleton
06.10.93	Graham McGrath DREW 6 Glasgow
25.10.93	James Drummond L RSC 2 Glasgow
19.02.94	Harald Geier L CO 3 Hamburg, Germany
22.09.94	Ady Lewis L RSC 3 Bury
29.10.94	Terry Gaskin W PTS 6 Cannock
21.11.94	Keith Knox L PTS 6 Glasgow
16.01.95	Keith Knox L PTS 6 Musselburgh
23.01.95	Ian Baillie W RTD 3 Glasgow
11.03.95	Terry Gaskin DREW 6 Barnsley
22.03.95	Terry Gaskin W PTS 8 Stoke
26.04.95	Shaun Norman DREW 6 Stoke
17.05.95	Mark Reynolds L PTS 6 Ipswich
01.06.95	Rowan Williams L PTS 8 Musselburgh
05.10.95	Shaun Hall W PTS 6 Glasgow
23.10.95	Richard Vowles L PTS 6 Glasgow
22.11.95	Steve Williams L PTS 6 Sheffield
07.12.95	Paul Quarmby W PTS 6 Sunderland
02.02.96	Philippe Desavoye L PTS 8 Dieppe, France
16.03.96	Noel Wilders L RTD 4 Sheffield
22.04.96	Anthony Hanna L PTS 6 Manchester
20.05.96	Andy Roberts W PTS 6 Bradford
24.06.96	Andy Roberts W PTS 6 Bradford
03.09.96	Dharmendra Singh Yadav L PTS 6 Bethnal Green
23.09.96	Garry Burrell L PTS 6 Glasgow
10.10.96	Colin Innes L PTS 6 Newcastle
03.12.96	Michael Gibbons L PTS 6 Yarm
17.12.96	Andy Roberts DREW 6 Doncaster
20.02.97	Steve Williams L PTS 8 Mansfield
17.03.97	Shaun Anderson L RTD 4 Glasgow

Career: 55 contests, won 14, drew 6, lost 35.

Elvis Parsley

Bloxwich. *Born* Walsall, 6 December, 1962
Featherweight. Ht. 5'7½"
Manager P. Cowdell/R. Gray

04.06.90	Phil Lashley W RSC 3 Birmingham
20.06.90	Mark Bates L CO 1 Basildon
27.09.90	Andrew Robinson W RTD 3 Birmingham
10.12.90	Karl Taylor W PTS 6 Birmingham
18.02.91	Peter Campbell W RSC 3 Derby
01.05.91	Neil Leitch W CO 2 Solihull
20.05.91	Neil Smith L RSC 5 Leicester
02.10.91	Muhammad Shaffique W CO 1 Solihull
29.04.92	Kelton McKenzie L RSC 5 Solihull *(Vacant Midlands Area Featherweight Title)*
28.04.93	Dean Amory L PTS 6 Solihull

12.10.93	Kid McAuley W PTS 6 Wolverhampton
30.11.93	Mike Deveney W PTS 6 Wolverhampton
16.12.93	Barry Jones L PTS 6 Newport
05.04.94	Kevin Middleton W RSC 4 Bethnal Green
23.01.95	Danny Lutaaya W RSC 3 Bethnal Green
24.03.95	Floyd Havard L RSC 6 Swansea
29.09.95	Paul Webster W RSC 5 Bethnal Green
18.12.95	Jonjo Irwin L RSC 8 Mayfair *(British Featherweight Title Challenge)*
07.05.96	Michael Brodie L RSC 1 Mayfair
25.06.96	Duke McKenzie L RSC 1 Mansfield
15.10.96	Miguel Matthews W PTS 8 Wolverhampton
04.12.96	Miguel Matthews W PTS 6 Stoke
25.02.97	Paul Griffin L PTS 8 Sheffield

Career: 23 contests, won 13, lost 10.

Andy Peach

Bloxwich. *Born* Bloxwich, 1 August, 1971
Welterweight. Ht. 5'8"
Manager Self

27.10.92	Stuart Dunn L RSC 3 Leicester
09.12.92	Jason Fores W PTS 6 Stoke
09.02.93	Ray Golding L PTS 6 Wolverhampton
11.03.93	Richard O'Brien L PTS 6 Walsall
06.05.93	Billy McDougall L PTS 6 Walsall
30.09.93	Ernie Locke L PTS 6 Walsall
04.11.93	Dennis Berry L PTS 6 Stafford
02.12.93	Ernie Locke L RTD 3 Walsall
08.02.94	Brian Coleman L PTS 6 Wolverhampton
04.03.94	Nicky Thurbin L PTS 6 Bethnal Green
14.03.94	Howard Eastman L PTS 6 Mayfair
18.04.94	Howard Clarke L PTS 6 Walsall
28.04.94	Scott Doyle L PTS 6 Mayfair
23.05.94	David Bain L RSC 6 Walsall
26.08.94	Cam Raeside L PTS 6 Barnsley
12.10.94	Prince Kasi Kaihau L PTS 6 Stoke
25.10.94	Howard Clarke L RSC 3 Edgbaston
29.11.94	Mark Antony W PTS 6 Wolverhampton
12.12.94	Prince Kasi Kaihau L PTS 6 Doncaster
18.01.95	John Stronach L RSC 5 Solihull
06.03.95	Norman Hutcheon W RSC 2 Leicester
22.03.95	Andrew Jervis L PTS 6 Stoke
05.05.95	Prince Kasi Kaihau L PTS 6 Doncaster
16.05.95	Brian Dunn W RSC 1 Cleethorpes
23.05.95	Steve Roberts L RSC 3 Potters Bar
06.07.95	Rick North W RSC 4 Hull
17.07.95	Neil Sinclair L RSC 1 Mayfair
08.11.95	Trevor Meikle L PTS 6 Scunthorpe
06.12.95	Trevor Meikle L RSC 3 Stoke
24.01.96	Adam Baldwin L PTS 6 Stoke
13.02.96	Paul Webb W PTS 6 Wolverhampton
22.02.96	Steve Levene L PTS 6 Walsall
26.03.96	Ozzy Orrock W RSC 2 Wolverhampton
29.03.96	Shaun Stokes L RSC 3 Doncaster
26.09.96	Paul Webb W PTS 6 Walsall
15.10.96	Steve Howden W RSC 6 Wolverhampton
24.10.96	Paul Webb L RSC 3 Birmingham
20.11.96	Harry Dhami L RTD 3 Wembley
19.03.97	Richard Inquieti W RSC 1 Stoke
12.04.97	James Hare L RSC 1 Sheffield

Career: 40 contests, won 10, lost 30.

Tommy Peacock

Liverpool. *Born* Liverpool, 24 October, 1969
Lightweight. Ht. 5'9"
Manager S. Vaughan

22.11.96	Wayne Jones W RSC 4 Liverpool
04.04.97	Craig Kelley W PTS 6 Liverpool

Career: 2 contests, won 2.

Robert Peel

Llandovery. *Born* Birmingham, 11 January, 1969
S. Middleweight. Ht. 5'10"
Manager Self

24.01.91	John Kaighin W PTS 6 Gorseinon
12.02.91	John Kaighin W PTS 6 Cardiff
13.03.91	Andrew Flute L PTS 6 Stoke
04.04.91	Clay O'Shea L PTS 6 Watford
12.04.91	Adrian Wright L RSC 6 Willenhall
15.05.91	John Kaighin L PTS 8 Swansea
29.10.91	Jason Matthews L RSC 6 Cardiff
03.02.92	Warren Stowe L PTS 6 Manchester
02.03.92	Steve Thomas DREW 6 Merthyr
11.05.92	Steve Thomas L PTS 6 Llanelli
04.06.92	Darren Pilling L PTS 6 Burnley
28.10.92	Barry Thorogood L PTS 6 Cardiff
24.03.93	Russell Washer W PTS 6 Cardiff
27.05.93	Dean Cooper L PTS 6 Bristol
14.08.93	Ensley Bingham L RTD 3 Hammersmith
22.09.93	Adrian Dodson L CO 1 Bethnal Green
10.11.93	Barry Thorogood L PTS 6 Ystrad
20.05.94	Geoff McCreesh L RSC 2 Acton
25.06.94	Dale Nixon L PTS 6 Cullompton
07.10.94	Dale Nixon L RSC 7 Taunton
29.11.94	Barry Thorogood L PTS 10 Cardiff *(Vacant Welsh Middleweight Title)*
03.03.95	David Larkin W PTS 6 Bethnal Green
12.04.95	Barry Thorogood L RSC 8 Llanelli *(Welsh Middleweight Title Challenge)*
17.05.95	Andy Ewen L RSC 4 Ipswich
04.04.97	Graham Townsend L PTS 6 Brighton
25.04.97	Mike Gormley L PTS 6 Mere

Career: 26 contests, won 4, drew 1, lost 21.

Chris Pegg

Newark. *Born* Newark, 10 January, 1967
L. Welterweight. Ht. 5'4½"
Manager J. Ashton

23.01.85	Dean Dickinson L PTS 4 Stoke
04.02.85	Dean Dickinson W PTS 6 Birmingham
07.03.85	Chubby Martin L PTS 6 Nottingham
26.03.85	Mickey Baird W PTS 6 Chorley
22.04.85	Peter Bowen L PTS 6 Birmingham
22.05.85	Si Holdcroft W PTS 6 Stoke
08.05.97	Dean Bramhald L PTS 6 Mansfield

Career: 7 contests, won 3, lost 4.

Danny Peters

Liverpool. *Born* Liverpool, 19 July, 1973
L. Heavyweight. Ht. 5'10"
Manager B. Devine

06.09.93	Steve Levene W RSC 4 Liverpool
25.10.93	Russell Washer W PTS 6 Liverpool
02.07.94	Spencer Alton W PTS 6 Liverpool
26.09.94	John Duckworth W PTS 6 Liverpool
20.04.95	Ernie Loveridge W PTS 6 Liverpool
30.06.95	Nick Ingram W RSC 6 Liverpool

29.09.95 Carlo Colarusso W PTS 6 Liverpool
04.11.95 Carl Smith W CO 3 Liverpool
26.10.96 Greg Scott-Briggs W PTS 6 Liverpool
03.12.96 Neil Simpson W PTS 6 Liverpool
Career: 10 contests, won 10.

Danny Peters   Les Clark

Stevie Pettit

Walsall. *Born* Birmingham, 28 April, 1969
Cruiserweight. Ht. 6'2"
Manager E. Cashmore

08.11.95 Chris Woollas L PTS 6 Walsall
22.02.96 Craig Jones W RSC 1 Walsall
21.05.96 Nigel Williams W RTD 3 Edgbaston
26.09.96 Slick Miller W PTS 6 Walsall
15.04.97 Patrick Lawrence W PTS 6 Edgbaston
Career: 5 contests, won 4, lost 1.

Jimmy Phelan

Hull. *Born* London, 18 June, 1971
Former Central Area Lightweight
Champion.
Ht. 5'9"
Manager Self

23.11.93 T. J. Smith L PTS 6 Kettering
16.12.93 Paul Bowen W PTS 6 Walsall
10.02.94 Micky Hall L PTS 6 Hull
11.10.94 Colin Dunne L PTS 6 Bethnal Green
31.10.94 George Naylor L PTS 6 Liverpool
16.03.95 Bobby Guynan W RSC 5 Basildon
01.07.95 A. M. Milton W PTS 6 Kensington
22.09.95 Tony Foster W PTS 10 Hull
    *(Central Area Lightweight Title
    Challenge)*
08.12.95 Yifru Retta L RSC 5 Bethnal Green
15.03.96 Carl Tilley L PTS 6 Hull
27.09.96 Wayne Rigby L PTS 10 Hull
    *(Central Area Lightweight Title
    Defence)*
03.02.97 Kelton McKenzie L RSC 5 Leicester
14.03.97 Kid McAuley W PTS 6 Hull
04.04.97 Scott Dixon L PTS 6 Glasgow
03.05.97 Mark Winters L PTS 4 Manchester
09.06.97 Malcolm Melvin L RSC 2 Birmingham
Career: 16 contests, won 5, lost 11.

Dean Phillips

Llanelli. *Born* Swansea, 1 February, 1976
S. Featherweight. Ht. 5'6"
Manager F. Warren

10.03.94 Paul Richards L PTS 6 Bristol
23.03.94 Phil Janes W RSC 1 Cardiff
27.08.94 Craig Kelley W RSC 4 Cardiff
21.09.94 Steve Edwards W RTD 4 Cardiff
02.11.94 Anthony Maynard L PTS 6
    Birmingham
04.02.95 Greg Upton W PTS 6 Cardiff
04.03.95 Mike Deveney W PTS 8 Livingston
24.03.95 Bamana Dibateza W PTS 6 Swansea
16.06.95 Danny Luutaya W RSC 2 Southwark
22.07.95 Colin McMillan L PTS 8 Millwall
20.09.95 Mervyn Bennett W PTS 6 Ystrad
16.03.96 Mike Anthony Brown W RSC 6
    Glasgow
26.04.96 Bamana Dibateza W PTS 6 Cardiff
19.09.96 Peter Judson L RSC 10 Manchester
    *(Vacant IBF Inter-Continental
    S. Featherweight Title)*
Career: 14 contests, won 10, lost 4.

Esham Pickering

Sheffield. *Born* Newark, 7 August, 1976
Featherweight. Ht. 5'5"
Manager B. Ingle

23.09.96 Brendan Bryce W RSC 5 Cleethorpes
24.10.96 Kevin Sheil W PTS 6 Lincoln
22.11.96 Amjed Mamond W RSC 2 Hull
09.12.96 Des Gargano W RTD 2 Chesterfield
16.12.96 Graham McGrath W PTS 6
    Cleethorpes
20.03.97 Robert Braddock W RSC 6 Newark
12.04.97 Graham Marsh W PTS 4 Sheffield
26.04.97 Mike Deveney W PTS 4 Swadlincote
16.05.97 Chris Price W PTS 6 Hull
26.06.97 Graham McGrath W PTS 6 Salford
Career: 10 contests, won 10.

(Warren) John Pierre

Newcastle. *Born* Newcastle, 22 April, 1966
Cruiserweight. Ht. 6'0"
Manager N. Fawcett

10.10.91 Gary Charlton W PTS 6 Gateshead
20.01.92 Art Stacey L PTS 6 Bradford
21.09.92 Albert Call L PTS 6 Cleethorpes
20.09.93 Martin Langtry L PTS 6 Cleethorpes
12.10.93 Richard Atkinson W PTS 6
    Wolverhampton
21.10.93 Alan Smiles L PTS 6 Glasgow
08.12.93 Art Stacey L PTS 6 Hull
19.12.93 Alan Smiles DREW 6 Glasgow
25.10.94 Richard Bango L RSC 3
    Middlesbrough
27.02.95 Kenley Price L PTS 6 Barrow
15.05.95 Declan Faherty L PTS 6 Bradford
12.06.95 Brian McDermott L PTS 6 Bradford
14.11.95 Jacklord Jacobs L PTS 6 Yarm
07.12.95 Sean Daly DREW 6 Hull
29.02.96 Chris Woollas DREW 6 Scunthorpe
16.03.96 Mark Prince L PTS 6 Glasgow
22.04.96 Colin Brown L PTS 6 Glasgow
23.05.96 Tim Redman W PTS 6 Queensferry
06.07.96 Kelly Oliver L PTS 4 Manchester
13.07.96 Danny Williams L PTS 4 Bethnal
    Green
16.08.96 Steve Bristow L PTS 6 Liverpool

14.09.96 John Keeton L PTS 4 Sheffield
13.06.97 Glen Liechti L RSC 1 Slagelse,
    Denmark
Career: 23 contests, won 3, drew 3, lost 17.

Michael Pinnock

Birmingham. *Born* Birmingham, 6 June,
1965
L. Heavyweight. Ht. 6'0"
Manager Self

19.05.95 David Flowers L PTS 6 Leeds
13.06.95 Mark Snipe L PTS 6 Basildon
20.06.95 Darren Sweeney L PTS 8 Birmingham
06.09.95 Steve Loftus L PTS 6 Stoke
21.09.95 Luan Morena L PTS 4 Battersea
24.10.95 Graham Townsend L PTS 4 Southwark
17.11.95 Graham Townsend L PTS 4 Bethnal
    Green
03.12.95 Neville Smith L RSC 5 Southwark
23.01.96 Butch Lesley L PTS 4 Bethnal Green
05.03.96 Panayiotis Panayiotiou L PTS 4
    Bethnal Green
16.03.96 Mark Hickey L PTS 6 Barnstaple
25.03.96 Lee Simpkin W PTS 6 Birmingham
03.04.96 Jason Hart L PTS 6 Bethnal Green
24.04.96 Gordon Behan L PTS 6 Solihull
03.05.96 David Larkin DREW 6 Sheffield
14.05.96 Mervyn Penniston L RSC 2 Dagenham
19.07.96 Chris Davies L PTS 6 Ystrad
29.07.96 Stuart Fleet L RSC 3 Skegness
04.10.96 Paul Bonson L PTS 6 Wakefield
28.10.96 Zak Goldman DREW 6 Leicester
14.11.96 Paul Bonson DREW 6 Sheffield
21.11.96 Darren Sweeney W RSC 5 Solihull
26.11.96 Mark Smallwood L PTS 6
    Wolverhampton
03.02.97 Neil Simpson L PTS 6 Leicester
09.06.97 Mark Hobson L PTS 6 Bradford
Career: 25 contests, won 2, drew 3, lost 20.

Michael Pinnock   Les Clark

Dean Pithie

Coventry. *Born* Coventry, 18 January 1974
S. Featherweight. Ht. 5'5"
Manager F. Warren/C. Magri

17.02.95	Kid McAuley W RSC 3 Cumbernauld
13.04.95	Kid McAuley W RSC 1 Bloomsbury
01.07.95	Pete Buckley W PTS 4 Kensington
22.07.95	G. G. Goddard W PTS 4 Millwall
21.10.95	Anthony Campbell W PTS 4 Bethnal Green
10.11.95	Kelton McKenzie DREW 6 Derby
26.04.96	Kelton McKenzie W PTS 6 Cardiff
25.06.96	Lewis Reynolds W RSC 2 Mansfield
14.09.96	Miguel Matthews W PTS 4 Sheffield
14.12.96	Marty Chestnut W RSC 3 Sheffield
18.01.97	Harry Escott W RSC 4 Swadlincote
25.02.97	Pete Buckley W PTS 4 Sheffield
26.04.97	David Morris W PTS 8 Swadlincote

Career: 13 contests, won 12, drew 1.

Steve Pollard

Hull. *Born* Hull, 18 December, 1957
Welterweight. Former Central Area
Featherweight Champion. Ht. 5'7"
Manager Self

28.04.80	Bryn Jones W PTS 6 Piccadilly
27.05.80	Pat Mallon W PTS 6 Glasgow
02.06.80	Andy Thomas W PTS 6 Piccadilly
02.10.80	Eddie Glass W PTS 6 Hull
03.11.80	Rocky Bantleman W CO 2 Piccadilly
01.12.80	Chris McCallum W PTS 6 Hull
17.02.81	Billy Laidman W PTS 6 Leeds
02.03.81	Bryn Jones W RSC 5 Piccadilly
30.03.81	John Sharkey L RSC 5 Glasgow
27.04.81	Ian McLeod L PTS 8 Piccadilly
01.06.81	Gary Lucas L PTS 8 Piccadilly
11.06.81	John Sharkey W PTS 8 Hull
08.03.82	Brian Hyslop DREW 8 Hamilton
22.04.82	Rocky Bantleman W RSC 8 Piccadilly
10.05.82	Lee Graham DREW 8 Piccadilly
26.05.82	Alan Tombs DREW 8 Piccadilly
23.09.82	Pat Doherty L PTS 8 Merton
26.10.82	Lee Halford L PTS 8 Hull
25.11.82	Kevin Howard L PTS 6 Sunderland
10.02.83	Keith Foreman L PTS 8 Sunderland
29.03.83	Steve Farnsworth W RSC 2 Hull *(Central Area Featherweight Title Challenge)*
18.06.83	Andre Blanco W PTS 8 Izegem, Belgium
04.10.83	Jim McDonnell L RSC 5 Bethnal Green
22.11.83	Joey Joynson L PTS 8 Wembley
22.01.84	Jean-Marc Renard L PTS 8 Izegem, Belgium
13.11.84	Jim McDonnell L RSC 6 Bethnal Green
17.12.84	John Doherty L PTS 10 Bradford *(Central Area Featherweight Title Defence)*
12.03.85	Mike Whalley L RSC 8 Manchester
20.01.86	Alex Dickson L RSC 7 Glasgow
10.03.86	Dave Savage L PTS 8 Glasgow
26.03.86	Peter Harris L RSC 3 Swansea
13.11.86	Dean Marsden L CO 7 Huddersfield
07.04.87	Darren Connellan W PTS 8 Batley
15.04.87	Paul Gadney L PTS 8 Lewisham
30.04.87	Gary Nickels L RSC 1 Wandsworth
22.09.87	Kevin Taylor L PTS 8 Oldham
18.11.87	Gary de Roux DREW 8 Peterborough
11.12.87	Gary Maxwell L PTS 8 Coalville
28.01.88	John Bennie L PTS 6 Bethnal Green
24.02.88	Craig Windsor L PTS 8 Glasgow
09.03.88	Peter Bradley L PTS 8 Wembley
30.03.88	Scott Durham W PTS 8 Bethnal Green
25.04.88	Colin Lynch W PTS 8 Birmingham
18.05.88	John Bennie W PTS 8 Lewisham
30.08.88	Mike Chapman W PTS 8 Kensington
15.11.88	Tony Foster L RSC 3 Hull
17.01.89	Peter Bradley L PTS 8 Chigwell
31.05.89	Carl Crook L RSC 4 Manchester
04.09.89	Michael Armstrong L PTS 8 Hull
10.10.89	Tony Foster L RSC 3 Hull
22.03.90	Chris Bennett W PTS 4 Gateshead
07.04.90	Frankie Dewinter L PTS 6 St Elois Vyve, Belgium
20.05.90	Mark Ramsey L PTS 6 Sheffield
30.11.90	Shaun Cooper L PTS 6 Birmingham
11.02.91	Dave Anderson L PTS 6 Glasgow
02.03.91	Allan Hall L PTS 6 Darlington
05.12.91	Shaun Cogan L PTS 6 Oakengates
18.01.92	Ian Honeywood L PTS 6 Kensington
30.03.92	J. T. Williams W PTS 6 Eltham
30.04.92	Jason Rowland L RSC 2 Kensington
10.09.92	Paul Charters L PTS 6 Sunderland
16.10.92	Kevin Toomey L RSC 7 Hull
12.11.93	Kevin Toomey W PTS 8 Hull
24.11.94	Dave Curtis W RTD 4 Hull
22.09.95	Dave Curtis W RSC 6 Hull
19.01.96	Peter Richardson L PTS 8 Bracknell
06.11.96	Trevor Meikle L RSC 6 Hull

Career: 67 contests, won 22, drew 4, lost 41.

Chris Pollock   Les Clark

Chris Pollock

Bedworth. *Born* Coventry, 2 October, 1972
Middleweight. Ht. 5'10½"
Manager R. Gray/P. Cowdell

17.06.93	Jamie Morris W RSC 2 Bedworth
03.11.93	Kenny Scott W PTS 6 Worcester
08.12.93	Brian Coleman L PTS 6 Stoke
08.03.94	Brian Coleman W PTS 6 Edgbaston
29.03.94	Gary Cogan L PTS 6 Wolverhampton
29.03.96	Prince Kasi Kaihau W RSC 2 Doncaster
25.04.96	Harry Dhami L PTS 6 Mayfair
29.01.97	Alex Mason L RSC 5 Stoke
19.03.97	Johnny Hooks W PTS 6 Stoke
29.04.97	Darren Swords W RSC 6 Manchester
22.05.97	Peter Federenko L CO 2 Solihull
30.06.97	Jason Ratcliff L RSC 1 Bethnal Green

Career: 12 contests, won 6, lost 6.

(Anthony) Tiny Pope

Wellingborough. *Born* Kettering, 7 August, 1974
Flyweight. Ht. 5'3"
Manager M. Shinfield

07.03.97	Willie Smith W PTS 6 Northampton

Career: 1 contest, won 1.

Dean Powell

Lewisham. *Born* Salisbury, 4 June, 1970
Middleweight. Ht. 5'9"
Manager A. Urry

17.12.96	Matthew Tait L PTS 6 Bethnal Green
11.02.97	Matthew Tait L RSC 4 Bethnal Green

Career: 2 contests, lost 2.

Dean Powell   Les Clark

Chris Price

Rotherham. *Born* Rotherham, 4 March, 1977
Lightweight. Ht. 5'9"
Manager B. Ingle

06.09.95	Shaun Gledhill L PTS 6 Stoke
23.10.95	Jason Squire L PTS 6 Leicester
14.11.95	Colin Innes W PTS 6 Yarm
03.02.96	Alex Moon L RSC 2 Liverpool
20.03.96	Johnny Miller L PTS 6 Stoke
15.05.96	Tommy Janes L RSC 4 Cardiff
22.08.96	John Briffa L RSC 2 Salford
22.11.96	Kid McAuley DREW 6 Hull
09.12.96	Robbie Sivyer DREW 6 Chesterfield
17.12.96	Dean Bramhald L PTS 6 Doncaster
20.02.97	David Kirk L PTS 6 Mansfield

135

20.03.97 Peter Gabbitus L PTS 6 Doncaster
29.04.97 Shaun Gledhill L PTS 6 Manchester
16.05.97 Esham Pickering L PTS 6 Hull
22.05.97 Ervine Blake L PTS 6 Solihull
13.06.97 Scott Dixon L PTS 6 Paisley
Career: 16 contests, won 1, drew 2, lost 13.

Chris Price   Les Clark

Mark Prince

Tottenham. *Born* London, 10 March, 1969
WBO Inter-Continental L. Heavyweight
Champion. Ht. 6'1"
Manager F. Warren/C. Carew

04.04.93 Bobby Mack W RSC 2 Brockley
23.05.93 John Kaighin W RSC 3 Brockley
25.06.93 Art Stacey W CO 2 Battersea
14.08.93 Simon McDougall W PTS 6
    Hammersmith
20.01.94 Zak Chelli W CO 1 Battersea
14.04.94 John Foreman W CO 3 Battersea
21.07.94 Tony Booth W RSC 3 Battersea
25.02.95 Kofi Quaye W RSC 7 Millwall
02.06.95 Steve Osborne W RSC 3 Bethnal Green
22.07.95 Tony Booth W RSC 2 Millwall
09.09.95 Scott Lindecker W RSC 2 Cork
27.10.95 Lenzie Morgan W PTS 8 Brighton
16.03.96 John Pierre W PTS 6 Glasgow
06.07.96 Maurice Core W RSC 7 Manchester
    (Vacant WBO Inter-Continental L.
    Heavyweight Title)
03.02.97 Michael Gale W RSC 6 Sunderland
    (Elim. British L. Heavyweight Title)
Career: 15 contests, won 15.

Byron Pryce (Price)

Newbridge. *Born* Newport, 16 May, 1978
Lightweight. Ht. 6'0"
Manager F. Warren

23.10.96 Fred Reeve W RSC 1 Halifax
21.06.97 Craig Kelley DREW 4 Cardiff
Career: 2 contests, won 1, drew 1.

Byron Pryce   Les Clark

Delroy Pryce (Price)

Newbridge. *Born* Newport, 25 May, 1979
Featherweight. Ht. 5'7"
Manager F. Warren

21.06.97 John Farrell DREW 4 Cardiff
Career: 1 contest, drew 1.

Chris Pyatt

Leicester. *Born* Islington, 3 July, 1963
L. Middleweight. Former WBO
Middleweight Champion. Former
Undefeated WBC International
Middleweight Champion. Former European
& Commonwealth L. Middleweight
Champion. Former Undefeated British L.
Middleweight Champion. Ht. 5'8½"
Manager Self

01.03.83 Paul Murray W RTD 2 Kensington
05.04.83 Billy Waith W RSC 8 Kensington
28.04.83 Lee Hartshorn W RSC 3 Leicester
27.09.83 Darwin Brewster W PTS 8 Wembley
08.10.83 Tyrone Demby W RSC 2 Atlantic City,
    USA
22.11.83 Tony Britton W RSC 4 Wembley
22.02.84 Judas Clottey W PTS 8 Kensington
15.03.84 Pat Thomas W PTS 10 Leicester
09.05.84 Franki Moro W CO 4 Leicester
23.05.84 Alfonso Redondo W RSC 3 Mayfair
16.10.84 John Ridgman W RSC 1 Kensington
16.11.84 Brian Anderson W PTS 12 Leicester
    (Final Elim. British L. Middleweight
    Title)
12.02.85 Helier Custos W RSC 5 Kensington
05.06.85 Graeme Ahmed W RSC 3 Kensington
01.07.85 Mosimo Maeleke W RSC 6 Mayfair
23.09.85 Sabiyala Diavilia L RSC 4 Mayfair
19.02.86 Prince Rodney W CO 9 Kensington
    (British L. Middleweight Title
    Challenge)
20.05.86 Thomas Smith W RSC 1 Wembley
17.09.86 John van Elteren W RSC 1 Kensington
    (Vacant European L. Middleweight
    Title)

25.10.86 Renaldo Hernandez W RSC 3 Paris,
    France
28.01.87 Gianfranco Rosi L PTS 12 Perugia,
    Italy
    (European L. Middleweight Title
    Defence)
18.04.87 Dennis Johnson W CO 2 Kensington
26.05.87 Sammy Floyd W RSC 2 Wembley
28.10.87 Gilbert Josamu W PTS 8 Wembley
28.05.88 Jose Duarte W RSC 4 Kensington
23.11.88 Eddie Hall W RSC 2 Bethnal Green
01.12.88 Knox Brown W RSC 2 Edmonton
14.12.88 Tyrone Moore W CO 1 Bethnal Green
15.02.89 Russell Mitchell W RSC 4 Bethnal
    Green
17.05.89 Daniel Dominguez W RSC 10 Millwall
11.10.89 Wayne Harris W RSC 3 Millwall
25.04.90 Daniel Sclarandi W RSC 2 Millwall
23.10.90 John David Jackson L PTS 12 Leicester
    (WBO L. Middleweight Title
    Challenge)
05.11.91 Craig Trotter W PTS 12 Leicester
    (Vacant Commonwealth L.
    Middleweight Title)
01.02.92 Ambrose Mlilo W RSC 3 Birmingham
    Commonwealth L. Middleweight Title
    Defence)
31.03.92 Melvyn Wynn W CO 3 Norwich
28.04.92 James Tapisha W RSC 1
    Wolverhampton
    (Commonwealth L. Middleweight Title
    Defence)
23.05.92 Ian Strudwick W PTS 10 Birmingham
27.10.92 Adolfo Caballero W CO 5 Leicester
    (Vacant WBC International
    Middleweight Title)
26.01.93 Danny Garcia W PTS 12 Leicester
    (WBC International Middleweight Title
    Defence)
23.02.93 Colin Manners W CO 3 Doncaster
16.03.93 Paul Wesley W PTS 10 Mayfair
10.05.93 Sumbu Kalambay W PTS 12 Leicester
    (Vacant WBO Middleweight Title)
18.09.93 Hugo Corti W CO 6 Leicester
    (WBO Middleweight Title Defence)
09.02.94 Mark Cameron W CO 1 Brentwood
    (WBO Middleweight Title Defence)
11.05.94 Steve Collins L RSC 5 Sheffield
    (WBO Middleweight Title Defence)
13.05.95 Anthony Ivory W PTS 8 Glasgow
02.09.95 James Mason W RSC 5 Wembley
16.12.95 Kevin Kelly W PTS 12 Cardiff
    (Commonwealth L. Middleweight Title
    Challenge)
06.07.96 Steve Foster L PTS 12 Manchester
    (Commonwealth L. Middleweight Title
    Defence. IBF Inter-Continental L.
    Middleweight Title Challenge)
03.05.97 Maurice Forbes W PTS 8 Manchester
Career: 51 contests, won 46, lost 5.

Danny Quacoe

Crawley. *Born* Hammersmith, 30
December, 1965
Welterweight. Ht. 5'10"
Manager Self

22.10.92 Joel Ani L CO 1 Bethnal Green
28.11.93 Roger Dean W RSC 3 Southwark
06.03.94 Prince Louis W RSC 2 Southwark
16.05.94 Dave Madden W RSC 4 Heathrow
19.11.94 Dennis Griffin W RSC 5 Heathrow
30.09.95 Kevin Lueshing L PTS 8 Cardiff

27.10.95 Leigh Wicks L RSC 4 Brighton
26.01.96 Paul Dyer L PTS 6 Brighton
09.03.96 Mark Winters L RSC 2 Millstreet
20.04.96 Georgie Smith L PTS 6 Brentwood
31.05.96 Frank Olsen L RSC 2 Copenhagen, Denmark
01.10.96 Spencer McCracken L RTD 3 Birmingham
05.11.96 Jim Rock L RSC 4 Belfast
15.02.97 Paul Miles L PTS 6 Tooting
25.03.97 Gilbert Eastman L RSC 3 Lewisham
30.06.97 Richard Williams L PTS 4 Bethnal Green

Career: 16 contests, won 4, lost 12.

Tommy Quinn

Tranent. *Born* Edinburgh, 2 November, 1975
Welterweight. Ht. 5'11"
Manager T. Gilmour

16.01.95 Billy McDougall W CO 5 Musselburgh
20.03.95 Paul Scott W RSC 4 Glasgow
24.04.95 Billy McDougall W RSC 3 Glasgow
01.06.95 Wayne Shepherd W PTS 6 Musselburgh
18.09.95 Shaun O'Neill W PTS 6 Glasgow
16.02.96 Richard O'Brien W CO 4 Irvine
16.03.96 Shamus Casey W PTS 4 Glasgow
03.06.96 Michael Alexander W PTS 6 Glasgow
18.01.97 Jimmy Vincent L RSC 1 Swadlincote

Career: 9 contests, won 8, lost 1.

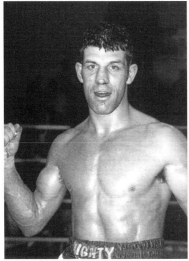

Willie Quinn   Les Clark

Willie Quinn

Tranent. *Born* Edinburgh, 17 February, 1972
WBO Inter-Continental Middleweight Champion. Ht. 5'11½"
Manager T. Gilmour

09.10.91 Mark Jay L PTS 6 Glasgow
27.01.92 Hugh Fury W RSC 3 Glasgow
18.03.92 Andy Manning W PTS 6 Glasgow
30.03.92 John McKenzie W RSC 4 Glasgow
19.09.92 Martin Rosamond W RSC 4 Glasgow
25.01.93 Mike Phillips W PTS 6 Glasgow

06.03.93 Steve Thomas W RSC 4 Glasgow
15.05.93 Dave Owens W PTS 6 Glasgow
30.11.93 Russell Washer W PTS 6 Cardiff
02.02.94 Marvin O'Brien W PTS 6 Glasgow
28.03.94 Spencer Alton W RTD 3 Musselburgh
06.06.94 Marvin O'Brien W RSC 4 Glasgow
20.09.94 Shamus Casey RSC 3 Musselburgh
23.11.94 Mark Jay W RSC 1 Irvine
16.01.95 Mark Jay W RSC 2 Musselburgh
17.02.95 Martin Jolley W CO 5 Cumbernauld
05.04.95 John Duckworth W PTS 8 Irvine
01.06.95 Paul Busby W RTD 8 Musselburgh
(Vacant WBO Inter-Continental Middleweight Title)
18.11.95 Peter Waudby W RTD 6 Glasgow
(WBO Inter-Continental Middleweight Title Defence)
16.03.96 Martin Jolley W RSC 4 Glasgow
18.01.97 Neville Brown L RSC 4 Swadlincote
(British Middleweight Title Challenge)
04.04.97 Stinger Mason W RSC 6 Glasgow
16.05.97 Colin Manners W PTS 6 Glasgow

Career: 23 contests, won 21, lost 2.

David Radford

Hemsworth. *Born* Hemsworth, 30 May, 1969
Middleweight. Ht. 6'0"
Manager T. Callighan

27.03.90 Tommy Warde L CO 3 Leicester
09.05.90 Chris Micolazczyk W PTS 6 Solihull
21.05.90 Brian Keating W PTS 6 Bradford
28.06.90 Paul Hanlon W RSC 2 Birmingham
03.09.90 Andre Wharton L RSC 5 Dudley
16.01.91 Tony Kosova W PTS 6 Stoke
21.02.91 Griff Jones L PTS 6 Leeds
15.04.91 Paul Burton L RTD 1 Wolverhampton
13.05.91 Pete Bowman W CO 2 Manchester
02.12.91 Dave Binsteed W RSC 6 Liverpool
14.12.91 Delroy Matthews L CO 1 Bexleyheath
24.02.92 Mark Jay L PTS 6 Bradford
09.03.92 Tyrone Eastmond DREW 6 Manchester
25.04.92 Warren Stowe L RSC 3 Manchester
11.03.95 Richard Munro W RSC 5 Barnsley
28.04.95 Thomas Hansvoll L PTS 6 Randers, Denmark
21.09.95 Dave Battey W PTS 6 Sheffield
20.10.95 Dave Battey W CO 1 Mansfield
22.11.95 Darren Swords W PTS 6 Sheffield
04.12.95 Rob Stevenson W CO 2 Manchester
14.02.96 Dave Johnson W RSC 5 Sunderland
04.06.96 Kevin Thompson L PTS 6 York
04.10.96 David Larkin W RSC 5 Wakefield
20.04.97 Martin Jolley W PTS 8 Leeds

Career: 24 contests, won 14, drew 1, lost 9.

Cam Raeside

Ilkeston. *Born* Toronto, Canada, 7 May, 1968
Midlands Area Welterweight Champion. Ht. 5'8"
Manager Self

02.12.93 Billy McDougall W RSC 5 Evesham
18.02.94 Brian Coleman W PTS 6 Leicester
26.08.94 Andy Peach W PTS 6 Barnsley
09.02.95 Gary Hiscox L RSC 5 Doncaster
30.10.95 Lee Murtagh W PTS 6 Bradford
29.02.96 Paul Webb W PTS 6 Scunthorpe
29.03.96 Michael Alexander W PTS 6 Doncaster
01.10.96 John Harrison W PTS 6 Birmingham

25.11.96 Brian Dunn W RSC 3 Cleethorpes
(Vacant Midlands Area Welterweight Title)
18.01.97 Junior Witter DREW 6 Swadlincote
10.05.97 Ray Newby W PTS 10 Nottingham
(Midlands Area Welterweight Title Defence)

Career: 11 contests, won 9, drew 1, lost 1.

Cam Raeside   Les Clark

Nigel Rafferty

Wolverhampton. *Born* Wolverhampton, 29 December, 1967
Former Midlands Area Cruiserweight Champion. Ht. 5'11"
Manager R. Gray

05.06.89 Carl Watson L PTS 6 Birmingham
28.06.89 Tony Hodge L PTS 6 Brentwood
06.07.89 Tony Hodge W PTS 6 Chigwell
04.09.89 Joe Frater L PTS 6 Grimsby
24.10.89 Paul Wesley W PTS 6 Wolverhampton
22.11.89 Paul Wesley W PTS 8 Stafford
28.11.89 Paul Wesley W PTS 6 Wolverhampton
04.12.89 Dean Murray W PTS 6 Grimsby
20.12.89 Paul Wright DREW 6 Kirkby
17.01.90 Gil Lewis L PTS 6 Stoke
31.01.90 Antoine Tarver L PTS 4 Bethnal Green
19.02.90 Paul Wesley W PTS 8 Birmingham
19.03.90 Terry Gilbey W PTS 6 Grimsby
01.05.90 Sean Heron L RSC 2 Oldham
13.09.90 Paul Murray W PTS 6 Watford
27.09.90 Paul Murray DREW 6 Birmingham
09.10.90 Paul Murray W PTS 6 Wolverhampton
24.10.90 Andrew Flute L CO 6 Dudley
27.11.90 Carlos Christie W PTS 8 Wolverhampton
06.12.90 Carlos Christie L PTS 6 Wolverhampton
28.01.91 Alan Richards DREW 8 Birmingham
04.03.91 Carlos Christie L PTS 8 Birmingham
26.03.91 Lee Prudden W PTS 6 Wolverhampton
13.05.91 Tony Behan W DIS 7 Birmingham
05.06.91 Lee Prudden W PTS 6 Wolverhampton
10.09.91 Paul Busby L RSC 2 Wolverhampton
20.11.91 Julian Johnson DREW 6 Cardiff

02.12.91	Kesem Clayton W PTS 8 Birmingham
21.01.92	Glenn Campbell L RSC 6 Stockport
30.03.92	Simon McDougall W PTS 8 Coventry
25.04.92	Sammy Storey L RSC 3 Belfast
16.06.92	Garry Delaney L CO 5 Dagenham
24.11.92	Graham Burton W PTS 8 Wolverhampton
02.12.92	John J. Cooke L PTS 6 Bardon
23.03.93	Stephen Wilson W RSC 3 Wolverhampton
14.04.93	Ole Klemetsen L RSC 2 Kensington
19.05.93	Zak Chelli L RSC 3 Leicester
22.09.93	Martin Jolley W PTS 6 Chesterfield
12.10.93	Carl Smallwood DREW 8 Wolverhampton
28.10.93	Lee Archer L PTS 8 Walsall
08.12.93	Darren Ashton L PTS 6 Stoke
26.01.94	Monty Wright L PTS 6 Birmingham
08.02.94	Greg Scott-Briggs W PTS 6 Wolverhampton
17.02.94	Glenn Campbell L RSC 7 Bury
18.04.94	Graham Burton W PTS 8 Walsall
23.05.94	Darren Ashton L PTS 6 Walsall
15.06.94	Darron Griffiths L RSC 4 Southwark
03.08.94	Leif Keiski L RSC 5 Bristol
20.10.94	John J. Cooke L RSC 7 Walsall
	(Midlands Area L. Heavyweight Title Challenge)
13.12.94	Paul Lawson L RSC 4 Ilford
20.03.95	John Foreman W PTS 10 Birmingham
	(Midlands Area Cruiserweight Title Challenge)
19.04.95	Bruce Scott L RSC 2 Bethnal Green
17.05.95	Ole Klemetsen L RSC 4 Ipswich
06.07.95	Tony Booth L RSC 7 Hull
26.08.95	Darren Corbett L PTS 6 Belfast
20.09.95	Darren Westover L PTS 6 Potters Bar
29.09.95	Paul Lawson L PTS 6 Bethnal Green
07.10.95	Darren Corbett L PTS 6 Belfast
25.10.95	Robert Norton L RSC 6 Telford
21.02.96	Martin Langtry L CO 4 Batley
	(Midlands Area Cruiserweight Title Defence)
20.05.96	Albert Call DREW 6 Cleethorpes
30.05.96	Tony Dowling L PTS 6 Lincoln
27.08.96	Chris Okoh L RSC 4 Windsor
26.09.96	Paul Wesley DREW 6 Walsall
09.10.96	Chris Woollas L PTS 6 Stoke
28.10.96	Neil Simpson L PTS 8 Leicester
12.11.96	Robert Norton L PTS 8 Dudley
30.11.96	Kelly Oliver L PTS 6 Tylorstown
14.12.96	John Keeton L RTD 3 Sheffield
28.01.97	Darren Corbett L PTS 10 Belfast
	(All-Ireland Cruiserweight Title Challenge)
04.03.97	Dominic Negus L PTS 4 Southwark
25.03.97	Tony Booth DREW 8 Wolverhampton
12.04.97	John Keeton L RSC 6 Sheffield
20.05.97	Dominic Negus L PTS 4 Edmonton

Career: 74 contests, won 20, drew 8, lost 46.

Mark Ramsey

Birmingham. *Born* Birmingham, 24 January, 1968
L. Welterweight. Ht. 5'7½"
Manager B. Ingle

15.11.89	Mick O'Donnell W RSC 1 Lewisham
08.12.89	Dave Pierre L RSC 2 Doncaster
22.02.90	Karl Taylor W RSC 4 Hull
10.04.90	George Jones W RSC 6 Doncaster
20.05.90	Steve Pollard W PTS 6 Sheffield
18.10.90	Neil Haddock L RSC 5 Birmingham

30.05.91	Colin Sinnott W PTS 6 Birmingham
05.12.91	Carl Hook W RSC 5 Oakengates
27.01.93	Andrew Jervis W PTS 6 Stoke
12.02.93	Reymond Deva W PTS 6 Aubervilliers, France
04.03.93	Dave Pierre L PTS 8 Peterborough
01.05.93	Vyacheslav Ianowski L PTS 8 Berlin, Germany
02.07.93	Andreas Panayi DREW 6 Liverpool
05.08.93	Jean Chiarelli W RSC 4 Ascona, Italy
01.10.93	Freddy Demeulenaere W RSC 3 Waregem, Belgium
26.03.94	James Osunsedo W RSC 4 Dortmund, Germany
07.05.94	Andrei Sinepupov L PTS 12 Dnepropetrousk, Ukraine
	(Vacant WBO Penta-Continental Lightweight Title)
30.11.94	Mark Elliot W RSC 10 Wolverhampton
	(Elim. British L. Welterweight Title)
20.05.95	Ahmet Katejev L RTD 5 Hamburg, Germany
	(WBC International Welterweight Title Challenge)
15.09.95	Paul Dyer L PTS 6 Mansfield
23.10.95	Stefan Scriggins L PTS 8 Leicester
12.02.96	Alan McDowall L PTS 8 Glasgow
16.03.96	Alan McDowall L PTS 6 Glasgow
28.06.96	Poli Diaz W RSC 4 Madrid, Spain
12.11.96	Paul Samuels L RSC 4 Dudley
24.02.97	Bobby Vanzie DREW 8 Glasgow
25.03.97	Joshua Clottey L PTS 8 Lewisham
30.04.97	Anthony Campbell L PTS 6 Acton
20.05.97	Peter Richardson L PTS 8 Edmonton

Career: 29 contests, won 13, drew 2, lost 14.

Mark Ramsey   Les Clark

Jason Ratcliff

Romford. *Born* Rush Green, 28 March, 1972
Middleweight. Ht. 5'9½"
Manager F. King

27.11.96	Ernie Loveridge W PTS 4 Bethnal Green
08.03.97	Andy Gray W PTS 4 Brentwood
08.04.97	Andy Ewen W RSC 4 Bethnal Green
27.05.97	Jeff Finlayson W PTS 4 Mayfair
30.06.97	Chris Pollock W RSC 1 Bethnal Green

Career: 5 contests, won 5.

Jason Ratcliff   Les Clark

Tim Redman

Dolgellau. *Born* Dolgellau, 1 May, 1970
Cruiserweight. Ht. 6'2"
Manager Self

07.07.95	Phill Day W RSC 2 Cardiff
16.10.95	Peter Oboh L RTD 2 Mayfair
16.11.95	Gypsy Carman L PTS 6 Evesham
05.02.96	Jacklord Jacobs DREW 6 Bexleyheath
23.05.96	John Pierre L PTS 6 Queensferry
04.10.96	Geoff Hunter W CO 5 Pentre Halkyn
27.11.96	John Kaighin W PTS 4 Swansea
31.01.97	Chris Woollas W PTS 6 Pentre Halkyn
16.04.97	Michael Sprott L CO 2 Bethnal Green

Career: 9 contests, won 4, drew 1, lost 4.

(Peter) Andrew Reed

Potters Bar. *Born* Egham, 22 November, 1962
Lightweight. Ht. 5'7"
Manager Self

09.12.93	Simon Frailing L PTS 6 Watford
29.01.94	Russell Rees L PTS 6 Cardiff
08.03.94	T. J. Smith L PTS 6 Kettering
05.04.94	Anthony Campbell L PTS 6 Bethnal Green
28.04.94	Marco Fattore DREW 6 Mayfair
27.05.94	Chris Francis L PTS 6 Ashford
04.06.94	Marcus McCrae L PTS 6 Cardiff
29.09.94	Lewis Reynolds L PTS 4 Bethnal Green
16.11.94	Greg Upton L PTS 6 Bloomsbury
23.01.95	Matt Brown L PTS 4 Bethnal Green
25.02.95	Marcus McCrae L RSC 4 Millwall
23.05.95	Mark O'Callaghan W PTS 4 Potters Bar
10.06.95	Paul Griffin L RSC 5 Manchester

09.12.95 Martin Holgate L RSC 1 Bethnal Green
27.11.96 Jason Cook L RSC 3 Bethnal Green
30.04.97 Brendan Kelly L PTS 6 Acton
Career: 16 contests, won 1, drew 1, lost 14.

Darren Rees
Batley. *Born* Batley, 19 May, 1969
Middleweight. Ht. 5'11"
Manager J. Celebanski

28.10.96 Lee Simpkin W PTS 6 Bradford
09.12.96 Roy Chipperfield W PTS 6 Bradford
17.02.97 Mike Thompson W PTS 6 Bradford
14.04.97 Raziq Ali L PTS 6 Bradford
09.06.97 Lee Simpkin W PTS 6 Bradford
Career: 5 contests, won 4, lost 1.

Fred Reeve
Hull. *Born* Hull, 14 April, 1969
S. Featherweight. Ht. 5'5½"
Manager Self

09.11.92 Tim Hill L CO 4 Bradford
14.12.92 Leo Turner L RSC 2 Bradford
19.03.93 Kevin Haidarah W RSC 2 Manchester
29.04.93 Marty Chestnut W PTS 6 Hull
07.10.93 Chip O'Neill L RSC 2 Hull
03.03.94 Ian Richardson L PTS 6 Newcastle
28.03.94 Dougie Fox W RSC 2 Cleethorpes
28.04.94 Ian Richardson L RSC 2 Hull
26.09.94 Jobie Tyers L PTS 6 Bradford
22.11.94 Tony Falcone L PTS 6 Bristol
07.12.94 Robert Grubb W RSC 3 Stoke
18.12.94 Brian Carr L CO 2 Glasgow
11.02.95 Stephen Smith L CO 1 Frankfurt, Germany
06.07.95 Paul Goode W RSC 2 Hull
05.10.95 Colin Innes W PTS 6 Hull
20.10.95 G. G. Goddard L PTS 6 Mansfield
07.12.95 Chris Lyons W PTS 6 Hull
06.03.96 Miguel Matthews L PTS 6 Solihull
09.04.96 Richard Evatt L RSC 1 Stevenage
17.05.96 Jason Squire DREW 6 Hull
20.09.96 Brian Carr L RSC 3 Glasgow
23.10.96 Byron Pryce L RSC 1 Halifax
03.12.96 Andy Green L CO 2 Yarm
Career: 23 contests, won 7, drew 1, lost 15.

Fred Reeve　　　　　　　　Les Clark

Pele Reid
Birmingham. *Born* Birmingham, 11 January, 1973
WBO Inter-Continental Heavyweight Champion. Ht. 6'3"
Manager B. Ingle/F. Warren

24.11.95 Gary Williams W RSC 1 Manchester
20.01.96 Joey Paladino W RSC 1 Mansfield
26.01.96 Vance Idiens W RSC 1 Brighton
11.05.96 Keith Fletcher W CO 1 Bethnal Green
25.06.96 Andy Lambert W CO 1 Mansfield
12.10.96 Eduardo Carranza W CO 2 Milan, Italy
02.11.96 Ricky Sullivan W RSC 2 Garmisch, Germany
25.02.97 Michael Murray W RSC 1 Sheffield
28.06.97 Ricardo Kennedy W RSC 1 Norwich
(Vacant WBO Inter-Continental Heavyweight Title)
Career: 9 contests, won 9.

Martin Renaghan
Keady. *Born* Craigavon, 12 October, 1974
Lightweight. Ht. 5'7"
Manager F. Warren

31.08.96 Andy Martin W RSC 2 Dublin
25.02.97 Simon Frailing W RSC 3 Sheffield
Career: 2 contests, won 2.

Gary Reyniers　　　　　　　　Les Clark

Gary Reyniers
Greenford. *Born* Hammersmith, 28 November, 1970
S. Middleweight. Ht. 6'2"
Manager D. Currivan

20.09.96 Dennis Doyley L RSC 2 Tooting
07.11.96 Simon Andrews DREW 6 Battersea
20.03.97 Edwin Cleary L PTS 6 Newark
Career: 3 contests, drew 1, lost 2.

Lewis Reynolds
Canning Town. *Born* Hatfield, 25 February, 1970
Lightweight. Ht. 5'8"
Manager D. Powell/F. Maloney

29.09.94 Andrew Reed W PTS 4 Bethnal Green
18.11.94 Jason Hutson L RSC 3 Bracknell
25.03.95 Vince Burns W RSC 4 Millwall
25.05.95 Simon Frailing W CO 1 Reading
16.06.95 Wayne Jones W PTS 4 Southwark
17.11.95 Simon Ford W RSC 3 Bethnal Green
25.06.96 Dean Pithie L RSC 2 Mansfield
27.11.96 Tommy Janes W RSC 1 Swansea
24.04.97 Colin Dunne L CO 4 Mayfair
(Southern Area Lightweight Title Challenge)
Career: 9 contests, won 6, lost 3.

Mark Reynolds
Sudbury. *Born* Sudbury, 27 July, 1969
Southern Area Flyweight Champion. Ht. 5'5½"
Manager F. Maloney

24.09.94 Shaun Norman W PTS 4 Wembley
12.11.94 Vince Feeney L PTS 6 Dublin
07.02.95 Danny Lawson W PTS 4 Ipswich
17.05.95 Neil Parry W PTS 6 Ipswich
04.06.95 Anthony Hanna W PTS 10 Bethnal Green
(Elim. British Flyweight Title)
14.09.95 Tiger Singh W RSC 3 Battersea
20.10.95 Ricky Beard W PTS 10 Ipswich
(Southern Area Flyweight Title Challenge)
15.12.95 Mzukisi Skali L RSC 2 Bethnal Green
(WBC International L. Flyweight Title Challenge)
21.03.96 Rowan Williams DREW 6 Southwark
09.07.96 Brendan Bryce W PTS 4 Bethnal Green
11.12.96 Anthony Hanna DREW 8 Southwark
08.05.97 Steve Williams W RTD 6 Mansfield
(Elim. British Flyweight Title)
27.05.97 Ady Lewis L PTS 12 Mayfair
(British Flyweight Title Challenge)
Career: 13 contests, won 8, drew 2, lost 3.

George Richards
Birmingham. *Born* Birmingham, 19 December, 1967
L. Middleweight. Ht. 5'9"
Manager P. Cowdell/R. Gray

06.12.95 Ozzy Orrocks W RSC 3 Stoke
17.01.96 Adam Baldwin W PTS 6 Solihull
13.02.96 Donovan Davey W PTS 6 Wolverhampton
22.02.96 Paul Murray W PTS 6 Walsall
06.03.96 Donovan Davey W PTS 6 Solihull
26.03.96 George Wilson W PTS 8 Wolverhampton
04.05.96 Steve Roberts L PTS 6 Dagenham
09.10.96 James McGee W PTS 6 Stoke
24.10.96 Prince Kasi Kaihau W PTS 6 Birmingham
26.11.96 Michael Alexander L PTS 8 Wolverhampton
16.01.97 Prince Kasi Kaihau W PTS 8 Solihull
03.03.97 Michael Alexander W PTS 8 Birmingham
25.03.97 David Bain W PTS 6 Wolverhampton
12.04.97 Jim Rock L PTS 6 Sheffield
22.05.97 Dave Andrews W PTS 6 Solihull
Career: 15 contests, won 12, lost 3.

Mark Richards

Wednesbury. *Born* Wednesbury, 30 March, 1972
Lightweight. Ht. 5'9"
Manager D. Bradley

01.10.96	Craig Hartwell W PTS 6 Birmingham
12.11.96	Marc Smith W PTS 6 Dudley
22.03.97	Mark Haslam DREW 4 Wythenshawe
19.04.97	Mark McGowan L PTS 6 Plymouth

Career: 4 contests, won 2, drew 1, lost 1.

(Mark) Liam Richardson

Wakefield. *Born* Barnsley, 15 December, 1967
L. Heavyweight. Ht. 6'1"
Manager C. Aston

17.03.97	Danny Southern L RSC 5 Glasgow
19.06.97	Lee Swaby L RSC 4 Scunthorpe

Career: 2 contests, lost 2.

Peter Richardson

Middlesbrough. *Born* Middlesbrough, 24 June, 1970
L. Welterweight. Ht. 5'9¼"
Manager F. Maloney

23.02.95	John O. Johnson W RSC 5 Southwark
27.04.95	Carl Roberts W RSC 1 Bethnal Green
25.05.95	Everald Williams W RSC 6 Reading
02.07.95	John Smith W PTS 6 Dublin
29.09.95	Tony Foster W RSC 1 Bethnal Green
15.12.95	Karl Taylor W PTS 8 Bethnal Green
19.01.96	Steve Pollard W PTS 8 Bracknell
21.03.96	Adrian Chase W RSC 2 Southwark
14.05.96	Trevor Meikle W RSC 2 Dagenham
29.06.96	Kevin McKillan W CO 2 Erith
07.10.96	Rimvidas Billius L RSC 6 Lewisham
11.01.97	Rimvidas Billius W PTS 10 Bethnal Green
01.03.97	John Smith W RSC 5 Liverpool
20.05.97	Mark Ramsey W PTS 8 Edmonton

Career: 14 contests, won 13, lost 1.

Wayne Rigby

Manchester. *Born* Manchester, 19 July, 1973
Central Area Lightweight Champion. Ht. 5'6"
Manager J. Trickett

27.02.92	Lee Fox L PTS 6 Liverpool
08.06.92	Leo Turner W PTS 6 Bradford
02.07.92	Leo Turner W CO 5 Middleton
05.10.92	Colin Innes W PTS 6 Manchester
01.12.92	John T. Kelly L PTS 6 Hartlepool
02.06.94	Kid McAuley W PTS 6 Middleton
13.06.94	Chris Clarkson W PTS 6 Liverpool
22.09.94	Mark Hargreaves W PTS 6 Bury
06.03.95	Kelton McKenzie L PTS 8 Leicester
18.05.95	John T. Kelly W PTS 6 Middleton
05.06.95	Hugh Collins W RSC 4 Glasgow
17.01.96	Kid McAuley W PTS 6 Solihull
24.03.96	Steve Tuckett W PTS 6 Shaw
27.09.96	Jimmy Phelan W PTS 10 Hull
	(Central Area Lightweight Title Challenge)
07.03.97	Alan Bosworth W RSC 5 Northampton

Career: 15 contests, won 12, lost 3.

Stuart Rimmer

St Helens. *Born* St Helens, 22 April, 1971
Lightweight. Ht. 5'6"
Manager P. Dwyer

13.02.90	Dave Croft W PTS 6 Wolverhampton
07.03.90	Mark Antony L RSC 1 Doncaster
23.04.90	Dave Croft W CO 2 Birmingham
01.05.90	Neil Foran L RSC 2 Oldham
04.06.90	Frankie Foster L PTS 6 Glasgow
27.06.90	Bernard McComiskey L PTS 6 Kensington
12.09.90	Steve Griffith W RSC 2 Bethnal Green
27.09.90	Andrew Morgan W PTS 6 Birmingham
09.10.90	Jim Lawler W CO 2 Wolverhampton
29.10.90	Tony Feliciello L RSC 5 Birmingham
27.11.90	Alan Peacock L RSC 4 Glasgow
12.02.91	Andrew Morgan L PTS 8 Wolverhampton
24.04.91	Steve Winstanley L PTS 6 Preston
04.06.91	Michael Ayers L CO 1 Bethnal Green
10.09.91	Shaun Cooper L RSC 2 Wolverhampton
27.03.96	Wayne Pardoe L RSC 3 Stoke
02.10.96	Vic Broomhead W CO 5 Stoke
29.11.96	Rocky Ferrari W RSC 5 Glasgow
04.12.96	David Kirk L PTS 6 Stoke

Career: 19 contests, won 7, lost 12.

Brian Robb

Telford. *Born* Liverpool, 5 April, 1967
S. Featherweight. Ht. 5'6"
Manager Self

14.02.89	Miguel Matthews L RSC 2 Wolverhampton
27.03.90	Neil Leitch W PTS 6 Wolverhampton
09.05.90	Peter Judson L PTS 6 Solihull
22.05.90	Nicky Lucas W PTS 6 Canvey Island
20.06.90	Paul Harvey L PTS 6 Basildon
09.10.90	Des Gargano W PTS 6 Wolverhampton
24.10.90	Paul Harvey L RSC 2 Dudley
23.01.91	Jason Primera L RSC 7 Solihull
04.03.91	Pete Buckley L RSC 7 Birmingham
05.06.91	Pete Buckley L PTS 10 Wolverhampton
	(Vacant Midlands Area S. Featherweight Title)
29.08.91	Renny Edwards W PTS 6 Oakengates
31.10.91	Miguel Matthews DREW 6 Oakengates
05.12.91	Neil Leitch W CO 2 Oakengates
20.02.92	Pete Buckley L RSC 10 Oakengates
	(Midlands Area S. Featherweight Title Challenge)
26.03.92	Kelton McKenzie L RSC 4 Telford
13.10.92	Paul Harvey L RSC 2 Mayfair
04.12.92	Kevin Middleton L RSC 1 Telford
22.02.95	Andrew Smith W PTS 6 Telford
21.04.95	Andrew Smith DREW 6 Dudley
23.06.95	Chris Francis L RSC 1 Bethnal Green
25.10.95	Robert Grubb W PTS 6 Telford
11.11.95	Jason Blanche L RSC 4 Halifax
31.01.96	Chris Lyons W PTS 6 Birmingham
05.03.96	Jay Levy W RTD 3 Bethnal Green
22.06.96	Stephen Smith L RSC 4 Dortmund, Germany
03.09.96	Paul Ingle L RSC 2 Bethnal Green
11.10.96	Jason Cook L RSC 2 Mayfair
27.11.96	Richard Evatt L RSC 2 Bethnal Green
08.03.97	Richard Evatt L CO 3 Brentwood

Career: 29 contests, won 9, drew 2, lost 18.

Andy Roberts

Doncaster. *Born* Doncaster, 4 March, 1976
Central Area Bantamweight Champion. Ht. 5'3"
Manager J. Rushton

20.10.94	Robert Grubb DREW 6 Walsall
12.12.94	Jason Morris W PTS 6 Doncaster
09.02.95	Robert Grubb DREW 6 Doncaster
22.03.95	Michael Edwards L PTS 6 Stoke
06.04.95	Steve Williams L PTS 6 Sheffield
05.05.95	Jason Morris W PTS 6 Doncaster
22.06.95	Paul Quarmby L PTS 6 Houghton le Spring
30.06.95	Stefy Bull L PTS 4 Doncaster
17.10.95	Robert Grubb L PTS 6 Wolverhampton
08.11.95	Graham McGrath W PTS 6 Scunthorpe
28.11.95	Graham McGrath L PTS 6 Wolverhampton
26.01.96	Darren Greaves W RSC 5 Doncaster
29.03.96	Graham McGrath L PTS 6 Doncaster
20.05.96	Neil Parry L PTS 6 Bradford
24.06.96	Neil Parry L PTS 6 Bradford
12.09.96	Steve Williams L PTS 6 Doncaster
23.09.96	Willie Smith W RSC 4 Bradford
03.10.96	Chip O'Neill W PTS 6 Sunderland
17.12.96	Neil Parry DREW 6 Doncaster
20.03.97	Marcus Duncan W PTS 10 Doncaster
	(Central Area Bantamweight Title Challenge)

Career: 20 contests, won 7, drew 3, lost 10.

Dewi Roberts

Dolgellau. *Born* Bangor, 11 September, 1968
Welterweight. Ht. 5'10"
Manager Self

28.11.91	Gavin Lane L PTS 6 Evesham
11.02.92	Edward Lloyd L RSC 1 Cardiff
11.05.92	Nigel Burder W CO 3 Llanelli
22.11.93	Steve McLevy L RSC 1 Glasgow
24.02.94	Paul Robinson W RSC 6 Walsall
04.03.94	Jason Rowland L RSC 1 Bethnal Green
17.06.94	Paul Dyer L PTS 6 Plymouth
25.06.94	Carl van Bailey W RSC 2 Cullompton
02.09.94	Keith Marner L PTS 6 Spitalfields
17.09.94	Paul Knights L PTS 6 Crawley
25.10.94	Everald Williams L PTS 6 Southwark
09.11.94	Jason Beard L RSC 4 Millwall
17.02.95	Georgie Smith L RSC 2 Crawley
05.10.95	Paul Salmon W PTS 6 Queensferry
20.10.95	Gary Beardsley L PTS 6 Mansfield
22.11.95	Dave Fallon DREW 6 Mayfair
01.05.97	Hughie Davey L PTS 6 Newcastle
21.06.97	Jason Williams L RSC 1 Cardiff

Career: 18 contests, won 4, drew 1, lost 13.

Steve Roberts

West Ham. *Born* Newham, 3 December, 1972
Southern Area L. Middleweight Champion. Ht. 5'11"
Manager B. Hearn

16.03.95	Julian Eavis W PTS 6 Basildon
23.05.95	Andy Peach W RSC 3 Potters Bar
13.06.95	Robbie Dunn W RSC 3 Basildon
20.09.95	Jason Hart W RSC 5 Potters Bar
30.09.95	Dick Hanns-Kat W CO 1 Basildon
25.11.95	Ernie Loveridge W PTS 4 Dagenham
23.01.96	Andrew Jervis W PTS 6 Bethnal Green
20.04.96	Peter Vosper W PTS 6 Brentwood

04.05.96 George Richards W PTS 6 Dagenham
27.09.96 Rob Stevenson W PTS 6 Stevenage
27.11.96 Lindon Scarlett W PTS 6 Bethnal Green
08.03.97 Adan Lugo W CO 4 Brentwood
08.04.97 Gilbert Jackson W PTS 10 Bethnal Green
(Vacant Southern Area L. Middleweight Title)
Career: 13 contests, won 13.

Andrew Robinson
Dudley. *Born* Birmingham, 6 November, 1965
S. Featherweight. Ht. 5'6"
Manager Self

14.06.88 Darryl Pettit DREW 6 Birmingham
29.09.88 Darryl Pettit W PTS 6 Stafford
17.10.88 Sean Hogg L PTS 6 Birmingham
01.12.88 Mark Antony L PTS 6 Stafford
12.12.88 Peter Bowen L CO 4 Birmingham
15.03.89 Phil Lashley W PTS 6 Stoke
10.10.89 Jamie Morris W PTS 6 Wolverhampton
07.03.90 Dean Bramhald W PTS 6 Doncaster
19.03.90 Peter Judson L PTS 6 Cleethorpes
11.04.90 Tony Silkstone L PTS 6 Dewsbury
26.04.90 Tony Silkstone L PTS 6 Halifax
30.05.90 Kruga Hydes L PTS 6 Stoke
21.06.90 Mark Antony L PTS 6 Alfreton
10.07.90 Bradley Stone L PTS 6 Canvey Island
27.09.90 Elvis Parsley L RTD 3 Birmingham
24.10.90 Richard Woolgar L RSC 3 Dudley
26.11.90 Sugar Free Somerville W PTS 6 Bethnal Green
15.04.91 Finn McCool DREW 6 Leicester
13.05.91 Dean Bramhald W RTD 1 Birmingham
16.05.91 Craig Dermody L PTS 6 Liverpool
29.04.92 Lee Fox L PTS 6 Stoke
04.12.95 Graham McGrath W PTS 6 Birmingham
17.01.96 Carl Allen W PTS 6 Solihull
30.01.96 Chris Francis L PTS 6 Barking
21.02.96 Thomas Padgett W PTS 6 Batley
25.10.96 Mark Haslam L RTD 4 Mere
02.12.96 Norman Dhalie L PTS 6 Birmingham
17.12.96 Richard Evatt L RSC 2 Doncaster
20.05.97 Tontcho Tontchev L RSC 2 Edmonton
Career: 29 contests, won 9, drew 2, lost 18.

(Edwin) Ed Robinson
Reading. *Born* Taplow, 21 October, 1971
L. Middleweight. Ht. 5'11"
Manager F. Maloney

02.04.96 Lee Simpkin W PTS 4 Southwark
04.03.97 Alvar Coppard L RSC 1 Southwark
Career: 2 contests, won 1, lost 1.

Jamie Robinson
West Ham. *Born* London, 12 September, 1968
L. Middleweight. Ht. 5'9"
Manager F. Maloney

17.08.90 Duke de Palma W PTS 4 Las Vegas, USA
04.10.90 Rodney Knox L RSC 1 Atlantic City, USA
23.10.91 Dave Whittle W RSC 4 Bethnal Green
13.11.91 Michael Oliver W PTS 6 Bethnal Green
11.02.92 Julian Eavis W PTS 6 Barking
02.04.92 Mark Jay W PTS 6 Basildon

22.10.92 Gary Pemberton W RSC 3 Bethnal Green
17.12.92 Lee Crocker W RTD 2 Barking
27.02.93 Russell Washer W PTS 6 Dagenham
31.03.93 John Duckworth W RSC 3 Barking
10.11.93 Stuart Dunn W PTS 6 Bethnal Green
17.02.94 Steve Scott W CO 2 Dagenham
21.09.94 Russell Washer L PTS 6 Cardiff
11.01.97 Wayne Appleton DREW 4 Bethnal Green
20.05.97 Anthony McFadden L PTS 8 Edmonton
Career: 15 contests, won 11, drew 1, lost 3.

Steve Robinson
Cardiff. *Born* Cardiff, 13 December, 1968
WBO Inter-Continental Featherweight Champion. Former WBO Featherweight Champion. Former Undefeated WBA Penta-Continental & Welsh Featherweight Champion. Ht. 5'8"
Manager D. Gardiner

01.03.89 Alan Roberts W PTS 6 Cardiff
13.03.89 Terry Smith W RTD 4 Piccadilly
06.04.89 Nicky Lucas L PTS 8 Cardiff
04.05.89 John Devine W PTS 6 Mayfair
19.08.89 Marcel Herbert L PTS 6 Cardiff
13.11.89 Shane Silvester W RSC 2 Brierley Hill
10.07.90 Mark Bates L PTS 6 Canvey Island
12.09.90 Tim Driscoll L PTS 8 Bethnal Green
26.09.90 Russell Davison W PTS 8 Manchester
03.10.90 Drew Docherty L PTS 8 Solihull
22.10.90 Alan McKay L PTS 6 Mayfair
19.11.90 Neil Haddock W RSC 9 Cardiff
19.12.90 Brian Roche DREW 6 Preston
24.04.91 Russell Davison W RTD 6 Preston
28.05.91 Colin Lynch W RSC 6 Cardiff
18.07.91 Peter Harris W PTS 10 Cardiff
(Welsh Featherweight Title Challenge)
31.01.92 Henry Armstrong L PTS 6 Manchester
11.05.92 Neil Haddock L PTS 10 Llanelli
(Vacant Welsh S. Featherweight Title)
07.10.92 Edward Lloyd W RTD 8 Barry
30.10.92 Stephane Haccoun W PTS 8 Istres, France
01.12.92 Dennis Oakes W RTD 2 Liverpool
19.01.93 Paul Harvey W PTS 12 Cardiff
(Vacant WBA Penta-Continental Featherweight Title)
13.02.93 Medhi Labdouni L PTS 8 Paris, France
17.04.93 John Davison W PTS 12 Washington
(Vacant WBO Featherweight Title)
10.07.93 Sean Murphy W CO 9 Cardiff
(WBO Featherweight Title Defence)
23.10.93 Colin McMillan W PTS 12 Cardiff
(WBO Featherweight Title Defence)
12.03.94 Paul Hodkinson W CO 12 Cardiff
(WBO Featherweight Title Defence)
04.06.94 Freddy Cruz W PTS 12 Cardiff
(WBO Featherweight Title Defence)
01.10.94 Duke McKenzie W CO 9 Cardiff
(WBO Featherweight Title Defence)
04.02.95 Domingo Damigella W PTS 12 Cardiff
(WBO Featherweight Title Defence)
07.07.95 Pedro Ferradas W RSC 9 Cardiff
(WBO Featherweight Title Defence)
30.09.95 Prince Naseem Hamed L RSC 8 Cardiff
(WBO Featherweight Title Defence)
18.09.96 Kelton McKenzie W PTS 8 Tylorstown
03.02.97 Billy Hardy L PTS 12 Sunderland
(European Featherweight Title Challenge)

08.03.97 Tomas Serrano W CO 1 Brentwood
(Vacant WBO Inter-Continental Featherweight Title)
08.05.97 Julio Cesar Sanchez W CO 7 Mansfield
(WBO Inter-Continental Featherweight Title Defence)
Career: 36 contests, won 24, drew 1, lost 11.

Steve Robinson   Les Clark

Derek Roche
Leeds. *Born* New Ross, 19 July 1972
Central Area Welterweight Champion. Ht. 5'9"
Manager J. Celebanski

26.09.94 Michael Alexander W RSC 6 Bradford
05.12.94 Shamus Casey W PTS 6 Bradford
30.01.95 Carl Smith W RSC 3 Bradford
23.02.95 Charlie Paine W CO 1 Hull
25.03.95 Rob Stevenson W PTS 6 Rothwell
12.06.95 Paul King W PTS 6 Bradford
25.09.95 Hughie Davey W PTS 6 Bradford
11.11.95 Rick North W RSC 2 Halifax
11.12.95 Kevin McKenzie W RSC 3 Bradford
13.01.96 Shamus Casey W PTS 6 Halifax
07.03.96 Wayne Shepherd W RSC 3 Bradford
23.09.96 Trevor Meikle W PTS 10 Bradford
(Central Area Welterweight Title Challenge)
23.10.96 Paul Miles W RSC 2 Halifax
09.12.96 Gary Beardsley W RSC 2 Bradford
17.02.97 Michael Alexander W DIS 4 Bradford
09.06.97 Chris Saunders W RSC 4 Bradford
(Central Area Welterweight Title Defence. Elim. British Welterweight Title)
Career: 16 contests, won 16.

Jim Rock
Dublin. *Born* Dublin, 12 March, 1972
L. Middleweight. Ht. 5'11"
Manager M. O'Callaghan

25.11.95 Craig Lynch W PTS 4 Dublin
09.03.96 Peter Mitchell W PTS 6 Millstreet

03.09.96 Rob Stevenson W PTS 6 Belfast
05.11.96 Danny Quacoe W RSC 4 Belfast
28.01.97 Roy Chipperfield W RTD 2 Belfast
12.04.97 George Richards W PTS 6 Sheffield
Career: 6 contests, won 6.

Vince Rose
Tottenham. *Born* London, 9 July, 1968
L. Middleweight. Ht. 5'8"
Manager B. Hearn

13.10.92 Ojay Abrahams W RSC 3 Mayfair
14.11.92 Marty Duke W PTS 6 Cardiff
30.01.93 Ojay Abrahams DREW 6 Brentwood
11.05.93 Gary Pemberton W PTS 6 Norwich
11.01.94 Warren Stephens W PTS 6 Bethnal
Green
09.02.94 Ojay Abrahams L PTS 6 Brentwood
28.06.94 Said Bennajem L PTS 6 Mayfair
27.08.94 Matthew Turner L RSC 4 Cardiff
07.11.94 Dennis Berry W PTS 6 Bethnal Green
21.02.95 Dave Johnson L PTS 8 Sunderland
14.04.95 Danny Juma L RSC 3 Belfast
23.06.95 Nicky Thurbin L PTS 10 Bethnal
Green
*(Vacant Southern Area L. Middleweight
Title)*
16.10.95 Ernie Loveridge W PTS 4 Heybridge
17.11.95 Joni Nyman DREW 8 Helsinki,
Finland
09.04.96 Geoff McCreesh L RSC 4 Stevenage
06.11.96 Dennis Berry L RSC 3 Hull
Career: 16 contests, won 7, drew 2, lost 7.

Andy Ross
Denbigh. *Born* Stoke, 30 November, 1974
S. Featherweight. Ht. 5'6¾"
Manager R. Jones

04.10.96 Keith Jones DREW 6 Pentre Halkyn
31.01.96 Nigel Leake L PTS 6 Pentre Halkyn
19.06.97 Gary Jenkinson L PTS 6 Scunthorpe
Career: 3 contests, drew 1, lost 2.

Jason Rowland
West Ham. *Born* London, 6 August, 1970
L. Welterweight. Ht. 5'9¾"
Manager F. Warren

19.09.89 Terry Smith W RSC 1 Millwall
15.11.89 Mike Morrison W PTS 6 Reading
14.02.90 Eamonn Payne W PTS 6 Millwall
17.04.90 Dave Jenkins W CO 1 Millwall
22.05.90 Mike Morrison W PTS 6 St Albans
12.02.91 Vaughan Carnegie W PTS 6 Basildon
07.03.91 Vaughan Carnegie W CO 2 Basildon
11.12.91 Brian Cullen W RSC 4 Basildon
30.04.92 Steve Pollard W RSC 2 Kensington
17.12.92 Jimmy Vincent W PTS 6 Wembley
10.02.93 Seth Jones W RSC 2 Lewisham
18.03.93 John Smith W PTS 6 Lewisham
04.03.94 Dewi Roberts W RSC 1 Bethnal Green
26.04.94 Ray Hood W CO 1 Bethnal Green
12.09.94 Steve Burton W RSC 1 Mayfair
11.10.94 Phil Found W RSC 4 Bethnal Green
09.11.94 Floyd Churchill W RSC 2 Millwall
09.12.94 Richard Swallow W RSC 2 Bethnal
Green
03.03.95 Nigel Bradley W RSC 3 Bethnal Green
29.11.95 Bernard Paul L CO 1 Bethnal Green
*(Southern Area L. Welterweight Title
Challenge. Elim. British
L. Welterweight Title)*
27.03.97 Kevin McKillan W PTS 8 Norwich
Career: 21 contests, won 20, lost 1.

Jason Rowland   Tony Fitch

Danny Ruegg   Les Clark

Danny Ruegg
Bournemouth. *Born* Poole, 28 November,
1974
Western Area S. Bantamweight Champion.
Ht. 5'5"
Manager J. Bishop

30.09.93 Johnny Simpson L PTS 6 Hayes
17.02.94 Paul Webster L PTS 4 Dagenham
04.03.94 Darren Greaves L PTS 6 Weston super
Mare
17.06.94 Danny Lawson L PTS 6 Plymouth
25.10.94 Jon Pegg W PTS 6 Edgbaston
16.11.94 Chris Lyons W PTS 6 Bloomsbury
18.02.95 Tony Falcone L PTS 10 Shepton
Mallet
*(Vacant Western Area S. Bantamweight
Title)*
13.05.95 James Murray L PTS 6 Glasgow
10.06.95 Michael Gomez L PTS 4 Manchester
02.10.95 Richard Vowles L PTS 4 Mayfair
24.11.95 Michael Gomez W PTS 4 Manchester
21.03.96 Patrick Mullings L RSC 3 Southwark
03.09.96 Tommy Waite L RSC 4 Belfast

18.10.96 Tony Falcone W PTS 10 Barnstaple
(*Western Area S. Bantamweight Title
Challenge*)
26.11.96 Carl Greaves L RTD 4 Sheffield
18.01.97 Clinton Beeby W RSC 2 Swadlincote
29.04.97 Paul Ireland L RSC 6 Belfast
Career: 17 contests, won 5, lost 12.

Charlie Rumbol
Camberwell. *Born* Lambeth, 24 November,
1977
Featherweight. Ht. 5'6½"
Manager Self

03.04.96 Robert Grubb W PTS 6 Bethnal Green
10.05.96 Lee Armstrong L PTS 6 Wembley
03.07.96 Martin Evans W PTS 6 Wembley
24.10.96 Simon Frailing L PTS 6 Wembley
11.02.97 Nigel Leake L RSC 3 Bethnal Green
Career: 5 contests, won 2, lost 3.

Brendan Ryan
Nottingham. *Born* Nottingham, 2
November, 1970
L. Middleweight. Ht. 5'9¼"
Manager M. Shinfield

06.03.89 Andy Rowbotham W RSC 2 Leicester
20.03.89 Pete Roberts W PTS 6 Nottingham
08.05.89 Andy Sweeney W PTS 6 Leicester
15.05.89 Andy Kent W PTS 6 Northampton
22.05.89 Andy Kent W PTS 6 Peterborough
05.06.89 John Ritchie L PTS 6 Glasgow
25.09.89 Lyn Davies L RSC 2 Leicester
20.11.89 Mick Mulcahy W PTS 6 Leicester
04.12.89 Wayne Windle DREW 6 Manchester
11.12.89 Paul Bowen W PTS 6 Nottingham
24.01.90 Brian Cullen L PTS 8 Stoke
05.02.90 Oliver Henry DREW 6 Leicester
19.02.90 Brian Cullen W PTS 8 Nottingham
26.02.90 James Jiora L PTS 6 Bradford
19.03.90 John Smith W PTS 6 Leicester
10.04.90 Mark Kelly L PTS 6 Doncaster
23.04.90 Pete Roberts W PTS 6 Bradford
14.05.90 Vaughan Carnegie L PTS 6 Leicester
21.05.90 Dean Bramhald DREW 6 Cleethorpes
04.06.90 Malcolm Melvin W RSC 7 Edgbaston
17.09.90 John Townsley DREW 8 Glasgow
13.11.90 Malcolm Melvin W PTS 10 Edgbaston
(*Vacant Midlands Area
L. Welterweight Title*)
24.04.91 Richard Joyce L PTS 8 Stoke
14.05.92 Carl Wright L PTS 4 Liverpool
16.06.92 Bernard Paul L CO 6 Dagenham
10.11.95 Steve Goodwin W RSC 4 Derby
29.11.95 Howard Eastman L RSC 2 Bethnal
Green
13.07.96 Kevin Adamson L RSC 2 Bethnal
Green
Career: 28 contests, won 12, drew 4, lost 12.

Danny Ryan
Donegal. *Born* Glasgow, 6 March, 1973
Middleweight. Ht. 5'10"
Manager B. Hearn

06.05.95 Paul Matthews W PTS 6 Shepton
Mallet
02.06.95 Peter Mitchell W PTS 6 Bethnal Green
09.09.95 Stinger Mason W PTS 6 Cork
25.11.95 Mark Dawson W PTS 4 Dublin
09.03.96 Marvin O'Brien W PTS 4 Millstreet

13.04.96 Michael Bowen L RSC 2
Wythenshawe
19.10.96 Jason Matthews L CO 5 Bristol
29.04.97 Peter Mitchell DREW 6 Belfast
02.06.97 Danny Juma W PTS 6 Belfast
Career: 9 contests, won 6, drew 1, lost 2.

Paul Ryan
Hackney. *Born* South Ockenham, 2
February, 1965
Welterweight. Former British &
Commonwealth L. Welterweight
Champion. Former Undefeated WBO Inter-
Continental L. Welterweight Champion.
Ht. 5'8"
Manager F. Warren

26.09.91 Chris Mylan W PTS 6 Dunstable
18.01.92 Alex Sterling W RSC 4 Kensington
25.03.92 Michael Clynch W RSC 4 Dagenham
16.05.92 Greg Egbuniwe W RSC 4 Muswell Hill
26.09.92 Korso Aleain W CO 4 Earls Court
17.12.92 Rick Bushell W RSC 1 Barking
03.02.93 Neil Smith W RSC 1 Earls Court
27.02.93 Mike Morrison W PTS 6 Dagenham
15.09.93 Shaun Cogan W RSC 3 Ashford
10.11.93 Steve Phillips W RSC 3 Bethnal Green
17.02.94 Rob Stewart W RSC 4 Dagenham
09.04.94 Carl Wright W RSC 8 Mansfield
17.08.94 John Smith W RTD 2 Sheffield
10.09.94 Dave Lovell W RSC 3 Birmingham
09.11.94 Massimo Bertozzi W RSC 2 San
Remo, Italy
04.02.95 George Wilson W RSC 4 Cardiff
25.02.95 Paul Denton W RSC 4 Millwall
13.05.95 Jorge Aquino W RSC 4 Glasgow
01.07.95 Oscar Palomino W RSC 8 Kensington
(*Vacant WBO Inter-Continental
L. Welterweight Title*)
02.09.95 Karl Taylor W RSC 3 Wembley
21.10.95 Eric Jakubowski W RSC 3 Bethnal
Green
(*WBO Inter-Continental L.
Welterweight Title Defence*)
09.12.95 Ross Hale W CO 1 Bethnal Green
(*British & Commonwealth L.
Welterweight Title Challenge. WBO
Inter-Continental L. Welterweight Title
Defence*)
13.02.96 Jonathan Thaxton L RSC 1 Bethnal
Green
13.07.96 Andy Holligan L CO 1 Bethnal Green
(*British & Commonwealth
L. Welterweight Title Defence*)
26.04.96 Michael Monaghan W RSC 2
Swadlincote
29.05.97 Ojay Abrahams W RSC 3 Mayfair
Career: 26 contests, won 24, lost 2.

Ricky Sackfield
Salford. *Born* Birmingham, 11 April, 1967
Welterweight. Ht. 5'7"
Managers F. Warren/N. Basso

30.04.91 Willie Yeardsley W PTS 4 Stockport
19.09.91 Seth Jones W RSC 1 Stockport
21.10.91 Rob Stewart L PTS 6 Bury
21.01.92 David Thompson W CO 1 Stockport
03.02.92 Scott Doyle W PTS 6 Manchester
09.03.92 John O. Johnson L PTS 6 Manchester
31.03.92 Carl Wright L RSC 1 Stockport
24.09.92 Mark Legg L PTS 6 Stockport
15.02.93 Robert Lloyd W RSC 4 Manchester

26.03.93 Soren Sondergaard L RSC 2
Copenhagen, Denmark
12.06.95 Wayne Windle W PTS 6 Manchester
13.01.96 John O. Johnson W PTS 6 Manchester
13.04.96 John Smith W PTS 4 Wythenshawe
22.08.96 Steve Howden L PTS 6 Salford
19.09.96 Brian Coleman L RSC 3 Manchester
Career: 15 contests, won 8, lost 7.

Paul Salmon
Plymouth. *Born* Plymouth, 27 March, 1971
L. Welterweight. Ht. 5'9½"
Manager Self

12.10.94 Anthony Huw Williams L RSC 4
Sheffield
18.11.94 Dennis Gardner L RSC 1 Bracknell
24.02.95 Billy McDougall W PTS 6 Weston
super Mare
28.04.95 Frank Olsen L RSC 2 Randers,
Denmark
05.10.95 Dewi Roberts L PTS 6 Queensferry
30.10.95 Nicky Bardle L CO 1 Heathrow
04.04.96 Dave Hinds W RTD 5 Plymouth
20.04.96 David Kehoe L PTS 6 Brentwood
16.05.96 Roger Hunte L RSC 5 Dunstable
14.09.96 James Hare L RSC 4 Sheffield
07.11.96 Pat Larner L PTS 6 Battersea
Career: 11 contests, won 2, lost 9.

Roger Sampson
Sheffield. *Born* Sheffield, 3 July, 1972
L. Welterweight. Ht. 5'7¼"
Manager G. Rhodes

26.06.97 Robbie Sivyer W PTS 6 Sheffield
Career: 1 contest, won 1.

Paul Samuels
Newport. *Born* Newport, 23 March, 1973
Welterweight. Ht. 6'0"
Manager F. Warren

11.11.95 Wayne Windle W RSC 2 Halifax
13.02.96 John Harrison W CO 1 Cardiff
05.03.96 Tom Welsh W RSC 3 Bethnal Green
13.03.96 Brian Coleman W PTS 6 Wembley
15.05.96 Gary Hiscox W RSC 3 Cardiff
12.11.96 Mark Ramsey W RSC 4 Dudley
21.06.97 Howard Clarke W PTS 8 Caridff
Career: 7 contests, won 7.

Sugar Raj Kumar Sangwan
Clapton. *Born* India, 20 August, 1969
Heavyweight. Ht. 6'2"
Manager F. Maloney

09.07.96 Gary Williams W PTS 4 Bethnal Green
Career: 1 contest, won 1.

Chris Saunders
Barnsley. *Born* Barnsley, 15 August, 1969
Former British Welterweight Champion.
Ht. 5'8"
Manager B. Ingle

22.02.90 Malcolm Melvin W PTS 4 Hull
10.04.90 Mike Morrison W PTS 6 Doncaster
20.05.90 Justin Graham W RSC 3 Sheffield
29.11.90 Ross Hale L PTS 6 Bayswater
05.03.91 Rocky Ferrari L PTS 4 Glasgow
19.03.91 Richard Woolgar W RSC 3 Leicester
26.03.91 Felix Kelly L PTS 6 Bethnal Green

17.04.91	Billy Schwer L RSC 1 Kensington
16.05.91	Richard Burton L PTS 6 Liverpool
06.06.91	Mark Tibbs W RSC 6 Barking
30.06.91	Billy Schwer L RSC 3 Southwark
01.08.91	James Jiora W PTS 6 Dewsbury
03.10.91	Gary Flear L PTS 6 Burton
24.10.91	Ron Shinkwin W PTS 6 Dunstable
21.11.91	J. P. Matthews L RSC 4 Burton
30.01.92	John O. Johnson L PTS 6 Southampton
11.02.92	Eddie King W RSC 4 Wolverhampton
27.02.92	Richard Burton L PTS 10 Liverpool
	(Vacant Central Area L. Welterweight Title)
09.09.92	John O. Johnson DREW 6 Stoke
01.10.92	Mark McCreath L RSC 4 Telford
01.12.92	Shea Neary L PTS 6 Liverpool
22.02.93	Cham Joof L PTS 4 Eltham
16.03.93	Mark Elliot L PTS 6 Wolverhampton
26.04.93	Dean Hollington W RSC 5 Lewisham
23.10.93	Michael Smyth L PTS 6 Cardiff
02.12.93	Rob Stewart L PTS 4 Sheffield
03.03.94	Kevin Lueshing W RSC 4 Ebbw Vale
04.06.94	Jose Varela W CO 2 Dortmund, Germany
26.08.94	Julian Eavis W PTS 6 Barnsley
26.09.94	Julian Eavis W PTS 6 Cleethorpes
26.10.94	Lindon Scarlett W PTS 8 Leeds
17.12.94	Roberto Welin W RSC 7 Cagliari, Italy
15.09.95	Del Bryan W PTS 12 Mansfield
	(British Welterweight Title Challenge)
13.02.96	Kevin Lueshing L RSC 3 Bethnal Green
	(British Welterweight Title Defence)
25.06.96	Michael Carruth L RSC 10 Mansfield
09.06.97	Derek Roche L RSC 4 Bradford
	(Central Area Welterweight Title Challenge. Elim. British Welterweight Title)

Career: 36 contests, won 16, drew 1, lost 19.

Mark Sawyers   Les Clark

Mark Sawyers

Cardiff. *Born* Bristol, 19 May, 1967
L. Middleweight. Ht. 5'8"
Manager D. Gardiner

11.02.97	Peter McCormack W RSC 2 Wolverhampton

07.03.97	Alex Mason L PTS 6 Weston super Mare
28.06.97	Spencer Fearon L PTS 4 Norwich

Career: 3 contests, won 1, lost 2.

Lindon Scarlett

Dudley. *Born* Dudley, 11 January, 1967
Former Undefeated Midlands Area
Welterweight Champion. Ht. 5'10"
Manager Self

22.04.87	Tommy Shiels L PTS 6 Kensington
07.05.87	Dusty Miller W PTS 6 Bayswater
09.11.87	Sean Heron L PTS 6 Glasgow
20.01.88	Simon Paul W PTS 6 Solihull
12.04.88	Ted Kershaw L RSC 7 Oldham
11.10.89	Carlo Colarusso W PTS 8 Stoke
22.11.89	Carlo Colarusso W PTS 8 Solihull
06.12.89	Julian Eavis W PTS 8 Stoke
14.02.90	Wayne Ellis DREW 6 Millwall
13.03.90	Romolo Casamonica L PTS 8 Milan, Italy
08.05.90	Mickey Lloyd L RSC 2 Brentford
18.10.90	Kevin Spratt W RSC 2 Birmingham
16.11.90	Tony Gibbs W PTS 6 Telford
19.03.91	Des Robinson W RSC 4 Birmingham
24.10.91	Razor Addo W PTS 8 Bayswater
22.01.92	Kelvin Mortimer W RSC 1 Solihull
08.02.92	Javier Castillejos L PTS 8 Madrid, Spain
23.05.92	Chris Peters DREW 8 Birmingham
15.02.93	Gordon Blair W CO 4 Mayfair
27.10.93	Chris Peters W PTS 8 West Bromwich
26.01.94	Rick North W RSC 6 Birmingham
	(Vacant Midlands Area Welterweight Title)
10.09.94	Del Bryan L PTS 12 Birmingham
	(British Welterweight Title Challenge)
26.10.94	Chris Saunders L PTS 8 Leeds
27.11.96	Steve Roberts L PTS 6 Bethnal Green
01.03.97	Dennis Berry W DIS 6 Liverpool
12.04.97	Ryan Rhodes L RSC 1 Sheffield
	(Vacant IBF Inter-Continental L. Middleweight Title)

Career: 26 contests, won 14, drew 2, lost 10.

Billy Schwer

Luton. *Born* Luton, 12 April, 1969
Former Commonwealth Lightweight
Champion. Former Undefeated British
Lightweight Champion. Ht. 5'8½"
Manager M. Duff

04.10.90	Pierre Conan W RSC 1 Bethnal Green
31.10.90	Mark Antony W RSC 2 Wembley
12.12.90	Sean Casey W RSC 1 Kensington
16.01.91	Dave Jenkins W PTS 6 Kensington
07.02.91	John Smith W RSC 2 Watford
06.03.91	Chubby Martin W RSC 3 Wembley
04.04.91	Andy Robins W RSC 2 Watford
17.04.91	Chris Saunders W RSC 1 Kensington
02.05.91	Karl Taylor W RSC 2 Northampton
30.06.91	Chris Saunders W RSC 3 Southwark
11.09.91	Tony Foster W PTS 8 Hammersmith
26.09.91	Felix Kelly W RSC 2 Dunstable
24.10.91	Patrick Kamy W CO 1 Dunstable
20.11.91	Marcel Herbert W PTS 8 Kensington
12.02.92	Tomas Quinones W CO 8 Wembley
25.03.92	Bobby Brewer W RSC 4 Kensington
03.09.92	Wayne Windle W CO 1 Dunstable

28.10.92	Carl Crook W RTD 9 Kensington
	(British & Commonwealth Lightweight Title Challenge)
17.12.92	Mauricio Aceves W RSC 3 Wembley
24.02.93	Paul Burke L RSC 7 Wembley
	(British & Commonwealth Lightweight Title Defence)
15.06.93	Farid Benredjeb W PTS 8 Hemel Hempstead
10.11.93	Paul Burke W PTS 12 Watford
	(British & Commonwealth Lightweight Title Challenge)
16.02.94	Sean Murphy W RSC 3 Stevenage
	(British & Commonwealth Lightweight Title Defence)
04.03.94	John Roby W RSC 2 Bethnal Green
22.03.94	Edgar Castro W CO 5 Bethnal Green
11.05.94	Howard Grant W RSC 9 Stevenage
	(Commonwealth Lightweight Title Defence)
09.11.94	Manuel Hernandez W CO 6 Millwall
28.01.95	Rafael Ruelas L RSC 8 Las Vegas, USA
	(IBF Lightweight Title Challenge)
12.05.95	Stephen Chungu W RSC 11 Bethnal Green
	(Commonwealth Lightweight Title Defence)
23.06.95	Bruno Rabanales W DIS 6 Bethnal Green
28.10.95	Ditau Molefyane W CO 8 Kensington
	(Commonwealth Lightweight Title Defence)
25.11.95	David Tetteh L RSC 12 Dagenham
	(Commonwealth Lightweight Title Defence)
15.03.96	Edward Lloyd W RTD 5 Dunstable
16.05.96	Gareth Jordan W RSC 3 Dunstable
24.10.96	Alan Temple W PTS 8 Wembley
20.11.96	Jean-Michel Moulun W RTD 7 Wembley

Career: 36 contests, won 33, lost 3.

Bruce Scott

Hackney. *Born* Jamaica, 16 August, 1969
L. Heavyweight. Ht. 5'9½"
Manager Self

25.04.91	Mark Bowen L PTS 6 Mayfair
16.09.91	Randy B. Powell W RSC 5 Mayfair
21.11.91	Steve Osborne W PTS 6 Burton
27.04.92	John Kaighin W CO 4 Mayfair
07.09.92	Lee Prudden W PTS 6 Bethnal Green
03.12.92	Mark Pain W RSC 5 Lewisham
15.02.93	Paul McCarthy W PTS 6 Mayfair
22.04.93	Sean O'Phoenix W RSC 3 Mayfair
14.06.93	John Oxenham W RSC 1 Bayswater
04.10.93	Simon McDougall W PTS 6 Mayfair
16.12.93	Bobby Mack W RSC 4 Newport
05.04.94	Steve Osborne W RSC 5 Bethnal Green
17.10.94	Bobbi Joe Edwards W PTS 8 Mayfair
09.12.94	John Keeton W CO 2 Bethnal Green
19.04.95	Nigel Rafferty W RSC 2 Bethnal Green
19.05.95	Cordwell Hylton W RSC 1 Southwark
11.11.95	Tony Booth W RSC 3 Halifax
05.03.96	Nick Manners W RSC 5 Bethnal Green
13.07.96	Tony Booth W PTS 8 Bethnal Green
30.11.96	Nicky Piper L RSC 7 Tylorstown
	(Commonwealth L. Heavyweight Title Challenge)
15.05.97	Grant Briggs W RSC 2 Reading

Career: 21 contests, won 19, lost 2.

Keith Scott

Newbiggin. *Born* Ashington, 17 September, 1975
Welterweight. Ht. 5'9"
Manager N. Fawcett

04.12.96 Mark Owens W PTS 6 Hartlepool
03.02.97 Shaun O'Neill W PTS 4 Sunderland
27.02.97 Dean Nicholas W PTS 6 Sunderland
01.05.97 Shaun O'Neill W PTS 6 Newcastle
Career: 4 contests, won 4.

Paul Scott

Newbiggin. *Born* Ashington, 27 November, 1969
L. Welterweight. Ht. 5'7"
Manager T. Conroy

06.10.94 Trevor George W PTS 6 Cramlington
24.10.94 James Jiora L PTS 6 Bradford
24.11.94 Ram Singh W PTS 6 Newcastle
20.03.95 Tommy Quinn L RSC 4 Glasgow
12.06.95 Lambsy Kayani L PTS 6 Bradford
29.07.95 Mark Allen W RSC 5 Whitley Bay
02.11.95 Dean Nicholas L PTS 6 Houghton le Spring
18.11.95 Mark Breslin L PTS 6 Glasgow
14.03.97 Mark Breslin L RTD 3 Irvine
01.05.97 Brian Booth L PTS 6 Newcastle
Career: 10 contests, won 3, lost 7.

Greg Scott-Briggs

Chesterfield. *Born* Swaziland, 6 February, 1966
L. Heavyweight. Ht. 6'1"
Manager J. Ashton

04.02.92 Mark McBiane W PTS 6 Alfreton
03.03.92 Tony Colclough W RSC 2 Cradley Heath
30.03.92 Carl Smallwood L PTS 6 Coventry
27.04.92 Richard Atkinson L PTS 6 Bradford
28.05.92 Steve Walton W PTS 6 Gosforth
04.06.92 Joe Frater L PTS 6 Cleethorpes
30.09.92 Carl Smallwood L PTS 6 Solihull
17.03.93 Carl Smallwood L PTS 8 Stoke
26.04.93 Tony Colclough W RSC 4 Glasgow
08.06.93 Peter Flint W RSC 1 Derby
07.09.93 Steve Loftus W RSC 2 Stoke
22.09.93 Paul Hanlon W PTS 6 Chesterfield
04.11.93 Lee Archer L PTS 8 Stafford
24.11.93 Tony Colclough W PTS 6 Solihull
08.12.93 Lee Archer W RTD 6 Stoke
08.02.94 Nigel Rafferty L PTS 6 Wolverhampton
17.02.94 Lee Archer L PTS 8 Walsall
11.03.94 Monty Wright L CO 1 Bethnal Green
26.09.94 Dave Battey W RSC 4 Cleethorpes
11.10.94 Mark Smallwood L PTS 8 Wolverhampton
29.10.94 Mark Smallwood L PTS 6 Cannock
12.11.94 Thomas Hansvold L PTS 4 Randers, Denmark
30.11.94 Monty Wright L PTS 6 Wolverhampton
06.03.95 Neil Simpson L RTD 5 Leicester
15.09.95 David Flowers L PTS 6 Darlington
29.11.95 Neil Simpson L DIS 7 Solihull
(Vacant Midlands Area L. Heavyweight Title)
20.03.96 Stinger Mason W PTS 6 Stoke
26.10.96 Danny Peters L PTS 6 Liverpool
13.06.97 Jamie Warters L RSC 5 Leeds
Career: 29 contests, won 11, lost 18.

Nigel Selby

Barnsley. *Born* Royston, 27 October, 1968
Cruiserweight. Ht. 6'2½"
Manager Self

20.05.91 Rocky Tyrrell W PTS 6 Bradford
27.06.91 Rocky Tyrrell W PTS 6 Leeds
11.04.97 Tim Brown W PTS 6 Barnsley
Career: 3 contests, won 3.

Kevin Sheil

Cardiff. *Born* Wexford, 8 May, 1972
Featherweight. Ht. 5'6"
Manager K. Hayde

28.11.95 Stefy Bull L PTS 6 Wolverhampton
18.12.95 Richard Evatt L RSC 1 Mayfair
30.05.96 Carl Greaves L PTS 6 Lincoln
18.09.96 Keith Jones L PTS 4 Tylorstown
02.10.96 Ian Turner L PTS 6 Cardiff
15.10.96 Stefy Bull DREW 6 Wolverhampton
24.10.96 Esham Pickering L PTS 6 Lincoln
03.03.97 Robert Grubb W DIS 3 Birmingham
20.03.97 Keith Jones DREW 8 Solihull
10.04.97 Carl Greaves L PTS 6 Sheffield
Career: 10 contests, won 1, drew 2, lost 7.

(Rufus) Rocky Shelly (Davies)

Mansfield. *Born* Oldham, 18 August, 1970
L. Heavyweight. Ht. 5'10½"
Manager Self

09.12.91 Stuart Fleet W RSC 1 Cleethorpes
26.12.91 Issa Moluh L RSC 2 Berne, Switzerland
05.03.92 Des Vaughan L RSC 5 Battersea
22.03.96 Carl Nicholson L RTD 3 Mansfield
02.10.96 Chris Woollas L RSC 4 Stoke
01.11.96 Ernie Loveridge L RTD 3 Mansfield
04.12.96 Johnny Hooks W RSC 6 Stoke
20.02.97 Clinton Woods L RSC 2 Mansfield
Career: 8 contests, won 2, lost 6.

Charles Shepherd

Carlisle. *Born* Burnley, 28 June, 1970
S. Featherweight. Ht. 5'4"
Manager J. Doughty/T. Gilmour

28.10.91 Chris Aston W PTS 6 Leicester
31.01.92 Alan McDowall L RSC 3 Glasgow
18.05.92 Mark Legg W PTS 6 Marton
25.09.92 George Naylor W RSC 4 Liverpool
22.10.92 Didier Hughes L PTS 4 Bethnal Green
13.02.93 Nigel Wenton W PTS 8 Manchester
23.05.93 Cham Joof W PTS 4 Brockley
21.10.93 Karl Taylor W RTD 5 Bayswater
09.02.94 Justin Juuko L RSC 5 Bethnal Green
21.04.94 Tony Foster L PTS 10 Hull
(Vacant Central Area Lightweight Title)
29.09.94 Frankie Foster W RSC 3 Tynemouth
08.03.95 Bamana Dibateza W PTS 8 Solihull
26.04.95 Kelton McKenzie W RSC 7 Solihull
23.05.95 Michael Ayers L RSC 3 Potters Bar
(British Lightweight Title Challenge)
14.11.95 John Stovin W RSC 4 Bury
22.04.96 Marc Smith W RSC 2 Crystal Palace
29.06.96 P. J. Gallagher L PTS 12 Erith
(British S. Featherweight Title Challenge)
28.10.96 Harry Escott W PTS 8 Glasgow
Career: 18 contests, won 12, lost 6.

Charles Shepherd　　　　Les Clark

Wayne Shepherd

Carlisle. *Born* Whiston, 3 June, 1959
Welterweight. Ht. 5'6"
Manager J. Doughty

07.10.91 Benji Joseph W PTS 6 Bradford
28.10.91 Noel Henry W PTS 6 Leicester
16.12.91 Dave Maj DREW 6 Manchester
03.02.92 Dave Maj L PTS 6 Manchester
30.03.92 Hughie Davey L PTS 6 Bradford
18.05.92 Dave Whittle W PTS 6 Marton
14.10.92 Richard Swallow L PTS 8 Stoke
31.10.92 George Scott L RSC 6 Earls Court
13.02.93 Delroy Waul L RSC 5 Manchester
31.03.93 Derek Grainger L RSC 4 Barking
11.06.93 Hughie Davey L PTS 6 Gateshead
06.09.93 Shea Neary L RTD 2 Liverpool
26.01.94 James McGee W PTS 6 Stoke
28.02.94 Craig Winter L PTS 6 Manchester
02.03.95 Denny Johnson L PTS 6 Cramlington
06.04.95 Shaun Stokes L PTS 6 Sheffield
22.05.95 Peter Varnavas W PTS 6 Morecambe
01.06.95 Tommy Quinn L PTS 6 Musselburgh
29.07.95 Shaun O'Neill L PTS 4 Whitley Bay
07.10.95 Neil Sinclair L PTS 6 Belfast
30.10.95 John Stronach L PTS 6 Bradford
11.12.95 Shamus Casey L PTS 6 Morecambe
07.03.96 Derek Roche L RSC 3 Bradford
22.04.96 Gilbert Eastman L PTS 4 Crystal Palace
25.06.96 Geoff McCreesh L PTS 4 Stevenage
26.09.96 John Docherty L PTS 6 Glasgow
10.11.96 John Docherty L PTS 6 Glasgow
22.12.96 Chris Barnett L PTS 6 Salford
16.03.97 C. J. Jackson L PTS 6 Shaw
Career: 29 contests, won 5, drew 1, lost 23.

Eddie Sica

Highbury. *Born* Islington, 5 September, 1968
Featherweight. Ht. 5'4½"
Manager F. Maloney

24.10.95 Chris Lyons W PTS 4 Southwark

29.11.95	Martin Evans L RSC 2 Southwark	
02.04.96	Benny May W RSC 1 Southwark	
07.10.96	Scott Harrison L RSC 2 Lewisham	
28.01.97	Wayne Jones W PTS 6 Piccadilly	
28.04.97	Rocky Turnbull DREW 4 Hull	

Career: 6 contests, won 3, drew 1, lost 2.

John Sillo (Sillitoe)

Liverpool. *Born* Oxford, 10 February, 1965
Featherweight. Ht. 5'5"
Manager S. Vaughan

28.09.93	Graham McGrath W PTS 6 Liverpool
11.12.93	Marty Chestnut W PTS 6 Liverpool
25.02.94	Craig Kelley W PTS 6 Chester
06.05.94	Chris Lyons W RSC 3 Liverpool
26.09.94	Pete Buckley W PTS 6 Liverpool
25.03.95	Garry Burrell W PTS 6 Chester
20.04.95	Pete Buckley W PTS 6 Liverpool
29.09.95	Alexander Tiranov L RTD 3 Liverpool
08.12.95	Jason Thomas W PTS 6 Liverpool
13.04.96	Michael Brodie L CO 1 Liverpool
22.11.96	Robert Grubb W RSC 2 Liverpool

Career: 11 contests, won 9, lost 2.

Justin Simmons

Plymouth. *Born* Plymouth, 3 November, 1974
Welterweight. Ht. 5'11½"
Manager G. Mitchell/C. Sanigar

19.09.95	Shamus Casey W PTS 6 Plymouth
13.11.95	John Janes W PTS 6 Barnstaple
29.11.95	Allan Gray W PTS 6 Bethnal Green
12.02.96	Dennis Gardner W RSC 3 Heathrow
04.04.96	Steve McGovern DREW 6 Plymouth
10.12.96	Steve McGovern W RSC 2 Plymouth
21.01.97	Paul Miles W PTS 4 Bristol
19.04.97	John Smith W RTD 5 Plymouth

Career: 8 contests, won 7, drew 1.

Lee Simpkin

Swadlincote. *Born* Ashby, 26 September, 1974
Middleweight. Ht. 6'1"
Manager Self

31.01.96	Scott Beasley L RSC 3 Stoke
25.03.96	Michael Pinnock L PTS 6 Birmingham
02.04.96	Ed Robinson L PTS 4 Southwark
09.05.96	Terry Morrill L RSC 5 Hull
23.09.96	Michael Monaghan L PTS 6 Cleethorpes
03.10.96	Shaun O'Neill L PTS 6 Sunderland
28.10.96	Darren Rees L PTS 6 Bradford
04.12.96	Peter McCormack W PTS 6 Stoke
09.12.96	Michael Monaghan L PTS 6 Chesterfield
16.01.97	Alex Mason L PTS 6 Solihull
14.04.97	Lee Murtagh L PTS 6 Bradford
01.05.97	Rob Stevenson L PTS 6 Hull
09.06.97	Darren Rees L PTS 6 Bradford

Career: 13 contests, won 1, lost 12.

Neil Simpson

Coventry. *Born* London, 5 July, 1970
Former Midlands Area L. Heavyweight Champion. Ht. 6'2"
Manager J. Griffin

04.10.94	Kenny Nevers W PTS 4 Mayfair
20.10.94	Johnny Hooks W RSC 2 Walsall

05.12.94	Chris Woollas L PTS 6 Cleethorpes
15.12.94	Paul Murray W PTS 6 Walsall
06.03.95	Greg Scott-Briggs W RTD 5 Leicester
17.03.95	Thomas Hansvold L PTS 4 Copenhagen, Denmark
26.04.95	Craig Joseph L PTS 6 Solihull
11.05.95	Andy McVeigh L CO 2 Dudley
24.06.95	Dave Owens W RSC 1 Cleethorpes
25.09.95	Tony Booth L PTS 8 Cleethorpes
11.10.95	Darren Ashton W RSC 3 Solihull
29.11.95	Greg Scott-Briggs W DIS 7 Solihull
	(Vacant Midlands Area L. Heavyweight Title)
19.02.96	Stephen Wilson L PTS 6 Glasgow
27.03.96	Tony Booth W PTS 6 Whitwick
26.04.96	Dean Francis L RSC 3 Cardiff
02.10.96	Chris Davies W PTS 4 Cardiff
28.10.96	Nigel Rafferty W PTS 8 Leicester
03.12.96	Danny Peters L PTS 6 Liverpool
03.02.97	Michael Pinnock W PTS 6 Leicester
25.04.97	Stuart Fleet L PTS 10 Cleethorpes
	(Midlands Area L. Heavyweight Title Defence)

Career: 20 contests, won 11, lost 9.

Neil Sinclair

Belfast. *Born* Belfast, 23 February, 1974
Welterweight. Ht. 5'10½"
Manager B. Hearn

14.04.95	Marty Duke W RSC 2 Belfast
27.05.95	Andrew Jervis L RSC 3 Belfast
17.07.95	Andy Peach W RSC 1 Mayfair
26.08.95	George Wilson W PTS 4 Belfast
07.10.95	Wayne Shepherd W PTS 6 Belfast
02.12.95	Brian Coleman W RTD 1 Belfast
13.04.96	Hughie Davey W PTS 6 Liverpool
28.05.96	Prince Kasi Kaihau W RSC 2 Belfast
03.09.96	Dennis Berry L PTS 6 Belfast

Career: 9 contests, won 7, lost 2.

Jimmy Singh

Sheffield. *Born* Walsall, 15 October, 1971
Lightweight. Ht. 5'8"
Manager B. Ingle

04.06.95	Nelson Ide L CO 1 Bethnal Green
26.09.96	Robert Grubb L RSC 2 Walsall

Career: 2 contests, lost 2.

(Raminderbir) Ram Singh

Wisbech. *Born* Crewe, 13 August, 1969
Lightweight. Ht. 5'11"
Manager Self

06.06.94	Wahid Fats L RSC 3 Manchester
26.09.94	Robert Howard W PTS 6 Morecambe
17.11.94	Terry Whittaker L PTS 6 Sheffield
24.11.94	Paul Scott L PTS 6 Newcastle
05.12.94	Liam Dineen L PTS 6 Houghton le Spring
12.01.95	Steve Tuckett L RSC 6 Leeds
21.02.95	Glen Hopkins L RSC 1 Sunderland
03.04.95	Dave Madden L PTS 6 Northampton
27.04.95	Paul Hamilton W RSC 2 Hull
14.06.95	Terry Whittaker L PTS 6 Batley
28.09.95	John T. Kelly L PTS 6 Sunderland
05.10.95	Garry Burrell L PTS 8 Glasgow
29.01.96	Marco Fattore DREW 6 Piccadilly
21.02.96	Dave Fallon L PTS 6 Piccadilly
19.03.96	Andy Green L PTS 6 Leeds
01.04.96	Hurricane Hughes W PTS 6 Bradford

22.04.96	John T. Kelly L PTS 6 Manchester
09.05.96	Liam Dineen L PTS 6 Sunderland
30.05.96	Steve Conway L PTS 6 Lincoln
13.06.96	Thomas Bradley L RSC 1 Sheffield
24.02.97	Phil Molyneux L PTS 6 Manchester

Career: 21 contests, won 3, drew 1, lost 17.

(Sukhdarshan) Tiger Singh (Mahal)

Peterborough. *Born* India, 28 October, 1970
Bantamweight. Ht. 5'8"
Manager Self

10.12.92	Ian Baillie W PTS 6 Corby
11.05.93	Anthony Hanna L PTS 6 Norwich
06.10.93	Anthony Hanna L PTS 6 Solihull
28.10.93	Nick Tooley L PTS 6 Torquay
30.11.93	Vince Feeney L PTS 6 Leicester
02.03.94	Lyndon Kershaw L PTS 6 Solihull
09.05.94	Terry Gaskin W RSC 2 Bradford
20.09.94	Keith Knox L PTS 6 Musselburgh
28.11.94	Terry Gaskin W PTS 6 Manchester
08.03.95	Lyndon Kershaw L PTS 6 Solihull
26.04.95	Darren Noble W PTS 6 Solihull
14.09.95	Mark Reynolds L RSC 3 Battersea
08.12.95	Shaun Hall W PTS 6 Leeds
04.10.96	Noel Wilders L PTS 6 Wakefield
01.11.96	Steve Williams L PTS 6 Mansfield

Career: 15 contests, won 5, lost 10.

Robbie Sivyer

Chesterfield. *Born* Chesterfield, 22 September, 1973
Lightweight. Ht. 5'9"
Manager M. Shinfield

26.04.93	Garry Burrell L PTS 6 Glasgow
07.06.93	Simon Hamblett W PTS 6 Walsall
29.06.93	Mark Allen L PTS 6 Edgbaston
22.09.93	John Stovin L PTS 6 Chesterfield
13.11.93	Wayne Jones L PTS 6 Cullompton
04.03.94	Wayne Jones L PTS 6 Weston super Mare
05.06.95	Trevor Royal W CO 5 Birmingham
02.10.95	T. J. Smith L RSC 4 Birmingham
04.12.95	Robert Grubb W PTS 6 Birmingham
16.03.96	Norman Dhalie W CO 4 Barnstaple
13.06.96	Kid McAuley W PTS 6 Sheffield
01.10.96	Simon Frailing W PTS 6 Birmingham
09.12.96	Chris Price DREW 6 Chesterfield
26.06.97	Roger Sampson L PTS 6 Sheffield

Career: 14 contests, won 6, drew 1, lost 7.

Trevor Small

Birmingham. *Born* Solihull, 26 February, 1968
Cruiserweight. Ht. 6'0"
Manager W. Swift

09.12.92	Sean O'Phoenix W PTS 6 Stoke
20.01.93	Art Stacey W PTS 6 Solihull
28.04.93	Tony Behan W PTS 6 Solihull
20.09.93	Albert Call DREW 6 Cleethorpes
06.10.93	Art Stacey W PTS 6 Solihull
02.11.93	Phil Soundy W RSC 6 Southwark
13.12.93	Albert Call L RSC 5 Cleethorpes
02.09.94	Andrew Benson L PTS 6 Spitalfields
20.12.94	Terry Dunstan L RTD 4 Bethnal Green
18.10.96	Patrick Akerlund L CO 2 Vejle, Denmark
30.11.96	James Branch W CO 1 Tylorstown

Career: 11 contests, won 6, drew 1, lost 4.

Mark Smallwood

Atherstone. *Born* Nuneaton, 30 January, 1975
S. Middleweight. Ht. 6'2"
Manager Self

22.02.93	John Dempsey W CO 1 Bedworth
17.03.93	Sean Smith W RSC 1 Stoke
10.05.93	Tim Robinson W RSC 4 Cleethorpes
17.06.93	Phil Ball W RSC 1 Bedworth
24.11.93	Darren Littlewood W PTS 8 Solihull
24.02.94	Jerry Mortimer W PTS 6 Walsall
18.04.94	Gil Lewis W RSC 5 Walsall
23.05.94	Dean Ashton W RTD 3 Walsall
11.10.94	Greg Scott-Briggs W PTS 8 Wolverhampton
29.10.94	Greg Scott-Briggs W PTS 6 Cannock
29.11.94	Paul Murray W PTS 8 Wolverhampton
18.01.95	Marvin O'Brien W PTS 6 Solihull
26.11.96	Michael Pinnock W PTS 6 Wolverhampton
16.01.97	Chris Woollas W PTS 8 Solihull

Career: 14 contests, won 14.

Georgie Smith

Basildon. *Born* Basildon, 29 August, 1971
Southern Area L. Welterweight Champion.
Ht. 5'10"
Manager B. Hearn

07.11.94	Malcolm Thomas W PTS 6 Bethnal Green
20.12.94	Stevie Bolt W RSC 2 Bethnal Green
17.02.95	Dewi Roberts W RSC 2 Crawley
16.03.95	Shaba Edwards W CO 2 Basildon
09.05.95	Wayne Jones W RSC 3 Basildon
13.06.95	Rudy Valentino W PTS 6 Basildon
28.10.95	Kevin McKillan W CO 2 Kensington
06.02.96	Gary Beardsley W RSC 1 Basildon
20.04.96	Danny Quacoe W PTS 6 Brentwood
08.03.97	Peter Nightingale W RSC 1 Brentwood
22.04.97	Brian Coleman W PTS 6 Bethnal Green
30.06.97	Richie Edwards W RSC 10 Bethnal Green
	(Vacant Southern Area L. Welterweight Title)

Career: 12 contests, won 12.

John Smith

Liverpool. *Born* Liverpool, 13 October, 1959
Welterweight. Ht. 5'9"
Manager Self

26.06.86	Ray Golding W PTS 6 Edgbaston
22.09.86	John Townsley W PTS 6 Edgbaston
06.11.86	Robert Harkin L PTS 8 Glasgow
20.11.86	John Best L PTS 6 Bredbury
08.12.86	Gary Sommerville DREW 8 Edgbaston
18.03.87	John Best L RSC 2 Solihull
24.04.87	Brian Wareing L PTS 8 Liverpool
24.09.87	John Dickson L PTS 6 Glasgow
01.02.88	Peter Crook L PTS 6 Manchester
17.03.88	Mick Mason DREW 8 Sunderland
29.03.88	Paul Seddon W RSC 4 Marton
17.06.88	Gary Sommerville W RSC 5 Edgbaston
28.11.88	Gary Sommerville L PTS 8 Edgbaston
24.01.89	Mark Kelly L PTS 8 Kings Heath
22.03.89	John Davies L PTS 8 Solihull
17.07.89	Richard Adams W RSC 3 Stanmore
08.09.89	Muhammad Lovelock W PTS 6 Liverpool

14.09.89	Roy Rowland L RSC 3 Basildon
17.10.89	Jim Talbot L PTS 6 Oldham
25.10.89	Kevin Plant L PTS 6 Doncaster
10.11.89	Seamus O'Sullivan L PTS 6 Battersea
30.11.89	Dave Pierre L PTS 6 Mayfair
08.12.89	Allan Hall L RSC 2 Doncaster
29.01.90	Darren Mount L PTS 8 Liverpool
08.03.90	Dave Pierre L PTS 6 Peterborough
19.03.90	Brendan Ryan L PTS 6 Leicester
05.04.90	Darren Mount L PTS 8 Liverpool
04.05.90	Pete Roberts L PTS 6 Liverpool
24.09.90	Mark Dinnadge W RTD 2 Lewisham
09.10.90	Pete Roberts W PTS 8 Liverpool
13.11.90	Paul Charters L RSC 4 Hartlepool
21.01.91	Kris McAdam L PTS 6 Glasgow
07.02.91	Billy Schwer L RSC 2 Watford
26.03.91	Andrew Morgan L RSC 4 Wolverhampton
24.04.91	Andrew Morgan L PTS 6 Aberavon
16.05.91	Kevin Toomey L PTS 6 Liverpool
13.06.91	Kevin Toomey L PTS 6 Hull
25.07.91	Robert McCracken L RTD 1 Dudley
07.10.91	Pete Roberts L PTS 8 Liverpool
23.10.91	Dean Hollington L PTS 6 Bethnal Green
12.11.91	Mark Elliot L PTS 6 Wolverhampton
21.11.91	Richard Burton L PTS 6 Burton
02.12.91	Mike Calderwood DREW 8 Liverpool
19.12.91	Richard Burton L PTS 6 Oldham
01.02.92	George Scott L RSC 3 Birmingham
03.03.92	Paul Charters L PTS 8 Houghton le Spring
12.05.92	Ross Hale L CO 1 Crystal Palace
03.09.92	Chris Mulcahy DREW 6 Liverpool
25.09.92	Kevin McKillan L PTS 6 Liverpool
07.10.92	Alan Peacock DREW 6 Glasgow
12.11.92	Mark Tibbs L RSC 6 Bayswater
18.03.93	Jason Rowland L PTS 6 Lewisham
29.03.93	Shea Neary L PTS 6 Liverpool
13.09.93	Rob Stewart DREW 6 Middleton
22.09.93	Jonathan Thaxton L PTS 6 Wembley
27.10.93	Mark McCreath L RSC 7 West Bromwich
25.11.93	Charlie Kane L PTS 6 Tynemouth
21.02.94	Alan Peacock L RSC 4 Glasgow
28.03.94	Charlie Kane L PTS 6 Musselburgh
10.04.94	Kris McAdam W PTS 8 Glasgow
28.06.94	Malcolm Melvin L PTS 6 Edgbaston
17.08.94	Paul Ryan L RTD 2 Sheffield
19.09.94	Alan Peacock L PTS 8 Glasgow
28.09.94	Shaun Cogan L RSC 3 Glasgow
17.11.94	Nigel Bradley L PTS 6 Sheffield
29.11.94	Shaun Cogan L RSC 4 Cannock
25.01.95	Shea Neary L RSC 5 Stoke
24.02.95	Steve McLevy L PTS 6 Irvine
20.04.95	Andreas Panayi L RSC 4 Liverpool
12.06.95	Wahid Fats W CO 3 Manchester
02.07.95	Peter Richardson L PTS 6 Dublin
09.09.95	Michael Carruth L PTS 8 Cork
20.09.95	Bernard Paul L PTS 6 Potters Bar
29.09.95	John Jones L PTS 6 Liverpool
24.10.95	Richie Edwards L PTS 4 Southwark
14.11.95	Bobby Vanzie L PTS 6 Bury
29.11.95	Paul Miles L PTS 4 Southwark
06.12.95	Gary Beardsley L PTS 8 Stoke
07.03.96	Bobby Vanzie L PTS 6 Bradford
15.03.96	John Stovin DREW 6 Hull
13.04.96	Ricky Sackfield L PTS 4 Wythenshawe
22.04.96	Dean Nicholas L PTS 6 Glasgow
25.06.96	Nicky Bardle L PTS 4 Stevenage
13.07.96	Martin Holgate L PTS 4 Bethnal Green
31.08.96	Mark Winters L PTS 4 Dublin
13.10.96	Scott Walker L PTS 6 Shaw
25.10.96	Chris Barnett L PTS 6 Mere

18.11.96	Steve McLevy L PTS 8 Glasgow
06.12.96	Steve Tuckett L RSC 4 Leeds
01.03.97	Peter Richardson L PTS 6 Liverpool
19.04.97	Justin Simmons L RTD 5 Plymouth
21.06.97	Darren Williams L PTS 4 Cardiff

Career: 92 contests, won 10, drew 7, lost 75.

Marc Smith

Swansea. *Born* Kingston, 31 August, 1974
Lightweight. Ht. 5'9"
Manager P. Boyce

20.05.94	Andrew Smith DREW 6 Neath
11.10.94	Mark Allen W PTS 6 Wolverhampton
20.10.94	Mark Allen L PTS 6 Walsall
09.03.95	Simon Hamblett L PTS 6 Walsall
16.03.95	Nelson Ide L RSC 4 Basildon
20.09.95	Craig Kelley W RSC 1 Ystrad
29.09.95	P. J. Gallagher L RSC 3 Bethnal Green
02.11.95	Anthony Campbell L PTS 6 Mayfair
22.11.95	Marco Fattore W PTS 6 Mayfair
12.02.96	Adrian Chase L CO 1 Heathrow
20.03.96	Tommy Janes W RSC 6 Cardiff
22.04.96	Charles Shepherd L RSC 2 Crystal Palace
12.11.96	Mark Richards L PTS 6 Dudley
22.12.96	Scott Dixon L PTS 6 Glasgow
03.03.97	Kelton McKenzie L PTS 8 Leicester
20.03.97	Vic Broomhead L PTS 6 Solihull
11.04.97	Steve Conway L PTS 4 Barnsley
10.05.97	John O.Johnson L PTS 5 Nottingham
27.05.97	Jason Cook L PTS 4 Mayfair

Career: 19 contests, won 4, drew 1, lost 14.

Marc Smith   Les Clark

Martin Smith

Huddersfield. *Born* London, 16 August, 1967
L. Middleweight. Ht. 6'0"
Manager Self

24.09.87	Tony Britland DREW 6 Crystal Palace
20.01.88	Danny Shinkwin W PTS 6 Hornsey

10.03.88 Cecil Branch W PTS 6 Croydon
13.04.88 Tony Britland W RSC 2 Gravesend
11.05.88 Simon Paul W RTD 5 Greenwich
28.05.88 Oliver Henry W PTS 6 Kensington
25.06.88 Damien Denny NC 5 Luton
16.02.89 Winston May DREW 6 Battersea
14.09.89 Brian Robinson L PTS 6 Basildon
19.10.89 Des Robinson W PTS 4 Manchester
13.11.89 Joni Nyman L PTS 8 Helsinki, Finland
25.11.89 Andre Kimbu L PTS 8 Gravelines, France
22.02.90 Robbie Harron W PTS 6 Hull
15.03.90 James Collins W PTS 6 Manchester
06.06.90 John Ogiste W RSC 2 Battersea
12.02.91 Rex Kortram W PTS 6 Rotterdam, Holland
19.03.91 Shaun Cummins DREW 8 Leicester
07.05.91 Danny Quigg W PTS 6 Glasgow
01.10.91 Mike Phillips W PTS 6 Sheffield
28.10.91 Gilbert Hallie DREW 8 Arnhem, Holland
10.01.92 Said Skouma W PTS 8 Vitrolles, France
14.04.92 Dave Owens W PTS 6 Mansfield
08.05.92 Freddie Demeulenaere DREW 8 Waregem, Belgium
24.04.93 Robert McCracken L RSC 10 Birmingham
 (Final Elim. British L. Middleweight Title)
02.12.96 Howard Clarke W PTS 8 Birmingham
Career: 25 contests, won 15, drew 5, lost 4, no contest 1.

Neville Smith

Cranford. *Born* Isleworth, 7 January, 1976
S. Middleweight. Ht. 6'2"
Manager H. Holland

03.12.95 Michael Pinnock W RSC 5 Southwark
12.02.96 Simon Andrews W RSC 3 Heathrow
20.09.96 Martin Jolley W RSC 3 Tooting
15.02.97 Simon Andrews W PTS 4 Tooting
Career: 4 contests, won 4.

Tony Smith

Sheffield. *Born* Sheffield, 15 August, 1967
Welterweight. Ht. 5'8"
Manager J. Rushton

12.03.97 Richard Inquieti L RSC 2 Stoke
25.04.97 Dean Bramhald L PTS 6 Cleethorpes
03.05.97 Anas Oweida L RSC 1 Manchester
09.06.97 Christian Brady L RSC 4 Birmingham
Career: 4 contests, lost 4.

(Paul) Willie Smith

Scunthorpe. *Born* Scunthorpe, 18 August, 1976
Bantamweight. Ht. 5'6"
Manager J. Rushton

23.09.96 Andy Roberts L RSC 4 Bradford
17.12.96 Sean Green L PTS 6 Doncaster
07.03.97 Tiny Pope L PTS 6 Northampton
14.03.97 David Coldwell L RSC 5 Hull
Career: 4 contests, lost 4.

Michael Smyth

Barry. *Born* Caerphilly, 22 February, 1970
Welterweight. Ht. 5'9¾"
Manager Self

02.05.91 Carl Brasier W RSC 2 Kensington
28.05.91 Rick North W RSC 1 Cardiff
18.07.91 Mike Morrison W RSC 2 Cardiff
03.09.91 Julian Eavis W PTS 6 Cardiff
20.11.91 Mike Russell W RSC 3 Cardiff
17.12.91 Julian Eavis W PTS 6 Cardiff
19.05.92 Ojay Abrahams W PTS 6 Cardiff
07.10.92 David Lake W CO 2 Barry
14.11.92 Des Robinson W PTS 6 Cardiff
10.07.93 Ernie Loveridge W RSC 6 Cardiff
23.10.93 Chris Saunders W PTS 6 Cardiff
12.03.94 Gordon Blair W RSC 4 Cardiff
21.07.94 Maurice Forbes W RSC 3 Battersea
24.09.94 Mike DeMoss W RSC 1 Wembley
25.10.94 Scott Doyle W CO 1 Southwark
25.01.95 Rick North W DIS 4 Cardiff
17.06.95 Kevin Lueshing L RSC 3 Cardiff
 (Final Elim. British Welterweight Title)
20.09.95 Howard Clarke DREW 6 Ystrad
25.10.95 Nigel Bradley W RSC 4 Cardiff
16.12.95 Geoff McCreesh W DIS 4 Cardiff
25.05.96 Maxim Nesterenko L RSC 5 St Petersburg, Russia
 (Vacant WBC International Welterweight Title)
19.07.96 Alexei Perevozchikov W RSC 5 Ystrad
02.10.96 Andrew Murray L PTS 12 Cardiff
 (Commonwealth Welterweight Title Challenge)
26.02.97 Paul King W CO 1 Cardiff
Career: 24 contests, won 20, drew 1, lost 3.

Neville Smith (right) blasts away at Simon Andrews on his way to a points win   Les Clark

Mark Snipe

Brighton. *Born* Brighton, 9 March, 1972
L. Heavyweight. Ht. 6'1"
Manager Self

13.06.95 Michael Pinnock W PTS 6 Basildon
27.10.95 Stinger Mason DREW 6 Brighton
26.01.96 Robert Harper W PTS 6 Brighton
13.04.96 Lee Whitehead W PTS 4 Wythenshawe
04.04.97 Darren Ashton L RSC 2 Brighton
Career: 5 contests, won 3, drew 1, lost 1.

Danny Southern

Barnsley. *Born* Barnsley, 6 April, 1978
Cruiserweight. Ht. 6'0"
Manager G. Rhodes

26.11.96 Pat Durkin W PTS 6 Sheffield
17.03.97 Liam Richardson W RSC 5 Glasgow
11.04.97 Kevin Mitchell W RSC 3 Barnsley
15.05.97 Ian Henry DREW 6 Sunderland
Career: 4 contests, won 3, drew 1.

Michael Sprott

Reading. *Born* Reading, 16 January, 1975
Heavyweight. Ht. 6'0¾"
Manager T. Lawless

20.11.96 Geoff Hunter W RSC 1 Wembley
19.02.97 Johnny Davison W CO 2 Acton
17.03.97 Slick Miller W CO 1 Mayfair
16.04.97 Tim Redman W CO 2 Bethnal Green
20.05.97 Waldeck Fransas W PTS 6 Edmonton
Career: 5 contests, won 5.

Jason Squire   Les Clark

Jason Squire

Leicester. *Born* Leicester, 18 June, 1975
Featherweight. Ht. 5'4½"
Manager J. Griffin

06.06.95 Michael Edwards W RSC 1 Leicester
11.10.95 Chris Lyons W PTS 6 Solihull
23.10.95 Chris Price W PTS 6 Leicester
29.11.95 Carl Allen W PTS 6 Solihull
27.03.96 Carl Allen DREW 6 Whitwick

17.05.96 Fred Reeve DREW 6 Hull
06.09.96 Alex Moon L PTS 4 Liverpool
28.10.96 Robert Braddock W PTS 6 Leicester
09.12.96 Graham McGrath W PTS 8 Leicester
03.02.97 Steve Conway L PTS 6 Leicester
03.03.97 Nicky Wilders W PTS 6 Leicester
19.03.97 Ervine Blake L RTD 6 Stoke
Career: 12 contests, won 7, drew 2, lost 3.

Paul Squire

Leicester. *Born* Leicester, 5 September, 1977
Flyweight. Ht. 5'6½"
Manager J. Griffin

12.05.97 Terry Gaskin DREW 6 Leicester
Career: 1 contest, drew 1.

Craig Stanley

Croydon. *Born* Croydon, 16 March, 1974
L. Welterweight. Ht. 5'6"
Manager F. Maloney

22.04.96 Jason Campbell W RSC 2 Crystal Palace
29.06.96 Arv Mittoo W PTS 4 Erith
11.12.96 Marco Fattore W PTS 4 Southwark
25.03.97 Brian Coleman DREW 4 Lewisham
22.05.97 Arv Mittoo L RSC 3 Southwark
Career: 5 contests, won 3, drew 1, lost 1.

Craig Stanley   Les Clark

Jimmy Steel

Stoke. *Born* Stoke, 22 June, 1970
L. Middleweight. Ht. 5'7"
Manager W. Swift

25.04.96 Andy Gray W PTS 6 Mayfair
13.10.96 Johnny Whiteside L RSC 2 Shaw
11.01.97 Enzo Giordano L PTS 4 Bethnal Green
04.04.97 Michael Thomas L PTS 6 Brighton
Career: 4 contests, won 1, lost 3.

Jimmy Steel   Les Clark

Danny Stevens

Margate. *Born* Lambeth, 16 September, 1973
L. Welterweight. Ht. 5'10"
Manager Self

09.12.94 Brian Coleman W RTD 2 Bethnal Green
14.02.95 Roy Dehara W RSC 6 Bethnal Green
03.03.95 Steve Howden W RSC 2 Bethnal Green
19.04.95 Dusty Miller L RSC 3 Bethnal Green
14.10.96 Craig Hartwell W CO 2 Mayfair
17.12.96 Kid McAuley W DIS 3 Bethnal Green
27.03.97 Martin Holgate L RSC 3 Norwich
Career: 7 contests, won 5, lost 2.

Rob Stevenson

Hull. *Born* Hull, 16 March, 1971
Middleweight. Ht. 5'9"
Manager Self

28.11.91 Matt Mowatt L PTS 6 Hull
26.03.92 Steve Scott W PTS 6 Hull
04.04.92 Chris Mulcahy L PTS 8 Cleethorpes
29.04.92 Alan Williams W PTS 6 Liverpool
01.06.92 Chris Mulcahy L PTS 6 Manchester
13.10.92 Dean Hiscox L PTS 6 Wolverhampton
26.11.92 Steve Scott L PTS 6 Hull
18.02.93 Warren Stephens W PTS 6 Hull
25.02.93 Ron Hopley DREW 6 Bradford
29.04.93 Billy McDougall DREW 6 Hull
01.07.93 Ron Hopley W PTS 6 York
02.12.93 Ian Noble W PTS 6 Hartlepool
13.12.93 Prince Kasi Kaihau L RSC 5 Doncaster
24.02.94 David Sumner W PTS 6 Hull
24.02.95 Billy Collins L PTS 6 Irvine
25.03.95 Derek Roche L PTS 6 Rothwell
01.07.95 Paul Carr L PTS 6 Kensington
22.09.95 Brian Dunn L PTS 6 Hull
03.11.95 David Bain L PTS 6 Dudley
25.11.95 Jim Webb L PTS 6 Dublin
04.12.95 David Radford L CO 2 Manchester
26.02.96 Shamus Casey W PTS 6 Hull
09.05.96 Carlton Williams L PTS 6 Hull

03.09.96 Jim Rock L PTS 6 Belfast
27.09.96 Steve Roberts L PTS 6 Stevenage
27.02.97 Roy Chipperfield W RSC 5 Hull
20.03.97 Phil Epton L PTS 6 Doncaster
01.05.97 Lee Simpkin W PTS 6 Hull
20.05.97 Ahmet Dottuev L CO 1 Edmonton
Career: 29 contests, won 9, drew 2, lost 18.

Rob Stevenson   Les Clark

Clayon Stewart

Paddington. *Born* London, 8 March, 1963
L. Middleweight. Ht. 5'10"
Manager Self

22.01.86 G. L. Booth L PTS 6 Stoke
17.04.86 Danny Garrison W CO 3 Wolverhampton
26.06.86 Victor Carvalho L CO 3 Hsboa, Portugal
01.10.86 Roy Horn W PTS 6 Bournemouth
11.11.86 Russell Burnett L PTS 6 Southampton
06.04.87 Russell Burnett L PTS 6 Southampton
26.11.90 Tony Wellington L PTS 6 Mayfair
08.12.90 Tony Wellington L RSC 1 Bristol
06.02.91 Gary Booker L PTS 6 Battersea
18.02.91 Darren Murphy L PTS 6 Windsor
10.11.93 Kevin Adamson L RSC 1 Bethnal Green
13.07.96 Paul Carr W RSC 1 Bethnal Green
27.08.96 Andy Edge W PTS 4 Windsor
04.03.97 Anthony McFadden L RSC 6 Southwark
Career: 14 contests, won 4, lost 10.

Shaun Stokes

Sheffield. *Born* Sheffield, 19 November, 1969
Welterweight. Ht. 5'7"
Manager J. Rushton

09.02.95 Gary Beardsley L RSC 3 Doncaster
22.03.95 Kenny Scott W RSC 1 Stoke
28.03.95 Patrick Parton W CO 1 Wolverhampton

06.04.95 Wayne Shepherd W PTS 6 Sheffield
05.05.95 Trevor Smith DREW 6 Doncaster
18.05.95 Kevin McKillan DREW 8 Middleton
06.07.95 Mark Allen W PTS 6 Hull
21.09.95 Darren Covill W PTS 6 Sheffield
11.10.95 Tony Swift L PTS 6 Solihull
23.10.95 Richard Swallow W PTS 6 Leicester
21.11.95 Shaun Cogan L PTS 8 Edgbaston
17.01.96 Richard Swallow L PTS 6 Solihull
04.03.96 Jyrki Vierela W RSC 4 Helsinki, Finland
29.03.96 Andy Peach W RSC 3 Doncaster
12.09.96 Ozzy Orrock W CO 1 Doncaster
23.09.96 Charlie Kane L RSC 6 Glasgow
23.10.96 Spencer McCracken L PTS 8 Halifax
05.11.96 Eamonn Magee L RSC 2 Belfast
24.02.97 Steve McLevy L RSC 1 Glasgow
04.04.97 John Jones L PTS 6 Liverpool
05.06.97 Ross Hale L PTS 8 Bristol
Career: 21 contests, won 9, drew 2, lost 10.

Shaun Stokes   Les Clark

Sammy Storey

Belfast. *Born* Belfast, 9 August, 1963
Former Undefeated British S. Middleweight
Champion. Former All-Ireland
Middleweight Champion. Ht. 6'0"
Manager B. Hearn

03.12.85 Nigel Shingles W RSC 6 Belfast
05.02.86 Sean O'Phoenix W PTS 6 Sheffield
22.04.86 Karl Barwise W PTS 6 Belfast
29.10.86 Jimmy Ellis W RSC 5 Belfast
25.04.87 Rocky McGran W PTS 10 Belfast
(Vacant All-Ireland Middleweight Title)
19.10.87 Shamus Casey W PTS 6 Belfast
05.12.87 Paul Mitchell W PTS 6 Doncaster
27.01.88 Steve Foster W RSC 4 Belfast
18.03.88 Steve Collins L PTS 10 Boston, USA
(All-Ireland Middleweight Title Defence)
19.10.88 Tony Lawrence W RSC 3 Belfast
07.12.88 Darren Hobson W RSC 6 Belfast
25.01.89 Abdul Amoru Sanda W RSC 8 Belfast
08.03.89 Kevin Roper W RSC 3 Belfast
19.09.89 Tony Burke W PTS 12 Belfast
(Vacant British S. Middleweight Title)

29.11.89 Noel Magee W RSC 9 Belfast
(British S. Middleweight Title Defence)
17.03.90 Simon Collins W CO 7 Belfast
30.10.90 James Cook L RSC 10 Belfast
(British S. Middleweight Title Defence)
31.05.91 Saldi Ali L PTS 8 Berlin, Germany
07.09.91 Johnny Melfah W PTS 8 Belfast
13.11.91 Karl Barwise W PTS 6 Belfast
25.04.92 Nigel Rafferty W RSC 3 Belfast
03.02.93 Graham Jenner W RSC 4 Earls Court
28.04.93 Carlos Christie W RSC 8 Dublin
22.09.93 John Kaighin W PTS 6 Bethnal Green
21.05.94 Fidel Castro W PTS 6 Belfast
27.08.94 Chris Eubank L RSC 7 Cardiff
(WBO S. Middleweight Title Challenge)
18.03.95 Colin Manners W PTS 8 Millstreet
27.04.95 Ali Forbes W PTS 12 Bethnal Green
(British S. Middleweight Title Challenge)
11.11.95 Henry Wharton L CO 4 Halifax
(European & Commonwealth S. Middleweight Title Challenge)
05.11.96 Butch Lesley W DIS 3 Belfast
08.04.97 David Starie L RSC 7 Bethnal Green
(Vacant British S. Middleweight Title)
Career: 31 contests, won 25, lost 6.

Adrian Strachan

Richmond. *Born* Bromley, 8 April, 1966
Middleweight. Ht. 5'10"
Manager Self

12.10.90 Lawrence Leonce L RSC 3 Cayenne, French Guiana
26.01.91 Zdravko Kostic L PTS 6 Pozaravac, Yugoslavia
04.06.91 Martin Rosamond W PTS 6 Bethnal Green
24.09.91 Martin Rosamond W PTS 6 Basildon
01.10.91 Gary Pemberton W RSC 2 Sheffield
19.11.91 Tracy Jocelyn W PTS 6 Norwich
26.11.91 Chris Richards W PTS 6 Bethnal Green
12.05.92 Horace Fleary W PTS 6 Crystal Palace
30.04.97 Carlton Williams W RSC 3 Acton
Career: 9 contests, won 7, lost 2.

Paul Street

Warrington. *Born* Stockport, 20 February, 1965
L. Middleweight. Ht. 5'7½"
Manager R. Jones

02.10.96 Ray Newby L CO 2 Stoke
Career: 1 contest, lost 1.

Lee Swaby

Manchester. *Born* Lincoln, 14 May, 1976
Cruiserweight. Ht. 6'2"
Manager N. Basso

29.04.97 Naveed Anwar W PTS 6 Manchester
19.06.97 Liam Richardson W RSC 4 Scunthorpe
Career: 2 contests, won 2.

Neil Swain

Gilfach Goch. *Born* Pontypridd, 4 September, 1971
Former Commonwealth S. Bantamweight
Champion. Ht. 5'5"
Manager D. Gardiner

29.04.93 Vince Feeney W PTS 6 Mayfair

27.05.93	Marcus Duncan W PTS 6 Burnley
01.10.93	Rowan Williams W PTS 6 Cardiff
16.10.93	Philippe Desavoye W PTS 6 Levallois, France
10.11.93	Barry Jones L PTS 6 Ystrad
29.01.94	Alan Ley W RSC 3 Cardiff
12.03.94	Ceri Farrell W CO 1 Cardiff
09.04.94	Vince Feeney L PTS 6 Mansfield
06.05.94	Peter Culshaw L PTS 6 Liverpool
25.05.94	Paul Ingle L CO 4 Bristol
30.07.94	Jose Lopez L RTD 4 Bethnal Green
21.09.94	Yusuf Vorajee W RTD 1 Cardiff
01.10.94	Richie Wenton W RTD 5 Cardiff
19.11.94	Dave Hardie W RSC 2 Cardiff
29.11.94	Pete Buckley W PTS 6 Cardiff
25.01.95	Rowan Williams W PTS 6 Cardiff
04.02.95	Chris Jickells W PTS 6 Cardiff
12.04.95	Mike Parris W RSC 20 Llanelli
	(Vacant Commonwealth S. Bantamweight Title)
28.07.95	Tony Falcone W RSC 5 Bristol
	(Commonwealth S. Bantamweight Title Defence)
20.09.95	Graham McGrath W RSC 1 Ystrad
04.11.95	Anton Gilmore L PTS 10 Sun City, South Africa
13.02.96	Nathan Sting W PTS 12 Cardiff
	(Vacant Commonwealth S. Bantamweight Title)
06.11.96	Pete Buckley W PTS 4 Tylorstown
22.03.97	Michael Brodie L RSC 10 Wythenshawe
	(Vacant British S. Bantamweight Title)

Career: 24 contests, won 17, lost 7.

Richard Swallow
Northampton. *Born* Northampton, 10 February, 1970
L. Welterweight. Ht. 5'8"
Manager J. Griffin

15.10.90	Richard O'Brien L RTD 1 Kettering
14.02.91	Dave Fallon W RSC 4 Southampton
06.03.91	Carl Brasier W PTS 6 Croydon
02.05.91	Mike Morrison W PTS 6 Northampton
24.03.92	Dean Bramhald W PTS 8 Wolverhampton
06.04.92	Dean Bramhald W PTS 6 Northampton
29.04.92	Chris Aston W RSC 3 Solihull
14.10.92	Wayne Shepherd W PTS 8 Stoke
24.11.92	Chris Mulcahy W PTS 6 Wolverhampton
20.01.93	Ray Newby W PTS 8 Solihull
03.03.93	Ray Newby W PTS 8 Solihull
11.06.93	Soren Sondergaard L RTD 3 Randers, Denmark
08.02.94	Billy McDougall W PTS 6 Wolverhampton
30.09.94	Bernard Paul W PTS 8 Bethnal Green
31.10.94	Carl Wright L PTS 6 Liverpool
09.12.94	Jason Rowland L RSC 2 Bethnal Green
14.02.95	Jason Beard L PTS 6 Bethnal Green
17.03.95	Frank Olsen L RSC 1 Copenhagen, Denmark
06.06.95	Anthony Maynard W RSC 2 Leicester
23.10.95	Shaun Stokes L PTS 6 Leicester
22.11.95	Gary Beardsley DREW 6 Sheffield
17.01.96	Shaun Stokes W PTS 6 Solihull
12.02.96	Nicky Bardle W RSC 4 Heathrow
28.10.96	Bobby Vanzie L PTS 6 Bradford
20.03.97	Anthony Maynard W RSC 6 Solihull
12.05.97	Nigel Bradley W PTS 6 Leicester

Career: 26 contests, won 15, drew 1, lost 10.

Darren Sweeney
Birmingham. *Born* London, 3 March, 1971
All-Ireland Middleweight Champion. Ht. 5'11"
Manager Self

28.06.94	Japhet Hans W PTS 6 Edgbaston
25.10.94	Dave Battey W CO 1 Edgbaston
15.12.94	Mark Hale W PTS 6 Walsall
07.03.95	Colin Pitters W PTS 6 Edgbaston
20.03.95	Carl Winstone W PTS 6 Birmingham
11.05.95	Martin Jolley W PTS 6 Dudley
20.06.95	Michael Pinnock W PTS 8 Birmingham
17.10.95	Shaun Hendry L RSC 1 Wolverhampton
21.11.95	Carl Winstone W PTS 6 Edgbaston
04.12.95	Peter Mitchell W PTS 8 Birmingham
06.03.96	David Larkin W PTS 6 Solihull
25.03.96	Roy Chipperfield W CO 1 Birmingham
21.05.96	Mark Hale W RSC 8 Edgbaston
24.10.96	Colin Manners W PTS 8 Birmingham
21.11.96	Michael Pinnock L RSC 5 Solihull
15.04.97	Michael Alexander W RSC 6 Edgbaston
	(Vacant All-Ireland Middleweight Title)

Career: 16 contests, won 14, lost 2.

Tony Swift
Solihull. *Born* Solihull, 29 June, 1968
L. Welterweight. Ht. 5'10"
Manager Self

25.09.86	Barry Bacon W PTS 6 Wolverhampton
06.10.86	Wil Halliday W PTS 6 Birmingham
23.10.86	Patrick Loftus W PTS 6 Birmingham
26.11.86	Adam Muir W PTS 6 Wolverhampton
08.12.86	George Baigrie W PTS 6 Birmingham
26.01.87	Dean Bramhald W PTS 8 Birmingham
04.03.87	Dean Bramhald W RSC 5 Dudley
25.03.87	Peter Bowen W PTS 8 Stafford
22.06.87	Peter Bowen W PTS 8 Stafford
07.10.87	Dean Bramhald W PTS 8 Stoke
19.10.87	Kevin Plant W PTS 8 Birmingham
02.12.87	Dean Bramhald W PTS 8 Stoke
16.03.88	Ron Shinkwin W PTS 8 Solihull
04.05.88	Kevin Plant DREW 8 Solihull
28.09.88	Kevin Plant DREW 8 Solihull
23.11.88	Lenny Gloster L PTS 8 Solihull
12.06.89	Humphrey Harrison W PTS 8 Manchester
28.11.89	Seamus O'Sullivan W RSC 1 Battersea
16.02.90	Ramses Evilio W PTS 6 Bilbao, Spain
30.05.90	Darren Mount W PTS 8 Stoke
05.09.90	Glyn Rhodes L RSC 7 Stoke
25.10.90	Jimmy Harrison L PTS 6 Battersea
19.04.91	Gary Barron DREW 8 Peterborough
12.11.91	Carlos Chase W PTS 6 Milton Keynes
03.03.92	Steve McGovern W RSC 4 Cradley Heath
10.04.92	Willie Beattie W PTS 10 Glasgow
	(Elim. British Welterweight Title)
29.09.92	Nigel Bradley W PTS 8 Stoke
05.10.93	Andrew Murray L RSC 6 Mayfair
	(Vacant Commonwealth Welterweight Title)
09.04.94	Andreas Panayi W PTS 8 Bethnal Green
11.06.94	Andreas Panayi L PTS 8 Bethnal Green
05.10.94	Mark Elliot L PTS 8 Wolverhampton
15.03.95	Shea Neary L RSC 3 Stoke
11.10.95	Shaun Stokes W PTS 6 Solihull

28.10.95	Paul Knights L PTS 6 Kensington
22.01.96	Steve McLevy W PTS 8 Glasgow
04.02.96	Naas Scheepers L PTS 8 Johannesburg, South Africa
27.09.96	Michael Ayers L RSC 5 Stevenage

Career: 37 contests, won 24, drew 3, lost 10.

(Danny) Darren Swords (Muir)
Manchester. *Born* Manchester, 7 July, 1968
S. Middleweight. Ht. 5'9½"
Manager J. Doughty

22.09.94	Roy Chipperfield W PTS 6 Bury
05.12.94	Paul Clarkson W RSC 3 Bradford
16.02.95	Shamus Casey W PTS 6 Bury
29.10.95	Shamus Casey W PTS 6 Shaw
22.11.95	David Radford L PTS 6 Sheffield
13.10.96	Johnny Hooks L PTS 6 Shaw
16.03.97	Mike Whittaker W PTS 6 Shaw
29.04.97	Chris Pollock L RSC 6 Manchester

Career: 8 contests, won 5, lost 3.

Matthew Tait
Harrow. *Born* Hillingdon, 15 April, 1973
L. Middleweight. Ht. 5'10½"
Manager D. Mancini

17.12.96	Dean Powell W PTS 6 Bethnal Green
29.01.97	Paul Webb W RTD 1 Bethnal Green
11.02.97	Dean Powell W RSC 4 Bethnal Green

Career: 3 contests, won 3.

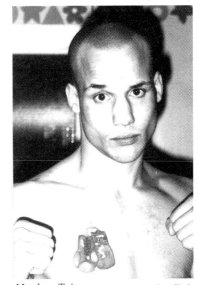

Matthew Tait   Les Clark

Karl Taylor
Birmingham. *Born* Birmingham, 5 January, 1966
L. Welterweight. Midlands Area Lightweight Champion. Ht. 5'5"
Manager Self

18.03.87	Steve Brown W PTS 6 Stoke
06.04.87	Paul Taylor L PTS 6 Southampton
12.06.87	Mark Begley W RSC 1 Leamington
18.11.87	Colin Lynch W RSC 4 Solihull
29.02.88	Peter Bradley L PTS 8 Birmingham
04.10.89	Mark Antony W CO 2 Stafford

30.10.89 Tony Feliciello L PTS 8 Birmingham
06.12.89 John Davison L PTS 8 Leicester
23.12.89 Regilio Tuur L RTD 1 Hoogvliet, Holland
22.02.90 Mark Ramsey L RSC 4 Hull
29.10.90 Steve Walker DREW 6 Birmingham
10.12.90 Elvis Parsley L PTS 6 Birmingham
16.01.91 Wayne Windle W PTS 8 Stoke
02.05.91 Billy Schwer L RSC 2 Northampton
25.07.91 Peter Till L RSC 4 Dudley
  (Midlands Area Lightweight Title Challenge)
24.02.92 Charlie Kane L PTS 8 Glasgow
28.04.92 Richard Woolgar W PTS 6 Wolverhampton
29.05.92 Alan McDowall L PTS 6 Glasgow
25.07.92 Michael Armstrong L RSC 3 Manchester
02.11.92 Hugh Forde L PTS 6 Wolverhampton
23.11.92 Dave McHale L PTS 8 Glasgow
22.12.92 Patrick Gallagher L RSC 3 Mayfair
13.02.93 Craig Dermody L RSC 5 Manchester
31.03.93 Craig Dermody W PTS 6 Barking
07.06.93 Mark Geraghty W PTS 8 Glasgow
13.08.93 Giorgio Campanella L CO 6 Arezzo, Italy
05.10.93 Paul Harvey W PTS 6 Mayfair
21.10.93 Charles Shepherd L RTD 5 Bayswater
21.12.93 Patrick Gallagher L PTS 6 Mayfair
09.02.94 Alan Levene W RSC 2 Brentwood
01.03.94 Shaun Cogan L PTS 6 Dudley
15.03.94 Patrick Gallagher L PTS 6 Mayfair
18.04.94 Peter Till W PTS 10 Walsall
  (Midlands Area Lightweight Title Challenge)
24.05.94 Michael Ayers DREW 8 Sunderland
12.11.94 P. J. Gallagher L PTS 6 Dublin
29.11.94 Dingaan Thobela W PTS 8 Cannock
31.03.95 Michael Ayers L RSC 8 Crystal Palace
  (British Lightweight Title Challenge)
06.05.95 Cham Joof W PTS 8 Shepton Mallet
23.06.95 Poli Diaz L PTS 8 Madrid, Spain
02.09.95 Paul Ryan L RSC 3 Wembley
04.11.95 Carl Wright L PTS 6 Liverpool
15.12.95 Peter Richardson L PTS 8 Bethnal Green
23.01.96 Paul Knights DREW 6 Bethnal Green
05.03.96 Andy Holligan L PTS 6 Barrow
20.03.96 Mervyn Bennett W PTS 8 Cardiff
21.05.96 Malcolm Melvin L PTS 10 Edgbaston
  (Midlands Area L. Welterweight Title Challenge)
07.10.96 Joshua Clottey L RSC 2 Lewisham
20.12.96 Anatoly Alexandrov L RSC 7 Bilbao, Spain
28.01.97 Eamonn Magee L PTS 6 Belfast
28.02.97 Mark Breslin L RSC 6 Kilmarnock
Career: 50 contests, won 14, drew 3, lost 33.

Alan Temple

Hartlepool. *Born* Hartlepool, 21 October, 1972.
Lightweight. Ht. 5'8"
Manager G. Robinson

29.09.94 Stevie Bolt W CO 2 Bethnal Green
22.11.94 Phil Found W PTS 6 Bristol
07.02.95 Brian Coleman W PTS 6 Ipswich
27.04.95 Everald Williams L PTS 6 Bethnal Green
29.09.95 Kevin McKillan W PTS 6 Hartlepool
23.11.95 Rudy Valentino L RSC 3 Marton
02.03.96 Tony Foster W PTS 6 Newcastle
08.06.96 Micky Hall W RSC 2 Newcastle

20.09.96 Scott Dixon L PTS 4 Glasgow
24.10.96 Billy Schwer L PTS 8 Wembley
04.12.96 Harry Escott W PTS 8 Hartlepool
12.02.97 Tanveer Ahmed L RSC 8 Glasgow
  (Elim. British Lightweight Title)
Career: 12 contests, won 7, lost 5.

Alan Temple   Les Clark

John Paul Temple

Islington. *Born* London, 30 May, 1973
Lightweight. Ht. 5'11"
Manager T. Toole

11.02.97 Mark O'Callaghan W PTS 6 Bethnal Green
17.03.97 Les Frost W CO 4 Mayfair
24.04.97 Chris Lyons W PTS 6 Mayfair
Career: 3 contests, won 3.

John Paul Temple   Les Clark

Jonathan Thaxton

Norwich. *Born* Norwich, 10 September, 1974
IBF & WBO Inter-Continental L. Welterweight Champion. Former Southern Area L. Welterweight Champion. Ht. 5'6"
Manager B. Ingle/F. Warren

09.12.92 Scott Smith W PTS 6 Stoke
03.03.93 Dean Hiscox W PTS 6 Solihull
17.03.93 John O. Johnson W PTS 6 Stoke
23.06.93 Brian Coleman W PTS 8 Gorleston
22.09.93 John Smith W PTS 6 Wembley
07.12.93 Dean Hollington W RSC 3 Bethnal Green
10.03.94 B. F. Williams W RSC 4 Watford
  (Vacant Southern Area L. Welterweight Title)
18.11.94 Keith Marner L PTS 10 Bracknell
  (Southern Area L. Welterweight Title Defence)
26.05.95 David Thompson W RSC 6 Norwich
23.06.95 Delroy Leslie W PTS 6 Bethnal Green
12.08.95 Rene Prins L PTS 8 Zaandam, Holland
08.12.95 Colin Dunne L RSC 5 Bethnal Green
  (Vacant Southern Area Lightweight Title)
20.01.96 John O. Johnson W RSC 4 Mansfield
13.02.96 Paul Ryan W RSC 1 Bethnal Green
25.06.96 Mark Elliot W CO 5 Mansfield
  (Vacant IBF Inter-Continental L. Welterweight Title)
14.09.96 Bernard Paul W PTS 12 Sheffield
  (Vacant WBO Inter-Continental L. Welterweight Title)
27.03.97 Paul Burke W RSC 9 Norwich
  (IBF & WBO Inter-Continental L. Welterweight Title Defences)
28.06.97 Gagik Chachatrian W RSC 2 Norwich
  (IBF & WBO Inter-Continental L. Welterweight Title Defences)
Career: 18 contests, won 15, lost 3.

Chris Thomas   Les Clark

Chris Thomas

Merthyr Tydfil. *Born* Merthyr Tydfil, 13 December, 1971
Flyweight. Ht. 5'3½"
Manager B. Ingle

15.03.95	Shaun Norman L RSC 2 Stoke	
28.11.95	Harry Woods L RSC 1 Cardiff	
23.10.96	Jason Whitaker L PTS 6 Halifax	

Career: 3 contests, lost 3.

(David) Danny Thomas

Telford. *Born* Telford, 18 January, 1971
S. Featherweight. Ht. 5'6"
Manager D. Bradley

01.10.96	David Morris L PTS 6 Birmingham
11.10.96	Jason Dee L RSC 3 Mayfair
17.03.97	Nicky Wilders W RSC 6 Mayfair

Career: 3 contests, won 1, lost 2.

Gareth Thomas

Salcombe. *Born* Widnes, 26 March, 1972
S. Middleweight. Ht. 5'10"
Manager N. Christian

03.09.96	Dominic Negus L RSC 2 Bethnal Green
18.10.96	Simon Andrews L RSC 5 Barnstaple
10.12.96	Simon Andrews L RSC 4 Plymouth

Career: 3 contests, lost 3.

Jason Thomas

Merthyr Tydfill. *Born* Pontypridd, 7 October, 1976
Bantamweight. Ht. 5'6"
Manager B. Ingle

28.11.95	Henry Jones W PTS 4 Cardiff
08.12.95	John Sillo L PTS 6 Liverpool
13.01.96	Paul Griffin L RSC 2 Manchester
02.10.96	Henry Jones L PTS 4 Cardiff
23.10.96	Noel Wilders L PTS 6 Halifax
27.11.96	Jason Booth L PTS 4 Swansea
02.06.97	Colin Moffett W RSC 3 Belfast

Career: 7 contests, won 2, lost 5.

Jason Thomas   Les Clark

Michael Thomas

Brighton. *Born* Nigeria, 14 September, 1971
L. Middleweight. Ht. 6'1"
Manager A. Barrow

04.04.97	Jimmy Steel W PTS 6 Brighton

Career: 1 contest, won 1.

(Adrian) Carl Thompson

Manchester. *Born* Manchester, 26 May, 1964
Former European Cruiserweight Champion.
Former Undefeated British & WBC International Cruiserweight Champion.
Ht. 6'0"
Manager N. Basso/F. Warren

06.06.88	Darren McKenna W RSC 2 Manchester
11.10.88	Paul Sheldon W PTS 6 Wolverhampton
13.02.89	Steve Osborne W PTS 6 Manchester
07.03.89	Sean O'Phoenix W RSC 4 Manchester
04.04.89	Keith Halliwell W RSC 1 Manchester
04.05.89	Tenko Ernie W CO 4 Mayfair
12.06.89	Steve Osborne W PTS 8 Manchester
11.07.89	Peter Brown W RSC 5 Batley
31.10.89	Crawford Ashley L RSC 6 Manchester *(Vacant Central Area L. Heavyweight Title)*
21.04.90	Francis Wanyama L PTS 6 St Amandsberg, Belgium
07.03.91	Terry Dixon W PTS 8 Basildon
01.04.91	Yawe Davis L RSC 2 Monaco, Monte Carlo
04.09.91	Nicky Piper W RSC 3 Bethnal Green
04.06.92	Steve Lewsam W RSC 8 Cleethorpes *(Vacant British Cruiserweight Title)*
17.02.93	Arthur Weathers W CO 2 Bethnal Green *(Vacant WBC International Cruiserweight Title)*
31.03.93	Steve Harvey W CO 1 Bethnal Green
25.07.93	Willie Jake W CO 3 Oldham
02.02.94	Massimiliano Duran W CO 8 Ferrara, Italy *(European Cruiserweight Title Challenge)*
14.06.94	Akim Tafer W RSC 6 Epernay, France *(European Cruiserweight Title Defence)*
10.09.94	Dionisio Lazario W RSC 1 Birmingham
13.10.94	Tim Knight W RSC 5 Paris, France
10.06.95	Ralf Rocchigiani L RSC 11 Germany *(Vacant WBO Cruiserweight Title)*
13.04.96	Albert Call W RTD 4 Wythenshawe
09.11.96	Jason Nicholson W PTS 8 Manchester
26.04.97	Keith McMurray W RSC 4 Zurich, Switzerland

Career: 25 contests, won 21, lost 4.

David Thompson

Hull. *Born* Hull, 14 March, 1969
L. Welterweight. Ht. 5'8"
Manager M. Brooks

26.03.90	Mark Conley W PTS 4 Bradford
09.04.90	Andy Rowbotham W PTS 6 Manchester
26.04.90	Andy Rowbotham DREW 6 Manchester
21.05.90	Johnny Walker L CO 1 Bradford
01.11.90	Colin Sinnott L PTS 6 Hull
16.11.90	Carl Tilley L CO 1 Telford
17.12.90	Eddie King W PTS 6 Manchester
18.02.91	Barry North W PTS 6 Birmingham
25.02.91	Steve Winstanley W RTD 4 Bradford
28.03.91	Shane Sheridan L CO 5 Alfreton
17.05.91	Jason Brattley DREW 6 Bury
13.06.91	James Jiora DREW 6 Hull
30.06.91	Nicky Lucas W PTS 6 Southwark
25.07.91	Shaun Cogan L CO 1 Dudley
13.11.91	Mark Tibbs L PTS 6 Bethnal Green
28.11.91	Kevin Toomey L PTS 6 Hull
09.12.91	Chris Aston L PTS 6 Bradford
21.01.92	Ricky Sackfield L CO 1 Stockport
30.03.92	Jason Brattley L PTS 6 Bradford
26.03.93	Tanveer Ahmed L PTS 6 Glasgow
09.12.94	Colin Dunne L RSC 3 Bethnal Green
23.01.95	P. J. Gallagher L RSC 1 Bethnal Green
20.02.95	Jay Mahoney L RSC 4 Manchester
26.05.95	Jonathan Thaxton L RSC 6 Norwich
22.09.95	Dean Nicholas L PTS 6 Hull
29.09.95	Rudy Valentino L RSC 1 Bloomsbury
23.11.95	Alan Bosworth L RSC 4 Tynemouth
01.05.97	Phil Molyneux L CO 1 Hull

Career: 28 contests, won 6, drew 3, lost 19.

Kevin Thompson   Les Clark

Kevin Thompson

Dudley. *Born* Wolverhampton, 11 February, 1967
L. Middleweight. Ht. 6'0"
Manager T. Petersen

09.04.87	Roy Horn W PTS 6 Piccadilly
13.10.87	Eddie Collins W CO 1 Wolverhampton
26.10.87	Dusty Miller W PTS 4 Piccadilly
11.11.87	Danny Shinkwin W CO 4 Stafford
09.12.87	Wil Halliday W PTS 6 Evesham
12.01.88	Frank McCord W RSC 6 Cardiff
09.03.88	Robert Armstrong W RSC 6 Stoke
15.09.89	Mickey Lloyd L CO 7 High Wycombe
02.12.89	Patrick Vungbo L PTS 8 Brussels, Belgium
13.02.90	Julian Eavis W PTS 8 Wolverhampton
14.02.91	Leigh Wicks L PTS 8 Southampton
04.12.92	Mickey Lerwill W PTS 6 Telford

05.03.96	Leigh Wicks W PTS 6 Bethnal Green
13.03.96	Geoff McCreesh L PTS 6 Wembley
09.04.96	Ojay Abrahams L RSC 3 Stevenage
04.06.96	David Radford W PTS 6 York
17.03.97	Steve McNess W RSC 1 Mayfair

Career: 17 contests, won 12, lost 5.

Mike Thompson

Northampton. *Born* Andover, 28 May, 1970
Middleweight. Ht. 6'1½"
Manager J. Weaver

17.02.97	Darren Rees L PTS 6 Bradford
15.04.97	Alex Mason L RSC 2 Edgbaston

Career: 2 contests, lost 2.

Gary Thornhill

Liverpool. *Born* Liverpool, 11 February,
1968
Central Area S. Featherweight Champion.
Ht. 5'6½"
Manager S. Vaughan

27.02.93	Brian Hickey W CO 4 Ellesmere Port
02.07.93	Dougie Fox W CO 1 Liverpool
30.10.93	Miguel Matthews W PTS 6 Chester
01.12.93	Wayne Windle W PTS 6 Stoke
25.02.94	Edward Lloyd DREW 6 Chester
06.05.94	Derek Amory W RSC 1 Liverpool
25.03.95	Craig Kelley W PTS 6 Chester
20.04.95	Michael Hermon W RSC 6 Liverpool
30.06.95	Chip O'Neill W RTD 3 Liverpool
04.11.95	Kid McAuley W PTS 6 Liverpool
08.12.95	Des Gargano W RTD 2 Liverpool
	(Vacant Central Area S. Featherweight Title)
13.04.96	Dominic McGuigan W RSC 3 Liverpool
25.06.96	Chris Jickells W PTS 6 Stevenage
11.12.96	Justin Juuko L RSC 8 Southwark
	(Commonwealth S. Featherweight Title Challenge)

Career: 14 contests, won 12, drew 1, lost 1.

Nicky Thurbin

Loughton. *Born* Ilford, 26 October, 1971
Former Undefeated Southern Area L.
Middleweight Champion. Ht. 5'10"
Manager M. Duff

07.12.93	John Rice W PTS 6 Bethnal Green
14.01.94	Delwyn Panayiotiou W RTD 3 Bethnal Green
16.02.94	Warren Stephens W PTS 6 Stevenage
04.03.94	Andy Peach W PTS 6 Bethnal Green
22.03.94	Carl Winstone W PTS 6 Bethnal Green
11.10.94	Billy McDougall W RSC 6 Bethnal Green
09.12.94	Julian Eavis W PTS 6 Bethnal Green
20.01.95	Marty Duke W PTS 6 Bethnal Green
19.04.95	Peter Mitchell W PTS 6 Bethnal Green
12.05.95	Marty Duke W RSC 3 Bethnal Green
19.05.95	Anthony Lawrence W PTS 6 Southwark
23.06.95	Vince Rose W PTS 10 Bethnal Green
	(Vacant Southern Area L. Middleweight Title)
27.09.95	Steve Goodwin W PTS 8 Bethnal Green
08.12.95	Harry Dhami W PTS 8 Bethnal Green
27.03.97	Kevin Adamson W PTS 8 Norwich
29.05.97	Leigh Wicks W PTS 8 Mayfair

Career: 16 contests, won 16.

Graham Townsend

Hailsham. *Born* Eastbourne, 9 March, 1971
Southern Area S. Middleweight Champion.
Ht. 6'0½"
Manager T. Lawless

24.10.95	Michael Pinnock W PTS 4 Southwark
17.11.95	Michael Pinnock W PTS 4 Bethnal Green
30.01.96	Eddie Knight L PTS 4 Barking
10.05.96	Simon Andrews W RSC 5 Wembley
25.06.96	Butch Lesley W PTS 6 Stevenage
24.10.96	Jason Hart W RSC 5 Mayfair
	(Vacant Southern Area S. Middleweight Title)
29.01.97	Hunter Clay W RSC 1 Bethnal Green
11.02.97	Ridha Sousi L RSC 7 Bethnal Green
04.04.97	Robert Peel W PTS 6 Brighton

Career: 9 contests, won 7, lost 2.

Joe Townsley

Cleland. *Born* Bellshill, 13 January, 1972
L. Middleweight. Ht. 5'9¼"
Manager T. Gilmour

20.03.95	Hughie Davey L PTS 6 Glasgow
05.04.95	Brian Dunn W RSC 3 Irvine
18.11.95	Kevin Toomey W RSC 6 Glasgow
14.02.96	Shamus Casey W PTS 6 Sunderland
18.03.96	Robbie Bell W PTS 6 Glasgow
03.06.96	Shamus Casey W PTS 6 Glasgow
26.09.96	Prince Kasi Kaihau W PTS 8 Glasgow
10.11.96	Michael Alexander W PTS 8 Glasgow
14.03.97	Michael Alexander W PTS 6 Irvine
02.06.97	Hughie Davey W PTS 8 Glasgow

Career: 10 contests, won 9, lost 1.

Steve Tuckett   Les Clark

Steve Tuckett

Wakefield. *Born* Leeds, 27 January, 1973
L. Welterweight. Ht. 5'9"
Manager G. Lockwood

12.01.95	Ram Singh W RSC 6 Leeds
20.02.95	Paul Hughes W PTS 6 Manchester
06.03.95	John T. Kelly W RSC 3 Bradford

26.04.95	George Wilson W PTS 6 Solihull
19.05.95	Micky Hall L RSC 2 Leeds
15.09.95	Mark Legg W PTS 6 Darlington
29.10.95	Bobby Vanzie L RSC 2 Shaw
24.03.96	Wayne Rigby L PTS 6 Shaw
14.11.96	Steve Howden W RSC 1 Sheffield
06.12.96	John Smith W RSC 4 Leeds
18.02.97	Nicky Bardle W CO 2 Cheshunt
24.03.97	Jyri Kjall L CO 1 Helsinki, Finland
13.06.97	Donovan Davey W PTS 6 Leeds

Career: 13 contests, won 9, lost 4.

(Robert) Rocky Turnbull

Bridlington. *Born* Darlington, 16 July, 1973
Featherweight. Ht. 5'4¾"
Manager S. Pollard

28.04.97	Eddie Sica DREW 4 Hull

Career: 1 contest, drew 1.

Rocky Turnbull   Les Clark

Ian Turner

Cardiff. *Born* Abergavenny, 6 November,
1975
Bantamweight. Ht. 5'8"
Manager D. Gardiner

29.05.96	Henry Jones W PTS 6 Ebbw Vale
19.07.96	Marty Chestnut W PTS 6 Ystrad
02.10.96	Kevin Sheil W PTS 6 Cardiff

Career: 3 contests, won 3.

Greg Upton

Teignmouth. *Born* Canada, 11 June, 1971
Featherweight. Western Area
S. Featherweight Champion. Ht. 5'5½"
Manager Self

28.11.91	Eunan Devenney W PTS 6 Evesham
29.04.92	Chris Morris W RSC 2 Liverpool
01.06.92	Graham McGrath W PTS 6 Solihull
19.11.92	Mark Hargreaves L RSC 3 Evesham
24.03.93	Barry Jones L RSC 2 Cardiff
27.05.93	Trevor Royal W CO 2 Bristol
	(Vacant Western Area S. Featherweight Title)

28.10.93	Graham McGrath W PTS 8 Torquay
03.03.94	Sean Knight L RSC 6 Ebbw Vale
25.06.94	Steve Edwards DREW 6 Cullompton
03.08.94	Pete Buckley W PTS 6 Bristol
07.10.94	Jason Hutson L RSC 1 Taunton
16.11.94	Andrew Reed W PTS 6 Bloomsbury
04.02.95	Dean Phillips L PTS 6 Cardiff
27.04.95	Paul Webster L RSC 1 Bethnal Green
15.09.95	Michael Gomez W PTS 4 Mansfield
16.11.95	G. G. Goddard DREW 6 Evesham
29.11.95	Ady Benton W PTS 6 Solihull
05.02.96	Paul Ingle L RSC 10 Bexleyheath
21.01.97	Keith Jones DREW 6 Bristol
26.02.97	Keith Jones W PTS 4 Cardiff
19.04.97	David Jeffrey W RSC 5 Plymouth

Career: 21 contests, won 11, drew 3, lost 7.

Rudy Valentino Les Clark

Rudy Valentino (Isaacs)

Hanwell. *Born* London, 6 July, 1964
Lightweight. Ht. 5'6"
Manager T. Toole

22.10.86	Mike Russell W PTS 6 Greenwich
26.11.86	Tim O'Keefe W PTS 6 Lewisham
19.03.87	Neil Haddock W PTS 6 Bethnal Green
30.04.87	Marvin P. Gray W PTS 6 Washington
15.09.87	Peter Crook L PTS 6 Kensington
18.11.87	Paul Burke L PTS 6 Bethnal Green
02.12.87	Mark Pearce W PTS 6 Piccadilly
18.01.88	John Dickson W PTS 6 Mayfair
08.03.88	James Jiora W PTS 6 Batley
05.04.88	Hugh Forde L RSC 2 Birmingham
18.05.88	Chubby Martin L RSC 5 Lewisham
08.02.89	Paul Moylett W RSC 2 Kensington
15.02.89	Richard Joyce L PTS 6 Stoke
24.04.89	Steve Topliss L PTS 6 Nottingham
21.06.89	Sugar Gibiluru W PTS 6 Eltham
04.09.89	Jose Tuominen L RSC 2 Helsinki, Finland
19.10.89	Harry Escott L RTD 4 Manchester
27.03.90	Peter Bradley L PTS 8 Mayfair
23.04.90	Lee Amass W RSC 6 Crystal Palace
28.05.90	Pierre Lorcy L PTS 8 Paris, France
20.10.90	Gianni di Napoli DREW 8 Leon, France

15.12.90	Angel Mona L PTS 8 Vichy, France
10.04.91	Marcel Herbert W RSC 3 Newport *((Elim. British Lightweight Title)*
17.07.91	Giovanni Parisi L PTS 8 Abbiategrasso, Italy
13.09.91	Giorgio Campanella L PTS 8 Gaggiano, Italy
19.02.92	Michael Ayers L RSC 7 Muswell Hill *(Southern Area Lightweight Title Challenge & Elim. British Lightweight Title)*
17.09.93	Soren Sondergaard L PTS 6 Copenhagen, Denmark
29.10.93	Racheed Lawal L CO 1 Korsoer, Denmark
04.10.94	Paul Burke L PTS 6 Mayfair
07.11.94	Patrick Gallagher L PTS 6 Bethnal Green
19.04.95	Colin Dunne L PTS 6 Bethnal Green
13.06.95	Georgie Smith L PTS 6 Basildon
29.09.95	David Thompson W RSC 1 Bloomsbury
23.11.95	Alan Temple W RSC 3 Marton
05.03.96	Colin Dunne L RSC 4 Bethnal Green
04.03.97	Andy Green L PTS 6 Yarm
24.04.97	Benny Jones W PTS 6 Mayfair
30.06.97	Matt Brown L PTS 10 Bethnal Green *(Southern Area S. Featherweight Title Challenge)*

Career: 38 contests, won 15, drew 1, lost 22.

Bobby Vanzie

Bradford. *Born* Bradford, 11 January, 1974
L. Welterweight. Ht. 5'5"
Manager J. Doughty/T. Gilmour

22.05.95	Alan Peacock W RSC 1 Morecambe
29.10.95	Steve Tuckett W RSC 2 Shaw
14.11.95	John Smith W PTS 6 Bury
07.03.96	John Smith W PTS 6 Bradford
02.06.96	Anthony Campbell W PTS 6 Shaw
28.10.96	Richard Swallow W PTS 6 Bradford
24.02.97	Mark Ramsey DREW 8 Glasgow
08.06.97	C. J. Jackson W RSC 3 Shaw

Career: 8 contests, won 7, drew 1.

Peter Varnavas

Burnley. *Born* Burnley, 27 March, 1974
L. Middleweight. Ht. 5'6"
Manager Self

03.10.94	Carl Smith L RSC 2 Manchester
02.11.94	Andy McVeigh L RSC 3 Birmingham
22.05.95	Wayne Shepherd L PTS 6 Morecambe
08.09.95	Paul Burns L RSC 3 Liverpool
09.10.95	Lee Power L PTS 6 Manchester
09.12.95	Michael Bowen L CO 3 Bethnal Green
13.01.96	Lee Murtagh L PTS 6 Halifax
02.03.96	Geoff McCreesh L PTS 4 Newcastle
15.03.96	Pat Wright L PTS 6 Dunstable
03.04.96	Panayiotis Panayiotiou L PTS 4 Bethnal Green
30.09.96	Richard Inquieti W CO 2 Manchester

Career: 11 contests, won 1, lost 10.

Chris Vassiliou

Margate. *Born* Hitchin, 18 June, 1963
L. Middleweight. Ht. 5'11"
Manager P. Byrne

22.02.93	Darren Blackford L RSC 1 Eltham
26.06.93	Glenn Catley L CO 2 Keynsham
27.05.94	Harry Dhamie L RSC 5 Ashford

24.01.95	Robbie Dunn W PTS 6 Piccadilly
07.02.95	Prince Louis L PTS 4 Ipswich
28.01.97	Alvar Coppard W RSC 6 Piccadilly
08.02.97	Anas Oweida L PTS 4 Millwall
25.04.97	G. L. Booth L PTS 6 Mere

Career: 8 contests, won 2, lost 6.

Louis Veitch

Blackpool. *Born* Glasgow, 9 March, 1963
Former Central Area Flyweight Champion.
Ht. 5'2"
Manager J. McMillan

09.10.91	Tucker Thomas W RSC 4 Marton
11.11.91	Shaun Norman L RSC 5 Bradford
12.03.92	Neil Armstrong L PTS 6 Glasgow
10.04.92	Mark Robertson L PTS 6 Glasgow
16.05.92	Mickey Cantwell L PTS 6 Muswell Hill
09.07.92	Paul Weir L PTS 6 Glasgow
11.09.92	Neil Armstrong L PTS 6 Glasgow
26.10.92	Nick Tooley L PTS 6 Cleethorpes
14.12.92	Lyndon Kershaw DREW 6 Bradford
29.01.93	Neil Armstrong L PTS 6 Glasgow
10.02.93	Mickey Cantwell DREW 8 Lewisham
29.03.93	Neil Parry W PTS 6 Glasgow
29.05.93	Neil Armstrong L PTS 10 Paisley
07.10.93	Lyndon Kershaw W PTS 10 Hull *(Vacant Central Area Flyweight Title)*
22.11.93	James Drummond L PTS 8 Glasgow
02.02.94	Ian Baillie W RSC 1 Glasgow
25.03.94	Jesper D. Jensen L PTS 6 Bornholme, Denmark
24.05.94	Vince Feeney L PTS 6 Leicester
02.11.94	Lyndon Kershaw W PTS 10 Solihull *(Central Area Flyweight Title Defence)*
21.01.95	James Murray L RSC 3 Glasgow *(Scottish Bantamweight Title Challenge)*
05.04.95	Keith Knox DREW 6 Irvine
14.06.95	Ady Benton W RSC 2 Batley
02.07.95	Vince Feeney L PTS 4 Dublin
20.11.95	Keith Knox L RSC 6 Glasgow *(Vacant Scottish Flyweight Title. Elim. British Flyweight Title)*
05.03.96	Peter Culshaw L RSC 3 Barrow *(Central Area Flyweight Title Defence)*
03.06.96	Paul Weir L CO 1 Glasgow
18.09.96	Harry Woods W DIS 4 Tylorstown
01.12.96	Ady Lewis L PTS 10 Shaw *(Vacant Central Area Flyweight Title)*
24.01.97	Jesper Jensen L PTS 8 Copenhagen, Denmark
28.02.97	Des Gargano W PTS 6 Kilmarnock
02.06.97	Tommy Waite L RSC 5 Belfast

Career: 31 contests, won 8, drew 3, lost 20.

Jimmy Vincent

Birmingham. *Born* Barnet, 5 June, 1969
L. Middleweight. Ht. 5'8"
Manager N. Nobbs

19.10.87	Roy Williams W PTS 6 Birmingham
11.11.87	Mick Greenwood W PTS 6 Stafford
19.11.87	Darryl Pettit W RSC 6 Ilkeston
24.11.87	Roy Williams W PTS 6 Wolverhampton
14.02.88	Niel Leggett L PTS 6 Peterborough
29.02.88	Billy Cawley W CO 1 Birmingham
13.04.88	Dave Croft W PTS 6 Wolverhampton
16.05.88	Barry North W PTS 6 Wolverhampton
14.06.88	Dean Dickinson W PTS 6 Birmingham
20.09.88	Henry Armstrong L PTS 6 Stoke

10.10.88 Henry Armstrong L PTS 6 Manchester
17.10.88 Dean Dickinson W PTS 6 Birmingham
14.11.88 Peter Gabbitus L PTS 6 Stratford upon Avon
22.11.88 Barry North W RSC 4 Wolverhampton
12.12.88 Tony Feliciello L PTS 8 Birmingham
09.09.92 Mark Dawson L PTS 6 Stoke
23.09.92 Mark Epton W RSC 6 Leeds
17.12.92 Jason Rowland L PTS 6 Wembley
06.03.93 Mark Tibbs W PTS 6 Glasgow
27.08.96 Geoff McCreesh L RSC 1 Windsor
26.09.96 David Bain W RSC 3 Walsall
28.10.96 Lee Murtagh W RSC 2 Bradford
18.01.97 Tommy Quinn W RSC 1 Swadlincote
25.02.97 Kevin Adamson W PTS 6 Sheffield
25.03.97 Gary Jacobs L RSC 1 Lewisham
Career: 25 contests, won 16, lost 9.

Jimmy Vincent   Les Clark

Peter Vosper

Plymouth. *Born* Plymouth, 6 October, 1966
Western Area L. Heavyweight Champion.
Ht. 5'10"
Manager Self

15.02.89 Mark White W PTS 6 Bethnal Green
01.03.89 Lester Jacobs L PTS 6 Bethnal Green
29.03.89 George Moody L PTS 6 Bethnal Green
09.05.89 Tony Cloak W RSC 2 Plymouth
20.06.89 Spencer Alton W PTS 6 Plymouth
17.10.89 Spencer Alton DREW 8 Plymouth
30.11.89 Ray Webb L PTS 6 Southwark
03.03.90 Michael Gale L RSC 2 Wembley
26.04.90 Michael Clarke L PTS 6 Wandsworth
21.05.90 Chris Walker W RSC 2 Mayfair
26.09.90 Ali Forbes L PTS 6 Mayfair
12.04.91 Frank Eubanks L RSC 1 Manchester
30.05.91 Russell Washer W PTS 6 Mayfair
06.06.91 John Kaighin DREW 6 Barking
27.06.91 Nick Manners L RSC 1 Leeds
16.12.91 Paul McCarthy L PTS 6 Southampton
25.02.92 Roland Ericsson L RSC 6 Crystal Palace
01.12.92 John Kaighin L RSC 4 Bristol
13.11.93 Martin Rosamond W PTS 6 Cullompton

04.03.94 Cliff Churchward W PTS 8 Weston super Mare
17.06.94 Paul Murray W PTS 8 Plymouth
07.10.94 Darren Dorrington L RSC 6 Taunton
(Vacant Western Area S. Middleweight Title)
13.01.95 Thomas Hansvold L PTS 6 Aalborg, Denmark
17.02.95 Mark Delaney L RSC 1 Crawley
25.03.95 Steve McNess L RSC 5 Millwall
23.05.95 Howard Eastman L RSC 1 Bethnal Green
19.09.95 Spencer Alton W RTD 3 Plymouth
13.11.95 Martin Jolley L PTS 6 Barnstaple
16.12.95 Glenn Catley L RSC 2 Cardiff
23.02.96 Barry Exton L PTS 6 Weston super Mare
04.04.96 Carl Winstone W PTS 6 Plymouth
20.04.96 Steve Roberts L PTS 6 Brentwood
11.05.96 Jason Matthews L RSC 1 Bethnal Green
29.06.96 Anthony McFadden L PTS 4 Erith
19.10.96 Darren Dorrington L RSC 3 Bristol
07.03.97 Peter Mitchell L PTS 8 Weston super Mare
19.04.97 Simon Andrews W PTS 10 Plymouth
(Vacant Western Area L. Heavyweight Title)
Career: 37 contests, won 11, drew 2, lost 24.

Tommy Waite

Belfast. *Born* Belfast, 11 March, 1972
Bantamweight. Ht. 5'4"
Manager B. Hearn

28.05.96 Graham McGrath W PTS 4 Belfast
03.09.96 Danny Ruegg W RSC 4 Belfast
05.11.96 Graham McGrath W PTS 4 Belfast
28.01.97 Rowan Williams W PTS 4 Belfast
29.04.97 Henry Jones W PTS 4 Belfast
02.06.97 Louis Veitch W RSC 5 Belfast
Career: 6 contests, won 6.

Ivan Walker

Newcastle. *Born* Blyth, 6 February, 1970
L. Welterweight. Ht. 5'8"
Manager N. Fawcett

01.05.97 Les Frost W CO 1 Newcastle
16.05.97 Scott McQueen W PTS 6 Glasgow
13.06.97 Gerard Murphy L PTS 6 Paisley
Career: 3 contests, won 2, lost 1.

Scott Walker

Oldham. *Born* Oldham, 5 December, 1970
L. Welterweight. Ht. 5'5"
Manager J. Doughty

18.04.94 Paul Bowen W PTS 6 Manchester
02.06.94 Brian Coleman W CO 1 Middleton
26.09.94 Carl Tilley W PTS 6 Morecambe
28.11.94 Wahid Fats L RSC 4 Manchester
16.02.95 John T. Kelly W PTS 6 Bury
08.03.95 Anthony Maynard L PTS 6 Solihull
18.05.95 Mark Allen W RSC 2 Middleton
29.10.95 T. J. Smith W PTS 6 Shaw
24.03.96 Alan Bosworth DREW 6 Shaw
02.06.96 Liam Dineen W RSC 1 Shaw
13.10.96 John Smith W PTS 6 Shaw
01.12.96 Anthony Campbell L RSC 4 Shaw
08.06.97 Brian Booth W PTS 6 Shaw
Career: 13 contests, won 9, drew 1, lost 3.

Tony Walton

Liverpool. *Born* Liverpool, 28 September, 1972
Middleweight. Ht. 5'10"
Manager Self

16.02.94 Geoff McCreesh L PTS 6 Stevenage
11.03.94 Steve McNess L PTS 4 Bethnal Green
14.10.96 Steve McNess L PTS 6 Mayfair
Career: 3 contests, lost 3.

Jamie Warters

York. *Born* York, 16 December, 1973
L. Heavyweight. Ht. 6'1"
Manager T. O'Neill

15.09.95 Phil Reid W RSC 5 Darlington
07.12.95 Scott Beasley W PTS 6 Hull
19.03.96 Declan Faherty W PTS 6 Leeds
13.06.97 Greg Scott-Briggs W RSC 5 Leeds
Career: 4 contests, won 4.

Mike Watson

Nottingham. *Born* Nottingham, 17 December, 1973
Welterweight. Ht. 5'9"
Manager W. Swift

25.01.95 Steve Howden L RSC 2 Stoke
08.03.95 Adam Baldwin W PTS 6 Bloomsbury
22.07.95 Martin Holgate L PTS 6 Millwall
01.09.95 Clayton Hollingsworth W PTS 6 Wolverhampton
18.09.95 Mark Breslin L PTS 6 Glasgow
05.10.95 Tom Welsh L CO 3 Queensferry
03.11.95 Gary Hiscox L PTS 6 Dudley
08.12.95 Allan Gray L PTS 6 Bethnal Green
15.03.96 Allan Gray DREW 6 Dunstable
29.04.96 Allan Gray L PTS 6 Mayfair
25.06.96 James Hare L PTS 4 Mansfield
25.10.96 John Briffa W RSC 1 Mere
11.01.97 Gilbert Eastman L RSC 1 Bethnal Green
20.03.97 Chris Barnett L RSC 2 Salford
Career: 14 contests, won 3, drew 1, lost 10.

Mike Watson   Les Clark

Peter Waudby

Hull. *Born* Hull, 18 November, 1970
Central Area L. Middleweight Champion.
Ht. 5'10½"
Manager L. Billany

21.09.92	Simon Fisher W RSC 2 Cleethorpes
16.10.92	Chris Mulcahy W RSC 4 Hull
14.12.92	Shamus Casey W PTS 6 Cleethorpes
10.05.93	Julian Eavis W PTS 6 Cleethorpes
27.05.93	Warren Stowe L PTS 6 Burnley
16.09.93	Shamus Casey W PTS 6 Hull
10.11.93	Roy Rowland W RSC 5 Watford
13.12.93	Chris Richards W PTS 6 Cleethorpes
17.03.94	Dave Johnson W PTS 6 Lincoln
15.04.94	Colin Pitters W PTS 8 Hull
16.05.94	Shamus Casey W PTS 6 Cleethorpes
25.10.94	Kevin Lueshing L RSC 2 Middlesbrough
24.11.94	Shamus Casey W PTS 6 Hull
16.02.95	Derek Wormald DREW 6 Bury
06.03.95	Paul Jones L PTS 6 Mayfair
22.09.95	Andrew Jervis W PTS 10 Hull *(Vacant Central Area L. Middleweight Title)*
18.11.95	Willie Quinn L RTD 6 Glasgow *(WBO Inter-Continental Middleweight Title Challenge)*
26.02.96	Earl Ling W PTS 6 Hull
09.05.96	Craig Winter W RSC 5 Hull *(Elim. British L. Middleweight Title)*
28.11.96	Trevor Meikle W PTS 8 Hull
25.02.97	Ryan Rhodes L CO 1 Sheffield *(British L. Middleweight Title Challenge)*

Career: 21 contests, won 15, drew 1, lost 5.

Paul Webb

Bulkington. *Born* Nuneaton, 5 July, 1970
L. Middleweight. Ht. 5'11"
Manager P. Byrne

08.03.95	Peter Mitchell L RSC 1 Bloomsbury
11.05.95	Robbie Bell L PTS 6 Sunderland
20.06.95	Steve Levene L PTS 6 Birmingham
24.01.96	Carlton Williams L PTS 6 Stoke
13.02.96	Andy Peach L PTS 6 Wolverhampton
29.02.96	Cam Raeside L PTS 6 Scunthorpe
27.03.96	Carlton Williams L PTS 6 Whitwick
22.04.96	Brian Dunn L PTS 6 Cleethorpes
29.04.96	Marty Duke L PTS 6 Hull
16.05.96	Marty Duke L PTS 6 Dunstable
04.06.96	Ron Hopley L PTS 6 York
03.07.96	Kevin McCarthy L RSC 2 Wembley
12.09.96	Robert Harper NC 2 Doncaster
26.09.96	Andy Peach L PTS 6 Walsall
07.10.96	Peter McCormack DREW 6 Birmingham
24.10.96	Andy Peach W RSC 3 Birmingham
21.11.96	Steve Levene L RSC 2 Solihull
29.01.97	Matthew Tait L RTD 1 Bethnal Green

Career: 18 contests, won 1, drew 1, lost 15, no contest 1.

Ray Webb

Stepney. *Born* Hackney, 10 March, 1966
S. Middleweight. Ht. 5'11"
Manager D. Powell

02.11.88	Doug Calderwood W RSC 6 Southwark
12.01.89	Robert Gomez W RSC 1 Southwark
30.11.89	Peter Vosper W PTS 6 Southwark
06.04.90	Carlo Colarusso L PTS 6 Telford

15.09.90	Ray Close L PTS 8 Belfast
06.11.90	Ahmet Canbakis W PTS 6 Mayfair
08.12.90	Franck Nicotra L PTS 8 Ferrara, Italy
10.01.91	Carlos Christie W PTS 6 Wandsworth
27.03.91	Silvio Branco L PTS 8 Mestre, Italy
30.05.91	Karl Barwise W PTS 8 Mayfair
11.12.91	Ian Strudwick L CO 8 Basildon *(Vacant Southern Area S. Middleweight Title)*
06.03.92	Oleg Volkov L PTS 8 Berlin, Germany
28.11.93	Karl Barwise W PTS 6 Southwark
06.03.94	Trevor Ambrose W RSC 6 Southwark
27.04.94	Darron Griffiths L RSC 6 Bethnal Green *(Elim. British S. Middleweight Title)*
20.02.95	Craig Joseph W PTS 6 Glasgow
29.11.95	Montell Griffin L RSC 6 Southwark
26.11.96	David Starie L RSC 6 Bethnal Green

Career: 18 contests, won 9, lost 9.

Greg Wedlake

Minehead. *Born* Bristol, 19 January, 1970
Heavyweight. Ht. 6'2¾"
Manager C. Sanigar

19.10.96	Lennox Williams W PTS 4 Bristol
09.12.96	Johnny Davison W PTS 6 Bristol
21.01.97	Johnny Davison W RSC 2 Bristol
05.06.97	David Jules W RSC 3 Bristol

Career: 4 contests, won 4.

Greg Wedlake   Les Clark

Paul Weir

Irvine. *Born* Glasgow, 16 September, 1967
Flyweight. Former WBO L. Flyweight
Champion. Former Undefeated WBO M.
Flyweight Champion. Ht. 5'3"
Manager T. Gilmour

27.04.92	Eduardo Vallejo W CO 2 Glasgow
09.07.92	Louis Veitch W PTS 6 Glasgow
21.09.92	Neil Parry W RSC 4 Glasgow
23.11.92	Shaun Norman W PTS 8 Glasgow
06.03.93	Kevin Jenkins W PTS 8 Glasgow
15.05.93	Fernando Martinez W RSC 7 Glasgow *(Vacant WBO M. Flyweight Title)*

25.10.93	Lindi Memani W PTS 12 Glasgow *(WBO M. Flyweight Title Defence)*
02.02.94	Josue Camacho L PTS 12 Glasgow *(WBO L. Flyweight Title Challenge)*
23.11.94	Paul Oulden W PTS 12 Irvine *(Vacant WBO L. Flyweight Title)*
05.04.95	Ric Magramo W PTS 12 Irvine *(WBO L. Flyweight Title Defence)*
29.07.95	Jose Luis Velarde W PTS 10 Whitley Bay
18.11.95	Jacob Matlala L TD 5 Glasgow *(WBO L. Flyweight Title Defence)*
13.04.96	Jacob Matlala L RSC 10 Liverpool *(WBO L. Flyweight Title Challenge)*
03.06.96	Louis Veitch W CO 1 Glasgow
11.10.96	Lyndon Kershaw W PTS 6 Mayfair
28.02.97	Anthony Hanna W PTS 8 Kilmarnock
02.05.97	Jesper Jensen L RSC 8 Randers, Denmark *(European Flyweight Title Challenge)*

Career: 17 contests, won 13, lost 4.

Paul Weir   Les Clark

Scott Welch

Shoreham. *Born* Yarmouth, 21 April, 1968
Former Undefeated British, Commonwealth
& WBO Inter-Continental Heavyweight
Champion. Former Undefeated Southern
Area Heavyweight Champion. Ht. 6'2"
Manager F. Warren

08.09.92	John Williams W RSC 5 Norwich
06.10.92	Gary Williams W PTS 4 Antwerp, Belgium
23.02.93	Gary Charlton L RSC 3 Doncaster
11.05.93	Denroy Bryan W RSC 4 Norwich
29.06.93	John Harewood W RSC 5 Mayfair
18.09.93	Des Vaughan W RSC 2 Leicester
28.09.93	Gypsy Carman W RSC 3 Bethnal Green
05.10.93	Cordwell Hylton W RSC 1 Mayfair
06.11.93	Joey Paladino W RSC 3 Bethnal Green
30.11.93	Chris Coughlan W CO 1 Cardiff
21.12.93	Carl Gaffney W RSC 3 Mayfair
15.03.94	Steve Garber W RSC 4 Mayfair

157

06.05.94 James Oyebola L CO 5 Atlantic City, USA
(Vacant WBC International Heavyweight Title)
17.09.94 R. F. McKenzie W RSC 1 Crawley
10.12.94 Michael Murray W PTS 8 Manchester
13.05.95 Eduardo Carranza W CO 1 Glasgow
01.07.95 Julius Francis W RSC 10 Kensington
(Southern Area Heavyweight Title Challenge. Final Elim. British Heavyweight Title)
27.10.95 James Oyebola W RSC 10 Brighton
(British Heavyweight Title Challenge. Vacant Commonwealth & WBO Inter-Continental Heavyweight Titles)
16.03.96 Joe Bugner W RSC 6 Berlin, Germany
(WBO Inter-Continental Heavyweight Title Defence)
08.06.96 Mike Sedillo W RSC 1 Newcastle
09.11.96 Daniel Netto W PTS 8 Las Vegas, USA
11.01.97 Henry Akinwande L PTS 12 Nashville, USA
(WBO Heavyweight Title Challenge)
28.06.97 Yuri Yelistratov W RSC 1 Norwich
Career: 23 contests, won 20, lost 3.

Nigel Wenton

Liverpool. *Born* Liverpool, 5 April, 1969
Welterweight. Ht. 5'7"
Manager Self

08.06.88 Steve Taggart W RSC 2 Sheffield
23.06.88 Rafael Saez W RSC 3 Panama City, Panama
19.10.88 Niel Leggett W RTD 2 Belfast
02.11.88 Kid Sumali W RTD 3 Southwark
15.11.88 Tony Graham W RSC 3 Piccadilly
07.12.88 John Bennie W RSC 5 Belfast
14.12.88 Young Joe Rafiu W RSC 1 Kirkby
18.01.89 Ian Honeywood W RSC 3 Kensington
25.01.89 Mark Perce W PTS 6 Belfast
08.03.89 Juan Torres W RTD 3 Belfast
12.04.89 Edwin Murillo W CO 2 Belfast
10.05.89 Nigel Senior W RSC 2 Kensington
07.06.89 Eamonn Payne W RSC 3 Wembley
28.07.89 Fabian Salazar L PTS 6 Isla Margarita, Venezuela
19.09.89 Sugar Gibiliru W PTS 8 Belfast
31.10.89 Tomas Arguelles W PTS 6 Belfast
13.12.89 Tony Dore W PTS 6 Kirkby
21.02.90 Luis Mendieta W RSC 3 Belfast
17.03.90 Scott de Pew W RSC 2 Belfast
29.04.90 Sharmba Mitchell L PTS 8 Atlantic City, USA
15.07.90 Bryant Paden DREW 10 Atlantic City, USA
07.09.91 Oliver Harrison W RTD 5 Belfast
13.11.91 Tony Richards W RSC 5 Belfast
11.12.91 Jeff Roberts W CO 2 Dublin
25.04.92 Ed Pollard W RTD 6 Belfast
10.12.92 Davy Robb W RSC 3 Bethnal Green
13.02.93 Charles Shepherd L PTS 8 Manchester
18.06.93 David Sample L PTS 10 Belfast
28.03.95 Kenny Louis W CO 2 Bay St Louis, USA
08.07.95 Walter Cowans W RSC 4 Laporte, USA
02.10.95 Howard Clarke W PTS 6 Mayfair
07.12.95 Scott Salaam W RSC 1 Hammond, USA
22.03.97 Wayne Boudreaux W PTS 8 Wythenshawe
19.04.97 Craig Houk W RSC 1 Milan, Italy
Career: 34 contests, won 29, drew 1, lost 4.

Richie Wenton

Liverpool. *Born* Liverpool, 28 October, 1967
Former Undefeated British & WBO Inter-Continental S. Bantamweight Champion.
Ht. 5'8"
Manager F. Warren

14.12.88 Miguel Matthews W CO 2 Kirkby
25.01.89 Sean Casey W PTS 4 Belfast
10.04.89 Stuart Carmichael W RSC 2 Mayfair
13.12.89 Joe Mullen W RSC 5 Kirkby
21.02.90 Ariel Cordova W PTS 6 Belfast
17.03.90 Mark Johnson W PTS 4 Belfast
28.03.90 Jose Luis Vasquez W PTS 6 Manchester
23.05.90 Graham O'Malley W PTS 6 Belfast
09.07.90 Eugene Pratt W CO 1 Miami Beach, USA
15.09.90 Graham O'Malley W PTS 6 Belfast
30.10.90 Alejandro Armenta W RSC 2 Belfast
12.02.91 Sean Casey W PTS 4 Belfast
31.03.92 Graham O'Malley W PTS 6 Stockport
25.07.92 Ramos Agare W RSC 3 Manchester
26.09.92 Floyd Churchill L RSC 2 Earls Court
28.04.93 Kelton McKenzie W PTS 8 Dublin
13.11.93 Des Gargano W PTS 8 Cullompton
26.04.94 Bradley Stone W RSC 10 Bethnal Green
(Vacant British S. Bantamweight Title)
01.10.94 Neil Swain L RTD 5 Cardiff
25.03.95 Paul Lloyd W RSC 5 Chester
(British S. Bantamweight Title Defence)
30.06.95 Mike Parris W PTS 12 Liverpool
(Vacant WBO Inter-Continental S. Bantamweight Title)
09.10.95 Vincenzo Belcastro L PTS 12 San Benedetto, Italy
(European S. Bantamweight Title Challenge)
06.02.96 Wilson Docherty W PTS 12 Basildon
(British S. Bantamweight Title Defence)
19.09.96 Efren Gonzalez W PTS 8 Manchester
Career: 24 contests, won 21, lost 3.

Paul Wesley

Birmingham. *Born* Birmingham, 2 May, 1962
Middleweight. Ht. 5'9"
Manager N. Nobbs

20.02.87 B. K. Bennett L PTS 6 Maidenhead
18.03.87 Darryl Ritchie DREW 4 Stoke
08.04.87 Dean Murray W PTS 6 Evesham
29.04.87 John Wright W PTS 4 Loughborough
12.06.87 Leon Thomas W RSC 2 Leamington
16.11.87 Steve McCarthy L CO 8 Southampton
25.01.88 Paul Murray W PTS 8 Birmingham
29.02.88 Paul Murray DREW 8 Birmingham
15.03.88 Johnny Williamson W CO 2 Bournemouth
09.04.88 Joe McKenzie W RSC 6 Bristol
10.05.88 Tony Meszaros W PTS 8 Edgbaston
21.03.89 Carlton Warren L CO 2 Wandsworth
10.05.89 Rod Douglas L CO 1 Kensington
24.10.89 Nigel Rafferty L PTS 6 Wolverhampton
22.11.89 Nigel Rafferty L PTS 8 Stafford
28.11.89 Nigel Rafferty L PTS 6 Wolverhampton
05.12.89 Ian Strudwick L PTS 6 Catford
24.01.90 Rocky Feliciello W PTS 6 Solihull
19.02.90 Nigel Rafferty L PTS 8 Birmingham
22.03.90 John Ashton L PTS 10 Wolverhampton
(Midlands Area Middleweight Title Challenge)
17.04.90 Winston May DREW 8 Millwall
09.05.90 Alan Richards W PTS 8 Solihull
04.06.90 Julian Eavis W PTS 8 Birmingham
18.09.90 Shaun Cummins L RSC 1 Wolverhampton
17.10.90 Julian Eavis W PTS 6 Stoke
23.01.91 Wally Swift Jnr L PTS 10 Solihull
(Midlands Area L. Middleweight Title Challenge)
20.03.91 Horace Fleary L RSC 5 Solihull
16.05.91 Delroy Waul L RSC 7 Liverpool
04.07.91 Neville Brown W RSC 1 Alfreton
31.07.91 Francesco dell'Aquila L PTS 8 Casella, Italy
03.10.91 Neville Brown L PTS 8 Burton
29.10.91 Tony Collins DREW 8 Kensington
03.03.92 Antonio Fernandez L PTS 10 Cradley Heath
(Vacant Midlands Area Middleweight Title)
10.04.92 Jean-Charles Meuret L PTS 8 Geneva, Switzerland
03.06.92 Sumbu Kalambay L PTS 10 Salice Terme, Italy
29.10.92 Ian Strudwick W RSC 1 Bayswater
14.11.92 Paul Busby L PTS 8 Cardiff
24.11.92 Paul Jones W RSC 2 Doncaster
16.03.93 Chris Pyatt L PTS 10 Mayfair
04.06.93 Jacques le Blanc L PTS 10 Moncton, Canada
28.07.93 Antonio Fernandez L RSC 3 Brixton
(Midlands Area Middleweight Title Challenge)
09.10.93 Warren Stowe W PTS 10 Manchester
(Elim. British L. Middleweight Title)
09.02.94 Steve Collins L PTS 8 Brentwood
10.02.95 Robert McCracken L PTS 12 Birmingham
(British L. Middleweight Title Challenge)
24.02.95 Scott Doyle W PTS 8 Weston super Mare
18.03.95 Crisanto Espana L PTS 6 Millstreet
21.04.95 Gilbert Jackson L RSC 6 Dudley
(Elim. British L. Middleweight Title)
31.01.96 Howard Eastman L RSC 1 Birmingham
21.03.96 Gary Logan L PTS 6 Southwark
13.04.96 Harry Simon L RTD 4 Wythenshawe
26.09.96 Nigel Rafferty DREW 6 Walsall
19.10.96 Glenn Catley L RSC 7 Bristol
25.03.97 Chris Johnson L CO 2 Lewisham
Career: 53 contests, won 16, drew 5, lost 32.

Darren Westover

Ilford. *Born* Plaistow, 3 September, 1968
Cruiserweight. Ht. 6'3"
Manager B. Hearn

04.10.89 Dave Furneaux W RSC 1 Kensington
25.10.89 David Haycock W RSC 2 Wembley
06.12.89 Kevin Roper W RSC 1 Wembley
03.03.90 Steve Osborne W RSC 6 Wembley
26.04.94 Newby Stevens W RSC 5 Bethnal Green
11.05.94 Art Stacey W PTS 6 Stevenage
09.05.95 Rob Albon W RSC 2 Basildon
13.06.95 Nicky Wadman W RSC 1 Basildon
17.07.95 Steve Osborne W RSC 5 Mayfair

20.09.95 Nigel Rafferty W PTS 6 Potters Bar
05.02.96 Chris Okoh L RSC 2 Bexleyheath
(Vacant WBO Inter-Continental Cruiserweight Title)
28.04.97 Chris Henry L RTD 4 Enfield
(Vacant Southern Area Cruiserweight Title)
05.06.97 Kelly Oliver L RTD 1 Bristol
Career: 13 contests, won 10, lost 3.

Jason Whitaker

Halifax. *Born* Halifax, 29 April, 1973
S. Bantamweight. Ht. 5'9"
Manager T. Callighan

23.10.96 Chris Thomas W PTS 6 Halifax
17.02.97 Sean Green L PTS 6 Bradford
02.06.97 Alston Buchanan L RSC 6 Glasgow
Career: 3 contests, won 1, lost 2.

Jason Whitaker   Les Clark

Lee Whitehead

Manchester. *Born* Barton, 16 July, 1965
S. Middleweight. Ht. 5'10¾"
Manager N. Basso

09.10.95 Roy Chipperfield W RSC 2 Manchester
04.12.95 Phil Ball W PTS 6 Manchester
13.01.96 Elwen Brooks W PTS 6 Manchester
26.02.96 Kevin Burton W PTS 6 Manchester
13.04.96 Mark Snipe L PTS 4 Wythenshawe
02.06.96 Andy Fletcher W RSC 2 Shaw
22.08.96 Peter Mason W PTS 6 Salford
19.09.96 Brian Galloway W PTS 4 Manchester
22.12.96 Martin Jolley DREW 6 Salford
18.01.97 Mark Dawson W PTS 6 Manchester
26.06.97 Martin Jolley W PTS 6 Salford
Career: 11 contests, won 9, drew 1, lost 1.

Johnny Whiteside

Preston. *Born* Preston, 14 September, 1973
S. Middleweight. Ht. 6'0½"
Manager J. Doughty

13.10.96 Jimmy Steel W RSC 2 Shaw
01.12.96 Andy Gray W PTS 6 Shaw
Career: 2 contests, won 2.

Mike Whittaker

Oldham. *Born* Rochdale, 9 January, 1968
S. Middleweight. Ht. 5'11½"
Manager J. Doughty

30.09.96 Pat Durkin W PTS 6 Manchester
01.12.96 Andy Fletcher W CO 1 Shaw
16.03.97 Darren Swords L PTS 6 Shaw
08.06.97 Lee Gordon W RSC 1 Shaw
Career: 4 contests, won 3, lost 1.

Terry Whittaker

Barnsley. *Born* Barnsley, 15 July, 1971
S. Featherweight. Ht. 5'6½"
Manager K. Tate

17.11.94 Ram Singh W PTS 6 Sheffield
14.06.95 Ram Singh W PTS 6 Batley
18.10.95 Kid McAuley W PTS 6 Batley
29.11.95 Kid McAuley DREW 6 Solihull
21.02.96 Miguel Matthews W PTS 6 Batley
20.05.96 Arv Mittoo W CO 5 Cleethorpes
30.05.96 Kid McAuley W PTS 6 Lincoln
06.11.96 Tommy Janes L RSC 4 Tylorstown
Career: 8 contests, won 6, drew 1, lost 1.

Leigh Wicks

Brighton. *Born* Worthing, 29 July, 1965
L. Middleweight. Ht. 5'6¼"
Manager H. Holland

29.04.87 Fidel Castro W PTS 6 Hastings
26.09.87 Jason Rowe W PTS 6 Hastings
18.11.87 Lou Ayres W PTS 6 Holborn
26.01.88 Theo Marius L PTS 8 Hove
15.02.88 Shamus Casey W PTS 6 Copthorne
26.04.88 Franki Moro DREW 8 Hove
04.05.88 Tony Britton W PTS 8 Wembley
18.05.88 Mark Howell W RSC 8 Portsmouth
25.05.88 Newton Barnett DREW 8 Hastings
22.11.88 Roy Callaghan L PTS 8 Basildon
16.03.89 Tony Britland W PTS 8 Southwark
12.10.89 Tony Gibbs W CO 2 Southwark
08.02.90 Ernie Noble W PTS 8 Southwark
26.04.90 Julian Eavis DREW 8 Mayfair
06.11.90 Gordon Blair W PTS 8 Mayfair
10.01.91 Barry Messam W PTS 6 Wandsworth
14.02.91 Kevin Thompson W PTS 8 Southampton
21.10.91 Tony Britland W RSC 3 Mayfair
20.02.92 Mick Duncan L PTS 8 Glasgow
30.04.92 Darren Morris DREW 6 Mayfair
19.10.92 Bozon Haule W PTS 8 Mayfair
20.01.93 Robert McCracken L PTS 8 Wolverhampton
17.02.93 Kevin Lueshing L PTS 6 Bethnal Green
22.04.93 Warren Stowe L PTS 6 Bury
27.10.95 Danny Quacoe W RSC 4 Brighton
18.11.95 Gary Jacobs L RTD 3 Glasgow
26.01.96 Wayne Appleton L PTS 6 Brighton
05.03.96 Kevin Thompson L PTS 6 Bethnal Green
24.03.97 Ross Hale L PTS 6 Bristol
08.04.97 Ahmet Dottuev W RSC 1 Bethnal Green
29.05.97 Nicky Thurbin L PTS 8 Mayfair
Career: 31 contests, won 16, drew 4, lost 11.

Nicky Wilders

Castleford. *Born* Castleford, 11 August, 1973
Featherweight. Ht. 5'6"
Manager T. Callighan

04.10.96 Shaune Danskin W PTS 6 Wakefield
06.12.96 Lyndon Kershaw W PTS 6 Leeds
03.03.97 Jason Squire L PTS 6 Leicester
17.03.97 Danny Thomas L RSC 6 Mayfair
Career: 4 contests, won 2, lost 2.

Noel Wilders

Castleford. *Born* Castleford, 4 January, 1975
Bantamweight. Ht. 5'5"
Manager T. Callighan

16.03.96 Neil Parry W RTD 4 Sheffield
04.06.96 Graham McGrath W PTS 6 York
04.10.96 Tiger Singh W PTS 6 Wakefield
23.10.96 Jason Thomas W PTS 6 Halifax
12.03.97 John Matthews W PTS 6 Stoke
20.04.97 Shaun Anderson W PTS 6 Leeds
Career: 6 contests, won 6.

Noel Wilders   Les Clark

Carlton Williams

Leicester. *Born* Kingston, Jamaica, 2 August, 1969
Middleweight. Ht. 5'11½"
Manager J. Griffin

26.10.95 Barry Exton DREW 6 Birmingham
11.12.95 Brian Dunn L RSC 4 Cleethorpes
24.01.96 Paul Webb W PTS 6 Stoke
27.03.96 Paul Webb W PTS 6 Whitwick
09.05.96 Rob Stevenson W PTS 6 Hull
02.06.96 Jeff Finlayson W PTS 6 Shaw
18.09.96 Grant Briggs L RTD 3 Tylorstown
09.12.96 Alex Mason W PTS 6 Leicester
16.12.96 Michael Monaghan L PTS 6 Cleethorpes
03.02.97 Brian Galloway L PTS 6 Leicester
03.03.97 Jeff Finlayson W PTS 6 Leicester

20.03.97 Alex Mason L PTS 6 Solihull
30.04.97 Adrian Strachan L RSC 3 Acton
09.06.97 Alex Carey DREW 6 Birmingham
Career: 14 contests, won 6, drew 2, lost 6.

Carlton Williams   Les Clark

Chris Williams

Merthyr. *Born* Merthyr, 25 December, 1977
S. Bantamweight. Ht. 5'6½"
Manager D. Gardiner

26.02.97 John Matthews L RSC 1 Cardiff
03.05.97 Michael Gomez W PTS 4 Manchester
Career: 2 contests, won 1, lost 1.

Chris Williams   Les Clark

Danny Williams

Brixton. *Born* London, 13 July, 1973
Heavyweight. Ht. 6'3"
Manager F. Warren

21.10.95 Vance Idiens W CO 2 Bethnal Green
09.12.95 Joey Paladino W RSC 1 Bethnal Green
13.02.96 Slick Miller W RSC 1 Bethnal Green
09.03.96 James Wilder W PTS 4 Millstreet
13.07.96 John Pierre W PTS 4 Bethnal Green
31.08.96 Andy Lambert W RSC 2 Dublin
09.11.96 Michael Murray W CO 1 Manchester
08.02.97 Shane Woollas W RSC 2 Millwall
03.05.97 Albert Call W RSC 4 Manchester
Career: 9 contests, won 9.

(Wayne) Darren Williams

Swansea. *Born* Swansea, 17 July, 1975
Welterweight. Ht. 5'8"
Manager C. Sanigar/F. Warren

21.06.97 John Smith W PTS 4 Cardiff
Career: 1 contest, won 1.

Gary Williams

Nottingham. *Born* Nottingham, 25
September, 1965
Heavyweight, Ht. 5'11½"
Manager W. Swift

27.04.92 Damien Caesar L RSC 4 Mayfair
07.09.92 J. A. Bugner L PTS 4 Bethnal Green
06.10.92 Scott Welch L PTS 4 Antwerp, Belgium
01.12.92 Kenny Sandison W PTS 6 Liverpool
27.01.93 Kenny Sandison DREW 6 Stoke
13.02.93 Kevin McBride L PTS 4 Manchester
01.03.93 Ashley Naylor DREW 4 Bradford
29.03.93 Kevin Cullinane W RSC 2 Liverpool
26.04.93 Ashley Naylor W PTS 6 Bradford
10.08.93 Peter Smith L RSC 4 Marula, South Africa
08.12.93 Graham Arnold L PTS 6 Hull
02.02.94 Vincenzo Cantatore L CO 2 Ferrara, Italy
17.03.94 Neil Kirkwood L RSC 1 Lincoln
10.09.94 Clayton Brown L PTS 4 Birmingham
04.10.94 Mike Holden L RSC 4 Mayfair
13.12.94 Damien Caesar L RSC 2 Ilford
18.03.95 Darren Corbett DREW 4 Millstreet
06.05.95 Clayton Brown L PTS 4 Shepton Mallet
10.06.95 Joey Paladino L PTS 6 Manchester
15.09.95 Adrian Kneeshaw W RSC 6 Mansfield
11.10.95 Shane Woollas L PTS 6 Solihull
03.11.95 Tony Henry W PTS 6 Dudley
24.11.95 Pele Reid L RSC 1 Manchester
12.01.96 John Pettersson DREW 4 Copenhagen, Denmark
31.01.96 Robert Norton L RSC 2 Birmingham
21.03.96 Mika Kihlstrom L PTS 4 Southwark
02.04.96 Doug Liggion L PTS 4 Southwark
22.04.96 Shane Woollas L PTS 10 Cleethorpes
(Vacant Midlands Area Heavyweight Title)
27.05.96 Jukka Jarvinen L PTS 6 Helsinki, Finland
09.07.96 Sugar Raj Kumar Sangwan L PTS 4 Bethnal Green
08.10.96 Owen Bartley L PTS 4 Battersea
26.11.96 Israel Ajose L CO 2 Bethnal Green
18.01.97 Craig Bowen-Price L CO 1 Manchester
28.04.97 Jarrod Corrigan W RSC 4 Hull
Career: 34 contests, won 6, drew 4, lost 24.

(Leon) Jason Williams

Swansea. *Born* Swansea, 11 July, 1974
Welterweight. Ht. 5'11"
Manager C. Sanigar/F. Warren

19.04.97 John Harrison L PTS 6 Plymouth
21.06.97 Dewi Roberts W RSC 1 Cardiff
Career: 2 contests, won 1, lost 1.

Lennox Williams

Leicester. *Born* Sheffield, 3 January, 1965
Heavyweight. Ht. 5'9½"
Manager W. Wigley

19.10.96 Greg Wedlake L PTS 4 Bristol
19.06.97 Shane Woollas L PTS 6 Scunthorpe
Career: 2 contests, lost 2.

Lennox Williams   Les Clark

Richard Williams

Streatham. *Born* London, 9 May, 1971
L. Middleweight. Ht. 5'9½"
Manager B. Hearn

08.03.97 Marty Duke W RSC 3 Brentwood
30.06.97 Danny Quacoe W PTS 4 Bethnal Green
Career: 2 contests, won 2.

Rowan Williams

Birmingham. *Born* Birmingham, 18 March, 1968
Midlands Area Bantamweight Champion.
Ht. 5'5½"
Manager Self

17.02.93 Nick Tooley W PTS 4 Bethnal Green
04.04.93 Des Gargano W PTS 4 Brockley
23.06.93 Graham McGrath W PTS 4 Edmonton
01.10.93 Neil Swain L PTS 6 Cardiff
10.02.94 Neil Armstrong L PTS 6 Glasgow
12.11.94 Jesper D. Jensen L PTS 6 Randers, Denmark
18.01.95 Graham McGrath W CO 6 Solihull
(Vacant Midlands Area Bantamweight Title)
25.01.95 Neil Swain L PTS 6 Cardiff
02.03.95 Donnie Hood L PTS 8 Glasgow

20.04.95	Peter Culshaw L CO 6 Liverpool
01.06.95	Neil Parry W PTS 8 Musselburgh
19.01.96	Dharmendra Singh Yadav L PTS 4 Bracknell
21.03.96	Mark Reynolds DREW 6 Southwark
30.03.96	Vince Feeney L RSC 6 Dublin
27.09.96	Spencer Oliver L RTD 3 Stevenage
06.11.96	Harry Woods L PTS 6 Tylorstown
27.11.96	Francis Ampofo L PTS 6 Bethnal Green
28.01.97	Tommy Waite L PTS 4 Belfast

Career: 18 contests, won 5, drew 1, lost 12.

Steve Williams

Mansfield. *Born* Worksop, 11 October, 1968
Flyweight. Ht. 5'7"
Manager J. Ashton

06.03.95	Shaun Hall DREW 6 Bradford
06.04.95	Andy Roberts W PTS 6 Sheffield
20.10.95	Terry Gaskin W PTS 6 Mansfield
22.11.95	Neil Parry W PTS 6 Sheffield
22.03.96	Darren Noble W PTS 6 Mansfield
12.09.96	Andy Roberts W PTS 6 Doncaster
01.11.96	Tiger Singh W PTS 6 Mansfield
20.02.97	Neil Parry W PTS 8 Mansfield
08.05.97	Mark Reynolds L RTD 6 Mansfield
	(Elim. British Flyweight Title)

Career: 9 contests, won 7, drew 1, lost 1.

George Wilson

Camberwell. *Born* London, 7 April, 1966
Welterweight. Ht. 5'10"
Manager Self

18.06.92	Sean Cave L PTS 6 Peterborough
07.07.92	Erwin Edwards L RSC 4 Bristol
08.09.92	Erwin Edwards L RSC 3 Southend
16.02.93	Derrick Daniel W PTS 6 Tooting
23.02.93	Sean Metherell W PTS 6 Kettering
29.03.93	Joel Ani L PTS 6 Mayfair
21.06.93	Jamie Davidson W RSC 4 Swindon
03.11.93	Sean Baker L RSC 2 Bristol
26.02.94	Michael Carruth L PTS 6 Earls Court
29.03.94	Mark Tibbs L RSC 6 Bethnal Green
27.10.94	Paul Dyer L PTS 4 Bayswater
04.02.95	Paul Ryan L RSC 4 Cardiff
26.04.95	Steve Tuckett L PTS 6 Solihull
12.05.95	Mohamed Boualleg L RSC 6 Rouen, France
28.07.95	Sean Baker L PTS 6 Bristol
26.08.95	Neil Sinclair L PTS 4 Belfast
15.09.95	James Donoghue L PTS 6 Darlington
27.09.95	Jason Beard L PTS 6 Bethnal Green
02.12.95	Frank Olsen L PTS 6 Belfast
26.03.96	George Richards L PTS 8 Wolverhampton
10.05.96	Geoff McCreesh L PTS 6 Wembley
28.09.96	Geoff McCreesh L PTS 4 Barking
02.11.96	Andrei Pestriaev L RSC 3 Paris, France
14.12.96	Stephane Galtier W PTS 6 Rouen les Sapins, France
31.01.97	Pascal Avit L PTS 6 Clemont Ferrand, France
01.03.97	Stephane Jacob L PTS 6 Paris, France
26.04.97	David Sarraille L PTS 6 Marcheprime, France
07.06.97	Stephane Jacob L PTS 8 Bruay la Brussiere, France

Career: 28 contests, won 4, lost 24.

John Wilson

Edinburgh. *Born* Edinburgh, 4 January, 1972
L. Heavyweight. Ht. 6'1"
Manager A. Morrison/F. Warren

18.11.94	Steve Yorath W PTS 6 Glasgow
18.12.94	Craig Byrne W RSC 2 Glasgow
21.01.95	Tim Robinson W RSC 1 Glasgow
04.03.95	Darren Ashton NC 3 Livingston
08.06.95	Art Stacey W PTS 6 Glasgow
01.09.95	Marvin O'Brien W PTS 6 Wolverhampton
15.09.95	Marvin O'Brien W PTS 6 Glasgow
17.12.95	Barrie Bessant W RSC 1 Glasgow
12.02.96	Declan Faherty W PTS 6 Glasgow
20.09.96	Kevin Morton W PTS 8 Glasgow
04.04.97	Tony Booth W PTS 6 Glasgow

Career: 11 contests, won 10, no contest 1.

Wayne Windle

Sheffield. *Born* Sheffield, 18 October, 1968
Central Area L. Welterweight Champion.
Former Central Area Lightweight
Champion. Ht. 5'8"
Manager B. Ingle

25.10.88	Mick Mulcahy L PTS 6 Cottingham
17.11.88	Dave Pratt L PTS 6 Ilkeston
02.02.89	Jeff Dobson L RSC 6 Croydon
04.04.89	John Ritchie DREW 4 Sheffield
05.10.89	Des Gargano L PTS 6 Middleton
16.10.89	Des Gargano W PTS 6 Manchester
16.11.89	Noel Carroll L PTS 6 Manchester
04.12.89	Brendan Ryan DREW 6 Manchester
29.01.90	Mike Close W PTS 6 Liverpool
05.02.90	Mike Close W PTS 6 Brierley Hill
12.03.90	Barry North W PTS 6 Hull
21.03.90	Neil Foran L PTS 6 Preston
29.05.90	Terry Collins L PTS 6 Bethnal Green
11.06.90	Muhammad Lovelock W PTS 6 Manchester
12.09.90	Brian Cullen W RSC 1 Stafford
22.09.90	Bernard McComiskey W PTS 6 Kensington
08.10.90	Johnny Walker DREW 6 Leicester
22.10.90	Mick Mulcahy W PTS 4 Cleethorpes
14.11.90	Andy Robins W PTS 6 Sheffield
26.11.90	Michael Driscoll L RSC 3 Bethnal Green
16.01.91	Karl Taylor L PTS 8 Stoke
06.02.91	Felix Kelly L PTS 6 Bethnal Green
12.03.91	Mark Antony W CO 1 Mansfield
24.04.91	Steve Foran L CO 3 Preston
13.06.91	Pete Roberts W RSC 7 Hull
	(Vacant Central Area Lightweight Title)
15.08.91	Suwanee Anukun L PTS 6 Marbella, Spain
21.09.91	George Scott L CO 2 Tottenham
10.12.91	Kevin Toomey W PTS 6 Sheffield
26.03.92	Kevin Toomey L DIS 8 Hull
	(Central Area Lightweight Title Defence)
03.09.92	Billy Schwer L CO 1 Dunstable
20.01.93	Mark Elliot L CO 3 Wolverhampton
01.06.93	Mick Mulcahy L PTS 6 Manchester
01.12.93	Gary Thornhill L PTS 6 Stoke
03.03.94	J. T. Williams L RSC 3 Ebbw Vale
01.10.94	Dave Anderson L RSC 2 Cardiff
14.04.95	Bernard McComiskey L RSC 5 Belfast

12.06.95	Ricky Sackfield L PTS 6 Manchester
11.11.95	Paul Samuels L RSC 2 Halifax
15.10.96	Norman Dhalie L PTS 6 Wolverhampton
06.11.96	Tony Foster W PTS 4 Hull
09.12.96	Brian Coleman W PTS 6 Chesterfield
20.03.97	Dean Bramhald W RSC 4 Doncaster
	(Vacant Central Area L. Welterweight Title)

Career: 42 contests, won 15, drew 3, lost 24.

Carl Winstone

Pontenewydd. *Born* Pontypool, 21 December, 1967
Middleweight. Ht. 6'0"
Manager Self

22.03.94	Nicky Thurbin L PTS 6 Bethnal Green
20.03.95	Darren Sweeney L PTS 6 Birmingham
12.04.95	Paul Matthews W PTS 6 Llanelli
08.07.95	David Larkin L RSC 2 York
13.11.95	Simon Andrews W PTS 6 Barnstaple
21.11.95	Darren Sweeney L PTS 6 Edgbaston
29.11.95	Paolo Roberto L PTS 4 Southwark
08.12.95	Jon Stocks L RSC 3 Liverpool
23.02.96	Ernie Loveridge L PTS 8 Weston super Mare
04.04.96	Peter Vosper L PTS 6 Plymouth
29.05.96	Paul Matthews L PTS 6 Ebbw Vale
07.10.96	Prince Kasi Kaihau L RSC 5 Birmingham

Career: 12 contests, won 2, lost 10.

Craig Winter

Denbigh. *Born* Aylesbury, 10 September, 1971
Middleweight. Ht. 5'10"
Manager T. Gilmour

19.12.93	Allan Logan W PTS 6 Glasgow
28.02.94	Wayne Shepherd W PTS 6 Manchester
18.04.94	John Duckworth W RSC 5 Manchester
26.09.94	Dave Whittle W PTS 6 Liverpool
10.12.94	Hughie Davey W PTS 6 Manchester
25.03.95	David Maw W RSC 3 Rothwell
20.04.95	Paul King W RSC 4 Liverpool
16.06.95	Ernie Loveridge W PTS 6 Liverpool
08.09.95	Ernie Loveridge W PTS 6 Liverpool
14.02.96	Mark Cichocki W PTS 6 Sunderland
09.05.96	Peter Waudby L RSC 5 Hull
	(Elim. British L. Middleweight Title)
04.10.96	Robert Harper W RSC 5 Pentre Halkyn
31.01.97	Martin Jolley W RSC 3 Pentre Halkyn

Career: 13 contests, won 12, lost 1.

Mark Winters

Antrim. *Born* Antrim, 29 December, 1971
L. Welterweight. Ht. 5'8"
Manager F. Warren

04.03.95	Trevor Smith W PTS 6 Livingston
10.06.95	Mark McGowan W PTS 6 Manchester
09.09.95	Anthony Campbell W PTS 4 Cork
25.11.95	John O. Johnson W RSC 2 Dublin
13.01.96	Rick North W PTS 4 Manchester
09.03.96	Danny Quacoe W RSC 2 Millstreet
08.06.96	Brian Coleman W PTS 4 Newcastle
31.08.96	John Smith W PTS 4 Dublin
30.11.96	Paul Dyer W PTS 6 Tylorstown
14.03.97	Paul Denton W PTS 8 Reading
03.05.97	Jimmy Phelan W PTS 4 Manchester

Career: 11 contests, won 11.

Mark Winters   Les Clark

Junior Witter

Bradford. *Born* Bradford, 10 March, 1974
Welterweight. Ht. 5'7"
Manager B. Ingle

18.01.97   Cam Raeside DREW 6 Swadlincote
04.03.97   John Green W PTS 6 Yarm
20.03.97   Lee Molyneux W RSC 6 Salford
25.04.97   Trevor Meikle W PTS 6 Mere
15.05.97   Andreas Panayi W RSC 5 Reading
Career: 5 contests, won 4, drew 1.

Junior Witter   Les Clark

Richie Woodhall

Telford. *Born* Birmingham, 17 April, 1968
Former Undefeated European &
Commonwealth Middleweight Champion.
Ht. 6'2"
Manager M. Duff

18.10.90   Kevin Hayde W RSC 3 Birmingham
30.11.90   Robbie Harron W RSC 2 Birmingham
16.01.91   Chris Haydon W RSC 3 Kensington
21.02.91   Shamus Casey W RSC 3 Walsall
30.05.91   Marty Duke W RSC 4 Birmingham
29.08.91   Nigel Moore W RSC 1 Oakengates
31.10.91   Colin Pitters W PTS 8 Oakengates
04.02.92   Graham Burton W RSC 2 Alfreton
26.03.92   Vito Gaudiosi W CO 1 Telford
     (Vacant Commonwealth Middleweight Title)
01.10.92   John Ashton W PTS 12 Telford
     (Commonwealth Middleweight Title Defence)
04.12.92   Horace Fleary W PTS 8 Telford
16.03.93   Carlo Colarusso W PTS 8 Wolverhampton
24.04.93   Royan Hammond W PTS 10 Birmingham
27.10.93   Garry Meekison W PTS 12 West Bromwich
     (Commonwealth Middleweight Title Defence)
01.03.94   Heath Todd W RSC 7 Dudley
16.03.94   Greg Lonon W RSC 6 Birmingham
05.10.94   Jacques le Blanc W PTS 12 Wolverhampton
     (Commonwealth Middleweight Title Defence)
30.11.94   Art Serwano W RSC 11 Wolverhampton
     (Commonwealth Middleweight Title Defence)
22.02.95   Silvio Branco W RSC 9 Telford
     (Vacant European Middleweight Title)
25.10.95   Zdravko Kostic W PTS 12 Telford
     (European Middleweight Title Defence)
31.01.96   Derek Wormald W RSC 10 Birmingham
     (European Middleweight Title Defence)
19.10.96   Keith Holmes L RSC 12 Upper Marlboro, USA
     (WBC Middleweight Title Challenge)
Career: 22 contests, won 21, lost 1.

Clinton Woods

Sheffield. *Born* Sheffield, 1 May, 1972
Central Area S. Middleweight Champion.
Ht. 6'2"
Manager D. Hobson

17.11.94   Dave Proctor W PTS 6 Sheffield
12.12.94   Earl Ling W RSC 5 Cleethorpes
23.02.95   Paul Clarkson W RSC 1 Hull
06.04.95   Japhet Hans W RSC 3 Sheffield
16.05.95   Kevin Burton W PTS 6 Cleethorpes
14.06.95   Kevin Burton W RSC 6 Batley
21.09.95   Paul Murray W PTS 6 Sheffield
20.10.95   Phil Ball W RSC 4 Mansfield
22.11.95   Andy Ewen W RSC 3 Sheffield
05.02.96   Chris Walker W RSC 6 Bradford
16.03.96   John Duckworth W PTS 8 Sheffield
13.06.96   Ernie Loveridge W PTS 6 Sheffield
14.11.96   Craig Joseph W PTS 10 Sheffield
     (Vacant Central Area S. Middleweight Title)
20.02.97   Rocky Shelly W RSC 2 Mansfield
10.04.97   Darren Littlewood W RSC 6 Sheffield
     (Central Area S. Middleweight Title Defence)
26.06.97   Darren Ashton W PTS 6 Sheffield
Career: 16 contests, won 16.

Harry Woods

Bargoed. *Born* Caerphilly, 13 February, 1975
Flyweight. Ht. 5'4"
Manager D. Gardiner

07.07.95   Henry Jones W PTS 4 Cardiff
29.09.95   Dave Martin DREW 4 Bloomsbury
25.10.95   Mark Hughes DREW 8 Cardiff
28.11.95   Chris Thomas W RSC 1 Cardiff
20.12.95   Dave Martin W CO 2 Usk
20.03.96   Anthony Hanna W PTS 6 Cardiff
29.05.96   Shaun Norman W RSC 5 Ebbw Vale
18.09.96   Louis Veitch L DIS 4 Tylorstown
02.10.96   Jose Ramon Bartolme W RSC 3 Cardiff
06.11.96   Rowan Williams W PTS 6 Tylorstown
27.11.96   Matthew Harris W PTS 8 Swansea
28.12.96   Alex Baba L PTS 12 Accra, Ghana
     (WBC International Flyweight Title Challenge)
26.02.97   Jose Antonio Lopez L RSC 5 Cardiff
Career: 13 contests, won 8, drew 2, lost 3.

Harry Woods   Les Clark

Chris Woollas

Epworth. *Born* Scunthorpe, 22 November, 1973
Cruiserweight. Ht. 5'11"
Manager J. Rushton

17.08.94   Darren Littlewood W RSC 4 Sheffield
05.10.94   Robert Norton DREW 6 Wolverhampton
05.12.94   Neil Simpson W PTS 6 Cleethorpes
10.02.95   Monty Wright L RSC 4 Birmingham
30.06.95   Kenny Nevers L RSC 2 Doncaster
25.09.95   Cliff Elden DREW 6 Cleethorpes
08.11.95   Stevie Pettit W PTS 6 Walsall
17.11.95   Markku Salminen L PTS 6 Helsinki, Finland
11.12.95   Cliff Elden DREW 6 Cleethorpes
15.02.96   Pele Lawrence W RSC 6 Sheffield
29.02.96   John Pierre DREW 6 Scunthorpe
16.03.96   David Jules W PTS 6 Sheffield

162

22.04.96	Jacklord Jacobs DREW 4 Crystal Palace
30.05.96	Martin Langtry L RSC 6 Lincoln *(Midlands Area Cruiserweight Title Challenge)*
03.09.96	Darren Corbett L RSC 7 Belfast
02.10.96	Rocky Shelly W RSC 6 Stoke
09.10.96	Nigel Rafferty W PTS 6 Stoke
28.10.96	Colin Brown L PTS 8 Glasgow
10.11.96	Michael Gale DREW 6 Glasgow
25.11.96	Albert Call L PTS 6 Cleethorpes
17.12.96	Darren Corbett L RSC 1 Doncaster
16.01.97	Mark Smallwood L PTS 8 Solihull
31.01.97	Tim Redman L PTS 6 Pentre Halkyn
14.03.97	Kelly Oliver L PTS 6 Reading
24.03.97	Mikael Lindblad L RSC 7 Helsinki, Finland
19.06.97	Ian Henry W PTS 6 Scunthorpe

Career: 26 contests, won 8, drew 6, lost 12.

Shane Woollas

Epworth. *Born* Scunthorpe, 28 July, 1972
Midlands Area Heavyweight Champion.
Ht. 6'2"
Manager J. Rushton

26.08.94	Neil Kirkwood L RSC 6 Barnsley
28.07.95	Rob Albon W RTD 4 Epworth
11.10.95	Gary Williams W PTS 6 Solihull
08.11.95	David Jules W PTS 6 Scunthorpe
26.01.96	Nigel Williams W RSC 2 Doncaster
31.01.96	David Jules L PTS 6 Stoke
22.04.96	Gary Williams W PTS 10 Cleethorpes *(Vacant Midlands Area Heavyweight Title)*
29.07.96	David Jules L PTS 6 Skegness
31.08.96	Willi Fischer L CO 2 Palma, Mallorca
08.10.96	Mika Kihlstrom L PTS 4 Battersea
06.11.96	Kevin McBride L RSC 2 Hull
08.02.97	Danny Williams L RSC 2 Millwall
19.06.97	Lennox Williams W PTS 6 Scunthorpe

Career: 13 contests, won 6, lost 7.

Carl Wright

Liverpool. *Born* Liverpoool, 19 February, 1969
L. Welterweight. Ht. 5'7"
Manager S. Vaughan

13.10.89	Mick Mulcahy W PTS 6 Preston
31.10.89	Mick Mulcahy W PTS 6 Manchester
24.01.90	Mike Morrison W PTS 6 Preston
19.12.90	Julian Eavis W PTS 6 Preston
31.03.92	Ricky Sackfield W RSC 1 Stockport
14.05.92	Brendan Ryan W PTS 4 Liverpool
12.06.92	Dean Bramhald W PTS 6 Liverpool
15.09.92	Wayne Panayiotiou W RSC 2 Liverpool
25.09.92	Mick Mulcahy W PTS 8 Liverpool
12.11.92	Jim Lawlor W RSC 3 Liverpool
29.04.93	Marcel Herbert W PTS 8 Mayfair
09.04.94	Paul Ryan L RSC 8 Mansfield
31.10.94	Richard Swallow W PTS 6 Liverpool
27.02.95	Hugh Forde W PTS 6 Barrow
20.04.95	John O. Johnson W PTS 6 Liverpool
04.11.95	Karl Taylor W PTS 6 Liverpool
10.05.96	Kevin McKillan W PTS 8 Liverpool
18.10.96	Soren Sondergaard L PTS 12 Vejle, Denmark *(European L. Welterweight Title Challenge)*

Career: 18 contests, won 16, lost 2.

Michael Wright

Chatham. *Born* Chatham, 2 April, 1974
S. Featherweight. Ht. 5'7"
Manager B. Hearn

30.09.95	Mark O'Callaghan L RSC 1 Basildon
25.11.95	Mark O'Callaghan W PTS 4 Dagenham
06.02.96	Wayne Jones W PTS 4 Basildon
09.07.96	Venkatesan Deverajan W RSC 3 Bethnal Green

Career: 4 contests, won 3, lost 1.

Monty Wright

Stevenage. *Born* Bedford, 1 November, 1969
Southern Area L. Heavyweight Champion. Ht. 5'9"
Manager M. Duff/T. Lawless

10.11.93	Steve Osborne W RSC 3 Watford
26.01.94	Nigel Rafferty W PTS 6 Birmingham
16.02.94	Bobby Mack W RSC 3 Stevenage
11.03.94	Greg Scott-Briggs W CO 1 Bethnal Green
05.04.94	Karl Barwise W PTS 6 Bethnal Green
11.05.94	Simon McDougall L PTS 6 Stevenage
12.09.94	L. A. Williams W RSC 1 Mayfair
11.10.94	Tim Robinson W CO 1 Bethnal Green
30.11.94	Greg Scott-Briggs W PTS 6 Wolverhampton
10.02.95	Chris Woollas W RSC 4 Birmingham
12.05.95	Nicky Wadman W CO 2 Bethnal Green
23.06.95	Art Stacey W RSC 2 Bethnal Green
27.09.95	Jerry Mortimer W RTD 3 Bethnal Green
03.11.95	John Keeton L RSC 4 Dudley
14.10.96	Luan Morena W RSC 5 Mayfair
17.12.96	Eddie Knight W RSC 5 Bethnal Green *(Vacant Southern Area L. Heavyweight Title)*
16.04.97	Luan Morena W DIS 2 Bethnal Green

Career: 17 contests, won 15, lost 2.

Pat Wright

Cambridge. *Born* Bedford, 23 July, 1973
Welterweight. Ht. 5'10¾"
Managers M. Duff/T. Lawless

15.03.96	Peter Varnavas W PTS 6 Dunstable
25.06.96	Robbie Dunn W RSC 2 Stevenage
24.10.96	Craig Lynch W PTS 6 Wembley
17.12.96	Gary Hiscox W PTS 6 Bethnal Green
29.01.97	Paul Miles W PTS 6 Bethnal Green

Career: 5 contests, won 5.

Paul Wright

Liverpool. *Born* Liverpool, 24 February, 1966
Central Area Middleweight Champion. Ht. 5'9¾"
Manager S. Vaughan

13.10.89	Andy Balfe W RSC 1 Preston
31.10.89	John Tipping W RSC 1 Manchester
20.12.89	Nigel Rafferty DREW 6 Kirkby
13.04.92	Shaun McCrory W PTS 6 Manchester
14.05.92	Chris Walker W PTS 6 Liverpool
15.09.92	John Kaighin W DIS 5 Liverpool
23.10.92	Jason McNeill W RSC 1 Liverpool

28.11.92	Russell Washer W PTS 8 Manchester
05.02.93	Sean Smith W RSC 2 Manchester
22.04.93	Glenn Campbell L RSC 4 Bury *(Elim. British S. Middleweight Title & Central Area S. Middleweight Title Challenge)*
06.09.93	Alan Baptiste W PTS 6 Liverpool
02.07.94	Shamus Casey W RSC 1 Liverpool
26.09.94	Carlos Christie W PTS 6 Liverpool
24.10.94	Stephen Wilson L PTS 10 Glasgow *(Elim. British S. Middleweight Title)*
27.02.95	John Duckworth DREW 6 Barrow
20.04.95	Chris Richards W PTS 6 Liverpool
29.09.95	Paul Murray W RSC 5 Liverpool
08.12.95	Carl Smith W RSC 2 Liverpool
05.03.96	Ernie Loveridge W PTS 6 Barrow
13.04.96	Mark Dawson W PTS 6 Liverpool
16.08.96	Colin Manners W PTS 10 Liverpool *(Vacant Central Area Middleweight Title)*
27.03.97	Jason Matthews L RSC 3 Norwich *(Vacant WBO Inter-Continental Middleweight Title)*

Career: 22 contests, won 17, drew 2, lost 3.

Dharmendra Singh Yadav

East Ham. *Born* New Delhi, India, 29 December, 1972
Bantamweight. Ht. 5'3"
Manager F. Maloney

29.11.95	Shaun Norman W PTS 4 Southwark
19.01.96	Rowan Williams W PTS 4 Bracknell
02.04.96	Brendan Bryce W PTS 4 Southwark
14.05.96	Anthony Hanna W PTS 4 Dagenham
09.07.96	Krasimir Tcholakov W RSC 1 Bethnal Green
03.09.96	Neil Parry W PTS 6 Bethnal Green

Career: 6 contests, won 6.

Pat Wright   Les Clark

163

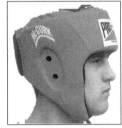

164

British Area Title Bouts During 1996-97

Central Area

Titleholders at 30 June 1997
Fly: *vacant.* **Bantam:** Andy Roberts. **S. Bantam:** *vacant.*
Feather: Stefy Bull. **S. Feather:** Gary Thornhill. **Light:** Wayne
Rigby. **L. Welter:** Wayne Windle. **Welter:** Derek Roche. **L.
Middle:** Peter Waudby. **Middle:** Paul Wright. **S. Middle:** Clinton
Woods. **L. Heavy:** Michael Gale. **Cruiser:** Denzil Browne.
Heavy: Neil Kirkwood.

16 August 1996	Paul Wright W PTS 10 Colin Manners, Liverpool (Vacant Middle)
23 September 1996	Trevor Meikle L PTS 10 Derek Roche, Bradford (Welter)
27 September 1996	Jimmy Phelan L PTS 10 Wayne Rigby, Hull (Light)
14 November 1996	Clinton Woods W PTS 10 Craig Joseph, Sheffield (Vacant S. Middle)
1 December 1996	Ady Lewis W PTS 10 Louis Veitch, Shaw (Vacant Fly)
17 December 1996	Stefy Bull W RSC 4 Robert Braddock, Doncaster (Vacant Feather)
20 March 1997	Marcus Duncan L PTS 10 Andy Roberts, Doncaster (Bantam)
20 March 1997	Wayne Windle W RSC 4 Dean Bramhald, Doncaster (Vacant L. Welter)
10 April 1997	Clinton Woods W RSC 6 Darren Littlewood, Sheffield (S. Middle)

During the above period, Ady Lewis (Fly), Paul Lloyd (S.
Bantam), and Shea Neary (L. Welter), relinquished their titles,
while Chris Jickells (Feather) retired.

Midlands Area

Titleholders at 30 June 1997
Fly: Anthony Hanna. **Bantam:** Rowan Williams. **S. Bantam:** Carl
Allen. **Feather:** Kelton McKenzie. **S. Feather:** *vacant.* **Light:**
Karl Taylor. **L. Welter:** Malcolm Melvin. **Welter:** Cam Raeside.
L. Middle: Steve Goodwin. **Middle:** *vacant.* **S. Middle:** *vacant.*
L. Heavy: Stuart Fleet. **Cruiser:** Martin Langtry. **Heavy:** Shane
Woollas.

26 September 1996	Matthew Harris L PTS 10 Carl Allen, Walsall (S. Bantam)
24 October 1996	Carlos Christie W PTS 10 Andrew Flute, London (S. Middle)
25 November 1996	Cam Raeside W RSC 3 Brian Dunn, Cleethorpes (Vacant Welter)
25 April 1997	Neil Simpson L PTS 10 Stuart Fleet, Cleethorpes (L. Heavy)
10 May 1997	Cam Raeside W PTS 10 Ray Newby, Nottingham (Welter)

During the above period, Richard O'Brien (Welter) relinquished
his title, while Antonio Fernandez (Middle) and Carlos Christie (S.
Middle) were stripped of theirs.

Northern Area

Titleholders at 30 June 1997
Fly: *vacant.* **Bantam:** *vacant.* **S. Bantam:** *vacant.* **Feather:** Colin
Innes. **S. Feather:** *vacant.* **Light:** *vacant.* **L. Welter:** *vacant.*
Welter: Paul King. **L. Middle:** Mark Cichocki. **Middle:** *vacant.*
S. Middle: *vacant.* **L. Heavy:** *vacant.* **Cruiser:** *vacant.* **Heavy:**
vacant.

| 10 October 1996 | Paul King W PTS 10 Hughie Davey, Newcastle (Welter) |

During the above period, both Dominic McGuigan (S. Feather)
and Terry French (L. Heavy) retired.

Northern Ireland Area

Titleholders at 30 June 1997 - None.

Scottish Area

Titleholders at 30 June 1997
Fly: Keith Knox. **Bantam:** *vacant.* **S. Bantam:** *vacant.* **Feather:**
Brian Carr. **S. Feather:** *vacant.* **Light:** *vacant.* **L. Welter:** Steve
McLevy. **Welter:** *vacant.* **L. Middle:** *vacant.* **Middle:** *vacant.* **S.
Middle:** *vacant.* **L. Heavy:** *vacant.* **Cruiser:** *vacant.* **Heavy:**
vacant.

| 6 November 1996 | Brian Carr W PTS 10 Mike Deveney, Glasgow (Feather) |

During the above period, Mark Geraghty (S. Feather) and Kris
McAdam (Light) retired.

*Steve Roberts, the new Southern Area light-middleweight
champion*   Les Clark

Southern Area

Titleholders at 30 June 1997
Fly: Mark Reynolds. **Bantam:** Vince Feeney. **S. Bantam:** *vacant.* **Feather:** *vacant.* **S. Feather:** Matt Brown. **Light:** Colin Dunne. **L. Welter:** Georgie Smith. **Welter:** Harry Dhami. **L. Middle:** Steve Roberts. **Middle:** Howard Eastman. **S. Middle:** Graham Townsend. **L. Heavy:** Monty Wright. **Cruiser:** Dominic Negus. **Heavy:** *vacant.*

28 September 1996	Julius Francis W RSC 5 James Oyebola, Barking (Heavy)
24 October 1996	Graham Townsend W RSC 5 Jason Hart, London (Vacant S. Middle)
11 December 1996	Howard Eastman W RSC 10 Sven Hamer, London (Vacant Middle)
11 December 1996	Matt Brown W RSC 9 Marcus McCrae, London (Vacant S. Feather)
17 December 1996	Monty Wright W RSC 5 Eddie Knight, London (Vacant L. Heavy)
18 February 1997	Bernard Paul W PTS 10 Richie Edwards, Cheshunt (Vacant L. Welter)
18 February 1997	Spencer Oliver W RSC 10 Patrick Mullings, Cheshunt (Vacant S. Bantam)
14 March 1997	Harry Dhami W PTS 10 Paul Dyer, Reading (Welter)
8 April 1997	Steve Roberts W PTS 10 Gilbert Jackson, London (Vacant L. Middle)
8 April 1997	Vince Feeney W PTS 10 Francis Ampofo, London (Vacant Bantam)
24 April 1997	Colin Dunne W CO 4 Lewis Reynolds, London (Light)
28 April 1997	Chris Henry W RTD 4 Darren Westover, Enfield (Vacant Cruiser)
20 May 1997	Harry Dhami W RTD 2 Paul Miles, Gillingham (Welter)
17 June 1997	Chris Henry L RSC 10 Dominic Negus, Cheshunt (Cruiser)
30 June 1997	Matt Brown W PTS 10 Rudy Valentino, London (S. Feather)
30 June 1997	Georgie Smith W RSC 10 Richie Edwards, London (Vacant L. Welter)

During the above period, Spencer Oliver (Bantam), Bernard Paul (L. Welter), Nicky Thurbin (L. Middle), Mark Baker (Middle), and Julius Francis (Heavy), relinquished their titles.

Welsh Area

Titleholders at 30 June 1997
Fly: *vacant.* **Bantam:** *vacant.* **S. Bantam:** *vacant.* **Feather:** Peter Harris. **S. Feather:** J. T. Williams. **Light:** *vacant.* **L. Welter:** *vacant.* **Welter:** *vacant.* **L. Middle:** *vacant.* **Middle:** Barry Thorogood. **S. Middle:** Darron Griffiths. **L. Heavy:** *vacant.* **Cruiser:** *vacant.* **Heavy:** *vacant.*

During the above period, Carlo Colarusso (L. Middle) retired.

Western Area

Titleholders at 30 June 1997
Fly: *vacant.* **Bantam:** *vacant.* **S. Bantam:** Danny Ruegg. **Feather:** *vacant.* **S. Feather:** Greg Upton. **Light:** *vacant.* **L. Welter:** *vacant.* **Welter:** *vacant.* **L. Middle:** *vacant.* **Middle:** *vacant.* **S. Middle:** Darren Dorrington. **L. Heavy:** Peter Vosper. **Cruiser:** *vacant.* **Heavy:** *vacant.*

18 October 1996	Tony Falcone L PTS 10 Danny Ruegg, Barnstaple (S. Bantam)
19 April 1997	Peter Vosper W PTS 10 Simon Andrews, Plymouth (Vacant L. Heavy)

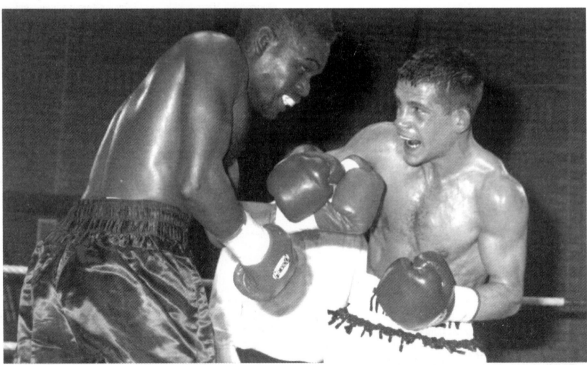

In one of last season's best contests, the up-and-coming Spencer Oliver (right) won the Southern Area super-bantamweight title by stopping Patrick Mullings in the tenth

Les Clark

British Title Bouts During 1996-97

All of last season's title bouts are shown in date order within their weight division and give the boxers' respective weights, along with the referee's scorecard if going to a decision. Every contest is summarised briefly and all referees are named.

Flyweight
27 January 1997   Ady Lewis 7.13½ (England) W PTS 12 Keith Knox 7.13½ (Scotland), Forte Post House Hotel, Glasgow. Following Mickey Cantwell's decision to hand back his belt in January 1997, at 4'10½", Lewis became the smallest champion in the history of British boxing after his narrow 117½-116½ points win over a tough opponent. Hardly unexpectedly, although the referee, Dave Parris, had no problems with the decision, others did, and a rematch is a distinct possibility. The post mortem recognised that although Knox was the busier of the two, Lewis' punches appeared to carry more authority and it was this factor that ultimately gained him the title.

27 May 1997   Ady Lewis 8.0 (England) W PTS 12 Mark Reynolds 7.12½ (England), Marriott Hotel, London. Despite being a clear winner at 119-116½ on Terry O'Connor's scorecard, Lewis, who had difficulty making the weight, failed to find the punch that would make the arithmetic unnecessary. For his part, Reynolds looked to make the body his target and his extra reach tell, but was never really allowed to settle and was generally outworked. Incidentally, this was Terry O'Connor's first British title bout following his upgrading to "A" Star referee.

Bantamweight
Drew Docherty (Scotland) did not defend the belt during the period.

S. Bantamweight
22 March 1997   Michael Brodie 8.9¾ (England) W RSC 10 Neil Swain 8.9½ (Wales), the Forum, Wythenshawe. Made for the vacant title, following Richie Wenton's decision to look for a world title shot, this was yet another contest deserving of Fight of the Year. Surprisingly, Swain's Commonwealth belt was not at stake but, following his brilliant victory, Brodie was in no doubt that he should be recognised as champion. The fight itself was a thriller, travelling at an almost inhuman pace, but, ultimately, it was Brodie's body work which slowed Swain down and set him up for the big finish at 1.15 of the tenth. That was when a thudding right hand crashed into Swain's head and rendered him unconscious, leaving the referee, Roy Francis, no alternative but to stop the action immediately.

Featherweight
11 January 1997   Colin McMillan 9.0 (England) L RSC 8 Paul Ingle 8.13 (England), York Hall, London. In what was undoubtedly an upset, Ingle scored a magnificent stoppage defeat over the former world champion. Although McMillan boxed well at times, the relentless challenger would never leave him alone, his face being a bloody mess by the eighth and, on being dropped from a left uppercut,

the referee, John Coyle, had no hesitation in waving it off with 1.42 of the round gone.

28 April 1997   Paul Ingle 8.13½ (England) W RTD 11 Michael Alldis 8.13½ (England), Ice Arena, Hull. Although putting up a game performance against the impressive Ingle, Alldis was ultimately no match for the brash young champion. Floored by a right hand over the top for a count of eight in the seventh, and twice more at the end of the 11th, having given it his best shot he was wisely retired by his corner following the bell to end the round.

S. Featherweight
P. J. Gallagher (England) forfeited the title in June 1997 due to inactivity.

Lightweight
20 November 1996   Michael Ayers 9.9 (England) W RSC 9 Colin Dunne 9.8¼ (England), Conference Centre, Wembley. Good enough to be the Fight of the Year, the pair put on a tremendous seesaw battle that had both men fighting at their very best. There was no doubt that Dunne believed he could win, but Ayers felt he could not lose. However, as the fight went past the halfway stage it was noticeable that the champion was getting stronger and, in the seventh, a cracking left to the ribs had Dunne down for five. The challenger somehow survived the eighth, but the day of reckoning was close at hand and with punches coming in from all angles, the referee, Dave Parris, rescued him in the ninth.

L. Welterweight
13 July 1996   Paul Ryan 9.13¾ (England) L CO 1 Andy Holligan 9.13¼ (England), York Hall, London. Also involving the Commonwealth title, Ryan slumped to a crashing defeat in a fight that was expected to end early, but in his favour. With nobody blinking in case they missed any of the action, Holligan took Ryan's blows without flinching, whereas two left hooks to the head saw the latter crashing to the canvas to be counted out by Larry O'Connell at 2.09 of the opening round. Holligan relinquished the title in June 1997 in order to concentrate on a crack at the European crown.

Welterweight
Kevin Lueshing (England) did not defend the title during the above period. *Stop Press:* Geoff McCreesh stopped Lueshing in the tenth round at the Wembley Arena on 19 July to become the new champion.

L. Middleweight
14 December 1996   Ryan Rhodes 10.13¼ (England) W RSC 8 Paul Jones 10.13¾ (England), Ponds Forge Leisure

Centre, Sheffield. Fighting for the title that had become vacant in November 1996 when Ensley Bingham signed for a WBO title shot at Ronald Wright, in winning, Rhodes became the youngest British champion since Eric Boon back in 1938. With both men knowing each other well, until the eighth there were few signs of anything dramatic as they both cancelled each other out. Then it happened. With Jones backed against the ropes, Rhodes stepped in with a chopping right hander that put him down for a count of eight and, on rising and unable to understand the referee, Richie Davies' instruction, the fight was stopped with just seven seconds of the round remaining.

25 February 1997   Ryan Rhodes 10.13 (England) W CO 1 Peter Waudby 10.13 (England), Hillsborough Leisure Centre, Sheffield. In what turned out to be a mismatch, Waudby was out of the fight almost from the first bell. Outspeeded and outpunched, he was floored two times in the opener before being counted out by referee, Mickey Vann, in the act of rising from a third knockdown at 1.58 of the round.

14 March 1997   Ryan Rhodes 10.13¾ (England) W RSC 7 Del Bryan 10.13¼ (England), Rivermead Leisure Centre, Reading. Having already been beaten by Rhodes earlier in the season, Bryan had no answer to the latter's variety, power, and movement, and was rescued by the referee, Roy Francis, at 1.54 of the seventh, having already been floored in the fourth and fifth, respectively. Already the youngest post-war champion, Rhodes also made the Lonsdale Belt his own property in record time – 90 days.

Middleweight

18 January 1997   Neville Brown 11.5¼ (England) W RSC 4 Willie Quinn 11.5½ (Scotland), Green Bank Leisure Centre, Swadlincote. As in nearly all of Brown's title defences, he made hard work of a fight he was expected to win easily, a point highlighted when he walked on to a right hand that left him deposited on the canvas for a count of seven in the second round. However, when the chips were down, Brown made his big effort. Under pressure again in the fourth, he hit back with a heavy right and, with Quinn struggling to survive, rained in blow after blow until Larry O'Connell rescued the unfortunate Scot at 2.10 of the round.

S. Middleweight

8 April 1997   David Starie 11.10¾ (England) W RSC 7 Sammy Storey 12.0 (Ireland), York Hall, London. Fighting for the title that had been vacated by Joe Calzaghe in January, following the latter's decision to channel his energies into a world championship attempt, Starie dominated as he worked Storey to head and body, his hand speed being too much for the veteran Irishman. It seemed to be just a matter of time before the younger man caught up with Storey. Eventually, in the seventh, a cracking right floored him for a count of nine and, upon rising, the referee, John Keane, stopped it with 2.17 of the round gone. *Stop Press:* Dean Francis won the title on 19 July at York Hall, Bethnal Green when halting Starie inside six rounds.

L. Heavyweight

Crawford Ashley (England) did not defend the title during the duration.

Cruiserweight

14 December 1996   Johnny Nelson 13.6 (England) W RSC 7 Dennis Andries 13.7½ (England), Ponds Forge Leisure Centre, Sheffield. Billed for the vacant title after Terry Dunstan had relinquished same in September 1996 to challenge for the European championship, Nelson breezed to an easy win over the once menacing Andries. The former world champion, who was just a shadow of his former self, and, at the age of 43, was surely taking part in his last title fight, was an easy target for his faster, more vital opponent and was rescued by John Keane at 1.50 of the seventh, despite not having been floored.

Heavyweight

Scott Welch (England) vacated the title in November 1996 in order to concentrate on a WBO world title challenge.

Hands held aloft, Andy Holligan celebrates the win over Paul Ryan that landed him the British and Commonwealth light-welterweight titles in July 1996
Les Clark

Lord Lonsdale Challenge Belts: Outright Winners

The original belts were donated to the National Sporting Club by Lord Lonsdale and did not bear his name, the inscription reading, "The National Sporting Club's Challenge Belt." It was not until the British Boxing Board of Control was formed that the emblems were reintroduced and the belts became known as the Lord Lonsdale Challenge Belts. The first contest involving the BBBoC belt was Benny Lynch versus Pat Palmer for the flyweight title on 16 September 1936. To win a belt outright, a champion must score three title match victories at the same weight, not necessarily consecutively.

Outright Winners of the National Sporting Club's Challenge Belt, 1909-1935 (20)

FLYWEIGHT	Jimmy Wilde; Jackie Brown
BANTAMWEIGHT	Digger Stanley; Joe Fox; Jim Higgins; Johnny Brown; Johnny King
FEATHERWEIGHT	Jim Driscoll; Tancy Lee; Johnny Cuthbert; Nel Tarleton
LIGHTWEIGHT	Freddie Welsh
WELTERWEIGHT	Johnny Basham; Jack Hood
MIDDLEWEIGHT	Pat O'Keefe; Len Harvey; Jock McAvoy
L. HEAVYWEIGHT	Dick Smith
HEAVYWEIGHT	Bombardier Billy Wells; Jack Petersen

Outright Winners of the BBBoC Lord Lonsdale Challenge Belt, 1936-1997 (96)

FLYWEIGHT	Jackie Paterson; Terry Allen; Walter McGowan; John McCluskey; Hugh Russell; Charlie Magri; Pat Clinton; Robbie Regan; Francis Ampofo
BANTAMWEIGHT	Johnny King; Peter Keenan (2); Freddie Gilroy; Alan Rudkin; Johnny Owen; Billy Hardy; Drew Docherty
S. BANTAMWEIGHT	Richie Wenton
FEATHERWEIGHT	Nel Tarleton; Ronnie Clayton (2); Charlie Hill; Howard Winstone (2); Evan Armstrong; Pat Cowdell; Robert Dickie; Paul Hodkinson; Colin McMillan; Sean Murphy
S. FEATHERWEIGHT	Jimmy Anderson; John Doherty; Floyd Havard
LIGHTWEIGHT	Eric Boon; Billy Thompson; Joe Lucy; Dave Charnley; Maurice Cullen; Ken Buchanan; Jim Watt; George Feeney; Tony Willis; Carl Crook; Billy Schwer; Michael Ayers
L. WELTERWEIGHT	Joey Singleton; Colin Power; Clinton McKenzie (2); Lloyd Christie; Andy Holligan; Ross Hale
WELTERWEIGHT	Ernie Roderick; Wally Thom; Brian Curvis (2); Ralph Charles; Colin Jones; Lloyd Honeyghan; Kirkland Laing; Del Bryan (2)
L. MIDDLEWEIGHT	Maurice Hope; Jimmy Batten; Pat Thomas; Prince Rodney; Andy Till; Robert McCracken; Ryan Rhodes
MIDDLEWEIGHT	Pat McAteer; Terry Downes; Johnny Pritchett; Bunny Sterling; Alan Minter; Kevin Finnegan; Roy Gumbs; Tony Sibson; Herol Graham; Neville Brown (2)
S. MIDDLEWEIGHT	Sammy Storey
L. HEAVYWEIGHT	Randy Turpin; Chic Calderwood; Chris Finnegan; Bunny Johnson; Tom Collins; Dennis Andries; Tony Wilson; Crawford Ashley
CRUISERWEIGHT	Johnny Nelson; Terry Dunstan
HEAVYWEIGHT	Henry Cooper (3); Horace Notice; Lennox Lewis

NOTES: Jim Driscoll was the first champion to win an NSC belt outright, whilst Eric Boon later became the first champion to put three notches on a BBBoC belt.

Nel Tarleton and Johnny King are the only champions to have won both belts outright.

Freddie Welsh and Johnny King, each with just two notches on an NSC Lonsdale Belt, were allowed to keep their spoils after winning British Empire titles, while Walter McGowan and Charlie Magri, with one notch on a BBBoC Lonsdale Belt, kept their awards under the three years/no available challengers ruling.

Henry Cooper holds the record number of belts won by a single fighter, three in all.

Chris and Kevin Finnegan are the only brothers to have won belts outright.

Jim Higgins holds the record for winning an NSC belt outright in the shortest time, 279 days, whilst Ryan Rhodes won a BBBoC belt in just 90 days, following a successful defence against Del Bryan last March.

British Champions Since Gloves, 1878-1997

The listings below show the tenure of all British champions at each weight since gloves (two ounces or more) were introduced to British rings under Queensberry Rules. Although Charley Davis (147 lbs) had beaten Charlie Napper (140 lbs) with gloves in 1873, we start with Denny Harrington, who defeated George Rooke for both the English and world middleweight titles in London on 12 March 1878. We also make a point of ignoring competition winners, apart from Anthony Diamond who beat Dido Plumb for the middles title over 12 rounds, basically because full championship conditions or finish fights of three minute rounds were not applied. Another point worth bearing in mind, is that prior to the 1880s there were only three weights – heavy, middle and light. Anything above 154 lbs, the middleweight limit, was classified a heavyweight contest, whereas below, say 133 lbs, was considered to be a lightweight bout. Therefore, to put things into current perspective, in many cases, we have had to ascertain the actual poundage of fighters concerned and relate them to the modern weight classes. Another point worth remembering is that men born outside Britain, who won open titles in this country, are not recorded for fear of added confusion, and, although many of the champions or claimants listed before 1909, were no more than English titleholders, having fought for the "championship of England", for our purposes they carry the "British" label.

Prior to 1909, the year that the Lord Lonsdale Challenge Belt was introduced and weight classes subsequently standardised, poundages within divisions could vary quite substantially, thus enabling men fighting at different weights to claim the same "title" at the same time. A brief history of the weight fluctuations between 1891 and 1909, shows:

Bantamweight   With the coming of gloves, the division did not really take off until Nunc Wallace established himself at 112 lbs on beating (small) Bill Goode after nine rounds in London on 12 March 1889. Later, with Wallace fighting above the weight, Billy Plimmer was generally recognised as the country's leading eight stoner, following victories over Charles Mansford and Jem Stevens, and became accepted as world champion when George Dixon, the number one in America's eyes, gradually increased his weight. In 1895 Pedlar Palmer took the British title at 112 lbs, but by 1900 he had developed into a 114 pounder. Between 1902 and 1904, Joe Bowker defended regularly at 116 lbs and in 1909 the NSC standardised the weight at 118 lbs, even though the USA continued for a short while to accept only 116 lbs.

Featherweight   Between 1886 and 1895, one of the most prestigious championship belts in this country was fought for at 126 lbs and, although George Dixon was recognised in the USA as world featherweight champion, gradually moving from 114 to 122 lbs, no major international contests took place in Britain during the above period at his weight. It was only in 1895, when Fred Johnson took the British title at 120 lbs, losing it to Ben Jordan two years later, that we came into line with the USA. Ben Jordan became an outstanding champion, who, between 1898 and 1899, was seen by the NSC as world champion at 120 lbs. However, first Harry Greenfield, then Jabez White and Will Curley, continued to claim the 126 lbs version of the British title and it was only in 1900, when Jack Roberts beat Curley, that the weight limit was finally standardised at nine stone.

Lightweight   Outstanding champions often carried their weights as they grew in size. A perfect example of this was Dick Burge, the British lightweight champion from 1891-1901, who gradually increased from 134 to 144 lbs, while still maintaining his right to the title. It was not until 1902 that Jabez White brought the division into line with the USA. Later, both White, and then Goldswain, carried their weight up to 140 lbs and it was left to Johnny Summers to set the current limit of 135 lbs.

Welterweight   The presence of Dick Burge fighting from 134 to 144 lbs plus up until 1900, explains quite adequately why the welterweight division, although very popular in the USA, did not take off in this country until 1902. The championship was contested between 142 and 146 lbs in those days and was not really supported by the NSC, but by 1909 with their backing it finally became established at 147 lbs.

Note that the Lonsdale Belt notches (title bout wins) relate to NSC, 1909-1935, and BBBoC, 1936-1997.

Champions in **bold** are accorded national recognition.

*Undefeated champions (Does not include men who forfeited titles).

Title Holder	Lonsdale Belt Notches	Tenure	Title Holder	Lonsdale Belt Notches	Tenure	Title Holder	Lonsdale Belt Notches	Tenure
Flyweight (112 lbs)			Jimmy Wilde		1914-1915	**Jackie Brown**	3	1931-1935
Sid Smith		1911	**Joe Symonds**	1	1915-1916	**Benny Lynch***	2	1935-1938
Sid Smith	1	1911-1913	**Jimmy Wilde***	3	1916-1923	**Jackie Paterson**	4	1939-1948
Bill Ladbury		1913-1914	**Elky Clark***	2	1924-1927	**Rinty Monaghan***	1	1948-1950
Percy Jones	1	1914	**Johnny Hill***	1	1927-1929	**Terry Allen**	1	1951-1952
Joe Symonds		1914	**Jackie Brown**		1929-1930	**Teddy Gardner***	1	1952
Tancy Lee	1	1914-1915	**Bert Kirby**	1	1930-1931	**Terry Allen***	2	1952-1954

Title Holder	Lonsdale Belt Notches	Tenure
Dai Dower*	1	1955-1957
Frankie Jones	2	1957-1960
Johnny Caldwell*	1	1960-1961
Jackie Brown	1	1962-1963
Walter McGowan*	1	1963-1966
John McCluskey*	3	1967-1977
Charlie Magri*	1	1977-1981
Kelvin Smart	1	1982-1984
Hugh Russell*	3	1984-1985
Duke McKenzie*	2	1985-1986
Dave Boy McAuley*	1	1986-1988
Pat Clinton*	3	1988-1991
Robbie Regan	1	1991
Francis Ampofo	1	1991
Robbie Regan*	2	1991-1992
Francis Ampofo	3	1992-1996
Mickey Cantwell*	1	1996-1997
Ady Lewis	2	1997-

Bantamweight (118 lbs)

Title Holder	Lonsdale Belt Notches	Tenure
Nunc Wallace*		1889-1891
Billy Plimmer		1891-1895
Tom Gardner		1892
Willie Smith		1892-1896
Nunc Wallace		1893-1895
George Corfield		1893-1896
Pedlar Palmer		1895-1900
Billy Plimmer		1896-1898
Harry Ware		1899-1900
Harry Ware		1900-1902
Andrew Tokell		1901-1902
Jim Williams		1902
Andrew Tokell		1902
Harry Ware		1902
Joe Bowker		1902-1910
Owen Moran		1905-1907
Digger Stanley		1906-1910
Digger Stanley	2	1910-1913
Bill Beynon	1	1913
Digger Stanley	1	1913-1914
Curley Walker*	1	1914-1915
Joe Fox*	3	1915-1917
Tommy Noble	1	1918-1919
Walter Ross*	1	1919-1920
Jim Higgins	3	1920-1922
Tommy Harrison		1922-1923
Bugler Harry Lake	1	1923
Johnny Brown	3	1923-1928
Alf Pattenden	2	1928-1929
Johnny Brown		1928
Teddy Baldock		1928-1929
Teddy Baldock*	1	1929-1931
Dick Corbett	1	1931-1932
Johnny King	1	1932-1934
Dick Corbett*	1	1934
Johnny King	1+2	1935-1947
Jackie Paterson	2	1947-1949
Stan Rowan*	1	1949
Danny O'Sullivan	1	1949-1951
Peter Keenan	3	1951-1953
John Kelly	1	1953-1954
Peter Keenan	3	1954-1959
Freddie Gilroy*	4	1959-1963
Johnny Caldwell	1	1964-1965
Alan Rudkin	1	1965-1966
Walter McGowan	1	1966-1968
Alan Rudkin*	4	1968-1972
Johnny Clark*	1	1973-1974
Dave Needham	1	1974-1975
Paddy Maguire	1	1975-1977
Johnny Owen*	4	1977-1980
John Feeney	1	1981-1983
Hugh Russell	1	1983
Davy Larmour	1	1983
John Feeney	1	1983-1985
Ray Gilbody	2	1985-1987
Billy Hardy*	5	1987-1991
Joe Kelly	1	1992
Drew Docherty	4	1992-

S. Bantamweight (122 lbs)

Title Holder	Lonsdale Belt Notches	Tenure
Richie Wenton*	3	1994-1996
Michael Brodie	1	1997-

Featherweight (126 lbs)

Title Holder	Lonsdale Belt Notches	Tenure
Bill Baxter		1884-1891
Harry Overton		1890-1891
Billy Reader		1891-1892
Fred Johnson		1891-1895
Harry Spurden		1892-1895
Jack Fitzpatrick		1895-1897
Fred Johnson		1895-1897
Harry Greenfield		1896-1899

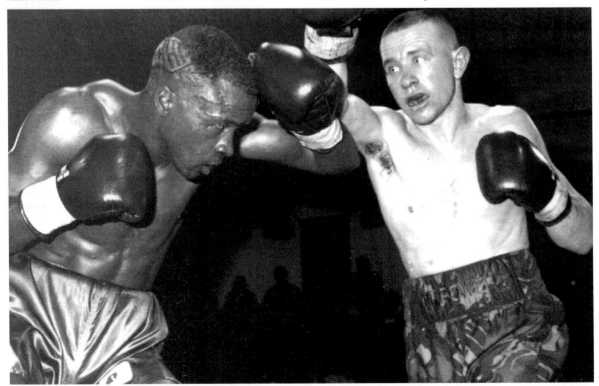

Paul Ingle (right) powered his way to the British featherweight title last January, via an eighth-round stoppage win over the defending champion, Colin McMillan

Les Clark

172

Title Holder	Lonsdale Belt Notches	Tenure
Ben Jordan*		1897-1900
Jabez White		1899-1900
Will Curley		1900-1901
Jack Roberts		1901-1902
Will Curley		1902-1903
Ben Jordan*		1902-1905
Joe Bowker		1905
Johnny Summers		1906
Joe Bowker		1905-1906
Jim Driscoll		1906-1907
Spike Robson		1906-1907
Jim Driscoll*	3	1907-1913
Spike Robson		1907-1910
Ted Kid Lewis*	1	1913-1914
Llew Edwards*	1	1915-1917
Charlie Hardcastle	1	1917
Tancy Lee*	3	1917-1919
Mike Honeyman	2	1920-1921
Joe Fox*	1	1921-1922
George McKenzie	2	1924-1925
Johnny Curley	2	1925-1927
Johnny Cuthbert	1	1927-1928
Harry Corbett	1	1928-1929
Johnny Cuthbert	2	1929-1931
Nel Tarleton	1	1931-1932
Seaman Tommy Watson	2	1932-1934
Nel Tarleton	2	1934-1936
Johnny McGrory	1	1936-1938
Jim Spider Kelly	1	1938-1939
Johnny Cusick	1	1939-1940
Nel Tarleton*	3	1940-1947
Ronnie Clayton	6	1947-1954
Sammy McCarthy	1	1954-1955
Billy Spider Kelly	1	1955-1956
Charlie Hill	3	1956-1959
Bobby Neill	1	1959-1960
Terry Spinks	2	1960-1961
Howard Winstone*	7	1961-1969
Jimmy Revie	2	1969-1971
Evan Armstrong	2	1971-1972
Tommy Glencross	1	1972-1973
Evan Armstrong*	2	1973-1975
Vernon Sollas	1	1975-1977
Alan Richardson	2	1977-1978
Dave Needham	2	1978-1979
Pat Cowdell*	3	1979-1982
Steve Sims*	1	1982-1983
Barry McGuigan*	2	1983-1986
Robert Dickie	3	1986-1988
Peter Harris	1	1988
Paul Hodkinson*	3	1988-1990
Sean Murphy	2	1990-1991
Gary de Roux	1	1991
Colin McMillan*	3	1991-1992
John Davison*	1	1992-1993
Sean Murphy	1	1993
Duke McKenzie*	1	1993-1994
Billy Hardy*	1	1994
Michael Deveney	1	1995
Jonjo Irwin	2	1995-1996
Colin McMillan	1	1996-1997
Paul Ingle	2	1997-

S. Featherweight (130 lbs)

Title Holder	Lonsdale Belt Notches	Tenure
Jimmy Anderson*	3	1968-1970
John Doherty	1	1986
Pat Cowdell	1	1986
Najib Daho	1	1986-1987
Pat Cowdell	1	1987-1988
Floyd Havard	1	1988-1989
John Doherty	1	1989-1990
Joey Jacobs	1	1990
Hugh Forde	1	1990
Kevin Pritchard	1	1990-1991
Robert Dickie	1	1991
Sugar Gibiliru	1	1991
John Doherty	1	1991-1992
Michael Armstrong	1	1992
Neil Haddock	2	1992-1994
Floyd Havard*	3	1994-1995
P. J. Gallagher	2	1996-1997

Lightweight (135 lbs)

Title Holder	Lonsdale Belt Notches	Tenure
Dick Burge		1891-1897
Harry Nickless		1891-1894
Tom Causer		1894-1897
Tom Causer		1897
Dick Burge		1897-1901
Jabez White		1902-1906
Jack Goldswain		1906-1908
Johnny Summers		1908-1909
Freddie Welsh	1	1909-1911
Matt Wells	1	1911-1912
Freddie Welsh*	1	1912-1919
Bob Marriott*	1	1919-1920
Ernie Rice	1	1921-1922
Seaman Nobby Hall		1922-1923
Harry Mason		1923-1924
Ernie Izzard	2	1924-1925
Harry Mason		1924-1925
Harry Mason*	1	1925-1928
Sam Steward		1928-1929
Fred Webster		1929-1930
Al Foreman	1	1930-1932
Johnny Cuthbert		1932-1934
Harry Mizler		1934
Jackie Kid Berg		1934-1936
Jimmy Walsh	1	1936-1938
Dave Crowley	1	1938
Eric Boon	3	1938-1944
Ronnie James*	1	1944-1947
Billy Thompson	3	1947-1951
Tommy McGovern	1	1951-1952
Frank Johnson	1	1952-1953
Joe Lucy	1	1953-1955
Frank Johnson	1	1955-1956
Joe Lucy	2	1956-1957
Dave Charnley*	3	1957-1965
Maurice Cullen	4	1965-1968
Ken Buchanan*	2	1968-1971
Willie Reilly*	1	1972
Jim Watt	1	1972-1973
Ken Buchanan*	1	1973-1974
Jim Watt*	2	1975-1977
Charlie Nash*	1	1978-1979
Ray Cattouse	2	1980-1982
George Feeney*	3	1982-1985
Tony Willis	3	1985-1987
Alex Dickson	1	1987-1988
Steve Boyle	2	1988-1990
Carl Crook	5	1990-1992
Billy Schwer	1	1992-1993
Paul Burke	1	1993
Billy Schwer	2	1993-1995
Michael Ayers	5	1995-

L. Welterweight (140 lbs)

Title Holder	Lonsdale Belt Notches	Tenure
Des Rea	1	1968-1969
Vic Andreetti*	2	1969-1970
Des Morrison	1	1973-1974
Pat McCormack	1	1974
Joey Singleton	3	1974-1976
Dave Boy Green*	1	1976-1977
Colin Power*	2	1977-1978
Clinton McKenzie	1	1978-1979
Colin Power	1	1979
Clinton McKenzie	5	1979-1984
Terry Marsh*	1	1984-1986
Tony Laing*	1	1986
Tony McKenzie	2	1986-1987
Lloyd Christie	3	1987-1989
Clinton McKenzie*	1	1989
Pat Barrett*	2	1989-1990
Tony Ekubia	1	1990-1991
Andy Holligan	3	1991-1994
Ross Hale	4	1994-1995
Paul Ryan	1	1995-1996
Andy Holligan*	1	1996-1997

Welterweight (147 lbs)

Title Holder	Lonsdale Belt Notches	Tenure
Charlie Allum		1903-1904
Charlie Knock		1904-1906
Curly Watson		1906-1910
Young Joseph		1908-1910
Young Joseph	1	1910-1911
Arthur Evernden		1911-1912
Johnny Summers		1912
Johnny Summers	2	1912-1914
Tom McCormick		1914
Matt Wells		1914
Johnny Basham	3	1914-1920
Matt Wells		1914-1919
Ted Kid Lewis		1920-1924
Tommy Milligan*		1924-1925
Hamilton Johnny Brown		1925
Harry Mason		1925-1926
Jack Hood*	3	1926-1934
Harry Mason		1934
Pat Butler*		1934-1936
Dave McCleave		1936
Jake Kilrain	1	1936-1939
Ernie Roderick	5	1939-1948
Henry Hall	1	1948-1949
Eddie Thomas	2	1949-1951
Wally Thom	1	1951-1952
Cliff Curvis*	1	1952-1953
Wally Thom	2	1953-1956
Peter Waterman*	2	1956-1958
Tommy Molloy	2	1958-1960
Wally Swift	1	1960
Brian Curvis*	7	1960-1966
Johnny Cooke	2	1967-1968
Ralph Charles*	3	1968-1972
Bobby Arthur	1	1972-1973
John H. Stracey*	1	1973-1975
Pat Thomas	2	1975-1976
Henry Rhiney	2	1976-1979
Kirkland Laing	1	1979-1980
Colin Jones*	3	1980-1982
Lloyd Honeyghan*	2	1983-1985
Kostas Petrou	1	1985
Sylvester Mittee	1	1985
Lloyd Honeyghan*	1	1985-1986
Kirkland Laing	4	1987-1991
Del Bryan	2	1991-1992
Gary Jacobs*	2	1992-1993
Del Bryan	4	1993-1995
Chris Saunders	1	1995-1996
Kevin Lueshing	1	1996-

L. Middleweight (154 lbs)

Title Holder	Lonsdale Belt Notches	Tenure
Larry Paul	2	1973-1974
Maurice Hope*	3	1974-1977
Jimmy Batten	3	1977-1979
Pat Thomas	3	1979-1981
Herol Graham*	2	1981-1983
Prince Rodney*	1	1983-1984
Jimmy Cable	2	1984-1985
Prince Rodney	2	1985-1986
Chris Pyatt*	1	1986
Lloyd Hibbert*	1	1987
Gary Cooper	1	1988
Gary Stretch	2	1988-1990
Wally Swift Jnr	2	1991-1992
Andy Till	3	1992-1994
Robert McCracken*	3	1994-1995
Ensley Bingham*	2	1996
Ryan Rhodes	3	1996-

Middleweight (160 lbs)

Title Holder	Lonsdale Belt Notches	Tenure
Denny Harrington		1876-1880
William Sheriff*		1880-1883
Bill Goode		1887-1890
Toff Wall*		1890
Ted Pritchard		1890-1895
Ted White		1893-1895
Ted White*		1895-1896
Anthony Diamond*		1898
Dick Burge*		1898-1900
Jack Palmer		1902-1903
Charlie Allum		1905-1906
Pat O'Keefe		1906
Tom Thomas	1	1906-1910
Jim Sullivan*	1	1910-1912
Jack Harrison*	1	1912-1913
Pat O'Keefe	2	1914-1916
Bandsman Jack Blake	1	1916-1918
Pat O'Keefe*	1	1918-1919
Ted Kid Lewis		1920-1921
Tom Gummer	1	1920-1921
Gus Platts		1921
Johnny Basham		1921
Ted Kid Lewis	2	1921-1923
Johnny Basham		1921
Roland Todd		1923-1925
Roland Todd		1925-1927
Tommy Milligan	1	1926-1928
Frank Moody		1927-1928
Alex Ireland		1928-1929
Len Harvey	5	1929-1933
Jock McAvoy	3+2	1933-1944
Ernie Roderick	1	1945-1946
Vince Hawkins	1	1946-1948
Dick Turpin	2	1948-1950
Albert Finch	1	1950
Randy Turpin*	1	1950-1954
Johnny Sullivan	1	1954-1955
Pat McAteer*	3	1955-1958
Terry Downes	1	1958-1959
John Cowboy McCormack	1	1959
Terry Downes	2	1959-1962
George Aldridge	1	1962-1963
Mick Leahy	1	1963-1964
Wally Swift	1	1964-1965
Johnny Pritchett*	4	1965-1969
Les McAteer	1	1969-1970
Mark Rowe	1	1970
Bunny Sterling	4	1970-1974
Kevin Finnegan*	1	1974
Bunny Sterling*	1	1975
Alan Minter	3	1975-1977
Kevin Finnegan	1	1977
Alan Minter*	1	1977-1978
Tony Sibson	1	1979
Kevin Finnegan*	1	1979-1980
Roy Gumbs	3	1981-1983
Mark Kaylor	1	1983-1984
Tony Sibson	1	1984
Herol Graham*	1	1985-1986
Brian Anderson	1	1986-1987
Tony Sibson	1	1987-1988
Herol Graham	4	1988-1992
Frank Grant	2	1992-1993
Neville Brown	6	1993-

S. Middleweight (168 lbs)

Title Holder	Lonsdale Belt Notches	Tenure
Sammy Storey	2	1989-1990
James Cook*	1	1990-1991
Fidel Castro	2	1991-1992
Henry Wharton*	1	1992-1993
James Cook	1	1993-1994
Cornelius Carr*	1	1994
Ali Forbes	1	1995
Sammy Storey*	1	1995
Joe Calzaghe*	2	1995-1997
David Starie	1	1997-

L. Heavyweight (175lbs)

Title Holder	Lonsdale Belt Notches	Tenure
Dennis Haugh		1913-1914
Dick Smith	2	1914-1916
Harry Reeve*	1	1916-1917
Dick Smith*	1	1918-1919
Boy McCormick*	1	1919-1921
Jack Bloomfield*	1	1922-1924
Tom Berry	1	1925-1927
Gipsy Daniels*	1	1927
Frank Moody	1	1927-1929
Harry Crossley	1	1929-1932
Jack Petersen*	1	1932
Len Harvey*	1	1933-1934
Eddie Phillips		1935-1937
Jock McAvoy	1	1937-1938
Len Harvey	2	1938-1942
Freddie Mills*	1	1942-1950
Don Cockell	2	1950-1952
Randy Turpin*	1	1952
Dennis Powell	1	1953
Alex Buxton	2	1953-1955
Randy Turpin*	1	1955
Ron Barton*	1	1956
Randy Turpin*	2	1956-1958
Chic Calderwood	3	1960-1963
Chic Calderwood*	1	1964-1966
Young John McCormack	2	1967-1969
Eddie Avoth	2	1969-1971
Chris Finnegan	2	1971-1973
John Conteh*	2	1973-1974
Johnny Frankham	1	1975
Chris Finnegan*	1	1975-1976
Tim Wood	1	1976-1977
Bunny Johnson	3	1977-1981
Tom Collins	3	1982-1984
Dennis Andries*	5	1984-1986
Tom Collins*	1	1987
Tony Wilson	3	1987-1989
Tom Collins	1	1989-1990
Steve McCarthy	1	1990-1991
Crawford Ashley*	3	1991-1992
Maurice Core*	2	1992-1994
Crawford Ashley	1	1994-

Cruiserweight (190 lbs)

Title Holder	Lonsdale Belt Notches	Tenure
Sam Reeson*	1	1985-1986
Andy Straughn	1	1986-1987
Roy Smith	1	1987
Tee Jay	1	1987-1988
Glenn McCrory*	2	1988
Andy Straughn	1	1988-1989
Johnny Nelson*	3	1989-1991
Derek Angol*	2	1991-1992
Carl Thompson*	1	1992-1994
Dennis Andries	1	1995
Terry Dunstan*	3	1995-1996
Johnny Nelson	1	1996-

Heavyweight (190 lbs +)

Title Holder	Lonsdale Belt Notches	Tenure
Tom Allen*		1878-1882
Charlie Mitchell*		1882-1894
Jem Smith		1889-1891
Ted Pritchard		1891-1895
Jem Smith		1895-1896
George Chrisp		1901
Jack Scales		1901-1902
Jack Palmer		1903-1906
Gunner Moir		1906-1909
Iron Hague		1909-1910
P.O. Curran		1910-1911
Iron Hague		1910-1911
Bombardier Billy Wells	3	1911-1919
Joe Beckett		1919
Frank Goddard	1	1919
Joe Beckett*	1	1919-1923
Frank Goddard		1923-1926
Phil Scott*		1926-1931
Reggie Meen		1931-1932
Jack Petersen	3	1932-1933
Len Harvey		1933-1934
Jack Petersen		1934-1936
Ben Foord		1936-1937
Tommy Farr*	1	1937-1938
Len Harvey*	1	1938-1942
Jack London	1	1944-1945
Bruce Woodcock	2	1945-1950
Jack Gardner	1	1950-1952
Johnny Williams	1	1952-1953
Don Cockell*	1	1953-1956
Joe Erskine	2	1956-1958
Brian London	1	1958-1959
Henry Cooper*	9	1959-1969
Jack Bodell	1	1969-1970
Henry Cooper	1	1970-1971
Joe Bugner	1	1971
Jack Bodell	1	1971-1972
Danny McAlinden	1	1972-1975
Bunny Johnson	1	1975
Richard Dunn	2	1975-1976
Joe Bugner*	1	1976-1977
John L. Gardner*	2	1978-1980
Gordon Ferris	1	1981
Neville Meade	1	1981-1983
David Pearce*	1	1983-1985
Hughroy Currie	1	1985-1986
Horace Notice*	4	1986-1988
Gary Mason	2	1989-1991
Lennox Lewis*	3	1991-1993
Herbie Hide*	1	1993-1994
James Oyebola	1	1994-1995
Scott Welch*	1	1995-1996

Don Cockell and High Wycombe Remembered

by Derek O'Dell

The research required to produce each year's British Boxing Yearbook presents a herculean task to editor, Barry Hugman. He needs co-operation from members of his team when deadlines approach and the preparation for the 1989 edition ran true to form.

"You live in Buckinghamshire", said Barry. "I need a list of every post-war promotion in your area and the name of each promoter."

It was, at first, a straightforward and routine task until shows held at Wycombe Town Hall became a stumbling block. I knew that a promotional group, Matt, with Benny Huntman as matchmaker, ran infrequent shows during the war years. A syndicate named Wycombe Boxing Promotions superseded that in which Huntman was involved but nobody was named as being licenseholder on the British Boxing Board of Controls' records. Some members of the earlier promotions group had been on the post-war syndicate but they were long dead.

Then, as often happens, lady luck smiled on me. I'd been sifting through the sports' section of the Bucks Free Press for 1946 when I saw an advertisement for a forthcoming evening's boxing. Not only did it reveal where tickets were available, it also gave a few names and the addresses of syndicate members. Bear in mind that telephones were the privilege of the well off in 1946, so it was common practice to reveal private addresses of ticket sellers.

Forty years had passed since the appearance of that paper, so it was a longshot - but it paid off. There was, and still is, one relative of the original syndicate resident at the very last address I contacted. I was informed that the one person who might be able to help me was very elderly but, remarkably, still alive.

Soon, I was engaged in an interesting and fruitful conversation with a nonagenarian whose failing memory had to be prodded and cajoled into recalling events that had taken place all those years ago.

"Let me think for a while", he mused. "We did indeed form a syndicate. There were five or six of us and it was a successful venture. When the war was over, those of us who survived decided to carry on. We started to lose money only when television became so popular an entertainment medium that people stayed at home. Eventually we disbanded. Our proudest achievement, if that is what it can correctly be termed, was in giving a 17-year-old young man his first paid fight and that he went on to fight for a world title in America."

"That boxer was Don Cockell, who was one of our very best post-war champions," I prompted.

"You've got it! That was his name. He missed the last train home and spent the night on High Wycombe station. We paid him three pounds and he was so delighted that he promised to box for us for nothing if he ever won a championship title. I'd almost forgotten about it when some years later, he offered to appear in an exhibition contest with his stablemate."

I reminded him that the stablemate was Jack Gardner, who was our heavyweight champion at the time. Cockell held the light-heavyweight title and they were both managed by John Simpson of Basingstoke.

"Yes, those two brought in a capacity crowd to our show. Cockell was still remembered - after all, he boxed for us quite often at the beginning of his career. The exhibition drew nobbins and that is a rarity. The fans loved him."

I checked Cockell's record. He fought eight times at Wycombe up to 1948. Only two contests went the distance, both against Jimmy Carroll, and there was just a single defeat against Sidcup's Jock Taylor. The Taylor setback was by a knockout and only two other men were to blot Don's record in that fashion were Aaron Wilson and Kitione Lave. Lave was to bring down the curtain on Cockell's career but, like a true pro, he put the Taylor and Wilson defeats behind him and got on with learning his trade. On both occasions he was quickly back in action with a win.

Coming back from adversity was a reassuring feature of Don's career. When he'd broken into the world ratings, rheumatic fever - severe enough to finish most sportsmen's ambitions - retarded his progress, but he overcame that considerable obstacle to put himself in line for a world-title shot. He was British and European champion with fine wins over top Americans, Nick Barone, Freddie Beshore and Lloyd Marshall. Then he went to pieces losing to unfancied Jimmy Slade in a "marking time" fight before he challenged Joey Maxim for the world title.

Randolph Turpin beat him two months later and future prospects looked decidely dim. I met him briefly soon after the Turpin debacle. That was in Weybridge, where he ran a hairdressing business. He looked ill, there was a nasty boil on his neck, he was fat, and a far cry from the jaunty, athletic scrapper who had cut a swathe through the light-heavyweight ranks. To add to those problems his prized Lonsdale Belt had been stolen. He said that getting down to the 12st 6lb limit for the Turpin fight was torture. Four months later he was 14 stone!

I thought him too short for a heavyweight. Realistically, he was, but Cockell had a deep well of courage and determination that counteracted his physical shortcomings. Promoter, Stan Baker, had faith in him. He gave Don his first chance to climb the heavyweight ladder and his judgement was rewarded when Don won the British and Empire titles and then ventured into world contention by licking Roland La Starza and Harry "Kid" Matthews. Matthews lost three out of three to Don, two of them in Seattle, which was the Kid's hometown!

In 1955, Don was top contender and he found himself opposing the great Rocky Marciano for boxing's biggest prize in a foreign ring, with all the odds piled high against him.

He was never in with a fair chance. The ring was of the smallest size permitted, which was a considerable advantage to the champion. The referee, Frank Brown, allowed Marciano to ignore the rule book. Don was butted, cut, elbowed, hit after the bell, and took a head punch when on one knee. Despite all of this, he put up a magnificent fight, taking Marciano's best shots until he had nothing left to give.

With a larger ring, and the chance of boxing from centre ground and to use his excellent footwork and ring craft, Don may have gone the full 15-rounds distance. I was expecting him to upset the odds and to win on points but, with the gift of hindsight, I know that Rocky's unflagging aggression would have won the day whatever the conditions were. We often hear of how modern champions would be too fast, too big, too everything for him, but we heard those same opinions when he was due to fight Louis, Walcott, Charles, and Moore etc. Rocky beat them all and they were never the same afterwards. Neither was Don Cockell. He'd given a career-best performance in a heart-stopping display of give and take.

In the late 1970s, Don was guest of honour at an ex-boxers' function. He was confined to a wheelchair and was suffering from throat cancer that was soon to kill him. Nobody had ever squeezed a single word of exuse or alibi from him following his defeat by Marciano. The nearest he ever came was a light-hearted quip that Rocky developed a strange deafness when the bell rang to end a round. Cockell did us proud that night and the old timers remembered him and gave him such a rousing ovation that Don was moved to tears. It was an emotional occasion and a reminder of how proud is the boxing fraternity of the man who began his career in Wycombe Town Hall.

That building, slightly to the east of the town centre, has a long history as a fight venue. In its halycon days in the 1930s, boxing was held there nearly every week during the season and even in summer, the promoters kept going with open-air tournaments at nearby showgrounds. Steve "Curly" Fay, a transplanted Welshman, was one of the early favourites. When he retired, on a winning note and to a packed house, Don Smith was developing as a local hero, but the 1939-45 war checked his progress and he never quite fulfilled that early promise in peacetime years to follow.

Despite the tough nature of the sport, there were humorous moments. That dour scrapper from Croydon, Pat Stribling, was, like Cockell, a neophyte pro, when he appeared at the Town Hall in 1948. In the opposite corner was the crafty veteran from Worksop, Allan Cooke, who proceeded to keep his man at bay with a well-oiled straight left. By round three, Pat had found the key to getting past Cooke's attacks and was weakening his opponent with body attacks. It was at this crucial stage that the referee noticed a smear of blood on Pat's forehead and he immediately stopped the contest and raised Cooke's arm.

A boxer cannot see a cut on his own face and is often unaware of how slight or how serious it is. Imagine Pat's chagrin when, in his dressing room, he saw that the so-called cut was merely a pimple on his forehead that had bled slightly. He was furious but the referee had left the building.

On the train home, Pat was looking for a seat when he noticed the official sitting in a packed compartment. He moved along to remonstrate, but the referee spoke first:

"Hello Pat. That was a lucky break for us when you were cut. Another round and we would have missed this train."

Pat was speechless. He would have preferred to be benighted on the bleak and inhospitable east-bound platform of High Wycombe's railway station than to lose a fight. All boxers have such pride, but the referee had taken the easy way out.

Nine years have passed since the last boxing promotion was held at the old Town Hall. I belonged to the syndicate that tried to revive local interest in the game. Our venture lasted to just two tournaments, but lack of money, rather than lack of support, is what caused us to disband. The palmy days of boxing in the town have gone. Through the doors of the Town Hall have passed many famous personalities - stars of stage and screen, dignitaries and politicians, sportsmen and entertainers. They, by their presence, brought honours to the town, but none did more so than the former blacksmith from Battersea, Don Cockell.

Don Cockell (right) will always be remembered for his brave performance against Rocky Marciano, seen here throwing a heavy left hand

Retired British Champions: Career Summary

Includes all British champions, and claimants, or British boxers who have won international titles since the introduction of gloves, and who had retired by July, 1997. It does not include champions still active (for their records see under Current British-Based Champions or Active British-Based Boxers). Although Joe Bugner, Ray Close, and Derek Williams continue to be active, they are unlikely to box in the UK again and, for our purposes, their details are recorded in this section. Please make allowances for some of the early British champions' records possibly being incomplete. Undefeated champions are those who relinquished their titles, not forfeited them.

George Aldridge British Middleweight Champion, 1962-1963. *Born* 01.02.36. *From* Market Harborough. *Pro Career* 1956-1963 (52 contests, won 36, drew 2, lost 14).

Terry Allen British Flyweight Champion, 1951-1952, and Undefeated British Flyweight Champion, 1952-1954. European and World Flyweight Champion, 1950. *Born* 18.06.24. *From* Islington. Birthname - Edward Govier. *Deceased* 1987. *Pro Career* 1942-1954 (74 contests, won 60, drew 1, lost 13).

Charlie Allum British Welterweight Champion, 1903-1904. British Middleweight Championship Claimant, 1905-1906. *Born* 23.04.1876. *From* Notting Hill. *Deceased* 1918. *Pro Career* 1903-1910 (44 contests, won 21, drew 5, lost 18).

Brian Anderson British Middleweight Champion, 1986-1987. *Born* 09.07.61. *From* Sheffield. *Pro Career* 1980-1987 (39 contests, won 27, drew 3, lost 9).

Jimmy Anderson Undefeated British S. Featherweight Champion, 1968-1970. *Born* 01.10.42. *From* Waltham Cross. *Pro Career* 1964-1971 (37 contests, won 27, drew 1, lost 9).

Vic Andreetti Undefeated British L. Welterweight Champion, 1969-1970. *Born* 29.01.42. *From* Hoxton. *Pro Career* 1961-1969 (67 contests, won 51, drew 3, lost 13).

Derek Angol Undefeated British Cruiserweight Champion, 1991-1992. Undefeated Commonwealth Cruiserweight Champion, 1989-1993. *Born* 28.11.64. *From* Camberwell. *Pro Career* 1986-1996 (31 contests, won 28, lost 3).

Evan Armstrong British Featherweight Champion, 1971-1972, and Undefeated British Featherweight Champion, 1973-1975. Commonwealth Featherweight Champion, 1974. *Born* 15.02.43. *From* Ayr. *Pro Career* 1963-1974 (54 contests, won 39, drew 1, lost 14).

Michael Armstrong British S. Featherweight Champion, 1992. *Born* 18.12.68. *From* Moston. Birthname - Morris. *Pro Career* 1987-1994 (26 contests, won 18, drew 1, lost 7).

Bobby Arthur British Welterweight Champion, 1972-1973. *Born* 25.07.47. *From* Coventry. *Pro Career* 1967-1976 (41 contests, won 26, lost 15).

Eddie Avoth British L. Heavyweight Champion, 1969-1971. Commonwealth L. Heavyweight Champion, 1970-1971. *Born* 02.05.45. *From* Cardiff. *Pro Career* 1963-1972 (53 contests, won 44, lost 9).

Teddy Baldock British Bantamweight Championship Claimant, 1928-1929. Undefeated British Bantamweight Champion, 1929-1931. British Empire Bantamweight Championship Claimant, 1928-1930. European Bantamweight Championship Claimant, 1928-1931. World Bantamweight Championship Claimant, 1927. *Born* 23.05.07. *From* Poplar. *Deceased* 1971. *Pro Career* 1921-1931 (80 contests, won 72, drew 3, lost 5).

Pat Barrett Undefeated British L. Welterweight Champion, 1989-1990. European L. Welterweight Champion, 1990-1992. *Born* 22.07.67. *From* Manchester. *Pro Career* 1987-1994 (42 contests, won 37, drew 1, lost 4).

Ron Barton Undefeated British L. Heavyweight Champion, 1956. *Born* 25.02.33. *From* West Ham. *Pro Career* 1954-1961 (31 contests, lost 5).

Johnny Basham British Welterweight Champion, 1914-1920. British Empire Welterweight Championship Claimant, 1919-1920. European Welterweight Championship Claimant, 1919-1920. British Middleweight Champion, 1921. British and European Middleweight Championship Claimant, 1921. *Born* 13.09.1890. *From* Newport. *Died* 1947. *Pro Career* 1910-1929 (87 contests, won 65, drew 7, lost 15).

Jimmy Batten British L. Middleweight Champion, 1977-1979. *Born* 07.11.55. *From* Millwall. *Pro Career* 1974-1983 (49 contests, won 40, lost 9).

Joe Beckett British Heavyweight Championship Claimant, 1919. Undefeated British Heavyweight Champion, 1919-1923. British Empire Heavyweight Championship Claimant, 1919-1923. *Born* 04.04.1892. *From* Southampton. *Deceased* 1965. *Pro Career* 1912-1923 (61 contests, won 49, drew 1, lost 11).

Jackie Kid Berg British Lightweight Champion, 1934-1936. World L. Welterweight Champion, 1930-1931 (NBA version). *Born* 28.06.09. *From* Stepney. Birthname - Judah Bergman. *Deceased* 1991. *Pro Career* 1924-1945 (192 contests, won 157, drew 9, lost 26).

Tom Berry British L. Heavyweight Champion, 1925-1927. British Empire L. Heavyweight Championship Claimant, 1927. *Born* 14.02.1890. *From* Custom House. *Deceased* 1943. *Pro Career* 1909-1931 (114 contests, won 67, drew 5, lost 41, no contest 1).

Bill Beynon British Bantamweight Champion, 1913. European Bantamweight Championship Claimant, 1913. *Born* 08.04.1891. *From* Taibach. *Deceased* 1932. *Pro Career* 1909-1931 (192 contests, won 70, drew 30, lost 91, no decision 1).

Bandsman Jack Blake British Middleweight Champion, 1916-1918. *Born* 1893. *From* Great Yarmouth. *Deceased* 1961. *Pro Career* 1910-1922 (64 contests, won 49, lost 14, no contest 1).

Jack Bloomfield Undefeated British L. Heavyweight Champion, 1922-1924. British Empire L. Heavyweight Championship Claimant, 1923-1924. *Born* 20.11.1899. *From* Islington. Birthname - Jack Blumenfeld. *Deceased* 1961. *Pro Career* 1918-1924 (38 contests, won 28, drew 1, lost 5, no decision 3, no contest 1).

Jack Bodell British Heavyweight Champion, 1969-1970 and 1971-1972. Commonwealth Heavyweight Champion, 1971-1972. European Heavyweight Champion, 1971. *Born* 11.08.40. *From* Swadlincote. *Pro Career* 1962-1972 (71 contests, won 58, lost 13).

Eric Boon British Lightweight Champion, 1938-1944. *Born* 28.12.19. *From* Chatteris. *Deceased* 1981. *Pro Career* 1935-1952 (122 contests, won 93, drew 5, lost 23. no contest 1).

Joe Bowker British Bantamweight Champion, 1902-1910. European Bantamweight Championship Claimant, 1910. World Bantamweight Champion, 1902-1904 (GB version). Undefeated World Bantamweight Champion, 1904-1905. British Featherweight Champion, 1905-1907. World Featherweight Champion, 1905-1907 (GB version). *Born* 20.07.1883. *From* Salford. Birthname - Tommy Mahon. *Deceased* 1955. *Pro Career* 1900-1919 (50 contests, won 39, drew 1, lost 8, no decision 2).

Steve Boyle British Lightweight Champion, 1988-1990. *Born* 28.11.62. *From* Glasgow. *Pro Career* 1983-1993 (33 contests, won 25, drew 2, lost 6).

Cornelius Boza-Edwards Undefeated European S. Featherweight Champion, 1982. World S. Featherweight Champion, 1981 (WBC version). *Born* Uganda, 27.05.56. *From* London. *Pro Career* 1976-1987 (53 contests, won 45, drew 1, lost 7).

Jim Brady British Empire Bantamweight Championship Claimant, 1941-1945. *From* Dundee. *Deceased* 1980. *Pro Career* 1932-1947 (169 contests, won 104, drew 15, lost 50).

Jackie Brown British and British Empire Flyweight Champion, 1962-1963. *Born* 02.03.35. *From* Edinburgh. *Pro Career* 1958-1966 (44 contests, won 32, drew 1, lost 10, no contest 1).

Jackie Brown British Flyweight Champion, 1929-1930 and 1931-1935. European Flyweight Championship Claimant, 1931-1935. World Flyweight Champion, 1932-1935 (NBA/IBU version). *Born* 29.11.09. *From* Manchester. *Deceased* 1971. *Pro Career* 1926-1939 (135 contests, won 103, drew 8, lost 24).

Hamilton Johnny Brown British Welterweight Champion, 1925. *Born* 1901. *From* Hamilton. Birthname - John Fleming. *Deceased* 1983. *Pro Career* 1920-1931 (55 contests, won 38, drew 2, lost 15).

Johnny Brown British Bantamweight Champion, 1923-1928. British Empire Bantamweight Championship Claimant, 1923-1928. British Bantamweight Championship Claimant, 1928. European Bantamweight Championship Claimant, 1923-1928. *Born* 18.07.02. *From* Stepney. Birthname - Phil Hackman. *Deceased* 1975. *Pro Career* 1919-1928 (99 contests, won 54, drew 5, lost 25, no decision 15).

Frank Bruno Undefeated European Heavyweight Champion, 1985-1986. WBC Heavyweight Champion, 1995-96. *Born* 16.11.61. *From* Wandsworth. *Pro Career* 1982-1996 (45 contests, won 40, lost 5).

Ken Buchanan Undefeated British Lightweight Champion, 1968-1971, and 1973-1974. Undefeated European Lightweight Champion, 1974-1975. World Lightweight Champion, 1970-1971. World Lightweight Champion, 1971-1972 (WBA version). *Born* 28.06.45. *From* Edinburgh. *Pro Career* 1965-1982 (69 contests, won 61, lost 8).

Joe Bugner British, Commonwealth and European Heavyweight Champion, 1971. Undefeated European Heavyweight Champion, 1972-1975. European Heavyweight Champion, 1976-1977. Undefeated British and Commonwealth Heavyweight Champion, 1976-1977. *Born* Hungary, 13.03.50. *From* Bedford. *Pro Career* 1967-1997 (79 contests, won 65, drew 1, lost 13).

Dick Burge British Lightweight Champion, 1891-1897. Undefeated British Lightweight Champion, 1897-1901. World Lightweight Champion, 1891-1896 (GB version). Undefeated British Middleweight Champion, 1898-1900. *Born* 19.02.1865. *From* Cheltenham. *Deceased* 1918. *Pro Career* 1882-1900 (25 contests, won 14, drew 2, lost 8, no decision 1).

Pat Butler Undefeated British Welterweight Champion, 1934-1936. *Born* 16.03.13. *From* Mountsorrel. *Pro Career* 1931-1936 (114 contests, won 65, drew 4, lost 44, no contest 1).

Alex Buxton British L. Heavyweight Champion, 1953-1955. *Born* 10.05.25. *From* Watford. *Pro Career* 1942-1963 (125 contests, won 78, drew 4, lost 43).

Jimmy Cable British L. Middleweight Champion, 1984-1985. European L. Middleweight Champion, 1984. *Born* 07.09.57. *From* Crawley. *Pro Career* 1980-1988 (41 contests, won 30, drew 2, lost 9).

Chic Calderwood British and British Empire L. Heavyweight Champion, 1960-1963. Undefeated British L. Heavyweight Champion, 1964-1966. *Born* 09.01.37. *From* Craigneuk. Birthname - Charles Calderwood. *Deceased* 1966. *Pro Career* 1957-1966 (55 contests, won 44, drew 1, lost 9, no contest 1).

Johnny Caldwell Undefeated British Flyweight Champion, 1960-1961. British and British Empire Bantamweight Champion, 1964-1965. World Bantamweight Champion, 1961-1962 (EBU version). *Born* 07.05.38. *From* Belfast. *Pro Career* 1958-1965 (35 contests, won 29, drew 1, lost 5).

Fidel Castro British S. Middleweight Champion, 1991-1992. *Born* 17.04.63. *From* Nottingham. Birthname - Smith. *Pro Career* 1987-1995 (30 contests, won 22, lost 8).

Ray Cattouse British Lightweight Champion, 1980-1982. *Born* 24.07.52. *From* Balham. *Pro Career* 1975-1983 (31 contests, won 26, drew 3, lost 2).

Tom Causer British Lightweight Championship Claimant, 1894-1897. British Lightweight Champion, 1897. *Born* 15.01.1872. *From* Bermondsey. *Deceased* 1918. *Pro Career* 1891-1898 (36 contests, won 31, drew 2, lost 3).

Ralph Charles Undefeated British and British Empire/Commonwealth Welterweight Champion, 1968-1972. European Welterweight Champion, 1970-1971. *Born* 05.02.43. *From* West Ham. *Pro Career* 1963-1972 (43 contests, won 39, lost 4).

Dave Charnley Undefeated British Lightweight Champion, 1957-1965. British Empire Lightweight Champion, 1959-1962. European Lightweight Champion, 1960-1963. *Born* 10.10.35. *From* Dartford. *Pro Career* 1954-1964 (61 contests, won 48, drew 1, lost 12).

George Chrisp British Heavyweight Championship Claimant, 1901. *Born* 23.02.1872. *From* Newcastle. *Deceased*. *Pro Career* 1889-1906 (23 contests, won 15, lost 8).

Lloyd Christie British L. Welterweight Champion, 1987-1989. *Born* 28.02.62. *From* Wolverhampton. *Pro Career* 1981-1989 (46 contests, won 24, drew 1, lost 21).

Elky Clark Undefeated British Flyweight Champion, 1924-1927. British Empire Bantamweight Championship Claimant, 1924-1927. Undefeated European Flyweight Champion, 1925-1927. *Born* 04.01.1898. *From* Glasgow. *Deceased* 1956. *Pro Career* 1921-1927 (45 contests, won 29, drew 4, lost 12).

Johnny Clark Undefeated British and European Bantamweight Champion, 1973-1974. *Born* 10.09.47. *From* Walworth. *Pro Career* 1966-1974 (43 contests, won 39, drew 1, lost 3).

Ronnie Clayton British Featherweight Champion, 1947-1954. British Empire Featherweight Championship Claimant, 1947-1951. European Featherweight Champion, 1947-1948. *Born* 09.02.23. *From* Blackpool. *Pro Career* 1941-1954 (113 contests, won 79, drew 8, lost 26).

Pat Clinton Undefeated British Flyweight Champion, 1988-1991. Undefeated European Flyweight Champion, 1990-1991. World Flyweight Champion, 1992-1993 (WBO version). *Born* 04.04.64. *From* Croy. *Pro Career* 1985-1992 (23 contests, won 20, lost 3).

Ray Close Undefeated European S. Middleweight Champion, 1993. *Born* 20.01.69. *From* Belfast. *Pro Career* 1988-1997 (29 contests, won 25, drew 1, lost 3).

Don Cockell British L. Heavyweight Champion, 1950-1952. Undefeated European L. Heavyweight Champion, 1951-1952. Undefeated British Heavyweight Champion, 1953-1956. British Empire Heavyweight Championship Claimant, 1953-1954. Undefeated British Empire Heavyweight Champion, 1954-1956. *Born* 22.09.28. *From* Battersea. *Deceased* 1983. *Pro Career* 1946-1956 (80 contests, won 65, drew 1, lost 14).

Tom Collins British L. Heavyweight Champion, 1982-1984. Undefeated British L. Heavyweight Champion, 1987 and 1989-1990. European L. Heavyweight Champion, 1987-1988 and 1990-1991. *Born* Curacao, 01.07.55. *From* Leeds. *Pro Career* 1977-1993 (50 contests, won 26, drew 2, lost 22).

John Conteh Undefeated British, Commonwealth and European L. Heavyweight Champion, 1973-1974. World L. Heavyweight Champion, 1974-1977 (WBC version). *Born* 27.05.51. *From* Liverpool. *Pro Career* 1971-1980 (39 contests, won 34, drew 1, lost 4).

James Cook Undefeated British S. Middleweight Champion, 1990-1991. British S. Middleweight Champion, 1993-1994. European S. Middleweight Champion, 1991-1992. *Born* Jamaica, 17.05.59. *From* Peckham. *Pro Career* 1982-1994 (35 contests, won 25, lost 10).

Johnny Cooke British and British Empire Welterweight Champion, 1967-1968. *Born* 17.12.34. *From* Bootle. *Pro Career* 1960-1971 (93 contests, won 52, drew 7, lost 34).

Gary Cooper British L. Middleweight Champion, 1988. *Born* 31.05.57. *From* Lymington. *Pro Career* 1978-1989 (27 contests, won 16, drew 2, lost 9).

Henry Cooper Undefeated British Heavyweight Champion, 1959-1969. British Heavyweight Champion, 1970-1971. British Empire/Commonwealth Heavyweight Champion, 1959-1971. Undefeated European Heavyweight Champion, 1964 and 1968-1969 and European Heavyweight Champion, 1970-1971. *Born* 03.05.34. *From* Bellingham. *Pro Career* 1954-1971 (55 contests, won 40, drew 1, lost 14).

Dick Corbett British Bantamweight Champion, 1931-1932 and Undefeated British Bantamweight Champion, 1934. British Empire Bantamweight Championship Claimant, 1930-1932 and 1934. *Born* 28.09.08. *From* Bethnal Green. Birthname - Dick Coleman. *Deceased* 1943. *Pro Career* 1926-1943 (183 contests, won 130, drew 17, lost 36).

Harry Corbett British Featherweight Champion, 1928-1929. European Lightweight Championship Claimant, 1930-1931. *Born* 14.02.04. *From* Bethnal Green. Birthname - Henry Coleman. *Deceased* 1957. *Pro Career* 1921-1936 (219 contests, won 141, drew 25, lost 50, no contest 3).

George Corfield British Bantamweight Championship Claimant, 1893-1896. *Born* 1874. *From* Sheffield. *Deceased*. *Pro Career* 1890-1902 (32 contests, won 18, drew 4, lost 10).

Henry Cooper

Pat Cowdell Undefeated British Featherweight Champion, 1979-1982. Undefeated European Featherweight Champion, 1982-1983. British S. Featherweight Champion, 1986 and 1987-1988. European S. Featherweight Champion, 1984-1985. *Born* 18.08.53. *From* Warley. *Pro Career* 1977-1988 (42 contests, won 36, lost 6).

Carl Crook British & Commonwealth Lightweight Champion, 1990-1992. *Born* 10.11.63. *From* Chorley. *Pro Career* 1985-1993 (31 contests, won 26, drew 1, lost 4).

Harry Crossley British L. Heavyweight Champion, 1929-1932. *Born* 04.05.01. *From* Mexborough. *Deceased* 1948. *Pro Career* 1924-1934 (87 contests, won 58, drew 8, lost 20, no decision 1).

Dave Crowley British Lightweight Champion, 1938. *Born* 04.05.10. *From* Clerkenwell. *Deceased* 1974. *Pro Career* 1928-1946 (183 contests, won 129, drew 11, lost 42, no decision 1).

Maurice Cullen British Lightweight Champion, 1965-1968. *Born* 30.12.37. *From* Shotton. *Pro Career* 1959-1970 (55 contests, won 45, drew 2, lost 8).

Johnny Curley British Featherweight Champion, 1925-1927. *Born* 09.11.1897. *From* Lambeth. *Deceased* 1982. *Pro Career* 1912-1931 (181 contests, won 129, drew 18, lost 33, no decision 1).

Will Curley British Featherweight Championship Claimant, 1900-1901 and 1902-1903. *Born* 16.08.1877. *From* Newcastle. *Deceased* 1973. *Pro Career* 1892-1903 (33 contests, won 26, drew 3, lost 4).

P. O. Curran British Heavyweight Championship Claimant, 1910-1911. British Empire Heavyweight Championship Claimant, 1911. *Born* 1882. *From* Clarefield Lideen. Birthname - Matthew Curran. *Deceased* 1938. *Pro Career* 1908-1920 (86 contests, won 45, drew 3, lost 33, no contest 5).

Hughroy Currie British Heavyweight Champion, 1985-1986. *Born* Jamaica, 09.02.59. *From* Catford. *Pro Career* 1981-1989 (29 contests, won 17, drew 1, lost 11).

Brian Curvis Undefeated British and British Empire Welterweight Champion, 1960-1966. *Born* 14.08.37. *From* Swansea. Birthname - Brian Nancurvis. *Pro Career* 1959-1966 (41 contests, won 37, lost 4).

Cliff Curvis Undefeated British Welterweight Champion, 1952-1953. British Empire Welterweight Championship Claimant, 1952. *Born* 02.11.27. *From* Swansea. Birthname - Cliff Nancurvis. *Pro Career* 1944-1953 (55 contests, won 42, drew 1, lost 12).

Johnny Cusick British Featherweight Champion, 1939-1940. British Empire Featherweight Championship Claimant, 1939-1940. *Born* 27.01.16. *From* Manchester. *Deceased* 1990. *Pro Career* 1932-1949 (79 contests, won 64, drew 3, lost 12).

Johnny Cuthbert British Featherweight Champion, 1927-1928 and 1929-1931. British Lightweight Champion, 1932-1934. *Born* 09.07.05. *From* Sheffield. *Deceased* 1987. *Pro Career* 1921-1934 (153 contests, won 110, drew 14, lost 29).

Najib Daho British S. Featherweight Champion, 1986-1987. Commonwealth Lightweight Champion, 1989-1990. *Born* Morocco, 13.01.59. *From* Manchester. *Deceased* 1993. *Pro Career* 1977-1991 (60 contests, won 34, drew 1, lost 25).

Gipsy Daniels Undefeated British L. Heavyweight Champion, 1927. British Empire L. Heavyweight Championship Claimant, 1927. *Born* 1902. *From* Newport. Birthname - Danny Thomas. *Deceased* 1967. *Pro Career* 1920-1938 (139 contests, won 87, drew 11, lost 41).

John Davison Undefeated British Featherweight Champion, 1992-1993. *Born* 30.09.58. *From* Newcastle. *Pro Career* 1988-1993 (20 contests, won 15, lost 5).

Gary DeRoux British Featherweight Champion, 1991. *Born* 04.11.62. *From* Peterborough. *Pro Career* 1986-1993 (22 contests, won 13, drew 1, lost 8).

Anthony Diamond Undefeated British Middleweight Champion, 1898. *Born* 13.11.1861. *From* Birmingham. *Deceased* 1930. *Pro Career* 1887-1898 (12 contests, won 10, lost 2).

Robert Dickie British Featherweight Champion, 1986-1988. British S. Featherweight Champion, 1991. *Born* 23.06.64. *From* Swansea. *Pro Career* 1983-1993 (28 contests, won 22, drew 2, lost 4).

Alex Dickson British Lightweight Champion, 1987-1988. *Born* 01.10.62. *From* Larkhall. *Pro Career* 1985-1989 (22 contests, won 18, drew 1, lost 3).

John Doherty British S. Featherweight Champion, 1986, 1989-1990 and 1991-1992. *Born* 17.07.62. *From* Bradford. *Pro Career* 1982-1992 (39 contests, won 28, drew 3, lost 8).

Pat Doherty Commonwealth Lightweight Champion, 1989. *Born* 12.04.62. *From* Croydon. *Pro Career* 1981-1989 (32 contests, won 18, drew 3, lost 11).

Dai Dower Undefeated British Flyweight Champion, 1955-1957. Undefeated British Empire Flyweight Champion, 1954-1957. European Flyweight Champion, 1955. *Born* 26.06.33. *From* Abercynon. *Pro Career* 1953-1958 (37 contests, won 34, lost 3).

Terry Downes British Middleweight Champion, 1958-1959 and 1959-1962. World Middleweight Champion, 1961-1962 (NY/EBU version). *Born* 09.05.36. *From* Paddington. *Pro Career* 1957-1964 (44 contests, won 35, lost 9).

Jim Driscoll British Featherweight Championship Claimant, 1906-1907. Undefeated British Featherweight Champion, 1907-1913. Undefeated European Featherweight Champion, 1912-1913. British Empire Featherweight Championship Claimant, 1908-1913. Undefeated World Featherweight Champion, 1907-1913 (GB version). *Born* 15.12.1880. *From* Cardiff. *Deceased* 1925. *Pro Career* 1901-1919 (71 contests, won 52, drew 6, lost 3, no decision 10).

Richard Dunn British and Commonwealth Heavyweight Champion, 1975-1976. European Heavyweight Champion, 1976. *Born* 19.01.45. *From* Bradford. *Pro Career* 1969-1977 (45 contests, won 33, lost 12).

Llew Edwards Undefeated British Featherweight Champion, 1915-1917. British Empire Featherweight Championship Claimant, 1915-1917. *Born* 1894. *From* Porth. *Deceased* 1965. *Pro Career* 1913-1922 (106 contests, won 85, drew 5, lost 13, no decision 3).

Tony Ekubia British L. Welterweight Champion, 1990-1991. Commonwealth L. Welterweight Champion, 1989-1991. *Born* Nigeria, 06.03.60. *From* Manchester. *Pro Career* 1986-1993 (25 contests, won 21, lost 4).

Joe Erskine British Heavyweight Champion, 1956-1958. British Empire Heavyweight Champion, 1957-1958. *Born* 26.01.34. *From* Cardiff. *Deceased* 1990. *Pro Career* 1954-1964 (54 contests, won 45, drew 1, lost 8).

Arthur Evernden British Welterweight Champion, 1911-1912. *Born* 19.01.1886. *From* Chatham. *Deceased*. *Pro Career* 1908-1917 (74 contests, won 45, drew 5, lost 22, no decision 2).

Tommy Farr Undefeated British Heavyweight Champion, 1937-1938.

British Empire Heavyweight Championship Claimant, 1937-1938. *Born* 12.03.14. *From* Tonypandy. *Deceased* 1986. Pro Career (125 contests, won 80, drew 13, lost 30, no decision 2).

George Feeney Undefeated British Lightweight Champion, 1982-1985. *Born* 09.02.57. *From* West Hartlepool. *Pro Career* 1977-1984 (29 contests, won 19, lost 10).

John Feeney British Bantamweight Champion, 1981-1983 and 1983-1985. *Born* 15.05.58. *From* West Hartlepool. *Pro Career* 1977-1987 (48 contests, won 35, lost 13).

Gordon Ferris British Heavyweight Champion, 1981. *Born* 21.11.52. *From* Enniskillen. *Pro Career* 1977-1982 (26 contests, won 20, lost 6).

Darren Fifield Commonwealth Flyweight Champion, 1993-1994. *Born* 09.10.69. *From* Henley. *Pro Career* 1992-1996 (13 contests, won 7, drew 2, lost 4).

Albert Finch British Middleweight Champion, 1950. *Born* 16.05.26. *From* Croydon. *Pro Career* 1945-1958 (103 contests, won 72, drew 9, lost 21, no contest 1).

Chris Finnegan British L. Heavyweight Champion, 1971-1973 and Undefeated British L. Heavyweight Champion, 1975-1976. Commonwealth L. Heavyweight Champion, 1971-1973. European L. Heavyweight Champion, 1972. *Born* 05.06.44. *From* Iver. *Pro Career* 1968-1975 (37 contests, won 29, drew 1, lost 7).

Kevin Finnegan British Middleweight Champion, 1977. Undefeated British Middleweight Champion, 1974 and 1979-1980. European Middleweight Champion, 1974-1975 and 1980. *Born* 18.04.48. *From* Iver. *Pro Career* 1970-1980 (47 contests, won 35, drew 1, lost 11).

Ben Foord British Heavyweight Champion, 1936-1937. British Empire Heavyweight Championship Claimant, 1936-1937. *Born* Vrede, South Africa, 21.01.13. *From* Leicester. *Deceased* 1942. *Pro Career* 1932-1940 (59 contests, won 40, drew 4, lost 15).

Ali Forbes British S. Middleweight Champion, 1995. *Born* 07.03.61. *From* Sydenham. *Pro Career* 1989-1995 (14 contests, won 11, drew 1, lost 2).

Hugh Forde British S. Featherweight Champion, 1990. Commonwealth S. Featherweight Champion, 1991. *Born* 07.05.64. *From* Birmingham. *Pro Career* 1986-1995 (31 contests, won 24, lost 7).

Al Foreman Undefeated British Lightweight Champion, 1930-1932. British Empire Lightweight Championship Claimant, 1930-1933 and 1933-1934. *Born* 03.11.04. *From* Bow. Birthname - Albert Harris. *Deceased* 1954. *Pro Career* 1920-1934 (164 contests, won 133, drew 11, lost 20).

Joe Fox Undefeated British Bantamweight Champion, 1915-1917. Undefeated British Featherweight Champion, 1921-1922. *Born* 08.02.1892. *From* Leeds. *Deceased* 1965. *Pro Career* 1910-1925 (117 contests, won 62, drew 11, lost 17, no contest 2, no decision 25).

Johnny Frankham British L. Heavyweight Champion, 1975. *Born* 06.06.48. *From* Reading. *Pro Career* 1970-1976 (40 contests, won 28, drew 1, lost 11).

Jack Gardner British Heavyweight Champion, 1950-1952. British Empire Heavyweight Championship Claimant, 1950-1952. European Heavyweight Champion, 1951. *Born* 06.11.26. *From* Market Harborough. *Deceased* 1978. *Pro Career* 1948-1956 (34 contests, won 28, lost 6).

John L. Gardner Undefeated British Heavyweight Champion, 1978-1980. Undefeated Commonwealth Heavyweight Champion, 1978-1981. Undefeated European Heavyweight Champion, 1980-1981. *Born* 19.03.53. *From* Hackney. *Pro Career* 1973-1983 (39 contests, won 35, lost 4).

Teddy Gardner Undefeated British and European Flyweight Champion, 1952. British Empire Flyweight Championship Claimant, 1952. *Born* 27.01.22. *From* West Hartlepool. *Deceased* 1977. *Pro Career* 1938-1952 (66 contests, won 55, drew 3, lost 8).

Tom Gardner British Bantamweight Championship Claimant, 1892. *Born* 27.06.1869. *From* Stepney. *Deceased* 1946. *Pro Career* 1886-1892 (27 contests, won 20, drew 1, lost 6).

Sugar Gibiliru British S. Featherweight Champion, 1991. *Born* 13.07.66. *From* Liverpool. *Pro Career* 1984-1995 (55 contests, won 16, drew 7, lost 32).

Ray Gilbody British Bantamweight Champion, 1985-1987. *Born* 21.03.60. *From* Warrington. *Pro Career* 1983-1987 (16 contests, won 11, drew 1, lost 4).

Freddie Gilroy Undefeated British and British Empire Bantamweight Champion, 1959-1963. European Bantamweight Champion, 1959-1960. *Born* 07.03.36. *From* Belfast. *Pro Career* 1957-1962 (31 contests, won 28, lost 3).

Tommy Glencross British Featherweight Champion, 1972-1973. *Born* 31.07.47. *From* Glasgow. *Pro Career* 1967-1978 (48 contests, won 31, drew 1, lost 16).

Frank Goddard British Heavyweight Champion, 1919 and 1923-1926. *Born* 27.11.1891. *From* Clapham. *Deceased* 1957. *Pro Career* 1912-1926 (55 contests, won 40, lost 15).

Jack Goldswain British Lightweight Champion, 1906-1908. *Born* 22.07.1878. *From* Bermondsey. *Deceased* 1954. *Pro Career* 1896-1919 (144 contests, won 79, drew 12, lost 52, no contest 1).

Frank Grant British Middleweight Champion, 1992-1993. *Born* 22.05.65. *From* Bradford. *Pro Career* 1986-1993 (26 contests, won 22, lost 4).

Dave Boy Green Undefeated British and European L. Welterweight Champion, 1976-1977. European Welterweight Champion, 1979. *Born* 02.06.53. *From* Chatteris. *Pro Career* 1974-1981 (41 contests, won 37, lost 4).

Harry Greenfield British Featherweight Championship Claimant, 1896-1899. *Born* 1873. *From* Camden Town. *Deceased* 1946. *Pro Career* 1889-1902 (50 contests, won 20, drew 5, lost 24, no decision 1).

Roy Gumbs British Middleweight Champion, 1981-1983. Commonwealth Middleweight Champion, 1983. *Born* St Kitts, 05.09.54. *From* Tottenham. *Pro Career* 1976-1985 (40 contests, won 26, drew 3, lost 11).

Tom Gummer British Middleweight Champion, 1920-1921. *Born* 04.12.1894. *From* Rotherham. *Deceased* 1982. *Pro Career* 1914-1922 (53 contests, won 39, drew 2, lost 12).

Neil Haddock British S. Featherweight Champion, 1992-1994. *Born* 22.06.64. *From* Llanelli. *Pro Career* 1987-1994 (26 contests, won 14, drew 1, lost 11).

Iron Hague British Heavyweight Champion, 1909-1910. British Heavyweight Championship Claimant, 1910-1911. *Born* 06.11.1885. *From* Mexborough. Birthname - William Hague. *Deceased* 1951. *Pro Career* 1904-1915 (37 contests, won 25, drew 1, lost 11).

Henry Hall British Welterweight Champion, 1948-1949. *Born* 06.09.22. *From* Sheffield. *Deceased* 1979. *Pro Career* 1945-1952 (66 contests, won 43, drew 3, lost 20).

Seaman Nobby Hall British Lightweight Champion, 1922-1923. European Lightweight Championship Claimant, 1922-1923. *Born* 15.10.1892. *From* Peebles. Birthname - James Hall. *Deceased* 1953. *Pro Career* 1909-1935 (165 contests, won 112, drew 12, lost 41).

Charlie Hardcastle British Featherweight Champion, 1917. *Born* 14.02.1894. *From* Barnsley, *Deceased* 1960. *Pro Career* 1911-1923 (66 contests, won 38, drew 5, lost 20, no decision 3).

Jack Harrison Undefeated British Middleweight Champion, 1912-1913. *Born* 15.10.1888. *From* Rushden. *Deceased* 1971. *Pro Career* 1905-1924 (32 contests, won 14, drew 3, lost 12, no decision 3).

Tommy Harrison British Bantamweight Champion, 1922-1923. British Empire Bantamweight Championship Claimant, 1922-1923. European Bantamweight Championship Claimant, 1921-1922. *Born* 17.08.1892. *From* Stoke. *Deceased* 1931. *Pro Career* 1909-1923 (83 contests, won 50, drew 7, lost 25, no decision 1).

Len Harvey British Middleweight Champion, 1929-1933. British Empire Middleweight Championship Claimant, 1929-1933. Undefeated British L. Heavyweight Champion, 1933-1934 and British L. Heavyweight Champion, 1938-1942. British Empire L. Heavyweight Championship Claimant, 1939-1942. World L. Heavyweight Champion, 1939-1942 (GB version). British Heavyweight Champion, 1933-1934 and Undefeated British Heavyweight Champion, 1938-1942. British Empire Heavyweight Championship Claimant, 1934 and 1939-1942. *Born* 11.07.07. *From* Callington. *Deceased* 1976. *Pro Career* 1920-1942 (134 contests, won 112, drew 9, lost 13).

Paul Harvey Commonwealth S. Featherweight Champion, 1991-1992. *Born* 10.11.64. *From* Ilford. *Pro Career* 1989-1994 (22 contests, won 16, drew 1, lost 5).

Dennis Haugh British L. Heavyweight Championship Claimant, 1913-1914. *From* Tipperary. *Deceased*. *Pro Career* 1909-1916 (50 contests, won 26, drew 4, lost 18, no contest 2).

Vince Hawkins British Middleweight Champion, 1946-1948. *Born* 15.04.23. *From* Eastleigh. *Pro Career* 1940-1950 (86 contests, won 75, drew 1, lost 10).

Lloyd Hibbert Undefeated British L. Middleweight Champion, 1987. Commonwealth L. Middleweight Champion, 1987. *Born* 29.06.59. *From* Birmingham. *Pro Career* 1979-1987 (23 contests, won 19, lost 4).

Jim Higgins British Bantamweight Champion, 1920-1922. British Empire Bantamweight Championship Claimant, 1920-1922. *Born* 25.10.1897. *From* Hamilton. *Deceased* 1964. *Pro Career* 1919-1930 (34 contests, won 18, drew 3, lost 13).

Charlie Hill British Featherweight Champion, 1956-1959. *Born* 20.06.30. *From* Cambuslang. *Pro Career* 1953-1959 (36 contests, won 31, lost 5).

Johnny Hill Undefeated British Flyweight Champion, 1927-1929. European Flyweight Championship Claimant, 1928-1929. World Flyweight Champion, 1928-1929 (GB version). *Born* 14.12.05. *From* Edinburgh. *Deceased* 1929. Pro Career 1926-1929 (23 contests, won 18, drew 3, lost 1, no contest 1).

Paul Hodkinson Undefeated British Featherweight Champion, 1988-1990. Undefeated European Featherweight Champion, 1989-1991. World Featherweight Champion, 1991-1993 (WBC version). *Born* 14.09.65. *From* Liverpool. *Pro Career* 1986-1994 (26 contests, won 22, drew 1, lost 3).

Lloyd Honeyghan Undefeated British Welterweight Champion, 1983-1985 & 1985-1986. Undefeated Commonwealth & European Champion, 1985-1986. World Welterweight Champion, 1986. WBC Welterweight Champion, 1986-1987 & 1988-1989. IBF Welterweight Champion, 1986-1987. Commonwealth L. Middleweight Champion, 1993-1994. *Born* 22.04.60, Jamaica. *From* Bermondsey. *Pro Career* 1980-1995 (48 contests, won 43, lost 5).

Mike Honeyman British Featherweight Champion, 1920-1921. *Born* 11.11.1896. *From* Woolwich. *Deceased* 1944. *Pro Career* 1913-1926 (167 contests, won 109, drew 18, lost 40).

Jack Hood Undefeated British Welterweight Champion, 1926-1934. Undefeated European Welterweight Champion, 1933. *Born* 17.12.02. *From* Birmingham. *Deceased* 1992. *Pro Career* 1921-1935 (81 contests, won 66, drew 7, lost 6, no contest 1, no decision 1).

Maurice Hope Undefeated British L. Middleweight Champion, 1974-1977. Undefeated Commonwealth L. Middleweight Champion, 1976-1979. Undefeated European L. Middleweight Champion, 1976-1978. World L. Middleweight Champion, 1979-1981 (WBC version). *Born* Antigua, 06.12.51. *From* Hackney. *Pro Career* 1973-1982 (35 contests, won 30, drew 1, lost 4).

Alf Howard European Lightweight Champion, 1930. *Born* 1907. *From* Liverpool. *Deceased* 1959. *Pro Career* 1923-1937 (87 contests, won 62, drew 3, lost 22).

Mickey Hughes Commonwealth L. Middleweight Champion, 1992-1993. *Born* 13.06.62. *From* St Pancras. *Pro Career* 1985-1993 (31 contests, won 24, lost 7).

Mo Hussein Commonwealth Lightweight Champion, 1987-1989. *Born* 17.11.62. *From* West Ham. *Pro Career* 1982-1989 (27 contests, won 23, lost 4).

Alex Ireland British Middleweight Champion, 1928-1929. British Empire and European Middleweight Championship Claimant, 1928-1929. *Born* 11.02.01. *From* Leith. *Deceased* 1966. *Pro Career* 1922-1930 (47 contests, won 34, drew 3, lost 10).

Ernie Izzard British Lightweight Champion, 1924-1925. *Born* 25.02.05. *From* Herne Hill. *Deceased* 1970. *Pro Career* 1920-1935 (120 contests, won 90, drew 9, lost 19, no decision 2).

Joey Jacobs British S. Featherweight Champion, 1990. *Born* 01.10.60. *From* Manchester. *Pro Career* 1986-1991 (15 contests, won 10, lost 5).

Ronnie James Undefeated British Lightweight Champion, 1944-1947. *Born* 08.10.17. *From* Swansea. *Deceased* 1977. *Pro Career* 1933-1947 (119 contests, won 98, drew 5, lost 16).

Tee Jay British Cruiserweight Champion, 1987-1988. *Born* Ghana, 21.01.62. Birthname - Taju Akay. *From* Notting Hill. *Pro Career* 1985-1991 (19 contests, won 14, drew 1, lost 4).

Bunny Johnson British and Commonwealth Heavyweight Champion, 1975. British L. Heavyweight Champion, 1977-1981. *Born* Jamaica, 10.05.47. *From* Birmingham. Birthname - Frank Johnson. *Pro Career* 1968-1981 (73 contests, won 55, drew 1, lost 17).

Frank Johnson British Lightweight Champion, 1952-1953 and 1955-1956. British Empire Lightweight Championship Claimant, 1953. *Born* 27.11.28. *From* Manchester. Birthname - Frank Williamson. *Deceased* 1970. *Pro Career* 1946-1957 (58 contests, won 47, lost 11).

Fred Johnson British Featherweight Championship Claimant, 1891-1895. British Featherweight Champion, 1895-1897. *Born* 03.10.1865. *From* Hackney. *Deceased*. *Pro Career* 1884-1901 (38 contests, won 27, drew 1, lost 10).

Len Johnson British Empire Middleweight Championship Claimant, 1926. European Middleweight Championship Claimant, 1928-1929. *Born* 16.10.02. *From* Manchester. *Deceased* 1974. *Pro Career* 1921-1933 (100 contests, won 70, drew 3, lost 27).

Colin Jones Undefeated British Welterweight Champion, 1980-1982. Undefeated Commonwealth Welterweight Champion, 1981-1984. Undefeated European Welterweight Champion, 1982-1983. *Born* 21.03.59. *From* Gorseinon. *Pro Career* 1977-1985 (30 contests, won 26, drew 1, lost 3).

Frankie Jones British Flyweight Champion, 1957-1960. British Empire Flyweight Champion, 1957. *Born* 12.02.33. *From* Plean. *Deceased* 1991. *Pro Career* 1955-1960 (25 contests, won 17, lost 8).

Percy Jones British and European Flyweight Champion, 1914. World Flyweight Champion, 1914 (GB/IBU version). *Born* 26.12.1892. *From* Porth. *Deceased* 1922. *Pro Career* 1910-1915 (51 contests, won 45, drew 3, lost 3).

Ben Jordan Undefeated British Featherweight Champion, 1897-1900 and 1902-1905. World Featherweight Champion, 1898-1905 (GB version). *Born* 01.04.1873. *From* Bermondsey. *Deceased* 1945. *Pro Career* 1892-1905 (42 contests, won 35, drew 1, lost 3, no contest 3).

Young Joseph British Welterweight Championship Claimant, 1908-1910. British Welterweight Champion, 1910-1911. European Welterweight Championship Claimant, 1910-1911. *Born* 12.02.1885. *From* Aldgate. Birthname - Aschel Joseph. *Deceased* 1952. *Pro Career* 1903-1914 (129 contests, won 83, drew 21, lost 25).

Peter Kane Undefeated World Flyweight Champion, 1938-1939. European Bantamweight Champion, 1947-1948. *Born* 28.04.18. *From* Golborne. Birthname - Peter Cain. *Deceased* 1991. *Pro Career* 1934-1948 (102 contests, won 92, drew 2, lost 7, no contest 1).

Mark Kaylor British and Commonwealth Middleweight Champion, 1983-1984. *Born* 11.05.61. *From* West Ham. *Pro Career* 1980-1991 (48 contests, won 40, drew 1, lost 7).

Peter Keenan British Bantamweight Champion, 1951-1953 and 1954-1959. British Empire Bantamweight Champion, 1955-1959. European Bantamweight Champion, 1951-1952 and 1953. *Born* 08.08.28. *From* Glasgow. *Pro Career* 1948-1959 (66 contests, won 54, drew 1, lost 11).

Billy Spider Kelly British Featherweight Champion, 1955-1956. British Empire Featherweight Championship Claimant, 1954. British Empire Featherweight Champion, 1954-1955. *Born* 21.04.32. *From* Londonderry. *Pro Career* 1950-1962 (83 contests, won 56, drew 4, lost 23).

Jim Spider Kelly British Featherweight Champion, 1938-1939. British Empire Featherweight Championship Claimant, 1938-1939. *Born* 25.02.12. *From* Londonderry. *Deceased* 1988. *Pro Career* 1928-1948 (150 contests, won 105, drew 12, lost 33).

Joe Kelly British Bantamweight Champion, 1992. *Born* 18.05.64. *From* Glasgow. *Pro Career* 1985-1992 (27 contests, won 18, drew 2, lost 7).

John Kelly British and European Bantamweight Champion, 1953-1954. *Born* 17.01.32. *From* Belfast. *Pro Career* 1951-1957 (28 contests, won 24, lost 4).

Jake Kilrain British Welterweight Champion, 1936-1939. *Born* 29.05.14. *From* Bellshill. Birthname - Harry Owens. *Deceased* 1984. *Pro Career* 1931-1949 (133 contests, won 103, drew 4, lost 26).

Johnny King British Bantamweight Champion, 1932-1934 and 1935-1947. British Empire Bantamweight Championship Claimant, 1932-1934. *Born* 08.01.12. *From* Manchester. *Deceased* 1963. *Pro Career* 1926-1947 (222 contests, won 158, drew 15, lost 48, no contest 1).

Bert Kirby British Flyweight Champion, 1930-1931. *Born* 02.12.08. *From* Birmingham. *Deceased* 1975. *Pro Career* 1926-1938 (187 contests, won 111, drew 14, lost 61, no contest 1).

181

Charlie Knock British Welterweight Champion, 1904-1906. *Born* 18.08.1880. *From* Stratford. *Deceased* 1939. *Pro Career* 1899-1910 (92 contests, won 59, drew 7, lost 25, no contest 1).

Bill Ladbury British and European Flyweight Champion, 1913-1914. World Flyweight Champion, 1913-1914 (GB/IBU version). *Born* 14.10.1891. *From* Deptford. *Deceased* 1917. *Pro Career* 1908-1917 (53 contests, won 31, drew 5, lost 17).

Kirkland Laing British Welterweight Champion, 1987-1991. European Welterweight Champion, 1990. *Born* 20.06.54, Jamaica. *From* Nottingham. *Pro Career* 1975-1994 (56 contests, won 43, drew 1, lost 12).

Tony Laing Undefeated British L. Welterweight Champion, 1986. Commonwealth L. Welterweight Champion, 1987-1988. *Born* 22.09.57. *From* Nottingham. *Pro Career* 1977-1988 (18 contests, won 13, drew 1, lost 4).

Bugler Harry Lake British and European Bantamweight Championship Claimant, 1923. British Empire Bantamweight Championship Claimant, 1923. *Born* 17.10.02. *From* Devonport. *Deceased* 1970. *Pro Career* 1917-1933 (172 contests, won 108, drew 16, lost 48).

Davy Larmour British Bantamweight Champion, 1983. *Born* 02.04.52. *From* Belfast. *Pro Career* 1977-1983 (18 contests, won 11, lost 7).

Mick Leahy British Middleweight Champion, 1963-1964. *Born* Cork, 12.03.35. *From* Coventry. *Pro Career* 1956-1965 (72 contests, won 46, drew 7, lost 19).

Tancy Lee British Flyweight Champion, 1914-1915. European Flyweight Champion, 1914-1916. World Flyweight Champion, 1915 (GB/IBU version). Undefeated British Featherweight Champion, 1917-1919. *Born* 31.01.1882. *From* Paisley. Birthname - James Lee. *Deceased* 1941. *Pro Career* 1910-1926 (60 contests, won 48, drew 2, lost 10).

Ted Kid Lewis Undefeated British Featherweight Champion, 1913-1914. Undefeated European Featherweight Champion, 1913-1914. British Welterweight Champion, 1920-1924. British Empire Welterweight Championship Claimant, 1920-1924. European Welterweight Championship Claimant, 1920-1924. World Welterweight Champion, 1915-1916 and 1917-1919. British Middleweight Championship Claimant, 1920-1921. British Middleweight Champion, 1921-1923. British Empire Middleweight Championship Claimant, 1922-1923. European Middleweight Championship Claimant, 1921-1923 and 1924-1925. *Born* 24.10.1894. *From* Aldgate. Birthname - Gershon Mendelhoff. *Deceased* 1970. *Pro Career* 1909-1929 (281 contests, won 170, drew 13, lost 30, no decision 68).

Stewart Lithgo Commonwealth Cruiserweight Champion, 1984. *Born* 02.06.57. *From* West Hartlepool. *Pro Career* 1977-1987 (30 contests, won 16, drew 2, lost 12).

Brian London British and British Empire Heavyweight Champion, 1958-1959. *Born* 19.06.34. *From* Blackpool. Birthname - Brian Harper. *Pro Career* 1955-1970 (58 contests, won 37, drew 1, lost 20).

Jack London British Heavyweight Champion, 1944-1945. British Empire Heavyweight Championship Claimant, 1944-1945. *Born* 23.06.13. *From* West Hartlepool. Birthname - Jack Harper. *Deceased* 1964. *Pro Career* 1931-1949 (141 contests, won 95, drew 5, lost 39, no contests 2).

Eamonn Loughran Undefeated Commonwealth Welterweight Champion, 1992-1993. WBO Welterweight Champion, 1993-1996. *Born* 05.06.70. *Fron* Ballymena. *Pro Career* 1987-1996 (30 contests, won 26, drew 1, lost 2, no contest 1).

Joe Lucy British Lightweight Champion, 1953-1955 and 1956-1957. *Born* 09.02.30. *From* Mile End. *Deceased* 1991. *Pro Career* 1950-1957 (37 contests, won 27, lost 10).

Benny Lynch Undefeated British Flyweight Champion, 1935-1938. European Flyweight Championship Claimant, 1935-1938. World Flyweight Champion, 1935-1937 (NBA version). *Born* 02.04.13. *From* Glasgow. *Deceased* 1946. *Pro Career* 1931-1938 (110 contests, won 82, drew 15, lost 13).

Danny McAlinden British and Commonwealth Heavyweight Champion, 1972-1975. *Born* Newry, 01.06.47. *From* Coventry. *Pro Career* 1969-1981 (45 contests, won 31, drew 2, lost 12).

Les McAteer British and British Empire Middleweight Champion, 1969-1970. *Born* 19.08.45. *From* Birkenhead. *Pro Career* 1965-1979 (39 contests, won 27, drew 2, lost 10).

Pat McAteer Undefeated British Middleweight Champion, 1955-1958.

British Empire Middleweight Champion, 1955-1958. *Born* 17.03.32. *From* Birkenhead. *Pro Career* 1952-1958 (57 contests, won 49, drew 2, lost 6).

Dave McAuley Undefeated British Flyweight Champion, 1986-1988. World Flyweight Champion, 1989-1992 (IBF version). *Born* 15.06.61. *From* Larne. *Pro Career* 1983-1992 (23 contests, won 18, drew 2, lost 3).

Jock McAvoy British Middleweight Champion, 1933-1944. British Empire Middleweight Championship Claimant, 1933-1939. British L. Heavyweight Champion, 1937-1938. *Born* 20.11.07. *From* Rochdale. Birthname - Joe Bamford. *Deceased* 1971. *Pro Career* 1927-1945 (148 contests, won 134, lost 14).

Sammy McCarthy British Featherweight Champion, 1954-1955. *Born* 05.11.31. *From* Stepney. *Pro Career* 1951-1957 (53 contests, won 44, drew 1, lost 8).

Steve McCarthy British L. Heavyweight Champion, 1990-1991. *Born* 30.07.62. *From* Southampton. *Pro Career* 1987-1994 (17 contests, won 12, drew 1, lost 4).

Dave McCleave British Welterweight Champion, 1936. *Born* 25.12.11. *From* Smithfield. *Deceased* 1988. *Pro Career* 1934-1945 (115 contests, won 84, drew 3, lost 28).

John McCluskey Undefeated British Flyweight Champion, 1967-1977. Commonwealth Flyweight Champion, 1970-1971. *Born* 23.01.44. *From* Hamilton. *Pro Career* 1965-1975 (38 contests, won 23, lost 15).

John Cowboy McCormack British Middleweight Champion, 1959. European Middleweight Champion, 1961-1962. *Born* 09.01.35. *From* Maryhill. *Pro Career* 1957-1966 (45 contests, won 38, lost 7).

Young John McCormack British L. Heavyweight Champion, 1967-1969. *Born* Dublin, 11.12.44. *From* Brixton. *Pro Career* 1963-1970 (42 contests, won 33, drew 1, lost 8).

Pat McCormack British L. Welterweight Champion, 1974. *Born* Dublin, 28.04.46. *From* Brixton. *Pro Career* 1968-1975 (49 contests, won 30, drew 1, lost 18).

Boy McCormick Undefeated British L. Heavyweight Champion, 1919-1921. *Born* 25.12.1899. *From* Dublin. Birthname - Noel McCormick. *Deceased* 1939. *Pro Career* 1916-1926 (39 contests, won 22, drew 1, lost 10, no decision 6).

Tom McCormick British Welterweight Champion, 1914. British Empire Welterweight Championship Claimant, 1914. *Born* 08.08.1890. *From* Dundalk. *Deceased* 1916. *Pro Career* 1911-1915 (46 contests, won 35, drew 2, lost 9).

Glenn McCrory Undefeated British Cruiserweight Champion, 1988. Undefeated Commonwealth Cruiserweight Champion, 1987-1989. World Cruiserweight Champion, 1989-1990 (IBF version). *Born* 23.09.64. *From* Annfield Plain. *Pro Career* 1984-1993 (39 contests, won 30, drew 1, lost 8).

Jim McDonnell Undefeated European Featherweight Champion, 1985-1987. *Born* 12.09.60. *From* Camden Town. *Pro Career* 1983-1990 (29 contests, won 26, lost 3).

Tommy McGovern British Lightweight Champion, 1951-1952. *Born* 05.02.24. *From* Bermondsey. *Deceased* 1989. *Pro Career* 1947-1953 (66 contests, won 45, drew 4, lost 17).

Walter McGowan Undefeated British Flyweight Champion, 1963-1966. Undefeated British Empire Flyweight Champion, 1963-1969. World Flyweight Champion, 1966 (WBC version). British and British Empire Bantamweight Champion, 1966-1968. *Born* 13.10.42. *From* Hamilton. *Pro Career* 1961-1969 (40 contests, won 32, drew 1, lost 7).

Johnny McGrory British Featherweight Champion, 1936-1938. British Empire Featherweight Championship Claimant, 1936-1938. *Born* 25.04.15. *From* Glasgow. *Pro Career* 1933-1943 (103 contests, won 72, drew 8, lost 23).

Barry McGuigan Undefeated British Featherweight Champion, 1983-1986. Undefeated European Featherweight Champion, 1983-1985. World Featherweight Champion, 1985-1986 (WBA version). *Born* 28.02.61. *From* Clones. *Pro Career* 1981-1989 (35 contests, won 32, lost 3).

Billy Mack European Welterweight Championship Claimant, 1923. *Born* 1900. *From* Liverpool. *Deceased* 1973. *Pro Career* 1919-1928 (72 contests, won 47, drew 6, lost 18, no contest 1).

Clinton McKenzie British L. Welterweight Champion, 1978-1979 and 1979-1984. Undefeated British L. Welterweight Champion, 1989. European

L. Welterweight Champion, 1981-1982. *Born* 15.09.55. *From* Croydon. *Pro Career* 1976-1989 (50 contests, won 36, lost 14).

George McKenzie British Featherweight Champion, 1924-1925. *Born* 22.09.1900. *From* Leith. *Deceased* 1941. *Pro Career* 1920-1929 (45 contests, won 36, drew 2, lost 7).

Tony McKenzie British L. Welterweight Champion, 1986-1987. *Born* 04.03.63. *From* Leicester. *Pro Career* 1983-1993 (34 contests, won 26, drew 1, lost 7).

Charlie Magri Undefeated British Flyweight Champion, 1977-1981. Undefeated European Flyweight Champion, 1979-1983 and 1984-1985. European Flyweight Champion, 1985-1986. World Flyweight Champion, 1983 (WBC version). *Born* Tunisia, 20.07.56. *From* Stepney. *Pro Career* 1977-1986 (35 contests, won 30, lost 5).

Paddy Maguire British Bantamweight Champion, 1975-1977. *Born* 26.09.48. *From* Belfast. *Pro Career* 1969-1977 (35 contests, won 26, drew 1, lost 8).

Bob Marriott Undefeated British Lightweight Champion, 1919-1920. *Born* 21.12.1891. *From* Bermondsey. *Deceased* 1970. *Pro Career* 1915-1920 (10 contests, won 8, lost 2).

Terry Marsh Undefeated British L. Welterweight Champion, 1984-1986. European L. Welterweight Champion, 1985-1986. Undefeated World L. Welterweight Champion, 1987 (IBF version). *Born* 07.02.58. *From* Basildon. *Pro Career* 1981-1987 (27 contests, won 26, drew 1).

Terry Marsh   Derek Rowe

Gary Mason British Heavyweight Champion, 1989-1991. *Born* Jamaica, 15.12.62. *From* Wandsworth. *Pro Career* 1984-1991 (36 contests, won 35, lost 1).

Harry Mason British Lightweight Champion, 1923-1924. Undefeated British Lightweight Champion, 1925-1928. European Lightweight Championship Claimant, 1923-1926. British Lightweight Championship Claimant, 1924-1925. British Welterweight Champion, 1925-1926 and 1934. *Born* 27.03.03. *From* Leeds. *Deceased* 1977. *Pro Career* 1920-1937 (208 contests, won 140, drew 14, lost 52, no decision 2).

Billy Matthews European Featherweight Championship Claimant, 1922. *Born* 13.04.01. *From* London. *Deceased* 1967. *Pro Career* 1917-1926 (64 contests, won 39, drew 3, lost 22).

Neville Meade British Heavyweight Champion, 1981-1983. *Born* Jamaica, 12.09.48. *From* Swansea. *Pro Career* 1974-1983 (34 contests, won 20, drew 1, lost 13).

Reggie Meen British Heavyweight Champion, 1931-1932. *Born* 20.11.07. *From* Desborough. *Deceased* 1984. *Pro Career* 1927-1939 (104 contests, won 57, drew 3, lost 44).

Tommy Milligan Undefeated British Welterweight Champion, 1924-1925. European Welterweight Championship Claimant, 1924-1925. British Empire Welterweight Championship Claimant, 1924-1925. British Middleweight Champion, 1926-1928. British Empire Middleweight Championship Claimant, 1926-1928. European Middleweight Championship Claimant, 1925-1928. *Born* 02.03.04. *From* Wishaw. Birthname - Tommy Mulligan. *Deceased* 1970. *Pro Career* 1921-1928 (51 contests, won 42, lost 9).

Freddie Mills Undefeated British L. Heavyweight Champion, 1942-1950. British Empire L. Heavyweight Championship Claimant, 1942-1950. Undefeated European L. Heavyweight Champion, 1947-1950. World L. Heavyweight Champion, 1942-1946 (GB version). World L. Heavyweight Champion, 1948-1950. *Born* 26.06.19. *From* Bournemouth. *Deceased* 1965. *Pro Career* 1936-1950 (101 contests, won 77, drew 6, lost 18).

Alan Minter British Middleweight Champion, 1975-1977. Undefeated British Middleweight Champion, 1977-1978. European Middleweight Champion, 1977. Undefeated European Middleweight Champion, 1978-1979. World Middleweight Champion, 1980. *Born* 17.08.51. *From* Crawley. *Pro Career* 1972-1981 (49 contests, won 39, lost 9, no contest 1).

Charlie Mitchell Undefeated British Heavyweight Champion, 1882-1894. *Born* 24.11.1861. *From* Birmingham. *Deceased* 1918.

Sylvester Mittee British Welterweight Champion, 1985. Commonwealth Welterweight Champion, 1984-1985. *Born* St Lucia, 29.10.56. *From* Bethnal Green. *Pro Career* 1977-1988 (33 contests, won 28, lost 5).

Harry Mizler British Lightweight Champion, 1934. *Born* 22.01.13. *From* Stepney. *Deceased* 1990. *Pro Career* 1933-1943 (81 contests, won 63, drew 2, lost 16).

Gunner Moir British Heavyweight Champion, 1906-1909. *Born* 17.04.1879. *From* Lambeth. Birthname - James Moir. *Deceased* 1939. *Pro Career* 1903-1913 (25 contests, won 14, lost 11).

Tommy Molloy British Welterweight Champion, 1958-1960. *Born* 02.02.34. *From* Birkenhead. *Pro Career* 1955-1963 (43 contests, won 34, drew 2, lost 6, no contest 1).

Rinty Monaghan Undefeated British and World Flyweight Champion, 1948-1950. British Empire Flyweight Championship Claimant, 1948-1950. Undefeated European Flyweight Champion, 1949-1950. World Flyweight Champion, 1947-1948 (NBA version). *Born* 21.08.20. *From* Belfast. Birthname - John Monaghan. *Deceased* 1984. *Pro Career* 1934-1949 (66 contests, won 51, drew 6, lost 9).

Frank Moody British Middleweight Championship Claimant, 1927-1928. British L. Heavyweight Champion, 1927-1929. *Born* 27.08.1900. *From* Pontypridd. *Deceased* 1963. *Pro Career* 1914-1936 (204 contests, won 129, drew 15, lost 51, no decision 9).

Owen Moran British Bantamweight Championship Claimant, 1905-1907. Undefeated World Bantamweight Champion, 1907 (GB version). *Born* 04.12.1884. *From* Birmingham. *Deceased* 1949. *Pro Career* 1900-1916 (110 contests, won 66, drew 6, lost 17, no decision 21).

Des Morrison British L. Welterweight Champion, 1973-1974. *Born* Jamaica, 01.02.50. *From* Bedford. *Pro Career* 1970-1982 (50 contests, won 36, drew 2, lost 12).

Sean Murphy British Featherweight Champion, 1990-1991 and 1993. *Born* 01.12.64. *From* St Albans. *Pro Career* 1986-1994 (27 contests, won 22, lost 5).

Charlie Nash Undefeated British Lightweight Champion, 1978-1979. Undefeated European Lightweight Champion, 1979-1980. European Lightweight Champion, 1980-1981. *Born* 10.05.51. *From* Derry. *Pro Career* 1975-1983 (30 contests, won 25, lost 5).

Dave Needham British Bantamweight Champion, 1974-1975. British Featherweight Champion, 1978-1979. *Born* 15.08.51. *From* Nottingham. *Pro Career* 1971-1980 (39 contests, won 30, drew 1, lost 8).

Bobby Neill British Featherweight Champion, 1959-1960. *Born* 10.10.33. *From* Edinburgh. *Pro Career* 1955-1960 (35 contests, won 28, lost 7).

Kid Nicholson European Bantamweight Championship Claimant, 1928. *Born* 1904. *From* Leeds. Birthname - George Nicholson. *Deceased* 1968. *Pro Career* 1919-1934 (105 contests, won 57, drew 7, lost 40, no contest 1).

Harry Nickless British Lightweight Championship Claimant, 1891-1894. *Born* 1866. *From* Kew. *Deceased* 1899. *Pro Career* 1888-1894 (14 contests, won 11, drew 1, lost 2).

Tommy Noble British Bantamweight Champion, 1918-1919. *Born* 04.03.1897. *From* Bermondsey. *Deceased* 1966. *Pro Career* 1915-1926 (179 contests, won 84, drew 19, lost 67, no decision 8, no contest 1).

Horace Notice Undefeated British and Commonwealth Heavyweight Champion, 1986-1988. *Born* 07.08.57. *From* Birmingham. *Pro Career* 1983-1988 (16 contests, won 16).

John O'Brien British Empire Featherweight Champion, 1967. *Born* 20.02.37. *From* Glasgow. *Deceased* 1979. *Pro Career* 1956-1971 (47 contests, won 30, lost 17).

Pat O'Keefe British Middleweight Championship Claimant, 1906. British Middleweight Champion, 1906 and 1914-1916. Undefeated British Middleweight Champion, 1918-1919. *Born* 17.03.1883. *From* Bromley by Bow. *Deceased* 1960. *Pro Career* 1901-1918 (99 contests, won 70, drew 4, lost 22, no decision 3).

Danny O'Sullivan British Bantamweight Champion, 1949-1951. *Born* 06.01.23. *From* Finsbury Park. *Deceased* 1990. *Pro Career* 1947-1951 (43 contests, won 33, drew 1, lost 9).

Johnny Owen Undefeated British Bantamweight Champion, 1977-1980. Undefeated Commonwealth Bantamweight Champion, 1978-1980. Undefeated European Bantamweight Champion, 1980. *Born* 07.01.56. *From* Merthyr. *Deceased* 1980. *Pro Career* 1976-1980 (28 contests, won 25, drew 1, lost 2).

Jack Palmer British Middleweight Champion, 1902-1903. British Heavyweight Champion, 1903-1906. *Born* 31.03.1878. *From* Newcastle. Birthname - Jack Liddell. *Deceased* 1928. *Pro Career* 1896-1916 (40 contests, won 26, drew 2, lost 12).

Pedlar Palmer British Bantamweight Champion, 1895-1900. World Bantamweight Champion, 1895-1899. World Bantamweight Championship Claimant, 1900. *Born* 19.01.1876. *From* Canning Town. Birthname - Tom Palmer. *Deceased* 1949. *Pro Career* 1891-1919 (64 contests, won 45, drew 4, lost 15).

Jackie Paterson British Flyweight Champion, 1939-1948. British Empire Flyweight Championship Claimant, 1940-1948. World Flyweight Champion, 1943-1947. World Flyweight Champion, 1947-1948 (GB/NY version). British Bantamweight Champion, 1947-1949. British Empire Bantamweight Championship Claimant, 1945-1949. European Bantamweight Champion, 1946. *Born* 05.09.20. *From* Springfield. *Deceased* 1966. *Pro Career* 1938-1950 (92 contests, won 64, drew 3, lost 25).

Alf Kid Pattenden British Bantamweight Champion, 1928-1929. *Born* 24.09.03. *From* Mile End. *Deceased* 1982. *Pro Career* 1926-1931 (66 contests, won 38, drew 4, lost 24).

Larry Paul British L. Middleweight Champion, 1973-1974. *Born* 19.04.52. *From* Wolverhampton. *Pro Career* 1973-1978 (40 contests, won 30, drew 1, lost 9).

David Pearce Undefeated British Heavyweight Champion, 1983-1985. *Born* 08.05.59. *From* Newport. *Pro Career* 1978-1984 (21 contests, won 17, drew 1, lost 3).

Jack Petersen Undefeated British L. Heavyweight Champion, 1932. British Heavyweight Champion, 1932-1933 and 1934-1936. British Empire Heavyweight Championship Claimant, 1934-1936. *Born* 02.09.11. *From* Cardiff. *Deceased* 1990. *Pro Career* 1931-1937 (38 contests, won 33, lost 5).

Kostas Petrou British Welterweight Champion, 1985. *Born* 17.04.59. *From* Birmingham. *Pro Career* 1981-1988 (37 contests, won 30, lost 7).

Tiger Al Phillips European Featherweight Champion, 1947. British Empire Featherweight Championship Claimant, 1947. *Born* 25.01.20. *From* Aldgate. *Pro Career* 1938-1951 (89 contests, won 72, drew 3, lost 14).

Eddie Phillips British L. Heavyweight Champion, 1935-1937. *Born* 1909. *From* Bow. *Deceased* 1995. *Pro Career* 1928-1945 (57 contests, won 47, drew 4, lost 6).

Gus Platts British Middleweight Champion, 1921. European Middleweight Championship Claimant, 1921. *Born* 24.10.1891. *From* Sheffield. *Deceased* 1943. *Pro Career* 1910-1927 (132 contests, won 87, drew 8, lost 30, no decision 7).

Billy Plimmer British Bantamweight Champion, 1891-1895. World Bantamweight Champion, 1892-1895. British Bantamweight Championship Claimant, 1896-1898. *Born* 06.02.1869. *From* Birmingham. *Deceased* 1929. *Pro Career* 1888-1900 (46 contests, won 33, drew 5, lost 5, no decision 3).

Dennis Powell British L. Heavyweight Champion, 1953. *Born* 12.12.24. *From* Four Crosses. *Deceased* 1993. *Pro Career* 1947-1954 (68 contests, won 42, drew 4, lost 22).

Colin Power Undefeated British L. Welterweight Champion, 1977-1978. British L. Welterweight Champion, 1979. European L. Welterweight Champion, 1978. *Born* 02.02.56. *From* Paddington. *Pro Career* 1975-1983 (34 contests, won 28, drew 1, lost 5).

Kevin Pritchard British S. Featherweight Champion, 1990-1991. *Born* 26.09.61. *From* Liverpool. *Pro Career* 1981-1991 (48 contests, won 23, drew 3, lost 22).

Ted Pritchard British Middleweight Champion, 1890-1895. British Heavyweight Championship Claimant, 1891-1895. *Born* 1866. *From* Lambeth. *Deceased* 1903. *Pro Career* 1887-1895 (16 contests, won 11, drew 1, lost 3, no decision 1).

Johnny Pritchett Undefeated British Middleweight Champion, 1965-1969. Undefeated British Empire Middleweight Champion, 1967-1969. *Born* 15.02.43. *From* Bingham. *Pro Career* 1963-1969 (34 contests, won 32, drew 1, lost 1).

Des Rea British L. Welterweight Champion, 1968-1969. *Born* 09.01.44. *From* Belfast. *Pro Career* 1964-1974 (69 contests, won 28, drew 5, lost 36).

Billy Reader British Featherweight Champion, 1891-1892. *From* Fulham. *Deceased*. *Pro Career* 1887-1892 (12 contests, won 8, lost 4).

Mark Reefer Undefeated Commonwealth S. Featherweight Champion, 1989-1990. *Born* 16.03.64. Birthname - Mark Thompson. *From* Dagenham. *Pro Career* 1983-1992 (32 contests, won 23, drew 1, lost 8).

Sam Reeson Undefeated British Cruiserweight Champion, 1985-1986. Undefeated European Cruiserweight Champion, 1987-1988. *Born* 05.01.63. *From* Battersea. *Pro Career* 1983-1989 (26 contests, won 24, lost 2).

Harry Reeve Undefeated British L. Heavyweight Champion, 1916-1917. *Born* 07.01.1893. *From* Stepney. *Deceased* 1958. *Pro Career* 1910-1934 (154 contests, won 83, drew 20, lost 49, no decision 2).

Willie Reilly Undefeated British Lightweight Champion, 1972. *Born* 25.03.47. *From* Glasgow. *Pro Career* 1968-1972 (23 contests, won 13, drew 3, lost 7).

Jimmy Revie British Featherweight Champion, 1969-1971. *Born* 08.07.47. *From* Stockwell. *Pro Career* 1966-1976 (48 contests, won 38, drew 1, lost 9).

Henry Rhiney British Welterweight Champion, 1976-1979. European Welterweight Champion, 1978-1979. *Born* Jamaica, 28.11.51. *From* Luton. *Pro Career* 1973-1980 (57 contests, won 32, drew 6, lost 19).

Ernie Rice British and European Lightweight Champion, 1921-1922. *Born* 17.11.1896. *From* Hounslow. *Deceased* 1979. *Pro Career* 1912-1930 (78 contests, won 51, drew 2, lost 24, no decision 1).

Alan Richardson British Featherweight Champion, 1977-1978. *Born* 04.11.48. *From* Fitzwilliam. *Pro Career* 1971-1978 (27 contests, won 17, drew 1, lost 9).

Dick Richardson European Heavyweight Champion, 1960-1962. *Born* 01.06.34. *From* Newport. *Pro Career* 1954-1963 (47 contests, won 31, drew 2, lost 14).

Jack Roberts British Featherweight Champion, 1901-1902. *Born* 11.11.1873. *From* Covent Garden. *Deceased*. *Pro Career* 1891-1910 (90 contests, won 51, drew 3, lost 36).

Spike Robson British Featherweight Champion, 1906-1907. British Featherweight Championship Claimant, 1907-1910. *Born* 05.11.1877. *From* South Shields. Birthname - Frank Robson. *Deceased* 1957. *Pro Career* 1896-1915 (77 contests, won 45, drew 3, lost 11, no decision 17, no contest 1).

Ernie Roderick British Welterweight Champion, 1939-1948. European Welterweight Champion, 1946-1947. British Middleweight Champion, 1945-1946. *Born* 25.01.14. *From* Liverpool. *Deceased* 1986. *Pro Career* 1931-1950 (142 contests, won 114, drew 4, lost 24).

Prince Rodney Undefeated British L. Middleweight Champion, 1983-1984. British L. Middleweight Champion, 1985-1986. *Born* 31.10.58. *From* Huddersfield. *Pro Career* 1977-1990 (41 contests, won 31, drew 1, lost 9).

Walter Ross Undefeated British Bantamweight Champion, 1919-1920. *Born* 03.07.1898. *From* Glasgow. *Deceased. Pro Career* 1915-1926 (62 contests, won 35, drew 6, lost 19, no decision 2).

Stan Rowan Undefeated British Bantamweight Champion, 1949. British Empire Bantamweight Championship Claimant, 1949. *Born* 06.09.24. *From* Liverpool. *Pro Career* 1942-1953 (67 contests, won 46, drew 5, lost 16).

Mark Rowe British and Commonwealth Middleweight Champion, 1970. *Born* 12.07.47. *Born* 12.07.47. *From* Camberwell. *Pro Career* 1966-1973 (47 contests, won 38, drew 1, lost 8).

Alan Rudkin British Bantamweight Champion, 1965-1966 and Undefeated British Bantamweight Champion, 1968-1972. British Empire Bantamweight Champion, 1965-1966 and 1968-1969. European Bantamweight Champion, 1971. Undefeated Commonwealth Bantamweight Champion, 1970-1972. *Born* 18.11.41. *From* Liverpool. *Pro Career* 1962-1972 (50 contests, won 42, lost 8).

Hugh Russell Undefeated British Flyweight Champion, 1984-1985. British Bantamweight Champion, 1983. *Born* 15.12.59. *From* Belfast. *Pro Career* 1981-1985 (19 contests, won 17, lost 2).

Jack Scales British Heavyweight Championship Claimant, 1901-1902. *Born* 20.09.1874. *From* Bethnal Green. *Deceased. Pro Career* 1898-1911 (77 contests, won 41, drew 5, lost 30, no decision 1).

Phil Scott Undefeated British Heavyweight Champion, 1926-1931. British Empire Heavyweight Championship Claimant, 1926-1931. *Born* 03.01.1900. *From* Marylebone. Birthname - Phil Suffling. *Deceased* 1983. *Pro Career* 1919-1931 (85 contests, won 65, drew 4, lost 14, no contest 2).

Tony Sibson British Middleweight Champion, 1979. Undefeated British Middleweight Champion, 1984 and 1987-1988. Undefeated Commonwealth Middleweight Champion, 1980-1983 and 1984-1988. Undefeated European Middleweight Champion, 1980-1982. European Middleweight Champion, 1984-1985. *Born* 09.04.58. *From* Leicester. *Pro Career* 1976-1988 (63 contests, won 55, drew 1, lost 7).

Steve Sims Undefeated British Featherweight Champion, 1982-1983. *Born* 10.10.58. *From* Newport. *Pro Career* 1977-1987 (29 contests, won 14, drew 1, lost 14).

Joey Singleton British L. Welterweight Champion, 1974-1976. *Born* 06.06.51. *From* Kirkby. *Pro Career* 1973-1982 (40 contests, won 27, drew 2, lost 11).

Kelvin Smart British Flyweight Champion, 1982-1984. *Born* 18.12.60. *From* Caerphilly. *Pro Career* 1979-1987 (29 contests, won 17, drew 2, lost 10).

Dick Smith British L. Heavyweight Champion, 1914-1916. Undefeated British L. Heavyweight Champion, 1918-1919. *Born* 10.02.1886. *From* Woolwich. *Deceased* 1950. *Pro Career* 1913-1924 (21 contests, won 7, drew 1, lost 13).

Jem Smith British Heavyweight Champion, 1895-1896. British Heavyweight Championship Claimant, 1889-1891. *Born* 21.01.1863. *From* Cripplegate. *Deceased* 1931. *Pro Career* 1885-1897 (11 contests, won 4, drew 3, lost 4).

Roy Smith British Cruiserweight Champion, 1987. *Born* 31.08.61. *From* Nottingham. *Pro Career* 1985-1991 (26 contests, won 18, lost 8).

Sid Smith British Flyweight Championship Claimant, 1911. British Flyweight Champion, 1911-1913. World Flyweight Champion, 1913 (GB/IBU version). European Flyweight Champion, 1913. *Born* 25.02.1889. *From* Bermondsey. *Deceased* 1948. *Pro Career* 1907-1919 (106 contests, won 82, drew 5, lost 18, no decision 1).

Willie Smith British Bantamweight Championship Claimant, 1892-1896. *Born* 1871. *From* Shoreditch. *Deceased. Pro Career* 1890-1901 (18 contests, won 10, lost 7, no decision 1).

Young Joey Smith European Featherweight Championship Claimant, 1911. *Born* 1894. *From* Mile End. *Pro Career* 1909-1914 (24 contests, won 18, drew 3, lost 3).

Vernon Sollas British Featherweight Champion, 1975-1977. *Born* 14.08.54. *From* Edinburgh. *Pro Career* 1973-1977 (33 contests, won 25, drew 1, lost 7).

Terry Spinks British Featherweight Champion, 1960-1961. *Born* 28.02.38. *From* Canning Town. *Pro Career* 1957-1962 (49 contests, won 41, drew 1, lost 7).

Harry Spurden British Featherweight Champion, 1892-1895. *Born* 06.02.1869. *From* Cambridge. *Deceased. Pro Career* 1888-1901 (27 contests, won 19, drew 1, lost 7).

Digger Stanley British Bantamweight Championship Claimant, 1906-1910. British Bantamweight Champion, 1910-1913 and 1913-1914. European Bantamweight Championship Claimant, 1910-1912. World Bantamweight Champion, 1909-1912 (GB version). *Born* 28.02.1883. *From* Norwich. Birthname - George Stanley. *Deceased* 1919. *Pro Career* 1899-1918 (86 contests, won 56, drew 7, lost 21, no decision 2).

Bunny Sterling British Middleweight Champion, 1970-1974 and Undefeated British Middleweight Champion, 1975. Commonwealth Middleweight Champion, 1970-1972. European Middleweight Champion, 1976. *Born* Jamaica, 04.04.48. *From* Finsbury Park. *Pro Career* 1966-1977 (57 contests, won 35, drew 4, lost 18).

Sam Steward British Lightweight Champion, 1928-1929. *Born* 1905. *From* Lewisham. *Deceased. Pro Career* 1923-1936 (118 contests, won 80, drew 20, lost 18).

John H. Stracey Undefeated British Welterweight Champion, 1973-1975. Undefeated European Welterweight Champion, 1975-1976. World Welterweight Champion, 1975-1976 (WBC version). *Born* 22.09.50. *From* Bethnal Green. *Pro Career* 1969-1978 (51 contests, won 45, drew 1, lost 5).

Andy Straughn British Cruiserweight Champion, 1986-1987 and 1988-1989. *Born* Barbados, 25.12.59. *From* Hitchin. *Pro Career* 1982-1990 (27 contests, won 18, drew 2, lost 7).

Gary Stretch British L. Middleweight Champion, 1988-1990. *Born* 04.11.65. *From* St Helens. *Pro Career* 1985-1993 (25 contests, won 23, lost 2).

Jim Sullivan Undefeated British Middleweight Champion, 1910-1912. *Born* 07.06.1886. *From* Bermondsey. *Deceased* 1949. *Pro Career* 1904-1920 (83 contests, won 56, drew 5, lost 22).

Johnny Sullivan British Empire Middleweight Championship Claimant, 1954. British and British Empire Middleweight Champion, 1954-1955. *Born* 19.12.32. *From* Preston. Birthname - John Hallmark. *Pro Career* 1948-1960 (97 contests, won 68, drew 3, lost 26).

Johnny Summers British Featherweight Champion, 1906. British Lightweight Champion, 1908-1909. British Welterweight Championship Claimant, 1912. British Welterweight Champion, 1912-1914. British Empire Welterweight Championship Claimant, 1912-1914. *Born* 21.01.1883. *From* Middlesbrough. Birthname - Johnny Somers. *Deceased* 1946. *Pro Career* 1900-1920 (179 contests, won 104, drew 29, lost 32, no contest 1, no decision 13).

Wally Swift British Welterweight Champion, 1960. British Middleweight Champion, 1964-1965. *Born* 10.08.36. *From* Nottingham. *Pro Career* 1957-1969 (88 contests, won 68, drew 3, lost 17).

Wally Swift Jnr British L. Middleweight Champion, 1991-1992. *Born* 17.02.66. *From* Birmingham. *Pro Career* 1985-1994 (38 contests, won 26, drew 1, lost 11).

Joe Symonds British and European Flyweight Championship Claimant, 1914. British Flyweight Champion, 1915-1916. World Flyweight Champion, 1915-1916 (GB/IBU version). *Born* 28.12.1894. *From* Plymouth. Birthname - Hubert Toms. *Deceased* 1953. *Pro Career* 1911-1924 (136 contests, won 97, drew 11, lost 27, no decision 1).

Nel Tarleton British Featherweight Champion, 1931-1932 and 1934-1936. Undefeated British Featherweight Champion, 1940-1947. Undefeated British Empire Featherweight Championship Claimant, 1940-1947. *Born* 14.01.06. *From* Liverpool. *Deceased* 1956. *Pro Career* 1926-1945 (144 contests, won 116, drew 8, lost 20).

Wally Thom British Welterweight Champion, 1951-1952 and 1953-1956. British Empire Welterweight Championship Claimant, 1951-1952. European Welterweight Champion, 1954-1955. *Born* 14.06.26. *From* Birkenhead. *Deceased* 1980. *Pro Career* 1949-1956 (54 contests, won 42, drew 1, lost 11).

Eddie Thomas British Welterweight Champion, 1949-1951. European Welterweight Champion, 1951. British Empire Welterweight Championship Claimant, 1951. *Born* 27.07.26. *From* Merthyr. *Deceased* 1997. *Pro Career* 1946-1954 (48 contests, won 40, drew 2, lost 6).

Pat Thomas British Welterweight Champion, 1975-1976. British L. Middleweight Champion, 1979-1981. *Born* St Kitts, 05.05.50. *From* Cardiff. *Pro Career* 1970-1984 (57 contests, won 35, drew 3, lost 18, no contest 1).

Tom Thomas British Middleweight Champion, 1906-1910. *Born* 19.04.1880. *From* Penygraig. *Deceased* 1911. *Pro Career* 1899-1911 (44 contests, won 41, lost 3).

Billy Thompson British Lightweight Champion, 1947-1951. European Lightweight Champion, 1948-1949. *Born* 20.12.25. *From* Hickleton Main. *Pro Career* 1945-1953 (63 contests, won 46, drew 4, lost 13).

Andy Till British L. Middleweight Champion, 1992-1994. *Born* 22.08.63. *From* Northolt. *Pro Career* 1986-1995 (24 contests, won 19, lost 5).

Andrew Tokell British Bantamweight Championship Claimant, 1901-1902. British Bantamweight Champion, 1902. World Bantamweight Champion, 1902 (GB version). *Born* 01.03.1878. *From* Jarrow. *Deceased* 1915. *Pro Career* 1897-1908 (36 contests, won 27, lost 8, no contest 1).

Roland Todd British Middleweight Champion, 1923-1925. British Empire Middleweight Championship Claimant, 1923-1925. British Middleweight Championship Claimant, 1925-1927. European Middleweight Championship Claimant, 1923-1924. *Born* 09.01.1900. *From* Doncaster. *Deceased* 1969. *Pro Career* 1917-1929 (116 contests, won 81, drew 6, lost 27, no decision 2).

Dick Turpin British Middleweight Champion, 1948-1950. British Empire Middleweight Championship Claimant, 1948-1949. *Born* 26.11.20. *From* Leamington Spa. *Deceased* 1990. *Pro Career* 1937-1950 (103 contests, won 76, drew 6, lost 20, no contest 1).

Randy Turpin Undefeated British Middleweight Champion, 1950-1954. British Empire Middleweight Championship Claimant, 1952-1954. European Middleweight Champion, 1951-1954. World Middleweight Champion, 1951. World Middleweight Champion, 1953 (EBU version). Undefeated British L. Heavyweight Champion, 1952, 1955 and 1956-1958. British Empire L. Heavyweight Championship Claimant, 1952-1954. Undefeated British Empire L. Heavyweight Champion, 1954-1955. *Born* 07.06.28. *From* Leamington Spa. *Deceased* 1966. *Pro Career* 1946-1958 (73 contests, won 64, drew 1, lost 8).

Curley Walker Undefeated British Bantamweight Champion, 1914-1915. *Born* 04.02.1894. *From* Lambeth. Birthname - Con Walker. *Deceased* 1973. *Pro Career* 1909-1923 (117 contests, won 64, drew 11, lost 42).

Keith Wallace Undefeated Commonwealth Flyweight Champion, 1983-1984. *Born* 29.03.61. *From* Liverpool. *Pro Career* 1982-1990 (25 contests, won 20, lost 5).

Nunc Wallace Undefeated British Bantamweight Champion, 1889-1891. British Bantamweight Championship Claimant, 1893-1895. *From* Birmingham. Birthname - Edward Wallace. *Deceased*. *Pro Career* 1886-1895 (27 contests, won 18, lost 9).

Jimmy Walsh British Lightweight Champion, 1936-1938. *Born* 1913. *From* Chester. *Deceased* 1964. *Pro Career* 1931-1940 (89 contests, won 67, drew 2, lost 19, no contest 1).

Harry Ware British Bantamweight Championship Claimant, 1899-1900. British Bantamweight Champion, 1900-1902 and 1902. World Bantamweight Champion, 1900-1902 (GB version). *Born* 1875. *From* Mile End. *Deceased*. *Pro Career* 1895-1911 (59 contests, won 33, drew 8, lost 18).

Peter Waterman Undefeated British Welterweight Champion, 1956-1958. Undefeated European Welterweight Champion, 1958. *Born* 08.12.34. *From* Clapham. *Deceased* 1986. *Pro Career* 1952-1958 (46 contests, won 41, drew 2, lost 3).

Curly Watson British Welterweight Champion, 1906-1910. *Born* 05.10.1884. *From* Barrow. Birthname - Robert Watson. *Deceased* 1910. *Pro Career* 1902-1910 (78 contests, won 41, drew 6, lost 30, no contest 1).

Michael Watson Undefeated Commonwealth Middleweight Champion, 1989-1991. *Born* 15.03.65. *From* Islington. *Pro Career* 1984-1991 (30 contests, won 25, drew 1, lost 4).

Seaman Tommy Watson British Featherweight Champion, 1932-1934. *Born* 02.06.08. *From* Newcastle. *Deceased* 1971. *Pro Career* 1927-1935 (116 contests, won 106, drew 1, lost 9).

Jim Watt British Lightweight Champion, 1972-1973 and Undefeated British Lightweight Champion, 1975-1977. Undefeated European Lightweight Champion, 1977-1979. World Lightweight Champion, 1979-1981 (WBC version). *Born* 18.07.48. *From* Glasgow. *Pro Career* 1968-1981 (46 contests, won 38, lost 8).

Fred Webster British Lightweight Champion, 1929-1930. *Born* 18.06.08. *From* Kentish Town. *Deceased* 1971. *Pro Career* 1928-1934 (65 contests, won 46, drew 5, lost 14).

Bombardier Billy Wells British Heavyweight Champion, 1911-1919. British Empire Heavyweight Championship Claimant, 1911-1919. *Born* 31.08.1889. *From* Mile End. *Deceased* 1967. *Pro Career* 1909-1925 (59 contests, won 48, lost 11).

Matt Wells British Lightweight Champion, 1911-1912. European Lightweight Championship Claimant, 1911-1912. British Welterweight Champion, 1914. British Welterweight Championship Claimant, 1914-1919. British Empire Welterweight Championship Claimant, 1914-1919. World Welterweight Champion, 1914-1915 (Australian version). *Born* 14.12.1886. *From* Walworth. *Deceased* 1953. *Pro Career* 1909-1922 (86 contests, won 34, drew 3, lost 19, no decision 30).

Freddie Welsh British Lightweight Champion, 1909-1911. Undefeated British Lightweight Champion, 1912-1919. European Lightweight Championship Claimant, 1909-1911. Undefeated European Lightweight Champion, 1912-1914. British Empire Lightweight Championship Claimant, 1912-1914. World Lightweight Champion, 1912-1914 (GB version). World Lightweight Champion, 1914-1917. *Born* 05.03.1886. *From* Pontypridd. Birthname - Frederick Thomas. *Deceased* 1927. *Pro Career* 1905-1922 (168 contests, won 76, drew 7, lost 4, no decision 81).

Jabez White British Featherweight Championship Claimant, 1899-1900. British Lightweight Champion, 1902-1906. World Lightweight Championship Claimant, 1902-1905 (GB version). *Born* 20.10.1873. *From* Birmingham. *Deceased* 1966. *Pro Career* 1895-1913 (40 contests, won 31, drew 1, lost 7, no decision 1).

Ted White British Middleweight Championship Claimant, 1893-1895. Undefeated British Middleweight Champion, 1895-1896. *Born* 18.05.1867. *From* Charing Cross. *Deceased*. *Pro Career* 1888-1896 (28 contests, won 22, lost 6).

Jimmy Wilde British and European Flyweight Championship Claimant, 1914-1915. Undefeated British and European Flyweight Champion, 1916-1923. World Flyweight Champion, 1916 (GB/IBU version). World Flyweight Champion, 1916-1923. *Born* 15.05.1892. *From* Tylorstown. *Deceased* 1969. *Pro Career* 1910-1923 (153 contests, won 132, drew 2, lost 6, no decision 13).

Derek Williams Commonwealth Heavyweight Champion, 1988-1992. European Heavyweight Champion, 1989-1992. *Born* 11.03.65. *From* Peckham. *Pro Career* 1984-1997 (29 contests, won 19, drew 1, lost 9).

Jim Williams British Bantamweight Championship Claimant, 1902. *Born* 01.08.1876. *From* Marylebone. *Deceased*. *Pro Career* 1892-1903 (45 contests, won 36, drew 1, lost 8).

Johnny Williams British Heavyweight Champion, 1952-1953. British Empire Heavyweight Championship Claimant, 1952-1953. *Born* 25.12.26. *From* Rugby. *Pro Career* 1946-1956 (75 contests, won 60, drew 4, lost 11).

Tony Willis British Lightweight Champion, 1985-1987. *Born* 17.06.60. *From* Liverpool. *Pro Career* 1981-1989 (29 contests, won 25, lost 4).

Nick Wilshire Commonwealth L. Middleweight Champion, 1985-1987. *Born* 03.11.61. *From* Bristol. *Pro Career* 1981-1987 (40 contests, won 36, lost 4).

Tony Wilson British L. Heavyweight Champion, 1987-1989. *Born* 25.04.64. *From* Wolverhampton. *Pro Career* 1985-1993 (29 contests, won 20, drew 1, lost 8).

Howard Winstone Undefeated British Featherweight Champion, 1961-1969. European Featherweight Champion, 1963-1967. World Featherweight Champion, 1968 (WBC version). *Born* 15.04.39. *From* Merthyr. *Pro Career* 1959-1968 (67 contests, won 61, lost 6).

Tim Wood British L. Heavyweight Champion, 1976-1977. *Born* 10.08.51. *From* Leicester. *Pro Career* 1972-1979 (31 contests, won 19, drew 1, lost 11).

Bruce Woodcock British Heavyweight Champion, 1945-1950. British Empire Heavyweight Championship Claimant, 1945-1950. European Heavyweight Champion, 1946-1949. *Born* 18.01.21. *From* Doncaster. *Pro Career* 1942-1950 (39 contests, won 35, lost 4).

Commonwealth Title Bouts During 1996-97

All of last season's title bouts are shown in date order within their weight division and give the boxers' respective weights, along with the referee's (and judges') scorecard if going to a decision. Every contest is summarised briefly and all British officials are named.

Flyweight

27 September 1996   Peter Culshaw 7.13½ (England) W RSC 7 James Wanene 7.13 (Kenya), Leisure Centre, Stevenage. Out of his depth, and finding life tough at this level, the 35-year-old Kenyan still made a nuisance of himself and, at the same time, proved that Culshaw still has a long way to go if he wants to be a world champion. However, after Culshaw found the range with his body punches in the seventh it was just a matter of time before Wanene succumbed and, following another big attack, referee, Mickey Vann, brought matters to a halt at 2.31 of the round.

Bantamweight

7 October 1996   Paul Lloyd 8.6 (England) W RSC 6 Nathan Sting 8.4½ (Australia), The Theatre, Lewisham. This fight was made to decide a new champion, John Armour having relinquished the title in July 1996 after being forced on to the sidelines due to out-of-ring activities. With both men making a cracking start, it was just a matter of time before the pace dropped and it was the Tasmanian, Sting, who wilted first. Lloyd, for his part, however, continued to pour it on and, by the sixth, was in complete command. Finally, the contest was called off by the referee, John Coyle, at 1.59 of the round, with Sting under severe pressure and badly cut on his left eye.

18 February 1997   Paul Lloyd 8.5½ (England) W CO 1 Lybo Nkoko 8.2 (South Africa), Grundy Park Leisure Centre, Cheshunt. In making the first defence of his newly-won title, Lloyd's plan to attack the body quickly paid dividends as Nkoko folded in the first round, a left hook doing the damage. Counted out by Richie Davies at 1.41 of the round, Nkoko, who had not boxed for nearly a year and had lost five of his previous seven fights, was just not prepared for what hit him.

16 April 1997   Paul Lloyd 8.5¼ (England) W RSC 11 Simphiwe Pamana 8.6 (South Africa), York Hall, London. Again making a fast start, as in his previous defence, Lloyd had Pamana down from hurtful body punches in both the first and sixth rounds before he too was sent crashing in the seventh, a left hook-right cross doing the trick. Up at six, Lloyd came back strongly to batter the little South African and force a stoppage at 1.05 of the 11th round, referee, John Coyle, bringing the contest to a close.

S. Bantamweight

Following a ten round kayo defeat at the hands of Michael Brodie for the vacant British title at the Wythenshawe Forum, Neil Swain forfeited his championship belt.

Featherweight

11 October 1996   Jonjo Irwin 8.13¾ (England) W PTS 12 Smith Odoom 8.13¾ (Ghana), Hilton Hotel, London. Following Billy Hardy's decision to relinquish the title in September 1996 in order to concentrate on other commitments, Irwin and Odoom came together to contest the vacant crown. The pattern of the fight was quickly set, with the stocky southpaw, Odoom, being the aggressor, and Irwin using his height and reach advantage to good effect, while picking up the points. At the finish, although Larry O'Connell had no hesitation in naming Irwin the winner, the 117½-117 scorecard showed the new champion winning by just one round - the last.

17 December 1996   Jonjo Irwin 9.0 (England) W PTS 12 Rick Raynor 8.13¾ (Australia), The Dome, Doncaster. An interesting contest that saw Irwin outbox the determined Australian to well warrant John Coyle's 120-114½ points' decision in his favour, also saw both men suffering cuts caused by the challenger's dangerous, at times, headwork. Strangely, Raynor, a tall featherweight at 5'10", rarely matched the champion for jabs, the very punch that ultimately decided the fight.

S. Featherweight

11 December 1996   Justin Juuko 9.4 (Uganda) W RSC 8 Gary Thornhill 9.3 (England), Elephant & Castle Leisure Centre, London. Having taken a beating in the first round, culminating in a count and being rescued by the bell, Thornhill came back impressively to force the action and give the champion all the problems he could handle when breaking up his rhythm. Unfortunately, for the "Scouser", a cut right eye, sustained in the third, worsened considerably and he had to be rescued by Roy Francis early in the eighth when unable to see the punches coming.

22 May 1997   Justin Juuko 9.3½ (Uganda) W PTS 12 David Ouma 9.4 (Kenya), Elephant & Castle Leisure Centre, London. In a fight that involved the vacant WBC International title, as well as that of the Commonwealth, the Kenyan surprised many good judges as he pushed Juuko all the way. While there was never any real doubt about the result, the tough Kenyan took all that was coming his way without flinching, leaving the champion to ponder on whether he has the punching power to succeed at the highest level. Scorecards: Richie Davies 118-111, Terry O'Connor 117-113, 117-112. Richie Davies also refereed.

Lightweight

12 October 1996   David Tetteh 9.9 (Ghana) L PTS 12 Billy Irwin 9.9 (Canada), Toronto, Canada. Scorecards: 114-114, 114-116, 111-117.

4 March 1997   Billy Irwin 9.9 (Canada) L PTS 12 David Tetteh 9.9 (Ghana), Toronto, Canada. Scorecards: 111-119, 112-118, 110-117.

L. Welterweight

13 July 1996   Paul Ryan 9.13¾ (England) L CO 1 Andy Holligan 9.13¼ (England), York Hall, London. Holligan forfeited the title in January 1997 when failing to defend within the stipulated period. For a summary, see under British Title Bouts During 1996-97.

22 April 1997   Bernard Paul 9.13$^{3}/_{4}$ (England) W PTS 12 Felix Bwalya 9.13 (Zambia), York Hall, London. In a contest that was shrouded in controversy, Paul won the vacant title 117-116$^{1}/_{2}$ on referee Larry O'Connell's scorecard, despite looking an obvious loser. However, it must be taken into consideration that had Bwalya always hit with the knuckle part of the glove there would have only been one winner, but he did not. Stop Press: Following the 30 July meeting at the offices of the BBBoC, Paul was ordered by the Commonwealth Committee to meet Bwalya in a return by the end of this coming October.

Welterweight

2 October 1996   Andrew Murray 10.6 (Guyana) W PTS 12 Michael Smyth 10.6$^{1}/_{2}$ (Wales), Sophia Gardens, Cardiff. Despite carrying a cut over the right eye from as early as the second round (Smyth was cut over the same eye in the third), the champion boxed well within himself to come home an impressive 119-116 points winner on referee, Richie Davies' scorecard. Seemingly impervious to Smyth's single shots, strangely there were no follow ups, the champion cruised through the last third to treat the paying customers to his skills. Stop Press: On 30 July, the Commonwealth Boxing Council announced that Murray had decided to relinquish the title following his inability to secure defences against the mandatory challengers.

L. Middleweight

6 July 1996   Chris Pyatt 10.13 (England) L PTS 12 Steve Foster 10.13 (England), Nynex Arena, Manchester. Having turned pro back in 1981, and having won just five of his first 15 contests, in winning, Foster struck a blow for every aspiring fighter as his perseverence and hard work finally paid off. Although many onlookers felt the decision could have gone either way, the judges gave it to Foster (judges were in use because the contest also involved Foster's IBF Inter-Continental belt). Scorecards: Roy Francis 116-112, Dave Parris 117-114, 116-113. Referee: John Coyle. Foster forfeited the title in April 1997 for failing to defend against Kevin Kelly within the stipulated period. Stop Press: Kevin Kelly regained the championship he had controversially lost to Pyatt back in 1995, when outpointing fellow-Australian, Sam Soliman, in Sydney on 15 August.

Middleweight

1 October 1996   Robert McCracken 11.5$^{1}/_{2}$ (England) W PTS 12 Fitzgerald Bruney 11.5 (Canada), Aston Villa Leisure Centre, Birmingham. Following on from their earlier controversial fight for the vacant title, this time round the Canadian did nothing at all to warrant the decision, going down by a wide 119$^{1}/_{2}$-115$^{1}/_{2}$ on Larry O'Connell's scorecard. Despite taking an injured left elbow into the ring with him, McCracken outboxed and hurt his challenger throughout and it was only Bruney's awkwardness that kept him in the contest.

S. Middleweight

23 October 1996   Henry Wharton 12.0 (England) W RSC 5 Rick Thornberry 11.12 (Australia), North Bridge Leisure Centre, Halifax. The Australian, showing good hand speed and movement, buzzed around for a couple of sessions before Wharton got the range, putting him down for counts of nine in the third and fourth rounds, respectively. Although frustrating the champion in the fifth, during the interval, Thornberry's corner advised the referee (John Coyle) that their man could not continue due to a damaged shoulder.

L. Heavyweight

30 November 1996   Nicky Piper 12.6$^{3}/_{4}$ (Wales) W RSC 7 Bruce Scott 12.5$^{1}/_{2}$ (Jamaica), Rhondda Fach Leisure Centre, Tylorstown. In making a false start, the English-based Jamaican, Scott, soon found himself on the deck after taking a cracking left hook counter from the champion. However, on rising at five, he bravely fought back to give Piper some nasty moments until his left eye began to swell and impair his vision. Come the seventh, time was beginning to run out for the challenger and 43 seconds into the round, the referee, John Keane, brought the contest to an end.

Cruiserweight

6 November 1996   Chris Okoh 13.6 (England) W PTS 12 Tosca Petrides 13.5 (Australia), Ice Arena, Hull. Although winning 118$^{1}/_{2}$-117 on Paul Thomas' scorecard, Okoh's limitations were exposed against the wild, swinging Australian, who, despite a lack of knowledge regarding the sweet science, gave the champion all sorts of problems. In fact, had Petrides not faded when running out of stamina an upset would have definitely been on the cards. For his part, Okoh was advised to go back to the drawing board.

25 March 1997   Chris Okoh 13.5$^{1}/_{2}$ (England) W PTS 12 Denzil Browne 13.8 (England), The Theatre, Lewisham. Again unimpressive, Okoh found it difficult to attain any kind of rhythm, while Browne showed no initiative, being content to spoil and negate any good work coming the way of the champion. At the finish of one of the most boring title fights on record, referee, Terry O'Connor, made it 118-117$^{1}/_{2}$ in favour of Okoh, who must have shaded it in view of his aggression.

2 June 1997   Chris Okoh 13.6$^{3}/_{4}$ (England) L RSC 3 Darren Corbett 13.7 (Ireland), Waterfront Hall, Belfast. Despite outboxing Corbett in the first, Okoh's world was turned upside down in the second. Twice smashed to the canvas, it was only the bell that saved him as he rose at the count of six and when another crashing left hook smashed into his bleeding right eye to dump him heavily in the third, Mickey Vann rescued a badly shaken ex-champion at 1.23 of the round, leaving Corbett and his fans celebrating long into the night.

Heavyweight

30 June 1997   Julius Francis 17.5$^{3}/_{4}$ (England) W PTS 12 Joseph Chingangu 16.2 (Zambia), York Hall, London. Fighting for the title that Scott Welch had forfeited in January 1997, for failing to defend within the stipulated period, Francis clearly won, John Coyle awarding him the 118$^{1}/_{2}$-116 points verdict, but, in doing so, failed to shine. Unfortunately, in knocking Chingangu down in the sixth, Francis claimed to have damaged his right hand and boxed on the retreat from thereon in order to protect his injury, whilst, at the same time, scoring from distance.

Commonwealth Champions, 1887-1997

Since the last edition, Harold Alderman's magnificent research into Imperial British Empire title fights (see elsewhere in the book) has introduced many more claimants/champions than were shown last time round. Prior to 12 October 1954, the date that the British Commonwealth and Empire Boxing Championships Committee was formed, there was no official body as such and the Australian and British promoters virtually ran the show with other members of the British Empire mainly out in the cold. We have also listed Canadian representatives, despite championship boxing in that country being contested over ten or 12 rounds at most, but they are not accorded the same kind of recognition that their British and Australian counterparts are. Reconstituted as the British Commonwealth Boxing Championships Committee on 22 November 1972, and with a current membership that includes Australia, Bahama, Ghana, Guyana, Jamaica, Kenya, New Zealand, Nigeria, South Africa, Tanzania, Trinidad and Tobago, Zambia, and Zimbabwe, in 1989 the "British" tag was dropped.

COMMONWEALTH COUNTRY CODE
A = Australia; BAH = Bahamas; BAR = Barbados; BER = Bermuda; C = Canada; E = England; F = Fiji; GH = Ghana; GU = Guyana; I = Ireland; J = Jamaica; K = Kenya; N = Nigeria; NZ = New Zealand; NI = Northern Ireland; PNG = Papua New Guinea; SA = South Africa; SAM = Samoa; S = Scotland; T = Tonga; TR = Trinidad; U = Uganda; W = Wales; ZA = Zambia; ZI = Zimbabwe.

Champions in **bold** denote those recognised by the British Commonwealth and Empire Boxing Championships Committee (1954 to date) and, prior to that, those with the best claims

*Undefeated champions (Does not include men who forfeited titles)

Title Holder	Country	Tenure	Title Holder	Country	Tenure	Title Holder	Country	Tenure
Flyweight (112 lbs)			**Johnny King**	E	1932-1934	Barney Wilshur	C	1923
Elky Clark*	S	1924-1927	**Dick Corbett**	E	1934	Benny Gould	C	1923-1924
Harry Hill	E	1929	Frankie Martin	C	1935-1937	**Billy Grime**	A	1924
Frenchy Belanger	C	1929	Baby Yack	C	1937	Leo Kid Roy	C	1924-1932
Vic White	A	1929-1930	Johnny Gaudes	C	1937-1939	**Johnny McGrory**	S	1936-1938
Teddy Green	A	1930-1931	Lefty Gwynn	C	1939	**Jim Spider Kelly**	NI	1938-1939
Jackie Paterson	S	1940-1948	Baby Yack	C	1939-1940	**Johnny Cusick**	E	1939-1940
Rinty Monaghan*	NI	1948-1950	**Jim Brady**	S	1941-1945	**Nel Tarleton**	E	1940-1947
Teddy Gardner	E	1952	**Jackie Paterson**	S	1945-1949	**Tiger Al Phillips**	E	1947
Jake Tuli	SA	1952-1954	**Stan Rowan**	E	1949	**Ronnie Clayton**	E	1947-1951
Dai Dower*	W	1954-1957	**Vic Toweel**	SA	1949-1952	**Roy Ankrah**	GH	1951-1954
Frankie Jones	S	1957	**Jimmy Carruthers***	A	1952-1954	**Billy Spider Kelly**	NI	1954-1955
Dennis Adams*	SA	1957-1962	**Peter Keenan**	S	1955-1959	**Hogan Kid Bassey***	N	1955-1957
Jackie Brown	S	1962-1963	**Freddie Gilroy***	NI	1959-1963	**Percy Lewis**	TR	1957-1960
Walter McGowan*	S	1963-1969	**Johnny Caldwell**	NI	1964-1965	**Floyd Robertson**	GH	1960-1967
John McCluskey	S	1970-1971	**Alan Rudkin**	E	1965-1966	**John O'Brien**	S	1967
Henry Nissen	A	1971-1974	**Walter McGowan**	S	1966-1968	**Johnny Famechon***	A	1967-1969
Big Jim West*	A	1974-1975	**Alan Rudkin**	E	1968-1969	**Toro George**	NZ	1970-1972
Patrick Mambwe	ZA	1976-1979	**Lionel Rose***	A	1969	**Bobby Dunne**	A	1972-1974
Ray Amoo	N	1980	**Alan Rudkin***	E	1970-1972	**Evan Armstrong**	S	1974
Steve Muchoki	K	1980-1983	**Paul Ferreri**	A	1972-1977	**David Kotey***	GH	1974-1975
Keith Wallace*	E	1983-1984	**Sulley Shittu**	GH	1977-1978	**Eddie Ndukwu**	N	1977-1980
Richard Clarke	J	1986-1987	**Johnny Owen***	W	1978-1980	**Pat Ford***	GU	1980-1981
Nana Yaw Konadu*	GH	1987-1989	**Paul Ferreri**	A	1981-1986	**Azumah Nelson***	GH	1981-1985
Alfred Kotey*	GH	1989-1993	**Ray Minus***	BAH	1986-1991	**Tyrone Downes**	BAR	1986-1988
Francis Ampofo*	E	1993	**John Armour***	E	1992-1996	**Thunder Aryeh**	GH	1988-1989
Daren Fifield	E	1993-1994	**Paul Lloyd**	E	1996-	**Oblitey Commey**	GH	1989-1990
Francis Ampofo	E	1994-1995				**Modest Napunyi**	K	1990-1991
Danny Ward	SA	1995-1996	**S. Bantamweight (122 lbs)**			**Barrington Francis***	C	1991
Peter Culshaw	E	1996-	**Neil Swain**	W	1995	**Colin McMillan***	E	1992
			Neil Swain	W	1996-1997	**Billy Hardy***	E	1992-1996
Bantamweight (118 lbs)						**Jonjo Irwin**	E	1996-
Digger Stanley	E	1904-1905	**Featherweight (126 lbs)**					
Owen Moran	E	1905	**Jim Driscoll***	W	1908-1913	**S. Featherweight (130 lbs)**		
Ted Green	A	1905-1911	**Llew Edwards**	W	1915-1916	**Billy Moeller**	A	1975-1977
Charlie Simpson*	A	1911-1912	**Charlie Simpson***	A	1916	**Johnny Aba***	PNG	1977-1982
Jim Higgins	S	1920-1922	Tommy Noble	E	1919-1921	**Langton Tinago**	ZI	1983-1984
Tommy Harrison	E	1922-1923	**Bert Spargo**	A	1921-1922	**John Sichula**	ZA	1984
Bugler Harry Lake	E	1923	**Bert McCarthy**	A	1922	**Lester Ellis***	A	1984-1985
Johnny Brown	E	1923-1928	**Bert Spargo**	A	1922-1923	**John Sichula**	ZA	1985-1986
Billy McAllister	A	1928-1930	**Billy Grime**	A	1923	**Sam Akromah**	GH	1986-1987
Teddy Baldock*	E	1928-1930	**Ernie Baxter**	A	1923	**John Sichula**	ZA	1987-1989
Johnny Peters	E	1930	Leo Kid Roy	C	1923	**Mark Reefer***	E	1989-1990
Dick Corbett	E	1930-1932	**Bert Ristuccia**	A	1923-1924	**Thunder Aryeh**	GH	1990-1991

Title Holder	Country	Tenure
Hugh Forde	E	1991
Paul Harvey	E	1991-1992
Tony Pep	C	1992-1995
Justin Juuko	U	1995-

Lightweight (135 lbs)

Title Holder	Country	Tenure
Jim Burge	A	1890
George Dawson*	A	1890
Harry Nickless	E	1892-1894
Arthur Valentine	E	1894-1895
Dick Burge*	E	1894-1895
Jim Murphy*	NZ	1894-1897
Eddie Connolly*	C	1896-1897
Jack Goldswain	E	1906-1908
Jack McGowan	A	1909
Hughie Mehegan	A	1909-1910
Johnny Summers*	E	1910
Hughie Mehegan	A	1911
Freddie Welsh*	W	1912-1914
Ernie Izzard	E	1928
Tommy Fairhall	A	1928-1930
Al Foreman	E	1930-1933
Jimmy Kelso	A	1933
Al Foreman*	E	1933-1934
Laurie Stevens*	SA	1936-1937
Dave Crowley	E	1938
Eric Boon	E	1938-1944
Ronnie James*	W	1944-1947
Arthur King	C	1948-1951
Frank Johnson	E	1953
Pat Ford	A	1953-1954
Ivor Germain	BAR	1954

Title Holder	Country	Tenure
Pat Ford	A	1954-1955
Johnny van Rensburg	SA	1955-1956
Willie Toweel	SA	1956-1959
Dave Charnley	E	1959-1962
Bunny Grant	J	1962-1967
Manny Santos*	NZ	1967
Love Allotey	GH	1967-1968
Percy Hayles	J	1968-1975
Jonathan Dele	N	1975-1977
Lennox Blackmore	GU	1977-1978
Hogan Jimoh	N	1978-1980
Langton Tinago	ZI	1980-1981
Barry Michael	A	1981-1982
Claude Noel	T	1982-1984
Graeme Brooke	A	1984-1985
Barry Michael*	A	1985-1986
Langton Tinago	ZI	1986-1987
Mo Hussein	E	1987-1989
Pat Doherty	E	1989
Najib Daho	E	1989-1990
Carl Crook	E	1990-1992
Billy Schwer	E	1992-1993
Paul Burke	E	1993
Billy Schwer	E	1993-1995
David Tetteh	GH	1995-1997
Billy Irwin	C	1997
David Tetteh	GH	1997-

L. Welterweight (140 lbs)

Title Holder	Country	Tenure
Joe Tetteh	GH	1972-1973
Hector Thompson	A	1973-1977

Title Holder	Country	Tenure
Baby Cassius Austin	A	1977-1978
Jeff Malcolm	A	1978-1979
Obisia Nwankpa	N	1979-1983
Billy Famous	N	1983-1986
Tony Laing	E	1987-1988
Lester Ellis	A	1988-1989
Steve Larrimore	BAH	1989
Tony Ekubia	E	1989-1991
Andy Holligan	E	1991-1994
Ross Hale	E	1994-1995
Paul Ryan	E	1995-1996
Andy Holligan	E	1996-1997
Bernard Paul	E	1997-

Welterweight (147 lbs)

Title Holder	Country	Tenure
Tom Williams	A	1892-1895
Dick Burge	E	1895-1897
Eddie Connelly*	C	1903-1905
Joe White*	C	1907-1909
Johnny Summers	E	1912-1914
Tom McCormick	I	1914
Matt Wells	E	1914-1919
Fred Kay	A	1915
Tommy Uren	A	1915-1916
Fritz Holland	A	1916
Tommy Uren	A	1916-1919
Fred Kay	A	1919-1920
Johnny Basham	W	1919-1920
Bermondsey Billy Wells	E	1922
Ted Kid Lewis	E	1920-1924
Tommy Milligan*	S	1924-1925
Jack Carroll	A	1928

Counted out at 1.41 of round one of his Commonwealth bantamweight title challenge against Paul Lloyd (left), this is one of the few pictures showing the South African, Lybo Nkoko, on his feet

Les Clark

Title Holder	Country	Tenure	Title Holder	Country	Tenure	Title Holder	Country	Tenure
Charlie Purdie	A	1928-1929	Ken Salisbury	A	1984-1985	Mick King	A	1914-1915
Wally Hancock	A	1929-1930	Nick Wilshire	E	1985-1987	Les Darcy*	A	1915-1917
Tommy Fairhall*	A	1930	Lloyd Hibbert	E	1987	Ted Kid Lewis	E	1922-1923
Jack Carroll	A	1934-1938	Troy Waters*	A	1987-1991	Roland Todd	E	1923-1926
Eddie Thomas	W	1951	Chris Pyatt*	E	1991-1992	Len Johnson	E	1926-1928
Wally Thom	E	1951-1952	Mickey Hughes	E	1992-1993	Tommy Milligan	S	1926-1928
Cliff Curvis	W	1952	Lloyd Honeyghan	E	1993-1994	Alex Ireland	S	1928-1929
Gerald Dreyer	SA	1952-1954	Leo Young	A	1994-1995	Len Harvey	E	1929-1933
Barry Brown	NZ	1954	Kevin Kelly	A	1995	Del Fontaine	C	1931
George Barnes	A	1954-1956	Chris Pyatt	E	1995-1996	Ted Moore	E	1931
Darby Brown	A	1956	Steve Foster	E	1996-1997	Jock McAvoy	E	1933-1939
George Barnes	A	1956-1958				Ron Richards*	A	1940
Johnny van Rensburg	SA	1958	**Middleweight (160 lbs)**			Ron Richards*	A	1941-1942
George Barnes	A	1958-1960	Chesterfield Goode	E	1887-1890	Bos Murphy	NZ	1948
Brian Curvis*	W	1960-1966	Toff Wall	E	1890-1891	Dick Turpin	E	1948-1949
Johnny Cooke	E	1967-1968	Jim Hall	A	1892-1893	Dave Sands*	A	1949-1952
Ralph Charles*	E	1968-1972	Lackie Thompson	S	1894	Randy Turpin	E	1952-1954
Clyde Gray	C	1973-1979	Bill Heffernan	NZ	1894-1896	Al Bourke	A	1952-1954
Chris Clarke	C	1979	Bill Doherty	A	1896-1897	Johnny Sullivan	E	1954-1955
Clyde Gray*	C	1979-1980	Billy Edwards	A	1897-1898	Pat McAteer	E	1955-1958
Colin Jones*	W	1981-1984	Dido Plumb*	E	1898-1901	Dick Tiger	N	1958-1960
Sylvester Mittee	E	1984-1985	Tom Duggan	A	1901-1903	Wilf Greaves	C	1960
Lloyd Honeyghan*	E	1985-1986	Jack Palmer*	E	1902-1904	Dick Tiger*	N	1960-1962
Brian Janssen	A	1987	Jewey Cooke	E	1903-1904	Gomeo Brennan	BAH	1963-1964
Wilf Gentzen	A	1987-1988	Tom Dingey	C	1904-1905	Tuna Scanlon*	NZ	1964
Gary Jacobs	S	1988-1989	Jack Lalor	SA	1905	Gomeo Brennan	BAH	1964-1966
Donovan Boucher	C	1989-1992	Ted Nelson	A	1905	Blair Richardson*	C	1966-1967
Eamonn Loughran*	NI	1992-1993	Tom Dingey	C	1905	Milo Calhoun	J	1967
Andrew Murray	GU	1993-	Sam Langford*	C	1907-1911	Johnny Pritchett*	E	1967-1969
			Ed Williams	A	1908-1910	Les McAteer	E	1969-1970
L. Middleweight (154 lbs)			Arthur Cripps	A	1910	Mark Rowe	E	1970
Charkey Ramon*	A	1972-1975	Dave Smith	A	1910-1911	Bunny Sterling	E	1970-1972
Maurice Hope*	E	1976-1979	Jerry Jerome	A	1913	Tony Mundine*	A	1972-1975
Kenny Bristol	GU	1979-1981	Arthur Evernden	E	1913-1914	Monty Betham	NZ	1975-1978
Herol Graham*	E	1981-1984						

Bernard Paul (right) thumps in a right to the head of Zambia's Felix Bwalya on his way to annexing the vacant Commonwealth light-welterweight title in April

Les Clark

Al Korovou	A	1978
Ayub Kalule	U	1978-1980
Tony Sibson*	E	1980-1983
Roy Gumbs	E	1983
Mark Kaylor	E	1983-1984
Tony Sibson*	E	1984-1988
Nigel Benn	E	1988-1989
Michael Watson*	E	1989-1991
Richie Woodhall*	E	1992-1995
Robert McCracken	E	1995-

S. Middleweight (168 lbs)

Rod Carr	A	1989-1990
Lou Cafaro	A	1990-1991
Henry Wharton	E	1991-

L. Heavyweight (175 lbs)

Dave Smith*	A	1911-1915
Jack Bloomfield*	E	1923-1924
Tom Berry	E	1927
Gipsy Daniels*	W	1927
Len Harvey	E	1939-1942
Freddie Mills*	E	1942-1950
Randy Turpin*	E	1952-1955
Gordon Wallace	C	1956-1957
Yvon Durelle*	C	1957-1959
Chic Calderwood	S	1960-1963
Bob Dunlop*	A	1968-1970
Eddie Avoth	W	1970-1971
Chris Finnegan	E	1971-1973
John Conteh*	E	1973-1974
Steve Aczel	A	1975

Tony Mundine	A	1975-1978
Gary Summerhays	C	1978-1979
Lottie Mwale	ZA	1979-1985
Leslie Stewart*	TR	1985-1987
Willie Featherstone	C	1987-1989
Guy Waters*	A	1989-1993
Brent Kosolofski	C	1993-1994
Garry Delaney	E	1994-1995
Noel Magee	I	1995
Nicky Piper	W	1995-

Cruiserweight (190 lbs)

Stewart Lithgo	E	1984
Chisanda Mutti	ZA	1984-1987
Glenn McCrory*	E	1987-1989
Apollo Sweet	A	1989
Derek Angol*	E	1989-1993
Francis Wanyama	U	1994-1995
Chris Okoh	E	1995-1997
Darren Corbett	NI	1997-

Heavyweight (190 lbs +)

Peter Jackson*	A	1889-1901
Dan Creedon	NZ	1896-1903
Billy McColl	A	1902-1905
Tim Murphy	A	1905-1906
Bill Squires	A	1906-1909
Bill Lang	A	1909-1910
Tommy Burns*	C	1910-1911
P.O. Curran	I	1911
Dan Flynn	I	1911
Bombardier Billy Wells	E	1911-1919
Bill Lang	A	1911-1913

Dave Smith	A	1913-1917
Joe Beckett*	E	1919-1923
Phil Scott	E	1926-1931
Larry Gains	C	1931-1934
Len Harvey	E	1934
Jack Petersen	W	1934-1936
Ben Foord	SA	1936-1937
Tommy Farr	W	1937
Len Harvey*	E	1939-1942
Jack London	E	1944-1945
Bruce Woodcock	E	1945-1950
Jack Gardner	E	1950-1952
Johnny Williams	W	1952-1953
Don Cockell	E	1953-1956
Joe Bygraves	J	1956-1957
Joe Erskine	W	1957-1958
Brian London	E	1958-1959
Henry Cooper	E	1959-1971
Joe Bugner	E	1971
Jack Bodell	E	1971-1972
Danny McAlinden	NI	1972-1975
Bunny Johnson	E	1975
Richard Dunn	E	1975-1976
Joe Bugner*	E	1976-1977
John L. Gardner*	E	1978-1981
Trevor Berbick	C	1981-1986
Horace Notice*	E	1986-1988
Derek Williams	E	1988-1992
Lennox Lewis*	E	1992-1993
Henry Akinwande	E	1993-1995
Scott Welch	E	1995-1997
Julius Francis	E	1997-

Nicky Piper (right) the Commonwealth light-heavyweight champion, successfully defended his title with a seventh-round stoppage win over Bruce Scott last November

Les Clark

Imperial British Empire Title Bouts, 1887-1954

by Harold Alderman

The Imperial British Empire title initially came about when the champions of England (Britain) met their Australian counterparts, the first recorded contest of this nature with gloves being Chesterfield Goode versus Tom Lees on 30 August 1887. In fact, it was only when the official champions of each country came together that the title was given any credence. Later, in the 1890s, the Canadians came more and more into the reckoning, as did New Zealand and South Africa.

The first ever championship belt for the Australian version of the title was awarded by the "Sydney Referee" to George Dawson, following his 12 August 1890 win over Shadow Maber at 130lbs. Dawson's original opponent was to have been Jim Burge, who refused to box for the £150 on offer, demanding £200, which was refused. Dawson put a second notch on the belt on 24 November, when beating Burge inside 31 rounds, and then made it his own property with a 17-round win over Dummy Mace on 28 April 1891. Later, Hugh D. McIntosh put up a heavyweight championship belt, which was duly won by Tommy Burns, following his 20-round points win over Bill Lang on 11 April 1910. When Burns retired, McIntosh awarded the same belt to Dave Smith after he knocked out Bill Squires in the tenth on 26 December 1916 and also presented two other belts, Hughie Mehegan (light) and Bill Lang (heavy) being the recipients. In February 1926, he announced that he would be making a new batch of championship belts, covering the bantam, feather, light, welter, and middleweight titles, with the latter going to Len Johnson, who had been prevented by the NSC Board of Control from contesting either the British or Empire titles because he was coloured. At the time, Johnson held the Australian version of the championship. The first fight that involved the Lord Lonsdale British Empire Championship Belt was contested on 12 June 1933 at Olympia, Johnny King defeating Canada's Bobby Leitham on points over 15 rounds.

Unfortunately, when the Imperial British Empire championships eventually began to take off and really mean something in terms of status, and in helping to secure world title fights against the leading Americans, the British promoters began to cultivate them at the expense of member countries by continually matching fellow Brits to fight each other, something that eventually led to the other countries doing likewise. Matters came to head in the early 1950s and, in July 1954, an exploratory meeting, held in London, led to a body being set up and named as the British Commonwealth and Empire Board, which was duly formed during its inaugural meeting at the BBBoC on 12 October 1954. At that meeting, Great Britain, South Africa, Trinidad, British Guyana, Canada, Nigeria, New Zealand, and Australia were all represented and a championship committee issued their list of champions, recognising Don Cockell (heavy), Randy Turpin (l. heavy), Johnny Sullivan (middle), Barry Brown (welter), Billy Spider Kelly (feather), and Jake Tuli (fly), with the light and bantam-weight divisions seen as vacant. It is everything prior to this that we include within these pages.

You should also note that the Canadian version of the title was never contested over more than ten or 12 rounds, the maximum limit of the day in that country. Unfortunately, due to that situation, fights that took place in the Dominion were not recognised in Australia or Britain as involving the championship.

Regarding weight limits for individual weight classes, where it differs from what has been recognised since 1909, when the NSC standardised weights that were accepted throughout the British Empire, it is shown in brackets immediately following the fight in question.

COUNTRY CODE
A = Australia; BAR = Barbados; C = Canada; E = England; GH = Ghana; GU = Guyana; I = Ireland; NZ = New Zealand; NI = Northern Ireland; SA = South Africa; S = Scotland; W = Wales.

Flyweight (112lbs)

6 September 1924   Elky Clark (S) W RSC 10 Jim Hanna (I), Hengler's Circus, Glasgow

19 April 1926   Elky Clark (S) W RSC 20, Kid Socks (E), NSC, London. Clark retired in April 1927, following an unsuccessful operation to save the sight of his right eye

17 April 1929   Harry Hill (E) W PTS 10 Frenchy Belanger (C), Montreal, Canada

13 May 1929   Harry Hill (E) L RSC 6 Frenchy Belanger (C), Toronto, Canada. Belanger lost any claim he had to the title when stripped of the Canadian crown in May 1929

24 August 1929   Vic White (A) W PTS 15 Young Siki (E), Sydney, Australia

16 July 1930   Vic White (A) L RSC 3 Teddy Green (A), Sydney, Australia. Green retired in April 1931. Later, in 1936, without success, Kid Tanner claimed the championship as no Empire fighters would accept his challenge

11 March 1940   Jackie Paterson (S) W PTS 15 Kid Tanner (GU), Belle Vue, Manchester

3 February 1941   Jackie Paterson (S) W CO 8 Paddy Ryan (E), Ice Rink, Nottingham

19 June 1943   Jackie Paterson (S) W CO 1 Peter Kane (E), Hampden Park, Glasgow

10 July 1946   Jackie Paterson (S) W PTS 15 Joe Curran (E), Hampden Park, Glasgow

23 March 1948   Jackie Paterson (S) L CO 7 Rinty Monaghan (NI), King's Hall, Belfast

30 September 1949   Rinty Monaghan (NI) DREW 15 Terry Allen (E), King's Hall, Belfast. Monaghan retired on 31 March 1950

17 March 1952   Teddy Gardner (E) W PTS 15 Terry Allen (E), St James' Hall, Newcastle

8 September 1952   Teddy Gardner (E) L RSC 12 Jake Tuli (SA), St James' Hall, Newcastle. Tuli lost the title on 19 October 1954, when outpointed over 15 rounds by Welshman, Dai Dower, at London's Harringay Arena

Bantamweight (118 lbs)

19 November 1904   Digger Stanley (E) W CO 4 Sid Wilmott (A), Newcastle, England (114lbs)

23 January 1905   Digger Stanley (E) L PTS 20 Owen Moran (E), NSC, London (114lbs). Moran never took the 114 lbs title seriously and his claim lapsed

11 November 1905   Ted Green (A) W CO 8 Jack Ladbury (E), Sydney, Australia (116 lbs)

10 February 1906   Ted Green (A) W CO 16 Jack Ladbury (E), Charters Towers, Australia (116 lbs)

2 June 1906   Ted Green (A) W CO 8 Jack Ladbury (E), Sydney, Australia (116 lbs)

28 September 1907   Ted Green (A) W CO 3 Jack Ladbury (E), Sydney, Australia

1909   Ted Green (A) W CO 6 Billy Elliott (E), Brisbane, Australia

20 October 1911   Ted Green (A) L PTS 20 Charlie Simpson (A), Melbourne, Australia

22 January 1912   Charlie Simpson (A) W CO 17 Ted Green (A), Melbourne, Australia. Simpson relinquished the title in 1912 when unable to make 118 lbs any longer

29 November 1920   Jim Higgins (S) W PTS 20 Vince Blackburn (A), NSC, London

29 November 1920   Jim Higgins (S) W PTS 20 Billy Eynon (W), NSC, London

31 January 1921   Jim Higgins (S) W PTS 20 Kid Symonds (E), NSC, London

26 June 1922   Jim Higgins (S) L CO 13 Tommy Harrison (E), The Stadium, Liverpool

26 February 1923   Tommy Harrison (E) L PTS 20 Bugler Harry Lake (E), NSC, London

26 November 1923   Bugler Harry Lake (E) L PTS 20 Johnny Brown (E), NSC London

23 February 1925   Johnny Brown (E) W RTD 16 Harry Corbett (E), NSC, London

19 October 1925   Johnny Brown (E) W CO 12 Mick Hill (E), NSC, London

7 July 1928   Billy McAllister (A) W PTS 15 Kid Socks (E), Melbourne, Australia. With Johnny Brown not recognised as the champion in Australia, this fight involved their version of the vacant title

29 August 1928   Teddy Baldock (E) W RSC 2 Johnny Brown (E), Clapton Stadium, London

16 May 1929   Teddy Baldock (E) W PTS 15 Alf Kid Pattenden (E), Olympia, London. Baldock retired in September 1931

14 June 1929   Billy McAllister (A) W DIS 7 Teddy Green (A), Leichardt, Australia

6 December 1929   Billy McAllister (A) NC 6 Vic White (A), Leichardt, Australia

31 January 1930   Billy McAllister (A) W RSC 14 Vic White (A), Leichardt, Australia

26 April 1930   Billy McAllister (A) DREW 15 Johnny Peters (E), Sydney, Australia

17 May 1930   Billy McAllister (A) L CO 12 Johnny Peters (E), Sydney, Australia

22 May 1930   Dick Corbett (E) W PTS 15 Willie Smith (SA), Olympia, London

7 June 1930   Johnny Peters (E) W RSC 14 Billy McAllister (A), Melbourne, Australia. Peters was never recognised in England and moved up to featherweight

21 December 1931   Dick Corbett (E) W PTS 15 Johnny King (E), Belle Vue, Manchester

10 October 1932   Dick Corbett (E) L PTS 15 Johnny King (E), Belle Vue, Manchester

12 June 1933   Johnny King (E) W PTS 15 Bobby Leitham (C), Olympia, London

12 February 1934   Johnny King (E) L PTS 15 Dick Corbett (E), Belle Vue, Manchester

20 August 1934   Dick Corbett (E) DREW 15 Johnny King (E), Clapton Stadium, London. Corbett forfeited title in October 1934. Following two eliminators in Montreal (w pts 10 Lefty Gwynn on 28 November 1934 and w pts 12 Harry Gerson on 7 October 1935), and the refusal of Johnny King to fight him, the Canadian, Frankie Martin, claimed the title

14 June 1937   Frankie Martin (C) L PTS 10 Baby Yack (C), Toronto, Canada

26 July 1937   Baby Yack (C) W PTS 10 Frankie Martin (C), Toronto Canada

7 December 1937   Baby Yack (C) W PTS 10 Mog Mason (W), Toronto, Canada

7 November 1937   Baby Yack (C) L PTS 10 Johnny Gaudes (C), Toronto, Canada

30 January 1939   Johnny Gaudes (C) L CO 5 Lefty Gwynn (C), Toronto, Canada

8 May 1939 Lefty Gwynn (C) L CO 5 Baby Yack (C), Toronto, Canada. Baby Yack retired in 1940, thus ending any Canadian claim to this title

1 January 1941 Jim Brady (S) W PTS 15 Kid Tanner (GU), Dens Park, Dundee

5 August 1941 Jim Brady (S) W PTS 15 Jackie Paterson (S), Hampden Park, Scotland

12 September 1945 Jim Brady (S) L PTS 15 Jackie Paterson (S), Hampden Park, Scotland

20 October 1947 Jackie Paterson (S) W CO 5 Norman Lewis (E), Harringay Arena, London

24 March 1949 Jackie Paterson (S) L PTS 15 Stan Rowan (E), Anfield, Liverpool

12 November 1949 Stan Rowan (E) L PTS 15 Vic Toweel (SA), Johannesburg, South Africa

8 April 1950 Vic Toweel (SA) W PTS 15 Fernando Gagnon (C), Johannesburg, South Africa

2 December 1950 Vic Toweel (SA) W RTD 10 Danny O'Sullivan (E), Johannesburg, South Africa

26 January 1952 Vic Toweel (SA) W PTS 15 Peter Keenan (S), Johannesburg, South Africa

15 November 1952 Vic Toweel (SA) L CO 1 Jimmy Carruthers (A), Johannesburg, South Africa

21 March 1953 Jimmy Carruthers (A) W CO 10 Vic Toweel (SA), Johannesburg, South Africa. Carruthers retired on 16 May 1954

Featherweight (126 lbs)

24 February 1908 Jim Driscoll (W) W PTS 20 Charlie Griffin (A), NSC, England

14 February 1910 Jim Driscoll (W) W RSC 6 Seaman Hayes (E), NSC, London

18 April 1910 Jim Driscoll (W) W CO 15 Spike Robson (E), NSC, London

30 January 1911 Jim Driscoll (W) W RSC 7 Spike Robson (E), NSC, London

30 January 1911 Jim Driscoll (W) DREW 20 Owen Moran (E), NSC, London. Driscoll retired in July 1913

18 December 1915 Llew Edwards (W) W RTD 13 Jimmy Hill (A), Sydney, Australia

23 January 1916 Llew Edwards (W) L PTS 20 Charlie Simpson (A), Melbourne, Australia. Simpson quickly outgrew the division and the title lapsed

27 November 1919 Tommy Noble (E) W CO 18 Young Tibby Watson (A), Holborn Stadium, London

29 January 1920 Tommy Noble (E) W PTS 20 Benny McNeill (E), Holborn Stadium, London

18 June 1921 Tommy Noble (E) L PTS 20 Bert Spargo (A), Sydney, Australia. Despite Noble being overweight, his fragile claim passed to Spargo

5 November 1921 Bert Spargo (A) W PTS 20 Jack Green (A), Melbourne, Australia

17 June 1922 Bert Spargo (A) W PTS 20 Jerry Sullivan (A), Melbourne, Australia

29 July 1922 Bert Spargo (A) L DIS 1 Bert McCarthy (A), Melbourne, Australia

26 August 1922 Bert McCarthy (A) L PTS 20 Bert Spargo (A), Melbourne, Australia

10 February 1923 Bert Spargo (A) L PTS 20 Billy Grime (A), Melbourne, Australia

14 July 1923 Billy Grime (A) L PTS 20 Ernie Baxter (A), Melbourne, Australia

5 August 1923 Leo Kid Roy (C) W PTS 10 Joe Fox (E), Montreal, Canada. With Roy recognised as one of the world's premier feathers, the Montreal boxing commission matched him against the undefeated 126 lbs British champion for their version of the title

3 November 1923 Ernie Baxter (A) L PTS 20 Bert Ristuccia (A), Melbourne, Australia

21 September 1923 Leo Kid Roy (C) L PTS 10 Barney Wishur (C), Toronto, Canada

2 November 1923 Barney Wilshur (C) L PTS 10 Benny Gould (C), Toronto, Canada

2 February 1924 Bert Ristuccia (A) L PTS 20 Billy Grime (A), Melbourne, Australia

25 March 1924 Benny Gould (C) L PTS 10 Leo Kid Roy (C), Toronto, Canada

28 May 1924 Leo Kid Roy (C) W PTS 10 Al Foreman (C), Montreal, Canada

13 September 1924 Billy Grime (A) W PTS 20 Joe Fox (E), Melbourne, Australia. Grime never bothered with his claim after winning the Australian lightweight title in November 1924

31 October 1926 Leo Kid Roy (C) W PTS 12 Vic Foley (C), Montreal, Canada

18 July 1928 Leo Kid Roy (C) W PTS 10 Vic Foley (C), Montreal, Canada

24 September 1928 Leo Kid Roy (C) W PTS 10 Ralph McNaughton (C), Quebec, Canada

5 November 1928 Leo Kid Roy (C) W PTS 12 Vic Foley (C), Vancouver, Canada

9 April 1930 Leo Kid Roy (C) W PTS 10 Sammy Hackett (C), Montreal, Canada. Roy forfeited his Canadian title and Empire claim on 23 February 1932 for failing to defend

26 December 1936   Johnny McGrory (S) W PTS 12 Willie Smith (SA), Johannesburg, South Africa. McGrory forfeited title on the scales on 17 August 1938, when overweight for his defence against Benny Caplan

23 November 1938   Jim Spider Kelly (NI) W PTS 15 Benny Caplan (E), King's Hall, Belfast

28 June 1939   Jim Spider Kelly (NI) L RSC 12 Johnny Cusick (E), King's Hall, Belfast

1 February 1940   Johnny Cusick (E) L PTS 15 Nel Tarleton (E), The Stadium, Liverpool

2 November 1940   Nel Tarleton (E) W PTS 15 Tom Smith (E), The Stadium, Liverpool

23 February 1945   Nel Tarleton (E) W PTS 15 Tiger Al Phillips (E), Belle Vue, Manchester. Tarleton retired on 14 February 1947

18 March 1947   Tiger Al Phillips (E) W PTS 15 Cliff Anderson (GU), Albert Hall, London

1 July 1947   Tiger Al Phillips (E) W DIS 8 Cliff Anderson (GU), Olympia, London

11 September 1947   Tiger Al Phillips (E) L PTS 15 Ronnie Clayton (E), Anfield, Liverpool

11 April 1949   Ronnie Clayton (E) W PTS 15 Johnny Molloy (E), Ice Rink, Nottingham

11 August 1949   Ronnie Clayton (E) W CO 12 Eddie Miller (A), The Stadium, Liverpool

28 November 1950   Ronnie Clayton (E) W PTS 15 Jim Kenny (S), Albert Hall, London

26 February 1951   Ronnie Clayton (E) W PTS 15 Tiger Al Phillips (E), Ice Rink, Nottingham

30 April 1951   Ronnie Clayton (E) L PTS 15 Roy Ankrah (GH), Empress Hall, London

25 February 1952   Roy Ankrah (GH) W RTD 13 Ronnie Clayton (E), Ice Rink, Nottingham

2 October 1954   Roy Ankrah (GH) L PTS 15 Billy Spider Kelly (NI), King's Hall, Belfast. Kelly, having outpointed England's Sammy McCarthy over 15 rounds at The King's Hall, Belfast on 22 January 1955, lost the title after being kayoed by Hogan Kid Bassey (Nigeria) at the same venue on 19 November 1955

Lightweight (135 lbs)

24 January 1890   Jim Burge (A) W RTD 22 Sam Baxter (E), Sydney, Australia (130 lbs)

28 April 1890   Jim Burge (A) DREW 50 George Dawson (A), Sydney, Australia (130 lbs). Burge forfeited belt when refusing to box for a purse less than £200

12 August 1890   George Dawson (A) W CO 20 Shadow Maber (A), Sydney, Australia (130 lbs)

24 November 1890   George Dawson (A) W RSC 31 Jim Burge (A), Sydney, Australia (130 lbs)

28 April 1891   George Dawson (A) W RSC 17 Dummy Mace (A), Sydney Australia (130 lbs). With this win, Dawson made the championship belt his own property and the title lapsed after he went to the USA in December 1891

19 March 1894   Arthur Valentine (E) W PTS 20 Jim Burge (A), Raglan Music Hall, London (132 lbs). Valentine never defended

4 May 1894   Harry Nickless (E) L CO 28 Dick Burge (E), Bolingbroke Club, London (140 lbs). Nickless had claimed the title on 14 June 1892 after the Australian, Tom Williams, had forfeited because of illness

30 August 1894   Jim Murphy (NZ) W PTS 20 Lackie Thompson (S), Johannesburg, South Africa (132 lbs)

15 September 1894   Jim Murphy (NZ) W DIS 24 Jim Burge (A), Johannesburg, South Africa (132 lbs)

25 January 1895   Dick Burge (E) W CO 4 Tom Williams (A), NSC London (140 lbs). The 140 lbs title lapsed when Burge moved up the weights

24 February 1895   Jim Murphy (NZ) DREW 35 Jim Burge (A), Johannesburg, South Africa (132 lbs). Contested with skin-tight gloves. In December 1897, Murphy died aged 25

24 November 1896   Eddie Connolly (C) W CO 5 Tom Causer (E), Olympic Club, Birmingham (134 lbs). Connolly never defended his claim at the weight

29 January 1906   Jack Goldswain (E) W CO 13 Fred Buckland (SA), NSC, London (140 lbs)

24 April 1906   Jack Goldswain (E) W PTS 20 Jabez White (E), NSC, London (140 lbs). With the 135 lbs beginning to be recognised throughout the British Empire as the premier lightweight limit around this time, this was the last major fight at the weight

24 May 1909   Jack McGowan (A) W PTS 20 Bob Greenshield (A), Melbourne, Australia

28 July 1909   Jack McGowan (A) W RSC 20 Bob Greenshields (A), Ballarat, Australia (140 lbs)

29 November 1909   Jack McGowan (A) L RSC 10 Hughie Mehegan (A), Melbourne, Australia

6 April 1910   Hughie Mehegan (A) L CO 19 Johnny Summers (E), Sydney, Australia. From then on, Summers boxed as a welter

20 October 1911   Hughie Mehegan (A) W RTD 14 Hock Keys (A), Sydney, Australia

16 September 1912   Hughie Mehegan (A) W PTS 15 Matt Wells (E), The Ring, London

16 December 1912   Hughie Mehegan (A) L PTS 20 Freddie Welsh (W), NSC, London. The title lapsed after

Welsh left for America, following his world title victory in July 1914

12 May 1928   Ernie Izzard (E) W PTS 15 Charlie Purdy (NZ), Sydney, Australia

2 June 1928   Ernie Izzard (E) L PTS 15 Tommy Fairhall (A), Sydney, Australia. Although failing to make 135 lbs again, Fairhall was still recognised in Australia as the champion until January 1930

21 May 1930   Al Foreman (E) W CO 1 Fred Webster (E), Premierland, London

20 October 1930   Al Foreman (E) W CO 6 George Rose (E), Belle Vue, Manchester

15 December 1930   Al Foreman (E) DREW 15 Johnny Cuthbert (E), Olympia, London

24 April 1933   Al Foreman (E) L PTS 15 Jimmy Kelso (A), Sydney, Australia. Kelso forfeited the title on the scales when weighing in for his defence against Foreman in Sydney on 22 May 1933. The fight went ahead, with Foreman successfully reclaiming the title following a third-round disqualification win

19 September 1933   Al Foreman (E) W PTS 10 Tommy Bland (C), Montreal, Canada. Foreman retired in July 1934

11 January 1936   Laurie Stevens (SA) W PTS 12 Jackie Kid Berg (E), Johannesburg, South Africa. Stevens retired with eye trouble on 30 November 1937

26 June 1938   Dave Crowley (E) W PTS 15 Jimmy Walsh (E), The Stadium, Liverpool. Not recognised by the BBBoC as a championship fight, despite the British title being involved, surprisingly, Australia recognised it as such due to the international reputation of both men

15 December 1938   Dave Crowley (E) L CO 13 Eric Boon (E), Harringay Arena, London

23 February 1939   Eric Boon (E) W RSC 14 Arthur Danahar (E), Harringay Arena, London

9 December 1939   Eric Boon (E) W CO 9 Dave Crowley (E), Harringay Arena, London

12 August 1944   Eric Boon (E) L CO 10 Ronnie James (W), Arms Park, Cardiff. No longer able to make the weight, James relinquished the title prior to defending against Vic Patrick in Sydney, Australia on 14 January 1947

1 October 1948   Arthur King (C) W RTD 7 Billy Thompson (E), Belle Vue, Manchester. King forfeited the title when becoming an American citizen in September 1951

23 January 1953   Frank Johnson (E) W RSC 10 Frank Flannery (A), Melbourne, Australia. According to the BBBoC, Johnson forfeited the title on the scales when he was overweight for a defence against Joe Lucy on 9 June

1953, the fight going ahead with Lucy winning on points over 12 rounds. Following that, he announced his retirement

28 August 1953   Pat Ford (A) W PTS 15 Frank Johnson (E), Melbourne, Australia. Technically a fight for the vacant title as Johnson was not recognised in Britain as the champion

9 October 1953   Pat Ford (A) W CO 13 Frank Johnson (E), Melbourne, Australia

9 April 1954   Pat Ford (A) L PTS 15 Ivor Germain (BAR), Melbourne, Australia

2 July 1954   Ivor Germain (BAR) L PTS 15 Pat Ford (A), Melbourne, Australia. Ford was not recognised as champion by the British Commonwealth and Empire Board on its formation, 12 October 1954, and the title was declared vacant

Welterweight (147 lbs)

2 May 1892   Tom Williams (A) W CO 1 Bill Hatcher (E), NSC, London (144 lbs)

11 December 1893   Tom Williams (A) DREW 20 Cock Robin (E), NSC, London (146 lbs)

21 January 1895   Dick Burge (E) W CO 4 Tom Williams (A), NSC, London (142 lbs)

28 January 1897   Dick Burge (E) DREW 10 Eddie Connolly (C), Olympic Club, Birmingham (144 lbs). In moving up the weights, Burge allowed the title to lapse

26 January 1903   Eddie Connolly (C) W PTS 15 Tom Woodley (E), NSC, London (146 lbs). Connolly retired in 1905

8 August 1907   Joe White (C) W PTS 20 Andrew Jeptha (SA), National Athletic Club, Merthyr (146 lbs). Following the introduction of standard weights in 1909, the limit became recognised as 147 lbs

11 June 1913   Johnny Summers (E) W PTS 20 Sid Burns (E), Sydney, Australia

11 October 1913   Johnny Summers (E) W PTS 20 Arthur Evernden (E), Sydney, Australia

10 January 1914   Johnny Summers (E) L PTS 20 Tom McCormick (I), Sydney, Australia

14 February 1914   Tom McCormick (I) W CO 1 Johnny Summers (E), Sydney, Australia

21 March 1914   Tom McCormick (I) L PTS 20 Matt Wells (E), Sydney, Australia

6 May 1915   Fred Kay (A) W CO 11 Fred Dyer (W), Melbourne, Australia. With Wells beginning an American campaign, and unavailable, Kay was matched against Dyer for the Australian version of the title

4 December 1915   Fred Kay (A) L RSC 12 Tommy Uren (A), Melbourne, Australia

4 March 1916   Tommy Uren (A) W CO 14 Frankie O'Connor (A), Sydney, Australia

15 April 1916   Tommy Uren (A) L PTS 20 Fritz Holland (A), Sydney Australia

19 August 1916   Fritz Holland (A) L PTS 20 Tommy Uren (A), Sydney, Australia

4 November 1916   Tommy Uren (A) W PTS 20 Herb McCoy (A), Melbourne, Australia

18 January 1919   Tommy Uren (A) L PTS 20 Fred Kay (A), Sydney, Australia

7 June 1919   Fred Kay (A) DREW 20 Fritz Holland (A), Sydney, Australia

13 November 1919   Matt Wells (E) L PTS 20 Johnny Basham (W), Holborn Stadium, London

12 April 1920   Johnny Basham (W) W PTS 20 Fred Kay (A), NSC, London

9 June 1920   Johnny Basham (W) L CO 9 Ted Kid Lewis (E), Olympia, London

19 November 1920   Ted Kid Lewis (E) W CO 10 Johnny Basham (W), Albert Hall, London

12 May 1922   Bermondsey Billy Wells (E) W PTS 10 Frank Barrieau (C), Montreal, Canada. Never recognised in Britain, Wells' claim immediately faded away

3 July 1924   Ted Kid Lewis (E) W PTS 20 Hamilton Johnny Brown (S), Albert Hall, London

26 November 1924   Ted Kid Lewis (E) L PTS 20 Tommy Milligan (S), Industrial Hall, Edinburgh. Milligan, unable to make the weight, relinquished the title following his European title win over Bruno Frattini in June 1925

20 October 1928   Jack Carroll (A) W PTS 15 Harry Mason (E), Sydney, Australia

1 December 1928   Jack Carroll (A) L DIS 11 Charlie Purdie (NZ), Sydney, Australia

7 June 1929   Charlie Purdie (NZ) L RSC 4 Wally Hancock (A), Leichardt, Australia

12 July 1929   Wally Hancock (A) W RSC 12 Charlie Purdie (NZ), Leichardt, Australia

7 January 1930   Wally Hancock (A) DREW 15 Tommy Fairhall (A), Leichardt, Australia

7 March 1930   Wally Hancock (A) L PTS 15 Tommy Fairhall (A), Leichardt, Australia

24 October 1930   Tommy Fairhall (A) W PTS 15 Wally Hancock (A), Leichardt, Australia. Fairhall relinquished his claim to the title in December 1930

21 April 1934   Jack Carroll (A) W RSC 9 Billy Townsend (C), Melbourne, Australia

19 November 1934   Jack Carroll (A) W PTS 15 Billy Martin (A), Sydney, Australia

16 September 1935   Jack Carroll (A) NC 6 Paul Schaffer (C), Sydney, Australia. Carroll retired in February 1938

27 January 1951   Eddie Thomas (W) W CO 13 Pat Patrick (SA), Johannesburg, South Africa

16 October 1951   Eddie Thomas (W) L PTS 15 Wally Thom (E), Harringay Arena, London

24 July 1952   Wally Thom (E) L CO 9 Cliff Curvis (W), The Stadium, Liverpool

8 December 1952   Cliff Curvis (W) L PTS 15 Gerald Dreyer (SA), Johannesburg, South Africa

15 January 1954   Gerald Dreyer (SA) L RSC 7 Barry Brown (NZ), Wellington, New Zealand. Brown lost the title when kayoed in the 11th round by Australia's George Barnes on 24 November 1954 in Sydney

Middleweight (160 lbs)

30 August 1887   Chesterfield Goode (E) W RTD 15 Tom Lees (A), Lambeth School of Arms, London (158 lbs)

7 February 1890   Chesterfield Goode (E) L PTS 12 Toff Wall (E), Pelican Club, London (158 lbs). Wall forfeited title on 19 October 1891 after walking out of a bout against Australian Billy McCarthy

20 August 1892   Jim Hall (A) W CO 4 Ted Pritchard (E), Nr Brighton (158 lbs). Hall was not recognised after March 1893, having moved up in weight to challenge Bob Fitzsimmons

20 April 1894   Lackie Thompson (S) W CO 1 Patsy Donovan (SA), Johannesburg, South Africa (154 lbs)

29 September 1894   Lackie Thompson (S) L CO 12 Bill Heffernan (NZ), Johannesburg, South Africa (154 lbs)

30 March 1895   Bill Heffernan (NZ) W CO 5 Billy Kelly (I), Johannesburg, South Africa (154 lbs)

2 May 1896   Bill Heffernan (NZ) W CO 13 Arthur Tully (A), Johannesburg, South Africa (154 lbs)

5 September 1896   Bill Heffernan (NZ) L CO 18 Bill Doherty (A), Johannesburg, South Africa (154 lbs)

3 October 1896   Bill Doherty (A) W CO 5 Tom Duggan (A), Johannesburg, South Africa (154 lbs). By the following year, Doherty had outgrown the division

7 August 1897   Billy Edwards (A) W PTS 25 Mick Dunn (A), Johannesburg, South Africa (154 lbs)

20 October 1897   Billy Edwards (A) W PTS 20 Jack Valentine (A), Johannesburg, South Africa (154 lbs)

27 December 1897   Billy Edwards (A) W RTD 11 Tom Duggan (A), Johannesburg, South Africa (154 lbs)

23 May 1898   Dido Plumb (E) W CO 4 Billy Edwards (A), NSC, London (154 lbs)

1 May 1899   Dido Plumb (E) W CO 9 Bill Heffernan (NZ), NSC, London (154 lbs)

19 March 1900   Dido Plumb (E) W RSC 8 Jem Ryan (A), NSC, London (154 lbs). Plumb retired in 1901

15 June 1901   Tom Duggan (A) W CO 10 Bill Heffernan (NZ), Durban, South Africa (154 lbs)

24 November 1902   Jack Palmer (E) W PTS 15 Eddie Connolly (C), NSC, London (158 lbs). After making 158 lbs for the last time on 7 May 1904, Palmer's title claim lapsed

8 April 1903   Tom Duggan (A) L PTS 20 Jewey Cooke (E), Johannesburg, South Africa (154 lbs)

4 July 1903   Jewey Cooke (E) W PTS 20 Jim Holloway (SA), Johannesburg, South Africa (154 lbs)

1 October 1904   Jewey Cooke (E) L PTS 20 Tom Dingey (C), Johannesburg, South Africa (154 lbs)

18 March 1905   Tom Dingey (C) L PTS 20 Jack Lalor (SA), Johannesburg, South Africa (154 lbs)

13 May 1905   Jack Lalor (SA) L PTS 20 Ted Nelson (A), Johannesburg, South Africa (154 lbs)

1 July 1905   Ted Nelson (A) L PTS 20 Tom Dingey (C), Johannesburg, South Africa (158 lbs)

11 November 1905   Tom Dingey (C) W PTS 20 Jewey Cooke (E), Johannesburg, South Africa (158 lbs). The South African version of the 154/158 lbs title petered out when Dingey left for Britain in November 1905

22 April 1907   Sam Langford (C) W CO 4 Tiger Smith (W), NSC, London (158 lbs). Unable to find suitable opposition at the weight, Langford's claim lapsed after February 1911

16 October 1908   Ed Williams (A) W RSC 15 Pat O'Keefe (E), Melbourne, Australia. Despite O'Keefe not being the current British champion, the Australian promoters still billed this for their version of the title

26 April 1909   Ed Williams (A) W PTS 20 Arthur Cripps (A), Melbourne, Australia

11 August 1909   Ed Williams (A) W PTS 20 Arthur Cripps (A), Brisbane, Australia

11 March 1910   Ed Williams (A) L PTS 20 Arthur Cripps (A), Sydney, Australia. With Williams overweight, following his victory, Cripps took over the former's claim

20 August 1910   Arthur Cripps (A) W PTS 20 Jerry Jerome (A), Brisbane, Australia

12 October 1910   Arthur Cripps (A) L PTS 20 Dave Smith (A), Brisbane, Australia. The Australian version of the title temporarily lapsed, with Smith moving up to light-heavy early in 1911

1 February 1913   Jerry Jerome (A) W RSC 12 Arthur Cripps (A), Brisbane, Australia

20 September 1913   Jerry Jerome (A) L PTS 20 Arthur Evernden (E), Brisbane, Australia

18 August 1914   Arthur Evernden (E) L DIS 10 Mick King (A), Brisbane, Australia

12 June 1915   Mick King (A) L CO 10 Les Darcy (A), Sydney, Australia

9 October 1915   Les Darcy (A) W RTD 6 Fred Dyer (W), Sydney, Australia. Darcy died on 24 March 1917

19 June 1922   Ted Kid Lewis (E) W CO 11 Frankie Burns (A), Holland Park Rink, London

20 November 1922   Ted Kid Lewis (E) W PTS 20 Roland Todd (E), Holland Park Rink, London

15 February 1923   Ted Kid Lewis (E) L PTS 20 Roland Todd (E), Albert Hall, London. Todd forfeited his title claim in June 1926, due to his continued absence in America

20 February 1926   Len Johnson (E) W PTS 20 Harry Collings (A), Sydney, Australia. Unable to fight for a title in Britain because of his colour, and with Australia not recognising Roland Todd as champion, Johnson was matched against Collings, the Australian champion, for the vacant crown

17 April 1926   Len Johnson (E) W CO 19 Alf Stewart (A), Sydney, Australia

8 May 1926   Len Johnson (E) W CO 11 Tommy Uren (A), Sydney, Australia

12 July 1926   Tommy Milligan (S) W RSC 14 George West (E), Holland Park Rink, London

10 September 1926   Len Johnson (E) W PTS 20 George West (E), Belle Vue, Manchester

7 October 1926   Tommy Milligan (S) W RSC 14 Ted Moore (E), Albert Hall, London

1 November 1926   Len Johnson (E) W PTS 20 George West (E), Belle Vue, Manchester

3 January 1927   Len Johnson (E) W PTS 20 Len Harvey (E), The Ring, London

27 January 1927   Tommy Milligan (S) W RSC 14 Ted Moore (E), Albert Hall, London

31 January 1927   Len Johnson (E) W PTS 15 George West (E), Westgate Street Hippodrome, Cardiff. Johnson relinquished his Australian title claim on 1 January 1928, when he announced that he was moving into the light-heavyweight division

14 March 1928   Tommy Milligan (S) L DIS 9 Alex Ireland (S), Waverley Market Hall, Edinburgh

17 September 1928   Alex Ireland, (S) W PTS 15 Frank Moody (W), Waverley Market Hall, Edinburgh

16 May 1929   Alex Ireland (S) L CO 7 Len Harvey (E), Olympia, London

21 October 1929   Len Harvey (E) W PTS 15 Jack Hood (E), Holborn Stadium, London

18 December 1929   Len Harvey (E) DREW 15 Jack Hood (E), Olympia, London

22 May 1930   Len Harvey (E) W RSC 9 Steve McCall (S), Olympia, London

24 May 1931   Del Fontaine (C) W PTS 10 Ted Moore (E), Sasakatton, Canada. Although billed for the Canadian version of the title, there was no real recognition forth-coming for the winner, even in Canada

19 June 1931   Del Fontaine (C) L CO 5 Ted Moore (E), Sasakatton, Canada. The Canadian version of the title lapsed, as Moore never fought again

22 June 1931   Len Harvey (E) W PTS 15 Jack Hood (E), Albert Hall, London

21 March 1932   Len Harvey (E) W PTS 15 Jock McAvoy (E), Belle Vue, Manchester

12 December 1932   Len Harvey (E) W PTS 15 Jack Casey (E), St James' Hall, Newcastle

10 April 1933   Len Harvey (E) L PTS 15 Jock McAvoy (E), Belle Vue, Manchester

9 October 1933   Jock McAvoy (E) W CO 10 Archie Sexton (E), Belle Vue, Manchester

24 June 1935   Jock McAvoy (E) W PTS 15 Al Burke (A), Belle Vue, Manchester

25 October 1937   Jock McAvoy (E) W RTD 11 Jack Hyams (E), Belle Vue, Manchester

22 May 1939   Jock McAvoy (E) W PTS 15 Ginger Sadd (E), Belle Vue, Manchester. With the BBBoC considering that the title had been vacant since 1926, this would be the last time McAvoy would defend his version of the championship, prior to retiring in September 1945

26 February 1940   Ron Richards (A) W DIS 11 Fred Henneberry (A), Sydney, Australia. Having arrived home from a trip to Britain, Henneberry was matched against the defending Australian champion, Richards, for the vacant Empire title. This after the BBBoC had refused to sanction Henneberry v Jack McAvoy as a championship fight on the grounds that the former was not a national champion

16 December 1940   Ron Richards (A) W DIS 12 Fred Henneberry (A), Sydney, Australia. Richards, having announced his retirement in January 1941, came back in September that year and was later matched to contest the

Australian version of the vacant championship against old rival, Fred Henneberry

27 November 1941   Ron Richards (A) W DIS 13 Fred Henneberry (A), Sydney, Australia. Richards retired in May 1942

26 January 1948   Bos Murphy (NZ) W PTS 15 Vince Hawkins (E), Albert Hall, London

18 May 1948   Bos Murphy (NZ) L CO 1 Dick Turpin (E), Highfield Road, Coventry

28 June 1948   Dick Turpin W PTS 15 Vince Hawkins (E), Villa Park, Birmingham

20 June 1949   Dick Turpin (E) W PTS 15 Albert Finch (E), St Andrew's, Birmingham

6 September 1949   Dick Turpin (E) L CO 1 Dave Sands (A), Harringay Arena, London

9 May 1952   Dave Sands (A) W CO 5 Al Bourke (A), Melbourne, Australia. Sands was killed in a road accident on 11 August 1952

21 October 1952   Randy Turpin (E) W PTS 15 George Angelo (SA), Harringay Arena, London. Turpin relinquished the title on 12 May 1954

12 December 1952   Al Bourke (A) W PTS 15 Ron Toohey (A), Melbourne, Australia. Billed for the title after the BBBoC ignored Australian claims that their champion should have been involved in any title shake up

17 April 1953   Al Bourke (A) W PTS 15 Alfie Sands (A), Melbourne, Australia

17 July 1953   Al Bourke (A) W RSC 11 Carlo Marchini (A), Melbourne, Australia

20 November 1953   Al Bourke (A) W CO 13 Graham Higham (A), Brisbane, Australia

18 December 1953   Al Bourke (A) W RTD 10 Don Johnson (A), Melbourne, Australia. Bourke retired on 1 January 1954

14 September 1954   Johnny Sullivan (E) W CO 1 Gordon Hazell (E), Harringay Arena, London. Sullivan lost the title to England's Pat McAteer on 16 June 1955, following a ninth-round disqualification defeat at the Liverpool Stadium

L.Heavyweight (175 lbs)

11 November 1911   Dave Smith (A) W PTS 20 Bandsman Rice (E) Sydney, Australia

15 April 1913   Dave Smith (A) W CO 18 Jerry Jerome (A), Sydney, Australia

13 August 1913   Dave Smith (A) W RTD 11 Jerry Jerome (A), Brisbane, Australia. Smith relinquished the title in March 1915

26 March 1923 Jack Bloomfield (E) W RTD 5 Horace Jones (C), NSC, London

17 May 1923 Jack Bloomfield (E) W RTD 13 Dave Magill (I), Olympia, London. Bloomfield retired in August 1924

31 January 1927 Tom Berry (E) W PTS 20 Dave Magill (I), Belle Vue, Manchester

25 April 1927 Tom Berry (E) L PTS 20 Gipsy Daniels (W), Holland Park Rink, London. Daniels relinquished the title in November 1927, when dissatisfied with the purse offer for his next defence

10 July 1939 Len Harvey (E) W PTS 15 Jock McAvoy (E), White City, London

20 June 1942 Len Harvey (E) L CO 2 Freddie Mills (E), White Hart Lane, London. Mills retired on 25 January 1950

10 June 1952 Randy Turpin (E) W RSC 11 Don Cockell (E), White City, London. Turpin relinquished the title on 3 November 1955, following a second-round kayo defence over Alex Buxton (England) at London's Harringay Arena on 26 April 1955

Heavyweight (175 lbs+)

11 November 1889 Peter Jackson (A) W DIS 2 Jem Smith (E), Pelican Club, London

20 October 1890 Peter Jackson (A) DREW 8 Joe Goddard (A), Melbourne, Australia

30 May 1892 Peter Jackson (A) W CO 10 Frank Slavin (A), NSC, London. Jackson retired temporarily in 1892

27 January 1896 Dan Creedon (NZ) W CO 2 Jem Smith (E), NSC, London. Really a middleweight, Creedon returned to the USA to challenge for the world 160 lbs title

2 December 1899 Peter Jackson (A) DREW 25 Cyclone Billy Warren (A), Melbourne, Australia. Jackson died on 13 July 1901

13 October 1902 Billy McColl (A) W CO 4 Bill Doherty (A), Sydney, Australia

3 March 1903 Billy McColl (A) W RSC 6 Dan Creedon (NZ), Sydney, Australia

9 September 1905 Billy McColl (A) L CO 11 Tim Murphy (A), Sydney, Australia

28 April 1906 Tim Murphy (A) L CO 3 Bill Squires (A), Melbourne, Australia

7 November 1906 Bill Squires (A) W CO 1 Bill Smith (A), Melbourne, Australia

22 December 1906 Bill Squires (A) W CO 1 Mike Williams (SA), Melbourne, Australia

30 April 1908 Bill Squires (A) W CO 1 Jem Roche (I), Dublin, Ireland

3 February 1909 Bill Squires (A) L CO 17 Bill Lang (A), Sydney, Australia

25 October 1909 Bill Lang (A) W CO 20 Bill Squires (A), Melbourne, Australia

27 December 1909 Bill Lang (A) W CO 12 Bob Fitzsimmons (A), Sydney, Australia

17 January 1910 Bill Lang (A) W CO 7 Bill Squires (A), Sydney, Australia

11 April 1910 Bill Lang (A) L PTS 20 Tommy Burns (C), Sydney, Australia. Burns announced his retirement in January 1911

18 January 1911 P.O. Curran (I) W DIS 1 Bill Lang (A), Olympia, London

24 February 1911 P.O. Curran (I) L DIS 2 Dan Flynn (I), Free Trade Hall, Manchester

8 March 1911 Dan Flynn (I) L PTS 20 Bombardier Billy Wells (E), Olympia, London

24 April 1911 Bombardier Billy Wells (E) W CO 6 Iron Hague (E), NSC, London

9 August 1911 Bill Lang (A) W CO 5 Bill Squires (A), Brisbane, Australia. Not recognising his disqualification defeat at the hands of P.O. Curran, and backed by the Australian authorities, Lang continued to claim the title

18 December 1911 Bombardier Billy Wells (E) W CO 11 Fred Storbeck (SA), NSC, London

6 December 1912 Bombardier Billy Wells (E) W CO 2 George Rodel (SA), King's Hall, London

3 May 1913 Bill Lang (A) W PTS 20 P.O. Curran (I), Sydney, Australia

6 June 1913 Bombardier Billy Wells (E) W CO 13 Packey Mahoney (I), NSC, London

14 August 1913 Bombardier Billy Wells (E) W CO 15 Pat O'Keefe (E), The Ring, London

16 August 1913 Bill Lang (A) W PTS 20 P.O. Curran (I), Sydney, Australia

10 September 1913 Bombardier Billy Wells (E) W CO 10 Gunner Moir (E), Canterbury Music Hall, London

5 November 1913 Bill Lang (A) L RSC 10 Dave Smith (A), Melbourne, Australia

14 January 1914 Bombardier Billy Wells (E) W RTD 10 Gunner Rawles (I), Theatre Royal, Belfast

3 March 1914 Bombardier Billy Wells (E) W CO 4 Bandsman Blake, The Palladium, London

30 April 1914 Bombardier Billy Wells (E) W PTS 20 Bandsman Rice (E), The Stadium, Liverpool

30 June 1914 Bombardier Billy Wells (E) W CO 2 Colin Bell (A), Olympia, London

24 February 1915   Bombardier Billy Wells (E) W CO 6 Bandsman Rice (E), Grand Opera House, Belfast

31 May 1915   Bombardier Billy Wells (E) W CO 9 Dick Smith (E), The Ring, London

27 December 1915   Bombardier Billy Wells (E) W CO 1 Bandsman Rice (E), The Stadium, Liverpool

21 February 1916   Bombardier Billy Wells (E) W CO 3 Dick Smith (E), Golders Green Hippodrome, London

31 March 1916   Bombardier Billy Wells (E) W CO 5 P.O. Curran (I), Old Cosmo Rink, Plymouth

26 August 1916   Bombardier Billy Wells (E) W RTD 9 Dick Smith (E), St James' Hall, Newcastle

12 December 1916   Bombardier Billy Wells (E) W RSC 2 Dan Voyles (I), NSC, London

26 December 1916   Dave Smith (A) W CO 10 Bill Squires (A), Sydney, Australia

17 April 1917   Dave Smith (A) W PTS 20 Albert Lloyd (A), Sydney, Australia. Smith retired in June 1917

27 February 1919   Bombardier Billy Wells (E) L CO 5 Joe Beckett (E), Holborn Stadium, London

17 June 1919   Joe Beckett (E) W CO 2 Frank Goddard (E), Olympia, London

5 March 1920   Joe Beckett (E) W CO 5 Dick Smith (E), Albert Hall, London

10 May 1920   Joe Beckett (E) W CO 3 Bombardier Billy Wells (E), Olympia, London

17 July 1920   Joe Beckett (E) W RTD 7 Tommy Burns (C), Albert Hall, London

12 September 1921   Joe Beckett (E) W RSC 12 Boy McCormick (I), Royal Opera House, London

10 April 1922   Joe Beckett (E) W DIS 6 George Cook (A), Holland Park Rink, London

14 March 1923   Joe Beckett (E) W CO 17 Dick Smith (E), Holland Park Rink, London. Beckett retired in October 1923

27 January 1926   Phil Scott (E) W DIS 17 George Cook (A), Industrial Hall, Edinburgh

18 March 1926   Phil Scott (E) W CO 3 Frank Goddard (E), Albert Hall, London

30 April 1926   Phil Scott (E) W RTD 10 Boy McCormick (I), Belle Vue, Manchester

10 July 1926   Phil Scott (E) W PTS 20 Tom Heeney (NZ), The Dell, Southampton

13 June 1931   Phil Scott (E) L CO 2 Larry Gains (C), Tiger's Ground, Leicester

20 September 1931   Larry Gains (C) W PTS 10 Jack Renault (C), Toronto, Canada

28 January 1932   Larry Gains (C) DREW 15 Don McCorkindale (SA), Albert Hall, London

3 March 1932   Larry Gains (C) W PTS 15 Don McCorkindale (SA), Albert Hall, London

18 May 1933   Larry Gains (C) W PTS 15 George Cook (A), Olympia, London

8 February 1934   Larry Gains (C) L PTS 15 Len Harvey (E), Albert Hall, London

4 June 1934   Len Harvey (E) L RTD 12 Jack Petersen (W), White City, London

10 September 1934   Jack Petersen (W) W RTD 13 Larry Gains (C), White City, London

17 December 1934   Jack Petersen (W) W PTS 15 George Cook (A), Albert Hall, London

29 January 1936   Jack Petersen (W) W PTS 15 Len Harvey (E), Empire Pool, Wembley

23 April 1936   Jack Petersen (W) W PTS 15 Jock McAvoy (E), Empress Hall, London

17 August 1936   Jack Petersen (W) L RSC 3 Ben Foord (SA), Tiger's Ground, Leicester

15 March 1937   Ben Foord (SA) L PTS 15 Tommy Farr (W), Harringay Arena, London. Farr forfeited title on 11 August 1937 after signing to fight Maurice Strickland in Toronto

10 March 1939   Len Harvey (E) W RTD 13 Larry Gains (C), Harringay Arena, London. Harvey retired on 21 November 1942

15 September 1944   Jack London (E) W PTS 15 Freddie Mills (E), Belle Vue, Manchester

17 July 1945   Jack London (E) L CO 6 Bruce Woodcock (E), White Hart Lane, London

26 March 1949   Bruce Woodcock (E) W CO 3 Johnny Ralph (SA), Johannesburg, South Africa

2 June 1949   Bruce Woodcock (E) W CO 14 Freddie Mills (E), White City, London

14 November 1950   Bruce Woodcock (E) L RTD 11 Jack Gardner (E), Earls Court Exhibition Centre, London

11 March 1952   Jack Gardner (E) L PTS 15 Johnny Williams (W), Earls Court Exhibition Centre, London

13 October 1952   Johnny Williams (W) W RTD 7 Johnny Arthur (SA), Granby Halls, Leicester

12 May 1953   Johnny Williams (W) L PTS 15 Don Cockell (E), Harringay Arena, London

30 January 1954   Don Cockell (E) W PTS 15 Johnny Arthur (SA), Johannesburg, South Africa. Cockell forfeited the title on 1 May 1956 for failing to defend

European Title Bouts During 1996-97

All of last season's title bouts are shown in date order within their weight division and give the boxers' respective weights, along with the scorecard, if going to a decision. There is also a short summary of any bout that involved a British contestant and British officials, where applicable, are listed.

Flyweight
13 September 1996   Jesper Jensen 7.13½ (Denmark) W PTS 12 Keith Knox 7.10¾ (Scotland), Ringsted, Denmark. In an extremely competitive fight, which Knox forced all the way, the clever southpaw champion was good value for his points win, his fast, accurate counters seeing him home. However, it takes two to make a fight and the challenger was given a good reception from a sporting crowd for his part in what was an invigorating contest.

15 November 1996   Jesper Jensen 8.0 (Denmark) W PTS 12 Luigi Camputaro 8.0 (Italy), Copenhagen, Denmark. Referee: Richie Davies. Judge: John Keane.

2 May 1997   Jesper Jensen 7.13½ (Denmark) W RSC 8 Paul Weir 7.13½ (Scotland), Randers, Denmark. Despite making a good start, Weir ultimately slumped to a disappointing eighth round stoppage defeat as he found the champion a shade too powerful for him. The end came at 1.24 of the session after he was bowled over for a mandatory eight count, the effects of a southpaw left cross, and again floored from a flurry of blows that left him a demoralised, beaten fighter.

13 June 1997   Jesper Jensen 7.13¾ (Denmark) L CO 10 David Guerault 7.13 (France), Slagelse, Denmark. Judge: Larry O'Connell.

Bantamweight
30 November 1996   Johnny Bredahl 8.5½ (Denmark) W RSC 5 Harold Geier 8.5½ (Austria), Wiener Neustadt, Austria.

14 March 1997   Johnny Bredahl 8.5¾ (Denmark) W RSC 3 Drew Docherty 8.5¾ (Scotland), Odense, Denmark. Using his left lead as a range finder for the right cross, Bredahl quickly got to his challenger, breaking and bloodying his nose in the first, while Docherty's only contribution came in the shape of a handful of left jabs. Although trying to turn things around in the third, the Scot was caught by a solid straight left and never really recovered, taking a mandatory eight count before being rescued by the referee.

S. Bantamweight
11 July 1996   Vincenzo Belcastro 8.9¾ (Italy) L RSC 8 Salim Medjkoune 8.8¾ (France), Pavia, Italy. Referee: Paul Thomas. Judge: John Keane.

29 December 1996   Salim Medkjoune 8.9¾ (France) L CO 1 Martin Krastev 8.9¾ (Bulgaria), Clermont Ferrand, France. Judge: Larry O'Connell.

20 May 1997   Martin Krastev 8.9¼ (Bulgaria) L CO 4 Spencer Oliver 8.9¾ (England), Lee Valley Leisure Centre, Edmonton, England. Following a tough first round when Oliver was shaken from the effects of a left hook, he tightened his defence up and never again allowed the dangerous Bulgarian another free shot, while, at the same time, putting his own punches together in winning fashion. Twice down in the second, Krastev soon knew what he was up against in terms of power and, following a chopping right hand to the side of the head, the champion went down to be counted out, despite getting to his feet at the count of seven.

Featherweight
3 February 1997   Billy Hardy 8.13 (England) W PTS 12 Steve Robinson 8.13 (Wales), Crowtree Leisure Centre, Sunderland, England. Scorecards: Paul Thomas 118-110, Richie Davies 119-110, Mickey Vann 117-112. Referee: Roy Francis. With both men looking for the win that might lead them to a fight with Prince Naseem Hamed, it was the champion who came out on top, despite being badly cut over the right eye. It was certainly rough and tough, both receiving several warnings, but the expected strong finish from Robinson, especially with the bodywork, failed to materialise and the fight ended with Hardy boxing his way home.

S. Featherweight
17 September 1996   Anatoly Alexandrov 9.3¾ (Kazakhstan) W RSC 10 Pedro Ferrados 9.4 (Spain), Porrino, Spain. Referee: John Coyle. Alexandrov relinquished the title in October 1996 to chase a world title shot.

2 November 1996   Julien Lorcy 9.3 (France) W RSC 7 Boris Sinitsin 9.3¾ (Russia), Levallois Perret, France. Referee: Mickey Vann. Lorcy relinquished the title immediately following his win in order to challenge for a world championship.

6 April 1997   Djamel Lifa 9.3 (France) W RSC 6 Moussa Sangare 9.3 (France), Thiais, France.

Lightweight
15 February 1997   Angel Mona 9.8¼ (France) L RSC 5 Manuel Carlos Fernandes 9.4 (France), Thiais, France.

29 March 1997   Manuel Carlos Fernandes 9.8½ (France) L RSC 11 Oscar Garcia Cano 9.8½ (Spain), Grande Synthe, France. Referee: Roy Francis. Judge: Richie Davies.

L. Welterweight
18 October 1996   Soren Sondergaard 9.12½ (Denmark) W PTS 12 Carl Wright 9.13 (England), Vejle, Denmark. Scorecards: 120-106, 120-106, 120-108. Despite losing on points by the proverbial mile, Wright produced a brave and determined performance to not only stay in the fight but to prove a danger until the final bell. While Sondergaard's

better boxing ultimately won the day, with both men cut on the left eyebrow and both down in a dramatic and exciting third round, the result could never be taken for granted and the challenger deserved all the credit that came his way.

24 January 1997 Soren Sondergaard 9.13¾ (Denmark) W RSC 7 Viktor Baranov 9.11¾ (Russia), Copenhagen, Denmark.

Welterweight
15 February 1997 Andrei Pestriaev 10.6 (Russia) W RSC 12 Jose Luis Navarro 10.5½ (Spain), Thiais, France. The title had been vacated in October 1996 when Patrick Charpentier decided to chase a world title shot.

L. Middleweight
28 September 1996 Faouzi Hattab 10.13 (France) W RSC 9 Ahmet Dottuev 10.12½ (Balkharia), Broadway Theatre, Barking, England. Judge: Richie Davies. The title had become vacant in May 1996 on Laurent Boudouani being given a crack at the WBA world championship.

20 December 1996 Faouzi Hattab 10.12¾ (France) L PTS 12 David Ciarlante 10.13¾ (Italy), Cagliari, Italy. Scorecards: 113-115, 114-115, 113-114. Referee: Roy Francis.

10 May 1997 David Ciarlante 10.13½ (Italy) W RSC 9 Javier Martinez 10.11 (Spain), Rome, Italy. Referee: John Coyle.

Middleweight
19 October 1996 Alexandre Zaitsev 11.5½ (Russia) L PTS 12 Hassine Cherifi 11.5½ (France), Berck sur Mer, France. Scorecards: Mickey Vann 111-118, Dave Parris 114-116, 110-120. Referee: Mickey Vann.

25 January 1997 Hassine Cherifi 11.5¾ (France) W PTS 12 Branco Sobot 11.5¾ (Croatia), Stuttgart, Germany. Scorecards: Paul Thomas 116-113, 115-113, 116-112.

26 April 1997 Hassine Cherifi 11.4½ (France) W RSC 6 Neville Brown 11.5¾ (England), Greenbank Leisure Centre, Swadlincote, England. Having knocked Cherifi down twice and imposed a standing count on his rival, Brown somehow let the fight slip away when allowing himself to be drawn into a tear up and, although seemingly still in control, he began to take unnecessary chances and was tagged more and more as the fight progressed. Then it happened. Into the sixth, a right uppercut and a left hook, followed by a big right hand, decked Brown for six and shortly afterwards, at 2.44 of the round, the referee called it off to save the latter from further punishment.

S. Middleweight
5 July 1996 Frederic Seillier 11.13½ (France) W PTS 12 Mauro Galvano 11.11 (Italy), Heyeres, France. Scorecards: Larry O'Connell 117-114, 117-111, 119-109. Referee: Roy Francis. Billed for the vacant title, following the abdication of Henry Wharton (promised a WBC title chance) in March 1996, Seillier himself gave up the belt in November 1996 in order to have a crack at WBO champion, Steve Collins.

15 March 1997 Andrei Shkalikov 12.0 (Russia) W RTD 8 Mauro Galvano 11.12½ (Italy), Mazara, Italy. Referee: Dave Parris. Judge: John Keane.

L. Heavyweight
1 March 1997 Crawford Ashley 12.7 (England) W CO 3 Roberto Dominguez 12.5 (Spain), Everton Park Sports Centre, Liverpool, England. Following Eddy Smulders' decision to vacate the title in November 1996, in order to concentrate on a world title challenge, Ashley was matched against the powerful Dominguez. Although fancied at home, the Spaniard was never in the hunt as the Englishman controlled the fight with solid jabs prior to unleashing a terrific right uppercut that sent Dominguez crashing to be counted out by the timekeeper at 1.08 of round three, while still being tended to by the referee.

31 May 1997 Crawford Ashley 12.6¼ (England) W PTS 12 Pascal Warusfel 12.5½ (France), Alfortville, France. Scorecards: 117-113, 116-112, 114-14. Affected by a badly damaged left hand, sustained in round three, Ashley's performance obviously suffered, while Warusfel gained in confidence to surprise a good many people with his display, especially during the latter stages. The champion made no excuses for his performance, being extremely critical of himself, but at the end of the day he had successfully defended the title away from home against an extremely durable opponent, despite being single handed.

Cruiserweight
22 February 1997 Johnny Nelson 13.8 (England) W RSC 7 Patrice Aouissi 13.8 (France), Berk sur Mer, France. The title had become vacant in January 1997, following the abdication of Akim Tafer, who looked to get a crack at the world championship. Taking the fight at two days notice after Terry Dunstan had been forced to withdraw, Nelson quickly got his act together to contain Aouissi before opening up with two left hands in the sixth to put the Frenchman down for a count of seven. Carrying on the good work in the seventh, Nelson again decked Aouissi, who, after getting up at six with his face in a bloody mess, was quickly rescued by the referee.

Heavyweight
2 November 1996 Zeljko Mavrovic 15.13 (Croatia) W RSC 2 Clifton Mitchell 16.8 (England), Garmisch Partenkirchen, Germany. Following a feeling out opening round, Mavrovic took over in the second, his big rights getting home and ultimately flooring Mitchell for counts of six and two, respectively, before the referee came to the challenger's rescue with 2.17 of the session completed. Although protesting vociferously, at the time of the stoppage, the Englishman had his back to Mavrovic and appeared to be on his way to a beating.

15 February 1997 Zeljko Mavrovic 16.0 (Croatia) W RSC 8 Julius Francis 16.7 (England), Vienna, Austria. Although making a bright start, by the fourth Francis was beginning to take a steady stream of punches from the fast-hitting champion, who was already controlling the fight from long range. Having taken a standing count in the seventh, he began to wilt in the eighth and a heavy left to the body put him down for a six count, prior to the referee waving it off.

European Champions, 1909-1997

Prior to 1946, the championship was contested under the auspices of the International Boxing Union, re-named that year as the European Boxing Union (EBU). The IBU had come into being when Victor Breyer, a Paris-based journalist and boxing referee who later edited the Annuaire du Ring (first edition in 1910), warmed to the idea of an organisation that controlled boxing right across Europe, regarding rules and championship fights between the champions of the respective countries. He first came to London at the end of 1909 to discuss the subject with the NSC, but went away disappointed. However, at a meeting between officials from Switzerland and France in March 1912, the IBU was initially formed and, by June of that year, had published their first ratings. By April 1914, Belgium had also joined the organisation, although it would not be until the war was over that the IBU really took off. Many of the early champions shown on the listings were the result of promoters, especially the NSC, billing their own championship fights. Although the (French dominated) IBU recognised certain champions, prior to being re-formed in May 1920, they did not find their administrative "feet" fully until other countries such as Italy (1922), Holland (1923), and Spain (1924), produced challengers for titles. Later in the 1920s, Germany (1926), Denmark (1928), Portugal (1929) and Romania (1929) also joined the fold. Unfortunately, for Britain, its representatives (Although the BBBoC, as we know it today, was formed in 1929, an earlier attempt to form a Board of Control had been initiated in April 1918 by the NSC and it was that body who were involved here) failed to reach agreement on the three judges' ruling, following several meetings with the IBU early in 1920 and, apart from Elky Clark (fly), Ernie Rice and Alf Howard (light), and Jack Hood (welter), who conformed to that stipulation, fighters from these shores would not be officially recognised as champions until the EBU was formed in 1946. This led to British fighters claiming the title after beating IBU titleholders, or their successors, under championship conditions in this country. The only men who did not come into this category were Kid Nicholson (bantam), and Ted Kid Lewis and Tommy Milligan (welter), who defeated men not recognised by the IBU. For the record, the first men recognised and authorised, respectively, as being champions of their weight classes by the IBU were: Sid Smith and Michel Montreuil (fly), Charles Ledoux (bantam), Jim Driscoll and Louis de Ponthieu (feather), Freddie Welsh and Georges Papin (light), Georges Carpentier and Albert Badoud (welter), Georges Carpentier and Ercole Balzac (middle), Georges Carpentier and Battling Siki (light-heavy and heavy).

EUROPEAN COUNTRY CODE

AU = Austria; BEL = Belgium; BUL = Bulgaria; CRO = Croatia; CZ = Czechoslovakia; DEN = Denmark; E = England; FIN = Finland; FR = France; GER = Germany; GRE = Greece; HOL = Holland; HUN = Hungary; ITA = Italy; KAZ = Kazakhstan; LUX = Luxembourg; NI = Northern Ireland; NOR = Norway; POR = Portugal; ROM = Romania; RUS = Russia; S = Scotland; SP = Spain; SWE = Sweden; SWI = Switzerland; TU = Turkey; UK = Ukraine; W = Wales; YUG = Yugoslavia.

Champions in **bold** denote those recognised by the IBU/EBU

*Undefeated champions (Does not include men who may have forfeited titles)

Title Holder	Country	Tenure	Title Holder	Country	Tenure	Title Holder	Country	Tenure
Flyweight (112 lbs)			**Louis Skena***	FR	1953-1954	Digger Stanley	E	1910-1912
Sid Smith	E	1913	**Nazzareno Giannelli**	ITA	1954-1955	**Charles Ledoux**	FR	1912-1921
Bill Ladbury	E	1913-1914	**Dai Dower**	W	1955	Bill Beynon	W	1913
Percy Jones	W	1914	**Young Martin**	SP	1955-1959	Tommy Harrison	E	1921-1922
Joe Symonds	E	1914	**Risto Luukkonen**	FIN	1959-1961	**Charles Ledoux**	FR	1922-1923
Tancy Lee	S	1914-1916	**Salvatore Burruni***	ITA	1961-1965	Bugler Harry Lake	E	1923
Jimmy Wilde	W	1914-1915	**Rene Libeer**	FR	1965-1966	Johnny Brown	E	1923-1928
Jimmy Wilde*	W	1916-1923	**Fernando Atzori**	ITA	1967-1972	**Henry Scillie***	BEL	1925-1928
Michel Montreuil	BEL	1923-1925	**Fritz Chervet**	SWI	1972-1973	Kid Nicholson	E	1928
Elky Clark*	S	1925-1927	**Fernando Atzori**	ITA	1973	Teddy Baldock	E	1928-1931
Victor Ferrand	SP	1927	**Fritz Chervet***	SWI	1973-1974	**Domenico Bernasconi**	ITA	1929
Emile Pladner	FR	1928-1929	**Franco Udella**	ITA	1974-1979	**Carlos Flix**	SP	1929-1931
Johnny Hill	S	1928-1929	**Charlie Magri***	E	1979-1983	**Lucien Popescu**	ROM	1931-1932
Eugene Huat	FR	1929	**Antoine Montero**	FR	1983-1984	**Domenico Bernasconi**	ITA	1932
Emile Degand	BEL	1929-1930	**Charlie Magri***	E	1984-1985	**Nicholas Biquet**	BEL	1932-1935
Kid Oliva	FR	1930	**Franco Cherchi**	ITA	1985	**Maurice Dubois**	SWI	1935-1936
Lucien Popescu	ROM	1930-1931	**Charlie Magri**	E	1985-1986	**Joseph Decico**	FR	1936
Jackie Brown	E	1931-1935	**Duke McKenzie***	E	1986-1988	**Aurel Toma**	ROM	1936-1937
Praxile Gyde	FR	1932-1935	**Eyup Can***	TU	1989-1990	**Nicholas Biquet**	BEL	1937-1938
Benny Lynch	S	1935-1938	**Pat Clinton***	S	1990-1991	**Aurel Toma**	ROM	1938-1939
Kid David*	BEL	1935-1936	**Salvatore Fanni**	ITA	1991-1992	**Ernst Weiss**	AU	1939
Ernst Weiss	AU	1936	**Robbie Regan***	W	1992-1993	**Gino Cattaneo**	ITA	1939-1941
Valentin Angelmann*	FR	1936-1938	**Luigi Camputaro**	ITA	1993-1994	**Gino Bondavalli***	ITA	1941-1943
Enrico Urbinati*	ITA	1938-1943	**Robbie Regan***	W	1994-1995	**Jackie Paterson**	S	1946
Raoul Degryse	BEL	1946-1947	**Luigi Camputaro***	ITA	1995-1996	**Theo Medina**	FR	1946-1947
Maurice Sandeyron	FR	1947-1949	**Jesper Jensen**	DEN	1996-1997	**Peter Kane**	E	1947-1948
Rinty Monaghan*	NI	1949-1950	**David Guerault**	FR	1997-	**Guido Ferracin**	ITA	1948-1949
Terry Allen	E	1950				**Luis Romero**	SP	1949-1951
Jean Sneyers*	BEL	1950-1951	**Bantamweight (118 lbs)**			**Peter Keenan**	S	1951-1952
Teddy Gardner*	E	1952	Joe Bowker	E	1910			

Title Holder	Country	Tenure
Jean Sneyers*	BEL	1952-1953
Peter Keenan	S	1953
John Kelly	NI	1953-1954
Robert Cohen*	FR	1954-1955
Mario D'Agata	ITA	1955-1958
Piero Rollo	ITA	1958-1959
Freddie Gilroy	NI	1959-1960
Pierre Cossemyns	BEL	1961-1962
Piero Rollo	ITA	1962
Alphonse Halimi	FR	1962
Piero Rollo	ITA	1962-1963
Mimoun Ben Ali	SP	1963
Risto Luukkonen	FIN	1963-1964
Mimoun Ben Ali	SP	1965
Tommaso Galli	ITA	1965-1966
Mimoun Ben Ali	SP	1966-1968
Salvatore Burruni*	ITA	1968-1969
Franco Zurlo	ITA	1969-1971
Alan Rudkin	E	1971
Agustin Senin*	SP	1971-1973
Johnny Clark*	E	1973-1974
Bob Allotey	SP	1974-1975
Daniel Trioulaire	FR	1975-1976
Salvatore Fabrizio	ITA	1976-1977
Franco Zurlo	ITA	1977-1978
Juan Francisco Rodriguez	SP	1978-1980
Johnny Owen*	W	1980
Valerio Nati	ITA	1980-1982
Giuseppe Fossati	ITA	1982-1983
Walter Giorgetti	ITA	1983-1984
Ciro de Leva*	ITA	1984-1986
Antoine Montero	FR	1986-1987
Louis Gomis*	FR	1987-1988
Fabrice Benichou	FR	1988
Vincenzo Belcastro*	ITA	1988-1990
Thierry Jacob*	FR	1990-1992
Johnny Bredahl*	DEN	1992
Vincenzo Belcastro	ITA	1993-1994
Prince Naseem Hamed*	E	1994-1995
John Armour*	E	1995-1996
Johnny Bredahl	DEN	1996-

S. Bantamweight (122 lbs)

Title Holder	Country	Tenure
Vincenzo Belcastro	ITA	1995-1996
Salim Medjkoune	FR	1996
Martin Krastev	BUL	1996-1997
Spencer Oliver	E	1997-

Featherweight (126 lbs)

Title Holder	Country	Tenure
Young Joey Smith	E	1911
Jean Poesy	FR	1911-1912
Jim Driscoll*	W	1912-1913
Ted Kid Lewis*	E	1913-1914
Louis de Ponthieu*	FR	1919-1920
Arthur Wyns	BEL	1920-1922
Billy Matthews	E	1922
Eugene Criqui*	FR	1922-1923
Edouard Mascart	FR	1923-1924
Charles Ledoux	FR	1924
Henri Hebrans	BEL	1924-1925
Antonio Ruiz	SP	1925-1928
Luigi Quadrini	ITA	1928-1929
Knud Larsen	DEN	1929
Jose Girones	SP	1929-1934
Maurice Holtzer*	FR	1935-1938
Phil Dolhem	BEL	1938-1939
Lucien Popescu	ROM	1939-1941
Ernst Weiss	AU	1941
Gino Bondavilli	ITA	1941-1945

Title Holder	Country	Tenure
Ermanno Bonetti*	ITA	1945-1946
Tiger Al Phillips	E	1947
Ronnie Clayton	E	1947-1948
Ray Famechon	FR	1948-1953
Jean Sneyers	BEL	1953-1954
Ray Famechon	FR	1954-1955
Fred Galiana*	SP	1955-1956
Cherif Hamia	FR	1957-1958
Sergio Caprari	ITA	1958-1959
Gracieux Lamperti	FR	1959-1962
Alberto Serti	ITA	1962-1963
Howard Winstone	W	1963-1967
Jose Legra*	SP	1967-1968
Manuel Calvo	SP	1968-1969
Tommaso Galli	ITA	1969-1970
Jose Legra*	SP	1970-1972
Gitano Jiminez	SP	1973-1975
Elio Cotena	ITA	1975-1976
Nino Jimenez	SP	1976-1977
Manuel Masso	SP	1977
Roberto Castanon*	SP	1977-1981
Salvatore Melluzzo	ITA	1981-1982
Pat Cowdell*	E	1982-1983
Loris Stecca*	ITA	1983
Barry McGuigan*	NI	1983-1985
Jim McDonnell*	E	1985-1987
Valerio Nati*	ITA	1987
Jean-Marc Renard*	BEL	1988-1989
Paul Hodkinson*	E	1989-1991
Fabrice Benichou	FR	1991-1992
Maurizio Stecca	ITA	1992-1993
Herve Jacob	FR	1993
Maurizio Stecca	ITA	1993
Stephane Haccoun	FR	1993-1994
Stefano Zoff	ITA	1994
Medhi Labdouni	FR	1994-1995
Billy Hardy	E	1995-

S. Featherweight (130 lbs)

Title Holder	Country	Tenure
Tommaso Galli	ITA	1971-1972
Domenico Chiloiro	ITA	1972
Lothar Abend	GER	1972-1974
Sven-Erik Paulsen*	NOR	1974-1976
Roland Cazeaux	FR	1976
Natale Vezzoli	ITA	1976-1979
Carlos Hernandez	SP	1979
Rodolfo Sanchez	SP	1979
Carlos Hernandez	SP	1979-1982
Cornelius Boza-Edwards*	E	1982
Roberto Castanon	SP	1982-1983
Alfredo Raininger	ITA	1983-1984
Jean-Marc Renard	BEL	1984
Pat Cowdell	E	1984-1985
Jean-Marc Renard*	BEL	1986-1987
Salvatore Curcetti	ITA	1987-1988
Piero Morello	ITA	1988
Lars Lund Jensen	DEN	1988
Racheed Lawal	DEN	1988-1989
Daniel Londas*	FR	1989-1991
Jimmy Bredahl*	DEN	1992
Regilio Tuur	HOL	1992-1993
Jacobin Yoma	FR	1993-1995
Anatoly Alexandrov*	KAZ	1995-1996
Julian Lorcy*	FR	1996
Djamel Lifa	FR	1997-

Lightweight (135 lbs)

Title Holder	Country	Tenure
Freddie Welsh	W	1909-1911
Matt Wells	E	1911-1912

Title Holder	Country	Tenure
Freddie Welsh*	W	1912-1914
Georges Papin	FR	1920-1921
Ernie Rice	E	1921-1922
Seaman Nobby Hall	E	1922-1923
Harry Mason	E	1923-1926
Fred Bretonnel	FR	1924
Lucien Vinez	FR	1924-1927
Luis Rayo*	SP	1927-1928
Aime Raphael	FR	1928-1929
Francois Sybille	BEL	1929-1930
Alf Howard	E	1930
Harry Corbett	E	1930-1931
Francois Sybille	BEL	1930-1931
Bep van Klaveren	HOL	1931-1932
Cleto Locatelli	ITA	1932
Francois Sybille	BEL	1932-1933
Cleto Locatelli*	ITA	1933
Francois Sybille	BEL	1934
Carlo Orlandi*	ITA	1934-1935
Enrico Venturi*	ITA	1935-1936
Vittorio Tamagnini	ITA	1936-1937
Maurice Arnault	FR	1937
Gustave Humery	FR	1937-1938
Aldo Spoldi*	ITA	1938-1939
Karl Blaho	AU	1940-1941
Bruno Bisterzo	ITA	1941
Ascenzo Botta	ITA	1941
Bruno Bisterzo	ITA	1941-1942
Ascenzo Botta	ITA	1942
Roberto Proietti	ITA	1942-1943
Bruno Bisterzo	ITA	1943-1946
Roberto Proietti*	ITA	1946
Emile Dicristo	FR	1946-1947
Kid Dussart	BEL	1947
Roberto Proietti	ITA	1947-1948
Billy Thompson	E	1948-1949
Kid Dussart	BEL	1949
Roberto Proietti*	ITA	1949-1950
Pierre Montane	FR	1951
Elis Ask	FIN	1951-1952
Jorgen Johansen	DEN	1952-1954
Duilio Loi*	ITA	1954-1959
Mario Vecchiatto	ITA	1959-1960
Dave Charnley	E	1960-1963
Conny Rudhof*	GER	1963-1964
Willi Quatuor*	GER	1964-1965
Franco Brondi	ITA	1965
Maurice Tavant	FR	1965-1966
Borge Krogh	DEN	1966-1967
Pedro Carrasco*	SP	1967-1969
Miguel Velazquez	SP	1970-1971
Antonio Puddu	ITA	1971-1974
Ken Buchanan*	S	1974-1975
Fernand Roelandts	BEL	1976
Perico Fernandez*	SP	1976-1977
Jim Watt*	S	1977-1979
Charlie Nash*	NI	1979-1980
Francisco Leon	SP	1980
Charlie Nash	NI	1980-1981
Joey Gibilisco	ITA	1981-1983
Lucio Cusma	ITA	1983-1984
Rene Weller	GER	1984-1986
Gert Bo Jacobsen	DEN	1986-1988
Rene Weller*	GER	1988
Policarpo Diaz*	SP	1988-1990
Antonio Renzo	ITA	1991-1992
Jean-Baptiste Mendy*	FR	1992-1994
Racheed Lawal	DEN	1994
Jean-Baptiste Mendy*	FR	1994-1995
Angel Mona	FR	1995-1997

Title Holder	Country	Tenure
Manuel Carlos Fernandes	FR	1997
Oscar Garcia Cano	SP	1997-

L. Welterweight (140 lbs)

Title Holder	Country	Tenure
Olli Maki	FIN	1964-1965
Juan Sombrita-Albornoz	SP	1965
Willi Quatuor*	GER	1965-1966
Conny Rudhof	GER	1967
Johann Orsolics	AU	1967-1968
Bruno Arcari*	ITA	1968-1970
Rene Roque	FR	1970-1971
Pedro Carrasco*	SP	1971-1972
Roger Zami	FR	1972
Cemal Kamaci	TU	1972-1973
Toni Ortiz	SP	1973-1974
Perico Fernandez*	SP	1974
Jose Ramon Gomez-Fouz	SP	1975
Cemal Kamaci*	TU	1975-1976
Dave Boy Green*	E	1976-1977
Primo Bandini	ITA	1977
Jean-Baptiste Piedvache	FR	1977-1978
Colin Power	E	1978
Fernando Sanchez	SP	1978-1979
Jose Luis Heredia	SP	1979
Jo Kimpuani	FR	1979-1980
Giuseppe Martinese	ITA	1980
Antonio Guinaldo	SP	1980-1981
Clinton McKenzie	E	1981-1982
Robert Gambini	FR	1982-1983
Patrizio Oliva*	ITA	1983-1985
Terry Marsh	E	1985-1986
Tusikoleta Nkalankete	FR	1987-1989
Efren Calamati	ITA	1989-1990
Pat Barrett	E	1990-1992
Valery Kayumba	ITA	1992-1993
Christian Merle	FR	1993-1994
Valery Kayumba	FR	1994
Khalid Rahilou*	FR	1994-1996
Soren Sondergaard	DEN	1996-

Welterweight (147 lbs)

Title Holder	Country	Tenure
Young Joseph	E	1910-1911
Georges Carpentier*	FR	1911-1912
Albert Badoud*	SWI	1915-1921
Johnny Basham	W	1919-1920
Ted Kid Lewis	E	1920-1924
Piet Hobin	BEL	1921-1925
Billy Mack	E	1923
Tommy Milligan	S	1924-1925
Mario Bosisio*	ITA	1925-1928
Leo Darton	BEL	1928
Alf Genon	BEL	1928-1929
Gustave Roth	BEL	1929-1932
Adrien Aneet	BEL	1932-1933
Jack Hood*	E	1933
Gustav Eder	GER	1934-1936
Felix Wouters	BEL	1936-1938
Saverio Turiello	ITA	1938-1939
Marcel Cerdan*	FR	1939-1942
Ernie Roderick	E	1946-1947
Robert Villemain*	FR	1947-1948
Livio Minelli	ITA	1949-1950
Michele Palermo	ITA	1950-1951
Eddie Thomas	W	1951
Charles Humez*	FR	1951-1952
Gilbert Lavoine	FR	1953-1954
Wally Thom	E	1954-1955
Idrissa Dione	FR	1955-1956
Emilio Marconi	ITA	1956-1958
Peter Waterman*	E	1958

Title Holder	Country	Tenure
Emilio Marconi	ITA	1958-1959
Duilio Loi*	ITA	1959-1963
Fortunato Manca*	ITA	1964-1965
Jean Josselin	FR	1966-1967
Carmelo Bossi	ITA	1967-1968
Fighting Mack	HOL	1968-1969
Silvano Bertini	ITA	1969
Jean Josselin	FR	1969
Johann Orsolics	AU	1969-1970
Ralph Charles	E	1970-1971
Roger Menetrey	FR	1971-1974
John H. Stracey*	E	1974-1975
Marco Scano	ITA	1976-1977
Jorgen Hansen	DEN	1977
Jorg Eipel	GER	1977
Alain Marion	FR	1977-1978
Jorgen Hansen	DEN	1978
Josef Pachler	AU	1978
Henry Rhiney	E	1978-1979
Dave Boy Green	E	1979
Jorgen Hansen*	DEN	1979-1981
Hans-Henrik Palm	DEN	1982
Colin Jones*	W	1982-1983
Gilles Elbilia	FR	1983-1984
Gianfranco Rosi	ITA	1984-1985
Lloyd Honeyghan*	E	1985-1986
Jose Varela	GER	1986-1987
Alfonso Redondo	SP	1987
Mauro Martelli*	SWI	1987-1988
Nino la Rocca	ITA	1989
Antoine Fernandez	FR	1989-1990
Kirkland Laing	E	1990
Patrizio Oliva*	ITA	1990-1992
Ludovic Proto	FR	1992-1993
Gary Jacobs*	S	1993-1994
Jose Luis Navarro	SP	1994-1995
Valery Kayumba	FR	1995
Patrick Charpentier*	FR	1995-1996
Andrei Pestriaev	RUS	1997-

L. Middleweight (154 lbs)

Title Holder	Country	Tenure
Bruno Visintin	ITA	1964-1966
Bo Hogberg	SWE	1966
Yolande Leveque	FR	1966
Sandro Mazzinghi*	ITA	1966-1968
Remo Golfarini	ITA	1968-1969
Gerhard Piaskowy	GER	1969-1970
Jose Hernandez	SP	1970-1972
Juan Carlos Duran	ITA	1972-1973
Jacques Kechichian	FR	1973-1974
Jose Duran	SP	1974-1975
Eckhard Dagge	GER	1975-1976
Vito Antuofermo	ITA	1976
Maurice Hope*	E	1976-1978
Gilbert Cohen	FR	1978-1979
Marijan Benes	YUG	1979-1981
Louis Acaries	FR	1981
Luigi Minchillo*	ITA	1981-1983
Herol Graham*	E	1983-1984
Jimmy Cable	E	1984
Georg Steinherr	GER	1984-1985
Said Skouma*	FR	1985-1986
Chris Pyatt	E	1986-1987
Gianfranco Rosi*	ITA	1987
Rene Jacquot*	FR	1988-1989
Edip Secovic	AU	1989
Giuseppe Leto	ITA	1989
Gilbert Dele*	FR	1989-1990
Said Skouma	FR	1991
Mourad Louati	HOL	1991

Title Holder	Country	Tenure
Jean-Claude Fontana	FR	1991-1992
Laurent Boudouani	FR	1992-1993
Bernard Razzano	FR	1993-1994
Javier Castillejos	SP	1994-1995
Laurent Boudouani*	FR	1995-1996
Faouzi Hattab	FR	1996
David Ciarlante	ITA	1996-

Middleweight (160 lbs)

Title Holder	Country	Tenure
Georges Carpentier*	FR	1912-1918
Ercole Balzac	FR	1920-1921
Gus Platts	E	1921
Johnny Basham	W	1921
Ted Kid Lewis	E	1921-1923
Roland Todd	E	1923-1924
Ted Kid Lewis	E	1924-1925
Bruno Frattini	ITA	1924-1925
Tommy Milligan	S	1925-1928
Rene Devos	BEL	1926-1927
Barthelemy Molina	FR	1928
Alex Ireland	S	1928-1929
Mario Bosisio	ITA	1928
Leone Jacovacci	ITA	1928-1929
Len Johnson	E	1928-1929
Marcel Thil	FR	1929-1930
Mario Bosisio	ITA	1930-1931
Poldi Steinbach	AU	1931
Hein Domgoergen	GER	1931-1932
Ignacio Ara	SP	1932-1933
Gustave Roth	BEL	1933-1934
Marcel Thil*	FR	1934-1938
Edouard Tenet	FR	1938
Bep van Klaveren	HOL	1938
Anton Christoforidis	GRE	1938-1939
Edouard Tenet	FR	1939
Josef Besselmann*	GER	1942-1943
Marcel Cerdan	FR	1947-1948
Cyrille Delannoit	BEL	1948
Marcel Cerdan*	FR	1948
Cyrille Delannoit	BEL	1948-1949
Tiberio Mitri*	ITA	1949-1950
Randy Turpin	E	1951-1954
Tiberio Mitri	ITA	1954
Charles Humez	FR	1954-1958
Gustav Scholz*	GER	1958-1961
John Cowboy McCormack	S	1961-1962
Chris Christensen	DEN	1962
Laszlo Papp*	HUN	1962-1965
Nino Benvenuti*	ITA	1965-1967
Juan Carlos Duran	ITA	1967-1969
Tom Bogs	DEN	1969-1970
Juan Carlos Duran	ITA	1970-1971
Jean-Claude Bouttier	FR	1971-1972
Tom Bogs*	DEN	1973
Elio Calcabrini	ITA	1973-1974
Jean-Claude Bouttier	FR	1974
Kevin Finnegan	E	1974-1975
Gratien Tonna*	FR	1975
Bunny Sterling	E	1976
Angelo Jacopucci	ITA	1976
Germano Valsecchi	ITA	1976-1977
Alan Minter	E	1977
Gratien Tonna	FR	1977-1978
Alan Minter*	E	1978-1979
Kevin Finnegan	E	1980
Matteo Salvemini	ITA	1980
Tony Sibson*	E	1980-1982
Louis Acaries	FR	1982-1984
Tony Sibson	E	1984-1985

Title Holder	Country	Tenure
Ayub Kalule	DEN	1985-1986
Herol Graham	E	1986-1987
Sumbu Kalambay*	ITA	1987
Pierre Joly	FR	1987-1988
Christophe Tiozzo*	FR	1988-1989
Francesco dell' Aquila	ITA	1989-1990
Sumbu Kalambay*	ITA	1990-1993
Agostino Cardamone*	ITA	1993-1994
Richie Woodhall*	E	1995-1996
Alexandre Zaitsev	RUS	1996
Hassine Cherifi	FR	1996-

S. Middleweight (168 lbs)

Title Holder	Country	Tenure
Mauro Galvano*	ITA	1990-1991
James Cook	E	1991-1992
Franck Nicotra*	FR	1992
Vincenzo Nardiello	ITA	1992-1993
Ray Close*	NI	1993
Vinzenzo Nardiello	ITA	1993-1994
Frederic Seillier*	FR	1994-1995
Henry Wharton*	E	1995-1996
Frederic Seillier*	FR	1996
Andrei Shkalikov	RUS	1997-

L. Heavyweight (175 lbs)

Title Holder	Country	Tenure
Georges Carpentier	FR	1913-1922
Battling Siki	FR	1922-1923
Emile Morelle	FR	1923
Raymond Bonnel	FR	1923-1924
Louis Clement	SWI	1924-1926
Herman van T'Hof	HOL	1926
Fernand Delarge	BEL	1926-1927
Max Schmeling*	GER	1927-1928
Michele Bonaglia*	ITA	1929-1930
Ernst Pistulla*	GER	1931-1932
Adolf Heuser	GER	1932
John Andersson	SWE	1933
Martinez de Alfara	SP	1934
Marcel Thil	FR	1934-1935
Merlo Preciso	ITA	1935
Hein Lazek	AU	1935-1936
Gustave Roth	BEL	1936-1938
Adolf Heuser*	GER	1938-1939

Title Holder	Country	Tenure
Luigi Musina*	ITA	1942-1943
Freddie Mills*	E	1947-1950
Albert Yvel	FR	1950-1951
Don Cockell*	E	1951-1952
Conny Rux*	GER	1952
Jacques Hairabedian	FR	1953-1954
Gerhard Hecht	GER	1954-1955
Willi Hoepner	GER	1955
Gerhard Hecht	GER	1955-1957
Artemio Calzavara	ITA	1957-1958
Willi Hoepner	GER	1958
Erich Schoeppner	GER	1958-1962
Giulio Rinaldi	ITA	1962-1964
Gustav Scholz*	GER	1964-1965
Giulio Rinaldi	ITA	1965-1966
Piero del Papa	ITA	1966-1967
Lothar Stengel	GER	1967-1968
Tom Bogs*	DEN	1968-1969
Yvan Prebeg	YUG	1969-1970
Piero del Papa	ITA	1970-1971
Conny Velensek	GER	1971-1972
Chris Finnegan	E	1972
Rudiger Schmidtke	GER	1972-1973
John Conteh*	E	1973-1974
Domenico Adinolfi	ITA	1974-1976
Mate Parlov*	YUG	1976-1977
Aldo Traversaro	ITA	1977-1979
Rudi Koopmans	HOL	1979-1984
Richard Caramonolis	FR	1984
Alex Blanchard	HOL	1984-1987
Tom Collins	E	1987-1988
Pedro van Raamsdonk	HOL	1988
Jan Lefeber	HOL	1988-1989
Eric Nicoletta	FR	1989-1990
Tom Collins	E	1990-1991
Graciano Rocchigiani*	GER	1991-1992
Eddie Smulders	HOL	1993-1994
Fabrice Tiozzo*	FR	1994-1995
Eddy Smulders	HOL	1995-1996
Crawford Ashley	E	1997-

Cruiserweight (190 lbs)

Title Holder	Country	Tenure
Sam Reeson*	E	1987-1988

Title Holder	Country	Tenure
Angelo Rottoli	ITA	1989
Anaclet Wamba*	FR	1989-1990
Johnny Nelson*	E	1990-1992
Akim Tafer*	FR	1992-1993
Massimiliano Duran	ITA	1993-1994
Carl Thompson	E	1994
Alexander Gurov	UK	1995
Patrice Aouissi	FR	1995
Alexander Gurov*	UK	1995-1996
Akim Tafer*	FR	1996-1997
Johnny Nelson	E	1997-

Heavyweight (190 lbs +)

Title Holder	Country	Tenure
Georges Carpentier	FR	1913-1922
Battling Siki	FR	1922-1923
Erminio Spalla	ITA	1923-1926
Paolino Uzcudun	SP	1926-1928
Pierre Charles	BEL	1929-1931
Hein Muller	GER	1931-1932
Pierre Charles	BEL	1932-1933
Paolino Uzcudun	SP	1933
Primo Carnera	ITA	1933-1935
Pierre Charles	BEL	1935-1937
Arno Kolblin	GER	1937-1938
Hein Lazek	AU	1938-1939
Adolf Heuser	GER	1939
Max Schmeling*	GER	1939-1941
Olle Tandberg	SWE	1943
Karel Sys*	BEL	1943-1946
Bruce Woodcock	E	1946-1949
Joe Weidin	AU	1950-1951
Jack Gardner	E	1951
Hein Ten Hoff	GER	1951-1952
Karel Sys	BEL	1952
Heinz Neuhaus	GER	1952-1955
Franco Cavicchi	ITA	1955-1956
Ingemar Johansson*	SWE	1956-1959
Dick Richardson	W	1960-1962
Ingemar Johansson*	SWE	1962-1963
Henry Cooper*	E	1964
Karl Mildenberger	GER	1964-1968
Henry Cooper*	E	1968-1969
Peter Weiland	GER	1969-1970
Jose Urtain	SP	1970
Henry Cooper	E	1970-1971
Joe Bugner	E	1971
Jack Bodell	E	1971
Jose Urtain	SP	1971-1972
Jurgen Blin	GER	1972
Joe Bugner*	E	1972-1975
Richard Dunn	E	1976
Joe Bugner	E	1976-1977
Jean-Pierre Coopman	BEL	1977
Lucien Rodriguez	FR	1977
Alfredo Evangelista	SP	1977-1979
Lorenzo Zanon*	SP	1979-1980
John L. Gardner*	E	1980-1981
Lucien Rodriguez	FR	1981-1984
Steffen Tangstad	NOR	1984-1985
Anders Eklund	SWE	1985
Frank Bruno*	E	1985-1986
Steffen Tangstad	NOR	1986
Alfredo Evangelista	SP	1987
Anders Eklund	SWE	1987
Francesco Damiani	ITA	1987-1989
Derek Williams	E	1989-1990
Jean Chanet	FR	1990
Lennox Lewis*	E	1990-1992
Henry Akinwande*	E	1993-1995
Zeljko Mavrovic	CRO	1995-

Crawford Ashley (left) seen on his way to winning the European light-heavyweight title, care of a three-round kayo of the Spaniard, Roberto Dominguez

Les Clark

A-Z of Current World Champions

by Eric Armit

Shows the record since 1 July 1996, plus career summary and pen-portrait, of all men holding IBF, WBA, WBC and WBO titles as at 30 June 1997. The author has also produced similar data for those who first won titles between 1 July 1996 and 30 June 1997, but were no longer champions at the end of the period in question. Incidentally, the place name given is the respective boxer's domicile and may not necessarily be his birthplace, while all nicknames are shown where applicable. Not included are British fighters, Steve Collins (WBO S. Middleweight champion), Prince Naseem Hamed (WBO & IBF Featherweight Champion), Herbie Hide (WBO Heavyweight Champion), Lennox Lewis (WBC Heavyweight Champion), Robbie Regan (WBO Bantamweight Champion), and Robin Reid (WBC Middleweight Champion). Their full records can be found in either the Current British-Based Champions or Active British-Based Boxers: Career Records' sections.

Rosendo Alvarez

Managua, Nicaragua. *Born* 6 May, 1970
WBA M. Flyweight Champion.
Former Undefeated Latin American M. Flyweight Champion

Major Amateur Honours: None known, claims 55 wins in 67 fights.
Turned Pro: December 1992
Significant Results: Chana Porpaoin W PTS 12 Kermin Guardia W CO 3, Eric Chavez W PTS 12.
Type/Style: Good boxer and skilful in-fighter with a fair punch.
Points of Interest: 5'5" tall. Only the third Nicaraguan to win a world title, he has beaten both of the Porpaoin twins, made four title defences, and boasts 16 wins inside the distance.

01.10.96	Takashi Shiohama W RSC 8 Kokura *(WBA M. Flyweight Title Defence)*
11.01.97	Songkram Porpaoin W RSC 11 Sakaew *(WBA M. Flyweight Title Defence)*

Career: 24 contests, won 24.

Yuri (Ebihara) Arbachakov

Kemerova, Armenia. *Born* 22 October, 1966
WBC Flyweight Champion. Former Undefeated Japanese Flyweight Champion

Major Amateur Honours: Gold medallist, 1989 World and European Championships. Russian Champion, 1989
Turned Pro: February 1990
Significant Results: Muangchai Kitikasem W CO 8, Ysaias Zamudio W PTS 12, Chatchai Sasakul W PTS 12, Raul Juarez W PTS 12
Type/Style: Cool, upright stylist.
Points of Interest: 5'4" tall. Nine title

defences and 16 wins by kayo or stoppage. Chatchai Sasakul is now established as the interim champion, with Yuri unable to defend his title due to injury.

26.08.96	Takato Toguchi W RSC 9 Tokyo *(WBC Flyweight Title Defence)*

Career: 23 contests, won 23.

Jose Bonilla

El Tigre, Venezuela. *Born* 19 November, 1967
WBA Flyweight Champion. Former Undefeated Venezuelan Flyweight Champion. Former WBA Latin American Flyweight Champion

Major Amateur Honours: None known
Turned Pro: March 1990
Significant Results: Edicson Torres W PTS 12, Jesus Rojas L RSC 11, Rosendo Alvarez L RSC 11, Carlos Rodriguez W PTS 12
Type/Style: An intelligent counter puncher, but not a heavy hitter.
Points of Interest: 5'2" tall. All loses have been inside the distance.

14.10.96	Gustavo Vera W RSC 5 Turmero *(Venezuelan L. Flyweight Title Defence)*
23.11.96	Saen Sorploenchit W PTS 12 Bangkok *(WBA Flyweight Title Challenge)*
25.02.97	Hiroki Ioka W RSC 7 Osaka *(WBA Flyweight Title Defence*

Career: 25 contests, won 22, lost 3.

Mbulelo Botile

East London, South Africa. *Born* 23 July, 1972
IBF Bantamweight Champion. Former Undefeated South African Bantamweight Champion

Major Amateur Honours: None known

Turned Pro: July 1989
Significant Results: Harold Mestre W CO 2, Sammy Stewart W PTS 12, Ancee Gedeon W CO 11
Type/Style: A fine boxer and good counter puncher.
Points of Interest: 5'5" tall. Stable-mate of Vuyani Bungu. Turned professional at 17 and has made five title defences.

26.11.96	Aristead Clayton W PTS 12 Baton Rouge *(IBF Bantamweight Title Defence)*

Career: 21 contests, won 21.

Laurent Boudouani   Les Clark

Laurent Boudouani

Sallanches, France. *Born* 29 January, 1966
WBA L. Middleweight Champion.
Former Undefeated European L. Middleweight Champion.

Major Amateur Honours: Silver medallist, 1988 Olympics. World Military Champion, 1985. French Champion, 1985-1988
Turned Pro: April 1989
Significant Results: Gilbert Baptist L RSC 8, Jean-Claude Fontana W CO 3, Bernard Razzano L RSC 8, Javier Castillejo W RSC 9
Type/Style: Strong orthodox boxer.
Points of Interest: 5'11" tall. Has 31 wins inside the distance.

05.07.96	Victor Fessetchko W RSC 3 Hyeres	
21.08.96	Julio Cesar Vasquez W CO 5 Le Cannet Rochville *(WBA L. Middleweight Title Challenge)*	
14.12.96	Benji Singleton W RSC 4 Atlantic City	
29.03.97	Carl Daniels W PTS 12 Las Vegas *(WBA L. Middleweight Title Defence)*	
Career: 37 contests, won 35, lost 2.		

Lonnie Bradley

New York, USA. *Born* 16 September, 1968
WBO Middleweight Champion

Major Amateur Honours: National Golden Gloves Champion, 1992. Three times New York Golden Gloves Champion
Turned Pro: November 1992
Significant Results: David Mendez W RSC 12, Dario Galindez W RSC 1, Lonnie Beasley W PTS 12.
Type/Style: Compact boxer with good jab
Points of Interest: Trained by Bobby Cassidy, he is the first Harlem-based world champion since Sugar Ray Robinson, boasting five title defences and 19 wins inside the distance.

30.08.96	Simon Brown W PTS 12 Reading *(WBO Middleweight Title Defence)*	
04.03.97	Otis Grant DREW 12 Las Vegas *(WBO Middleweight Title Defence)*	
28.06.97	John Williams W RSC 8 Las Vegas *(WBO Middleweight Title Defence)*	
Career: 27 contests, won 26, drew 1.		

Charles (The Hatchet) Brewer

Philadelphia, USA. *Born* 15 October, 1969
IBF S. Middleweight Champion. Former Undefeated USBA S. Middleweight Champion

Major Amateur Honours: None
Turned Pro: August 1989

Significant Results: Carl Sullivan W CO 6, Lonnie Beasley L CO 1, Rodney Toney L PTS 10, Adam Garland W RSC 4, Frank Rhodes W PTS 12
Type/Style: Strong, big right-hand puncher
Points of Interest: Trained by former pro, Bobby Watts. Retired in disgust at one point of his career. Has 20 wins inside the distance.

04.10.96	Fermin Chirino W PTS 8 New York	
18.02.97	Greg Wright W PTS 12 Philadelphia *(USBA S. Middleweight Title Defence)*	
21.06.97	Gary Ballard W RSC 5 Tampa *(Vacant IBF S. Middleweight Title)*	
Career: 34 contests, won 29, lost 5.		

Vuyani (The Beast) Bungu

Mdantsane, South Africa. *Born* 26 February, 1967
IBF S. Bantamweight Champion. Former Undefeated South African S. Bantamweight Champion

Major Amateur Honours: None
Turned Pro: April 1987
Significant Results: Fransie Badenhorst L PTS 12, Felix Camacho W PTS 12, Kennedy McKinney W PTS 12, Jesus Salud W PTS 12
Type/Style: Strong, with excellent stamina and a good left hook
Points of Interest: 5'5" tall. Eight title defences.

20.08.96	Jesus Salud W PTS 12 Hammanskraal *(IBF S. Bantamweight Title Defence)*	
05.04.97	Kennedy McKinney W PTS 12 Hammanskraal *(IBF S. Bantamweight Title Defence)*	
Career: 34 contests, won 32, lost 2.		

Antonio (Goloso) Cermeno

Miranda, Venezuela. *Born* 6 March, 1969
WBA S. Bantamweight Champion. Former Undefeated Latin American S. Bantamweight Champion

Major Amateur Honours: Gold medallist, 1989 Central American Championships
Turned Pro: September 1990
Significant Results: Ramon Guzman W RSC 4, Jae-Won Choi L PTS 12, Wilfredo Vasquez W PTS 12, Jesus Salud W PTS 12
Type/Style: Strong, awkward, but effective, and a good puncher

Points of Interest: 5'10" tall. Five defences. Has 16 wins inside the distance.

09.11.96	Eddy Saenz W RTD 5 Las Vegas *(WBA S. Bantamweight Title Defence)*	
21.12.96	Yuichi Kasai W PTS 12 Las Vegas *(WBA S. Bantamweight Title Defence)*	
10.05.97	Angel Chacon W PTS 12 Miami *(WBA S. Bantamweight Title Defence)*	
Career: 28 contests, won 27, lost 1.		

Yong-Soo Choi

South Korea. *Born* 20 August, 1972
WBA S. Featherweight Champion. Former Undefeated OPBF S. Featherweight Champion

Major Amateur Honours: None
Turned Pro: November 1990
Significant Results: Victor Hugo Paz W RSC 10, Orlando Soto W RSC 8
Type/Style: A tough, game infighter who uses the peek-boo-style.
Points of Interest: 5'5" tall. Unbeaten since 1991.

13.10.96	Yamato Mitani W PTS 12 Tokyo *(WBA S. Featherweight Title Defence)*	
01.02.97	Lavka Sim W PTS 12 Seoul *(WBA S. Featherweight Title Defence)*	
24.05.97	Koji Matsumoto W PTS 12 Seoul *(WBA S. Featherweight Title Defence)*	
Career: 25 contests, won 23, lost 2.		

Jesus (El Tigre) Chong

Gomez Palacio, Mexico. *Born* 7 January, 1965
WBO L. Flyweight Champion. Former Undefeated NABF L. Flyweight Champion. Former Mexican L. Flyweight Champion.

Major Amateur Honours: Silver medallist, 1986 Mexican Olympic Festival
Turned Pro: September 1987
Significant Results: Johnny Tapia L PTS 8 Cuauhtemoc Gomez W PTS 10, Michael Carbajal L PTS 10, Eric Griffin W CO 7
Type/Style: Hard punching and brave, with a good chin
Points of Interest: 5'2" tall. Comes from a fighting family.

01.01.97	Diego Andrade W RSC 10 Gomez Palacio	
31.05.97	Eric Griffin W RSC 2 Las Vegas *(Vacant WBO L. Flyweight Title)*	
Career: 38 contests, won 31, lost 7.		

Pichitnoi Chor Siriwat

Chaiyaphum, Thailand. *Born* 31 January, 1975
WBA L. Flyweight Champion.

Major Amateur Honours: None
Turned Pro: August 1993
Significant Results: Silvio Gamez L RSC 6, Ric Magramo W CO 3, Roger Espanola W RSC 12.
Type/Style: Southpaw with a hard right hook
Points of Interest: Brother Pichit is a former undefeated IBF flyweight champion.

03.12.96	Keiji Yamaguchi W RSC 2 Osaka
	(WBA L. Flyweight Title Challenge)
Career: 18 contests, won 17, lost 1.	

Oscar de la Hoya

Montebello, USA. *Born* 4 February, 1973
WBC Welterweight Champion. Former Undefeated WBC L. Welterweight. Former Undefeated IBF & WBO Lightweight Champion. Former Undefeated WBO S. Featherweight Champion

Major Amateur Honours: Gold medallist 1992 Olympic Games. USBA Champion, 1990-1991, National Golden Gloves Champion, 1989
Turned Pro: November 1992
Significant Results: Juan Molina W PTS 12, Rafael Ruelas W RSC 2, Genaro Hernandez W RSC 6, Jesse Leija W RSC 2, Julio Cesar Chavez W RSC 4
Type/Style: Smooth boxer who is fast and accurate and a hard puncher
Points of Interest: 5'11" tall. Has beaten ten world or former world champions, with 21 wins inside the distance. Has won five versions of the world title in three years. Boxing since the age of six.

18.01.97	Miguel Angel Gonzalez W PTS 12 Las Vegas
	(WBC L. Welterweight Title Defence)
12.04.97	Pernell Whitaker W PTS 12 Las Vegas
	(WBC Welterweight Title Challenge)
14.06.97	David Kamau W CO 2 San Antonio
	(WBC Welterweight Title Defence)
Career: 25 contests, won 25.	

Osca de la Hoya

Marcelo Dominguez

Buenos Aires, Argentina. *Born* 15 January, 1970
WBC Cruiserweight Champion. Former Undefeated Argentinian Cruiserweight Champion

Major Amateur Honours: None
Turned Pro: October 1991
Significant Results: Nestor Giovannini W DIS 4, Anaclet Wamba L PTS 12, Akim Tafer W RSC 9, Sergei Kobozev W PTS 12
Type/Style: Tough, stocky and durable
Points of Interest: 5'10" tall. 36-3-3 as an amateur. Was WBC interim champion.

05.07.96	Patrice Aouissi W RTD 9 Hyeres
	(WBC Cruiserweight Title Defence)
06.12.96	Jose Arimatea Da Silva W RTD 7 Buenos Aires
	(WBC Cruiserweight Title Defence)
Career: 23 contests, won 21, drew 1, lost 1.	

Luisito (Golden Boy) Espinosa

Manila, Philippines. *Born* 26 June, 1967
WBC Featherweight Champion. Former WBA Bantamweight Champion

Major Amateur Honours: None
Turned Pro: May 1984
Significant Results: Kaokor Galaxy W CO 1, Israel Contreras L RSC 5, Manuel Medina W PTS 12, Alejandro Gonzalez W CO 4
Type/Style: Good jab and a hard left hook
Points of Interest: 5'7" tall. Nephew of former top pro, Leo Espinosa. Made two defences of WBA title and has made four defences of the WBC crown.

06.07.96	Cesar Soto W PTS 12 Manila
	(WBA Featherweight Title Defence)
02.11.96	Nobutoshi Hiranaka W RSC 8 Fukuoka
	(WBA Featherweight Title Defence)
17.05.97	Manuel Medina W TD 7 Manila
	(WBC Featherweight Title Defence)
Career: 48 contests, won 41, lost 7.	

Arturo (Thunder) Gatti

New Jersey, USA. *Born* Canada, 15 April, 1972
IBF S. Featherweight Champion. Former Undefeated USBA S. Featherweight Champion

Major Amateur Honours: Three times Canadian Golden Gloves Champion
Turned Pro: June 1991
Significant Results: King Solomon L PTS 6, Tracy Harris Patterson W PTS 12, Jose Sanabria W PTS 12, Wilson Rodriguez W RSC 6
Type/Style: Although a fast starter and big hitter, his defence is not too great
Points of Interest: 5'8" tall. Brother Joe is also a pro. Has 23 wins inside the distance, 14 in the first round.

11.07.96	Feliciano Correa W RSC 3 New York
22.02.97	Tracy Harris Patterson W PTS 12 Atlantic City
	(IBF S. Featherweight Title Defence)
04.05.97	Calvin Grove W RTD 7 Atlantic City
Career: 29 contests, won 28, lost 1.	

Uriah (The Boss) Grant

Kingston, Jamaica. *Born* 21 January, 1962
IBF Cruiserweight Champion. Former Undefeated Fecarbox Cruiserweight Champion

Major Amateur Honours: None
Turned Pro: June 1984
Significant Results: Matthew Saad Muhammad W PTS 10, Bobby Czyz L PTS 10, Alfred Cole L PTS 12 (2)
Type/Style: Solid boxer with a good chin
Points of Interest: Failed in two previous attempts at the IBF title. Has not had more than three fights in any year since 1991. His record shows 24 wins inside the distance.

06.08.96	Chris Byrd L PTS 10 Flint
07.12.96	Saul Montana W RSC 3 Indio
21.06.97	Adolpho Washington W PTS 12 Tampa
	(IBF Cruiserweight Title Challenge)
Career: 38 contests, won 26, lost 12.	

Montell Griffin

Chicago, USA. *Born* 6 June, 1970
WBC L. Heavyweight Champion.
Former Undefeated NABF L.
Heavyweight Champion

Major Amateur Honours: Competed in 1992 Olympics. 1992 US Champion. Gold medallist Canada Cup, 1991
Turned Pro: February 1993
Significant Results: David Vedder W PTS 10, Ray Lathon W PTS 12, James Toney W PTS 12.
Type/Style: Aggressive switch hitter
Points of Interest: 5'7" tall. Dad owned Windy City gym in Chicago.

11.07.96	Matthew Charleston W RSC 11 New York *(Vacant NABF L. Heavyweight Title)*
29.08.96	Melvin Wynn W CO 2 Worley
18.10.96	Russell Mitchell W RSC 1 Dolton
06.12.96	James Toney W PTS 12 Reno
21.03.97	Roy Jones W DIS 9 Atlantic City *(WBC L. Heavyweight Title Challenge)*
Career: 27 contests, won 27.	

Montell Griffin   Les Clark

Artur (Atuiz) Grigorian

Tashkent, Uzbekistan. *Born* 20 October, 1967
WBO Lightweight Champion

Major Amateur Honours: Silver medallist, 1991 World Championships. Competed in 1992 Olympics and 1993 World Championships.
Turned Pro: April 1994
Significant Results: Paul Kaoma W

PTS 8, Antonio Rivera W CO 12
Type/Style: Southpaw, stylish boxer
Points of Interest: 5'9" tall. Former interim champion, with 13 wins inside the distance. Based in Germany.

21.09.96	Gene Reed W CO 2 Berlin *(WBO Lightweight Title Defence)*
16.11.96	Marty Jakubowski W PTS 12 Hamburg *(WBO Lightweight Title Defence)*
22.02.97	Raul Balbi W RSC 11 Hamburg *(WBO Lightweight Title Defence)*
Career: 22 contests, won 22.	

Genaro (Chicanito) Hernandez

Los Angeles, USA. *Born* 10 May, 1966
WBC S. Featherweight Champion.
Former Undefeated WBA S.
Featherweight Champion

Major Amateur Honours: None
Turned Pro: September 1984
Significant Results: Daniel Londas W RSC 9, Raul Perez W CO 9, Jorge Paez W RSC 8, Oscar De La Hoya L RSC 6
Type/Style: An excellent intelligent boxer
Points of Interest: 5'10" tall. Brother Rudy a pro. Plagued by hand problems and suffered a broken nose against De La Hoya. Made eight defences of WBA title.

28.09.96	Antonio Hernandez W PTS 10 Fort Worth
22.03.97	Azumah Nelson W PTS 12 Corpus Christi *(WBC S. Featherweight Title Challenge)*
14.06.97	Anatoly Alexandrov W PTS 12 San Antonio *(WBC S. Featherweight Title Defence)*
Career: 38 contests, won 36, drew 1, lost 1.	

Phillip Holiday

Benoni, South Africa. *Born* 23 May, 1970
IBF Lightweight Champion

Major Amateur Honours: None
Turned Pro: April 1991
Significant Results: Sugar Baby Rojas W PTS 10, Miguel Julio W RTD 10, Jeff Fenech W RSC 2
Type/Style: Although a neat boxer with a busy style, he is a slow starter
Points of Interest: 5'7" tall. Trained by Harold Volbrecht, he has made six title defences.

19.10.96	Joel Diaz W PTS 12 Johannesburg *(IBF Lightweight Title Defence)*
21.12.96	Ivan Robinson W PTS 12 Uncasville *(IBF Lightweight Title Defence)*
16.05.97	Pete Taliaferro W PTS 12 Hammaskraal *(IBF Lightweight Title Defence)*
Career: 31 contests, won 31.	

Keith Holmes

Washington, USA. *Born* 30 March, 1969
WBC Middleweight Champion.
Former Undefeated USBA L.
Middleweight Champion

Major Amateur Honours: Runner-up in 1988 National Golden Gloves
Turned Pro: October 1989
Significant Results: Ron Hammond L PTS 6, Kelcie Banks W RSC 3, Andy Council W PTS 12
Type/Style: A hard-punching southpaw with a sound defence
Points of Interest: 6'2" tall. Career held up when accused of a drive-by shooting. Unbeaten in his last 22 fights, he has had one unsanctioned fight that does not appear on his record.

19.10.96	Richie Woodhall W RSC 12 Upper Marlboro *(WBC Middleweight Title Defence)*
Career: 30 contests, won 29, lost 1.	

Evander (The Real Deal) Holyfield

Atmore, USA. *Born* 19 October, 1962
WBA Heavyweight Champion.
Former WBC & IBF Heavyweight Champion. Former Undefeated WBC, IBF & WBA Cruiserweight Champion. Former Undefeated WBC Con Am Heavyweight Champion

Major Amateur Honours: Bronze medallist, 1984 Olympic Games. National Golden Gloves Champion, 1984. Silver medallist, 1983 Pan American Games
Turned Pro: November 1984
Significant Results: James Douglas W CO 3, George Foreman W PTS 12, Riddick Bowe L PTS 12, Riddick Bowe W PTS 12, Michael Moorer L PTS 12, Riddick Bowe L RSC 8
Type/Style: A tough, brave, compact boxer
Points of Interest: 6'2" tall. Has taken part in 15 world title fights and has 24

Evander Holyfield

Chris Farina

wins by stoppage or kayo. Career almost finished by heart problem diagnosis.

09.11.96	Mike Tyson W RSC 11 Las Vegas *(WBA Heavyweight Title Challenge)*
28.06.97	Mike Tyson W DIS 3 Las Vegas *(WBA Heavyweight Title Defence)*
Career: 37 contests, won 34, lost 3.	

Bernard (The Executioner) Hopkins

Philadelphia, USA. *Born* 15 January, 1965

IBF Middleweight Champion. Former Undefeated USBA Middleweight Champion

Major Amateur Honours: None
Turned Pro: October 1988
Significant Results: Roy Jones L PTS 12, Lupe Aquino W PTS 12, Segundo Mercado DREW 12, Segundo Mercado W PTS 12
Type/Style: Power puncher with fast hands
Points of Interest: 6'0" tall. Nephew of former pro, Art McCloud. Spent five years in jail. Enters ring wearing executioner's mask and a cape. Has 23 wins inside the distance.

16.07.96	Bo James W RSC 11 Atlantic City *(IBF Middleweight Title Defence)*
19.04.97	John David Jackson W RSC 7 Shreveport *(IBF Middleweight Title Defence)*
Career: 34 contests, won 31, drew 1, lost 2.	

Mark (Too Sharp) Johnson

Washington, USA. *Born* 13 August, 1971

IBF Flyweight Champion

Major Amateur Honours: National Golden Gloves Champion, 1989
Turned Pro: February 1990
Significant Results: Richie Wenton L PTS 4, Alberto Jimenez W PTS 12, Ancee Gedeon W PTS 10, Francisco Tejedor W CO 1
Type/Style: A strong, aggressive, fast-handed southpaw
Points of Interest: 5'3" tall. Unbeaten in his last 31 fights.

05.08.96	Raul Juarez W RSC 8 Los Angeles *(IBF Flyweight Title Defence)*
10.02.97	Alejandro Montiel W PTS 12 Los Angeles *(IBF Flyweight Title Defence)*
01.06.97	Cecilio Espino W CO 2 Uncasville *(IBF Flyweight Title Defence)*
Career: 33 contests, won 32, lost 1.	

Steve (Little but Bad) Johnston

Denver, USA. *Born* 28 September, 1972

WBC Lightweight Champion. Former Undefeated NABF Lightweight Champion

Major Amateur Honours: Gold medallist, 1991 Pan-American Games. 1990 US/ABF Champion
Turned Pro: February 1993
Significant Results: Corey Johnson W CO 8, Howard Grant W RSC 9, Jesus Rodriguez W RSC 10
Type/Style: A fast and slick southpaw
Points of Interest: 5'7" tall. Has 13 wins inside the distance.

| 18.01.97 | Jose Luis Baltazar W PTS 10 Las Vegas |
| 01.03.97 | Jean-Baptiste Mendy W PTS 12 Paris *(WBC Lightweight Title Challenge)* |

Career: 21 contests, won 21.

Junior (Poison) Ivey Jones

New York, USA. *Born* 19 December, 1970
WBO S. Bantamweight Champion. Former WBA Bantamweight Champion. Former Undefeated USBA Bantamweight Champion

Major Amateur Honours: Twice New York Golden Gloves Champion
Turned Pro: June 1989
Significant Results: Jose Quirino W RSC 3, Jorge Elicer Julio W PTS 12, James Michael Johnson L RSC 11, Orlando Canizales W PTS 12
Type/Style: An elegant, talented boxer, with a big right-hand punch
Points of Interest: 5'8" tall. Started boxing at nine to stop his sister beating him up.

20.08.96	Wilson Santos W PTS 10 New York
10.09.96	Tommy Parks W RSC 5 New York
22.11.96	Marco Antonio Barrera W RSC 5 Tampa *(WBO S. Bantamweight Title Challenge)*
18.04.97	Marco Antonio Barrera W PTS 12 Las Vegas *(WBO S. Bantamweight Title Defence)*

Career: 46 contests, won 44, lost 2.

Junior Jones

William Joppy

Tacoma Park, USA. *Born* 11 September, 1970
WBA Middleweight Champion

Major Amateur Honours: Olympic Triallist and National Golden Gloves semi-finalist
Turned Pro: February 1993
Significant Results: Rodney Toney DREW 12, Joaquin Velasquez W PTS 10, Shinji Takenhara W RSC 9
Type/Style: Quick hands, slick footwork, and a good combination puncher
Points of Interest: 5'9" tall. Started boxing at 14 and has 18 wins inside the distance.

| 19.10.96 | Ray McElroy W RSC 6 Upper Marlboro *(WBA Middleweight Title Defence)* |
| 10.05.97 | Peter Venancio W PTS 12 Miami *(WBA Middleweight Title Defence)* |

Career: 25 contests, won 24, drew 1.

William Joppy   Les Clark

Nana Yaw Konadu

Sunyani, Ghana. *Born* 14 February, 1965
WBA Bantamweight Champion. Former WBC S. Flyweight Champion. Former Undefeated WBC International S. Flyweight Champion. Former Undefeated Commonwealth & ABC Flyweight Champion. Former Undefeated ABC Bantamweight Champion.

Major Amateur Honours: Won 37 of 38 fights
Turned Pro: May 1985
Significant Results: Gilberto Roman W PTS 12, Sung-Kil Moon L TD 9, Sung-Kil Moon L RSC 4, Juan Polo Perez W PTS 12, Veeraphol Sahaprom W RSC 2
Type/Style: Fast, stylish boxer and hard puncher
Points of Interest: 5'8" tall. Good at all sports, he started boxing at ten. All losses have involved cuts.

| 27.10.96 | Daorung Chuwatana L TD 9 Bangkok *(WBA Bantamweight Title Defence)* |
| 21.06.97 | Daorung Chuwatana W RSC 7 Tampa *(WBA Bantamweight Title Challenge)* |

Career: 41 contests, won 37, drew 1, lost 3.

Frank Liles   Les Clark

Frank (Fabulous) Liles

Syracuse, USA. *Born* 15 February, 1965
WBA S. Middleweight Champion. Former Undefeated NABF S. Middleweight Champion

Major Amateur Honours: Silver medallist, 1987 Pan-American Games. National Golden Gloves Champion, 1986. US/ABF Champion, 1988
Turned Pro: August 1989
Significant Results: Tim Littles L PTS 12, Steve Little L PTS 12, Michael Nunn W PTS 12, Frederic Seillier W RSC 6
Type/Style: Clever southpaw with a sharp jab

Points of Interest: 6'3" tall. Five title defences and 21 wins inside the distance.

19.04.97	Segundo Mercado W RSC 5 Shreveport
	(WBA S. Middleweight Title Defence)
Career: 32 contests, won 30, lost 1, no contest 1.	

Michael Loewe

Leverkusen, Germany. *Born* Romania, 13 February, 1969
WBO Welterweight Champion

Major Amateur Honours: World Junior Champion, 1987
Turned Pro: September 1991
Significant Results: None
Type/Style: Fine boxer, but not a puncher
Points of Interest: Real name Mihai Leu. Boxed for Romania as an amateur.

19.10.96	Jorge Ramirez W PTS 8 Frankfurt
16.11.96	Eric Jakubowski W RSC 5 Hamburg
22.02.97	Santiago Samaniego W PTS 12 Hamburg
	(Vacant WBO Welterweight Title)
Career: 27 contests, won 27.	

Ricardo (Finito) Lopez

Cuernavaca, Mexico. *Born* 25 July, 1966
WBC M. Flyweight Champion.
Former Undefeated WBC Con Am M. Flyweight Champion

Major Amateur Honours: Mexican Golden Gloves Champion, 1984
Turned Pro: January 1985
Significant Results: Rocky Lim W CO 2, Saman Sorjaturong W RSC 2, Kermin Guardia W PTS 12, Ala Villamor W CO 8
Type/Style: A dazzling craftsman and a fast, accurate and hard puncher, he has it all
Points of Interest: 5'4" tall. Division record 19 title defences and has 34 wins inside the distance.

09.11.96	Morgan Ndumo W RSC 6 Las Vegas
	(WBC M. Flyweight Title Defence)
07.12.96	Myung-Sup Park W RSC 1 Indio
	(WBC M. Flyweight Title Defence)
29.03.97	Mongol Jor Charoen W PTS 12 Las Vegas
	(WBC M. Flyweight Title Defence)
Career: 45 contests, won 45.	

Raul (The Diamond) Marquez

Houston, USA. *Born* Mexico, 28 August, 1971
IBF L. Middleweight Champion.
Former Undefeated USBA L. Middleweight Champion

Major Amateur Honours: Competed in 1992 Olympic Games. US/ABF Champion, 1992. Silver medallist, 1991 World Championships
Turned Pro: October 1992
Significant Results: Alex Rios W CO 1, Jorge Vaca W PTS 10, Skipper Kelp W PTS 10
Type/Style: A fast, aggressive pressure fighting southpaw
Points of Interest: 5'10" tall. Has 19 wins inside the distance.

06.12.96	Scotty Smith W CO 2 Reno
10.01.97	Rafael Williams W RTD 5 Uncasville
	(USBA L. Middleweight Title Defence)
12.04.97	Anthony Stephens W RSC 9 Las Vegas
	(Vacant IBF L. Middleweight Title)
Career: 26 contests, won 26.	

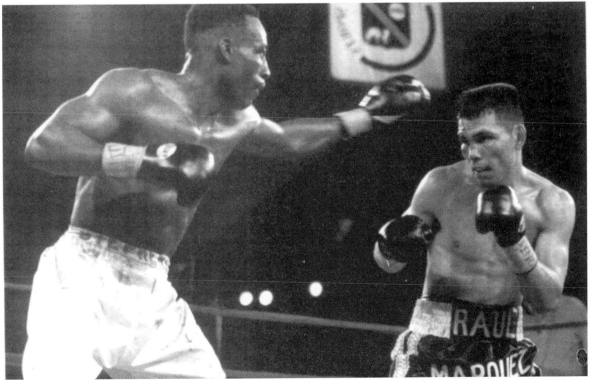

Raul Marquez (right) picked up the vacant IBF light-middleweight title following a ninth-round stoppage win over Anthony Stephens

Dariusz Michalczewski

Hamburg, Germany. *Born* Gdansk, Poland, 5 May, 1968
WBA and WBO L. Heavyweight Champion. Former Undefeated IBF L. Heavyweight Champion. Former Undefeated WBO Cruiserweight Champion

Major Amateur Honours: Bronze medallist, 1986 European Junior Championships. Silver medallist, 1989 European Championships. Gold medallist, 1991 European Champion-ships
Turned Pro: September 1991
Significant Results: Leonzer Barber W PTS 12, Nestor Giovannini W CO 10
Type/Style: Hard punching and aggressive pressure fighter. Has a solid jab, but defence is not too sound
Points of Interest: Won championships for both Poland and Germany as an amateur. Has 24 wins by stoppage or knock out. Relinquished the IBF title without defending it.

10.08.96	Graciano Rocchigiani W DIS 7 Hamburg *(WBO L. Heavyweight Title Defence)*
13.12.96	Christophe Girard W RSC 8 Hannover *(WBO L. Heavyweight Title Defence)*
13.06.97	Virgil Hill W PTS 12 Oberhausen *(WBA & IBF L. Heavyweight Title Challenge)*

Career: 34 contests, won 34.

Nate Miller

Philadelphia, USA. *Born* 3 August, 1963
WBA Cruiserweight Champion. Former NABF Cruiserweight Champion

Major Amateur Honours: USA amateur international
Turned Pro: September 1986
Significant Results: Al Cole L PTS 12, Jade Scott W RSC 7, Dwight Muhammad Qawi W RSC 7, Orlin Norris W CO 8
Type/Style: Tall, durable and strong with a solid jab
Points of Interest: 6'2" tall. Trained by Buster Drayton. A late bloomer, winning title at the age of 32, he has 26 wins by stoppage or kayo. Four title defences.

31.08.96	James Heath W RSC 7 Dublin *(WBA Cruiserweight Title Defence)*
22.02.97	Alexander Gurov W RSC 2 Fort Lauderdale *(WBA Cruiserweight Title Defence)*

Career: 34 contests, won 30, lost 4.

Michael Moorer

New York, USA. *Born* 12 November, 1967
IBF Heavyweight Champion. Former WBA Heavyweight Champion. Former Undefeated WBO L. Heavyweight Champion

Major Amateur Honours: US/ABF Champion, 1986, and Runner up in 1985
Turned Pro: March 1988
Significant Results: Bert Cooper W RSC 5, Evander Holyfield W PTS 12, George Foreman L CO 10, Axel Schulz W PTS 12
Type/Style: Good southpaw boxer with a strong jab, but plodding methodical approach
Points of Interest: 6'2" tall. Made nine defences of WBO L. Heavyweight crown but never defended WBO heavyweight title. Has 31 wins by knockout or stoppage.

09.11.96	Frans Botha W RSC 12 Las Vegas *(IBF Heavyweight Title Defence)*
29.03.97	Vaughn Bean W PTS 12 Las Vegas *(IBF Heavyweight Title Defence)*

Career: 40 contests, won 39, lost 1.

Vincenzo Nardiello

Ostia, Italy. *Born* Germany, 11 June, 1966
Former WBC & European S. Middleweight Champion

Major Amateur Honours: Competed in 1988 Olympic Games. Italian Champion, 1984, 1986, and 1987
Turned Pro: December 1988
Significant Results: Fidel Castro Smith W PTS 12, Mauro Galvano W PTS 12, Nigel Benn L RSC 8, Henry Wharton L RSC 6
Type/Style: A strong, awkward southpaw
Points of Interest: 5'10" tall. Brother Giovanni is Italian champion at the same weight.

06.07.96	Thulani Malinga W PTS 12 Manchester *(WBC S. Middleweight Title Challenge)*
12.10.96	Robin Reid L CO 7 Milan *(WBC S. Middleweight Title Defence)*
10.05.97	Tim Bryan W CO 2 Rome

Career: 37 contests, won 31, lost 6.

Orzubek (Gussie) Nazarov

Kant, Kyrghyzstan. *Born* 30 August, 1966
WBA Lightweight Champion. Former Undefeated OPBF & Japanese Lightweight Champion

Major Amateur Honours: Gold medallist, 1984 and 1987 European Championships. Russian Champion, 1985, 1987, and 1988
Turned Pro: February 1990
Significant Results: Dingaan Thobela W PTS 12 (2), Joey Gamache W CO 2
Type/Style: A very strong, damaging body-punching southpaw
Points of Interest: Bus driver's son who started boxing at 11 years of age, turning pro in Japan. Six WBA title defences. Has 18 wins by knockout or stoppage.

10.05.97	Leavander Johnson W RSC 7 Miami *(WBA Lightweight Title Defence)*

Career: 24 contests, won 24.

Terry Norris

Lubbock, USA. *Born* 17 June, 1967
WBC L. Middleweight Champion. Former Undefeated IBF L. Middleweight Champion. Former Undefeated NABF L. Middleweight Champion

Major Amateur Honours: None
Turned Pro: August 1986
Significant Results: Julian Jackson L RSC 2, John Mugabi W CO 1, Ray Leonard W PTS 12, Donald Curry W CO 9, Vince Pettway W CO 8
Type/Style: An excellent boxer with fast hands and a hard punch, but suspect chin
Points of Interest: 5'10" tall. Relinquished IBF title. Brother Orlin is a former WBA cruiserweight champion. Has taken part in 22 world title fights and lost three times on disqualification.

07.09.96	Alex Rios W RSC 5 Las Vegas
	(WBC & IBF L. Middleweight Title
	Defences)
11.01.97	Nick Rupa W RSC 10 Nashville
	(WBC & IBF L. Middleweight Title
	Defences)

Career: 51 contests, won 45, lost 6.

Giovanni Parisi

Vibo Valencia, Italy. *Born* 2 December, 1967
WBO L. Welterweight Champion. Former WBO Lightweight Champion. Former Undefeated Italian Lightweight Champion

Major Amateur Honours: Gold medallist, 1988 Olympic Games. Italian Champion, 1985 and 1986
Turned Pro: February 1989
Significant Results: Antonio Rivera W PTS 12, Julio Cesar Chavez L PTS 12, Sammy Fuentes W RSC 8, Carlos Gonzalez DREW 12
Type/Style: Stylish switch hitter
Points of Interest: 5'8" tall. Made two defences of the WBO lightweight title and has made three at light-welterweight.

12.10.96	Sergio Rey Revilla W RSC 4 Milan
	(WBO L. Welterweight Title Defence)
19.04.97	Harold Miller W RSC 8 Milan
	(WBO L. Welterweight Title Defence)

Career: 37 contests, won 34, drew 1, lost 2.

Mauricio (Indio) Pastrana

Sincelejo, Colombia. *Born* 20 January, 1973
Former Undefeated IBF L. Flyweight Champion

Major Amateur Honours: None
Turned Pro: October 1991
Significant Results: Fidel Julio W CO 3, Livaniel Alvarez W RSC 8
Type/Style: Busy and a good counter puncher. Also has a sound chin
Points of Interest: 5'2" tall. Stripped of the IBF title when he refused to weigh in for a defence, he has 12 wins on knockout or stoppage.

16.08.96	Luis Doria W RSC 6 Monteria
18.01.97	Michael Carbajal W PTS 12 Las Vegas
	(IBF L. Flyweight Title Challenge)

Career: 16 contests, won 16.

Gerry Penalosa

Cebu City, Philippines. *Born* 7 August, 1971
WBC S. Flyweight Champion. Former Undefeated IBF L. Flyweight Champion

Major Amateur Honours: None
Turned Pro: May 1989
Significant Results: Sammy Duran L PTS 12, Rolando Bohol W PTS 10, Rolando Pascua W CO 9
Type/Style: A hard-punching southpaw
Points of Interest: 5'6" tall. Brother Dodie is a former IBF light-flyweight champion. Has 22 wins by kayo or stoppage.

14.09.96	Kapchul Choi W RSC 3 Mandaue City
09.11.96	Prasob Jaimuang W RSC 5 Manila
20.02.97	Hiroshi Kawashima W PTS 12 Tokyo
	(WBC S. Flyweight Title Challenge)
14.06.97	Seung-Koo Lee W RSC 9 Mactan
	(WBC S. Flyweight Title Defence)

Career: 39 contests, won 37, drew 1, lost 1.

Vince Phillips

Pensacola, USA. *Born* 23 July, 1963
IBF L. Welterweight Champion

Major Amateur Honours: US/ABF champion, 1985 and 1986
Turned Pro: February 1989
Significant Results: Harold Brazier W

Vince Phillips

217

PTS 12, Anthony Jones L RSC 7, Rene Herrera W PTS 10, Ike Quartey L RSC 3

Type/Style: Has an aggressive style with a sharp right-hand punch, but is subject to cuts and swellings around the eyes

Points of Interest: Turned career around after battle against drug addiction. A stablemate of Roy Jones, he moved back down from welterweight to win the IBF title. Has 24 wins by stoppage or kayo.

28.10.96	Juan Rodriguez W RSC 5 Los Angeles
11.01.97	Romalis Ellis L PTS 10 Boston
31.05.97	Konstantin Tszyu W RSC 10 Atlantic City
	(IBF L. Welterweight Title Challenge)
Career: 39 contests, won 36, lost 3.	

Ike (Bazooka) Quartey

Accra, Ghana. *Born* 27 November, 1969
WBA Welterweight Champion. Former Undefeated Ghanaian, ABC and WBC International Welterweight Champion

Major Amateur Honours: Competed in 1988 Olympic Games. Bronze medallist, World Junior Championships
Turned Pro: November 1988
Significant Results: Lonnie Smith W PTS 10, Cristano Espana W RSC 11, Andrew Murray W RSC 4
Type/Style: Strong and powerful puncher with either hand
Points of Interest: 5'8" tall. Six title defences. Has 29 wins by kayo or stoppage.

04.10.96	Oba Carr W PTS 12 New York City
	(WBA Welterweight Title Defence)
18.04.97	Ralph Jones W RSC 5 Las Vegas
	(WBA Welterweight Title Defence)
Career: 34 contests, won 34.	

Khalid Rahilou

Conflans, France. *Born* 19 June, 1966
WBA L. Welterweight Champion. Former Undefeated French & European L. Welterweight Champion

Major Amateur Honours: French amateur champion, 1988 and 1989. Competed in 1988 Olympic Games
Turned Pro: December 1988
Significant Results: Christian Merle L RSC 8, Valery Kayumba W PTS 12,

Gert Bo Jacobsen W RSC 3, Gert Bo Jacobsen W RSC 9, Soren Sondergaard W RSC 9

Type/Style: A smart, cagey boxer with a good jab
Points of Interest: Former kick-boxing champion. Made five defences of the European title.

21.08.96	Angel Fernandez W CO 3 Le Cannet
11.01.97	Frankie Randall W RSC 11 Nashville
	(WBA L. Welterweight Title Challenge)
Career: 31 contests, won 29, lost 2.	

Ralf Rocchigiani

Rheinhausen, Germany. *Born* 13 March, 1963
WBO Cruiserweight Champion. Former German Cruiserweight Champion

Major Amateur Honours: Bronze medallist, 1982 European Junior Championships
Turned Pro: November 1983
Significant Results: Marvin Camel W PTS 10, Tyrone Booze L PTS 12, Torsten May L PTS 10, Carl Thompson W RSC 11
Type/Style: Although a good boxer, he is not a heavy puncher
Points of Interest: 6'0" tall. Brother Graciano is a former light-heavyweight, cum heavyweight. Has made six title defences.

13.07.96	Bashiru Ali W PTS 12 Essen
	(WBO Cruiserweight Title Defence)
13.12.96	Stefan Angehrn W PTS 12 Hannover
	(WBO Cruiserweight Title Defence)
26.04.97	Stefan Angehrn W PTS 12 Zurich
	(WBO Cruiserweight Title Defence)
Career: 55 contests, won 40, drew 7, lost 8.	

Danny Romero

Albuquerque, USA. *Born* 12 July, 1974
IBF S. Flyweight Champion. Former IBF FLyweight Champion. Former Undefeated NABF S. Flyweight Champion

Major Amateur Honours: US Junior Champion, 1989
Turned Pro: August 1992
Significant Results: Manuel Jesus Herrera W RSC 12, Francisco Tejedor W PTS 12, Miguel Martinez W CO 6, Willy Salazar L RSC 8

Type/Style: A hard punching, aggressive fighter
Points of Interest: 5'5" tall. Has 27 wins by kayo or stoppage. Suffered a fractured eye socket against Willy Salazar.

24.08.96	Harold Grey W CO 2 Albuquerque
	(IBF S. Flyweight Title Challenge)
01.11.96	Hipolito Saucedo W RSC 12 Indio Springs
	(IBF S. Flyweight Title Defence)
08.03.97	Jaji Sibali W RSC 6 Albuquerque
	(IBF S. Flyweight Title Defence)
Career: 31 contests, won 30, lost 1.	

Carlos Salazar

Buenos Aires, Argentina. *Born* 5 September, 1964
WBO Flyweight Champion. Former IBF S. Flyweight Champion. Former Undefeated South American Flyweight Champion. Former Argentinian Flyweight Champion

Major Amateur Honours: Selected for the 1984 Olympic team, but failed to make the weight
Turned Pro: December 1985
Significant Results: Sung-Il Moon L PTS 12, Marco Antonio Barrera L PTS 10, Harold Grey W PTS 12
Type/Style: Is a skilful southpaw
Points of Interest: 5'1" tall. Failed in three attempts to win WBC titles.

20.07.96	Jorge Calfin W PTS 10 Maldonado
06.09.96	Alberto Jimenez DREW 12 Buenos Aires
	(WBO Flyweight Title Challenge)
13.12.96	Alberto Jimenez W RSC 10 Buenos Aires
	(WBO Flyweight Title Challenge)
08.03.97	Antonio Ruiz DREW 12 Mexicali
	(WBO Flyweight Title Defence)
23.05.97	Antonio Ruiz W PTS 12 Roque Saenz Pena
	(WBO Flyweight Title Defence)
Career: 54 contests, won 44, drew 3, lost 7.	

Alex (Nene) Sanchez

Playa Ponce, Puerto Rico. *Born* 5 June, 1975
WBO M. Flyweight Champion

Major Amateur Honours: None
Turned Pro: October 1991
Significant Results: Rafael Orozco W PTS 12, Tomas Rivera W PTS 12
Type/Style: A speedy stylist and a good puncher
Points of Interest: 5'0" tall. Turned pro

at the age of 16. Had a two year period of inactivity, but has 18 wins by kayo or stoppage, ten in the first round.

22.02.97	Edgar Cardenas L PTS 10 Condado
29.03.97	Victor Burgos W PTS 12 Las Vegas
	(WBO M. Flyweight Title Defence)
Career: 26 contests, won 25, lost 1.	

Chatchai (Dutchboygym) Sasakul

Bangkok, Thailand. *Born* 5 February, 1970
WBC Interim Flyweight Champion. Former Undefeated WBC International Flyweight Champion

Major Amateur Honours: Competed in the 1988 Olympic Games. Gold medallist, 1988-1990 Kings Cup
Turned Pro: August 1991
Type/Style: Good hand and foot speed, but stamina questionable
Points of Interest: 5'3" tall. Has 21 wins by kayo or stoppage. Given an interim title shot due to injury to champion, Yuri Arbachakov, he has also fought under the name Chatchai Elitegym.

31.07.96	Jimmy Aguirre W CO 4 Bangkok
23.08.96	Ricky Ocoy W RSC 6 Suratani
08.11.96	Allan Morre W CO 7 Bangkok
30.01.97	Rami Gevero W CO 5 Chumpon
09.05.97	Ysaias Zamudio W PTS 12 Bangkok
	(Vacant WBC Interim Flyweight Title)
Career: 29 contests, won 28, lost 1.	

Sirimongkol Singmanassak

Bangkok, Thailand. *Born* 2 March, 1977
WBC Bantamweight Champion

Major Amateur Honours: None
Turned Pro: May 1994
Significant Results: Thalernsak Sitbaobey W RSC 3, Jose Luis Bueno W CO 6
Type/Style: A strong, stand-up boxer, but not a big puncher
Points of Interest: 5'7" tall. Only six wins inside the distance. Is a former WBU champion.

10.08.96	Jose Luis Bueno W RSC 5 Bangkok
	(Vacant Interim WBC Bantamweight Title)
15.02.97	Jesus Sarabia W PTS 12 Nakhon Phanom
	(WBC Bantamweight Title Defence)
26.04.97	Javier Campanario W RSC 4 Phuket
	(WBC Bantamweight Title Defence)
Career: 15 contests, won 15.	

Yokthai Sith-Oar

Chiengrai, Thailand. *Born* 25 December, 1975
WBA S. Flyweight Champion

Major Amateur Honours: None
Turned Pro: October 1994
Significant Results: Juan Antonio Torres W PTS 10, Abdi Pohan W RSC 5
Type/Style: An aggressive, hard body puncher, but short on stamina
Points of Interest: Former star kickboxer. Won the WBA title in only his 11th bout and has eight wins by kayo or stoppage.

24.08.96	Alimi Goitia W RSC 8 Kamphaeng Phet
	(WBA S. Flyweight Title Challenge)
10.11.96	Jack Siahaya W CO 2 Phichit
	(WBA S. Flyweight Title Defence)
01.03.97	Aquiles Guzman W PTS 12 Chachoensao
	(WBA S. Flyweight Title Defence)
29.04.97	Satoshi Iida DREW 12 Nagoya
	(WBA S. Flyweight Title Defence)
Career: 14 contests, won 13, drew 1.	

Saman Sorjaturong

Kampangsaen, Thailand. *Born* 2 August, 1969
WBC L. Flyweight Champion. Former Undefeated IBF L. Flyweight Champion

Major Amateur Honours: None
Turned Pro: December 1989
Significant Results: Ricardo Lopez L RSC 2, Humberto Gonzalez W RSC 7, Yuichi Hosono W RSC 4
Type/Style: Although a brave, aggressive puncher with a great left hook, he is let down by a poor defence
Points of Interest: 5'3" tall. Real name Saman Sriprataet. Relinquished the IBF title. Has eight title defences to his name and 28 wins by kayo or stoppage.

10.08.96	Shiro Yahiro W RSC 9 Phitsanulok
	(WBC L. Flyweight Title Defence)
19.10.96	Ali Galvez W CO 2 Samut Prakan
	(WBC L. Flyweight Title Defence)
15.12.96	Manuel Jesus Herrera W PTS 12 Changrai
	(WBC L. Flyweight Title Defence)
13.04.97	Julio Coronel W RSC 7 Chaiyaphum
	(WBC L. Flyweight Title Defence)
31.05.97	Mzukisi Marali W RSC 4 Petchaboon
	(WBC L. Flyweight Title Defence)
Career: 39 contests, won 36, drew 1, lost 2.	

Saman Sorjaturong

Ratanapol Sowvoraphin

Dankoonthod, Thailand. *Born* 6 June, 1973
IBF M. Flyweight Champion. Former Undefeated IBF Inter-Continental M. Flyweight Champion

Major Amateur Honours: None
Turned Pro: October 1990
Significant Results: Manny Melchor W PTS 12, Ala Villamor W RTD 7, Ronnie Magramo W PTS 12
Type/Style: Is a fast, slick southpaw
Points of Interest: 5'4" tall. Made 12 defences, but was then stripped of the title when he failed to make the weight. Regained the title two months later.

13.07.96	Jun Orhaliza W CO 3 Chiangmai
	(IBF M. Flyweight Title Defence)
28.09.96	Oscar Andrade W CO 5 Prachuabirikhan
	(IBF M. Flyweight Title Defence)
24.11.96	Gustavo Vera W CO 2 Udonthani
	(IBF M. Flyweight Title Defence)
18.01.97	Eddie Felisardo W CO 5 Nongbualampoo
22.03.97	Luis Doria W RSC 4 Saraburi
14.06.97	Juan Herrera W PTS 12 Bangkok
	(IBF M. Flyweight Title Defence)
Career: 36 contests, won 33, drew 1, lost 2.	

Johnny (Tap Tap) Tapia
Albuquerque, USA. *Born* 13 February, 1967
WBO S. Flyweight Champion. Former Undefeated USBA & NABF S. Flyweight Champion

Major Amateur Honours: Golden Gloves Champion, 1983 and 1985
Turned Pro: March 1988
Significant Results: Henry Martinez W RSC 11, Arthur Johnson W PTS 12, Ricardo Vargas T Draw 8
Type/Style: Is a cool, composed, slick boxer and a hard puncher
Points of Interest: Has had a constant battle against drugs and alcohol. Out of the sport for two years after 1985 Golden Gloves victory, his record shows ten title defences and 24 wins by kayo or stoppage.

17.08.96	Hugo Soto W PTS 12 Albuquerque *(WBO S. Flyweight Title Defence)*	
11.10.96	Sammy Stewart W RSC 7 Las Vegas *(WBO S. Flyweight Title Defence)*	
30.11.96	Adonis Cruz W PTS 12 Albuquerque *(WBO S. Flyweight Title Defence)*	
08.03.97	Jorge Barrera W RSC 3 Albuquerque *(WBO S. Flyweight Title Defence)*	
Career: 42 contests, won 40, drew 2.		

Felix Juan (Tito) Trinidad
Cupoy Alto, Puerto Rico. *Born* 10 January, 1973
IBF Welterweight Champion

Major Amateur Honours: None
Turned Pro: March 1990
Significant Results: Maurice Blocker W CO 2, Hector Camacho W PTS 12, Yori Boy Campas W RSC 4, Oba Carr W RSC 8
Type/Style: Despite being an explosive puncher with either hand, he has a vulnerable chin
Points of Interest: 5'10" tall. Has 11 title defences and 27 wins by kayo or stoppage. Dad was a pro.

07.09.96	Ray Lovato W RSC 6 Las Vegas *(IBF Welterweight Title Defence)*	
11.01.97	Kevin Lueshing W RSC 3 Nashville *(IBF Welterweight Title Defence)*	
Career: 31 contests, won 31.		

Wilfredo Vasquez
Bayamon, Puerto Rico. *Born* 2 August, 1961

WBA Featherweight Champion. Former WBA Bantamweight Champion. Former WBA S. Bantamweight Champion. Former Undefeated Puerto Rican Bantamweight Champion. Former Undefeated Latin American Featherweight Champion

Major Amateur Honours: None
Turned Pro: June 1981
Significant Results: Israel Contreras L CO 1, Raul Perez W RSC 3, Luis Mendoza W PTS 12, Orlando Canizales L PTS 12, Antonio Cermeno L PTS 12, Eloy Rojas W RSC 11
Type/Style: Is a sharp boxer with power in both hands
Points of Interest: 5'5" tall. Has taken part in 18 world title fights and has 37 wins by kayo or stoppage.

07.12.96	Bernardo Mendoza W RSC 5 Indio *(WBA Featherweight Title Defence)*	
30.03.97	Yuji Watanabe W RSC 5 Tokyo *(WBA Featherweight Title Defence)*	
Career: 58 contests, won 48, drew 3, lost 7.		

Adolpho Washington
Lexington, USA. *Born* 7 September, 1967
Former IBF Cruiserweight Champion. Former Undefeated NABF Cruiserweight Champion

Major Amateur Honours: None
Turned Pro: March 1989
Significant Results: Virgil Hill L TD 11, Anaclet Wamba DREW 12, Orlin Norris L PTS 12
Type/Style: Is a skilful boxer with a sharp jab
Points of Interest: The loss to Virgil Hill was due to a cut received from a ringside camera. Beat Riddick Bowe as a junior.

31.08.96	Torsten May W PTS 12 Palma de Mallorca *(Vacant IBF Cruiserweight Title)*	
21.06.97	Uriah Grant L PTS 12 Tampa *(IBF Cruiserweight Title Defence)*	
Career: 32 contests, won 26, drew 2, lost 4.		

Ronald (Winkie) Wright
St Petersburg, USA. *Born* 26 November, 1971

WBO L. Middleweight Champion. Former Undefeated NABF L. Middleweight Champion

Major Amateur Honours: Gold medallist, 1990 Olympic Festival
Turned Pro: October 1990
Significant Results: Julio Cesar Vazquez L PTS 12, Tony Marshall W PTS 12, Bronco McKart W PTS 12
Type/Style: Is a slick, clever southpaw
Points of Interest: 5'10" tall. Floored six times by Julio Cesar Vazquez.

09.11.96	Ensley Bingham W PTS 12 Manchester *(WBO L. Middleweight Title Defence)*	
03.05.97	Steve Foster W RSC 6 Manchester *(WBO L. Middleweight Title Defence)*	
Career: 38 contests, won 37, lost 1.		

Daniel Zaragoza
Mexico City, Mexico. *Born* 11 December, 1957
WBC S. Bantamweight Champion. Former WBC Bantamweight Champion. Former Undefeated Mexican Bantamweight Champion. Former Undefeated NABF S. Bantamweight Champion

Major Amateur Honours: Gold medallist, 1979 Pan American Games. Mexican Golden Gloves Champion, 1978
Turned Pro: October 1980
Significant Results: Carlos Zarate W RSC 10, Mike Ayala W RSC 7, Tracy Harris Patterson DREW 12, Hector Acero W PTS 12
Type/Style: A rugged, crafty and courageous southpaw, who is a good tactician but prone to cuts
Points of Interest: 5'6" tall. Has taken part in 21 WBC title fights and boasts 27 wins by kayo or stoppage.

20.07.96	Tsuyoshi Hamada W RSC 7 Osaka *(WBC S. Bantamweight Title Defence)*	
11.01.97	Wayne McCullough W PTS 12 Boston *(WBC S. Bantamweight Title Defence)*	
14.04.97	Joichiro Tatsuyoshi W PTS 12 Osaka *(WBC S. Bantamweight Title Defence)*	
Career: 65 contests, won 55, drew 3, lost 7.		

World Title Bouts During 1996-97

by Bob Yalen

All of last season's title bouts for the IBF, WBA, WBC, and WBO are shown in date order within their weight division and give the boxers' respective weights, along with the scorecard, if going to a decision. There is also a short summary of every bout that involved a British contestant and British officials, where applicable, are listed. Again, as in 1995-96, there was not one contest that involved the WORLD TITLE, a sad indictment of the modern era. The nearest anyone came to unifying a division, and that excludes other commissions such as the WBU, was when Dariusz Michalczewski, the WBO light-heavyweight champion defeated Virgil Hill for the IBF and WBA championships. Sadly, due to politics, the German has since relinquished the IBF version when a fight against the winner of Montell Griffin v Roy Jones for the WBC title, could have brought about a single champion.

M. Flyweight

IBF
13 July 1996 Ratanapol Sowvoraphin 7.6½ (Thailand) W CO 3 Jun Orhaliza 7.6 (Philippines), Chiangmai, Thailand.
28 September 1996 Ratanapol Sowvoraphin 7.6½ (Thailand) W CO 5 Oscar Andrade 7.6½ (Mexico), Prajuabirikhan, Thailand.
24 November 1996 Ratanapol Sowvoraphin 7.6 (Thailand) W CO 2 Gustavo Vera 7.6 (Venezuela), Udonthani, Thailand.
22 March 1997 Ratanapol Sowvoraphin 7.6 (Thailand) W RSC 4 Luis Doria 7.5½ (Colombia), Sabaruri, Thailand.
14 June 1997 Ratanapol Sowvoraphin 7.7 (Thailand) W PTS 12 Juan Herrera 7.7 (Colombia), Bangkok, Thailand. Scorecards: 115-113, 116-111, 117-109.

WBA
1 October 1996 Rosendo Alvarez 7.7 (Nicaragua) W RSC 8 Takashi Shiohama 7.6¼ (Japan), Kokura, Japan.
11 January 1997 Rosendo Alvarez 7.7 (Nicaragua) W RSC 11 Songkram Porpaoin 7.7 (Thailand), Sakaew, Thailand.

WBC
9 November 1996 Ricardo Lopez 7.7 (Mexico) W RSC 6 Morgan Ndumo 7.7 (South Africa), Las Vegas, USA.
7 December 1996 Ricardo Lopez 7.5¾ (Mexico) W RSC 1 Myung-Sup Park 7.5 (South Korea), Indio, USA.
29 December 1996 Ricardo Lopez 7.7 (Mexico) W PTS 12 Mongol Jor Charoen 7.7 (Thailand), Las Vegas, USA. Scorecards: 120-107, 119-108, 120-107.

WBO
29 March 1997 Alex Sanchez 7.7 (Puerto Rico) W PTS 12 Victor Burgos 7.7 (Mexico), Las Vegas, USA. Scorecards: 115-110, 113-112, 114-111.

L. Flyweight

IBF
13 September 1996 Michael Carbajal 7.9½ (USA) W RSC 8 Julio Coronel 7.10 (Colombia), Des Moines, USA.
12 October 1996 Michael Carbajal 7.10 (USA) W RSC 5 Tomas Rivera 7.10 (Mexico), Anaheim, USA.
18 January 1997 Michael Carbajal 7.10 (USA) L PTS 12 Mauricio Pastrana 7.8½ (Colombia), Las Vegas, USA. Scorecards: 116-112, 113-115, 114-115. Pastrana forfeited the title for failing to attend a weigh in for a defence against Manuel Herrera on 10 May.

WBA
13 August 1996 Keiji Yamaguchi 7.10 (Japan) W PTS 12 Carlos Murillo 7.9¾ (Panama), Osaka, Japan. Scorecards: 119-109, 119-111, 115-113.
3 December 1996 Keiji Yamaguchi 7.9¾ (Japan) L RSC 2 Pichitnoi Chor Siriwat 7.8¾ (Thailand), Osaka, Japan.
29 June 1997 Pichitnoi Chor Siriwat 7.10 (Thailand) W PTS 12 Sang-Chul Lee 8.10 (South Korea), Bangkok, Thailand. Scorecards: 119-110, 118-109, 118-109.

WBC
10 August 1996 Saman Sorjaturong 7.9½ (Thailand) W RSC 9 Shiro Yahiro 7.9¾ (Japan), Phitsanulok, Thailand.
19 October 1996 Saman Sorjaturong 7.8¾ (Thailand) W CO 2 Ali Galvez 7.9½ (Chile), Samut Prakan, Thailand.
15 December 1996 Saman Sorjaturong 7.10 (Thailand) W PTS 12 Manuel Jesus Herrera 7.9¼ (Dominican Republic), Changrai, Thailand. Scorecards: 116-112, 114-113, 115-113.
13 April 1997 Saman Sorjaturong 7.8 (Thailand) W RSC 7 Julio Coronel 7.10 (Colombia), Chaiyaphum, Thailand.
31 May 1997 Saman Sorjaturong 7.9½ (Thailand) W RSC 4 Mzukisi Marali 7.9½ (South Africa), Petchaboon, Thailand.

WBO
8 February 1997 Jacob Matlala 7.10 (South Africa) W PTS 12 Mickey Cantwell 7.9 (England), London Arena, London, England. Scorecards: 116-112, 116-112, 113-115. Despite being cut on the left eye following a clash of heads in the third, Cantwell's defensive skill and jab negated a lot of the champion's aggression and it was only in the latter stages that he began to wilt. However, it was a great effort and he will be looking to be involved in any title shake up, especially after Matlala relinquished the title in May 1997 when he was not allowed by the organisation to fight Michael Carbajal.
31 May 1997 Jesus Chong 7.9½ (Mexico) W RSC 2 Eric Griffin 7.10 (USA), Las Vegas, USA.

Flyweight

IBF
5 August 1996 Mark Johnson 7.13 (USA) W RSC 8 Raul Juarez 7.13½ (Mexico), Los Angeles, USA.
10 February 1997 Mark Johnson 8.0 (USA) W PTS 12 Alejandro Montiel 8.0 (Mexico), Los Angeles, USA. Scorecards: 119-107, 118-108, 118-108.
1 June 1997 Mark Johnson 8.0 (USA) W CO 2 Cecilio Espino 8.0 (Mexico), Uncasville, USA.

WBA
8 September 1996 Saen Sorploenchit 8.0 (Thailand) W PTS 12 Alexander Makhmoutov 8.0 (Russia), Nakhon

Phanom, Thailand. Scorecards: 118-113, 118-110, 119-111.
23 November 1996   Saen Sorploenchit 8.0 (Thailand) L PTS 12 Jose Bonilla 8.0 (Venezuela), Bangkok, Thailand. Scorecards: 111-117, 114-117, 111-117.
25 February 1997   Jose Bonilla 7.13½ (Venezuela) W RSC 7 Hiroki Ioka 8.0 (Japan), Osaka, Japan.

WBC
26 August 1996   Yuri Arbachakov 8.0 (Russia) W RSC 9 Takato Toguchi 8.0 (Japan), Tokyo, Japan. With Arbachakov sidelined with a fractured wrist since the above fight, an interim title meet was arranged between Chatchai Sasakul and Ysaias Zamudio.
9 May 1997   Chatchai Sasakul 8.0 (Thailand) W PTS 12 Ysaias Zamudio 7.13 (USA), Bangkok, Thailand. Scorecards: 116-112, 118-112, 117-113.

WBO
6 September 1996   Alberto Jimenez 7.13¼ (Mexico) DREW 12 Carlos Salazar 8.0 (Argentine), Buenos Aires, Argentina. Scorecards: 114-114, 115-113, 115-118.
13 December 1996   Alberto Jimenez 8.0 (Mexico) L RSC 10 Carlos Salazar 7.13½ (Argentine), Buenos Aires, Argentina.
8 March 1997   Carlos Salazar 8.0 (Argentine) DREW 12 Antonio Ruiz 8.0 (Mexico), Mexicali, Mexico. Scorecards: 114-114, 117-111, 114-114.
23 May 1997   Carlos Salazar 8.0 (Argentine) W PTS 12 Antonio Ruiz 8.0 (Mexico), Roque Saenz Pena, Argentina. Scorecards: 117-113, 117-112, 118-112.

S. Flyweight
IBF
24 August 1996   Harold Grey 8.3 (Colombia) L CO 2 Danny Romero 8.2¾ (USA), Albuquerque, USA.
1 November 1996   Danny Romero 8.3 (USA) W RSC 12 Hipolito Saucedo 8.3 (USA), Indio Springs, USA.
8 March 1997   Danny Romero 8.2¼ (USA) W RSC 6 Jaji Sibali 8.2¼ (South Africa), Albuquerque, USA. *Stop Press:* Romero lost his title on a points decision to the WBO champion, Johnny Tapia, in Las Vegas, USA, on 18 July.

WBA
24 August 1996   Alimi Goitia 8.3 (Venezuela) L RSC 8 Yokthai Sith-Oar 8.3 (Thailand), Kamphaeng Phet, Thailand.
10 November 1996   Yokthai Sith-Oar 8.3 (Thailand) W CO 2 Jack Siahaya 8.3 (Indonesia), Phichit, Thailand.
1 March 1997   Yokthai Sith-Oar 8.3 (Thailand) W PTS 12 Aquiles Guzman 8.3 (Venezuela), Chachoensao, Thailand. Scorecards: 119-111, 118-112, 115-113.
29 April 1997   Yokthai Sith-Oar 8.2½ (Thailand) DREW 12 Satoshi Iida 8.3 (Japan), Nagoya, Japan. Scorecards: 114-114, 115-115, 113-116.

WBC
12 October 1996   Hiroshi Kawashima 8.3 (Japan) W RSC 2 Domingo Sosa 8.3 (Dominican Republic), Tokyo, Japan.
20 February 1997   Hiroshi Kawashima 8.3 (Japan) L PTS 12 Gerry Penalosa 8.2½ (Philippines), Tokyo, Japan. Scorecards: 112-116, 114-115, 115-114.
14 June 1997   Gerry Penalosa 8.3 (Philippines) W RSC 9 Seung-Koo Lee 8.3 (South Korea), Mactan, Philippines.

WBO
17 August 1996   Johnny Tapia 8.2½ (USA) W PTS 12 Hugo Soto 8.2 (Argentine), Albuquerque, USA. Scorecards: 119-110, 118-110, 118-110.
11 October 1996   Johnny Tapia 8.3 W RSC 7 Sammy Stewart 8.1½ (USA), Las Vegas, USA.
30 November 1996   Johnny Tapia 8.2 (USA) W PTS 12 Adonis Cruz 8.2½ (Nicaragua), Albuquerque, USA. Scorecards: 117-111, 116-113, 119-113.
8 March 1997   Johnny Tapia 8.3 (USA) W RSC 3 Jorge Barrera 8.3 (Mexico), Albuquerque, USA. *Stop Press:* Tapia added the IBF title to his collection when he outpointed Danny Romero in Las Vegas, USA, on 18 July.

Bantamweight
IBF
26 November 1996   Mbulelo Botile 8.5½ (South Africa) W PTS 12 Aristead Clayton 8.6 (USA), Baton Rouge, USA. Scorecards: 120-106, 117-111, 116-112. *Stop Press:* Timothy Austin (USA) won the title on 19 July in Austin, USA, when he stopped Botile at 2.20 of the eighth round.

WBA
27 October 1996   Nana Yaw Konadu 8.6 (Ghana) L TD 9 Daorung Chuwatana 8.6 (Thailand), Bangkok, Thailand. Scorecards: 96-97, 94-97, 94-98.
15 March 1997   Daorung Chuwatana 8.6 (Thailand) W PTS 12 Felix Machado 8.6 (Venezuela), Satul Province, Thailand. Scorecards: 114-113, 115-113, 113-115.
21 June 1997   Daorung Chuwatana 8.4¾ (Thailand) L RSC 7 Nana Yaw Konadu 8.5¼ (Ghana), Tampa, USA.

WBC
10 August 1996   Sirimongkol Singmanassak 8.6 (Thailand) W RSC 5 Jose Luis Bueno 8.5½ (Mexico), Phitsanulok, Thailand. With Wayne McCullough having difficulty making the weight, this was billed for the vacant interim title. Later, in early February, the Irishman forfeited the title, leaving Singmanassak as the recognised champion.
15 February 1997   Sirimongkol Singmanassak 8.6 (Thailand) W PTS 12 Jesus Sarabia 8.6 (Mexico), Nakhon Phanom, Thailand. Scorecards: 115-111, 115-110, 115-111.
26 April 1997   Sirimongkol Singmanassak 8.6 (Thailand) W RSC 4 Javier Campanario 8.6 (Spain), Phuket, Thailand.

WBO
There were no title bouts at the weight during 1996-97 due to the champion, Robbie Regan, being injured.

S. Bantamweight
IBF
20 August 1996   Vuyani Bungu 8.10 (South Africa) W PTS 12 Jesus Salud 8.10 (USA), Hammanskraal, South Africa. Scorecards: 117-111, 118-109, 118-110.
5 April 1997   Vuyani Bungu 8.10 (South Africa) W PTS 12 Kennedy McKinney 8.9¾ (USA), Hammanskraal, South Africa. Scorecards: 115-113, 113-115, 117-113.

WBA
9 November 1996   Antonio Cermeno 8.9 (Venezuela) W RTD 5 Eddy Saenz 8.10 (Nicaragua), Las Vegas, USA.
21 December 1996   Antonio Cermeno 8.9 (Venezuela) W PTS 12 Yuichi Kasai 8.9½ (Japan), Las Vegas, USA. Scorecards: 118-109, 117-112, 117-112.

10 May 1997   Antonio Cermeno 8.9$^1/_2$ (Venezuela) W PTS 12 Angel Chacon 8.10 (Puerto Rico), Miami, USA. Scorecards: 115-112, 118-112, 118-111.

WBC

20 July 1996   Daniel Zaragoza 8.10 (Mexico) W RSC 7 Tsuyoshi Harada 8.9$^1/_4$ (Japan), Osaka, Japan.
11 January 1997   Daniel Zaragoza 8.9$^1/_2$ (Mexico) W PTS 12 Wayne McCullough 8.8 (Ireland), Boston, USA. Scorecards: 116-112, 116-112, 114-115.

Featherweight
IBF

31 August 1996   Tom Johnson 9.0 (USA) W PTS 12 Ramon Guzman 8.13$^1/_4$ (Venezuela), Dublin, Ireland. Scorecards: Dave Parris 115-107, 118-107, 116-109.
8 February 1997   Tom Johnson 8.13$^1/_2$ (USA) L RSC 8 Prince Naseem Hamed 9.0 (England), London Arena, London, England. By his win, Hamed, already the holder of the WBO version of the title, became a double champion. Although performing at a shade below his best, Hamed was always going better than Johnson, who, by a mixture of good skills and cunning, somehow held the Englishman off for seven rounds. However, into the eighth a right uppercut all but unhinged Johnson and despite rising at the count of eight the referee had seen enough, waving it off at 2.29 of the round.
3 May 1997   Prince Naseem Hamed 125$^3/_4$ (England) W RSC 1 Billy Hardy 126 (England), Nynex Arena, Manchester, England. Referee: Paul Thomas. Judges: Roy Francis, Mickey Vann, Dave Parris. Hamed's WBO title was also at stake. Stopped after just 1.33 of the first round, Hardy had already been subjected to a count of seven from a straight right lead, before a cracking right hook sent him down for six and brought the referee to his rescue.

WBA

7 December 1996   Wilfredo Vasquez 9.0 (Puerto Rico) W RSC 5 Bernardo Mendoza 8.11 (Chile), Indio, USA.
30 March 1997   Wilfredo Vasquez 9.0 (Puerto Rico) W RSC 5 Yuji Watanabe 8.13$^1/_4$ (Japan), Tokyo, Japan. Referee: John Coyle.

WBC

6 July 1996   Luisito Espinosa 8.13 (Philippines) W PTS 12 Cesar Soto 8.13$^1/_2$ (Mexico), Manila, Philippines. Scorecards: 117-112, 115-112, 115-112.
2 November 1996   Luisito Espinosa 8.13$^3/_4$ (Philippines) W RSC 8 Nobutoshi Hiranaka 8.13$^3/_4$ (Japan), Fukuoka, Japan.
17 May 1997   Luisito Espinosa 8.13$^3/_4$ (Philippines) W TD 7 Manuel Medina 9.0 (Mexico), Manila, Philippines. Scorecards: 78-73, 78-73, 77-75.

WBO

31 August 1996   Prince Naseem Hamed 9.0 (England) W RTD 11 Manuel Medina 8.13$^3/_4$ (Mexico), Dublin, Ireland. Carrying a bit of a cold, Hamed made heavy weather of his best opponent to date and, despite flooring Medina three times, in the first and twice in the ninth, the champion's timing was all at sea, leaving him missing badly at times and also easy to hit. However, even on a bad night the last thing you lose is your power and eventually it told on the challenger. At the end of the 11th round, cut and all in, Medina was taken out of the fight after the referee had seen enough.

9 November 1996   Prince Naseem Hamed 8.13$^3/_4$ (England) W RSC 2 Remigio Molina 8.13$^1/_4$ (Argentine), Nynex Arena, Manchester, England. Having spent a feeling out first round and looking to finish his rival in the next, Hamed unleashed a right-left that dropped Molina for seven. Jumping in immediately, on Molina rising, a tremendous right uppercut sent the Argentinian stumbling and effectively ended the fight as the referee rescued him at 2.32 of the session.
8 February 1997   Prince Naseem Hamed 9.0 (England) W RSC 8 Tom Johnson 8.13$^1/_2$ (USA), London Arena, London, England. The fight also involved Johnson's IBF title.
3 May 1997   Prince Naseem Hamed 8.13$^3/_4$ (England) W RSC 1 Billy Hardy 9.0 (England), Nynex Arena, Manchester, England. Referee: Paul Thomas. Judges: Roy Francis, Mickey Vann, Dave Parris. Hamed's IBF title was also at stake.

S. Featherweight
IBF

22 February 1997   Arturo Gatti 9.4 (Canada) W PTS 12 Tracy Harris Patterson 9.4 (USA), Atlantic City, USA. Scorecards: 118-108, 117-109, 116-110.

WBA

13 October 1996   Yong-Soo Choi 9.4 (South Korea) W PTS 12 Yamato Mitani 9.4 (Japan), Tokyo, Japan. Scorecards: 115-114, 115-113, 115-112.
1 February 1997   Yong-Soo Choi 9.3$^1/_2$ (South Korea) W PTS 12 Lakva Sim 9.3$^1/_2$ (Mongolia), Seoul, South Korea. Scorecards: 115-113, 114-113, 113-115.
24 May 1997   Yong-Soo Choi 9.4 (South Korea) W PTS 12 Koji Matsumoto 9.4 (Japan), Seoul, South Korea. Scorecards: 116-112, 117-114, 115-113.

WBC

22 March 1997   Azumah Nelson 9.3 (Ghana) L PTS 12 Genaro Hernandez 9.3$^3/_4$ (USA), Corpus Christi, USA. Scorecards: Richie Davies 110-118, 113-115, 114-113.
14 June 1997   Genaro Hernandez 9.3$^3/_4$ (USA) W PTS 12 Anatoly Alexandrov 9.3$^3/_4$ (Russia), San Antonio, USA. Scorecards: 116-113, 116-113, 113-115.

WBO

6 September 1996   Regilio Tuur 9.4 (Holland) W CO 1 Jose Vida Ramos 9.4 (Dominican Republic), Atlantic City, USA. Tuur retired in January 1997.
1 March 1997   Julien Lorcy 9.3$^1/_2$ (France) DREW 12 Arnulfo Castillo 9.3 (Mexico), Paris, France. Scorecards: 112-112, 116-112, 113-113.

Lightweight
IBF

19 October 1996   Phillip Holiday 9.7$^3/_4$ (South Africa) W PTS 12 Joel Diaz 9.8$^1/_2$ (USA), Johannesburg, South Africa. Scorecards: 119-109, 119-110, 119-110.
21 December 1996   Phillip Holiday 9.9 (South Africa) W PTS 12 Ivan Robinson 9.8$^3/_4$ (USA), Uncasville, USA. Scorecards: 118-110, 117-111, 116-112.
16 May 1997   Phillip Holiday 9.9 (South Africa) W PTS 12 Pete Taliaferro 9.9 (USA), Hammanskraal, South Africa. Scorecards: 115-111, 111-115, 115-111. *Stop Press:* Shane Mosley (USA) won the title when outpointing Phillip Holiday in Montville, USA, on 2 August.

WBA
10 May 1997   Orzubek Nazarov 9.8 (Kyrghyzstan) W RSC 7 Leavander Johnson 9.6 (USA), Miami, USA.

WBC
1 March 1997   Jean-Baptiste Mendy 9.7$^1/_2$ (France) L PTS 12 Steve Johnston 9.8$^1/_2$ (USA), Paris, France. Scorecards: 113-116, 114-113, 113-115.

WBO
21 September 1996   Artur Grigorian 9.8$^1/_2$ (Uzbekistan) W CO 2 Gene Reed 9.8$^3/_4$ (USA), Berlin, Germany.
16 November 1996   Artur Grigorian 9.8$^3/_4$ (Uzbekistan) W PTS 12 Marty Jakubowski 9.8 (USA), Hamburg, Germany. Scorecards: 120-106, 119-109, 119-109.
22 February 1997   Artur Grigorian 9.8 (Uzbekistan) W RSC 11 Raul Balbi 9.8$^1/_2$ (Argentine), Hamburg, Germany.

L. Welterweight
IBF
14 September 1996   Konstantin Tszyu 9.13$^1/_2$ (Russia) W CO 6 Jan Bergman 9.13$^3/_4$ (South Africa), Newcastle, Australia.
18 January 1997   Konstantin Tszyu 9.13 (Russia) TD 1 Leonardo Mas 10.0 (Puerto Rico), Las Vegas, USA.
31 May 1997   Konstantin Tszyu 10.0 (Russia) L RSC 10 Vince Phillips 10.0 (USA), Atlantic City, USA.

WBA
16 August 1996   Juan M. Coggi 10.0 (Argentine) L PTS 12 Frankie Randall 10.0 (USA), Buenos Aires, Argentine. Scorecards: 112-115, 113-114, 111-117. Referee: John Coyle.
11 January 1997   Frankie Randall 9.13$^1/_2$ (USA) L RSC 11 Khalid Rahilou 9.13 (France), Nashville, USA.

WBC
18 January 1997   Oscar de la Hoya 10.0 (USA) W PTS 12 Miguel Gonzalez 10.0 (Mexico), Las Vegas, USA. Scorecards: John Keane 117-110, 117-111, 117-109. De la Hoya relinquished the title on winning the WBC welter crown in April 1997.

WBO
12 October 1996   Giovanni Parisi 9.13$^1/_2$ (Italy) W RSC 4 Sergio Rey Revilla 9.10$^3/_4$ (Spain), Milan, Italy. Judge: Paul Thomas.
19 April 1997   Giovanni Parisi 9.12$^1/_4$ (Italy) W RSC 8 Harold Miller 9.12$^1/_4$ (USA), Milan, Italy.

Welterweight
IBF
7 September 1996   Felix Trinidad 10.7 (Puerto Rico) W RSC 6 Ray Lovato 10.6$^1/_2$ (USA), Las Vegas, USA.
11 January 1997   Felix Trinidad 10.7 (Puerto Rico) W RSC 3 Kevin Lueshing 10.6$^1/_4$ (England), Nashville, USA. For a moment in the second it looked as though Lueshing was on the verge of scoring a huge upset when two left hooks floored and hurt the champion. Unfortunately for the challenger, however, Trinidad was quickly up and in the third session began to demonstrate his power. After twice flooring the Englishman with heavy left hooks, a smashing right cross sent him crashing down for the third time and this time the referee did not even bother to pick up the count, stopping the action at 2.59 of the round.

WBA
5 October 1996   Ike Quartey 10.7 (Ghana) W PTS 12 Oba Carr 10.7 (USA), New York City, USA. Scorecards: 112-112, 116-109, 117-109.
18 April 1997   Ike Quartey 10.6$^1/_2$ (Ghana) W RSC 5 Ralph Jones 10.7 (USA), Las Vegas, USA.

WBC
20 September 1996   Pernell Whitaker 10.7 (USA) W PTS 12 Wilfredo Rivera 10.7 (Puerto Rico), Miami, USA. Scorecards: John Keane 115-111, 113-112, 115-113.
24 January 1997   Pernell Whitaker 10.7 (USA) W RSC 11 Diobelys Hurtado 10.6 (Cuba), Atlantic City, USA.
12 April 1997   Pernell Whitaker 10.6$^1/_2$ (USA) L PTS 12 Oscar de la Hoya 10.6$^1/_2$ (USA), Las Vegas, USA. Scorecards: 111-115, 110-116, 110-116.
14 June 1997   Oscar de la Hoya 10.7 (USA) W CO 2 David Kamau 10.6$^3/_4$ (Kenya), San Antonio, USA.

WBO
6 October 1996   Jose Luis Lopez 10.7 (Mexico) W RTD 5 Ramon Campas 10.7 (Mexico), Los Angeles, USA. Lopez forfeited the title in January 1997 after being tested positive for marijuana.
22 February 1997   Michael Loewe 10.5$^1/_2$ (Romania) W PTS 12 Santiago Samaniego 10.5 (Panama), Hamburg, Germany. Scorecards: 114-113, 117-110, 116-112.

L. Middleweight
IBF
7 September 1996   Terry Norris 10.13 (USA) W RSC 5 Alex Rios 10.13$^1/_2$ (USA), Las Vegas, USA. Norris' WBC title was also on the line.
11 January 1997   Terry Norris 11.0 (USA) W RSC 10 Nick Rupa 10.12$^1/_4$ (USA), Nashville, USA. Norris, whose WBC belt was also at stake, forfeited the title in February 1997, when unable to fulfil his mandatory requirements.
12 April 1997   Raul Marquez 10.13 (USA) W RSC 9 Anthony Stephens 11.0 (USA), Las Vegas, USA.

WBA
21 August 1996   Julio Cesar Vasquez 11.0 (Argentine) L CO 5 Laurent Boudouani 10.13 (France), Le Cannet Rocheville, France.
29 March 1997   Laurent Boudouani 11.0 (France) W PTS 12 Carl Daniels 11.0 (USA), Las Vegas, USA. Scorecards: 118-108, 115-111, 117-109.

WBC
7 September 1996   Terry Norris 10.13 (USA) W RSC 5 Alex Rios 10.13$^1/_2$ (USA), Las Vegas, USA.
11 January 1997   Terry Norris 11.0 (USA) W RSC 10 Nick Rupa 10.12$^1/_4$ (USA), Nashville, USA.

WBO
9 November 1996   Ronald Wright 10.12$^3/_4$ (USA) W PTS 12 Ensley Bingham 11.0 (England), Nynex Arena, Manchester, England. Scorecards: 119-109, 119-110, 119-110. Thought to stand a fair chance of success prior to the fight, unfortunately, at the final bell, Bingham had been found wanting, having neither the speed or ringcraft to get close enough to land his heavy punches on the adroit champion. To his credit, he continued to force the action, but it was a tactic which allowed Wright to highlight all of his skills, notably the excellent southpaw jab.

3 May 1997   Ronald Wright 11.0 (USA) W RSC 6 Steve Foster 10.13³/₄ (England), Nynex Arena, Manchester, England. Judge: Paul Thomas. Back in town for another defence, Wright merely emphasised the fact that he was a cut above our best men when he chopped down the Salford hard man inside six rounds of a one-sided tanking. The end came at 2.52 after Foster had twice been sent crashing following accurate body shots and, after praising the winner, he announced his retirement from the ring.

Middleweight
IBF
16 July 1996   Bernard Hopkins 11.4¹/₄ (USA) W RSC 11 Bo James 11.4 (USA), Atlantic City, USA.
19 April 1997   Bernard Hopkins 11.2¹/₂ (USA) W RSC 7 John David Jackson 11.2 (USA), Shreveport, USA.

WBA
19 October 1996   William Joppy 11.5 (USA) W RSC 6 Ray McElroy 11.2¹/₂ (USA), Upper Marlboro, USA.
10 May 1997 William Joppy 11.5 (USA) W PTS 12 Peter Venancio 11.5 (Brazil), Miami, USA. Scorecards: 114-113, 115-112, 114-112.

WBC
19 October 1996   Keith Holmes 11.3 (USA) W RSC 12 Richie Woodhall 11.4 (England), Upper Marlboro, USA. Unfortunately, Woodhall lost his chance of winning the title 12 days before the fight when he underwent keyhole surgery to his right elbow. However, he bravely made a fight of it, despite being unable to land straight punches, until running out of steam and being floored by short left hooks in the 12th round. On rising at nine, the challenger took another dozen or so punches without reply before the referee called a halt to the proceedings with 28 seconds of the fight left, leaving the disappointed Englishman to ponder on what might have been.

WBO
30 August 1996   Lonnie Bradley 11.5³/₄ (USA) W PTS 12 Simon Brown 11.3³/₄ (USA), Reading, USA. Scorecards: 117-111, 117-113, 117-111.
4 March 1997   Lonnie Bradley 11.6 (USA) DREW 12 Otis Grant 11.6 (Canada), Las Vegas, USA.
28 June 1997   Lonnie Bradley 11.6 (USA) W RSC 8 John Williams 11.5¹/₂ (USA), Las Vegas, USA.

S. Middleweight
IBF
5 October 1996   Roy Jones 12.0 (USA) W RSC 2 Bryant Brannon 12.0 (USA), New York City, USA. Roy Jones relinquished the title in March 1997 after being recognised as the WBC light-heavyweight champion.
21 June 1997   Charles Brewer 11.11 (USA) W RSC 5 Gary Ballard 11.13¹/₄ (South Africa), Tampa, USA.

WBA
19 April 1997   Frank Liles 12.0 (USA) W RSC 5 Segundo Mercado 11.12³/₄ (Ecuador), Shreveport, USA.

WBC
6 July 1996   Thulani Malinga 11.11³/₄ (South Africa) L PTS 12 Vincenzo Nardiello 11.13 (Italy), Nynex Arena, Manchester, England. Referee: Mickey Vann. Scorecards: John Keane 112-116, 116-111, 112-114.

12 October 1996   Vincenzo Nardiello 12.0 (Itlay) L CO 7 Robin Reid 11.13¹/₄ (England), Milan, Italy. In winning, Reid became the third British fighter to bring back a world title from Italy, but it was not until round five that the challenger really began to pressure Nardiello, putting him on the deck. Somehow, he let the champion off the hook until catching up with him again in the seventh, a thudding left hook to the ribs finishing off some useful body punches and forcing the full count out at 2.58 of the round.
8 February 1997   Robin Reid 11.12¹/₂ (England) W CO 7 Giovani Pretorius 11.12 (South Africa), London Arena, London, England. Judge: John Keane. Despite producing a tremendous first round, which included a knockdown, and cutting the South African over both eyes and dropping him again in the fifth, it took Reid until the seventh before a heavy right to the head finally put the challenger down and out at 2.10 of the session. Although showing some bad habits, once again the champion's power delivered the victory.
3 May 1997   Robin Reid 11.12¹/₄ (England) W PTS 12 Henry Wharton 12.0 (England), Nynex Arena, Manchester, England. Scorecards: Richie Davies 116-111, 117-113, 114-114. Referee: Larry O'Connell. Boxing well, mainly on the back foot, Reid countered all that that the challenger threw and seemed well worth his points win, despite one of the judges scoring it even. To be fair to Wharton, he was the one who forced the fight, but the champion boxed superbly to instructions and proved that he had the stamina and durability to go a hard 12 rounds.

WBO
6 July 1996   Steve Collins 11.11³/₄ (Ireland) W RSC 4 Nigel Benn 11.13¹/₂ (England), Nynex Arena, Manchester, England. Following a mauling opening two rounds, Benn got going with his heavy punches, but they merely bounced off the champion's head and, with Collins also beginning to get the bit between the teeth in the fourth, it was obvious the fight would not last. Then it happened. Missing with a wild right, Benn crashed to the canvas, twisting his right ankle in the process and was stopped moments later, at 2.46 of the round, when it was obvious he could not continue.
9 November 1996   Steve Collins 12.0 (Ireland) W RTD 6 Nigel Benn 11.13 (England), Nynex Arena, Manchester, England. Referee: Paul Thomas. Judge: Roy Francis. Competing well for three rounds before Collins got on top, Benn was retired on his stool at the end of the sixth after it had become patently obvious that the challenger had made his big effort only for his punches to have no effect on the durable champion. Announcing his retirement from the ring, it was a sad exit for a proud fighter, but there was only ever going to be one winner and that was Collins.
8 February 1997   Steve Collins 11.13¹/₂ (Ireland) W RSC 5 Frederic Seillier 11.13¹/₂ (France), London Arena, London, England. Judges: Roy Francis and Paul Thomas. Noted for being prone to cuts, as early as the second round Seillier was carrying severe damage to the left eye and in the fifth his nose was badly gashed, prompting the referee to call it off at 2.20 of the round. Although putting up game resistance, looking mainly to counter, the champion carried too much power and strength for the Frenchman and never looked likely to lose.

L. Heavyweight
IBF
23 November 1996   Henry Maske 12.6¹/₄ (Germany) L PTS 12 Virgil Hill 12.6³/₄ (USA), Munich, Germany.

Scorecards: 116-112, 113-116, 113-115. Hill's WBA title was also on the line.

13 June 1997   Virgil Hill 12.5^1/$_2$ (USA) L PTS 12 Dariusz Michalczewski 12.6 (Germany), Oberhausen, Germany. Scorecards: 112-117, 113-116, 110-118. Referee: John Coyle. The fight also involved the WBA belt. Michalczewski relinquished the IBF version a week later, rather than defend against William Guthrie by 19 July. *Stop Press:* William Guthrie became the IBF champion on 19 July in Indio, USA, when he stopped Darin Allen in the third round.

WBA
23 November 1996   Virgil Hill 12.6^3/$_4$ (USA) W PTS 12 Henry Maske 12.6^1/$_4$ (Germany), Munich, Germany. Scorecards: 112-116, 116-113, 115-113. With his win, Hill also took over the IBF championship.

13 June 1997   Virgil Hill 12.5^1/$_2$ (USA) L PTS 12 Dariusz Michalczewski 12.6 (Germany), Oberhausen, Germany. Scorecards: 112-117, 113-116, 110-118. Referee: John Coyle. Billed as an IBF/WBA title fight, following his win, Michalczewski, already the WBO titleholder, became a three-time champion.

WBC
22 November 1996   Roy Jones 12.5 (USA) W PTS 12 Mike McCallum 12.7 (Jamaica), Tampa, USA. Scorecards: 116-111, 117-110, 119-108. With Fabrice Tiozzo inactive, this was billed for the vacant interim title. Jones was named as champion in February 1997 after Tiozzo forfeited due to inactivity.

21 March 1997   Roy Jones 12.7 (USA) L DIS 9 Montell Griffin 12.7 (USA), Atlantic City, USA. *Stop Press:* Jones regained his title when knocking Griffin out in the first round on 7 August in Pensacola, USA.

WBO
10 August 1996   Dariusz Michalczewski 12.7 (Germany) W DIS 7 Graciano Rocchigiani 12.6 (Germany), Hamburg, Germany.

13 December 1996   Dariusz Michalczewski 12.7 (Germany) W RSC 8 Christophe Girard 12.6^1/$_2$ (France), Hannover, Germany.

Cruiserweight
IBF
31 August 1996   Adolpho Washington 13.7^3/$_4$ (USA) W PTS 12 Torsten May 13.6^1/$_2$ (Germany), Palma de Mallorca, Spain. Scorecards: 115-114, 117-111, 116-112. Billed for the vacant title after Al Cole relinquished in June 1996 when unable to make the weight.

21 June 1997   Adolpho Washington 13.8 (USA) L PTS 12 Uriah Grant 13.5^1/$_4$ (USA), Tampa, USA. Scorecards: 112-116, 114-114, 112-116.

WBA
31 August 1996   Nate Miller 13.7^1/$_2$ (USA) W RSC 7 James Heath 13.5^1/$_2$ (USA), Dublin, Ireland.

22 February 1997   Nate Miller 13.6 (USA) W RSC 2 Alexander Gurov 13.8 (Ukraine), Fort Lauderdale, USA.

WBC
5 July 1996   Marcelo Dominguez 13.8 (Argentine) W RTD 9 Patrice Aouissi 13.6 (France), Hyeres, France.

6 December 1996   Marcelo Dominguez 13.7^1/$_4$ (Argentine) W RTD 7 Jose Arimatea da Silva 13.6^1/$_2$ (Spain), Buenos Aires, Argentine.

WBO
13 July 1996   Ralf Rocchigiani 13.6^1/$_2$ (Germany) W PTS 12 Bashiru Ali 13.8 (Nigeria), Essen, Germany. Scorecards: 115-113, 116-112, 116-112.

13 December 1996   Ralf Rocchigiani 13.5^1/$_2$ (Germany) W PTS 12 Stefan Angehrn 13.4^1/$_2$ (Switzerland), Hannover, Germany. Scorecards: 119-109, 117-112, 118-110.

26 April 1997   Ralf Rocchigiani 13.5^1/$_4$ (Germany) W PTS 12 Stefan Angehrn 13.5^1/$_4$ (Switzerland), Zurich, Switzerland).

Heavyweight
IBF
9 November 1996   Michael Moorer 15.9 (USA) W RSC 12 Frans Botha 16.0 (South Africa), Las Vegas, USA.

29 March 1997   Michael Moorer 15.2 (USA) W PTS 12 Vaughn Bean 15.2 (USA), Las Vegas. Scorecards: 114-114, 116-113, 115-113.

WBA
7 September 1996   Bruce Seldon 16.5 (USA) L RSC 1 Mike Tyson 15.9 (USA), Las Vegas, USA.

9 November 1996   Mike Tyson 15.12 (USA) L RSC 11 Evander Holyfield 15.5 (USA), Las Vegas, USA.

28 June 1997   Evander Holyfield 15.8 (USA) W DIS 3 Mike Tyson 15.8 (USA), Las Vegas, USA.

WBC
7 February 1997   Lennox Lewis 17.13 (England) W RSC 5 Oliver McCall 16.13 (USA), Las Vegas, USA. Judge: Larry O'Connell. Billed for the vacant title after Mike Tyson forfeited in September 1996 for failing to defend against the leading challenger, Lennox Lewis, the latter recaptured his old crown when McCall was stopped after 55 seconds of the fifth round when refusing to protect himself. Having recently been in drug rehabilitation, it was all too much for the American who switched off towards the end of the third round and spent the remainder of the fight in floods of tears.

WBO
9 November 1996   Henry Akinwande 17.0 (England) W RSC 10 Alexander Zolkin 16.11 (Russia), Las Vegas, USA. Floored in the fourth from a big right, the Russian southpaw was easy meat for Akinwande's jab and was cut over both eyes from the sixth onwards. With the damage worsening and Zolkin shipping punches, the referee wisely waved it off after 2.32 of the tenth.

11 January 1997   Henry Akinwande 16.8^1/$_2$ (England) W PTS 12 Scott Welch 16.5 (England), Nashville, USA. Scorecards: 120-108, 120-108, 119-110. In an all-British title joust, despite his pre-fight brashness, the challenger could find no fight once the action had started, leaving Akinwande in total charge. Unfortunately, the champion, although able to land almost at will, was drawn into the lethargy and, unable to really hurt Welsh, ultimately settled for a points win. In February 1997, he relinquished the title in order to maintain his high rating with the WBC and obtain a contest against Lennox Lewis.

28 June 1997   Herbie Hide 15.4^3/$_4$ (England) W RSC 2 Tony Tucker 17.5^1/$_4$ (USA), Sports Village, Norwich, England. Floored three times in the second for an automatic stoppage defeat at 2.45 of the round, Tucker proved to be too old and too slow for his speedy opponent. Following a tentative start, once the younger man started to put his punches together it was obvious to most that it was just a matter of time and so it proved to be.

The American Invasion of Bombardier Billy Wells

by Bob Soderman

If you had been an inveterate moviegoer during the years 1935 through 1946, you were probably lucky enough to have included several of the British J. Arthur Rank Organisation films among your cinema viewing pleasures.

You must recall those classic films, such as "The 39 Steps", starring Robert Donat and Madeleine Carroll; "The Lady Vanishes", starring Michael Redgrave and Margaret Lockwood; "King Solomon's Mines", starring Paul Robeson and Roland Young; "Pygmalion", starring Leslie Howard and Wendy Hiller; plus countless other memorable Rank Organisation films. All of these films, every one of them, dramatically came on the screen showing a huge and very muscular man swinging a very large mallet against an immense gong; the sound from which reverberated to the very rafters of the cinema theatres. This was the trademark of the Rank Organisation; a visual symbol of what the public soon came to anticipate as enjoyable and very entertaining films.

Those inveterate film patrons probably were not aware of just who that gong-striking muscular man was. However, the man who swung that mallet, and sounded that gong at the beginning of all those films, was one of England's greatest and most popular sporting athletes of the 20th Century. More than likely, neither today's cinema patrons nor sports adherents know the name Bombardier Billy Wells, and it is of one brief part of his career that we would like to review here.

Bombardier Billy Wells became the heavyweight champion of Great Britain in 1911, at the age of 23, and held that championship until 1919. Gifted with a magnificent physique, his exploits in the ring during his career, which spanned the years 1909 to 1925, thrilled the boxing fans of three continents and he was a handsome and personable man besides.

Wells revolutionised the attitude of the British public toward the sport of boxing, transforming it from a spectacle attracting the so-called baser elements of society, to a respectable sport that commanded widespread respect and admiration. He invariably drew capacity gatherings to any arena he was booked to fight in.

Promoters soon came to realise that the good-looking Englishman was also attracting splendidly dressed middle-class ladies, who were making up a good part of the ringside seat section at all of his bouts. Very few of these ladies were interested in the art of prize fighting. Their prime interest was in Wells alone, in his 6 foot 2$^1/_2$ inch and 190 pound frame, and these admiring ladies soon coined their own name for him – "Beautiful Billy".

It was not his physical beauty that British men admired, it was his physical attributes, his remarkable speed for such a big man and his power to knock an opponent unconscious with one blow. This was what the men admired, and flocked eagerly to see the action, whenever the Bombardier was booked to fight.

Bombardier Billy Wells

227

Billy had come out of the British Army in 1910, having won the All-India heavyweight championship, and scored an impressive run of victories in London rings through 1911, culminating with his winning of the heavyweight championship of Britain, on 24 April, 1911, when he knocked out the then champion, Iron Hague, in six rounds.

The world's heavyweight champion at this time was the negro, Jack Johnson, who had won the title in 1908 and had ever since built up the enmity of the fistic and social world through his arrogance and flamboyant tactics.

As a consequence, in the United States, a thriving new industry had arisen. It was the feverish search for a white fighter to come along and eventually meet the detested Johnson in the ring to regain the championship for the White Race.

Fight managers, promoters, newspapermen, all were frantically engaged in seeking out, developing, promoting, and writing about this new breed of fighter – the "White Hope". In America there had sprung up dozens of these men and England's Bombardier Billy Wells became a prominent name added to the list. An elimination tournament of sorts had just begun, to crown the "White Heavyweight Champion", and an offer was made to Wells to come to New York for a series of bouts.

Al Palzer

Wells set sail for New York in May 1912 and, on arrival, set up his training camp well away from the city, in the small town of Rye. He was booked to meet his first American foe, Al Palzer, a big Iowa farm boy, on Friday 28 June, 1912, at New York's Madison Square Garden. The dozen or so New York sporting writers who visited Wells' camp and watched him box, were extremely impressed with him and their glowing reports in their newspapers helped to build a great deal of public interest in the forthcoming bout.

Al Palzer, Wells' first American opponent, was equally as tall as Wells, being 6 foot 3 inches, and he generally weighed around 220 pounds for his bouts. He was also no stranger to New York fistic audiences, having rolled up an impressive string of victories, including wins over some of America's leading heavyweights.

The styles of the two fighters were diametrically opposed. Palzer was a slugger, pure and simple, and thought nothing of absorbing two blows to get in one of his own, while Wells relied on cleverness of hand and foot, and was a standup boxer in the classic, British and European manner.

When they entered the ring on 28 June, the weights were announced as $228\frac{1}{4}$ for Palzer, and $188\frac{1}{2}$ for Wells. As the men stood in the centre of the ring for their instructions from the referee, Wells looked like a slender middle-weight contrasted to the herculean appearance of Palzer, his legs being thin compared to the huge limbs of his opponent.

At the opening bell Palzer landed a light left to the face and Wells followed with his own light left, and then they fell into a clinch. Billy then began to dance around his foe, shooting straight lefts and rights, making Al look clumsy and slow.

Palzer rushed and tried to get in close and, during one of these rushes, Wells ripped in a right uppercut as he bored in, starting the blood flowing from Al's mouth. "Go for the stomach," cried Palzer's corner, but the British champion was too fast and clever on the defence. The fans marvelled at the rare exhibition they were watching. Not since the heyday of James J. Corbett had anyone seen such brilliant boxing and clever defensive work.

Wells' attack employed every suitable weapon, hooks, jabs, uppercuts, straight lefts, and straight rights and Palzer's head was being jarred back and forth, but he still kept coming forward. Late in the round, Palzer crouched low and rushed at Wells. Billy stepped back a half-step and measured his man with perfection. A terrific right uppercut caught the rushing Palzer coming forward and down the Iowa farm boy went, crashing to the canvas.

Al barely got to his feet at the count of nine and staggered across the ring. Wells followed cautiously, wary of what might be a trick on the part of Palzer, to entice him close enough to let fly a desperation punch. Although Palzer reached out and grabbed Wells, Billy managed to land a few more punches after the clinch was broken before the bell ended the round.

The buzz of excited approval from the crowd persisted all during the one minute rest for the fighters, before the bell for round two sent them into action once again. Round two, at least for the first two minutes, was more of the same. Wells was absolutely brilliant, dancing rings around Palzer, methodically cutting him to ribbons. Al could only swing wildly, and was missing by wide margins as Billy moved in closer to gain more leverage for what he considered would be the final punches to ensure his apparent victory.

As Wells moved confidently in on Palzer, Al uncorked another wild right, but this time all the luck was on the American's side. The punch landed with shocking, full force on Wells' jaw, and down went Billy. Wells was down for a count of nine, but, on rising, was able to retreat and keep Palzer at bay with a sterling display of boxing. The crowd was in an uproar. For the rest of round two it was a determined Palzer stalking a cleverly retreating Wells. It had been a long, long time since the Garden had seen such an exciting battle between two big men.

The third round started out with both men a trifle subdued in their attack. Palzer was not rushing in aimlessly, as he had been, and Wells was keeping his distance and treating Palzer with a great deal of wary respect.

The knockdown of Wells had given Palzer a big surge of confidence and he was watching carefully for another opportunity to land one more hefty right. Al did land a hard right, but it was not the real big one he had hoped for, although it forced Billy to move into a clinch. At that point, some ringsiders observed that Wells' facial expression showed him to be undergoing considerable strain and it was becoming obvious that the unexpected knockdown he had suffered had greatly changed the complexion of the fight.

Wells was fighting purely on the defensive now and his early confidence seemed to be oozing away as the seconds ticked by. Palzer, on the other hand, was gaining in confidence and was now assuming the dominant role in the fight, brushing off Wells' now feeble leads and marching in relentlessly, his every punch sapping Billy's fast-ebbing spirit. Al got in close and swung a right hook to the jaw. Down went Wells once more. Billy barely made it to his feet at the count of nine, this time.

Wells walked around the ring, sidling away from Palzer, while a puzzled Palzer followed carefully, suspecting a ruse on Billy's part. Suddenly, Wells wheeled and landed a smashing left on Palzer's jaw. The punch sent Al's head back and was followed by a clinch. The respite was all too brief for Wells, for as soon as they broke Palzer landed a right hook to the stomach, forcing Billy's mouth to drop open, and down he went for the third time.

Wells just managed to regain his feet at the count of nine, but he was plainly a beaten man, all his initial strength seeming to have drained out of him. Walking around the ring, not attempting to throw a punch, he managed to duck under a right swing, moved forward in an attempt to clinch and hold on, before falling face forward to the floor.

Referee Billy Joh once more started to count, as the stunned fans looked on in wonderment at the Englishman lying as still as death on the canvas, but when the count had reached eight, Wells' corner threw a sponge into the ring in token of surrender.

It took several minutes of smelling salts and furious fanning with towels before he was recovered enough to leave the ring. The crowd, most of which had waited until Wells was revived, gave him a tremendous cheer of appreciation for his efforts, the cheers being every bit equal to that the crowd had given to the victorious Palzer. To anyone who had not witnessed the fight, and just seeing the two fighters as they exited the ring, it looked like Al Palzer had lost the bout, his left eye closed, his nose slightly off kilter, and his lips being puffy and cut. Wells, on the other hand, bore no marks of battle and his face showed no evidence of cuts or bruises.

Promoters for the Garden Athletic Club, after seeing the tremendous newspaper coverage following the bout with Al Palzer, and the unstinting praise for Bombardier Billy Wells, were quick to bring Wells back for another bout in Madison Square Garden. This time they obtained Tom Kennedy as the opponent. Kennedy was a top-rated heavyweight and had scored a victory over Al Palzer in one of his recent bouts. On 18 July, 1912, another large and enthusiastic crowd filled the arena for another look at the heavyweight champion of Great Britain.

Tom Kennedy was a much better boxer than Al Palzer, although not as hard a hitter, and it was felt that he would offer a more effective defence for Wells' undoubted cleverness, and would not be as easy to hit as was Palzer. Wells, even with his loss to Palzer, was the betting favourite on the night of the fight, but there was a last-minute surge of Kennedy money which brought the odds down to even money at fight time.

On this occasion, Billy Wells fought a much better fight. The Garden audience, many of whom had been present to see Wells land the many devastating first round punches that almost put Al Palzer into the land of nod, may not have agreed with that assessment. This time, Billy was careful to husband his strength and not lavish it all on an attempt to score a one-round knockout.

Tom Kennedy, a much different fighter than the wild-swinging Al Palzer, was a clever and careful boxer, with a keen and watchful eye in the ring. He was not a man who ignored his defences and, like Billy Wells, he was quick on his feet.

The fortunate ones in the Garden that night would undoubtedly remember this bout for a long time to come. Seldom would the Garden present a bout in which two big heavyweights, they both weighed in at ringside at 191$\frac{1}{2}$, give such a dazzling exhibition of cleverness and speed. To the spectators, it appeared as if they were watching a pair of dazzling lightweights, displaying wondrous speed of foot and of hand.

In the first minute of round one, Wells brought the crowd to its feet, expecting another wild melee, when he floored Kennedy with a beautifully-timed straight right to the jaw. Kennedy, on falling, reached up and grabbed Wells and pulled Billy down after him. By the time they both were back on their feet, the chance of a fast knockout had gone fleetingly by.

Kennedy seemed to match Wells in brilliance and cleverness in the first two rounds, but, from that point on in the bout, it was obvious that Wells was far superior in speed and cleverness to the American boxer. Billy was most careful not to make the same sort of mistakes he had made against Al Palzer, taking his time, and placing his punches where they would do the most good, while guarding against any unexpected punches that might find a chink in his armour.

In round three, Wells stunned Kennedy, forcing him to drop his hands to his sides, and quickly landed several hard rights to the jaw. Both the crowd, and Wells, expected to see Kennedy topple to the canvas, but Tom did not even stagger. Indeed, the last hard right seemed to wake Kennedy up, and he mounted his own attack which forced Wells to back up and give ground.

Wells' corner exhorted him to take it easy and not wear himself out with an unceasing attack. So Billy relied on his straight left jab; a jab which constantly sent Kennedy's head back and gradually wore him down. As the fight progressed, Kennedy absorbed more and more punishment, although he managed to keep the fight interesting with his sporadic rallies, rallies which worried Billy even though he was piling up points with his own unceasing attack.

In round eight, Kennedy was finally able to temporarily take the play away from Wells, getting home with his own straight jabs as Billy showed signs of tiring. It proved a temporary lapse for Wells, however, as he quickly regained the initiative by countering with a left hook to the stomach, followed by a right to the jaw, sending Kennedy down for the second time in the bout.

Tom took a nine count and was dazed when he regained his feet. Wasting no time in taking advantage of a greatly weakened Kennedy, Wells again hooked his left to the stomach, bringing Tom's guard down, and then shot another hard right to the jaw. Kennedy fell heavily and it was apparent that this time he would not get up. The referee had reached seven in his count when Kennedy's chief second threw a sponge into the ring to acknowledge defeat.

Ringside pundits, in their post-fight analysis, agreed that Wells had shown signs, again, of his inability to withstand too much punishment. On several occasions during the bout, Billy had been handed blows to the stomach which had forced him to back up, or fall into a clinch. Kennedy's own corner had shouted to him continually during the bout to "go after the stomach", but Tom would not, or could not, carry out these instructions. One reason of course, was the steady stream of stiff and very damaging left jabs that Kennedy was forced to absorb, punches that kept him back on his heels throughout almost every round of the fight.

Wells returned to England on 23 July, the day after he had been the guest of honour at a dinner hosted by Billy Gibson, manager of the Garden Athletic Club, at the Hotel St Denis. Thirty persons were present for the occasion, one of whom was the New York State Senator, James J. Frawley, who had been the leader in steering New York's present boxing bill through the State legislature for passage.

Wells' powerful jab can be seen to good advantage as he sets up Arthur Townley for the finisher

Wells delivered a short speech, promising he would return to New York in a few months, where he hoped to dispose of all the leading white heavyweights in order to force Jack Johnson into a match. At the dinner, Wells had been lauded for his excellent deportment, in and out of the ring, and was proclaimed by several of the speakers as a credit to the sport of boxing.

Back in England, Wells opted to take a long rest from the rigours of his boxing career, before returning to action on 6 December, 1912, at the King's Hall in London, and knocking out George (Boer) Rodel, of South Africa, in two rounds.

On 1 February, 1913, Wells and an entourage consisting of his wife, his brother, Sidney, and his manager, Jim Maloney, set sail for his return to the United States. He was supposedly matched with Luther McCarty, the now recognised "White Heavyweight Champion", for a March bout in Madison Square Garden in New York. McCarty, who had just knocked out Al Palzer, on 1 January, 1913, for some inexplicable reason then refused to sign for the match.

As a substitute for McCarty, the Madison Square Garden promoters signed Gunboat Smith, of California, to be the opponent. Gunboat was no stranger to New York fistic audiences, having appeared in local rings more than a dozen times in the last year and never having tasted defeat. Smith had been fighting since 1906, and was 5 feet 11 inches tall and weighed around 180 pounds.

Wells was the betting favourite for the Friday 14 March, 1913 match and was figured to be too clever and hard hitting for Smith to handle. Overlooked in the calculation of these odds, however, was the fact that Gunboat was quite a knockout puncher himself, having notched ten such triumphs in the last year alone. Also, Smith had not lost a bout for over a year and had suffered just three defeats in his entire career.

Wells, whose habit was to train with boxing gloves of regulation five or six ounce weight, instead of the usual big ten or 12 ounce gloves generally used in training camps, had his usual trouble in obtaining and keeping sparring partners. The sparmates had a tendency to quit after they had been knocked out in sparring session. They did not take too kindly to Wells' hard punching, despite the Englishman not being too vicious when in training. All-out sparring sessions were his usual style, his notion being that he wanted to duplicate the feeling and circumstances of the actual matches themselves, the better to condition himself.

Again, the visiting newsmen to Wells' camp were dutifully impressed. They went away convinced that he was the cleverest big man of the time and they were impressed with his hitting ability, especially when they saw him floor sparmate, Jack McFarland, a 200-pounder from Long Island City, who had fought Gunboat Smith the previous year. The newsmen were awed also by Wells' speed; "like a featherweight", they said, and then by his punch, "like the kick of a mule", they reported.

Smith will have to come to Wells, was the consensus of the experts. He will not be able to match Wells in boxing ability, and in coming in he will face the risk of running into one of Billy's devastating right hands. Again,

however, overlooked was the fact that Smith was a fairly good boxer himself and that he was possessed of a very good right-hand knockout punch of his own. The Gunboat's stamina was not in question, but some of the newsmen questioned that factor in Wells' make-up, citing his sudden deterioration in the match against Palzer. Against Tom Kennedy though, Billy had seemed more in control of himself, pacing his actions very nicely and showing no signs of weakness or fatigue.

An even larger crowd poured into the Garden that night, to see the British fighter they had so taken to their hearts emerge triumphant. Alas, that wish was not to be.

Wells weighed in at 192 and Smith 182$\frac{1}{2}$. Even though Billy was heavier and taller than his opponent, when they stood together in the ring centre to receive their instructions, Wells looked almost delicate compared with Smith's rugged appearance.

The first round was similar to the bout with Al Palzer, in that an alert Wells scored with straight lefts and rights to Smith's face and easily evaded Gunboat's wild swings. The pattern repeated itself all through the opening round, Smith rushing, Wells stabbing him with straight punches, and making his foe look like the veriest tyro. It was well into the second minute of the contest before Smith was able to land a punch, and then it was just a light straight left to the face. It was all Wells in round one.

Wells was quick to come out for round two and shot out a straight left, but Smith was rushing forward and they fell into a clinch. Coming out of the clinch, Smith again rushed and threw a wild right. It missed, but he quickly threw another one, and, inexplicably, it landed flush on the jaw, putting Wells down.

A group at the Ring in 1914, shows the Bombardier standing sixth from the left in the top row. Also in the picture are other champions or former champions such as Young Joseph, Harry Reeve, Billy Baxter, Charlie Mitchell, Jim Carney, Sid Smith, Jim Sullivan, Dick Smith, and Johnny Summers. See if you can spot them!

A greatly stunned Billy climbed to his feet at the count of nine. His countenance was clouded and he was weak. Worse, his speed seemed to have suddenly left him. He stood off and tried to box, but the Gunboat tore in, discarding any pretence at defence for Wells' now impotent punches, raining blows in from all angles and battering down his feeble attempts.

A looping right-hand smash landed just over Wells' left eye and down went Billy again! He made it to his feet at nine, but it was obvious to all in the crowd, that the fight had gone out of Billy Wells.

Wells was on his feet, yes, but he was now just a caricature of that brilliant boxer from round one. Smith threw another looping right that caught Billy on the point of the chin and, as Wells sank, he was out like the proverbial light even before he landed on the canvas.

This time it took more than a few minutes to revive him and have him depart the ring for his dressing room. And yet, the great crowd stayed around and gave him another hearty cheer as well as lavish rounds of applause. Wells' popularity appeared undiminished, but it was agreed by all the fight experts around New York that this defeat marked the end of Bombardier Billy Wells' career, as far as New York or the United States was concerned.

It was agreed that he was possessed of a full knowledge of all the finer aspects of the boxing profession. He boxed like a Corbett, he punched as hard as any man in the ring, he had speed, he had ring generalship, but he lacked two things, two essential things that every championship fighter must possess – stamina and brute instinct.

Against Al Palzer, Billy had been just one punch away from scoring a quick and decisive knockout, but he turned cautious and let the opportunity get away. Here it was not so much that caution took over. Rather, it was that lack of a brute instinct. Certainly, Palzer nor Smith hesitated when they had sensed that Wells was ready for the kill.

Wells would go on for the rest of his long career having his better nature take over at critical junctures, in fights that this better nature would prevent his winning and would allow opponents to turn the tide and result in his defeat.

For all his devotion to intensive training, at least in his three American bouts, Wells never could seem to muster that reserve of stamina that would have pulled him through to victory. He was plagued with a variety of weaknesses that interfered with him becoming the outstanding world success he should have been, even though he was such a resoundingly popular figure in his native Great Britain.

Perhaps it was, after all, the fact that Bombardier Billy Wells was much too intelligent a man in the ring to be the success, and world heavyweight champion, he might have been. He worried too much, whereas American opponents, Al Palzer and Gunboat Smith, worried not at all once they got inside the ring. Their only thought was landing that one crushing blow that would end it decisively. Wells was too much the stylist, too much the thinker, too much the worrier, to be what so many thought he should have been.

So, on 18 March, 1913, just four days after the un-expected knockout defeat at the hands of Gunboat Smith,

the Wells' group set sail for home, aboard the German liner, the Kaiser Wilhelm II. Bombardier Billy Wells never returned to America, although he continued fighting in England and in Europe until the year 1925. He retained the British heavyweight championship he had won in 1912, until 1919.

A rather strange fate awaited the first of Billy Wells' American opponents, Al Palzer. After Al's knockout win over Wells he then went on to suffer knockout defeats himself, at the hands of Luther McCarty, Frank Moran, and Dan Dailey, all in the year 1913, before being murdered on 26 July, 1914, by his own father, at their home in Minnesota.

An equally sad fate befell Luther McCarty, the recognised "White Heavyweight Champion", who had been slated to meet Wells, but who had backed out of the fight, with Gunboat Smith taking his place. McCarty was knocked out in the first round, on 24 May, 1913, at Calgary, Saskatchewan, in Canada, by Arthur Pelkey. He was carried from the ring and died eight minutes later. A coroner's jury determined later that McCarty had died of a haemorrhage of the brain, but not from any blow in the ring delivered by Pelkey.

What of Tom Kennedy and Gunboat Smith? Kennedy's career lasted into 1916, and he even fought in London in 1914. Later, he embarked on a second career, moving to Hollywood, California, and becoming a star of cinema comedies. Kennedy died in 1965, aged 80, in Woodland Hills, California.

Gunboat Smith carried on into the year 1921, and even fought Jack Dempsey three times, twice in 1917, and once in 1918. Smith also boxed one time in London, on 16 July, 1914, engaging in one of the most controversial heavyweight fights ever fought in England. On that night, he was disqualified in the sixth round of his bout against Georges Carpentier, for striking the latter when he was down. The jury is still out on that fight, 83 years later. Gunboat Smith also lived to a ripe old age, passing away on 6 August, 1974, in Leesburg, Florida, at the age of 87.

Bombardier Billy Wells also lived to a good age, just missing by two months the venerable figure of 80 years, when passing away on 12 June, 1967, in London. Billy was almost as popular in his later years as he had been during his prime. A few months before his death he had been the guest at a dinner sponsored by the British Boxing Writers, in London, after being reluctant to appear, fearing that no one would remember him. In this he was wrong. On being introduced, he was given a roaring, standing ovation, a tribute that brought tears to his eyes.

What might have happened, possibly, if Bombardier Billy Wells had not lost to both Al Palzer and to Gunboat Smith in America and had won instead? Might he not have gone on to face, and to beat Jack Johnson, for the world heavyweight championship? With just a little bit of luck, and a much kinder stroke of fate, Bombardier Billy Wells might have been included in that roster of fabled heavyweight champions of the world.

World Title Bouts Since Gloves: Addendum and Appendages

This section is the follow-up to the last three Yearbooks, which set out to provide a history of world championship boxing, fight by fight, in the most comprehensive form ever published. Where new information has come to hand, the title entry has been re-written, while an (+) following the date determines a fight never previously recorded as involving the championship. There is still much work to do, especially after it was discovered that champions in America during the no-decision era, more often than not, defended their title claims in bouts of that nature. Six men, Georges Carpentier (light-heavy), George Chip, Al McCoy, Mike O'Dowd (middles), Jack Britton (welter) and Benny Leonard (light), actually won their so-called championships in no-decision bouts, while the first million dollar gate, Dempsey v Carpentier in Jersey City, was articled as a fight where the referee would not be called upon to render a points verdict if it went the full distance. The most persistent abuser of the system appears to be former featherweight champion, Johnny Kilbane, who consistently asked his opponents to make the championship weight of 122 lbs, thus allowing the promoter to bill accordingly, while he would invariably come to the ring at around 130 lbs with his own referee in tow. However, conversely, Benny Leonard seemed quite happy to fight two ten rounders a week in different towns against men inside the limit as long as he was able to make as near to 135 lbs as he could manage without having to boil down. Although the opposition had to win inside the distance to stand any chance of being accorded championship status, both men continuously risked their title claims in these affairs, as did all the other leading men at the time. While no-decision boxing was a euphemism for exhibitions, and a way round the State laws during the early part of the century, without it the noble art in America would have died. That is why it must be considered of the utmost importance.

Country Code (Codes relate to place of domicile, not necessarily birthplace)
A-Australia; ARG-Argentina; ARM-Armenia; AU-Austria; BAH-Bahamas; BAR-Barbados; BEL-Belgium; BR-Brazil; C-Canada; CH-Chile; COL-Colombia; CR-Costa Rica; CUB-Cuba; CZ-Czechoslovakia; DEN-Denmark; DOM-Dominican Republic; EC-Ecuador; FIN-Finland; FR-France; GB-Great Britain; GER-Germany; GH-Ghana; GRE-Greece; GU-Guyana; HA-Hawaii; HOL-Holland; I-Ireland; IC-Ivory Coast; INDON-Indonesia; ITA-Italy; J-Jamaica; JAP-Japan; K-Kenya; MEX-Mexico; MOR-Morocco; N-Nigeria; NIC-Nicaragua; NOR-Norway; NZ-New Zealand; PAN-Panama; PAR-Paraguay; PE-Peru; PH-Philippines; PNG-Papua New Guinea; PR-Puerto Rico; SA-South Africa; SK-South Korea; SP-Spain; SWE-Sweden; SWI-Switzerland; TH-Thailand; TO-Togo; TR-Trinidad; TUN-Tunisia; U-Uganda; UR-Uruguay; USA-United States of America; VEN-Venezuela; YUG-Yugoslavia; ZA-Zambia.

Flyweight (112 lbs)

Established by the National Sporting Club in Britain in 1909, it was introduced in order to protect men who were just too small to be fighting at the ever-increasing bantamweight limit. The first sign of interest in the new weight division came when Johnny Coulon, who held the American 112 lbs bantamweight crown, claimed the American title, but within weeks he had moved up to 116 lbs. Eventually, in Britain, Sid Smith was matched for the vacant British title against Stoker Hoskyne at the Ring, Blackfriars on 25 September 1911. Although winning on points over 20 rounds and then outscoring Louis Ruddick over the same distance at Liverpool Stadium on 19 October 1911, there was little recognition for Smith, especially as the Hoskyne fight had been contested over two minute rounds and it was left to the NSC to match him against Joe Wilson with the Lonsdale Belt as an added extra, Smith winning on points over 20 rounds on 4 December 1912.

19.09.12+ Sid Smith (GB) W PTS 20 Curley Walker (GB), The Ring, London - GB. *Contested under full championship conditions, this fight was billed for the world 112 lbs title.*

19.10.14 Tancy Lee (GB) W RSC 14 Percy Jones (GB), NSC, London. *Although the fight went ahead at catchweights, Jones had already forfeited the GB/IBU version of the title on the scales, leaving Lee and Jimmy Wilde, who had outpointed Joe Symonds over 15 rounds at the NSC on 16 November 1914, to contest the vacant title.*

16.11.14 Jimmy Wilde (GB) W PTS 15 Joe Symonds (GB), The Ring, London. *Although shown in early record books as involving the British version of the title, it did not. However, with both men inside the weight, the winner went forward to meet Tancy Lee.*

03.12.14 Jimmy Wilde (GB) W CO 9 Sid Smith (GB), The Stadium, Liverpool. *With both men under 112 lbs, this was yet another fight that was incorrectly shown in early record books as involving the British version of the title.*

29.04.18 **Jimmy Wilde** (GB) W RSC 2 Dick Heasman (GB), NSC, London. *Although not billed as a world title fight, or even as one that involved the British and European championships, because the match was made at 102 lbs, with Wilde scaling 100¼ to Heasman's 102, had the champion lost, in all probability he*

would have forfeited his titles. Earlier, on the other side of the Atlantic, Johnny Rosner had claimed the vacant American title when knocking out the Young Zulu Kid inside seven rounds on 28 September 1917 in Brooklyn, but Wilde had already defeated both men and there was little recognition forthcoming. However, with the little Welshman fighting mainly in the bantamweight division, there was renewed interest in the States to find a worthy challenger for the title after Young Montreal outpointed Rosner over 12 rounds in Providence on 10 April 1919, but he too soon decided to campaign among the bantams.

12.04.20 **Jimmy Wilde** (GB) ND-W PTS 10 Young Zulu Kid (USA), Windsor. *According to the Chicago Tribune (newspaper), Wilde was never in any danger of losing his title. Recent research has shown that the title was never at risk, with the weight class limit standing at 112 lbs and the Kid scaling 114.*

24.05.20 **Jimmy Wilde** (GB) W PTS 10 Patsy Wallace (USA), Toronto. *Billed as a title fight, it being announced that the contest had been made at 116 lbs, according to the Toronto Daily Mail (Newspaper), Wilde and Wallace weighed 105 and 110 lbs, respectively. Following Wilde's defeat at the hands of world bantam champion, Pete Herman, and in order to find an American titleholder, Johnny Buff (112 lbs) outpointed Frankie Mason (108 lbs) over 15 rounds in New Orleans on 11 February 1921, despite the match having been made at 116 lbs. Fighting over 15 rounds in New York City, Buff then went on to kayo Abe Goldstein inside two rounds on 31 March 1921, with both men weighing in at 110 lbs, before he, in turn, was knocked out in the 11th by Pancho Villa on 14 September 1922. Although Villa (109½ lbs) lost the American title to Frankie Genaro (110½ lbs) over the same distance in New York City on 1 March 1923, when the promoter, Tex Rickard, lulled Wilde out of semi-retirement for a title defence, it was not Genaro who was selected to meet the little Welshman, but Villa, on the grounds that he was bigger box-office.*

08.02.24 **Pancho Villa** (USA) W PTS 15 Georgie Marks (USA), New York City. *Despite being billed as a title fight, the championship was ultimately not at stake when Marks came to the ring at 116½ lbs. The reason for restating this entry is the discovery that it was Georgie Marks, not Georgie Rivers, who was Villa's opponent.*

22.08.25 Fidel la Barba (USA) W PTS 10 Frankie Genaro (USA), Los Angeles – NBA/CALIFORNIA. *Although the fight was billed for*

Pancho Villa (left), the world flyweight champion, 1923-1925, shown prior to his clash with Johnny Buff

the vacant world championship, it was only Genaro's American title that passed to la Barba, as far as Europe was concerned. Also, it went unrecognised in New York.

08.07.26 Fidel la Barba (USA) W PTS 10 Georgie Rivers (MEX), Los Angeles – NBA/CALIFORNIA. *Billed as la Barba's first defence of the world title, the champion scaled 111¼ to Rivers' 110¾. Seven over the weight contests later, la Barba was matched against the European champion, Elky Clark, in order to unify the title.*

29.08.28 Johnny Hill (GB) W PTS 15 Newsboy Brown (USA), Clapton Stadium, London. *Although billed as a world title fight by the promoters, while Brown certainly lost his Californian recognition on the result, support was not totally forthcoming for Hill in Britain, let alone Europe, where the IBU stood by Emile Pladner, despite his defeat at the hands of Hill.*

21.03.29 Johnny Hill (GB) W PTS 15 Ernie Jarvis (GB), Albert Hall, London. *Advertised as a British and European title bout only as the powers that be did not recognise Hill's Californian title claim.*

29.06.29 Johnny Hill (GB) W DIS 10 Ernie Jarvis (GB), Cartyne Greyhound Track, Glasgow. *As in their first fight, with Hill's Californian title claim lacking credibility, the fight was billed for the British and European titles only.*

21.03.30 Midget Wolgast (USA) W PTS 15 Black Bill (CUB), New York City - NY. *Five days later, concurring with the NYSAC ruling, Wolgast was acclaimed as world champion by the Pennsylvanian Boxing Commission, an authority who had failed to recognise any fighter as a champion following the demise of Pancho Villa.*

Bantamweight (118 lbs)

28.12.92 **Billy Plimmer** (GB) W RSC 8 Joe McGrath (I), New York City (110 lbs). *Although we had earlier stated that Plimmer's right to be called champion was challenged by Jimmy Barry, that remark should now be discarded. Further research among the bantamweights makes clear the fact that Jimmy Barry was really considered as a light-bantam (five pounds below the recognised bantam limit) and not a rival to Plimmer. Therefore, his fights against Casper Leon (15 September 1894, 30 March 1895, 30 May 1898 and 29 December 1898), Jack Madden (21 October 1895), Jack Ward (1 March 1897), and Walter Croot (6 December 1897), should be removed from this section. Other fights, now considered to be at light-bantam, that need removing from the section are Patsy Donovan v Casper Leon (3 June 1899), Clarence Forbes v Casper Leon (9 June 1899), Steve Flanagan v Casper Leon (4 October 1899 and 27 October 1899), Dan Dougherty v Tommy Feltz (26 May 1900 and 4 August 1900), Digger Stanley v Jimmy Walsh (18 April 1904 and 6 June 1904), Digger Stanley v Ike Bradley (20 January 1906), Johnny Coulon v George Kitson (15 January 1910), Johnny Coulon v Earl Denning (29 January 1910), and Johnny Coulon v Jim Kenrick (19 February 1910), while Steve Flanagan v Dan Dougherty (19 February 1898 and 12 March 1900), Kid Murphy v Johnny Coulon (1 March 1907, 8 January 1908, 29 January 1908 and 11 February 1909), Kid Murphy v Young Britt (3 July 1907), Johnny Coulon v Cooney Kelly (20 February 1908), and Johnny Coulon v Young Terry McGovern (13 March 1908), should be recognised as paperweight title bouts. Following this judgement, at a later date, I will strive to produce a list of fights* *covering the paperweights and light-bantams, a weight class eventually recognised as the flyweight division, prior to 1911 when the flyweight division finally took off.*

30.09.98 Steve Flanagan (USA) DREW 25 Casper Leon (USA), New York City. *Confirmation that this was billed for the world 105 lbs title, and that both men made the weight, was discovered in the New York Evening Telegram (newspaper) fight report. This contest should now be recognised as involving the paperweight title.*

01.04.99+ Casper Leon (USA) DREW 20 Dan Dougherty (USA), New York City. *With Jimmy Barry inactive, and following two 20 round draws between the pair, Leon laid claim to the 110 lbs title. The Brooklyn Standard Union (newspaper), while not confirming Leon's claim, reported that both men were inside 108 lbs.*

23.06.99 Clarence Forbes (USA) DREW 12 Casper Leon (USA), St Louis. *Having already fought for the American version of the 112 lbs title some two weeks previously at the same venue, this time the pair were matched for the 115 lbs championship. Following the result, and taking into account Leon coming in at 118 lbs, Forbes (115) claimed the title.*

16.09.99+ Casper Leon (USA) DREW 20 Dan Dougherty (USA), New York City. *Leon was still claiming the 110 lbs title despite his loss to Patsy Donovan, and it was at that weight this was contested. This contest, along with their fight of 1 April 1899, should be seen as another light-bantamweight instalment.*

13.06.02+ Harry Forbes (USA) W PTS 10 Young Devanney (USA), Denver - USA. *Although billed for the bantamweight championship of the world, unfortunately, the Rocky Mountain Herald (newspaper) failed to note the weight.*

Jimmy Walsh, bantamweight claimant, 1905-1911

29.03.05 Jimmy Walsh (USA) ND-W RSC 6 Monte Attell (USA), Philadelphia. *Despite Joe Bowker being recognised as the bantam champion on both sides of the Atlantic, following this win at 116 lbs, Walsh laid claim to the title, but could only find support in New England.*

23.05.05 Jimmy Walsh (USA) W PTS 15 Willie Gibbs (USA), Chelsea. *Prior to the fight, the New England boxing community were claiming the 116 lbs championship for Walsh despite the fact that Frankie Neil was still recognised as the American champion throughout most of America. Detailed research of the Boston papers has uncovered that it was made at 115 lbs and, with both men inside the weight, it should be seen as a defence of Walsh's claim.*

08.03.07+ Jimmy Walsh (USA) W PTS 10 Eddie Menney (USA), Los Angeles. *According to Gary Phillips, the boxing historian, Walsh claimed the title in California as a result of this win at 115 lbs.*

09.10.08 Jimmy Walsh (USA) W PTS 15 Young Britt (USA), Baltimore. *Previously recorded as a title fight, this should now be discarded. Although the Baltimore Sun (newspaper) reported it as being billed as such, in fact, the ;match was made at 118 lbs, two pounds above the then recognised American class limit.*

30.12.09+ Monte Attell (USA) ND-DREW 10 Jimmy Carroll (USA), Portland. *Attell was introduced as the 116 lbs champion and having a pull in the weights. The Morning Oregonian (newspaper) reported that Carroll would be inside the bantam limit, despite the weights not being announced.*

15.03.10+ Jimmy Walsh (USA) DREW 8 Al Delmont (USA), Boston. *Although the Boston Post (newspaper) failed to report weights, something they did with unfailing regularity, Walsh was recognised on the east coast as the 116 lbs champion at this time and the paper added that the winner should meet Frankie Conley to decide the best man at the weight in America.*

08.04.10+ Jimmy Walsh (USA) ND-W PTS 10 Eddie Grunwald (USA), Milwaukee. *The Milwaukee Sentinel (newspaper) reported that title claimant Walsh met Grunwald at 115 lbs.*

23.11.10+ Monte Attell (USA) W PTS 10 Jimmy Walsh (USA), Kansas City. *Well documented in the San Francisco Chronicle (newspaper), Walsh refused to weigh in, while Attell, who scaled 116 lbs, immediately laid claim to the title.*

30.01.11+ Monte Attell (USA) ND-L PTS 10 Phil McGovern (USA), New York City. *With both men inside 116 lbs, Attell's resurrected claim was on the line.*

25.04.11+ Johnny Coulon (C) DREW 10 Eddie O'Keefe (USA), Kansas City. *The Kansas City Star (newspaper) reported that, with both men inside 116 lbs, Coulon's title claim was on the line.*

16.05.11 Jimmy Walsh (USA) DREW 12 Al Delmont (USA), Boston. *Although Walsh was still claiming the 116 lbs title, following his defeat at the hands of Monte Attell in Kansas City on 23 November 1910 support for him, even in his own neck of the woods, had been greatly impaired and this fight should be discarded as having any effect on the championship.*

25.05.11 Johnny Coulon (C) ND-W PTS 10 Johnny Daly (USA), Fort Wayne. *Made at 115 lbs, with both men inside an hour before the fight, according to the Chicago Tribune (newspaper), Coulon's title claim was automatically at risk.*

02.10.11+ Monte Attell (USA) W PTS 10 Johnny Daly (USA), New Orleans. *Having lost in over the weight contests against Young Britt and Al Delmont (2) since defeating Jimmy Walsh, Attell's so-called 116 lbs claim was, by now, considerably weakened, but he was still pushing for a fight against Johnny Coulon. Made at 116 lbs, with both inside, this fight took him a step closer, but on being outpointed over ten rounds at the same venue by Frankie Burns on 23 October 1911, despite the match being made at 118 lbs, Attell finally dropped out of contention.*

20.11.12+ Charles Ledoux (FR) ND-W PTS 10 Battling Reddy (USA), New York City. *As the holder of the IBU version of the world 118 lbs title, Ledoux (117¹/₂ lbs) technically risked his honours when allowing Reddy to come to the ring at 116 lbs.*

30.04.13+ Johnny Coulon (C) ND-W CO 4 Tommy Hudson (USA), Windsor - USA. *Made at 116 lbs (3.0 pm weigh-in).*

03.10.13+ Kid Williams (USA) ND-W CO 2 Mickey Dunn, Balitmore. *According to the Baltimore Evening Sun (newspaper), this was a 15 round title fight at 116 lbs.*

27.11.13+ Kid Williams (USA) ND-W PTS 10 Dick Loadman (USA), Milwaukee. *Williams defended his 116 lbs title claim reported the Milwaukee Sentinel (newspaper).*

06.01.14+ Kid Williams (USA) ND-W RSC 7 Chick Hayes (USA), Baltimore. *Made at 116 lbs, this was another defence of Williams' title claim at that weight.*

28.09.14 Kid Williams (USA) ND-W CO 4 Kid Herman (USA), Philadelphia. *Reported in the Philadelphia Ledger (newspaper), Herman was safely inside the 116 lbs mark, while Williams weighed in at 116¹/₄.*

23.03.15 Kid Williams (USA) ND-W PTS 10 Freddie Diggins (USA), Baltimore. *Earlier reported as involving the title, the author discovered that the fight never took place even though recorded in the Ring Record Book. The possibility remains that it got confused with their bout of 23 March 1914.*

04.06.15+ Kid **Williams** (USA) ND-W PTS 10 Jimmy Murray (USA), Baltimore. *The Baltimore Evening Sun (newspaper) reported that, with the match made at 118 lbs, Murray had every chance of landing the title, despite the fact that 116 lbs was the recognised limit in America at that time.*

08.11.15+ Johnny Ertle (USA) ND-W PTS 10 Abe Friedman (USA), New York City. *In defence of his title claim, Ertle scaled 114¾ lbs to Friedman's 114½.*

15.11.15+ Johnny Ertle (USA) ND-W PTS 10 Johnny Solsberg (USA), New York City. *With Solsberg weighing 114 lbs, Ertle (114¾) made another successful defence of his claim.*

09.02.16+ Johnny Ertle (USA) ND-W PTS 10 Terry Martin (USA), Brooklyn. *Shown as Teddy Martin in last year's Yearbook, the challenger's name has now been corrected.*

22.02.16+ Johnny Ertle (USA) DREW 12 Al Shubert (USA), New Bedford. *Both men were within the prescribed 116 lbs, according to the Boston Post (newspaper).*

11.04.16+ Kid Williams (USA) ND-W PTS 10 Battling Lahn (USA), Baltimore. *Made at 118 lbs, the Baltimore Sun (newspaper) stated that Lahn expected to win the title.*

09.05.16+ Johnny Ertle (USA) ND-W RSC 4 Bobby Burns (USA), St Paul. *The St Paul Pioneer Press (newspaper) reported that Ertle was still champion at the end of the fight. According to them, Burns was inside 116 lbs.*

15.05.16+ Kid Williams (USA) ND-W PTS 10 Billy Bevan (USA), Wilkes Barre. *Both men were announced as being inside 118 lbs, reported the Wilkes Barre Times-Leader (newspaper).*

30.05.16+ Kid Williams (USA) ND-W RSC 7 Benny McCoy (USA), Baltimore. *With the match made at 118 lbs, Williams' title claim was again at stake.*

17.06.16+ Johnny Ertle (USA) ND-W PTS 10 Johnny Ritchie (USA), St Louis. *Made at 116 lbs, Ertle's title claim would have been on the line in this one.*

28.08.16+ Kid Williams (USA) ND-W RSC 5 Young Mendo (USA), Buffalo. *The Buffalo Boxing Record handout gave Williams as scaling 118 lbs to Mendo's 116.*

04.09.16+ Kid Williams (USA) ND-W PTS 10 Frankie Brown (USA), Baltimore. *The Baltimore Evening Sun (newspaper) reported that Williams was called upon to defend at 118 lbs.*

04.09.16+ Johnny Ertle (USA) ND-L PTS 6 Benny Kaufman (USA), Philadelphia. *Both men were inside 116 lbs, according to the Philadelphia Ledger (newspaper), with Ertle scaling 116 to Kaufman's 114½.*

15.09.16+ Kid Williams (USA) ND-W PTS 10 Dick Loadman (USA), Buffalo. *Williams scaled 118½ lbs to Loadman's 118, according to the Buffalo Boxing Record.*

10.10.16+ Johnny Ertle (USA) ND-DREW 10 Joe Lynch (USA), New York City. *Ertle scaled 115 lbs to Lynch's 116.*

27.11.16+ Johnny Ertle (USA) ND-L PTS 10 Dick Loadman (USA), Baltimore. *Articled at 116 lbs, Ertle was inside, but Loadman insisted on making 118, the recognised limit. From hereon, Ertle would defend his claim at 116, 117 or 118 lbs.*

16.02.17+ Johnny Ertle (USA) ND-W PTS 10 Kid Herman (USA), Milwaukee. *The match was made at 118 lbs ringside, thus ensuring Ertle's claim was up for grabs.*

20.02.17+ Pete Herman (USA) ND-W PTS 10 Harry Kabakoff (USA), St Louis. *In a fight made at 118 lbs, the St Louis Post-Dispatch (newspaper) quoted that Herman was happy to risk his title against Kabakoff.*

06.03.17+ Pete Herman (USA) ND-W PTS 10 Jabez White (USA), Albany. *Reported as a championship battle in the Albany Evening Journal (newspaper), White came in at 116½ lbs to Herman's 117¾.*

27.04.17+ Pete Herman (USA) ND-W PTS 10 Kid Herman, Peoria. *There was no mention of the title in the Peoria Star or Journal (newspapers), but the Pekin Kid weighed in at 117 lbs, making sure the champion's belt was at risk. Although failing to weigh in, Pete Herman was adjudged to have been about four pounds heavier.*

03.05.17+ Pete Herman (USA) ND-W PTS 10 Harry Coulin (USA), Buffalo. *The Buffalo Boxing Record gave both men inside 118 lbs.*

14.05.17+ Johnny Ertle (USA) ND-L PTS 6 Tony Barone (USA), Pittsburgh. *Both men easily made the required 118 lbs.*

13.06.17+ Johnny Ertle (USA) ND-W RSC 9 Jack Douglas (USA), Dubuque. *According to the Dubuque Telegraph Herald (newspaper), both men scaled inside 117 lbs, thus putting Ertle's claim at risk.*

03.07.17+ Johnny Ertle (USA) ND-W PTS 15 Sammy Sandow (USA), Cincinnati. *Made at 117 lbs according to the Cincinnati Enquirer (newspaper).*

31.07.17+ Johnny Ertle (USA) ND-W PTS 10 Roy Moore (USA), St Paul. *The St Paul Pioneer Press (newspaper) reported the fight at 117 lbs.*

28.09.17+ Johnny Ertle (USA) ND-W PTS 10 Tony Barone (USA), Waterloo. *Barone, a natural bantam, was well inside 118 lbs for his second assault on Ertle's title claim.*

07.12.17+ Johnny Ertle (USA) ND-L PTS 10 Jack Kid Wolfe (USA), Cleveland. *Matched over ten rounds at 118 lbs, the Cleveland Plain Dealer (newspaper) stated that Wolfe had a few pounds to spare.*

10.12.17+ Pete Herman (USA) ND-W PTS 6 Joe Tuber (USA), Philadelphia. *Made at 118 lbs, both men were inside.*

17.12.17+ Johnny Ertle (USA) DREW 12 Kid Williams (USA), Baltimore. *Both men weighed in at 118 lbs (10.0am).*

25.01.18+ Johnny Ertle (USA) ND-L PTS 10 Jack Kid Wolfe (USA), Cleveland. *The Cleveland Plain Dealer (newspaper) reported Ertle and Wolfe weighing in at 117 lbs ringside.*

10.04.18 Pal Moore (USA) W PTS 15 Johnny Ertle (USA), Baltimore. *Although Pete Herman was generally recognised, with both men inside 116 lbs, it did not stop Moore self-styling himself as champion at the weight following his win over Ertle.*

29.04.18+ Pal Moore (USA) W PTS 8 Earl Puryear (USA), Memphis. *Moore defended his title claim at 118 lbs ringside reported the Memphis Daily Appeal (newspaper).*

06.05.18+ Pal Moore (USA) W PTS 12 Eddie Wimler (USA), Baltimore. *Both men weighed in at 118 lbs (3.0 pm).*

20.05.18+ Pal Moore (USA) W PTS 8 Earl Puryear (USA), Memphis. *The Memphis Daily Appeal (newspaper) reported Moore's 118 lbs title claim being up for grabs in this one, with Puryear well inside the limit.*

05.08.18+ Pal Moore (USA) ND-W PTS 8 Jackie Sharkey (USA), Jersey City. *Both men weighed in at 117 lbs ringside according to the Jersey Journal (newspaper).*

06.09.18 Pete Herman (USA) ND-W PTS 8 Young Zulu Kid (USA), Jersey City. *Although, on occasion, reported as involving Herman's title, the match was made at 119 lbs, a pound above the recognised class limit.*

31.01.19+ Pal Moore (USA) W PTS 12 Young McGovern (USA), Baltimore. *Made at 116 lbs, Moore, who claimed this to be his best fighting weight, defended his claim.*

03.02.19+ Pal Moore (USA) ND-W PTS 10 Dick Loadman (USA), Buffalo. *Moore weighed 116 lbs to Loadman's 118.*

10.02.19+ Pal Moore (USA) ND-W PTS 10 Earl Puryear (USA), Peoria. *Although there was no mention of the weight in the Peoria Star (newspaper), Moore was billed as the international champion and, with Puryear well inside 118 lbs, the former's claim would have been at risk.*

10.02.19+ Pete Herman (USA) ND-W PTS 10 Patsy Scanlon (USA), Pittsburgh. *Herman's title claim was on the line, with Scanlon articled to scale down inside 118 lbs.*

17.02.19+ Pal Moore (USA) W PTS 8 Johnny Ritchie (USA), Memphis. *The Memphis Daily Appeal (newspaper) reported the match at 118 lbs.*

08.04.19 Pete Herman (USA) ND-L PTS 10 Al Shubert (USA), Baltimore. *Despite the Pittsburgh Gazette (newspaper) reporting that the title did not change hands because Shubert, inside 118 lbs, could not land a kayo punch, further research shows that the fight was contracted for 122 lbs and that Herman's crown was safe before the fight even took place.*

14.04.19+ Pal Moore (USA) ND-W PTS 8 Sammy Sandow (USA), Memphis. *Made at 118 lbs, Sandow was inside 116 according to the Memphis Daily Appeal (newspaper). Two fights later, Moore's claim evaporated when he was outpointed by Jimmy Wilde over 20 rounds of a 116 lbs non-title fight at the NSC in London on 17 July 1919. With the world flyweight champion, who found it difficult to make 112 lbs let alone the bantam limit, declining to make an assault on the heavier division, Pete Herman was recognised as the undisputed champion from hereon.*

12.05.19+ Pete Herman (USA) ND-W PTS 10 Johnny Solsberg (USA), Syracuse. *The Syracuse Post-Standard (newspaper) reported this as a billed 118 lbs title fight.*

09.06.19+ Pete Herman (USA) ND-W PTS 10 Terry McHugh (USA), Allentown. *Although the Allentown Morning Call (newspaper) named McHugh as challenging for Herman's title, they somehow missed giving out the weights.*

04.07.19 Joe Burman (USA) ND-W CO 7 Pete Herman (USA), Benton Harbor. *Early record books showed this to be a defeat for the champion, despite him fighting Dick Griffin on the same day at Fort Wayne. Following recent research, the mystery has now been solved - Burman's opponent being Kid Herman.*

15.08.19+ Pete Herman (USA) ND-L PTS 10 Jackie Sharkey (USA), Milwaukee. *Billed as a title fight at 118 lbs according to the Milwaukee Sentinel (newspaper).*

15.09.19+ Pete Herman (USA) ND-DREW 10 Jackie Sharkey (USA), Detroit. *The Detroit News (newspaper) reported the title being at stake after Sharkey was allowed to come to the ring at 118 lbs. Herman agreed to make 121 lbs.*

12.11.19+ Pete Herman (USA) ND-W PTS 6 Joe Lynch (USA), Philadelphia. *Both men were inside the articled 118 lbs, reported the Philadelphia Public Ledger (newspaper).*

24.11.19+ Pete Herman (USA) ND-DREW 8 Johnny Buff (USA), Trenton. *Herman weighed 118 lbs to Buff's 114.*

10.02.20+ Pete Herman (USA) ND-W PTS 8 Johnny Solsberg (USA), St Louis. *Made at 118 lbs, Herman risked his title in this one.*

19.03.20+ Pete Herman (USA) ND-W CO 8 Lew Angelo (USA), Paterson. *Herman (119) risked his title by allowing Angelo to weigh in at 116½ lbs.*

19.08.20+ Pete Herman (USA) ND-W PTS 10 Roy Moore (USA), Colorado Springs. *The Colorado Springs Gazette (newspaper) reported that Herman retained his title, both men having weighed in at 116 lbs (3.0 pm).*

04.09.20+ Pete Herman (USA) ND-W PTS 10 George Lee (USA), New Orleans. *Lee was well inside 118 lbs according to the New Orleans Daily Picayune (newspaper).*

21.09.20+ Pete Herman (USA) ND-W PTS 10 Jimmy Kelly (USA), Beardstown. *The Daily Illinois News (newspaper), although not reporting weights, called Kelly a sensational challenger for Herman in a championship boxing show.*

09.02.21+ Joe Lynch (USA) ND-DREW 8 Jabez White (USA), St Louis. *White weighed 117¼ lbs to Lynch's 118½.*

28.03.21+ Joe Lynch (USA) ND-W PTS 10 Eddie Pichot (USA), Pittsburgh. *Pichot weighed 118 lbs and Lynch, 119.*

04.09.22 Joe Lynch (USA) ND-W PTS 10 Pal Moore (USA), Michigan City. *According to the New York Times (newspaper) report, Lynch's title was at risk in this, a fight articled at 118 lbs.*

27.02.23+ Joe Lynch (USA) ND-W PTS 8 Pete Husic (USA), Harrisburgh. *The Harrisburgh Patriot (newspaper) reported it as a billed title fight at 118 lbs.*

10.04.23+ Joe Lynch (USA) ND-W PTS 12 Joe O'Donnell (USA), Portland. *In back-to-back six rounders, this was an opportunity for O'Donnell to win the 118 lbs title claimed the Portland Press Herald (newspaper).*

09.07.23+ Joe Lynch (USA) ND-W PTS 8 Bobby Wolgast (USA), Philadelphia. *Wolgast came in at 117 lbs according to the Philadelphia Record (newspaper).*

23.11.23+ Joe Lynch (USA) ND-W CO 5 Frankie Murray (USA), Peoria. *The Peoria Star (newspaper) reported this as a title defence, however, with the match made at 120 lbs, it should not be recognised as one.*

23.01.24+ Joe Lynch (USA) ND-W CO 2 Parky Owens (USA), El Dorado. *According to the El Dorado News-Times (newspaper), with Owens scaling 116 lbs to Lynch's 118, the latter's title was technically on the line, albeit in a no-decision contest. This information was uncovered by boxing historian, Bob Soderman.*

05.05.24+ Abe Goldstein (USA) ND-W PTS 10 Clarence Rosen (USA), Detroit. *Made at 118 lbs, the Detroit News (newspaper) inferred that the title was on the line.*

16.02.25+ Eddie Martin (USA) ND-W PTS 12 Willie Spencer (USA), Portland. *The Portland Press Herald (newspaper) reported this affair to involve Martin's 118 lbs title. This was another instance of two six rounders being fought back-to-back.*

Super-Bantamweight (122 lbs)

On 21 September 1922, in a fight billed by the promoter as being for the vacant 122 lbs junior-featherweight title, Jack Kid Wolfe outpointed Joe Lynch over 15 rounds in New York City. The contest was not given official backing in New York, however, as the commission simply did not recognise the weight class at that time. Wolfe did not hang around to argue with the State officials, instead, looking to earn some money from his newly won "title", he received a 12 round "press" decision over Mickey Dillon at 122 lbs in Erie, Pennsylvania on 8 December 1922, before losing on points over ten rounds in Toronto on 26 December 1922 to the Russian-Canadian, Benny Gould. While the fight was billed for the title it is difficult to ascertain whether it had official backing, but regardless of that, Gould does not appear to fight at the weight again and no more is heard of the 122 lbs title until a little known body calling themselves the American Federation of Boxing started the ball rolling again with a series of eight rounders in New

York City. After appointing Lou Barbetta as their champion, he was outpointed by Davey Crawford (22 July 1941), before Crawford befell a similar fate himself at the hands of Aaron Seltzer (2 September 1941). His successor was Joey Iannotti, who, after outscoring Seltzer (6 October 1941), held on to his laurels next time out with a draw against Johnny Compo (29 January 1942), before going down on points to Seltzer (17 February 1942) in a rematch that turned out to be the last contest held under the auspices of the ABF. Resurrected as the super-bantamweight division by the World Boxing Council in 1976, the weight class is currently recognised as the junior featherweight division by the World Boxing Association, the International Boxing Federation, and the World Boxing Organisation.

Featherweight (126 lbs)

08.11.97 Will Curley (GB) W PTS 20 Patsy Haley (USA), Standard Theatre, Gateshead. *Although winning a bout billed for the world 116 lbs featherweight title, Curley received little recognition away from his native north-east.*

28.02.98+ Will Curley (GB) W CO 12 Billy Murphy (NZ), Ginnett's Circus, Newcastle. *In a contest billed for the world 116 lbs title, Curley (116) successfully defended his claim against Murphy (115½).*

15.05.99 George Dixon (C) W PTS 20 Kid Broad (USA), Buffalo. *Having been recorded as a title fight in record books many years ago, it can now be reported, as per the Buffalo Tribune (newspaper), that the match was made at 124 lbs. Although both men were inside the weight, the class limit was considered to be 122 lbs at that time and, as suspected, the fight did not carry title billing.*

03.07.99+ George Dixon (C) W CO 3 Sam Bolen (USA), Louisville. *According to the Louisville Courier-Journal (newspaper), this was the first championship battle ever for Louisville, despite the fact that it was articled for 128 lbs and Bolen came in at 129. Dixon, however, scaled 121 lbs.*

29.01.00+ Terry McGovern (USA) W CO 1 Jack Ward (USA), Baltimore. *The Baltimore Sun (newspaper) stated that the match was made at 118 lbs. The paper went on to say that McGovern looked to be at least 125 lbs and there was no mention of the championship being involved, despite 118 lbs being the weight for Dixon v McGovern 20 days earlier.*

01.02.04 Abe Attell (USA) W CO 5 Harry Forbes (USA), St Louis. *With both men inside the stipulated 120 lbs, the Chicago Tribune (newspaper) reported that, in their view, Attell should now be considered the rightful featherweight champion following his victory, a view which was generally shared after Young Corbett had been defeated by Jimmy Britt on 25 March 1904.*

08.12.04+ Abe Attell (USA) W PTS 15 Tommy Feltz (USA), St Louis - USA. *The St Louis Post-Dispatch (newspaper) gave this one at 122 lbs. Despite his defeat to Sullivan at 124 lbs, Attell was still recognised by many as the best at 122 lbs.*

28.01.05+ Abe Attell (USA) ND-W PTS 6 Tommy Murphy (USA), Philadelphia - USA. *According to the Baltimore Sun (newspaper), Attell firmed up his featherweight claim after beating Murphy at 122 lbs.*

03.02.05+ Abe Attell (USA) W PTS 15 Tommy Feltz (USA), Baltimore - USA. *Reported in the Baltimore Sun (newspaper) at 122 lbs, Attell's title claim would have been on the line.*

22.02.05 Abe Attell (USA) DREW 15 Kid Goodman (USA), Chelsea. *Although shown in the Boxing News Annual as a title fight, it was not, with the match articled at 126 lbs and both men agreeing beforehand to a drawn decision.*

10.05.05+ Abe Attell (USA) W PTS 10 Harry Forbes (USA), Detroit - USA. *Although both men were inside 122 lbs, therefore putting Attell's title claim technically at risk, the Detroit News (newspaper) reported this fight as a fake.*

16.01.06+ Abe Attell (USA) DREW 15 Chester Goodwin (USA), Chelsea - USA. *Despite the fight being made at catchweights, the Boston Post (newspaper) reported that Goodwin had a good chance of winning the title. The Boston papers often wrote in such terms and until weights become available it is probably best to treat the fight in similar vein to that of Attell v Goodman at the same venue the previous year.*

12.09.07+ Abe Attell (USA) W PTS 10 Jimmy Walsh (USA), Indianapolis - USA. *Both men were inside the required 122 lbs according to the Indianapolis News (newspaper).*

18.03.09+ Abe Attell (USA) ND-W PTS 10 Patsy Kline (USA), New York City - USA. *Kline easily made 122 lbs reported the New York World (newspaper).*

14.09.09 Abe Attell (USA) W PTS 12 Tommy O'Toole (USA), Boston -

USA. *Advertised as a world title defence for Attell in the Boston Post (newspaper), and recorded as such in last year's Yearbook, at the time of going to press no weights were available. However, further research of the Boston papers have uncovered that articles were signed for 122 lbs and that both were inside.*

22.11.09+ Abe Attell (USA) W PTS 8 Johnny Moran (USA), Memphis - USA. *The Memphis Daily Appeal (newspaper) gave this as a title fight at 122 lbs (6.0 pm weigh-in).*

06.12.09+ Abe Attell (USA) W PTS 8 Charley White (USA), Memphis - USA. *White and Attell were both inside the articled 122 lbs ringside, according to the Memphis Daily Appeal (newspaper) report.*

01.01.10+ Abe Attell (USA) W CO 5 Eddie Kelly (USA), Savanah - USA. *Reported in the Savanah Morning News (newspaper) as a billed title fight over 15 rounds at 122 lbs.*

16.09.10+ Abe Attell (USA) ND-W PTS 10 Charley White (USA), Milwaukee - USA. *Made at 122 lbs, Attell's title claim was on the line in this one, as stated in the Milwaukee Sentinel (newspaper).*

10.10.10 **Abe Attell** (USA) ND-W PTS 15 Jack White (USA), Winnipeg. *Despite the Winnipeg Telegram (newspaper) reporting this to be a championship go, other local papers showed it to be a fight at catchweights between the champion and a natural lightweight. Incidentally, White's brother was the more famous "left-hook" Charley.*

24.10.10 Abe Attell (USA) W PTS 10 Johnny Kilbane (USA), Kansas City - USA. *According to the Kansas City Star (newspaper), it was a billed title fight at 122 lbs, with both men inside.*

13.01.11 Abe Attell (USA) ND-W PTS 10 Patsy Kline (USA), New York City - USA. *According to the New York Times (newspaper), Kline, inside the weight, was again trying to relieve Attell of the 122 lbs title.*

19.06.11+ Joe Mandot (USA) W PTS 8 Joe Coster (USA), Memphis. *Despite the pronouncement in the Boston Post (newspaper) that, in winning, Mandot took over Coster's 122 lbs featherweight title claim, the truth of the matter was that the winner came in at 125 lbs and was soon to be ranked among the leading lightweights.*

23.12.11+ Johnny Kilbane (USA) ND-W PTS 12 Charley White (USA), Cleveland. *Made at 122 lbs, White was compelled to make the weight at the 3.0 pm weigh-in, according to the Cleveland Plain Dealer (newspaper).*

04.07.12 Johnny Kilbane (USA) ND-W PTS 12 Tommy Dixon (USA), Cleveland - USA. *The Cleveland Plain Dealer (newspaper) gave this as an articled title fight at 122 lbs, with both men inside.*

14.10.12 Johnny Kilbane (USA) ND-W PTS 12 Eddie O'Keefe (USA), Cleveland - USA. *Further research of the Cleveland Plain Dealer (newspaper), finds a statement by the champion that he was more than happy to have contracted to allow his next two Cleveland opponents to make 122 lbs. This information supports the paper's claim that O'Keefe would win the title if he could spring an inside-the-distance victory over Kilbane.*

29.10.12+ Johnny Kilbane (USA) ND-W CO 4 Tommy Duggan (USA), Johnstown - USA. *The Johnstown Tribune (newspaper) reported that Duggan, who scaled inside 122 lbs, had much to gain if he could win inside the distance.*

03.12.12 Johnny Kilbane (USA) ND-W RSC 9 Monte Attell (USA), Cleveland - USA. *As in Kilbane v O'Keefe on 14 October 1912, Attell was inside 122 lbs for this one.*

01.01.13+ Johnny Kilbane (USA) ND-W CO 2 Oliver Kirk (USA), St Louis - USA. *The St Louis Post-Dispatch (newspaper) reported the fight at catchweights, with Kilbane above the title limit and Kirk coming to the ring inside the required 122 lbs.*

10.11.13 Johnny Kilbane (USA) ND-W CO 1 Eddie O'Keefe (USA), Philadelphia - USA. *Made at 122 lbs, with O'Keefe inside, although only a no-decision six rounder, Kilbane's title was technically at risk. So reported the Philadelphia Inquirer (newspaper).*

29.05.14 Johnny Kilbane (USA) ND-W CO 2 Benny Chavez (USA), Denver - USA. *Further scrutiny of the Rocky Mountain Herald (newspaper), shows the match to have been made at catchweights, 122 lbs (Chavez) and 124 (Kilbane) being the prescribed weights. Thus, when Chavez made 122 lbs, the title was effectively on the line.*

02.12.15 Johnny Kilbane (USA) ND-W PTS 10 Patsy Brannigan (USA), Scranton - USA. *With several States recognising 125 lbs as being the new limit for the weight class, this was billed for the title, despite Kilbane stating that his title was only at risk when the opponent was allowed to make 122 lbs. That aside, Brannigan scaled 124 lbs, according to the Scranton Times (newspaper), and would have undoubtedly claimed the crown if successful.*

16.02.16+ Johnny Kilbane (USA) ND-W PTS 10 Johnny Creely, Hot Springs - USA. *While billed as a title defence for Kilbane in the*

Little Rock Gazette (newspaper), there was no mention of the weights.

19.04.17+ Johnny Kilbane (USA) ND-W PTS 10 Matt Brock (USA), Cleveland - USA. *With the weight class recognised in Cleveland as being 125 lbs (Kilbane still argued that if anyone wished to take his title it would have to be at 122 lbs), Brock was contracted to make 124 lbs and did so.*

12.04.19+ Johnny Kilbane (USA) ND-W PTS 10 Jack Lawlor (USA), Charleston - USA. *Although made at 128 lbs with no title billing, the Charleston Gazette (newspaper) claimed that Lawlor would come to the ring at 125 lbs (the State recognised featherweight limit) with a view to claiming Kilbane's crown if successful. In the event, this ruse came to nothing and should not be treated as involving the title.*

14.03.36+ Freddie Miller (USA) W PTS 10 Filio Echeverria (CUB), Havana - NBA. *Billed as a world title fight, according to the Havana Post (newspaper), Echeverria came in at 127 lbs. However, Alabama's Birmingham News (newspaper) gave it as Miller scaling 125¼ lbs to his opponent's 126.*

15.05.40 Petey Scalzo (USA) W RSC 6 Frankie Covelli (USA), Washington - NBA. *Originally thought not to involve the NBA version of the title, it was actually Scalzo's first defence of the championship that had been handed to him on 1 May 1940.*

Super-Featherweight (130 lbs)

28.07.22+ Johnny Dundee (USA) ND-W PTS 12 Kid Koster (USA), Houston. *Although the weight division was hardly recognised outside New York, Dundee (128 lbs) defended the title against Koster (128 lbs), according to the Houston Post-Dispatch (newspaper), even though it is unclear whether support was forthcoming from the NBA.*

30.05.25+ Mike Ballerino (USA) ND-W PTS 10 Frankie Callahan (USA), Columbus - NY/NBA. *The Ohio State Journal (newspaper) reported this as a 130 lbs defence for Ballerino, who held on despite the efforts of Callahan.*

Lightweight (135 lbs)

29.10.97 **George Lavigne** (USA) W RTD 12 Joe Walcott (USA), San Francisco. *In a return match, this time made at 135 lbs, Walcott, who was billed as the world welterweight champion, struggled to make the weight and, although inside on the night, weakened himself considerably. Following his victory, Lavigne had a fair claim to the welter title as well as holding on to his lightweight belt.*

25.11.98 **George Lavigne** (USA) W PTS 20 Tom Tracy (A), San Francisco. *Recorded as a lightweight title fight in the 1995 Yearbook, recent research shows that it had nothing to do with the 133 lbs championship and belongs in the welter division as a defence of Lavigne's claim at 142 lbs.*

20.11.02+ Jim Maloney (GB) W PTS 20 Bobby Dobbs (USA), National Athletic Club, London. *Made at 140 lbs, and considered to be a lightweight contest, this fight was incorrectly shown in the welter division in the 1995 Yearbook. Billed for the world title, Maloney (139³/₄ lbs) put the memory of his loss to Frank Erne five months earlier behind him in beating Dobbs (139 lbs).*

01.01.03 Joe Gans (USA) W DIS 11 Gus Gardner (USA), New Britain. *Billed for the title over 20 rounds at 136 lbs, a weight that Gans was more comfortable with at this stage of his career, both men were inside.*

09.02.03+ Spike Sullivan (USA) W CO 1 Jim Maloney (GB), NSC, London. *In a billed 15 rounder, with both men inside 140 lbs, the American took over Maloney's claim at the weight following his 61 second kayo win. Sullivan's claim goes nowhere, especially in the light of his second defeat at the hands of Jabez White, a 15 round points loss at the NSC on 20 April 1903 at 137 lbs.*

10.11.03 Jimmy Britt (USA) W RSC 20 Charley Sieger (USA), San Francisco. *Shown as a points win for Britt in last year's Yearbook, boxing historian, Paul Zabala, has recently informed me that it was a stoppage victory.*

01.04.08 **Joe Gans** (USA) ND-W CO 3 Spike Robson (GB), Philadelphia. *With Robson, a natural 126 pounder and safely inside 133 lbs, Gans' title was therefore techncially at risk.*

16.10.12+ Ad Wolgast (USA) ND-W PTS 6 Teddy Maloney (USA), Philadelphia. *Only a six round no-decision fight, but both fighters were inside 133 lbs.*

26.11.14+ **Freddie Welsh** (GB) ND-W PTS 10 Young Abe Brown (USA), Syracuse. *Made at 135 lbs, according to the Syracuse Post-Standard (newspaper).*

15.02.15+ **Freddie Welsh** (GB) ND-W PTS 6 Jimmy Anderson (USA), Grand Rapids. *The Boston Post (newspaper) gave this one as being articled at 135 lbs.*

18.06.15 **Freddie Welsh** (GB) ND-W PTS 10 Johnny Lustig (USA), New York City. *Shown as involving Welsh's title in last year's Yearbook, it did not, with Lustig scaling 137 lbs to the champion's 136¹/₂.*

08.06.16 **Freddie Welsh** (GB) W PTS 10 Tommy Lowe (USA), Washington. *Confirmation of this being a title fight came in the Washington Evening Star (newspaper), where it was reported that the match was made at 135 lbs and that Lowe was inside.*

24.04.17+ **Freddie Welsh** (GB) ND-L PTS 10 Chick Simler (USA), Scranton. *Billed for the title, the Scranton Times (newspaper) reported that Simler was inside 135 lbs.*

Benny Leonard (right), the world lightweight champion, 1917-1925, squares up to Richie Mitchell

14.09.17+ **Benny Leonard** (USA) ND-W RSC 2 Phil Bloom (USA), Pittsburgh. *Given the opportunity to challenge Leonard for the 135 lbs title, albeit in a no-decision contest, Bloom was just not up to the task.*

28.11.17+ **Benny Leonard** (USA) ND-W CO 1 Frankie Kirk (USA), Denver. *A ten rounder made at 135 lbs, as reported in the Rocky Mountain News (newspaper), the paper went on to say that Kirk expects to land the title.*

05.12.17+ **Benny Leonard** (USA) W RSC 8 Gene Delmont (USA), St Paul. *According to the Milwaukee Free Press (newspaper), Leonard weighed 134 lbs and Delmont 130.*

12.12.17+ **Benny Leonard** (USA) ND-W PTS 6 Patsy Cline (USA), Philadelphia. *Leonard made 134¹/₄ lbs to Cline's 134¹/₂.*

17.12.17+ **Benny Leonard** (USA) W RSC 5 Chick Brown (USA), New Haven. *Billed for the title and scheduled for ten rounds, the New Haven Journal (newspaper) reported that Brown was not to enter the ring weighing more than 135 lbs, something he did not need reminding of.*

22.07.18+ **Benny Leonard** (USA) ND-W RSC 5 Willie Gradwell (USA), Jersey City. *An eight rounder, with Leonard (136) allowing Gradwell to come to the ring at 132¹/₂ lbs.*

08.09.19+ **Benny Leonard** (USA) ND-W PTS 10 Johnny Clinton (USA), Syracuse. *Reported in the Syracuse Post-Standard (newspaper) as a title defence for Leonard at 135 lbs.*

15.10.19+ **Benny Leonard** (USA) ND-W PTS 10 Phil Bloom (USA), Detroit. *The Detroit News (newspaper) stated that Leonard, who was allowing Bloom to come in under the championship limit, was expected to scale 136 lbs.*

19.12.19+ **Benny Leonard** (USA) ND-W CO 6 Red Herring (USA), Memphis. *Herring was named the challenger in the Memphis Daily Appeal (newspaper). Offered the chance of a title shot, Leonard stipulated that Herring should make no more than 137 lbs and be under 135 lbs if he so wished. Needless to say, Herring was inside 135 lbs on the night.*

05.03.26+ **Rocky Kansas** (USA) W CO 6 Freddie Jacks (GB), Tampa. *Although no weights were given, the Tampa Morning Tribune (newspaper) reported the fight as a battle for the 135 lbs championship.*

08.10.26+ **Sammy Mandell** (USA) ND-W PTS 10 Joe Jawson (USA), Rockford. *The Rockford Daily Register-Gazette (newspaper) gave this as a championship bout at 135 lbs.*

29.10.26+ **Sammy Mandell** (USA) W PTS 10 Clausine Vincent (USA), Oklahoma City. *The Daily Oklahoman (newspaper) reported this to be a ten round championship fight at 135 lbs.*

11.04.27+ **Sammy Mandell** (USA) ND-W CO 2 Johnny Valdez (USA), Tucson. *The Tucson Daily Citizen (newspaper) reported this as a title defence for Mandell at 135 lbs.*

L. Welterweight (140 lbs)

Came into being in 1922 when Pinkey Mitchell was proclaimed world champion on 15 November, after the result of a "poll" taken by a weekly boxing magazine in Minneapolis called the Boxing Blade. There had been 20 names in the hat and 700,000 casting votes, many of them coming from outside America, but it was Mitchell who led the way with 100,000 to Harvey Thorpe's 40,000. Also known as the junior-welterweight and super-lightweight division, the NBA stated that an emblematic belt would be presented to Mitchell and that they would require him to defend it every six months against a selected opponent. However, Mitchell only ever defended the belt in no-decision affairs and it would not be until 1927 that the NYSAC recognised the weight division.

30.01.23+ Pinkey Mitchell (USA) ND-W PTS 10 Bud Logan (USA), Milwaukee - NBA. *With both men inside 140 lbs, Mitchell scaled 139³/₄ lbs to Logan's 137¹/₄.*

18.05.23+ Pinkey Mitchell (USA) ND-W CO 6 Tim Droney (USA), Louisville - NBA. *Scheduled for 12 rounds, Mitchell weighed 139¹/₂ lbs to Droney's 139.*

09.07.23+ Pinkey Mitchell (USA) ND-W PTS 8 Nate Goldman (USA), Philadelphia - NBA. *Goldman scaled 140 lbs to Mitchell's 139.*

14.12.23+ Pinkey Mitchell (USA) ND-W DIS 4 Nate Goldman (USA), Milwaukee - NBA. *Goldman scaled 137³/₄ lbs to Mitchell's 140¹/₂.*

08.04.24+ Pinkey Mitchell (USA) ND-W PTS 10 Bobby Harper (USA), Portland - NBA. *Despite being recorded on occasion as involving Mitchell's 140 lbs title, the Portland Oregonian (newspaper) tells us that with Harper weighing in at 142³/₄ lbs it did not.*

10.06.24+ Pinkey Mitchell (USA) ND-W PTS 10 Al van Ryan (USA), Sioux City - NBA. *Despite weighing 142 lbs, Mitchell's title was at stake after Ryan came to the ring inside 140 lbs.*

06.12.32+ Sammy Fuller (USA) W PTS 10 Billy Wallace (USA), Cleveland. *With Wallace weighing in at 135 lbs, Fuller (136) defended his claim (recognised by the Ring Magazine) to the title in this one.*

27.06.41 Harry Weekly (USA) W PTS 10 Carmelo Fenoy (USA), Birmingham. *Prior to the fight, the Louisiana Boxing Commission had agreed to name Weekly as world light-welterweight champion and, according to the Birmingham News (newspaper), it was initially felt that Weekly v Fenoy would re-launch the weight class. However, although the paper intimated the fight would be made at 140 lbs, it was actually made at catchweights.*

Welterweight (147 lbs)

30.07.92+ Tommy Ryan (USA) W CO 17 Jack Wilkes (USA), Omaha. *The Omaha World-Herald (newspaper) reported this as a billed American title fight, with both men inside 141 lbs.*

13.09.94+ Tommy Ryan (USA) W CO 4 Billy Layton (USA), near St Joseph. *Reported in the New York Herald (newspaper) as a welterweight defence for Ryan, despite both men weighing in at 146 lbs, the fight took place on a sandbank (neutral territory) in the Missouri River after being banned from St Joseph.*

17.03.97 George Green (USA) W CO 12 Mysterious Billy Smith (USA), Carson City. *With Tommy Ryan moving inexorably towards the full middleweight ranks, according to the Police Gazette (newspaper), Green claimed the title following his victory over Smith at 145 lbs.*

21.06.97+ Tommy Ryan (USA) W CO 2 Tom Williams (A), Syracuse. *Reported as being billed for the welterweight championship of the world by the Syracuse Herald (newspaper), despite the absence of weights.*

20.12.97+ Tommy Ryan (USA) W CO 3 Bill Heffernan (SA), Buffalo. *Although the match was made at 150 lbs, according to the Buffalo Courier (newspaper), it was billed as a defence of Ryan's world welter title, despite being eight pounds over the "popular" limit.*

03.10.98 Mysterious Billy Smith (USA) W CO 20 Jim Judge (USA), Scranton. *According to the Scranton Times (newspaper), both men were inside the prescribed 142 lbs at the 3.0 pm weigh-in.*

25.11.98+ George Lavigne (USA) W PTS 20 Tom Tracy (A), San Francisco. *Recorded as a lightweight title fight in the Ring Record Book, the San Francisco Chronicle (newspaper) reported that it was made at 142 lbs, with Lavigne expected to scale 134 lbs to Tracy's 138/140. What is now apparent is that this fight was a defence of Lavigne's Californian welterweight title claim at that weight.*

01.03.99+ Tommy Ryan (USA) W CO 8 Charles Johnson (USA), Hot Springs. *Set for 20 rounds at 150 lbs, according to Paul Zabala's researches of the Chicago Tribune (newspaper), with Ryan claiming both the welter title at 152 lbs and the 158 lbs middleweight championship, this match would have placed both of those claims at risk.*

04.05.00+ Matty Matthews (USA) DREW 10 Kid Parker (USA), Denver. *The Rocky Mountain News (newspaper) showed this to be billed for the world welter title, with both men inside the articled 140 lbs.*

20.11.02 Jim Maloney (GB) W PTS 20 Bobby Dobbs (USA), National Athletic Club, London. *Shown in the 1996 Yearbook as a welterweight fight, it belongs to the lightweight division.*

31.08.03 Martin Duffy (USA) DREW 10 Gus Gardner (USA), Fort Huron. *Although a catchweight contest, with Gardner well inside 142 lbs, despite being outweighed by some 15 lbs, Duffy's title claim was on the line.*

26.02.04 Martin Duffy (USA) W PTS 20 Rube Ferns (USA), Hot Springs. *Shown occasionally as a "white" title defence, further examination of the Chicago Tribune (newspaper) showed the fight to have been articled at 148 lbs, some six pounds heavier than their contest of 28 May 1903 and well over the class limit of the day.*

10.06.04+ Young Peter Jackson (USA) W CO 4 Joe Walcott (USA), Baltimore. *Following his win over the 142 lbs champion in a catchweight contest at 148 lbs, Jackson claimed the world welterweight title at that weight and immediately took his claim to England before coming home at the end of 1905. On his return, too heavy to be a genuine welter, Jackson took his claim up a division where he was twice defeated by Philadelphia Jack O'Brien.*

13.06.04 Honey Mellody (USA) DREW 20 Jack O'Keefe (USA), Butte. *With both men inside 142 lbs, the Anaconda Standard (newspaper) reported the fight as involving Mellody's "white" welter title.*

09.12.04+ Sam Langford (C) DREW 15 Jack Blackburn (USA), Marlboro. *Following the enforced retirement of Joe Walcott, Langford, having drawn with the latter over 15 rounds at 142 lbs on 5 September 1904 in Manchester, claimed the title with some justification, being called the legitimate champion in certain boxing circles. Made at 142 lbs, with neither tipping the beam and with both on their feet at the final bell, according to Articles of Agreement, it was declared a draw.*

13.02.05+ Sam Langford (C) DREW 15 Dave Holly (USA), Salem. *Made at 142 lbs, Holly came in at 137½, while Langford, unable to make the weight, was forced to pay forfeit.*

04.07.05 Buddy Ryan (USA) W CO 11 George Herberts (USA), Butte. *Billed for the 145 lbs title, and contested over 20 rounds, Ryan weighed in at 142 lbs to Herbert's 143½.*

20.09.05+ Sam Langford (C) DREW 10 Jack Blackburn (USA), Allentown. *The Allentown Morning Call (newspaper) gave it at 138 lbs with Langford having a slight advantage, but, from hereon, the latter appears to box at a heavier weight. Later, in 1908, prior to serving a prison sentence for manslaughter between 1909 and 1914, Blackburn claimed the 142 lbs welter title. Supported by the TS Andrews' Annual, the claim seems to be based on his fights against Langford and a 12 round points win over Jimmy Gardner (at the time, widely acclaimed as the best man in America at 142 lbs) in Boston back on 2 January 1904.*

24.11.05 Mike Twin Sullivan (USA) W PTS 20 Jimmy Gardner (USA), San Francisco. *Decided at catchweights, but with both men still inside 142 lbs, despite Sullivan being the bigger of the two, Gardner, reported in the San Francisco Chronicle (newspaper) prior to the fight as being the legitimate holder of the "white" 142 lbs title, forfeited his claim to that on the result.*

21.05.07+ Jimmy Gardner (USA) W PTS 10 Harry Lewis (USA), Denver. *Gardner's latest title claim stemmed from this, a fight made at 142 lbs, and following his win he challenged the world at the weight.*

27.11.07 Mike Twin Sullivan (USA) W CO 13 Kid Farmer (USA), Los Angeles. *Advertised as a title fight in the Los Angeles Times (newspaper), in essence it was contested at catchweights, with Farmer inside the welter limit of 142 lbs.*

07.01.08+ Jimmy Gardner (USA) W PTS 12 Joe Walcott (USA), Boston. *Prior to the fight, the Boston Post (newspaper) stated that Gardner should be recognised as the best 142 pounder in the world, a title he was still claiming following his victory. For the record, Walcott weighed in over 142 lbs.*

27.04.08+ Harry Lewis (USA) ND-W CO 3 Larry Conley (USA), Augusta. *The Daily Kenebee Journal (newspaper) gave this as a six rounder, with Conley articled and making 142 lbs.*

23.06.08+ Harry Lewis (USA) W PTS 12 Larry Temple (USA), Boston. *Articled at 145 lbs for the world welterweight title, further scrutiny of the Boston Post (newspaper) uncovered that while Lewis came in over the weight, Temple, who had worked hard to get in shape for the fight, was inside.*

14.12.08+ Harry Lewis (USA) DREW 12 Willie Lewis (USA), New Haven. *According to the New Haven Evening Register (newspaper), prior to the fight, the American title looked likely to change hands. However, they failed to mention the articled weights, while the statement was hardly supported when Willie Lewis said that he expected to make 158 lbs.*

11.01.10+ Harry Lewis (USA) W PTS 10 Howard Baker (USA), Denver. *Made at 145 lbs, the Rocky Mountain News (newspaper) reported that Lewis' title claim was on the line.*

05.05.10 Jimmy Clabby (USA) ND-W PTS 10 Dixie Kid (USA), New York City. *After receiving the "press decision" over the Kid, who still saw himself as champion, Clabby (139 lbs) claimed the title, while the loser moved his base to Europe. Made at 147 lbs, the Kid was right on the limit.*

29.11.11+ Ray Bronson (USA) ND-W PTS 10 Tommy Howell (USA), Indianapolis. *Made at 142 lbs, with both men inside, and with all the top Americans campaigning abroad, Bronson assumed the role of champion following the "press decision" in his favour.*

27.02.12+ Ray Bronson (USA) ND-W PTS 10 Young Erne (USA), Indianapolis. *Billed for the 142 lbs title, both men safely made the weight.*

01.04.12 Ray Bronson (USA) W PTS 15 Clarence English (USA), St Joseph. *Following his win over English at 142 lbs, Bronson put up forfeit, without takers, to fight anyone for the title in America at 142 lbs or 145 ringside.*

29.06.12+ Ray Bronson (USA) ND-W PTS 10 Harry Brewer (USA), Indianapolis. *Brewer and Bronson were both inside the articled 142 lbs, the Indianapolis News (newspaper) report tells us.*

02.09.12+ Ray Bronson (USA) ND-DREW 10 Wildcat Ferns (USA), Indianapolis. *The Indianapolis Star (newspaper) reported that both men made the required 142 lbs.*

29.10.12+ Ray Bronson (USA) ND-W PTS 8 Clarence English (USA), St Louis. *Made at 142 lbs, Bronson's claim was at risk, stated the St Louis Post-Dispatch (newspaper).*

13.11.12+ Wildcat Ferns (USA) ND-L PTS 10 Tommy Howell (USA), Indianapolis. *The Indianapolis News (newspaper) stated that both men would come to the ring inside 145 lbs.*

01.01.13+ Wildcat Ferns (USA) W PTS 10 Harry Brewer (USA), Kansas City. *According to the Kansas City Star (newspaper), both men made the prescribed 145 lbs.*

29.01.13+ Ray Bronson (USA) ND-W PTS 10 Jimmy Perry (USA), Indianapolis. *Bronson risked his title claim against Perry in an articled 142 pounder.*

10.03.13 Wildcat Ferns (USA) W PTS 10 Spike Kelly (USA), Kansas City. *Both men made the required 145 lbs, thus putting their claims at the weight at risk.*

18.03.13 Wildcat Ferns (USA) DREW 10 Jimmy Perry (USA), Atlanta. *Billed as one of a series of eliminators to decide the 145 lbs welter title, Ferns put his claim on the line.*

24.03.13+ Spike Kelly (USA) W CO 2 Jack Foreman (USA), Memphis. *Kelly put his title claim at risk in a fight made at 145 lbs, stated the Memphis Daily Appeal (newspaper) report. That was despite his recent points loss to Wildcat Ferns.*

05.04.13 Wildcat Ferns (USA) W PTS 10 Jimmy Perry (USA), Kansas City. *The Kansas City Star (newspaper) fails to make mention of the above fight and the author feels sure that it has become confused with their bout of 6 May 1913 in the same city.*

14.04.13+ Ray Bronson (USA) ND-DREW 10 Billy Griffith (USA), Cincinnati. *The Cincinnati Enquirer (newspaper) gave both men as being inside the stipulated 142 lbs.*

16.04.13+ Wildcat Ferns (USA) DREW 10 Tommy Howell (USA), Kansas City. *The Kansas City Star (newspaper) gave this one at catchweights, but with both fighters inside 145 lbs.*

23.04.13+ Ray Bronson (USA) ND-W PTS 10 Hilliard Lang (C), Indianapolis. *Made at 142 lbs, with both inside, the Indianapolis News (newspaper) reported that Bronson proved himself a real claimant.*

05.05.13+ Wildcat Ferns (USA) W PTS 10 Jimmy Perry (USA), Kansas City. *According to the Kansas City Star (newspaper), both men made the prescribed 145 lbs.*

09.09.13+ Spike Kelly (USA) ND-W PTS 10 Tommy Sheehan (USA), Superior. *The Milwaukee Sentinel (newspaper) reported this one at 145 lbs (6.0 am weigh-in).*

29.09.13+ Mike Glover (USA) ND-W PTS 10 Young Denny (USA), New Orleans. *With both men inside 142 lbs, as per the New Orleans Daily Picayune (newspaper) report, Glover's title claim had to be at stake.*

17.11.13+ Wildcat Ferns (USA) DREW 15 Johnny McCarthy (USA), Denver. *With the weight set at 145 lbs, the Rocky Mountain Herald (newspaper) claimed that both men made it easily.*

07.07.14+ Mike Glover (USA) ND-L PTS 12 Kid Graves (USA), New York City. *Graves weighed in at 143¾ lbs, while Glover scaled 147¼.*

29.12.14+ Kid Graves (USA) ND-DREW 10 Soldier Bartfield (USA), New York City. *Graves scaled 146¼ lbs to Bartfield's 144.*

12.01.15+ Kid Graves (USA) ND-W PTS 10 Kid Alberts (USA), Albany. *Both men made 142 lbs, according to the Albany Evening Journal (newspaper) report.*

30.01.15+ Kid Graves (USA) ND-L PTS 10 Jack Britton (USA), New York City. *Although Graves was over three pounds heavier than his rival, Britton was well inside 145 lbs.*

04.12.16+ Jack Britton (USA) ND-L PTS 10 Steve Latzo (USA), Wilkes Barre. *Latzo scaled 144 lbs to Britton's 147.*

17.12.17 **Ted Kid Lewis** (GB) ND-W PTS 12 Bryan Downey (USA), Columbus. *Although the Chicago Tribune (newspaper) reported that Downey was challenging for the title, the Columbus Ohio State Journal (newspaper) showed them to be outside the weight class, with Lewis scaling 145½ lbs to Downey's 145¾.*

17.08.18+ **Ted Kid Lewis** (GB) ND-W PTS 8 Walter Mohr (USA), Jersey City. *Lewis scaled 143 lbs to Mohr's 140.*

12.05.19+ **Jack Britton** (USA) ND-W PTS 12 Johnny Tillman, Baltimore. *Britton could not lose his title unless kayoed, reported the Baltimore Evening Sun (newspaper).*

09.07.19+ **Jack Britton** (USA) ND-W RSC 2 Al Doty (USA), Connellsville. *No weights were given, despite the Connellsville Daily Courier (newspaper) reporting it to involve the title.*

25.11.19+ **Jack Britton** (USA) ND-W PTS 10 Harvey Thorpe (USA), Buffalo. *The Buffalo Boxing Record handout gave Thorpe as 140 lbs to Britton's 144, ensuring that the latter's title was at risk.*

06.01.20 **Jack Britton** (USA) ND-W PTS 8 Johnny Alberts (USA), Bayonne. *Despite the title billing given in the Bayonne Evening News (newspaper), the fight was made at 150 lbs and each man weighed 148½ lbs.*

30.01.20+ **Jack Britton** (USA) W PTS 12 Jimmy Conway (USA), Savanah. *According to the Savanah Morning News (newspaper), this was a billed title fight with both men inside 145 lbs.*

08.03.20+ **Jack Britton** (USA) ND-W PTS 10 Dave Palitz (USA), Hartford. *The Hartford Courant (newspaper) gave Palitz at 143 lbs to Britton's 146. Although no title billing was attached, had Palitz won inside the distance Britton would have forfeited the championship.*

01.07.20+ **Jack Britton** (USA) ND-W PTS 12 Eddie Shevlin, Portland. *Britton had no trouble at all in holding on to his title in what was billed as a twin six round feature. The Daily Eastern Argus (newspaper) went on to explain that it was a way of getting around the six round State limit.*

23.11.20+ **Jack Britton** (USA) ND-W PTS 10 Bud Logan (USA), San Antonio. *No weights were reported in the San Antonio Express (newspaper), although the fight was accorded championship billing.*

29.11.20+ **Jack Britton** (USA) W PTS 10 Jake Abel (USA), Atlanta. *With Abel making 144 lbs, the Atlanta Constitution (newspaper) reported the world title to be at stake, despite the fact that Britton came into the ring decidedly over 150 lbs and the fight was articled to be in excess of 147 lbs.*

05.05.22 **Jack Britton** (USA) ND-W PTS 10 Cowboy Padgett (USA), Omaha. *Reported to be a title bout by the Vancouver Daily Province (newspaper), the Omaha World Herald (newspaper) stated that, in a fight set at 150 lbs, both men scaled 148½ lbs.*

16.05.22+ **Jack Britton** (USA) W CO 5 Morris Lux (USA), Tulsa. *The Tulsa World (newspaper) stated that this was a billed championship 15 rounder at 147 lbs.*

26.05.22+ **Jack Britton** (USA) DREW 12 Ray Long (USA), Oklahoma City. *Scheduled for 148 lbs, and billed as Oklahoma's first world title bout, despite the weight limit standing at 147, the Daily Oklahoman (newspaper) claimed Long made 144 lbs.*

23.02.23 **Mickey Walker** (USA) ND-W PTS 10 Johnny Griffiths (USA), Scranton. *According to the Scranton Times (newspaper), with Griffiths inside 147 lbs, Walker's title was up for grabs in this one.*

04.04.23+ **Mickey Walker** (USA) ND-W CO 2 Johnny Riley (USA), Wilkes Barre. *Reported to be for the 147 lbs title and scheduled*

for ten rounds, the Wilkes Barre Times-Leader (newspaper) stated that Riley was down to weight on the day of the fight.

20.09.23+ **Mickey Walker** (USA) ND-W CO 8 Bobby Green (USA), Davenport. *A recent discovery made by Bob Soderman, when perusing the Davenport Democrat and Leader (newspaper), was in uncovering the fact that Walker defended his title against Green at 147 lbs in this one.*

18.02.27+ Pete Latzo (USA) ND-L PTS 10 Billy Piltz (USA), Oklahoma City. *Billed for the world 147 lbs title, despite an absence of individual weights in the Daily Oklahoman (newspaper) report of the fight.*

Middleweight (160 lbs)

26.05.97+ Kid McCoy (USA) W RSC 10 Dick O'Brien (USA), New York City. *In a match made at 158 lbs, and scheduled for 25 rounds, the New York Herald (newspaper) reported that, by his victory, McCoy had proved to be a candidate for the championship. Regardless, this should be seen as a defence of his claim to the title.*

31.05.97+ Kid McCoy (USA) ND-W PTS 6 Jack Bonner (USA), Philadelphia. *Made at 158 lbs, the Philadelphia Inquirer (newspaper) reported McCoy as the world middleweight champion.*

08.09.97+ Kid McCoy (USA) NC 5 Tommy Ryan (USA), Syracuse. *The Syracuse Evening News (newspaper) reported that Ryan, although at his best at 145 lbs, surprisingly agreed to enter the ring at 154 lbs with McCoy weighing somewhere between 156 and the limit set at 158 lbs.*

15.11.97+ Kid McCoy (USA) W CO 2 Billy Smith (A), Chicago. *Despite both men being inside the required 158 lbs, the Chicago Tribune (newspaper) made no reference to McCoy's title claim.*

17.12.97 Kid McCoy (USA) W RTD 15 Dan Creedon (NZ), Long Island. *With Bob Fitzsimmons recognised as being unable to make 158 lbs anymore, the promoters billed this fight as a battle for the middleweight championship. Surprisingly made at catchweights, and over the 25 round route, despite the fact that the New York Herald (newspaper) called this one, at an earlier stage, hardly legitimate, they later reclassified it as being one of the most important fights in the region since the days of Jack, the Nonpareil, Dempsey. Despite pre-fight newspaper reports stating that McCoy was expected to make 160 lbs to Creedon's 165, the official announcement gave the weights as 155½ and 157, respectively. Early in 1898, with McCoy fighting mainly among the heavier men, Ryan again carried his welter claim into the middleweight division, declaring himself to be the best man in America at 152/154 lbs.*

23.12.98+ Tommy Ryan (USA) W CO 14 Dick O'Brien (USA), Hartford. *With the weights given as 148 lbs for Ryan and 158 for O'Brien, in the Philadelphia Item (newspaper), the former's title claim would have been on the line in this one.*

01.03.99+ Tommy Ryan (USA) W CO 8 Charles Johnson (USA), Hot Springs. *Made at 150 lbs, Ryan's 158 lbs title claim was automatically at stake.*

05.09.99+ Kid McCoy (USA) W CO 3 Geoff Thorne (GB), New York City. *Made at 158 lbs and scheduled for 20 rounds, with both men inside at the 3.0 pm weigh-in, McCoy's claim at the weight had to be at stake, even though there was no mention of that in the New York Times (newspaper) report. From hereon, however, McCoy appears to leave the middleweights in the possession of Tommy Ryan as he concentrated on the bigger men.*

10.11.00+ Tommy Ryan (USA) W CO 3 Geoff Thorne (GB), Chicago. *Although only a six rounder, but with both men inside 152 lbs, the Englishman was looking to unload Ryan of his title claim.*

10.10.01 George Green (USA) W DIS 6 Tommy Ryan (USA), Kansas City. *Made at 158 lbs, with both men inside (Green scaling 147), Ryan was winning easily until accidentally striking Green with his knee and being ruled out. Scheduled for ten rounds, until a decision was reached, the Kansas City Star (newspaper) made no mention that Ryan's title claim was involved, but at the contracted weight it had to be.*

30.01.02 Tommy Ryan (USA) W CO 7 George Green (USA), Kansas City. *If Green ever took his title claim seriously, and nobody else appeared to do so, with the Philadelphia Item (newspaper) and others continuing to refer to Ryan as the champion, this result put the record straight. However, for Green, also known as Young Corbett, this was to be his final contest before retirement beckoned.*

26.05.02+ Tommy Ryan (USA) W CO 4 Jimmy Handler (USA), Kansas City. *The Kansas City Star (newspaper) reported that had Handler, inside 158 lbs, won he would have claimed the title.*

20.04.03+ Jack O'Brien (USA) DREW 10 Joe Walcott (USA), Boston. *Reported in the Boston Post (newspaper) as the biggest* *middleweight bout ever seen in the city and, while not announcing weights, Walcott was well inside the limit. The paper went on to say that O'Brien should be recognised as the world champion.*

29.12.03+ Jack O'Brien (USA) DREW 10 Hugo Kelly (USA), Kansas City. *According to the Kansas City Star (newspaper), both O'Brien and Kelly were inside the articled 158 lbs.*

24.03.05+ Jack O'Brien (USA) W DIS 2 Young Peter Jackson (USA), Baltimore. *With the weights calling for 158 lbs, Jackson tipped the beam at 152.*

17.10.05+ Jack Twin Sullivan (USA) W PTS 20 Tommy Burns (C), Los Angeles. *Taking into account his 20 round points victory over Hugo Kelly in Kansas City on 6 April 1904, Sullivan (153 lbs) claimed the title following his defeat of Burns.*

11.09.06+ Hugo Kelly (USA) W RSC 5 Jack Burke (USA), Boston. *The Boston Post (newspaper) gave Kelly as a leading claimant in a match made at 158 lbs (6.0 pm weigh-in).*

22.04.07+ Sam Langford (C) W CO 4 Tiger Smith (GB), NSC, London. *Billed for the English open 158 lbs middleweight title, following his victory over Smith (151 lbs), Langford (154 lbs) challenged anyone in the world at 158. Meanwhile, in June 1907, Young Peter Jackson challenged the world at 154 lbs, Langford preferred.*

27.08.07+ Sam Langford (C) W PTS 10 Larry Temple (USA), Chelsea. *Prior to the fight, the Boston Post (newspaper) described Langford as the best 150 lbs fighter in the world and that this would be one of the few occasions where an opponent would weigh less than him. Despite Langford carrying surplus, with Temple well inside the middleweight limit, his claim was at stake in this one.*

12.11.07+ Sam Langford (C) W PTS 20 Young Peter Jackson (USA), Los Angeles. *Made at 158 lbs, with both inside the weight, Langford cemented his claim to the title by his victory, Jackson retiring from the ring one fight later.*

30.12.07 Hugo Kelly (USA) DREW 10 Billy Papke (USA), Milwaukee. *Made at 154 lbs (3.0 pm weigh-in), with both men inside, Kelly just about held on to his title claim. Prior to the fight, the Chicago Tribune (newspaper) reported that the winner would have a realistic claim to the championship.*

11.03.08+ Sam Langford (C) W PTS 8 Larry Temple (USA), Boston. *Again the Boston Post (newspaper) pronounced Langford as the best middleweight in the world and, despite him coming in slightly over the limit for this one, Temple, looking to claim the "black" title, was well inside. Continuing to challenge all and sundry, in January 1909, the Mirror of Life (newspaper) declared Langford to be the world champion because Tom Thomas, Stanley Ketchel and Billy Papke were all drawing the colour bar. Langford immediately challenged Ketchel and undertook to stop him inside ten rounds or forfeit his purse and deposited £200 with that intent. In July 1909, having signed articles to meet Langford, Ketchel refused to defend his title and asked for ten rounds at catchweights, instead.*

28.09.09+ Sam Langford (C) W RSC 5 Dixie Kid (USA), Boston. *Because the Dixie Kid was well inside 158 lbs, Langford's title claim was automatically at stake in this 12 rounder.*

10.01.10+ Sam Langford (C) W CO 3 Dixie Kid (USA), Memphis. *In a return match, the Dixie Kid was again well inside the middleweight limit, thus putting Langford's claim at risk. Meantime, the 158 lbs title was again publicly sought by Langford and Papke after Ketchel claimed that he could no longer make the weight. Eventually, with Papke refusing Langford at all costs and Ketchel deciding to stay in the middleweight division, promoter, Tex Rickard, promised to deliver a title bout between Langford and Ketchel. Despite all the promises, the nearest Langford got to Ketchel was a six round "press" decision loss in Philadelphia on 27 April 1910, Langford, by all accounts, allowing the champion off the hook in order to procure a championship match. Following Ketchel's murder in October 1910, Langford filed a claim with all the major boxing papers for the world 158 lbs title, which was restated in February 1911, but with no fighters interested in taking the bait, he concentrated on the heavier men from then on.*

20.12.10 Hugo Kelly (USA) W PTS 12 Frank Klaus (USA), Boston. *The Boston Daily Advertiser (newspaper) reported that, by his defeat of Klaus at 158 lbs, Kelly fully justified his title claim.*

21.09.11+ Leo Houck (USA) ND-W PTS 10 Frank Mantell (USA), New York City. *Made at 160 lbs, with both men inside, Houck successfully defended his title claim. Although the New York Times (newspaper) reported it as such, with 158 lbs recognised as the class limit at the time, Houck's title claim would have been safe.*

31.10.11 Bob Moha (USA) W PTS 12 Billy Papke (USA), Boston. *Recorded in the 1996 Yearbook as a title fight, closer scrutiny*

shows both men to have come in well over 158 lbs. Billed as a fight with a title in prospect, it ended up as one of the worst fakes ever seen in Boston.

08.02.12+ Jack Dillon (USA) ND-W PTS 10 Paddy Lavin (USA), Buffalo. *The Buffalo Courier (newspaper) reported the fight to have been made at 156 lbs, thus ensuring Dillon's title claim was at stake.*

21.02.12+ Hugo Kelly (USA) ND-W PTS 10 K. O. Brown (USA), Kenosha. *Made at 158 lbs, with Brown scaling 155 to Kelly's 158, the fight had some bearing on the title, according to the Chicago Tribune (newspaper) report.*

20.03.12+ Hugo Kelly (USA) ND-L PTS 10 Eddie McGoorty (USA), Kenosha. *With Kelly's 158 lbs title claim at stake, McGoorty weighed 157 to the former's 156½.*

09.04.12 Frank Mantell (USA) W CO 8 Russell Kane (USA), Marysville. *Made at catchweights, Mantell was 12 lbs heavier than Kane, who came to the ring inside 158 lbs.*

03.05.12+ Frank Klaus (USA) ND-W PTS 10 Jack Dillon (USA), New York City. *Made at 158 lbs in defence of Klaus' title claim, strangely, the ringside scales showed both men to be ten pounds adrift. Klaus was adamant that he had been 157½ earlier that afternoon, while Dillon claimed to have been 158½ at the same time.*

03.07.12+ Frank Mantell (USA) DREW 20 Cyclone Johnny Thompson (USA), Sacramento. *According to Gary Phillips, the local fight historian, the Sacramento papers had the contest billed for the 158 lbs title claimed by both men.*

08.11.12+ Jack Dillon (USA) W PTS 8 Jimmy Howard (USA), Memphis. *The Memphis Daily Appeal (newspaper) reported this to be the start of a middleweight series at 158 lbs. That aside, it was a successful defence of Dillon's claim.*

11.12.12+ Jack Dillon (USA) ND-W PTS 10 Gus Christie (USA), Indianapolis. *According to the Indianapolis Star (newspaper), both men made the required 158 lbs at the 3.0 pm weigh-in.*

19.12.12+ Jack Dillon (USA) ND-DREW 10 Harry Ramsay (USA), Cincinnati. *Made at 158 lbs, the Cincinnati Enquirer (newspaper) qualified that Dillon had again re-stated his claim to the title at that weight on 6 December.*

01.01.13+ Jack Dillon (USA) ND-DREW 10 Gus Christie (USA), Indianapolis. *A defence of Dillon's 158 lbs title claim.*

10.02.13+ Jack Dillon (USA) DREW 15 Bill McKinnon (USA), Providence. *With the State middleweight limit standing at 160 lbs, Dillon's title claim was on the line at that poundage.*

19.02.13+ Jack Dillon (USA) ND-W CO 2 Jack Denning (USA), Indianapolis. *A successful defence of Dillon's title claim at 158 lbs.*

27.02.13+ Eddie McGoorty (USA) ND-DREW 10 Gus Christie (USA), Fond du Lac. *The Milwaukee Sentinel (newspaper) reported that Christie was well inside the 158 lbs required to enforce McGoorty to defend his title claim.*

12.03.13+ Jack Dillon (USA) ND-W PTS 10 K. O. Brennan (USA), Indianapolis. *Dillon made yet another successful defence of his 158 lbs title claim in this one.*

24.03.13+ Eddie McGoorty (USA) ND-DREW 10 Bob Moha (USA), Millwaukee. *Made at 160 lbs, the Milwaukee Sentinel (newspaper) reported this to be the middleweight championship of Wisconsin, if not the world.*

14.04.13 Pat O'Keefe (GB) W PTS 20 Frank Mantell (USA), The Ring, London. *Announced as a title fight at 160 lbs, with both men reported as being inside, the billing was meaningless in the light of Mantell's defeat at the hands of Dillon.*

16.04.13+ Eddie McGoorty (USA) ND-W PTS 8 Freddie Hicks (USA), Windsor. *The Detroit Free Press (newspaper) reported that both men made the required 158 lbs.*

28.04.13+ Eddie McGoorty (USA) ND-W PTS 10 Bob Moha (USA), Milwaukee. *Reported in the Milwaukee Sentinel (newspaper) as a match at 160 lbs, this fight is yet another that should be considered as a defence of Dillon's title claim at the higher poundage.*

29.05.13+ Jack Dillon (USA) ND-W PTS 10 Frank Klaus (USA), Indianapolis. *Made at 160 lbs, both men were claiming the title at that weight at the time.*

01.07.13 Frank Klaus (USA) W CO 3 Jimmy Gardner (USA), Boston - USA. *Billed as a title fight in the Boston papers, while there was no mention that Klaus made 158 lbs, there was no doubt that Gardner was inside the championship weight on the night.*

03.07.13+ Jack Dillon (USA) ND-W CO 10 Bill McKinnon (USA), Indianapolis. *Dillon's 160 lbs title claim was on the line in this one, with McKinnon making the weight.*

02.08.13+ Jimmy Clabby (USA) DREW 12 Freddie Hicks (USA), Butte. *Reported as the champion by the Anaconda Standard (newspaper), Clabby was thought to weigh inside 154 lbs, while Hicks met the stipulated 158 lbs.*

01.09.13+ Jimmy Clabby (USA) W PTS 20 Sailor Grande (USA), Sacramento. *Made at 158 lbs, Clabby weighed in at 152 with Grande five pounds heavier.*

03.11.13+ Jack Dillon (USA) ND-W PTS 10 Gus Christie (USA), Milwaukee. *Made at 160 lbs according to the Milwaukee Sentinel (newspaper).*

15.11.13 George Chip (USA) ND-L PTS 6 Leo Houck (USA), Philadelphia - USA. *According to the Philadelphia Inquirer (newspaper), with Houck inside 158 lbs and despite it being a mere six rounder, Chip's title claim was at risk in a fight articled at the weight.*

27.11.13+ Jimmy Clabby (USA) W CO 14 Frank Logan (USA), San Francisco. *The San Francisco Chronicle (newspaper) gave this one at 158 lbs.*

27.11.13+ Jack Dillon (USA) W PTS 12 Sailor Petroskey (USA), Butte. *With the weigh-in set for 160 lbs, the recognised middles limit in Montana at the time, both men came in under 158, according to the Anaconda Standard (newspaper) report.*

01.01.14+ Jack Dillon (USA) ND-W PTS 10 Gus Christie (USA), Indianapolis. *Both men were down to the required 158 lbs, according to the Indianapolis Star (newspaper) report.*

04.02.14+ Jack Dillon (USA) ND-DREW 8 Freddie Hicks (USA), Windsor. *The Detroit Free Press (newspaper) gave this as a match contested at 158 lbs.*

23.03.14+ Jack Dillon (USA) W PTS 8 K. O. Brown (USA), Memphis. *Although Dillon scaled around the 170 lbs mark, the Memphis Commercial Appeal (newspaper) reported that Brown weighed in at 159.*

03.04.14+ Jimmy Clabby (USA) DREW 20 Billy Murray (USA), San Francisco. *With the match made at 158 lbs, Clabby's title claim would have been at stake.*

08.05.14 Al McCoy (USA) ND-W CO 1 George Pearsall (USA), South Norwalk - USA. *Reported in the Norwalk Hour (newspaper) as being a 158 lbs title fight, Pearsall, who undoubtedly made the weight, posed no risk to the man dubbed a "cheese champion".*

03.07.14+ Jack Dillon (USA) W PTS 10 Sailor Petroskey (USA), Kansas City. *The Kansas City Star (newspaper) gave this one at 160 lbs with a heavy forfeit if not adhered to, thus putting Dillon's title claim at the weight at risk.*

21.07.14+ Jack Dillon (USA) ND-W PTS 10 K. O. Brown (USA), Terre Haute. *Announced as being for the middleweight championship of the world, Dillon scaled 168 lbs to Brown's 157. All that and more was reported in the Indianapolis News (newspaper).*

07.09.14+ Jack Dillon (USA) ND-W PTS 10 Sailor Einert (USA), Terre Haute. *The Indianapolis News (newspaper) reported this to be a defence of Dillon's middleweight claim, despite the fact that he also considered himself to be the light-heavyweight champion. No weights were reported.*

17.11.14 Al McCoy (USA) ND-W PTS 10 Jack McCarron (USA), Pottsville - USA. *Recent research has uncovered that this was a fight between Al Thiel, "the new Al McCoy", and McCarron, not the Al McCoy then claiming the title. The misunderstanding came about after a former manager of the title claimant, upon being sacked, decided to rename Thiel, another of his charges and also a middleweight, as McCoy.*

04.12.14 Al McCoy (USA) ND-W PTS 10 Kid Wagner (USA), Wilkes Barre - USA. *Occasionally shown as a title bout, it was not, with both men scaling over 160 lbs. For the record, McCoy came in at 161 lbs, with Wagner fractionally above the 160 mark.*

01.01.15 Jack Dillon (USA) ND-DREW 6 Young Ahearn (GB), Philadelphia. *Dillon weighed 164 lbs to Ahearn's 156½.*

21.01.15+ Jimmy Clabby (USA) ND-L PTS 10 Mike Gibbons (USA), Milwaukee. *Billed for the championship at 158 lbs, the Milwaukee Sentinel (newspaper) referred to Clabby as the champion.*

20.03.15+ Young Ahearn (GB) ND-W PTS 10 Panama Joe Gans (USA), New York City. *Both men scaled 156 lbs.*

06.04.15+ Jack Dillon (USA) ND-W PTS 10 Billy Murray (USA), Hudson. *Made at 160 lbs, Murray was well inside, while Dillon was said to weigh 159.*

05.07.15+ Jack Dillon (USA) DREW 10 George Chip (USA), Kansas City. *Made at 158 lbs, and with both men inside, according to the Kansas City Star (newspaper), Dillon's title claim had to be at risk.*

12.07.15+ Jack Dillon (USA) ND-W PTS 10 Johnny Howard (USA), Rockaway. *Although Dillon scaled 170 lbs, with Howard coming in at 160, the former's title claim at 160 lbs had all but disintegrated, and obviously unable to make 158/160 lbs anymore, he campaigned at light-heavy from hereon.*

23.10.15 Al McCoy (USA) ND-DREW 10 Soldier Bartfield (USA), New York City - USA. *With Bartfield well inside 158 lbs, McCoy's title claim at the weight was undoubtedly at risk.*

25.11.15 Al McCoy (USA) ND-L PTS 15 Silent Martin (USA), Waterbury - USA. *According to the Waterbury Herald (newspaper), with Martin inside 158 lbs, McCoy's title claim was automatically on the line.*

22.05.16+ Al McCoy (USA) DREW 20 Al Ross (C), New Haven. *Made at 158 lbs ringside, according to the New Haven Evening Register (newspaper).*

28.09.16 Al McCoy (USA) ND-L PTS 10 Jackie Clark (USA), Scranton - USA. *The Scranton Times (newspaper) report carried title billing and claimed that Clark easily made the required 158 lbs.*

28.11.16 Al McCoy (USA) ND-W PTS 10 Jack McCarron (USA), Allentown - USA. *The Allentown Morning Call (newspaper) reported McCarron to be inside 158 lbs, with McCoy, much heavier, not articled to weigh in.*

30.04.17 Al McCoy (USA) ND-L PTS 10 Harry Greb (USA), Pittsburgh - USA. *Although the Pittsburgh Gazette (newspaper) reported that Greb was expected to weigh in at around 160 lbs, the same paper concluded that if either man was within 10 lbs of that weight it would be a miracle. On that basis, one should accept that McCoy's title claim was not at stake in this one.*

04.07.17 Al McCoy (USA) ND-L PTS 10 Jackie Clark (USA), Lonaconing - USA. *According to the Baltimore American (newspaper) and several other Maryland newspapers, Clark, inside 158 lbs, was challenging McCoy's right to the championship.*

21.07.19+ Mike O'Dowd (USA) ND-W CO 5 Young Fisher (USA), Syracuse. *Although no weights were reported in the Syracuse Post-Standard, the newspaper went on to say that, having been billed as such, the 158 lbs title had been at stake.*

10.11.19 Mike O'Dowd (USA) ND-W CO 2 Jimmy O'Hagen (USA), Detroit. *The Grand Rapids Herald (newspaper) reported that the 158 lbs title was not at stake with O'Dowd scaling 158½ lbs to O'Hagen's 159½.*

26.01.20+ Mike O'Dowd (USA) ND-W CO 8 Young Fisher (USA), Syracuse. *Fisher was reported to be well inside the required 158 lbs by the Syracuse Post-Standard (newspaper).*

12.03.20+ Mike O'Dowd (USA) W CO 3 Tommy Madden (USA), Denver. *Billed for 12 rounds to a decision, the Rocky Mountain News (newspaper), despite not mentioning the weights, reported that O'Dowd was risking his title.*

14.04.20+ Mike O'Dowd (USA) W CO 6 Walter Laurette (USA), Bridgeport. *Reported by the Bridgeport Evening Post (newspaper) to be a title fight scheduled for ten rounds, O'Dowd scaled 155 lbs to Laurette's 153.*

Harry Greb (left) weighs in for his meeting with Tiger Flowers, prior to losing the world middleweight title

01.07.20 **Johnny Wilson** (USA) ND-W PTS 12 Soldier Bartfield (USA), Newark. *In making his first title defence, the Boston Post (newspaper) reported Wilson to scale 157¾ lbs to Bartfield's 147½, thus giving him a huge pull in the weights.*

20.07.20+ **Johnny Wilson** (USA) ND-DREW 10 Young Fisher (USA), Syracuse. *The Syracuse Post-Standard (newspaper) gave this one as a billed title fight at 158 lbs.*

02.08.20+ **Johnny Wilson** (USA) ND-W CO 5 Steve Choynski (USA), Buffalo. *According to the Buffalo Morning Express (newspaper), this was a billed title fight at 158 lbs.*

21.04.22+ Johnny Wilson (USA) ND-NC 4 K.O. Jaffe (USA), Hazleton - NBA/NY. *Billed for the title and scheduled for ten rounds, the Hazleton Standard-Sentinal (newspaper) reported that Jaffe was well inside 158 lbs.*

15.09.24+ **Harry Greb** (USA) ND-W RSC 8 Billy Hirsch (USA), Mingo Junction. *Research by James E. Cashman shows Hirsch coming in at 155 lbs, as opposed to Greb's 172, thus creating a title risk for the champion.*

04.08.25+ **Harry Greb** (USA) ND-W CO 4 Ed Smith (USA), Kansas City. *With Smith making 160 lbs, according to James E. Cashman, despite Greb coming in at 169 it had to be a risk fight.*

30.07.30 Mickey Walker (USA) W CO 3 Willie Oster (USA), Newark. *Inadvertently recorded by the Boxing News Annual as being a title fight, it was not, with Walker weighing 163 lbs to Oster's 168. Stripped by the NBA on 14 February 1931 for failing to defend within the stipulated time, Walker vacated the NYSAC version of the title four months later on 19 June, having outgrown the weight class and deciding to campaign among the heavyweights.*

11.06.32 Marcel Thil (FR) W DIS 11 Gorilla Jones (USA), Paris - NBA/IBU. *Despite the 1996 Yearbook stating that the fight was not recognised by the NBA, facts that have recently come to light show that while the NBA were not happy with the result, Thil was not officially stripped until August 1933.*

04.07.32 Marcel Thil (FR) W PTS 15 Len Harvey (GB), White City, London - NBA/IBU. *Following Lou Brouillard's win over Ben Jeby for the NYSAC version of the title on 9 August 1933, within days, the NBA had stripped Gorilla Jones of his American title and put their weight behind Brouillard at Thil's expense.*

09.08.33 Lou Brouillard (C) W CO 7 Ben Jeby (USA), New York City - NY. *Shown in the 1996 Yearbook to be supported by both the NYSAC and the NBA, Brouillard only became recognised by the NBA following his win over Jeby.*

22.02.38+ Young Corbett III (USA) W PTS 10 Fred Apostoli (USA), San Francisco. *Although not a billed title fight, with Freddie Steele recognised by both the NBA and NYSAC, Apostoli (160¼ lbs) was claiming the title as a result of his win over the IBU titleholder, Marcel Thil, and, following the above result, Corbett (159½ lbs) was proclaimed world champion by the Californian State Commission in April 1938. In his next contest, on 25 May in Salt Lake City, Corbett (157 lbs) outpointed Jack Burke (149 lbs), but, outside of California, there was no recognition forthcoming.*

19.07.38+ Young Corbett III (USA) W PTS 10 Glen Lee (USA), Fresno - CALIFORNIA. *Billed for the Californian version of the world middleweight title, according to the San Francisco Chronicle (newspaper), Corbett scaled 160 lbs to Lee's 156.*

Light-Heavyweight (175 lbs)

28.04.14 Jack Dillon (USA) W PTS 10 Al Norton (USA), Kansas City. *Billed as a title bout, the Kansas City Star (newspaper) gave Norton as being well inside 175 lbs to Dillon's 168.*

03.07.14 Jack Dillon (USA) W PTS 10 Sailor Petroskey (USA), Kansas City. *Although recognised primarily as a middles fight, with the match made at 160 lbs and a heavy forfeit to be paid if not adherred to, Dillon's 175 lbs claim was also undoubtedly at stake.*

21.07.14+ Jack Dillon (USA) ND-W PTS 10 K.O. Brown (USA), Terre Haute. *Although billed for the world middleweight title, according to the Indianapolis News (newspaper), the fact that both Dillon (168) and Brown (157) were inside the light-heavyweight limit, the former's 175 lbs title claim was also at risk.*

07.09.14+ Jack Dillon (USA) ND-W PTS 10 Sailor Einert (USA), Terre Haute. *Although billed specifically for the middleweight championship, Dillon's 175 lbs title claim would also have been on the line.*

14.10.14+ Jack Dillon (USA) ND-NC 3 K.O. Brown (USA), St Louis. *This is yet another fight for Dillon that was considered not only to involve his middleweight claim, but his light-heavyweight title as well.*

01.01.15+ Jack Dillon (USA) ND-DREW 6 Young Ahearn (GB), Philadelphia. *Had Ahearn (156½ lbs) won, apart from picking up*

Dillon's middleweight claim, he may well have decided to latch on to the latter's 175 lbs claim also.

25.01.15+ Jack Dillon (USA) W RSC 4 Larry English (USA), Memphis. *The Memphis Daily Appeal (newspaper) reported that both weighed in the region of 170 lbs, but less than 175.*

20.02.15 Jack Dillon (USA) ND-W PTS 10 Frank Mantell (USA), New York City. *With Dillon scaling 173 lbs to Mantell's 171, the former's 175 lbs title claim was at stake in this one.*

06.04.15 Jack Dillon (USA) ND-W PTS 10 Billy Murray (USA), Hudson. *Basically another defence of his middles claim, being made at 160 lbs and Dillon claiming to have scaled 159 lbs with Murray well inside. It should also be recognised as another fight involving his light-heavyweight claim.*

05.07.15 Jack Dillon (USA) DREW 10 George Chip (USA), Kansas City. *Although made at 158 lbs, with both men claiming to have made the weight, in defence of his middles claim, Dillon's 175 lbs title claim was also obviously at risk.*

12.07.15 Jack Dillon (USA) ND-W PTS 10 Johnny Howard (USA), Rockaway. *With Howard scaling 160 lbs to Dillon's 170, both the latter's 160 and 175 lb claims were up for grabs.*

14.02.16+ Jack Dillon (USA) ND-W PTS 8 Vic Hanson (USA), Memphis. *Reported as a championship tryst by the Memphis Daily Appeal, the newspaper went on to say that the ringside weigh-in was set for 170 lbs.*

14.04.16 Jack Dillon (USA) ND-W PTS 10 Billy Miske (USA), St Paul. *Both men were inside 175 lbs, with Dillon scaling around 165 lbs and Miske 167.*

31.10.17 Battling Levinsky (USA) ND-W PTS 10 Zulu Kid (USA), Montreal. *The Montreal Herald (newspaper) poured cold water on Levinsky's title claim when recognising the Kid as a middleweight (well inside 175 lbs), by stating that if only the challenger carried a punch he would surely be a champion.*

28.04.19 Battling Levinsky (USA) ND-L PTS 12 Harry Greb (USA), Canton. *Levinsky's title claim was at stake in this one, with Greb well inside 175 lbs.*

23.01.20 Battling Levinsky (USA) ND-W PTS 8 Johnny Howard (USA), Perth Amboy. *The Perth Amboy Evening News (newspaper) reported that Levinsky scaled 178 lbs to Howard's 163, thus putting his title claim at risk despite the huge weight advantage.*

29.10.24+ **Mike McTigue** (USA) W RSC 6 Frank Carpenter (USA), Providence. *The Providence Evening Bulletin (newspaper) announced this to be a 12 round title bout at 175 lbs, with the contestants well inside the mark.*

26.12.24+ **Mike McTigue** (USA) W CO 4 Jimmy King (USA), Atlanta. *With King well inside 175 lbs at 162, the Atlanta Constitution (newspaper) had earlier reported that McTigue was not figuring on losing the title in this one.*

Mike McTigue (left), the world light-heavyweight champion, 1923-1925, seen here winning the title from Battling Siki

World Champions Since Gloves, 1889-1997

Since I began to carry out extensive research into world championship boxing from the very beginnings of gloved action, I discovered much that needed to be amended regarding the historical listings as we know them, especially prior to the 1920s. Although yet to finalise my researches, despite making considerable changes, the listings are the most comprehensive ever published. Bearing all that in mind, and using a wide range of American newspapers, the aim has been to discover just who had claims, valid or otherwise. Studying the records of all the recognised champions, supplied by Professor Luckett Davis and his team, fights against all opposition has been analysed to produce the ultimate data. Because there were no boxing commissions as such in America prior to the 1920s, the yardstick used to determine valid claims were victories over the leading fighters of the day and recognition given within the newspapers. Only where that criteria has been met have I adjusted previous information.

Championship Status Code:

AU = Austria; AUST = Australia; CALIF = California; CAN = Canada; CLE = Cleveland Boxing Commission; EBU = European Boxing Union; FR = France; GB = Great Britain; IBF = International Boxing Federation; IBU = International Boxing Union; ILL = Illinois; LOUIS = Louisiana; MARY = Maryland; MASS = Massachusetts; MICH = Michigan; NBA = National Boxing Association; NY = New York; PEN = Pennsylvania; SA = South Africa; TBC = Territorial Boxing Commission; USA = United States; WBA = World Boxing Association; WBC = World Boxing Council; WBO = World Boxing Organisation.

Champions in **bold** are accorded universal recognition.

*Undefeated champions (Does not include men who forfeited titles).

Title Holder	Birthplace	Tenure	Status
M. Flyweight (105 lbs)			
Kyung-Yung Lee*	S Korea	1987	IBF
Hiroki Ioka	Japan	1987-1988	WBC
Silvio Gamez*	Venezuela	1988-1989	WBA
Samuth Sithnaruepol	Thailand	1988-1989	IBF
Napa Kiatwanchai	Thailand	1988-1989	WBC
Bong-Jun Kim	S Korea	1989-1991	WBA
Nico Thomas	Indonesia	1989	IBF
Rafael Torres	Dom Republic	1989-1992	WBO
Eric Chavez	Philippines	1989-1990	IBF
Jum-Hwan Choi	S Korea	1989-1990	WBC
Hideyuki Ohashi	Japan	1990	WBC
Fahlan Lukmingkwan	Thailand	1990-1992	IBF
Ricardo Lopez	Mexico	1990-	WBC
Hi-Yon Choi	S Korea	1991-1992	WBA
Manny Melchor	Philippines	1992	IBF
Hideyuki Ohashi	Japan	1992-1993	WBA
Ratanapol Sowvoraphin	Thailand	1992-1996	IBF
Chana Porpaoin	Thailand	1993-1995	WBA
Paul Weir*	Scotland	1993-1994	WBO
Alex Sanchez	Puerto Rico	1993-	WBO
Rosendo Alvarez	Nicaragua	1995-	WBA
Ratanapol Sowvoraphin	Thailand	1996-	IBF
L. Flyweight (108 lbs)			
Franco Udella	Italy	1975	WBC
Jaime Rios	Panama	1975-1976	WBA
Luis Estaba	Venezuela	1975-1978	WBC
Juan Guzman	Dom Republic	1976	WBA
Yoko Gushiken	Japan	1976-1981	WBA
Freddie Castillo	Mexico	1978	WBC
Sor Vorasingh	Thailand	1978	WBC
Sun-Jun Kim	S Korea	1978-1980	WBC
Shigeo Nakajima	Japan	1980	WBC
Hilario Zapata	Panama	1980-1982	WBC
Pedro Flores	Mexico	1981	WBA
Hwan-Jin Kim	S Korea	1981	WBA
Katsuo Tokashiki	Japan	1981-1983	WBA
Amado Ursua	Mexico	1982	WBC
Tadashi Tomori	Japan	1982	WBC
Hilario Zapata	Panama	1982-1983	WBC

Title Holder	Birthplace	Tenure	Status
Jung-Koo Chang*	S Korea	1983-1988	WBC
Lupe Madera	Mexico	1983-1984	WBA
Dodie Penalosa	Philippines	1983-1986	IBF
Francisco Quiroz	Dom Republic	1984-1985	WBA
Joey Olivo	USA	1985	WBA
Myung-Woo Yuh	S Korea	1985-1991	WBA
Jum-Hwan Choi	S Korea	1986-1988	IBF
Tacy Macalos	Philippines	1988-1989	IBF
German Torres	Mexico	1988-1989	WBC
Yul-Woo Lee	S Korea	1989	WBC
Muangchai Kitikasem	Thailand	1989-1990	IBF
Jose de Jesus	Puerto Rico	1989-1992	WBO
Humberto Gonzalez	Mexico	1989-1990	WBC
Michael Carbajal	USA	1990-1993	IBF
Rolando Pascua	Philippines	1990-1991	WBC
Melchor Cob Castro	Mexico	1991	WBC
Humberto Gonzalez	Mexico	1991-1993	WBC
Hiroki Ioka	Japan	1991-1992	WBA
Josue Camacho	Puerto Rico	1992-1994	WBO
Myung-Woo Yuh*	S Korea	1992-1993	WBA
Michael Carbajal	USA	1993-1994	IBF/WBC
Silvio Gamez	Venezuela	1993-1995	WBA
Humberto Gonzalez	Mexico	1994-1995	WBC/IBF
Michael Carbajal*	USA	1994	WBO
Paul Weir	Scotland	1994-1995	WBO
Hi-Yong Choi	S Korea	1995-1996	WBA
Saman Sorjaturong	Thailand	1995	WBC/IBF
Jacob Matlala*	South Africa	1995-1997	WBO
Saman Sorjaturong	Thailand	1995-	WBC
Carlos Murillo	Panama	1996	WBA
Michael Carbajal	USA	1996-1997	IBF
Keiji Yamaguchi	Japan	1996	WBA
Pichitnoi Chor Siriwat	Thailand	1996-	WBA
Mauricio Pastrana	Colombia	1997	IBF
Jesus Chong	Mexico	1997-	WBO
Flyweight (112 lbs)			
Johnny Coulon	Canada	1910	USA
Sid Smith	England	1911-1913	GB
Sid Smith	England	1913	GB/IBU
Bill Ladbury	England	1913-1914	GB/IBU

Title Holder	Birthplace	Tenure	Status	Title Holder	Birthplace	Tenure	Status
Percy Jones	Wales	1914	GB/IBU	Freddie Castillo	Mexico	1982	WBC
Tancy Lee	Scotland	1915	GB/IBU	Eleonicio Mercedes	Dom Republic	1982-1983	WBC
Joe Symonds	England	1915-1916	GB/IBU	Charlie Magri	Tunisia	1983	WBC
Jimmy Wilde	Wales	1916	GB/IBU	Frank Cedeno	Philippines	1983-1984	WBC
Jimmy Wilde	Wales	1916-1923		Soon-Chun Kwon	S Korea	1983-1985	IBF
Pancho Villa*	Philippines	1923-1925		Koji Kobayashi	Japan	1984	WBC
Fidel la Barba	USA	1925-1927	NBA/CALIF	Gabriel Bernal	Mexico	1984	WBC
Fidel la Barba*	USA	1927		Sot Chitalada	Thailand	1984-1988	WBC
Johnny McCoy	USA	1927-1928	CALIF	Hilario Zapata	Panama	1985-1987	WBA
Izzy Schwartz	USA	1927-1929	NY	Chong-Kwan Chung	S Korea	1985-1986	IBF
Frenchy Belanger	Canada	1927-1928	NBA	Bi-Won Chung	S Korea	1986	IBF
Newsboy Brown	Russia	1928	CALIF	Hi-Sup Shin	S Korea	1986-1987	IBF
Frankie Genaro	USA	1928-1929	NBA	Fidel Bassa	Colombia	1987-1989	WBA
Emile Pladner	France	1929	NBA/IBU	Dodie Penalosa	Philippines	1987	IBF
Frankie Genaro	USA	1929-1931	NBA/IBU	Chang-Ho Choi	S Korea	1987-1988	IBF
Midget Wolgast	USA	1930-1935	NY	Rolando Bohol	Philippines	1988	IBF
Young Perez	Tunisia	1931-1932	NBA/IBU	Yong-Kang Kim	S Korea	1988-1989	WBC
Jackie Brown	England	1932-1935	NBA/IBU	Duke McKenzie	England	1988-1989	IBF
Jackie Brown	England	1935	GB/NBA	Elvis Alvarez*	Colombia	1989	WBO
Benny Lynch	Scotland	1935-1937	GB/NBA	Sot Chitalada	Thailand	1989-1991	WBC
Small Montana	Philippines	1935-1937	NY/CALIF	Dave McAuley	Ireland	1989-1992	IBF
Valentin Angelmann	France	1936-1938	IBU	Jesus Rojas	Venezuela	1989-1990	WBA
Peter Kane*	England	1938-1939	NBA/NY/GB/IBU	Yukihito Tamakuma	Japan	1990-1991	WBA
Little Dado	Philippines	1938-1939	CALIF	Isidro Perez	Mexico	1990-1992	WBO
Little Dado	Philippines	1939-1943	NBA/CALIF	Yul-Woo Lee	S Korea	1990	WBA
Jackie Paterson	Scotland	1943-1947		Muangchai Kitikasem	Thailand	1991-1992	WBC
Jackie Paterson	Scotland	1947-1948	GB/NY	Elvis Alvarez	Colombia	1991	WBA
Rinty Monaghan	Ireland	1947-1948	NBA	Yong-Kang Kim	S Korea	1991-1992	WBA
Rinty Monaghan*	Ireland	1948-1950		Pat Clinton	Scotland	1992-1993	WBO
Terry Allen	England	1950		Rodolfo Blanco	Colombia	1992	IBF
Dado Marino	Hawaii	1950-1952		Yuri Arbachakov	Russia	1992-	WBC
Yoshio Shirai	Japan	1952-1954		Aquiles Guzman	Venezuela	1992	WBA
Pascual Perez	Argentine	1954-1960		Pichit Sitbangprachan*	Thailand	1992-1994	IBF
Pone Kingpetch	Thailand	1960-1962		David Griman	Venezuela	1992-1994	WBA
Fighting Harada	Japan	1962-1963		Jacob Matlala	S Africa	1993-1995	WBO
Pone Kingpetch	Thailand	1963		Saen Sorploenchit	Thailand	1994-1996	WBA
Hiroyuki Ebihara	Japan	1963-1964		Alberto Jimenez	Mexico	1995-1996	WBO
Pone Kingpetch	Thailand	1964-1965		Francisco Tejedor	Colombia	1995	IBF
Salvatore Burruni	Italy	1965		Danny Romero*	USA	1995-1996	IBF
Salvatore Burruni	Italy	1965-1966	WBC	Mark Johnson	USA	1996-	IBF
Horacio Accavallo*	Argentine	1966-1968	WBA	Jose Bonilla	Venezuela	1996-	WBA
Walter McGowan	Scotland	1966	WBC	Carlos Salazar	Argentine	1996-	WBO
Chartchai Chionoi	Thailand	1966-1969	WBC				
Efren Torres	Mexico	1969-1970	WBC	**S. Flyweight (115 lbs)**			
Hiroyuki Ebihara	Japan	1969	WBA	Rafael Orono	Venezuela	1980-1981	WBC
Bernabe Villacampo	Philippines	1969-1970	WBA	Chul-Ho Kim	S Korea	1981-1982	WBC
Chartchai Chionoi	Thailand	1970	WBC	Gustavo Ballas	Argentine	1981	WBA
Berkrerk Chartvanchai	Thailand	1970	WBA	Rafael Pedroza	Panama	1981-1982	WBA
Masao Ohba*	Japan	1970-1973	WBA	Jiro Watanabe	Japan	1982-1984	WBA
Erbito Salavarria	Philippines	1970-1971	WBC	Rafael Orono	Venezuela	1982-1983	WBC
Betulio Gonzalez	Venezuela	1971-1972	WBC	Payao Poontarat	Thailand	1983-1984	WBC
Venice Borkorsor*	Thailand	1972-1973	WBC	Joo-Do Chun	S Korea	1983-1985	IBF
Chartchai Chionoi	Thailand	1973-1974	WBA	Jiro Watanabe	Japan	1984-1986	WBC
Betulio Gonzalez	Venezuela	1973-1974	WBC	Kaosai Galaxy*	Thailand	1984-1992	WBA
Shoji Oguma	Japan	1974-1975	WBC	Elly Pical	Indonesia	1985-1986	IBF
Susumu Hanagata	Japan	1974-1975	WBA	Cesar Polanco	Dom Republic	1986	IBF
Miguel Canto	Mexico	1975-1979	WBC	Gilberto Roman	Mexico	1986-1987	WBC
Erbito Salavarria	Philippines	1975-1976	WBA	Elly Pical	Indonesia	1986-1987	IBF
Alfonso Lopez	Panama	1976	WBA	Santos Laciar	Argentine	1987	WBC
Guty Espadas	Mexico	1976-1978	WBA	Tae-Il Chang	S Korea	1987	IBF
Betulio Gonzalez	Venezuela	1978-1979	WBA	Jesus Rojas	Colombia	1987-1988	WBC
Chan-Hee Park	S Korea	1979-1980	WBC	Elly Pical	Indonesia	1987-1989	IBF
Luis Ibarra	Panama	1979-1980	WBA	Gilberto Roman	Mexico	1988-1989	WBC
Tae-Shik Kim	S Korea	1980	WBA	Jose Ruiz	Puerto Rico	1989-1992	WBO
Shoji Oguma	Japan	1980-1981	WBC	Juan Polo Perez	Colombia	1989-1990	IBF
Peter Mathebula	S Africa	1980-1981	WBA	Nana Yaw Konadu	Ghana	1989-1990	WBC
Santos Laciar	Argentine	1981	WBA	Sung-Il Moon	S Korea	1990-1993	WBC
Antonio Avelar	Mexico	1981-1982	WBC	Robert Quiroga	USA	1990-1993	IBF
Luis Ibarra	Panama	1981	WBA	Jose Quirino	Mexico	1992	WBO
Juan Herrera	Mexico	1981-1982	WBA	Katsuya Onizuka	Japan	1992-1994	WBA
Prudencio Cardona	Colombia	1982	WBC	Johnny Bredahl	Denmark	1992-1994	WBO
Santos Laciar*	Argentine	1982-1985	WBA	Julio Cesar Borboa	Mexico	1993-1994	IBF

Title Holder	Birthplace	Tenure	Status
Jose Luis Bueno	Mexico	1993-1994	WBC
Hiroshi Kawashima	Japan	1994-1997	WBC
Harold Grey	Colombia	1994-1995	IBF
Hyung-Chul Lee	S Korea	1994-1995	WBA
Johnny Tapia	USA	1994-	WBO
Alimi Goitia	Venezuela	1995-1996	WBA
Carlos Salazar	Argentine	1995-1996	IBF
Harold Grey	Colombia	1996	IBF
Yokthai Sith-Oar	Thailand	1996-	WBA
Danny Romero	USA	1996-	IBF
Gerry Penalosa	Philippines	1997-	WBC

Bantamweight (118 lbs)

Title Holder	Birthplace	Tenure	Status
Tommy Kelly	USA	1889	
George Dixon	Canada	1889-1890	
Chappie Moran	England	1889-1890	
Tommy Kelly	USA	1890-1892	
Billy Plimmer	England	1892-1895	
Pedlar Palmer	England	1895-1899	
Terry McGovern	USA	1899	
Pedlar Palmer	England	1899-1900	GB
Terry McGovern*	USA	1899-1900	
Clarence Forbes	USA	1900	
Johnny Reagan	USA	1900-1902	
Harry Ware	England	1900-1902	GB
Harry Harris	USA	1901	
Harry Forbes	USA	1901-1902	
Kid McFadden	USA	1901	
Dan Dougherty	USA	1901	
Andrew Tokell	England	1902	GB
Harry Ware	England	1902	GB
Harry Forbes	USA	1902-1903	USA
Joe Bowker	England	1902-1904	GB
Frankie Neil	USA	1903-1904	USA
Joe Bowker*	England	1904-1905	
Frankie Neil	USA	1905	USA
Digger Stanley	England	1905-1907	
Owen Moran	England	1905-1907	
Jimmy Walsh	USA	1905-1908	USA
Owen Moran	England	1907	GB
Monte Attell	USA	1908-1910	
Jimmy Walsh	USA	1908-1911	
Digger Stanley	England	1909-1912	GB
Frankie Conley	Italy	1910-1911	
Johnny Coulon	Canada	1910-1911	
Monte Attell	USA	1910-1911	
Johnny Coulon	Canada	1911-1913	USA
Charles Ledoux	France	1912-1913	GB/IBU
Eddie Campi	USA	1913-1914	
Johnny Coulon	Canada	1913-1914	
Kid Williams	Denmark	1913-1914	
Kid Williams	Denmark	1914-1915	
Kid Williams	Denmark	1915-1917	
Johnny Ertle	USA	1915-1918	
Pete Herman	USA	1917-1919	
Pal Moore	USA	1918-1919	
Pete Herman	USA	1919-1920	
Joe Lynch	USA	1920-1921	
Pete Herman	USA	1921	
Johnny Buff	USA	1921-1922	
Joe Lynch	USA	1922-1923	
Joe Lynch	USA	1923-1924	NBA
Joe Burman	England	1923	NY
Abe Goldstein	USA	1923-1924	NY
Joe Lynch	USA	1924	
Abe Goldstein	USA	1924	
Eddie Martin	USA	1924-1925	
Charley Rosenberg	USA	1925-1926	
Charley Rosenberg	USA	1926-1927	NY
Bud Taylor*	USA	1926-1928	NBA
Bushy Graham*	Italy	1928-1929	NY
Al Brown	Panama	1929-1931	
Al Brown	Panama	1931	NY/IBU
Pete Sanstol	Norway	1931	CAN
Al Brown	Panama	1931-1933	
Al Brown	Panama	1933-1934	NY/NBA/IBU
Speedy Dado	Philippines	1933	CALIF
Baby Casanova	Mexico	1933-1934	CALIF
Sixto Escobar	Puerto Rico	1934	CAN
Sixto Escobar	Puerto Rico	1934-1935	NBA
Al Brown	Panama	1934-1935	NY/IBU
Lou Salica	USA	1935	CALIF
Baltazar Sangchilli	Spain	1935-1938	IBU
Lou Salica	USA	1935	NBA/NY
Sixto Escobar	Puerto Rico	1935-1937	NBA/NY
Harry Jeffra	USA	1937-1938	NY/NBA
Sixto Escobar	Puerto Rico	1938	NY/NBA
Al Brown	Panama	1938	IBU
Sixto Escobar	Puerto Rico	1938-1939	
George Pace	USA	1939-1940	NBA
Lou Salica	USA	1939	CALIF
Tony Olivera	USA	1939-1940	CALIF
Little Dado	Philippines	1940-1941	CALIF
Lou Salica	USA	1940-1942	NY/NBA
Lou Salica	USA	1941	
Kenny Lindsay	Canada	1941	CAN
Lou Salica	USA	1941-1942	
Lou Salica	USA	1942	NY
Manuel Ortiz	USA	1942-1943	NBA
Manuel Ortiz	USA	1943-1945	NY/NBA
Kui Kong Young	Hawaai	1943	TBC
Rush Dalma	Philippines	1943-1945	TBC
Manuel Ortiz	USA	1945-1947	
Harold Dade	USA	1947	
Manuel Ortiz	USA	1947-1950	
Vic Toweel	S Africa	1950-1952	
Jimmy Carruthers*	Australia	1952-1954	
Robert Cohen	Algeria	1954	
Robert Cohen	Algeria	1954-1956	NY/EBU
Raton Macias	Mexico	1955-1957	NBA
Mario D'Agata	Italy	1956-1957	NY/EBU
Alphonse Halimi	Algeria	1957	NY/EBU
Alphonse Halimi	Algeria	1957-1959	
Joe Becerra*	Mexico	1959-1960	
Alphonse Halimi	Algeria	1960-1961	EBU
Eder Jofre	Brazil	1960-1962	NBA
Johnny Caldwell	Ireland	1961-1962	EBU
Eder Jofre	Brazil	1962-1965	
Fighting Harada	Japan	1965-1968	
Lionel Rose	Australia	1968-1969	
Ruben Olivares	Mexico	1969-1970	
Chuchu Castillo	Mexico	1970-1971	
Ruben Olivares	Mexico	1971-1972	
Rafael Herrera	Mexico	1972	
Enrique Pinder	Panama	1972	
Enrique Pinder	Panama	1972-1973	WBC
Romeo Anaya	Mexico	1973	WBA
Rafael Herrera	Mexico	1973-1974	WBC
Arnold Taylor	S Africa	1973-1974	WBA
Soo-Hwan Hong	S Korea	1974-1975	WBA
Rodolfo Martinez	Mexico	1974-1976	WBC
Alfonso Zamora	Mexico	1975-1977	WBA
Carlos Zarate	Mexico	1976-1979	WBC
Jorge Lujan	Panama	1977-1980	WBA
Lupe Pintor*	Mexico	1979-1983	WBC
Julian Solis	Puerto Rico	1980	WBA
Jeff Chandler	USA	1980-1984	WBA
Albert Davila	USA	1983-1985	WBC
Richard Sandoval	USA	1984-1986	WBA
Satoshi Shingaki	Japan	1984-1985	IBF
Jeff Fenech*	Australia	1985-1987	IBF
Daniel Zaragoza	Mexico	1985	WBC
Miguel Lora	Colombia	1985-1988	WBC
Gaby Canizales	USA	1986	WBA

Title Holder	Birthplace	Tenure	Status
Bernardo Pinango*	Venezuela	1986-1987	WBA
Takuya Muguruma	Japan	1987	WBA
Kelvin Seabrooks	USA	1987-1988	IBF
Chang-Yung Park	S Korea	1987	WBA
Wilfredo Vasquez	Puerto Rico	1987-1988	WBA
Kaokor Galaxy	Thailand	1988	WBA
Orlando Canizales*	USA	1988-1994	IBF
Sung-Il Moon	S Korea	1988-1989	WBA
Raul Perez	Mexico	1988-1991	WBC
Israel Contrerras*	Venezuela	1989-1991	WBO
Kaokor Galaxy	Thailand	1989	WBA
Luisito Espinosa	Philippines	1989-1991	WBA
Greg Richardson	USA	1991	WBC
Gaby Canizales	USA	1991	WBO
Duke McKenzie	England	1991-1992	WBO
Joichiro Tatsuyushi*	Japan	1991-1992	WBC
Israel Contrerras	Venezuela	1991-1992	WBA
Eddie Cook	USA	1992	WBA
Victor Rabanales	Mexico	1992-1993	WBC
Rafael del Valle	Puerto Rico	1992-1994	WBO
Jorge Elicier Julio	Colombia	1992-1993	WBA
Il-Jung Byun	S Korea	1993	WBC
Junior Jones	USA	1993-1994	WBA
Yasuei Yakushiji	Japan	1993-1995	WBC
John Michael Johnson	USA	1994	WBA
Daorung Chuwatana	Thailand	1994-1995	WBA
Alfred Kotey	Ghana	1994-1995	WBO
Harold Mestre	Colombia	1995	IBF
Mbulelo Botile	S Africa	1995-	IBF
Wayne McCullough	Ireland	1995-1997	WBC
Veeraphol Sahaprom	Thailand	1995-1996	WBA
Daniel Jimenez	Puerto Rico	1995-1996	WBO
Nana Yaw Konadu	Ghana	1996	WBA
Robbie Regan	Wales	1996-	WBO
Daorung Chuwatana	Thailand	1996-1997	WBA
Sirimongkol Singmanassak	Thailand	1997-	WBC
Nana Yaw Konadu	Ghana	1997-	WBC

S. Bantamweight (122 lbs)

Title Holder	Birthplace	Tenure	Status
Rigoberto Riasco	Panama	1976	WBC
Royal Kobayashi	Japan	1976	WBC
Dong-Kyun Yum	S Korea	1976-1977	WBC
Wilfredo Gomez*	Puerto Rico	1977-1983	WBC
Soo-Hwan Hong	S Korea	1977-1978	WBA
Ricardo Cardona	Colombia	1978-1980	WBA
Leo Randolph	USA	1980	WBA
Sergio Palma	Argentine	1980-1982	WBA
Leonardo Cruz	Dom Republic	1982-1984	WBA
Jaime Garza	USA	1983-1984	WBC
Bobby Berna	Philippines	1983-1984	IBF
Loris Stecca	Italy	1984	WBA
Seung-In Suh	S Korea	1984-1985	IBF
Victor Callejas	Puerto Rico	1984-1986	WBA
Juan Meza	Mexico	1984-1985	WBC
Ji-Won Kim*	S Korea	1985-1986	IBF
Lupe Pintor	Mexico	1985-1986	WBC
Samart Payakarun	Thailand	1986-1987	WBC
Louie Espinosa	USA	1987	WBA
Seung-Hoon Lee*	S Korea	1987-1988	IBF
Jeff Fenech*	Australia	1987-1988	WBC
Julio Gervacio	Dom Republic	1987-1988	WBA
Bernardo Pinango	Venezuela	1988	WBA
Daniel Zaragoza	Mexico	1988-1990	WBC
Jose Sanabria	Venezuela	1988-1989	IBF
Juan J. Estrada	Mexico	1988-1989	WBA
Fabrice Benichou	Spain	1989-1990	IBF
Kenny Mitchell	USA	1989	WBO
Valerio Nati	Italy	1989-1990	WBO
Jesus Salud	USA	1989-1990	WBA
Welcome Ncita	S Africa	1990-1992	IBF
Paul Banke	USA	1990	WBC
Orlando Fernandez	Puerto Rico	1990-1991	WBO

Title Holder	Birthplace	Tenure	Status
Luis Mendoza	Colombia	1990-1991	WBA
Pedro Decima	Argentine	1990-1991	WBC
Kiyoshi Hatanaka	Japan	1991	WBC
Jesse Benavides	USA	1991-1992	WBO
Daniel Zaragoza	Mexico	1991-1992	WBC
Raul Perez	Mexico	1991-1992	WBA
Thierry Jacob	France	1992	WBC
Wilfredo Vasquez	Puerto Rico	1992-1995	WBA
Tracy Harris Patterson	USA	1992-1994	WBC
Duke McKenzie	England	1992-1993	WBO
Kennedy McKinney	USA	1992-1994	IBF
Daniel Jimenez	Puerto Rico	1993-1995	WBO
Vuyani Bungu	S Africa	1994-	IBF
Hector Acero-Sanchez	Dom Republic	1994-1995	WBC
Marco Antonio Barrera	Mexico	1995-1996	WBO
Antonio Cermeno	Venezuela	1995-	WBA
Daniel Zaragoza	Mexico	1995-	WBC
Junior Jones	USA	1996-	WBO

Featherweight (126 lbs)

Title Holder	Birthplace	Tenure	Status
Ike Weir	Ireland	1889-1890	
Billy Murphy	New Zealand	1890-1893	
George Dixon	Canada	1890-1893	
Young Griffo	Australia	1890-1893	
Johnny Griffin	USA	1891-1893	
Solly Smith	USA	1893	
George Dixon	Canada	1893-1896	
Solly Smith	USA	1896-1898	
Frank Erne	USA	1896-1897	
George Dixon	Canada	1896-1900	
Harry Greenfield	England	1897-1899	
Ben Jordan	England	1897-1899	
Will Curley	England	1897-1899	
Dave Sullivan	Ireland	1898	
Ben Jordan	England	1899-1905	GB
Eddie Santry	USA	1899-1900	
Terry McGovern	USA	1900	
Terry McGovern	USA	1900-1901	USA
Young Corbett II	USA	1901-1903	USA
Eddie Hanlon	USA	1903	
Young Corbett II	USA	1903-1904	
Abe Attell	USA	1903-1904	
Abe Attell	USA	1904-1911	USA
Joe Bowker	England	1905-1907	GB
Jim Driscoll	Wales	1907-1912	GB
Abe Attell	USA	1911-1912	
Joe Coster	USA	1911	
Joe Rivers	Mexico	1911	
Johnny Kilbane	USA	1911-1912	
Jim Driscoll*	Wales	1912-1913	GB/IBU
Johnny Kilbane	USA	1912-1922	USA
Johnny Kilbane	USA	1922-1923	NBA
Johnny Dundee	Italy	1922-1923	NY
Eugene Criqui	France	1923	
Johnny Dundee*	Italy	1923-1924	
Kid Kaplan	Russia	1925	NY
Kid Kaplan*	Russia	1925-1926	
Honeyboy Finnegan	USA	1926-1927	MASS
Benny Bass	Russia	1927-1928	NBA
Tony Canzoneri	USA	1927-1928	NY
Tony Canzoneri	USA	1928	
Andre Routis	France	1928-1929	
Bat Battalino	USA	1929-1932	
Bat Battalino	USA	1932	NBA
Tommy Paul	USA	1932-1933	NBA
Kid Chocolate*	Cuba	1932-1934	NY
Baby Arizmendi	Mexico	1932-1933	CALIF
Freddie Miller	USA	1933-1936	NBA
Baby Arizmendi	Mexico	1934-1935	NY
Baby Arizmendi	Mexico	1935-1936	NY/MEX
Baby Arizmendi	Mexico	1936	MEX
Petey Sarron	USA	1936-1937	NBA

Title Holder	Birthplace	Tenure	Status
Henry Armstrong	USA	1936-1937	CALIF/MEX
Mike Belloise	USA	1936	NY
Maurice Holtzer	France	1937-1938	IBU
Henry Armstrong*	USA	1937-1938	NBA/NY
Leo Rodak	USA	1938	MARY
Joey Archibald	USA	1938-1939	NY
Leo Rodak	USA	1938-1939	NBA
Joey Archibald	USA	1939-1940	
Joey Archibald	USA	1940	NY
Petey Scalzo	USA	1940-1941	NBA
Jimmy Perrin	USA	1940	LOUIS
Harry Jeffra	USA	1940-1941	NY/MARY
Joey Archibald	USA	1941	NY/MARY
Richie Lemos	USA	1941	NBA
Chalky Wright	Mexico	1941-1942	NY/MARY
Jackie Wilson	USA	1941-1943	NBA
Willie Pep	USA	1942-1946	NY
Jackie Callura	Canada	1943	NBA
Phil Terranova	USA	1943-1944	NBA
Sal Bartolo	USA	1944-1946	NBA
Willie Pep	USA	1946-1948	
Sandy Saddler	USA	1948-1949	
Willie Pep	USA	1949-1950	
Sandy Saddler*	USA	1950-1957	
Hogan Kid Bassey	Nigeria	1957-1959	
Davey Moore	USA	1959-1963	
Sugar Ramos	Cuba	1963-1964	
Vicente Saldivar*	Mexico	1964-1967	
Raul Rojas	USA	1967	CALIF
Howard Winstone	Wales	1968	WBC
Raul Rojas	USA	1968	WBA
Johnny Famechon	France	1968-1969	AUST
Jose Legra	Cuba	1968-1969	WBC
Shozo Saijyo	Japan	1968-1971	WBA
Johnny Famechon	France	1969-1970	WBC
Vicente Saldivar	Mexico	1970	WBC
Kuniaki Shibata	Japan	1970-1972	WBC
Antonio Gomez	Venezuela	1971-1972	WBA
Clemente Sanchez	Mexico	1972	WBC
Ernesto Marcel*	Panama	1972-1974	WBA
Jose Legra	Cuba	1972-1973	WBC
Eder Jofre	Brazil	1973-1974	WBC
Ruben Olivares	Mexico	1974	WBA
Bobby Chacon	USA	1974-1975	WBC
Alexis Arguello*	Nicaragua	1974-1977	WBA
Ruben Olivares	Mexico	1975	WBC
David Kotey	Ghana	1975-1976	WBC
Danny Lopez	USA	1976-1980	WBC
Rafael Ortega	Panama	1977	WBA
Cecilio Lastra	Spain	1977-1978	WBA
Eusebio Pedroza	Panama	1978-1985	WBA
Salvador Sanchez*	Mexico	1980-1982	WBC
Juan Laporte	Puerto Rico	1982-1984	WBC
Min-Keun Oh	S Korea	1984-1985	IBF
Wilfredo Gomez	Puerto Rico	1984	WBC
Azumah Nelson*	Ghana	1984-1988	WBC
Barry McGuigan	Ireland	1985-1986	WBA
Ki-Yung Chung	S Korea	1985-1986	IBF
Steve Cruz	USA	1986-1987	WBA
Antonio Rivera	Puerto Rico	1986-1988	IBF
Antonio Esparragoza	Venezuela	1987-1991	WBA
Calvin Grove	USA	1988	IBF
Jeff Fenech*	Australia	1988-1989	WBC
Jorge Paez	Mexico	1988-1990	IBF
Maurizio Stecca	Italy	1989	WBO
Louie Espinosa	USA	1989-1990	WBO
Jorge Paez*	Mexico	1990-1991	IBF/WBO
Marcos Villasana	Mexico	1990-1991	WBC
Kyun-Yung Park	S Korea	1991-1993	WBA
Troy Dorsey	USA	1991	IBF
Maurizio Stecca	Italy	1991-1992	WBO
Manuel Medina	Mexico	1991-1993	IBF

Title Holder	Birthplace	Tenure	Status
Paul Hodkinson	England	1991-1993	WBC
Colin McMillan	England	1992	WBO
Ruben Palacio	Colombia	1992-1993	WBO
Tom Johnson	USA	1993-1997	IBF
Steve Robinson	Wales	1993-1995	WBO
Gregorio Vargas	Mexico	1993	WBC
Kevin Kelley	USA	1993-1995	WBC
Eloy Rojas	Venezuela	1993-1996	WBA
Alejandro Gonzalez	Mexico	1995	WBC
Manuel Medina	Mexico	1995	WBC
Prince Naseem Hamed	England	1995-1997	WBO
Luisito Espinosa	Philippines	1995-	WBC
Wilfredo Vasquez	Puerto Rico	1996-	WBA
Prince Naseem Hamed	England	1997-	WBO/IBF

S. Featherweight (130 lbs)

Title Holder	Birthplace	Tenure	Status
Johnny Dundee	Italy	1921-1923	NY
Jack Bernstein	USA	1923	NY
Jack Bernstein	USA	1923	NBA/NY
Johnny Dundee	Italy	1923-1924	NBA/NY
Kid Sullivan	USA	1924-1925	NBA/NY
Mike Ballerino	USA	1925	NBA/NY
Tod Morgan	USA	1925-1929	NBA/NY
Benny Bass	Russia	1929-1930	NBA/NY
Benny Bass	Russia	1930-1931	NBA
Kid Chocolate	Cuba	1931-1933	NBA
Frankie Klick	USA	1933-1934	NBA
Sandy Saddler	USA	1949-1950	NBA
Sandy Saddler	USA	1950-1951	CLE
Harold Gomes	USA	1959-1960	NBA
Flash Elorde	Philippines	1960-1962	NBA
Flash Elorde	Philippines	1962-1967	WBA
Raul Rojas	USA	1967	CALIF
Yoshiaki Numata	Japan	1967	WBA
Hiroshi Kobayashi	Japan	1967-1971	WBA
Rene Barrientos	Philippines	1969-1970	WBC
Yoshiaki Numata	Japan	1970-1971	WBC
Alfredo Marcano	Venezuela	1971-1972	WBA
Ricardo Arredondo	Mexico	1971-1974	WBC
Ben Villaflor	Philippines	1972-1973	WBA
Kuniaki Shibata	Japan	1973	WBA
Ben Villaflor	Philippines	1973-1976	WBA
Kuniaki Shibata	Japan	1974-1975	WBC
Alfredo Escalera	Puerto Rico	1975-1978	WBC
Sam Serrano	Puerto Rico	1976-1980	WBA
Alexis Arguello*	Nicaragua	1978-1980	WBC
Yasutsune Uehara	Japan	1980-1981	WBA
Rafael Limon	Mexico	1980-1981	WBC
Cornelius Boza-Edwards	Uganda	1981	WBC
Sam Serrano	Puerto Rico	1981-1983	WBA
Rolando Navarrete	Philippines	1981-1982	WBC
Rafael Limon	Mexico	1982	WBC
Bobby Chacon	USA	1982-1983	WBC
Roger Mayweather	USA	1983-1984	WBA
Hector Camacho*	Puerto Rico	1983-1984	WBC
Rocky Lockridge	USA	1984-1985	WBA
Hwan-Kil Yuh	S Korea	1984-1985	IBF
Julio Cesar Chavez*	Mexico	1984-1987	WBC
Lester Ellis	England	1985	IBF
Wilfredo Gomez	Puerto Rico	1985-1986	WBA
Barry Michael	England	1985-1987	IBF
Alfredo Layne	Panama	1986	WBA
Brian Mitchell*	S Africa	1986-1991	WBA
Rocky Lockridge	USA	1987-1988	IBF
Azumah Nelson	Ghana	1988-1994	WBC
Tony Lopez	USA	1988-1989	IBF
Juan Molina*	Puerto Rico	1989	WBO
Juan Molina	Puerto Rico	1989-1990	IBF
Kamel Bou Ali	Tunisia	1989-1992	WBO
Tony Lopez	USA	1990-1991	IBF
Joey Gamache*	USA	1991	WBA
Brian Mitchell*	S Africa	1991-1992	IBF

Title Holder	Birthplace	Tenure	Status
Genaro Hernandez	USA	1991-1995	WBA
Juan Molina*	Puerto Rico	1992-1995	IBF
Daniel Londas	France	1992	WBO
Jimmy Bredahl	Denmark	1992-1994	WBO
Oscar de la Hoya*	USA	1994	WBO
James Leija	USA	1994	WBC
Gabriel Ruelas	USA	1994-1995	WBC
Regilio Tuur*	Surinam	1994-1997	WBO
Eddie Hopson	USA	1995	IBF
Tracy Harris Patterson	USA	1995	IBF
Yong-Soo Choi	S Korea	1995-	WBA
Arturo Gatti	Canada	1995-	IBF
Azumah Nelson	Ghana	1996-1997	WBC
Genaro Hernandez	USA	1997-	WBC

Lightweight (135 lbs)

Title Holder	Birthplace	Tenure	Status
Jack McAuliffe	Ireland	1889-1894	USA
Jem Carney	England	1889-1891	
Jimmy Carroll	England	1889-1891	
Dick Burge	England	1891-1896	GB
George Lavigne	USA	1894-1896	USA
George Lavigne	USA	1896	
George Lavigne	USA	1896-1897	
Eddie Connolly	Canada	1896-1897	
George Lavigne	USA	1897-1899	
Frank Erne	Switzerland	1899-1902	
Joe Gans	USA	1902	
Joe Gans	USA	1902-1906	
Jabez White	England	1902-1905	GB
Jimmy Britt	USA	1902-1905	
Battling Nelson	Denmark	1905-1907	
Joe Gans	USA	1906-1908	
Battling Nelson	Denmark	1908-1910	
Ad Wolgast	USA	1910-1912	
Willie Ritchie	USA	1912	
Freddie Welsh	Wales	1912-1914	GB
Willie Ritchie	USA	1912-1914	USA
Freddie Welsh	Wales	1914-1917	
Benny Leonard*	USA	1917-1925	
Jimmy Goodrich	USA	1925	NY
Rocky Kansas	USA	1925-1926	
Sammy Mandell	USA	1926-1930	
Al Singer	USA	1930	
Tony Canzoneri	USA	1930-1933	
Barney Ross*	USA	1933-1935	
Tony Canzoneri	USA	1935-1936	
Lou Ambers	USA	1936-1938	
Henry Armstrong	USA	1938-1939	
Lou Ambers	USA	1939-1940	
Sammy Angott	USA	1940-1941	NBA
Lew Jenkins	USA	1940-1941	NY
Sammy Angott*	USA	1941-1942	
Beau Jack	USA	1942-1943	NY
Slugger White	USA	1943	MARY
Bob Montgomery	USA	1943	NY
Sammy Angott	USA	1943-1944	NBA
Beau Jack	USA	1943-1944	NY
Bob Montgomery	USA	1944-1947	NY
Juan Zurita	Mexico	1944-1945	NBA
Ike Williams	USA	1945-1947	NBA
Ike Williams	USA	1947-1951	
Jimmy Carter	USA	1951-1952	
Lauro Salas	Mexico	1952	
Jimmy Carter	USA	1952-1954	
Paddy de Marco	USA	1954	
Jimmy Carter	USA	1954-1955	
Wallace Bud Smith	USA	1955-1956	
Joe Brown	USA	1956-1962	
Carlos Ortiz	Puerto Rico	1962-1963	
Carlos Ortiz	Puerto Rico	1963-1964	WBA/WBC
Kenny Lane	USA	1963-1964	MICH
Carlos Ortiz	Puerto Rico	1964-1965	

Title Holder	Birthplace	Tenure	Status
Ismael Laguna	Panama	1965	
Carlos Ortiz	Puerto Rico	1965-1966	
Carlos Ortiz	Puerto Rico	1966-1967	WBA
Carlos Ortiz	Puerto Rico	1967-1968	
Carlos Teo Cruz	Dom Republic	1968-1969	
Mando Ramos	USA	1969-1970	
Ismael Laguna	Panama	1970	
Ismael Laguna	Panama	1970	WBA
Ken Buchanan	Scotland	1970-1971	WBA
Ken Buchanan	Scotland	1971	
Ken Buchanan	Scotland	1971-1972	WBA
Pedro Carrasco	Spain	1971-1972	WBC
Mando Ramos	USA	1972	WBC
Roberto Duran	Panama	1972-1978	WBA
Chango Carmona	Mexico	1972	WBC
Rodolfo Gonzalez	Mexico	1972-1974	WBC
Guts Ishimatsu	Japan	1974-1976	WBC
Esteban de Jesus	Puerto Rico	1976-1978	WBC
Roberto Duran*	Panama	1978-1979	
Jim Watt	Scotland	1979-1981	WBC
Ernesto Espana	Venezuela	1979-1980	WBA
Hilmer Kenty	USA	1980-1981	WBA
Sean O'Grady	USA	1981	WBA
Alexis Arguello*	Nicaragua	1981-1983	WBC
Claude Noel	Trinidad	1981	WBA
Arturo Frias	USA	1981-1982	WBA
Ray Mancini	USA	1982-1984	WBA
Edwin Rosario	Puerto Rico	1983-1984	WBC
Charlie Choo Choo Brown	USA	1984	IBF
Harry Arroyo	USA	1984-1985	IBF
Livingstone Bramble	USA	1984-1986	WBA
Jose Luis Ramirez	Mexico	1984-1985	WBC
Jimmy Paul	USA	1985-1986	IBF
Hector Camacho*	Puerto Rico	1985-1987	WBC
Edwin Rosario	Puerto Rico	1986-1987	WBA
Greg Haugen	USA	1986-1987	IBF
Vinny Pazienza	USA	1987-1988	IBF
Jose Luis Ramirez	Mexico	1987-1988	WBC
Julio Cesar Chavez	Mexico	1987-1988	WBA
Greg Haugen	USA	1988-1989	IBF
Julio Cesar Chavez*	Mexico	1988-1989	WBA/WBC
Mauricio Aceves	Mexico	1989-1990	WBO
Pernell Whitaker	USA	1989	IBF
Edwin Rosario	Puerto Rico	1989-1990	WBA
Pernell Whitaker	USA	1989-1990	IBF/WBC
Juan Nazario	Puerto Rico	1990	WBA
Pernell Whitaker*	USA	1990-1992	IBF/WBC/WBA
Dingaan Thobela*	S Africa	1990-1992	WBO
Joey Gamache	USA	1992	WBA
Miguel Gonzalez*	Mexico	1992-1996	WBC
Giovanni Parisi*	Italy	1992-1994	WBO
Tony Lopez	USA	1992-1993	WBA
Fred Pendleton	USA	1993-1994	IBF
Dingaan Thobela	S Africa	1993	WBA
Orzubek Nazarov	Kyrghyzstan	1993-	WBA
Rafael Ruelas	USA	1994-1995	IBF
Oscar de la Hoya	USA	1994-1995	WBO
Oscar de la Hoya*	USA	1995	WBO/IBF
Oscar de la Hoya*	USA	1995-1996	WBO
Phillip Holiday	S Africa	1995-	IBF
Jean-Baptiste Mendy	France	1996-1997	WBC
Artur Grigorian	Uzbekistan	1996-	WBO
Steve Johnston	USA	1997-	WBC

L. Welterweight (140 lbs)

Title Holder	Birthplace	Tenure	Status
Pinkey Mitchell	USA	1922-1926	NBA
Mushy Callahan	USA	1926-1927	NBA
Mushy Callahan	USA	1927-1930	NBA/NY
Mushy Callahan	USA	1930	NBA
Jackie Kid Berg	England	1930-1931	NBA
Tony Canzoneri	USA	1931-1932	NBA
Johnny Jadick	USA	1932	NBA

Title Holder	Birthplace	Tenure	Status
Johnny Jadick	USA	1932-1933	PEN
Battling Shaw	Mexico	1933	LOUIS
Tony Canzoneri	USA	1933	LOUIS
Barney Ross*	USA	1933-1935	ILL
Maxie Berger	Canada	1939	CAN
Harry Weekly	USA	1941-1942	LOUIS
Tippy Larkin	USA	1946-1947	NY/NBA
Carlos Ortiz	Puerto Rico	1959-1960	NBA
Duilio Loi	Italy	1960-1962	NBA
Duilio Loi	Italy	1962	WBA
Eddie Perkins	USA	1962	WBA
Duilio Loi*	Italy	1962-1963	WBA
Roberto Cruz	Philippines	1963	WBA
Eddie Perkins	USA	1963-1965	WBA
Carlos Hernandez	Venezuela	1965-1966	WBA
Sandro Lopopolo	Italy	1966-1967	WBA
Paul Fujii	Hawaii	1967-1968	WBA
Nicolino Loche	Argentine	1968-1972	WBA
Pedro Adigue	Philippines	1968-1970	WBC
Bruno Arcari*	Italy	1970-1974	WBC
Alfonso Frazer	Panama	1972	WBA
Antonio Cervantes	Colombia	1972-1976	WBA
Perico Fernandez	Spain	1974-1975	WBC
Saensak Muangsurin	Thailand	1975-1976	WBC
Wilfred Benitez	USA	1976	WBA
Miguel Velasquez	Spain	1976	WBC
Saensak Muangsurin	Thailand	1976-1978	WBC
Antonio Cervantes	Colombia	1977-1980	WBA
Wilfred Benitez*	USA	1977-1978	NY
Sang-Hyun Kim	S Korea	1978-1980	WBC
Saoul Mamby	USA	1980-1982	WBC
Aaron Pryor*	USA	1980-1984	WBA
Leroy Haley	USA	1982-1983	WBC
Bruce Curry	USA	1983-1984	WBC
Johnny Bumphus	USA	1984	WBA
Bill Costello	USA	1984-1985	WBC
Gene Hatcher	USA	1984-1985	WBA
Aaron Pryor	USA	1984-1985	IBF
Ubaldo Sacco	Argentine	1985-1986	WBA
Lonnie Smith	USA	1985-1986	WBC
Patrizio Oliva	Italy	1986-1987	WBA
Gary Hinton	USA	1986	IBF
Rene Arredondo	Mexico	1986	WBC
Tsuyoshi Hamada	Japan	1986-1987	WBC
Joe Manley	USA	1986-1987	IBF
Terry Marsh*	England	1987	IBF
Juan M. Coggi	Argentine	1987-1990	WBA
Rene Arredondo	Mexico	1987	WBC
Roger Mayweather	USA	1987-1989	WBC
James McGirt	USA	1988	IBF
Meldrick Taylor	USA	1988-1990	IBF
Hector Camacho	Puerto Rico	1989-1991	WBO
Julio Cesar Chavez	Mexico	1989-1990	WBC
Julio Cesar Chavez	Mexico	1990-1991	IBF/WBC
Loreto Garza	USA	1990-1991	WBA
Greg Haugen	USA	1991	WBO
Hector Camacho	Puerto Rico	1991-1992	WBO
Edwin Rosario	Puerto Rico	1991-1992	WBA
Julio Cesar Chavez	Mexico	1991-1994	WBC
Rafael Pineda	Colombia	1991-1992	IBF
Akinobu Hiranaka	Japan	1992	WBA
Carlos Gonzalez	Mexico	1992-1993	WBO
Pernell Whitaker*	USA	1992-1993	IBF
Morris East	Philippines	1992-1993	WBA
Juan M. Coggi	Argentine	1993-1994	WBA
Charles Murray	USA	1993-1994	IBF
Zack Padilla*	USA	1993-1994	WBO
Frankie Randall	USA	1994	WBC
Jake Rodriguez	USA	1994-1995	IBF
Julio Cesar Chavez	Mexico	1994-1996	WBC
Frankie Randall	USA	1994-1996	WBA
Konstantin Tszyu	Russia	1995-1997	IBF

Title Holder	Birthplace	Tenure	Status
Sammy Fuentes	Puerto Rico	1995-1996	WBO
Juan M. Coggi	Argentine	1996	WBA
Giovanni Parisi	Italy	1996-	WBO
Oscar de la Hoya*	USA	1996-1997	WBC
Frankie Randall	USA	1996-1997	WBA
Khalid Rahilou	France	1997-	WBA
Vince Phillips	USA	1997-	IBF

Welterweight (147 lbs)

Title Holder	Birthplace	Tenure	Status
Paddy Duffy	USA	1889-1890	
Tommy Ryan	USA	1891-1894	
Mysterious Billy Smith	USA	1892-1894	
Tommy Ryan	USA	1894-1897	USA
Tommy Ryan	USA	1897-1899	
Dick Burge	GB	1897	
George Green	USA	1897	
Tom Causer	GB	1897	
Joe Walcott	Barbados	1897	
George Lavigne	USA	1897-1899	
Dick Burge	GB	1897-1898	
Mysterious Billy Smith	USA	1898-1900	
Bobby Dobbs	USA	1898-1902	
Rube Ferns	USA	1900	
Matty Matthews	USA	1900	
Eddie Connolly	Canada	1900	
Matty Matthews	USA	1900-1901	
Rube Ferns	USA	1901	
Joe Walcott	Barbados	1901-1906	
Eddie Connolly	Canada	1902-1903	GB
Matty Matthews	USA	1902-1903	
Rube Ferns	USA	1903	
Martin Duffy	USA	1903-1904	
Honey Mellody	USA	1904	
Jack Clancy	USA	1904-1905	GB
Dixie Kid	USA	1904-1905	
Buddy Ryan	USA	1904-1905	
Sam Langford	Canada	1904-1905	
George Petersen	USA	1905	
Jimmy Gardner	USA	1905	
Mike Twin Sullivan	USA	1905-1906	
Joe Gans	USA	1906	
Joe Walcott	Barbados	1906	USA
Honey Mellody	USA	1906	USA
Honey Mellody	USA	1906-1907	
Joe Thomas	USA	1906-1907	
Mike Twin Sullivan	USA	1907-1911	
Jimmy Gardner	USA	1907-1908	
Frank Mantell	USA	1907-1908	
Harry Lewis	USA	1908-1910	
Jack Blackburn	USA	1908	
Jimmy Gardner	USA	1908-1909	
Willie Lewis	USA	1909-1910	
Harry Lewis	USA	1910-1911	GB/FR
Jimmy Clabby	USA	1910-1911	
Dixie Kid	USA	1911-1912	GB/FR
Ray Bronson	USA	1911-1914	
Marcel Thomas	France	1912-1913	FR
Wildcat Ferns	USA	1912-1913	
Spike Kelly	USA	1913-1914	
Mike Glover	USA	1913-1915	
Mike Gibbons	USA	1913-1914	
Waldemar Holberg	Denmark	1914	
Tom McCormick	Ireland	1914	
Matt Wells	England	1914-1915	AUSTR
Kid Graves	USA	1914-1917	
Jack Britton	USA	1915	
Ted Kid Lewis	England	1915-1916	
Jack Britton	USA	1916-1917	
Ted Kid Lewis	England	1917	
Ted Kid Lewis	England	1917-1919	
Jack Britton	USA	1919-1922	
Mickey Walker	USA	1922-1923	

251

Title Holder	Birthplace	Tenure	Status
Mickey Walker	USA	1923-1924	NBA
Dave Shade	USA	1923	NY
Jimmy Jones	USA	1923	NY/MASS
Mickey Walker	USA	1924-1926	
Pete Latzo	USA	1926-1927	
Joe Dundee	Italy	1927-1928	
Joe Dundee	Italy	1928-1929	NY
Jackie Fields	USA	1929	NBA
Jackie Fields	USA	1929-1930	
Young Jack Thompson	USA	1930	
Tommy Freeman	USA	1930-1931	
Young Jack Thompson	USA	1930	
Lou Brouillard	Canada	1931-1932	
Jackie Fields	USA	1932-1933	
Young Corbett III	Italy	1933	
Jimmy McLarnin	Ireland	1933-1934	
Barney Ross	USA	1934	
Jimmy McLarnin	Ireland	1934-1935	
Barney Ross	USA	1935-1938	
Barney Ross	USA	1938	NY/NBA
Felix Wouters	Belgium	1938	IBU
Henry Armstrong	USA	1938-1940	
Fritzie Zivic	USA	1940	
Fritzie Zivic	USA	1940-1941	NY/NBA
Izzy Jannazzo	USA	1940-1942	MARY
Red Cochrane	USA	1941-1942	NY/NBA
Red Cochrane	USA	1942-1946	
Marty Servo	USA	1946	
Sugar Ray Robinson*	USA	1946-1951	
Johnny Bratton	USA	1951	NBA
Kid Gavilan	Cuba	1951-1952	NBA/NY
Kid Gavilan	Cuba	1952-1954	
Johnny Saxton	USA	1954-1955	
Tony de Marco	USA	1955	
Carmen Basilio	USA	1955-1956	
Johnny Saxton	USA	1956	
Carmen Basilio*	USA	1956-1957	
Virgil Akins	USA	1957-1958	MASS
Virgil Akins	USA	1958	
Don Jordan	Dom Republic	1958-1960	
Benny Kid Paret	Cuba	1960-1961	
Emile Griffith	Virgin Islands	1961	
Benny Kid Paret	Cuba	1961-1962	
Emile Griffith	Virgin Islands	1962-1963	
Luis Rodriguez	Cuba	1963	
Emile Griffith*	Virgin Islands	1963-1966	
Willie Ludick	S Africa	1966-1968	SA
Curtis Cokes	USA	1966	WBA
Curtis Cokes	USA	1966-1967	WBA/WBC
Charley Shipes	USA	1966-1967	CALIF
Curtis Cokes	USA	1968-1969	
Jose Napoles	Cuba	1969-1970	
Billy Backus	USA	1970-1971	
Jose Napoles	Cuba	1971-1972	
Jose Napoles	Cuba	1972-1974	WBA/WBC
Hedgemon Lewis	USA	1972-1974	NY
Jose Napoles	Cuba	1974-1975	
Jose Napoles	Cuba	1975	WBC
Angel Espada	Puerto Rico	1975-1976	WBA
John H. Stracey	England	1975-1976	WBC
Carlos Palomino	Mexico	1976-1979	WBC
Pipino Cuevas	Mexico	1976-1980	WBA
Wilfred Benitez	USA	1979	WBC
Sugar Ray Leonard	USA	1979-1980	WBC
Roberto Duran	Panama	1980	WBC
Thomas Hearns	USA	1980-1981	WBA
Sugar Ray Leonard	USA	1980-1981	WBC
Sugar Ray Leonard*	USA	1981-1982	
Don Curry	USA	1983-1984	WBA
Milton McCrory	USA	1983-1985	WBC
Don Curry	USA	1984-1985	WBA/IBF
Don Curry	USA	1985-1986	

Title Holder	Birthplace	Tenure	Status
Lloyd Honeyghan	Jamaica	1986	
Lloyd Honeyghan	Jamaica	1986-1987	WBC/IBF
Mark Breland	USA	1987	WBA
Marlon Starling	USA	1987-1988	WBA
Jorge Vaca	Mexico	1987-1988	WBC
Lloyd Honeyghan	Jamaica	1988-1989	WBC
Simon Brown	Jamaica	1988-1991	IBF
Tomas Molinares	Colombia	1988-1989	WBA
Mark Breland	USA	1989-1990	WBA
Marlon Starling	USA	1989-1990	WBC
Genaro Leon	Mexico	1989	WBO
Manning Galloway	USA	1989-1993	WBO
Aaron Davis	USA	1990-1991	WBA
Maurice Blocker	USA	1990-1991	WBC
Meldrick Taylor	USA	1991-1992	WBA
Simon Brown	Jamaica	1991	WBC/IBF
Simon Brown	Jamaica	1991	WBC
Maurice Blocker	USA	1991-1993	IBF
James McGirt	USA	1991-1993	WBC
Crisanto Espana	Venezuela	1992-1994	WBA
Gert Bo Jacobsen*	Denmark	1993	WBO
Pernell Whitaker	USA	1993-1997	WBC
Felix Trinidad	Puerto Rico	1993-	IBF
Eamonn Loughran	Ireland	1993-1996	WBO
Ike Quartey	Ghana	1994-	WBA
Jose Luis Lopez	Mexico	1996-1997	WBO
Michael Loewe	Romania	1997-	WBO
Oscar de la Hoya	USA	1997-	WBC

L. Middleweight (154 lbs)

Title Holder	Birthplace	Tenure	Status
Emile Griffith*	USA	1962-1963	AU
Denny Moyer	USA	1962-1963	WBA
Ralph Dupas	USA	1963	WBA
Sandro Mazzinghi	Italy	1963-1965	WBA
Nino Benvenuti	Italy	1965-1966	WBA
Ki-Soo Kim	S Korea	1966-1968	WBA
Sandro Mazzinghi	Italy	1968-1969	WBA
Freddie Little	USA	1969-1970	WBA
Carmelo Bossi	Italy	1970-1971	WBA
Koichi Wajima	Japan	1971-1974	WBA
Oscar Albarado	USA	1974-1975	WBA
Koichi Wajima	Japan	1975	WBA
Miguel de Oliveira	Brazil	1975	WBC
Jae-Do Yuh	S Korea	1975-1976	WBA
Elisha Obed	Bahamas	1975-1976	WBC
Koichi Wajima	Japan	1976	WBA
Jose Duran	Spain	1976	WBA
Eckhard Dagge	Germany	1976-1977	WBC
Miguel Castellini	Argentine	1976-1977	WBA
Eddie Gazo	Nicaragua	1977-1978	WBA
Rocky Mattioli	Italy	1977-1979	WBC
Masashi Kudo	Japan	1978-1979	WBA
Maurice Hope	Antigua	1979-1981	WBC
Ayub Kalule	Uganda	1979-1981	WBA
Wilfred Benitez	USA	1981-1982	WBC
Sugar Ray Leonard*	USA	1981	WBA
Tadashi Mihara	Japan	1981-1982	WBA
Davey Moore	USA	1982-1983	WBA
Thomas Hearns*	USA	1982-1986	WBC
Roberto Duran*	Panama	1983-1984	WBA
Mark Medal	USA	1984	IBF
Mike McCallum*	Jamaica	1984-1987	WBA
Carlos Santos	Puerto Rico	1984-1986	IBF
Buster Drayton	USA	1986-1987	IBF
Duane Thomas	USA	1986-1987	WBC
Matthew Hilton	Canada	1987-1988	IBF
Lupe Aquino	Mexico	1987	WBC
Gianfranco Rosi	Italy	1987-1988	WBC
Julian Jackson*	Virgin Islands	1987-1990	WBA
Don Curry	USA	1988-1989	WBC
Robert Hines	USA	1988-1989	IBF
John David Jackson*	USA	1988-1993	WBO

Title Holder	Birthplace	Tenure	Status
Darrin van Horn	USA	1989	IBF
Rene Jacqot	France	1989	WBC
John Mugabi	Uganda	1989-1990	WBC
Gianfranco Rosi	Italy	1989-1994	IBF
Terry Norris	USA	1990-1993	WBC
Gilbert Dele	France	1991	WBA
Vinny Pazienza*	USA	1991-1992	WBA
Julio Cesar Vasquez	Argentine	1992-1995	WBA
Verno Phillips	USA	1993-1995	WBO
Simon Brown	USA	1993-1994	WBC
Terry Norris	USA	1994	WBC
Vince Pettway	USA	1994-1995	IBF
Luis Santana	Dom Republic	1994-1995	WBC
Pernell Whitaker*	USA	1995	WBA
Gianfranco Rosi	Italy	1995	WBO
Carl Daniels	USA	1995	WBA
Verno Phillips	USA	1995	WBO
Paul Vaden	USA	1995	IBF
Terry Norris	USA	1995	WBC
Paul Jones	England	1995-1996	WBO
Terry Norris	USA	1995-1997	IBF/WBC
Julio Cesar Vasquez	Argentine	1995-1996	WBA
Bronco McKart	USA	1996	WBO
Ronald Wright	USA	1996-	WBO
Laurent Boudouani	France	1996-	WBA
Terry Norris	USA	1997-	WBC
Raul Marquez	USA	1997-	IBF

Middleweight (160 lbs)

Title Holder	Birthplace	Tenure	Status
Nonpareil Jack Dempsey	Ireland	1889-1891	USA
Bob Fitzsimmons	England	1891-1893	USA
Jim Hall	Australia	1892-1893	GB
Bob Fitzsimmons	England	1893-1894	
Bob Fitzsimmons	England	1894-1899	
Frank Craig	USA	1894-1895	GB
Dan Creedon	New Zealand	1895-1897	GB
Tommy Ryan	USA	1895-1896	
Kid McCoy	USA	1896-1898	
Tommy Ryan	USA	1898-1905	
Charley McKeever	USA	1900-1902	
George Gardner	USA	1901-1902	
Jack O'Brien	USA	1901-1905	
George Green	USA	1901-1902	
Jack Palmer	England	1902-1903	GB
Hugo Kelly	USA	1905-1908	
Jack Twin Sullivan	USA	1905-1908	
Sam Langford	Canada	1907-1911	
Billy Papke	USA	1908	
Stanley Ketchel	USA	1908	
Billy Papke	USA	1908	
Stanley Ketchel	USA	1908-1910	
Billy Papke	USA	1910-1913	
Stanley Ketchel*	USA	1910	
Hugo Kelly	USA	1910-1912	
Cyclone Johnny Thompson	USA	1911-1912	
Harry Lewis	USA	1911	
Leo Houck	USA	1911-1912	
Georges Carpentier	France	1911-1912	
Jack Dillon	USA	1912	
Frank Mantell	USA	1912-1913	
Frank Klaus	USA	1912-1913	
Georges Carpentier	France	1912	IBU
Jack Dillon	USA	1912-1915	
Eddie McGoorty	USA	1912-1913	
Frank Klaus	USA	1913	IBU
Jimmy Clabby	USA	1913-1914	
George Chip	USA	1913-1914	
Joe Borrell	USA	1913-1914	
Jeff Smith	USA	1913-1914	
Eddie McGoorty	USA	1914	AUSTR
Jeff Smith	USA	1914	AUSTR
Al McCoy	USA	1914-1917	

Title Holder	Birthplace	Tenure	Status
Jimmy Clabby	USA	1914-1915	
Mick King	Australia	1914	AUSTR
Jeff Smith	USA	1914-1915	AUSTR
Young Ahearn	England	1915-1916	
Les Darcy*	Australia	1915-1917	AUSTR
Mike Gibbons	USA	1916-1917	
Mike O'Dowd	USA	1917-1920	
Johnny Wilson	USA	1920-1921	
Johnny Wilson	USA	1921-1922	NBA/NY
Bryan Downey	USA	1921-1922	OHIO
Johnny Wilson	USA	1922-1923	NBA
Dave Rosenberg	USA	1922	NY
Jock Malone	USA	1922-1923	OHIO
Mike O'Dowd	USA	1922-1923	NY
Johnny Wilson	USA	1923	
Harry Greb	USA	1923-1926	
Tiger Flowers	USA	1926	
Mickey Walker	USA	1926-1931	
Gorilla Jones	USA	1932	NBA
Marcel Thil	France	1932-1933	NBA/IBU
Marcel Thil	France	1933-1937	IBU
Ben Jeby	USA	1933	NY
Lou Brouillard	Canada	1933	NY
Lou Brouillard	Canada	1933	NY/NBA
Vearl Whitehead	USA	1933	CALIF
Teddy Yarosz	USA	1933-1934	PEN
Vince Dundee	USA	1933-1934	NY/NBA
Teddy Yarosz	USA	1934-1935	NY/NBA
Babe Risko	USA	1935-1936	NY/NBA
Freddie Steele	USA	1936-1938	NY/NBA
Fred Apostoli	USA	1937-1938	IBU
Edouard Tenet	France	1938	IBU
Young Corbett III	Italy	1938	CALIF
Freddie Steele	USA	1938	NBA
Al Hostak	USA	1938	NBA
Solly Krieger	USA	1938-1939	NBA
Fred Apostoli	USA	1938-1939	NY
Al Hostak	USA	1939-1940	NBA
Ceferino Garcia	Philippines	1939-1940	NY
Ken Overlin	USA	1940-1941	NY
Tony Zale	USA	1940-1941	NBA
Billy Soose	USA	1941	NY
Tony Zale	USA	1941-1947	
Rocky Graziano	USA	1947-1948	
Tony Zale	USA	1948	
Marcel Cerdan	Algeria	1948-1949	
Jake la Motta	USA	1949-1950	
Jake la Motta	USA	1950-1951	NY/NBA
Sugar Ray Robinson	USA	1950-1951	PEN
Sugar Ray Robinson	USA	1951	
Randy Turpin	England	1951	
Sugar Ray Robinson*	USA	1951-1952	
Randy Turpin	England	1953	GB/EBU
Carl Bobo Olson	Hawaii	1953-1955	
Sugar Ray Robinson	USA	1955-1957	
Gene Fullmer	USA	1957	
Sugar Ray Robinson	USA	1957	
Carmen Basilio	USA	1957-1958	
Sugar Ray Robinson	USA	1958-1959	
Sugar Ray Robinson	USA	1959-1960	NY/EBU
Gene Fullmer	USA	1959-1962	NBA
Paul Pender	USA	1960-1961	NY/EBU
Terry Downes	England	1961-1962	NY/EBU
Paul Pender	USA	1962	NY/EBU
Dick Tiger	Nigeria	1962-1963	NBA
Dick Tiger	Nigeria	1963	
Joey Giardello	USA	1963-1965	
Dick Tiger	Nigeria	1965-1966	
Emile Griffith	Virgin Islands	1966-1967	
Nino Benvenuti	Italy	1967	
Emile Griffith	Virgin Islands	1967-1968	
Nino Benvenuti	Italy	1968-1970	

Title Holder	Birthplace	Tenure	Status	Title Holder	Birthplace	Tenure	Status
Carlos Monzon	Argentine	1970-1974		Jack O'Brien	USA	1905-1911	
Carlos Monzon	Argentine	1974-1976	WBA	Sam Langford	Canada	1911-1913	
Rodrigo Valdez	Colombia	1974-1976	WBC	Georges Carpentier	France	1913-1920	IBU
Carlos Monzon*	Argentine	1976-1977		Jack Dillon	USA	1914-1916	USA
Rodrigo Valdez	Colombia	1977-1978		Battling Levinsky	USA	1916-1920	USA
Hugo Corro	Argentine	1978-1979		**Georges Carpentier**	France	1920-1922	
Vito Antuofermo	Italy	1979-1980		**Battling Siki**	Senegal	1922-1923	
Alan Minter	England	1980		**Mike McTigue**	Ireland	1923-1925	
Marvin Hagler	USA	1980-1987		**Paul Berlenbach**	USA	1925-1926	
Marvin Hagler	USA	1987	WBC/IBF	**Jack Delaney***	Canada	1926-1927	
Sugar Ray Leonard	USA	1987	WBC	Jimmy Slattery	USA	1927	NBA
Frank Tate	USA	1987-1988	IBF	Tommy Loughran	USA	1927	NY
Sumbu Kalambay	Zaire	1987-1989	WBA	**Tommy Loughran***	USA	1927-1929	
Thomas Hearns	USA	1987-1988	WBC	Jimmy Slattery	USA	1930	NY
Iran Barkley	USA	1988-1989	WBC	**Maxie Rosenbloom**	USA	1930-1931	
Michael Nunn	USA	1988-1991	IBF	Maxie Rosenbloom	USA	1931-1933	NY
Roberto Duran	Panama	1989-1990	WBC	George Nichols	USA	1932	NBA
Doug de Witt	USA	1989-1990	WBO	Bob Godwin	USA	1933	NBA
Mike McCallum	Jamaica	1989-1991	WBA	**Maxie Rosenbloom**	USA	1933-1934	
Nigel Benn	England	1990	WBO	**Bob Olin**	USA	1934-1935	
Chris Eubank*	England	1990-1991	WBO	Al McCoy	Canada	1935	CAN
Julian Jackson	Virgin Islands	1990-1993	WBC	Bob Olin	USA	1935	NY/NBA
James Toney*	USA	1991-1993	IBF	John Henry Lewis	USA	1935-1938	NY/NBA
Gerald McClellan*	USA	1991-1993	WBO	Gustav Roth	Belgium	1936-1938	IBU
Reggie Johnson	USA	1992-1993	WBA	Ad Heuser	Germany	1938	IBU
Gerald McClellan*	USA	1993-1995	WBC	**John Henry Lewis**	USA	1938	
Chris Pyatt	England	1993-1994	WBO	John Henry Lewis	USA	1938-1939	NBA
Roy Jones*	USA	1993-1994	IBF	Melio Bettina	USA	1939	NY
John David Jackson	USA	1993-1994	WBO	Len Harvey	England	1939-1942	GB
Steve Collins*	Ireland	1994-1995	WBO	Billy Conn	USA	1939-1940	NY/NBA
Jorge Castro	Argentine	1994	WBA	Anton Christoforidis	Greece	1941	NBA
Julian Jackson	Virgin Islands	1995	WBC	Gus Lesnevich	USA	1941	NBA
Bernard Hopkins	USA	1995-	IBF	Gus Lesnevich	USA	1941-1946	NY/NBA
Lonnie Bradley	USA	1995-	WBO	Freddie Mills	England	1942-1946	GB
Quincy Taylor	USA	1995-1996	WBC	**Gus Lesnevich**	USA	1946-1948	
Shinji Takehara	Japan	1995-1996	WBA	**Freddie Mills**	England	1948-1950	
Keith Holmes	USA	1996-	WBC	**Joey Maxim**	USA	1950-1952	
William Joppy	USA	1996-	WBA	**Archie Moore**	USA	1952-1960	
				Archie Moore	USA	1960-1962	NY/EBU
S. Middleweight (168 lbs)				Harold Johnson	USA	1961-1962	NBA
Murray Sutherland	Scotland	1984	IBF	**Harold Johnson**	USA	1962-1963	
Chong-Pal Park*	S Korea	1984-1987	IBF	**Willie Pastrano**	USA	1963	
Chong-Pal Park	S Korea	1987-1988	WBA	Willie Pastrano	USA	1963-1964	WBA/WBC
Graciano Rocchigiani*	Germany	1988-1989	IBF	Eddie Cotton	USA	1963-1964	MICH
Fully Obelmejias	Venezuela	1988-1989	WBA	**Willie Pastrano**	USA	1964-1965	
Sugar Ray Leonard*	USA	1988-1990	WBC	**Jose Torres**	Puerto Rico	1965-1966	
Thomas Hearns*	USA	1988-1991	WBO	**Dick Tiger**	Nigeria	1966-1968	
In-Chul Baek	S Korea	1989-1990	WBA	**Bob Foster**	USA	1968-1970	
Lindell Holmes	USA	1990-1991	IBF	Bob Foster	USA	1970-1972	WBC
Christophe Tiozzo	France	1990-1991	WBA	Vicente Rondon	Venezuela	1971-1972	WBA
Mauro Galvano	Italy	1990-1992	WBC	**Bob Foster***	USA	1972-1974	
Victor Cordoba	Panama	1991-1992	WBA	John Conteh	England	1974-1977	WBC
Darrin van Horn	USA	1991-1992	IBF	Victor Galindez	Argentine	1974-1978	WBA
Chris Eubank	England	1991-1995	WBO	Miguel Cuello	Argentine	1977-1978	WBC
Iran Barkley	USA	1992-1993	IBF	Mate Parlov	Yugoslavia	1978	WBC
Michael Nunn	USA	1992-1994	WBA	Mike Rossman	USA	1978-1979	WBA
Nigel Benn	England	1992-1996	WBC	Marvin Johnson	USA	1978-1979	WBC
James Toney	USA	1993-1994	IBF	Victor Galindez	Argentine	1979	WBA
Steve Little	USA	1994	WBA	Matt Saad Muhammad	USA	1979-1981	WBC
Frank Liles	USA	1994-	WBA	Marvin Johnson	USA	1979-1980	WBA
Roy Jones*	USA	1994-1997	IBF	Mustafa Muhammad	USA	1980-1981	WBA
Steve Collins	Ireland	1995-	WBO	Michael Spinks	USA	1981-1983	WBA
Thulani Malinga	S Africa	1996	WBC	Dwight Muhammad Qawi	USA	1981-1983	WBC
Vincenzo Nardiello	Italy	1996	WBC	**Michael Spinks***	USA	1983-1985	
Robin Reid	England	1996-	WBC	J. B. Williamson	USA	1985-1986	WBC
Charles Brewer	USA	1997-	IBF	Slobodan Kacar	Yugoslavia	1985-1986	IBF
				Marvin Johnson	USA	1986-1987	WBA
L. Heavyweight (175 lbs)				Dennis Andries	Guyana	1986-1987	WBC
Jack Root	Austria	1903		Bobby Czyz	USA	1986-1987	IBF
George Gardner	Ireland	1903		Thomas Hearns*	USA	1987	WBC
George Gardner	Ireland	1903	USA	Leslie Stewart	Trinidad	1987	WBA
Bob Fitzsimmons	England	1903-1905	USA	Virgil Hill	USA	1987-1991	WBA

Title Holder	Birthplace	Tenure	Status
Charles Williams	USA	1987-1993	IBF
Don Lalonde	Canada	1987-1988	WBC
Sugar Ray Leonard*	USA	1988	WBC
Michael Moorer*	USA	1988-1991	WBO
Dennis Andries	Guyana	1989	WBC
Jeff Harding	Australia	1989-1990	WBC
Dennis Andries	Guyana	1990-1991	WBC
Leonzer Barber	USA	1991-1994	WBO
Thomas Hearns	USA	1991-1992	WBA
Jeff Harding	Australia	1991-1994	WBC
Iran Barkley*	USA	1992	WBA
Virgil Hill	USA	1992	WBA
Henry Maske	Germany	1993-1996	IBF
Mike McCallum	Jamaica	1994-1995	WBC
Dariusz Michalczewski	Poland	1994-	WBO
Fabrice Tiozzo	France	1995-1997	WBC
Virgil Hill	USA	1996-1997	IBF/WBA
Roy Jones	USA	1997	WBC
Montell Griffin	USA	1997-	WBC
Dariusz Michalczewski*	Poland	1997	WBO/IBF/WBA
Dariusz Michalczewski	Poland	1997-	WBO/WBA

Cruiserweight (190 lbs)

Title Holder	Birthplace	Tenure	Status
Marvin Camel	USA	1979-1980	WBC
Carlos de Leon	Puerto Rico	1980-1982	WBC
Ossie Ocasio	Puerto Rico	1982-1984	WBA
S. T. Gordon	USA	1982-1983	WBC
Marvin Camel	USA	1983-1984	IBF
Carlos de Leon	Puerto Rico	1983-1985	WBC
Lee Roy Murphy	USA	1984-1986	IBF
Piet Crous	S Africa	1984-1985	WBA
Alfonso Ratliff	USA	1985	WBC
Dwight Muhammad Qawi	USA	1985-1986	WBA
Bernard Benton	USA	1985-1986	WBC
Carlos de Leon	Puerto Rico	1986-1988	WBC
Evander Holyfield	USA	1986-1987	WBA
Rickey Parkey	USA	1986-1987	IBF
Evander Holyfield	USA	1987-1988	WBA/IBF
Evander Holyfield*	USA	1988	
Taoufik Belbouli*	France	1989	WBA
Carlos de Leon	Puerto Rico	1989-1990	WBC
Glenn McCrory	England	1989-1990	IBF
Robert Daniels	USA	1989-1991	WBA
Boone Pultz	USA	1989-1990	WBO
Jeff Lampkin*	USA	1990-1991	IBF
Magne Havnaa*	Norway	1990-1992	WBO
Masimilliano Duran	Italy	1990-1991	WBC
Bobby Czyz	USA	1991-1993	WBA
Anaclet Wamba	Congo	1991-1995	WBC
James Warring	USA	1991-1992	IBF
Tyrone Booze	USA	1992-1993	WBO
Al Cole*	USA	1992-1996	IBF
Marcus Bott	Germany	1993	WBO
Nestor Giovannini	Argentine	1993-1994	WBO
Orlin Norris	USA	1993-1995	WBA
Dariusz Michalczewski*	Poland	1994-1995	WBO
Ralf Rocchigiani	Germany	1995-	WBO
Nate Miller	USA	1995-	WBA
Marcelo Dominguez	Argentine	1995-	WBC
Adolpho Washington	USA	1996-1997	IBF
Uriah Grant	USA	1997-	IBF

Heavyweight (190 lbs+)

Title Holder	Birthplace	Tenure	Status
John L. Sullivan	USA	1889-1892	USA
Peter Jackson	Australia	1889-1892	
Frank Slavin	Australia	1890-1892	GB/AUST
Peter Jackson	Australia	1892-1893	GB/AUST
James J. Corbett	USA	1892-1894	USA
James J. Corbett	USA	1894-1895	
James J. Corbett	USA	1895-1897	
Peter Maher	Ireland	1895-1896	
Bob Fitzsimmons	England	1896-1897	

Title Holder	Birthplace	Tenure	Status
Bob Fitzsimmons	England	1897-1899	
James J. Jeffries	USA	1899-1902	
James J. Jeffries	USA	1902-1905	
Denver Ed Martin	USA	1902-1903	
Jack Johnson	USA	1902-1908	
Bob Fitzsimmons	England	1905	
Marvin Hart	USA	1905-1906	
Jack O'Brien	USA	1905-1906	
Tommy Burns	Canada	1906-1908	
Jack Johnson	USA	1908-1909	
Jack Johnson	USA	1909-1915	
Sam Langford	USA	1909-1911	
Sam McVey	USA	1911-1912	
Sam Langford	USA	1912-1914	
Luther McCarty	USA	1913	
Arthur Pelkey	Canada	1913-1914	
Gunboat Smith	USA	1914	
Harry Wills	USA	1914	
Georges Carpentier	France	1914	
Sam Langford	USA	1914-1915	
Jess Willard	USA	1915-1919	
Joe Jeannette	USA	1915	
Sam McVey	USA	1915	
Harry Wills	USA	1915-1916	
Sam Langford	USA	1916-1917	
Bill Tate	USA	1917	
Sam Langford	USA	1917-1918	
Harry Wills	USA	1918-1926	
Jack Dempsey	USA	1919-1926	
Gene Tunney*	USA	1926-1928	
Max Schmeling	Germany	1930-1932	
Jack Sharkey	USA	1932-1933	
Primo Carnera	Italy	1933-1934	
Max Baer	USA	1934-1935	
James J. Braddock	USA	1935	
James J. Braddock	USA	1935-1936	NY/NBA
George Godfrey	USA	1935-1936	IBU
James J. Braddock	USA	1936-1937	
Joe Louis*	USA	1937-1949	
Ezzard Charles	USA	1949-1950	NBA
Lee Savold	USA	1950-1951	GB/EBU
Ezzard Charles	USA	1950-1951	NY/NBA
Joe Louis	USA	1951	GB/EBU
Jersey Joe Walcott	USA	1951	NY/NBA
Jersey Joe Walcott	USA	1951-1952	
Rocky Marciano*	USA	1952-1956	
Floyd Patterson	USA	1956-1959	
Ingemar Johansson	Sweden	1959-1960	
Floyd Patterson	USA	1960-1962	
Sonny Liston	USA	1962-1964	
Muhammad Ali	USA	1964	
Muhammad Ali	USA	1964-1967	WBC
Ernie Terrell	USA	1965-1967	WBA
Muhammad Ali	USA	1967	
Joe Frazier	USA	1968-1970	WBC
Jimmy Ellis	USA	1968-1970	WBA
Joe Frazier	USA	1970-1973	
George Foreman	USA	1973-1974	
Muhammad Ali	USA	1974-1978	
Leon Spinks	USA	1978	
Leon Spinks	USA	1978	WBA
Larry Holmes*	USA	1978-1983	WBC
Muhammad Ali*	USA	1978-1979	WBA
John Tate	USA	1979-1980	WBA
Mike Weaver	USA	1980-1982	WBA
Michael Dokes	USA	1982-1983	WBA
Gerrie Coetzee	S Africa	1983-1984	WBA
Larry Holmes	USA	1983-1985	IBF
Tim Witherspoon	USA	1984	WBC
Pinklon Thomas	USA	1984-1986	WBC
Greg Page	USA	1984-1985	WBA
Tony Tubbs	USA	1985-1986	WBA

WORLD CHAMPIONS SINCE GLOVES, 1889-1997

Title Holder	Birthplace	Tenure	Status	Title Holder	Birthplace	Tenure	Status
Michael Spinks	USA	1985-1987	IBF	Michael Bentt	England	1993-1994	WBO
Tim Witherspoon	USA	1986	WBA	Evander Holyfield	USA	1993-1994	WBA/IBF
Trevor Berbick	Jamaica	1986	WBC	Herbie Hide	England	1994-1995	WBO
Mike Tyson	USA	1986-1987	WBC	Michael Moorer	USA	1994	WBA/IBF
James Smith	USA	1986-1987	WBA	Oliver McCall	USA	1994-1995	WBC
Mike Tyson	USA	1987	WBA/WBC	George Foreman	USA	1994-1995	WBA/IBF
Tony Tucker	USA	1987	IBF	Riddick Bowe*	USA	1995-1996	WBO
Mike Tyson	USA	1987-1989		George Foreman*	USA	1995	IBF
Mike Tyson	USA	1989-1990	IBF/WBA/WBC	Bruce Seldon	USA	1995-1996	WBA
Francesco Damiani	Italy	1989-1991	WBO	Frank Bruno	England	1995-1996	WBC
James Douglas	USA	1990	IBF/WBA/WBC	Frans Botha	S Africa	1995-1996	IBF
Evander Holyfield	USA	1990-1992	IBF/WBA/WBC	Mike Tyson	USA	1996	WBC
Ray Mercer	USA	1991-1992	WBO	Michael Moorer	USA	1996-	IBF
Michael Moorer*	USA	1992-1993	WBO	Henry Akinwande*	England	1996-1997	WBO
Riddick Bowe	USA	1992	IBF/WBA/WBC	Mike Tyson	USA	1996	WBA
Riddick Bowe	USA	1992-1993	IBF/WBA	Evander Holyfield	USA	1996-	WBA
Lennox Lewis	England	1992-1994	WBC	Lennox Lewis	England	1997-	WBC
Tommy Morrison	USA	1993	WBO	Herbie Hide	England	1997-	WBO

Herbie Hide (right) setting up Tony Tucker last June, on his way to regaining the WBO heavyweight title he lost to Riddick Bowe

Les Clark

Highlights From the 1996-97 Amateur Season

by David Prior

England were soon back in the medals just a few weeks after the disappointment of the Olympic Games in Atlanta, when Richard Hatton won a bronze in the World U19 Championships in Havana, Cuba (3-10 November 1996). Hatton, from the Sale West Club in Manchester, won his first three bouts in the light-welterweight division, including a victory over Cuban, Roberto Guerra Rivera, but there was an astonishing decision against him in the semi-finals when the eventual gold medallist, Timar Mergadze (Russia), was declared the winner. There were no medals for Hatton's three fellow countrymen, or for the four boxers from Ireland. Not surprisingly, the Cubans monopolised the winner's rostrum, as they had done in practically every tournament since 1983, with an incredible eight gold medals. Well behind were Russia (two gold medals), Germany, and Ukraine (one each).

The second international title event of the season was the European U19 Championships in Birmingham (1-8 June 1997). Incidentally, it was the first time that an international championship fixture had been held in this country since the Olympic Games in London, way back in 1948. The Russians dominated the gold medals - seven in total - but England made their mark with a well deserved silver for bantamweight, Scott Miller, and bronze for Stephen Burke (feather), Michael Dean (middle) and Paul Pierson (heavy). Ireland's Marvin Lee also won bronze at light-middleweight, but there were no medals for Scotland and Wales. Completing the East European tally of gold were Ukraine (two) and Lithuania (one), with Germany producing two titleholders.

In team events, England seniors lost their opening match against America 5-2 in London (November 1996) and in the following month were beaten twice by Denmark in a two-match tour - 6-5 in Horsens and 4-2 in Odense. There was also a 5-3 defeat by Austria in Innsbruck (April). Earlier, it had been back on the winning trail for England against Scotland in Motherwell in December, with a 7-3 scoreline, plus a win each in two U17 contests. Scotland had won the previous meeting 5-3 in London in February 1995. In their only outing of the season the England U19 squad drew 3-3 against America in London (February).

Scotland and Wales met three times and honours were equally divided. In December it was 4-4 in Dundee and the same scoreline at Queensferry in January. These events had involved boxers from the Amateur Boxing Associations of the two countries, but a third meeting in Glasgow (December), which also ended level at 5-5, featured boxers from the Scottish Amateur Boxing Federation and their Welsh counterparts. The two federations had been formed as separate entities to the existing associations.

In October, Wales had also drawn with Ireland (5-5) in Swansea, with the Irish team then losing twice to Sweden - 6-4 (Dublin) in November and 5-4 (Timra) in April. Ireland also lost 5-2 to Italy in Dublin (March), but in the same month a long trip to New Zealand, to celebrate the centenary of Bob Fitzsimmons winning the world heavyweight title from James J Corbett, ended with two wins. It was 4-2 in Auckland and 5-1 in Timaru, which was the adopted home of Fitzsimmons. At the back end of the season (July) in Dublin, Ireland defeated Canada 5-4.

Some multi-national tournaments took on a new dimension as the qualifying process for the European Senior Championships to be held in Minsk, Belarus in May 1998. Entries in the championships would be limited to 16 boxers in each of the 12 weights, with the four medallists from the eight qualifying tournaments (involving six weight classes each time) qualifying a country for the Minsk fixture.

In Constanza, Romania (in May 1997), Ian Napa earned England a championship entry at light-flyweight, which was followed by a place at bantamweight when Stephen Oates won a gold medal in the International Festival of Amateur Boxing in Liverpool (23-28 June). Ireland also booked a trip to Minsk at middleweight when Olympian, Brian Magee, won gold in Liverpool, while Scotland also ensured their attendance in the championships at welter and middleweight when Colin McNeil (silver) and Allan Foster (bronze) worked their way through to the medal stages.

In its fourth year, the Liverpool event saw Ukraine (two gold medals), Georgia, and Germany (one each) join England and Ireland on the winner's rostrum.

There were no medals, or places in Minsk, for the home countries in the third qualifier - the Acropolis Cup in Athens, Greece (21-25 May). This long established fixture made history as the first international tournament for women boxers; 24 entries from six countries, but not from England, Ireland, Scotland or Wales, yet! The previous Acropolis Cup event in 1996 (May/June) had provided silver medals for Ireland's Tommy Donnelly and Ted Clifford, and bronze for Glen McClarnon, as well as bronze for John Smith from Wales.

Just before the Atlanta Olympics, Tony Dodson (England) and Dermot Hamill from Ireland had won gold medals in a Junior Olympic multi-national in Marquette, Michigan (8-14 July). Robert O'Connor (Ireland), a silver, and Leigh Hallett (England), who won a bronze, were also among the medallists in this seven-nation tournament where the host country, America, won 12 of the 17 gold medals.

The 1996-97 season proper really started in September 1997, with England's Bobby Beck and James Rooney winning a bronze medal each in an U19 multi-national in Sebastopol, Ukraine. Also, in the same month, in a senior event in Tallinn, Estonia, there were silver medals for Ronnie Mercer (England) and Alex Arthur (Scotland), while Carl Wall and Russell Laing took third-place bronze medals for England and Scotland, respectively.

More medals were won by England in the Tammer tournament in Tampere, Finland (24-27 October); gold for Andy Lowe and bronze for Michael Jones and Kelvin Wing. Ireland's Alo Kelly was a gold medallist in a junior multi-national in Yugoslavia, with Irish youngsters also scheduled to appear in a similar tournament in Belgrade in October. About this time, Irish senior boxers were due to compete in the Wiener Neustadt multi-national in Austria and in the Copenhagen Box Cup in Denmark (November/December).

Andy Lowe won another gold medal in the Commonwealth Federation Championships in Mmbatho (formerly Mafeking), South Africa in November, as did Damaen Kelly and Stephen Kirk from Northern Ireland. This was only the second time these championships have been staged; the first being in Belfast in September 1983. There were silver medals for Michael Blaney and Adrian Patterson (Northern Ireland), and for Russell Laing (Scotland) and Kevin Short (Wales), while bronze medals went to Courtney Fry and Michael Jones (England), Alex Arthur and Graham McLevy (Scotland), and Kevin McCormack (Wales). In addition to the three champions from the United Kingdom, South Africa (three) topped the gold medals table, followed by Canada and Kenya (two each), and Australia and Zambia, with a medal apiece.

Completing the 1996-97 international scene there were two bronze medals for Ireland in the European U17 Cadet title event in Bitola, Macedonia (4-12 July).

At the start of the season there had been moves from the London ABA to withdraw from the national body because of their dissatisfaction with the way things were being run, but in the end all remained intact, unlike Scotland and Wales. Meanwhile, there are still some rumblings of discontent. There were, however, a number of changes in operational matters - the use of ten ounce gloves by all boxers, the introduction of 5 x 2 minute rounds at international and national level, and a new minimum age of ten years for boxers. That quickly reverted back to the previous minimum of 11 years. By far the most momentous change, certainly for amateur boxing, came from the ABAE decision to permit women to spar and from 1 October 1997 to box competitively, but not against men. This followed the AIBA's ruling to allow women to box, 114 years after the beginning of amateur boxing with the formation of the Amateur Boxing Association.

The senior domestic championships in all four home countries were completed in the month of March and once again many "new faces" emerged as titleholders. England had 11, with Ireland and Wales (seven each), and Scotland (five), making a total of 30 debut titleholders in the 48 finals.

England were first off the mark (5 March) at the National Indoor Arena in Birmingham. There had been new pairings at the quarter-final stages and all bouts, from the preliminaries through to the finals, were boxed over the new 5 x 2 minute distance.

Audley Harrison stops Nick Kendall to win the ABA super-heavyweight title

Les Clark

Paul Rogers, after years of persevering, finally gets to win the ABA light-heavyweight trophy in 1997

Les Clark

The first seven weights featured brand new champions, with Ian Napa (Crown & Manor) at light-fly, who outpointed Frannie Norton (New Astley), and Michael Hunter (Hartlepool Boys Welfare), who stopped Nicky Bell (Brighton) in the second to add the flyweight division to his previous Boys' Club title win in January. Repton Boys' bantamweight, Stephen Oates, captured that category by outscoring Levi Pattison (Hunslet Boys), while Steven Bell (Louvolite) made it at featherweight with a third round stoppage of Michael Walsh from Portsmouth University, the 1996 finalist being ruled out because of a damaged nose. At lightweight, Mark Hawthorne (Lowestoft) went 2-1 up in championship bouts against Bell Green's Roy Rutherford with a points decision. Rutherford had won the title in 1995. Light-welterweight, Richard Hatton (Sale West), followed up his World U19 bronze medal with a full distance win over former welterweight champion, Michael Hall, from Darlington, while Irishman and Olympian, Francis Barrett (Trojan Police), took the welterweight division. He outpointed Tim Smith (Handsworth). The Army's Chris Bessey, having been to Buckingham Palace the previous day for his MBE award, completed a trio of

ABA title wins by outpointing Michael Jones (Gemini) at light-middleweight, and the 1996 light-middle finalist, Ian Cooper, from Hartlepool Boys Welfare, went one better than last year with a points verdict over Jim Twite (Triumph) at middleweight, thus completing a 1997 double for his club. Popular west country light-heavyweight, Paul Rogers (Penhill RBL), made national title status at his fourth attempt when Mark Krence (St Michaels) was disqualified in round four. Blue Stevens (Pinewood Starr) followed in his father's (Les) footsteps by winning at heavyweight, outpointing the only defending champion, Tony Oakey (Leigh Park). Les had won at the same weight in 1971. And finally, at super-heavyweight, Audley Harrison made the double for Repton Boys with a first-round victory over Nick Kendall (Apollo).

There were seven new titleholders in the Irish finals at the National Stadium, Dublin (7 March), when all 12 contests went the full route for points decisions. At light-fly, Jim Rooney (Star) was successful, as was flyweight, Liam Cunningham (Saints), and featherweight, Pat O'Donnell (Dockers). They defeated Jim Prior (Darndale), Donal Hosford (Greenmount) and Aodh Carlyle (Sacred Heart), respectively. Lightweight Eugene McEneaney (Dealgan) outscored Declan Barrett (Rylane), Sunnyside's Michael Roche won against Tom Fitzgerald (Ballyvolane) in the light-middle category and moving up to heavy and super-heavyweight it was John Kiely (Limerick/Corpus Christi) and Stephen Reynolds (St Josephs). They were victorious against James Clancy (Phoenix) and Brendan Kirrane (Limerick/Corpus Christi). A move up to bantamweight proved successful for Damaen Kelly (Holy Trinity), in winning a fourth consecutive title, this time with a decision over Damien McKenna (Holy Family), while Neil Gough (St Pauls) won for the fifth time (his fourth at welterweight) when he defeated Bill Cowan (Monkstown). Glen McClarnon (Holy Family) achieved the double at light-welterweight with a win over Patrick Walsh (St Colmans), while middleweight, Brian Magee (Holy Trinity), and light-heavy, Stephen Kirk (Cairn Lodge), both made title status for the third year running, Cyprian Petrea Surugiu (Drimnagh) and Adrian Sheerin (Swinford) being in the opposite and losing corners.

There were no punches exchanged at all in the first three weight classes in Wales - finals at the Welsh Institute of Sport (13 March). The light-flyweight division was devoid of any contenders (for the third year running), while Darren Hayde (Splott Adventure) and Nathan Probert (Pembroke) won the fly and bantamweight titles on walkovers. Hayde and Probert were both first-time champions as were William Connors (Splott Adventure) at featherweight and Alwyn Evans (Carmarthen) in the light-welter category. Connors outpointed Jason Edwards (Flax), while Evans knocked out clubmate, Tino Meli, in the fifth round. Three more made it as debut champions - Anthony Smith (Highfield) at welterweight with a decision over Craig Maddocks (Llay), Sean Pepperall (Vale) who outpointed Darren Haines (Whitland) for the middleweight honours, and heavyweight, Keith Evans (Carmarthen), with a shock win over Scott Gammer (Pembroke). Defending light-heavyweight champion, Stephen Donaldson (Highfield), won again with a decision over Mark McAuley (Pontypridd) and it was the same again for 1996 super-heavyweight supremo, Kevin McCormack (Royal Navy), on a walkover. It was McCormack's record-breaking 11th Welsh title. Former lightweight champion, Vince Powell, (Army), was successful again at the weight, knocking out Paul Dennis (Aberkenfig) in the third. And Powell's fellow soldier, Kevin Short (also from Aberkenfig), a former ABA champion, won his first Welsh title with a fourth-round retirement win over Frank Sparano (Splott Adventure) at light-middleweight.

Scotland's five new champions - at the Time Capsule, Coatbridge (21 March), were Chris McLean (Barn), Peter Court (Springhill Boys), Allan Foster (Blantyre Miners), Lee Ramsey (Kingdom), and Paul Geddes (Elgin). McLean won at light-fly by default, Court took the light-middle-weight class by outscoring Alan Wolecki (St Francis), and Foster won at middleweight with a decision over Joe Gillon (Forgewood). Ramsey became the light-heavyweight champion, outpointing Darren Hamilton (Sparta), while Geddes won the heavyweight division with a points win over Willie Cane (Four Isles). It was the third championship win at lightweight for Jamie Coyle (Bannockburn), who outpointed Casey Nachman (Denbeath), and a similar tally for Sparta's Paul Shepherd, a former two-time flyweight champion, but now winning at bantamweight, with a points decision over Craig Docherty (Bellahouston). There was also a successful move up a weight (to featherweight) for Alex Arthur, from Leith Victoria, who beat Rhys Silverstein (Selkirk) on points. Defending flyweight titleholder, Russell Laing (Haddington), won again by stopping Paul Robertson (Sparta) in the first, while Graham McLevy (Clydeview) did the same at light-welterweight, outpointing Jerry Howett (St Francis). Super-heavyweight, John Cowie (Bannockburn), and welterweight, Colin McNeil (Springhill Boys), also kept their 1996 crowns, Cowie outpointing Kevin Cummings (Kirkintilloch) and McNeil taking a points decision over Lee Sharp (Leith Victoria).

The ABAE senior novice finals were held for the second time in May, at York Hall, Bethnal Green. Although London boxers were once again missing from the line-up there were some likely-looking prospects in action.

American light-heavyweight, Calvin Caldwell, boxing for Dennistoun, was among the titleholders at the inaugural Scottish Amateur Federation senior championships held in Motherwell (3 May).

After winning titles in the NABC-CYP and Schools Championships earlier in the season, Stephen Truscott (South Bank) completed a rare treble with a victory in Class 5 of the Junior ABAE finals at the Fox Hollies Leisure Centre, Birmingham, in May. Andrew Buchanan (Birtley) and Tony Dodson (Gemini) also won titles, which earned them a place in the European U19 title line-up. In class 6, Nicky Cook (Hornchurch & Elm Park) and Scott Miller (St Pauls) won again to add to their Class 5 title wins in 1996 and, at the same time, booked their places in the European Junior Championships. Also making the

European team were Stephen Burke (Salisbury), Stephen Smith (Repton Boys), Gavin Wake (Hunslet Boys), and Michael Dean (Long Lane), following their success in winning Class 6 titles.

Several schoolboy champions from the past were present at the Jubilee championships at the Aston Villa Leisure Centre, Birmingham (22 March), when Michael Grant (New Enterprise) made an impressive start in championship events by winning a Schools Junior "A" title. Adding to previous title wins were Grant Brotherton and Ross Murray (Newbiggin Dolphin), Ricky Ecclestone (Gemini), Daniel Lanigan (Mottram & Hattersley), Craig Lyon (Wigan), Chris Pratt (Bracknell Boys), David Robson (Hartlepool Catholic Boys) and Bobby Wood (Pleck). There were third-time wins for Scott MacDonald (St Josephs), Martin O'Donnell (Dale Youth), Sammy Price (Pinewood Starr), and Devlin Spensley (Shildon), while Partington's David Smith completed a clean sweep of everything by taking a Senior class (and fourth) title.

On the schoolboy international scene, England were successful in two out of three team fixtures against South Africa, winning 9-3 at Malvern and 5-4 at Barnsley, but losing 6-4 in London.

Daniel Hunt (Repton Boys) defeated Thomas Hamill (All Saints) in the NAB-CYP (Boys' Clubs) Class "A" finals at Winter Gardens, Blackpool (10 January), and the pair were later selected "best winner" and "best runner-up", while the best "stylist" of the night was Michael Maitchell from Darlington. The "best winner" in the Class "C" finals at the Grosvenor House Hotel, London (13 January) was Michael Dean (Long Lane), the best "runner-up" was Willenhall's Wesley Reid, who lost to Newham's Paul Souter, while the "stylist" of the tournament was Billy Johnson from Desborough. The "most courageous" special award went to Neil Tidman (Bulkington). The "stylist" of the night in the Boys' Club Class "B" finals at the Cutler's Hall, Sheffield (17 January), was Harry Cunningham (Saints), while the "best winner" was Matthew Thirwell (Fisher Downside), with Robert Nelson, from Batley & Dewsbury, chosen as the "best runner-up".

The 1997-98 season - the halfway stage between the Olympics - is certainly a busy one on the international scene. There are the rest of the European Championship qualifying tournaments in Finland, Ukraine, Turkey, Germany, and Italy, the world seniors title event in Budapest (October 1997), the European fixture in Minsk, Belarus (May 1998), followed by the Commonwealth Games in Kuala Lumpur (September 1998).

Given the money, and a slow-down in the defections to the paid ranks, there is much that our boxers can do - Havana, Birmingham and Liverpool prove that - and the next 12 months will tell whether prospects for medals in Sydney are a reality, or not.

(David Prior formerly wrote on amateur boxing in Boxing News/Amateur Boxing Scene and is the author of "Ringside with the Amateurs". He is also the Press Liaison Officer for the Amateur Boxing Association of England Limited.)

ABA National Championships, 1996-97

Combined Services v North-East Counties

Combined Services

RAF, RN & Army Championships   Maida Gymnasium, Aldershot - 11 & 12 December
L. Fly: no entries. **Fly:** *final:* D. Fox (RAF) w pts A. Jessiman (Army). **Bantam:** *final:* O. Spensley (RAF) wo. **Feather:** *final:* D. Dugan (Army) wo. **Light:** *final:* D. Williams (Army) wo. **L. Welter:** *final:* K. Bennett (Army) w co 2 S. Mackay (RAF). **Welter:** *final:* S. Brown (Army) wo. **L. Middle:** *final:* C. Bessey (Army) wo. **Middle:** *final:* D. Edwards (RN) w pts M. Barker (Army). **L. Heavy:** *semi-finals:* V. Jones (Army) wo, J. Gosling (RAF) w rsc 5 M. Kavanagh (RN); *final:* V. Jones w rsc 3 J. Gosling. **Heavy:** *semi-finals:* P. Vella (Army) wo, N. Hoskins (RAF) w rsc 4 A. Walton (RN); *final:* N. Hoskins w rsc 1 P. Vella. **S. Heavy:** *final:* D. Watts (Army) w rsc 4 P. Fiske (RAF).

North-East Counties

Yorkshire & Humberside Divisions   Manor Social Club, Sheffield - 16 January
L. Fly: no entries. **Fly:** *final:* M. Cairns (St Paul's) wo. **Bantam:** *final:* L. Pattison (Hunslet) wo. **Feather:** *final:* J. Betts (St Paul's) w rsc 3 D. Murdoch (Croft House). **Light:** *final:* A. Spenceley (St Patrick's) wo. **L. Welter:** *final:* M. MacIvor (Batley & Dewsbury) w dis 5 G. Williams (Sedbergh). **Welter:** *semi-finals:* G. Matsell (Hull Fish Trades) wo, T. Smith (Handsworth) w rsc 1 A. Wharton (Scarborough); *final:* T. Smith w pts G. Matsell. **L. Middle:** no entries. **Middle:** *semi-finals:* D. Rhodes (Hunslet) w rsc 2 J. Godbehere (Croft House), D. Smillie (Sedbergh) w dis 3 P. Carragher (Tom Hill); *final:* D. Smillie w pts D. Rhodes. **L. Heavy:** *final:* M. Hannon (Handsworth) wo. **Heavy:** *final:* M. Afsar (Sedbergh) wo. **S. Heavy:** *final:* G. Fitzgerald (Sacred Heart) wo.

North-East Division   Northumbria Centre, Washington - 17 January
L. Fly: no entries. **Fly:** *final:* M. Hunter (Hartlepool BW) wo. **Bantam:** *final:* M. Bunney (Lingdale) wo. **Feather:** *final:* J. Rooney (Hartlepool Catholic) w rsc 3 M. Thompson (Phil Thomas SoB). **Light:** *semi-finals:* A. McLean (Birtley) w co 1 P. Watson (Sunderland), G. Williams (Hartlepool BW) w dis 3 G. Hodgson (Spennymoor); *final:* G. Williams w pts A. McLean. **L. Welter:** *semi-finals:* M. Hall (Darlington) w pts M. Teesdale (Wellington), J. Donkin (Hylton Castle) w rsc 3 J. Bowery (Deerness); *final:* M. Hall w pts J. Donkin. **Welter:** *semi-finals:* N. Patterson (Shildon) wo, M. McLean (Birtley) w rsc 1 M. Draboczy (Lingdale); *final:* N. Patterson w pts M. McLean. **L. Middle:** *semi-finals:* S. McCrone (Spennymoor) wo, S. McCready (Birtley) w pts W. Mason (Lambton Street); *final:* S. McCready w pts S. McCrone. **Middle:** *final:* I. Cooper (Hartlepool BW) w pts J. Pearce (Wellington). **L. Heavy:** *semi-finals:* M. White (Birtley) wo, M. Thompson (Spennymoor) w rsc 2 M. Ferguson (Benton); *final:* M. Thompson w pts M. White. **Heavy:** *semi-finals:* K. Duke (Sunderland) wo, M. Chandler (Darlington) w pts D. Wilson (Wellington); *final:* K. Duke w pts M. Chandler. **S. Heavy:** *final:* M. McGhin (Sunderland) wo.

North-East Counties Finals   Manor Social Club, Sheffield - 30 January
L. Fly: no entries. **Fly:** M. Hunter (Hartlepool BW) w rsc 5 M. Cairns (St Paul's). **Bantam:** L. Pattison (Hunslet) wo M. Bunney (Lingdale). **Feather:** J. Betts (St Paul's) w co 2 J. Rooney (Hartlepool Catholic). **Light:** G. Williams (Hartlepool BW) w rsc 4 A. Spenceley (St Patrick's). **L. Welter:** M. Hall (Darlington) w pts M. MacIvor (Batley & Dewsbury). **Welter:** T. Smith (Handsworth) w dis 2 N. Patterson (Shildon). **L. Middle:** S. McCready (Birtley) wo. **Middle:** I. Cooper (Hartlepool BW) w pts D. Smillie (Sedbergh). **L. Heavy:** M. Thompson (Spennymoor) w rtd 1 M. Hannon (Handsworth). **Heavy:** K. Duke (Sunderland) w rsc 5 M. Afsar (Sedbergh). **S. Heavy:** G. McGhin (Sunderland) w rsc 2 G. Fitzgerald (Sacred Heart).

Combined Services v North-East Counties

Manor Social Club, Sheffield - 6 February
L. Fly: no entries. **Fly:** M. Hunter (Hartlepool BW) wo D. Fox (RAF). **Bantam:** L. Pattison (Hunslet) w pts O. Spensley (RAF). **Feather:** D. Dugan (Army) w rsc 4 J. Betts (St. Paul's). **Light:** D. Williams (Army) w rsc 2 G. Williams (Hartlepool BW). **L. Welter:** M. Hall (Darlington) w pts K. Bennett (Army). **Welter:** T. Smith (Handsworth) w pts S. Brown (Army). **L. Middle:** C. Bessey (Army) w pts S. McCready (Birtley). **Middle:** I. Cooper (Hartlepool BW) w pts D. Edwards (RN). **L. Heavy:** M. Thompson (Spennymoor) w rsc 3 V. Jones (Army). **Heavy:** K. Duke (Sunderland) w pts N. Hoskins (RAF). **S. Heavy:** G. McGhin (Sunderland) w rsc 1 D. Watts (Army)

London v North-West Counties

London

North-East Division   York Hall, Bethnal Green - 9 January
L. Fly: *final:* I. Napa (Crown & Manor) wo. **Fly:** *final:* M. Donoghue (Lion) wo. **Bantam:** *semi-finals:* L. Jared (Gator) w rsc 3 M. Cahill (Lion), S. Oates w rsc 5 W. Quinn (Newham); *final:* S. Oates w pts L. Jared. **Feather:** *semi-finals:* B. Murughan (Ruskin) wo, D. Adams (Repton) w dis 4 M. O'Callaghan (Newham); *final:* D. Adams w pts B. Murughan. **Light:** *final:* K. Wing (Repton) w pts A. Spelling (St George's). **L. Welter:** *final:* D. Happe (Repton) wo. **Welter:** *semi-finals:* E. Omar (Repton) wo, T. Cesay (Repton) w pts C. Lynes (Hornchurch & Elm Park); *final:* T. Cesay w pts E. Omar. **L. Middle:** *semi-finals:* G. Robshaw (West Ham) w pts I. Okoronkwo (Repton), A. Kirkbride (Newham) w pts E. Monteith (Gator); *final:* G. Robshaw w rsc 3 A. Kirkbride. **Middle:** *final:* A. Lowe (Repton) w pts S. Smith (Crown & Manor). **L. Heavy:** *final:* M. James (Repton) wo. **Heavy:** *final:* M. Lee (Repton) wo. **S. Heavy:** *final:* A. Harrison (Repton) w rsc 2 M. Potter (Five Star).

North-West Division   Irish Centre, Camden Town - 10 December
L. Fly: no entries. **Fly:** no entries. **Bantam:** *final:* P. Black (Dale) wo. **Feather:** *final:* M. Alexander (Islington) w pts J. Waters (Trojan). **Light:** *final:* D. Browne (Northolt) w rsc 1 T. Mongon (Trojan). **L. Welter:** *semi-finals:* J. Gallagher (Finchley) so, K. Nytasah (Trojan) w pts A. Hunt (Northolt); *final:* J. Gallagher w pts K. Nytasah. **Welter:** *final:* F. Barrett (Trojan) w rsc 4 A. Neunie (Islington). **L. Middle:** *semi-finals:* G. Uberio (Trojan) w dis 3 C. Officer (Dale), R. Brown (St Pancras) w pts C. Ifekoya

(Ruislip); *final:* R. Brown w pts G. Uberio. **Middle:** *final:* J. Tiftik (Trojan) w co 3 S. Tobin (Trojan). **L. Heavy:** *semi-finals:* M. Fallon (Trojan) wo, R. Ogodo (Trojan) w rsc 1 G. Foley (Islington); *final:* R. Ogodo w co 4 M. Fallon. **Heavy:** *final:* W. Barima (Northolt) wo. **S. Heavy:** no entries.

South-East Division   National Sports Centre, Crystal Palace - 19 December

L. Fly: no entries. **Fly:** no entries. **Bantam:** no entries. **Feather:** *semi-finals:* M. Bowden (Fisher) wo, E. Lam (Fitzroy Lodge) w rtd 2 N. Francis (Lynn); *final:* M. Bowden w pts E. Lam. **Light:** *semi-finals:* A. Wyatt (Lynn) wo, P. McCabe (Fitzroy Lodge) w rsc 4 L. Kerrigan (Lynn); *final:* P. McCabe w rsc 3 A. Wyatt. **L. Welter:** *semi-finals:* P. Buckley (Eltham) wo, D. Walker (Fisher) w rsc 3 D. Banjo (Lynn); *final:* D. Walker w pts P. Buckley. **Welter:** *semi-finals:* D. Morgan (Fitzroy Lodge) w pts M. Reigate (Fitzroy Lodge), A. Martin (Fitzroy Lodge) w dis 4 M. Clark (Lynn); *final:* D. Morgan w pts A. Martin. **L. Middle:** *final:* T. Thirwell (Fisher) w dis 4 S. Fearon (Lynn). **Middle:** no entries. **L. Heavy:** *semi-finals:* J. Sawicki (Eltham) wo, D. Archibald (Lynn) w pts A. Abdul (Lynn); *final:* D. Archibald w rsc 5 J. Sawicki. **Heavy:** *semi-finals:* T. Cullam (Lynn) wo, O. Yezerskyi (Fitzroy Lodge) w pts S. Hewitt (Fitzroy Lodge); *final:* T. Cullam w co 1 O. Yezerskyi. **S. Heavy:** no entries.

South-West Division   Town Hall, Battersea - 18 December

L. Fly: no entries. **Fly:** no entries. **Bantam:** no entries. **Feather:** no entries. **Light:** no entries. **L. Welter:** *final:* C. Williams (Balham) wo. **Welter:** *final:* A. Hussain (Balham) wo. **L. Middle:** *final:* K. Hassine (Balham) w dis 2 M. Barr (Kingston). **Middle:** *final:* P. Campbell (Balham) wo. **L. Heavy:** *final:* W. Barnes (Battersea) w rsc 2 D. Nairn (Battersea). **Heavy:** no entries. **S. Heavy:** *final:* P. Thompson (Balham) wo.

London Semi-Finals & Finals   York Hall, Bethnal Green - 23 & 30 January

L. Fly: *final:* I. Napa (Crown & Manor) wo. **Fly:** *final:* M. Donaghue (Lion) wo. **Bantam:** *final:* S. Oates (Repton) w co 2 P. Black (Dale). **Feather:** *semi-finals:* M. Bowden (Fisher) wo, D. Adams (Repton) w pts M. Alexander (Islington); *final:* M. Bowden w pts D. Adams. **Light:** *semi-finals:* P. McCabe (Fitzroy Lodge) wo, K. Wing (Repton) w rsc 5 D. Browne (Northolt); *final:* P. McCabe w rsc 4 K. Wing. **L. Welter:** *semi-finals:* J. Gallagher (Finchley) w rsc 4 C. Williams (Balham), D. Walker (Fisher) w pts D. Happe (Repton); *final:* J. Gallagher w pts D. Walker. **Welter:** *semi-finals:* T. Cesay (Repton) w rsc 5 A. Hussain (Balham), F. Barrett (Trojan) w pts D. Morgan (Fitzroy Lodge); *final:* F. Barrett w rtd 3 T. Cesay. **L. Middle:** *semi-finals:* G. Robshaw (West Ham) w pts R. Brown (St Pancras), K. Hassine (Balham) w co 5 T. Thirwell (Fisher); *final:* G. Robshaw w pts K. Hassine. **Middle:** *semi-finals:* P. Campbell (Balham) wo, A. Lowe (Repton) w pts J. Tiftik (Trojan); *final:* A. Lowe w pts P. Campbell. **L. Heavy:** *semi-finals:* M. James (Repton) w rsc 3 R. Ogodo (Trojan), W. Barnes (Battersea) w pts D. Archibald (Lynn); *final:* W. Barnes w pts M. James. **Heavy:** *semi-finals:* M. Lee (Repton) wo, W. Barima (Northolt) w co 3 T. Cullam (Lynn); *final:* W. Barima w co 3 M. Lee. **S. Heavy:** *final:* A. Harrison (Repton) w pts P. Thompson (Balham).

North-West Counties

East Lancashire & Cheshire Division   The Willows, Salford - 16 & 23 January

L. Fly: *final:* no entries. **Fly:** no entries. **Bantam:** *final:* A. Gribben (Ardwick) wo. **Feather:** *final:* S. Bell (Louvolite) wo. **Light:** *final:* R. Francis (Preston & Fulwood) wo. **L. Welter:** *semi-finals:* J. Spence (Ardwick) wo, R. Hatton (Sale West) w co 2 S. Sweeting (Droylsden); *final:* R. Hatton w rsc 2 J. Spence. **Welter:** *final:* J. Barrow (Sandygate) wo. **L. Middle:** *final:* A. Page (Louvolite) w rsc 3 A. Peck (Preston & Fulwood). **Middle:** *final:* C. Marshall (Sale West) w co 1 C. Crook (Lancs Constabulary). **L. Heavy:** *final:* S. Robinson (Sandygate) w pts J. Dixon (Carlisle). **Heavy:** *final:* V. Docherty (Lancs Constabulary) wo. **S. Heavy:** no entries.

West Lancashire & Cheshire Division   Everton Park Sports Centre, Liverpool - 17 & 24 January

L. Fly: *final:* G. Jones (Sefton) wo. **Fly:** *final:* W. Toohey (Gemini) w pts S. Warbrick (Gemini). **Bantam:** *final:* C. Toohey (Gemini) w pts D. Vlasman (Salisbury). **Feather:** *semi-finals:* M. Parker (Kirkby) w pts K. Roberts (Gemini), P. McCormack (St Theresa's) w pts P. Allen (Willaston); *final:* M. Parker w rtd 3 P. McCormack (St Theresa's). **Light:** *final:* L. Eedle (Gemini) w pts E. Roberts (Gemini). **L. Welter:** *semi-finals:* D. Keir (Long Lane) wo, C. Wall (Gemini) w pts J. Vlasman (Salisbury); *final:* C. Wall w pts D. Keir. **Welter:** *semi-finals:* S. Spence (Rotunda) w co 3 R. Murray (Gemini), M. Jennings (Wigan) w pts T. Maher (Sefton); *final:* M. Jennings w pts S. Spence. **L. Middle:** *final:* M. Jones (Gemini) w rtd 3 S. Garrett (Stanley). **Middle:** *semi-finals:* A. Mulcahy (Higherside) w pts S. Miller (Runcorn), L. Molloy (Salisbury) w pts M. Brooks (Campion Transport); *final:* A. Mulcahy w pts L. Molloy. **L. Heavy:** *final:* L. Cuddy (Campion Transport) wo. **Heavy:** *semi-finals:* D. Kehoe (Gemini) wo, D. Chubbs (Kirkby) w co 2 B. Kilbride (Willaston); *final:* D. Kehoe wo D. Chubbs. **S. Heavy:** no entries.

North-West Counties Finals   Everton Park Sports Centre, Liverpool - 31 January

L. Fly: G. Jones (Sefton) wo. **Fly:** W. Toohey (Gemini) wo. **Bantam:** C. Toohey (Gemini) w pts A. Gribben (Ardwick). **Feather:** S. Bell (Louvolite) w rsc 3 M. Parker (Kirkby). **Light:** E. Roberts (Gemini) - replaced L. Eedle (Gemini) - w pts R. Francis (Preston & Fulwood). **L. Welter:** R. Hatton (Sale West) w pts C. Wall (Gemini). **Welter:** M. Jennings (Wigan) w rsc 5 J. Barrow (Sandygate). **L. Middle:** M. Jones (Gemini) wo A. Page (Louvolite). **Middle:** C. Marshall (Sale West) w pts A. Mulcahy (Higherside). **L. Heavy:** L. Cuddy (Campion Transport) w pts S. Robinson (Sandygate). **Heavy:** D. Kehoe (Gemini) w co 2 V. Docherty (Lancs Constabulary). **S. Heavy:** no entries.

London v North-West Counties

York Hall, Bethnal Green - 7 February

L. Fly: I. Napa (Crown & Manor) w pts G. Jones (Sefton). **Fly:** M. Donaghue (Lion) w pts W. Toohey (Gemini). **Bantam:** S. Oates (Repton) w rsc 1 C. Toohey (Gemini). **Feather:** S. Bell (Louvolite) w rsc 5 M. Bowden (Fisher). **Light:** E. Roberts (Gemini) w rsc 2 P. McCabe (Fitzroy Lodge). **L. Welter:** R. Hatton (Sale West) w pts J. Gallagher (Finchley). **Welter:** F. Barrett (Trojan) w pts M. Jennings (Wigan). **L. Middle:** M. Jones (Gemini) w co 2 G. Robshaw (West Ham). **Middle:** P. Campbell (Balham) - replaced A. Lowe (Repton) - w co 2 C. Marshall (Sale West). **L. Heavy:** L. Cuddy (Campion Transport) w pts W. Barnes (Battersea). **Heavy:** D. Kehoe (Gemini) w co 1 W. Barima (Northolt). **S. Heavy:** A. Harrison (Repton) wo.

Midland Counties v Southern Counties

Midland Counties

Derbyshire Division   Pennine Hotel, Derby - 9 January
L. Fly: no entries. **Fly:** no entries. **Bantam:** no entries. **Feather:** no entries. **Light:** *final:* C. Spacie (St Michael's) w pts C. Rowland (Merlin). **L. Welter:** *final:* S. Williamson (Merlin) wo. **Welter:** *final:* G. Down (Chesterfield) wo. **L. Middle:** *final:* A. Palmer (Trinity) w pts L. Smith (Matlock). **Middle:** no entries. **L. Heavy:** *final:* M. Krence (St Michael's) wo. **Heavy:** *final:* A. Aziz (Derby) wo. **S. Heavy:** no entries.

Leicester, Rutland & Northamptonshire Division   Belgrave WMC - 5 December
L. Fly: no entries. **Fly:** no entries. **Bantam:** no entries. **Feather:** no entries. **Light:** no entries. **L. Welter:** no entries. **Welter:** *final:* L. Walsh (Braunstone) wo. **L. Middle:** *final:* N. Linford (Belgrave) wo. **Middle:** *final:* A. Foster (Kingsthorpe) w pts G. Jacques (Belgrave). **L. Heavy:** *final:* T. Taylor (Central) wo. **Heavy:** *final:* C. Thomas (Belgrave) wo. **S. Heavy:** *final:* D. McCafferty (Kettering) w rsc 5 S. Lansdowne (Belgrave).

Nottinghamshire & Lincolnshire Division   Town Hall, Louth - 11 January
L. Fly: no entries. **Fly:** no entries. **Bantam:** no entries. **Feather:** *final:* K. Gerowski (Cotgrave) wo. **Light:** no entries. **L. Welter:** *final:* D. Revill (Hughwaite) wo. **Welter:** *final:* J. Khaliq (Meadows & Ruddington) wo. **L. Middle:** no entries. **Middle:** no entries. **L. Heavy:** *final:* A. Kerr (Bingham) w pts M. Lacey (Louth). **Heavy:** no entries. **S. Heavy:** *final:* D. Castle (Radford) wo.

Warwickshire Division   Coventry Colliery Club, Keresley - 10 January
L. Fly: no entries. **Fly:** no entries. **Bantam:** *final:* G. Payne (Bell Green) wo. **Feather:** *final:* M. Payne (Bell Green) wo. **Light:** *final:* R. Rutherford (Bell Green) wo. **L. Welter:** *final:* I. Carroll (Triumph) w pts T. Feecham (Coventry Boys). **Welter:** no entries. **L. Middle:** no entries. **Middle:** *final:* J. Twite (Triumph) wo. **L. Heavy:** no entries. **Heavy:** *final:* D. Bendall (Triumph) wo. **S. Heavy:** *final:* D. Abbott (Stratford on Avon) wo.

Midland Counties (North Zone) Semi-Finals & Finals
Coventry Colliery Club, Keresley - 17 January, Harworth Colliery WMC, Harworth - 18 January, & Belgrave WMC, Leicester - 23 January
L. Fly: no entries. **Fly:** no entries. **Bantam:** *final:* G. Payne (Bell Green) wo. **Feather:** *final:* K. Gerowski (Cotgrave) wo M. Payne (Bell Green). **Light:** *final:* R. Rutherford (Bell Green) w pts C. Spacie (St Michael's). **L. Welter:** *semi-finals:* T. Carroll (Triumph) wo, D. Revill (Huthwaite) w pts S. Williamson (Merlin); *final:* I. Carroll w pts D. Revill. **Welter:** *semi-finals:* L. Walsh (Braunstone) wo, J. Khaliq (Meadows & Ruddington) w pts G. Down (Chesterfield); *final:* J. Khaliq w pts L. Walsh. **L. Middle:** *final:* N. Linford (Belgrave) w co 3 A. Palmer (Trinity). **Middle:** *final:* J. Twite (Triumph) w pts A. Foster (Kingsthorpe). **L. Heavy:** *semi-finals:* T. Taylor (Central) wo, M. Krence (St Michael's) w pts A. Kerr (Bingham); *final:* M. Krence w pts T. Taylor. **Heavy:** *semi-finals:* A. Aziz (Derby) wo, C. Thomas (Belgrave) w pts D. Bendall (Triumph); *final:* A. Aziz w pts C. Thomas. **S. Heavy:** *semi-finals:* D. Castle (Radford) wo, D. McCafferty (Kettering) w rsc 3 D. Abbott (Stratford on Avon);

final: D. McCafferty w co 1 D. Castle.

Birmingham Division   Irish Centre, Digbeth & North Road Club, Wolverhampton - 5 & 9 January
L. Fly: *final:* A. Odud (Birmingham City) wo. **Fly:** *final:* J. Hegney (Castle Vale) wo. **Bantam:** *final:* D. Ward (Small Heath) w rsc 4 T. Jukes (Birmingham City). **Feather:** no entries. **Light:** *final:* T. Adams (Ladywood) wo. **L. Welter:** *final:* G. Simpson (Birmingham City) wo. **Welter:** *final:* J. Scanlon (Birmingham City) wo. **L. Middle:** *semi-finals:* D. Harkin (Small Heath) wo, G. Harris (Rover) w pts G. Deakin (Birmingham City); *final:* D. Harkin w pts G. Harris. **Middle:** no entries. **L. Heavy:** no entries. **Heavy:** no entries. **S. Heavy:** *final:* L. Durrell (Small Heath) w pts D. Redmond (Rover).

North Staffordshire Division   Bidds Country Club, Stoke - 10 January
L. Fly: no entries. **Fly:** no entries. **Bantam:** *final:* D. Simpkin (Brownhills) wo. **Feather:** no entries. **Light:** *final:* M. Abbott (Hulton Abbey) wo. **L. Welter:** *final:* S. Lawton (Queensberry) wo. **Welter:** no entries. **L. Middle:** *final:* D. Steel (Stoke) wo. **Middle:** *final:* G. Gaylor (Burton on Trent) wo. **L. Heavy:** *final:* P. Scope (Burton on Trent) wo. **Heavy:** *final:* I. Thomas (Queensberry) wo. **S. Heavy:** no entries.

South Staffordshire Division   North Road Club, Wolverhampton - 9 January
L. Fly: no entries. **Fly:** no entries. **Bantam:** *final:* I. Read (Graisley) wo. **Feather:** *final:* S. Chinnock (Rugeley) wo. **Light:** no entries. **L. Welter:** *final:* C. Foxall (Silver Street) wo. **Welter:** *final:* J. Gould (Wednesbury) wo. **L. Middle:** *final:* M. Hough (Pleck) wo. **Middle:** *final:* K. Lang (Silver Street) wo. **L. Heavy:** *final:* A. Houldey (Wednesbury) wo. **Heavy:** *final:* M. Pugh (Silver Street) w pts A. Laddington (Wednesbury). **S. Heavy:** no entries.

West Mercia Division   Heath Hotel, Bewdley - 8 & 10 January
L. Fly: no entries. **Fly:** no entries. **Bantam:** *final:* T. Davies (Donnington) wo. **Feather:** *final:* N. Marsden (Shrewsbury Severnside) wo. **Light:** no entries. **L. Welter:** *final:* G. Reid (Shrewsbury) wo. **Welter:** no entries. **L. Middle:** *final:* D. Woodley (Tudorville) wo. **Middle:** *semi-finals:* D. Smith (Donnington) w pts S. Martin (Shrewsbury), I. Rogers (Shrewsbury Severnside) w pts H. Butler (Worcester City); *final:* D. Smith wo I. Rogers. **L. Heavy:** *final:* D. Norton (Stourbridge) wo. **Heavy:** no entries. **S. Heavy:** no entries.

Midland Counties (South Zone) Semi-Finals & Finals   Heath Hotel, Bewdley - 13 January, Ind Coope Social Club, Burton on Trent - 17 January, & Gala Baths, West Bromwich - 24 January
L. Fly: *final:* A. Odud (Birmingham City) wo. **Fly:** *final:* J. Hegney (Castle Vale) wo. **Bantam:** *semi-finals:* D. Simpkin (Brownhills) w rsc 2 I. Read (Graisley), T. Davies (Donnington) w pts D. Ward (Small Heath); *final:* T. Davies wo D. Simpkin. **Feather:** *final:* S. Chinnock (Rugeley) w pts N. Marsden (Shrewsbury Severnside). **Light:** *final:* T. Adams (Ladywood) w rsc 4 M. Abbott (Hulton Abbey). **L. Welter:** *semi-finals:* S. Lawton (Queensberry) w pts C. Foxall (Silver Street), G. Reid (Shrewsbury) w rtd 1 G. Simpson (Birmingham City); *final:* G. Reid w co 2 S. Lawton. **Welter:** *final:* J. Scanlon (Birmingham City) w pts J. Gould (Wednesbury). **L. Middle:** *semi-finals:* D. Steel (Stoke) w pts M. Hough (Pleck), D. Harkin (Small Heath) w pts D. Woodley (Tudorville); *final:* D. Harkin w pts D. Steel. **Middle:** *semi-finals:* D. Smith (Donnington) wo, G. Gaylor

(Burton on Trent) w co 1 K. Lang (Silver Street); *final:* D. Smith w pts G. Gaylor. **L. Heavy:** *semi-finals:* D. Norton (Stourbridge) wo, A. Houldey (Wednesbury) w pts P. Scope (Burton on Trent); *final:* A. Houldey w pts D. Norton. **Heavy:** *final:* M. Pugh (Silver Street) w pts I. Thomas (Queensberry). **S. Heavy:** *final:* L. Durrell (Small Heath) wo.

Midland Counties Finals   The University, Nottingham - 1 February

L. Fly: A. Odud (Birmingham City) wo. **Fly:** J. Hegney (Castle Vale) wo. **Bantam:** G. Payne (Bell Green) w pts T. Davies (Donnington). **Feather:** S. Chinnock (Rugeley) w pts K. Gerowski (Cotgrave). **Light:** R. Rutherford (Bell Green) w co 3 T. Adams (Ladywood). **L. Welter:** G. Reid (Shrewsbury) w co 3 I. Carroll (Triumph). **Welter:** J. Khaliq (Meadows & Ruddington) w pts J. Scanlon (Birmingham City). **L. Middle:** N. Linford (Belgrave) w pts D. Harkin (Small Heath). **Middle:** J. Twite (Triumph) w pts D. Smith (Donnington). **L. Heavy:** M. Krence (St Michael's) w pts A. Houldey (Wednesbury). **Heavy:** M. Pugh (Silver Street) w pts A. Aziz (Derby). **S. Heavy:** D. McCafferty (Kettering) w pts L. Durrell (Small Heath).

Southern Counties

Hampshire, Kent, Surrey & Sussex Divisions   Sports Centre, Sandwich - 18 January & Winter Gardens, Margate - 25 January

L. Fly: no entries. **Fly:** *final:* N. Bell (Brighton) w pts T. Craig (Basingstoke). **Bantam:** *final:* D. Western (Leigh Park) wo. **Feather:** *final:* M. Walsh (Portsmouth University) w pts B. Davidson (Leigh Park). **Light:** *final:* B. Urquhart (Westree) w rsc 1 P. Bedford (Basingstoke). **L. Welter:** *semi-finals:* A. Walsh (Portsmouth University) w rsc 3 C. Bourne (Shepway), R. Cox (Brighton) w rsc 5 J. Ball (Onslow); *final:* A. Walsh w pts R. Cox. **Welter:** *semi-finals:* J. Honey (Basingstoke) w pts J. Sale (Seaford), N. Philpott (Leigh Park) w pts G. Jones (Horsham); *final:* N. Philpott w pts J. Honey. **L. Middle:** *quarter-finals:* S. Laitt (Southampton) wo, S. Evans (Shepway) wo, A. Coates (Medway GG) ► wo, A. Gilbert (Crawley) w pts S. James (Broadstairs); *semi-final:* A. Coates w rsc 4 A. Gilbert, S. Laitt w rsc 4 S. Evans; *final:* A. Coates w rsc 4 S. Laitt. **Middle:** *final:* J. Weeks (Gravesham) wo. **L. Heavy:** *semi-finals:* M. Michael (Birchington) wo, L. Sale (Seaford w co 3 A. Wilford (Faversham); *final:* M. Michael w rsc 4 L. Sale. **Heavy:** *final:* T. Oakey (Leigh Park) wo. **S. Heavy:** *quarter-finals:* S. Makepeace (Snodland) wo, D. French (Gosport) wo, K. Davies (Camberley) wo, J. Flisher (Shepway) w rsc 3 M. Brown (Ryde); *semi-finals:* S. Makepeace w pts D. French, K. Davies w pts J. Flisher; *final:* K. Davies w rsc 2 S. Makepeace.

Midland Counties v Southern Counties

Willenhall Social Club, Coventry - 8 February

L. Fly: A. Odud (Birmingham City) wo. **Fly:** N. Bell (Brighton) w pts J. Hegney (Castle Vale). **Bantam:** G. Payne (Bell Green) w pts D. Western (Leigh Park). **Feather:** M. Walsh (Portsmouth University) w pts S. Chinnock (Rugeley). **Light:** R. Rutherford (Bell Green) w pts B. Urquhart (Westree). **L. Welter:** G. Reid (Shrewsbury) w rsc 3 A. Walsh (Portsmouth University). **Welter:** N. Philpott (Leigh Park) wo J. Khaliq (Meadows & Ruddington). **L. Middle:** A. Coates (Medway GG) w pts D. Harkin (Small Heath) - replaced N. Linford (Belgrave). **Middle:** J. Twite

(Triumph) w rsc 5 J. Weeks (Gravesham). **L. Heavy:** M. Krence (St Michael's) w rsc 3 M. Michael (Birchington). **Heavy:** T. Oakway (Leigh Park) w pts M. Pugh (Silver Street). **S. Heavy:** D. McCafferty (Kettering) w pts K. Davies (Camberley).

Western Counties v Eastern/Home Counties

Western Counties

Northern Division   Royal British Legion Club, Taunton - 11 January

L. Fly: no entries. **Fly:** no entries. **Bantam:** no entries. **Feather:** no entries. **Light:** *final:* R. Scutt (Sydenham) wo. **L. Welter:** *semi-finals:* S. Lucas (Walcot) wo, C. Thomas (Viking) w pts A. Berkley (Synwell); *final:* S. Lucas w rsc 1 C. Thomas. **Welter:** *semi-finals:* A. Cummings (National Smelting) wo, J. Turley (Penhill RBL) w pts N. Thomas (Kingswood); *final:* J. Turley w rsc 4 A. Cummings. **L. Middle:** *semi-finals:* D. Kelly (Gloucester) wo, A. Derrick (Taunton) w pts C. Johnson (Empire); *final:* A. Derrick w pts D. Kelly. **Middle:** *final:* D. Holder (Gloucester) w rsc 5 K. Chaffer (Viking). **L. Heavy:** *final:* P. Rogers (Penhill RBL) w pts H. Smith (Empire). **Heavy:** *semi-finals:* P. Lewis (Taunton) wo, S. Gray (Penhill RBL) w rtd 3 D. Beatty (Frome); *final:* P. Lewis w rsc 5 S. Gray. **S. Heavy:** *final:* B. Harding (Penhill RBL) wo.

Southern Division   Hendra Holiday Park, Newquay - 30 November

L. Fly: no entries. **Fly:** *final:* D. Barriball (Launceston) wo. **Bantam:** no entries. **Feather:** *final:* S. Gawron (Devonport) wo. **Light:** *semi-finals:* W. Nurrah (Devonport) wo, R. Petherick (Dawlish) w pts J. Leando (Pisces); *final:* W. Nurrah w pts R. Petherick. **L. Welter:** *semi-finals:* G. Turner (Poole) w pts D. Saunders (Dawlish), R. Warman (Truro) w co 2 A. Kennedy (Devonport); *final:* R. Warman w rsc 3 G. Turner. **Welter:** *final:* M. Pickard (Weymouth) wo. **L. Middle:** *semi-finals:* G. McGahey (Exeter) wo, G. Wharton (Bournemouth) w rsc 2 P. Swords (Pisces); *final:* G. McGahey w pts G. Wharton. **Middle:** *semi-finals:* B. White (Apollo) wo, S. Blackford (Truro) w rsc 2 R. Cox (Exmouth); *final:* S. Blackford w pts B. White. **L. Heavy:** *semi-finals:* S. Ashford (Exeter) wo, I. Tennant (Truro) w pts S. Butler (Brixham); *final:* S. Ashford w pts I. Tennant. **Heavy:** *final:* A. Stables (Devonport) w rtd 3 C. Thomas (Camborne). **S. Heavy:** *final:* N. Kendall (Apollo) wo.

Western Counties Finals   Littledown Leisure Centre, Bournemouth - 25 January

L. Fly: no entries. **Fly:** D. Barriball (Launceston) wo. **Bantam:** no entries. **Feather:** S. Gawron (Devonport) wo. **Light:** R. Scutt (Sydenham) wo W. Nurrah (Devonport). **L. Welter:** S. Lucas (Walcot) w rsc 4 R. Warman (Truro). **Welter:** J. Turley (Penhill RBL) w pts M. Pickard (Weymouth). **L. Middle:** A. Derrick (Taunton) w pts G. McGahey (Exeter). **Middle:** D. Holder (Gloucester) w rsc 3 S. Blackford (Truro). **L. Heavy:** P. Rogers (Penhill RBL) w rsc 2 S. Ashford (Exeter). **Heavy:** P. Lewis (Taunton) w pts A. Stables (Devonport). **S. Heavy:** N. Kendall (Apollo) wo B. Harding (Penhill RBL).

Eastern Counties

Essex Division   Civic Hall, Grays - 17 January

L. Fly: no entries. **Fly:** no entries. **Bantam:** *final:* T. Brocklebank (Canvey) wo. **Feather:** *final:* D. Dainty (Canvey) wo. **Light:**

final: D. Smith (Canvey) wo. **L. Welter:** *final:* M. Saliu (Colchester) wo. **Welter:** *final:* D. Bruce (Belhus Park) w rsc 3 D. Groome (Berry Boys). **L. Middle:** *final:* R. Hadley (Canvey) wo. **Middle:** *final:* D. Doyle (Belhus Park) w pts P. Turner (Halstead). **L. Heavy:** *semi-finals:* J. Veal (Colchester) wo, M. Quirey (Berry Boys) w rsc 3 J. Warren (Canvey); *final:* M. Quirey w co 3 J. Veal. **Heavy:** *final:* A. Batista (Billericay) wo. **S. Heavy:** no entries.

Mid-Anglia Division   Community Centre, Cambridge - 24 November
L. Fly: no entries. **Fly:** no entries. **Bantam:** no entries. **Feather:** no entries. **Light:** no entries. **L. Welter:** no entries. **Welter:** *final:* P. Gill (Chatteris) wo. **L. Middle:** no entries. **Middle:** no entries. **L. Heavy:** no entries. **Heavy:** no entries. **S. Heavy:** no entries.

Norfolk Division   Jubilee Hall, East Tuddenham - 11 January
L. Fly: no entries.**Fly:** no entries. **Bantam:** no entries. **Feather:** no entries. **Light:** no entries. **L. Welter:** *final:* R. Mann (Kingfisher) w pts A. Drummond (Norwich Lads). **Welter:** no entries. **L. Middle:** *final:* J. Lambert (Aylsham) w pts L. York (Kings Lynn). **Middle:** *final:* C. Saunders (Norwich City) wo. **L. Heavy:** no entries. **Heavy:** *final:* J. Carrara (Norwich City) w dis 5 C. Lewer (Dereham). **S. Heavy:** *final:* P. Eastman (Kings Lynn) wo.

Suffolk Division   Lucky Break Snooker & Leisure Club, Bury St Edmunds - 13 December
L. Fly: *final:* F. Norton (New Astley) wo. **Fly:** no entries. **Bantam:** no entries. **Feather:** no entries. **Light:** *final:* M. Hawthorne (Lowestoft) wo. **L. Welter:** *final:* J. Taylor (Ipswich) wo. **Welter:** *final:* W. Asker (Bury St Edmunds) wo. **L. Middle:** no entries. **Middle:** no entries. **L. Heavy:** *final:* M. Redhead (New Astley) w pts S. Mann (Sudbury). **Heavy:** *final:* S. Smith (Hurstlea & Kerridge) wo. **S. Heavy:** no entries.

Eastern Counties Semi-Finals & Finals   Corn Exchange, Bury St Edmunds - 25 January
L. Fly: *final:* F. Norton (New Astley) wo. **Fly:** no entries. **Bantam:** *final:* T. Brocklebank (Canvey) wo. **Feather:** *final:* D. Dainty (Canvey) wo. **Light:** *final:* M. Hawthorne (Lowestoft) w pts D. Smith (Canvey). **L. Welter:** *semi-finals:* J. Taylor (Ipswich) wo, M. Saliu (Colchester) w pts R. Mann (Kingfisher); *final:* M. Saliu w pts J. Taylor. **Welter:** *semi-finals:* W. Asker (Bury St Edmunds) wo, D. Bruce (Belhus Park) w co 1 P. Gill (Chatteris); *final:* W. Asker w pts D. Bruce. **L. Middle:** *final:* R. Hadley (Canvey) w rsc 4 J. Lambert (Aylsham). **Middle:** *final:* D. Doyle (Belhus Park) w co 3 C. Saunders (Norwich City). **L. Heavy:** *final:* M. Quirey (Berry Boys) wo M. Redhead (New Astley). **Heavy:** J. Carrara (Norwich City) withdrew; *final:* S. Smith (Hurstlea & Kerridge) w rtd 5 A. Batista (Billericay). **S. Heavy:** *final:* P. Eastman (Kings Lynn) wo.

Home Counties

Bedfordshire, Hertfordshire & North Buckinghamshire & Oxfordshire, Berkshire & South Buckinghamshire Divisions Campus West, Welwyn Garden City - 10 December & Molin's Recreation Club, Saunderton - 25 Janaury
L. Fly: no entries. **Fly:** no entries. **Bantam:** *final:* M. Bell (Mo's) wo. **Feather:** *semi-finals:* D. Maher (Marlow) wo, S. Morgan (Farley) w pts L. Dibsdall (Wolvercote); *final:* D. Maher w pts S. Morgan. **Light:** *semi-finals:* P. Cremin (Luton Hightown) wo, A. Phaltis (Luton Hightown) w pts I Reading (Hitchin); *final:* P.

Cremin wo A. Phaltis. **L. Welter:** *semi-finals:* D. Curran (Luton Irish) w dis 3 M. Calvert (Stevenage), D. Holt (Farley) w pts I. Eldridge (Watford); *final:* D. Holt w pts D. Curran. **Welter:** *final:* S. Thind (Bedford) w pts A. Smith (Watford). **L. Middle:** *final:* E. Randall (Bushey) wo. **Middle:** *final:* B. Bangher (Bedford) w rsc 3 D. Moore (Stevenage). **L. Heavy:** *final:* I. Khumalo (Chesham) w co 3 R. Baptiste (Lewsey). **Heavy:** *semi-finals:* M. Godfrey (Hitchin) wo, B. Stevens (Pinewood Starr) w pts P. Reading (Hitchin); *final:* B. Stevens w pts M. Godfrey. **S. Heavy:** no entries.

Eastern Counties v Home Counties

Molin's Recreation Club, Saunderton - 1 February
L. Fly: F. Norton (New Astley) wo. **Fly:** no entries. **Bantam:** T. Brocklebank (Canvey) w pts M. Bell (Mo's). **Feather:** D. Maher (Marlow) w pts D. Dainty (Canvey). **Light:** M. Hawthorne (Lowestoft) w rsc 5 P. Cremin (Luton Hightown). **L. Welter:** D. Holt (Farley) w pts M. Saliu (Colchester). **Welter:** S. Thind (Bedford) w pts W. Asker (Bury St Edmunds). **L. Middle:** R. Hadley (Canvey) w pts E. Randall (Bushey). **Middle:** D. Doyle (Belhus Park) w pts B. Bangher (Bedford). **L. Heavy:** M. Quirey (Berry Boys) w rsc 1 I. Khumalo (Chesham). **Heavy:** B. Stevens (Pinewood Starr) w dis 5 S. Smith (Hurstlea & Kerridge). **S. Heavy:** P. Eastman (Kings Lynn) wo.

Western Counties v Eastern Counties / Home

Counties

The Pavilion, Exmouth - 8 February
L. Fly: F. Norton (New Astley) wo. **Fly:** D. Barriball (Launceston) wo. **Bantam:** T. Brocklebank (Canvey) wo. **Feather:** S. Gawron (Devonport) w pts D. Maher (Marlow). **Light:** M. Hawthorne (Lowestoft) w rsc 1 R. Scutt (Sydenham). **L. Welter:** S. Lucas (Walcot) w pts D. Holt (Farley). **Welter:** S. Thind (Bedford) w pts J. Turley (Penhill RBL). **L. Middle:** A. Derrick (Taunton) w pts R. Hadley (Canvey). **Middle:** D. Doyle (Belhus Park) w pts D. Holder (Gloucester). **L. Heavy:** P. Rogers (Penhill RBL) w rsc 4 M. Quirey (Berry Boys). **Heavy:** B. Stevens (Pinewood Starr) w pts P. Lewis (Taunton). **S. Heavy:** N. Kendall (Apollo) w co 3 P. Eastman (Kings Lynn).

English ABA Semi-Finals & Finals

Cocks Moors Woods Leisure Centre, Birmingham - 17 February, HMS Nelson, Portsmouth - 18 February, & National Indoor Arena, Birmingham - 5 March
L. Fly *semi-finals:* F. Norton (New Astley) wo, I. Napa (Crown & Manor) w pts A. Odud (Birmingham); *final:* I. Napa w pts F. Norton. **Fly:** *semi-finals:* M. Hunter (Hartlepool BW) w rsc 2 M. Donaghue (Lion), N. Bell (Brighton) w pts D. Barriball (Launceston); *final:* M. Hunter w rsc 2 N. Bell. **Bantam:** *semi-finals:* S. Oates (Repton) w pts G. Payne (Bell Green), L. Pattison (Hunslet) w pts T. Brocklebank (Canvey); *final:* S. Oates w pts L. Pattison. **Feather:** *semi-finals:* S. Bell (Louvolite) w rsc 5 D. Dugan (Army), M. Walsh (Portsmouth University) w pts S. Gawron (Devonport); *final:* S. Bell w rsc 3 M. Walsh. **Light:** *semi-finals:* R. Rutherford (Bell Green) w pts D. Williams (Army), M. Hawthorne (Lowestoft) w rsc 3 E. Roberts (Gemini); *final:* M. Hawthorne w pts R. Rutherford. **L. Welter:** *semi-finals:* M. Hall

(Darlington) w pts D. Holt (Farley) - replaced S. Lucas (Walcot), R. Hatton (Sale West) w rsc 2 G. Reid (Shrewsbury); *final:* R. Hatton w pts M. Hall. **Welter:** *semi-finals:* F. Barrett (Trojan) w pts N. Philpott (Leigh Park), T. Smith (Handsworth) wo S. Thind (Bedford); *final:* F. Barrett w pts T. Smith. **L. Middle:** *semi-finals:* C. Bessey (Army) w rsc 5 A. Derrick (Taunton), M. Jones (Gemini) w pts A. Gilbert (Crawley) - replaced A. Coates (Medway GG); *final:* C. Bessey w pts M. Jones. **Middle:** *semi-finals:* J. Twite (Triumph) w pts P. Campbell (Balham), I. Cooper (Hartlepool BW) w pts D. Doyle (Belhus Park); *final:* I. Cooper w pts J. Twite. **L. Heavy:** *semi-finals:* P. Rogers (Penhill RBL) w pts M. Thompson (Spennymoor), M. Krence (St Michael's) w pts L. Cuddy (Campion Transport); *final:* P. Rogers w dis 4 P. Krence. **Heavy:** *semi-finals:* B. Stevens (Pinewood Starr) w pts K. Duke (Sunderland), T. Oakey (Leigh Park) w pts D. Kehoe (Gemini); *final:* B. Stevens w pts T. Oakey. **S. Heavy:** *semi-finals:* A. Harrison (Repton) w pts G. McGhin (Sunderland), N. Kendall (Apollo) w rsc 2 D. McCafferty (Kettering); *final:* A. Harrison w rsc 1 N. Kendall.

Steven Bell, the 1997 ABA featherweight champion.

Les Clark

Francis Barrett (right), formerly an Irish Olympian and now boxing for Trojan ABC, won the ABA welter title with a points win over Tim Smith

Les Clark

Irish Championships, 1996-97

Senior Tournament

The National Stadium, Dublin - 21 & 28 February & 7 March
L. Fly: *semi-finals:* J. Prior (Darndale, Dublin) wo, J. Rooney (Star, Belfast) w co 2 G. McManus (Immaculata, Belfast); *final:* J. Rooney w pts J. Prior. **Fly:** *semi-finals:* D. Hosford (Greenmount, Cork) w pts M. Murphy (St Paul's, Waterford), L. Cunningham (Saints, Belfast) w pts K. Moore (St Francis, Limerick); *final:* L. Cunningham w pts D. Hosford. **Bantam:** *semi-finals:* D. McKenna (Holy Family, Belfast) w pts N. Hazlett (St Brigid's, Dublin), D. Kelly (Holy Trinity, Belfast) w pts W. Valentine (St Saviour's, Dublin); *final:* D. Kelly w pts D. McKenna. **Feather:** *quarter-finals:* P. O'Donnell (Dockers, Belfast) wo, R. Kane (Bishop Kelly, Omagh) wo, M. Prunty (Portmarnock, Dublin) w pts D. Lowry (Albert Foundry, Belfast), A. Carlyle (Sacred Heart, Dublin) w pts J. Conlon (Holy Family, Belfast); *semi-finals:* P. O'Donnell w pts R. Kane, A. Carlyle w pts M. Prunty; *final:* P. O'Donnell w pts A. Carlyle. **Light:** *prelims:* N. Monteith (Dockers, Belfast) wo, P. Conlon (Holy Trinity, Belfast) wo, M. Hobbs (Arklow, Wicklow) wo, T. Carlyle (Sacred Heart, Dublin) wo, S. Redmond (St Luke's, Dublin) wo, E. McEneaney (Dealgan, Louth) wo, A. Maher (Crumlin, Dublin) wo, D. Barrett (Rylane, Cork) w pts P. Whelan (Neilstown, Dublin); *quarter finals:* N. Monteith w rsc 4 P. Conlon, M. Hobbs w pts T. Carlyle, D. Barrett w pts S. Redmond, E. McEneaney w pts A. Maher; *semi-finals:* D. Barrett w pts M. Hobbs, E. McEneaney w pts N. Monteith; *final:* E. McEneaney w pts D. Barrett; *final:* E. McEneaney w pts D. Barrett. **L. Welter:** *quarter-finals:* J. Morrissey (Sunnyside, Cork) w pts O. Montague (Dockers, Belfast), P. Walsh (St Colman's, Cork) w pts M. Sweeney (Crumlin, Dublin), S. Cowman (St Paul's, Waterford) w pts M. Kelly (Dealgan, Louth), G. McClarnon (Holy Family, Belfast) w pts M. Wickham (St Anthony's/St Patrick's, Wexford); *semi-finals:* P. Walsh w pts J. Morrisey, G. McClarnon w pts S. Cowman; *final:* G. McClarnon w pts P. Walsh. **Welter:** *quarter-finals:* N. Gough (St Paul's, Waterford) wo, S. Barrett (Rylane, Cork) w pts R. Murray (St Matthew's, Belfast), W. Cowan (Monkstown, Belfast) w pts M. Blaney (Holy Trinity, Belfast), F. Barrett (Olympic, Galway) w pts S. Spence (Holy Family, Belfast); *semi-finals:* N. Gough w pts S. Barrett, W. Cowan w pts F. Barrett; *final:* N. Gough w pts W. Cowan. **L. Middle:** *Prelims:* J. Kelly (Manorhamilton, Leitrim) wo, S. Keeler (St Saviour's, Dublin) wo, M. Roche (Sunnyside, Cork) wo, R. Brannigan (Dockers, Belfast) wo, T. Shehan (St Michael's, Athy) w pts F. Webb (Holy Trinity, Belfast), E. Fisher (Holy Trinity, Belfast) w pts B. Geraghty (Crumlin, Dublin), T. Fitzgerald (Ballyvolane, Cork) w pts B. Kerr (Lisburn, Antrim), F. O'Brien (Ballyduff, Kerry) w pts R. Heagney (Mark Heagney, Cookstown); *quarter-finals:* J. Kelly w pts S. Keeler, M. Roche w pts R. Brannigan, E. Fisher w pts T. Shehan, T. Fitzgerald w pts F. O'Brien; *semi-finals:* M. Roche w pts J. Kelly, T. Fitzgerald w pts E. Fisher; *final:* M. Roche w pts T. Fitzgerald. **Middle:** *quarter-finals:* C. Surugiu (Drimnagh, Dublin) wo, B. Magee (Holy Trinity, Belfast) w pts A. Kelly (Brosna, Offaly), T. Donnelly (Mark Heagney, Cookstown) w pts R. Fox (Phibsboro, Dublin), D. Galvin (St Saviour's, Dublin) w rsc 4 P. Dunne (Phibsboro, Dublin); *semi-finals:* B. Magee w rsc 5 T. Donnelly, C. Surugiu w pts D. Galvin; *final:* B. Magee w pts C. Surugiu. **L. Heavy:** *quarter-finals:* S. Kirk (Cairn Lodge, Belfast) wo, S. Dawson (Crumlin, Dublin) wo, A. Sheerin (Swinford, Mayo) w rsc 4 M. Fallon (Trojan, London), S. Lawlor (Grangecon, Kildare) w pts J. O'Leary (Rylane, Cork); *semi-finals:* S. Kirk w rsc 3 S. Dawson, A. Sheerin w rsc 3 S. Lawlor; *final:* S. Kirk w pts A. Sheerin.

Heavy: *quarter-finals:* J. Clancy (Phoenix, Dublin) wo, A. McGee (Trim, Meath) w rsc 3 T. Corcoran (Brosna, Offaly), J. Kiely (Limerick/Corpus Christi, Limerick) w rsc 2 P. Doran (Phibsboro, Dublin), H. McNally (Randalstown, Antrim) w rsc 3 J. Gildea (Donegal Town, Donegal); *semi-finals:* J. Clancy w rsc 2 A. McGee, J. Kiely w pts H. McNally; *final:* J. Kiely w pts J. Clancy. **S. Heavy:** *prelims:* D. Ward (Ballymun, Dublin) wo, S. Murphy (St Michael's, Wexford) wo, S. Reynolds (St Joseph's, Sligo) wo, D. Greene (Trim, Meath) wo, B. Kirrane (Limerick/Corpus Christi, Limerick) wo, D. Redmond (Austin Rover, Birmingham) wo, T. Clare (Buncrana, Donegal) wo, J. Kinsella (Crumlin, Dublin) w rsc 4 D. Horan (Dunboyne, Meath); *quarter-finals:* D. Ward w pts S. Murphy, S. Reynolds w rsc 3 D. Greene, B. Kirrane w pts D. Redmond, T. Clare w pts J. Kinsella; *semi-finals:* S. Reynolds w pts D. Ward, B. Kirrane w rsc 5 T. Clare; *final:* S. Reynolds w pts B. Kirrane.

Intermediate Finals

The National Stadium, Dublin - 6 December
L. Fly: J. Rooney (Star, Belfast) w rsc 3 M. Rodgers (Rosses, Donegal). **Fly:** A. McGahon (Togher, Louth) w rsc 2 G. Ryan (Liscarroll, Cork). **Bantam:** N. Hazlett (St Brigid's, Dublin) w pts M. Burke (Gorey, Wexford). **Feather:** M. Prunty (Portmarnock, Dublin) w pts R. Kane (Bishop Kelly, Omagh). **Light:** P. O'Donnell (Dockers, Belfast) w pts L. McLoughlin (Ring, Derry). **L. Welter:** P. McCloskey (St Canice's, Derry) w pts J. Harkin (Dunfanaghy, Donegal). **Welter:** J. Keohane (Dungarvan, Waterford) w pts D. Conlon (Lough Glynn, Roscommon). **L. Middle:** F. O'Brien (Ballyduff, Kerry) w pts K. Whelan (St Saviour's, Dublin, and Crystal, Waterford). **Middle:** P. Smyth (Keady, Armagh) w pts S. McHale (St Joseph's, Sligo). **L. Heavy:** P. Breathnach (Rosmuc/Camus, Galway) w pts S. O'Grady (St Saviour's, Dublin). **Heavy:** T. Crampton (St Broughan's, Offaly) w pts P. Byrne (Swinford, Mayo). **S. Heavy:** S. Reynolds (St Joseph's, Sligo) w pts J. White (St Pat's, Newry).

Junior Finals

The National Stadium, Dublin - 25 April
L. Fly: H. Cunningham (South Belfast) w pts D. Campbell (Glin, Dublin). **Fly:** B. Dunne (CIE, Dublin) w rsc 1 J. O'Neill (Golden Cobra, Dublin). **Bantam:** J. Chishum (Greenmount, Cork) w pts J. P. Campbell (South Meath, Meath). **Feather:** A. Carlyle (Sacred Heart, Dublin) w pts E. Gillen (Antrim). **Light:** O. Kelly (Loughglynn, Roscommon) w pts K. Clifford (Grangecon, Kildare). **L. Welter:** P. Stephens (CIE, Dublin) w rsc 4 J. McDonagh (Galway). **Welter:** C. Carmichael (Holy Trinity, Belfast) w pts P. Colgan (Avona, Dublin). **L. Middle:** M. Lee (Oughterard, Galway) w pts I. Timms (Quarryvale, Dublin). **Middle:** T. Sheahan (St Michael's, Athy) w pts M. McAllister (Dockers, Belfast). **L. Heavy:** P. Sharkey (Rosses, Donegal) w pts S. Reddy (Arklow, Wicklow). **Heavy:** C. McMonagle (Letterkenny, Donegal) w rsc 2 S. Breathnach (Rosmuc/Camus, Galway).

Irish Senior Titles: Record Wins

10: Jim O'Sullivan, 1980-1990. **9:** Gerry O'Colmain, 1943-1952; Harry Perry, 1952-1962. **8:** Mick Dowling, 1968-1975; Ernie Smyth, 1932-1940. **7:** Jack Chase, 1926-1932; Jim McCourt, 1963-1972; Billy Walsh, 1983-1991.

Scottish and Welsh Senior Championships, 1996-97

Scotland

Monklands Time Capsule, Coatbridge - 1 & 21 March, Fairfield Club, Glasgow - 10 March & Hydro Hotel, Dunblane - 14 March

L. Fly: *final:* C McLean (Barn) wo. **Fly:** *final:* R. Laing (Haddington) w rsc 1 P. Robertson (Sparta). **Bantam:** *semi-finals:* C. Docherty (Bellahouston) w pts B. Hawthorne (Port Glasgow), P. Shepherd (Sparta) w pts P. Muir (Meadowbank); *final:* P. Shepherd w pts C. Docherty. **Feather:** *semi-finals:* A. Arthur (Leith Victoria) w pts H. McCutcheon (North West), R. Silverstein (Selkirk) w rsc 2 S. Bartlett (Elgin); *final:* A. Arthur w pts R. Silverstein. **Light:** *quarter-finals:* J. Coyle (Bannockburn) wo, S. Hay (Barn) w rsc 3 J. Keatings (Cambusnethan), M. Gowans (Selkirk) w pts R. Snaith (Haddington), C. Naichman (Denbeath) w co 3 P. Roy (Elgin); *semi-finals:* J. Coyle w pts S. Hay, C. Naichman w pts M. Gowans; *final:* J. Coyle w pts C. Naichman. **L. Welter:** *quarter-finals:* G. McLevy (Clydeview) wo, K. McIntyre (Paisley) w pts G. Fernie (Bonnyrigg), J. Howett (St Francis) w pts W. Leckie (Haddington), P. Evans (Barn) w pts D. Hendry (Port Glasgow); *semi-finals:* G. McLevy w pts K. McIntyre, J. Howett w pts P. Evans; *final:* G. McLevy w pts J. Howett. **Welter:** *quarter-finals:* C. McNeill (Springhill) wo, T. Kennedy (Barn) wo, L. Sharp (Leith Victoria) wo, P. Munro (Astoria) w pts L. Smith (Aberdeen); *semi-finals:* C. McNeill w rsc 2 T. Kennedy, L. Sharp w pts P. Munro; *final:* C. McNeill w pts L. Sharp. **L. Middle:** *quarter-finals:* L. Murphy (Forgewood) wo, A. Wolecki (St Francis) wo, S. Fallon (Camelon) wo, P. Court (Springhill) w pts M. Black (Chirnside); *semi-finals:* A. Wolecki w rsc 2 S. Fallon, P. Court w pts L. Murphy; *final:* P. Court w pts A. Wolecki. **Middle:** *prelims:* D. Feeney (Phoenix) wo, B. Laidlaw (Cardenden) wo, W. Clark (Denbeath) wo, J. Day (Pride) wo, J. Gillon (Forgewood) wo, A. Howett (St Francis) wo, A. Keddie (Kincorth) w pts J. Gilhaney (Cleland), A. Foster (Blantyre) w pts M. Fleming (Kingdom); *quarter-finals:* D. Feeney w pts B. Laidlaw, W. Clark w pts J. Day, J. Gillon w rsc 2 A. Howett, A. Foster w pts A. Keddie; *semi-finals:* J. Gillon w rsc 2 W. Clark, A. Foster wo D. Feeney; *final:* A. Foster w pts J. Gillon. **L. Heavy:** *quarter-finals:* L. Ramsay (Kingdom) wo, A. Fleming (Kingdom) w pts P. Grainger (Sparta), D. Hamilton (Sparta) w pts A. Barron (Elgin), A. Kelly (Meadowbank) w rsc 1 K. Martin (Wellmeadow); *semi-finals:* D. Hamilton w rsc 3 A. Fleming, L. Ramsay w pts A. Kelly; *final:* L. Ramsay w pts D. Hamilton. **Heavy:** *semi-finals:* W. Cane (Four Isles) wo, P. Geddes (Elgin) w pts B. McFadden (Bannockburn); *final:* P. Geddes w pts W. Cane. **S. Heavy:** *semi-finals:* J. Cowie (Bannockburn) w pts K. Gault (Port Glasgow), K. Cummings (Kirkintilloch) w rsc 3 F. Smith (Springhill); *final:* J. Cowie w pts K. Cummings.

Wales

The Afan Lido, Port Talbot - 8 February, Holme View Leisure Centre, Barry - 23 February, Bay View Centre, Port Talbot - 28 February, & The Welsh Institute of Sport, Cardiff - 13 March

L. Fly: no entries. **Fly:** *final:* D. Hayde (Splott Adventure) wo. **Bantam:** *final:* N. Probert (Pembroke) wo. **Feather:** *semi-finals:* W. Connors (Splott Adventure) w rsc 3 L. Jones (Gilfach Goch), J. Edwards (Flax) w co 1 L. Walsh (St Joseph's East); *final:* W. Connors w pts J. Edwards. **Light:** *semi-finals:* P. Dennis (Aberkenfig) w pts P. Williams (Bangor), V. Powell (Army) w rsc 2 K. Evans (Newtown); *final:* V. Powell w co 3 P. Dennis. **L. Welter:** *quarter-finals:* T. Meli (Carmarthen) wo, M. Allison (Whitland) wo, M. Woodward (Highfield) w pts R. Williams (Aberaman), A. Evans (Carmarthen) w rsc 2 C. Brophy (Premier); *semi-finals:* T. Meli w rsc 2 M. Allison, A. Evans w co 1 M. Woodward; *final:* A. Evans w co 5 T. Meli. **Welter:** *quarter-finals:* C. Maddocks .(Llay) w pts J. Clark (Duffryn), D. Edwards (Aberkenfig) w co 2 C. Hughes (Bangor), A. Smith (Highfield) w pts K. Thomas (Pontypridd), J. Williams (Gwent) w pts R. Weston (Splott Adventure); *semi-finals:* A. Smith wo J. Williams, C. Maddocks w rsc 4 D. Edwards; *final:* A. Smith w pts C. Maddocks. **L. Middle:** *semi-finals:* F. Sparano (Splott Adventure) w pts J. Cheal (Whitland), K. Short (Aberkenfig) w pts M. Gammer (Pembroke); *final:* K. Short w rtd 4 F. Sparano. **Middle:** *prelims:* N. Pearce (Splott Adventure) wo, M. Hiscock (Cwmavon) wo, D. Haines (Whitland) wo, K. Shucker (Newtown) wo, S. Pepperall (Vale) wo, L. Lewis (Pembroke) wo, S. Mattan (Highfield) wo, G. Williams (Gilfach Goch) w pts M. Phillips (Carmarthen); *quarter-finals:* N. Pearce w rsc 4 M. Hiscock, D. Haines w rsc 1 K. Shucker, S. Pepperall w pts L. Lewis, S. Mattan w pts C. Williams; *semi-finals:* S. Pepperall w rsc 3 S. Mattan, D. Haines w pts N. Pearce; *final:* S. Pepperall w pts D. Haines. **L. Heavy:** *quarter-finals:* S. Donaldson (Highfield) wo, A. Irvine (Cwmavon) wo, M. McAuley (Pontypridd) wo, H. Williams (Newtown) w pts M. Tolton (Cwmavon); *semi-finals:* S. Donaldson w dis 2 A. Irvine, M. McAuley w pts H. Williams; *final:* S. Donaldson w pts M. McAuley. **Heavy:** *semi-finals:* S. Gammer (Pembroke) w pts J. Smith (Highfield), K. Evans (Carmarthen) w rsc 2 G. Davies (Gilfach Goch); *final:* K. Evans w pts S. Gammer. **S. Heavy:** *final:* K. McCormack (Royal Marines) wo.

Vince Powell (Army), the 1997 Welsh lightweight champion   Les Clark

British and Irish International Matches and Championships, 1996-97

Internationals

Wales (5) v Ireland (5)   The Ritzy Nightclub, Swansea - 15 October
(Welsh names first): **Feather:** J. Edwards l rsc 3 T. Carlyle, A. Dummer l pts J. Conlon. **Welter:** C. Thomas l pts M. Blaney, M. Gammer l rsc 3 F. Barrett. **L. Middle:** K. Short w rsc 2 S. Gibson, D. Williams w pts F. Webb. **Middle:** D. Haines w pts A. Kelly. **L. Heavy:** S. Thomas l rsc 2 S. Collier. **Heavy:** S. Gammer w rsc 2 P. Deane, J. Smith w pts J. Kiely.

Ireland (4) v Sweden (6)   National Stadium, Dublin - 15 November
(Irish names first): **Bantam:** D. McKenna w pts D. Olsson. **Feather:** T. Carlyle l pts J. H. Larbi. **L. Welter:** J. Morrissey l rsc 3 T. Semakala, M. Dillon l pts T. Acar. **Welter:** N. Gough w co 1 J. Antman, S. Barrett l pts A. Khattab. **L. Heavy:** A. Sheerin w pts S. Gasper, T. Donnelly l pts J. Karzoumi. **Heavy:** P. Deane w pts J. Applegren, C. O'Grady l rtd 1 R. Mukiibi.

England (2) v America (5)   Hilton Hotel, London - 18 November
(English names first): **L. Fly:** I. Napa w pts B. Martinez. **Light:** K. Wing l co 3 D. Jackson. **L. Welter:** C. Wall l pts L. Shepherd. **L. Middle:** C. Bessey w pts B. Lewis. **Middle:** D. Rhodes l pts R. Wells. **L. Heavy:** P. Rogers l rsc 1 L. Young. **Heavy:** T. Oakey l pts C. Brock.

Scotland (3) v England (7)   Civic Centre, Motherwell - 7 December
(Scottish names first): **Bantam:** R. Laing w rsc 3 J. Hegney. **Feather:** D. Campbell l pts M. Walsh. **Light:** D. Stewart w pts R. Beck. **L. Welter:** G. McLevy l pts D. Walker, K. McIntyre l rsc 1 R. Hatton. **Welter:** C. McNeill w pts T. Cesay. **L. Middle:** A. Wolecki l pts A. Page. **Middle:** J. Daley l rsc 1 J. Pearce. **L. Heavy:** L. Ramsey l pts M. Thompson. **Heavy:** W. Cane l pts T. Oakey.

Scotland (4) v Wales (4)   Stakis Earl Grey Hotel, Dundee - 17 December
(Scottish names first): **Fly:** R. Laing w pts D. Fox. **Light:** J. Coyle l pts V. Powell. **L. Welter:** K. McIntyre w pts C. Maddocks, J. Howett w co 1 J. Gethin. **Welter:** T. Cunningham l pts F. Borg. **L. Middle:** A. Wolecki l pts K. Short. **Middle:** A. Howett w pts G. Williams. **S. Heavy:** D. McCafferty l pts K. McCormack.

England (5) v Denmark (6)   Horsens, Denmark - 19 December
(English names first): **Bantam:** D. Vlasman l pts M. Mollenberg. **Feather:** L. Eedle w pts R. Idrissi. **Light:** K. Bennett l pts M. Eraslan. **L. Welter:** C. Wall l pts A. Vester. **Welter:** R. Murray w rsc 4 J. Yrtoft, J. Khaliq l rtd 2 T. Damgaard. **L. Middle:** C. Bessey w pts C. Bladt, A. Page w pts M. Kessler. **L. Heavy:** M. Thompson w pts A. Lika. **Heavy:** T. Oakey l rsc 2 T. B. Thomsen, W. Barima l rtd 4 O. A. Nielsen.

England (2) v Denmark (4)   Odense, Denmark - 20 December
(English names first): **Bantam:** D. Vlasman l pts M. Mollenberg. **Feather:** L. Eedle l rsc 4 R. Idrissi. **Light:** K. Bennett l pts M. Eraslan. **Welter:** J. Khaliq w pts J. Yrtoft. **L. Middle:** A. Page l pts F. Nasir. **L. Heavy:** M. Thompson w pts A. Lika.

Wales (4) v Scotland (4)   Styles Nightclub, Queensferry - 23 January
(Welsh names first): **Bantam:** P. Crewe l pts C. Docherty. **Feather:** J. Edwards w rsc 2 R. Silverstein. **L. Welter:** C. Maddocks l pts K. McIntyre. **Welter:** A. Mitchell l rsc 1 C. McNeill. **L. Middle:** J. Clarke w co 1 P. Munro. **Middle:** S. Thomas w pts A. Howett. **L. Heavy:** D. Williams l rsc 3 J. Campbell. **S. Heavy:** S. Gammer w dis 3 J. Cowie.

Young England (3) v Young USA (3)   Royal Lancaster Hotel, London - 3 February
(English names first): **Fly:** S. Miller w pts R. Benitez. **Light:** A. Buchanan l pts L. Mosley. **L. Welter:** L. Maltby l rtd 2 K. Kemp.

Welter: G. Wake w pts R. Mason. **L. Middle:** A. Larkins w pts J. Johnson. **L. Heavy:** D. Short l rtd 1 A. Sarmiento.

Ireland (2) v Italy (4)   National Stadium, Dublin - 28 March
(Irish names first): **Bantam:** D. McKenna l pts G. Bergantino. **Feather:** A. Carlyle w pts P. Caoine. **L. Welter:** P. Walsh l pts C. Di Corcia. **Welter:** M. Wickham l pts A. Diurno. **L. Middle:** E. McEaney l pts A. Letizia. **Heavy:** J. Kiely w pts G. Mocerino.

England (3) v Austria (5)   Innsbruck, Austria - 11 April
(English names first): **Light:** R. Rutherford w pts G. Gadzie. **L. Welter:** M. Hall l co 2 A. Suteu. **Welter:** S. Kuchler. **L. Middle:** S. Whyte l pts H. Salzburger. **Middle:** J. Pearce w rsc 3 R. Moser. **L. Heavy:** C. Fry w pts H. Dominik, M. Krence l pts Z. Dimitrivjevic. **Heavy:** P. Anderson l pts A. Stragenegg.

Ireland (4) v Sweden (5)   Sundvall, Sweden - 14 April
(Irish names first): **L. Fly:** J. Rooney w pts A. Adaan. **Fly:** L. Cunningham l pts F. Mtabinwa. **Feather:** P. O'Donnell l pts J. H. Larbi, A. Carlyle w pts B. Bagdare. **Light:** E. McEaney w pts V. Wartanian. **L. Middle:** T. Fitzgerald w pts C. Abrahamson. **L. Heavy:** A. Sheerin l pts I. Karzoumi. **Heavy:** J. Clancy l pts K. Turkson. **S. Heavy:** S. Reynolds l pts T. Asklos.

Championships

World Juniors   Havana, Cuba - 3 to 10 November
Fly: J. Hegney (England) l pts E. Lutsker (Ukraine); C. Nash (Ireland) l pts R. Monsouri (Algeria). **Bantam:** J. Rooney (England) w pts S. Ekinci (Turkey), l pts O. Bobarnat (Romania). **Feather:** A. Carlyle (Ireland) w pts N. C. Hernandez (Colombia), w pts A. Santos (Mexico), l pts S. Digrazia (Italy). **Light:** M. Dillon (Ireland) w rsc 3 N. Saito (Japan), l pts T. Hakobiyan (Armenia); R. Beck (Ireland) w pts C. Brisson (Canada), l pts W. Blain (France). **L. Welter:** R. Hatton (England) w rsc 1 O. Nabaccie (Georgia), w pts G. Rivera (Cuba), w pts K. Kemp (USA), l pts T. Mergadze (Russia). **Middle:** A. Kelly (Ireland) w pts T. Johnson (USA), l pts M. Golovinznin (Ukraine).

European Juniors   Birmingham, England - 1 to 8 June
L. Fly: H. Cunningham (Ireland) w pts I. Tugulea (Moldova), l pts J. Thomas (France). **Fly:** D. Hayde (Wales) l pts R. Zhuravsky (Belarus); N. Cook (England) l pts K. Dzhamoloudinov (Russia); B. Dunne (Ireland) w pts R. Lundby (Sweden), l pts K. Dzhamoloudinov (Russia). **Bantam:** C. Docherty (Scotland) l pts M. Tamulis (Lithuania); J. Chisholm (Ireland) w pts V. Osipenko (Estonia), w pts B. Badarni (Israel), l pts S. Miller (England); S. Miller (England) w pts V. Pashkov (Belarus), w pts A. Baran (Turkey), w pts J. Chisholm (Ireland), w pts J. Hamalainen (Finland), l rsc 3 A. Shaiduline (Russia). **Feather:** B. Morrison (Scotland) w pts G. Vinciguerra (Italy), l rsc 4 F. Bouricha (France); A. Carlyle (Ireland) w rsc 5 L. Snober (Israel), w pts H. Torosyan (Armenia), l pts A. Kozlovsky (Russia); S. Burke (England) w pts V. Puiu (Romania), w pts N. Schuster (Germany), l pts A. Kozlovsky (Russia). **Light:** S. Smith (England) l pts O. Akdi (Turkey); C. Nachman (Scotland) l rsc 2 D. Taranta (Belarus); O. Kelly (Ireland) l rsc 4 V. Kasym (Moldova). **L. Welter:** A. Buchanan (England) w pts S. Bagirov (Azerbaijan); J. Hull (Wales) l pts D. Covaliciuk (Moldova); P. Stephens (Ireland) w pts M. Bicer (Turkey), w pts H. Mahroum (Israel), l pts A. Mishine (Russia). **Welter:** G. Wale (England) w pts G. Tsekvava (Russia), l pts D. Sartison (Germany). **L. Middle:** A. Larkins (England) l pts A. Catic (Germany); M. Lee (Ireland) w rsc 4 A. Movsesyan (Armenia), w pts M. Muntean (Moldova), w pts P. Kavaliauskas (Lithuania), l rsc 3 E. Kazantsev (Russia). **Middle:** B. Connell (Scotland) w pts T. Buric (Croatia), l pts M. Dean (England); M. Dean (England) w pts N. Borovcahin (Yugoslavia), w rsc 5 B. Connell, l co 1 G. Hidvegi (Hungary); T. Sheahan (Ireland) w pts R. Gerrits (Holland), l pts H. Kilic (Turkey). **L. Heavy:** T. Dodson (England) w co 2 Z. Lole (Hungary), l pts S. Kretschmann (Germany). **Heavy:** P. Pierson (England) w rsc 5 I. Klonis (Greece), w pts P. Dimovska (Macedonia), l rtd 1 A. Yatsenko (Ukraine).

British Junior Championship Finals, 1996-97

National Association of Boys' Clubs

Winter Gardens, Blackpool - 10 January

Class A: 42 kg: D. Cook (Hornchurch & Elm Park) w rtd 3 P. Murray (Marsh Lane). 45 kg: M. Maitchell (Darlington) w pts D. Langley (Hollington). 48 kg: D. Robson (Hartlepool Catholic) w co 2 S. Langley (Hollington). 51 kg: D. Hunt (Repton) w pts T. Hamill (All Saints). 54 kg: S. Mann (Benchill) w pts J. O'Reilly (Newham). 57 kg: S. Birch (St Helens) w pts R. Schofield (St Joseph's). 60 kg: M. Weatherhead (Dale) w pts R. Hughes (Hartlepool Boys Welfare). 63.5 kg: D. Holland (Tower Hill) w rsc 1 J. Venner (Saxon). 67 kg: P. McDermott (St Agnes) w rsc 2 J. Smith (Pinewood Starr). 71 kg: S. Price (Pinewood Starr) w pts S. McGuire (Lambton Street).

Cutler's Hall, Sheffield - 17 January

Class B: 45 kg: D. Hamill (All Saints) w pts S. Symes (West Hill). 48 kg: H. Cunningham (Saints) w pts T. Chapman (Newham). 51 kg: M. Power (St Pancras) w pts R. Nelson (Batley & Dewsbury). 54 kg: S. Truscott (South Bank) w pts M. Burke (Newham). 57 kg: P. Humphrey (New Astley) w co 2 T. Khan (Sedbergh). 60 kg: T. McDonagh (Collyhurst) w pts T. Stanhope (Lynn). 63.5 kg: M. Thirwell (Fisher Downside) w rsc 1 L. Hallett (Pleck). 67 kg: D. Cadman (Repton) w co 1 K. Concepcion (Belgrave). 71 kg: P. Gardner (Birtley) w pts L. King (Shepway). 74 kg: S. Mullins (Didcott) w pts N. Thompson (Wellington). 77 kg: T. Dodson (Gemini) wo D. Haye (Fitzroy Lodge).

Grosvenor House, London - 13 January

Class C: 48 kg: no entries. 51 kg: M. Hunter (Hartlepool Boys Welfare) w rsc 3 N. Cook (Hornchurch & Elm Park). 54 kg: W. Johnson (Desborough) w pts G. Steadman (West Ham). 57 kg: T. Rowley (Hartlepool Boys Welfare) w rtd 3 A. Lever (Newport Pagnell). 60 kg: L. Daws (Rosehill) w rsc 4 N. Wright (Shildon). 63.5 kg: S. Hodgson (Shildon) w pts M. Lomax (West Ham). 67 kg: A. Farnell (Collyhurst & Moston) w rsc 4 J. Benson (Chadwell St Mary). 71 kg: N. Tidman (Bulkington) w pts A. Larkins (Bracknell). 75 kg: M. Dean (Long Lane) w rsc 4 S. Lee (West Ham). 81 kg: P. Souter (Newham) w pts W. Reid (Willenhall). 91 kg: T. Foy (Belhus Park) wo T. Ahmad (Venture).

Schools

Aston Villa Leisure Centre, Birmingham - 22 March

Junior A: 32 kg: N. McDonald (West Wirral) w pts B. Burns (Devonport). 34 kg: M. Stead (Darlington) w pts T. McCarthy (Newham). 36 kg: M. Meads (Old Vic) w pts T. Marshall (Devonport). 39 kg: D. Lawrence (Northolt) w pts L. Bottom (RHP). 42 kg: L. Grice (Doncaster Plant) w pts R. Smith (Newham). 45 kg: E. Ives (Medway Golden Gloves) w rsc 3 J. Thompson (Sunderland). 48 kg: M. Grant (New Enterprise) w pts J. Bottom (RHP). 51 kg: J. Sweeney (Trojan Police) w pts K. Connelly (Collyhurst & Moston). 54 kg: no entires. 57 kg: A. Gibbens (Bognor) w pts S. Blackburn (Tower Hill).

Junior B: 36 kg: D. Lanigan (Mottram & Hattersley) w pts B. Dodd (Hornchurch & Elm Park). 39 kg: J. Shotter (West Ham) w pts T. Khan (Bradford Police). 42 kg: R. Barrett (Eltham) w pts J. Fletcher (Karmand Centre). 45 kg: A. Gardner (Medway Golden Gloves) w pts M. Kilroy (Keighley). 48 kg: G. Brotherton (Newbiggin Dolphin) w pts W. Killick (Marvels Lane). 51 kg: L. Pointing (Princess Royal) w pts L. Cadman (Repton). 54 kg: P. Smith (Rotunda) w rsc 3 A. Hatrey (Devonport). 57 kg: C. Pratt (Bracknell) w pts A. Sherwood (Aldercar & Langley). 60 kg: J. Bateman (Princess Royal) w pts S. Coughlan (Northolt). 63 kg: D. Teasdale (Unity) w rsc 1 R. Doroba (Kingfisher). 66 kg: S. Denham (Aycliffe) w dis 1 A. Squires (New Astley).

Intermediate: 39 kg: S. MacDonald (St Joseph's) w pts D. Lambert (Karmand Centre). 42 kg: C. Lyon (Wigan) w pts E. Hewlett (Hollington). 45 kg: M. Moran (Golden Gloves) wo K. Tiller (Hornchurch & Elm Park). 48 kg: R. Ecclestone (Gemini) w pts M. Coveney (West Ham). 51 kg: J. Stewart (Lynn) w pts F. Fehintola (Karmand Centre). 54 kg: L. Beavis (Dale) w pts T. Fletcher (Karmand Centre). 57 kg: M. O'Donnell (Dale) w pts L. Ryan (Coleshill). 60 kg: R. Murray (Newbiggin Dolphin) w pts K. Groves (Alma). 63 kg: D. Spensley (Shildon) w pts M. Corcoran (East Ham Boleyn). 66 kg: J. Varney (Karmand Centre) w dis 3 J. McDonagh (Wolvercote). 69 kg: K. Wilkinson (Focus) w rsc 1 J. Culshaw (Doncaster Plant).

Senior: 42 kg: D. Cook (Hornchurch & Elm Park) w rsc 2 D. O'Grady (Fox). 45 kg: M. Maitchell (Darlington) w rsc 2 N. May (Newham). 48 kg: D. Robson (Hartlepool Catholic Boys) w pts J. Convey (St Mary's). 51 kg: J. Garforth (Batley & Dewsbury) w pts M. Zaman (Newham). 54 kg: S. Truscott (South Bank) w pts J. O'Reilly (Newham). 57 kg: M. Concepcion (Belgrave) w pts S. O'Donnell (Dale). 60 kg: M. Weatherhead (Dale) w pts T. McDonagh (Collyhurst & Moston). 63.5 kg: D. Smith (Partington) w rsc 2 M. Welsh (Swanley). 67 kg: B. Wood (Pleck) w pts A. Barrett (Newham). 71 kg: M. Briggs (Tower Hill) w pts C. Cartwright (Fisher Downside). 75 kg: S. Price (Pinewood Starr) w rsc 1 A. Khan (Unity).

ABA Youth

Fox Hollies Leisure Centre, Birmingham - 12 April

Class 5 (born 1980): 42 kg: no entries. 45 kg: S. Symes (West Hill) wo J. Coffey (Lewsey). 48 kg: D. Robinson (Parks) w pts J. Convey (St Mary's). 51 kg: T. Chapman (Newham) w pts G. Wilshaw (Brownhills) – replaced R. Nelson (Batley & Dewsbury). 54 kg: S. Truscott (South Bank) w pts N. Booth (Walsall Wood). 57 kg: P. Humphrey (New Astley) w co 1 D. Wyatt (Golden Ring). 60 kg: T. McDonagh (Collyhurst & Moston) w pts S. Rushton (Penhill RBL). 63.5 kg: A. Buchanan (Birtley) w pts L. Delaney (Dale). 67 kg: D. Cadman (Repton) w rsc 1 B. Jackson (Sacred Heart). 71 kg: P. Gardner (Birtley) w pts M. Briggs (Tower Hill). 75 kg: J. Smith (Empire) wo S. Mullins (Didcot). 81 kg: T. Dodson (Gemini) w dis 2 S. Clay (Rugeley Police). 91 kg: no entries.

Class 6 (born 1979): 45 kg: no entries. 48 kg: no entries. 51 kg: N. Cook (Hornchurch & Elm Park) w rsc 2 I. Snowling (Halstead). 54 kg: S. Miller (St Paul's) w pts D. Mulholland (Transport). 57 kg: S. Burke (Salisbury) w rsc 1 L. O'Reilly (St Mary's). 60 kg: S. Smith (Repton) w pts N. Wright (Shildon). 63.5kg: S. Yates (Dawlish) w pts J. McKeever (Cavendish). 67 kg: G. Wake (Hunslet) w pts K. Mitchell (Camborne & Redruth). 71 kg: D. Kemp (Beccles) w pts W. Fleming (West Wirral). 75 kg: M. Dean (Long Lane) w pts L. Coates (Medway Golden Gloves). 81 kg: R. Walls (Sporting Ring) w pts J. Ainscough (Kirkdale). 91 kg: D. Dolan (Plains Farm) w pts P. Souter (Newham).

ABA Champions, 1881-1997

L. Flyweight
1971 M. Abrams
1972 M. Abrams
1973 M. Abrams
1974 C. Magri
1975 M. Lawless
1976 P. Fletcher
1977 P. Fletcher
1978 J. Dawson
1979 J. Dawson
1980 T. Barker
1981 J. Lyon
1982 J. Lyon
1983 J. Lyon
1984 J. Lyon
1985 M. Epton
1986 M. Epton
1987 M. Epton
1988 M. Cantwell
1989 M. Cantwell
1990 N. Tooley
1991 P. Culshaw
1992 D. Fifield
1993 M. Hughes
1994 G. Jones
1995 D. Fox
1996 R. Mercer
1997 I. Napa

I. Napa (Repton ABC), the 1997 ABA light-flyweight champion.   Les Clark

Flyweight
1920 H. Groves
1921 W. Cuthbertson
1922 E. Warwick
1923 L. Tarrant
1924 E. Warwick
1925 E. Warwick
1926 J. Hill
1927 J. Roland
1928 C. Taylor
1929 T. Pardoe
1930 T. Pardoe
1931 T. Pardoe
1932 T. Pardoe
1933 T. Pardoe
1934 P. Palmer
1935 G. Fayaud
1936 G. Fayaud
1937 P. O'Donaghue
1938 A. Russell
1939 D. McKay
1944 J. Clinton
1945 J. Bryce
1946 R. Gallacher
1947 J. Clinton
1948 H. Carpenter
1949 H. Riley
1950 A. Jones
1951 G. John
1952 D. Dower
1953 R. Currie
1954 R. Currie
1955 D. Lloyd
1956 T. Spinks
1957 R. Davies
1958 J. Brown
1959 M. Gushlow
1960 D. Lee
1961 W. McGowan
1962 M. Pye
1963 M. Laud
1964 J. McCluskey
1965 J. McCluskey
1966 P. Maguire
1967 S. Curtis
1968 J. McGonigle
1969 D. Needham
1970 D. Needham
1971 P. Wakefield
1972 M. O'Sullivan
1973 R. Hilton
1974 M. O'Sullivan
1975 C. Magri
1976 C. Magri
1977 C. Magri
1978 G. Nickels
1979 R. Gilbody
1980 K. Wallace
1981 K. Wallace
1982 J. Kelly
1983 S. Nolan
1984 P. Clinton
1985 P. Clinton
1986 J. Lyon
1987 J. Lyon
1988 J. Lyon
1989 J. Lyon
1990 J. Armour
1991 P. Ingle
1992 K. Knox
1993 P. Ingle
1994 D. Costello
1995 D. Costello
1996 D. Costello
1997 M. Hunter

Bantamweight
1884 A. Woodward
1885 A. Woodward
1886 T. Isley
1887 T. Isley
1888 H. Oakman
1889 H. Brown
1890 J. Rowe
1891 E. Moore
1892 F. Godbold
1893 E. Watson
1894 P. Jones
1895 P. Jones
1896 P. Jones
1897 C. Lamb
1898 F. Herring
1899 A. Avent
1900 J. Freeman
1901 W. Morgan
1902 A. Miner
1903 H. Perry
1904 H. Perry
1905 W. Webb
1906 T. Ringer
1907 E. Adams
1908 H. Thomas
1909 J. Condon
1910 W. Webb
1911 W. Allen
1912 W. Allen
1913 A. Wye
1914 W. Allen
1919 W. Allen
1920 G. McKenzie
1921 L. Tarrant
1922 W. Boulding
1923 A. Smith
1924 L. Tarrant
1925 A. Goom
1926 F. Webster
1927 E. Warwick
1928 J. Garland
1929 F. Bennett
1930 H. Mizler
1931 F. Bennett
1932 J. Treadaway
1933 G. Johnston
1934 A. Barnes
1935 L. Case
1936 A. Barnes
1937 A. Barnes
1938 J. Pottinger
1939 R. Watson
1944 R. Bissell
1945 P. Brander
1946 C. Squire
1947 D. O'Sullivan
1948 T. Profitt
1949 T. Miller
1950 K. Lawrence
1951 T. Nicholls
1952 T. Nicholls
1953 J. Smillie
1954 J. Smillie
1955 G. Dormer
1956 O. Reilly
1957 J. Morrissey
1958 H. Winstone
1959 D. Weller
1960 F. Taylor
1961 P. Benneyworth
1962 P. Benneyworth
1963 B. Packer
1964 B. Packer
1965 R. Mallon
1966 J. Clark
1967 M. Carter
1968 M. Carter
1969 M. Piner
1970 A. Oxley
1971 G. Turpin
1972 G. Turpin
1973 P. Cowdell
1974 S. Ogilvie
1975 S. Ogilvie
1976 J. Bambrick
1977 T. Turner
1978 J. Turner
1979 R. Ashton
1980 R. Gilbody
1981 P. Jones
1982 R. Gilbody
1983 J. Hyland
1984 J. Hyland
1985 S. Murphy
1986 S. Murphy
1987 J. Sillitoe
1988 K. Howlett
1989 K. Howlett
1990 P. Lloyd
1991 D. Hardie
1992 P. Mullings
1993 R. Evatt
1994 S. Oliver
1995 N. Wilders
1996 L. Eedle
1997 S. Oates

Featherweight
1881 T. Hill
1882 T. Hill
1883 T. Hill
1884 E. Hutchings
1885 J. Pennell
1886 T. McNeil
1887 J. Pennell
1888 J. Taylor
1889 G. Belsey
1890 G. Belsey
1891 F. Curtis
1892 F. Curtis
1893 T. Davidson
1894 R. Gunn
1895 R. Gunn
1896 R. Gunn
1897 N. Smith
1898 P. Lunn
1899 J. Scholes
1900 R. Lee
1901 C. Clarke
1902 C. Clarke
1903 J. Godfrey
1904 C. Morris
1905 H. Holmes
1906 A. Miner
1907 C. Morris
1908 T. Ringer
1909 A. Lambert
1910 C. Houghton
1911 H. Bowers
1912 G. Baker
1913 G. Baker
1914 G. Baker
1919 G. Baker
1920 J. Fleming
1921 G. Baker
1922 E. Swash
1923 E. Swash
1924 A. Beavis
1925 A. Beavis
1926 R. Minshull
1927 F. Webster
1928 F. Meachem
1929 F. Meachem
1930 J. Duffield
1931 B. Caplan
1932 H. Mizler
1933 J. Walters
1934 J. Treadaway
1935 E. Ryan
1936 J. Treadaway
1937 A. Harper
1938 C. Gallie
1939 C. Gallie
1944 D. Sullivan
1945 J. Carter
1946 P. Brander
1947 S. Evans
1948 P. Brander
1949 H. Gilliland
1950 P. Brander
1951 J. Travers

1952 P. Lewis
1953 P. Lewis
1954 D. Charnley
1955 T. Nicholls
1956 T. Nicholls
1957 M. Collins
1958 M. Collins
1959 G. Judge
1960 P. Lundgren
1961 P. Cheevers
1962 B. Wilson
1963 A. Riley
1964 R. Smith
1965 K. Buchanan
1966 H. Baxter
1967 K. Cooper
1968 J. Cheshire
1969 A. Richardson
1970 D. Polak
1971 T. Wright
1972 K. Laing
1973 J. Lynch
1974 G. Gilbody
1975 R. Beaumont
1976 P. Cowdell
1977 P. Cowdell
1978 M. O'Brien
1979 P. Hanlon
1980 M. Hanif
1981 P. Hanlon
1982 H. Henry
1983 P. Bradley
1984 K. Taylor
1985 F. Havard
1986 P. Hodkinson
1987 P. English
1988 D. Anderson
1989 P. Richardson
1990 B. Carr
1991 J. Irwin
1992 A. Temple
1993 J. Cook
1994 D. Pithie
1995 D. Burrows
1996 T. Mulholland
1997 S. Bell

Lightweight
1881 F. Hobday
1882 A. Bettinson
1883 A. Diamond
1884 A. Diamond
1885 A. Diamond
1886 G. Roberts
1887 J. Hair
1888 A. Newton
1889 W. Neale
1890 A. Newton
1891 E. Dettmer
1892 E. Dettmer
1893 W. Campbell
1894 W. Campbell
1895 A. Randall
1896 A. Vanderhout
1897 A. Vanderhout
1898 H. Marks
1899 H. Brewer
1900 G. Humphries
1901 A. Warner

1902 A. Warner
1903 H. Fergus
1904 M. Wells
1905 M. Wells
1906 M. Wells
1907 M. Wells
1908 H. Holmes
1909 F. Grace
1910 T. Tees
1911 A. Spenceley
1912 R. Marriott
1913 R. Grace
1914 R. Marriott
1919 F. Grace
1920 F. Grace
1921 G. Shorter
1922 G. Renouf
1923 G. Shorter
1924 W. White
1925 E. Viney
1926 T. Slater
1927 W. Hunt
1928 F. Webster
1929 W. Hunt
1930 J. Waples
1931 D. McCleave
1932 F. Meachem
1933 H. Mizler
1934 J. Rolland
1935 F. Frost
1936 F. Simpson
1937 A. Danahar
1938 T. McGrath
1939 H. Groves
1944 W. Thompson
1945 J. Williamson
1946 E. Thomas
1947 C. Morrissey
1948 R. Cooper
1949 A. Smith
1950 R. Latham
1951 R. Hinson
1952 F. Reardon
1953 D. Hinson
1954 G. Whelan
1955 S. Coffey
1956 R. McTaggart
1957 J. Kidd
1958 R. McTaggart
1959 P. Warwick
1960 R. McTaggart
1961 P. Warwick
1962 B. Whelan
1963 B. O'Sullivan
1964 J. Dunne
1965 A. White
1966 J. Head
1967 T. Waller
1968 J. Watt
1969 H. Hayes
1970 N. Cole
1971 J. Singleton
1972 N. Cole
1973 T. Dunn
1974 J. Lynch
1975 P. Cowdell
1976 S. Mittee
1977 G. Gilbody
1978 T. Marsh

1979 G. Gilbody
1980 G. Gilbody
1981 G. Gilbody
1982 J. McDonnell
1983 K. Willis
1984 A. Dickson
1985 E. McAuley
1986 J. Jacobs
1987 M. Ayers
1988 C. Kane
1989 M. Ramsey
1990 P. Gallagher
1991 P. Ramsey
1992 D. Amory
1993 B. Welsh
1994 A. Green
1995 R. Rutherford
1996 K. Wing
1997 M. Hawthorne

L. Welterweight
1951 W. Connor
1952 P. Waterman
1953 D. Hughes
1954 G. Martin
1955 F. McQuillan
1956 D. Stone
1957 D. Stone
1958 R. Kane
1959 R. Kane
1960 R. Day
1961 B. Brazier
1962 B. Brazier
1963 R. McTaggart
1964 R. Taylor
1965 R. McTaggart
1966 W. Hiatt
1967 B. Hudspeth
1968 E. Cole
1969 J. Stracey
1970 D. Davies
1971 M. Kingwell
1972 T. Waller
1973 N. Cole
1974 P. Kelly
1975 J. Zeraschi
1976 C. McKenzie
1977 J. Douglas
1978 D. Williams
1979 E. Copeland
1980 A. Willis
1981 A. Willis
1982 A. Adams
1983 D. Dent
1984 D. Griffiths
1985 I. Mustafa
1986 J. Alsop
1987 A. Holligan
1988 A. Hall
1989 A. Hall
1990 J. Pender
1991 J. Matthews
1992 D. McCarrick
1993 P. Richardson
1994 A. Temple
1995 A. Vaughan
1996 C. Wall
1997 R. Hatton

Welterweight
1920 F. Whitbread
1921 A. Ireland
1922 E. White
1923 P. Green
1924 P. O'Hanrahan
1925 P. O'Hanrahan
1926 B. Marshall
1927 H. Dunn
1928 H. Bone
1929 T. Wigmore
1930 F. Brooman
1931 J. Barry
1932 D. McCleave
1933 P. Peters
1934 D. McCleave
1935 D. Lynch
1936 W. Pack
1937 D. Lynch
1938 C. Webster
1939 R. Thomas
1944 H. Hall
1945 R. Turpin
1946 J. Ryan
1947 J. Ryan
1948 M. Shacklady
1949 A. Buxton
1950 T. Ratcliffe
1951 J. Maloney
1952 J. Maloney
1953 L. Morgan
1954 N. Gargano
1955 N. Gargano
1956 N. Gargano
1957 R. Warnes
1958 B. Nancurvis
1959 J. McGrail
1960 C. Humphries
1961 A. Lewis
1962 J. Pritchett
1963 J. Pritchett
1964 M. Varley
1965 P. Henderson
1966 P. Cragg
1967 D. Cranswick
1968 A. Tottoh
1969 T. Henderson
1970 T. Waller
1971 D. Davies
1972 T. Francis
1973 T. Waller
1974 T. Waller
1975 W. Bennett
1976 C. Jones
1977 C. Jones
1978 E. Byrne
1979 J. Frost
1980 T. Marsh
1981 T. Marsh
1982 C. Pyatt
1983 R. McKenley
1984 M. Hughes
1985 E. McDonald
1986 D. Dyer
1987 M. Elliot
1988 M. McCreath
1989 M. Elliot
1990 A. Carew
1991 J. Calzaghe

1992 M. Santini
1993 C. Bessey
1994 K. Short
1995 M. Hall
1996 J. Khaliq
1997 F. Barrett

L. Middleweight
1951 A. Lay
1952 B. Foster
1953 B. Wells
1954 B. Wells
1955 B. Foster
1956 J. McCormack
1957 J. Cunningham
1958 S. Pearson
1959 S. Pearson
1960 W. Fisher
1961 J. Gamble
1962 J. Lloyd
1963 A. Wyper
1964 W. Robinson
1965 P. Dwyer
1966 T. Imrie
1967 A. Edwards
1968 E. Blake
1969 T. Imrie
1970 D. Simmonds
1971 A. Edwards
1972 L. Paul
1973 R. Maxwell
1974 R. Maxwell
1975 A. Harrison
1976 W. Lauder
1977 C. Malarkey
1978 E. Henderson
1979 D. Brewster
1980 J. Price
1981 E. Christie
1982 D. Milligan
1983 R. Douglas
1984 R. Douglas
1985 R. Douglas
1986 T. Velinor
1987 N. Brown
1988 W. Ellis
1989 N. Brown
1990 T. Taylor
1991 T. Taylor
1992 J. Calzaghe
1993 D. Starie
1994 W. Alexander
1995 C. Bessey
1996 S. Dann
1997 C. Bessey

Middleweight
1881 T. Bellhouse
1882 A. H. Curnick
1883 A. J. Curnick
1884 W. Brown
1885 M. Salmon
1886 W. King
1887 R. Hair
1888 R. Hair
1889 G. Sykes
1890 J. Hoare
1891 J. Steers
1892 J. Steers

Ian Cooper of Hartlepool Boys Welfare ABC (left) landed his first ABA title when outpointing Triumph's Jim Twite in the 1997 middleweight final.

Les Clark

1893 J. Steers	1927 F. P. Crawley	1962 A. Matthews	1993 J. Calzaghe	1948 D. Scott
1894 W. Sykes	1928 F. Mallin	1963 A. Matthews	1994 D. Starie	1949 *Declared no contest*
1895 G. Townsend	1929 F. Mallin	1964 W. Stack	1995 J. Matthews	1950 P. Messervy
1896 W. Ross	1930 F. Mallin	1965 W. Robinson	1996 J. Pearce	1951 G. Walker
1897 W. Dees	1931 F. Mallin	1966 C. Finnegan	1997 I. Cooper	1952 H. Cooper
1898 G. Townsend	1932 F. Mallin	1967 A. Ball		1953 H. Cooper
1899 R. Warnes	1933 A. Shawyer	1968 P. McCann	**L. Heavyweight**	1954 A. Madigan
1900 E. Mann	1934 J. Magill	1969 D. Wallington	1920 H. Franks	1955 D. Rent
1901 R. Warnes	1935 J. Magill	1970 J. Conteh	1921 L. Collett	1956 D. Mooney
1902 E. Mann	1936 A. Harrington	1971 A. Minter	1922 H. Mitchell	1957 T. Green
1903 R. Warnes	1937 M. Dennis	1972 F. Lucas	1923 H. Mitchell	1958 J. Leeming
1904 E. Mann	1938 H. Tiller	1973 F. Lucas	1924 H. Mitchell	1959 J. Ould
1905 J. Douglas	1939 H. Davies	1974 D. Odwell	1925 H. Mitchell	1960 J. Ould
1906 A. Murdock	1944 J. Hockley	1975 D. Odwell	1926 D. McCorkindale	1961 J. Bodell
1907 R. Warnes	1945 R. Parker	1976 E. Burke	1927 A. Jackson	1962 J. Hendrickson
1908 W. Child	1946 R. Turpin	1977 R. Davies	1928 A. Jackson	1963 P. Murphy
1909 W. Child	1947 R. Agland	1978 H. Graham	1929 J. Goyder	1964 J. Fisher
1910 R. Warnes	1948 J. Wright	1979 N. Wilshire	1930 J. Murphy	1965 E. Whistler
1911 W. Child	1949 S. Lewis	1980 M. Kaylor	1931 J. Petersen	1966 R. Tighe
1912 E. Chandler	1950 P. Longo	1981 B. Schumacher	1932 J. Goyder	1967 M. Smith
1913 W. Bradley	1951 E. Ludlam	1982 J. Price	1933 G. Brennan	1968 R. Brittle
1914 H. Brown	1952 T. Gooding	1983 T. Forbes	1934 G. Brennan	1969 J. Frankham
1919 H. Mallin	1953 R. Barton	1984 B. Schumacher	1935 R. Hearns	1970 J. Rafferty
1920 H. Mallin	1954 K. Phillips	1985 D. Cronin	1936 J. Magill	1971 J. Conteh
1921 H. Mallin	1955 F. Hope	1986 N. Benn	1937 J. Wilby	1972 W. Knight
1922 H. Mallin	1956 R. Redrup	1987 R. Douglas	1938 A. S. Brown	1973 W. Knight
1923 H. Mallin	1957 P. Burke	1988 M. Edwards	1939 B. Woodcock	1974 W. Knight
1924 J. Elliot	1958 P. Hill	1989 S. Johnson	1944 E. Shackleton	1975 M. Heath
1925 J. Elliot	1959 F. Elderfield	1990 S. Wilson	1945 A. Watson	1976 G. Evans
1926 F. P. Crawley	1960 R. Addison	1991 M. Edwards	1946 J. Taylor	1977 C. Lawson
	1961 J. Caiger	1992 L. Woolcock	1947 A. Watson	1978 V. Smith

1979 A. Straughn	1889 A. Bowman	1923 E. Eagan	1957 D. Thomas	1987 J. Moran
1980 A. Straughn	1890 J. Steers	1924 A. Clifton	1958 D. Thomas	1988 H. Akinwande
1981 A. Straughn	1891 V. Barker	1925 D. Lister	1959 D. Thomas	1989 H. Akinwande
1982 G. Crawford	1892 J. Steers	1926 T. Petersen	1960 L. Hobbs	1990 K. Inglis
1983 A. Wilson	1893 J. Steers	1927 C. Capper	1961 W. Walker	1991 P. Lawson
1984 A. Wilson	1894 H. King	1928 J. L. Driscoll	1962 R. Dryden	1992 S. Welch
1985 J. Beckles	1895 W. E. Johnstone	1929 P. Floyd	1963 R. Sanders	1993 P. Lawson
1986 J. Moran	1896 W. E. Johnstone	1930 V. Stuart	1964 C. Woodhouse	1994 S. Burford
1987 J. Beckles	1897 G. Townsend	1931 M. Flanagan	1965 W. Wells	1995 M. Ellis
1988 H. Lawson	1898 G. Townsend	1932 V. Stuart	1966 A. Brogan	1996 T. Oakey
1989 N. Piper	1899 F. Parks	1933 C. O'Grady	1967 P. Boddington	1997 B. Stevens
1990 J. McCluskey	1900 W. Dees	1934 P. Floyd	1968 W. Wells	
1991 A. Todd	1901 F. Parks	1935 P. Floyd	1969 A. Burton	
1992 K. Oliver	1902 F. Parks	1936 V. Stuart	1970 J. Gilmour	**S. Heavyweight**
1993 K. Oliver	1903 F. Dickson	1937 V. Stuart	1971 L. Stevens	1982 A. Elliott
1994 K. Oliver	1904 A. Horner	1938 G. Preston	1972 T. Wood	1983 K. Ferdinand
1995 K. Oliver	1905 F. Parks	1939 A. Porter	1973 G. McEwan	1984 R. Wells
1996 C. Fry	1906 F. Parks	1944 M. Hart	1974 N. Meade	1985 G. Williamson
1997 P. Rogers	1907 H. Brewer	1945 D. Scott	1975 G. McEwan	1986 J. Oyebola
	1908 S. Evans	1946 P. Floyd	1976 J. Rafferty	1987 J. Oyebola
	1909 C. Brown	1947 G. Scriven	1977 G. Adair	1988 K. McCormack
Heavyweight	1910 F. Storbeck	1948 J. Gardner	1978 J. Awome	1989 P. Passley
1881 R. Frost-Smith	1911 W. Hazell	1949 A. Worrall	1979 A. Palmer	1990 K. McCormack
1882 H. Dearsley	1912 R. Smith	1950 P. Toch	1980 F. Bruno	1991 K. McCormack
1883 H. Dearsley	1913 R. Smith	1951 A. Halsey	1981 A. Elliott	1992 M. Hopper
1884 H. Dearsley	1914 E. Chandler	1952 E. Hearn	1982 H. Hylton	1993 M. McKenzie
1885 W. West	1919 H. Brown	1953 J. Erskine	1983 H. Notice	1994 D. Watts
1886 A. Diamond	1920 R. Rawson	1954 B. Harper	1984 D. Young	1995 R. Allen
1887 E. White	1921 R. Rawson	1955 D. Rowe	1985 H. Hylton	1996 D. Watts
1888 W. King	1922 T. Evans	1956 D. Rent	1986 E. Cardouza	1997 A. Harrison

The son of the 1971 ABA heavyweight champion, Les Stevens, Blue (left) took the same title in 1997 when outpointing Tony Oakey, the previous year's winner.

Les Clark

International Amateur Champions, 1904-1997

Shows all Olympic, World, European & Commonwealth champions since 1904. British silver and bronze medal winners are shown throughout, where applicable.

Country Code

ALG = Algeria; ARG = Argentine; ARM = Armenia; AUS = Australia; AUT = Austria; AZE = Azerbaijan; BEL = Belgium; BUL = Bulgaria; CAN = Canada; CEY = Ceylon (now Sri Lanka); CI = Channel Islands; CUB = Cuba; DEN = Denmark; DOM = Dominican Republic; ENG = England; ESP = Spain; EST = Estonia; FIJ = Fiji Islands; FIN = Finland; FRA = France; GBR = United Kingdom; GDR = German Democratic Republic; GEO = Georgia; GER = Germany (but West Germany only from 1968-1990); GHA = Ghana; GUY = Guyana; HOL = Netherlands; HUN = Hungary; IRL = Ireland; ITA = Italy; JAM = Jamaica; JPN = Japan; KAZ = Kazakhstan; KEN = Kenya; LIT = Lithuania; MEX = Mexico; NKO = North Korea; NIG = Nigeria; NIR = Northern Ireland; NOR = Norway; NZL = New Zealand; POL = Poland; PUR = Puerto Rico; ROM = Romania; RUS = Russia; SAF = South Africa; SCO = Scotland; SKO = South Korea; SR = Southern Rhodesia; STV = St Vincent; SWE = Sweden; TCH = Czechoslovakia; THA = Thailand; TUR = Turkey; UGA = Uganda; UKR = Ukraine; URS = USSR; USA = United States of America; VEN = Venezuela; WAL = Wales; YUG = Yugoslavia; ZAM =

Olympic Champions, 1904-1996

St Louis, USA - 1904
Fly: G. Finnegan (USA). **Bantam:** O. Kirk (USA). **Feather:** O. Kirk (USA). **Light:** H. Spangler (USA). **Welter:** A. Young (USA). **Middle:** C. May (USA). **Heavy:** S. Berger (USA).

London, England - 1908
Bantam: H. Thomas (GBR). **Feather:** R. Gunn (GBR). **Light:** F. Grace (GBR). **Middle:** J.W.H.T. Douglas (GBR). **Heavy:** A. Oldman (GBR).
Silver medals: J. Condon (GBR), C. Morris (GBR), F. Spiller (GBR), S. Evans (GBR).
Bronze medals: W. Webb (GBR), H. Rodding (GBR), T. Ringer (GBR), H. Johnson (GBR), R. Warnes (GBR), W. Philo (GBR), F. Parks (GBR).

Antwerp, Belgium - 1920
Fly: F. Genaro (USA). **Bantam:** C. Walker (SAF). **Feather:** R. Fritsch (FRA). **Light:** S. Mossberg (USA). **Welter:** T. Schneider (CAN). **Middle:** H. Mallin (GBR). **L. Heavy:** E. Eagan (USA). **Heavy:** R. Rawson (GBR).
Silver medal: A. Ireland (GBR).
Bronze medals: W. Cuthbertson (GBR), G. McKenzie (GBR), H. Franks (GBR).

Paris, France - 1924
Fly: F. la Barba (USA). **Bantam:** W. Smith (SAF). **Feather:** J. Fields (USA). **Light:** H. Nielson (DEN). **Welter:** J. Delarge (BEL). **Middle:** H. Mallin (GBR). **L. Heavy:** H. Mitchell (GBR). **Heavy:** O. von Porat (NOR).
Silver medals: J. McKenzie (GBR), J. Elliot (GBR).

Amsterdam, Holland - 1928
Fly: A. Kocsis (HUN). **Bantam:** V. Tamagnini (ITA). **Feather:** B. van Klaveren (HOL). **Light:** C. Orlando (ITA). **Welter:** E. Morgan (NZL). **Middle:** P. Toscani (ITA). **L. Heavy:** V. Avendano (ARG). **Heavy:** A. Rodriguez Jurado (ARG).

Los Angeles, USA - 1932
Fly: I. Enekes (HUN). **Bantam:** H. Gwynne (CAN). **Feather:** C. Robledo (ARG). **Light:** L. Stevens (SAF). **Welter:** E. Flynn (USA). **Middle:** C. Barth (USA). **L. Heavy:** D. Carstens (SAF). **Heavy:** A. Lovell (ARG).

Berlin, West Germany - 1936
Fly: W. Kaiser (GER). **Bantam:** U. Sergo (ITA). **Feather:** O. Casanova (ARG). **Light:** I. Harangi (HUN). **Welter:** S. Suvio (FIN). **Middle:** J. Despeaux (FRA). **L. Heavy:** R. Michelot (FRA). **Heavy:** H. Runge (GER).

London, England - 1948
Fly: P. Perez (ARG). **Bantam:** T. Csik (HUN). **Feather:** E. Formenti (ITA). **Light:** G. Dreyer (SAF). **Welter:** J. Torma (TCH). **Middle:** L. Papp (HUN). **L. Heavy:** G. Hunter (SAF). **Heavy:** R. Iglesas (ARG).
Silver medals: J. Wright (GBR), D. Scott (GBR).

Helsinki, Finland - 1952
Fly: N. Brooks (USA). **Bantam:** P. Hamalainen (FIN). **Feather:** J. Zachara

(TCH). **Light:** A. Bolognesi (ITA). **L. Welter:** C. Adkins (USA). **Welter:** Z. Chychla (POL). **L. Middle:** L. Papp (HUN). **Middle:** F. Patterson (USA). **L. Heavy:** N. Lee (USA). **Heavy:** E. Sanders (USA).
Silver medal: J. McNally (IRL).

Melbourne, Australia - 1956
Fly: T. Spinks (GBR). **Bantam:** W. Behrendt (GER). **Feather:** V. Safronov (URS). **Light:** R. McTaggart (GBR). **L. Welter:** V. Jengibarian (URS). **Welter:** N. Linca (ROM). **L. Middle:** L. Papp (HUN). **Middle:** G. Schatkov (URS). **L. Heavy:** J. Boyd (USA). **Heavy:** P. Rademacher (USA).
Silver medals: T. Nicholls (GBR), F. Tiedt (IRL).
Bronze medals: J. Caldwell (IRL), F. Gilroy (IRL), A. Bryne (IRL), N. Gargano (GBR), J. McCormack (GBR).

Rome, Italy - 1960
Fly: G. Torok (HUN). **Bantam:** O. Grigoryev (URS). **Feather:** F. Musso (ITA). **Light:** K. Pazdzior (POL). **L. Welter:** B. Nemecek (TCH). **Welter:** N. Benvenuti (ITA). **L. Middle:** W. McClure (USA). **Middle:** E. Crook (USA). **L. Heavy:** C. Clay (USA). **Heavy:** F. de Piccoli (ITA).
Bronze medals: R. McTaggart (GBR), J. Lloyd (GBR), W. Fisher (GBR).

Tokyo, Japan - 1964
Fly: F. Atzori (ITA). **Bantam:** T. Sakurai (JPN). **Feather:** S. Stepashkin (URS). **Light:** J. Grudzien (POL). **L. Welter:** J. Kulej (POL). **Welter:** M. Kasprzyk (POL). **L. Middle:** B. Lagutin (URS). **Middle:** V. Popenchenko (URS). **L. Heavy:** C. Pinto (ITA). **Heavy:** J. Frazier (USA).
Bronze medal: J. McCourt (IRL).

Mexico City, Mexico - 1968
L. Fly: F. Rodriguez (VEN). **Fly:** R. Delgado (MEX). **Bantam:** V. Sokolov (URS). **Feather:** A. Roldan (MEX). **Light:** R. Harris (USA). **L. Welter:** J. Kulej (POL). **Welter:** M. Wolke (GDR). **L. Middle:** B. Lagutin (URS). **Middle:** C. Finnegan (GBR). **L. Heavy:** D. Poznyak (URS). **Heavy:** G. Foreman (USA).

Munich, West Germany - 1972
L. Fly: G. Gedo (HUN). **Fly:** G. Kostadinov (BUL). **Bantam:** O. Martinez (CUB). **Feather:** B. Kusnetsov (URS). **Light:** J. Szczepanski (POL). **L. Welter:** R. Seales (USA). **Welter:** E. Correa (CUB). **L. Middle:** D. Kottysch (GER). **Middle:** V. Lemeschev (URS). **L. Heavy:** M. Parlov (YUG). **Heavy:** T. Stevenson (CUB).
Bronze medals: R. Evans (GBR), G. Turpin (GBR), A. Minter (GBR).

Montreal, Canada - 1976
L. Fly: J. Hernandez (CUB). **Fly:** L. Randolph (USA). **Bantam:** Y-J. Gu (NKO). **Feather:** A. Herrera (CUB). **Light:** H. Davis (USA). **L. Welter:** R. Leonard (USA). **Welter:** J. Bachfield (GDR). **L. Middle:** J. Rybicki (POL). **Middle:** M. Spinks (USA). **L. Heavy:** L. Spinks (USA). **Heavy:** T. Stevenson (CUB).
Bronze medal: P. Cowdell (GBR).

Moscow, USSR - 1980
L. Fly: S. Sabirov (URS). **Fly:** P. Lessov (BUL). **Bantam:** J. Hernandez

(CUB). **Feather:** R. Fink (GDR). **Light:** A. Herrera (CUB). **L. Welter:** P. Oliva (ITA). **Welter:** A. Aldama (CUB). **L. Middle:** A. Martinez (CUB). **Middle:** J. Gomez (CUB). **L. Heavy:** S. Kacar (YUG). **Heavy:** T. Stevenson (CUB).
Bronze medals: H. Russell (IRL), A. Willis (GBR).

Los Angeles, USA - 1984
L. Fly: P. Gonzalez (USA). **Fly:** S. McCrory (USA). **Bantam:** M. Stecca (ITA). **Feather:** M. Taylor (USA). **Light:** P. Whitaker (USA). **L. Welter:** J. Page (USA). **Welter:** M. Breland (USA). **L. Middle:** F. Tate (USA). **Middle:** J-S. Shin (SKO). **L. Heavy:** A. Josipovic (YUG). **Heavy:** H. Tillman (USA). **S. Heavy:** T. Biggs (USA).
Bronze medal: B. Wells (GBR).

Seoul, South Korea - 1988
L. Fly: I. Mustafov (BUL). **Fly:** H-S. Kim (SKO). **Bantam:** K. McKinney (USA). **Feather:** G. Parisi (ITA). **Light:** A. Zuelow (GDR). **L. Welter:** V. Yanovsky (URS). **Welter:** R. Wangila (KEN). **L. Middle:** S-H. Park (SKO). **Middle:** H. Maske (GDR). **L. Heavy:** A. Maynard (USA). **Heavy:** R. Mercer (USA). **S. Heavy:** L. Lewis (CAN).
Bronze medal: R. Woodhall (GBR).

Barcelona, Spain - 1992
L. Fly: R. Marcelo (CUB). **Fly:** C-C. Su (NKO). **Bantam:** J. Casamayor (CUB). **Feather:** A. Tews (GER). **Light:** O. de la Hoya (USA). **L. Welter:** H. Vinent (CUB). **Welter:** M. Carruth (IRL). **L. Middle:** J. Lemus (CUB). **Middle:** A. Hernandez (CUB). **L. Heavy:** T. May (GER). **Heavy:** F. Savon (CUB). **S. Heavy:** R. Balado (CUB).
Silver medal: W. McCullough (IRL).
Bronze medal: R. Reid (GBR).

Atlanta, USA - 1996
L. Fly: D. Petrov (BUL). **Fly:** M. Romero (CUB). **Bantam:** I. Kovaks (HUN). **Feather:** S. Kamsing (THA). **Light:** H. Soltani (ALG). **L. Welter:** H. Vinent (CUB). **Welter:** O. Saitov (RUS). **L. Middle:** D. Reid (USA). **Middle:** A. Hernandez (CUB). **L. Heavy:** V. Jirov (KAZ). **Heavy:** F. Savon (CUB). **S. Heavy:** V. Klitchko (UKR).

World Champions, 1974-1995

Havana, Cuba - 1974
L. Fly: J. Hernandez (CUB). **Fly:** D. Rodriguez (CUB). **Bantam:** W. Gomez (PUR). **Feather:** H. Davis (USA). **Light:** V. Solomin (URS). **L. Welter:** A. Kalule (UGA). **Welter:** E. Correa (CUB). **L. Middle:** R. Garbey (CUB). **Middle:** R. Riskiev (URS). **L. Heavy:** M. Parlov (YUG). **Heavy:** T. Stevenson (CUB).

Belgrade, Yugoslavia - 1978
L. Fly: S. Muchoki (KEN). **Fly:** H. Strednicki (POL). **Bantam:** A. Horta (CUB). **Feather:** A. Herrera (CUB). **Light:** D. Andeh (NIG). **L. Welter:** V. Lvov (URS). **Welter:** V. Rachkov (URS). **L. Middle:** V. Savchenko (URS). **Middle:** J. Gomez (CUB). **L. Heavy:** S. Soria (CUB). **Heavy:** T. Stevenson (CUB).

Munich, West Germany - 1982
L. Fly: I. Mustafov (BUL). **Fly:** Y. Alexandrov (URS). **Bantam:** F. Favors (USA). **Feather:** A. Horta (CUB). **Light:** A. Herrera (CUB). **L. Welter:** C. Garcia (CUB). **Welter:** M. Breland (USA). **L. Middle:** A. Koshkin (URS). **Middle:** B. Comas (CUB). **L. Heavy:** P. Romero (CUB). **Heavy:** A. Jagubkin (URS). **S. Heavy:** T. Biggs (USA).
Bronze medal: T. Corr (IRL).

Reno, USA - 1986
L. Fly: J. Odelin (CUB). **Fly:** P. Reyes (CUB). **Bantam:** S-I. Moon (SKO). **Feather:** K. Banks (USA). **Light:** A. Horta (CUB). **L. Welter:** V. Shishov (URS). **Welter:** K. Gould (USA). **L. Middle:** A. Espinosa (CUB). **Middle:** D. Allen (USA). **L. Heavy:** P. Romero (CUB). **Heavy:** F. Savon (CUB). **S. Heavy:** T. Stevenson (CUB).

Moscow, USSR - 1989
L. Fly: E. Griffin (USA). **Fly:** Y. Arbachakov (URS). **Bantam:** E. Carrion (CUB). **Feather:** A. Khamatov (URS). **Light:** J. Gonzalez (CUB). **L.**

Welter: I. Ruzinkov (URS). **Welter:** F. Vastag. **L. Middle:** I. Akopokhian (URS). **Middle:** A. Kurniavka (URS). **L. Heavy:** H. Maske (GDR). **Heavy:** F. Savon (CUB). **S. Heavy:** R. Balado (CUB).
Bronze medal: M. Carruth (IRL).

Sydney, Australia - 1991
L. Fly: E. Griffin (USA). **Fly:** I. Kovacs (HUN). **Bantam:** S. Todorov (BUL). **Feather:** K. Kirkorov (BUL). **Light:** M. Rudolph (GER). **L. Welter:** K. Tsziu (URS). **Welter:** J. Hernandez (CUB). **L. Middle:** J. Lemus (CUB). **Middle:** T. Russo (ITA). **L. Heavy:** T. May (GER). **Heavy:** F. Savon (CUB). **S. Heavy:** R. Balado (CUB).

Tampere, Finland - 1993
L. Fly: N. Munchian (ARM). **Fly:** W. Font (CUB). **Bantam:** A. Christov (BUL). **Feather:** S. Todorov (BUL). **Light:** D. Austin (CUB). **L. Welter:** H. Vinent (CUB). **Welter:** J. Hernandez (CUB). **L. Middle:** F. Vastag (ROM). **Middle:** A. Hernandez (CUB). **L. Heavy:** R. Garbey (CUB). **Heavy:** F. Savon (CUB). **S. Heavy:** R. Balado (CUB).
Bronze medal: D. Kelly (IRL).

Berlin, Germany - 1995
L. Fly: D. Petrov (BUL). **Fly:** Z. Lunka (GER). **Bantam:** R. Malachbekov (RUS). **Feather:** S. Todorov (BUL). **Light:** L. Doroftel (ROM). **L. Welter:** H. Vinent (CUB). **Welter:** J. Hernandez (CUB). **L. Middle:** F. Vastag (ROM). **Middle:** A. Hernandez (CUB). **L. Heavy:** A. Tarver (USA). **Heavy:** F. Savon (CUB). **S. Heavy:** A. Lezin (RUS).

World Junior Champions, 1979-1996

Yokohama, Japan - 1979
L. Fly: R. Shannon (USA). **Fly:** P. Lessov (BUL). **Bantam:** P-K. Choi (SKO). **Feather:** Y. Gladychev (URS). **Light:** R. Blake (USA). **L. Welter:** I. Akopokhian (URS). **Welter:** M. McCrory (USA). **L. Middle:** A. Mayes (USA). **Middle:** A. Milov (URS). **L. Heavy:** A. Lebedev (URS). **Heavy:** M. Frazier (USA).
Silver medals: N. Wilshire (ENG), D. Cross (ENG).
Bronze medal: I. Scott (SCO).

Santa Domingo, Dominican Republic - 1983
L. Fly: M. Herrera (DOM). **Fly:** J. Gonzalez (CUB). **Bantam:** J. Molina (PUR). **Feather:** A. Miesses (DOM). **Light:** A. Beltre (DOM). **L. Welter:** A. Espinoza (CUB). **Welter:** M. Watkins (USA). **L. Middle:** U. Castillo (CUB). **Middle:** R. Batista (CUB). **L. Heavy:** O. Pought (USA). **Heavy:** A. Williams (USA). **S. Heavy:** L. Lewis (CAN).

Bucharest, Romania - 1985
L. Fly: R-S. Hwang (SKO). **Fly:** T. Marcelica (ROM). **Bantam:** R. Diaz (CUB). **Feather:** D. Maeran (ROM). **Light:** J. Teiche (GDR). **L. Welter:** W. Saeger (GDR). **Welter:** A. Stoianov (BUL). **L. Middle:** M. Franek (TCH). **Middle:** O. Zahalotskih (URS). **L. Heavy:** B. Riddick (USA). **Heavy:** F. Savon (CUB). **S. Heavy:** A. Prianichnikov (URS).

Havana, Cuba - 1987
L. Fly: E. Paisan (CUB). **Fly:** C. Daniels (USA). **Bantam:** A. Moya (CUB). **Feather:** G. Iliyasov (URS). **Light:** J. Hernandez (CUB). **L. Welter:** L. Mihai (ROM). **Welter:** F. Vastag (ROM). **L. Middle:** A. Lobsyak (URS). **Middle:** W. Martinez (CUB). **L. Heavy:** D. Yeliseyev (URS). **Heavy:** R. Balado (CUB). **S. Heavy:** L. Martinez (CUB).
Silver medal: E. Loughran (IRL).
Bronze medal: D. Galvin (IRL).

San Juan, Puerto Rico - 1989
L. Fly: D. Petrov (BUL). **Fly:** N. Monchai (FRA). **Bantam:** J. Casamayor (CUB). **Feather:** C. Febres (PUR). **Light:** A. Acevedo (PUR). **L. Welter:** E. Berger (GDR). **Welter:** A. Hernandez (CUB). **L. Middle:** L. Bedey (CUB). **Middle:** R. Garbey (CUB). **L. Heavy:** R. Alvarez (CUB). **Heavy:** K. Johnson (CAN). **S. Heavy:** A. Burdiantz (URS).
Silver medals: E. Magee (IRL), R. Reid (ENG), S. Wilson (SCO).

Lima, Peru - 1990
L. Fly: D. Alicea (PUR). **Fly:** K. Pielert (GDR). **Bantam:** K. Baravi (URS). **Feather:** A. Vaughan (ENG). **Light:** J. Mendez (CUB). **L. Welter:** H.

Vinent (CUB). **Welter:** A. Hernandez (CUB). **L. Middle:** A. Kakauridze (URS). **Middle:** J. Gomez (CUB). **L. Heavy:** B. Torsten (GDR). **Heavy:** I. Andreev (URS). **S. Heavy:** J. Quesada (CUB).
Bronze medal: P. Ingle (ENG).

Montreal, Canada - 1992
L. Fly: W. Font (CUB). **Fly:** J. Oragon (CUB). **Bantam:** N. Machado (CUB). **Feather:** M. Stewart (CAN). **Light:** D. Austin (CUB). **L. Welter:** O. Saitov (RUS). **Welter:** L. Brors (GER). **L. Middle:** J. Acosta (CUB). **Middle:** I. Arsangaliev (RUS). **L. Heavy:** S. Samilsan (TUR). **Heavy:** G. Kandeliaki (GEO). **S. Heavy:** M. Porchnev (RUS).
Bronze medal: N. Sinclair (IRL).

Istanbul, Turkey - 1994
L. Fly: J. Turunen (FIN). **Fly:** A. Jimenez (CUB). **Bantam:** J. Despaigne (CUB). **Feather:** D. Simion (ROM). **Light:** L. Diogenes (CUB). **L. Welter:** V. Romero (CUB). **Welter:** E. Aslan (TUR). **L. Middle:** G. Ledsvanys (CUB). **Middle:** M. Genc (TUR). **L. Heavy:** P. Aurino (ITA). **Heavy:** M. Lopez (CUB). **S. Heavy:** P. Carrion (CUB).

Havana, Cuba - 1996
L. Fly: L. Hernandez (CUB). **Fly:** L. Cabrera (CUB). **Bantam:** P. Miradal (CUB). **Feather:** E. Rodriguez (CUB). **Light:** R. Vaillan (CUB). **L. Welter:** T. Mergadze (RUS). **Welter:** J. Brahmer (GER). **L. Middle:** L. Mezquia (CUB). **Middle:** V. Pletniov (RUS). **L. Heavy:** O. Simon (CUB). **Heavy:** A. Yatsenko (UKR). **S. Heavy:** S. Fabre (CUB).
Bronze medal: R. Hatton (ENG).

European Champions, 1924-1996

Paris, France - 1924
Fly: J. McKenzie (GBR). **Bantam:** J. Ces (FRA). **Feather:** R. de Vergnie (BEL). **Light:** N. Nielsen (DEN). **Welter:** J. Delarge (BEL). **Middle:** H. Mallin (GBR). **L. Heavy:** H. Mitchell (GBR). **Heavy:** O. von Porat (NOR).

Stockholm, Sweden - 1925
Fly: E. Pladner (FRA). **Bantam:** A. Rule (GBR). **Feather:** P. Andren (SWE). **Light:** S. Johanssen (SWE). **Welter:** H. Nielsen (DEN). **Middle:** F. Crawley (GBR). **L. Heavy:** T. Petersen (DEN). **Heavy:** B. Persson (SWE).
Silver medals: J. James (GBR), E. Viney (GBR), D. Lister (GBR).

Berlin, Germany - 1927
Fly: L. Boman (SWE). **Bantam:** K. Dalchow (GER). **Feather:** F. Dubbers (GER). **Light:** H. Domgoergen (GER). **Welter:** R. Caneva (ITA). **Middle:** J. Christensen (NOR). **L. Heavy:** H. Muller (GER). **Heavy:** N. Ramm (SWE).

Amsterdam, Holland - 1928
Fly: A. Kocsis (HUN). **Bantam:** V. Tamagnini (ITA). **Feather:** B. van Klaveren (HOL). **Light:** C. Orlandi (ITA). **Welter:** R. Galataud (FRA). **Middle:** P. Toscani (ITA). **L. Heavy:** E. Pistulla (GER). **Heavy:** N. Ramm (SWE).

Budapest, Hungary - 1930
Fly: I. Enekes (HUN). **Bantam:** J. Szeles (HUN). **Feather:** G. Szabo (HUN). **Light:** M. Bianchini (ITA). **Welter:** J. Besselmann (GER). **Middle:** C. Meroni (ITA). **L. Heavy:** T. Petersen (DEN). **Heavy:** J. Michaelson (DEN).

Los Angeles, USA - 1932
Fly: I. Enekes (HUN). **Bantam:** H. Ziglarski (GER). **Feather:** J. Schleinkofer (GER). **Light:** T. Ahlqvist (SWE). **Welter:** E. Campe (GER). **Middle:** R. Michelot (FRA). **L. Heavy:** G. Rossi (ITA). **Heavy:** L. Rovati (ITA).

Budapest, Hungary - 1934
Fly: P. Palmer (GBR). **Bantam:** I. Enekes (HUN). **Feather:** O. Kaestner GER). **Light:** E. Facchini (ITA). **Welter:** D. McCleave (GBR). **Middle:** S. Szigetti (HUN). **L. Heavy:** P. Zehetmayer (AUT). **Heavy:** G. Baerlund (FIN).
Bronze medal: P. Floyd (GBR).

Milan, Italy - 1937
Fly: I. Enekes (HUN). **Bantam:** U. Sergo (ITA). **Feather:** A. Polus (POL). **Light:** H. Nuremberg (GER). **Welter:** M. Murach (GER). **Middle:** H. Chmielewski (POL). **L. Heavy:** S. Szigetti (HUN). **Heavy:** O. Tandberg (SWE).

Dublin, Eire - 1939
Fly: J. Ingle (IRL). **Bantam:** U. Sergo (ITA). **Feather:** P. Dowdall (IRL). **Light:** H. Nuremberg (GER). **Welter:** A. Kolczyski (POL). **Middle:** A. Raedek (EST). **L. Heavy:** L. Musina (ITA). **Heavy:** O. Tandberg (SWE).
Bronze medal: C. Evenden (IRL).

Dublin, Eire - 1947
Fly: L. Martinez (ESP). **Bantam:** L. Bogacs (HUN). **Feather:** K. Kreuger (SWE). **Light:** J. Vissers (BEL). **Welter:** J. Ryan (ENG). **Middle:** A. Escudie (FRA). **L. Heavy:** H. Quentemeyer (HOL). **Heavy:** G. O'Colmain (IRL).
Silver medals: J. Clinton (SCO), P. Maguire (IRL), W. Thom (ENG), G. Scriven (ENG).
Bronze medals: J. Dwyer (SCO), A. Sanderson (ENG), W. Frith (SCO), E. Cantwell (IRL), K. Wyatt (ENG).

Oslo, Norway - 1949
Fly: J. Kasperczak (POL). **Bantam:** G. Zuddas (ITA). **Feather:** J. Bataille (FRA). **Light:** M. McCullagh (IRL). **Welter:** J. Torma (TCH). **Middle:** L. Papp (HUN). **L. Heavy:** G. di Segni (ITA). **Heavy:** L. Bene (HUN).
Bronze medal: D. Connell (IRL).

Milan, Italy - 1951
Fly: A. Pozzali (ITA). **Bantam:** V. Dall'Osso (ITA). **Feather:** J. Ventaja (FRA). **Light:** B. Visintin (ITA). **L. Welter:** H. Schelling (GER). **Welter:** Z. Chychla (POL). **L. Middle:** L. Papp (HUN). **Middle:** S. Sjolin (SWE). **L. Heavy:** M. Limage (BEL). **Heavy:** G. di Segni (ITA).
Silver medal: J. Kelly (IRL).
Bronze medals: D. Connell (IRL), T. Milligan (IRL), A. Lay (ENG).

Warsaw, Poland - 1953
Fly: H. Kukier (POL). **Bantam:** Z. Stefaniuk (POL). **Feather:** J. Kruza (POL). **Light:** V. Jengibarian (URS). **L. Welter:** L. Drogosz (POL). **Welter:** Z. Chychla (POL). **L. Middle:** B. Wells (ENG). **Middle:** D. Wemhoner (GER). **L. Heavy:** U. Nietchke (GER). **Heavy:** A. Schotzikas (URS).
Silver medal: T. Milligan (IRL).
Bronze medals: J. McNally (IRL), R. Barton (ENG).

Berlin, West Germany - 1955
Fly: E. Basel (GER). **Bantam:** Z. Stefaniuk (POL). **Feather:** T. Nicholls (ENG). **Light:** H. Kurschat (GER). **L. Welter:** L. Drogosz (POL). **Welter:** N. Gargano (ENG). **L. Middle:** Z. Pietrzykowski (POL). **Middle:** G. Schatkov (URS). **L. Heavy:** E. Schoeppner (GER). **Heavy:** A. Schotzikas (URS).

Prague, Czechoslovakia - 1957
Fly: M. Homberg (GER). **Bantam:** O. Grigoryev (URS). **Feather:** D. Venilov (BUL). **Light:** K. Pazdzior (POL). **L. Welter:** V. Jengibarian (URS). **Welter:** M. Graus (GER). **L. Middle:** N. Benvenuti (ITA). **Middle:** Z. Pietrzykowski (POL). **L. Heavy:** G. Negrea (ROM). **Heavy:** A. Abramov (URS).
Bronze medals: R. Davies (WAL), J. Morrissey (SCO), J. Kidd (SCO), F. Teidt (IRL).

Lucerne, Switzerland - 1959
Fly: M. Homberg (GER). **Bantam:** H. Rascher (GER). **Feather:** J. Adamski (POL). **Light:** O. Maki (FIN). **L. Welter:** V. Jengibarian (URS). **Welter:** L. Drogosz (POL). **L. Middle:** N. Benvenuti (ITA). **Middle:** G. Schatkov (URS). **L. Heavy:** Z. Pietrzykowski (POL). **Heavy:** A. Abramov (URS).
Silver medal: D. Thomas (ENG).
Bronze medals: A. McClean (IRL), H. Perry (IRL), C. McCoy (IRL), H. Scott (ENG).

Belgrade, Yugoslavia - 1961
Fly: P. Vacca (ITA). **Bantam:** S. Sivko (URS). **Feather:** F. Taylor (ENG).

Light: R. McTaggart (SCO). **L. Welter:** A. Tamulis (URS). **Welter:** R. Tamulis (URS). **L. Middle:** B. Lagutin (URS). **Middle:** T. Walasek (POL). **L. Heavy:** G. Saraudi (ITA). **Heavy:** A. Abramov (URS).
Bronze medals: P. Warwick (ENG), I. McKenzie (SCO), J. Bodell (ENG).

Moscow, USSR - 1963
Fly: V. Bystrov (URS). **Bantam:** O. Grigoryev (URS). **Feather:** S. Stepashkin (URS). **Light:** J. Kajdi (HUN). **L. Welter:** J. Kulej (POL). **Welter:** R. Tamulis (URS). **L. Middle:** B. Lagutin (URS). **Middle:** V. Popenchenko (URS). **L. Heavy:** Z. Pietrzykowski (POL). **Heavy:** J. Nemec (TCH).
Silver medal: A. Wyper (SCO).

Berlin, East Germany - 1965
Fly: H. Freisdadt (GER). **Bantam:** O. Grigoryev (URS). **Feather:** S. Stepashkin (URS). **Light:** V. Barranikov (URS). **L. Welter:** J. Kulej (POL). **Welter:** R. Tamulis (URS). **L. Middle:** V. Ageyev (URS). **Middle:** V. Popenchenko (URS). **L. Heavy:** D. Poznyak (URS). **Heavy:** A. Isosimov (URS).
Silver medal: B. Robinson (ENG).
Bronze medals: J. McCluskey (SCO), K. Buchanan (SCO), J. McCourt (IRL).

Rome, Italy - 1967
Fly: H. Skrzyczak (POL). **Bantam:** N. Giju (ROM). **Feather:** R. Petek (POL). **Light:** J. Grudzien (POL). **L. Welter:** V. Frolov (URS). **Welter:** B. Nemecek (TCH). **L. Middle:** V. Ageyev (URS). **Middle:** M. Casati (ITA). **L. Heavy:** D. Poznyak (URS). **Heavy:** M. Baruzzi (ITA).
Silver medal: P. Boddington (ENG).

Bucharest, Romania - 1969
L. Fly: G. Gedo (HUN). **Fly:** C. Ciuca (ROM). **Bantam:** A. Dumitrescu (ROM). **Feather:** J. Orban (ROM). **Light:** S. Cutov (ROM). **L. Welter:** V. Frolov (URS). **Welter:** G. Meier (GER). **L. Middle:** V. Tregubov (URS). **Middle:** V. Tarasenkov (URS). **L. Heavy:** D. Poznyak (URS). **Heavy:** I. Alexe (ROM).
Bronze medals: M. Dowling (IRL), M. Piner (ENG), A. Richardson (ENG), T. Imrie (SCO).

Madrid, Spain - 1971
L. Fly: G. Gedo (HUN). **Fly:** J. Rodriguez (ESP). **Bantam:** T. Badar (HUN). **Feather:** R. Tomczyk (POL). **Light:** J. Szczepanski (POL). **L. Welter:** U. Beyer (GDR). **Welter:** J. Kajdi (HUN). **L. Middle:** V. Tregubov (URS). **Middle:** J. Juotsiavitchus (URS). **L. Heavy:** M. Parlov (YUG). **Heavy:** V. Tchernishev (URS).
Bronze medals: N. McLaughlin (IRL), M. Dowling (IRL), B. McCarthy (IRL), M. Kingwell (ENG), L. Stevens (ENG).

Belgrade, Yugoslavia - 1973
L. Fly: V. Zasypko (URS). **Fly:** C. Gruescu (ROM). **Bantam:** A. Cosentino (FRA). **Feather:** S. Forster (GDR). **Light:** S. Cutov (ROM). **L. Welter:** M. Benes (YUG). **Welter:** S. Csjef (HUN). **L. Middle:** A. Klimanov (URS). **Middle:** V. Lemechev (URS). **L. Heavy:** M. Parlov (YUG). **Heavy:** V. Ulyanich (URS).
Bronze medal: J. Bambrick (SCO).

Katowice, Poland - 1975
L. Fly: A. Tkachenko (URS). **Fly:** V. Zasypko (URS). **Bantam:** V. Rybakov (URS). **Feather:** T. Badari (HUN). **Light:** S. Cutov (ROM). **L. Welter:** V. Limasov (URS). **Welter:** K. Marjaama (FIN). **L. Middle:** W. Rudnowski (POL). **Middle:** V. Lemechev (URS). **L. Heavy:** A. Klimanov (URS). **Heavy:** A. Biegalski (POL).
Bronze medals: C. Magri (ENG), P. Cowdell (ENG), G. McEwan (ENG).

Halle, East Germany - 1977
L. Fly: H. Srednicki (POL). **Fly:** L. Blazynski (POL). **Bantam:** S. Forster (GDR). **Feather:** R. Nowakowski (GDR). **Light:** A. Rusevski (YUG). **L. Welter:** B. Gajda (POL). **Welter:** V. Limasov (URS). **L. Middle:** V. Saychenko (URS). **Middle:** I. Shaposhnikov (URS). **L. Heavy:** D. Kvachadze (URS). **Heavy:** E. Gorstkov (URS).
Bronze medal: P. Sutcliffe (IRL).

Cologne, West Germany - 1979
L. Fly: S. Sabirov (URS). **Fly:** H. Strednicki (POL). **Bantam:** N. Khrapzov

(URS). **Feather:** V. Rybakov (URS). **Light.** V. Demianenko (URS). **L. Welter:** S. Konakbaev (URS). **Welter:** E. Muller (GER). **L. Middle:** M. Perunovic (YUG). **Middle:** T. Uusiverta (FIN). **L. Heavy:** A. Nikolyan (URS). **Heavy:** E. Gorstkov (URS). **S. Heavy:** P. Hussing (GER).
Bronze medal: P. Sutcliffe (IRL).

Tampere, Finland - 1981
L. Fly: I. Mustafov (BUL). **Fly:** P. Lessov (BUL). **Bantam:** V. Miroschnichenko (URS). **Feather:** R. Nowakowski (GDR). **Light:** V. Rybakov (URS). **L. Welter:** V. Shisov (URS). **Welter:** S. Konakvbaev (URS). **L. Middle:** A. Koshkin (URS). **Middle:** J. Torbek (URS). **L. Heavy:** A Krupin (URS). **Heavy:** A. Jagupkin (URS). **S. Heavy:** F. Damiani (ITA).
Bronze medal: G. Hawkins (IRL).

Varna, Bulgaria - 1983
L. Fly: I. Mustafov (BUL). **Fly:** P. Lessov (BUL). **Bantam:** Y. Alexandrov (URS). **Feather:** S. Nurkazov (URS). **Light:** E. Chuprenski (BUL). **L. Welter:** V. Shishov (URS). **Welter:** P. Galkin (URS). **L. Middle:** V. Laptev (URS). **Middle:** V. Melnik (URS). **L. Heavy:** V. Kokhanovski (URS). **Heavy:** A. Jagubkin (URS). **S. Heavy:** F. Damiani (ITA).
Bronze medal: K. Joyce (IRL).

Budapest, Hungary - 1985
L. Fly: R. Breitbarth (GDR). **Fly:** D. Berg (GDR). **Bantam:** L. Simic (YUG). **Feather:** S. Khachatrian (URS). **Light:** E. Chuprenski (BUL) **L. Welter:** S. Mehnert (GDR). **Welter:** I. Akopokhian (URS). **L. Middle:** M. Timm (GDR). **Middle:** H. Maske (GDR). **L. Heavy:** N. Shanavasov (URS). **Heavy:** A. Jagubkin (URS). **S. Heavy:** F. Somodi (HUN).
Bronze medals: S. Casey (IRL), J. Beckles (ENG).

Turin, Italy - 1987
L. Fly: N. Munchyan (URS). **Fly:** A. Tews (GDR). **Bantam:** A. Hristov (BUL). **Feather:** M. Kazaryan (URS). **Light:** O. Nazarov (URS). **L. Welter:** B. Abadjier (BUL). **Welter:** V. Shishov (URS). **L. Middle:** E. Richter (GDR). **Middle:** H. Maske (GDR). **L. Heavy:** Y. Vaulin (URS). **Heavy:** A. Vanderlijde (HOL). **S. Heavy:** U. Kaden (GDR).
Bronze medal: N. Brown (ENG).

Athens, Greece - 1989
L. Fly: I.Mustafov (BUL). **Fly:** Y. Arbachakov (URS). **Bantam:** S. Todorov (BUL). **Feather:** K. Kirkorov (BUL). **Light:** K. Tsziu (URS). **L. Welter:** I. Ruznikov (URS). **Welter:** S. Mehnert (GDR). **L. Middle:** I. Akopokhian (URS). **Middle:** H. Maske (GDR). **L. Heavy:** S. Lange (GDR). **Heavy:** A. Vanderlijde (HOL). **S. Heavy:** U. Kaden (GDR).
Bronze Medal: D. Anderson (SCO).

Gothenburg, Sweden - 1991
L. Fly: I. Marinov (BUL). **Fly:** I. Kovacs (HUN). **Bantam:** S. Todorov (BUL). **Feather:** P. Griffin (IRL). **Light:** V. Nistor (ROM). **L. Welter:** K. Tsziu (URS). **Welter:** R. Welin (SWE). **L. Middle:** I. Akopokhian (URS). **Middle:** S. Otke (GER). **L. Heavy:** D. Michalczewski (GER). **Heavy:** A. Vanderlijde (HOL). **S. Heavy:** E. Beloussov (URS).
Bronze medals: P. Weir (SCO), A. Vaughan (ENG).

Bursa, Turkey - 1993
L. Fly: D. Petrov (BUL). **Fly:** R. Husseinov (AZE). **Bantam:** R. Malakhbetov (URS). **Feather:** S. Todorov (BUL). **Light:** J. Bielski (POL). **L. Welter:** N. Suleymanogiu (TUR). **Welter:** V. Karpaclauskas (LIT). **L. Middle:** F. Vastag (ROM). **Middle:** D. Eigenbrodt (GER). **L. Heavy:** I. Kshinin (RUS). **Heavy:** G. Kandelaki (GEO). **S. Heavy:** S. Rusinov (BUL).
Bronze medals: P. Griffin (IRL), D. Williams (ENG), K. McCormack (WAL).

Vejle, Denmark - 1996
L. Fly: D. Petrov (BUL). **Fly:** A. Pakeev (RUS). **Bantam:** I. Kovacs (HUN). **Feather:** R. Paliani (RUS). **Light:** L. Doroftei (ROM). **L. Welter:** O. Urkal (GER). **Welter:** H. Al (DEN). **L. Middle:** F. Vastag (ROM). **Middle:** S. Ottke (GER). **L. Heavy:** P. Aurino (ITA). **Heavy:** L. Krasniqi (GER). **S. Heavy:** A. Lezin (RUS).
Bronze medals: S. Harrison (SCO), D. Burke (ENG), D. Kelly (IRL).

Note: Gold medals were awarded to the Europeans who went the furthest in the Olympic Games of 1924, 1928 & 1932.

European Junior Champions, 1970-1997

Miskolc, Hungary - 1970

L. Fly: Gluck (HUN). **Fly:** Z. Kismeneth (HUN). **Bantam:** A. Levitschev (URS). **Feather:** Andrianov (URS). **Light:** L. Juhasz (HUN). **L. Welter:** K. Nemec (HUN). **Welter:** Davidov (URS). **L. Middle:** A. Lemeschev (URS). **Middle:** N. Anfimov (URS). **L. Heavy:** O. Sasche (GDR). **Heavy:** J. Reder (HUN).
Bronze medals: D. Needham (ENG), R. Barlow (ENG), L. Stevens (ENG).

Bucharest, Romania - 1972

L. Fly: A. Turei (ROM). **Fly:** Condurat (ROM). **Bantam:** V. Solomin (URS). **Feather:** V. Lvov (URS). **Light:** S. Cutov (ROM). **L. Welter:** K. Pierwieniecki (POL). **Welter:** Zorov (URS). **L. Middle:** Babescu (ROM). **Middle:** V. Lemeschev (URS). **L. Heavy:** Mirounik (URS). **Heavy:** Subutin (URS).
Bronze medals: J. Gale (ENG), R. Maxwell (ENG), D. Odwell (ENG).

Kiev, Russia - 1974

L. Fly: A. Tkachenko (URS). **Fly:** V. Rybakov (URS). **Bantam:** C. Andreikovski (BUL). **Feather:** V. Sorokin (URS). **Light:** V. Limasov (URS). **L. Welter:** N. Sigov (URS). **Welter:** M. Bychkov (URS). **L. Middle:** V. Danshin (URS). **Middle:** D. Jende (GDR). **L. Heavy:** K. Dafinoiu (ROM). **Heavy:** K. Mashev (BUL).
Silver medal: C. Magri (ENG).
Bronze medals: G. Gilbody (ENG), K. Laing (ENG).

Izmir, Turkey - 1976

L. Fly: C. Seican (ROM). **Fly:** G. Khratsov (URS). **Bantam:** M. Navros (URS). **Feather:** V. Demoianeko (URS). **Light:** M. Puzovic (YUG). **L. Welter:** V. Zverev (URS). **Welter:** K. Ozoglouz (TUR). **L. Middle:** W. Lauder (SCO). **Middle:** H. Lenhart (GER). **L. Heavy:** I. Yantchauskas (URS). **Heavy:** B. Enjenyan (URS).
Silver medal: J. Decker (ENG).
Bronze medals: I. McLeod (SCO), N. Croombes (ENG).

Dublin, Ireland - 1978

L. Fly: R. Marx (GDR). **Fly:** D. Radu (ROM). **Bantam:** S. Khatchatrian (URS). **Feather:** H. Loukmanov (URS). **Light:** P. Oliva (ITA). **L. Welter:** V. Laptiev (URS). **Welter:** R. Filimanov (URS). **L. Middle:** A. Beliave (URS). **Middle:** G. Zinkovitch (URS). **L. Heavy:** I. Jolta (ROM). **Heavy:** P. Stoimenov (BUL).
Silver medals: M. Holmes (IRL), P. Hanlon (ENG), M. Courtney (ENG).
Bronze medals: T. Thompson (IRL), J. Turner (ENG), M. Bennett (WAL), J. McAllister (SCO), C. Devine (ENG).

Rimini, Italy - 1980

L. Fly: A. Mikoulin (URS). **Fly:** J. Varadi (HUN). **Bantam:** F. Rauschning (GDR). **Feather:** J. Gladychev (URS). **Light:** V. Shishov (URS). **L. Welter:** R. Lomski (BUL). **Welter:** T. Holonics (GDR). **L. Middle:** N. Wilshire (ENG). **Middle:** S. Laptiev (URS). **L. Heavy:** V. Dolgoun (URS). **Heavy:** V. Tioumentsev (URS). **S. Heavy:** S. Kormihtsine (URS).
Bronze medals: N. Potter (ENG), B. McGuigan (IRL), M. Brereton (IRL), D. Cross (ENG).

Schwerin, East Germany - 1982

L. Fly: R. Kabirov (URS). **Fly:** I. Filchev (BUL). **Bantam:** M. Stecca (ITA). **Feather:** B. Blagoev (BUL). **Light:** E. Chakimov (URS). **L. Welter:** S. Mehnert (GDR). **Welter:** T. Schmitz (GDR). **L. Middle:** B. Shararov (URS). **Middle:** E. Christie (ENG). **L. Heavy:** Y. Waulin (URS). **Heavy:** A. Popov (URS). **S. Heavy:** V. Aldoshin (URS).
Silver medal: D. Kenny (ENG).
Bronze medal: O. Jones (ENG).

Tampere, Finland - 1984

L. Fly: R. Breitbart (GDR). **Fly:** D. Berg (GDR). **Bantam:** K. Khdrian (URS). **Feather:** O. Nazarov (URS). **Light:** C. Furnikov (BUL). **L. Welter:** W. Schmidt (GDR). **Welter:** K. Doinov (BUL). **L. Middle:** O. Volkov (URS). **Middle:** R. Ryll (GDR). **L. Heavy:** G. Peskov (URS). **Heavy:** R. Draskovic (YUG). **S. Heavy:** L. Kamenov (BUL).
Bronze medals: J. Lowey (IRL), F. Harding (ENG), N. Moore (ENG).

Copenhagen, Denmark - 1986

L. Fly: S. Todorov (BUL). **Fly:** S. Galotian (URS). **Bantam:** D. Drumm (GDR). **Feather:** K. Tsziu (URS). **Light:** G. Akopkhian (URS). **L. Welter:** F. Vastag (ROM). **Welter:** S. Karavayev (URS). **L. Middle:** E. Elibaev (URS). **Middle:** A. Kurnabka (URS). **L. Heavy:** A. Schultz (GDR). **Heavy:** A. Golota (POL). **S. Heavy:** A. Prianichnikov (URS).

Gdansk, Poland - 1988

L. Fly: I. Kovacs (HUN). **Fly:** M. Beyer (GDR). **Bantam:** M. Aitzanov (URS). **Feather:** M. Rudolph (GDR). **Light:** M. Shaburov (URS). **L. Welter:** G. Campanella (ITA). **Welter:** D. Konsun (URS). **L. Middle:** K. Kiselev (URS). **Middle:** A. Rudenko (URS). **L. Heavy:** O. Velikanov (URS). **Heavy:** A. Ter-Okopian (URS). **S. Heavy:** E. Belusov (URS).
Bronze medals: P. Ramsey (ENG), M. Smyth (WAL).

Usti Nad Labem, Czechoslovakia - 1990

L. Fly: Z. Paliani (URS). **Fly:** K. Pielert (GDR). **Bantam:** K. Baravi (URS). **Feather:** P. Gvasalia (URS). **Light:** J. Hildenbrandt (GDR). **L. Welter:** N. Smanov (URS). **Welter:** A. Preda (ROM). **L. Middle:** A. Kakauridze (URS). **Middle:** J. Schwank (GDR). **L. Heavy:** Iljin (URS). **Heavy:** I. Andrejev (URS). **S. Heavy:** W. Fischer (GDR).
Silver medal: A. Todd (ENG).
Bronze medal: P. Craig (ENG).

Edinburgh, Scotland - 1992

L. Fly: M. Ismailov (URS). **Fly:** F. Brennfuhrer (GER). **Bantam:** S. Kuchler (GER). **Feather:** M. Silantiev (URS). **Light:** S. Shcherbakov (URS). **L. Welter:** O. Saitov (URS). **Welter:** H. Kurlumaz (TUR). **L. Middle:** Z. Erdie (HUN). **Middle:** V. Zhirov (URS). **L. Heavy:** D. Gorbachev (URS). **Heavy:** L. Achkasov (URS). **S. Heavy:** A. Mamedov (URS).
Silver medals: M. Hall (ENG), B. Jones (WAL).
Bronze medals: F. Slane (IRL), G. Stephens (IRL), C. Davies (WAL).

Salonika, Greece - 1993

L. Fly: O. Kiroukhine (UKR). **Fly:** R. Husseinov (AZE). **Bantam:** M. Kulbe (GER). **Feather:** E. Zakharov (RUS). **Light:** O. Sergeev (RUS). **L. Welter:** A. Selihanov (RUS). **Welter:** O. Kudinov (UKR). **L. Middle:** E. Makarenko (RUS). **Middle:** D. Droukovski (RUS). **L. Heavy:** A. Voida (RUS). **Heavy:** V. Klitchko (UKR). **S. Heavy:** A. Moiseev (RUS).
Bronze medal: D. Costello (ENG).

Sifok, Hungary - 1995

L. Fly: D. Gaissine (RUS). **Fly:** A. Kotelnik (UKR). **Bantam:** A. Loutsenko (UKR). **Feather:** S. Harrison (SCO). **Light:** D. Simon (ROM). **L. Welter:** B. Ulusoy (TUR). **Welter:** O. Bouts (UKR). **L. Middle:** O. Bukalo (UKR). **Middle:** V. Plettnev (RUS). **L. Heavy:** A. Derevtsov (RUS). **Heavy:** C. O'Grady (IRL). **S. Heavy:** D. Savvine (RUS).
Silver medal: G. Murphy (SCO).
Bronze medal: N. Linford (ENG).

Birmingham, England - 1997

L. Fly: G. Balakshine (RUS). **Fly:** K. Dzhamoloudinov (RUS). **Bantam:** A. Shaiduline (RUS). **Feather:** D. Marciukaitis (LIT). **Light:** D. Baranov (RUS). **L. Welter:** A. Mishine (RUS). **Welter:** D. Yuldashev (UKR). **L. Middle:** A. Catic (GER). **Middle:** D. Lebedev (RUS). **L. Heavy:** V. Uzelkov (UKR). **Heavy:** S. Koeber (GBR). **S. Heavy:** D. Pirozhenko (RUS).
Silver medal: S. Miller (ENG).
Bronze medals: S. Burke (ENG), M. Dean (ENG), P. Pierson (ENG), M. Lee (IRE).

Note: The age limit for the championships were reduced from 21 to 19 in 1976.

Commonwealth Champions, 1930-1994

Hamilton, Canada - 1930

Fly: W. Smith (SAF). **Bantam:** H. Mizler (ENG). **Feather:** F. Meacham (ENG). **Light:** J. Rolland (SCO). **Welter:** L. Hall (SAF). **Middle:** F. Mallin

(ENG). **L. Heavy:** J. Goyder (ENG). **Heavy:** V. Stuart (ENG).
Silver medals: T. Pardoe (ENG), T. Holt (SCO).
Bronze medals: A. Lyons (SCO), A. Love (ENG), F. Breeman (ENG).

Wembley, England - 1934

Fly: P. Palmer (ENG). **Bantam:** F. Ryan (ENG). **Feather:** C. Cattarall (SAF). **Light:** L. Cook (AUS). **Welter:** D. McCleave (ENG). **Middle:** A. Shawyer (ENG). **L. Heavy:** G. Brennan (ENG). **Heavy:** P. Floyd (ENG).
Silver medals: A. Barnes (WAL), J. Jones (WAL), F. Taylor (WAL), J. Holton (SCO).
Bronze medals: J. Pottinger (WAL), T. Wells (SCO), H. Moy (ENG), W. Duncan (NIR), J. Magill (NIR), Lord D. Douglas-Hamilton (SCO).

Melbourne, Australia - 1938

Fly: J. Joubert (SAF). **Bantam:** W. Butler (ENG). **Feather:** A. Henricus (CEY). **Light:** H. Groves (ENG). **Welter:** W. Smith (AUS). **Middle:** D. Reardon (WAL). **L. Heavy:** N. Wolmarans (SAF). **Heavy:** T. Osborne (CAN).
Silver medals: J. Watson (SCO), M. Dennis (ENG).
Bronze medals: H. Cameron (SCO), J. Wilby (ENG).

Auckland, New Zealand - 1950

Fly: H. Riley (SCO). **Bantam:** J. van Rensburg (SAF). **Feather:** H. Gilliland (SCO). **Light:** R. Latham (ENG). **Welter:** T. Ratcliffe (ENG). **Middle:** T. van Schalkwyk (SAF). **L. Heavy:** D. Scott (ENG). **Heavy:** F. Creagh (NZL).
Bronze medal: P. Brander (ENG).

Vancouver, Canada - 1954

Fly: R. Currie (SCO). **Bantam:** J. Smillie (SCO). **Feather:** L. Leisching (SAF). **Light:** P. van Staden (SR). **L. Welter:** M. Bergin (CAN). **Welter:** N. Gargano (ENG). **L. Middle:** W. Greaves (CAN). **Middle:** J. van de Kolff (SAF). **L. Heavy:** P. van Vuuren (SAF). **Heavy:** B. Harper (ENG).
Silver medals: M. Collins (WAL), F. McQuillan (SCO).
Bronze medals: D. Charnley (ENG), B. Wells (ENG).

Cardiff, Wales - 1958

Fly: J. Brown (SCO). **Bantam:** H. Winstone (WAL). **Feather:** W. Taylor (AUS). **Light:** R. McTaggart (SCO). **L. Welter:** H. Loubscher (SAF). **Welter:** J. Greyling (SAF). **L. Middle:** G. Webster (SAF). **Middle:** T. Milligan (NIR). **L. Heavy:** A. Madigan (AUS). **Heavy:** D. Bekker (SAF).
Silver medals: T. Bache (ENG), M. Collins (WAL), J. Jordan (NIR), R. Kane (SCO), S. Pearson (ENG), A. Higgins (WAL), D. Thomas (ENG).
Bronze medals: P. Lavery (NIR), D. Braithwaite (WAL), R. Hanna (NIR), A. Owen (SCO), J. McClory (NIR), J. Cooke (ENG), J. Jacobs (ENG), B. Nancurvis (ENG), R. Scott (SCO), W. Brown (WAL), J. Caiger (ENG), W. Bannon (SCO), R. Pleace (WAL).

Perth, Australia - 1962

Fly: R. Mallon (SCO). **Bantam:** J. Dynevor (AUS). **Feather:** J. McDermott (SCO). **Light:** E. Blay (GHA). **L. Welter:** C. Quartey (GHA). **Welter:** W. Coe (NZL). **L. Middle:** H. Mann (CAN). **Middle:** M. Calhoun (JAM). **L. Heavy:** A. Madigan (AUS). **Heavy:** G. Oywello (UGA).
Silver medals: R. McTaggart (SCO), J. Pritchett (ENG).
Bronze medals: M. Pye (ENG), P. Benneyworth (ENG), B. Whelan (ENG), B. Brazier (ENG), C. Rice (NIR), T. Menzies (SCO), H. Christie (NIR), A. Turmel (CI).

Kingston, Jamaica - 1966

Fly: S. Shittu (GHA). **Bantam:** E. Ndukwu (NIG). **Feather:** P. Waruinge (KEN). **Light:** A. Andeh (NIG). **L. Welter:** J. McCourt (NIR). **Welter:** E. Blay (GHA). **L. Middle:** M. Rowe (ENG). **Middle:** J. Darkey (GHA). **L. Heavy:** R. Tighe (ENG). **Heavy:** W. Kini (NZL).
Silver medals: P. Maguire (NIR), R. Thurston (ENG), R. Arthur (ENG), T. Imrie (SCO).
Bronze medals: S. Lockhart (NIR), A. Peace (SCO), F. Young (NIR), J. Turpin (ENG), D. McAlinden (NIR).

Edinburgh, Scotland - 1970

L. Fly: J. Odwori (UGA). **Fly:** D. Needham (ENG). **Bantam:** S. Shittu (GHA). **Feather:** P. Waruinge (KEN). **Light:** A. Adeyemi (NIG). **L. Welter:** M. Muruli (UGA). **Welter:** E. Ankudey (GHA). **L. Middle:** T.

Imrie (SCO). **Middle:** J. Conteh (ENG). **L. Heavy:** F. Ayinla (NIG). **Heavy:** B. Masanda (UGA).
Silver medals: T. Davies (WAL), J. Gillan (SCO), D. Davies (WAL), J. McKinty (NIR).
Bronze medals: M. Abrams (ENG), A. McHugh (SCO), D. Larmour (NIR), S. Oglivie (SCO), A. Richardson (ENG), T. Joyce (SCO), P. Doherty (NIR), J. Rafferty (SCO), L. Stevens (ENG).

Christchurch, New Zealand - 1974

L. Fly: S. Muchoki (KEN). **Fly:** D. Larmour (NIR). **Bantam:** P. Cowdell (ENG). **Feather:** E. Ndukwu (NIG). **Light:** A. Kalule (UGA). **L. Welter:** O. Nwankpa (NIG). **Welter:** M. Muruli (UGA). **L. Middle:** L. Mwale (ZAM). **L. Heavy:** W. Knight (ENG). **Heavy:** N. Meade (ENG).
Silver medals: E. McKenzie (WAL), A. Harrison (SCO).
Bronze medals: J. Bambrick (SCO), J. Douglas (SCO), J. Rodgers (NIR), S. Cooney (SCO), R. Davies (ENG), C. Speare (ENG), G. Ferris (NIR).

Edmonton, Canada - 1978

L. Fly: S. Muchoki (KEN). **Fly:** M. Irungu (KEN). **Bantam:** B. McGuigan (NIR). **Feather:** A. Nelson (GHA). **Light:** G. Hamill (NIR). **L. Welter:** W. Braithwaite (GUY). **Welter:** M. McCallum (JAM). **L. Middle:** K. Perlette (CAN). **Middle:** P. McElwaine (AUS). **L. Heavy:** R. Fortin (CAN). **Heavy:** J. Awome (ENG).
Silver medals: J. Douglas (SCO), K. Beattie (NIR), D. Parkes (ENG), V. Smith (ENG).
Bronze medals: H. Russell (NIR), M. O'Brien (ENG), J. McAllister (SCO), T. Feal (WAL).

Brisbane, Australia - 1982

L. Fly: A. Wachire (KEN). **Fly:** M. Mutua (KEN). **Bantam:** J. Orewa (NIG). **Feather:** P. Konyegwachie (NIG). **Light:** H. Khalili (KEN). **L. Welter:** C. Ossai (NIG). **Welter:** C. Pyatt (ENG). **L. Middle:** S. O'Sullivan (CAN). **Middle:** J. Price (ENG). **L. Heavy:** F. Sani (FIJ). **Heavy:** W. de Wit (CAN).
Silver medals: J. Lyon (ENG), J. Kelly (SCO), R. Webb (NIR), P. Hanlon (ENG), J. McDonnell (ENG), N. Croombes (ENG), H. Hylton (ENG).
Bronze medals: R. Gilbody (ENG), C. McIntosh (ENG), R. Corr (NIR).

Edinburgh, Scotland - 1986

L. Fly: S. Olson (CAN). **Fly:** J. Lyon (ENG). **Bantam:** S. Murphy (ENG). **Feather:** B. Downey (CAN). **Light:** A. Dar (CAN). **L. Welter:** H. Grant (CAN). **Welter:** D. Dyer (ENG). **L. Middle:** D. Sherry (CAN). **Middle:** R. Douglas (ENG). **L. Heavy:** J. Moran (ENG). **Heavy:** J. Peau (NZL). **S. Heavy:** L. Lewis (CAN).
Silver medals: M. Epton (ENG), R. Nash (NIR), P. English (ENG), N. Haddock (WAL), J. McAlister (SCO), H. Lawson (SCO), D. Young (SCO), A. Evans (WAL).
Bronze medals: W. Docherty (SCO), J. Todd (NIR), K. Webber (WAL), G. Brooks (SCO), J. Wallace (SCO), C. Carleton (NIR), J. Jacobs (ENG), B. Lowe (NIR), D. Denny (NIR), G. Thomas (WAL), A. Mullen (SCO), G. Ferrie (SCO), P. Tinney (NIR), B. Pullen (WAL), E. Cardouza (ENG), J. Oyebola (ENG), J. Sillitoe (CI).

Auckland, New Zealand - 1990

L. Fly: J. Juuko (UGA). **Fly:** W. McCullough (NIR). **Bantam:** S. Mohammed (NIG). **Feather:** J. Irwin (ENG). **Light:** G. Nyakana (UGA). **L. Welter:** C. Kane (SCO). **Welter:** D. Defiagbon (NIG). **L. Middle:** R. Woodhall (ENG). **Middle:** C. Johnson (CAN). **L. Heavy:** J. Akhasamba (KEN). **Heavy:** G. Onyango (KEN). **S. Heavy:** M. Kenny (NZL).
Bronze medals: D. Anderson (SCO), M. Edwards (ENG), P. Douglas (NIR).

Victoria, Canada - 1994

L. Fly: H. Ramadhani (KEN). **Fly:** P. Shepherd (SCO). **Bantam:** R. Peden (AUS). **Feather:** C. Patton (CAN). **Light:** M. Strange (CAN). **L. Welter:** P. Richardson (ENG). **Welter:** N. Sinclair (NIR). **L. Middle:** J. Webb (NIR). **Middle:** R. Donaldson (CAN). **L. Heavy:** D. Brown (CAN). **Heavy:** O. Ahmed (KEN). **S. Heavy:** D. Dokiwari (NIG).
Silver medals: S. Oliver (ENG), J. Cook (WAL), M. Renaghan (NIR), M. Winters (NIR), J. Wilson (SCO).
Bronze medals: D. Costello (ENG), J. Townsley (SCO), D. Williams (ENG).

The Triple Hitters' Boxing Quiz (Part Two)

Compiled by Ralph Oates

QUESTIONS

1. Jack Johnson won the world heavyweight title when he stopped defending champion, Tommy Burns, in round 14 on 26 December 1908. Who was the referee of this contest?
   A. Hugh McIntosh.   B. H.C. Nathan.   C. Jack Welch.

2. Arnold Raymond Cream was the real name of which former world heavyweight champion?
   A. Ezzard Charles.   B. Max Baer.
   C. Jersey Joe Walcott.

3. Which former world light-heavyweight champion was nicknamed "The Orchid Man"?
   A. Tommy Loughran.   B. Georges Carpentier.
   C. Maxie Rosenbloom.

4. To win the world light-heavyweight title, Freddie Mills defeated defending champion, Gus Lesnevich, on 26 July 1948. By which method?
   A. Fourth-round knockout.   B. Ninth-round stoppage.
   C. Fifteen-round points decision.

5. Carlos Monzon retained his world middleweight title on 17 June 1972 when the challenger, Jean-Claude Bouttier, retired in round 12. In which country did this contest take place?
   A. Argentina.   B. France.   C. Denmark.

6. John H. Stracey won the WBC version of the world welterweight title when he stopped defending champion, Jose Napoles, in round six, in a contest which took place on 6 December 1975. Who was the referee of this bout?
   A. Waldemar Schmidt.   B. Octavio Meyran.
   C. Carlos Berrocal.

7. What was the nationality of former world welterweight champion, Curtis Cokes?
   A. Cuban.   B. American.   C. Canadian.

8. In which year did Scotland's Jim Watt win the WBC world lightweight title?
   A. 1978.   B. 1979.   C. 1980.

9. On 25 November 1995, Billy Schwer lost his Commonwealth lightweight title to David Tetteh when he was stopped. In which round?
   A. 10.   B. 11.   C. 12.

10. Who was the first holder of the European super-featherweight title?
    A. Tommaso Galli.   B. Lothar Abend.
    C. Cornelius Boza-Edwards.

11. Which one of these fighters boxed in the southpaw stance?

A. Charlie Magri.   B. Alan Minter.   C. Alan Rudkin.

12. Prince Naseem Hamed made the second defence of the WBO world featherweight title on 8 June 1996 and thus retained his crown by stopping challenger, Daniel Alicea, in round two. Where did this contest take place?
    A. Liverpool.   B. Manchester.   C. Newcastle.

13. How many professional contests did former world, European, and British featherweight champion, Howard Winstone, win in the first round?
    A. One.   B. Two.   C. None.

14. On 6 February 1996, Richie Wenton made the second defence of his British super-bantamweight title against Wilson Docherty and retained his crown. By which method?
    A. Fifth-round knockout.   B. Eighth-round stoppage.
    C. Twelve-round points decision.

15. During his pro career, former European, British, and Commonwealth bantamweight champion, Alan Rudkin, had how many contests?
    A. 49.   B. 50.   C. 51.

16. To win the Commonwealth flyweight crown, Peter Culshaw stopped defending champion, Danny Ward, in which round?
A. One.   B. Two.   C. Three.

17. To win the vacant WBU light-welterweight title, Shea Neary outpointed Darryl Tyson over 12 rounds on 26 October 1996. Who was the referee for this contest?
A. Mills Lane.   B. Steve Smoger.   C. Lou Fillipo.

18. In which year was former world, European, British and Commonwealth light-heavyweight champion, John Conteh, born?
A. 1951.   B. 1952.   C. 1953.

19. In defence of his Commonwealth light-heavyweight crown on 30 November 1996, Nicky Piper stopped challenger, Bruce Scott. Name the round?
A. Seven.   B. Eight.   C. Nine.

20. Paul Ingle won the British featherweight crown when he stopped defending champion, Colin McMillan, in round eight on 11 January 1997. Who was the referee of this contest?
A. Roy Francis.   B. John Coyle.   C. Mickey Vann.

21. During his pro career, which heavyweight title did Frank Bruno not hold?
A. European.   B. World.   C. British.

22. Who is nicknamed "The Grim Reaper"?
A. Dean Pithie.   B. Robin Reid.   C. Pele Reid.

23. Which boxer is not from Wales?

A. Charlie Magri.   B. Tommy Farr.   C. Brian Curvis.

24. Which boxer did Eddie Thomas not manage during his career?
A. Ken Buchanan.   B. Howard Winstone.
C. Maurice Hope.

25. Which punch was former European, British and Commonwealth heavyweight champion, Henry Cooper, famous for?
A. The uppercut.   B. Right cross.   C. Left hook.

26. Which boxer did Terry Lawless manage during his career?
A. John H. Stracey.   B. Alan Rudkin.   C. Jack Bodell.

27. On 7 February 1997, Lennox Lewis became the first British-born boxer to regain the world heavyweight championship when he stopped Oliver McCall in round five for the vacant WBC title. In which part of America did the above contest take place?
A. Las Vegas.   B. San Francisco.   C. Boston.

28. How tall is former British flyweight champion, Mickey Cantwell?
A. 5ft.   B. 5ft.1in.   C. 5ft.2$\frac{1}{2}$in.

29. Who was the first man to defeat Nicky Piper in the pro ranks when stopping him in the third round on 4 September 1991?
A. Maurice Core.   B. Nigel Benn.   C. Carl Thompson.

30. How many world middleweight title bouts did former champion, Terry Downes, have during his career?
A. Two.   B. Three.   C. Four.

31. Which version of the world featherweight crown did Paul Hodkinson once hold?
A. WBA.   B. WBC.   C. IBF.

32. Who is not from Scotland?
A. Katherine Morrison.   B. Johnny Nelson.
C. Gary Jacobs.

33. In which year was former world welterweight and middleweight champion, Emile Griffith, born?
A. 1938.   B. 1939.   C. 1940.

34. Which world title did Japan's Masahiko "Fighting" Harada not hold during his pro career?
A. Flyweight.   B. Bantamweight.   C. Featherweight.

35. On 14 December 1996, Ryan Rhodes won the vacant British light-middleweight crown when he stopped former world title holder, Paul "Silky" Jones, in round eight. Which version of the world light-middleweight championship did Jones once hold?
A. WBC.   B. WBO.   C. WBA.

36. Samam Sorjaturong retained his WBC light-flyweight title on 14 December 1996 when he defeated the challenger, Manuel Herrera. By which method was victory achieved?
A. Fifth-round knockout.   B. Eighth-round stoppage.
C. Twelve-round points decision.

37. Who hosts the TV series "Ringside Boxing"?
    A. Reg Gutteridge.   B. Tania Follett.
    C. Paul Dempsey.

38. Which boxer was nicknamed "Homicide Hank"?

    A. Henry Hank.   B. Henry Armstrong.
    C. Henry Nissen.

39. Heavyweight Pele Reid stopped his opponent, Michael Murray, in the first round on 25 February 1997 and thus recorded the quickest ever win at that time in the history of British boxing. How many seconds did the contest last?
    A. Nine.   B. Ten.   C. Eleven.

40. Guglielmo Papaleo boxed under which name in the pro ranks?
    A. Jackie Wilson.   B. Willie Pep.   C. Phil Terranova.

41. On a Mike Barrett promotion which took place on 6 December 1966, Billy Walker stopped American opponent, Ray Patterson, in round eight. True or false? Ray was the brother of former two-time world heavyweight champion, Floyd Patterson.

42. Who was the Commonwealth super-middleweight champion prior to Henry Wharton?
    A. Lou Cafaro.   B. Rod Carr.   C. Sipho Moyo.

43. In the Olympic Games of 1984, Pernell Whitaker won a gold medal, but in which weight division?
    A. Featherweight.   B. Lightweight.
    C. Light-Welterweight.

44. In which year did Dennis Andries have his first pro contest?
    A. 1976.   B. 1977.   C. 1978.

45. Who is associated with Panix Promotions?
    A. Mickey Duff.   B. Frank Maloney.   C. Barry Hearn.

46. On 8 February 1997, Prince Naseem Hamed added the IBF world featherweight title to his WBO crown when he stopped Tom "Boom Boom" Johnson in round eight of a unification contest. Who was the referee of this championship bout?
    A. Lou Filippo.   B. Rudy Battle.   C. Joe Cortez.

47. On 1 March 1997, Hector "Macho" Camacho defended his IBC middleweight crown against "Sugar" Ray Leonard and stopped him. In which round?
    A. Five.   B. Six.   C. Seven.

48. On 27 January 1993, Barry Jones outpointed future British featherweight champion, Mike Deveney, over six rounds. Where did this contest take place?
    A. Newport.   B. Llanelli.   C. Cardiff.

49. In 1988, Michael Moorer had 12 bouts. How many of them did he win in the first round?
    A. Five.   B. Six.   C. Seven.

50. Who was the first holder of the Commonwealth light-middleweight title?
    A. Kenny Bristol.   B. Maurice Hope.
    C. Charkey Ramon.

ANSWERS

1: Hugh McIntosh. 2: Jersey Joe Walcott. 3: Georges Carpentier. 4: Fifteen-round points decision. 5: France. 6: Octavio Meyran. 7: American. 8: 1979. 9: 12. 10: Tommaso Galli. 11: Alan Minter. 12: Newcastle. 13: None. 14: Twelve-round points decision. 15: 50. 16: Three. 17: Steve Smoger. 18: 1951. 19: Seven. 20: John Coyle. 21: British. 22: Robin Reid. 23: Charlie Magri. 24: Maurice Hope. 25: Left hook. 26: John H. Stracey. 27: Las Vegas. 28: 5ft.2½in. 29: Carl Thompson. 30: Three. 31: WBC. 32: Johnny Nelson. 33: 1938. 34: Featherweight. 35: WBO. 36: Twelve-round points decision. 37: Paul Dempsey. 38: Henry Armstrong. 39: Nine. 40: Willie Pep. 41: True. 42: Lou Cafaro. 43: Lightweight. 44: 1978. 45: Frank Maloney. 46: Rudy Battle. 47: Five. 48: Cardiff. 49: Five. 50: Charkey Ramon.

Directory of Ex-Boxers' Associations

by Ron Olver

BIRMINGHAM Founded 1985. Disbanded. Re-formed 1995. HQ: Emerald Club, Green Lane, Birmingham. Ernie Cashmore (P); Paddy Maguire (C), 265 Mackadown Lane, Tilecross, Birmingham. Bobby Sexton (T); Tom Byrne (S).

BOURNEMOUTH Founded 1980. HQ: Mallard Road Bus Services Social Club, Bournemouth. Dai Dower (P); Peter Fay (C & S); Percy Singer (T); Ken Wells (VC).

CORK Founded 1973. HQ: Acra House, Maylor Street, Cork. Johnny Fitzgerald (P & C); John Cronin (VC); Eamer Coughlan (T); Tim O'Sullivan (S & PRO), Acra House, Maylor Street, Dublin.

CORNWALL Founded 1989. HQ: St Austell British Legion and Royal Hotel, Camborne in alternate months. Roy Coote (P); Len Magee (C), Fred Edwards (VC); Jimmy Miller (T); Bill Matthews (S), 33 Victoria Road, St Austell, Cornwall PL25 4QF.

CROYDON Founded 1982. HQ: The Prince Of Wales, Thornton Heath. Tom Powell, BEM (P); Martin Olney (C), Chris Wood (VC); Bill Flemington (T); Richard Evans (PRO); Gilbert Allnutt (S), 37 Braemar Avenue, Thornton Heath, Croydon CR9 7RJ.

EASTERN AREA Founded 1973. HQ: Norfolk Dumpling, Cattle Market, Hall Road, Norwich. Brian Fitzmaurice (P); Alfred Smith (C); Clive Campling (VC); Eric Middleton (T & S), 48 City Road, Norwich NR1 3AU.

IPSWICH Founded 1970. HQ: Flying Horse, Waterford Road, Ipswich. Alby Kingham (P); Frank Webb (C); Vic Thurlow (T); Nigel Wheeler (PRO & S); 20 Stratford Road, Ipswich 1PL 6OF.

IRISH Founded 1973. HQ: National Boxing Stadium, South Circular Road, Dublin. Maxie McCullagh (P); Jack O'Rourke (C); Willie Duggan (VC); Tommy Butler (T); Denis Morrison (S), 55 Philipsburgh Terrace, Marino, Dublin.

KENT Founded 1967. HQ: Chatham WMC, New Road, Chatham. Teddy Bryant (P); Bill Warner (C & T); Mick Smith (VC); Ray Lambert (PRO); Paul Nihill MBE, (S), 59 Balfour Road, Rochester, Kent.

KINGSTON UPON HULL & EAST YORKSHIRE Founded 1996. HQ: The Whittington & Cat, Commercial Road, Old Town, Hull HU1 2SA. Wally Mays (C); Stan Gossip (VC); Bert Smith (T); Gilbert Johnson (S); Mike Ulyatt (PRO), 28 Blackthorn Lane, Willerby, East Yorkshire HU10 6RD.

LEEDS Founded 1952. HQ: North Leeds WMC, Burmantofts, Lincoln Green, Leeds 9. Johnny Durkin (P); Greg Steene (HP); Frankie Brown (C); Alan Alster (T); Steve Butler (PRO); Malcolm Bean (S), 11 Crawshaw Gardens, Pudsey, Leeds LS28 7 BW

LEFT-HOOK CLUB Betty Faux (S), 144 Longmoor Lane, Aintree, Liverpool. No regular meetings. Formed specifically with the aim of holding functions to raise money in order to help former boxers in need.

LEICESTER Founded 1972. HQ: Belgrave WMC, Checketts Road, Leicester. Pat Butler (P); Mick Greaves (C); Mrs Rita Jones (T); Norman Jones (S), 60 Dumbleton Avenue, Leicester LE3 2EG.

LONDON Founded 1971. HQ; St Pancras Conservative Club, Argyle Square, London. Stephen Powell (P); Micky O'Sullivan (C); Andy Williamson (VC); Ron Olver (PRO); Ray Caulfield (T); Mrs Mary Powell (S), 36 St Peters Street, Islington, London N1 8JT.

MANCHESTER Founded 1968. HQ: British Rail Social Club, Store Street, Manchester. Jackie Braddock (P); Jack Jamieson (AP); Tommy Proffitt (C); Jack Edwards (VC); Eddie Lillis (T); John Fleming (S), 24 Oakbank Avenue, Moston, Manchester M9 1EX.

MERSEYSIDE (Liverpool) Founded 1973. HQ: Transport Drivers Club, Hockenhall Alley, Liverpool. Johnny Cooke (P); Terry Riley (C); Jim Boyd (VC); Jim Jenkinson (T); Sandy Manuel (S), 26 Cantsfield Street, Wavertree, Liverpool L7 4JZ.

NORTHAMPTONSHIRE Founded 1981. HQ: Exclusive Club, Gold Street, Northampton. Joe Grundler (P); Dick Rogers (C); Paddy Hyland (VC); Robin Murray-Basham (T); Sid Green (S), 8 Friars Close, Delapre, Northampton NN4 8PU.

NORTHERN FEDERATION Founded 1974. Several member EBAs. Annual Gala. Eddie Monahan (S), 16 Braemar Avenue, Marshside, Southport.

NORTHERN IRELAND Founded 1970. HQ: Ulster Sports Club, Belfast. Derek Wade (P); Benny Vaughan (C); Sammy Cosgrove (VC & PRO); Sammy Thompson (T); Al Gibson (S), 900 Crumlin Road, Belfast.

NORTH STAFFS & SOUTH CHESHIRE Founded 1969. HQ: The Saggar Makers Bottom Knocker, Market Place, Burslem, Stoke on Trent. Tut Whalley (P); Roy Simms (VC); Les Dean (S); John Greatbach (T); Billy Tudor (C & PRO), 133 Sprinkbank Road, Chell Heath, Stoke on Trent, Staffs ST6 6HW.

NORWICH HQ: West End Retreat, Brown Street, Norwich. Les King (P); John Pipe (C); Jack Wakefield (T); Dick Sadd (S), 76 Orchard Street, Norwich.

NOTTINGHAM Founded 1979. HQ: The Lion Hotel, Clumber Street, Nottingham. Frank Parkes (P); Len Chorley (C); Mrs B. Booker (T); Graham Rooksby (S), 42 Spinney Road, Heworth, Notts NG12 5LN.

PLYMOUTH Founded 1982. HQ: Exmouth Road Social Club, Stoke, Plymouth. George Borg (P); Tom Pryce-Davies (C); Doug Halliday (VC); Arthur Willis (T); Buck Taylor (S), 15 Greenbank Avenue, St Judes, Plymouth PL4 9BT.

PRESTON Founded 1973. HQ: County Arms Hotel, Deepdale Road, Preston. Harry Finch (P); John Allen (C); Brian Atkinson (T & S), County Arms Hotel, Preston.

ST HELENS Founded 1983. HQ: Travellers Rest Hotel, Crab Street, St Helens. Johnny Molloy (P); George Thomas (C); Jimmy O'Keefe (VC); Tommy McNamara (T); Paul Britch (S), 40 Ashtons Green Drive, Parr, St Helens.

SCOTTISH Founded 1997. Frank O'Donnell (S), 14 Dougrie Drive, Castlemilk, Glasgow G45 9AD.

SLOUGH Founded 1973. HQ: Faraday Hall Ex-Servicemens' Club, Slough. Max Quartermain (P); Ken Curtis (C); Gordon Jones (T); Ernie Watkins (S), 5 Sunbury Road, Eton, Windsor.

SQUARE RING Founded 1978. HQ: Torquay Social Club. George Pook (P); Maxie Beech (VC); Johnny Mudge (S); Jim Banks (T); Paul King (C), 10 Pine Court Apartments, Middle Warberry Road, Torquay.

SUNDERLAND Founded 1959. HQ: Hendon Gardens, Sunderland. Jack Wilson (P); Terry Lynn (C); Joe Riley (PRO); Wilf Lawrence (T); Les Simm (S), 21 Orchard Street, Pallion, Sunderland SR4 6QL.

SUSSEX Founded 1974. HQ: Brighton & Hove Sports & Social Club, Conway Street, Hove. Geoff Williams (P & T); Bert Hollows (C); Eric Moulson (S), 43 Ruskin Road, Hove EN3 5HA.

SWANSEA & SOUTH WEST WALES Founded 1983. HQ: Villiers Arms, Neath Road, Hafod, Swansea. Cliff Curvis (P); Gordon Pape (C); Ernie Wallis (T); Len Smith (S), Cockett Inn, Cockett, Swansea SA2 0GB.

TRAMORE Founded 1981. HQ: Robinson Bar, Main Street, Tramore, Co Waterford. T. Flynn (P); J. Dunne (C); C. O'Reilly (VC); W. Hutchinson (T); Peter Graham (S), 3 Riverstown, Tramore.

TYNESIDE Founded 1970. HQ: Pelaw Social Club, Heworth, Pelaw. Billy Charlton (P); Maxie Walsh (C); Gordon Smith (VC); Malcolm Dinning (T); Bill Wilkie (S & PRO), 60 Calderdale Avenue, Walker, Newcastle NE6 4HN.
WELSH Founded 1976. HQ: Rhydyfelin Rugby Club, Pontypridd. Howard Winstone (P); Terry Pudge (C); Llew Miles (T & PRO); Johnny Jones (S), 1 Meadow Street, Garden Village, Gilfach Goch CF39 8TA.
The above information is set at the time of going to press and no responsibility can be taken for any changes in officers or addresses of HQs that may happen between then and publication or changes that have not been notified to me.

ABBREVIATIONS
P - President. HP - Honorary President. AP - Acting President. C - Chairman. VC - Vice Chairman. T - Treasurer. S - Secretary. PRO - Public Relations Officer and/or Press Officer.

Ron Olver (left) pictured at the launch of the 1995 British Boxing Yearbook. Also in the frame (left to right) are Jonathan Ticehurst, Simon Block, Dr Ossie Ross, and in the foreground, John Morris Tony Fitch

Obituaries

by Ron Olver

It is impossible to list everyone, but I have again done my best to include final tributes for as many of the well-known boxers and other familiar names within the sport, who have passed away since the 1997 Yearbook was published. We honour them and will remember them.

ARCHER Fred *From* Hucknall. *Died* July 1997, aged 69. Noted for his power of punch, among his victims were Tommy Hewson (first round), Les Dallison (first), Teddy Wilson (first), Mick Straw (second), Barry Leonard (first), and Johnny Hunt (fourth). After being stopped by Frank Priest (1950), he retired for two years before coming back to win an open competition at Derby. Managed and trained by top record compiler, Vic Hardwicke, after retiring he became a councillor with Hucknall District Council. Also took up road running and won many events all over Britain.

ARNOLD George *From* Dublin. *Died* May 1997, aged 65. Former Irish champion and international. Settled in Luton, joining Electrolux, and powered his way to the London welter title in 1954 before going out at the penultimate stage of the ABA championships to the legendary Nicky Gargano on points. Could have become a professional singer, but preferred to retain his amateur status. Later became a member of the London Ex-Boxers' Association.

ATKINSON Charles *From* Liverpool. *Died* 17 December 1996, aged 83. An outstanding coach and trainer, he coached Frank Hope to the ABA middleweight title (1955), Liverpool's first, and stayed in the amateurs until Joey Singleton and Tony Byrne turned pro and persuaded him to go with them. Was involved with all Liverpool's world champions and looked after John Conteh from the age of ten until he turned pro. Also looked after Paul Hodkinson. He died two months after preparing Shea Neary for his winning bout over Darryl Tyson in their WBU light-welterweight title fight. Son, Charles junior, along with brother Mike, promoted at the now-demolished Liverpool Stadium and is now ITV's boxing adviser, as well as a trainer and cornerman.

BARTER Ted *From* Kingston. *Died* 19 December 1996, aged 81. With a real name of Henry Farman Littleproud, which was too long for boxing bills and too much of a mouthful for MCs, he turned pro at 15 and averaged 20 fights a year throughout his career. While confessing he most enjoyed his stints with Alf Stewart's booth, as a licensed pro, his victims included R. H. S. Clouston, Bob Scally, Ben Smith, Jim Toohig, Jack Daly, Pat Mulcahy, Billy Bird, Dixie Cullen, and Paddy Bennett. Joining the RAF in World War II, the first fighter of note that he ever saw was Ted Kid Lewis, and a dream came true when Ted was in his corner when he boxed at RAF Duxford. Continued to box during the war years, his victims included Gene Fowler, Albert O'Brien, Jack Barr, Jimmy Hockley, and Jack Lewis. Also met Freddie Mills, Albert Finch, Johnny Williams, and Mark Hart. On retiring,

moved into amateur boxing, receiving an ABA Coaching Certificate with Kingson BC (1969), and rose to Clerk of Works for the local council. A member of London, Croydon and Sussex EBAs, in 1980 he travelled to New York with a group of ex-boxers to attend Ring 8 of the Veteran Boxers' Association.

BETTINA Melio *From* Bridgeport, Connecticut, USA. *Died* 20 December 1996, aged 80. A pro between 1934-1948, Melio won the New York version of the world light-heavyweight title by defeating Tiger Jack Fox (1939). Beaten by Billy Conn for the world title (1939), two months later he was again beaten by Conn in a world title fight (1939), before losing to Anton Christoforidis for the vacant NBA version of world title (1941). Other victims included Bob Godwin, Fred Apostoli, Solly Krieger, Red Burman, Jimmy Bivins, Gus Dorazio, and Eddie Blunt. His career record read, 99 bouts, 82 wins (36 inside the distance), three draws, 13 defeats, and one no contest.

BRANCHINI Umberto *From* Italy. *Died* March 1997. A leading Italian manager in the 1960s and 1970s, looking after Salvatore Burruni, Rocky Mattioli, Sandro Lopopolo, and Loris Stecca, he also brought to Europe, South American stars like Horacio Accavallo, Helenio Ferreira, Everaldo Costa Azevedo, and Miguel Cuello.

BROWN Charlie *From* Belfast. *Died* October 1996. Pro 1937-1951. At 5 foot 8 inches, Charlie was the tallest bantamweight of his era in Britain, beating Kid Tanner, and was the first Irish boxer to defeat Jackie Paterson. Other men he beat were Johnny Boom, Joe Boy Collins, Jimmy Stewart, Jackie Horseman, and Peter Maguire. Also met Eddie Carson, Ronnie Draper, and Stan Rowan.

BURTON Rocky *From* Bedworth. *Died* October 1996, aged 37. Pro 1977-1992. Boxing unsuccessfully for the Midlands Area title on three occasions, his career record was 47 bouts, winning 22, losing 24 and drawing one. Campaigned abroad against good-class opposition like Anders Eklund and Anaclet Wamba.

CLANSEY Jack *From* Sunderland. *Died* June 1997, aged 83. Pro 1932-1943. Beat Jack London, and met Jack Casey and Jack Strongbow. Having been out of action for a while, he made a comeback in 1943 to box for the war effort.

CLARK ex-Stoker Fred *From* Luton. *Died* January 1997. Pro 1941-1950. Remembered as Bruce Woodcock's first professional opponent (1942), the Stoker beat Gene Fowler (twice), Jim O'Connor, Jack Stanley, Charlie Collett, and

Jim Gully. Also met Dom Lydon, Charlie Bundy, Mark Hart, and Al Marson. In later years was a member of London Ex-Boxers' Association.

COLLINS Joe "Boy" *From* Dublin. *Died* April 1997. Predominately a bantamweight as a pro, Joe won the Irish amateur flyweight title in 1943, before turning to the paid ranks. Fighting between 1945 and 1950, he numbered among his victims Tommy Madine, Max Brady, and Johnny Boom, while losing to the likes of Jimmy Webster, Jackie Bryce, Stan Rowan, Norman Lewis, Eddie Magee, Charlie Brown, and Jimmy Green. Having made an abortive attempt to land the Irish bantamweight title, losing to Bunty Doran (1947), his career was ended by Manny Kid Francis (1950), having earlier drawn with the man from the Gold Coast (now Ghana).

COULTER Billy *From* Woolwich, London. *Died* 17 April 1997. Pro 1950-1956. Defeated Dudley Cox, Fred Balio, Alf Lay (2), but lost to Lew Lazar, Ken Wittey, and Lay.

DALY George *From* Lambeth, London. *Died* January 1997, aged 82. Pro 1929-1951. Managed by Ted Broadribb and trained by Archie "Doc" Watson, he became the office-boy to famous promoter, Jeff Dickson. With just one defeat in 1932, against Pat Cassidy, there followed an unbeaten run of over 50 bouts to March 1935 when he outpointed Boyo Rees in a British lightweight title eliminator. After outscoring Jimmy Walsh in a semi-final eliminator, George should have met Seaman Tommy Watson in a final eliminator, but their respective managers could not agree on purse money. Beat Watson in a non-title fight, but the Board of Control ignored this and matched Walsh with Kid Berg for the title. George boxed on for another 15 years, but never got another chance. Accompanying Tommy Farr to America (1937), winning five and losing two, he beat Len Wickwar twice, once via a knockout, and also met champions, Chalky Wright, Harry Mizler, and Tommy McGovern. Outpointed by Tommy Barnham in a final eliminator for the South-Eastern Area title (1950), the Londoner ended his career by beating two area champions, Harry Hughes and Roy Coote (1951). Dubbed "The Last of the Mechanics" because of his skilful boxing, he became a second, then a manager, before being the coach to the RAF for eight years. In 1965 he was appointed trainer/instructor at the newly-opened Board of Control Gym at Haverstock Hill, staying there until it closed in the late 1970s. A film extra for many years, holding an Equity card, and a lifelong supporter of Millwall FC, George also became a vice-president of the London Ex-Boxers' Association. Possessing a wonderful sense of humour, he and brother Tommy were a great double act, and in a career of 150 bouts (George reckoned another 50 went unrecorded), he was never knocked out. Following his father being killed in World War I, a month before George was born, he never married, concentrating on looking after his mother, instead.

DALY Terry *From* Battersea, London. *Died* December 1996. Pro 1966-1969. In 1967, he won six out of seven, four in the first round. Although losing to Rocky James (2) and Bunny Johnson, he numbered Derek Groombridge, Bernard Pollard, Charlie Wilson (2), Dennis Avoth, Vic Moore, and Rudolph Vaughan, among his victims.

DAVIS Harry *From* Bethnal Green, London. *Died* 23 March 1997, aged 81. Pro 1933-1949. Although defeated by Arthur Danahar for the Southern Area welterweight title (1945), he beat Jack Kid Berg, Johnny Softley, Billy Jones, George Merritt, Arthur Danahar, Dick Shields, Willie Whyte, Ric Sanders, and Bob Cleaver. Worked in Covent Garden, before becoming a cab driver, he also acted as a Board of Control whip at many venues.

DUBS Harvey *From* Toronto, Canada. *Died* May 1997, aged 75. Famous for flooring Sugar Ray Robinson, despite Ray getting up to stop him in the same round (1942), with 73 wins (45 inside the distance) in 80 fights, he was elected to the Canadian Hall of Fame (1974).

EVANS Arthur "Titch" *From* Trealaw. *Died* 25 March 1997, aged 78. In a short career of 24 bouts, Titch met Welsh champions, Jack Kiley and Ronnie Bishop. In the same stable as Ivor Drew, Matt Powell, and Dick Owen, he served in World War II and had his last serious bout, for the Army against the Navy at the United Services Club, in Cairo (1941). After the war he performed with Ron Taylor's booth. Later became a member of the Welsh EBA.

EVANS Jackie *From* Pontypool. *Died* March 1997. A good-class flyweight who met Terry Allen, Tim Mahoney, Ronnie Bishop, Mickey Colbert, and Ivor Gravell, Jackie later managed Mike Manley and Andrew Williams.

FIELDING Bobby *From* Wrexham. *Died* 25 March 1997, aged 85. One of six brothers who all boxed, four were on the same bill at Wrexham Drill Hall (1931), and all were miners. Father fought as Billy Fielding, but was gassed in World War I. Bobby, a pro between 1929-1942, won the Welsh flyweight title by beating Freddie Morgan (1932). He also beat Arthur Billington, Bert Wallace, Charlie Hazell, Benny Howells, Gwyn Thomas, Cliff Peregrine, Percy Dexter, Tut Whalley, and Syd Parker. After retiring, he did a bit of coaching before becoming a professional gardener. In the Medical Corps in World War II, and a Life Member of the Burma Star Association, Bobby concentrated on looking after his mother and never married. His passion was dogs and he made a short film entitled "Three Wise Dogs", which was shown in schools. While training 50,000 dogs in the Wrexham area, he was employed by the Clwyd Mold Road Safety Committee, teaching children the right way to cross the road.

HARRINGTON Stan *From* Honolulu, Hawaii. *Died* 17 January 1997, aged 63. A pro from 1953, he was beaten by Denny Moyer for the WBA junior-middleweight crown (1963), prior to being defeated by Kim-Ki Soo for the same title (1966). With most of his fights taking place in Honolulu, big names such as Carlos Chavez, L. C. Morgan, Chico Vejar, Joe Miceli, Tony Dupas, Paddy DeMarco, Rudell Stitch, Rocky Kalingo, Isaac Logart, Denny Moyer,

Rubin Carter, Charlie Scott, Gaspar Ortega, and Manuel Gonzalez, failed to get the better of him. Twice beat the legendary Sugar Ray Robinson in 1965.

Stan Harrington

HAYES Frank *From* Birmingham. *Died* January 1997. Pro 1939-1950. Although beaten by Alex Woods for the vacant Northern Ireland light-heavyweight title (1944), Frank defeated Bert Hyland, Reg Crofts, Dixie Moore, and Kid Mallabone. Also went the distance with Albert Finch and Dick Turpin. In later years he became a member of Nottingham EBA.

HURST Jackie *From* St Georges, London. *Died* 20 May 1997, aged 80. Pro 1934-1940. Lost to champions Johnny McGrory, Johnny King and Spider Kelly, but beat men of the quality of Jackie Rankin, Mickey Summers, Jack Gubbins, Tony Butcher, George Marsden, Johnny Holt, Johnny Peters, and Cuthbert Taylor. Also had a spell in the States prior to the war.

INGLE Johnny *From* Dublin. *Died* April 1997. Pro 1943-1949. The brother of Jimmy Ingle, the former European flyweight amateur champion who developed into a top-class professional welter and middleweight, and also of Brendan Ingle, also a former pro who now looks after Prince Naseem Hamed, Johnny was the Eire lightweight champion. Among his victims were Jimmy Smith, Dan McAllister, Johnny Ward, and Paddy Burgin.

INGRAM Bert *From* Sunderland. *Died* 20 May 1997, aged 75. Pro 1944-1950. A coal miner, he met George Casson four times, including once for the Northern Area middleweight title, and also fought Sammy Sullivan, Doug Mansfield, and Gene Devlin, whom he bested twice. Among those he beat were Joe Myers, Albert Rendle, Patsy Dodds, and Henry Smart. Became chairman, then president of Sunderland EBA, as well as being a member of Tyneside EBA, raising a lot of money for charity.

JOHNSTON Tom *From* Belfast. *Died* 25 April 1997, aged 67. Having won the British ATC title in 1949, Tom turned to the paid ranks in 1950 and remained unbeaten in 15 contests until stopped by the future British middleweight champion, Johnny Sullivan, in October 1951. Also defeated by Tom Meli, a man he had already beaten, and then Jackie Scott, Tom won his next four fights before being stopped in the sixth by Pat McAteer, another future British champion, after leading all the way. Less than four weeks later, his career came to a close following another inside the distance defeat, this time at the hands of Roy Agland. Listed among his victims were Jackie Brown, Joe Baillie, Sammy Hamilton, Kit Pompey, Ken Richardson, Les Kirk, and Frank Priest.

JORDAN Don *From* Los Angeles, USA. *Died* April 1997, aged 62. Pro 1953-1962. Won the world welterweight title by beating Virgil Akins (1958), and successfully defended against Akins and Denny Moyer (1959), before losing it to Benny Paret (1960). Also beat Lauro Salas, Joe Miceli, Paddy DeMarco, Isaac Logart, Gaspar Ortega, and Tony DeMarco. Prior to winning the championship, in his one and only bout in Britain, he was outscored by Dave Charnley (1958) in a lightweight battle. In 75 contests, he won 50 (17 inside the distance), drew one, and lost 23, with one no decision.

Don Jordan

JOYCE Willie *From* Chicago, USA. *Died* 5 December 1996. Pro 1937-1947. Had three successive fights with Lew Jenkins, drawing the first and winning the other two (1939), and also won and lost to Henry Armstrong in successive fights (1943). Won the California lightweight title by beating Ray Lunny (1944) and the same year had six fights in six months, beating Chester Slider (twice), Ike Williams, Henry Armstrong, and losing to Armstrong and Willie Pep. He started 1945, beating Chalky Wright and Ike Williams (twice), and losing to Williams and Wright. Other world champions he met, included Beau Jack and Johnny Bratton. Beaten by Tippy Larkin for the vacant world junior-welterweight title (April 1946), he was again outscored by Larkin for the championship five months later, before bowing out of boxing the following year.

KELLY Terry *From* Manchester. *Died* August 1996. Following in the footsteps of his father and two brothers, who were also pros, he beat Ernie Vickers, Ernie Thompson, Bert Hornby, Ginger Ward, Bob Blair, and Ernie Foden. Also met Terry Ratcliffe, Terry Cullen, Billy Exley, and Stan Hawthorne, before emigrating to Australia.

KIM Ki-Soo *From* South Korea. *Died* 10 June 1997, aged 57. Pro 1961-1969. Won the Orient and Pacific middleweight titles (1965), prior to moving down to win the WBA junior-middleweight crown when outpointing Nino Benvenuti over 15 rounds in Seoul on 25 June 1966. Held the championship just under two years, successfully defending against Stan Harrington and Freddie Little, until venturing to Milan and being defeated by Sandro Mazzinghi. He next lost the Orient middleweight title to Hisao Minami (1968), before regaining it in March 1969 and announcing his retirement six months later. Totalled 37 bouts, winning 33 (18 inside the distance), drawing two, and losing two.

LAWAL Rachid *From* Denmark. *Born* Sierra Leone. *Died* 25 November 1996, aged 30, after being stabbed while working as a doorman at a disco. Won the European super-featherweight title in 1988, beating Lars Lund Jensen and successfully defended same against John Doherty and Mike Whalley, before losing it to Daniel Londas, all contests taking place in 1989. Stopped in seven rounds by Manning Galloway in a WBO welterweight championship bid (1991), he came back to win the vacant European light-weight crown in 1994, beating Paul Burke, being dispossessed by Jean-Baptiste Mendy later that year. Scored 13 kayoes in his 25 wins.

LEARMOUTH Wally *From* Poplar. *Died* February 1997. Pro 1937-1945. A finalist in an open welterweight competition at Holborn Stadium, he went on to beat Bert Goddard, Johnny Francis, Billy Waterman, Johnny Clark, and Sid Fitzhugh. Inactive during World War II, there was a comeback in 1945, defeating Tommy Leahy, before retirement beckoned.

LEGGE Harry *From* Bournemouth. *Died* 25 August 1997, aged 77. Pro 1943-1954. Contracted polio at the age of five. Both legs were affected, the left leg developed, the right did not, being thin, due to no muscular development. He overcame this handicap and in time perfected a natural balance. Rejected by the Armed Services in World War II because of his deformed leg, he worked as a laboratory assistant at a Cordite factory where nitro-glycerine was made. After a brief amateur career, Harry turned pro with manager, Jack Turner, in 1943 and from October 1944 to November 1945 had an unbeaten run of 19 bouts, which included only three draws. In 1945-46, Harry crammed in 44 contests, followed by 35 in 1947. Every summer he joined the booths, something which he really enjoyed. Had seven bouts with Cornishman, Roy Coote, of which Roy won four and Harry three, including two South-West Area lightweight title fights, Roy winning both. They also met twice for the Western Area title, Harry winning the first (1951) and losing the return (1952). Harry was also beaten by Hal Bagwell for the South Central Area title. Never knocked out in 166 official bouts, of which he won 86 and drew 26, he later became secretary of the Bournemouth EBA, wrote a regular boxing column for the *Bournemouth Echo,* and wrote two books which proved very popular, entitled *Penny A Punch* and *A Few Punches More.* He also broadcast on local radio from time to time, wrote articles in a freelance capacity, and, after he retired from boxing, became a manager and gym proprietor. All in all, he made a major contribution to the sport he loved.

McAREE Jimmy *From* Belfast. *Died* October 1996, aged 79. The Ulster amateur champion (1939), he later became the trainer/coach to six champions who won the same flyweight title that he did. Managed Freddie Gilroy from the time he turned pro at the beginning of 1957, guiding him to British, European, and Empire bantamweight titles, and just failing to win the world title together. Was an upholsterer by trade, but spent up to six nights per week coaching his club. Boxing was his life.

MONTANEZ Pedro *From* Puerto Rico. *Died* 27 June 1996, aged 83. Turned pro in 1931, campaigning in Europe during the early 1930s, principally in France, but had three fights in London, beating George Odwell and Harry Brooks. Then went to America, defeating Aldo Spoldi and Frankie Klick, before outpointing Lou Ambers, world lightweight champion, in a ten-round non-title fight (April 1937). Outpointed by Ambers in a world title fight (September 1937), he moved up to welter to take on the great Henry Armstrong (1940), only to be stopped inside nine rounds.

MORGAN Adrian *Died* 21 January 1997, aged 68. An 'A' Star referee for over a decade prior to reaching the retirement age of 65 in 1993, Adrian continued to work as a judge right up until his death. John Morris, the General Secretary of the BBBoC, said "He was a fine official, having officiated all over the world for the WBC and the EBU, and one of the nicest men in boxing". As a member of the BBBoC Referees' Committee, he had recently accepted a post as a Board inspector in Wales.

MORRIS George *From* Battersea, London. *Died* March 1997. Pro 1933-1937. Met Johnny McGrory, Charlie Bint, and Jimmy Toohig, and beat Jackie Stayton, Tommy Fox, Morrie Goldstein, and Tom Sullivan. After leaving the ring, George turned to coaching lads at the Polytechnic, Devas, and Firestone clubs, training Ernie Woodman and Ray Moore among others. In later years, he became a member of London and Croydon EBAs.

O'NEILL Jim *From* Cambuslang. *Died* 31 October 1996, aged 84. Pro 1930-1936. The Scottish bantamweight champion in 1933, after beating Mickey Summers, he lost the title to Jimmy Knowles (1934). Beat Dan McGoldrick and met quality opponents such as Jim Campbell, Jim Maharg, and Teddy O'Neill, before retiring from the paid ranks and moving into the amateur game. Having coached Hoover BC from 1950-1986 (until the club closed its doors), when it re-opened in 1996 it was re-named O'Neill BC.

PARDOE Wayne *From* Walsall. *Died* 9 October 1996, aged 26. Had four pro fights, winning three and losing one, after starting boxing at the age of 12 and representing Young England as an amateur. Fell through a skylight while working on a building site, he died a fortnight later.

PELLONE Tony *From* New York City, USA. Real name Jimmy Pell. *Died* April 1996. Pro 1943-1952. In a career that fell just short of a world title shot, Tony won and lost against Bob Montgomery and was outpointed by Ike Williams, Kid Gavilan, and Johnny Saxton, all champions. Other big names on his record were Lulu Constantino (won), Billy Graham (won and lost), Tony Janiro (lost), Maxie Shapiro (won), Johnny Greco (won), Chuck Taylor (won and lost), Charlie Fusari (won and lost), Paddy Young (won), Joe Miceli (won), Lester Felton (drew), and Vince Foster (lost).

PETERSEN Craig *From* Australia. *Died* 15 April 1997, aged 26. Following a loss to Apollo Sweet for the Commonwealth cruiserweight title (1989), he moved up to heavy the following year to outpoint Jimmy Thunder for the Australian heavyweight crown, before losing same to Thunder in a return and then being stopped by Herbie Hide for the WBC International title in 1992. With 22 wins and one draw from 29 contests, his last fight was against Chris Byrd in Michigan in January. His death was thought to have been drug-related.

POMPEY Kit *From* British Guiana (now Guyana). *Died* February 1997, aged 70. Pro 1951-1957. Settling in Britain, he beat Alf Danahar, Jack Baker, and Jimmy Brogden, and tackled champions, Eddie Thomas and Wally Thom within two months, going the distance with both. Sandwiched in between was a win over Rocco King. Also went the course with Martin Hansen, the scourge of British middleweights, and beat Tommy Armour, Billy Ambrose, and George Roe. After retiring from Rolls Royce (Barnoldswick plant), Kit became a doorman at hotels and clubs.

PUDNEY Ron *From* Croydon. *Died* 22 June 1997, aged 74. Pro 1947-1954. Won two Boxing News Certificates of Merit, beating Bert Hyland (1950) and Alex Buxton to annex the Southern Area middleweight title (1951). Successfully defended same against Les Allen (1951), before losing it to Wally Beckett (1953). Also beat Eric McQuade, Harry Davis, Bob Cleaver, Wally Beckett, Bert Sanders, Ginger Sadd, Freddie Webb, George Dilkes, and Bruce Crawford, and drawing with Johnny Sullivan. Became a trainer, eventually opening his own gym, then did nothing for five years until coming back to the sport as a Board of Control inspector, a position which he carried out successfully for 20 years. During World War II, Ron was in the Royal Air Force, serving as a rear gunner and wireless operator, mainly in North Africa. Was also a member of the London Ex-Boxers' Association and Croydon EBA.

RAMEY Wesley *From* Everett, Michigan, USA. *Died* 10 March 1997, aged 88. Turned pro in 1928 and averaged 20 bouts per year throughout his long career, beating Johnny Jadick, Benny Bass, Battling Shaw, and Tony Canzoneri, all champions, before campaigning in Australia (1934). Then he travelled to South Africa (1934), during which he was twice defeated by the legendary Laurie Stevens, before coming to Britain to beat Boyo Rees and Harry Brooks. The following year he beat Tommy John, but was beaten by Jimmy Walsh (disqualification), both in London, before returning to America. In successive fights he beat champions, Lew Jenkins and Sammy Angott, prior to defeating Jenkins again during the same year (1938). Continued to box until 1941, when he outpointed Maurice Arnault.

ROSSITER Tony *From* Lewisham, London. *Died* July 1996, aged 26. A top-class amateur with the St Joseph's club in Deptford, Tony never turned pro, winning South East London Divisional titles in 1989, 1993, and 1995. Coming into the sport at the age of 11, he reached the 1987 NABC Class "B" 48 kg final, before moving up to senior level when his high spot came when winning a London title in 1989 by outpointing the ill-fated Bradley Stone.

SACCO Ubaldo *From* Mar de Plata, Argentina. *Died* 28 May 1997, aged 41. A clever boxer with an excellent jab and solid punch, Ubaldo turned pro in 1978, losing just once in 27 contests before beating Robert Alfaro for the national light-welterweight title (1981), prior to adding the South American title at the weight to his collection a year later when outpointing the same man. Stripped of both belts in October 1984, having made defences against Hugo Luero (1981) and Jose da Silva Rodriguez (1983), in his very next contest he took the WBA crown from the head of Gene Hatcher a couple of months later, before losing it to Patrizio Oliva the following March. With problems outside the ring, that was it and in 52 fights he lost just four, scoring 23 inside the distance wins. Although the official cause of death was meningitis, there had been a history of drug and alcohol abuse in the past few years.

SNIPE Jack *From* South Yorkshire. *Died* 15 October 1996. Boxed in the Royal Artillery, rising to the rank of captain, and later joined the police force in Doncaster before settling in Peacehaven and becoming a Board of Control referee. Brother Roy is also a referee, and son Mark is a pro fighter, who, at one time, was a sparring-partner to Chris Eubank.

STEENE Alex *From* Leeds. *Died* May 1997. With an English mother and Russian father, Alex excelled at soccer, snooker, and boxing, for Hunslet BC, before leaving school at 14. During World War II, he served in the Royal Marines and Royal Navy, and also the Merchant Navy. Arrived in London in 1950 and although his boxing career had been cut short by the war he was involved in other aspects of the sport for which he had a great passion. Alex was delighted when his son, Greg, became a promoter 16 years ago, and gave him every support, loving to have boxers and ex-boxers around him. Among those who worked for him were Alex Buxton and Bruce Wells. Made honorary president of Leeds and also vice-president of LEBA, he was a great benefactor of both EBAs and did a lot of good work for various charities. Alex and his family became great friends of the late LEBA president, Jack Powell, and his family, and on 15 November 1996, at LEBA's 25th Anniversary Dinner LEBA, president, Stephen Powell (Jack's son), presented Alex with the Jack Powell Award for his services and support to LEBA.

STRAUB Charlie *From* Lanark. *Died* October 1996, aged 69. The British Railways champion (1950), Charlie eventually became a trainer at Lanarkshire Welfare Club, a post he held for 30 years. Trained Chic Calderwood, Tommy McGuinness, Willie Fisher, Bobby Fisher, Dave Douglas, Tommy Cook, and James Murray.

STUBBS Jimmy *From* Runcorn. *Died* March 1997, aged 76. Pro 1936-1947. Turned pro before he was 16, weighing 6 stone 12 lbs, beating Jim Brady, Kid Tanner, Joe Curran, Tiny Bostock, Johnny Boom, Jim McCann, and Tommy Farricker, and taking Peter Kane to a disputed verdict. Also gave weight to Jackie Paterson, but went the full distance. Although working in the Cammell Laird shipyard, Jimmy came back in 1945 to beat Danny Woods and Johnny Molloy, before losing to John Cusick. As a youngster he showed so much potential that Liverpool promoter, Johnny Best, signed a seven-year option on his services and it is difficult to understand why he never got a shot at a national or even an area title.

TANDBERG Olle *From* Stockholm, Sweden. *Died* February 1997, aged 77. As an amateur, Olle carried off Swedish and European heavyweight titles before turning pro in 1941. After eight fights, he won the vacant European heavyweight title by beating Karel Sys (1943), but lost it to Sys six months later. Although his greatest victory came in a ten round points win over Joe Baksi (1947), other good men he defeated included Stephane Olek, Luigi Musina, Heinz Lazek, and Aaron Wilson. Also met world champions Jersey Joe Walcott and Joey Maxim. Took on

several British opponents, beating Jock Porter, Jack London, and Ken Shaw, after losing to Eddie Phillips.

TEMPLAR Simon *From* Burton. *Died* 10 July 1997, aged 71. Pro 1948-1955. Came from Jamaica as an aircraft engineer with the RAF and settled in Britain, his real name being Andy Pinkney. Surprisingly, his ring name did not emanate from the ficticious film figure who was nicknamed "The Saint", but from a wild west character in a film. Having launched his career from a gym in a Derby Street pub (1948), he met several top heavyweights, including Joe Erskine and Joe Bygraves. Was also a good club cricketer. Highly respected as a real gentleman, one of the "gentle giants", he beat Tom Kennedy, Jock Thoms, Matt Hardy, Gordon Day, Noel Reid, George Stern, Paddy Slavin, and Frank Bell.

Eddie Thomas

THOMAS Eddie *From* Merthyr. *Died* 2 June 1997, aged 71. Having been the Welsh junior champion, ABA junior champion, and ABA lightweight champion (1946), Eddie turned pro in 1946, winning the Welsh welterweight title by beating Gwyn Williams (1948). Won the British title, beating Henry Hall (1949), and successfully defended it against Cliff Curvis (1950). Everything happened in 1951, however. He won the Empire crown by beating Pat Patrick, won the European title by beating Michele Palermo, but then lost the latter to Charles Humez, before losing his two other titles to Wally Thom. Was then inactive for 18 months, due to an injury sustained while playing soccer.

During his pro career, Eddie took part in several British title eliminating bouts, losing to Gwyn Williams (1948), beating Stan Hawthorne and Ernie Roderick (1949), drawing with Bunty Adamson (1953), and losing to Adamson (1954). After retiring, he became a successful manager and trainer, guiding Ken Buchanan and Howard Winstone to world titles, and Colin Jones to a championship crack. Also highly regarded as a "cuts" expert, when the Welsh Area Council celebrated 50 years, Eddie was honoured as the man who had done most for Welsh boxing (1980). Starting life as a miner, and eventually owning his own mine, he was elected Mayor to Merthyr (1994), having already been made a Freeman of the Borough (1992). Was instrumental in providing help in the Aberfan disaster and did a lot of charity work, being awarded the MBE in 1984.

THURLEY Charlie *Died* October 1996, aged 82. The Board of Control's senior inspector, Charlie had been a good-class amateur middleweight who won an Army title. His wife, Dinky, was an Olympic swimming coach and his son, Charlie, was coach of the Welsh water polo team.

VOLANTE Vince A son of Italian immigrants who settled in Liverpool, and the brother of top pro, Dom Volante, Vince's boxing career was curtailed through illness after he had won a Catholic Schools' title. The founder member of the Merseyside EBA, and chairman of their Benevolent Committee, he was also vice chairman of the Northern Federation.

WALLS Earl *From* Toronto, Canada. *Died* 15 December 1996, aged 68. Having turned pro in 1948, he won the Canadian heavyweight title by beating Vern Escoe (1952), and successfully defended it against Escoe the following month. Came to Britain in 1949, beating Ken Shaw, Piet Wilde, Kurt Schiegl, and losing to Lloyd Barnett and Alf Gallagher (disqualification). Most of his fights were in Edmonton, Alberta, and his victims included Res Layne (twice), Joe Kahut, Bernie Reynolds, Freddie Beshore, and Edgardo Romero. In March 1955, Earl retained his Canadian title by drawing with James J. Parker and retired from boxing.

WARUSFEL Ilde. French Military champion 1949. *Died* May 1996, aged 65. Had around 50 bouts as a pro. His younger brother, Jean-Claude, lost in a European title challenge against Vito Antuofermo and his son, Georges, lost in EBU fights against Marijan Benes and Hans-Henrik Palm. Fought Leen Jansen and Artemio Calzavara among others.

WEISS Ernst *From* Austria. *Died* May 1997, aged 85. A three-time European champion at fly, bantam and feather, Ernst won the 112 lbs title when defeating Fortunato Ortega (1936), only to lose it after just two months to Valentin Angelmann in a bout recognised as involving the world championship by the IBU, but by no other recognised body. His next title, this time at 118 lbs, was secured following a 12-round kayo win over Aurel Toma (1939), while the featherweight crown was lifted thanks to‚

a points victory over Lucien Popescu (1941). Both titles were snatched immediately, by Gino Cattaneo and Gino Bondavilli, respectively. Boxed in Britain against Jackie Brown and Peter Kane (twice), losing all three contests.

ZALE Tony *From* Gary, Indiana, USA. *Died* 21 March 1997, aged 83. Pro 1934-1948. Worked in the steel mills as a youngster and, as a pro, was appropriately nicknamed the "Man of Steel". Won the NBA middleweight title by beating Al Hostak (1940) and retained it against Steve Mamakos (1941) and Hostak (1941), before winning the vacant world championship when beating Georgie Abrams (1941). Having served in the American Navy during World War II, remaining inactive until 1946, he came back to retain the title by beating Rocky Graziano in the first of three memorable title fights. He then lost the title to Rocky (1947), before regaining it in 1948, none of the bouts going the full distance. Three months after the third bout with Graziano, Tony lost the crown to Marcel Cerdan. Elected to the Boxing Hall of Fame (1958), his record showed 87 bouts, with 67 wins (44 inside the distance), two draws, and 18 losses.

Tony Zale

ZUDDAS Gianni *From* Cagliari, Italy. *Died* October 1996, aged 68. Turned pro in 1949 after winning a silver at bantamweight in the 1948 Wembley Olympic Games and was soon on the trail of the Italian 118 lbs title, going unbeaten in 34 contests. However, in six title shots he would only win the championship once, against Amleto Falcinelli (1952), drawing against Alvaro Nuvoloni (1951), and losing to Mario D'Agata, in 1953 and 1954, and Federico Scarponi twice in 1959. Beat Tino Cardinale, Armand Deianna, Mickey McKay, Calistro Etter, Theo Nolten, Theo Medina, Andre Valignat, and Emile Chemama and, later on in his career, went the distance with Eder Jofre in Sao Paulo (1959), the year before the Brazilian won the world title.

MUNRO & HYLAND BROS

PROMOTIONS

INTERNATIONAL BOXING PROMOTERS AND MANAGERS
LIVERPOOL, ENGLAND

TEAM FOR 1997

Danny 'Boy' Peters
Super-Middleweight

Paul Burns
Welterweight

Alex Moon - *Lightning*
Featherweight

Shea Neary 'The Shamrock Express'
WBU Light-Welterweight Champion of the World

'Magic' Matthew Ellis
The Blackpool Rock
Heavyweight

Danny Costello
Flyweight

Gary Lockett
Light-Middleweight

Gary Ryder
Light-Welterweight

David Burke
Super-Featherweight

TRAINERS: Kevin Sanders, Kenny Willis, George Schofield

MATCHMAKER: John Gaynor

THE MORTON SUITE, THE MOAT HOUSE HOTEL, 1 PARADISE STREET, LIVERPOOL, ENGLAND L1 8JD
TELEPHONE: 0151-708 8331 • FAX: 0151-708 6701
Licensed by The British Boxing Board of Control

A Boxing Quiz With a Few Below the Belt (Part Two)

Compiled by Les Clark

QUESTIONS

1. Former British light-middleweight champion, Jimmy Batten, had 49 professional fights losing only nine. Can you name the only man to beat him twice?

2. Prior to winning the WBC junior-lightweight title, Cornelius Boza Edwards had lost only two bouts, one being to Alexis Arguello. To whom was the other?

3. Vic Andretti fought two men for a British title. How many times in all did Vic contest a British title?

4. Who successfully defended his world title against Chic Calderwood?

5. Can you remember the name of England's featherweight Olympian in Atlanta?

6. How many times did Ken Buchanan contest the world lightweight title?

7. Who did Billy "Spider" Kelly outpoint in 1953, only to lose to in a return with his British Empire title at stake?

8. When was the British heavyweight title last contested between two Welshmen and who were they?

9. Who was the first man to beat former British and Commonwealth champion, Mark Kaylor, in the pro ring?

10. This boxer won the same ABA title that his father had won 26 years previously. Can you name him?

11. Can you name the first boxer to stop former British, Commonwealth, and world featherweight champion, Colin McMillan?

12. Who successfully defended his Commonwealth title on seven occasions and his British title six times, despite losing in attempts for the European and world titles?

13. Name a Scottish boxer who held a version of the world super-middleweight title?

14. Can you recall the venue used for the Rocky Marciano v Don Cockell fight?

15. What was significant about Steve Collins' win over Frederic Seillier in the London Arena?

16. Maurice Hope contested the world title on six occasions. How many did he lose?

17. In what year were the 109th ABA finals held and how did they differ from previous years?

18. Who was the first boxer to beat Barry McGuigan in the pro ring?

19. How many European title bouts did Henry Cooper participate in?

20. Name the Welsh middleweight who twice lost to Terry Downes in British title attempts?

21. Who was the last Irish-born boxer to hold the British heavyweight title?

22. Can you name a former European heavyweight champion who beat Ezzard Charles, but lost to Willie Pastrano, Nino Valdes, and Cleveland Williams?

23. How many times did Sugar Ray Robinson fight in Britain?

24. Can you name a South African boxer who became British and Commonwealth heavyweight champion?

25. Which British boxer has contested the most world title fights at one weight?

26. Rinty Monaghan retained his British, European, and world titles with a draw in Belfast. Against whom?

27. Did the former world heavyweight champion, Leon Spinks, ever fight in the UK?

28. What have Bob Fitzsimmons and Duke McKenzie in common?

29. The referee for Steve Collins v Frederic Seillier was Joe Cortez. Can you name the three judges?

30. How many times have the ABA finals been held in Birmingham's Indoor Arena?

31. Can you name the last Liverpool boxer to win a Lonsdale Belt outright in the lightweight division?

32. This former undefeated British and Commonwealth champion was counted out in Buenos Aires in a world title challenge. Can you name him?

33. Which one of the Finnigan brothers won the most professional championship contests?

34. Former British and Commonwealth heavyweight champion, Danny McAlinden, won points' decisions on only three occasions from 45 bouts. Can you name the opponents in these three bouts?

35. Can you name a German who held the world WBC light-flyweight title?

36. Can you name a British flyweight who never fought for the British title, but twice challenged Maurice Sandeyron for the European belt, drawing one and losing the other?

37. The Thomas A'Becket pub has now closed. Can you name the man who first opened the famous gym above it?

38. Which of the following boxers did not fight for the European title – Jack Bodell, Danny McAlinden, Tommy Farr, or Billy Aird?

39. Do you know the first British title fight that Harry Gibbs refereed?

40. Colin Jones took the British welterweight title from Kirkland Laing at which venue – Wembley Arena, Empire Pool, Wembley, or Wembley Grand Hall?

41. To whom did manager and trainer of the Bristol Boy's, Chris Sanigar, lose his Southern Area light-welterweight belt to?

42. Dave Charnley lost 12 contests. How many of those were title bouts?

43. How many times did Primo Carnera fight in the UK?

44. Willie Pastrano fought in the UK on seven occasions, losing three times. Can you name the men who inflicted these losses?

45. The Wembley Arena was once known as the Empire Pool. Can you name the boxers who first topped the bill at this venue?

46. Which of the following boxers fought for the European heavyweight title - Don Cockell, Richard Dunn, Jack Petersen, or Joe Erskine?

47. Who was the former world middle and light-heavyweight champion, Dick Tiger's last opponent in the ring?

48. Tim Witherspoon boxed in the UK prior to facing Frank Bruno. Can you name his opponent and where he fought?

49. How many times did Joe Bugner contest the European heavyweight title and on how many of these occasions did he lose?

50. At which venue did Harry Gibbs referee his last fight before retiring from the British ring?

296

Leading BBBoC License Holders: Names and Addresses

Licensed Promoters

Sam Adair
Ashfield House
Ashford
Barnstable
Devon
01271 46872

Michael Andrew
38 Kennedy Avenue
Laindon West
Basildon
Essex
01268 651581

John Ashton
1 Charters Close
Kirkby in Ashfield
Nottinghamshire
NG17 8PF
01623 721278

Lance Billany
32 Beaconsfield Carrs
Meadow
Withernsea
HU19 2EP
01964 613578

Pat Brogan
112 Crewe Road
Haslington
Crewe
Cheshire
01270 874825

Harry Burgess
25 Calthorpe Street
London
WC1X 0JX

Trevor Callighan
40 Prescott Street
Halifax
West Yorkshire
HX1 2QW
01422 366004

Roy Cameron
5 Birbeck Road
Acton
London W3 6BG
0181 2482816

Carlton Carew
18 Mordaunt Street
Stockwell
London
SW9 9RB
0171 7385180

Eva Christian
80 Alma Road
Plymouth
Devon PL3 4HU
01752 252753

Annette Conroy
144 High Street East
Sunderland
Tyne and Wear
SR1 2BL
0191 5676871

Pat Cowdell
129a Moat Road
Oldbury
Warley
W. Midlands
0121 5528082

John Cox
11 Fulford Drive
Links View
Northampton
01604 712107

Denis Cross
6 Partington Street
Newton Heath
Manchester M40 2AQ
0161 2056651

Michael Dalton
16 Edward Street
Grimsby
South Humberside
01472 310288

John Robert Davies
5 Welsh Road
Garden City
Deeside
Clwyd
01244 821173

Shaun Doyle
15 Jermyn Croft
Dodworth
Barnsley
South Yorkshire
01226 298492

Eastwood Promotions
Bernard Eastwood
Eastwood House
2-4 Chapel Lane
Belfast 1
Northern Ireland
01232 238005

James Evans
88 Windsor Road
Bray
Berkshire
SL6 2DJ
01628 23640

Evesham Sporting Club
Mike Goodall
Schiller
Gibbs Lane
Offenham
Evesham WR11 5RR

Norman Fawcett
4 Wydsail Place
Gosforth
Newcastle upon Tyne
NE3 4QP
0191 2131294

John Forbes
5 Durham Road
Sedgefield
Stockton on Tees
Cleveland
TS21 3DW
01740 21054

Joe Frater
The Cottage
Main Road
Grainthorpe
Louth
Lincolnshire
01472 343194

Dai Gardiner
13 Hengoed Hall Drive
Cefn Hengoed
Hengoed
Mid Glamorgan
CF8 7JW
01443 812971

Harold Gorton
Gorton House
4 Hollius Road
Oldham
Lancashire
0161 6788833

Ron Gray
Ingrams Oak
19 Hatherton Road
Cannock
Staffordshire
01543 502279

Johnny Griffin
Leicester
LE1 2GN
0116 2629287

Clive Hall
23 Linnett Drive
Barton Seagrave
Kettering
Northamptonshire
01536 726037

Jess Harding
70 Hatfield Road
Potters Bar
Hertfordshire
01707 642982

Dennis Hobson
The Lodge
Stone Lane
Woodhouse
Sheffield
Yorkshire
S13 7BR
01742 540270

Steve Holdsworth
85 Sussex Road
Watford
Hertfordshire
WD2 5HR
01923 252949

Harry Holland
62 Roseberry
Hounslow
Middlesex
0181 7374886

Hull & District Sporting Club
Mick Toomey
25 Purton Grove
Bransholme
Hull HU7 4QD
01482 216813

Alma Ingle
26 Newman Road
Wincobank
Sheffield S9 1LP
0114 2811277

Owen McMahon
3 Atlantic Avenue
Belfast
BT15 2HN
01232 743535

Matchroom
Barry Hearn
10 Western Road
Romford
Essex RM1 3JT
01708 788771

Katherine Morrison
85 Sydney Street
Glasgow G31 2ND
0141 5548895

Munro & Hyland Bros
The Morton Suite
The Moat House Hotel
1 Paradise Street
Liverpool L1 8JD
0151 7088331

National Promotions
National House
60-66 Wardour Street
London W1V 3HP
0171 4375956

Noble Art Promotions
Greg Steene/Bruce Baker
150 Brick Lane
London E1 6RU
0181 5333699

North Staffs Sporting Club
J Baddeley
29 Redwood Avenue
Stone
Staffordshire ST15 0DB
01782 202242

Panix Promotions
Frank Maloney
99 Middlesex Street
London E1 7DA
0171 2471999

Peacock Promotions
Anthony Bowers
Peacock Gym
Caxton Street North
Canning Town
London E16 1JR
0171 5113799

Phoenix Camp Promotions
Middlewood Street
Salford
Manchester
0161 8394070

Queensberry Yeo Ltd
(Special Licence)
1 Concorde Drive
5(c) Business Centre
Clevedon
Avon
BS21 6UH
01275 879520

Gus Robinson
Stranton House
Westview Road
Hartlepool
TS24 0BB
01429 234221

Round One Boxing
Promotions
Dave Furneaux
251 Embankment Road
Prince Rock
Plymouth
Cornwall
PL4 9JH
01752 265546

Christine Rushton
20 Alverley Lane
Balby
Doncaster
Yorkshire
DN4 9AS
01302 310919

St Andrews Sporting
Club
Tommy Gilmour
Anderson Suite
Forte Crest Hotel
Bothwell Street
Glasgow
G2 7EN
0141 2485461

Chris Sanigar
Dorset House
Dorset End Road
Kingswood
Bristol
BS15 1SE
0117 9496699

Mike Shinfield
126 Birchwood Lane
Somercotes
Derbyshire
DE55 4NE
01773 603124

John Spensley
The Black Swan Hotel
Tremholme Bar
Near Stokesley
North Yorkshire
DL6 3JY
01642 850717

Sports Network
Frank Warren
Centurion House
Bircherley Green
Hertford
Hertfordshire
SG14 1AP
01992 505550

Sporting Club of Wales
Paul Boyce
Brynamlwg
2 Pant Howell Ddu
Ynysmerdy
Briton Ferry
Neath SA11 2TU

Sportsman Promotions
Frank Quinlan
Hollinthorpe Low Farm
Swillington Lane
Leeds
Yorkshire
LS26 8BZ
0113 2870167

Tara Promotions
Jack Doughty
Grains Road
Shaw
Oldham
Lancashire OL2 8JB
01706 841460

Team Promotions
David Gregory
Contract House
Split Crow Road
Gateshead
Tyne and Wear
NE10 9JX
0191 4774871

Jack Trickett
Acton Court Hotel
187 Buxton Road
Stockport
Cheshire
0161 4836172

UK Pro Box
Promotions
David Matthews
22 Copt Royd Grove
Yeadon
Leeds
Yorkshire
LS19 7HQ
01532 506328

Michael Edward
Ulyatt
28 Blackthorn Lane
Willerby
Hull
01482 657200

Stephen Vaughan
Lombard Chambers
Ormond Street
Liverpool L3 9NA
0151 2863092

Wolverhampton
Sporting Club
J R Mills
24 Perton Road
Wightwick
Wolverhampton
Staffordshire WV6 8DN
0121 5052141

Stephen Mark Wood
29 Falconwood Chase
Worsley
Manchester
0161 7902579

David Woolas
Tudor Lodge
Bellshaw Lane
Belton
Nr Doncaster
Yorkshire DN9 1PF
01427 874266

Yorkshire Executive
Sporting Club
John Celebanski
87 Crowtree Lane
Bradford
01274 824015

Licensed Managers

Isola Akay
129 Portnall Road
Paddington
London
W9 3BN
0181 9607724

John Ashton
1 Charters Close
Kirkby in Ashfield
Nottinghamshire
NG17 8PF
01623 721278

Chris Aston
23 Juniper Grove Mews
Netherton
Huddersfield
West Yorkshire
HD4 7WG
01484 667824

Albert Barrow
236 Frenchfield Road
Brighton
BN2 2YG
01273 695749

Nat Basso
38 Windsor Road
Prestwich
Lancashire
M25 8FF
0161 7403998

John Baxter
1 Ivatt Close
Leicester
LE7 9UT
0116 2432325

Lance Billany
32 Beaconsfield
Carrs Meadow
Withernsea
North Humberside
HU19 2EP
01964 613578

Jack Bishop
76 Gordon Road
Fareham
Hampshire
PO16 7SS
01329 284708

Tony Borg
3 Francis Street
Newport
Gwent
Wales
01633 243917

Gerald Bousted
4 Firlands Road
Barton
Torquay
Devon
TQ2 8EW

Jackie Bowers
36 Drew Road
Silvertown
London E10
0171 4765530

Paul Boyce
Brynamlwg
2 Pant Howell Ddu
Ynysmerdy
Briton Ferry
Neath
SA11 2TU

David Bradley
The Dovecote
Aston Hall
Claverley
WV5 7DZ
01746 710287

Colin Breen
31 Penlan Road
Treboeth
Swansea
West Glamorgan
01792 791109

Mike Brennan
2 Canon Avenue
Chadwell Heath
Romford
Essex
0181 5994588

Fred Britton
71 Henrietta Street
Leigh
Lancashire
WN7 1LH
01942 678667

Michael Brooks
114 Gildane
Orchard Park Estate
Hull HU6 9AY
01482 857237

Winston Burnett
6 Faber Way
City Gardens
Sloper Road
Grangetown
Cardiff CF1 8DN
01222 237332

Steve Butler
107 Cambridge Street
Normanton
West Yorkshire
WF6 1ES
01924 891097

Paddy Byrne
70 Benfield Way
Portslade by Sea
Sussex
BN4 2DL
01273 412498

Trevor Callighan
40 Prescott Street
Halifax
West Yorkshire
HX1 2QW
01422 366004

Enzo Calzaghe
51 Caerbryn
Pentwynmawr
Newbridge
Gwent
South Wates
01495 248988

Carlton Carew
18 Mordaunt Street
Brixton
London
SW9 9RB
0171 7385180

Ernest Cashmore
4 Beech Court
Birmingham B43 6AB
0121 3575841

John Cheshire
38 Achilles Close
St James Place
Rolls Road
London SE1
0171 2320887

Nigel Christian
80 Alma Road
Plymouth
Devon
PL3 4HU
01752 252753

Peter Coleman
29 The Ring Road
Leeds
Yorkshire
LS14 1NH

William Connelly
72 Clincart Road
Mount Florida
Glasgow G42

Tommy Conroy
144 High Street East
Sunderland
Tyne and Wear
0191 5676871

Chris Coughlan
27 Maes Yr Haf
Llansamlet
Swansea
Wales
SA7 9ST
01792 310133

Pat Cowdell
129a Moat Road
Oldbury
Warley
West Midlands
B68 8EE
0121 5528082

John Cox
11 Fulford Drive
Links View
Northampton
NN2 7NX
01604 712107

Dave Currivan
15 Northolt Avenue
South Ruislip
Middlesex
0181 8419933

David Davies
10 Bryngelli
Carmel
Llanelli
Dyfed
SA14 7EL
01269 843204

Glyn Davies
63 Parc Brynmawr
Felinfoel
Llanelli
Dyfed
SA15 4PG
01554 756282

John Davies
5 Kent Road
Connah's Quay
Deeside
Clywd
Wales
01244 821173

Ronnie Davies
3 Vallensdean Cottages
Hangleton Lane
Portslade
Sussex
01273 416497

Brian Dawson
30 Presdales Drive
Ware
Hertfordshire
SG12 9NN
01920 485390

Peter Defreitas
13 Electric Parade
Seven Kings
Essex
IG3 8BY
0181 252 5883

Brendan Devine
12 Birkdale Close
Clubmoor
Liverpool
L6 0DL
0151 2631179

John Donnelly
15 Birkdale Avenue
St Annes on Sea
Lancshire
01253 712612

Jack Doughty
Tara Sports & Leisure
Ltd
Grains Road
Shaw
Near Oldham
Lancashire
OL2 8JB
01706 841460

Shaun Doyle
15 Jermyn Croft
Dodworth
Barnsley
South Yorkshire
S75 3LR
01226 298492

Phil Duckworth
The Hampton Hotel
Longclose Lane
Richmond Hill
Leeds LS9 8NP

Mickey Duff
National House
60-66 Wardour Street
London
W1V 3HP
0171 4375956

Pat Dwyer
93 Keir Hardie Avenue
Bootle
Liverpool 20
Merseyside
L20 0DN
0151 5253456

Bernard Eastwood
Eastwood House
2-4 Chapel Lane
Belfast 1
Northern Ireland
01232 238005

Greg Evans
21 Portman Road
Liverpool
Merseyside
L15 2HH

Jim Evans
88 Windsor Road
Maidenhead
Berkshire SL6 2DJ
01628 23640

Michael Fawcett
44 Rawstone Walk
Plaistow
London E13
0181 5545613

Norman Fawcett
4 Wydsail Place
Gosforth
Newcastle upon Tyne
NE3 4QP
0191 2846874

Colin Flute
84 Summerhill Road
Coseley
West Midlands
WV14 8RE
01902 402699

Tania Follett
123 Calfrious Way
Bracknell
Berkshire
RG12 3HD
01344 55547

Steve Foster
62 Overdale
Swinton
Salford M27 5WZ
0161 7941723

George Francis
11 Hillway
Holly Lodge Estate
London N6
0181 3482898

David Fry
91 Dugdell Close
Tricketts Cross
Ferndown
Dorset BH22 8BJ
01202 891725

Dai Gardiner
13 Hengoed Hall Drive
Cefn Hengoed
Mid Glamorgan
01633 284810

John Gaynor
7 Westhorne Fold
Counthill Drive
Brooklands Road
Crumpsall
Manchester M8 4JN
0161 7406993

Anthony Gee
Flat 1
Sunnyside
61 Ridge Road
Crouch End
London N8 9LJ
0181 3748952

Jimmy Gill
45 Blandford Road
Chilwell
Nottingham NG9 4GY
0115 9229957

Tommy Gilmour
Forte Crest Hotel
Bothwell Street
Glasgow G2 7EN
0141 2485461

Billy Graham
76 Aston Avenue
Fallowfield
Manchester
0161 2263218

Ron Gray
Ingrams Oak
19 Hatherton Road
Cannock
Staffordshire
01543 502279

Dave Gregory
10 Mill Farm Road
Hamsterley Mill
Nr Rowlands Gill
Tyne & Wear
0191 4774871

Johnny Griffin
Leicester
LE1 2GN
0116 2629287

Carl Gunns
Flat 2
Heathcliffe
469 Loughborough
Road
Birstall
Leicester

Jess Harding
70 Hatfield Road
Potters Bar
Hertfordshire
01707 270440

Billy Hardy
24 Dene Park
Castletown
Sunderland
SR5 3AG
0191 5491514

Frank Harrington
178 Kingsway
Heysham
Lancashire
LA3 2EG
01524 859953

Kevin Hayde
93 St Mary Street
Cardiff
CF1 1DW
01222 227606

Howard Hayes
No 9, Flat 3
Barrell Lane
Warsworth
Doncaster
South Yorkshire
DN4 9JR
01302 856209

Patrick Healy
1 Cranley Buildings
Brookes Market
Holborn
London EC1
0171 2428121

Barry Hearn
Matchroom
10 Western Road
Romford
Essex
RM1 3JT
01708 730480

George Hill
52 Hathaway
Marton
Blackpool
Lancashire
FY4 4AB

Dennis Hobson
Oarhouse
The Ford
Ridgeway
Sheffield
S12 7YD
01246 431116

Steve Holdsworth
85 Sussex Road
Watford
Hertfordshire
WD2 5HR
01923 252949

Harry Holland
12 Kendall Close
Feltham
Middlesex
0181 7374886

Gordon Holmes
15 Robert Andrew
Close
Morley St Botolph
Wymondham
Norfolk
NR18 9AA
01953 607887

Lloyd Honeyghan
22 Risborough
Deacon Way
Walworth Road
London
SE17
0171 7012435

John Hyland
The Morton Suite
The Moat House Hotel
1 Paradise Street
Liverpool
L1 8JD
0151 7088331

Brendan Ingle
26 Newman Road
Wincobank
Sheffield
S9 1LP
0114 2811277

Dominic Ingle
26 Newman Road
Sheffield
S9 1LP
0114 2811277

John Ingle
20 Rockmount Road
Wincobank
Sheffield S9
0114 2617934

Derek Isaamen
179 Liverpool Road
South
Maghill
Liverpool
L31 8AA

Richard Jones
1 Churchfields
Croft
Warrington
Cheshire WA3 7JR
01925 765167

Billy Kane
17 Bamburn Terrace
Byker
Newcastle upon Tyne
NE6 2GH
0191 2655493

Freddie King
7 St Charles Road
Brentwood
Essex
CM14 4TS
01277 230545

Johnny Kramer
115 Crofton Road
Plaistow
London E13

Terry Lawless
National House
60-66 Wardour Street
London W1V 3HP
0171 4375956

Brian Lawrence
50 Willow Vale
London W12
0181 7230182

Buddy Lee
The Walnuts
Roman Bank
Leverington
Wisbech
Cambridgeshire
PE13 5AR
01945 583266

Paul Lister
7 Murrayfield
Seghill
Northumberland

Graham Lockwood
106 Burnside Avenue
Skipton
Yorkshire
BB23 2DB
01756 792726

Brian Lynch
53 Hall Lane
Upminster
Essex
01708 223432

Pat Lynch
Gotherinton
68 Kelsey Lane
Balsall Common
Near Coventry
West Midlands
01676 33374

Burt McCarthy
Danecourt
Copt Hill
Danbury
Essex
CM3 4NW
01245 225383

John McIntyre
941 Aikenhead Road
Glasgow
G44 4QE
0141 8486468

Owen McMahon
3 Atlantic Avenue
Belfast
BT15
01232 743535

Jim McMillan
21 Langcliffe Road
Preston
Lancashire
PR2 6UE
01772 700665

Charlie Magri
345 Bethnal Green Road
London
E2 6LG
0171 7399035

Frank Maloney
Panix Promotions
99 Middlesex Street
London
E1 7DA
0171 2471999

Dennie Mancini
16 Rosedew Road
Off Fulham Palace Road
London
W6 9ET
0171 4371526

Terry Marsh
141 Great Gregorie
Basildon
Essex

Gary Mason
18 Camberwell Church
Street
Camberwell Green
London
SE5
0171 7032324

Arthur Melrose
33 Easterhill Street
Glasgow
G32 8LN
0141 7784127

Tommy Miller
128 Clapton Mount
King Cross Road
Halifax
West Yorkshire
01422 361147

Glyn Mitchell
28 Furneaux Road
Milehouse
Plymouth
Devon
01752 562054

Alex Morrison
39 Armour Street
Glasgow
G31 2ND
0141 5548704

Graham Moughton
1 Hedgemans Way
Dagenham
Essex
RM9 6DB
0181 5174070

James Murray
87 Spean Street
Glasgow
G44 4DS
0141 6377926

Herbert Myers
The Lodge
Lower House Lane
Burnley
Lancashire
01282 779300

David Nelson
29 Linley Drive
Stirchley Park
Telford
Shropshire
TF3 1RQ
01952 594690

Paul Newman
8 Teg Close
Downs Park Estate
Portslade
Sussex
BN41 2GZ
01273 419777

Norman Nobbs
364 Kings Road
Kingstanding
Birmingham
B44 0UG
0121 3555341

Terry O'Neill
48 Kirkfield View
Colton Village
Leeds
LS15 9DX
0113 2256140

Bob Paget
8 Masterman House
New Church Road
London
SE5 7HU

George Patrick
84 Wooler Road
Edmonton
London
N18 2JS
0181 8035609

Billy Pearce
Flat D
36 Courtfield Gardens
South Kensington
London
SW5 0PJ
0171 3702144

Terry Petersen
54 Green Leafe Avenue
Wheatley Hills
Doncaster
South Yorkshire
DN2 5RF
01302 368333

Des Piercy
190 Harrington Road
South Norwood
London
SE25 4NE
0181 6563290

Steve Pollard
899 Beverley High
Road
Hull
HU6 9NJ
01482 226698

Dean Powell
10 Cuddington
Deacon Way
Heygate Estate
Walworth
London
SE17 1SP
0171 2471999

Howard Rainey
55 Colwyn House
Hercules Road
London SE1
0171 7713251

Glyn Rhodes
8 Valentine Crescent
Shine Green
Sheffield
S5 0NW
0114 2492699

Ken Richardson
15 East Walk
North Road Estate
Retford
Nottinghamshire
DN22 7YF
01777 702770

Fred Rix
14 Broom Road
Shirley
Croydon
Surrey CR0 8NE
0181 7770233

Gus Robinson
Stranton House
Westview Road
Hartlepool
TS24 0BB
01429 234221

Ronnie Rush
4 Marcross Road
Ely
Cardiff
South Glamorgan
CF5 4RP
01222 593902

John Rushton
20 Alverley Lane
Balby
Doncaster
DN4 9AS
01302 31099

Joe Ryan
22B Adeyfield House
Cranwood Street
City Road
London EC1V 9NX

Chris Sanigar
Dorset House
Down End Road
Kingswood
Bristol
BS15 1SE
0117 9496699

Mike Shinfield
126 Birchwood Lane
Somercotes
Derbyshire
DE55 4NE
01773 603124

Steve Sims
132 Chepstow Road
Newport
Gwent
01633 213062

Len Slater
78 Sutcliffe Avenue
Nunsthorpe
Grimsby
Lincolnshire
01472 879862

Darkie Smith
21 Northumberland
House
Gaisford Street
London NW5
0171 2676805

Brian Snagg
The Heath Hotel
Green Hill Road
Allerton
Liverpool

Les Southey
Oakhouse
Park Way
Hillingdon
Middlesex
01895 54714

Greg Steene
22 Welbeck Street
London
W1M 7PG
0181 3600720

Danny Sullivan
29 Mount Gould
Avenue
Mount Gould
Plymouth
Devon
PL4 9HA
01752 660752

Norrie Sweeney
3 Saucehill Terrace
Paisley
Scotland
PA2 6SY
0141 8898798

Wally Swift
Grove House
54 Grove Road
Knowle
Solihull
West Midlands
B93 0PJ
01564 775140

Amos Talbot
70 Edenfield Road
Rochdale
OL11 5AE
01706 30662

Keith Tate
214 Dick Lane
Tyersal
Bradford
BD4 8JH
01274 779164

Glenroy Taylor
95 Devon Close
Perivale
Middlesex

Jimmy Tibbs
44 Gylingdune
Gardens
Seven Kings
Essex
0181 5990693

Roy Tindall
17 Tavistock Drive
Chadderton
Oldham
Lancashire
0161 3451386

Terry Toole
6 Churchwell Close
Chipping Onger
Essex
CM5 9BH
01277 362372

Mick Toomey
25 Purton Grove
Bransholme
Hull
HU7 4QD
01482 824476

Jack Trickett
Acton Court Hotel
187 Buxton Road
Stockport
Cheshire
0161 4836172

Frankie Turner
67 Camden High Street
London
NW1
0171 3801470

Bill Tyler
Northcroft House
Chorley
Lichfield
Staffordshire
WS13 8DL
01922 711160

Danny Urry
26 Nella Road
Hammersmith
London
W6
0171 4856523

Stephen Vaughan
Lombard Chambers
Ormond Street
Liverpool
L3 9NA
0151 2817861

Frank Warren
Centurion House
Bircherley Green
Hertford
Hertfordshire
SG14 1AP
01992 505550

Robert Watt
32 Dowanhill Street
Glasgow
G11

Gerry Watts
20 Taunton Crescent
Llanrumney
Cardiff
South Glamorgan
01443 778649

Jack Weaver
301 Coventry Road
Hinckley
Leicestershire
LE10 0NE
01455 619066

Ken Whitney
38 Shakespeare Way
Corby
Northamptonshire
NN17 2ND
01536 201194

William Wigley
4 Renfrew Drive
Wollaton
Nottinghamshire
NG8 2FX
0115 9162694

Mick Williamson
34a St Marys Grove
Cannonbury
London N1
0171 354739

Licensed Matchmakers

Neil Bowers
59 Carson Road
Canning Town
London
E16 4BD
0171 4735631

Steve Foster
62 Overdale
Swinton
Salford
M27 5WZ
0161 7941723

John Gaynor
7 Westhorne Fold
Counthill Drive
Brooklands Road
Crumpsall
Manchester
M8 4JN
0161 7406993

Ron Gray
Ingrams Oak
19 Hatherton Road
Cannock
Staffordshire
01543 502279

Bobby Holder
17 Merredene Street
Brixton
London SW9 6LR
0171 7385180

Steve Holdsworth
85 Sussex Road
Watford
Herts WD2 5HR
01923 252949

John Ingle
20 Rockmount Road
Wincobank
Sheffield S9 1LP
0114 2617934

Jason King
27 Rowan Road
Ingatestone
Essex
CM4 9AA
01708 730480

Graham Lockwood
106 Burnside Avenue
Skipton
N. Yorkshire
BD23 2DB
01756 792726

Dennie Mancini
16 Rosedew Road
Off Fulham Palace Road
Hammersmith
London
W6 9ET
0171 4371526

Tommy Miller
128 Clapton Mount
King Cross Road
Halifax
West Yorkshire
01422 361147

Norman Nobbs
364 Kings Road
Kingstanding
Birmingham
B44 0UG
0121 3555341

Dean Powell
10 Cuddington
Deacon Way
Heygate Estate
Walworth
London
SE17 1SP
0171 2471999

Len Slater
78 Sutcliffe Avenue
Nunsthorpe
Grimsby
Lincolnshire
01472 879862

Darkie Smith
21 Northumberland
House
Gaisford Street
London NW5
0171 2676805

Terry Toole
6 Churchwell Close
Chipping Onger
Essex CM5 9BH
01277 362372

Frank Turner
67 Camden High Street
London NW1
0171 3801470

Licensed BBBoC Referees, Timekeepers, Ringwhips, and Inspectors

Licensed Referees

Class 'B'

Terence Cole	Northern Area
Lee John Cook	Midlands Area
Kenneth Curtis	Southern Area
Phillip Edwards	Central Area
Keith Garner	Central Area
Mark Green	Southern Area
Jeffrey Hinds	Southern Area
Al Hutcheon	Scottish Area
David Irving	Northern Ireland
Christopher Kelly	Central Area
Philip Moyse	Midlands Area
Roy Snipe	Central Area
Grant Wallis	Western Area

Class 'A'

Ivor Bassett	Welsh Area
Arnold Bryson	Northern Area
Phil Cowsill	Central Area
Roddy Evans	Welsh Area
Anthony Green	Central Area
Michael Heatherwick	Welsh Area
Ian John-Lewis	Southern Area
Wynford Jones	Welsh Area
Denzil Lewis	Western Area
Marcus McDonnell	Southern Area
Len Mullen	Scottish Area
James Pridding	Midlands Area
Lawrence Thompson	Northern Area
Anthony Walker	Southern Area
Gerald Watson	Northern Area
Barney Wilson	Northern Ireland

Class 'A' Star

John Coyle	Midlands Area
Richard Davies	Southern Area
Roy Francis	Southern Area
John Keane	Midlands Area
Larry O'Connell	Southern Area
Terry O'Connor	Midlands Area
Dave Parris	Southern Area
Paul Thomas	Midlands Area
Mickey Vann	Central Area

Licensed Timekeepers

Alan Archbold	Northern Area
Roy Bicknell	Midlands Area
Roger Bowden	Western Area
Arnold Bryson	Northern Area
Neil Burder	Welsh Area
Ivor Campbell	Welsh Area
Frank Capewell	Central Area
Robert Edgeworth	Southern Area
Dale Elliott	Northern Ireland

Harry Foxall	Midlands Area
Eric Gilmour	Scottish Area
Brian Heath	Midlands Area
Ken Honiball	Western Area
Greg Hue	Southern Area
Winston Hughes	Midlands Area
Albert Kelleher	Northern Area
Michael McCann	Southern Area
Peter McCann	Southern Area
Norman Maddox	Midlands Area
Tommy Miller	Central Area
Gordon Pape	Welsh Area
Daniel Peacock	Southern Area
Barry Pinder	Central Area
Raymond Rice	Southern Area
Tommy Rice	Southern Area
Colin Roberts	Central Area
Russell Routledge	Northern Area
James Russell	Scottish Area
Nick White	Southern Area

Licensed Ringwhips

Bob Ainsley-Matthews	Southern Area
George Andrews	Central Area
Bernard Baggley	Midlands Area
Bob Batey	Northern Area
Robert Brazier	Southern Area
Albert Brewer	Southern Area
Michael Burke	Scottish Area
Steve Butler	Central Area
Alan Caffell	Southern Area
Theodore Christian	Western Area
John Davis	Southern Area
Ernie Draper	Southern Area
Wayne Elliott	Welsh Area
Jack Forbes	Northern Area
Colin Gallagher	Central Area
Danny Gill	Midlands Area
Chris Gilmore	Scottish Area
Mike Goodall	Midlands Area
Simon Goodall	Midlands Area
Peter Gray	Midlands Area
Arran Lee Grinnell	Midlands Area
David Hall	Central Area
Peter Hallberg	Midlands Area
Thomas Hallett	Northern Area
John Hardwick	Southern Area
Frank Hutchinson	Northern Area
Keith Jackson	Midlands Area
James McGinnis	Scottish Area
Alun Martin	Welsh Area
Tommy Miller (Jnr)	Central Area
Linton O'Brien	Northern Area
Dennis Pinching	Southern Area
Sandy Risley	Southern Area

Neil Sinclair	Southern Area
John Vary	Southern Area
Paul Wainwright	Northern Area
James Wallace	Scottish Area

Inspectors

Alan Alster	Central Area
William Ball	Southern Area
Michael Barnett	Central Area
Don Bartlett	Midlands Area
Jeffrey Bowden	Western Area
Fred Breyer	Southern Area
David Brown	Western Area
Ray Chichester	Welsh Area
Geoff Collier	Midlands Area
Julian Courtney	Welsh Area
Albert Cresswell	Midlands Area
John Crowe	Midlands Area
Jaswinder Dhaliwal	Midlands Area
Les Dean	Midlands Area
Robert Edgar	Central Area
Kevin Fulthorpe	Welsh Area
Bob Galloway	Southern Area
Paul Gooding	Northern Area
John Hall	Central Area
Eric Higgins	Scottish Area
Richard Hingston	Western Area
Jonathan Hooper	Western Area
Terry Hutcheon	Scottish Area
David Hughes	Welsh Area
Freddie King	Southern Area
Eddie Lillis	Central Area
Bob Lonkhurst	Southern Area
Tom McElhinney	Western Area
Stuart Meiklejohn	Central Area
David Ogilvie	Northern Area
Charlie Payne	Southern Area
Fred Potter	Northern Area
Les Potts	Midlands Area
David Renicke	Western Area
Bob Rice	Midlands Area
John Shaw	Western Area
J. Shea Jnr	Scottish Area
Bert Smith	Central Area
David Stone	Southern Area
Reg Thompson	Southern Area
John Toner	Northern Ireland
Nigel Underwood	Midlands Area
Ernie Wallis	Welsh Area
Robert Warner	Central Area
William Wilkins	Welsh Area
Clive Williams	Western Area
Geoff Williams	Midlands Area
David Wilson	Southern Area
Paul Woollard	Scottish Area

JIM EVANS PROMOTIONS

Licensed to British Boxing Board of Control

88 WINDSOR ROAD
MAIDENHEAD
BERKS SL6 2DJ
Tel & Fax: (01628) 23640

Manager / Coach Jim Evans

BOXERS:

Geoff McCreesh (British Welterweight Champion)
Ridha Soussi (Super-Middleweight) 8 x 3
Adrian Riley (Light-Middleweight) 6 or 8 x 3
Allan Gilbert (Light-Middleweight) 6 x 2
Colin Clarke (Light-Middleweight) 6 x 2
Alvar Coppard (Light-Middleweight) 6 x 2
Andy Edge (Light-Middleweight) 6 x 2
Lewis Reynolds (Lightweight) 6 or 8 x 3
Brendan Kelly (Lightweight) 6 x 3
John Matthews (Bantamweight) 6 or 8 x 3
Shane Mallon (Flyweight) 6 x 2

Trainers: **Johnny Bloomfield, Richard Dimmock,**

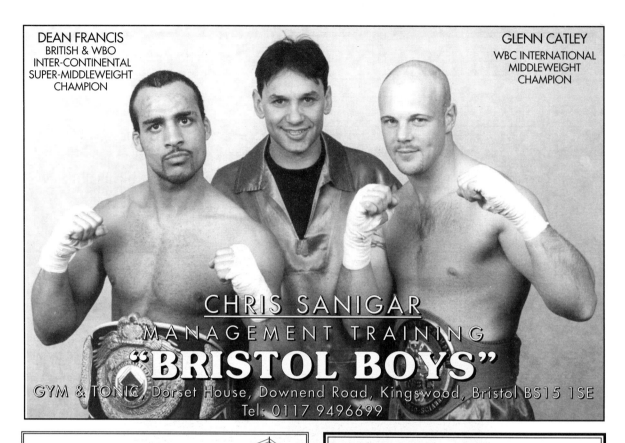

DEAN FRANCIS
BRITISH & WBO
INTER-CONTINENTAL
SUPER-MIDDLEWEIGHT
CHAMPION

GLENN CATLEY
WBC INTERNATIONAL
MIDDLEWEIGHT
CHAMPION

CHRIS SANIGAR
MANAGEMENT TRAINING
"BRISTOL BOYS"
GYM & TONIC, Dorset House, Downend Road, Kingswood, Bristol BS15 1SE
Tel: 0117 9496699

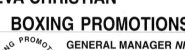

306

Stephen Vaughan
International Promoter / Manager
Lombard Chambers, Ormond Street, Liverpool L3 9NA

TEL / FAX: 0151 281 7861   **MOBILE: 0370 568978**

HEAD TRAINER
GEORGE VAUGHAN

trainer **Danny Vaughan**   trainer **John Smith**

Flyweight
Peter Culshaw - Commonwealth Champion WBA No 2

Super Bantamweight
Tony Mulholland - 1996 ABA Featherweight Champion

Featherweight
John Sillo
Chris Ainscough - Unbeaten

Super Featherweight
Gary Thornhill - Central Area Champion
Tommy Peacock - Unbeaten

Light Welterweight
Andy Holligan - Former Undefeated British Champion
Carl Wright

Welterweight
Andreas Panayi
Tony Mock
John Jones - Ex England International

Light Middleweight
Andrew Jervis

Middleweight
Paul Wright - Central Area Champion
John Stocks

Cruiserweight
Steve Bristow - Unbeaten

Matchmaker
JOHN GAYNOR

General Manager
LEE MALONEY

Ring Whip
COLIN GALLAGHER

Boxers' Record Index

Alito Color Group of Companies

Wish Barry Hugman
every success in producing
THE BRITISH BOXING YEARBOOK 1998.
*Once again you can count on our supporting
this valuable publication for the Boxing
fraternity.*

**Terry Brady
Chairman**